Invitation to the Life Span

Contemporary artist Andrea Cobb portrays three people, each distinct in age, ethnicity, and sexuality but all full-face and wide-eyed, appreciating one multicolored butterfly. Note that the three people are intimately connected, not only head to head but also clothed and surrounded by a unifying blue, with one unbroken line that cups each chin. Throughout the life span, each person and each moment is distinct, yet all of them together make up the human experience.

Invitation to the Life Span

KATHLEEN STASSEN BERGER

Bronx Community College
City University of New York

WORTH PUBLISHERS

Publisher: Catherine Woods

Executive Editor: Jessica Bayne

Developmental Editors: Cecilia Gardner, Tom Churchill

Marketing Manager: Amy Shefferd

Supplements and Media Editor: Sharon Prevost

Associate Managing Editor: Tracey Kuehn

Project Editor: Vivien Weiss

Art Director: Barbara Reingold

Interior Designer: Lissi Sigillo

Layout Designer: Paul Lacy

Associate Designer: Lyndall Culbertson

Senior Illustration Coordinator: Bill Page

Illustrations: Todd Buck Illustration, MPS Limited

Photo Editor: Cecilia Varas

Photo Researchers: Christina Micek, Donna Ranieri

Production Manager: Barbara Anne Seixas

Composition: MPS Limited

Printing and Binding: Quad/Graphics Versailles

Cover Art: Illustration © Andrea Cobb/www.i2iart.com

Library of Congress Control Number: 2009932476

ISBN-13: 978-07167-5466-4

ISBN-10: 0-7167-5466-5

Sixth printing

Worth Publishers

41 Madison Avenue

New York, NY 10010

www.worthpublishers.com

Credit is given to the following sources for permission to use the photos indicated:

Part Openers

David M. Phillips/Photo Researchers, pp. vi, xxiv

Scott Hancock/www.jupiterimages.com, pp. vi, 82

© Craig Pershouse/Lonely Planet Images, pp. vi, 156

Eric Wheater/Lonely Planet Images, pp. vi, 230

© Grove Pashley/Corbis, pp. vii, 306

Andrew Burke/Lonely Planet Images, pp. vii, 382

Bloom Works Inc./Alamy, pp. vii, 494

Chapter Openers

© Erin Moroney LaBelle/The Image Works, p. 2

© Clare Marsh/John Birdsall Archive/The Image Works, p. 42

Rayes/Getty Images, pp. viii, 84

© Dinodia/The Image Works, pp. ix, 122

© Guntmar Fritz/zefa/Corbis, pp. ix, 158

Daniel Boag/Lonely Planet Images, p. 196

© Floresco Productions/Corbis, pp. x, 232

Susan Barr/www.jupiterimages.com, pp. x, 270

www.jupiterimages.com, p. 308

© Buero Monaco/zefa/Corbis, pp. xi, 346

www.jupiterimages.com, pp. xi, 384

www.jupiterimages.com, p. 418

Yellow Dog Productions Inc./Getty Images, pp. xii, 454

Punchstock, pp. xii, 496

Getty Images, p. 528

© Buddhika Weerasinghe/Reuters/Corbis, p. 564

About the Author

Kathleen Stassen Berger completed her undergraduate education at Stanford University and Radcliffe College, earned her M.A.T. from Harvard University, and received her M.S. and Ph.D. from Yeshiva University. Her broad range of experience as an educator includes directing a preschool, teaching philosophy and humanities at the United Nations International School, teaching child and adolescent development to graduate students at Fordham University, teaching inmates earning paralegal degrees at Sing Sing Prison, and teaching undergraduates at both Montclair State University and Quinnipiac University. She has also been involved in education as the president of Community School Board District Two in Manhattan.

For over three decades, Berger has taught human development at Bronx Community College of the City University of New York. The students she teaches every year—who come from diverse ethnic, economic, and educational backgrounds and who represent a wide range of interests—consistently honor her with the highest instructor evaluations.

Berger's developmental texts are currently being used at nearly 700 colleges and universities worldwide and have been translated into a dozen languages. Her research interests include adolescent identity, sibling relationships, and bullying. As the mother of four daughters and as a new grandmother, she brings to her teaching and writing ample firsthand experience with human development.

Brief Contents

Contents

85

157
Part III Early Childhood

Preface

"Translational" is a new buzz word in *Science* magazine, as scientists strive to apply laboratory research to everyday life. "From bench to bedside" is how the biologists describe it, "What works?" is the question educators ask, and politicians study "public perception." Many experiments in developmental science—such as studies proving that 6-month-old babies can distinguish between French and English or that underfed mice live longer than well-fed ones—are not readily applied to daily life or are misinterpreted.

Translation is needed, so that people worldwide can understand and benefit from discoveries that originate in science laboratories. *Invitation to the Life Span* (and every teacher) is a translator. My goal in writing it is to increase access, examining the results of small-scale, controlled research and explaining them to a wider audience.

Readers who know my other textbooks regard this *Invitation* as past due. Again and again, colleagues at teaching conferences told me they did not cover critical aspects of development because my book was too long. Some instructors left out theories, others omitted middle age, and many covered late adulthood and death in a single week. I came to understand that many instructors needed an accessible yet comprehensive text.

This new book covers all the major topics of life-span development in 15 chapters and 589 pages. I have carefully organized and thought through the material, including current research, fresh images and examples, and extensive multicultural data. This translation from the laboratory to real life does not sacrifice any core content or shortchange any age.

My life—as girl, woman, daughter, wife, mother, and now grandmother—furnishes anecdotes that facilitate the translation. At the same time, as is evident in my analyses of the most recent research on everything from Alzheimer disease to zygotes, teaching and learning are my life's work and passion.

Because I am both a scholar and an ordinary person, this text is challenging as well as accessible. My own students have inspired me. They deserve a book that respects their intellect and their experiences, as do all students. I hope this book will enable all of us to be wiser, more compassionate, and more effective as we enjoy every year, even every moment, of life.

The Same, Yet Different Curiosity is universal among humans, as the faces of these children show. They are in a tent camp for refugees of a major earthquake in Pakistan in 2005. As their varying reactions to the experience demonstrate, each person is unique.

ZORIAH / THE IMAGE WORKS

Features

This new book shares many features with my other development texts. Unique elements include questions that aid critical thinking ("For Deeper Reflection," in the margins next to relevant text discussions), mathematical analysis ("Understanding the Numbers," in the margins), and recall of concepts (two-page charts called "Concept Reviews," which appear at the end of each part).

What's for Dinner? Markets are universal, but each culture has a unique mix of products, stores, and salespeople. Compare this floating food market in Bangkok, Thailand, with a North American supermarket.

JUPITER IMAGES

Writing That Communicates the Excitement and Challenge of the Field

The same hallmark features of my other textbooks are here, too: current research, compelling personal narratives, and culturally diverse presentation. The voice of this book makes developmental psychology clear, compelling, and easy to grasp by relating to the reader's personal experience. An overview of the science of human development should be intriguing, just as people are. Each sentence conveys tone as well as content. Chapter-opening vignettes bring student readers into the immediacy of development. Examples and explanations abound, connecting theory, research, and students' own experiences.

Concise Format

At fewer than 600 pages, and with just 15 chapters, the text covers the essentials in a format that fits easily into a one-term syllabus. The organization is topical within a chronological framework, providing students with a scaffold for understanding the interplay between age and domain.

The first two chapters focus on definitions, theories, research, genetics, and life before birth. This introductory part of the book provides the structure for understanding the life-span perspective, including plasticity, nature and nurture, cultural awareness, family bonding, and many other concepts. The other six parts correspond to the major periods of child and adult development, including a separate chapter on emerging adulthood.

Coverage of Diversity

Multicultural and international, rich and poor, infant and grandparent, male and female, gay and straight, normal and pathological—an understanding of, and respect for, all these words and concepts are vital to an appreciation of development. Research finds surprising commonalities and notable differences. We are all the same, yet each of us is unique.

Beginning with the discussion of "all kinds of people" in Chapter 1, each chapter highlights the possibilities and variations of human life across the life span. New findings about family structure, bilingualism, and bereavement are among the many topics that illustrate, and encourage respect for, human differences. Examples and research results from many parts of the world are not presented as peripheral highlights or set apart in boxes but are integrated throughout the text, as the following list of topics makes clear:

Inclusion of all kinds of people in the study of development, pp. 5–6

Ethnicity, race, and culture defined, pp. 11–12

Cultural differences in incidence of twin births, p. 47

Male and female chromosomes, pp. 47–48

Sex-chromosome abnormalities, pp. 50–51

Sex-selection policies in China, India, and other countries, p. 56

Birthing practices in various cultures, pp. 64–67

Rates of cesarean births in different countries, pp. 65–66

Low-birthweight rates in different countries, pp. 67–69

Nature–nurture interaction in nearsightedness among children in Britain, Africa, and Asia, p. 72

Sleeping Beauty At 3 months, most babies—like this infant in Mongolia—can sleep soundly amid noisy human activity.

SEAN SPRAGUE / THE IMAGE WORKS

Getting Ready Her shape, hairstyle, eye makeup, and boa are those of a mature woman, but this girl is actually just 13 years old. Her emotional maturity is harder to gauge than her physical development.

Trio at Play Sex differences are apparent by age 3, not only in haircuts and clothing but also in physical closeness (girls hold hands) and preferred activities (boys more readily take risks).

Keep Smiling Good humor seems to be a cause of longevity, and vice versa. This is as true among the elderly in nations where few reach old age as it is in countries where the aged outnumber the young.

© ANDREAS LANDER / DPA / CORBIS

Up-to-Date Coverage

My mentors taught me to be curious, creative, and skeptical. My students provide me with new perspectives. Consequently, I eagerly read and evaluate thousands of journal articles and books on everything from autism to zygosity. The recent explosion of research in neuroscience and genetics has challenged me, once again, first to understand and then to translate complex facts and provocative speculations.

Like all other sciences, life-span development is built on past learning. This book necessarily explains many facts and concepts—stages and ages, norms and variations, dangers and diversities, classic theories and creative applications. At the same time, we know much more now than we did a decade, or even a year, ago. This book describes cutting-edge research on everything from epigenetics to end-of-life care. The following list of examples from just one area, brain research, illustrates the kinds of connections between classic ideas and current insights that are made throughout the text.

Dunedin study of correlation between neurotransmitter production and violent crime in adolescent boys, p. 13

A View from Science feature on mirror neurons, p. 14

Brain activity as a measure of depression, p. 16

Brain development in infancy, pp. 88–93

A View from Science feature on the effect of social deprivation on brain growth, p. 92

Piaget's sensorimotor intelligence, pp. 105–108

Information-processing theory on infant cognition, pp. 108–111

Chomsky's hypothesis of a language acquisition device, p. 117

Brain maturation and emotional development in infancy, pp. 127–128

Brain development in early childhood, pp. 166–170

Brain maturation as basis for theory of mind, p. 177

Development of prefrontal cortex and emotional regulation, p. 201

Boy brains, girl brains, and emotional regulation, pp. 202–203

Brain development in middle childhood, pp. 242–246

Brain development in adolescence, pp. 324–326

Flexible use of brain by young adults to combine subjective and objective thought, p. 396

The aging brain in adulthood, pp. 435–436

The aging brain in late adulthood, pp. 512–513

Information processing in the elderly, pp. 514–517

Dementia (Alzheimer disease, vascular dementia, frontal lobe dementia), pp. 517–522

New cognitive development in late adulthood, pp. 522–525

Brain death, pp. 577–578

Pedagogical Support

This book was designed for today's students. Each chapter begins with a brief real-life vignette to help students connect to the chapter content. Key terms appear in boldface type in the text; they are defined in the margins and again in a glossary at the back of the book. The outline on the first page of each chapter and the system of major and minor subheads facilitate the survey-question-read-write-review (SQ3R) approach. Chapters end with a brief summary, a list of key terms, and key questions for review. Then application exercises suggest ways to apply concepts to everyday life. **After each part, two-page Concept Reviews visually connect key ideas.**

Each major section of a chapter closes with "Key Points," allowing students to pause and reflect on what they've just read. Active learning is stressed in "Observation Quizzes," which inspire readers to look more closely at photographs, tables, and graphs, and in "Especially for . . ." questions in the margins. Each "Especially for . . ." question is addressed to a specific population—such as parents, nurses, educators, psychologists, or social workers—who are asked to apply what they have just read. Furthermore, I chose each photograph and wrote each caption with the expectation that students will learn from it. (This Preface offers a selection of the photographs that appear in the book.)

New Tricks With a grandchild as a patient tutor, this woman, like many other older people, is delighted to learn how to use a laptop computer.

Critical thinking is encouraged throughout, as every chapter challenges myths, research designs, and cultural assumptions. A series of marginal questions called "For Deeper Reflection" encourage students to think more deeply. Another series, called "Understanding the Numbers," allow students to use their quantitative reasoning skills. Features called "A View from Science" apply the research that shapes theory, practice, and application.

Supplements

As an instructor myself, I know that supplements can make or break a class. Students are now media savvy, and instructors use tools that did not exist when they were in college. Many supplements are available for both students and professors.

DevelopmentPortal

DevelopmentPortal is the complete online gateway to all student and instructor resources available with the textbook. It brings together the Video Tool Kit, the eBook, and powerful assessment tools. Created by psychologists and master teachers, DevelopmentPortal includes robust diagnostic quizzes to focus study where it is needed most and an assignment engine that allows instructors to conduct and administer quizzes and tests, with more than 80 questions per chapter for ongoing assessment, distinct from the test bank questions.

Video Tool Kit

The Video Tool Kit is available online. Its 80-plus student activities range from classic experiments (like the visual cliff and the Strange Situation) to observations on children's play and adolescent risk-taking. Dozens of video clips include classic historical footage from Harry Harlow and riveting footage on children in war as well as the genetics of Alzheimer disease.

The Video Tool Kit was prepared by a talented team of instructors, including Victoria Cross (University of California, Davis), Sheridan DeWolf (Grossmont College), Pamela B. Hill (San Antonio College), Lisa Huffman (Ball State University), Thomas Ludwig (Hope College), Cathleen McGreal (Michigan State University), Amy Obegi (Grossmont College), Michelle L. Pilati (Rio Hondo College), Tanya Renner (Kapiolani Community College), Catherine Robertson (Grossmont College), S. Stavros Valenti (Hofstra University), and Pauline Zeece (University of Nebraska, Lincoln).

eBook

The eBook integrates the complete text and its interactive study tools in a format that instructors and students can customize—all at a significantly lower price than the printed text. It offers access from any Internet-connected computer; quick, intuitive navigation to any section, subsection, or printed book page; a Notes feature that allows any page to be customized; a full-text search; text highlighting; and a searchable glossary. Some students may prefer this format over the printed book.

Companion Web Site

The companion Web site at **www.worthpublishers.com/berger** is a free online educational home for students and instructors. Tools on the site include: interactive flashcards in both English and Spanish; a Spanish-language glossary; quizzes; Internet exercises and case studies; and Frequently Asked Questions about Development. A password-protected Instructor Site offers a full array of teaching resources.

The companion Web site was edited by Catherine Robertson (Grossmont College).

Study Guide

The *Study Guide* by Richard O. Straub (University of Michigan, Dearborn) helps students evaluate their understanding and retain their learning longer. Each chapter includes a review of key concepts, guided study questions, and section reviews that encourage students' active participation in the learning process. Two practice tests and a challenge test help them assess their mastery of the material.

For Instructors

In addition to the electronic and printed resources designed for both students and faculty members, *Invitation to the Life Span* offers tools specifically for instructors.

Videos

A Tool Kit is available that includes more than 400 closed-captioned video clips and animations, along with discussion starters and PowerPoint slides, which can easily be downloaded and assigned to students. A selection of the most popular video clips is also available on CD or DVD.

In addition to the Tool Kit, instructors can ask their sales representative about video packages, including *Journey Through the Life Span,* a series that contains vivid footage of people of all ages from around the world. The 8- to 10-minute clips for each chapter and observational modules provide an overview of major developmental topics.

Transitions through the Life Span, a telecourse developed by Coast Learning Systems and Worth Publishers, teaches the fundamentals of life-span development. The course explores many contexts that influence development. Each video lesson includes examples interwoven with experts' commentary.

Instructor's Resources

This collection of resources written by Richard O. Straub has been hailed as the richest collection of instructor's resources in the field of development. It features chapter-by-chapter previews and lecture guides, learning objectives, springboard topics for discussion and debate, handouts for student projects, and supplementary readings from journal articles. Course-planning suggestions, ideas for term projects, and a guide to audiovisual and software materials are also included.

Sustained by Mother Nature One of the favorite activities of many retirees is caring for their own home. Gardening in particular becomes more popular.

PowerPoint Slides

Many presentation slides are available on the companion Web site or in the Tool Kit. There are two prebuilt Power-Point slide sets for each text chapter—one featuring chapter outlines, the other featuring all chapter art and illustrations. Both can be customized to fit a particular class. Video presentation slides provide an easy way to connect chapter content to the selected video clips and follow-up questions. In addition, Martin Wolfger and Michael James (Ivy Tech Community College, Bloomington) have produced a set of enhanced lecture slides focusing on key themes from the text and featuring tables, graphs, and figures.

Test Bank and Computerized Test Bank

The test bank, prepared by Susan Higgins (University of Kansas), includes at least 90 multiple-choice and 70 fill-in, true-false, and essay questions for each chapter. Each question is keyed to the textbook by topic, page number, and level of difficulty. The Diploma computerized test bank, available on a dual-platform CD-ROM for Windows and Macintosh, guides instructors step-by-step through the process of creating a test and allows them to quickly add questions; to edit, scramble, or resequence items; to format a test; and to include pictures, equations, and media links. The accompanying gradebook enables instructors to record students' grades throughout the course and includes the capacity to sort student records, view detailed analyses of test items, curve tests, generate reports, add weights to grades, and more.

The CD-ROM is also the access point for Diploma Online Testing, which allows instructors to create and administer secure exams over a network or over the Internet. In addition, Diploma has the ability to restrict tests to specific computers or time blocks. Blackboard- and WebCT-formatted versions of each item in the Test Bank are available on the CD-ROM.

Appreciation

I am very grateful for the help and advice of many academic reviewers, including:

Eileen J. Achorn, *University of Texas, San Antonio*

Susan Allen, *University of Mississippi*

Paula Avioli, *Kean University*

Esther Barkat, *Waynesburg University*

Patrick Bowman, *University of Louisiana, Lafayette*

Ralph Braithwaite, *University of Hartford*

Jennifer Braverman, *College of New Jersey*

William Brinnier, *Central Piedmont Community College*

Kathryn Caldwell, *Ithaca College*

Elaine Cassel, *Lord Fairfax Community College*

Kimberly Clayton-Code, *Northern Kentucky University*

Molly B. Connelly, *University of New Hampshire*

Victoria Cooke, *Erie Community College*

Pamela G. Costa, *Tacoma Community College*

Eric De Vos, *Saginaw Valley State University*

Frank DeCaria, *West Virginia Northern Community College*

John DeFrancesco, *American International College*

Allison R. Hollingsworth Deming, *Ferrum College*

Meliksah Demir, *Northern Arizona University*

Kimberly Desmond, *Indiana University of Pennsylvania*

Rock Edward Doddridge, *Asheville–Buncombe Technical Community College*

Ranjana Dutta, *Saginaw Valley State University*

Anne B. Edwards, *Purdue University, Calumet*

Mary-Jane Eisen, *St. Joseph College*

Celeste Favela, *El Paso Community College*

Jacki Fitzpatrick, *Texas Tech University*

Donna Fletcher, *Florida State University*

Rod Fowers, *Highline Community College*

Tony Fowler, *Florence–Darlington Technical College*

Laura Garofoli, *Fitchburg State College*

Erica Gelven, *Three Rivers Community College*

Dan Grangaard, *Austin Community College*

Jerry Green, *Tarrant County College, Northwest Campus*

Christine Grela, *McHenry County College*

Janelle Grellner, *University of Central Oklahoma*

Laura Gruntmeir, *Redlands Community College*

Rea Gubler, *Southern Utah University*

Trudie Guffey, *Gadsden State Community College*

Anne Gutshall, *College of Charleston*

Debbie Handy, *Washington State University*

Mary Beth Hartshorn, *Diablo Valley College*

Constance Hayes, *University of Texas, Brownsville*

Jennifer J. Higa, *Honolulu Community College*

Valerie Holland, *Warren County Community College*

Bette Hollis, *Dominican University of California*

Tasha Howe, *Humboldt State University*

Alycia Hund, *Illinois State University*

Holly Hunt, *Montana State University*

Jane Hyche, *Gwinnett Technical College*

Benetha Jackson, *Angelina College*

Susan Johns, *St. Joseph College*

Saliwe Kawewe, *Southern Illinois University*

Thomas Keenan, *Niagara College*

Jennifer King-Cooper, *Sinclair Community College*

Marvin Lee, *Tennessee State University*

Cynthia Lofaso, *Central Valley Community College*

Kenneth Luke, *Tyler Junior College*

Christine MacDonald, *Indiana State University*

Tammy Mahan, *College of the Canyons*

Sara Martino, *The Richard Stockton College of New Jersey*

Mary McGlamery, *Angelo State University*

Joshua Mersky, *University of Wisconsin, Milwaukee*

Judith Luna Meyer, *Beaufort County Community College*

Marcie Miller, *South Plains College*

Diana Moore, *Shenandoah University*

Pat Moretti, *Santa Clara University*

Edward Morris, *Owensboro Community and Technical College*

Ronald Mossler, *Los Angeles Valley College*

Debra Nelson, *Washington State University*

Christine Newcombe, *Dominican College*

Shirley O'Brien, *Eastern Kentucky University*

Sandra Osborne, *Montana State University*

Pete Peterson, *Johnson County Community College*

Linda Petroff, *Central Community College*

Joseph Pickard, *University of Missouri, St. Louis*

Linda Pinney, *J. Sargeant Reynolds Community College*

Justina Powers, *Cameron University*

David Price, *Kettering College of Medical Arts*

Pat Puccio, *College of DuPage*

Rodney Raasch, *Normandale Community College*

Lillian Range, *Our Lady of Holy Cross College*

Nancy Rankin, *University of New England*

Amy Reesing, *Arizona State University*

Judy Reilly, *San Diego State University*

Alesia Richardson, *Chicago State University*

Maureen Riley-Behringer, *Case Western Reserve University*

Tovah Sands, *California State University, Northridge*

Cheryl Sawyer, *University of Houston, Clear Lake*

Patty Sawyer, *Middlesex Community College*

Peggy Skinner, *South Plains College*

Nancy Smuckler, *University of Wisconsin, Milwaukee*

Stephen Soreff, *Southern New Hampshire University*

Meredith Stanford, *University of Massachusetts, Lowell*

O'Ann Steere, *College of DuPage*

Chris Thomas, *Florence–Darlington Technical College*

Jeffrey Turner, *Mitchell College*

Sharon Votel, *St. Mary's University of Minnesota*

Tricia Waters, *Colorado College*

Belinda Wholeben, *Rockford College*

Wanda A. Willard, *Monroe Community College*

Lois Willoughby, *Miami Dade College*

Thomas Wilson, *Bellarmine University*

Mahbubeh Yektaparast, *Central Piedmont Community College*

The editorial, production, sales, and marketing people at Worth Publishers are dedicated to meeting the highest standards of excellence. They devote time, effort, and talent to every aspect of publishing, as is evident on every page. I particularly would like to thank: Stacey Alexander, Jessica Bayne, Tom Chao, Tom Churchill, Lyndall Culbertson, Emily Ernst, Adam Frese, Cele Gardner, Tom Kling, Tracey Kuehn, Paul Lacy, Christina Micek, Katherine Nurre, Sharon Prevost, Donna Ranieri, Babs Reingold, Barbara Seixas, Amy Shefferd, Walter Shih, Carlise Sternbridge, Ted Szczepanski, Cecilia Varas, Vivien Weiss, and Catherine Woods.

Dedication

To Tom Kling and Bill Davis, superstars in the Worth galaxy of sales representatives. They believed in this text long before anyone else. Without them, this book would not be.

Kathleen Stassen Berger
September 2009

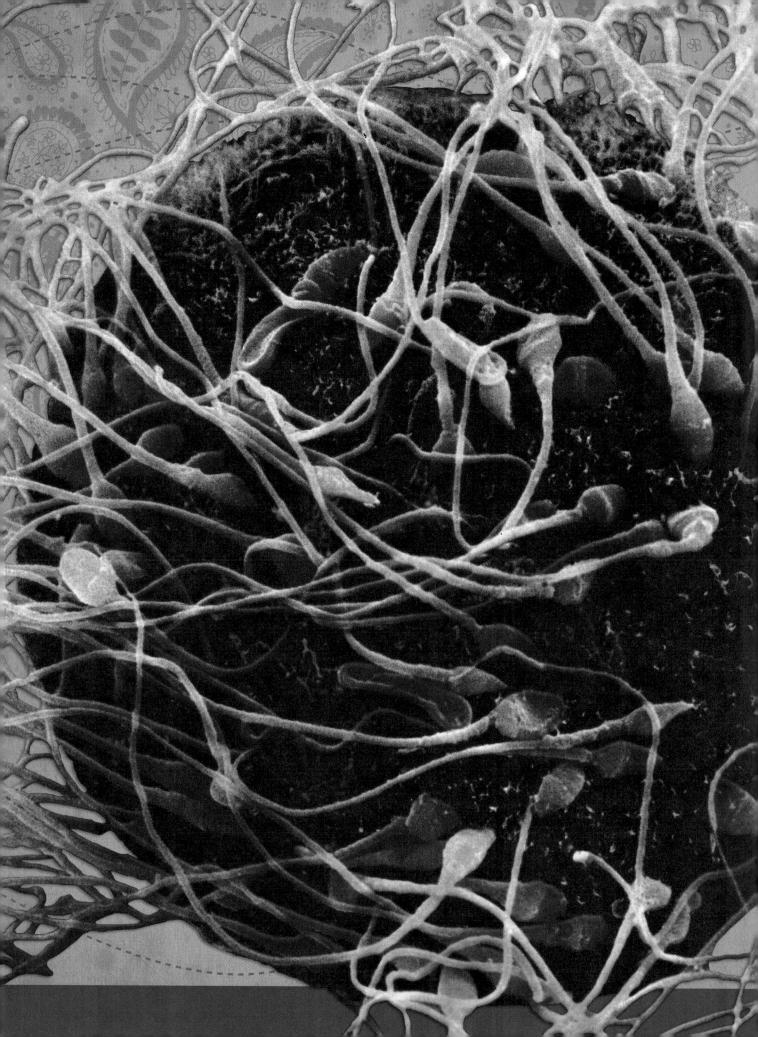

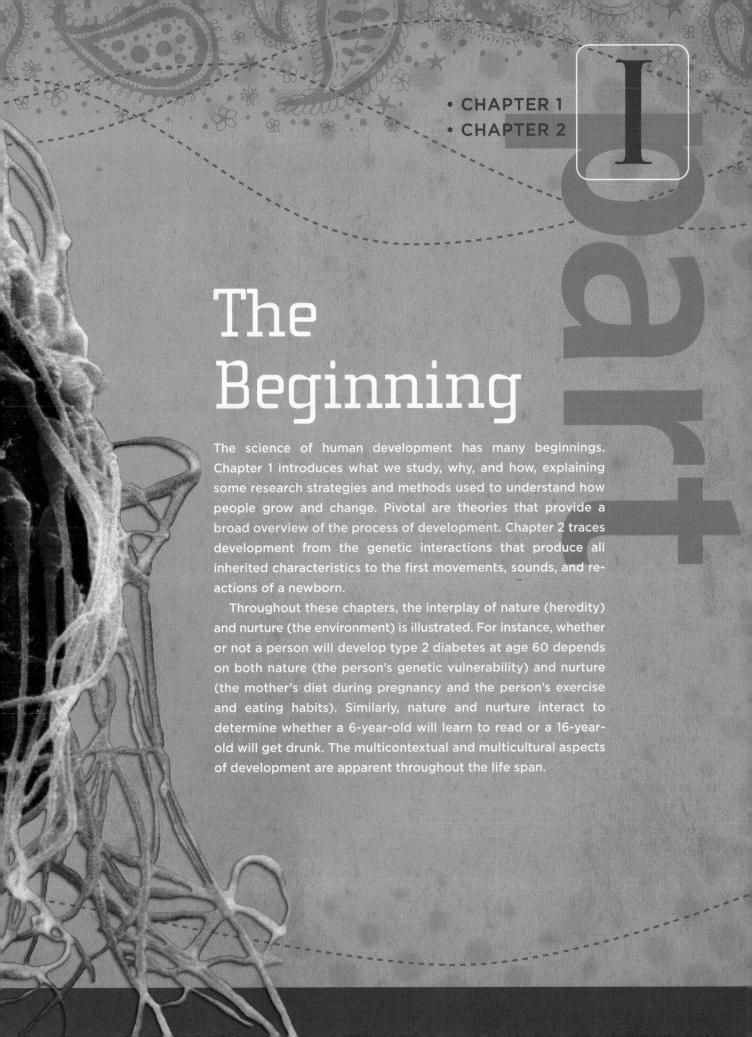

The Beginning

The science of human development has many beginnings. Chapter 1 introduces what we study, why, and how, explaining some research strategies and methods used to understand how people grow and change. Pivotal are theories that provide a broad overview of the process of development. Chapter 2 traces development from the genetic interactions that produce all inherited characteristics to the first movements, sounds, and reactions of a newborn.

Throughout these chapters, the interplay of nature (heredity) and nurture (the environment) is illustrated. For instance, whether or not a person will develop type 2 diabetes at age 60 depends on both nature (the person's genetic vulnerability) and nurture (the mother's diet during pregnancy and the person's exercise and eating habits). Similarly, nature and nurture interact to determine whether a 6-year-old will learn to read or a 16-year-old will get drunk. The multicontextual and multicultural aspects of development are apparent throughout the life span.

CHAPTER OUTLINE

THE SCIENCE OF
Development

"We had our baby," my brother phoned me one November day in 1967.

"Wonderful. Boy or girl?" I said.

"Boy. David. [*Long sigh*] He has some problems. He is scheduled for heart surgery tomorrow. Both eyes have thick cataracts. And more."

"Oh, no. I am so sorry."

"Don't worry. It's not genetic. Dot had rubella when he was an embryo. We had suspected that, but we didn't tell you because the doctor wasn't sure and we didn't want to worry you. They now found rubella virus in him. It doesn't affect you."

I was heartsick for my brother and his wife. But he was concerned about me. I was six months pregnant with our first child, and he thought I might be frightened for my fetus. It is true that pregnant women are prone to irrational fears, anxieties, and other emotions, but at that moment I was much more worried about his baby than mine.

My concerns were valid. Over the next four years, it became clear that our child, Bethany, was fine but David was not. I watched him slowly and painstakingly learn to chew, to walk, to hum, and finally, at age 4, to talk. Hundreds of special doctors, nurses, teachers, and neighbors aided his development. Thousands of researchers also helped him indirectly by describing how children like him can grow.

Decades have passed since that first phone call. David—at right in the photograph, with his brothers Mike and Bill—recently turned 40. He told me:

> I am generally quite happy, but secretly a little happier lately, especially since November, because I have been consistently getting a pretty good vibrato when I am singing, not only by myself but also in congregational hymns in church. [*He explained vibrato:*] When a note bounces up and down within a quartertone either way of concert pitch, optimally between 5.5 and 8.2 times per second.

So David is knowledgeable as well as happy.

He also has a wry sense of humor. When I complained that my writing wasn't progressing as fast

as I wanted it to, David replied, "That sounds just like a certain father I know." This was an acute observation: David's dad and I live thousands of miles apart, but we share half our genes and most of our childhood. Because of that, we are similar in many ways. ●

THIS CHAPTER BEGINS to detail the myriad influences on human life, including genes and childhood experiences. It introduces the science of development over the life span and includes definitions, perspectives, methods, and ethics—all crucial concepts for everyone who seeks to master this subject. But it is also important to know that the goal of our study is to enable David and Bethany, and all the other 6.2 billion people on Earth, to fulfill their potential throughout their lives.

David's life continues to be amazing, filled with joys and sorrows. So is yours. This chapter, and those that follow, trace that reality.

Defining Development

science of human development
The science that seeks to understand how and why people of all ages and circumstances change or remain the same over time.

The **science of human development** *seeks to understand how and why people—all kinds of people, everywhere, of every age—change over time.* Developmentalists recognize that growth is *multidirectional, multicontextual, multicultural, multidisciplinary,* and *plastic.* All these terms will be explained in this chapter, but first we need to delve deeper into the elements of the basic definition of developmental science: the how and why of development, the inclusion of all kinds of people, and the observation of change over time.

Understanding How and Why

● **FOR DEEPER REFLECTION** Beyond science, how else can people learn about human development?

First, developmental study is a *science* (Bornstein & Lamb, 2005). It depends on theories, data, analysis, critical thinking (or deeper reflection), and sound methodology—just like every other science. And like all scientists, developmentalists ask questions and seek answers, trying to ascertain "how and why"—that is, trying to discover the processes of development and the reasons for those processes.

People disagree about how children should be raised; whether emerging adults should marry; when adults should divorce, or retire, or die. Such subjective opinions arise from emotions and upbringing, not necessarily from evidence. Scientists seek to move past subjectivity, to progress from opinion to truth, from wishes to outcomes. To avoid unexamined opinions and to rein in personal biases, scientists follow the five basic steps of the **scientific method**:

scientific method
A way to answer questions that requires empirical research and data-based conclusions.

1. *Begin with curiosity.* On the basis of theory, prior research, or a personal observation, pose a question.
2. *Develop a hypothesis.* Shape the question into a hypothesis, a specific prediction that can be tested.
3. *Test the hypothesis.* Design and conduct research to gather empirical evidence (data).
4. *Draw conclusions.* Use the evidence to support or refute the hypothesis.
5. *Report the results.* Share the data and conclusions, as well as alternative explanations. Each new finding extends or clarifies earlier work.

replication
The repetition of a study, using different participants.

Developmentalists begin with curiosity and then seek the facts, drawing conclusions only after careful research and analysis of data. **Replication**—the repetition of a study, using different participants—often follows the fifth step; it is needed before the scientific community accepts the study's conclusions.

Including All Kinds of People

As the second element of our definition indicates, developmental science includes *all kinds of people*—young and old; rich and poor; of every ethnicity, background, sexual orientation, culture, and nationality. The challenge is to identify universalities and differences and then describe them in ways that simultaneously unify humanity and distinguish each human being.

Both the universal and the unique are evident in each developing person. For example, your father's father's father was once a boy who never sent a text message, was not vaccinated against chicken pox, and did not fear nuclear war. That much is universal, relevant to understanding great-grandfathers. Also universal is that his life affects you, even if you never knew him. All of his descendants are influenced (for better or worse) by his values and behavior. Furthermore, about 12 percent of your genes were his as well, including, if you are male, his Y chromosome.

Yet your great-grandfather was (or is) unique. No one exactly like him will ever live again. His effect on you depends on dozens of other factors, which again are unique to you and may include rebellion against his example. Your study of development will help you discover his influence, but you cannot be certain of every aspect of that influence. More science is needed.

ZORIAH / THE IMAGE WORKS

The Same, Yet Different Curiosity is universal among humans, as the faces of these children show. They are in a tent camp for refugees of a major earthquake in Pakistan in 2005. As their varying reactions to the experience demonstrate, each person is unique.

THE NATURE–NURTURE DEBATE This example highlights a great puzzle of development, the *nature–nurture debate*. **Nature** refers to the influence of genes that people inherit. **Nurture** refers to environmental influences, beginning with the health and diet of the embryo's mother and continuing lifelong, including family, school, community, and society.

The nature–nurture debate has many other names, among them *heredity–environment* and *maturation–learning*. Under whatever name, the basic question is: How much of any characteristic, behavior, or emotion is the result of genes and how much is the result of experience?

Note that the question is "how much," not "which," because both genes and the environment affect every characteristic. Thus, nature always affects nurture, and then nurture affects nature (Moffitt et al., 2006; Reiss et al., 2000).

nature
A general term for the traits, capacities, and limitations that each individual inherits genetically from his or her parents at the moment of conception.

nurture
A general term for all the environmental influences that affect development after an individual is conceived.

CRITICAL AND SENSITIVE PERIODS The fact that nature and nurture always interact helps clarify another question: whether or not certain times of life are critical for later development. A **critical period** is a time when certain things *must* occur for normal development.

For example, a human fetus develops arms and legs, hands and feet, fingers and toes, each on a particular day between 28 and 54 days after conception. If this critical period for limb development is disrupted, then the child never develops normal limbs. Between 1957 and 1961, thousands of pregnant women in 30 nations took a new prescription sedative called thalidomide during this critical period, and their babies were born with missing or deformed arms, hands, legs, or feet. The specific deformity depended on which critical day the drug disrupted development (K. L. Moore & Persaud, 2003).

At certain points during early childhood, there may be a **sensitive period**, when a particular development occurs most easily. One example is language. If

critical period
A time when a particular type of developmental growth (in body or behavior) must happen if it is ever going to happen.

sensitive period
A time when a certain type of development is most likely to happen or happens most easily, although it may still happen later with more difficulty. For example, early childhood is considered a sensitive period for language learning.

children do not master a first language during the sensitive period between ages 1 and 3, they may still do so later (hence this is not a critical period), but they will have more difficulty. Similarly, some (but not all) researchers believe that the years before puberty are a sensitive period for learning a second or third language, although not every scholar agrees (Birdsong, 2006; Herschensohn, 2007).

Note that both of these examples involve nature *and* nurture. Developmentalists agree that no period is either critical or sensitive unless a combination of genetic and environmental factors makes it so. Most of the time, for most people, development proceeds smoothly. Almost every human develops toes, language, and everything else that characterizes our species. Even though people may look, act, or talk in ways that are unlike your way or my way, they are usually developing well.

difference-equals-deficit error
The mistaken belief that a deviation from some norm is necessarily inferior to behavior or characteristics that meet the standard.

DEFICIT, OR JUST DIFFERENCE? To assume otherwise—to conclude that someone who is different from us is inferior—is to commit a mistake known as the **difference-equals-deficit error**. Such mistakes are one reason we need science. Differences are not necessarily wrong or right, better or worse; the scientific method is needed for accurate assessments of deviations from the norm. In fact, a difference may be an asset, not a liability, in many areas of life (Marschark & Spencer, 2003).

The error of assuming that a difference is a deficit may be made clearer with an example. It was once assumed that deaf children were not only different, but deficient—unable to learn what hearing children could. It was assumed that that was simply their nature; they were thus nurtured accordingly, excluded from most schools. As a result, deaf children could not talk, read, or even think as well as other children could.

Their problems were particularly glaring with regard to reading. Since fluency in language precedes fluid reading, deaf children could not recognize words when they saw them on the page. If they were admitted to school, their teachers tried to make them as similar to hearing children as possible: Normal language (speech) was taught, and the use of sign language was forbidden.

However, when researchers stopped assuming that differences were deficits, they discovered that sign language activates the language areas of the brain and that deaf children can communicate as well, and as quickly, as hearing children. If they are taught appropriately, their intellect matches that of other children and adults (Schick et al., 2007). They can become fluent in reading the printed word (Goldin-Meadow & Mayberry, 2001).

Researchers find that all children learn better when they use gestures as well as words (S. W. Cook et al., 2008). Education is being transformed by such discoveries—advances that were not expected when differences were assumed to be deficits and when the role of nurture was ignored.

SUSAN MEISELAS / MAGNUM PHOTOS

Just Different, Not Deficient A student uses Nicaraguan Sign Language, invented in the 1970s by children at the school for the deaf that she attends in Managua. Sign language conveys meaning perfectly well and is not inferior to speech, as most educators once assumed.

● **FOR DEEPER REFLECTION** How can you decide whether a difference really is a deficit?

Observing Changes over Time

The third crucial element in the definition of developmental science is the issue of whether individuals *change or remain the same over time*. The science of human development studies all the transformations and consistencies of human life, from conception until death.

The fact that change is lifelong is obvious now, but 50 years ago the study of development was primarily the study of children, who were thought to grow in stages (infancy, toddlerhood, early childhood, and so on). It was thought that once people were fully grown, they stopped changing; puberty was considered the final stage.

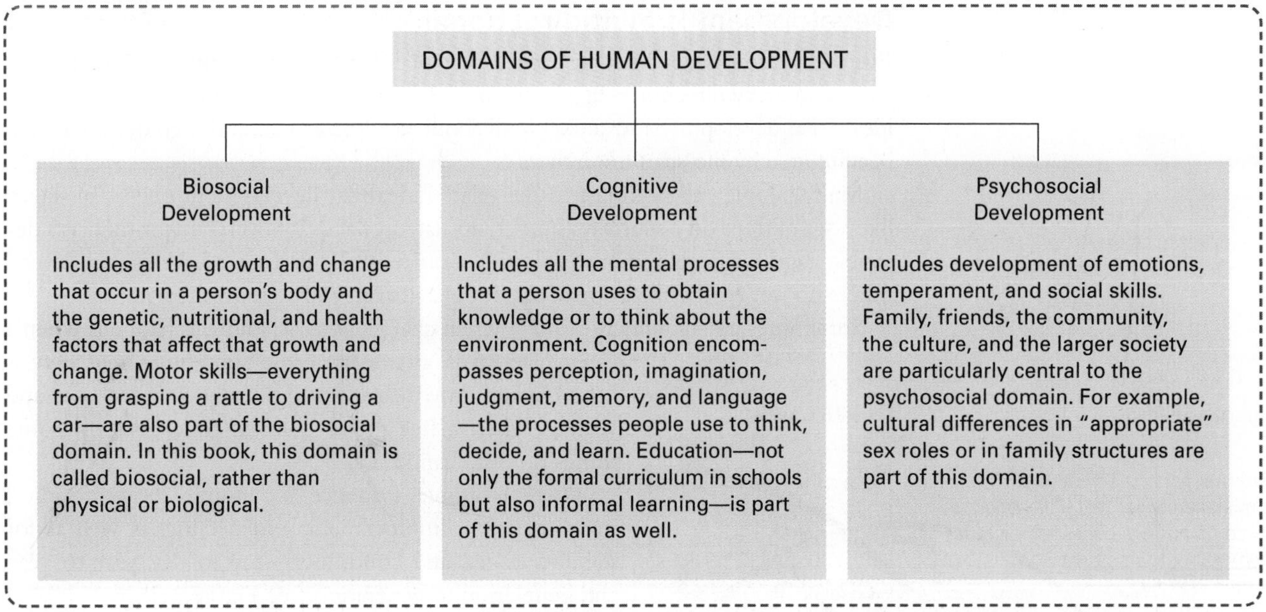

DOMAINS OF HUMAN DEVELOPMENT

Biosocial Development

Includes all the growth and change that occur in a person's body and the genetic, nutritional, and health factors that affect that growth and change. Motor skills—everything from grasping a rattle to driving a car—are also part of the biosocial domain. In this book, this domain is called biosocial, rather than physical or biological.

Cognitive Development

Includes all the mental processes that a person uses to obtain knowledge or to think about the environment. Cognition encompasses perception, imagination, judgment, memory, and language—the processes people use to think, decide, and learn. Education—not only the formal curriculum in schools but also informal learning—is part of this domain as well.

Psychosocial Development

Includes development of emotions, temperament, and social skills. Family, friends, the community, the culture, and the larger society are particularly central to the psychosocial domain. For example, cultural differences in "appropriate" sex roles or in family structures are part of this domain.

FIGURE 1.1 The Three Domains The division of human development into three domains makes it easier to study, but remember that very few factors belong exclusively to one domain or another. Development is not piecemeal but holistic: Each aspect of development is related to all three domains.

Furthermore, each developmental advance was thought to build on previous development in that specific area: Running evolved from walking, talking from babbling, and so on. To make it easier to study, development was often segmented into stages and three domains—physical, intellectual, and social (or, as in this book, *biosocial, cognitive,* and *psychosocial*; see Figure 1.1), each of which was divided into many specific substages and subdomains.

Such divisions are useful because it is impossible to consider all ages and domains simultaneously. All developmental scholars and textbooks use ages and topics to organize and focus their study. Yet developmentalists recognize that each domain and each stage affects the others in a "reciprocal connection" (P. B. Baltes et al., 2006, p. 644).

KEYPoints

- Developmental study is a science, following the five steps of the scientific method.
- All kinds of developing persons are studied, to learn what is universal as well as what is unique to each individual.
- Some periods of life are critical or sensitive for certain developments.
- Differences among people do not indicate that one way is better than another.

The Life-Span Perspective

The **life-span perspective**, as first set forth by Paul and Margaret Baltes and their associates (P. B. Baltes et al., 2006; Staudinger & Lindenberger, 2003), is an approach to the study of human development that takes into account all phases of life, not just childhood or adulthood. The life-span perspective notes that development throughout life is (1) multidirectional, (2) multicontextual, (3) multicultural, (4) multidisciplinary, and (5) plastic. Each of these five insights into the nature of development merits further explanation here.

life-span perspective An approach to the study of human development that takes into account all phases of life, not just childhood or adulthood.

Development Is Multidirectional

Every direction is apparent in each aspect of life. Over time, human characteristics change in every direction—up, down, or straight across as time goes on. The traditional idea—that development advanced until about age 20, steadied, and then declined—has been refuted by life-span research.

Many people still hold fast to the related idea that development occurs in stages, like a set of steps on a stairway (up, flat, up, flat, up, flat . . .). Several major theorists describe stages of development (you will soon read about three of them), but several others do not (you will also read about behaviorism and systems theories).

Sometimes *discontinuity* is evident, when change occurs rapidly, as happens when a caterpillar turns into a butterfly. Sometimes *continuity* is found, when growth happens gradually over each day and year, as when a tree grows taller as time goes by. Some things do not change at all.

There is ample evidence for simple growth, radical transformation, improvement, and decline, as well as for stability, stages, and continuity—day to day, year to year, and generation to generation (see Figure 1.2).

As the Baltes team emphasized, a multidirectional perspective enables researchers to recognize that gains and losses often occur together as people age and that losses may lead to gains, or vice versa (P. B. Baltes et al., 2006). Furthermore, changes in one area may spread to other areas of development, and thus interactions between domains must be considered.

This idea is reflected by the use of the term *multidimensional* to describe development. For example, when a man's wife dies, his physical, intellectual, and social well-being often declines. One study found that, in the month after their spouse died, widowers entered nursing homes three times more often than other men of similar age, education, and health (Nihtilä & Martikainen, 2008). Some widowers, in contrast, expand their social worlds after a period of mourning, and that change may trigger changes in the direction of other dimensions of life.

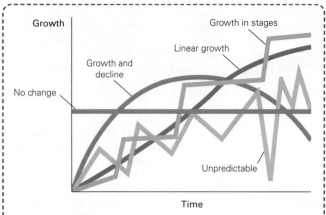

FIGURE 1.2 Patterns of Developmental Growth Many patterns of developmental growth have been discovered by careful research. Although linear (or near-linear) progress seems most common, scientists now find that almost no aspect of human change follows the linear pattern exactly.

What Will He Do Without Her? With the death of his wife, life has suddenly changed for this man. The direction that change will take is difficult to predict. Compared with other men their age, widowers are more likely to die *or* to marry.

Development Is Multicontextual

The second insight from the life-span perspective is that development is multicontextual. It takes place within many contexts, including physical surroundings (climate, noise, population density, etc.) and family patterns. The impact of various contexts is explained throughout this book.

Developmentalists who study the life span take dozens of contexts into account. Here we highlight two social contexts whose influence may not ordinarily be obvious: the historical and the economic contexts.

THE HISTORICAL CONTEXT All persons born within a few years of one another are said to be a **cohort**, a group defined by its members' shared age, which means that they travel through life together. Each member of a cohort is affected by the values, events, technologies, and culture of his or her era. For example, attitudes about war differ for the cohorts who came of age in the United States during World War II, the Vietnam War, the Gulf War, and the Iraq War.

Sometimes demographic characteristics rather than headline-making events constitute the historical context. For example, the cohort born between 1946 and 1964, called the baby-boom generation because it represented a sizable spike in the birth rate, will experience quite a different old age than did earlier cohorts. Their large numbers are influencing government policies regarding Social Security, Medicare, and other programs for the elderly.

If you doubt that national trends and events touch individuals, consider your first name—a word chosen especially for you. Look at Table 1.1, which lists the most popular names for boys and girls born into cohorts 20 years apart, beginning in 1928. Your name and your reaction to it are influenced by the era.

"And this is Charles, our web-master."

Computer Expert in a Baseball Cap Cohort differences become most apparent when new technology appears. Which age group is most likely to download music onto iPods or to send text messages on cell phones?

cohort
A group defined by the shared age of its members, who, because they were born at about the same time, move through life together, experiencing the same historical events and cultural shifts.

TABLE 1.1 Which First Names for U.S. Girls and Boys Were Most Popular in 1928, 1948, 1968, 1988, and 2008?

Year	Top Five Girls' Names	Top Five Boys' Names
———	Mary, Betty, Dorothy, Helen, Margaret	Robert, John, James, William, Charles
———	Lisa, Michelle, Kimberly, Jennifer, Mary	Michael, David, John, James, Robert
———	Emma, Isabella, Emily, Madison, Ava	Jacob, Michael, Ethan, Joshua, Daniel
———	Linda, Mary, Barbara, Patricia, Susan	James, Robert, John, William, David
———	Jessica, Ashley, Amanda, Sarah, Jennifer	Michael, Christopher, Matthew, Joshua, Andrew

Source: Social Security Administration Web site (http://www.ssa.gov/OACT/babynames), retrieved June 1, 2009.

Guess First If your answers, in order from top to bottom, were 1928, 1968, 2008, 1948, and 1988, you are excellent at detecting cohort influences. If you made a mistake, perhaps that's because the data are compiled from applications for Social Security numbers, so the names of those who did not get a Social Security number are omitted.

Not the Typical Path This woman's lifelong ambition is to walk the 2,160-mile Appalachian Trail from Maine to Georgia. She is considerably more active than the average member of her cohort.

AP PHOTO / CHARLES REX ARBOGAST

The Culture of Poverty In this southern Illinois neighborhood, littered yards are part of a "culture of poverty" that also includes poor nutrition, substandard housing, and an average life expectancy of 52 years.

OBSERVATION QUIZ
A 13-year-old is shown in this photo, trying to garden. Can you find her? (see answer, page 12) →

socioeconomic status (SES)
A person's position in society as determined by income, wealth, occupation, education, and place of residence. (Sometimes called *social class*.)

THE SOCIOECONOMIC CONTEXT Another influential context of development is the socioeconomic one, reflected in a person's **socioeconomic status**, abbreviated **SES**. Sometimes SES is called *social class* (as in *middle class* or *working class*). SES reflects income, wealth, occupation, education, and place of residence.

Suppose a family in the United States is made up of an infant, an unemployed mother, and a father who earns $15,000 a year. Their SES would be considered low if the wage earner was an illiterate dishwasher living in an urban slum, but it would be considered much higher if the wage earner was a postdoctoral student living on campus and teaching part time.

As this example illustrates, SES brings advantages and disadvantages, opportunities and limitations—all affecting housing, nutrition, knowledge, and habits. Although low income obviously limits a person, other factors (such as education) can make poverty better or worse. Indeed, annual wages may be an inadequate measure of wealth: One study found that financial assets over a longer period affected children's learning more than their parents' current income did (Yeung & Conley, 2008).

A question for developmentalists is: When does low SES do most damage to human development? In infancy, a family's low SES often means inferior medical care and malnutrition, which could stunt a baby's brain development; in adulthood, job and marriage prospects are reduced as SES falls; in late adulthood, accumulated stress (called *allostatic load*, explained later) overwhelms the body's reserves, causing disease and death. Which of these effects is worst? The answer is not clear; SES is a powerful influence on development at every age.

Development Is Multicultural

When social scientists use the term *culture*, they are referring to the "patterns of behavior that are passed from one generation to the next . . . [and] that serve as the resources for the current life of a social group" (Cole, 2005, p. 49). The social group may be citizens of a nation, residents of a region within a nation, members of an ethnic group, people living in one neighborhood, or even students in a college class.

Any group may have its own culture—its own values, customs, clothes, dwellings, cuisine, and assumptions. Culture affects every action—indeed, every thought. Thus, to understand anyone's development, scientists consider the culture in which that person is immersed. Have you ever wondered why some of your fellow students use highlighters, study in the library, or call professors by their first names, while others do not? The answer may have to do with the culture of the college, of students' hometowns, or of students' families.

The fact that there is a culture of college has practical implications. Especially for those who are first in their families to attend college, it may take time to understand the routines and expectations of higher education.

I have a bright and conscientious friend who sobbed when she failed her first semester at Wesleyan University. Her parents had not attended college, but they believed that education could transform her life; consequently, they had always checked her homework. It was hard for her to take responsibility for the completeness and correctness of her own work when she left home to attend college.

Fortunately, after two semesters at less demanding colleges, my friend was readmitted to Wesleyan and graduated three years later. Similarly, if students living at home can survive their first year at college, adjusting their family culture to the college culture, they are likely to stay to complete their degree.

Another practical application of the multicultural perspective arises for students who study in other nations. If they ignore cultural variations or consider differences to be deficits, they may be inadvertently rude or insulting.

LEARNING WITHIN A CULTURE Russian developmentalist Lev Vygotsky (1896–1934) was a leader in describing the interaction between culture and education (Wertsch & Tulviste, 2005). Vygotsky noted how members of each of the many cultures in his native land (which included Asians and Europeans, of many religions) taught their children the beliefs and habits they would need as adults.

Vygotsky (whose views are discussed in more detail in Chapter 5) believed that *guided participation*, the process by which mentors guide novices to master the skills and habits expected within a culture, is universal. Guided participation can occur via direct instruction in school but more often happens informally, through "mutual involvement in several widespread cultural practices with great importance for learning: narratives, routines, and play" (Rogoff, 2003, p. 285).

Barbara Rogoff, who studies cultural transmission in Guatemalan, Mexican, Chinese, and U.S. families, has conducted research inspired by Vygotsky. She cites many examples of how adults guide children, noting that clashes may occur between parents and teachers of different cultures. In one such misunderstanding, a teacher praised a student to his mother:

> **Teacher:** Your son is talking well in class. He is speaking up a lot.
> **Mother:** I am sorry.

[Rogoff, 2003, p. 311; from Crago, 1992, p. 496]

ETHNICITY, RACE, AND CULTURE Confusion arises whenever people—scientists or nonscientists—refer to *ethnic groups, races,* and *cultures.* Each of these terms has a distinct meaning, although many people confuse them. The following definitions may help to dispel this confusion.

People of an **ethnic group** share certain attributes, almost always including ancestral heritage and often national origin, religion, culture, and language (Whitfield & McClearn, 2005). Although people of a particular ethnicity may share a culture, this is not always so; by the same token, people could share a culture without having the same ancestors.

JUPITER IMAGES

What's for Dinner? Markets are universal, but each culture has a unique mix of products, stores, and salespeople. Compare this floating food market in Bangkok, Thailand, with a North American supermarket.

ethnic group
People whose ancestors were born in the same region and who often share a language, culture, and religion.

ZHOU GUANGLI / XINHUA PRESS / CORBIS

Heritage Aloft At least 10 major ethnic groups make up China's population of 1.3 billion. This man shows his grandson the multicolored lanterns displayed on Lantern Day in Hangzhou. Other nations, and other parts of China, have no Lantern Day festival, but all have special traditional celebrations of their own.

social construction
An idea that is based on shared perceptions, not on objective reality. Many age-related terms, such as *childhood*, *adolescence*, *yuppie*, and *senior citizen*, are social constructions.

ANSWER TO OBSERVATION QUIZ
(from page 10) Carolyn Whitaker, in an orange shirt, is at the far left. ●

epigenetic
Referring to the effects of environmental forces on the expression of an individual's, or a species', genetic inheritance.

The term *race* has been used to categorize people on the basis of biology, particularly outward appearance. However, appearance is not a reliable indicator of biological differences or developmental traits. For instance, about 95 percent of the genetic differences between one person and another occur *within*, not between, supposed racial groups. Skin color is often considered the most salient racial marker, but genetic variation is particularly apparent among dark-skinned people whose ancestors were African (Tishkoff et al., 2009).

Thus, race is misleading as a biological category. Instead, race is a **social construction**, an idea created by society. Unlike biology, social constructions can change within a few years, affecting the development of each cohort.

Social constructions are not without power. Perceived racial differences lead to discrimination, and racial self-concept affects cognition (see the discussion of *stereotype threat* in Chapter 11). As one team of psychologists expressed it, "Race is a social construction wherein individuals [who are] labeled as being of different races on the basis of physical characteristics are often treated as though they belong to biologically defined groups" (Goldston et al., 2008, p. 14). Differential treatment is a potent influence on development.

Development Is Multidisciplinary

Scientists often specialize, studying one phenomenon in one species within one domain at one age. Such specialization provides a deeper understanding of the rhythms of vocalization among 3-month-old infants, for instance, or of the effects of alcohol on adolescent mice, or of widows' relationships with their grown children. (The results of these studies inform later sections of this book.)

However, human development is such a vast subject that it requires insight and information from many scientists, past and present, in many disciplines. As one expert explains, "The study of development is a huge community enterprise that spans generations and many disciplines" (C. L. Moore, 2002, p. 74). Almost every topic in human development has benefited from multidisciplinary research. Examples follow, showing the impact of research in genetics and neuroscience, two relatively new disciplines useful to developmentalists.

GENETICS AND AN EPIGENETIC UNDERSTANDING The importance of multidisciplinary research became particularly apparent with the onset of genetic analysis. The final decades of the twentieth century witnessed dozens of surprising genetic discoveries, leading to a momentous accomplishment in the twenty-first century: The Human Genome Project mapped all the genes that make up a person. To the surprise of many developmentalists, every trait—psychological as well as physical—is influenced by genes (see Chapter 2).

At first, some scientists thought that genes *determined* everything, that humans became whatever their genes destined them to be—crusaders, killers, or ordinary people. But multidisciplinary research has quickly revealed the limitations of this hypothesis. Yes, genes affect every aspect of behavior. But even identical twins, who have exactly the same genes as each other, are not truly identical—biologically, psychologically, or socially (Poulsen et al., 2007).

The fact that genes alone do not determine development soon led to the realization that all important human characteristics are **epigenetic**. In "epigenetic programming . . . health and behavior are mediated through altered gene expression" (Moffitt et al., 2006, p. 6).

The prefix *epi-* means "with," "around," "before," "after," "beyond," or "near." The word *epigenetic,* therefore, refers to the environmental factors that surround the genes, affecting genetic expression. Some "epi" influences occur in the first hours of life, as biochemical elements silence certain genes in a process called *methylation*. Other epigenetic influences occur later, including some that impede development (e.g., injury, temperature extremes, drug abuse, and crowding) as well as some that facilitate it (e.g., nourishing food, loving care, and active play).

The inevitable epigenetic interaction between genes and the environment (nature and nurture) is illustrated in Figure 1.3. That simple diagram, with arrows going up and down over time, has been redrawn and reprinted dozens of times to emphasize that genes interact with environmental conditions again and again in each person's life (A. Gottlieb, 2003).

Much epigenetic research has focused on serious diseases that are known to be genetic, including cancer, schizophrenia, and autism (Saey, 2008). No social scientist doubts that the discipline of biology, particularly genetics, helps predict, diagnose, and treat every disease. Yet even medical doctors, trained in biology and chemistry, recognize that many other disciplines provide insight and understanding. They acknowledge that "epigenetics [is] at the epicenter of modern medicine" (Feinberg, 2008, p. 1345).

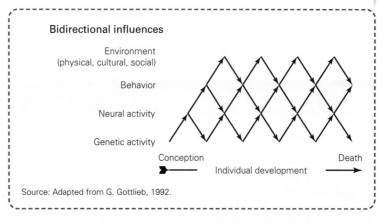

FIGURE 1.3 An Epigenetic Model of Development Notice that there are as many arrows going down as going up, at all levels. Although development begins with genes at conception, it requires that all four factors interact.

NEUROSCIENCE MEETS THE BOYS OF NEW ZEALAND One of the human problems that developmentalists continually seek to understand is the fact that some young people become violent, hurting others as well as themselves. Sociologists, psychologists, and economists have found some clues to youth violence. Many factors in the social context contribute, including past child abuse and current SES. The violent delinquent is often a boy who was beaten in childhood and who now lives in a violent, drug-filled, crowded neighborhood (Maas et al., 2008).

Yet some boys who live in such conditions never become violent. A fourth discipline—biology—suggests why. One genetic variant occurs in the code for the enzyme monoamine oxidase A (MAOA), which affects chemicals in the brain called *neurotransmitters*. This gene comes in two versions, one producing higher levels of the enzyme than the other. Both versions are quite normal; about one-third of all people whose genes have been analyzed have the lower-MAOA version.

A famous developmental study began with virtually every child born in Dunedin, New Zealand, between April 1, 1972, and March 31, 1973. The children and their families were examined on dozens of measures from early childhood on, providing a wealth of developmental data. One measure was how the children were treated; another measure was which variant of the MAOA gene they had inherited.

The Dunedin study found that boys who were mistreated by their parents were about twice as likely to be overly aggressive (to develop a conduct disorder and to be violent, antisocial, and eventually convicted of a violent crime) if, *and only if*, they had the low-MAOA gene instead of the high-MAOA one (Caspi et al., 2002).

Does this mean that becoming a violent criminal is inevitable for those with less of that enzyme? No. As Figure 1.4 shows, *if* they were not maltreated, boys with the low-MAOA gene were even more likely than those with the high-MAOA gene to become law-abiding, peaceable adults.

In practical terms, this means that many factors, noted by many disciplines, combine to protect or undermine a person's healthy development. Often researchers in one discipline discover something

FIGURE 1.4 Genetic Origins for Violent Crime Two variables—parental treatment and a variant of the gene that produces the enzyme MAOA—interact to affect the likelihood that a child will commit a violent crime. Of the boys in the "probable maltreatment" category, 10 percent were convicted of a violent crime if their MAOA level was high, but 26 percent were convicted if their MAOA was low.

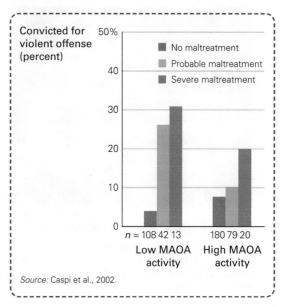

that intrigues scientists in other fields. An important recent example of this process is research on *mirror neurons*. These are brain cells that allow a person to vicariously experience what he or she actually only observes, as the following explains.

A VIEW FROM SCIENCE

Mirror Neurons

About a decade ago, neuroscientists were surprised to realize that certain parts of a monkey's brain responded to actions the monkey observed as if the monkey had actually performed those actions itself. For example, when a monkey saw a monkey in another cage reach for a banana, the same brain areas were activated (lit up in brain scans) in both monkeys.

The next step was to find exactly where in the monkey's brain the activated area was located. The researchers found certain neurons, which they dubbed **mirror neurons**, in the F5 area of the premotor cortex. Once they had located these neurons in monkeys, they found them in humans as well (Rizzolatti & Craighero, 2004).

Human brains seem to mirror much more than actions like reaching for a banana. Scientists "turned to the human brain and found neural activity that mirrors not only the movement but also the intentions, sensations, and emotions of those around us" (G. Miller, 2005, p. 945). Indeed, "The human mirror neuron system may allow us to go beyond imitating the observed motor acts of others to infer their intentions and perhaps even their states of mind" (Coward, 2008, p. 1494).

Scientists in many disciplines continue to explore the implications of this discovery (Rizzolatti & Sinigaglia, 2008; Soekadar et al., 2008):

- Anthropologists think that mirror neurons might explain cultural transmission and social organization (Adenzato & Garbarini, 2006; Morrison, 2002).

- Psychopathologists connect autism with lost mirror neurons (J. H. G. Williams et al., 2006).

- Psychiatrists believe that abnormalities in this part of the brain may be involved in some symptoms of schizophrenia (Buccino & Amore, 2008).

- Linguists wonder whether mirror neurons aid language learning (Buccino et al., 2004).

- Social psychologists think that mirror neurons help people understand one another's intentions and pain (J. C. Harris, 2003; Iacoboni, 2009).

- Cognitive psychologists suggest that mirror neurons explain newborns' ability to imitate what they see (Diamond & Amso, 2008).

Although scientists are excited by these multidisciplinary possibilities, they are cautious as well. Researchers in none of these disciplines consider mirror neurons a *proven* explanation.

Research on human brains is notoriously difficult. Neural networks are complex; mirror neurons alone certainly do not explain all of human learning or social responsiveness (Wheatley et al., 2007). Yet because developmental research is multidisciplinary, thousands of scientists in a wide variety of fields are studying implications suggested by the discovery of mirror neurons in a monkey's brain.

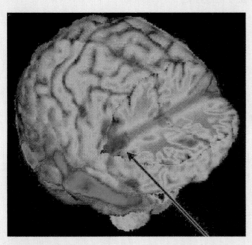

NATACHA PISARENKO / AP

Lighting Up In the photograph at left, the arrow points to a web of neurons that are activated not only when a monkey uses motor abilities (as in reaching for a banana) but also when the monkey sees another perform that action. At right, these toddlers in Buenos Aires may be exhibiting mirror neurons at work as they get ready to join other fans in cheering on Argentina's soccer team in a match against Peru.

Development Is Plastic

The term *plasticity* denotes two complementary aspects of development: Human traits can be molded (as plastic can be), yet people maintain a certain durability of identity (as plastic does). The concept of plasticity in development provides both hope and realism—hope because change is possible, and realism because development builds on what has come before.

PLASTICITY AND DAVID'S FUTURE In some ways, plasticity underlies all the other four characteristics of development. My nephew David, whose story opened this chapter, required heart surgery two days after he was born and again at age 5. His first eye surgery, at 6 months, destroyed one eye. As he grew older, malformations of his thumbs, ankles, feet, teeth, spine, and brain became evident. Predictions were dire: Some people wondered why his parents did not place him in an institution. As a young child, David was severely retarded.

Plasticity is evident in David's development over the decades. Remember, plasticity cannot erase a person's genetic endowment, childhood experiences, or permanent damage. David's disabilities are always with him (he still lives at home), and he may be losing vision in his remaining eye. But by age 10, David had skipped a year of school and was a fifth-grader, reading at the 11th-grade level. He learned a second and a third language. In young adulthood, after one failing semester, he earned several As and graduated from college.

David now works as a translator of German texts, which he enjoys because "I like providing a service to scholars, giving them access to something they would otherwise not have" (personal communication, 2007). As his aunt, I have seen him repeatedly defy pessimistic predictions. All five of the characteristics of the life-span perspective are evident in David's life, as summarized in Table 1.2.

mirror neurons Cells in an observer's brain that respond to an action performed by someone else in the same way they would if the observer had actually performed that action.

TABLE 1.2 Five Characteristics of Development

Characteristic	Application in David's Story
Multidirectional. Change occurs in every direction, not always in a straight line. Gains and losses, predictable growth, and unexpected transformations are evident.	David's development seemed static (or even regressive, as when early surgery destroyed one eye) but then accelerated each time he entered a new school or college.
Multidisciplinary. Numerous academic fields—especially psychology, biology, education, and sociology, but also neuroscience, economics, religion, anthropology, history, medicine, genetics, and many more—contribute insights.	Two disciplines were particularly critical: medicine (David would have died without advances in surgery on newborns) and education (special educators guided him and his parents many times).
Multicontextual. Human lives are embedded in many contexts, including historical conditions, economic constraints, and family patterns.	The high SES of David's family made it possible for him to receive daily medical and educational care. His two older brothers protected him.
Multicultural. Many cultures—not just between nations but also within them—affect how people develop.	Appalachia, where David and his family lived, has a particular culture, including acceptance of people with disabilities and willingness to help families in need. Those aspects of that culture benefited David and his family.
Plasticity. Every individual, and every trait within each individual, can be altered at any point in the life span. Change is ongoing, although neither random nor easy.	David's measured IQ changed from about 40 (severely mentally retarded) to about 130 (far above average), and his physical disabilities became less crippling as he matured.

PLASTICITY AND DEPRESSION IN PARENT AND CHILD Even in traits that originate with genes, such as depression, plasticity is evident. Indeed, one reason that ongoing discoveries in genetics and neuroscience are thrilling to many developmentalists is that they reveal plasticity. This may seem paradoxical, because every person's genes are set at conception, 38 weeks before birth, and because basic brain structures are formed prenatally, beginning in the third week after conception.

But the same research that has found the power of the 20,000 or so human genes (half of them for brain development) also finds that nutrition, education, and child rearing are crucial; epigenetic factors enhance or dampen the effect of every gene. This is especially true for emotions, impulses, and anxieties, all of which originate in the brain and develop during childhood (Fries & Pollak, 2007; M. H. Johnson, 2007).

There is no doubt that depression is partly genetic—a matter of brain chemicals that make some people feel sad and uninterested in life. There is also no doubt that depression is developmental, with rates of depression increasing and decreasing at certain points of the life span (Kapornai & Vetró, 2008). For instance, the incidence of clinical depression suddenly increases in early adolescence, particularly among girls.

Child-rearing practices have an impact as well. Typically, depressed mothers smile and talk to their infants less, and the infants become less active and verbal. A researcher who has investigated mother–infant interaction for decades relates that he once asked nondepressed mothers of 3-month-old infants to simulate depression for three minutes:

> The mothers were asked to speak in a monotone, to keep their faces flat and expressionless, to slouch back in their chair, to minimize touch, and to imagine that they felt tired and blue. The infants . . . reacted strongly, . . . cycling among states of wariness, disengagement, and distress with brief bids to their mother to resume her normal affective state. Importantly, the infants continued to be distressed and disengaged . . . after the mothers resumed normal interactive behavior.
>
> *[Tronick, 2007, p. 306]*

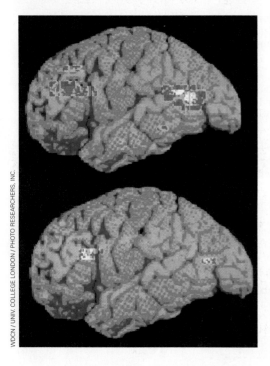

Red Means Stop At top, the red areas on this PET scan show abnormally low metabolic activity and blood flow in a depressed person's brain, in contrast to the normal brain at bottom.

WDCN / UNIV. COLLEGE LONDON / PHOTO RESEARCHERS, INC.

Nevertheless, research over the years of early childhood finds plasticity in depression. A 1-year-old who is depressed is likely to also be depressed at age 6 if the mother is still sad but is likely to be much happier if the mother's mood has lifted.

One detailed study traced this connection in multiple ways (Ashman et al., 2008). Various measures, including heart and brain activity, were first taken when the children were 14 months old and then repeated at ages 2, 3½, 4½, and 6½.

Physiological, psychological, and social data showed that the mother's depression over the years had a major impact. Children of mothers whose depression decreased were less aggressive (as rated by their kindergarten teachers on such observations as "hits other children") than children whose mothers were continually depressed.

The researchers note that "consistent with previous research, contextual risk factors such as low marital satisfaction and high family conflict were found to mediate the relationship between maternal depression and child behavior measures" (Ashman et al., 2008, p. 74). They suggest that the child's home environment might change "children's patterns of brain activity as well as their behavioral outcomes" (p. 73). This is evidence of plasticity in each domain—the biosocial, the cognitive, and the psychosocial.

Similar conclusions arise from research on adults with depression: Many genetic, biochemical, and neurological factors distinguish them from other adults (Gotlib & Hamilton, 2008). However, their moods and behaviors are powerfully affected by experiences and cognitions (Gotlib & Hammen, 2002; Monroe et al., 2007).

KEY Points

- Development is multidirectional, with gains and losses evident at every stage and in every domain.
- Among the many contexts of development are historical circumstances and economic conditions.
- Culture always influences development, which must be studied using many academic disciplines.
- Each person's development is plastic, connected to prior events but also open to change.

Theories of Human Development

As you read earlier in this chapter, the scientific method begins with observations, questions, and theories (step 1). These lead to specific hypotheses that can be tested (step 2). A *theory* is a comprehensive and organized explanation of many phenomena; a *hypothesis* is more limited and may be proven false. Theories are generalities; hypotheses are specific. Data are collected through research (step 3), conclusions are drawn (step 4), and the results are reported (step 5).

Although developmental scientists are intrigued by all their observations, they use theories to sharpen their perceptions and to organize the thousands of behaviors they observe every day.

Thus, a **developmental theory** is a systematic statement of principles and generalizations that provides a framework for understanding how and why people change as they grow older. Theorists "try to make sense out of observations . . . [and] construct a story of the human journey from infancy through childhood or adulthood" (P. H. Miller, 2002, p. 2). Theories connect facts with patterns, weaving the details of life into a meaningful whole.

Imagine building a house. A person could have a heap of lumber, nails, and other materials, but without a plan and workers, the heap cannot become a home. Likewise, observations of human development are essential raw materials, but theories put them together. Kurt Lewin (1943) once quipped, "Nothing is as practical as a good theory."

You will encounter dozens of theories throughout this text, each one useful in organizing data and developing hypotheses. Four theories that apply to the entire life span are introduced here; more details about each of them appear later in this text.

Psychoanalytic Theory

Inner drives and motives are the foundation of **psychoanalytic theory**. These basic underlying forces are thought to influence every aspect of thinking and behavior, from the smallest details of daily life to the crucial choices of a lifetime (Dijksterhuis & Nordgren, 2006).

FREUD'S STAGES Psychoanalytic theory originated with Sigmund Freud (1856–1939), an Austrian physician who treated patients suffering from mental illness. He listened to their accounts of dreams and fantasies and constructed an elaborate, multifaceted theory.

developmental theory
A group of ideas, assumptions, and generalizations that interpret and illuminate the thousands of observations that have been made about human growth. A developmental theory provides a framework for explaining the patterns and problems of development.

psychoanalytic theory
A theory of human development that holds that irrational, unconscious drives and motives, often originating in childhood, underlie human behavior.

Freud at Work In addition to being the world's first psychoanalyst, Sigmund Freud was a prolific writer. His many papers and case histories, primarily descriptions of his patients' bizarre symptoms and unconscious sexual urges, helped make the psychoanalytic perspective a dominant force for much of the twentieth century.

AKG / PHOTO RESEARCHERS, INC.

According to Freud, development in the first six years occurs in three stages, each characterized by sexual pleasure centered on a particular part of the body. Infants experience the *oral stage*, so named because the erotic body part is the mouth, followed by the *anal stage* in early childhood, with the focus on the anus. In the preschool years (the *phallic stage*), the penis becomes a source of pride and fear for boys and a reason for sadness and envy for girls.

In middle childhood comes *latency*, a quiet period that ends when one enters the *genital stage* at puberty. Freud was the most famous theorist who thought that development stopped after puberty and that the genital stage continued throughout adulthood (see Table 1.3).

Freud maintained that at each stage, sensual satisfaction (from stimulation of the mouth, anus, or genitals) is linked to developmental needs, challenges, and conflicts. How people experience and resolve these conflicts—especially those related to weaning (oral), toilet training (anal), male roles (phallic), and sexual pleasure (genital)—determines personality patterns, because "the early stages provide the foundation for adult behavior" (Salkind, 2004, p. 125).

ERIKSON'S STAGES Many of Freud's followers became famous theorists themselves. The most notable in human development was Erik Erikson (1902–1994), who described eight developmental stages, each characterized by a challenging developmental crisis (summarized in Table 1.3). Although Erikson's first five stages build on Freud's theory, he also described three adult stages, perhaps because in his own adult life he made several dramatic moves. He was a wandering artist in Italy, a teacher in Austria, and a Harvard professor in the United States.

Erikson named two polarities at each stage (which is why the word *versus* is used in the name of each one), but he recognized the possibility of many outcomes between these opposites (Erikson, 1963). For most people, development at each stage leads to neither extreme. For instance, the generativity-versus-stagnation stage of adulthood rarely involves a person who is completely stagnant—no children, no work, no creativity. Instead, it is a matter of degree: Most people are at least somewhat generative.

Erikson, like Freud, believed that problems of adult life echo the conflicts of childhood. For example, an adult who has difficulty establishing a secure, close rela-

CORBIS

What's in a Name?—Erik Erikson
As a young man, this neo-Freudian changed his last name to the one we know him by. What do you think his choice means? (See the caption to the next photograph.)

Who Are We? The most famous of Erikson's eight crises is the identity crisis, during adolescence, when young people find their own answer to the question "Who am I?" Erikson did this for himself by choosing a last name that, with his first name, implies "son of myself" (Erik, Erik's son). These children in Northern Ireland may be smoking because their search for identity is taking place in a sociocultural context that allows an unhealthy path toward adulthood.

GIDEON MENDEL / CORBIS

TABLE 1.3 Comparison of Freud's Psychosexual and Erikson's Psychosocial Stages

Approximate Age	Freud (Psychosexual)	Erikson (Psychosocial)
Birth to 1 year	*Oral Stage* The lips, tongue, and gums are the focus of pleasurable sensations in the baby's body, and sucking and feeding are the most stimulating activities.	*Trust vs. Mistrust* Babies either trust that others will care for their basic needs, including nourishment, warmth, cleanliness, and physical contact, *or* develop mistrust about the care of others.
1–3 years	*Anal Stage* The anus is the focus of pleasurable sensations in the baby's body, and toilet training is the most important activity.	*Autonomy vs. Shame and Doubt* Children either become self-sufficient in many activities, including toileting, feeding, walking, exploring, and talking, *or* doubt their own abilities.
3–6 years	*Phallic Stage* The phallus, or penis, is the most important body part, and pleasure is derived from genital stimulation. Boys are proud of their penises; girls wonder why they don't have one.	*Initiative vs. Guilt* Children either want to undertake many adultlike activities *or* internalize the limits and prohibitions set by parents. They feel either adventurous *or* guilty.
6–11 years	*Latency* Not really a stage, latency is an interlude during which sexual needs are quiet and children put psychic energy into conventional activities like schoolwork and sports.	*Industry vs. Inferiority* Children busily learn to be competent and productive in mastering new skills *or* feel inferior, unable to do anything as well as they wish they could.
Adolescence	*Genital Stage* The genitals are the focus of pleasurable sensations, and the young person seeks sexual stimulation and sexual satisfaction in heterosexual relationships.	*Identity vs. Role Confusion* Adolescents try to figure out "Who am I?" They establish sexual, political, and vocational identities *or* are confused about what roles to play.
Adulthood	Freud believed that the genital stage lasts throughout adulthood. He also said that the goal of a healthy life is "to love and to work."	*Intimacy vs. Isolation* Young adults seek companionship and love *or* become isolated from others because they fear rejection and disappointment. *Generativity vs. Stagnation* Middle-aged adults contribute to the next generation through meaningful work, creative activities, and raising a family, *or* they stagnate. *Integrity vs. Despair* Older adults try to make sense out of their lives, either seeing life as a meaningful whole *or* despairing at goals never reached.

tionship with a life partner (intimacy versus isolation) may never have resolved the first crisis of early infancy (trust versus mistrust). Erikson believed that earlier crises leave their imprint, even in old age.

However, Erikson's stages differ significantly from Freud's in that they emphasize family and culture, not sexual urges. He called his theory *epigenetic,* partly to stress that the expression of genes, as well as of biological impulses, is powerfully influenced by the social environment.

Behaviorism

Another theory, **behaviorism**, arose in direct opposition to the psychoanalytic emphasis on unconscious, hidden urges (described in Table 1.4). Early in the twentieth century, John B. Watson (1878–1958) argued that, if psychology was to be a science, psychologists should examine only what they could see and measure. According to Watson, if psychologists focus on behavior, they will realize that anything can be learned. He wrote:

behaviorism
A theory of human development that studies observable behavior. Behaviorism is also called *learning theory,* because it describes the laws and processes by which behavior is learned.

An Early Behaviorist John Watson was an early proponent of learning theory. His ideas are still influential and controversial today.

conditioning
According to behaviorism, the processes by which responses become linked to particular stimuli and learning takes place. The word *conditioning* is used to emphasize the importance of repeated practice, as when an athlete *conditions* his or her body to perform well by training for a long time.

classical conditioning
A learning process in which a meaningful stimulus (such as the smell of food to a hungry animal) gradually comes to be connected with a neutral stimulus (such as a particular sound) that had no special meaning before the learning process began. (Also called *respondent conditioning*.)

Give me a dozen healthy infants, well-formed, and my own specified world to bring them up in and I'll guarantee to take any one at random and train him to become any type of specialist I might select—doctor, lawyer, artist, merchant chief, and yes, even beggar-man and thief, regardless of his talents, penchants, tendencies, abilities, vocations, and race.

[Watson, 1924/1998, p. 82]

Many other psychologists, especially in the United States, agreed. They found that the unconscious motives and drives that Freud described were difficult (or impossible) to verify via the scientific method (Uttal, 2000). Researchers found that the parents' approach to toilet training, for instance, did not determine a child's later personality.

For every individual at every age, from newborn to centenarian, behaviorists identify laws that govern how simple actions and environmental responses shape behavior. This includes all behavior, from reading a book to robbing a bank, from saying "Good morning" to a stranger to saying "I love you" to a spouse. They contend that, for the most part, external responses determine personality. Behaviorists are also called *learning theorists* because they believe that all behavior is learned, step by step.

LAWS OF BEHAVIOR The specific laws of learning apply to **conditioning**, the processes by which responses become linked to particular stimuli. There are two types of conditioning: classical and operant.

More than a century ago, Ivan Pavlov (1849–1936), a Russian scientist who won a Nobel Prize for his work on animal digestion, noticed that his experimental dogs drooled not only when they saw and smelled food but also when they heard the footsteps of the attendants who brought the food. This observation led Pavlov to perform experiments in which he conditioned dogs to salivate when they heard a specific sound.

Pavlov began by sounding a tone just before presenting food. After a number of repetitions of the sound-then-food sequence, dogs began salivating at the sound, even when there was no food. This simple experiment demonstrated **classical conditioning** (also called *respondent conditioning*), a process in which a person or animal learns to associate a neutral stimulus with a meaningful stimulus, gradually reacting to the neutral stimulus with the same response as to the meaningful one.

The most influential North American behaviorist was B. F. Skinner (1904–1990). Skinner agreed with Watson that psychology should focus on the scientific study of behavior, and he agreed with Pavlov that classical conditioning explains some

TABLE 1.4 Psychoanalytic Theory vs. Behaviorism

Area of Disagreement	Psychoanalytic Theory	Behaviorism
The unconscious	Emphasizes unconscious wishes and urges, unknown to the person but powerful all the same	Holds that the unconscious not only is unknowable but also may be a destructive fiction that keeps people from changing
Observable behavior	Holds that observable behavior is a symptom, not the cause—the tip of an iceberg, with the bulk of the problem submerged	Looks only at observable behavior—what a person does rather than what a person thinks, feels, or imagines
Importance of childhood	Stresses that early childhood, including infancy, is critical; even if a person does not remember what happened, the early legacy lingers throughout life	Holds that current conditioning is crucial; early habits and patterns can be unlearned, even reversed, if appropriate reinforcements and punishments are used
Scientific status	Holds that most aspects of human development are beyond the reach of scientific experiment; uses ancient myths, the words of disturbed adults, dreams, play, and poetry as raw material	Is proud to be a science, dependent on verifiable data and carefully controlled experiments; discards ideas that sound good but are not proven

behavior. However, Skinner believed that another type of conditioning, **operant conditioning** (also called *instrumental conditioning*), is crucial.

In operant conditioning, animals perform some action and a response occurs. If the response is useful or pleasurable, the animal is likely to repeat the action. If the response is painful, the animal is not likely to repeat the action.

Pleasant consequences are sometimes called *rewards,* and unpleasant consequences are sometimes called *punishments.* Behaviorists hesitate to use those words, however, because what people commonly think of as a punishment can actually be a reward, and vice versa.

For example, parents punish their children by withholding dessert, by spanking them, by not letting them play, by speaking harshly to them, and so on. But if a particular child dislikes the dessert, being deprived of it is actually a reward, not a punishment. Another child might not mind a spanking, especially if he or she craves parental attention. In that family, the intended punishment (spanking) is actually a reward (attention).

Any consequence that follows a behavior and makes the person (or animal) likely to repeat that behavior is called a **reinforcement**, not a reward. Once a behavior has been conditioned, humans and other creatures will repeat it even if reinforcement occurs only occasionally.

Similarly, punishment makes a creature less likely to repeat a certain action. Almost all daily behavior, from combing your hair to joking with friends, can be understood as a result of past operant conditioning, according to behaviorists.

This insight has practical application for parents: Early parenting is considered crucial for children's future development because it teaches habits that may endure. For instance, if parents want their child to share, and their infant offers them a gummy, half-eaten cracker, they should take the gift with apparent delight and then return it, smiling.

The science of human development has benefited from behaviorism. The theory's emphasis on the origins and consequences of observed behavior led researchers to realize that many actions that seem to be genetic, or to result from deeply rooted emotional problems, are actually learned. And if something is learned, it can be unlearned. No longer are "the events of infancy and early childhood . . . the foundation for adult personality and psychopathology," as psychoanalysts believed (Cairns & Cairns, 2006, p. 117). People *can* change, even in old age.

A Contemporary of Freud Ivan Pavlov was a physiologist who received the Nobel Prize in 1904 for his research on digestive processes. It was this line of study that led to his discovery of classical conditioning.

OBSERVATION QUIZ

In appearance, how is Pavlov similar to Freud, and how do both look different from the other theorists pictured? (see answer, page 24) →

operant conditioning
The learning process in which a particular action is followed either by something desired (which makes the person or animal more likely to repeat the action) or by something unwanted (which makes the action less likely to be repeated). (Also called *instrumental conditioning.*)

reinforcement
A technique for conditioning behavior in which that behavior is followed by something desired, such as food for a hungry animal or a welcoming smile for a lonely person.

Rats, Pigeons, and People B. F. Skinner is best known for his experiments with rats and pigeons, but he also applied his knowledge to human problems. For his daughter, he designed a glass-enclosed crib in which temperature, humidity, and perceptual stimulation could be controlled to make her time in the crib enjoyable and educational. He wrote about an ideal society based on principles of operant conditioning, where, for example, workers in less desirable jobs would earn greater rewards.

Social Learning in Action Social learning validates the old maxim "Actions speak louder than words." If the moment here is typical for this child, she is likely to grow up with a ready sense of the importance of this particular chore of infant care.

OBSERVATION QUIZ

What shows that this child imitates her mother? (see answer, page 24) →

social learning theory
An extension of behaviorism that emphasizes the influence that other people have over a person's behavior. The theory's basic principle is that even without specific reinforcement, every individual learns many things through observation and imitation of other people.

cognitive theory
A theory of human development that focuses on changes in how people think over time. According to this theory, our thoughts shape our attitudes, beliefs, and behaviors.

Would You Talk to This Man? Children loved talking to Jean Piaget, and he learned by listening carefully—especially to their incorrect explanations, which no one had paid much attention to before. All his life, Piaget was absorbed with studying the way children think. He called himself a "genetic epistemologist"—one who studies how children gain knowledge about the world as they grow up.

SOCIAL LEARNING THEORY A major extension of behaviorism is **social learning theory**, which was first described by Albert Bandura (b. 1925), a scientist who continues to study and write (e.g., Bandura, 2006). This theory notes that, because humans are social beings, they learn from observing others, even without personally receiving any reinforcement.

Social learning is often called *modeling,* because people learn by observing other people and then copying them. For example, extensive developmental research finds that children learn from witnessing domestic violence as well as from being abused themselves. As the multicultural approach would predict, what they learn varies, depending on the social context.

In a family in which one parent hit the other, one son might identify with the abuser and another with the victim. Later in adulthood, because of their past social learning, one man might be quick to slap his wife and spank his children, while his brother might be fearful and apologetic at home, cowed by criticism. The two brothers learned opposite lessons from observing the same childhood events.

As this example shows, social learning is connected to perceptions and interpretations. It is also related to self-understanding, social reflection, and *self-efficacy* (how effective people think they are when it comes to changing themselves or altering their social context).

High self-efficacy can lead to high aspirations and notable achievements (Bandura et al., 2001). Both of these result from learning and are not inborn attributes, according to social learning theory. For instance, an emerging adult who starts a business and then works day and night, believing it will succeed, is high in self-efficacy.

Cognitive Theory

In a third theory, each person's ideas and beliefs are of central importance. According to **cognitive theory**, thoughts and expectations profoundly affect actions. Cognitive theory has dominated psychology since about 1980 and has branched into many versions, each adding insights about human development. The word *cognitive* refers not just to thinking but also to attitudes, beliefs, and assumptions.

The most famous cognitive theorist was a Swiss scientist, Jean Piaget (1896–1980). Unlike other scientists of the early twentieth century, Piaget realized that babies are curious and thoughtful, creating their own *schema* (Piaget's word for minitheories) about their world. Piaget began by observing his own three infants; later he studied thousands of older children (Inhelder & Piaget, 1958).

From this work, Piaget developed the central thesis of cognitive theory: How people think (not just what they know) changes with time and experience, and human thinking influences human actions. Piaget maintained that cognitive development occurs in four major age-related

TABLE 1.5 Piaget's Periods of Cognitive Development

Age Range	Name of Period	Characteristics of the Period	Major Gains During the Period
Birth to 2 years	Sensorimotor	Infants use senses and motor abilities to understand the world. Learning is active; there is no conceptual or reflective thought.	Infants learn that an object still exists when it is out of sight (*object permanence*) and begin to think through mental actions.
2–6 years	Preoperational	Children think magically and poetically, using language to understand the world. Thinking is *egocentric,* causing children to perceive the world from their own perspective.	The imagination flourishes, and language becomes a significant means of self-expression and of influence from others.
6–11 years	Concrete operational	Children understand and apply logical operations, or principles, to interpret experiences objectively and rationally. Their thinking is limited to what they can personally see, hear, touch, and experience.	By applying logical abilities, children learn to understand concepts of conservation, number, classification, and many other scientific ideas.
12 years through adulthood	Formal operational	Adolescents and adults think about abstractions and hypothetical concepts and reason analytically, not just emotionally. They can be logical about things they have never experienced.	Ethics, politics, and social and moral issues become fascinating as adolescents and adults take a broader and more theoretical approach to experience.

periods, or stages: *sensorimotor, preoperational, concrete operational,* and *formal operational* (see Table 1.5).

Intellectual advancement occurs lifelong because humans seek *cognitive equilibrium*—that is, a state of mental balance. An easy way to achieve this balance is to interpret new experiences through the lens of preexisting ideas. For example, infants discover that new objects can be grasped in the same way as familiar objects; adolescents explain the day's headlines as evidence that supports their existing worldviews; older adults speak fondly of the good old days as embodying values that should endure.

Sometimes, however, a new experience is jarring and incomprehensible. The resulting experience is one of *cognitive disequilibrium,* an imbalance that initially creates confusion. As Figure 1.5 illustrates, disequilibrium leads to cognitive growth because it forces people to adapt their old concepts. Piaget describes two types of adaptation:

● *Assimilation,* in which new experiences are interpreted to fit into, or assimilate with, old ideas

● *Accommodation,* in which old ideas are restructured to include, or accommodate, new experiences

Accommodation requires more mental energy than assimilation, but it is sometimes necessary because new ideas and experiences may not fit into existing cognitive structures. Accommodation produces significant intellectual growth.

Ideally, when people disagree, adaptation is mutual. For example, parents are often startled by their adolescents' strong opinions—say, that heroin should be legalized or that cigarettes should be outlawed. Parents may grow intellectually if they revise their concepts to accommodate such ideas, and adolescents may grow if they incorporate their parents' opinions.

Another influential cognitive theory, called *information processing,* differs from Piaget's theory. Many researchers (in addition to those influenced by information-processing theory) now think that some of Piaget's conclusions were mistaken, but all appreciate his basic insight: Thoughts influence emotions and actions.

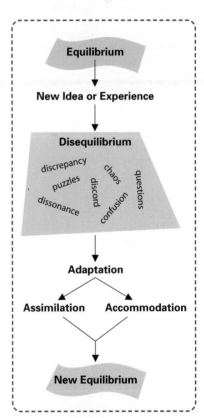

FIGURE 1.5 Challenge Me Most of us, most of the time, prefer the comfort of our conventional conclusions. According to Piaget, however, when new ideas disturb our thinking, we have an opportunity to expand our cognition with a broader and deeper understanding.

ecological-systems approach
The view that in the study of human development, the person should be considered in all the contexts and interactions that constitute a life. (Later renamed *bioecological theory*.)

dynamic-systems theory
A view of human development as an ongoing, ever-changing interaction between the physical and emotional being and between the person and every aspect of his or her environment, including the family and society.

Systems Theories

Many useful twenty-first-century developmental theories describe systems that involve the interaction of various forces and people. The word *systems* captures the idea that a change in one part of a person, family, or society affects every aspect of development because each part is connected to all the other parts (Spencer et al., 2006).

To pick an everyday example, an automobile is a system for transporting people and things from one place to another, a system that depends on the interaction of many moving parts. If one part malfunctions, the car may or may not still move; it depends on whether the part is a broken taillight, a flat tire, a dead battery, or a burned-out engine.

In the same way, human development depends on systems. Consider examples from the three domains of development. Some systems are physiological, such as the immune system, which includes many kinds of immune cells. Some systems are cognitive, such as language, with sounds, words, and grammar all working together to produce communication. And some are social, such as the members of a family, workers in a factory, or citizens of a town. Minor dysfunctions can be overcome, but a major dysfunction can bring the whole system to a dead stop.

ECOLOGICAL SYSTEMS Just as a naturalist studying an organism examines the ecology, or the interrelationship between the organism and its environment, Urie Bronfenbrenner (1917–2005) recommended that developmentalists take an **ecological-systems approach** when studying human development (Bronfenbrenner & Morris, 2006). He believed that each person is affected by many systemic contexts and interactions.

Bronfenbrenner described three nested levels that surround individuals and affect their development: *microsystems* (elements of the person's immediate surroundings, such as family and peer group), *exosystems* (local institutions such as school and church), and *macrosystems* (the larger social setting, including cultural values, economic policies, and political processes).

Recognizing the importance of historical conditions, Bronfenbrenner also described the *chronosystem* (literally, "time system"), which affects the other three systems. Because he appreciated the dynamic interaction of the microsystem, exosystem, and macrosystem, he named a fifth system, the *mesosystem,* consisting of the connections among the other systems.

One example of a mesosystem is the interface between home and school, including various communication processes between a child's parents and teachers (such as letters home, parent–teacher conferences, phone calls, back-to-school nights). Another mesosystem is made up of all the connections between a person's work and family life. These connections include not only the direct impact of family leave, retirement, and shift work but also such indirect macrosystem impacts as unemployment rates, minimum-wage standards, and hiring practices—each of which affects everyone in a family microsystem.

Throughout his life, Bronfenbrenner emphasized the study of humans in natural settings, as they actually live their lives, and the need to take their physical well-being into account. He renamed his approach *bioecological theory* to highlight the important role of biology, recognizing that biological systems affect all the other systems (Bronfenbrenner & Morris, 2006).

DYNAMIC SYSTEMS A related approach is called **dynamic-systems theory**, which stresses fluctuations and transitions, "the dynamic synthesis of multiple levels of analysis" (Lerner et al., 2005, p. 38). The application of dynamic-systems theory to human development is "relatively new" (Thelen & Smith, 2006, p. 258), but it follows the approach that natural scientists have used for over 50 years. Systemic change over time is the nature of life:

> [S]easons change in ordered measure, clouds assemble and disperse, trees grow to a certain shape and size, snowflakes form and melt, minute plants and animals pass through elaborate life cycles that are invisible to us, and social groups come together and disband.
>
> [Thelen & Smith, 2006, p. 271]

A crucial tenet of this theory is that development is *dynamic*, which means that the interaction between the physical and emotional being, and between the person and every aspect of the environment, is always in flux, always changing. When scientists approach any developmental topic or problem, dynamic-systems theory urges them to delve more deeply into the components of the topic as well as to broaden their focus and consider changing social and cultural factors.

Accordingly, over the past few decades developmentalists have begun to explore developing persons in greater depth and to look more broadly at the contexts around them. It is as if they are adjusting a camera lens or a computer screen to zoom in on the neurons and genes within each person and to zoom out to the surrounding contexts.

Each of the theories we have been examining—psychoanalytic theory, behaviorism, cognitive theory, and systems theory—has hundreds of applications and variations, many of which you will encounter later in this text. The power of genes, for example, is a major topic of the next chapter; the stages set forth by Freud, Erikson, and Piaget are described at each age when they are relevant.

All theories lead to specific hypotheses, such as that breast-feeding fosters bonding between mother and child (psychoanalytic), that imprisoning teenagers increases crime (behaviorism), that college education reduces prejudice (cognitive), and that a high unemployment rate impairs the health of adults (dynamic systems). Scientific research has explored each of these hypotheses.

AP PHOTO / JIM MONE

Dynamic Interaction A dynamic-systems approach highlights the ever-changing impact that each part of a system has on all the other parts. This classroom scene reflects the eagerness for education felt by many immigrants, the reticence of some boys in an academic context, and a global perspective (as demonstrated by the world map). These facets emerge from various systems—family, gender, and culture—and they have interacted to produce this moment.

OBSERVATION QUIZ
What country is this? (see answer, page 26) ➜

ESPECIALLY FOR Future Teachers
Does the classroom furniture shown in the photograph above affect instruction? (see response, page 27) ➜

KEY Points

- Developmental theories organize observations and lead to hypotheses.
- Psychoanalytic theory, as developed by Freud, emphasizes unconscious urges, beginning in childhood. Erikson added a psychosocial, lifelong perspective.
- Behaviorism stresses learning by means of reinforcement.
- Cognitive theory, as developed by Piaget, emphasizes the influence of ideas and beliefs.
- Systems theories, such as the bioecological approach of Bronfenbrenner, stress the dynamic interaction of many levels of development.

scientific observation
A method of testing a hypothesis by unobtrusively watching and recording participants' behavior in a systematic and objective manner—in a natural setting, in a laboratory, or in searches of archival data.

Using the Scientific Method

Thus far, we have focused on the first step of the scientific method: forming a question, which may begin with a theory. Remember that in step 2, the question is turned into a hypothesis. The hypothesis is tested in step 3, and then conclusions are drawn in step 4. In step 5, scientists publish specific details about their methods and participants in order to enable other scientists to replicate their research and confirm, extend, qualify, or refute their conclusions.

There are hundreds of ways to design scientific studies and analyze their results, and researchers continually try to make sure that their data are valid and convincing. Often statistical measures help scientists discover relationships between various aspects of the data. (Some statistical perspectives are presented in Table 1.6). Every research design, method, and statistical measure has strengths as well as weaknesses. Now we describe three basic strategies for conducting research.

Observation

Scientific observation requires the researcher to record behavior systematically and objectively. Observations often occur in a naturalistic setting (such as a home, school, or public place) where people are likely to behave as they usually do. Observation can also occur in a laboratory, with more standardized circumstances. And sometimes scientists study data that was originally collected for some other purpose, observing trends that have significance for human development.

Analysis of decades of medical data on weight (an example of observations recorded for some other reason) shows an increase in obesity as well as an increase in related

TABLE 1.6 Statistical Measures Often Used to Analyze Research Results

Measure	Use
Effect size	Indicates how much one variable affects another. Effect size ranges from 0 to 1: An effect size of 0.2 is called small, 0.5 moderate, and 0.8 large.
Significance	Indicates whether the results might have occurred by chance. A finding that chance would produce the results less than 5 times in 100 is significant at the 0.05 level. A finding that chance would produce the results once in 100 times is significant at 0.01; once in 1,000 times is significant at 0.001.
Cost-benefit analysis	Calculates how much a particular independent variable costs versus how much it saves. This is particularly useful to analyze public spending. For instance, one cost-benefit analysis showed that an expensive preschool program cost $15,166 per child (in 2000 dollars) but saved $215,000 by age 40, in reduced costs of special education, unemployment, prison, and other public expenses (Belfield et al., 2006).
Odds ratio	Indicates how a particular variable compares to a standard, set at 1. For example, one study found that, although less than 1 percent of all child homicides occurred at school, the odds were similar for public and private schools. The odds of such deaths occurring in high schools, however, were 18.47 times that of elementary or middle schools (set at 1.0) (MMWR, January 18, 2008).
Factor analysis	Hundreds of variables could affect any given behavior. In addition, many variables (such as family income and parental education) may overlap. To take this into account, analysis reveals variables that can be clustered together to form a factor, which is a composite of many variables. For example, SES might become one factor, child personality another.
Meta-analysis	A "study of studies." Researchers use statistical tools to synthesize the results of previous, separate studies. Then they analyze the accumulated results, using criteria that weight each study fairly. This approach improves data analysis by combining the results of studies that used so few participants that the conclusions did not reach significance.

Sources: Alasuutari et al., 2008; Duncan & Magnuson, 2007; Hubbard & Lindsay, 2008.

Who Participates? For all these measures, the characteristics of the people who participate in the study (formerly called the *subjects*, now called the *participants*) are important, as is the number of people who are studied. Even a tiny effect size that could be applied to a large population may indicate a useful benefit. For example, the effect size of exercise on heart health is small, but millions of lives would be saved if everyone walked at least an hour a day.

ALAMY

Can They See Her? No, and they cannot hear each other. This scientist is observing three deaf boys through a window that is a mirror on the other side. Her observations will help them learn to communicate.

problems, including heart disease and diabetes. An article in a leading medical journal suggests that, given the increase in the incidence of obesity in the United States, the current generation of children may be the first to die at younger ages than their parents (Devi, 2008).

Although genes are part of the reason some individuals are overweight, genes do not change much from one generation to the next, so the recent increase must be caused by some nongenetic factor. Dozens of hypotheses have been suggested, including bigger portion sizes in restaurants, greater consumption of high-calorie fast food, school policies, desk work, more fat (or carbohydrates, or artificial sweeteners, or soft drinks) in the diet.

One team of researchers posed a specific hypothesis: Children are gaining weight because they get too little exercise, and one reason is that they are driven to school (Sirard et al., 2005). To test their hypothesis, observers went to eight elementary schools (some rural, some urban) in South Carolina, noting how the children arrived at school.

They tried to make their observations objective. For example, to make sure that they accounted for all the ways children got to school, they arrived before the first children did and continued to tally the children's modes of transportation until all the latecomers had arrived. To make sure they would catch any fluctuations by day of the week, they observed for five consecutive days. They found that almost all (95 percent) the children arrived by car or school bus (see Figure 1.6; Sirard et al., 2005).

This is an excellent example of an observational study. People tend to think that they already know the facts, but sometimes trends are not perceived until data are collected and published. For instance, obesity has been increasing over the past 30 years, but few realized it until national data were reported.

Likewise, many more parents in a nationwide survey said that their children walk to school than the researchers tallied in this particular study. As in this study, observers record what actually occurs, not what other people tell them.

RESPONSE FOR Future Teachers (from page 25) Yes. Every aspect of the environment affects what happens within that space. In this classroom, tables and movable chairs foster group collaboration and conversation—potent learning methods that are difficult to achieve when desks and seats are bolted to the floor in rows and the teacher sits or stands at the front of the room. ●

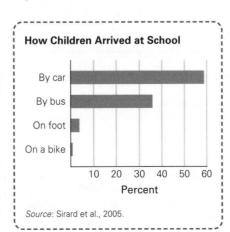

How Children Arrived at School

Source: Sirard et al., 2005.

FIGURE 1.6 Why Walk When You Can Ride? An observational study of eight South Carolina elementary schools found that only 5 percent of the children rode their bikes or walked to school. Such a study could not explain *why* so few children got to school under their own steam. For that, an experiment would be needed.

Observational studies have a major limitation: They do not indicate what causes people to do what they do. In this example, it may not be the case that children are overweight because they are driven to school; rather, parents may drive their children to school because the children are overweight and find it hard to walk or ride a bike. Observation cannot tell us whether inactivity causes obesity or vice versa.

The Experiment

The **experiment** is the usual research method used to establish what causes what. In the social sciences, experimenters typically impose a particular treatment on a group of volunteer participants (formerly referred to as *subjects*) or expose them to a specific condition and then note whether their behavior changes.

In technical terms, the experimenters manipulate an **independent variable**, which is the imposed treatment or special condition (also called the *experimental variable*; a *variable* is anything that can vary). They note whether this independent variable affects whatever they are studying, called the **dependent variable** (which *depends* on the independent variable). Thus, the independent variable is the new, special treatment; any change in the dependent variable is the result.

The purpose of an experiment is to find out whether an independent variable affects the dependent variable. In a typical experiment (as diagrammed in Figure 1.7), two groups of participants are studied. One group is called the *experimental group*, which gets a particular treatment (the independent variable). The other group is the *comparison group* (also called a *control group*), which does not.

Let us look now at an experiment designed to determine the cause of obesity. Experiments using children are difficult to design, partly because ethical guidelines are particularly stringent when children are involved. Therefore, to understand the relationship between movement and obesity, investigators recruited inactive adults.

experiment
A research method in which the researcher tries to determine the cause-and-effect relationship between two variables by manipulating one (called the *independent variable)* and then observing and recording the ensuing changes in the other (called the *dependent variable).*

independent variable
In an experiment, the variable that is introduced to see what effect it has on the dependent variable. (Also called *experimental variable.*)

dependent variable
In an experiment, the variable that may change as a result of whatever new condition or situation the experimenter adds. In other words, the dependent variable *depends* on the independent variable.

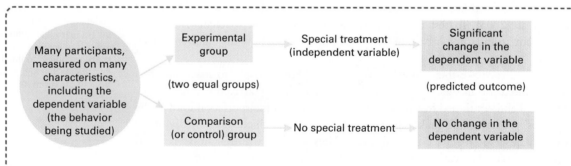

Procedure:

1. Divide participants into two groups that are matched on important characteristics, especially the behavior that is the dependent variable on which this study is focused.

2. Give special treatment, or intervention (the independent variable), to one group (the experimental group).

3. Compare the groups on the dependent variable. If they now differ, the cause of the difference was probably the independent variable.

4. Publish the results.

OBSERVATION QUIZ

Does the experimental group always change? (see answer, page 30) ➞

FIGURE 1.7 How to Conduct an Experiment The basic sequence diagrammed here applies to all experiments. Many additional features, especially the statistical measures listed in Table 1.6 and various ways of reducing experimenter bias, affect whether step 4, publication, occurs. (Scientific journals reject reports of experiments that were not rigorous in method and analysis.)

Self-described adult "couch potatoes" agreed to follow a strict diet and to wear electronic monitoring equipment to record their bodily movements (Levine et al., 2005). Movement was automatically recorded 120 times each minute, 24 hours a day. Half the volunteers were overweight and half were underweight.

In the first phase of this study, the electronic monitors recorded that the lean adults moved significantly more than the heavy adults did. For instance, the underweight participants averaged nine hours a day standing or walking; the overweight ones spent only six hours doing so. So far this is merely observation, aided by technology.

Then came the experiment. Both groups were put on food regimens, either to gain or to lose weight, for two months. The diets worked. The overweight participants lost an average of 20 pounds (8 kg), and the lean ones gained about 10 pounds (4 kg). (The change was temporary; most people returned to their usual weight when they stopped the experimental diets.)

The crucial question was: When their weight changed after the diet, did the formerly lean people still move more than the formerly fat ones did? Or did the weight change affect the frequency of movement? In other words, did the independent variable (the new weight) affect the dependent variable (the frequency of movement)?

The answer was no. The monitors recorded no significant change after people gained or lost weight. The fact that movement patterns overall were stable helps developmentalists understand why people, on average, are heavier now than they were 30 years ago. People exercise less today than they did then, and that is a cause of overweight, not a result.

The Survey

A third research method is the **survey**. Information is collected from a large number of people by interview, questionnaire, or some other means. This is a quick, direct way to obtain data.

Acquiring valid survey data is not easy. For example, when pollsters try to predict elections, they hope that the people they survey will vote as they say they will, that undecided people will follow the trends, and that people who refuse to tell their opinion, or who are not included, will be similar to those surveyed. Researchers know that none of this is certain. Some people lie, some change their minds, some (especially those who don't have phones or who never talk to strangers) are never surveyed.

Furthermore, survey answers are influenced by the wording and the sequence of the questions. Respondents present themselves as they would like to be, especially when they are questioned directly.

Survey answers are particularly likely to be distorted when the truth might be troubling. When asked how often high school seniors in the United States smoke marijuana, for instance, teachers, the police, and parents answer differently than do the teenagers themselves. In a nationwide survey of 14,000 high school students throughout the United States, 49 percent of seniors said they had tried marijuana (MMWR, June 6, 2008); most parents, however, believe that their teenage children have never used illegal drugs.

Surveys exploring sexual behavior can yield similarly paradoxical findings. Every year since 1991, the same U.S. survey has asked high school students if they had intercourse before age 13. About twice as many ninth-graders (14 percent in 2007) as twelfth-graders (7 percent) always say yes. Do twelfth-graders forget what happened before they were in ninth grade, or do ninth-graders lie?

Flaws characterize other common research methods such as case studies, in which just one person is examined, and historical studies, in which published accounts of past events are analyzed. That is one reason developmental study is multidisciplinary: Each discipline favors particular methods.

ESPECIALLY FOR Nurses In the field of medicine, why are experiments conducted to test new drugs and treatments? (see response, page 30) →

● **UNDERSTANDING THE NUMBERS**
Did the diets work better for the heavy ones who lost 20 pounds than for the lean ones who gained 10 pounds?

Answer Not necessarily. The original body weight is crucial. If the heavy ones originally weighed twice as much, then dieting worked equally well for the two groups. Thus, if a 200-pound person lost 20 pounds and a 100-pound person gained 10, both changed by 10 percent.

survey
A research method in which information is collected from a large number of people by interviews, written questionnaires, or some other means.

ANSWER TO OBSERVATION QUIZ (from page 28) No. Note the word *predicted.* The hypothesis is that change will occur for the experimental group but not the control group, but the reason for doing the experiment is to discover whether that prediction does indeed come true. ●

cross-sectional research
A research design that compares groups of people who differ in age but are similar in other important characteristics.

RESPONSE FOR Nurses (from page 29) Experiments are the only way to determine cause-and-effect relationships. If we want to be sure that a new drug or treatment is safe and effective, an experiment must be conducted to establish that the drug or treatment improves health. ●

Studying Development over the Life Span

In addition to conducting observations, experiments, and surveys, developmentalists must measure how people *change or remain the same over time,* as our definition of the *science of human development* stressed. To do so, developmental researchers use one of three basic research designs: cross-sectional, longitudinal, or cross-sequential (see Figure 1.8).

CROSS-SECTIONAL RESEARCH The most convenient (quickest and least expensive) way to study development is with **cross-sectional research.** Groups of people of one age are compared with people of another age. For instance, in the United States in 2006, 92 percent of men aged 25 to 34 were in the labor force, but only 70 percent of those aged 55 to 64 were (U.S. Bureau of the Census, 2008). From those facts one might conclude that almost one out of every four men stops working between age 30 and age 60.

Cross-sectional design seems simple. However, it is difficult to ensure that the various groups being compared are similar in every way except age. In this example, the younger U.S. men, on average, had more education than the older ones. Thus, what seems to be the result of age might actually have to do with schooling: Perhaps education, not age, accounted for the higher employment rates of the younger adults.

A related problem is that historical change might affect one cohort more than another. An example of this would be the number of people in a cohort. Look at the two population charts in Figure 1.9. Perhaps the 60-year-old men had more trouble finding work because there are so many of them. If so, that is a cohort effect that might mistakenly be considered an age effect.

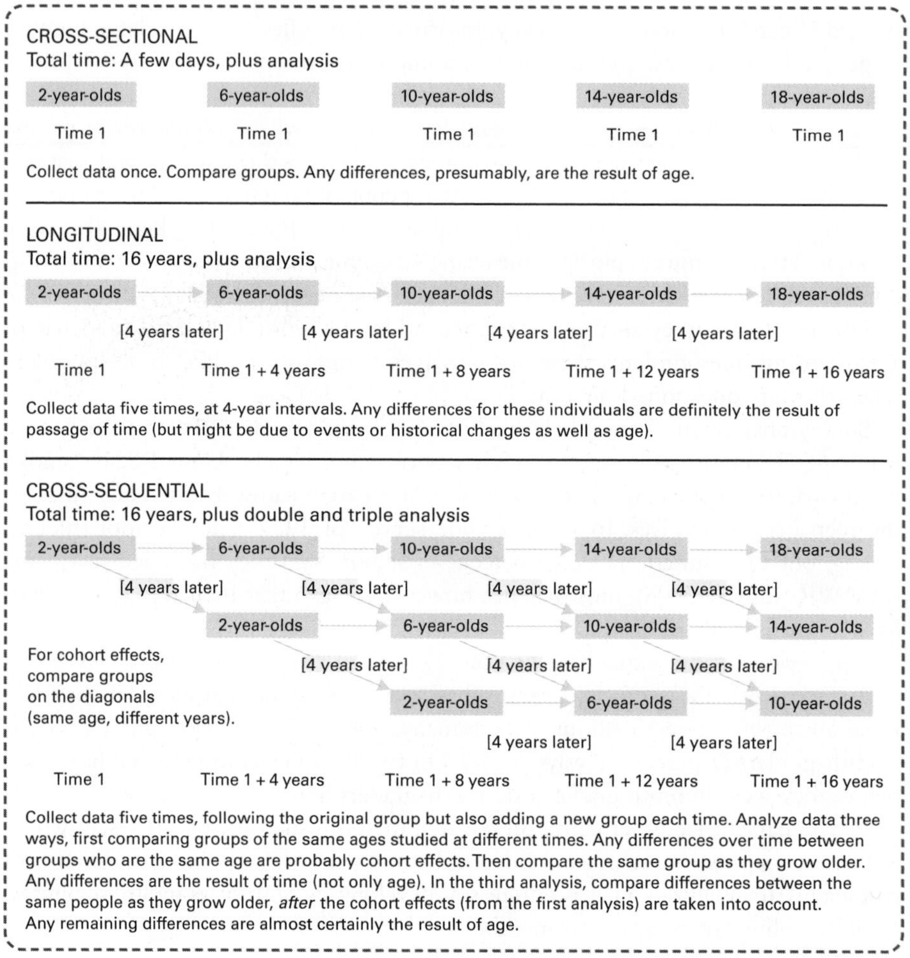
CROSS-SECTIONAL
Total time: A few days, plus analysis
2-year-olds
6-year-olds
10-year-olds
14-year-olds
18-year-olds
Time 1
Time 1
Time 1
Time 1
Time 1
Collect data once. Compare groups. Any differences, presumably, are the result of age.
LONGITUDINAL
Total time: 16 years, plus analysis
2-year-olds
6-year-olds
10-year-olds
14-year-olds
18-year-olds
[4 years later]
[4 years later]
[4 years later]
[4 years later]
Time 1
Time 1 + 4 years
Time 1 + 8 years
Time 1 + 12 years
Time 1 + 16 years
Collect data five times, at 4-year intervals. Any differences for these individuals are definitely the result of passage of time (but might be due to events or historical changes as well as age).
CROSS-SEQUENTIAL
Total time: 16 years, plus double and triple analysis
2-year-olds
6-year-olds
10-year-olds
14-year-olds
18-year-olds
[4 years later]
[4 years later]
[4 years later]
[4 years later]
2-year-olds
6-year-olds
10-year-olds
14-year-olds
For cohort effects, compare groups on the diagonals (same age, different years).
[4 years later]
[4 years later]
[4 years later]
2-year-olds
6-year-olds
10-year-olds
[4 years later]
[4 years later]
Time 1
Time 1 + 4 years
Time 1 + 8 years
Time 1 + 12 years
Time 1 + 16 years
Collect data five times, following the original group but also adding a new group each time. Analyze data three ways, first comparing groups of the same ages studied at different times. Any differences over time between groups who are the same age are probably cohort effects. Then compare the same group as they grow older. Any differences are the result of time (not only age). In the third analysis, compare differences between the same people as they grow older, *after* the cohort effects (from the first analysis) are taken into account. Any remaining differences are almost certainly the result of age.

FIGURE 1.8 Which Approach Is Best? Cross-sequential research is the most time-consuming and most complex approach, but it also yields the best information about development. This is one reason why hundreds of scientists conduct research on the same topics, replicating one another's work—to gain some of the advantages of cross-sequential research without having to wait all those years.

Age Structure of the U.S. Population, 1920 and 2010 (population in millions)

1920	Years	2015 (projected)
0.5	85+	6.2
0.7	80–84	5.6
1.2	75–79	7.9
1.7	70–74	11.1
2.2	65–69	15.8
3.0	60–64	18.8
3.6	55–59	21.6
4.7	50–54	22.3
5.8	45–49	21.0
6.3	40–44	20.4
7.8	35–39	20.8
8.1	30–34	22.0
9.1	25–29	22.4
9.3	20–24	22.3
9.4	15–19	21.2
10.6	10–14	21.6
11.4	5–9	21.7
11.6	0–4	22.0

Sources: U.S. Bureau of the Census,1975 *(left)*; U.S. Bureau of the Census, 2008 *(right)*.

FIGURE 1.9 The Baby-Boom Population Bulge Unlike earlier times, when each generation was slightly smaller than the one that followed, each cohort today has a unique position, determined by the reproductive patterns of the preceding generation and by the medical advances developed during their own lifetime. As a result, the baby boomers, born between 1947 and 1964, represent a huge bulge in the U.S. population. In another three decades, the leading edge of the baby-boom generation, largely intact, will begin moving into the upper age group.

Compare These with Those The apparent similarity of these two groups in gender and ethnic composition makes them candidates for cross-sectional research. Before we could be sure that any difference between the two groups is the result of age, we would have to be sure the groups are alike in other ways, such as socioeconomic status and religious affiliation. Even if two groups seem identical in everything but age, there may be unknown differences.

Six Stages of Life These photos show Sarah-Maria, born in 1980 in Switzerland, at six stages of her life: infancy (age 1), early childhood (age 3), middle childhood (age 8), adolescence (age 15), emerging adulthood (age 19), and adulthood (age 29).

longitudinal research
A research design in which the same individuals are followed over time and their development is repeatedly assessed.

LONGITUDINAL RESEARCH To help discover whether age itself, not cohort differences, causes a developmental change, scientists undertake **longitudinal research**. This research design involves collecting data repeatedly on the same individuals as they age. Longitudinal research is particularly useful in studying development over the years of a long age span (Elder & Shanahan, 2006).

You already read about the links among the MAOA gene, child maltreatment, and adult criminality. That was one of hundreds of findings from a longitudinal study of an entire cohort in Dunedin, New Zealand. Some other surprising findings of longitudinal research are given in Table 1.7.

Longitudinal research has several drawbacks. Over time, participants may withdraw, move to an unknown address, or die. These losses can skew the final results if those who disappear are unlike those who stay, as is usually the case. Another problem is that participants become increasingly aware of the questions or the goals of the study and therefore may change in ways that most other people do not.

Probably the biggest problem comes from the changing historical context. Science, popular culture, and politics alter life experiences, and those changes limit the current relevance of data collected on people born decades ago. Results from longitudinal studies of people born in 1900, as they made their way through childhood, adulthood, and old age, may not be relevant to people born in 2000.

TABLE 1.7 Some Findings from Longitudinal Research

- *Adjustment to parents' divorce.* Negative effects linger, sometimes even into middle age, but not for everyone (Amato & Afifi, 2006; Hetherington & Kelly, 2002).

- *Preventing delinquency.* Patient parenting at age 5, using conversation rather than physical punishment, decreases the likelihood of delinquency 10 years later (Pettit, 2004).

- *The effects of day care.* The quality and extent of nonmaternal care in infancy and early childhood are less influential than the mother's warmth and responsiveness or coldness and rejection (NICHD, 2005).

- *Parenting difficult babies.* Although some babies are difficult (crying, irregular), responsive and encouraging parenting results in better than average development for them by first grade (Belsky et al., 2007; Stright et al., 2008).

- *The stability of personality.* Early temperament and childhood personality predict later personality in adolescence and beyond, although some change is always possible (Kagan, 2007; McCrae & Costa, 2003; Roberts et al., 2007).

SARAH-MARIA VISCHER / THE IMAGE WORKS

Furthermore, the need to wait decades for conclusions from longitudinal research makes it difficult to apply findings to current problems. For example, because of alarm about the possible harm decades later caused by ingesting industrial compounds called *phthalates* in the plastic of baby bottles and infant toys, many parents now use glass baby bottles. But perhaps the risk of occasional shattered glass causes more harm than chemicals in plastic. Parents need the answer now, not in 50 years.

CROSS-SEQUENTIAL RESEARCH As you see, cross-sectional and longitudinal research each have advantages that compensate for the other's disadvantages. Scientists have discovered a third strategy that uses these two together, often with complex statistical analysis (Hartmann & Pelzel, 2005). This combination is called **cross-sequential research** (also referred to as *cohort-sequential* or *time-sequential research*). With this design, researchers study several groups of people of different ages (a cross-sectional approach) and follow them over the years (a longitudinal approach).

A cross-sequential design lets researchers compare findings for a group of, say, 18-year-olds with findings for the same individuals at age 8, as well as with findings for groups who were 18 a decade or two earlier and with findings for groups who are currently 8 years old (see Figure 1.8). Cross-sequential research thus allows scientists to disentangle chronological age and historical period.

One well-known cross-sequential study (the Seattle Longitudinal Study) found that some intellectual abilities—including the ability to build one's vocabulary—increase throughout adulthood, whereas others—such as speed of thinking—start to decline at about age 30 (Schaie, 2005). This study also discovered that declines in math ability are related more closely to education than to age, a finding that neither cross-sectional nor longitudinal research alone could reveal.

cross-sequential research
A hybrid research design in which researchers first study several groups of people of different ages (a cross-sectional approach) and then follow those groups over the years (a longitudinal approach). (Also called *cohort-sequential research* or *time-sequential research*.)

ESPECIALLY FOR Future Researchers What is the best method for collecting data? (see response, page 35) →

KEY Points

- Developmentalists use many research methods.
- Observational research requires careful and systematic recording of whatever actually occurs.
- Experiments seek the relationship between cause and effect, as revealed by change in the dependent variable.
- To study change over time, cross-sectional and longitudinal research are both useful, but a cross-sequential combination of the two is best.

Cautions from Science

There is no doubt that the scientific method illuminates and illustrates human development as nothing else does. Facts, hypotheses, and possibilities have all emerged that would not be known without science—and people of all ages are healthier and more capable than people of previous generations because of it.

For example, infectious diseases in children, illiteracy in adults, depression in late adulthood, and racism and sexism at every age are much less prevalent today than a century ago. Science is one reason for all these declines.

Developmental scientists have also discovered unexpected sources of harm. Video games, cigarettes, television, shift work, and automobiles are all less benign than people first thought.

Although the benefits of science are many, so are the pitfalls if research is wrongly done or misinterpreted. We now discuss three potential hazards: misinterpreting correlation, depending too heavily on numbers, and ignoring ethics.

Correlation and Causation

correlation
A number that indicates the degree of relationship between two variables, expressed in terms of the likelihood that one variable will (or will not) occur when the other variable does (or does not). A correlation indicates only that two variables are related, not that one variable causes the other to occur.

Probably the most common mistake in interpreting research is the confusion of correlation with causation. A **correlation** exists between two variables if one variable is more (or less) likely to occur when the other does. A correlation is *positive* if both variables tend to increase together or decrease together, *negative* if one variable tends to increase while the other decreases, and *zero* if no connection is evident.

To illustrate: From birth to age 9, there is a positive correlation between age and height (children grow taller as they grow older), a negative correlation between age and amount of sleep (children sleep less as they grow older), and zero correlation between age and number of toes (children do not have more or fewer toes as they grow older). (Now try taking the quiz on correlation in Table 1.8.)

TABLE 1.8 Quiz on Correlation

Two Variables	Positive, Negative, or Zero Correlation?	Why? (Third Variable)
1. Ice cream sales and murder rate	_____	_____
2. Learning to read and number of baby teeth	_____	_____
3. Adult gender and number of offspring	_____	_____

For each of these three pairs of variables, indicate whether the correlation between them is positive, negative, or nonexistent. Then try to think of a third variable that would determine the direction of the correlation. The correct answers are printed upside down below.

Expressed in numerical terms, correlations vary from +1 (the most positive correlation) to −1 (the most negative correlation). Correlations are almost never that high; usually a correlation of +0.3 or −0.3 is noteworthy; a correlation of +0.8 or −0.8 is amazingly high.

Many correlations are unexpected. For instance, first-born children are more likely to develop asthma than are later-born children, teenage girls have higher rates of mental health problems than do teenage boys, and newborns born to immigrants weigh more than do newborns of nonimmigrants. (All these correlations are discussed later.)

Answers:
1. Positive; third variable: heat
2. Negative; third variable: age
3. Zero; each child must have a parent of each sex; no third variable

TABLE 1.9 Correlates of First Sexual Intercourse Before Age 20

Variable	Correlation
Listening to degrading sexual music	0.36*
Having friends who will approve of sex	0.39
Having parents who know where teen is	−0.30
Engaging in heavy petting before age 15	0.47

*The correlation between music and first intercourse was lower but remained significant and positive after all other measured factors were taken into account.
Source: Martino et al., 2006.

Correlations are easy to misinterpret. The truth that *correlation is not causation* is drummed into every social scientist, yet researchers are still tempted to assume that one variable causes another. For instance, a longitudinal study found a correlation between teenagers' listening to song lyrics with degrading sex themes (with males depicted as sexually insatiable studs and women as mindless sex objects) and sexual intercourse before age 20 (see Table 1.9). The authors of this study say that, because correlation is not causation, they cannot be certain of the direction of effects. Nevertheless, they write that

> reducing the amount of degrading sexual content in popular music, or reducing young people's exposure to music with this type of content, could delay initiation of intercourse. . . . Intervention possibilities include reaching out to parents of adolescents, to teens, and to the recording industry.
>
> *[Martino et al., 2006, p. 439]*

The researchers suggest that lyrics glorifying degrading sex encourage teenagers to have sex without first building a relationship. Some readers of this study objected. One criminal justice professor at the University of Massachusetts wrote: "The fact that sexually active kids listen to music with a sexual content should not be surprising. Did we expect they would listen to Mozart's Requiem?" (L. Siegel, 2006).

With correlation, there is always the possibility that the direction of causality is the opposite of the one hypothesized or that a third variable may be the underlying cause. Alternative explanations from each domain of development for the connection between having early sex and listening to sex-themed music include the following:

- *Biosocial.* Some teenagers have high levels of testosterone (a hormone that increases in adolescence, especially for boys), which drives them to seek sexual experiences and explicitly sexual music. Sexual intercourse may be the result of those hormones (a third variable).

- *Cognitive.* Some teenagers seek sexual experiences, and they find music to reinforce their values. (This explanation for the correlation suggests the opposite causal direction from the authors' assumption.)

- *Psychosocial.* Teenagers idolize some music stars—going to their concerts, watching their videos, buying their posters. Because of social learning, they emulate their idol's lifestyle, which may include sexual activities. Listening to music is a by-product of this admiration (a third variable).

Each of these three explanations is possible, as is the original one. Many other hypotheses could be formulated.

RESPONSE FOR Future Researchers (from page 33) There is no best method for collecting data. The method used depends on many factors, such as the age of participants (infants can't complete questionnaires), the question being researched, and the time frame. ●

Quantity and Quality

A second caution concerns how heavily scientists should rely on data produced by **quantitative research** (from the word *quantity*). Quantitative research data can be categorized, ranked, or numbered and thus can be easily translated across cultures and for diverse populations. One example of quantitative research is the use of children's school achievement scores to measure the effectiveness of education.

Since quantities can be easily summarized, compared, charted, and replicated, many scientists prefer quantitative research. Statistics require numbers. Quantitative data are said to provide "rigorous, empirically testable representations" (Nesselroade & Molenaar, 2003, p. 635).

However, when data are reduced to categories and numbers, some nuances and individual distinctions are lost. Many developmental researchers thus turn to **qualitative research** (from *quality*)—asking open-ended questions, reporting answers in narrative (not numerical) form, and generating "a rich description of the phenomena of interest" (Hartmann & Pelzel, 2005, p. 163). Qualitative research reflects cultural and contextual diversity and complexity. But it is also more vulnerable to bias and harder to replicate.

Developmentalists use both quantitative and qualitative methods. Sometimes they translate qualitative research into quantifiable data; sometimes they use qualitative studies to suggest hypotheses for quantitative research. One caution applies especially to qualitative research: Scientists must take care not to leap to conclusions on the basis of one small study (Hartmann & Pelzel, 2005).

Ethics

The most important caution for all scientists, especially for those studying humans, is to uphold ethical standards in their research. Each academic discipline and professional society involved in the study of human development has a *code of ethics* (a set of moral principles) and specific practices within a scientific culture to protect the integrity of research.

Ethical standards and codes are increasingly stringent. Most educational and medical institutions have an *Institutional Research Board* (IRB), a group that permits only research that follows certain guidelines. Although IRBs often slow down scientific study, some research conducted before they were established was clearly unethical, especially when the participants were children, members of minority groups, prisoners, or animals (Blum, 2002; Washington, 2006).

PROTECTION OF RESEARCH PARTICIPANTS Researchers must ensure that participation is voluntary, confidential, and harmless. In Western nations, this entails the *informed consent* of the participants—that is, the participants' understanding of the research procedures and of any risks involved. If children are involved, consent must be obtained from the parents as well as the children, and the children must be allowed to end their participation at any time. In some other nations, ethical standards require consent of the village elders and heads of families, as well as of the research participants themselves (Doumbo, 2005).

Protection of participants may conflict with the goals of science. The Canadian Psychological Association suggests ways to resolve this conflict. Its four guiding principles are "respect for the dignity of persons," "responsible caring," "integrity in relationships," and "responsibility to society." All four should be followed, if possible, but they are ranked in order of importance: Respect for individuals is most important (Canadian Psychological Association, 2000).

IMPLICATIONS OF RESEARCH RESULTS Once a study has been completed, additional issues arise. Scientists are obligated to "promote accuracy, honesty, and truthfulness" (American Psychological Association, 2002).

Deliberate falsification is rare. When it does occur, it leads to ostracism from the scientific community, dismissal from a teaching or research position, and, sometimes, criminal prosecution. Another obvious breach of ethics is to "cook" the data, or distort one's findings, in order to make a particular conclusion seem to be the only reasonable one.

Insidious dangers include unintentionally slanting the conclusions and withholding publication of a result, especially when there is "ferocious . . . pressure from commercial funders to ignore good scientific practice" (Bateson, 2005, p. 645). Even nonprofit research groups and academic institutions may put undue pressure on scientists to produce publishable results.

For this reason, scientific training, collaboration, and replication are crucial. Precautions are built into scientific methodology. In addition, reports in professional journals include (1) affiliation and funding of the researchers, (2) details for replication, (3) the limitations of the findings, and (4) alternative interpretations. For example, the study of listening to sexually degrading lyrics (Martino et al., 2006) was funded by the RAND Corporation, a nonprofit group that tends to be critical of contemporary culture. That fact triggered suspicions in some other scientists.

Ethical standards cannot be taken for granted. As stressed in the beginning of this chapter, researchers, like all other humans, have strong opinions, which they expect research to confirm. Therefore, they might try (sometimes without even realizing it) to achieve the results they want. One researcher in animal behavior explains: "Desirable modes of scientific conduct require considerable self-awareness as well as a reaffirmation of the old virtues of honesty, skepticism, and integrity" (Bateson, 2005, p. 645). Such virtues are essential for every scholar, writer, and student of human development.

WHAT SHOULD WE STUDY? For developmentalists, the most important ethical concern of all is to study issues that will help humans live satisfying and productive lives. Consider these questions, for instance:

- Do we know enough about prenatal drug abuse to protect every fetus?

- Do we know enough about the effects of poverty to enable everyone to be healthy?

- Do we know enough about sexual urges to eliminate AIDS, unwanted pregnancy, and sexual abuse?

- Do we know enough about dying to enable everyone to die with dignity?

The answer to all these questions is a resounding *NO*. The reasons are many, but a major one is that these topics are controversial. Some researchers avoid them, fearing unwelcome and uninformed publicity (Kempner et al., 2005). Few funders are eager to support scientific studies of drug abuse, poverty, sex, or death, partly because people have strong opinions on these issues that may conflict with scientific findings and conclusions. Yet developmentalists have an obligation to study topics that are important for the human family.

The next cohort of developmental scientists will build on what is known, mindful of what issues need to be explored. Remember that the goal is to help all 6.2 billion people on Earth fulfill their potential. Much more needs to be learned. The next 14 chapters are a beginning.

RESPONSE FOR People Who Have Applied to College or Graduate School (from page 36) Most institutions of higher education emphasize quantitative data—the SAT, GRE, GPA, class rank, and so on. Decide for yourself whether this is fairer than a more qualitative approach. ●

KEYpoints

- Correlation is not causation. Two variables may be related not because one causes the other but because of the influence of a third variable.
- Quantitative research is easier to analyze and compare, but qualitative study captures more nuances.
- Research ethics require that the participants be respected; they must give informed consent, and confidentiality must be ensured.
- Scientists need to study and report data on many issues that are crucial for the optimal development of all humans.

SUMMARY

Defining Development

1. The study of human development is a science that seeks to understand how people change or remain the same over time. As a science, it begins with questions and hypotheses, gathers empirical data, and reports results.

2. All kinds of people, of every age, culture, and background, are studied by developmental scientists. One goal is to find the universal patterns of human growth, while recognizing that each person is unique.

The Life-Span Perspective

3. The life-span approach recognizes that development is multidirectional, multicontextual, multicultural, multidisciplinary, and plastic.

4. Change is *multidirectional*: Both continuity (sameness) and discontinuity (sudden shifts) are evident.

5. A *multicontextual* approach to development recognizes that certain experiences or innovations shape people of each cohort and generation. A person's socioeconomic status (SES) also affects development lifelong.

6. The *multicultural* approach recognizes that culture has a profound effect on development.

7. Understanding development requires research and insights from many academic disciplines. This *multidisciplinary* approach recognizes that human behavior is best understood by using many perspectives.

8. Human development is *plastic*, which means that it is possible for individuals to change in important ways.

Theories of Human Development

9. Psychoanalytic theory emphasizes that human actions and thoughts originate from unconscious impulses and childhood conflicts.

10. Erikson's version of psychoanalytic theory emphasizes psychosocial development, specifically as societies, cultures, and parents respond to individuals. Erikson described eight successive stages of psychosocial development, each involving a developmental crisis that occurs as people mature within their context.

11. Behaviorists, or learning theorists, believe that scientists should study observable and measurable behavior. Behaviorism emphasizes conditioning—a learning process. Social learning theory recognizes that much of human behavior is learned by observing the behavior of others.

12. Cognitive theorists believe that thought processes are powerful influences on human attitudes, behavior, and development. Piaget proposed that children's thinking develops through four age-related periods.

13. Systems theories emphasize the interactions among numerous influences on each person. Ecological systems include community and cultural influences; dynamic systems stress that change is pervasive.

Using the Scientific Method

14. Commonly used research methods are scientific observation, the experiment, and the survey. Each method has strengths and weaknesses.

15. To study change over time, scientists use three research designs: cross-sectional research (comparing people of different ages), longitudinal research (studying the same people over time), and cross-sequential research (combining the other two methods).

Cautions from Science

16. A correlation shows that two variables are related. However, it does not prove that one variable causes the other.

17. In qualitative research, information is reported without being quantified and thus is not translated into numbers. Qualitative research best captures the nuances of individual lives, but quantitative research is easier to replicate, interpret, and verify.

18. Ethical behavior is crucial in all the sciences. Not only must participants be protected and their identities kept confidential, but results must be clearly reported and interpreted. The most important ethical question is whether scientists are designing, conducting, analyzing, publishing, and applying the research that is most critically needed.

KEY TERMS

science of human development (p. 4)
scientific method (p. 4)
replication (p. 4)
nature (p. 5)
nurture (p. 5)
critical period (p. 5)
sensitive period (p. 5)
difference-equals-deficit error (p. 6)
life-span perspective (p. 7)

cohort (p. 9)
socioeconomic status (SES) (p. 10)
ethnic group (p. 11)
social construction (p. 12)
epigenetic (p. 12)
mirror neurons (p. 15)
developmental theory (p. 17)
psychoanalytic theory (p. 17)
behaviorism (p. 19)
conditioning (p. 20)

classical conditioning (p. 20)
operant conditioning (p. 21)
reinforcement (p. 21)
social learning theory (p. 22)
cognitive theory (p. 22)
ecological-systems approach (p. 24)
dynamic-systems theory (p. 24)
scientific observation (p. 26)
experiment (p. 28)
independent variable (p. 28)

dependent variable (p. 28)
survey (p. 29)
cross-sectional research (p. 30)
longitudinal research (p. 32)
cross-sequential research (p. 33)
correlation (p. 34)
quantitative research (p. 36)
qualitative research (p. 36)

KEY QUESTIONS

1. What does it mean to say that the study of human development is a science?

2. Give an example of a social construction. Why is it a construction, not a fact?

3. What are some cohort differences between you and your parents?

4. How can behaviorism be seen as a reaction to psychoanalytic theory?

5. How does the exosystem affect your life today?

6. How does a theory differ from a hypothesis?

7. What are the differences between scientific observation, ordinary observation, and experiment?

8. Why would a scientist conduct a cross-sectional study?

9. What are the disadvantages and advantages of qualitative research?

10. What is one additional question about development that should be answered?

APPLICATIONS

1. It is said that culture is pervasive but that people are unaware of it. List 30 things you did *today* that you might have done differently in another culture.

2. How would your life be different if your parents were much higher or lower in SES than they are? What if you had been born in another cohort?

3. Design an experiment to answer a question you have about human development. Specify the question and the hypothesis and then describe the experiment, including the sample size and the variables. (Look first at Appendix B.)

RESPONSE FOR Future Researchers and Science Writers (from page 36) Yes. Anyone you write about must give consent and be fully informed about your intentions. They can be identified by name only if they give permission. For example, family members gave permission before anecdotes about them were included in this text. My nephew David read the first draft of his story (see pages 3–4) and is proud to have his experiences used to teach others. ●

The Science of Development

MULTICULTURAL

Local cultures
Example: College

Ethnicity
National origin
Language
Religion

Social constructions confused with biology
Examples:
Race, gender

Differences thought to be deficits
Example:
Deaf children

MULTIDIRECTIONAL

Continuity

Discontinuity
Stages
Crises

Gains in later adulthood not recognized

> **"HOW AND WHY PEOPLE CHANGE OVER TIME"**
> BOTH NATURE (GENES) AND NURTURE (ENVIRONMENT)

MULTICONTEXTUAL

Socioeconomic status (SES)
Education and income
Rich and poor

History
Cohort
Generation
Old and young

Poverty reduces possibilities

PLASTIC

Nephew David
Mute toddler →
multilingual adult

Emotions
Nature and nurture
Depression over time

Some disabilities are lifelong

MULTIDISCIPLINARY

Traditional
Disciplines:
Biology,
psychology,
sociology
Domains:
Biosocial,
cognitive,
psychosocial

Epigenetic (genes and environment)
Examples:
Teenage delinquency,
mirror neurons

Newer disciplines
Neuroscience (brain)
Genetics (heredity)
Economics (SES)

Overly broad generalization

Overly narrow specialization

THE SCIENTIFIC METHOD

Over the life span
Cross-sectional
(one time)
Longitudinal
(repeated)
Cross-sequential
(combination)

Five steps
Question
Hypothesis
Research
Conclusions
Share findings

Research methods
Observation
Experiments
Surveys

Replication needed

Developmental research takes decades

CAUTIONS AND COMPLICATIONS

Ethics of research
IRB (Institutional Review Board)
Informed consent and confidentiality
Protection of participants

Correlation versus cause

Qualitative and quantitative

Erroneous implications

Correlation confused with causation

Critical questions not asked

THEORIES

Systems
Interactions within and between systems
Bronfenbrenner:
Bioecological
Dynamic systems:
Always changing

Behaviorism
Laws of learning: Reinforcement
Conditioning: Pavlov and Skinner

Psychoanalytic
Childhood influences on adulthood
Freud's and Erikson's stages

Cognitive
Piaget: Stages
Adaptation to new experiences and ideas

Theories need to be tested

KEY
Major topic
Related topic
Potential problem

CHAPTER OUTLINE

GENES AND PRENATAL
Development

I was picking up my daughter Rachel from kindergarten when another mother, Stephanie, pulled me aside. She whispered that she had seen Rachel fall on the sidewalk; her little finger was slightly bent and might need medical attention. A month earlier, Stephanie said, her son had fallen. He had had a similarly bent finger, which turned out to be broken.

Rachel was playing happily, but I saw that her finger was indeed crooked. I walked her home and consulted my husband. He smiled and spread out his hands, revealing a similarly bent little finger. Aha! An inherited abnormality, not an injury. I was relieved that we could avoid the emergency room, but I faulted myself for not noticing that finger earlier. ●

STEPHANIE AND I HAD BOTH mistaken a genetic quirk (heredity) for a potentially serious injury (environment). Many people experience this kind of confusion because they don't think about genes unless a problem appears.

As you remember, both genes and the environment affect every human characteristic. In this chapter, we begin with genetics. We then look at prenatal growth and the miracle of birth. We conclude with the interaction between nature and nurture in nearsightedness, alcoholism, and certain birth defects.

Problems are not the main theme of the chapter, however. Above all, this chapter describes an amazing process—how a single tiny cell becomes a wiggling, squalling, 7-pound human being.

The Beginning of Life

Every person starts life as a single cell, which from the beginning is distinct from all other cells. As this section describes, conception is a prime example of both the universal processes and the unique characteristics that are evident in human life.

Chromosomes and Genes

All living things are composed of cells that promote growth and sustain life according to instructions in their molecules of **DNA (deoxyribonucleic acid).** Each molecule of DNA is called a **chromosome** (see Figure 2.1). Human cells have 46 chromosomes arranged in 23 pairs, with one important exception.

That exception is the reproductive cell, called a **gamete.** Each gamete—*sperm* in a man and *ovum* in a woman—has only 23 chromosomes, one from each of a person's 23 pairs of chromosomes. Each man or woman can produce 2^{23} different gametes, or more than 8 million versions of their 46 chromosomes.

DNA (deoxyribonucleic acid)
The molecule that contains the chemical instructions for cells to manufacture various proteins.

chromosome
One of the 46 molecules of DNA (in 23 pairs) that each cell of the human body contains and that, together, contain all the genes. Other species have more or fewer chromosomes.

gamete
A reproductive cell; that is, a sperm or an ovum that can produce a new individual if it combines with a gamete from the other sex to form a zygote.

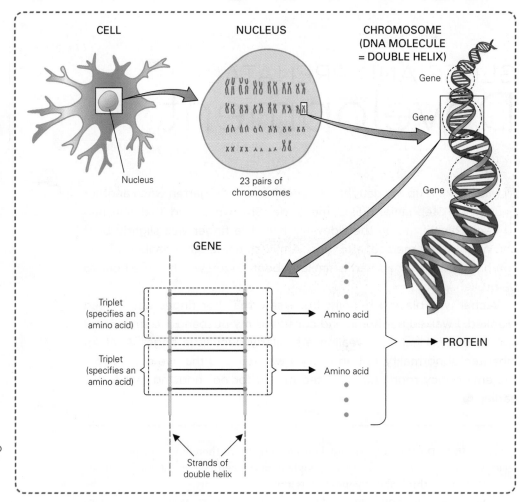

CELL NUCLEUS CHROMOSOME (DNA MOLECULE = DOUBLE HELIX)

Gene

Gene

Nucleus

23 pairs of chromosomes

Gene

GENE

Triplet (specifies an amino acid)

Triplet (specifies an amino acid)

Amino acid

Amino acid

PROTEIN

Strands of double helix

FIGURE 2.1 How Proteins Are Made The genes on the chromosomes in the nucleus of each cell instruct the cell to manufacture the proteins needed to sustain life and development.

zygote
The single cell that is formed from the fusing of two gametes, a sperm and an ovum.

gene
A section of a chromosome and the basic unit for the transmission of heredity, consisting of a string of chemicals that are instructions for the cell to manufacture certain proteins.

genotype
An organism's entire genetic inheritance, or genetic potential.

phenotype
The observable characteristics of a person, including appearance, personality, intelligence, and all other traits.

When a sperm and an ovum combine, they create a new cell in which each of the 23 chromosomes from one parent is paired with a gamete with 23 from the other, for a total of 46 chromosomes. This new cell is called a **zygote.** In each zygote, half the chromosomes are from the mother and half are from the father. Each person began as a zygote, with all the DNA instructions for development contained in that one cell.

These instructions are organized into units called **genes,** with each gene located on a particular one of the 46 chromosomes. Thus, every gene is a separate section of a chromosome, and each gene contains certain instructions for development.

Genes carry their instructions via four chemicals, whose names are abbreviated A, T, C, and G. These four chemicals occur in four possible pairs—AT, TA, CG, and GC—that are strung together in triplets (sets of three pairs) resembling the rungs of a ladder. Each person has about 3 billion pairs, which carry the instructions to form that person.

GENETIC VARIATIONS AND SIMILARITIES Genes are passed down from generation to generation. Half of a person's genes come from each parent, which means one-fourth come from each grandparent, one-eighth from each great-grandparent, and so on.

Together, all the genes make up the organism's genetic inheritance, or **genotype**, which is unique for each person. The genotype is quite different from the **phenotype,** which is a person's actual appearance and manifest behavior.

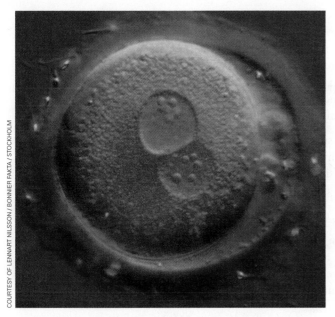

The Moment of Conception This ovum is about to become a zygote. It has been penetrated by a single sperm, whose nucleus now lies next to the nucleus of the ovum. Soon, the two nuclei will fuse, bringing together about 20,000 genes to guide development.

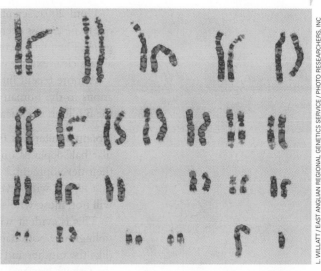

Mapping the Karyotype A *karyotype* portrays a person's chromosomes. To create a karyotype, a cell is grown in a laboratory, magnified, and then usually photographed. The photo is cut into pieces and rearranged so that the matched pairs of chromosomes are lined up from largest (*top left*) to smallest (*bottom row, fourth pair from the left*). Shown at the bottom right is the 23rd chromosome pair: These two do not match, meaning that this karyotype shows a male (XY).

Many genes are identical for every human being. However, some genes vary slightly in their codes from one person to another. Each such variation of a gene is called an **allele.** For example, the two versions of the MAOA gene you read about in Chapter 1 are alleles of the same gene. Some alleles result in life-threatening conditions, others merely differentiate one person from another, and still others have no effect on the phenotype that scientists can detect (Marcus, 2004).

The Human Genome Genetic diversity not only distinguishes each person (you can immediately spot a close friend in a crowd) but also teaches us to appreciate human differences. As one expert said, "What's cool is that we are a mosaic of pieces of genomes. None of us is truly normal" (Eichler, quoted in J. Cohen, 2007b, p. 1315).

Moreover, genetic diversity enables the human species to adapt to many climates, from the frigid Arctic to the steamy tropics. Even devastating diseases do not necessarily kill us all, because of our diverse genes. For instance, a few people have an allele that protects them from the HIV virus that causes AIDS (E. Gonzalez et al., 2005). Similarly, genotype differences allowed some of our ancestors to survive tuberculosis, malaria, the Black Death, and other scourges.

The entire packet of instructions to make a living organism is the **genome.** There is a genome for every species, even for every kind of plant. The human genome is 99.5 percent identical for any two persons (J. Cohen, 2007b); the genomes for humans and chimpanzees are 98 percent the same; the genomes for humans and every other mammal are at least 90 percent the same. All these shared genes allow scientists to learn about human genetics from other creatures, especially mice, by transposing, deactivating, enhancing, and duplicating their genes.

The more scientists experiment with genes, the more they are amazed. A worldwide effort to map all the human genes led to the *Human Genome Project*, which was virtually completed in 2003 and which continues to reveal surprises. One surprise was the discovery of how many genes humans actually have.

allele
Any of the possible forms in which a gene for a particular trait can occur.

genome
The full set of genes that are the instructions to make an individual member of a certain species.

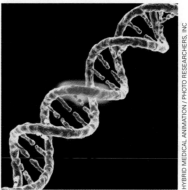

Twelve of 3 Billion Pairs This is a computer illustration of a small segment of one gene, with several triplets. Even a small difference in one gene, such as a few extra triplets, can cause major changes in a person's phenotype.

Until 2001, scientists thought humans had about 100,000 genes, but that turned out to be a gross overestimate. The Human Genome Project found only about 20,000 genes. The precise count is still unknown, partly because of another surprise: It is not always clear exactly where one gene ends and another begins (Pennisi, 2007).

A more recent international project, called the *HapMap,* aims to spot all the variations in the human genome. The HapMap has noted 11 million variations among the 3 billion chemical pairs that constitute the human genome (Hinds et al., 2005).

Sibling Similarities Full siblings get half their genes from each parent, but the particular half depends on which of the millions of possible gametes combined to start their development. Two siblings may have the exact same gene (a 50/50 chance), but in a family with several children, about half will have that particular gene and half will not; those who share one gene do not necessarily share the next one.

This is evident when looking at a family with many children. For example, two siblings may both happen to inherit their father's red hair, but one may have blue eyes (like the mother and the father's father) and the other, brown eyes (like the father and the father's mother). Given that each child has about 10,000 genes from each parent, with half a million common variations and millions more uncommon ones, billions of combinations are possible.

Of course, both parents might have some identical gene pairs; thus, all their children will have the same pair, one from each parent. For instance, if both parents have a pair of blue-eye genes, both will have blue eyes—and so will all their children. But for the many genes and alleles that differ, full siblings are not necessarily alike, even though they all come from the same man and woman.

Twins There is one major exception to genetic diversity. Although every zygote is genetically unique, about once in every 250 human conceptions, the zygote not only duplicates but splits apart completely, creating two, or four, or even eight separate zygotes, each identical to that first single cell. If each of those separated cells implants and grows, multiple births occur. One separation results in **monozygotic twins,** from one *(mono)* zygote (also called *identical twins*). Two or three separations create monozygotic quadruplets or octuplets. (An incomplete split creates *conjoined twins,* formerly called Siamese twins.)

Because monozygotic multiples originate from the same zygote, they have the same genotype, with identical genetic instructions for physical appearance, psychological traits, vulnerability to diseases, and everything else. However, because nurture always affects nature, even before birth, identical twins do not have exactly the same phenotype.

monozygotic twins
Twins who originate from one zygote that splits apart very early in development. (Also called *identical twins.*)

Same Birthday, Same (or Different?) Genes Twins who are of different sexes or who have obvious differences in personality are dizygotic, sharing only half of their genes. Many same-sex twins with similar temperaments are dizygotic as well. One of these twin pairs is dizygotic; the other is monozygotic.

OBSERVATION QUIZ
Can you tell which pair is monozygotic? (see answer, page 48) →

DAVID YOUNG-WOLFF / PHOTOEDIT

JOHNER IMAGES / GETTY IMAGES

Dizygotic twins, also called *fraternal twins,* occur about twice as often as monozygotic twins. They began life as two *(di)* zygotes created by two ova fertilized by two sperm at roughly the same time. (Usually, only one ovum leaves the ovaries per month, but sometimes two or more ova are released.) Triplets can be trizygotic, and so on.

Dizygotic twins, like any other siblings, have half their genes in common. They can look quite different (about half are male/female pairs) or they can look quite similar, again like other siblings.

The incidence of dizygotic twins is genetic, because some women inherit the tendency to release more than one ovum when they ovulate. This genetic tendency varies by ethnicity. For example, dizygotic twins occur about once in every 11 births among the Yoruba in Nigeria, once in 100 among the British, and once in 700 among the Japanese (Gall, 1996; Piontelli, 2002). On the contrary, the incidence of monozygotic twins is not genetic; they are equally rare in every ethnic group.

Age also matters. Older women are more likely to release more than one ovum at a time and thus to have dizygotic twins.

MALE AND FEMALE In 22 of the 23 pairs of human chromosomes that each person inherits, the chromosomes of each pair are closely matched. These 44 chromosomes are called *autosomes,* which means that they are not connected to the sex chromosomes (the other two).

The 23rd pair of chromosomes is a special case. In females, it is composed of two large X-shaped chromosomes. Accordingly, it is designated **XX.** In males, the 23rd pair has one large X-shaped chromosome and one smaller Y-shaped chromosome. It is called **XY.**

Because a female's 23rd pair is XX, every ovum that her body creates contains either one X or the other—but always an X. Because a male's 23rd pair is XY, half of his sperm carry an X chromosome and half carry a Y. The Y chromosome has a gene that directs the developing fetus to make male organs. Thus, the sex of the developing organism depends on which sperm penetrates the ovum—either an X sperm, which creates a girl (XX), or a Y sperm, which creates a boy (XY) (see Figure 2.2).

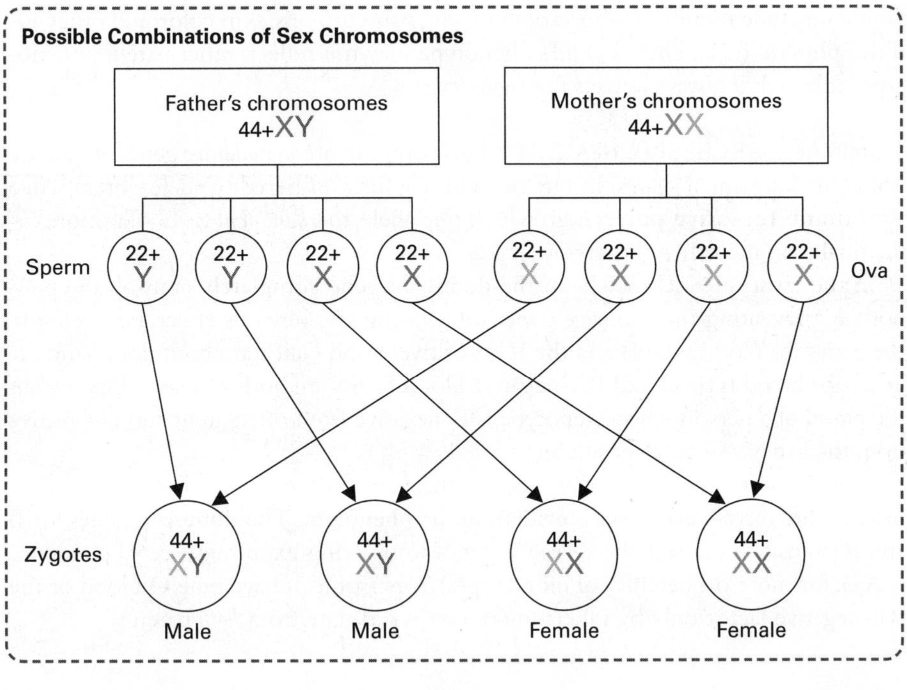

dizygotic twins
Twins who are formed when two separate ova are fertilized by two separate sperm at roughly the same time. (Also called *fraternal twins.*)

XX
A 23rd chromosome pair that consists of two X-shaped chromosomes, one each from the mother and the father. XX zygotes become females.

XY
A 23rd chromosome pair that consists of an X-shaped chromosome from the mother and a Y-shaped chromosome from the father. XY zygotes become males.

Possible Combinations of Sex Chromosomes

FIGURE 2.2 Determining a Zygote's Sex Any given couple can produce four possible combinations of sex chromosomes; two lead to female children and two, to male. In terms of the future person's sex, it does not matter which of the mother's Xs the zygote inherited. All that matters is whether the father's Y sperm or X sperm fertilized the ovum. However, for X-linked conditions, it matters a great deal because typically one, but not both, of the mother's Xs carries the trait.

ANSWER TO OBSERVATION QUIZ
(from page 46) The Japanese American girls are the monozygotic twins. If you were not sure, look at their teeth, their eyebrows, and the shape of their faces, compared with the ears and chins of the boys. ●

polygenic
Referring to a trait that is influenced by many genes.

multifactorial
Referring to a trait that is affected by many factors, both genetic and environmental.

regulator gene
A gene that directs the interactions of other genes, controlling their expression, duplication, and transcription.

additive gene
A gene that adds something to some aspect of the phenotype. Its contribution depends on additions from the other genes, which may come from either the same or the other parent.

ESPECIALLY FOR Future Parents
Suppose you wanted your daughters to be short and your sons to be tall. Could you achieve that? (see response, page 50) →

dominant–recessive pattern
The interaction of a pair of alleles in such a way that the phenotype reveals the influence of one allele (the dominant gene) more than that of the other (the recessive gene).

The natural sex ratio at conception is close to 50/50, since each sperm has one chromosome of the father's 23rd pair of chromosomes, equally often a Y and an X. The sex ratio at birth is affected by serious adversity (such as famine) because males are more likely to be spontaneously aborted early in prenatal development.

Notice that if the 23rd pair is XY (male), it includes genes that are not paired. In XX (female) zygotes as well, one of the two X chromosomes is deactivated early in prenatal development, so genes on one X cannot pair with those on the other X.

Likewise, autosomes can carry genes that are not paired, or that dominate the other member of the pair, or that are activated only if particular other genes or nongenetic influences (the nutrients and transcription factors surrounding each gene) are present. Thus, for many reasons, the interaction among and between genes varies. Some of these variations are now described.

Genetic Interactions

No gene functions alone. Almost every trait is **polygenic** (affected by many genes) and **multifactorial** (influenced by many factors). The same gene produces the legs of butterflies, cats, centipedes, and humans. Similarly, the eyes of flies, mice, and people all originate from one gene, called *Pax6*. Other genes direct the human fetus to grow only two legs and to develop human visual acuity.

To differentiate humans from other animals, the action of those other genes, called **regulator genes,** is crucial. Regulator genes direct polygenic interactions, controlling the genetic expression, duplication, and transcription of the other genes (Marcus, 2004). Human regulator genes allow distinctively human modes of talking, walking, and thinking to spring from the same genes that control the equivalent functions in other creatures.

ADDITIVE HEREDITY Some genes are **additive genes.** Their effects *add up* to make the phenotype. When genes interact additively, the phenotype reflects all the genes that are involved. Height, hair curliness, and skin color, for instance, are influenced by additive genes. Indeed, height is affected by an estimated 100 genes, each contributing a small amount (Little, 2002). (Of course, nutrition and illness also affect the phenotype for height.)

Centuries of marriage between people with different ancestries means that most families include members who vary in height, hair curliness, skin color, and other additive physical traits. Thus, a child's phenotype may not reflect either parent's phenotype, although it always reflects their genotype.

DOMINANT-RECESSIVE HEREDITY Less common are *nonadditive* genes, which do not contribute equal shares. In one nonadditive form of heredity, alleles interact in a **dominant–recessive pattern,** in which one allele, the *dominant gene*, is far more influential than the other, the *recessive gene*.

In the most unequal match-up, the dominant gene completely controls the phenotype, preventing the recessive gene from having any obvious effect. For example, the genes for blood type B and the Rh-positive blood factor are both dominant; the genes for blood type O and Rh-negative blood factor are both recessive. That means the blood of a person whose genotype is B-negative from one parent and O-positive from the other will be B-positive.

The reason for the B-positive blood is that, since the genes for both O and Rh-negative are recessive, neither is evident in the phenotype. The dominant genes for B and Rh-positive prevent the recessive genes from being expressed (see Appendix A, p. A-3, for more on heredity of blood types). A person can have type O blood or the Rh-negative factor only by inheriting the recessive gene from *both* parents.

Contrary to this example, however, many recessive genes are not *completely* hidden when paired with a dominant gene. For example, because the gene for brown eyes is dominant and the gene for blue eyes is recessive, most people who have one gene for blue eyes and one for brown end up with brown eyes. However, some people with this pairing have hazel eyes, a color that hints at their recessive blue-eye gene.

Carriers and Genetic Expression

As you learn more about the interactions among genetic and nongenetic influences on development, remember to distinguish between a person's *genotype,* or genetic *potential*, and *phenotype,* or the actual *expression* of that genetic inheritance in physical appearance, health, intelligence, and actions.

Everyone has many recessive genes in his or her genotype that are not expressed in the phenotype. In genetic terms, each of us is a **carrier** of unexpressed genes; that is, we "carry" a gene that will be transmitted to half our sperm or ova. Because we are merely carriers, we do not express that trait in our phenotype.

Since each gamete (reproductive cell) has half of each parent's genes, there is a 50/50 chance that a carried gene will be passed on to a child. If a child inherits a carried gene, whether or not that gene is expressed depends on many other genetic and nongenetic factors. Thus, the child could also be just a carrier, with the gene unexpressed, or could express that gene in the phenotype.

Heritability is a statistical term that indicates what portion of the variation in a particular trait within a particular population is inherited. Height, for instance, is highly heritable. Thus, when children are well nourished, about 90 percent of the height differences among children of the same age is genetic. Making a short 5-year-old drink his milk and eat his dinner will never make him a tall adult (unless he has tall genes but was previously severely malnourished).

Heritability is a useful measure within a population. But it is not accurate when applied from one population to another, or even to one individual in a particular population. For example, Rachel's bent little finger, mentioned in the chapter's opening, is the product of genes; finger shape is highly heritable. However, nurture always affects nature. As her mother, I wonder if that anomaly appeared because of something I did during early pregnancy, perhaps involving my diet, or stress, or sleep. I know that she inherited her finger from her father, but I will never know how much nurture affected heritability in that one case.

There is a general point to be made here. Every trait, action, and attitude has a genetic component: Without genes, no behavior could exist. But without environment, no gene could be expressed. The specifics are complicated, requiring longitudinal and multicultural research. Heritability is useful, but prediction in any one instance is not entirely certain.

carrier
A person whose genotype includes a gene that is not expressed in the phenotype. Such an unexpressed gene occurs in half the carrier's gametes and thus is passed on to half the carrier's children, who will most likely be carriers, too. Generally, the characteristic appears in the phenotype only when such a gene is inherited from both parents.

heritability
A statistic that indicates what percentage of the variation in a particular trait within a particular population, in a particular context and era, can be traced to genes.

CORBIS / THE PURCELL TEAM

Shyness Is Universal Inhibition is a psychological trait that is influenced by genetics. It is more common at some ages (late infancy and early adolescence) and in some gene pools (natives of northern Europe and East Asia) than others. But every community includes some individuals who are unmistakably shy, such as this toddler in Woleai, more than 3,000 miles west of Hawaii.

KEY points

- Humans have 46 chromosomes that match up in 23 pairs and about 20,000 genes.
- Genetic diversity is protective of the human species. Full siblings (except monozygotic twins) have only half their genes in common.
- Both parents' genes contribute equally to a child's genotype, but only sperm, not ova, determine the child's sex.
- Genes interact in many ways; the phenotype differs from the genotype. Everyone is a carrier of genes for some traits that are not expressed in the phenotype. Heritability is a useful statistic for a population group, but it does not predict individual differences.

RESPONSE FOR Future Parents (from page 48) Yes, but you wouldn't want to. You would have to choose one mate for your sons and another for your daughters, and you would have to use sex-selection methods. Even so, it might not work, given all the genes on your genotype. More important, the effort would be unethical, unnatural, and possibly illegal. ●

Down syndrome
A condition in which a person has 47 chromosomes instead of the usual 46, with three rather than two chromosomes at the 21st position. People with Down syndrome typically have distinctive characteristics, including unusual facial features (thick tongue, round face, slanted eyes), heart abnormalities, and language difficulties. (Also called *trisomy-21*.)

Universal Happiness All young children delight in painting brightly colored pictures on a big canvas, but this scene is unusual for two reasons: Daniel has trisomy-21, and this photograph was taken at the only school in Chile where normal and special-needs children share classrooms.

REUTERS / CLAUDIA DAUT

Genetic Problems

The chromosomal and genetic interactions just described are fascinating in themselves, but this knowledge has very practical implications. Sometimes a part of a gene has too many repetitions of a base pair; or a recessive allele pairs with another, similar allele; or a zygote does not have exactly 23 chromosomes. These anomalies can cause various disorders, some of which are discussed here.

Chromosomal Abnormalities

Gametes (sperm or ova) may have more or fewer than 23 chromosomes. This happens for many reasons, both inherited and environmental (such as a parent's exposure to radiation). The variable that most often correlates with chromosomal abnormalities is the age of the mother, presumably because ova become increasingly fragile by midlife. The father's age is also relevant (Crow, 2003).

Most abnormal zygotes formed by such gametes do not duplicate, divide, and differentiate (K. L. Moore & Persaud, 2003) or are spontaneously aborted early in pregnancy. Nonetheless, about once in every 200 births, an infant is born with 45, 47, or even 48 or 49 chromosomes instead of the usual 46.

Each chromosomal abnormality produces a recognizable *syndrome,* a cluster of distinct characteristics that occur together. Typically, the cause is that three chromosomes, instead of the usual two, occupy a particular location—a condition called a *trisomy.* Traditionally, such problems were recognized by physical signs such as malformed eyes, hands, or inner organs, but now chromosomal analysis can detect anomalies that do not affect appearance (Hamerton & Evans, 2005).

DOWN SYNDROME Most embryos with chromosomal abnormalities are aborted spontaneously. Among those that survive, however, the most notable problem is three copies of chromosome 21, which results in **Down syndrome** (also called *trisomy-21*). Most individuals with Down syndrome have specific facial characteristics (thick tongue, round face, slanted eyes). Many also have hearing losses, heart abnormalities, muscle weakness, and short stature. All are slow to develop language.

Adults with Down syndrome age faster than other adults. By age 40, most have one or more problems of aging, including cataracts, dementia, and certain forms of cancer. Nonetheless, children and young adults with Down syndrome can live for many happy years. One such person advised others with Down syndrome:

> You may have to work hard, but don't ever give up. Always remember that you are important. You are special in your own unique way. And one of the best ways to feel good about yourself is to share yourself with someone else.
>
> [*Christi Todd, quoted in Hassold & Patterson, 1999*]

ABNORMALITIES OF THE SEX CHROMOSOMES About 1 in every 500 infants has only one X and no Y chromosome (the X stands alone) or has three or more sex chromosomes, not just a pair. Although the normal 22 pairs of autosomes allow fetal growth and newborn survival, these abnormalities at the 23rd pair hinder cognitive and psychosocial development as well as sexual maturation.

A newborn with only one X has *Turner syndrome.* As a result, she is unusually short, her female organs are underdeveloped, and she cannot conceive and bear children. Usually she is slow to develop, particularly in spatial understanding.

If there are three, four, or five sex chromosomes instead of two, a child may seem normal until puberty. If he is XXY, he has *Klinefelter syndrome*, whose symptoms include learning problems. Klinefelter syndrome may not be recognized until puberty, when the double X keeps a boy's penis from growing and fat accumulates around his breasts. Sometimes the condition is not recognized until adulthood, when a man discovers that he is infertile.

Many people with sex-chromosome abnormalities have "productive and healthy lives" (Hamerton & Evans, 2005, p. 631). Hormone therapy, special education, and psychological counseling for them and their families can help these people develop normally.

Gene Disorders

Everyone carries genes or alleles that *could* produce serious diseases or handicaps in the next generation (see Table 2.1 on pages 52–53). Given that most genetic disorders are polygenic and that the mapping of the human genome is recent, the exact impact of each allele is not yet known (Hinds et al., 2005). However, single-gene disorders have been studied for decades (S. M. Miller et al., 2006).

DOMINANT DISORDERS Most of the 7,000 *known* single-gene disorders are dominant and easy to identify as such: Half the offspring of parents with a dominant disorder will also have the disorder (in other words, it will be expressed in their phenotype). If the condition is fatal in childhood, it will, of course, never be transmitted. Thus, all the dominant disorders either begin in adulthood or have relatively mild or variable symptoms.

One example of a disorder thought to be dominant is *Tourette syndrome.* Some who inherit the Tourette gene exhibit uncontrollable tics and explosive outbursts of verbal obscenities. But most have milder symptoms, such as an occasional twitch that is barely noticeable or a postponable impulse to speak inappropriately (Olson, 2004).

RECESSIVE DISORDERS The number of recessive conditions is probably in the millions. Recessive genes are usually carried on the autosomes, which means that men and women are equally likely to carry them and offspring of both sexes are equally likely to inherit them. For example, cystic fibrosis, thalassemia, and sickle-cell anemia are equally devastating in both sexes and are also fairly common; about 1 in 12 North Americans is a carrier for one of them.

Lethal recessive conditions are usually rare. The three conditions just mentioned are exceptions. Carriers of the recessive gene for cystic fibrosis, thalassemia, or sickle-cell anemia are likely to survive and reproduce because the very gene that causes illness when two recessive genes are inherited is protective if a person is only a carrier.

For example, carriers of the sickle-cell trait have some protection against malaria, a deadly killer in central Africa. As a result, over the centuries, African carriers were more likely than noncarriers to survive. Similarly, the single cystic fibrosis gene is more common among people whose ancestors came from northern Europe because carriers of that gene may have been protected against cholera.

Some recessive conditions are sex-linked, usually carried on the X chromosome. Males are more likely to be affected by such conditions because they have no second X with a healthy dominant gene (see Table 2.2 on page 54).

One X-linked condition, called **fragile X syndrome,** is caused by a single gene that has more than 200 repetitions of a triplet (Plomin et al., 2008). (It is normal to have some repetitions, but not this many.) Fragile X syndrome is the most common form of *inherited* mental retardation (many other forms are not inherited). In addition

fragile X syndrome
A genetic disorder in which part of the X chromosome seems to be attached to the rest of it by a very thin string of molecules. The cause is a single gene that has more than 200 repetitions of one triplet.

On the Autism Spectrum Ryan, age 11, prefers his action figures to real people. He has Asperger syndrome, a pervasive developmental disorder that is largely inherited, especially by boys. Ryan's two older brothers have it, too.

JOHN AMIS / AP

TABLE 2.1 Common Genetic Diseases and Conditions

Name	Description	Prognosis	Probable Inheritance	Incidence*	Carrier Detection?†	Prenatal Detection?
Albinism	No melanin; person is very blond and pale	Normal, but must avoid sun damage	Recessive	Rare overall; 1 in 8 Hopi Indians is a carrier	No	No
Alzheimer disease	Loss of memory and increasing mental impairment	Eventual death, often after years of dependency	Early onset—dominant; after age 60—multifactorial	Fewer than 1 in 100 middle-aged adults; perhaps 25 percent of all adults over age 85	Yes, for some genes; ApoE4 allele increases incidence	No
Cancer	Tumors that can spread	With early diagnosis and treatment, most are cured; without them, death usually within 3 years	Multifactorial; almost all cancers have a genetic component	More than half of all people develop some form of cancer; about one-fourth die of it	No	No
Cleft palate, cleft lip	The two sides of the upper lip or palate are not joined	Correctable by surgery	Multifactorial	1 in every 700 births; more common in Asian Americans and American Indians	No	Yes
Club foot	The foot and ankle are twisted	Correctable by surgery	Multifactorial	1 in every 200 births; more common in boys	No	Yes
Cystic fibrosis	Mucous obstructions, especially in lungs and digestive organs	Most live to middle adulthood	Recessive gene; also spontaneous mutations	1 in 3,200; 1 in 25 European Americans is a carrier	Sometimes	Yes, in most cases
Diabetes	Abnormal sugar metabolism because of insufficient insulin	Early onset (type 1) fatal without insulin; for later onset (type 2), variable risks	Multifactorial; for later onset, body weight is significant	Type 1: 1 in 500 births; more common in American Indians and African Americans. Type 2: 1 adult in 6 by age 60	No	No
Deafness (congenital)	Inability to hear from birth on	Cochlear implants and/or sign language contribute to leading a normal life	Multifactorial; some forms are recessive	1 in 1,000 births; more common in people from Middle East	No	No
Hemophilia	Absence of clotting factor in blood	Death from internal bleeding; blood transfusions prevent damage	X-linked recessive; also spontaneous mutations	1 in 10,000 males; royal families of England, Russia, and Germany had it	Yes	Yes
Hydrocephalus	Obstruction causes excess fluid in the brain	Brain damage and death; surgery can make normal life possible	Multifactorial	1 in every 100 births	No	Yes
Muscular dystrophy (30 diseases)	Weakening of muscles	Inability to walk, move; wasting away and sometimes death	Recessive, x-linked, or multifactorial	1 in every 3,500 males develops Duchenne's	Yes, for some forms	Yes, for some forms

OBSERVATION QUIZ

Is there any ethnic group that does not have a genetic condition that is more common among its members than among the general population? (see answer, page 54) ➜

to having cognitive problems, children with fragile X often have muscle weakness and are shy, with poor social skills (Hagerman, 2002).

Another sex-linked condition is *hemophilia*, in which the blood does not clot normally. In the past such children often bled to death; today blood transfusions can save their lives.

The most common X-linked condition is *color blindness*, an inability to distinguish certain hues, especially red and green. The reason color blindness is so common is that the condition is not debilitating and thus is often passed down from father to

TABLE 2.1 (Continued)

Name	Description	Prognosis	Probable Inheritance	Incidence*	Carrier Detection?[†]	Prenatal Detection?
Neural-tube defects (open spine)	Anencephaly (parts of the brain missing) or spina bifida (lower spine not closed)	Anencephalic—severe retardation; spina bifida—poor lower body control	Multifactorial; folic acid deficit and genes	Anencephaly—1 in 1,000 births; spina bifida—3 in 1,000; more common in Welsh and Scots	No	Yes
Phenylketo-nuria (PKU)	Abnormal digestion of protein	Mental retardation, preventable by diet begun by 10 days after birth	Recessive	1 in 100 European Americans is a carrier, especially Norwegians and Irish	Yes	Yes
Pyloric stenosis	Overgrowth of muscle in intestine	Vomiting, loss of weight, eventual death; correctable by surgery	Multifactorial	1 male in 200, 1 female in 1,000; less common in African Americans	No	No
Rett syndrome	Neurological developmental disorder	Boys die at birth. At 6–18 months, girls lose communication and motor skills	X-linked	1 in 10,000 female births	No	Some-times
Schizophrenia	Severely distorted thought processes	No cure; drugs, hospitalization, psychotherapy ease symptoms	Multifactorial	1 in 100 people develop it by early adulthood	No	No
Sickle-cell anemia	Abnormal blood cells	Possible painful "crisis"; heart and kidney failure; treatable with drugs	Recessive	1 in 11 African Americans and 1 in 20 Latinos are carriers	Yes	Yes
Tay-Sachs disease	Enzyme disease	Healthy infant becomes weaker, usually dying by age 5	Recessive	1 in 30 American Jews and 1 in 20 French Canadians are carriers	Yes	Yes
Thalassemia	Abnormal blood cells	Paleness and listlessness, low resistance to infections, slow growth	Usually recessive, occasionally dominant	1 in 10 Americans from southern Europe, northern Africa, or south Asia is a carrier	Yes	Yes
Tourette syndrome	Uncontrollable tics, body jerking, verbal outbursts	Appears at about age 5; worsens and then improves with age	Dominant, but variable penetrance	1 in 250 children	Sometimes	No

*Incidence statistics vary from country to country; those given here are for the United States. All these diseases can occur in any ethnic group. Many affected groups limit transmission through genetic counseling; for example, the incidence of Tay-Sachs disease is declining because many Jewish young adults obtain testing and counseling before marriage.

[†]"Yes" refers to carrier detection. Family history can also reveal genetic risk.

Sources: Benacerraf, 2007; Briley & Sulser, 2001; M. G. Butler & Meaney, 2005; Haydon, 2007; Hemminki et al., 2008; Klug et al., 2008; McKusick, 2007; Mange & Mange, 1999; K. L. Moore & Persaud, 2007; Shahin et al., 2002.

daughter and then from mother to son. All these conditions are much more common in boys than girls, because girls are likely to be protected by their second X.

Advising Prospective Parents

Genetic counseling helps people know how likely they are to conceive a child with a severe genetic or chromosomal condition. Counselors need to be carefully trained, because emotional reactions to such information can lead many clients to misinterpret the words *facts, risk,* and *probability* (O'Doherty, 2006).

genetic counseling
Consultation and testing by trained experts that enable individuals to learn about their genetic heritage, including harmful conditions that they might pass along to any children they conceive.

ANSWER TO OBSERVATION QUIZ
(from page 52) No. As you see, many major ethnic groups are mentioned in Table 2.1. In fact, even much smaller groups whose members tend to marry within the group also have higher rates of particular conditions. ●

ESPECIALLY FOR Historians Some genetic diseases may have changed the course of history. For instance, the last czar of Russia had four healthy daughters and one son with hemophilia. Once called the royal disease, hemophilia is X-linked. How could this rare condition have affected the monarchies of Russia, England, Austria, Germany, and Spain? (see response, page 56) ➜

TABLE 2.2 The 23rd Pair and X-Linked Color Blindness

X indicates an X chromosome with the X-linked gene for color blindness

23rd Pair	Phenotype	Genotype	Next Generation
1. XX	Normal woman	Not a carrier	No color blindness from mother
2. XY	Normal man	Normal X from mother	No color blindness from father
3. XX	Normal woman	Carrier from father	Half her children will inherit her X. The girls with her X will be carriers; the boys with her X will be color-blind.
4. XX	Normal woman	Carrier from mother	Half her children will inherit her X. The girls with her X will be carriers; the boys with her X will be color-blind.
5. XY	Color-blind man	Inherited from mother	All his daughters will have his X. None of his sons will have his X. All his children will have normal vision, unless their mother also had an X for color blindness.
6. XX	Color-blind woman (rare)	Inherited from both parents	Every child will have one X from her. Therefore, every son will be color-blind. Daughters will be only carriers, unless they also inherit an X from the father, as their mother did.

"The Hardest Decision I Ever Had to Make" That's how this woman described her decision to terminate her third pregnancy when genetic testing revealed that the fetus had Down syndrome. She soon became pregnant again with a male fetus that had the normal 46 chromosomes, as did her two daughters and her fourth child, not yet born when this photo was taken. Many personal factors influence such decisions. Do you think she and her husband would have made the same choice if they had had no other children?

ROBERT SPENCER /THE NEW YORK TIMES

Genetic counselors try to follow two ethical guidelines: (1) Their clients' test results are kept confidential, beyond the reach of insurance companies and public records, and (2) decisions regarding sterilization, adoption, abortion, or carrying a pregnancy to term are made by the clients, not by the counselor.

PRESENTING THE FACTS Genetic counselors must present facts, not opinions, but facts are not always straightforward. If one parent has a dominant gene for a particular disease or if both members of a couple carry the same recessive gene, odds are that half their children will inherit the dominant gene or that one out of four will have the double recessive. But before conception, those are merely odds. Some, all, or none of their offspring *could* inherit the disease. Each pregnancy is a risk, another roll of the same dice.

To add to the uncertainty, the specific effects of many regulator genes are not yet known, and medical treatments for many conditions are not yet proven effective (Gustafson, 2006). Prospective parents need to decide when to take the risk, when to wait, when to avoid pregnancy, and when to opt for prenatal testing.

More problems arise because tests during pregnancy often merely reveal that more tests are needed (see Table 2.3). For instance, the level of alpha-fetoprotein (AFP, found via a blood test) may be too high (possibly indicating a neural-tube defect) or too low (possibly indicating Down syndrome), but high and low levels are usually false alarms. Amniocentesis and chorionic villi sampling (CVS) are more definitive, but they are more invasive.

Furthermore, amniocentesis may reveal not an extra chromosome with known effects but a small segment that is added to a chromosome—with unknown implications. Modern technology often finds

TABLE 2.3 Methods of Postconception Testing

Method	Description	Risks, Concerns, and Indications
Pre-implantation testing	After in vitro fertilization, one cell is removed from each zygote at the four- or eight-cell stage and analyzed.	Not entirely accurate. Requires surgery, in vitro fertilization, and rapid assessment. This delays implantation and reduces the likelihood of successful birth. It is used only when couples are at high risk of known, testable genetic disorders.
Tests for pregnancy-associated plasma protein (PAPPA) and human chorionic gonadotropin	Blood tests are usually done at about 11 weeks to indicate levels of these substances.	Indicate normal pregnancy, but false-positive or false-negative results sometimes occur.
Alpha-fetoprotein assay	The mother's blood is tested for the level of alpha-fetoprotein (AFP). Now usually done at mid-pregnancy; often combined with other blood tests and repeat sonogram.	Indicates neural-tube defects, multiple embryos (both cause high AFP), or Down syndrome (low AFP). Normal levels change each week; interpretation requires accurate dating of conception.
Sonogram (ultrasound)	High-frequency sound waves are used to produce a "picture" of the fetus as early as 6 weeks. Sonograms are more accurate later in pregnancy to detect less apparent problems, to confirm earlier suspicions, and to anticipate birth complications.	Reveals problems such as a small head or other body malformations, excess fluid accumulating on the brain, Down syndrome (detected by expert, looking at neck of fetus), and several diseases (for instance, of the kidneys). Estimates fetal age and reveals multiple fetuses, placental position, and fetal growth, all of which are useful to know in every pregnancy. Sometimes sex is apparent. No known risks, unlike the X-rays that it has replaced.
Chorionic villi sampling (CVS)	A sample of the chorion (part of the placenta) is obtained (via sonogram and syringe) at about 10 weeks and analyzed. Since the cells of the placenta are genetically identical to the cells of the fetus, this can indicate many chromosomal or genetic abnormalities.	Provides the same information as amniocentesis but can be performed earlier. Not 100 percent accurate. Can cause spontaneous abortion (rare).
Amniocentesis	About half an ounce of the fluid inside the placenta is withdrawn (via sonogram and syringe) at about 16 weeks. The cells are cultured and analyzed.	Spontaneous abortion is rare (less than 0.05 percent). Detects chromosomal abnormalities and other genetic and prenatal problems. Is done later in pregnancy than other tests, and it takes a week before results are known.

Sources: Eddleman et al., 2006; Malone et al., 2005; K. L. Moore & Persaud, 2003; Reece & Hobbins, 2007; D. Wright et al., 2006.

problems that were previously undetectable. Some test results are *false positives,* suggesting an abnormality that is not actually present. Others are *false negatives,* providing unfounded reassurance when a fetus is actually impaired.

Newborns are also tested for many genetic diseases; here, too, false positives cause needless worry. Moreover, accurate results (true positives) may reveal a problem for which no treatment exists, or a marriage may be strained if a spouse is told that he or she is, or is not, a carrier (F. A. Miller et al., 2009). Nonetheless, most health professionals, and many organizations that are concerned with children's health (such as the March of Dimes), advocate the testing of prospective parents and newborns for dozens of conditions (N. S. Green et al., 2006).

PKU: A SUCCESS STORY One routine test is for **phenylketonuria (PKU),** a recessive condition for which northern Europeans are particularly at risk (Welsh & Pennington, 2000). (The incidence is 26 times higher among the Irish than among the Japanese.) Newborns with the double-recessive PKU gene become severely retarded if they consume phenylalanine, an amino acid found in many foods. Parents of a baby with PKU need to feed their child a special diet.

phenylketonuria (PKU)
A genetic disorder in which a child's body is unable to metabolize an amino acid called phenylalanine. The resulting buildup of phenylalanine in body fluids causes brain damage, progressive mental retardation, and other symptoms.

RESPONSE FOR Historians (from page 54): Hemophilia is a painful chronic disease that (before blood transfusions became feasible) killed a boy before adulthood. Though rare, it ran in European royal families, whose members often intermarried, which meant that many queens (including England's Queen Victoria) were carriers of hemophilia and thus were destined to watch half their sons die of it. All families, even rulers of nations, are distracted from their work when they have a child with a mysterious and lethal illness. Some historians believe that hemophilia among European royalty was an underlying cause of the Russian Revolution of 1917 as well as of the spread of democracy in the nineteenth and twentieth centuries. ●

Thousands of children who would have died in institutions now live fairly normal lives because of early testing and this special diet. A full-grown adult with PKU may eat foods containing phenylalanine; the exception is that a woman with PKU who wishes to become pregnant must go back to the special diet in order not to harm her embryo (Plomin et al., 2008).

The PKU case is straightforward: No professional would suggest skipping PKU testing, nor would any parent potentially cause damage to the baby's brain by refusing testing. The test for PKU is quite accurate, the treatment is fairly simple, and the result is a normal child instead of a severely impaired one.

However, PKU has many variants, some of which cause mild retardation even when the diet is followed. Some other consequences were not anticipated by the scientists who discovered the PKU gene; for example, some couples with a PKU child avoid a second pregnancy, and some children with PKU rebel and eat forbidden food, while others become overly dependent on their parents.

Despite these problems, a cost-benefit analysis makes it obvious that PKU testing is wise. However, the situation is not always so clear-cut for other conditions. Often the diagnosis is less certain and the consequences more variable (Sandel, 2007), as the following explains.

A VIEW FROM SCIENCE

Genetic Testing and Parental Choice

At the moment, genetic testing occurs primarily when there is a known risk of a particular condition that would result in the birth of a severely impaired child, often one who would become less and less capable and die before reaching adulthood. However, as more genetic traits are discovered, prospective parents may seek testing in order to abort those embryos that do not have the exact traits that they prefer.

This practice was common in China and India because a sonogram or amniocentesis can easily discover the sex of a fetus. In some cities in China, selective abortions became an unexpected consequence of a government policy begun in 1979 (Greenhalgh, 2008). A "one child per couple" campaign reduced poverty but led to abortions of female fetuses because many parents wanted their only child to be a boy.

Since 1993, the Chinese government has allowed many families to have a second child and forbidden prenatal testing to determine sex. But that "law has been spottily enforced": In one city with careful records (Guiyang), 75 girls are born for every 100 boys (H. W. French, 2005). Similar imbalances have occurred in other nations.

The United Nations opposes prenatal sex selection. Some nations allow it, but others—including China, India, Australia, and Canada—outlaw it except to prevent the birth of a child with severe disabilities (such as hemophilia, which affects only boys).

If you were a prospective parent, would you welcome a baby who had the following genetic tendencies?

● *Diseases:* heart attack, constricted arteries, diabetes, high blood pressure, Alzheimer disease

"Save the Girl Child" That's the slogan on this poster, which appears on the wall outside a New Delhi hospital. Sex selection, while illegal, is still widespread in India. In 2008, in response to the threat of a lawsuit, Google and Yahoo removed all advertisements for sex-selection products and services from their Indian connections.

PEDRO UGARTE / AFP / GETTY IMAGES

● *Responses to substances:* general substance abuse, alcoholism, tobacco addiction, lactose intolerance (poor digestion of milk)

● *Personality:* seeks novelty, evening preference, antisocial behavior, conduct disorder

● *Appearance:* male, blue eyes, fair skin, sticky earwax

An embryo with genes for all these traits would become a difficult, curious, and hard-to-control boy, likely to become a risk-taking drug addict and then to develop heart disease. If he survived to old age, he might become demented.

All these traits did, in fact, exist in one person, although when he was in the uterus, genetic testing was not yet available. True to his genetic heritage, he was a troublesome, disobedient boy who became a rebellious adolescent. As a young adult, he was drafted to fight in Vietnam. To avoid front-line combat, he got himself assigned to a field hospital, where he treated many soldiers who later died. He once tried to commit suicide by swimming out into the China Sea, but he changed his mind and swam back to shore. His father had a fatal heart attack at age 59 (J. Cohen, 2007b; Wade, 2007).

Eventually, this man's military experiences convinced him that he needed more education. He earned a PhD and began to do research in genetics. He soon antagonized other scientists, who bristled at his enormous ego and his maverick ways. With a combination of brilliance, charm, and perseverance (all partly genetic traits, although the genes that predict them are not yet known), he founded a company called Celera Genomics, which succeeded at deciphering the human genome in a commercial project that ran parallel to the Human Genome Project.

This man's name is Craig Venter. He was one of five people whose DNA was used to generate the complete sequence of the human genome—which is how the information about his genetic tendencies was obtained. The entire world is benefiting from his work. The timing of events in his life helped him: Not only did his service in Vietnam change his direction, but his own genome was unknown before he became famous and successful. If it had been known, his fate might have been quite different.

Thanks partly to Venter, it will soon be possible to decode a person's genome for $1,000 (Winstein, 2007). That possibility raises many ethical questions. Some parents may knowingly risk having children with crippling diseases or severe mental illness. That may be unfair to the children or to the society that pays for their care; but it may also be unfair for anyone to prevent adults from bearing as many children, with or without genetic diseases, as they choose.

No reputable scientist advocates abortion of fetuses with the kinds of traits indicated in Venter's genome. Indeed, pediatricians whose patients suffer from conditions that are thought to be genetic often hesitate to advise the parents to be tested, having in mind the ethical implications for those parents' subsequent pregnancies (Pagon & Trotter, 2007).

Experts are well aware of these and other moral risks of genetic testing (Ekberg, 2007). Many doctors in clinics that offer pre-implantation testing would like more guidance about when not to test (Baruch et al., 2008). Now is the time for these ethical questions to be debated, before all the possibilities become realities.

KEY points

- Everyone carries some genetic problems. The impact and inheritance patterns are variable: Some are dominant, some recessive, some additive.

- Chromosomal abnormalities include Down syndrome (trisomy-21) and an unusual number of sex chromosomes. Some people with such problems develop well.

- Gene disorders may be either dominant (e.g., probably Tourette syndrome) or recessive (e.g., cystic fibrosis, thalassemia, sickle-cell anemia). Some recessive gene disorders are sex-linked (e.g., fragile X, hemophilia, color blindness).

- Genetic testing can determine the risk of conceiving a child with many serious diseases and conditions. Decisions are made by parents, not professionals.

From Zygote to Newborn

The beginning of human life is astonishing. A tiny cell, smaller than the period at the end of this sentence, turns into a person in a mere nine months. In less than a year, the most extensive transformation of the entire life span occurs.

To make it easier to study, prenatal development is often divided into three main periods. The first two weeks are called the **germinal period;** the third through the eighth week is called the **embryonic period;** the longest stretch, from the ninth week until birth, is called the **fetal period.** (For alternative terms, see Table 2.4.)

● **FOR DEEPER REFLECTION** Why might someone want to know a baby's sex before birth?

germinal period
The first two weeks of prenatal development after conception, characterized by rapid cell division and the beginning of cell differentiation.

embryonic period
The stage of prenatal development from approximately the third through the eighth week after conception, during which the basic forms of all body structures, including internal organs, develop.

fetal period
The stage of prenatal development from the ninth week after conception until birth, during which the fetus grows in size and matures in functioning.

TABLE 2.4 Timing and Terminology

Popular and professional books use various phrases to segment pregnancy. The following comments may help to clarify the phrases used.

- *Beginning of pregnancy:* Pregnancy begins at conception, which is also the starting point of *gestational age.* However, the organism does not become an embryo until about two weeks later, and pregnancy does not affect the woman (and cannot be confirmed by blood or urine testing) until implantation. Paradoxically, many obstetricians date the onset of pregnancy from the date of the woman's last menstrual period (LMP), about 14 days *before* conception.

- *Length of pregnancy:* Full-term pregnancies last 266 days, or 38 weeks, or 9 months. If the LMP is used as the starting time, pregnancy lasts 40 weeks, sometimes expressed as 10 lunar months. (A lunar month is 28 days long.)

- *Trimesters:* Instead of *germinal period, embryonic period,* and *fetal period,* some writers divide pregnancy into three-month periods called *trimesters.* Months 1, 2, and 3 are called the *first trimester;* months 4, 5, and 6, the *second trimester;* and months 7, 8, and 9, the *third trimester.*

- *Due date:* Although doctors assign a specific due date (based on the woman's LMP), only 5 percent of babies are born on that exact date. Babies born between three weeks before and two weeks after that date are considered "full term" or "on time." Babies born earlier are called *preterm;* babies born later are called *post-term.* The words *preterm* and *post-term* are more accurate than *premature* and *postmature.*

The Germinal Period: The First Two Weeks

Within hours after conception, the zygote begins *duplication and division.* First, the original 23 pairs of chromosomes duplicate and the single cell divides into two cells, each of which contains a complete set of chromosomes. Those two cells soon duplicate and divide, becoming four identical cells. Those four duplicate and divide, becoming eight, and so on.

In the process of becoming a baby, the one-celled zygote multiplies into about 10 trillion cells. By adulthood, the number of cells in a human body increases to more than 100 trillion. Almost every one of those cells carries an exact copy of the complete genetic instructions inherited by the zygote. This explains why DNA testing of any cell, even from a drop of blood or a snip of hair, can identify "the real father," or "the guilty criminal," or "the long-lost brother."

Until about the eight-cell stage, the organism consists of *stem cells,* which could develop into any body part. But then a third process, *differentiation,* is added to duplication and division. Following genetic instructions, cells begin to specialize, taking different forms and reproducing at various rates, depending on where they are

First Stages of the Germinal Period The original zygote as it divides into (a) two cells, (b) four cells, and (c) eight cells. Occasionally at this early stage, the cells separate completely, forming the beginning of monozygotic twins, quadruplets, or octuplets.

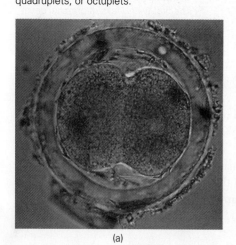
(a)

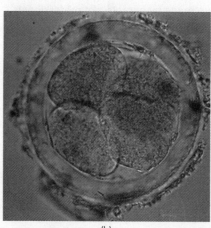
(b)

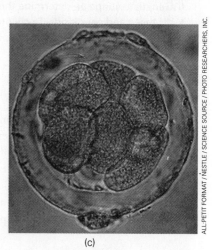
(c)

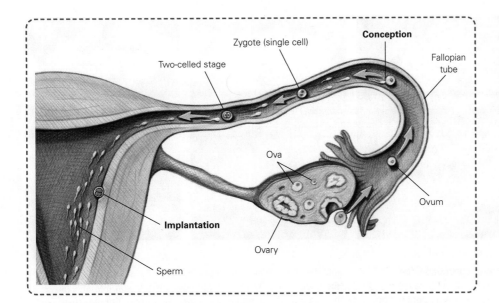

FIGURE 2.3 **The Most Dangerous Journey** In the first 10 days after conception, the organism does not increase in size because it is not yet nourished by the mother. However, the number of cells increases rapidly as the organism prepares for implantation, which occurs successfully about less than half the time.

located. As one expert explains the impact of specialization, "We are sitting with parts of our body that could have been used for thinking" (G. Gottlieb, 1992/2002, p. 172).

One consequence of differentiation is that cells on the outer side of the developing mass become the **placenta,** the organ that will support the developing life. **Implantation,** the process by which the developing placenta connects to the nurturing environment of the uterus (see Figure 2.3), usually begins about 10 days after conception and takes about a week (K. L. Moore & Persaud, 2003).

About 60 percent of all conceptions *in vivo* (literally, "in life," inside the woman's body) and 70 percent of all conceptions *in vitro* (literally, "in glass," outside the body) fail to implant (see Table 2.5). Typically, a woman is unaware of a failed implantation; her period might merely arrive a few days later than usual.

If implantation is successful, the organism begins to grow in size because the placenta is connected to the umbilical cord, which brings nourishment and carries away waste. The first noticeable signs of pregnancy occur after implantation, when substances begin to enter a pregnant woman's body via the placenta, affecting her hormones and digestion. Pregnancy tests at that point (but not earlier) may detect new chemicals in her urine. After implantation, the woman is literally eating and urinating for two.

placenta
The organ that surrounds the developing embryo and fetus, sustaining life via the umbilical cord. The placenta is attached to the wall of the pregnant woman's uterus.

implantation
The process, beginning about 10 days after conception, in which the developing organism burrows into the placenta that lines the uterus, where it can be nourished and protected as it continues to develop.

TABLE 2.5 Vulnerability During Prenatal Development

The Germinal Period
An estimated 60 percent of all developing organisms fail to grow or implant properly and thus do not survive the germinal period. Most of these organisms are grossly abnormal.

The Embryonic Period
About 20 percent of all embryos are aborted spontaneously, most often because of chromosomal abnormalities.

The Fetal Period
About 5 percent of all fetuses are aborted spontaneously before viability at 22 weeks or are stillborn, defined as born dead after 22 weeks.

Birth
About 31 percent of all zygotes grow and survive to become living newborn babies.

Sources: Bentley & Mascie-Taylor, 2000; K. L. Moore & Persaud, 2003.

● UNDERSTANDING THE NUMBERS
If the numbers in the table are added up (60 + 20 + 5 = 85), it appears that only 15 percent of zygotes survive. Why does the table say 31 percent?

Answer The later rates are percentages of those who have already survived to that point. The 5 percent of fetal deaths refer to the 36 percent that have reached week 8, which is 1.8 percent of those conceived.

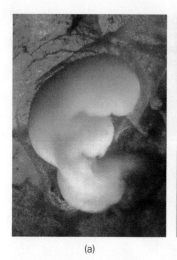

(a)

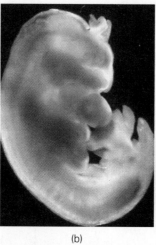

(b)

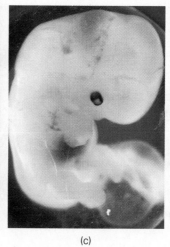

(c)

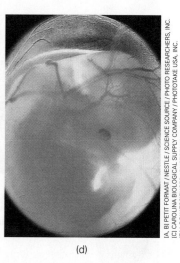

(d)

The Embryonic Period (*a*) At 4 weeks after conception, the embryo is only about ⅛ inch (3 millimeters) long, but already the head (*top right*) has taken shape. (*b*) At 5 weeks after conception, the embryo has grown to twice the size it was at 4 weeks. Its primitive heart, which has been pulsing for a week now, is visible, as is what appears to be a primitive tail, which will soon be enclosed by skin and protective tissue at the tip of the backbone (the coccyx). (*c*) By 7 weeks, the organism is somewhat less than an inch (2½ centimeters) long. Eyes, nose, the digestive system, and even the first stage of leg formation can be seen. (*d*) At 8 weeks, the 1-inch-long organism is clearly recognizable as a human fetus.

The Embryonic Period: From Two Through Eight Weeks

About two weeks after conception, the inner cells of the developing organism (now surrounded by the placenta) show the first sign of body shape and structure when a thin line called the *primitive streak* appears down the middle of the cell mass. That event occasions a new name for the developing organism: **embryo.** The primitive streak becomes the *neural tube* 22 days after conception, eventually becoming the brain and spine of the central nervous system (K. L. Moore & Persaud, 2003).

The head begins to take shape in the fourth week, as eyes, ears, nose, and mouth form. Also in the fourth week, a minuscule blood vessel that will become the heart begins to pulsate, making the cardiovascular system the first part of the embryo to show any activity. At that point, the embryo appears to have a tail because the spine is not yet enclosed.

Soon the body systems and parts grow, according to the schedule set by the genes. For example, by the fifth week, buds that will become arms and legs emerge. Upper arms and then forearms form, followed by hands, then palms, and finally webbed fingers. Legs, feet, and webbed toes, in that order, emerge a few days later, each with the beginning of a skeletal structure. At the end of the embryonic period, the fingers and toes separate (52 and 54 days after conception, respectively). At this point, the entire sexual–reproductive system is similar in both sexes, preparing to produce gametes and developing the body structures necessary to eliminate waste.

The Fetal Period: From Nine Weeks Until Birth

At eight weeks after conception, all the body structures except the sex organs are formed, and the embryo is called by a new name, the **fetus.** If the fetus is male, a gene (called the

embryo
The name for a developing human organism from about the third through the eighth week after conception.

fetus
The name for a developing human organism from the start of the ninth week after conception until birth.

The Fetus At the end of 4 months, the fetus, now 6 inches long, looks fully formed but out of proportion—the distance from the top of the skull to the neck is almost as long as that from the neck to the rump. For many more weeks, the fetus must depend on the translucent membranes of the placenta and umbilical cord (the long white object in the foreground) for survival.

OBSERVATION QUIZ

Can you see eyebrows, fingernails, and genitals? (see answer, page 62) →

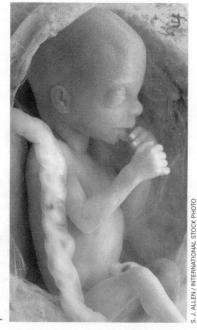

SRY gene) soon commands male sexual organs to develop outside the body; otherwise, female organs develop within. Thus, two tiny regions in the body of the embryo become ovaries or testicles early in the fetal period.

By the twelfth week, the genitals are fully formed and begin sending hormones to the developing brain. Most functions of the brain are gender neutral, but these sex hormones cause some differences in fetal brain organization (Neave, 2008).

By the end of the third month, the fetus has all its structures and the overall shape of a human, although the head is far bigger and the arms and legs much smaller than in newborns, who themselves are disproportionate to adults. In general, the head develops first, in a pattern called *cephalocaudal* (literally, "from head to tail") growth; the extremities develop last, in a pattern called *proximodistal* ("from near to far") growth. The tail is enclosed at the end of the spine; sex organs are present and may be visible to an expert reading a **sonogram** (an image similar to an X-ray, except that it uses sound waves instead of radiation; also called *ultrasound*).

The 3-month-old fetus weighs about 3 ounces (87 grams) and is about 3 inches (7.5 centimeters) long (K. L. Moore & Persaud, 2003). These numbers—3 months, 3 ounces, 3 inches—are rounded off for easy recollection. (For those on the metric system, "100 days, 100 grams, 100 millimeters" is similarly imprecise but useful.)

In the fourth, fifth, and sixth months, the cardiovascular system becomes more active. During a prenatal checkup, the fetal heartbeat is audible by stethoscope or with a hand-held amplifier. Digestive, respiratory, and excretory systems develop, and organs begin to function. Fingernails, toenails, and buds for teeth form, and hair grows (including eyelashes).

Up to half a million neurons (brain cells) per minute are created at peak growth during mid-pregnancy (Dowling, 2004). Neurons move to designated spots within the brain, from back to front: first to the brain stem above the back of the neck, then to the midbrain, and finally to the cortex. Although the cortex undergoes extensive development before birth, the prefrontal cortex (at the forehead) is not fully mature until the end of adolescence or later (Stiles, 2008).

Advances in brain function are crucial for the **age of viability,** the point in development when a preterm newborn can survive. That's because the brain regulates

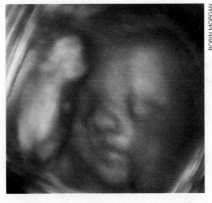

There's Your Baby For many parents, their first glimpse of their future child is an ultrasound image. This is Alice Morgan, 63 days before birth.

sonogram
An image of an unborn fetus (or an internal organ) produced by scanning it with high-frequency sound waves. (Also called *ultrasound*.)

age of viability
The age (about 22 weeks after conception) at which a fetus may survive outside the mother's uterus if specialized medical care is available.

One of the Tiniest Rumaisa Rahman was born after 26 weeks and 6 days weighing only 8.6 ounces (244 grams). Nevertheless, she has a good chance of living a full, normal life. Rumaisa gained 5 pounds (2,270 grams) in the hospital and then, 6 months after her birth, went home. Her twin sister, Hiba, who weighed 1.3 pounds (590 grams) at birth, had gone home two months earlier. At their one-year birthday, the twins seemed normal, with Rumaisa weighing 15 pounds (6,800 grams) and Hiba 17 (7,711 grams) (CBS News, 2005).

Can He Hear? A fetus, just about at the age of viability, is shown fingering his ear. Such gestures are probably random; but, yes, he can hear.

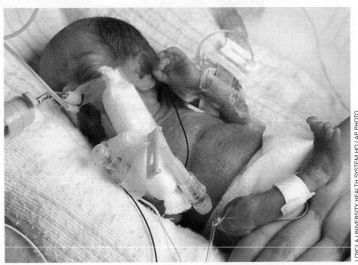

ESPECIALLY FOR Biologists Many people believe that the differences between the sexes are primarily socio-cultural, not biological. Is there any prenatal support for that view? (see response, page 64) →

ANSWER TO OBSERVATION QUIZ (from page 60) Yes, yes, and no. Genitals are formed, but they are not visible in this photo. The object grow-ing from the lower belly is the umbilical cord. ●

basic body functions, including breathing. With advanced medical care, the age of viability is 22 weeks after conception; most babies born this early weigh under a pound (less than 450 grams).

This 22-week barrier has not been overcome by even the most sophisticated res-pirators and heart regulators, because maintaining life requires some brain response. The chance of survival at birth increases with each day after the 22-week mark. Advanced neonatal care saves about 65 percent of those born at 23 to 26 weeks after conception (M. M. Kelly, 2006; Wilson-Costello et al., 2007).

In the last three months of pregnancy, the fetus gains about 5 pounds (2¼ kilo-grams), the heart and lungs mature, and the digestive system begins to function as the fetus swallows amniotic fluid. Brain growth makes the cortex develop layers, folding several times in order to fit within the skull (see Figure 2.4).

A newborn's brain weighs about 400 grams, so it is far bigger than any other part of the baby (an aspect of cephalocaudal growth) and proportionally far larger than the brain of any other animal. The brain distinguishes humans from other creatures, none of which have the multilayered, wrinkled cortex of newborn humans.

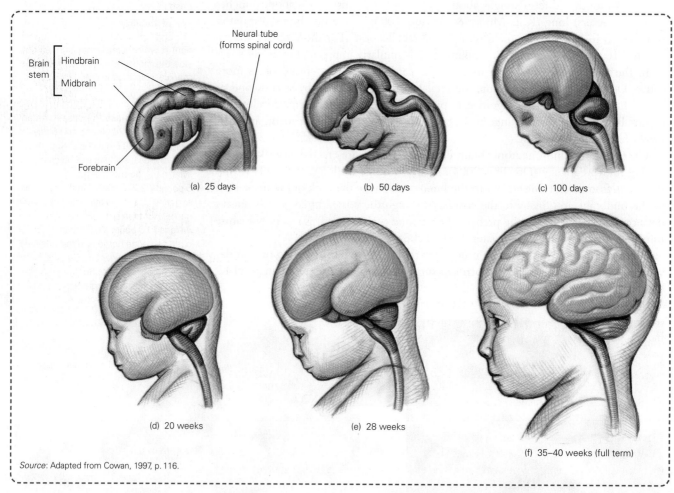

Source: Adapted from Cowan, 1997, p. 116.

FIGURE 2.4 Prenatal Growth of the Brain Just 25 days after conception (*a*), the central nerv-ous system is already evident. The brain looks distinctly human by day 100 (*c*). By the 28th week of gestation (*e*), at the very time brain activity begins, the various sections of the brain are recog-nizable. When the fetus is full term (*f*), all the parts of the brain, including the cortex (the outer layer), are formed, folding over one another and becoming more convoluted, or wrinkled, as the number of brain cells increases.

Birth

For a full-term fetus and a healthy mother, birth can be simple and quick. At some time during the last month of pregnancy, most fetuses change position, turning upside down so that the head is low in the mother's pelvic cavity. They are now in position to be born in the usual way, head first.

The Process of Birth

At about 38 weeks after conception, the fetal brain signals the release of hormones to trigger the woman's uterine muscles to begin contracting and relaxing. This is the start of *labor,* the birth process. A first baby is born, on average, 12 hours later (K. L. Moore & Persaud, 2003), although it is not unusual for labor to take twice, or half, that long. Labor is usually quicker for later-born babies, especially if the mother is still relatively young (under age 30).

The same hormones that trigger labor also protect the fetal brain (Tyzio et al., 2006). The typical head-first delivery enables newborns to breathe before they have fully emerged. (Some babies end up in the *breech* position, with the buttocks or, rarely, the feet first. To prevent anoxia [oxygen deprivation], breech babies are often delivered via cesarean section.)

The first breaths of oxygen cause the infant's color to change from bluish to pinkish. ("Bluish" and "pinkish" refer to the blood color, visible beneath the skin, and apply to newborns of all skin colors.) The eyes open wide; the tiny fingers grab; the tinier toes stretch and retract. The newcomer is instantly, zestfully ready for life.

Although many newborns have misshapen heads, body bruises, and splotchy skin, appearance is not a reliable indicator of health. Beyond a birthweight of at least 5½ pounds (2,500 grams), the quickest measure of newborn vitality is the **Apgar scale** (see Table 2.6). The examiner checks five vital signs—heart rate, breathing, muscle tone, color, and reflexes—at one minute and again at five minutes after birth, assigning each a score of 0, 1, or 2 (Moster et al., 2001).

Oxygen level affects color, and at one minute, many healthy newborns are bluish, scoring a 0 or 1. The oxygen level quickly rises (Kamlin et al., 2006). If the five-minute Apgar total is 7 or above, all is well.

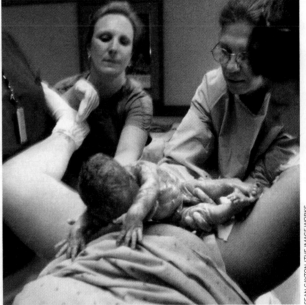

SEAN CAYTON / THE IMAGE WORKS

No Doctor Needed In this Colorado Springs birthing center, most babies are delivered with the help of nurse-midwives. This newborn's bloody appearance and bluish fingers are completely normal; an Apgar test at five minutes revealed that the baby's heart was beating steadily and that the body was "entirely pink."

Apgar scale
A quick assessment of a newborn's body functioning. The baby's heart rate, respiratory effort, muscle tone, color, and reflexes are given a score of 0, 1, or 2 twice—at one minute and five minutes after birth—and each time the total of all five scores is compared with the ideal score of 10 (which is rarely attained).

TABLE 2.6 Criteria and Scoring of the Apgar Scale

	Five Vital Signs				
Score	Color	Heartbeat	Reflex Irritability	Muscle Tone	Respiratory Effort
0	Blue, pale	Absent	No response	Flaccid, limp	Absent
1	Body pink, extremities blue	Slow (below 100)	Grimace	Weak, inactive	Irregular, slow
2	Entirely pink	Rapid (over 100)	Coughing, sneezing, crying	Strong, active	Good; baby is crying

Source: Apgar, 1953.

RESPONSE FOR Biologists (from page 62) Only one of the 46 human chromosomes determines sex, and the genitals develop last in the prenatal sequence. Sex differences are apparent before birth, but they are relatively minor. ●

The Same Situation, Many Miles Apart: Preparing for Birth Both of these pregnant women are carrying twins, but their prognoses are quite different. The American woman in Lamaze class (*left*) is practicing breathing during labor. The pregnant woman in Afghanistan (*right*) and her doctors discuss why labor will be induced: One of her twins is not developing normally. Neither of her babies is expected to live. Virtually all newborns in developed nations survive; the Afghan woman has already lost two children at birth.

OBSERVATION QUIZ

Is the woman at left in the left-hand photo the pregnant woman's doctor?
(see answer, page 66) →

Traditional and Modern Birthing Practices

As modern medicine is introduced in the developing areas of the world, a conflict may arise between traditional home births attended by a midwife and hospital births attended by an obstetrician. Home births risk complications, and hospital births risk too much intervention. All too often, women must choose one or the other, rather than combining the best features of each. It need not be so, as in this example from the Inuit people of northern Canada:

> Until thirty or forty years ago every woman, and most men, learned midwifery skills and knew what to do to help at a birth if they were needed. . . . Since the 1950s, as the medical system took control in the belief that hospital birth was safer, more and more pregnant women were evacuated by air to deliver in large hospitals in Winnipeg and other cities. . . .
>
> Around three weeks before her due date, a woman is flown south to wait in bed and breakfast accommodation for labor to start, and to have it induced if the baby does not arrive when expected. Anxious about their children left at home, mothers become bored and depressed. . . . Women . . . deliver in a supine position [on their back] instead of an upright one, which was part of their tradition, and also describe being tied up while giving birth. Many women say that children who have been born in a hospital are different and no longer fit into the Inuit lifestyle. . . .
>
> Several new birth centres have now been created [in the Inuit homeland] and nurse–midwives are bringing in traditional midwives as assistants during childbirth, training some Inuit midwives to work alongside them, and at the same time learning some of the old Inuit ways themselves.

[Kitzinger, 2001, pp. 160–161]

Another example of a traditional custom incorporated into a modern birth is the **doula.** Long a fixture in many Latin American countries, a doula is a woman who helps with labor, delivery, breast-feeding, and newborn care. Traditionally, doulas were the only attendants at birth, but today they often work alongside the medical staff in hospitals.

In North as well as South America, many prospective parents find a doula to help at birth. Recently, a study enlisted middle-class couples in which the husbands planned to be with their wives during labor. Half were randomly assigned to be accompanied by a doula, while the other half had only the usual nurses and doctors. Not only were all the husbands and wives happy to have doulas with them, but the births were easier, as evidenced by a significantly lower rate of cesarean sections (McGrath & Kennell, 2008).

Every culture has some birthing practices that are beneficial and some that are destructive. From a developmental perspective, combining traditional and modern birthing practices is likely to be an improvement over wholesale adoption or rejection of either.

doula
A woman who helps with the birth process. Doulas are trained to offer support to new mothers, including massage and suggestions for breast-feeding positions.

Not Waiting for Nature

Under some circumstances, birth may occur before spontaneous labor begins. Prenatal checkups sometimes discover something seriously amiss, such as high blood pressure in the mother, slow fetal growth, or twins that are destroying each other (called twin transfusion syndrome). Sometimes medical professionals deliver babies by inducing labor (starting it before hormones do so naturally) or by performing surgery.

CESAREAN SECTION In a **cesarean section (c-section),** the fetus is removed through surgery (B. Hamilton et al., 2004). Such births may occur if labor has begun but does not progress. More often, a cesarean is scheduled before the first contraction.

The rate of surgical birth varies markedly from place to place (see Figure 2.5). In the poorest nations, cesareans are performed only in an emergency. In richer nations, possible problems are anticipated and cesarean sections are planned. Some c-sections are performed for the convenience of the mother or the obstetrician—a practice widely regarded as dangerous (Jukelevics, 2008). About one-third of births in the United States are via c-section, a rate that has been rising for decades.

A c-section means less trauma for the newborn, who can immediately receive advanced care. However, surgery and anesthesia slow down the mother's recuperation,

cesarean section (c-section)
A surgical birth, in which incisions through the mother's abdomen and uterus allow the fetus to be removed quickly, instead of being delivered through the vagina.

DOUGLAS ENGLE / MCT

From Day One For various reasons, some countries have much higher rates of cesarean deliveries than others. These new mothers in Brazil, which has a high cesarean rate, have safely delivered their babies and, with the encouragement of the hospital, are breast-feeding them from the very beginning.

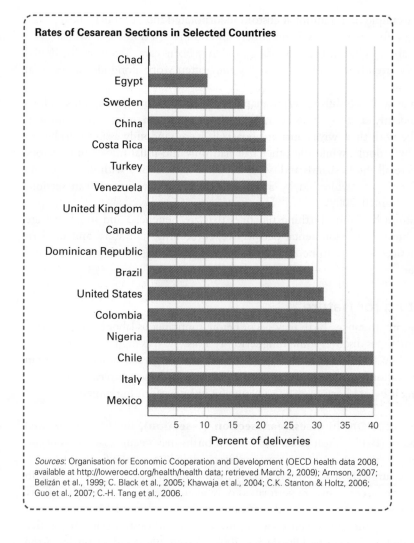

Rates of Cesarean Sections in Selected Countries

Chad
Egypt
Sweden
China
Costa Rica
Turkey
Venezuela
United Kingdom
Canada
Dominican Republic
Brazil
United States
Colombia
Nigeria
Chile
Italy
Mexico

5 10 15 20 25 30 35 40

Percent of deliveries

Sources: Organisation for Economic Cooperation and Development (OECD health data 2008, available at http://loweroecd.org/health/health data; retrieved March 2, 2009); Armson, 2007; Belizán et al., 1999; C. Black et al., 2005; Khawaja et al., 2004; C.K. Stanton & Holtz, 2006; Guo et al., 2007; C.-H. Tang et al., 2006.

FIGURE 2.5 Too Many Cesareans or Too Few? Rates of cesarean deliveries vary widely from nation to nation. In general, cesarean births are declining in North America and increasing in Africa. Latin America has the highest rates in the world (note that 40 percent of all births in Chile and Mexico are by cesarean), and sub-Saharan Africa has the lowest (the rate in Chad is less than half of 1 percent). The underlying issue is whether some women who should have cesareans do not get them, while other women have unnecessary cesareans.

● **FOR DEEPER REFLECTION** Do people's attitudes about medical intervention at birth reflect their attitudes about medicine at other points in the life span, in such areas as assisted reproductive technology (ART), immunization, and life support?

ANSWER TO OBSERVATION QUIZ
(from page 64) No; she is the pregnant woman's mother. Doctors are unlikely to attend their patients' Lamaze classes, but every pregnant woman in the class is supposed to have a helper—usually the baby's father, but sometimes a close relative or friend. ●

and this delay may impair her ability to breast-feed and care for the baby. Another possible drawback is that once a woman has had a cesarean, subsequent deliveries may also be by cesarean; this idea is controversial (Landon et al., 2004).

MEDICAL INTERVENTION A similar dilemma arises with every type of intervention. For instance, microsurgery in the days before and after birth on tiny, malformed hearts, lungs, and digestive systems prevents death. Eighty years ago, my nephew David (whose story is told in Chapter 1) would have died, as did 5 percent of all babies born in the United States in 1900 (De Lee, 1938). Now fewer than 1 newborn in 200 dies.

Every year, obstetricians, midwives, and nurses save millions of lives. A lack of medical attention during birth and during illegal abortions is the major reason motherhood is still hazardous in the least developed nations; about 1 in 20 women in the poorest nations die from complications of pregnancy (Daulaire et al., 2002).

However, while modern medical care during childbirth has undeniable benefits, it also puts healthy women in hospitals, with attendants, equipment (such as an IV), birth positions, and surgery that may not be in their best interest (Jukelevics, 2008). For example, in Pelotas, Brazil, most births are by cesarean (82 percent for private patients in 2004); furthermore, the rate of low-birthweight infants in Pelotas is rising (from 11 to 16 percent in 10 years), because many infants are born before they are ready (Barros et al., 2005).

As an example of the alternative to hospital deliveries, consider this account of a home birth in Ghana:

> Huddled in a corner of the hut, she was lying on the floor. . . . She lay curled into a small ball on her left side, her pregnant and contracting uterus protruding from her thin frame. No sound came from her. No sound came from the midwife either. She was seated in the corner of the dark, hot hut, waiting. Suddenly, Emefa gave a low whimper and hauled herself into a sitting and then squatting position. The midwife crept over to her and gently supported Emefa's back as she bore down. No words, no commands, no yelling. . . . The baby's head appeared gradually, slowly making its progress into the world. How did the midwife know that it was time? . . . A soft whoosh and the baby's body was born into the steady and confident hands of the midwife. And still there was no sound. The baby did not cry, not because there was any problem, but because it was a gentle birth. The baby was breathing as he was handed to his mother.
>
> *[Hillier, 2003, p. 3]*

The idea of a "gentle birth" is appealing, but this newborn may have been lucky. The infant mortality rate in Ghana is 10 times that of the United States, where 99 percent of births take place in hospitals or birth centers, with emergency help at the ready. What is needed is a balance between nature and intervention. One sign of balance will be a decrease in the number of low-birthweight newborns.

Low Birthweight

Low birthweight (LBW) is defined internationally as a body weight of less than 2,500 grams (5½ pounds) at birth. In the United States, low birthweight has slowly increased over the past 25 years (see Figure 2.6) and is now the leading cause of infant mortality. About 8 percent of all newborns in the United States are seriously underweight—not the world's highest rate, but far from the lowest (see Figure 2.7).

Low birthweight increases the danger of harm from prenatal teratogens (discussed later), adds to birth risks, and makes survival less certain. Every extra gram of weight at birth is protective (unless birthweight is over 4,000 grams, almost 10 pounds).

The LBW babies at greatest risk are the smallest. To focus on them, some underweight newborns are classified as **very low birthweight (VLBW)**, under 1,500 grams (3 pounds, 5 ounces), or **extremely low birthweight (ELBW)**, under 1,000 grams (2 pounds, 3 ounces).

Thinking About Her Baby This woman may be more fortunate than others in Ghana, which has a high death rate among mothers and babies from birth complications. The wooden structure behind her is a field hospital, so she will receive medical care when she gives birth.

low birthweight (LBW)
A body weight at birth of less than 5½ pounds (2,500 grams).

very low birthweight (VLBW)
A body weight at birth of less than 3 pounds, 5 ounces (1,500 grams).

extremely low birthweight (ELBW)
A body weight at birth of less than 2 pounds, 3 ounces (1,000 grams).

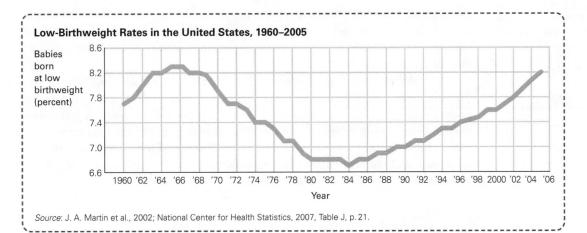

Low-Birthweight Rates in the United States, 1960–2005

Babies born at low birthweight (percent)

Source: J. A. Martin et al., 2002; National Center for Health Statistics, 2007, Table J, p. 21.

FIGURE 2.6 What Is Changing? Several changes have occurred in the United States over the past 25 years that should reduce the rate of low birthweight, including fewer teen parents, more Mexican immigrants, and better prenatal care. However, the rate has increased instead, so other factors must be at work. Possible causes are drug use, more multiple births, and environmental pollution.

FIGURE 2.7 Some Better, Some Worse Some of these nations (e.g., Mexico, Bangladesh) have far fewer low-birthweight newborns than they did 25 years ago, and some have more (e.g., United States). The changes as well as the range indicate that birthweight is affected more by nurture than by nature. Very few newborns weigh less than 5½ pounds (2,500 grams) because most are genetically destined to have a healthy weight.

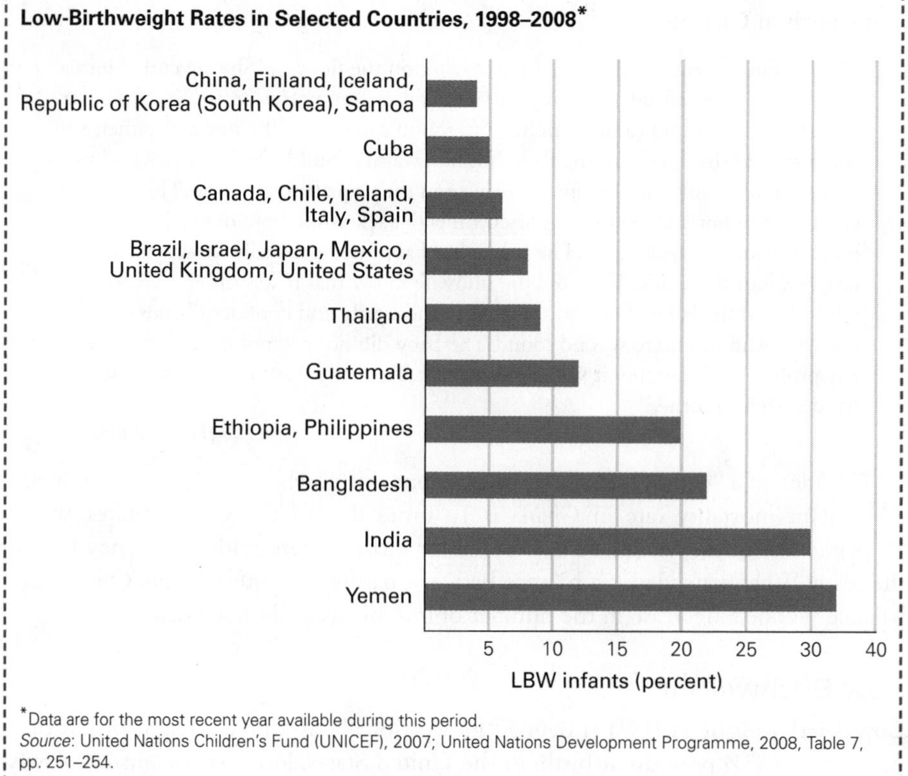

Low-Birthweight Rates in Selected Countries, 1998–2008*

China, Finland, Iceland, Republic of Korea (South Korea), Samoa
Cuba
Canada, Chile, Ireland, Italy, Spain
Brazil, Israel, Japan, Mexico, United Kingdom, United States
Thailand
Guatemala
Ethiopia, Philippines
Bangladesh
India
Yemen

LBW infants (percent)
5 10 15 20 25 30 40

*Data are for the most recent year available during this period.
Source: United Nations Children's Fund (UNICEF), 2007; United Nations Development Programme, 2008, Table 7, pp. 251–254.

preterm birth
A birth that occurs 3 or more weeks before the full 38 weeks of the typical pregnancy have elapsed—that is, at 35 or fewer weeks after conception.

small for gestational age (SGA)
Having a body weight at birth that is significantly lower than expected, given the time since conception. For example, a 5-pound (2,265-gram) newborn is considered SGA if born on time but not SGA if born two months early. (Also called *small-for-dates*.)

PRETERM OR SLOW-GROWING? There are two reasons a newborn might be too small. If birth occurs early, before 35 weeks of gestation instead of at the usual 38, the baby is **preterm** and usually (though not always) weighs less than 2,500 grams (5½ pounds). Babies born before 32 weeks are always low birthweight.

The second reason for low birthweight is slow gain throughout pregnancy. Such infants are described as *small-for-dates,* or **small for gestational age (SGA),** meaning that the baby's birthweight is significantly lower than expected, given the time since conception. SGA suggests impairment throughout prenatal development—a sign that something is seriously amiss.

CAUSES OF LOW BIRTHWEIGHT Behind these two reasons for low birthweight are a wide variety of specific causes. Some are genetic; for example, small women tend to have small babies. However, nurture, not nature, is responsible for almost all cases of low birthweight.

Maternal illness, exhaustion, infection, and malnutrition all cause low birthweight. The importance of nutrition is starkly evident in data from Gambia, one of the poorest nations in Africa. Preterm births are highest (17 percent) in July, when women usually work long hours in the fields. However, SGA births are more common (31 percent) in November, the end of the "hungry season," when most women have been undernourished for three months or more (Rayco-Solon et al., 2005). November newborns are most likely to die.

Severe malnutrition during pregnancy is rare in developed nations, where prenatal care is readily available; weighing the pregnant woman is part of every prenatal visit, and underweight women are encouraged to eat more. This advice is particularly important if the woman is under age 16 and still growing herself. Note, however, that the U.S. teen pregnancy rate has been falling while low birthweight has been increasing; young pregnancy is not the most common cause.

Instead, drug use may be to blame for most low-birthweight newborns in the United States. Fetal growth is slowed by every psychoactive drug, including tobacco, which is the most prevalent.

Another common reason for LBW is multiple births, which now often result from assisted reproduction (discussed in Chapter 12). Many doctors note that singletons are healthier; still, many infertile couples welcome multiple births.

Mothers, Fathers, and a Good Start

Fathers, other relatives, neighbors, and cultures can help to reduce the incidence of birth complications. Consider statistics about low birthweight in the United States. For mothers born in Mexico, the rate of LBW is only 5 percent, compared with 7 percent for mothers of Mexican or European heritage who were born in the United States (a significant difference, since the statistics are based on the total number of recorded births).

Why does a low-income group have fewer LBW infants than a high-income group? The probable reason is that the partners and families of pregnant Mexican-born women encourage them to eat well and avoid drugs (Lara et al., 2005).

THE FATHER'S ROLE As is shown by Mexican American husbands who safeguard their wives' pregnancies, a supportive father-to-be helps a mother-to-be stay healthy, well nourished, and drug-free. For example, a woman's education level and employment status do not correlate with decreased alcohol consumption during pregnancy, but her marital status does (MMWR, April 5, 2002).

Not only through the example of their behavior but also more directly, fathers and other family members can decrease or increase a mother's stress, which in turn affects her circulation, diet, rest, digestion, and, ultimately, the fetus. One study in northern India found that 18 percent of fathers abused their wives during pregnancy; the result was a doubling of the rate of fragile newborns and infant death (Ahmed et al., 2006).

Another way to interpret this research is that, even in a poor nation, 82 percent of fathers took good care of their wives. In fact, worldwide, many men are solicitous and helpful to their pregnant wives, who might be demanding or tearful.

The need for social support is mutual. Fathers need reassurance, just as mothers do. Levels of cortisol, a stress hormone, correlate between expectant fathers and mothers: When one parent is stressed, often the other is, too (S. J. Berg & Wynne-Edwards, 2002). Pregnant women should encourage fathers to feel fetal movement, listen to the heartbeat, participate in labor, hold the newborn. A close father–infant connection helps every member of the family.

THE IMPORTANCE OF CLOSE CONTACT Birth complications can have a lingering impact. Low-birthweight babies, for example, are more likely to become adults who are overweight, diabetic, and have disorders of the heart (Hack et al., 2002). Infants in intensive care have higher levels of stress hormones, and their parents treat them differently than they treat newborns who go home soon after birth, ready to eat, sleep, and react without any special equipment.

Once developmentalists became aware of these differences, policies changed. If a newborn must stay in the hospital for weeks after birth, both mother and father are encouraged to help with early caregiving. Doing so benefits both the baby and the parents, who are understandably deprived, depressed, stressed, or angry (Eriksson & Pehrsson, 2005).

One technique for developing close parental involvement is **kangaroo care,** in which the mother of a low-birthweight infant holds her newborn between her

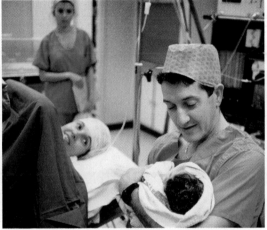

BUBBLES PHOTOLIBRARY / ALAMY

His Baby, Too This new father's evident joy in his baby illustrates a truism that developmental research has only recently reflected: Fathers contribute much more than just half their child's genes.

OBSERVATION QUIZ
Why is a green sheet draped in front of this new mother's face? (see answer, page 71) ➔

kangaroo care
A child-care technique in which the mother of a low-birthweight infant holds the baby between her breasts, like a kangaroo that carries her immature newborn in a pouch on her abdomen.

ALEX BALUYUT / ONASIA.COM

A Beneficial Beginning These new mothers in a maternity ward in Manila are providing their babies with kangaroo care.

postpartum depression
The sadness and inadequacy felt by some new mothers in the days and weeks after giving birth.

parent–infant bond
The strong, loving connection that forms as parents hold, examine, and feed their newborn.

SHEHZAD NOORANI / PETER ARNOLD, INC.

A Teenage Mother This week-old baby, born in a poor village in Myanmar (Burma), has a better chance of survival than he might otherwise have had because his 18-year-old mother has bonded with him.

breasts, skin-to-skin, allowing the tiny baby to hear her heartbeat and feel her body heat. Fathers can also benefit their newborn and themselves by cradling the baby next to their chests (Magill-Evans et al., 2006).

A comparison study (Feldman et al., 2002) found that newborns given kangaroo care slept more deeply and spent more time alert than did those in standard care. At 6 months, infants who had received kangaroo care were more responsive. Other research confirms the benefits of kangaroo care (Ludington-Hoe et al., 2006; Tallandini & Scalembra, 2006).

Another way parents can help their premature newborn is by regularly performing massage therapy, gently stroking the baby several times a day. Tiny babies who are caressed seem less irritable and more relaxed (Hernandez-Reif et al., 2007). Such soothing massage of tiny babies is routine in India; it is a radical innovation in the United States.

POSTPARTUM DEPRESSION In the days and weeks after birth, between 8 and 15 percent of mothers experience **postpartum depression,** a sense of inadequacy and sadness (called *baby blues* in the mild version and *postpartum psychosis* in the most severe form) (Perfetti et al., 2004). These rates are for the United States; other nations may have higher rates. For example, a standard postpartum scale found rates of 36 percent in Pakistan (Husain et al., 2006).

Depressed mothers find baby care—feeding, diapering, bathing—burdensome. They may think about mistreating the infant. Postpartum depression can have a long-term impact on the child; it should be promptly treated.

When a mother experiences postpartum depression, the father plays a particularly crucial role. His active caregiving allows the baby to thrive and the mother to recover. Unfortunately, some fathers become depressed themselves. One study found that, even when the mothers were not depressed, if fathers were depressed after birth, their sons had notable behavior problems as toddlers (Ramchandani et al., 2005).

From a developmental perspective, some causes of depression predate the pregnancy; others occur during pregnancy; and still others arise from coping with a newborn who has health, feeding, or sleeping difficulties. Birth itself—with its accompanying anesthesia, changing hormones, and pain—can precipitate depression (Ashman & Dawson, 2002; I. Jones, 2006). No matter what the cause, someone must help new parents adjust.

BONDING Focusing on the parents' emotions raises the question: Are the first hours crucial for formation of the **parent–infant bond,** the strong, loving connection that forms as parents hold, examine, and feed their newborn? Some claim that this bond must develop soon after birth when a mother touches her naked baby, just as sheep and goats must immediately smell and nuzzle their newborns if they are to nurture them (M. H. Klaus & Kennell, 1976).

However, research does not find that early skin-to-skin contact is essential for humans (Eyer, 1992; Lamb, 1982). Unlike sheep and goats, most mammals do not need immediate contact for parents to nurture their offspring. In fact, substantial research on monkeys focuses on *cross-fostering,* in which newborns are removed from their biological mothers in the first days of life and raised by another female or even a male. A strong and beneficial relationship does sometimes develop (Suomi, 2002).

KEY Points

- After about 38 weeks of gestation, birth occurs. A healthy newborn should weigh at least 5½ pounds (2,500 grams) and score at least 7 out of 10 on the Apgar scale.

- Medical intervention during pregnancy and birth is sometimes necessary to save lives, but it may occur too soon or too intensely.

- Prenatal care reduces the incidence of low birthweight, which is associated with poor nutrition, multiple births, and drug use.

- The newborn's well-being is affected by the father's participation, close physical contact with the parents, and postpartum depression in the mother. The parent–infant connection begins before birth and endures throughout life.

ESPECIALLY FOR Scientists Research with animals can benefit people, but it is sometimes used too quickly to support conclusions about people. When does that happen? (see response, page 72) →

Nature, Nurture, and the Phenotype

One goal of this chapter is to enable readers to understand the interaction between genes and experiences. As you remember, *nature* refers to genotype, a person's genetic inheritance. *Nurture* refers to everything that surrounds the person, including the prenatal environment. For every trait, scientists try to figure out how much of the phenotype results from nature and how much from nurture.

Hundreds of researchers in dozens of nations have studied thousands of twins—monozygotic and dizygotic, some raised together and others raised in different homes—and tens of thousands of other siblings, including stepsiblings, adopted siblings, and biological siblings. Furthermore, taking a multidisciplinary approach, biologists and biochemists have analyzed the molecules of DNA. The results of all their research have led to four general conclusions (B. J. Ellis & Bjorklund, 2005; Gottesman & Hanson, 2005; Plomin et al., 2003):

COURTESY OF EDNA MORLOK.

Too Cute? This portrait of the Genain sisters was taken 20 years before they all developed schizophrenia. However, from their identical hair ribbons to the identical position of their feet, it is apparent that their unusual status as quadruplets set them apart as curiosities. Could their life in the spotlight have nurtured their potential for schizophrenia? There is no way to know for sure.

- Genes affect every aspect of human behavior, including personality and learning.

- Nongenetic influences begin at conception and continue lifelong, sometimes altering genetic instructions.

- Most environmental influences on children raised in the same home are *not* shared, partly because parents treat each child differently.

- Children, adolescents, and, especially, adults "niche-pick," choosing environments that are compatible with their genetic inheritance.

In this section, to illustrate these conclusions and to highlight the central role that the nature–nurture interaction plays in development, we examine its influence on three conditions: nearsightedness, alcoholism, and birth defects caused by prenatal teratogens.

Nearsightedness

How well people can see depends on many factors, among them age, nutrition, and experience. Genes are certainly crucial. Nearsightedness, or *myopia*, is evident in more than 150 genetic syndromes (I. G. Morgan, 2003). Often the problem is "high" nearsightedness, which is very severe. More common among the general population is

ANSWER TO OBSERVATION QUIZ
(from page 69) The drape prevents the mother from watching as her doctor stitches up the incision of a c-section. The sight is likely to be upsetting to many women, even though anesthesia allows them to remain awake without feeling pain. ●

Good Students These young Korean children are already learning to read a second language, Chinese. They are probably also advanced in math and science, compared with 8-year-olds in the United States. Their accomplishments may have come at a price: Many of them are nearsighted.

RESPONSE FOR Scientists (from page 71) Animal research tends to be used too quickly whenever it supports an assertion that is popular but has not been substantiated by research data, as in the social construction about physical contact being crucial for parent–infant bonding. ●

ESPECIALLY FOR Future Drug Counselors Is the wish for excitement likely to lead to addiction? (see response, page 75) →

"low" nearsightedness, which renders distant objects blurry. Low nearsightedness runs in families, which indicates that it may be genetic.

A study of British twins found that minor variations in the Pax6 gene are a common cause of low nearsightedness (Hammond et al., 2004). This research found the heritability of myopia to be about 90 percent, which means that if one monozygotic twin is nearsighted, the other twin is almost always nearsighted, too.

But we must interpret that 90 percent carefully. Remember from page 49 that heritability is determined by calculating inherited variations *within* a particular group, in this case British twins. When we study only one group, all from the same era and region, it may seem as if genes are the major cause of poor vision (Farbrother & Guggenheim, 2001). However, historical and multicultural research finds that environment plays a powerful role.

A dramatic example comes from Africa, where at least 100,000 people have poor eyesight because their diet (and their mothers' diet during pregnancy) lacks sufficient vitamin A. For them, the heritability of nearsightedness is low because their environment is so influential. Scientists are working to develop a strain of maize (a staple of the African diet) that is high in vitamin A (Harjes et al., 2008). If they succeed, and if everyone eats the new strain, not only will eyesight improve among Africans but the heritability of nearsightedness will also increase.

Nearsightedness among well-nourished children may also be affected by the environment. Among East Asian schoolchildren, nearsightedness has increased dramatically over the past two decades: from 12 to 84 percent among children in Taiwan; from 28 to 44 percent in Singapore; from 10 to 60 percent in Hong Kong (cited in Grosvenor, 2003). These numbers from cross-sectional samples have been confirmed by a sequential study in Singapore. The eyesight of every 17-year-old male in that city-state is tested as part of the exam for military service. In 1980, 26 percent of them were nearsighted; in 1990, 43 percent were (Tay et al., 1992).

Parents of these children are less often nearsighted. Since a Pax6 allelle makes a person vulnerable, and since children have the same genes as their parents, something in the children's environment must have interacted with their Pax6 genes.

Schoolwork is one possibility. Fifty years ago, most East Asian children did not attend school; now most spend long hours studying. As their young eyes focus on their books, they may lose acuity for objects far away, becoming nearsighted.

Ophthalmologists suggest that if these children spent more time outside playing, fewer would need glasses (Goss, 2002; Grosvenor, 2003; I. G. Morgan, 2003). This explanation may be wrong, but something in nurture, not just nature, affects visual acuity.

Alcoholism

Alcoholism was once thought to be a sinful habit, a sign of moral weakness (Kobler, 1973/1993). Today, however, most people realize that alcoholism is a disease that originates with the genes. Instead of blaming alcoholics for a lack of moral fiber, developmentalists now blame their biochemistry. Genes can cause an overpowering addictive pull in some people (Heath et al., 2003).

As with most other genetic conditions, alcoholism is "likely to be conferred by multiple genes of small to modest effects, possibly only apparent in gene–environment interactions" (Enoch, 2006, p. 193). Those multiple genes include some that affect the body, influencing how the person metabolizes and digests alcohol, and some that affect the mind.

Certain genetic traits (a quick temper, sensation seeking, high anxiety) in certain contexts make it hard to abstain; conversely, other traits (such as a need for self-control) and other contexts (such as a church social in a "dry" county) make it hard to drink. Note that context is crucial: Alcoholism is genetic, but the environment interacts with the genes. This is apparent even before birth.

In 1973, scientists first realized that some pregnant women who drank heavily had babies with distorted facial features, including small eyes and thin upper lips. Those infants had what is now known as **fetal alcohol syndrome (FAS);** as children, they were mentally retarded, impulsive, and hyperactive (Calhoun & Warren, 2007).

Alcohol is definitely the cause of FAS, but some infants born to drinking mothers seem unharmed. One reason they are protected is genetic, as is indicated when dizygotic twins are affected differently before birth by their mother's drinking. Because it is impossible to predict which fetuses will and will not be affected, almost all obstetricians in the United States (fewer in Europe) advise women who are, or may become, pregnant to abstain from alcohol completely.

Since 1998, four states have authorized "involuntary commitment" (jail or forced residential treatment) for pregnant women who do not stop drinking. Advocates for women consider such laws discriminatory, especially since they are more often enforced for minority women. Some experts believe that the threat of jail may cause women who most need prenatal care to avoid getting it. In that case, nurture would intensify, rather than moderate, the effects of nature.

Genes are crucial in cultures where alcohol is readily available and being drunk is considered acceptable, but they are irrelevant for people who live where alcohol is unavailable (rural Saudi Arabia, for instance). In such places, no one can become an active alcoholic, so it does not matter what genes a person has for alcohol metabolism. Nature *and* nurture must combine to create an alcoholic.

Consider the story of baseball superstar Mickey Mantle. He mistakenly thought his family's genetic patterns were destiny, not a warning (Jaffe, 2004). Several of his male relatives died before middle age, including Mantle's father, who died of cancer at age 39. Many relatives on both sides of his family were heavy drinkers of alcohol. Knowing his genetic background, Mantle might have chosen to avoid alcohol. Instead, he became "a notorious alcoholic [because he] believed a family history of early mortality meant he would die young" (Jaffe, 2004, p. 37). At age 46, Mantle purportedly said, "If I knew I was going to live this long, I would have taken better care of myself." He kept on drinking. Despite a liver transplant, liver damage killed him at age 63, 15 years short of the life expectancy for men of his time.

Prenatal Teratogens

Most pregnant women in the modern world are exposed to **teratogens.** Teratogens are substances (such as drugs and pollutants) and conditions (such as severe malnutrition and extreme stress) that increase the risk of prenatal abnormalities. For many reasons, the risks are much higher for some pregnancies than for others. Table 2.7 on pages 74–75 lists some teratogens and their effects, as well as protective measures.

The possible harm that a teratogen may do to a developing organism (whether zygote, embryo, or fetus) is more extensive than people once thought. Structural abnormalities (such as malformed faces) are obvious at birth, but many substances are *behavioral teratogens.* These affect the child's developing brain, making him or her slow to talk, hyperactive, or learning-disabled. The effects of behavioral teratogens do not become evident until months or years after birth.

Pregnant women in the twenty-first century cannot avoid all teratogens: At some point during pregnancy, everyone is exposed to a virus, or breathes a pollutant, or is emotionally stressed. Through the mother, these circumstances may affect the fetus; the specifics depend on both nature and nurture.

© DAVID H. WELLS / CORBIS

Yes, But . . . An adopted boy points out something to his father—a positive interaction between the two. The shapes of the boy's eyes, ears, and upper lip indicate that he was born with fetal alcohol syndrome (FAS). Scientists disagree about the strength of the correlation between FAS and drinking alcohol during pregnancy.

● **FOR DEEPER REFLECTION** How much protection, if any, should the legal system provide for fetuses? Should alcoholic women who are pregnant be jailed to prevent them from drinking? What about people who enable them to drink, such as their partners, their parents, bar owners, bartenders?

fetal alcohol syndrome (FAS)
A cluster of birth defects, including abnormal facial characteristics, slow physical growth, and retarded mental development, that may occur in the child of a woman who drinks alcohol while pregnant.

teratogens
Agents and conditions, including viruses, drugs, and chemicals, that can impair prenatal development and result in birth defects or even death.

● **UNDERSTANDING THE NUMBERS** What was the average life expectancy for men when Mickey Mantle died?

Answer Age 78 (63 + 15), the average for U.S. men who had reached age 50. Mantle may have misunderstood cohort effects as well as genetics. When he was born in 1931, the average male life span was 63 because one of every 15 boys died in infancy, and his father's early death was not unusual. When Mantle died in 1995, the average newborn lived to age 70, and most men his age lived to 80.

TABLE 2.7 Teratogens: Effects of Exposure and Prevention of Damage

Teratogens	Effects on Child of Exposure	Measures for Preventing Damage
Diseases		
Rubella (German measles)	In embryonic period, causes blindness and deafness; in first and second trimesters, causes brain damage	Get immunized before becoming pregnant
Toxoplasmosis	Brain damage, loss of vision, mental retardation	Avoid eating undercooked meat and handling cat feces, garden dirt
Measles, chicken pox, influenza	May impair brain functioning	Get immunized before getting pregnant; avoid infected people during pregnancy
Syphilis	Baby is born with syphilis, which, untreated, leads to brain and bone damage and eventual death	Early prenatal diagnosis and treatment with antibiotics
AIDS	Baby may catch the virus. Without treatment, illness and death are likely during childhood.	Prenatal drugs and cesarean birth make AIDS transmission rare
Other sexually transmitted infections, including gonorrhea and chlamydia	Not usually harmful during pregnancy but may cause blindness and infections if transmitted during birth	Early diagnosis and treatment; if necessary, cesarean section, treatment of newborn
Infections, including infections of urinary tract, gums, and teeth	May cause premature labor, which increases vulnerability to brain damage	Get infection treated, preferably before becoming pregnant
Pollutants		
Lead, mercury, PCBs (polychlorinated biphenyls), dioxin, and some pesticides, herbicides, and cleaning compounds	May cause spontaneous abortion, preterm labor, and brain damage	Most common substances are harmless in small doses, but pregnant women should avoid regular and direct exposure, such as drinking well water, eating unwashed fruits or vegetables, using chemical compounds, eating fish from polluted waters
Radiation		
Massive or repeated exposure to radiation, as in medical X-rays	In the embryonic period, may cause abnormally small head (microcephaly) and mental retardation; in the fetal period, suspected but not proven to cause brain damage. Exposure to background radiation, as from power plants, is usually too low to have an effect.	Get sonograms, not X-rays, during pregnancy; pregnant women who work directly with radiation need special protection or temporary assignment to another job
Social and Behavioral Factors		
Very high stress	Early in pregnancy, may cause cleft lip or cleft palate, spontaneous abortion, or preterm labor	Get adequate relaxation, rest, and sleep; reduce hours of employment; get help with housework and child care
Malnutrition	When severe, may interfere with conception, implantation, normal fetal development, and full-term birth	Eat a balanced diet (with adequate vitamins and minerals, including, especially, folic acid, iron, and vitamin A); achieve normal weight before getting pregnant, then gain 25–35 lbs (10–15 kg) during pregnancy
Excessive, exhausting exercise	Can affect fetal development when it interferes with pregnant woman's sleep, digestion, or nutrition	Get regular, moderate exercise
Medicinal Drugs		
Lithium	Can cause heart abnormalities	Avoid all medicines, whether prescription or over-the-counter, during pregnancy unless they are approved by a medical professional who knows about the pregnancy and is aware of the most recent research
Tetracycline	Can harm the teeth	
Retinoic acid	Can cause limb deformities	
Streptomycin	Can cause deafness	
ACE inhibitors	Can harm digestive organs	
Phenobarbital	Can affect brain development	
Thalidomide	Can stop ear and limb formation	

TABLE 2.7 (Continued)

Teratogens	Effects on Child of Exposure	Measures for Preventing Damage
Psychoactive Drugs		
Caffeine	Normal use poses no problem	Avoid excessive use: Drink no more than three cups a day of beverages containing caffeine (coffee, tea, cola drinks, hot chocolate)
Alcohol	May cause fetal alcohol syndrome (FAS) or fetal alcohol effects (FAE)	Stop or severely limit alcohol consumption during pregnancy; especially dangerous are three or more drinks a day or four or more drinks on one occasion
Tobacco	Reduces birthweight, increases risk of malformations of limbs and urinary tract, and may affect the baby's lungs	Stop smoking before and during pregnancy
Marijuana	Heavy exposure may affect the central nervous system; when smoked, may hinder fetal growth	Avoid or strictly limit marijuana consumption
Heroin	Slows fetal growth and may cause premature labor; newborns with heroin in their bloodstream require medical treatment to prevent the pain and convulsions of withdrawal	Get treated for heroin addiction before becoming pregnant; if already pregnant, gradual withdrawal on methadone is better than continued use of heroin
Cocaine	May cause slow fetal growth, premature labor, and learning problems in the first years of life	Stop using cocaine before pregnancy; babies of cocaine-using mothers may need special medical and educational attention in their first years of life
Inhaled solvents (glue or aerosol)	May cause abnormally small head, crossed eyes, and other indications of brain damage	Stop sniffing inhalants before becoming pregnant; be aware that serious damage can occur before a woman knows she is pregnant

Note: This table summarizes some relatively common teratogenic effects. As the text makes clear, many individual factors in each pregnancy affect whether a given teratogen will actually cause damage and what that damage might be. This is a general summary of what is known; new evidence is reported almost daily, so some of these generalities will change. Pregnant women or women who want to become pregnant should consult with their physicians.
Sources: Mann & Andrews, 2007; O'Rahilly & Müller, 2001; Reece & Hobbins, 2007; Shepard & Lemire, 2004; L. T. Singer et al., 2002.

GENETIC VULNERABILITY Some zygotes carry genes that make them vulnerable. For example, Japan has excellent preconception and prenatal care and, consequently, lower-than-average rates of almost every birth defect. However, babies with cleft lip are born in Japan at three times the rate in Canada (World Health Organization, 2003), suggesting that cleft lip is influenced by genes and that those genes are more common in Japanese people than in Canadians.

The neural tube, which develops into the central nervous system, is the first part of the embryo to form. Neural-tube defects, which lead to abnormalities of the spine and brain, are caused by abnormally low levels of folic acid in a pregnant woman's body. This deficiency is often dietary, but it may also have a genetic cause: Some women do not metabolize folic acid well.

A woman would not know about her metabolism of folic acid, so all women are urged to take vitamin supplements containing folic acid *before* becoming pregnant. However, only one-third of U.S. women of childbearing age do so (Suellentrop et al., 2006). In response, folic acid is now added to many foods in the United States and Canada, and the rate of spina bifida (a serious condition in which the spinal column is not completely closed) has decreased.

TIMING OF EXPOSURE Each body part has a *critical period* when that body part develops, followed by a *sensitive period* when teratogens can interfere with recent growth (see Figure 2.8). Teratogens are most harmful to whatever part of the embryo is forming at the time of exposure (K. L. Moore & Persaud, 2003).

RESPONSE FOR Future Drug Counselors (from page 72): Maybe. Some people who love risk become addicts; others develop a healthy lifestyle that includes adventure, new people, and exotic places. Any trait can lead in various directions. You need to be aware of the connection so that you can steer your clients toward healthy adventures. ●

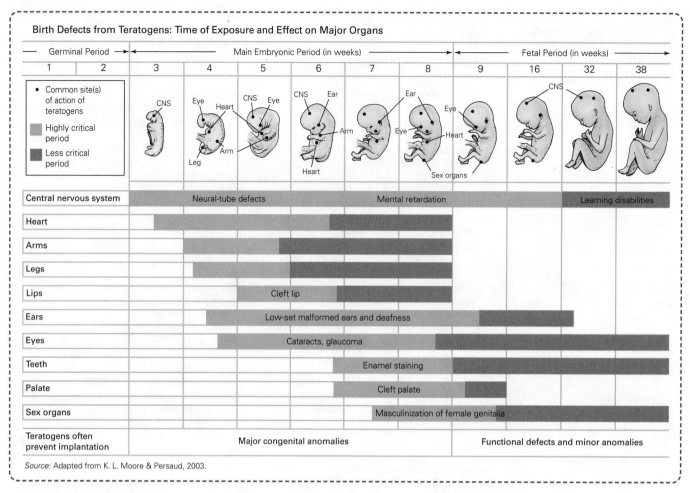

Birth Defects from Teratogens: Time of Exposure and Effect on Major Organs

Source: Adapted from K. L. Moore & Persaud, 2003.

FIGURE 2.8 Critical Periods in Human Development The most serious damage from teratogens (*orange bars*) is likely to occur early in prenatal development. However, significant damage (*purple bars*) to many vital parts of the body, including the central nervous system (CNS, the brain and spinal cord), eyes, and genitals, can occur during the last months of pregnancy as well.

threshold effect
A situation in which a certain teratogen is relatively harmless in small doses but becomes harmful once exposure reaches a certain level (the threshold).

For structural abnormalities, the critical period is the first two months, often before the woman knows that she is pregnant. This is also when most spontaneous abortions occur, typically because something is severely amiss.

However, body functioning and the cortex continue to mature throughout the embryonic and fetal stages of development. Consequently, teratogens that cause preterm birth (notably cigarettes) are particularly harmful in the second half of pregnancy; others (notably psychoactive drugs) are harmful to the brain at any time, even in the last weeks before birth.

AMOUNT OF EXPOSURE The critical period is an aspect of heredity (nature); the other crucial factor causing birth defects is the amount of exposure to a teratogen (nurture). Some teratogens have a **threshold effect;** they are virtually harmless until exposure reaches a certain level, when they "cross the threshold" and become damaging (O'Rahilly & Müller, 2001).

For instance, bisphenol A (BPA) is a chemical compound used to make clear plastic. Everyone has trace amounts in their bodies; that seems harmless. But too much is teratogenic in mice, causing infertility, obesity, diabetes, and cancer. Scientists do not know the threshold for humans, but some advise pregnant women to avoid plastic containers and plastic dishware, since the embryo and the fetus are more vulnerable than the adult (Vandenberg et al., 2007).

Similar uncertainties exist for dozens of other chemicals that were unknown 50 years ago, including several of the plasticizing chemical compounds known as phthalates and dozens of chemicals found in pesticides, prescription drugs, cosmetics, and herbicides. Note that these substances are found in most modern societies. The *nature* of prenatal development has not changed much for thousands of years, but *nurture,* or environmental influences, includes many new substances.

Some teratogens reach the threshold of harm only when a pregnant woman ingests them. Accordingly, pregnant women should avoid taking prescription drugs unless their doctor is aware that they are pregnant, is familiar with the research on the drug's effects, and is convinced that the drug is necessary. Exposure to other teratogens is literally unavoidable because they are present in the air and water. Trace amounts are harmless, but it is not known when a trace becomes a teratogen.

Indeed, some substances are beneficial up to a point but are fiercely teratogenic in large quantities. For example, vitamin A is an essential part of the prenatal diet, but 50,000 or more daily units of vitamin A can cause the development of abnormal body structures in the fetus. Some of the nutrients in fish are beneficial to fetal brain development; but fish may also contain pollutants that are harmful when ingested in sufficient quantities.

Only research on pregnant humans—thousands of them, studied longitudinally—can determine the exact threshold for a specific teratogen. Such a study would need to be comprehensive, since substances interact to raise or lower the risk. Furthermore, since each woman and each fetus is unique, the threshold varies from one person to another.

Resolving Uncertainties

This point highlights a problem with all advice and warnings about nature and nurture. Pregnancy need not be an anxious time, filled with restrictions and fears about diet, diseases, drugs, and other possible dangers. The anxiety itself may reduce sleep, impair digestion, and raise blood pressure—all of which may hinder development.

Good prenatal care teaches women what they can do—what vitamins to take, what drugs to avoid, what foods to eat—to help ensure that they will have healthy babies. Pregnant women who drink and smoke, for instance, are more likely to quit or at least cut down with professional medical advice than without it.

Sometimes prenatal care literally saves a life. For example, if testing in the first two months discovers maternal syphilis or HIV, treatment can prevent transmission of the virus to the fetus. Prenatal care can also protect the fetus if a woman is anemic, has high blood pressure, or develops gestational diabetes.

Ideally, prenatal care reassures prospective parents that all is well, thus helping to ensure a healthy pregnancy by reducing stress (see Table 2.8). Both future parents can listen

---

TABLE 2.8 Before Pregnancy

What Prospective Mothers Should Do	What Prospective Mothers Really Do (U.S. data)
1. Plan the pregnancy.	1. About 60 percent of pregnancies are intended.
2. Take a daily multivitamin with folic acid.	2. About 40 percent of women aged 18 to 45 take vitamins.
3. Avoid binge drinking (defined as four or more drinks in a row).	3. One-eighth of all women who might become pregnant binge-drink.
4. Update immunizations against all teratogenic viruses, especially rubella.	4. Because of laws regarding school admission, most young women in the United States are well immunized.
5. Gain or lose weight, as appropriate.	5. Babies born to underweight women are at risk for low birthweight. Babies born to obese women have three times the usual rate of birth complications. About half of all women begin pregnancy at an appropriate weight.
6. Reassess use of prescription drugs.	6. Eighty-five percent of pregnant women take prescription drugs (not counting vitamins).
7. Maintain exercise habits.	7. Most women do not exercise, especially in the third trimester.

Sources: Downs & Hausenblas, 2007; Suellentrop et al., 2006; Tsai et al., 2007.

to the heartbeat and view a sonogram of the fetus. Hearing and seeing their developing baby are likely to increase their motivation to reduce the fetus's exposure to risks. Thus, one more developing person will be ready for 80 years or so of life on Earth.

KEY Points

- Nature and nurture always interact; neither operates in isolation.
- Virtually all physical and psychological conditions—including nearsightedness, alcoholism, and the effects of prenatal teratogens—have genetic roots.
- Environmental influences allow genes to affect the phenotype or not—as when a genetic tendency toward alcoholism is irrelevant because the person never drinks.
- Good prenatal care can help to ensure a healthy baby, assure the prospective parents that all is well, and even save lives.

SUMMARY

The Beginning of Life

1. Genes are the foundation for all development. Human conception occurs when two gametes (an ovum and a sperm, each with 23 chromosomes) combine to form a zygote, 46 chromosomes in a single cell.

2. Every cell of every human being has a unique genetic code made up of about 20,000 genes, some in variations called alleles. The environment interacts with the genetic instructions for every trait.

3. The sex of an embryo depends on the sperm: A Y sperm creates an XY (male) embryo; an X sperm creates an XX (female) embryo. Twins occur if a zygote splits in two (monozygotic, or identical, twins) or if two ova are fertilized by two sperm (dizygotic, or fraternal, twins).

4. Genes interact in various ways; sometimes additively, with multiple genes contributing to a trait, and sometimes in a dominant–recessive pattern. Heritability refers to the impact of genes on a trait within a specific population, not necessarily within an individual.

Genetic Problems

5. Often a zygote has more or fewer than 46 chromosomes. Such zygotes usually do not develop; the main exceptions are those with three chromosomes at the 21st location (Down syndrome, or trisomy-21) or an odd number of sex chromosomes.

6. Genetic testing and counseling can help many couples learn whether their future children are at risk for a chromosomal or genetic abnormality. The odds depend on what types of genes are involved (dominant, recessive, or additive). The final decisions are made by the couple after learning the facts and possibilities.

From Zygote to Newborn

7. The first two weeks of prenatal growth are called the germinal period. The cells differentiate, as the developing organism implants itself in the lining of the uterus.

8. The period from the third through the eighth week after conception is called the embryonic period. The heart begins to beat, and the eyes, ears, nose, and mouth form. By the eighth week, the embryo has the basic organs and features of a human, with the exception of the sex organs.

9. The fetal period extends from the ninth week until birth. By the 12th week, all the organs and body structures have formed. The fetus attains viability at 22 weeks, when the brain is sufficiently mature to regulate basic body functions.

10. The average fetus gains approximately 4½ pounds (2,000 grams) during the last three months of pregnancy. Maturation of brain, lungs, and heart ensures survival of virtually all full-term babies.

Birth

11. Medical intervention can speed contractions, dull pain, measure health via the Apgar scale, and save lives, but it is sometimes impersonal and unnecessary. The goal is a balance, protecting the baby but also allowing parental involvement and control.

12. Birth complications, such as unusually long and stressful labor that includes anoxia (a lack of oxygen to the fetus), have many causes. Low birthweight (under 5½ pounds, or 2,500 grams) may arise from multiple births, placental problems, maternal illness, malnutrition, smoking, drinking, drug use, and age.

13. Kangaroo care is helpful when the newborn is of low birthweight. Mother–newborn interaction should be encouraged, although the parent–infant bond depends on many factors in addition to birth practices.

14. Many women feel unhappy, incompetent, or unwell after giving birth. Postpartum depression gradually disappears with appropriate help; fathers are particularly crucial to the well-being of mother and child, although they, too, are vulnerable to depression.

Nature, Nurture, and the Phenotype

15. Nature and nurture interact to cause virtually all human problems, including alcoholism and nearsightedness. Whether a teratogen harms an embryo or fetus depends not only on genes but also on timing and amount of exposure.

KEY TERMS

DNA (deoxyribonucleic acid) (p. 43)
chromosome (p. 43)
gamete (p. 43)
zygote (p. 44)
gene (p. 44)
genotype (p. 44)
phenotype (p. 44)
allele (p. 45)
genome (p. 45)
monozygotic twins (p. 46)
dizygotic twins (p. 47)
XX (p. 47)
XY (p. 47)

polygenic (p. 48)
multifactorial (p. 48)
regulator gene (p. 48)
additive gene (p. 48)
dominant–recessive pattern (p. 48)
carrier (p. 49)
heritability (p. 49)
Down syndrome (p. 50)
fragile X syndrome (p. 51)
genetic counseling (p. 53)
phenylketonuria (PKU) (p. 55)
germinal period (p. 57)
embryonic period (p. 57)

fetal period (p. 57)
placenta (p. 59)
implantation (p. 59)
embryo (p. 60)
fetus (p. 60)
sonogram (p. 61)
age of viability (p. 61)
Apgar scale (p. 63)
doula (p. 65)
cesarean section (c-section) (p. 65)
low birthweight (LBW) (p. 67)
very low birthweight (VLBW) (p. 67)

extremely low birthweight (ELBW) (p. 67)
preterm birth (p. 68)
small for gestational age (SGA) (p. 68)
kangaroo care (p. 69)
postpartum depression (p. 70)
parent–infant bond (p. 70)
fetal alcohol syndrome (FAS) (p. 73)
teratogens (p. 73)
threshold effect (p. 76)

KEY QUESTIONS

1. How and when is the sex of a zygote determined?

2. Genetically speaking, what are the similarities and differences between individuals and between humans and other animals?

3. What are the differences among monozygotic twins, dizygotic twins, and other siblings?

4. What are the causes and effects of a zygote with more or fewer than 46 chromosomes?

5. Genetic testing for various diseases is much more common now than it once was. What are the advantages and disadvantages?

6. What are the major differences between an embryo at 2 weeks and at 8 weeks after conception?

7. Since almost all fetuses born at 30 weeks survive, why don't women have an elective cesarean at that time?

8. How and when does a pregnant woman's husband influence pregnancy?

9. How have medical procedures helped *and* harmed the birth process?

10. Why do hospitals encourage parents of fragile newborns to provide some care, even if the newborn is in critical condition?

11. Name four causes of low birthweight. What can be done to prevent each one?

12. What can be done to relieve the effects of postpartum depression on the mother, the father, and the infant?

APPLICATIONS

1. Pick one of your traits, and explain the influences that both nature *and* nurture have on it. For example, if you have a short temper, explain its origins in your genetics, your culture, and your childhood experiences.

2. Draw a genetic chart of your biological relatives, going back as many generations as you can, listing all serious illnesses and causes of death. Include ancestors who died in infancy. Do you see any genetic susceptibility? If so, how can you overcome it?

3. Go to a nearby greeting-card store and analyze the cards about pregnancy and birth. Do you see any cultural attitudes (e.g., vari-ations depending on the sex of the newborn or of the parent)? If possible, compare those cards with cards from a store that caters to another economic or cultural group.

4. Interview three mothers of varied backgrounds about their birth experiences. Make your interviews open-ended—let them choose what to tell you, as long as they give at least a 10-minute description. Then compare and contrast the three accounts, not-ing especially any influences of culture, personality, circumstances, or cohort.

Genes and Prenatal Development

THE HUMAN GENOME

Male or female
Sperm are X or Y, creating female (XX) or male (XY)

Pairs of genes interact in many ways
Additive
Dominant-Recessive

Uniqueness and Diversity
Only monozygotic twins have exactly the same genes

Usual for humans: 46 chromosomes, about 20,000 genes
Some genes occur in various configurations (allelles)

"NONE OF US IS TRULY NORMAL"
EACH PERSON IS UNIQUE—GENETICALLY, PRENATALLY, AND IN BIRTH

Abortion of embryos that are not the desired sex

FROM ZYGOTE TO NEWBORN

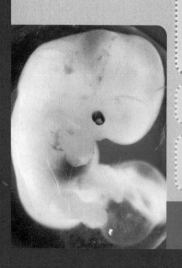

Germinal period: From conception to 2 weeks
Implantation—very hazardous

Embryo: From 2 to 8 weeks
Formation of organs and structures

Fetus: From 8 weeks to birth
Brain development
Viability at 22 weeks

Premature birth

Spontaneous abortion (miscarriage)

INHERITED DISORDERS

Chromosomal miscounts (more or fewer than 46)
Down syndrome (trisomy-21)
23rd pair (XO, XXY, XYY, others)
Most others do not survive

Genetic conditions
Carriers (one recessive gene)
Recessive (two recessive genes)
Dominant (half of all offspring)

Genetic testing and counseling
Decisions made by parents

Tests not competely accurate

LOW BIRTHWEIGHT (UNDER 2,500 GRAMS/ 5½ POUNDS)

Many types
Preterm
Slow growth (SGA)
Very low birthweight (VLBW)
Extremely low birth-weight (ELBW)

Many causes
Undernourished mother
Drug-using mother
Multiple births

Slower language development

Death (especially with ELBW)

Days or weeks in hospital

Brain damage

NURTURE AFFECTS NATURE

Phenotype (actual characteristics) is not just genotype (genes)

Teratogens
Genetic vulnerability
Drugs, pollutants, diseases
Impact affected by dose and timing

Alcoholism
Partly genetic
Metabolism, risk taking
Culture, age

Nearsightedness

BIRTH

Full term at 38 weeks

Parents after birth
Kangaroo care helps fragile newborns
Early contact not necessary for bonding but helps
Fathers may be crucial

Cesarean section
About 35 percent in the United States

Postpartum depression (about 20 perent)

Practices vary by culture and medical care

KEY
■ Major topic
■ Related topic
■ Potential problem

The First Two Years

Adults don't change much in a year or two. Their hair might grow longer, grayer, or thinner; they might be a little fatter; or they might learn something new. But if you saw friends you hadn't seen for two years, you'd recognize them immediately.

By contrast, if you cared for a newborn every single day for a month, went away for two years, and then came back, you might not recognize him or her. The baby would have quadrupled in weight, grown taller by more than a foot, and sprouted a new head of hair. The child's behavior would have changed, too, with much less crying, but some laughter and fear—including fear of you.

A year or two is not much compared with the 80 or so years of the average life span. However, in two years newborns reach half their adult height, learn to talk in sentences, and come to express almost every emotion—not just joy and fear but also love, jealousy, and shame. The next two chapters describe these dramatic changes.

CHAPTER OUTLINE

THE FIRST TWO YEARS
Body and Brain

By the time our first child, Bethany, reached 14 months, she was talking and laughing—early for babies her age, and much to her parents' delight. But she still held on to tables and chairs as she walked, although she should have been taking independent steps, according to the norms for 12-month-olds. I was not only a young mother; I was also a graduate student. That led me to study variations in the norms for age of walking. The data were reassuring: Babies in Paris are among the latest walkers in the world, and my grandmother was French.

Two months later, Bethany was walking and I concluded that her heritage was the reason for her early talking and late walking. My students from many nations provided additional testimony. Those from Jamaica, Guatemala, and Nigeria expected babies to walk earlier than those from Russia, China, and Korea. And babies from each background met the expectations of their parents.

All this could have been the result of either nature or nurture, but I chose to believe that the timetable was dictated by genetics. I was not surprised when our second child, Rachel, didn't take her first steps until 15 months. Our third child, Elissa, also walked later than the average baby—though on schedule for a Berger child with French ancestry. By then, Bethany had become the fastest runner in her kindergarten; my earlier worries had disappeared.

By the time Sarah was born, I was an established professor and author, able to afford a full-time caregiver, Mrs. Todd, from Jamaica. She thought Sarah was the brightest, most advanced baby she had ever seen, except, perhaps, for her own daughter Gillian. I agreed, but I cautioned her that Berger children walk late.

"She'll be walking by a year," Mrs. Todd told me. "Maybe sooner. Gillian walked at 10 months."

"We'll see," I replied, confident in my genetic interpretation.

I underestimated Mrs. Todd. By the time Sarah was 8 months old, Mrs. Todd was already spending a good deal of time bent

HAZEL HANKIN

My Youngest at 8 Months When I look at this photo of Sarah, I see evidence of Mrs. Todd's devotion. Sarah's hair is washed and carefully brushed, her jumper and blouse are clean and pressed, and the carpet and stepstool are perfect equipment for standing practice. Sarah's legs—chubby and far apart—indicate that she is not about to walk early; but, given all these signs of Mrs. Todd's attention to caregiving, it is not surprising, in hindsight, that my fourth daughter was my earliest walker.

over behind her, holding her up by both hands to help her practice walking—to Sarah's great delight. Lo and behold, Sarah took her first step at exactly 1 year—late for a Todd, but amazingly early for a Berger.

As a scientist, I know that a single case proves nothing. The genetic influences on Sarah differ from those on her sisters. Furthermore, she is only one-eighth French, a fraction I had ignored when I sought reassurance regarding Bethany.

Nonetheless, as you read about infant development, remember that caregiving practices enable babies to grow, move, and learn. Development is never quite as straightforward and automatic, or as genetically determined, as it once seemed. The multidirectional and multicontextual perspectives, explained in Chapter 1, are evident. ●

THIS CHAPTER TRACES EARLY DEVELOPMENT, from the first movements of the newborn to the first sentences of the toddler. You will learn about body growth, brain maturation, sitting, walking, thinking, and talking—each accomplishment impressive in its own right.

The entire set of accomplishments is interactive: Progress in body movement allows advances in thinking, and vice versa. There is a "bidirectional link between action, on the one hand, and perception and cognition, on the other" (Rakison & Woodward, 2008, p. 1209).

It will become apparent, as we describe the first two years, that babies are innately propelled to achieve, but caregivers and cultural practices are pivotal influences. Caregivers can encourage early skills, safeguard health with immunizations, provide ideal nutrition with breast milk, talk to babies for months before babies can talk back, and direct the infant's boundless curiosity away from danger and toward the wonders of our world—all in a way that is consistent with their particular culture.

● **UNDERSTANDING THE NUMBERS**
In terms of brain volume, what does the increase in head circumference from 14 inches at birth to 19 inches at age 2 mean?

Answer Since the formula for circumference is πr^2 and the one for volume is πr^3, the numbers must be cubed. The proportions would be the same for radius, diameter, or circumference, so the volume increases by about 250 percent (e.g., $14^3 = 2,744$; $19^3 = 6,859$; $6,859/2,744 = 2.499$). Actually, brain volume increases more than that, since the head becomes slightly more oval and the top half increases more than the bottom half (as you can see in the photos of Juwan, opposite).

norm
An average, or standard, measurement, calculated from the measurements of many individuals within a specific group or population.

Body Changes

Some aspects of infant development seem automatic. Newborns cry in hunger, suck whatever touches their lips, resist overfeeding, and consume enough to grow in body and brain. Sensory and movement skills are immature at birth and develop over the first year according to a genetic timetable. Yet even these natural impulses and schedules are affected by culture, as you will soon see.

Height and Weight

At birth, the average infant weighs about 7½ pounds (3.4 kilograms) and measures about 20 inches (51 centimeters). That's less than the weight of a gallon of milk and as long as the distance from a large man's elbow to the tips of his fingers.

Newborns often lose some weight in the first few days and then gain rapidly. Normally, birthweight doubles by the fourth month, triples by the first birthday, and quadruples by age 2. In those first two years, humans grow about a foot (about 30 centimeters). By age 2, most children are half their adult height (see Figure 3.1 and Appendix A, pp. A-6, A-7).

These numbers are *norms,* a term already used in the first paragraph of this chapter. A **norm** is an average, or standard, for a particular population. The "particular population" for the norms just cited is North American infants. Some perfectly healthy newborns are genetically smaller or larger than the norm. Some parents encourage infants to eat too much—a common mistake, and one that can result in an overweight toddler.

As you remember, newborns who weigh only 6 pounds are not low-birthweight. A small newborn may be genetically destined to be small. Or, especially if the father is tall, that baby may evidence a "birth catch-up," eating voraciously and gaining especially quickly, doubling in weight by 3 months instead of 4.

At each well-baby checkup (monthly at first), a doctor or nurse measures the baby's growth and compares the results to the norms as well as to that baby's previous numbers. Measurements include not only height and weight but also head circumference, which indicates brain development. Abnormal growth may be the first indication of a physical or psychological problem, and that is why such checkups are vital.

Teething or the sniffles can temporarily interfere with weight gain, but stored fat allows the head circumference to keep increasing, a phenomenon called **head-sparing** (Georgieff & Rao, 2001). In head-sparing, nature safeguards the most important part of the infant's growth—not the chubby legs or fat cheeks that grandparents like to pinch, but the brain. Brains triple in weight during the first two years: The norm for head circumference increases from 14 to 19 inches (about 36 to 48 centimeters).

In Just the First Two Years . . .

Percentage of adult size

FIGURE 3.1 **Growing Up** Two-year-olds are barely talking and are totally dependent on adults, but they have already reached half their adult height and three-fourths of their adult brain size. This is dramatic evidence that biosocial growth is the foundation for cognitive and social maturity.

head-sparing
A biological mechanism that protects the brain when malnutrition disrupts body growth. The brain is the last part of the body to be damaged by malnutrition.

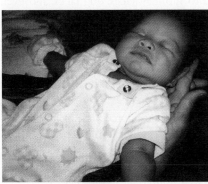

Both Amazing and Average Juwan's growth from (a) 4 months to (b) 12 months to (c) 24 months is a surprise and delight to everyone who knows him. At age 2, this Filipino American toddler seems to have become a self-assured, outgoing individual, obviously unique. Yet the norms indicate that he is developing right on schedule—weight, teeth, motor skills, and all.

(a)   (b)   (c)

ALL: INES YVETTE LAURAYA-ERESE

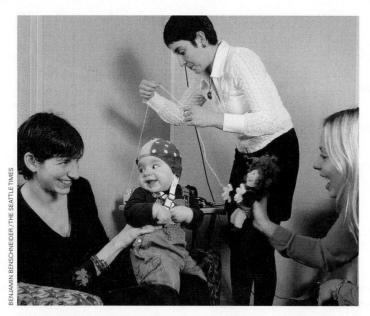

BENJAMIN BENSCHNEIDER / THE SEATTLE TIMES

Electric Excitement Milo's delight at his mother's facial expressions is visible, not just in his eyes and mouth but also in the neurons of the outer layer of his cortex. Electrodes map his brain activation region by region and moment by moment. Every month of life up to age 2 shows increased electrical excitement.

neuron
One of billions of nerve cells in the central nervous system, especially in the brain.

cortex
The outer layers of the brain in humans and other mammals. Most thinking, feeling, and sensing involve the cortex. (Sometimes called the *neocortex*.)

axon
A fiber that extends from a neuron and transmits electrochemical impulses from that neuron to the dendrites of other neurons.

dendrite
A fiber that extends from a neuron and receives electrochemical impulses transmitted from other neurons via their axons.

synapse
The intersection between the axon of one neuron and the dendrites of other neurons.

neurotransmitter
A brain chemical that carries information from the axon of a sending neuron to the dendrites of a receiving neuron.

Brain Development

Lifelong, no body part is more important than the brain. No transplant or artificial organ can replace it. Brain maturation is the crucial factor in viability of the fetus (as you saw in Chapter 2), and decades later death is defined by lack of normal neurological activity (as you will see in the Epilogue). Accordingly, you will read more about the brain in almost every chapter. We start here with the basics.

BASIC BRAIN STRUCTURES The newborn's brain has billions of **neurons**, as brain cells are called. About 70 percent of neurons are in the **cortex**, the brain's six outer layers (see Figure 3.2); it is sometimes called the *neocortex* (Kolb & Whishaw, 2008).

Every brain area specializes in particular functions. For instance, seeing is located in the visual cortex, and hearing is located in the auditory cortex. This does not mean that only one part of the cortex is activated at a time: Most tasks require activation of many areas of the brain, each of which plays a particular role in coordination with the others.

Within and between brain areas, neurons are connected to other neurons by intricate networks of nerve fibers called **axons** and **dendrites** (see Figure 3.3). Each neuron has a single axon and numerous dendrites, with the latter spreading out like the branches of a tree. The axon of one neuron meets—but does not touch—the dendrites of other neurons at intersections called **synapses,** which are critical communication links within the brain.

To be more specific, a neuron communicates by sending electrical impulses through its axon. Along the way, the electrical signal is turned into a chemical signal, or **neurotransmitter,** and sent across the synapse, to be picked up by the dendrites of another neuron. The dendrites bring the message to the cell body of their neuron, where it is translated back into an electrical signal and conveyed via the axon to other neurons. This process is much slower in infancy than later on, for reasons explained in Chapter 5.

During the first months and years, rapid growth and refinement occur in axons, dendrites, and synapses, especially in the cortex. Dendrite growth is the major reason that brain weight triples in the first two years (Johnson, 2005).

The particulars of brain structure and growth depend on both genes and experience. For example, one part of the brain is dedicated to faces. In newborns, this area is activated by anything that looks like a face (e.g., a simple drawing with two dots for eyes). Very young humans seem to attend to monkey faces, dog faces, and even doll faces as avidly as to human faces. But experience refines perception, and soon infants become discriminating observers, focusing on people.

By 6 months, using both the visual cortex and the face region, infants immediately recognize the faces of their caregivers (even in a photograph) and closely examine the facial expressions of strangers. They no longer stare intently at monkey faces or simple drawings (Johnson, 2005).

Throughout life, that face area of the brain allows acute perception of tiny details. That is why you can recognize your best friends from high school even if you have not seen them for a decade, or why a glance at a face in a crowd makes you think, "I know that person from somewhere," perhaps wracking your brain (the non–face areas) to remember where and when you met that individual.

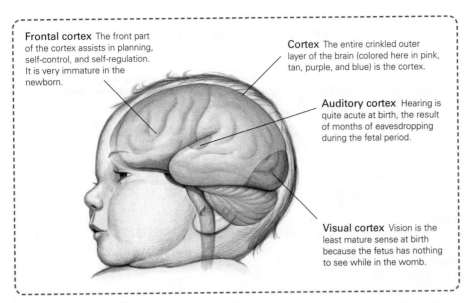

Frontal cortex The front part of the cortex assists in planning, self-control, and self-regulation. It is very immature in the newborn.

Cortex The entire crinkled outer layer of the brain (colored here in pink, tan, purple, and blue) is the cortex.

Auditory cortex Hearing is quite acute at birth, the result of months of eavesdropping during the fetal period.

Visual cortex Vision is the least mature sense at birth because the fetus has nothing to see while in the womb.

FIGURE 3.2 **The Developing Cortex** The infant's cortex consists of four to six thin layers of tissue that cover the brain. It contains virtually all the neurons that make conscious thought possible. Some areas of the cortex, such as those devoted to the basic senses, mature relatively early. Others, such as the frontal cortex, mature quite late.

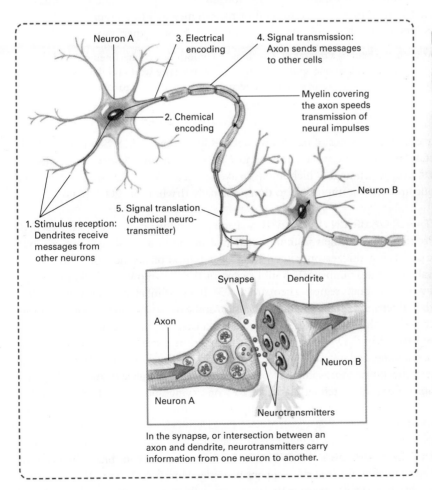

Neuron A

3. Electrical encoding

4. Signal transmission: Axon sends messages to other cells

Myelin covering the axon speeds transmission of neural impulses

2. Chemical encoding

1. Stimulus reception: Dendrites receive messages from other neurons

5. Signal translation (chemical neuro-transmitter)

Neuron B

Synapse Dendrite

Axon

Neuron B

Neuron A

Neurotransmitters

In the synapse, or intersection between an axon and dendrite, neurotransmitters carry information from one neuron to another.

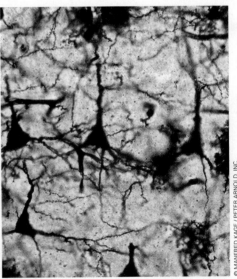

© MANFRED KAGE / PETER ARNOLD, INC.

FIGURE 3.3 **How Two Neurons Communicate** The link between one neuron and another is shown in the simplified diagram at left. The infant brain actually contains billions of neurons, each with one axon and many dendrites. Every electro-chemical message to or from the brain causes thousands of neurons to fire simultaneously, each transmitting the message across the synapse to neighboring neurons. The electron micrograph directly above shows several neurons, greatly magnified, with their tangled but highly organized and well-coordinated sets of dendrites and axons.

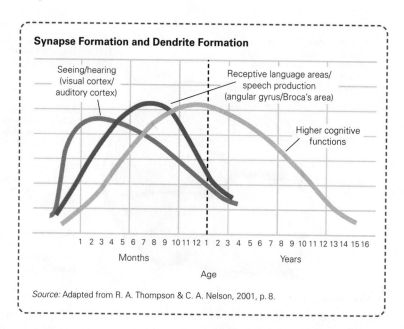

FIGURE 3.4 Brain Growth in Response to Experience These curves show the rapid rate of synapse formation for three functions of the brain (senses, language, and planning). After the initial increase, the underused neurons are gradually pruned, or inactivated, as no functioning dendrites are formed from them.

Neurons and synapses *proliferate* (increase rapidly in number) before birth. This increase continues at a fast pace after birth, but soon an opposite phenomenon occurs: the elimination, or *pruning*, of unnecessary connections (C. A. Nelson et al., 2006). Unused dendrites, axons, synapses (and probably neurons) shrink and die because no experience has activated them to send or receive messages (see Figure 3.4). Pruning occurs lifelong, but it is most intense before age 2. As one expert says:

> At birth, the brain is a thicket of branching extensions that connect neurons and allow them to talk to one another. Early in life, experience works on this tangle like a bonsai master, pruning away connections that don't play a part in working neuronal circuits and reinforcing those that do.
>
> [G. Miller, 2003, p. 78]

Paradoxically, this loss of dendrites increases brain power (L. S. Scott et al., 2007). In fact, fragile X syndrome (mentioned in Chapter 2) involves "a persistent failure of normal synapse pruning," which results in axons and dendrites that are too dense and too long and make it impossible to think normally (Irwin et al., 2002, p. 194).

TIMETABLE OF BRAIN MATURATION Each part of the brain develops on a schedule. Proliferation and then pruning occur first in the visual and auditory cortexes, before age 1. For this reason, remediation of blindness or deafness (such as cataract removal or cochlear implants) should occur in the first months of life, to prevent atrophy of those brain regions (Leonard, 2003). If a deaf infant's deficit is recognized at birth and repaired, language comprehension and expression will be more advanced than those of a child whose deafness was noticed later (Kennedy et al., 2006).

The last part of the brain to mature is the **prefrontal cortex,** the area for anticipation, planning, and impulse control. It is virtually undeveloped in early infancy and gradually becomes more efficient over the years of childhood and adolescence (Luciana, 2003). Thus, telling an infant to stop crying and go to sleep is pointless because the infant cannot decide to comply; such self-control requires brain capacity that is not yet present.

prefrontal cortex
The area of the cortex at the front of the brain that specializes in anticipation, planning, and impulse control.

STIMULATION AND BRAIN DEVELOPMENT Is it necessary for brain circuits to be activated in infancy? Yes, but this happens naturally. Most parents provide all the stimulation that is needed, caressing the newborn, talking to the preverbal infant, and

TABLE 3.1 Some Techniques Used by Neuroscientists to Understand Brain Function

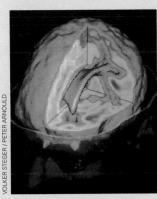

EEG, normal brain

Technique
EEG (electroencephalogram)

Use
Measures electrical activity in the outer layers of the brain, where the cortex is.

Limitations
Especially in infancy, much brain activity of interest occurs below the cortex.

ERP when listening

Technique
ERP (event-related potential)

Use
Notes the amplitude and frequency of electrical activity (as shown by brain waves) in specific parts of the cortex in reaction to various stimuli.

Limitations
Reaction within the cortex signifies perception, but interpretation of the amplitude and timing of brain waves is not straightforward.

fMRI when talking

Technique
fMRI (functional magnetic resonance imaging)

Use
Measures changes in blood flow anywhere in the brain (not just the outer layers).

Limitations
Signifies brain activity, but infants are notoriously active, which can make fMRIs useless.

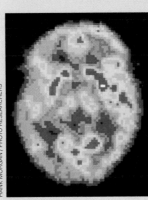

PET scan of sleep

Technique
PET (positron emission tomography)

Use
Also (like fMRI) reveals activity in various parts of the brain. Locations can be pinpointed with precision, but PET requires injection of radioactive dye to light up the active parts of the brain.

Limitations
Many parents and researchers hesitate to inject radioactive dye into an infant's brain unless a serious abnormality is suspected.

For both practical and ethical reasons, these techniques have not been used with large, representative samples of normal infants. One of the challenges of neuroscience is to develop methods that are harmless, easy to use, and comprehensive for the study of normal children. A more immediate challenge is to depict the data in ways that are easy to interpret.

showing affection toward a small person. No special toys are required, because infant brains are adaptive (C. A. Nelson et al., 2007). They show plasticity in that they grow in the way that their experiences allow.

This does not mean that infant brains are impervious to harm. Early in life, brains notice what occurs and adapt their neurons and dendrites. That much is known, but thousands of scientists are using various techniques to try to understand precisely how areas of the brain function in the early months (see Table 3.1).

Some causes of brain damage are known. An impatient caregiver may shake a baby, sharply and quickly, to make him or her stop crying. Shaken babies become quiet because of ruptured blood vessels in the brain. This results in broken neural connections, the mark of **shaken baby syndrome.** In the United States, more than one in five of all children hospitalized for maltreatment have suffered this kind of brain damage, according to sensitive brain scans (Rovi et al., 2004).

Even without such evident damage, the brains of terrified babies produce a flood of cortisol and other stress hormones that may disrupt normal reactions lifelong, causing a person to be hypervigilant (always alert) or emotionally flat (never happy, sad, or angry). Furthermore, depriving a baby of normal social contact can also impair the brain, as the following explains.

shaken baby syndrome
A life-threatening injury that occurs when an infant is forcefully shaken back and forth, a motion that ruptures blood vessels in the brain and breaks neural connections.

A VIEW FROM SCIENCE

The Effect of Social Deprivation on Brain Growth

What effect does early stimulation—or lack of it—have on the brain's development? To explore that question, Marion Diamond, William Greenough, and their colleagues raised some rats in a social playground—large cages with other rats and many stimulating objects. Some of their litter mates (who were from the same gene pool) were raised alone, in small, barren cages. Autopsies on rats from both groups found that the brains of the "enriched" rats were larger and heavier and had more dendrites than the brains of the "deprived" rats (Diamond et al., 1988; Greenough & Volkmar, 1973).

Using many other species of animals, researchers have confirmed that early experiences do affect brain growth. Isolation and sensory deprivation harm the developing brain, and a complex social environment enhances neurological growth (Curtis & Nelson, 2003). Note that this experimental deprivation was extreme: Every animal raised in the wild has many social and environmental experiences.

Such experiments are unthinkable with humans, but a chilling natural experiment began in Romania in the 1980s, when dictator Nicolae Ceausescu forbade birth control and outlawed abortions except for mothers who already had five or more children. Parents were paid for every birth but received no financial support for raising their children.

As a result of these policies, unwanted births and infant mortality rose; illegal abortions became the leading cause of death for women age 15–45 (Verona, 2003). More than 100,000 children were abandoned to crowded institutions, forced to endure "severe and pervasive restriction of human interactions, play, conversation, and experiences" (Rutter & O'Connor, 2004, p. 91).

A Fortunate Pair Elaine Himelfarb (shown in the background), of San Diego, California, is shown here in Bucharest to adopt 22-month-old Maria.

Ceausescu was ousted and killed in 1989. In the following years, North American and western European couples adopted thousands of the institutionalized Romanian children. They hoped that "lots of love and good food would change the skinny, floppy waif they found in the orphanage into the child of their dreams" (D. E. Johnson, 2000, p. 154).

All the Romanian adoptees experienced catch-up growth, becoming taller and gaining weight until they reached the norms for their age (Rutter & O'Connor, 2004). However, many showed signs of emotional damage. They were too friendly to strangers, or too angry without reason, or too frightened of normal events (Chisholm, 1998).

By age 11, most of those who had been adopted before they were 6 months old seemed normal, but those adopted when they were older than a year averaged 15 points below normal on IQ tests. Their deficits were especially evident in abilities controlled by the prefrontal cortex, including social interaction and impulse control (C. A. Nelson, 2007).

Further research in Romania has found that infants develop best in their own families, second best in foster families, and much worse in institutions (C. A. Nelson et al., 2007). This is confirmed by recent data on a group of Romanian children who had lived in institutions until about age 2 (Romania no longer permits international adoptions). These institutionalized 2-year-olds were then randomly assigned to foster homes in Romania or to ongoing institutional care. By age 4, the fostered children were smarter (by about 10 IQ points) than those who had remained institutionalized, although their IQ scores were still below those of children who had been cared for by their parents since birth (C. A. Nelson et al., 2007).

Developmentalists are convinced that infants in frightening homes or impersonal institutions are at risk for lifelong brain damage (Maclean, 2003). Many governments ignore this danger. More than a million children in central and eastern Europe live in institutions. Some of these institutions provide excellent physical care but nonetheless harm infants because their caregiving staff do not respond to the babies as individuals (St. Petersburg–U.S.A. Orphanage Research Team, 2008).

Fewer infants are institutionalized in North America. However, another problem occurs: Authorities should, but do not, "move children into permanent homes more quickly or remove them from abusive homes sooner" (C. A. Nelson, 2007, p. 17).

It is apparent that all infants need love and stimulation to become the persons their genes enable them to be. Head-sparing, plasticity, and catch-up growth compensate for the many limitations, imperfections, and lapses of human parenting, but they cannot overcome prolonged early deprivation. Impairment increases the longer stress or isolation goes on.

SLEEP PATTERNS One consequence of brain maturation is the ability to sleep for several uninterrupted hours. Newborns cannot do this. In the early months, parents need to adjust their schedules to accommodate their babies, since the reverse is impossible. Normally, newborns sleep about 17 hours a day, in one- to three-hour segments. Spending so much time sleeping helps them use most of their energy for the doubling of birthweight, as described earlier.

Newborns' sleep is primarily *active sleep*, as opposed to *quiet sleep*. That means they are often dozing, able to awaken if someone rouses them, but also able to go back to sleep quickly if they wake up, cry, and are comforted. In such sleep (but not in quiet sleep, with slow brain waves and slow breathing), infants wake themselves up if their oxygen level falls (H. L. Richardson et al., 2006). They then breathe rapidly, protecting themselves from *anoxia* (lack of oxygen).

A curious aspect of early sleep patterns is that newborns have a high proportion of **REM (rapid eye movement) sleep,** with flickering eyes and rapid brain waves. When adults are awakened during REM sleep, they report that they had been dreaming; presumably infants would say the same thing if they could talk. The content of infant dreams is not known, but experts agree that dreaming helps consolidate memories and that infant sleep patterns generally are adaptive.

Over the first months, the proportion of time spent in each type of sleep changes. REM sleep declines, as does "transitional sleep," the dozing, half-awake stage. At 3 or 4 months, quiet sleep (also called *slow-wave sleep*) increases markedly (Salzarulo & Fagioli, 1999).

The various states of waking and sleeping become more evident with age, as brain maturation allows a more definite cycle, with longer periods of sleeping, eating, and playing at a stretch. Thus, although many newborns rarely seem sound asleep or wide awake, by 3 months most babies have periods of alertness (when they are neither hungry nor sleepy) and periods of deep sleep (when household noises do not wake them). By 12 months, infants take naps, usually two a day, and then sleep longer at night.

ESPECIALLY FOR Social Workers An infertile couple in their late 30s asks for your help in adopting a child from eastern Europe. They particularly want an older child. How do you respond? (see response, page 95) →

REM (rapid eye movement) sleep A stage of sleep characterized by flickering eyes behind closed lids, dreaming, and rapid brain waves.

SEAN SPRAGUE / THE IMAGE WORKS

Sleeping Beauty At 3 months, most babies—like this infant in Mongolia—can sleep soundly amid noisy human activity.

KEY points

- Weight and height increase markedly in the first two years; the norms are three times the birthweight by age 1 and 12 inches (30 centimeters) taller than birth height by age 2.
- Brain development is rapid during infancy, particularly development of the axons, dendrites, and synapses within the cortex.
- Experience shapes the infant brain, as pruning eliminates unused connections.
- Early sleep patterns originate from brain impulses and are adaptive.

Moving and Perceiving

Brain development cannot be directly observed. Various brain scans highlight neurological activity in special cases, but for most infants, brain maturation is invisible. However, brain growth is evident in the progression of many skills involved in movement and awareness of the surrounding environment.

Motor Skills

Motor skills are the abilities needed to move and control the body (Adolph & Berger, 2006). Just as the motor of a car is the crucial part that allows it to go, the motor skills of people and other animals allow them to move their bodies. To make the car actually travel, a driver, gas, and various connections to the motor are needed; in the human body, the brain directs movement, and nutrition is needed to fuel the muscles.

REFLEXES Normal newborns are active. They curl their toes, grasp with their fingers, screw up their faces, and so on. Even at birth, these movement abilities indicate brain functioning. This is evident in the Apgar scale and many other tests of newborn functioning, such as the *Brazelton Neonatal Behavioral Assessment Scale*, which elicits reflexes and assesses newborns' senses and reactions to discern how well the brain is functioning.

Strictly speaking, the first movements are not *skills* but **reflexes,** involuntary responses to a particular stimulus. The reflexes that are part of the Apgar and Brazelton scales (and other measures of an infant's health) are particularly significant if the infant is preterm or if brain damage is suspected, as is often indicated by the absence of reflexes. Reflexes are also useful to demonstrate to parents that their tiny baby is already a capable young person (Lawhon & Hedlund, 2008).

Newborns normally have dozens of reflexes, 18 of which are mentioned in *italics* below. There are three sets of reflexes that are critical for survival:

● Reflexes that maintain oxygen supply. The *breathing reflex* begins in normal newborns even before the umbilical cord, with its supply of oxygen, is cut. Additional reflexes that maintain oxygen are reflexive *hiccups* and *sneezes,* as well as *thrashing* (moving the arms and legs about) to escape something that covers the face.

● Reflexes that maintain constant body temperature. When infants are cold, they *cry, shiver,* and *tuck in their legs* close to their bodies, thereby helping to keep themselves warm. When they are hot, they try to *push away* blankets and then stay still.

● Reflexes that facilitate feeding. The *sucking reflex* causes newborns to suck anything that touches their lips—fingers, toes, blankets, and rattles, as well as natural and artificial nipples of various textures and shapes. The *rooting reflex* causes babies to turn their mouths toward anything that brushes against their cheeks—a reflexive search for a nipple—and start to suck. *Swallowing* is another important reflex that aids feeding, as are *crying* when the stomach is empty and *spitting up* when too much has been swallowed too quickly.

reflex
An unlearned, involuntary action or movement emitted in response to a particular stimulus. A reflex is an automatic response that is built into the nervous system and occurs without conscious thought.

Never Underestimate the Power of a Reflex For developmentalists, newborn reflexes are mechanisms for survival, indicators of brain maturation, and vestiges of evolutionary history. For parents, they are mostly delightful and sometimes amazing. Both of these viewpoints are demonstrated by three star performers: A 1-day-old girl stepping eagerly forward on legs too tiny to support her body, a newborn boy grasping so tightly that his legs dangle in space, and another newborn boy sucking on the doctor's finger.

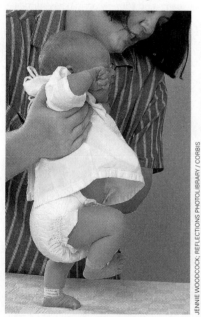

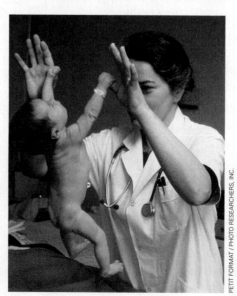

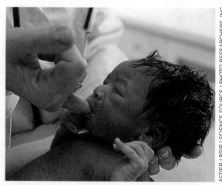

Other reflexes are not necessary for survival but are important signs of normal brain and body functioning. Among them are the following:

- *Babinski reflex*. When infants' feet are stroked, their toes fan upward.
- *Stepping reflex*. When infants are held upright with their feet touching a flat surface, they move their legs as if to walk.
- *Swimming reflex*. When they are laid horizontally on their stomachs, infants stretch out their arms and legs.
- *Palmar grasping reflex*. When something touches infants' palms, they grip it tightly.
- *Moro reflex*. When someone startles them, perhaps by banging on the table they are lying on, infants fling their arms outward and then bring them together on their chests, as if to hold on to something, while crying with wide-open eyes.

Cultural differences *may* originate from temperamental differences in the strength of various reflexes. For instance, some researchers report that reflexive thrashing and crying when a cloth covers the face are typical for European infants but not Chinese ones, who often will simply turn their heads to escape the cloth. In general, Chinese infants are less active than European babies in their reflexive responses; it is not known whether the difference is primarily genetic or environmental. Some alleles are more common among Chinese infants, but prenatal care, birth practices, diet, and early postnatal care differ as well (Kagan & Snidman, 2004).

GROSS MOTOR SKILLS Deliberate, coordinated actions that produce large movements, usually involving several parts of the body, are called **gross motor skills.** These emerge from reflexes.

Crawling is one example. As babies gain muscle strength, they start to wiggle, attempting to move forward by pushing their shoulders and upper bodies against whatever surface they are lying on. Usually by 5 months or so, they use their arms, and then legs, to inch forward on their bellies. Between 8 and 10 months, most infants can lift their midsections and crawl (or *creep,* as the British call it) on "all fours," coordinating their hands, elbows, knees, and feet in a smooth, balanced manner (Adolph et al., 1998).

Sitting is another gross motor skill that develops gradually, as muscles mature to steady the top half of the body. By 3 months, most infants have enough muscle control to be lap-sitters if the lap's owner provides back support. By 6 months, they can usually sit unsupported. If an 8-month-old cannot sit, it is a sign that something is seriously amiss with the child's brain as well as body.

Walking progresses from reflexive, hesitant, adult-supported stepping to a smooth, coordinated gait. Most infants can walk while holding on at 9 months, can stand alone at 10 months, and can walk independently at 12 months.

Once maturation of the muscles and brain allows it, infants become passionate walkers, logging long hours of practice on foot.

> Walking infants practice keeping balance in upright stance and locomotion for more than 6 accumulated hours per day. They average between 500 and 1,500 walking steps per hour so that by the end of each day, they have taken 9,000 walking steps and traveled the length of 29 football fields.
>
> [*Adolph et al., 2003, p. 494*]

They take all these steps on many surfaces, with bare feet or wearing socks, slippers, or shoes. They do not want to be held or pushed in their strollers.

RESPONSE FOR Social Workers (from page 93) Tell them that such a child would require extra time and commitment. Ask whether both are prepared to meet with other parents of international adoptees; to obtain professional help (for speech, nutrition, physical development, and/or family therapy); and to help the child with schoolwork, play dates, and so on. You might ask them to adopt a special-needs child from their own area, to become foster parents, or to volunteer at least 10 hours a week at a day-care center. Their response would indicate their willingness to help a real—not imagined—child. Then you might help them adopt the child they want. ●

gross motor skills
Physical abilities involving large body movements, such as walking and jumping. (The word *gross* here means "big.")

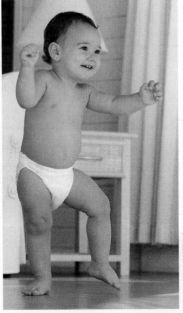

Bossa Nova Baby?
This boy in Brazil demonstrates his joy at acquiring the gross motor skill of walking, which quickly becomes dancing whenever music plays.

RICK GOMEZ / MASTERFILE

fine motor skills
Physical abilities involving small body movements, especially of the hands and fingers, such as drawing and picking up a coin. (The word *fine* here means "small.")

FINE MOTOR SKILLS Small body movements are called **fine motor skills.** Finger movements are fine motor skills, enabling humans to write, draw, type, tie, and so on. Movements of the tongue, jaw, lips, and toes are fine movements, too. Mouth skills precede finger skills by many months, and skillful grabbing with the feet sometimes precedes grabbing with the hands (Adolph & Berger, 2005). However, hand skills are most praised. (Skill at spitting, chewing, or flexing the toes is rarely noted or valued.)

Regarding finger skills, newborns have a strong reflexive grasp but lack control. During their first 2 months, babies excitedly wave their arms at objects dangling in front of them. By 3 months of age, they can usually touch something within reach, but limited eye–hand coordination prevents them from grabbing, holding on, and letting go. When babies were fitted with "sticky mittens" that allowed them to capture objects earlier than they normally could, their reaching and grabbing were speeded up; this is further evidence that experience affects motor skills (Heathcock et al., 2008).

By 4 months, infants usually grab, but their timing is off: They are likely to close their hands too early or too late. Finally, by 6 months, with a concentrated, deliberate stare, most babies can reach for and grasp any object of the right size. They can hold a bottle, shake a rattle, and yank a sister's braids. Once this maneuver is possible, they practice it: "From 6 to 9 months, reaching appears as a quite compulsive behavior for small objects presented within arm's reach" (Atkinson & Braddick, 2003, p. 58).

Toward the end of the first year and throughout the second, finger skills improve. Babies master the *pincer movement* (using thumb and forefinger to pick up tiny objects) and feed themselves, first with hands, then fingers, then utensils. By about age 2, thinking may precede grabbing (Atkinson & Braddick, 2003). A toddler may decide against grabbing Mommy's earrings or Daddy's glasses . . . but the parents shouldn't count on it.

ELIZABETH CREWS / THE IMAGE WORKS

What Next? This 7-month-old is focused on grabbing, but her reach seems off-target, her overalls seem restrictive, and she is too young to crawl; she may soon be crying in frustration as the ball rolls out of reach. But there are other signs that her motor skills are advanced, so she may be on the verge of a major new achievement.

OBSERVATION QUIZ
Which of these skills has the greatest variation in age of acquisition? Why? (see answer, page 98) ➡

ETHNIC VARIATIONS All healthy infants develop skills in the same sequence, but the timing varies. Table 3.2 shows age norms for gross motor skills, based on a large, multiethnic sample of U.S. infants. When infants are grouped by ethnicity, the average African American is ahead of the Latino, who is ahead of the European American—but individual differences often outweigh ethnic differences.

What accounts for this variation? It is at least partly genetic. Monozygotic twins walk on the same day more often than dizygotic twins do. Striking individual differences are apparent in infant strategies, effort, and concentration, again suggesting something inborn in motor-skill achievements (Thelen & Corbetta, 2002).

Cultural patterns of child rearing are also influential, as is apparent from the opening of this chapter. Early reflexes are less likely to fade if culture and conditions allow extensive practice. This has been demonstrated with legs (the stepping reflex), hands (the grasping reflex), and crawling (the swimming reflex). Thus, motor skills are an example of a complex and dynamic system in which practice counts, as discussed in Chapter 1 (Thelen & Corbetta, 2002).

TABLE 3.2 AT ABOUT THIS TIME: Age Norms (in Months) for Gross Motor Skills

Skill	When 50% of All Babies Master the Skill	When 95% of All Babies Master the Skill
Sit, head steady	3 months	4 months
Sit, unsupported	6	7
Pull to stand (holding on)	9	10
Stand alone	12	14
Walk well	13	15
Walk backward	15	17
Run	18	20
Jump up	26	29

Note: As the text explains, age norms are approximate and are affected by culture and cohort. These are U.S. norms, mostly for European American children. Mastering skills a few weeks earlier or later is not an indication of health or intelligence. Mastering them very late, however, is a cause for concern.
Source: Coovadia & Wittenberg, 2004; based primarily on Denver II (Frankenburg et al., 1992).

Some cultures promote more practice than others. For example, Jamaican caregivers (such as Mrs. Todd) provide rhythmic and stretching exercises for their infants as part of daily care; their infants are among the youngest walkers (Adolph & Berger, 2005).

Other cultures discourage or even prevent infants from crawling or walking. The people of Bali, Indonesia, never let their infants crawl, for babies are considered divine and crawling is for animals (M. Diener, 2000). In colonial America, "standing stools" were designed for babies to strengthen their walking muscles without crawling (Calvert, 2003). Infants were tightly swaddled and tied in their cradles day and night to prevent movement, because

> parents and physicians alike viewed crawling on all fours, not as a natural stage of human development, but as a bad habit that, if not thwarted, would remain the baby's primary form of locomotion for the rest of its life.... As the common form of locomotion for most animals, crawling raised too many fears and negative associations.
>
> *[Calvert, 2003, p. 65]*

By contrast, the Beng people of the Ivory Coast are proud when their babies crawl but do not let them walk until they are at least 1 year old. Although the Beng do not recognize the connection, one reason for this prohibition may be birth control: Beng mothers do not resume sexual relations until their baby begins walking (Gottlieb, 2000).

Sensation and Perception

The motor skills just described reflect brain development. The senses we now describe typically *precede* intellectual and motor development, making it possible. Newborns have open eyes, sensitive ears, and responsive noses, tongues, and skin, all of which are used to perceive and then understand their experiences.

Since all of a newborn's senses function, why do newborns seem to perceive very little? They might look at their mother's face and then look away, staring longer at a light. They might hear a loud noise and startle, crying and moving their limbs. The reason for such imperceptive reactions is that perception requires experience. Let us clarify the difference between sensation and perception.

Sensation occurs when a sensory system detects a stimulus, as when the inner ear reverberates with sound or the retina and pupil of the eye intercept light. Thus, sensations begin when an outer organ (eye, ear, skin, tongue, or nose) meets something that can be seen, heard, touched, tasted, or smelled.

Perception occurs when the brain processes a sensation. Perception results when a message from one of the sensing organs reaches the brain, and then past experiences and neurological connections suggest that a particular sensation merits processing. Without experience, newborns stare at lights, startle at noises, and consider every face the same. By 6 months, they are far more discerning.

HEARING The sense of hearing develops during the last trimester of pregnancy and is already quite acute at birth; it is the most advanced of the newborn's senses (Saffran et al., 2006). Certain sounds trigger reflexes in newborns, even without conscious perception. Sudden noises startle them, making them cry; rhythmic sounds, such as a lullaby or a heartbeat, soothe them and put them to sleep.

A newborn's hearing can be checked with advanced equipment. This practice is standard at most hospitals in North America and Europe, since early remediation is

MIKE GREENLAR / THE IMAGE WORKS

Safe and Secure Like this Algonquin baby in Quebec, many American Indian infants spend happy hours each day on a cradle board. The discovery in the 1950s that Native American children walk at about the same age as European American children suggested that maturation, not practice, led to motor skills. Later research found that Native American infants undergo exercise sessions each day, an indication that practice is important, too.

sensation
The response of a sensory system (eyes, ears, skin, tongue, nose) when it detects a stimulus.

perception
The mental processing of sensory information when the brain interprets a sensation.

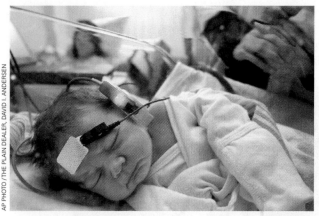

Before Leaving the Hospital As mandated by a 2004 Ohio law, 1-day-old Henry has his hearing tested via vibrations of the inner ear in response to various tones. The computer interprets the data and signals any need for more tests—as is the case for about 1 baby in 100. Normal newborns hear quite well; Henry's hearing was fine.

binocular vision
The ability to focus the two eyes in a coordinated manner in order to see one image.

ANSWER TO OBSERVATION QUIZ
(from page 96) Jumping up, with a three-month age range for acquisition. The reason is that the older an infant is, the more impact culture has. ●

needed for those infants (less than 1 percent) who would benefit (Calevo et al., 2007). Normally, even in the first days of life, infants turn their heads toward the source of a sound. It takes some learning before they can accurately pinpoint where the sound came from, but they already sense and begin to perceive what they hear (Saffran et al., 2006).

Young infants are particularly attentive to the human voice, developing rapid comprehension of the rhythm, segmentation, and cadence of spoken words long before comprehension of their meaning. As time goes on, sensitive hearing combines with the developing brain to distinguish patterns of sounds and syllables.

Infants become accustomed to the rules of their language, such as which syllable is usually stressed (various English dialects have different rules), whether changing voice tone is significant (as in Chinese), whether certain sound combinations are repeated, and so on. All this is based on very careful listening to human speech, even speech not directed toward them or speech that is uttered in a language they do not yet understand.

SEEING Vision is the least mature sense at birth. Newborns focus only on objects between 4 and 30 inches (10 and 75 centimeters) away (Bornstein et al., 2005). If an object in front of them moves, they might not track (follow) it with their eyes. Instead, they lose sight of it, even though it is just a few inches to the left or right.

Soon experience combines with brain maturation to improve visual ability. By 3 months, infants might look intently at a human face and, tentatively and fleetingly, smile when they realize that those eyes, nose, and mouth are, indeed, a face. They can also track a slowly moving object, such as a rattle, in front of them.

Over time, visual scanning becomes more efficient. For example, 3-month-olds look closely at the parts of a face—the eyes and mouth—that contain the most information. They much prefer photos of real faces over photos of faces with the eyes blanked out. Even better from the infants' perspective are faces that move: Parents typically bob their heads, open their mouths wide, and raise their eyebrows to get their infants to smile. The reason for such parental foolishness is that infants reward it with evident delight.

Binocular vision is the ability to coordinate the two eyes to see one image. Because using both eyes together is impossible in the womb, many newborns temporarily seem wall-eyed or cross-eyed. At about 3 months, binocular vision appears, and infants focus both eyes on one thing (Atkinson & Braddick, 2003). This is seen with tracking: Moving an object slowly in front of an infant reveals that both eyes follow it from one side to another. Such evidence of binocular vision is absent in newborns but usually present by 4 months.

Is sensation essential for the visual cortex to develop? Yes, according to a series of classic experiments (Hubel & Wiesel, 2005). Kittens' eyes were sutured shut for several weeks, and then the stitches were removed. The anatomy of their eyes was normal, but some of the neural pathways of the visual cortex had atrophied. Their vision was diminished for life. When adult cats experienced the same temporary blindness, no visual impairment occurred.

Worse were the effects on one eye when it was blindfolded and the other eye was not. In that situation, no neural connections could build to that eye. The kitten's other eye was normal, but without both eyes, binocular vision never became activated in the brain. When the blinded eye was opened, it became obvious that the other eye had taken over the entire visual cortex (unlike when both eyes were blindfolded, and the visual cortex was unused and therefore underdeveloped). Because binocular vision is essential for depth perception, those cats could not safely leap from one surface to another. Instead, they sometimes fell to the floor.

Such experiments would never be done with humans, and current guidelines for ethical research now forbid similar studies in cats. However, when human adults who were blind from birth become able to see, their lack of early visual experience is evident (Sacks, 1995). Typically, they do not perceive tiny visual details in the same way as a person who could see from birth, and their spatial navigation is impaired because vision aids the early development of many gross motor skills.

SMELLING, TASTING, AND TOUCHING As with vision and hearing, the senses of smell, taste, and touch function at birth and rapidly adapt to the social world. For example, one study found that a taste of sugar is a good pain reliever for newborns (Gradin et al., 2002), but another study found that it had no effect on 4-week-olds—unless the sugar was accompanied by a reassuring look from a caregiver (Zeifman et al., 1996).

ALL: CINDY CHARLES / PHOTOEDIT, INC.

Learning About a Lime As with every other normal infant, Jacqueline's curiosity leads to taste and then to a slow reaction, from puzzlement to tongue-out disgust. Jacqueline's responses demonstrate that the sense of taste is acute in infancy and that quick brain reactions are still to come.

Similar adaptation occurs for the other senses. Breast-fed babies can differentiate the smell as well as the taste of their own mother's milk.

Touch seems especially sensitive in the early months. The ability to be comforted by touch is one of the important "skills" tested in the Brazelton Neonatal Behavioral Assessment Scale. Although almost all newborns respond to massage and cuddling, over time they perceive whose touch it is and what it communicates. For instance, 12-month-olds respond differently to their mother's touch, depending on whether the touch is tense or relaxed (Hertenstein & Campos, 2001).

As babies learn to recognize their caregiver's smell and handling, they relax only when cradled by that caregiver, even when their eyes are closed. This discrimination is familiar to every adult, who might regard a pat from a loved one as reassuring but the same gesture from a stranger as intrusive, perhaps even insulting and hostile.

THE SENSES AND SOCIAL PERCEPTIONS Infants perceive the most important experiences with all their senses. Breast milk, for instance, is a mild sedative, so the newborn literally feels happier at the mother's breast, connecting pleasure with taste, touch, smell, and sight.

The entire package of the five senses furthers two goals: social interaction (to respond to familiar caregivers) and comfort (to be soothed amid the disturbances of infant life). Infants similarly adapt their awareness of pain and motion to aid their socialization and comfort.

ESPECIALLY FOR Parents of Grown Children Suppose you realize that you seldom talked to your children until they talked to you and that you often put them in cribs and playpens. Did you limit their brain growth and their sensory capacity? (see response, page 100) ➤

RESPONSE FOR Parents of Grown Children (from page 99) Probably not. Brain development is programmed to occur for all infants, requiring only the stimulation that virtually all families provide—warmth, reassuring touch, overheard conversation, facial expressions, movement. Extras such as baby talk, music, exercise, mobiles, and massage may be beneficial but are not essential. ●

Infants respond to motion as well as to sights and sounds, so many new parents soothe their baby's distress by rocking, carrying, or even driving (with the baby in a safety seat) while humming a lullaby; here again, infant comfort is connected with social interaction and the senses. Another soothing activity is to put the infant in a sling and vacuum the carpet: Steady noise, movement, and touch combine to soothe distress.

In sum, infants' senses are immature, but they function quite well to help babies join the human family.

KEY points

- Motor skills develop over the first two years, indicating brain maturation and enabling the infant to learn.

- Newborns demonstrate many reflexes, some of which aid survival.

- Gross and fine motor skills follow a genetic timetable for maturation; they are also affected by practice and experience.

- All the senses function at birth, with hearing the most acute sense and vision the least developed. Every sense allows perception to develop and furthers social interaction, as caregivers are recognized by sight, touch, smell, and voice.

---

immunization
A process that stimulates the body's immune system to defend against attack by a particular contagious disease. Immunization may be accomplished either naturally (by having the disease) or through vaccination (often by having an injection). (Also called *inoculation* or *vaccination*.)

FIGURE 3.5 More Babies Are Surviving Improvements in public health—better nutrition, cleaner water, more widespread immunization—over the past three decades have meant millions of survivors.

Surviving in Good Health

Although precise worldwide statistics are unavailable, about 10 billion children were born between 1950 and 2007. About 3 billion of them died before age 5. As high as this figure is, the death toll would have been twice that without public health measures that have become widespread in the past 100 years.

Most children now live to adulthood. In the healthiest nations, 99.9 percent of babies who survive the first month (when the sickest and smallest newborns sometimes die) live at least to age 15 (UNICEF, 2006). Even in the least healthy nations, about three-quarters of newborns survive, whereas a few decades ago half the population died in childhood (see Figure 3.5 for examples of this dramatic improvement). Improved public health practices (clean water, adequate food, early immunization, treated sleeping nets in malarial areas, oral rehydration) are the main reason.

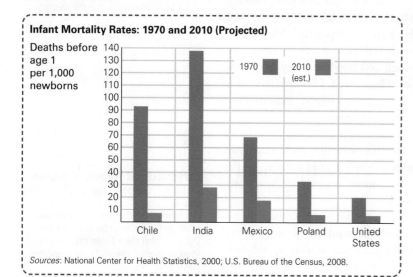

Infant Mortality Rates: 1970 and 2010 (Projected)

Deaths before age 1 per 1,000 newborns

Sources: National Center for Health Statistics, 2000; U.S. Bureau of the Census, 2008.

Immunization

Measles, whooping cough, pneumonia, and other illnesses were once common childhood killers. These diseases can still be fatal, especially for malnourished children, but they are much less prevalent today. Children are protected from them through **immunization** (also called *inoculation* or *vaccination*), which primes the immune system to defend the body against a specific contagious disease. Immunization has justly been called medicine's greatest lifesaver (A. Allen, 2007). (Information about various vaccines is given in Table 3.3.)

Many parents worry about possible side effects of vaccinations. However, risk analysis (explained in Chapter 2) reveals that the risks of the diseases

TABLE 3.3 Details About Vaccinations: United States

Vaccine	Year of Introduction*	Peak Annual Disease Total*	2007 Total[†]	Worst Consequences of Natural Disease*[†]	Percent of Children Vaccinated (U.S.)[†]	Known Vaccine Side Effects[†]
Chicken pox (varicella)	1995	4 million (est.)	34,507	Encephalitis (2 in 10,000 cases), bacterial skin infections, shingles (300,000 per year)	90.0	Fever (1 in 10 doses); mild rash (1 in 20 doses)
DTaP (diphtheria, tetanus, and pertussis)					84.5	Seizures (1 in 14,000), crying for 3 hours or more (1 in 1,000), fever of 105°F or higher (1 in 16,000)
Diphtheria	1923	206,939	0	Death (5 to 10 in 100 cases), muscle paralysis, heart failure		Adult Td (tetanus and diphtheria) vaccine may cause deep, aching pain and muscle wasting in upper arms
Tetanus	1927	1,560 (est.)	20	Death (1 in 10 cases), fractured bones, pneumonia		
Pertussis	1926 (whole cell) 1991 (acellular)	265,269	8,739	Death (2 in 1,000 cases), pneumonia (10 in 100 cases), seizures (1 to 2 in 100 cases)		Brain disease (0 to 10 in 1 million doses—whole-cell vaccine only)
H. influenzae (Type B) (childhood) (all serotypes)	1985	20,000 (est.)	2,231	Death (2 to 3 in 100 cases), meningitis, pneumonia, blood poisoning, inflammation of epiglottis, skin or bone infections	92.6	Redness, warmth, or swelling at injection site (1 in 4); fever of 101°F or higher (1 in 20)
IPV (inactivated) polio vaccine)	1955; improved version used in U.S. since 1987	21,269	0	Death (2 to 5 in 100 cases in children), respiratory failure, paralysis, postpolio syndrome	92.6	Soreness and redness at injection site
MMR (measles, mumps, and rubella)					92.3	Seizure caused by fever (1 in 3,000 doses); low platelet count (1 in 30,000 doses)
Measles	1963	894,134	30	Encephalitis (1 in 1,000 cases), pneumonia (6 in 100 cases), death (1 to 2 in 1,000 cases), seizure (6 to 7 in 1,000 cases)		Temporary joint pain and stiffness (1 in 4 teenaged girls and women)
Mumps	1967	152,209	715	Deafness (1 in 20,000 cases), inflamed testicles (20 to 50 in 100 postpubertal males)		
Rubella	1969	56,686	11	Blindness, deafness, heart defects, and/or mental retardation in 85 percent of children born to mothers infected in early pregnancy		
PCV7 (pneumococcal conjugate vaccine)[†] (childhood)	2000	93,000 (est.)	20,000 (2005 est.)	Death or serious illness caused by meningitis, pneumonia, blood poisoning, ear infections		Fever over 100.4°F (1 in 3); redness, tenderness, or swelling at injection site (1 in 4)

Sources: *Lieu et al., 2000; [†]Centers for Disease Control and Prevention, 2009.

STEVEN RUBIN / THE IMAGE WORKS

Look Away! The benefits of immunization justify the baby's brief discomfort, but many parents still do not appreciate the importance of following the recommended schedule of immunizations.

ESPECIALLY FOR Nurses and Pediatricians A mother refuses to have her baby immunized because she wants to prevent side effects. She wants your signature for a religious exemption. What should you do? (see response, page 105) ➜

Sleeping Like a Baby It's best to lay babies on their backs to sleep—even if it's in a hammock in a Cambodian temple.

JOHN VINK / MAGNUM PHOTOS

that vaccines can prevent are far greater than the risks from immunization (A. Allen, 2007). The hypothesis that immunization causes brain damage, particularly autism, has been disproven many times (Offit, 2008). Polio had almost been eliminated worldwide when fear of the vaccine halted immunization in northern Nigeria in 2003. As a result, the virus spread to 20 other nations, and hundreds of children were paralyzed for life (L. Roberts, 2009).

One stunning success story has been the fight against the form of measles called rubeola (not rubella, or German measles). Thanks to a vaccine developed in 1963, fewer than 100 cases of rubeola occurred in 2003 in North and South America, down from 53,683 in 1997 (MMWR, June 13, 2003). Such success cannot be taken for granted. Because immunization levels fell recently in some U.S. states, there were 131 cases of measles in the United States in the first seven months of 2008, far more than the 12-month average of the previous 10 years (MMWR, August 22, 2008).

The disease has not yet been conquered worldwide: 125,000 African children had measles in 2005 (down from 500,000 in 1999) (Wiysonge et al., 2006). In India in 2005, 100,000 died from rubeola (Dugger, 2006).

Some of the victims in such epidemics are too young (under 3 months) to be immunized themselves. Very young infants and those whose immune systems are not functioning properly can be protected against infectious diseases by what is called *herd immunization*. The idea is that if about 90 percent of older infants and children are immunized, infectious disease will not spread in a community (the "herd"), because if one person contracts it, the chances are very slim that anyone else will catch it (R. Anderson & Moore, 2006).

Preventing Sudden Infant Death Syndrome

A global approach to health measures not only brings immunization to developing nations but can also spread sound health practices in the opposite direction. An Asian practice has come to the West that allows thousands of infants to survive who would have died 20 years ago.

In 1990, about 5,000 babies died of **sudden infant death syndrome (SIDS)** in the United States, as did thousands in other American and European nations. SIDS is "sudden" because it occurs with no warning: A seemingly healthy infant, usually 2 to 6 months old, is put to sleep but never wakes up.

BACK TO SLEEP Today, only half as many babies die of SIDS as did two decades ago. The main reason is that observant scientists noted that few healthy Chinese infants died suddenly, of no apparent cause. Some genetic weakness was the first hypothesis that occurred to the scientists. Current research continues to suggest that some infants are indeed genetically more vulnerable to SIDS.

Anthropologists, however, noticed that most Asian infants were put to sleep face up, not on their stomachs, whereas most other infants were put to sleep face down. This observation led to experiments in which some Western parents were told to put their infants to sleep on their backs. The data showed that "back to sleep" (as the public-awareness campaign slogan puts it) reduced SIDS dramatically among infants of every ethnicity.

The actual cause of SIDS is still unknown: low birthweight, heavy clothing, soft bedding, teenage parenthood, and, particularly, maternal smoking are risk factors (M. Anderson et al., 2005). Putting infants to sleep on their backs reduces the risk but does not eliminate it.

CO-SLEEPING One other risk factor for SIDS may be relevant. There is a correlation between SIDS and **co-sleeping,** or *bed-sharing,* a practice in which infants sleep in the same bed as their parents. This correlation has led many pediatricians to advise against co-sleeping. At the same time, some say that co-sleeping encourages breast-feeding, which is known to reduce the rate of SIDS.

Most North American and European babies sleep in a separate room from their parents, while Asian, African, and Latin American infants sleep beside or between their parents. Increasingly, however, Western parents allow co-sleeping, at least in the first months (Blair & Ball, 2004). In the United States, co-sleeping is common in immigrant and African American families.

As you remember from Chapter 1, it is difficult for researchers to isolate the effects of ethnicity, socioeconomic status (SES), and other factors in order to conclude which cultural practices are beneficial and which are not. A difference does not equal a deficit.

Many parents and some professionals believe that co-sleeping is not harmful unless the adult is drugged or drunk—and thus in danger of "overlying" the baby. According to one report:

> Mothers instinctively take up a protective posture when sharing a bed with their infants, lying in a fetal position with their lower arm above the infant's head and the infant lying within around 20–30 centimeters [about 10 inches] from the mother's chest. The position of the mother's thighs prevents the baby from sliding down the bed.

[*Wailoo et al., 2004, p. 1083*]

Although a videotape analysis found that co-sleeping infants wake up six times a night and solo sleepers only three times, co-sleepers get as much sleep because they go back to sleep quickly (Mao et al., 2004). However, co-sleeping correlates with poverty, preterm birth, and maternal cigarette smoking, as well as with SIDS. Is the correlation with SIDS spurious, a reflection of poverty rather than co-sleeping? The answer is not yet known.

There is another consideration: family peace of mind. Infants with anxious mothers wake up more often (Scher, 2008), and 60 percent of all new mothers have anxiety dreams about their babies (T. Nielsen & Paquette, 2007). One common dream is that the baby is lost; many mothers awaken to check on their sleeping infants.

Bed-sharing, or at least room-sharing, seems to be a logical solution for these anxious mothers. Since more and more U.S. mothers are having only one or two children, and are having them later in life, increased rates of co-sleeping may be a natural outcome of increased maternal concern for each infant.

Infant brain patterns adjust to experiences. Thus, infants who sleep with their parents become children who want their parents nearby at night. Parents who would rather not have their older children crawl into their bed at midnight may want to think twice about putting their infants to sleep beside them.

Adequate Nutrition

For every infant disease (including SIDS), breast-feeding reduces risk and malnutrition increases it, stunting growth of body and brain.

Infant nursing formulas in cans or bottles and pureed food in tiny jars are heavily advertised, but, as the slogan says, *breast is best.* Breast milk has so many advantages that it seems to be a miracle food (see Table 3.4).

ESPECIALLY FOR Police Officers and Social Workers If an infant died suddenly, what would you look for to distinguish SIDS from homicide? (see response, page 105) →

sudden infant death syndrome (SIDS)
A situation in which a seemingly healthy infant, at least 2 months of age, suddenly stops breathing and dies unexpectedly while asleep.

co-sleeping
A custom in which parents and their children (usually infants) sleep together in the same bed. (Also called *bed-sharing.*)

STEPHEN CHIANG / JUPITERIMAGES

Danger or Safety? Will Susan roll over on newborn Anisa as they sleep? Some physicians fear that co-sleeping poses a risk of suffocation, but others believe that it is protective.

ESPECIALLY FOR New Parents You are aware of cultural differences in sleeping practices, and this raises a very practical issue: Should your newborn sleep in bed with you? (see response, page 105) →

TABLE 3.4 The Benefits of Breast-Feeding

For the Baby

Balance of nutrition (fat, protein, etc.) adjusts to age of baby

Breast milk has micronutrients not found in formula

Less infant illness, including allergies, ear infections, stomach upsets

Less childhood asthma

Better childhood vision

Less adult illness, including diabetes, cancer, heart disease

Protection against measles and all other childhood diseases, since breast milk contains antibodies

Stronger jaws, fewer cavities, advanced breathing reflexes (less SIDS)

Higher IQ, less likely to drop out of school, more likely to attend college

Later puberty, less prone to teenage pregnancy

Less likely to become obese, hypertensive by age 12

For the Mother

Easier bonding with baby

Reduced risk of breast cancer and osteoporosis

Natural contraception (with exclusive breast-feeding, for several months)

Pleasure of breast stimulation

Satisfaction of meeting infant's basic need

No formula to prepare; no sterilization

Easier travel with the baby

For the Family

Increased survival of other children (because of spacing of births)

Increased family income (because formula and medical care are expensive)

Less stress on father, especially at night (he cannot be expected to feed the baby)

Sources: Beilin & Huang, 2008; DiGirolamo et al., 2005; Oddy, 2004; Riordan, 2009.

Breast milk is always sterile and at body temperature, it contains more iron and vitamins C and A than does cow's milk, and it provides all the immunity against disease that the mother has. The fats and sugars in breast milk make it digestible and better for brain growth (Riordan, 2009). The health benefits may last lifelong: Breast-fed babies are less likely to develop allergies, asthma, obesity, and heart disease (Oddy, 2004).

Breast milk adjusts to the age of the baby. For newborns, the breasts secrete *colostrum,* a thick, high-calorie fluid. After three days, the breasts produce less-concentrated milk, which is perfect for the very young child. As the infant gets older, the composition of breast milk adjusts to the baby's changing nutritional needs. Quantity increases or decreases to meet demand: Twins and even triplets can gain weight on schedule when they are breast-fed (Riordan, 2009).

No one doubts the health benefits, but more research is needed before developmentalists can be convinced that breast-feeding improves intelligence (Soliday, 2007) or that every mother should breast-feed. If a mother is HIV-positive or uses toxic drugs, it may be wise for her to avoid breast-feeding. HIV-positive mothers in areas without reliable sources of clean water may be better advised to breast-feed, however, because it is difficult to ensure that infant formula is sterile. Experts disagree about the risks and benefits of breast-feeding for HIV-positive mothers of HIV-negative babies (J. Cohen, 2007a).

The Same Situation, Many Miles Apart: Breast-Feeding Breast-feeding is universal. None of us would exist if our foremothers had not successfully breast-fed their babies for millennia. Currently, breast-feeding is practiced worldwide, but it is no longer the only way to feed infants, and each culture has particular practices.

OBSERVATION QUIZ

What three differences do you see between these two breast-feeding women—one in the United States and one in Madagascar? (see answer, page 106) ➡

© JENNIE HART / ALAMY

© W. LAYER / PETER ARNOLD, INC.

Virtually all international health organizations recommend that infants be fed only breast milk for the first four to six months. Many experts, however, recommend that supplements of certain vitamins (notably vitamin D) are needed if breast milk is the prime food for a year or more (Stokstad, 2003).

In industrialized nations, formula can be sterile, convenient, and relatively inexpensive, but many women in those countries still choose breast-feeding for the health of their infants. In the United States, 74 percent of all newborns are breast-fed (a marked increase from a few decades ago), although only 43 percent are still being breast-fed at 6 months (Centers for Disease Control and Prevention, 2008; see Appendix A, p. A-5). The mother's comfort and convenience are the main reasons for stopping breast-feeding early; cultural and social forces (employers, fathers, other relatives) may also discourage breast-feeding.

KEY Points

- Various public health measures have saved millions of infants in recent decades.
- Immunization not only protects those who are inoculated but also helps to stop the spread of contagious diseases.
- Far fewer infants now die of SIDS (sudden infant death syndrome) than previously because most parents now put their infants to sleep on their backs, not on their stomachs.
- Breast milk is the ideal infant food; breast-feeding reduces malnutrition and diseases.

Infant Cognition

While every developmentalist and every parent is rightly awed by the rapid physical growth of the human infant, intellectual growth during infancy is even more impressive. Concepts, memories, and sentences—nonexistent in newborns—are evident by age 1 and consolidated by age 2. To describe this intellectual progression over the first two years, we begin with the framework devised by Jean Piaget, who was "arguably the most influential researcher of all time within the area of cognitive developmental psychology" (Birney et al., 2005, p. 328).

Sensorimotor Intelligence

You read earlier that throughout their first year, infants use their senses to sort and classify every experience. They grab things, shake them, taste them, and inspect them closely. It is said that "infants spend the better part of their first year merely looking around" (Rovee-Collier, 2001, p. 35).

Piaget, who was introduced in Chapter 1, was the first to recognize that "merely looking around" is the stuff of intellectual development. Contrary to the popular idea of his day, Piaget realized that infants are smart and active learners, adapting their thoughts to assimilate and accommodate to whatever their senses and motor skills let them experience.

Of the four distinct periods of cognitive development described by Piaget, the first begins at birth and ends at about 24 months. Piaget referred to cognition during this period as **sensorimotor intelligence** because intellectual advancement closely follows the progression of sensory and motor skills described earlier. Sensorimotor intelligence develops in six stages, according to Piaget (see Table 3.5).

RESPONSE FOR Nurses and Pediatricians (from page 102) It is difficult to convince people that their method of child rearing is wrong, although you should try. In this case, listen respectfully and then describe specific instances of serious illness or death from a childhood disease. Suggest that the mother ask her grandparents if they knew anyone who had polio, tuberculosis, or tetanus (they probably did). If you cannot convince this mother, do not despair: Vaccination of 95 percent of toddlers helps protect the other 5 percent. If the mother has religious reasons, talk to her clergy adviser. ●

RESPONSE FOR Police Officers and Social Workers (from page 103) An autopsy, or at least a speedy and careful examination by a medical pathologist, is needed. Suspected foul play must be either substantiated or firmly rejected—so that the parents can be arrested, warned about conditions that caused an accident, or allowed to mourn. The immediate circumstances—such as the infant's body position when discovered, the position of the mattress and blankets, the warmth and humidity of the room, and the baby's health—are crucial. Furthermore, although SIDS victims sometimes turn blue and seem bruised, they rarely display signs of specific injury or neglect, such as a broken limb, a scarred face, an angry rash, or a skinny body. ●

RESPONSE FOR New Parents (from page 103) From the psychological and cultural perspectives, babies can sleep anywhere as long as the parents can hear them if they cry. The main consideration is safety: Infants should not sleep on a mattress that is too soft, nor beside an adult who is drunk or drugged. Otherwise, the family should decide for itself. ●

sensorimotor intelligence
Piaget's term for the way infants think—by using their senses and motor skills—during the first period of cognitive development.

ANSWER TO OBSERVATION QUIZ
(from page 104) The babies' ages, the settings, and the mothers' apparent attitudes. The U.S. mother *(left)* is indoors in a hospital and seems attentive to whether she is feeding her infant the right way. The mother in Madagascar *(right)* seems confident and content as she feeds her older baby in a public place, enjoying the social scene. ●

TABLE 3.5 The Six Stages of Sensorimotor Intelligence

For an overview of the stages of sensorimotor thought, it helps to group the six stages into pairs. The first two stages involve the infant's responses to his or her own body.

Primary Circular Reactions

Stage One (birth to 1 month)	*Reflexes:* sucking, grasping, staring, listening.
Stage Two (1–4 months)	*The first acquired adaptations:* accommodation and coordination of reflexes. Examples: sucking a pacifier differently from a nipple; grabbing a bottle to suck it.

The next two stages involve the infant's responses to objects and people.

Secondary Circular Reactions

Stage Three (4–8 months)	*Making interesting sights last:* responding to people and objects. Example: clapping hands when mother says "patty-cake."
Stage Four (8–12 months)	*New adaptation and anticipation:* becoming more deliberate and purposeful in responding to people and objects. Example: putting mother's hands together in order to make her start playing patty-cake.

The last two stages are the most creative, first with action and then with ideas.

Tertiary Circular Reactions

Stage Five (12–18 months)	*New means through active experimentation:* experimentation and creativity in the actions of the "little scientist." Example: putting a teddy bear in the toilet and flushing it.
Stage Six (18–24 months)	*New means through mental combinations:* considering before doing provides the child with new ways of achieving a goal without resorting to trial-and-error experiments. Example: before flushing, remembering that the toilet overflowed the last time, and hesitating.

STAGES ONE AND TWO Stage one, called the *stage of reflexes,* lasts a month. The infant's repeated awareness of reflexes and sensations provides information about what the body can do, allowing movements to become deliberate instead of reflexive and allowing sensation to become perception. That enables the infant to move on to stage two, *first acquired adaptations* (also called the *stage of first habits*), from months 1 to 4.

According to Piaget, when people of any age encounter new experiences, they adapt by either accommodating or assimilating. **Assimilation** occurs when a new experience is simply incorporated into old concepts and perceptions; **accommodation** requires changing one's perceptions and assumptions to adjust to new experiences. Both begin at birth.

Consider an infant in stages one and two. One of the strongest early reflexes is the sucking reflex. Newborns suck anything that touches their lips: nipples of any shape and material, fingers of any person, pacifiers of any type, shoulders, blankets, and so on—whatever touches their mouth or cheek. That is assimilation: Everything is for sucking.

By about 1 month, the first acquired adaptations become evident. Infants suck pacifiers without the reflexive tongue-pushing and swallowing that bottle nipples require. This adaptation is a sign that infants have begun to organize their perceptions; as they accommodate to pacifiers, they are using their minds to think about their experiences.

assimilation
Piaget's term for a type of adaptation in which new experiences are interpreted to fit into, or assimilate with, old ideas.

accommodation
Piaget's term for a type of adaptation in which old ideas are restructured to include, or accommodate, new experiences.

Time for Adaptation Sucking is a reflex at first, but adaptation begins as soon as an infant differentiates a pacifier from her mother's breast or realizes that her hand has grown too big to fit into her mouth. This infant's expression of concentration suggests that she is about to make that adaptation and suck just her thumb from now on.

FSTOP / PUNCHSTOCK

Soon more accommodation is apparent. Infants suck breast or bottle nipples when hungry, suck specific things for comfort (rejecting pacifiers of an unfamiliar type or rejecting all pacifiers if thumbs, fingers, or knuckles have been accommodated), and never suck other things (fuzzy blankets, large balls). All this indicates thought.

STAGES THREE AND FOUR During stage three (4 to 8 months), infants seek to *make interesting events last.* Realizing that rattles make noise, for example, they wave their arms and laugh whenever someone puts a rattle in their hand. Seeing something that normally delights them—a favorite toy, a smiling parent—triggers active efforts for interaction. If a mother kisses an infant's belly, the 6-month-old is likely not only to laugh but also to pull the mother's head down to encourage another kiss.

ESPECIALLY FOR New Parents
When should parents decide whether to feed their baby only by breast, only by bottle, or using some combination? When should they decide whether or not to let their baby use a pacifier? (see response, page 109) ➡

Stage four (8 months to 1 year) is called *new adaptation and anticipation,* or "the means to the end," because babies now think about a goal and begin to understand how to reach it. Thinking is more innovative in stage four than it was in stage three. Stage-three babies merely understand how to continue an experience. Stage-four babies anticipate.

As an example of such anticipation, a 10-month-old girl who enjoys playing in the bathtub might crawl over to her mother with a bar of soap as a signal to start her bath, remove her clothes to make her wishes crystal clear, and squeal with delight when the bath water is turned on. Similarly, if a 10-month-old boy sees his mother putting on her coat, he might try to stop her from leaving or drag over his own jacket to signal that he wants to go with her.

These examples reveal *goal-directed behavior*—that is, purposeful action. The baby's goal-directedness stems from awareness of cause and effect, from memory for actions already completed, and from understanding of other people's intentions (Behne et al., 2005; Willatts, 1999).

Piaget thought that the concept of **object permanence,** the awareness that objects or people continue to exist when they are no longer in sight, emerges at about 8 months. As evidence for this, he noticed what happens when a toy falls from a baby's crib, rolls under a couch, or is covered by a cloth. Babies under 8 months do not search for it. Piaget believed that this failure to search for an object that is no longer seen means that infants lack the concept of object permanence.

Talk to Me This 4-month-old is learning how to make interesting sights last: The best way to get Daddy to respond is to vocalize, stare, smile, and pat his cheek.

object permanence
The realization that objects (including people) still exist when they can no longer be seen, touched, or heard.

Peek-a-Boo The best hidden object is Mom under an easily moved blanket, as 7-month-old Elias has discovered. Peek-a-boo is fun from about 7 to 12 months. In another month, Elias will search for more conventionally hidden objects. In a year or two, his surprise and delight at finding Mom will fade.

Contemporary scientists disagree. They believe that other immaturities, such as imperfect motor skills, prevent infants under 8 months from demonstrating the concept of object permanence (L. B. Cohen & Cashon, 2006; Ruffman et al., 2005). As one infant researcher explains, "Amid his acute observation and brilliant theorizing, Piaget . . . mistook infants' motor incompetence for conceptual incompetence" (Mandler, 2004, p. 17). A series of clever experiments, in which objects seemed to disappear behind a screen while researchers traced eye movements and brain activity, reveal some inkling of object permanence in infants as young as 4½ months (Baillargeon & DeVos, 1991; Spelke, 1993).

STAGES FIVE AND SIX Stage five (age 12 to 18 months), is called *new means through active experimentation*. This builds on the goal-directedness of stage four, but stage-five actions are expansive, purposeful, and creative. One-year-olds are active explorers, delighted to squeeze toothpaste out of the tube, dismantle the iPod, flush the overflowing toilet again and again.

Piaget referred to the stage-five toddler as a **"little scientist"** who "experiments in order to see." Their scientific method is trial and error. Their devotion to discovery is familiar to every adult scientist—and to every parent.

Finally, in the sixth stage (age 18 to 24 months), toddlers begin to anticipate and imagine by using *mental combinations*, an intellectual experimentation that supersedes the active experimentation of stage five.

Stage-six toddlers think about consequences, hesitating a moment before yanking the cat's tail or dropping a raw egg on the floor. They can also repeat what they have seen a few days before, an ability called *deferred imitation,* which requires toddlers to combine what they witnessed earlier with a new opportunity to repeat what they saw. A classic example is Piaget's daughter, Jacqueline, who observed another child

> who got into a terrible temper. He screamed as he tried to get out of a playpen and pushed it backward, stamping his feet. Jacqueline stood watching him in amazement, never having witnessed such a scene before. The next day, she herself screamed in her playpen and tried to move it, stamping her foot lightly several times in succession.
>
> *[Piaget, 1962, p. 63]*

Mental combinations are possible after 18 months, but not always apparent. Stage-six toddlers' strong impulse to discover sometimes overwhelms the new ability of reflection; they do not always choose wisely. Nor do they always defer imitation. Sometimes they repeat what they see immediately; sometimes they seem to forget completely. But at least thought sometimes precedes action; pretending is possible; memories can be stored.

Information Processing

Piaget's stage-based overview contrasts with **information-processing theory,** a perspective modeled on computer functioning. Information-processing theorists believe that a step-by-step description of the mechanisms of thought adds insight to our understanding of cognition at every age.

Information-processing research has overturned some of Piaget's conclusions—including the concept of object permanence. Many concepts and categories seem to develop in the infant brain between 4 and 12 months, with none of the discontinuity implied in theories like Piaget's (L. B. Cohen & Cashon, 2006; Mandler, 2004; Quinn, 2004).

When discontinuity appears, instead of assuming that a new stage has arrived, information-processing models analyze exactly what underlying components have come together for the new advance (Munakata, 2006). Active information process-

"little scientist"
The stage-five toddler (age 12 to 18 months) who experiments without anticipating the results, using trial and error in active and creative exploration.

ESPECIALLY FOR Parents of Toddlers
One parent wants to put all the breakable or dangerous objects away because a toddler is now able to move around independently. The other parent says that the baby should learn not to touch certain things. Who is right? (see response, page 111) ➔

information-processing theory
A perspective that compares human thinking processes, by analogy, to computer analysis of data, including sensory input, connections, stored memories, and output.

ing, benefiting from maturing senses and brain connections, is evident throughout the first year.

For example, in one experiment, infants of various ages were shown eight displays on a TV screen (Courage et al., 2006). Three-month-olds looked at a display of static dots for an average of 10 seconds before they looked away, but maturation allowed the older babies to figure out what they saw, decide it was uninteresting, and thus look more briefly. By 12 months, the babies stared at the static dots for only 5 seconds before glancing away. The older babies were more likely to glance back, perhaps to see if new information was available to process, but only for a moment.

Another display was of an active *Sesame Street* scene (Courage et al., 2006). Again, older babies looked more briefly, but the contrast was not as great as for the static dots, presumably because the babies were watching the movement. This experiment finds evidence of ongoing information processing, affected by both maturation and the particulars of the input (e.g., dots versus *Sesame Street*). Advances in the brains of older babies allowed more efficient attention.

SUDDEN DROPS The fact that both experience and maturing intellectual processes affect what infants understand is quite apparent in studies of depth perception. This research began with an apparatus called the **visual cliff,** which was designed to provide the illusion of a sudden dropoff between one horizontal surface and another (see the photograph at right). Mothers were able to urge their 6-month-olds to wiggle forward over the supposed edge of the cliff, but 10-month-olds fearfully refused to budge (E. Gibson & Walk, 1960).

At first, researchers hypothesized that inadequate depth perception kept the younger babies from seeing the drop and that maturation of the visual cortex allowed older babies to see depth and therefore refuse to move. However, later research (with more advanced technology) found that interpretation to be wrong. Even 3-month-olds noticed a drop: Their heart rate slowed and their eyes opened wide when they were placed over a visual cliff. But noncrawlers did not realize that they could fall. Processing, not input—perception, not sensation—made the difference.

The same progress is evident with walking: Novice walkers are fearless and reckless; experienced walkers are more careful (Adolph & Berger, 2005). For instance, in another study, toddlers and adults walked along a solid surface that suddenly gave way (it became soft foam), making them fall (Joh & Adolph, 2006). The researchers made the following observations:

● The adults fell once and then, having noted exactly where the surface changed, adjusted their balance. They did not fall when they walked that path again.

● Most of the toddlers fell numerous times before they perceived that falling was imminent, and then they balked at following that path.

● Three-year-olds, once they realized that the foam meant falling, sometimes dived into the foam and scrambled to reach the other side, a strategy no adult used.

Thus, individuals of every age process the information they acquire (in this case, information about falling), but what they do with that information depends on the dynamic system of motor skills and perceptions. (Dynamic systems are discussed in Chapter 1.)

EARLY MEMORY One important part of information processing is memory, since people cannot interpret information that they have forgotten. According to classic developmental theory, infants store no memories in their first year (Freud called this *infantile amnesia*) and do not remember things that occurred a day or two earlier until they are 1½ years old (Piaget called this *deferred imitation*).

RESPONSE FOR New Parents (from page 107) Both decisions should be made within the first month, during the stage of reflexes. If parents wait until the infant is 4 months or older, they may discover that they are too late. It is difficult to introduce a bottle to a 4-month-old who has been exclusively breast-fed or a pacifier to a baby who has already adapted the sucking reflex to a thumb. ●

visual cliff
An experimental apparatus that gives an illusion of a sudden dropoff between one horizontal surface and another.

MARK RICHARDS / PHOTOEDIT

Depth Perception This toddler in a laboratory in Berkeley, California, is crawling on the experimental apparatus called a visual cliff. She stops at the edge of what she perceives as a dropoff.

CALVIN AND HOBBES

YOU KNOW WHAT'S WEIRD? I DON'T REMEMBER MUCH OF ANYTHING UNTIL I WAS THREE YEARS OLD.

HALF OF MY LIFE IS A COMPLETE BLANK! I MUST'VE BEEN BRAINWASHED!

GOOD HEAVENS, WHAT KIND OF SICKO WOULD BRAINWASH AN INFANT?! AND WHAT DID I KNOW THAT SOMEONE WANTED ME TO FORGET??

BOY, AM I MYSTERIOUS.

I SEEM TO RECALL YOU SPENT MOST OF THE TIME BURPING UP.

© 1989 Universal Press Syndicate

WATERSON 8-1

© 1989 UNIVERSAL PRESS SYNDICATE

Selective Amnesia As we grow older, we forget about spitting up, nursing, crying, and almost everything else from our early years. However, strong emotions (love, fear, mistrust) may leave lifelong traces.

He Remembers! In this demonstration of Rovee-Collier's experiment, a young infant immediately remembers how to make the familiar mobile move. (Unfamiliar mobiles do not provoke the same reaction.) He kicks his right leg and flails both arms, just as he learned to do several weeks ago.

OBSERVATION QUIZ
How and why is this mobile unlike those usually sold for babies? (see answer, page 113) →

MICHAEL NEWMAN / PHOTOEDIT

On the basis of a series of experiments, however, developmentalists now agree that very young infants *can* remember *if* the following conditions are met:

● Experimental conditions are similar to real life.
● Motivation is high.
● Special measures aid memory retrieval.

The most dramatic evidence for infant memory comes from a series of innovative experiments in which 3-month-olds were taught to make a mobile move by kicking their legs (Rovee-Collier, 1987, 1990). These experiments began with infants who lay on their backs, in their own cribs, connected to a mobile by means of a ribbon tied to one foot. Virtually all the infants made occasional kicks (as well as random arm movements and noises) and realized, after a while, that kicking made the mobile move. They then kicked more vigorously and frequently, sometimes laughing at their accomplishment.

So far, this is no surprise—self-activated movement is highly reinforcing to infants, and 3-month-olds are at Piaget's stage two of sensorimotor intelligence, able to adapt their reflexes. When some infants had the mobile-and-ribbon apparatus reinstalled in their cribs *one week later,* most started to kick immediately; this reaction indicated that they remembered their previous experience. But when other infants were tested *two weeks later,* they began with only random kicks. Apparently they had forgotten what they had learned—evidence that memory is fragile early in life.

Now comes the surprise. The lead researcher, Carolyn Rovee-Collier, developed a set of innovative experiments that demonstrated that 3-month-old infants could remember after two weeks *if* they had a brief **reminder session** before being retested (Rovee-Collier & Hayne, 1987). (A reminder session is any perceptual experience that might make a person recollect an idea or thing.)

In the experimental reminder session, infants were positioned so that they could *not* kick and were allowed to watch the mobile move, but they were *not* tied to it. The next day, when they were again connected to the mobile and could move their legs, they kicked as they had learned to do two weeks earlier.

Apparently, watching the mobile move on the previous day revived their faded memory. They had stored in their brains the memory of how to make the mobile move; they just needed some processing time, provided by the reminder session, to recall it. Overall, some early memories can be "highly enduring, and become even more so after repeated encounters with reminders" (Rovee-Collier & Gerhardstein, 1997).

TODDLER MEMORY As each month passes, infants can retain information for a longer time than when they were younger, with less training or reminding. Toward the end of the first year, many kinds of memory, including deferred imitation, are apparent (Meltzoff & Moore, 1999). For example, suppose a 10-month-old watches someone playing with a toy the baby has never seen. The next day, if given that toy, 10-month-olds play with it in the same way as they had observed. (Younger infants do not.)

By the middle of the second year, toddlers can remember and reenact more complex sequences. In one study, 16- and 20-month-olds watched an experimenter perform various activities, such as putting a doll to bed, making a party hat, and cleaning a table (Bauer & Dow, 1994). For each activity, the experimenter used props and gave a brief "instruction" for performing each step. For instance, to clean the table, the experimenter wet it with water from a white spray bottle, saying, "Put on the water"; wiped it with a paper towel, saying, "Wipe it"; and placed the towel in a wooden trash basket, saying, "Toss it."

A week later, most toddlers remembered how to carry out the sequence when they heard "Put on the water. Wipe it. Toss it." Hearing those words enabled them to do what they had seen, not only with the same props but also with different props (for instance, a clear spray bottle, a sponge, and a plastic garbage can). This result shows that infants develop concepts that they then remember, a much more advanced cognitive accomplishment than mindless imitation (Mandler, 2004).

Many other experiments also show that toddlers think conceptually and process information more quickly than Piaget's stages suggest. As with the example just cited, language helps encode memories (R. Richardson & Hayne, 2007).

> **reminder session**
> A perceptual experience that is intended to help a person recollect an idea, a thing, or an experience, without testing whether the person remembers it at the moment.

NANCY SHEEHAN / PHOTOEDIT

Memory Aid Personal motivation and action are crucial to early memory, and that is why Noel has no trouble remembering which shape covers the photograph of herself as a baby.

KEY Points

- Infants demonstrate cognitive advances throughout their first years.
- Piaget described cognition in the first two years as sensorimotor development, a period that has six stages, from reflexes to new exploration and deferred imitation.
- Piaget said that object permanence begins at 8 months, but more recent research finds that it starts earlier.
- Information-processing theory traces the step-by-step learning of infants. Each advance is seen as the accumulation of many small advances, not as a new stage.
- Very young infants can store memories, especially if they are given reminder sessions.

RESPONSE FOR Parents of Toddlers (from page 108) It is easier and safer to babyproof the house because toddlers, being "little scientists," want to explore. However, both parents should encourage and guide the baby. A couple may leave out a few untouchable items if that will prevent a major conflict between husband and wife. ●

Language Learning

Many people consider language the distinguishing human characteristic, the means by which people learn from one another and thus allow the human species to survive and thrive. Table 3.6 summarizes language development during the first two years. Children learn language with amazing speed; 2-year-olds speak in sentences, some of them in more than one language. How does this proficiency happen?

TABLE 3.6 AT ABOUT THIS TIME: The Development of Spoken Language in the First Two Years

Age*	Means of Communication
Newborn	Reflexive communication—cries, movements, facial expressions
2 months	A range of meaningful noises—cooing, fussing, crying, laughing
3–6 months	New sounds, including squeals, growls, croons, trills, vowel sounds
6–9 months	Babbling, including both consonant and vowel sounds repeated in syllables
10–12 months	Comprehension of simple words; speechlike intonations; specific vocalizations that have meaning to those who know the infant well. Deaf babies express their first signs; hearing babies also use specific gestures (e.g., pointing) to communicate.
12 months	First spoken words that are recognizably part of the native language
13–18 months	Slow growth of vocabulary, up to about 50 words
18 months	Naming explosion—three or more words learned per day. Much variation: Some toddlers do not yet speak.
21 months	First two-word sentence
24 months	Multiword sentences. Half the toddler's utterances are two or more words long.

*The ages of accomplishment in this table reflect norms. Many healthy children with normal intelligence attain these steps in language development earlier or later than indicated here.
Sources: Bloom, 1993, 1998; Fenson et al., 2000; Lenneberg, 1967; Saffran et al., 2006.

Early Communication

child-directed speech
The high-pitched, simplified, and repetitive way adults speak to infants. (Also called *baby talk* or *motherese*.)

As with other aspects of infant cognition, communication begins with the senses and motor skills. The most obvious sense for language is audition; infants need to hear speech in order to learn the particular language, out of the world's 6,000 languages, that their family uses.

Evidence for astute early listening abounds (Saffran et al., 2006). Indeed, even fetuses listen and remember what they hear: Newborns recognize their mothers' voices at birth.

STOCK CONNECTION DISTRIBUTION / ALAMY

Lip-Reading Communication begins in early infancy. Infants closely watch speakers' mouth movements and facial expressions. By this baby's age, 5 months, bilingual infants can tell by looking who is speaking French and who is speaking English.

Throughout infancy, babies prefer to hear speech over other sounds, and they like high-pitched, simplified, and repetitive spoken sounds. This preferred pattern of speech is called *baby talk* or *motherese*, since mothers all over the world speak it. Both these terms have misleading implications, however, so scientists prefer the more formal term **child-directed speech.**

To be specific, child-directed speech is rich in many sounds that capture infants' attention and make them feel comforted, happy, or excited (G. A. Bryant & Barrett, 2007). It is inaccurate to call it *motherese* because men can use it as well as women, and people speak it whether or not they are parents. Babies communicate with cries, gurgles, smiles, and pouts, all of which are understood by attentive humans of any age or gender.

Long before age 1, infants demonstrate that they understand the rhythm, syllables, sounds, and cadence of spoken words (Saffran et al., 2006). By

Happy Talk Ty's mother and the teacher demonstrate the sign for *more* in a sign-language class at the public library in Hudson, Florida. Ty takes the lesson very seriously: Learning language in any form is crucial for 1-year-olds.

6 months, infants can distinguish, just by looking at someone's mouth movements (without sound), whether or not someone is speaking their native language (Weikum et al., 2007).

From 6 to 9 months, babies repeat certain syllables (*ma-ma-ma, da-da-da, ba-ba-ba*), a phenomenon referred to as **babbling** because of the way it sounds. Responding with child-directed speech encourages them; deaf babies stop babbling because they hear no replies. Hearing babies make more noises as they grow older, pausing to listen and babbling more when their caregivers answer. Babies wave their arms as they babble, again in response to encouragement (Iverson & Fagan, 2004).

Toward the end of the first year, babbling begins to sound like the native language as infants imitate what they hear. Deaf children whose parents address them in sign language use distinctive hand gestures—which resemble the signs their parents use—in a repetitive manner similar to babbling.

Hearing babies understand and express concepts with their hands sooner than with sounds (Goldin-Meadow, 2006). Almost all 10-month-old infants point, lift their arms to be picked up, push away a spoon with unwanted food on it, and so on. All these gestures are communications. Some parents deliberately teach their infants additional gestures and signs. For example, if an adult signs "I love you" with a smile of affection, a baby will soon sign it back. Such signing advances early communication (Goodwyn et al., 2000). Some people believe that it also accelerates infant speech, but that is not yet proven.

First Words

At about 1 year, babies speak a few words. Spoken vocabulary increases gradually (about one or two new words a week). Infants learn meanings more rapidly; they comprehend about 10 times more words than they say (Schafer, 2005; D. Snow, 2006).

Once spoken vocabulary reaches about 50 words, it builds quickly, at a rate of 50 to 100 words per month. Typically, 21-month-olds talk twice as much as 18-month-olds do (Adamson & Bakeman, 2006). This language spurt is called the **naming explosion** because the first words include mostly nouns (Gentner & Boroditsky, 2001).

Although cultural differences are evident in the first words infants say, infants between 12 and 18 months old, in almost every language, name each significant caregiver (often *dada, mama, nana, papa, baba, tata*), each sibling, and sometimes each pet (Bloom, 1998; Tardif et al., 2008; see Appendix A, p. A-4). Other frequently uttered

babbling
The extended repetition of certain syllables, such as *ba-ba-ba*, that begins when babies are between 6 and 9 months old.

ESPECIALLY FOR Nurses and Pediatricians The parents of a 6-month-old have just been told that their child is deaf. They don't believe it because, as they tell you, the baby babbles as much as their other children did. What do you tell them? (see response, page 115) ➤

ANSWER TO OBSERVATION QUIZ (from page 110) It is black and white, with larger objects—designed to be particularly attractive to infants, not to adult shoppers.

naming explosion
A sudden increase in an infant's vocabulary, especially in the number of nouns, that begins at about 18 months of age.

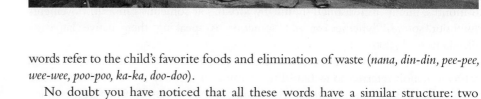

Cultural Values If they are typical of most families in the relatively taciturn Otavalo culture of Ecuador, these three children hear significantly less conversation than children elsewhere. In most Western cultures, that might be called maltreatment. However, verbal fluency is not a priority in this community. In fact, people who talk too much are ostracized and those who keep secrets are valued, so encouragement of talking may constitute maltreatment in the Otavalo culture.

ESPECIALLY FOR Caregivers A toddler calls two people "Mama." Is this a sign of confusion? (see response, page 116) ➞

holophrase
A single word that is used to express a complete, meaningful thought.

words refer to the child's favorite foods and elimination of waste (*nana, din-din, pee-pee, wee-wee, poo-poo, ka-ka, doo-doo*).

No doubt you have noticed that all these words have a similar structure: two identical syllables, each a consonant followed by a vowel sound. These are easier for infants to say, and that is why *father* becomes *dada* or *papa*.

The first words soon take on nuances of tone, loudness, and cadence that are precursors of the first grammar, because a single word can convey many messages by the way that it is spoken. Imagine three meaningful sentences encapsulated in "Dada!" "Dada?" and "Dada." Each is a **holophrase,** a single word spoken in such a way that it expresses an entire thought (Tomasello, 2006).

Cultural Differences in Language Use

All new talkers say names and utter holophrases. However, infants differ in their use of various parts of speech, depending on the language they are learning (Bornstein et al., 2004). For instance, by 18 months, English-speaking infants use more nouns but fewer verbs than Chinese or Korean infants do. Why?

One explanation goes back to the language itself. Chinese and Korean are called *verb-friendly languages,* in that verbs are placed at the beginning or end of sentences, which makes them easier to notice and learn. In English, not only do verbs occur in various positions within sentences but also their forms change in illogical ways (e.g., *go, went, gone*). This irregularity of position and form makes English verbs harder to learn than English nouns (Gentner & Boroditsky, 2001).

An alternative explanation considers the entire social context: Playing with a variety of toys and learning about dozens of objects are crucial experiences in North American culture, whereas East Asian cultures emphasize human interactions. Accordingly, North American infants are encouraged to name many inanimate things, whereas Asian infants learn words for social interactions and activities. Thus, the Chinese toddler might learn *come, play, love, carry, run,* and so on before the Canadian baby does. (This difference is the result of experience, not genes. A toddler of Chinese heritage, growing up in an English-speaking Canadian home, will have the language-learning patterns of other Canadian toddlers.)

Certain concepts as well as parts of speech are harder in some languages than in others. For example, learning adjectives is simpler in Italian and Spanish than in English or French because patterns in those languages allow adjectives to stand by themselves without the nouns (Waxman & Lidz, 2006). If you want a blue cup from a group of multicolored cups, you would ask for "a blue cup" or "a blue one" in English but simply "uno azul" ("a blue") in Spanish. It is not surprising that children with equal exposure learn *azul* faster than *blue*.

Each language has some prepositions that are difficult. English-speaking infants confuse *before* and *after*; Dutch-speaking infants misuse *out* when it refers to taking off clothes; Korean infants need to learn two meanings of *in* (Mandler, 2004). In every language, however, infants are quick and efficient in learning both vocabulary and grammar (Bornstein et al., 2004).

Acquiring Grammar

Grammar includes all the devices by which words communicate meaning. Sequence, prefixes, suffixes, intonation, loudness, verb forms, pronouns, negations, prepositions, and articles—all of these are aspects of grammar.

Grammar is present in holophrases—indicated by intonations and gestures—but becomes obvious at about 21 months, when word combinations begin. Toddlers show their knowledge of grammar when they follow accepted word order, such as "Baby cry" or "More juice," rather than the reverse. Soon three words combine in the sequence subject/verb/object—as in "Mommy read book," rather than any of the five other possible combinations of those three words.

In the first few years, a child's grasp of grammar correlates with the size of his or her vocabulary. The child who says "Baby is crying" is ahead of the child who says "Baby crying" or simply "Baby" (Dionne et al., 2003). Comprehension advances as well. Grammar helps toddlers understand what others are saying (Kedar et al., 2006).

Listening to two languages does not necessarily slow down the acquisition of grammar, as some people believe. However, "development in each language proceeds separately and in a language-specific manner" (Conboy & Thal, 2006, p. 727). If children hear the word *milk* 20 times a day from four different people, they learn that word faster than if they hear it 10 times from two people and hear *leche* or *lait* 10 times from two other people. With time, bilingual children learn both names for that white liquid.

Children need vocabulary to master grammar; thus, bilingual children may learn grammar slowly unless they are exposed to more speech than is typical. They can catch up, however. (Bilingual education is discussed later.)

Hypotheses About Language Development

Worldwide, people who are not yet 2 years old already use language well. Their acquisition of language is so impressive that, by adolescence, some of them compose lyrics or deliver orations that move thousands of their co-linguists.

How is language learned so quickly? Answers come from three schools of thought. The first says that infants learn language because they are directly taught, the second that infants naturally understand language, and the third that social impulses propel infants to communicate. Parents and teachers want children to speak fluently, but no one wants to waste time teaching something that infants either cannot learn or will learn on their own. Which perspective should guide them?

HYPOTHESIS ONE: INFANTS NEED TO BE TAUGHT The seeds of the first approach were planted more than 50 years ago, when the dominant theory in North American psychology was behaviorism, or learning theory. The essential idea was that all learning is acquired, step by step, through association and reinforcement.

RESPONSE FOR Nurses and Pediatricians (from page 113) Urge the parents to begin learning sign language and investigate the possibility of cochlear implants. Babbling has a biological basis and begins at a specified time, in deaf as well as hearing babies. If their infant can hear, sign language does no harm. If the child is deaf, however, non-communication may be destructive. ●

ESPECIALLY FOR Educators An infant day-care center has a new child whose parents speak a language other than the one the teachers speak. Should the teachers learn basic words in the new language, or should they expect the baby to learn their language? (see response, page 117) →

RESPONSE FOR Caregivers (from page 114) Not at all. Toddlers hear several people called "Mama" (their own mother, their grandmothers, their cousins' and friends' mothers) and experience mothering from several people, so it is not surprising if they use "Mama" too broadly. They will eventually narrow the label down to the one correct person. ●

ESPECIALLY FOR Nurses and Pediatricians Bob and Joan have been reading about language development in children. Because they are convinced that language is "hardwired," they believe they don't need to talk to their 6-month-old son. How do you respond? (see response, page 118) →

● **FOR DEEPER REFLECTION** Some parents never speak to their infants. When is this silence a deficit, and when is it merely a difference?

B. F. Skinner (1957) noticed that spontaneous babbling is usually reinforced. Typically, every time a baby says "ma-ma-ma-ma," a grinning mother appears, repeating the sound as well as showering her baby with attention, praise, and perhaps food. This is exactly what infants want. To achieve that response again, babies repeat those sounds; thus, via operant conditioning, talking begins.

Most parents worldwide are excellent instructors, responding to their infants' gestures and sounds (Gros-Louis et al., 2006). Even in preliterate societies, parents use child-directed speech, responding quickly with a high-pitched voice, short sentences, stressed nouns, and simple grammar—exactly the techniques that behaviorists would recommend. The core ideas of this hypothesis about language learning are the following:

● Parents are expert teachers, and other caregivers help them teach children to speak.

● Frequent repetition of words is instructive, especially when the words are linked to the pleasures of daily life.

● Well-taught infants become well-spoken children.

Behaviorists note that some 3-year-olds converse in elaborate sentences; others just barely put one simple word with another. Such variations correlate with the amount of language teaching the child receives and, eventually, with adult intelligence (Fagan et al., 2007). Parents of the most verbally adept children teach language throughout infancy—singing, explaining, listening, responding, and reading to their children every day, even before age 1 (Raikes et al., 2006).

In one large study in Australia, parents who provided extensive language exposure before age 1 had children who spoke early and well (Reilly et al., 2006). Similarly, in a detailed U.S. study, researchers analyzed the language that mothers (all middle class) used with their preverbal infants, aged 9 to 17 months (Tamis-Lamonda et al., 2001).

In both studies, variation was evident in how much the parents interacted with their children. In the U.S. study, one mother never imitated her infant's babbling; another mother imitated 21 times in 10 minutes, babbling back as if in conversation. Overall, U.S. mothers were most likely to describe things or actions (e.g., "That is a spoon you are holding—spoon"), as would be expected in a culture that encourages the naming of objects.

The frequency of maternal responsiveness at 9 months predicted infants' language ability many months later (see Figure 3.6). It was not that noisy infants (who might have had a genetic inclination that would soon make them start talking) elicited

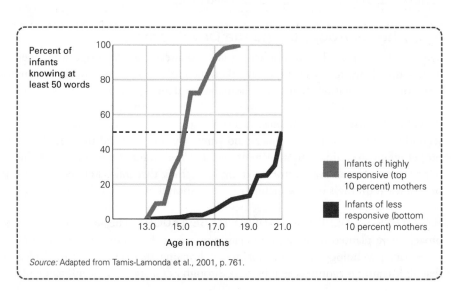

FIGURE 3.6 Maternal Responsiveness and Infants' Language Acquisition Learning the first 50 words is a milestone in early language acquisition, as it predicts the arrival of the naming explosion and the multiword sentence a few weeks later. Researchers found that the 9-month-old infants of highly responsive mothers (top 10 percent) reached this milestone as early as 15 months. The infants of nonresponsive mothers (bottom 10 percent) lagged significantly behind.

Source: Adapted from Tamis-Lamonda et al., 2001, p. 761.

more talk. Some quiet infants had mothers who talked a lot—suggesting play activities, describing things, and asking questions. Quiet infants with talkative mothers usually became talkative later on.

This research is in keeping with the behaviorist hypothesis that adults teach language and infants learn it. According to this perspective, if adults want children who speak, understand, and (later) read well, they must talk to their babies.

HYPOTHESIS TWO: INFANTS TEACH THEMSELVES

A contrary hypothesis holds that language learning is innate; adults need not teach it. The seeds of this perspective were planted soon after Skinner proposed his theory of verbal learning. Noam Chomsky (1968, 1980) and his followers believe that language is too complex to be mastered merely through step-by-step conditioning.

While behaviorists focused on variations among children in their vocabulary size, Chomsky focused on similarities in language acquisition. Noting that all young children master basic grammar at about the same age, Chomsky cited this *universal grammar* as evidence that humans are born with a mental structure that prepares them to incorporate some elements of human language—for example, the use of a raised tone at the end of an utterance to indicate a question.

Chomsky labeled this hypothesized mental structure the **language acquisition device (LAD).** The LAD enables children to derive the rules of grammar quickly and effectively from the speech they hear every day, regardless of whether their native language is English, Thai, or Urdu.

Other scholars agree with Chomsky that infants are innately ready to use their minds to understand and speak whatever language is offered. The various languages of the world are all logical, coherent, and systematic, and that is what makes it possible for babies to learn them quickly.

This idea does not strip languages and cultures of various differences in sounds, grammar, and almost everything else; the point is that "language is a window on human nature, exposing deep and universal features of our thoughts and feelings" (Pinker, 2007, p. 148). Infants are primed to grasp the particular language they are exposed to, making caregiver speech "not a 'trigger' but a 'nutrient'" (Slobin, 2001, p. 438).

There is no need for a trigger, according to this hypothesis, because the developing brain is searching for language. The LAD quickly and efficiently connects neurons and creates dendrites to support whichever particular language the infant hears.

Research supports this perspective as well. As you remember, newborns are primed to listen to speech (Vouloumanos & Werker, 2007), and all infants babble *ma-ma* and *da-da* sounds (not yet referring to mother or father). No reinforcement or teaching is needed; infants merely need dendrites to grow, mouth muscles to strengthen, neurons to connect, and speech to be heard.

Nature also provides for deaf infants. All 6-month-olds, hearing or not, would rather look at sign language than at nonlinguistic pantomime. For hearing infants, this preference disappears by 10 months because their affinity for gestural language is no longer needed (Krentz & Corina, 2008). Deaf infants are signing by then.

HYPOTHESIS THREE: SOCIAL IMPULSES FOSTER INFANT LANGUAGE LEARNING

The third hypothesis is *social-pragmatic*. It holds that the crucial starting point for language learning is neither vocabulary reinforcement (Skinner) nor innate verbal understanding (Chomsky) but rather a social impulse toward communication. According to this perspective, infants communicate in every way they can because humans are social beings, dependent on one another for survival, well-being, and joy.

Evidence to support this notion is that by 9 months, infant brain patterns and heart rates indicate attention when people talk to them, without understanding content

RESPONSE FOR Educators (from page 115) Probably both. Infants love to communicate, and they seek every possible way to do so. Therefore, the teachers should try to understand the baby, and the baby's parents, but they can also teach another language. ●

language acquisition device (LAD) Chomsky's term for a hypothesized mental structure that enables humans to learn language, including the basic aspects of grammar, vocabulary, and intonation.

MICHELLE D. BRIDWELL / PHOTOEDIT

Show Me Where Pointing is one of the earliest forms of communication, emerging at about 10 months. As Carlos's mother demonstrates, accurate pointing requires a basic understanding of social interaction, because the pointer needs to take the observer's angle of vision into account.

but with awareness and pleasure that they are the focus of attention (Santesso et al., 2007). It is the emotional message of speech, not the words, that propels infants to learn language. In one study, people who had never heard English (Shuar hunter-farmers living in remote foothills of the Andes Mountains in Ecuador) listened to tapes of North American mothers talking to their babies. The Shuar successfully distinguished among utterances conveying comfort, approval, attention, and prohibition, without knowing any of the English words (G. A. Bryant & Barrett, 2007).

It is easy to believe that early communication is primarily social. Before age 1, infants vocalize, babble, gesture, listen, and point—with an outstretched little index finger that is soon accompanied by a very sophisticated glance to see if the other person is looking at the right spot (Tomasello et al., 2007). This social impulse is a human trait; other animals do not understand pointing. These and many other examples show that communication is the servant of social interaction (Bloom, 1998; Hoehl et al., 2008).

Here is an experiment. Suppose an 18-month-old is playing with an unnamed toy and an adult utters a word. Does the child connect that word to the toy? Not necessarily. When toddlers played with a fascinating toy and adults said a word, the toddlers looked up, figured out what the adults were looking at, and assigned the new word to that, not to the fascinating toy (Baldwin, 1993). This supports hypothesis three: The toddlers were socially focused.

Another study also suggests social learning. Many 1-year-olds enjoy watching television, becoming absorbed in programs like *Teletubbies,* but they probably do not learn much from it. In a controlled experiment, 1-year-olds learned vocabulary much better when someone taught them in person rather than on a video. This suggests social language acquisition, not impersonal learning (Krcmar et al., 2007).

This research indicates that social impulses, not explicit teaching (hypothesis one) or brain maturation (hypothesis two), lead infants to learn language, "as part of the package of being a human social animal" (Hollich et al., 2000, p. 11). They seek to understand what others want and intend; therefore, "Children acquire linguistic symbols as a kind of by-product of social action with adults" (Tomasello, 2001, p. 135).

COMBINING ALL THREE APPROACHES Each of these three positions has been supported by research. As a result, scholars have tried to integrate all of them. In a monograph based on 12 experiments designed by eight researchers (Hollich et al., 2000), the authors presented a hybrid perspective that incorporated aspects of the previous hypotheses.

They began by noting that children learn language for many reasons—to indicate intention, to call objects by name, to get what they want, to talk to family members, to sing to themselves, to express their wishes, to remember the past, to make friends, and much more. Therefore, mastering various aspects of language may be best explained by different hypotheses at different ages. For example, the name of the family dog may be learned as family members, and eventually the dog itself, reinforce the name—a behaviorist process (hypothesis one). However, the distinction between *cat* and *dog* may reflect a neurological predilection, a brain capacity that is genetic (hypothesis two). Furthermore, infants who allow themselves to be licked by the dog may reflect an inborn joy in social interaction (hypothesis three).

After intensive study, another group of scientists agreed that there are many explanations for how language is learned. The ability to hear differences in sounds leads to proficient speech, because "multiple attentional, social and linguistic cues" contribute to early language (Tsao et al., 2004, p. 1081).

RESPONSE FOR Nurses and Pediatricians (from page 116) While much of language development is indeed hard-wired, many experts assert that exposure to language is required. You don't need to convince Bob and Joan of this point, though—just convince them that their baby will be happier if they talk to him. ●

In another study supporting the hybrid explanation, 10-month-old infants looked at pairs of objects that they had never seen before. One of each pair was fascinating to babies and the other was boring, specifically "a blue sparkle wand . . . [paired with] a white cabinet latch . . . a red, green, and pink party clacker . . . [paired with] a beige bottle opener" (Pruden et al., 2006, p. 267). The experimenter said a made-up name (not an actual word), and then the infants were tested to see if they assigned the word to the object that had the experimenter's attention (the dull one) or to the fascinating one.

Remember that 18-month-old toddlers in a similar experiment chose the object that the adults looked at (Baldwin, 1993). However, this time 10-month-olds seemed to assign the word to the fascinating object, not the dull one. These researchers interpreted their experiment as supporting the idea that *how* language is learned depends on the age of the child as well as on the particular circumstances.

Too Young for Language? No. The early stages of language are communication through noises, gestures, and facial expressions, very evident here between this !Kung grandmother and granddaughter.

This set of experiments suggests that behaviorist reinforcement explains some language acquisition in young children, whereas social learning explains it in slightly older ones. As the research team expressed it, "The perceptually driven 10-month-old becomes the socially aware 19-month-old" (Pruden et al., 2006, p. 278).

It makes logical and practical sense for nature to provide several paths toward language learning (Sebastián-Gallés, 2007). Indeed, although child-directed speech is an ideal way for children to learn, some cultures do not encourage adults to talk to preverbal infants. Fortunately, an alternate route is available: Babies learn from overhearing adults speak to one another (Floor & Akhtar, 2006; Soderstrom, 2007).

Each mode of learning may be preferred or more efficient in some stages, cultures, and families. Nonetheless, virtually all children learn to communicate using the words and grammar of their native tongue (Bornstein et al., 2004). Language acquisition researchers need to take all kinds of development into account. Many do. As one expert concludes:

> In the current view, our best hope for unraveling some of the mysteries of language acquisition rests with approaches that incorporate multiple factors, that is, with approaches that incorporate not only some explicit linguistic model, but also the full range of biological, cultural, and psycholinguistic processes involved.
>
> *[Tomasello, 2006, pp. 292–293]*

Infants are active learners not only of language (as just outlined) and of perceptions and motor skills (as explained in the first half of this chapter) but also of everything else in their experience. In the next chapter, you will read more examples of the social and emotional understanding that infants acquire.

KEYPoints

- Infants learn rapidly to communicate and to speak, starting with cries in the first weeks and progressing to words by 1 year and sentences before age 2.

- Some experts emphasize the importance of adult reinforcement of early speech; others suggest that language learning is innate; others believe it is a by-product of social impulses.

- A hybrid explanation suggests that language learning occurs in many ways, depending on the specific age, culture, and goals of the infant.

SUMMARY

Body Changes

1. In the first two years of life, infants grow taller, gain weight, and increase in head circumference—all indicative of development. The norm at birth is 7½ pounds in weight and 20 inches in lengh (about 3.4 kilograms, 51 centimeters). Birthweight doubles by 4 months, triples by 1 year, and quadruples by 2 years.

2. The brain increases dramatically in size and complexity, with rapid growth of neurons, development of dendrites, and formation of synapses.

3. Experience is vital for dendrites and synapses to link neurons. In the first year, the parts of the cortex dedicated to the senses and motor skills mature. If neurons are unused, dendrites are cut back and brain regions are rededicated to processing other sensations.

4. Sleep gradually decreases over the first two years. As with all areas of development, variations in sleep patterns are normal.

Moving and Perceiving

5. Newborns have many reflexes, including the survival reflexes of sucking and breathing. Gross motor skills are soon evident, from rolling over to sitting up (at about 6 months), from standing to walking (at about 1 year), from climbing to running (before age 2).

6. Fine motor skills are difficult for infants, but babies gradually develop the hand and finger control needed to grab, aim, and manipulate almost anything within reach. Experience, time, and motivation allow infants to advance in all their motor skills.

7. At birth, the senses already respond to stimuli. Prenatal experience makes hearing the most mature sense. Vision is the least mature at birth, but it improves quickly. Infants use their senses to strengthen their early social interactions.

Surviving in Good Health

8. About 3 billion infant deaths have been prevented in the past half-century because of improved health care. One major innovation is immunization, which has eradicated smallpox and virtually eliminated polio and measles in developed nations.

9. Sudden infant death syndrome (SIDS) once killed about 5,000 infants per year in the United States and thousands more worldwide. This number has been reduced by half since 1990, primarily because researchers discovered that putting infants to sleep on their backs makes SIDS less likely.

10. Breast-feeding is best for infants. Breast milk helps them resist disease and promotes growth of every kind.

Infant Cognition

11. Piaget believed that sensorimotor intelligence develops in six stages—three pairs of two stages each—beginning with reflexes and ending with the toddler's active exploration and use of mental combinations. Infants become more goal-oriented, creative, and experimental as "little scientists."

12. Infants gradually develop an understanding of objects in their first two years. As shown in Piaget's classic experiment, infants understand object permanence and begin to search for hidden objects at about 8 months. Other research finds that Piaget underestimated the cognition of young infants.

13. Another approach to understanding infant cognition is information-processing theory, which looks at each step of the thinking process, from input to output.

14. Infant memory is fragile but not completely absent. Reminder sessions help trigger memories, and young brains learn motor sequences long before they can remember with words.

Language Learning

15. Eager attempts to communicate are apparent in the first year. Infants babble at about 6 to 9 months, understand words and gestures by 10 months, and speak their first words at about 1 year.

16. Vocabulary begins to build very slowly until the infant knows approximately 50 words. Then a naming explosion begins. Toward the end of the second year, toddlers begin putting two words together, showing by their word order that they understand the rudiments of grammar.

17. Various theories attempt to explain how infants learn language as quickly as they do. The three main theories emphasize that infants must be taught, or that their brains are genetically attuned to language, or that their social impulses foster language learning. The challenge for developmental scientists has been to formulate a hybrid theory that uses all the insights and research on early language learning.

KEY TERMS

norm (p. 86)
head-sparing (p. 87)
neuron (p. 88)
cortex (p. 88)
axon (p. 88)
dendrite (p. 88)
synapse (p. 88)
neurotransmitter (p. 88)
prefrontal cortex (p. 90)
shaken baby syndrome (p. 91)

REM (rapid eye movement) sleep (p. 93)
reflex (p. 94)
gross motor skills (p. 95)
fine motor skills (p. 96)
sensation (p. 97)
perception (p. 97)
binocular vision (p. 98)
immunization (p. 100)

sudden infant death syndrome (SIDS) (p. 103)
co-sleeping (p. 103)
sensorimotor intelligence (p. 105)
assimilation (p. 106)
accommodation (p. 106)
object permanence (p. 107)
"little scientist" (p. 108)

information-processing theory (p. 108)
visual cliff (p. 109)
reminder session (p. 110)
child-directed speech (p. 112)
babbling (p. 113)
naming explosion (p. 113)
holophrase (p. 114)
language acquisition device (LAD) (p. 117)

KEY QUESTIONS

1. Why is pruning an essential part of brain development?

2. What are the differences in the visual abilities of a newborn and a 3-month-old?

3. In what ways does herd immunity save lives?

4. Since breast-feeding is best, why do most North American mothers bottle-feed their 6-month-olds?

5. Why is Piaget's first period of cognitive development called sensorimotor intelligence? Give examples.

6. What does the active experimentation of the stage-five toddler suggest for parents?

7. Why would a person remember very little about experiences in infancy?

8. What indicates that toddlers use some grammar?

9. How do deaf and hearing babies compare in early language learning?

10. How would a caregiver who subscribes to the behaviorist theory of language learning respond when an infant babbles?

11. According to the sociocultural theory of language learning, what might explain why an 18-month-old is not yet talking?

12. What does the hybrid model of language learning suggest to caregivers?

APPLICATIONS

1. Immunization regulations and practices vary, partly for social and political reasons. Ask at least two faculty or administrative staff members what immunizations students at your college must have and why. If you hear, "It's a law," ask why.

2. Observe three infants (whom you do not know) in public places such as a store, playground, or bus. Look closely at body size and motor skills, especially how much control each baby has over legs and hands. From that, estimate the age in months, then ask the caregiver how old the infant is.

3. Many educators recommend that parents read to babies even before the babies begin talking. How would advocates of each of the three hypotheses about language development respond to this advice?

4. Test an infant's ability to search for a hidden object. Ideally, the infant should be about 7 or 8 months old, and you should retest over a period of weeks. If the infant can immediately find the object, make the task harder by pausing between the hiding and the searching or by secretly moving the object from one hiding place to another. Describe this experiment in detail.

CHAPTER OUTLINE

THE FIRST TWO YEARS
Psychosocial Development

As I sat on a crowded subway car, a young woman boarded with an infant, about 8 months old, in one arm and a heavy shopping bag on the other. She stood in front of me, trying to steady herself as the train started to move. "Can I help?" I asked. Wordlessly, she handed me . . . the baby!

I began softly singing a children's song. The baby was quiet, neither crying nor smiling, keeping her eyes intently on her mother. We traveled for about 10 minutes, as I wondered why I was holding a living human being rather than the mother's shopping bag.

Both the mother and I were expressing our cultural and personal values as we attended to the baby; the baby, like every other infant, had her own emotional reaction as well. I was happy she was quiet, and I welcomed the chance to sing a lullaby again. The infant did not smile; nor did I expect her to, as she was about the age when she would know a stranger when she saw one.

That moment on the subway signified psychosocial development for the three of us. We were all part of a psychosocial interaction; our reactions to the situation were affected by our ages, past experiences, and circumstances. ●

THIS CHAPTER OPENS by tracing infants' emotions as their brains mature and their experiences accumulate over the first two years. Then we review the four major theories that were first described in Chapter 1, focusing on how each describes psychosocial development during infancy. Toilet training, temperament, and ethnotheories are included in that section.

Theories lead to an exploration of caregiver–infant interaction, particularly the concepts of *synchrony, attachment,* and *social referencing*—all pivotal to psychosocial development. For each of these interactions, we consider fathers as well as mothers.

Both parents are important for infants, but often other caregivers affect their development as well. The pros and cons of infant day care are discussed, with special attention to the impact of nonparental care on psychosocial development. The chapter ends with practical suggestions for stimulating the healthy emotional growth of infants. That mother on the subway may have made a wise choice in handing me her baby—just not the choice I expected.

Emotional Development

Within the first two years, infants progress from reactive pain and pleasure to complex patterns of social awareness (see Table 4.1). This period of life is characterized by "high emotional responsiveness" (Izard et al., 2002, p. 767). This is evident even in infancy with speedy, uncensored reactions—crying, startling, laughing, raging—and, by toddlerhood, with more complex responses, from self-satisfied grins to mournful pouts.

Infants' Emotions

At first there is pleasure and pain. Newborns look happy and relaxed when they have just been fed and are drifting off to sleep. They cry when they are hurt or hungry, are tired or frightened (as by a loud noise or a sudden loss of support), or are suffering from *colic*, the recurrent bouts of uncontrollable crying and irritability that afflict about one-third of all infants in the early months.

SMILING AND LAUGHING The relaxed pleasure of the newborn infant soon develops into more varied positive reactions (Lavelli & Fogel, 2005). Curiosity is evident as infants distinguish the unusual from the familiar. Happiness is expressed by the **social smile,** a smile evoked by a human face at about 6 weeks. Soon laughter appears, at about 3 or 4 months.

Infants worldwide express social joy between 2 and 4 months (Konner, 2007). The sound of a baby's laugh pleases most adults, which is one reason parents, and even adept strangers, encourage it. Among the Navajo, whoever brings forth that first laugh gives a feast to celebrate that the baby is becoming a person (Rogoff, 2003). Laughter builds as curiosity does; a typical 6-month-old laughs loudly upon discovering new things, particularly social experiences that have the right balance between familiarity and surprise, such as Daddy making a funny face.

ANGER AND SADNESS Infants express anger, usually triggered by frustration, by the time they are 6 months old. Anger is most apparent when infants are prevented from reaching a graspable object they want or from moving as they wish (Plutchik, 2003). Infants hate to be strapped in, caged in, closed in, or even just held tightly on someone's lap when they want to explore.

social smile
A smile evoked by a human face, normally first evident in infants about 6 weeks after birth.

©AZIZUR RAHIM PEU / DRIK / MAJORITY WORLD /THE IMAGE WORKS

Shared Joy This woman and her baby in Bangladesh demonstrate that, long before infants are able to express their emotions in words, they smile and laugh to show their joy when their mother expresses delight in them.

As always, culture and experience influence the norms of development. This is especially true for emotional development after the first 8 months.

TABLE 4.1 AT ABOUT THIS TIME: Ages When Emotions Emerge

Age	Emotional Expression
Birth	Crying; contentment
6 weeks	Social smile
3 months	Laughter; curiosity
4 months	Full, responsive smiles
4–8 months	Anger
9–14 months	Fear of social events (strangers, separation from caregiver)
12 months	Fear of unexpected sights and sounds
18 months	Self-awareness; pride; shame; embarrassment

Anger in infancy is a healthy response to frustration—unlike sadness, which also appears in the first months. Sadness indicates withdrawal and is accompanied by an increase in the body's production of *cortisol,* a stress hormone (Lewis & Ramsay, 2005).

It is more difficult to conduct reliable hormone analyses with infants than with older people, so not all the hormonal changes that accompany infant emotions are known. However, the fact that sadness is accompanied by elevated levels of cortisol indicates that sorrow is stressful for infants. Many researchers believe that the infant brain is shaped by the early social emotions, particularly sadness and fear (Fries & Pollak, 2007; M. H. Johnson, 2007).

FEAR Fully formed fear in response to some person, thing, or situation (not just distress at a surprise) emerges at about 9 months. Fear rapidly becomes more frequent as well as more apparent (Witherington et al., 2004). Two kinds of social fear are obvious:

- **Stranger wariness** is expressed when an infant no longer smiles at any friendly face but instead cries or looks frightened when an unfamiliar person moves too close, too quickly.

- **Separation anxiety** is expressed in tears, dismay, or anger when a familiar caregiver leaves. Separation anxiety is normal at age 1, intensifies by age 2, and usually subsides after that. If it remains strong after age 3, it may be considered an emotional disorder (Silverman & Dick-Niederhauser, 2004).

Many 1-year-olds fear not just strangers but also anything unexpected, from the flush of a toilet to the pop of a jack-in-the-box, from the closing of elevator doors to the tail-wagging approach of a dog. With repeated experiences and caregiver reassurance, older infants might enjoy flushing the toilet themselves (again and again) or calling the dog (and crying if the dog does *not* come).

stranger wariness
An infant's expression of concern—a quiet stare when clinging to a familiar person, or a look of sadness—when a stranger appears.

separation anxiety
An infant's distress when a familiar caregiver leaves, most obvious between 9 and 14 months.

Toddlers' Emotions

Emotions that emerge in the first months of life take on new strength at about age 1 (Kagan, 2002). Throughout the second year and beyond, anger and fear typically become less frequent but more focused, targeted toward infuriating or terrifying experiences. Similarly, laughing and crying become louder and more discriminating.

In addition, new emotions appear toward the end of the second year: pride, shame, embarrassment, and guilt (Witherington et al., 2004). These emotions require an awareness of other people. They emerge from family interactions, influenced by the culture (Mesquita & Leu, 2007). For example, North American families generally encourage pride in toddlers ("You did it all by yourself"—even when that is untrue), but Asian families discourage pride, instead cultivating modesty and shame (Rogoff, 2003).

In every culture, families reinforce the emotions that will best prepare the toddler for life in that society. These preferences are cultural, not genetic. Infants of Chinese heritage adopted by European American parents reflect the emotions favored by their adopted culture more than the ones expected from Asian infants (Camras et al., 2006).

By age 2, children can display the entire spectrum of emotional reactions. They have been taught which expressions of emotion are acceptable in their culture and which are not (Saarni et al., 2006). Such teaching occurs many times a day. For example, if a toddler holds on tightly to his mother's skirt and hides his face when a

Stranger Wariness Becomes Santa Terror For toddlers, even a friendly stranger is cause for alarm, especially if Mom's protective arms are withdrawn. The most frightening strangers are men who are unusually dressed and who act as if they might take the child away. Ironically, therefore, Santa Claus remains terrifying until children are about 3 years old.

ESPECIALLY FOR Nurses and Pediatricians Parents come to you concerned that their 1-year-old hides her face and holds onto them tightly whenever a stranger appears. What do you tell them? (see response, page 128) →

self-awareness
A person's realization that he or she is a distinct individual whose body, mind, and actions are separate from those of other people.

friendly but strange dog approaches, the mother could either hastily pick the child up or bend down to pet the dog. The mother's response encourages the child to express either fear or happiness the next time a dog appears.

Self-Awareness

In addition to social interactions, another foundation for emotional growth is **self-awareness,** the realization that one's body, mind, and actions are separate from those of other people (R. A. Thompson, 2006). At about age 1, an emerging sense of "me" and "mine" leads to a new consciousness of others. As one developmentalist explains:

> With the emergence of consciousness in the second year of life, we see vast changes in both children's emotional life and the nature of their social relationships. . . . The child can feel . . . self-conscious emotions, like pride at a job well done or shame over a failure.
>
> [M. Lewis, 1997, p. 132]

Very young infants have no sense of self—at least as most people define *self* (Harter, 2006). In fact, a prominent psychoanalyst, Margaret Mahler, theorized that for the first four months of life infants see themselves as part of their mothers. They "hatch" at about 5 months and spend the next several months developing an awareness of themselves as separate from their mothers (Mahler et al., 1975). The period from 15 to 18 months "is noteworthy for the emergence of the *Me-self,* the sense of self as the *object* of one's knowledge" (Harter, 1998, p. 562).

MIRROR RECOGNITION In a classic experiment (M. Lewis & Brooks, 1978), babies aged 9–24 months looked into a mirror after a dot of rouge had been surreptitiously put on their noses. If the babies reacted by touching their noses, that meant they knew the mirror showed their own faces. None of the babies younger than 12 months old reacted as if they knew the mark was on them (they sometimes smiled and touched the dot on the "other" baby in the mirror). However, those between 15 and 24 months usually showed self-awareness, touching their own noses with curiosity and puzzlement.

Self-recognition in the mirror test as well as in photographs usually emerges at about 18 months. This is the same age at which two other advances occur: pretending and using first-person pronouns (*I, me, mine, myself, my*).

Some developmentalists connect self-recognition with self-understanding (e.g., Gallup et al., 2002), although "the interpretation of this seemingly simple task [the mirror recognition] is plagued by controversy" (M. Nielsen et al., 2006, p. 176). For example, one study found that self-recognition in the mirror test *negatively* correlated with embarrassment when a doll's leg fell off (it had been rigged to do so) as each

Mirror, Mirror This toddler clearly recognizes herself in the reflection in the mirror, and her careful combing indicates that she also knows that her culture admires long hair in females.

OBSERVATION QUIZ

This little girl may end up tangling her hair instead of smoothing it. Besides the comb, what else do you see that she might misuse? (see answer, page 128) →

ELYSE LEWIN / BRAND X / CORBIS

toddler played with it (K. C. Barrett, 2005). Particularly for boys, 17-month-olds who recognized themselves were *less* embarrassed at this mishap and more likely to tell the examiner about it.

Does a sense of self at this age diminish shame as it increases pride? Perhaps. Pride seems to be linked to the toddler's maturing self-concept, not necessarily to other people's opinions or actions (K. C. Barrett, 2005). If someone tells a 2-year-old, "You're very smart," the child may smile but usually already feels smart—and thus is pleased and proud, but not surprised. In fact, telling toddlers that they are smart, strong, or beautiful may even be unhelpful (S. A. Kelley et al., 2000). It may undercut their self-awareness, making it seem as if pride comes from pleasing other people.

BRAIN MATURATION AND THE EMOTIONS Brain maturation is involved in all the emotional developments just described. There is no doubt that varied experiences, as well as good nutrition, promote both brain maturation and emotional development. Nor is there any doubt that emotional reactions begin in the brain (M. H. Johnson, 2007). Infants' understanding of themselves, demonstrated in their use of personal pronouns and in the mirror test, is related to maturation of a particular part of the brain (the left temporoparietal junction) (Lewis & Carmody, 2008).

Scans of infant brains are notoriously difficult, expensive, and open to various interpretations, so it is difficult to prove any specific neurological explanation of emotional development. Consequently, theories about the more subtle connections between brain architecture and emotional expression, as in the role of mirror neurons (see Chapter 1) or as in fear responses to stress, are still speculative.

Developmentalists do agree that infants' emotional development—specifically, social awareness and reactions to stress—is directly tied to brain development. As for more advanced emotions, research has not yet pinned down the connections, sequences, or ages at which advances in brain development might foster them (although 3 months and 8 months have been suggested as pivotal times).

Synesthesia One topic of great interest is the relationship between brain maturation and the ability to express each emotion or sensation in an appropriate way, not confusing fear and anger, for instance, or a loud sound with the color red. Research on infant senses suggests that such differentiation originates in the brain.

For older children and adults, it is known that *synesthesia*—the stimulation of one sensory stimulus to the brain (sound, sight, touch, taste, or smell) by another—is at least partly genetic. In older children and adults, synesthesia is often connected to creativity and is unusual (K. J. Barnett et al., 2008). For infants, however, synesthesia seems common, because the boundaries between the sensory parts of the cortex are less distinct. For a newborn, textures seem associated with vision and sounds with smells; and the infant's own body seems associated with the bodies of others. Such sensory connections are called *cross-modal perception,* and they may become the basis for early social understanding (Meltzoff, 2007).

The tendency of one part of the brain to activate another also seems to occur with the emotions. An infant's cry can be triggered by pain, fear, tiredness, or excitement; laughter can turn to tears for reasons that adults do not understand. Older children and adults have a quite different pattern, usually crying only in sadness (and sometimes not even then).

Infants' emotions are less predictable than adult ones because of the way their brains are activated. Compared with infants, the toddlers' targeted and self-aware emotions (described earlier) may result from their advances in brain specialization.

Social Impulses Most developmentalists agree that the social smile and the first laughter appear as the cortex of the brain matures (Konner, 2007). The same is probably true for nonreflexive fear, self-awareness, and anger. The maturation of a particular part of the cortex (the anterior cingulate gyrus) is directly connected to emotional self-regulation, which allows the child to moderate these emotions (Posner et al., 2007).

As you have seen, one important aspect of the infant's emotional development is that particular people (typically the ones whom the infant sees most often) begin to arouse specific emotions. This is almost certainly related to brain development, as neurons that fire together become more closely and quickly connected. Infant emotional reactions depend partly on memory, which, as Chapter 3 explained, is fragile in the first months and gradually improves as dendrites and axons connect.

No wonder toddlers (but not young infants) quickly get angry when a teasing older sibling approaches them or react with fear when entering the doctor's office. Now they are able to remember the last time big brother prevented them from doing what they wanted or the shot the doctor gave them last month.

STRESS As mentioned in Chapter 3, excessive stress impairs the brain, particularly in areas associated with emotional development (E. K. Adam et al., 2007). Brain imagery and cortisol measurements have proven that the hypothalamus, the part of the brain that regulates various bodily functions and hormone production, is affected by chronic early stress; it may grow more slowly in stressed than in non-stressed infants. (The hypothalamus is discussed further in Chapter 5.)

Abuse—one form of chronic stress—has long-term consequences for a child's emotional development, and high levels of stress hormones are one sign of emotional impairment. However, the specifics of harm to the infant brain are difficult to prove because it is ethically impossible to compare the effects of maltreatment in one group of infants with another group who are similar in every way except maltreatment.

Nevertheless, it is known that the brains of older children who have been maltreated respond abnormally to stress and even to photographs of frightened people (Gordis et al., 2008; C. L. Masten et al., 2008). Such abnormal neurological responses begin in infancy. This research has important applications: Everything should be done to prevent excessive stress in infants, even when no evidence of maltreatment exists.

One obvious way families and societies can keep infants from experiencing high levels of stress is to provide new mothers with abundant help and emotional support. The father's involvement affects an infant's well-being as well. When the father of a baby delivered via cesarean section provides *kangaroo care,* holding the newborn against his naked chest (see Chapter 2), that baby tends to cry less and to be more relaxed (Erlandsson et al., 2007). Throughout an infant's early development, the father's behavior toward the mother affects her stress level, and her state of high or low stress is then transmitted to the baby (Talge et al., 2007).

On Top of His World This boy's blissful expression is evidence that fathers can prevent or relieve stress in infants, protecting a baby's brain and promoting the mother's peace of mind.

A Case of Abnormal Emotional Development

The developmental progression just reviewed describes the usual sequence, which is the result of caregivers' attention and an infant's brain maturation. The usual, however, is not inevitable. One father writes about his third child, Jacob.

> [My wife, Rebecca, and I] were convinced that we were set. We had surpassed our quota of 2.6 children and were ready to engage parental autopilot. I had just begun a prestigious job and was working 10–11 hours a day. The children would be fine. We hired a nanny to watch Jacob during the day. As each of Jacob's early milestones passed, we felt that we had taken another step toward our goal of having three normal children. We were on our way to the perfect American family. Yet, somewhere back in our minds we had some doubts. Jacob seemed different than the girls. He had some unusual attributes. There were times when we would be holding him and he would arch his back and scream so loud that it was painful for us.
>
> [Jacob's father, 1997, p. 59]

As an infant, Jacob did not relate to his parents (or to anyone else). His parents paid little heed to his emotional difficulties, focusing instead on his physical development. They noted that Jacob sat up and walked on schedule, and whenever they "had some doubts," they found excuses, telling themselves that "boys are different." As time went on, however, their excuses fell short. His father continues:

> Jacob had become increasingly isolated [by age 2]. I'm not a psychologist, but I believe that he just stopped trying. It was too hard, perhaps too scary. He couldn't figure out what was expected of him. The world had become too confusing, and so he withdrew from it. He would seek out the comfort of quiet, dark places and sit by himself. He would lose himself in the bright, colorful images of cartoons and animated movies.
>
> [Jacob's father, 1997, p. 62]

RESPONSE FOR Nurses and Pediatricians (from page 126) Stranger wariness is normal up to about 14 months. This baby's behavior actually sounds like secure attachment! ●

ANSWER TO OBSERVATION QUIZ (from page 126) Perfume. She might splash too much of her mother's perfume on herself, reeking instead of wafting. ●

Jacob's parents eventually realized something had to be done. When Jacob was 3, they took him to be evaluated at a major teaching hospital. He was seen by at least 10 experts, none of whom were encouraging.

The diagnosis was "pervasive developmental disorder," a catchall diagnosis of emotional abnormalities that can include autism (discussed in Chapter 7). The despairing parents were advised to consider residential placement because Jacob would always need special care and, with Jacob living elsewhere, they would not be constantly reminded of their "failure." This recommendation did not take into account the commitment that Jacob's parents, like most parents, felt toward their child.

Yet, despite their commitment, it was apparent that they had ignored signs of trouble, overlooking their son's sometimes violent reaction to being held. The absence of smiling and of social reactions should have raised an alarm. The father's use of the word *autopilot* to describe his and his wife's approach to parenting shows that he realized this in hindsight. Later in this chapter, you will learn the outcome.

KEY Points

- Newborns express distress and contentment, and soon infants also display curiosity and joy, with social smiles and laughter.
- Expressions of anger and fear become increasingly evident as babies reach 12 months of age.
- In toddlerhood, self-awareness underlies the expression of pride, shame, embarrassment, and guilt.
- Brain maturation makes all these emotions possible. Extreme stress impairs the brain and emotional growth.

Theories of Infant Psychosocial Development

Each of the four major theories described in Chapter 1 has its own perspective on the origin of infants' emotions. This section shows how theories have sparked research in three current and crucial areas: toilet training, temperament, and ethnotheories. All three of these topics are outgrowths of theories, and consideration of each topic illustrates the application of theories.

Psychoanalytic Theory

Psychoanalytic theory connects biosocial and psychosocial development, emphasizing the need for responsive maternal care. Both major psychoanalytic theorists, Sigmund Freud and Erik Erikson, described two distinct early stages of development. Freud (1935, 1940/1964) wrote about the *oral stage* and the *anal stage*; Erikson (1963) called his first stages *trust versus mistrust* and *autonomy versus shame and doubt.*

FREUD: THE ORAL AND ANAL STAGES According to Freud (1935), the first year of life is the *oral stage,* so named because the mouth is the young infant's primary source of gratification. In the second year, with the *anal stage,* the infant's main pleasure comes from the anus—particularly from the sensual pleasure of bowel movements and, eventually, the psychological pleasure of controlling them.

Freud believed that both the oral and anal stages are fraught with potential conflicts that have long-term consequences. If a mother frustrates her infant's urge to suck—by weaning the infant too early, for example, or preventing the child from sucking on fingers or toes—the child may become distressed and anxious, eventually

ESPECIALLY FOR Nursing Mothers You have heard that if you wean your child too early, he or she will overeat or become an alcoholic. Is it true? (see response, page 130) →

RESPONSE FOR Nursing Mothers (from page 129) Freud thought so, but there is no experimental evidence that weaning, even when ill timed, has such dire long-term effects. ●

becoming an adult with an *oral fixation*. Such a person is stuck (fixated) at the oral stage and therefore eats, drinks, chews, bites, or talks excessively, in quest of the mouth-related pleasure that was denied in infancy.

Similarly, if toilet training is overly strict or if it begins too early, parent–infant interaction may become locked into conflict over the toddler's refusal or inability to comply. The child becomes fixated and develops an *anal personality*—as an adult, seeking self-control with an unusually strong need for regularity and cleanliness in all aspects of life. With such adults, everything is neat, even the sock drawer: Every sock is matched, rolled, and in place.

Freud's ideas about the connection between the infant's anal stage and the adult's anal personality have been studied in detail and refuted, according to behaviorists (R. R. Sears et al., 1976). Other ideas about the optimal timing and method of toilet training, and their impact on a child, are discussed in the following.

A VIEW FROM SCIENCE

Toilet Training: How and When?

A century ago, parents in the United States often began toilet training infants in the first month of life (Accardo, 2006). By the middle of the twentieth century, toilet training did not begin until 12 months or later. One reason for the change was psychoanalytic theory, which persuaded parents to postpone toilet training until the child was ready, thus avoiding conflict and the potential development of an anal personality. The child was supposed to be allowed to decide when to begin and how quickly to proceed.

Toward the end of the twentieth century, many U.S. scientists rejected that psychoanalytic view. Some proposed an alternative plan based on behaviorist principles; this plan was said to make it possible to complete toilet training in a day (Azrin & Foxx, 1974). In this method, children drink quantities of their favorite juice; sit on the potty with a parent nearby to keep them happy, entertained, and in place; then, when the inevitable occurs, they are praised and rewarded. This reinforcement is supposed to teach children to head for the potty whenever the need arises.

A comparison study found that this behaviorist approach was often effective for older children with serious disabilities. However, this study also found that many other methods of toilet training succeeded with normal children. Contrary to psychoanalytic predictions, no method seemed to result in marked negative emotional consequences (Klassen et al., 2006).

Waiting until the child is ready—that is, physiologically mature and cognitively capable (knowing some words and having a sense of self)—makes sense to many parents. Research finds that later training, initiated by the child,

tends to succeed more quickly. One study followed hundreds of toddlers whose parents began toilet training them when they were between 18 months and 3 years of age. Early starters took about a year to be completely toilet-trained (doing everything without help); later starters took only about three months (Blum et al., 2003).

Psychoanalytic theory on toilet training has been further undermined by cross-cultural surveys. Researchers have found that toilet training occurs "in very diverse ways . . . at different ages, with different degrees of attention and harshness" (Rozin, 2007, p. 405). In some cultures, parents are expected to toilet-train their infants by 6 months; in others, parents do not train their children at all—toddlers train themselves by watching slightly older children and imitating what they do.

All Together, Now Toddlers in an employees' day-care program at a flower farm in Colombia learn to use the potty on a schedule.

REUTERS / JOSE MIGUEL GOMEZ / LANDOV

Variations are also evident within cultures. A survey found that some U.S. parents thought toilet training should begin as early as 6 months; others, as late as 4 years. The preferred age was affected by the parents' level of education: More years of education correlated with later training (I. B. Horn et al., 2006). Other research in industrialized nations found that the age of success depends more on the child's bladder size and sleep habits (which vary a great deal among children) than on the culture (Jansson et al., 2005).

Berry Brazelton is a leading U.S. pediatrician who writes about child development. (You read about the Brazelton Neonatal Behavioral Assessment Scale in Chapter 2.) He believes that toilet training should begin when the child is cognitively, emotionally, and biologically ready. That is usually around age 2 for daytime training and age 3 or older for nighttime dryness (Brazelton & Sparrow, 2006).

As with many other child-rearing issues, Brazelton realizes that many toilet-training recommendations and practices reflect value judgments. He writes:

As a society, we are far too concerned about pushing children to be toilet trained early. I don't even like the phrase "toilet training." It really should be toilet learning.

[*Brazelton & Sparrow, 2006, p. 193*]

Rejecting this relaxed, child-centered approach, some Western parents prefer to start potty training very early. One U.S. mother began training her baby just 33 days after birth. She would notice when her son was about to defecate and hold him above the toilet; she claimed that he was trained by 6 months (M. Sun & Rugolotto, 2004).

The view from contemporary science is that the "best" age to start toilet training depends on what the goal is. If the goal is to foster the child's independence and autonomy, with as little parental interference as possible, then it makes sense to wait until the sense of self is well developed, perhaps at age 2. But if the goal is to have a compliant infant, and if the parents are patient and willing to respond to subtle signs that defecation is imminent, then starting earlier makes sense (Accardo, 2006).

ERIKSON: TRUST AND AUTONOMY According to Erikson, the first crisis of life is **trust versus mistrust,** when infants learn whether the world can be trusted to satisfy their basic needs. Babies feel secure when food and comfort are provided with "consistency, continuity, and sameness of experience" (Erikson, 1963, p. 247). If social interaction inspires trust and security, the child (and later the adult) will confidently explore the social world.

The next crisis is called **autonomy versus shame and doubt.** Toddlers want autonomy (self-rule) over their own actions and bodies. If they fail to gain it, they feel ashamed of their actions and doubtful about their abilities.

Like Freud, Erikson believed that problems arising in early infancy could last a lifetime, creating an adult who is suspicious and pessimistic (mistrusting) or who is easily shamed (insufficient autonomy). These traits could be destructive or not, depending on the norms and expectations of the culture.

Erikson is seen as insightful because he took culture into account. He was aware that some cultures (including that of the United States) encourage independence and autonomy, but he may not have realized that in others (e.g., China), "shame is a normative emotion that develops as parents use explicit shaming techniques" to encourage children's loyalty and harmony within their families (Mascolo et al., 2003, p. 402).

Westerners expect toddlers to go through the stubborn and defiant "terrible twos"; parents elsewhere expect toddlers to be docile and obedient. Thus, autonomy is prized in the United States, but it is considered immature by many other peoples of the world (Morelli & Rothbaum, 2007). Contemporary developmentalists hesitate to say that one way or the other is best for the infants' emotional health.

trust versus mistrust
Erikson's first crisis of psychosocial development. Infants learn basic trust if the world is a secure place where their basic needs (for food, comfort, attention, and so on) are met.

autonomy versus shame and doubt
Erikson's second crisis of psychosocial development. Toddlers either succeed or fail in gaining a sense of self-rule over their actions and their bodies.

A Mother's Dilemma Infants are wonderfully curious, as this little boy demonstrates. Parents, however, must guide as well as encourage the drive toward autonomy. Notice this mother's expression as she makes sure her son does not crush or eat the flower.

JOSE LUIS PELEAZ, INC. / CORBIS

Behaviorism

From the perspective of behaviorism, parents mold an infant's emotions and personality as they reinforce or punish the child's spontaneous behaviors (as explained in Chapter 1). Behaviorists believe that if parents smile and pick up their infant at every glimmer of a grin, he or she will become a child—and later an adult—with a sunny disposition. They believe that the opposite is also true. The early behaviorist John Watson expressed this idea in strong terms:

> Failure to bring up a happy child, a well-adjusted child—assuming bodily health— falls squarely upon the parents' shoulders. [By the time the child is 3,] parents have already determined . . . [whether the child] is to grow into a happy person, wholesome and good-natured, whether he is to be a whining, complaining neurotic, an anger-driven, vindictive, over-bearing slave driver, or one whose every move in life is definitely controlled by fear.
>
> *[Watson, 1928, pp. 7, 45]*

social learning
The acquisition of behavior patterns by observing the behavior of others.

Later behaviorists noted infant **social learning,** which (as you remember) is learning via observing others. The power of social learning for children is evident in a classic experiment by Albert Bandura: Children watched an adult hitting a rubber Bobo clown with a mallet and then treated the doll the same way (Bandura, 1977).

Social learning is strongest in certain contexts. In Bandura's experiment, 4-year-old children had good reason to attack Bobo: They had been deliberately frustrated by being told they could not play with some attractive toys. They were then left alone with a mallet and the large rubber doll. Both boys and girls pounded and kicked Bobo, as they had just seen an adult do.

COPYRIGHT ALBERT BANDURA

Hammering Bobo These images are stills from the film of Bandura's original study of social learning, in which frustrated 4-year-olds imitated the behavior they had observed an adult perform. The children used the same weapon as the adult, with the same intent— whether that involved hitting the doll with a hammer, shooting it with a toy gun, or throwing a large ball at it.

Since that experiment, hundreds of developmentalists have demonstrated that social learning occurs throughout infancy and childhood (A. S. Morris et al., 2007; M. Nielsen, 2006). In many families, toddlers express emotions in various ways—from giggling to cursing—and their particular expression is similar to that of their parents or older siblings. A boy might develop a hot temper, for instance, if his father's outbursts seem to win respect from his mother.

Behaviorist theory emphasizes the role of parents, especially mothers, as does psychoanalytic theory. Freud thought that the mother is the young child's first and most enduring "love object," and behaviorists stress the power that a mother has over her children. In retrospect, this focus on the mother seems too narrow.

Cognitive Theory

You learned in Chapter 1 that cognitive theory holds that thoughts and values determine a person's perspective. Thinking is affected both by the person's age and by cultural values, and thoughts affect emotions. Cognition guides parents as well as infants.

THE INFANT'S WORKING MODEL According to cognitive theory, early experiences are important because beliefs, perceptions, and memories make them so, not because they are buried in the unconscious (psychoanalytic theory) or burned into the brain (behaviorism). Infants use their early relationships to develop a **working model,** a set of assumptions that become a frame of reference to be called on later in life (Bretherton & Munholland, 1999; R. A. Thompson & Raikes, 2003). To use Piaget's terminology, people develop cognitive *schema* to organize their perceptions of other people.

This frame of reference is called a *model* because early relationships form a proto-type, or blueprint, for later relationships; it is called *working* because, while usable, it is not necessarily fixed or final. Ideally, infants develop "a working model of the self as valued, loved, and competent" and "a working model of parents as emotionally avail-able, loving, sensitive and supportive" (Harter, 2006, p. 519).

Of course, reality does not always conform to this ideal. For instance, a 1-year-old girl whose parents are inconsistent might develop a working model of people as unpredictable and not to be trusted. All her life, she will apply that model to every new person she meets: Her childhood relationships will be insecure; as a schoolchild, she will be suspicious of teachers; and in adulthood, she may always be on guard against further disappointment. The opposite working model would develop if the girl's parents were consistently delighted with her.

According to cognitive theory, it is a child's *interpretation* of early experiences that is crucial, not necessarily the experiences themselves (Schaffer, 2000). The hopeful message from cognitive theory is that people can rethink and reorganize their thoughts, developing new working models that are more positive than their original ones. Our mistrustful girl can learn to trust if her later experiences—such as mar-riage to a faithful and loving husband—provide a new model.

ETHNOTHEORIES Thus far, we have focused on the working model that a particu-lar person might hold, but cognitive theory also takes into consideration the social constructions, or cultural beliefs, of the entire community. Such ideas make up an **ethnotheory,** a set of ideas in which the values and practices of a particular culture or ethnic group are embedded.

Group members are usually unaware that theories underlie their customs. However, as you have already seen with breast-feeding, immunization, and co-sleeping in Chap-ter 3, many child-rearing practices arise from ethnotheories (H. Keller et al., 2006).

This is also true for emotional development. For example, if a culture's ethnotheory includes the idea that ancestors are reincar-nated in the younger generation, then "children are not expected to show respect for adults, but adults [are expected to show respect] for their reborn ancestors." Such cultures favor indulgent child-rearing practices, with no harsh punishments. "Western people perceive [these cultures] as extremely lenient" (Dasen, 2003, pp. 149–150).

Remember from Chapter 1 that cultures change over time, in response to changing contexts. This was confirmed by a study of the ethnotheories of grandmothers and mothers of 3-month-olds (Lamm et al., 2008). The grandmother–mother pairs were from four contexts: urban Germany, urban India, urban Cameroon, and rural Cameroon. The women held ethnotheories that differed by culture and by generation, with the mothers valuing autonomy more than the grandmothers did.

The generation gap was smallest in the two cultures that were the most different. In urban Germany, the grandmothers tended to agree with the mothers in valuing autonomy; among rural West Africans, the mothers tended to agree with the grandmothers in valuing compliance.

The greatest gap in grandmother–mother attitudes occurred in urban Cameroon, probably because social change had been most

working model
In cognitive theory, a set of assump-tions that the individual uses to organ-ize perceptions and experiences. For example, a person might assume that other people are trustworthy and be surprised by evidence that this work-ing model of human behavior is erroneous.

ethnotheory
A theory that underlies the values and practices of a culture but is not usually apparent to the people within the culture.

Which Sister Has a Personality Problem? In Mongolia, females are expected to display shyness as a sign of respect to elders and strangers. Consequently, if the younger of these sisters is as shy as she seems, her parents are less likely to be distressed about her withdrawn behavior than the typical North American parent would be. Conversely, they may worry about the boldness of her older sister.

LEONG KATAI / MATERIAL WORLD

ESPECIALLY FOR Linguists and Writers U.S. culture has given rise to the term *empty nest,* signifying an ethnotheory about mothers whose children have grown up and left home. What cultural values are expressed by that term? (see response, page 136) →

temperament
Inborn differences between one person and another in emotions, activity, and self-regulation. Temperament is epigenetic, originating in the genes but affected by child-rearing practices.

recent and dramatic in that cultural context. The mothers tended to value autonomy much more than the grandmothers did. Overall, the cognitive perspective of the grandmothers was much more influenced by traditional Cameroon values and that of the mothers, by more modern ethnotheories (Lamm et al., 2008).

Systems Theory

You learned in Chapter 1 that systems theory incorporates many factors, both genetic and learned, all of which change over time and influence one another. Every inherited trait affects the social context and vice versa, all in a systematic, interactive way. This systems view is an epigenetic approach to development, using all five characteristics of the life-span perspective (multidirectional, multicontextual, multicultural, multidisciplinary, and plastic). Systems theory is especially insightful in interpreting temperament.

TEMPERAMENT A child might be anxious not only because of early experiences but also because of inborn predispositions that evoke anxiety and protectiveness in the parents and because of sociocultural forces that encourage particular emotions. The same could be true for a child who is naturally happy, angry, or fearful.

In infants, **temperament** begins as "constitutionally based individual differences" in emotions, activity, and self-regulation (Rothbart & Bates, 2006, p. 100). "Constitutionally based" means that these traits originate with nature (genes), although they are influenced by nurture.

Some researchers believe that personality and temperament overlap, making it difficult to distinguish one from the other (e.g., Caspi & Shiner, 2006). Generally, however, personality traits (e.g., honesty and humility) are considered to originate from learning, whereas temperament traits (e.g., shyness and aggression) are considered to originate from the genes. Systems theories stress that the boundaries between temperament and personality are porous, since genes, child rearing, and culture all influence one another (Rothbart & Bates, 2006).

The New York Longitudinal Study In some laboratory studies of temperament, researchers expose infants to events that have been designed to be frightening and observe how the babies react. Four-month-olds might see spinning mobiles or hear unusual sounds; older babies might confront a noisy, moving robot or a clown who quickly moves close. At such experiences, some children laugh (and are classified as "easy"), some cry ("difficult"), and some are quiet ("slow to warm up") (Fox et al., 2001; Kagan & Snidman, 2004).

These three categories come from a classic study called the *New York Longitudinal Study* (NYLS). Begun in the 1960s, the NYLS was the first among many large studies to recognize that each newborn has distinct inborn traits that then evoke responses from the parents.

Although temperament probably begins in the brain, it is difficult to detect via brain scans, so most researchers use parents' reports and direct observation. In order to avoid merely reflecting the parents' hopes and biases, researchers ask for specific details, seeking what are called *operational definitions.* As the NYLS researchers explain:

> If a mother said that her child did not like his first solid food, we . . . were satisfied only when she gave a description such as "When I put the food into his mouth he cried loudly, twisted his head away, and let it drool out."
>
> *[Chess et al., 1965, p. 26]*

According to the NYLS, by 3 months, infants manifest nine temperamental traits that can be clustered into four categories (the three noted above and a fourth category of "hard to classify" infants). The proportion of infants in each category was as follows:

- Easy, 40 percent
- Difficult, 10 percent
- Slow to warm up, 15 percent
- Hard to classify, 35 percent

The NYLS found that temperament often changes in the early weeks but becomes increasingly stable by age 3 or so, partly because parents and culture encourage certain traits. The research finds that 3-year-olds with extreme temperaments (perhaps very difficult or very easy) are likely to have the same traits in adolescence and young adulthood (Guerin et al., 2003).

True to systems theory, however, research on genetic predispositions and later traits finds that parenting practices may be crucial, as you remember from the MAOA research on the New Zealand boys, reported in Chapter 1. Systems theory always acknowledges that things change with time; temperament is no exception.

The Big Five Other researchers began by studying adult personality traits and came up with the **Big Five** (whose first letters form the memorable acronym *OCEAN*). These five traits are listed here with the characteristics that define them:

- Openness: imaginative, curious, welcoming new experiences
- Conscientiousness: organized, deliberate, conforming
- Extroversion: outgoing, assertive, active
- Agreeableness: kind, helpful, easygoing
- Neuroticism: anxious, moody, self-critical

Big Five

The five basic clusters of personality traits that remain quite stable throughout life: openness, conscientiousness, extroversion, agreeableness, and neuroticism.

The Big Five traits are found in many cultures and among people of all ages, although the proportions in each category differ by age and nationality (McCrae & Costa, 2003). The Big Five are more complex than the easy/difficult/slow-to-warm-up/hard-to-classify categories; but an infant high in agreeableness might be classified as easy, one high in neuroticism would be difficult, and so on.

Again, the social context matters. Although everyone can be rated on all five traits, the proportion of people in a community who are high or low in each trait varies. In the United States, each state has a different profile (Rentfrow et al., 2008). According to an Internet survey of 619,397 people, New York is highest in openness, New Mexico in conscientiousness, North Dakota in both extroversion and agreeableness, and West Virginia in neuroticism. Lowest in each of these traits, respectively, are North Dakota, Alaska, Maryland, Alaska (again), and Utah. Obviously, not everyone in those states fits the profile, but social norms and institutions, as well as the geographic setting, might have some influence on everyone, of every age (Rentfrow et al., 2008).

Other studies of temperament from infancy throughout childhood show both change and continuity, with each trait affecting the others and ongoing maturation affecting the entire constellation (Janson & Mathiesen, 2008). In other words, an individual child might be temperamentally shy, but over the next several years that trait might either continue (about half the time) or change as other aspects of temperament, experiences, age, and regional culture systematically affect each trait.

One longitudinal study of infant temperament (Fox et al., 2001) identified and grouped 4-month-old participants into three distinct types—positive (exuberant), negative, and inhibited (fearful). The researchers followed each group, taking laboratory measures, mothers' reports, and brain scans at 9, 14, 24, and 48 months.

A little more than half the children did not change much, reacting the same way and having similar brain-wave patterns when confronted with frightening experiences all four times they were tested. A little less than half altered their responses as they grew older. Fearful infants were most likely to change and exuberant infants,

FIGURE 4.1 Do Babies' Temperaments Change? The data suggest that fearful babies are not necessarily fated to remain that way. Adults who are reassuring and do not act frightened themselves can help children overcome an innate fearfulness. Some fearful children do not change, however, and it is not known whether that's because their parents are not sufficiently reassuring (nurture) or because they are temperamentally more fearful (nature).

OBSERVATION QUIZ

Out of 100 4-month-olds who react positively to noises and other experiences, how many are fearful at later times in early childhood? (see answer, page 138) ➔

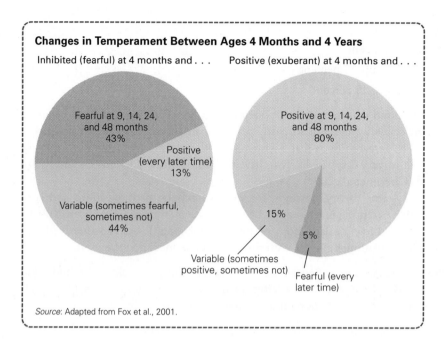

Changes in Temperament Between Ages 4 Months and 4 Years

Inhibited (fearful) at 4 months and . . .

Fearful at 9, 14, 24, and 48 months
43%

Positive (every later time)
13%

Variable (sometimes fearful, sometimes not)
44%

Positive (exuberant) at 4 months and . . .

Positive at 9, 14, 24, and 48 months
80%

15%

5%

Variable (sometimes positive, sometimes not)

Fearful (every later time)

Source: Adapted from Fox et al., 2001.

proximal parenting
Caregiving practices that involve being physically close to the baby, with frequent holding and touching.

distal parenting
Caregiving practices that involve remaining distant from the baby, providing toys, food, and face-to-face communication with minimal holding and touching.

RESPONSE FOR Linguists and Writers (from page 134) The implication is that human mothers are like sad birds, bereft of their fledglings, who have flown away. ●

least likely (see Figure 4.1). That speaks to the influence of maturation and child rearing on inborn temperament: Adults coax frightened children to be braver and encourage exuberant children to stay happy.

THE EFFECTS OF PARENTING The role of parents is discussed repeatedly in this text because parents are influential in many important ways. Parenting patterns affect infant emotions and vice versa, as described by systems theory, which takes into account the mutual influence of family members. For instance, parents of a difficult infant need to provide much more guidance than do parents of an easy infant.

Here we highlight one aspect of parenting that seems to have a significant influence on the self-awareness of toddlers: how much the parents carry and cuddle their infant. **Proximal parenting** involves being physically close to the baby, often holding and touching the child. **Distal parenting** involves keeping some distance from the baby—providing toys, feeding by putting finger food within reach, and talking face-to-face instead of communicating by touch.

As you read in Chapter 3, parents who talk often to their infants tend to have more verbal children. In middle-class North America, verbal fluency is prized. As the systems approach stresses, each value is part of a larger social system. Not every culture values verbal fluency; some value quiet thoughtfulness instead. Thus, values affect the parents' behavior, which influences infants to fit into the social system that will support them.

Now let's look at a longitudinal study that compared proximal and distal parenting among the Nso people of rural Cameroon and among Greeks in the city of Athens (H. Keller et al., 2004). The researchers videotaped 78 mothers as they played with their 3-month-olds. Coders (who did not know the study's hypothesis) rated the style of play as either proximal (e.g., carrying, swinging, caressing, exercising the child's body) or distal (e.g., face-to-face talking) (see Table 4.2).

The Nso mothers were proximal parents, holding their babies all the time and almost never using toys or bottles. The Greek mothers were distal parents, using objects almost half the time and holding their babies less than the Nso parents did.

The researchers hypothesized that proximal parenting would result in toddlers who were less self-aware but more compliant—traits needed in an interdependent

TABLE 4.2 Play Patterns in Rural Cameroon and Urban Greece

Age of Babies	Type of Play	Nso, Cameroon	Athens, Greece
		Amount of Time Spent in Play (percent)	
3 months	Held by mother	100	31
3 months	Object play	3	40
	Toddler Behavior Measured		
18 months	Self-recognition	3	68
18 months	Compliance (without prompting)	72	2

Source: Adapted from H. Keller et al., 2004.

ESPECIALLY FOR Statisticians Note the sizes of the samples: 78 mother–infant pairs in Cameroon and Greece and 12 pairs in Costa Rica. Are these samples big enough to draw conclusions from? (see answer, page 138) →

and cooperative society such as rural Cameroon. By contrast, distal parenting might result in toddlers who were self-aware but less obedient—traits needed in modern Athens, where independence, self-reliance, and competition are highly valued.

The hypothesis proved to be accurate. At 18 months, these children were tested on self-awareness (via the rouge test) and obedience to their parents' instructions. The African toddlers did not recognize themselves in the mirror but were compliant; the opposite was true of the Greek children.

Replicating their own work, these researchers studied a dozen mother–infant pairs in Costa Rica. In that Central American nation, mother–infant distance was midway between that of the Nso and of the Greeks, as was later toddler behavior. The researchers reanalyzed all their data, child by child. They found that, even apart from culture, proximal or distal play at 3 months was highly predictive of toddler behavior. In other words, Greek mothers who, unlike most of their peers, were proximal parents had more obedient toddlers (H. Keller et al., 2004).

The same results were found by a longitudinal study of German fathers (Borke et al., 2007). As this research suggests, every aspect of early emotional development is part of a social system, interacting with social values that fit into the society.

You already read that separation anxiety is apparent at about 1 year. However, as you would expect from a systems perspective, the strength of this anxiety is affected by the parents' behavior. Separation anxiety is more evident in Japan than in Germany because Japanese infants "have very few experiences with separation from the mother," whereas in Germany "infants are frequently left alone outside of stores or supermarkets" while their mothers shop (Saarni et al., 2006, p. 237).

PARENTING IN A PROXIMAL CULTURE We noted earlier that infants become angry when they are restrained. Some Western parents rarely hold their infants except to restrain them (and the purpose of the restraint is often to enforce a separation between the parent and the infant). Parents force protesting toddlers to sit in strollers, to ride in car seats, to stay in cribs and playpens or behind gates—all examples of distal parenting. If toddlers do not lie down quietly to allow diapers to be quickly changed (and few do), some parents simply hold down the protesting child to get the task done quickly.

By contrast, Mayan parents from Mexico and Guatemala believe that children should not be forced to obey their parents; they use affectionate touch to teach children to comply with social norms. In one example, 18 month-old Roberto did not

No Distance Between Them This Namibian mother holds her child very close and has massaged his whole body with butterfat and red ochre. Touch and caress, more than words and toys, express love in a proximal culture.

ESPECIALLY FOR Pediatricians A parent complains that her child refuses to stay in the car seat, spits out disliked foods, and almost never does what she says. How should you respond? (see response, page 138) →

ANSWER TO OBSERVATION QUIZ (from page 136) Out of 100 4-month-olds, 20 are fearful at least occasionally later in childhood, but only 5 are consistently fearful. ●

RESPONSE FOR Statisticians (from page 137) Probably not. These studies are reported here because the results were dramatic (see Table 4.2) and because the two studies pointed in the same direction. Nevertheless, replication by other researchers is needed. ●

RESPONSE FOR Pediatricians (from page 137) Remember the origins of the misbehavior—probably a combination of the child's inborn temperament and the parent's distal parenting. Blended with ethnotheory, all contribute to the child's being stubborn and independent. Acceptance is more warranted than anger. On the other hand, this parent may be expressing hostility toward the child—a sign that intervention may be needed. Find out. ●

want to get dressed. His mother tried to persuade him: "Let's put on your diaper . . . Let's go to Grandma's . . . We're going to do an errand." When this did not work, his mother then invited Roberto to nurse, as she swiftly slipped the diaper on him with the father's assistance. The father announced, "It's over" (Rogoff, 2003, p. 204).

Roberto's mother then tackled the task of getting Roberto to put on pants. He wiggled and refused to stand still to allow his pants to be pulled up. Roberto became interested in a ball, and his mother raised the stakes: "Do you want another toy?" she asked.

> They [the parents] continued to try to talk Roberto into cooperating, and handed him various objects, which Roberto enjoyed. But still he stubbornly refused to cooperate with dressing. They left him alone for a while. When his father asked if he was ready, Roberto pouted "nono!"
>
> After a bit, the mother told Roberto that she was leaving and waved goodbye. "Are you going with me?" Roberto sat quietly with a worried look [separation anxiety]. "Then put on your pants, put on your pants to go up the hill." Roberto stared into space, seeming to consider the alternatives. His mother started to walk away. "OK then, I'm going. Goodbye." Roberto started to cry, and his father persuaded, "Put on your pants then!" and his mother asked, "Are you going with me?"
>
> Roberto looked down worriedly, one arm outstretched in half a take-me gesture.
>
> "Come on, then," his mother offered the pants and Roberto let his father lift him to a stand and cooperated in putting his legs into the pants and in standing to have them fastened. His mother did not intend to leave; instead she suggested that Roberto dance for the audience. Roberto did a baby version of a traditional dance.
>
> *[Rogoff, 2003, p. 204]*

The ethnotheory of this culture holds that "elders protect and guide rather than giving orders or dominating" (Rogoff, 2003, p. 205).

KEY Points

- Psychoanalytic theory stresses the mother's responses to the infant's needs for food and elimination (Freud, who described the oral and anal stages) or for security and independence (Erikson, who identified trust versus mistrust and autonomy versus shame and doubt as the first two crises of life).
- Behaviorism also stresses caregiving—especially as parents reinforce and model behavior.
- Cognitive theory emphasizes mental frameworks that affect emotions and actions, both the working models held by individuals and the ethnotheories developed by societies.
- Systems theory emphasizes the interactions of genes, child-rearing practices, and culture, as in the development of temperamental traits and in the proximal or distal approach to parenting.

The Development of Social Bonds

All the theories of development agree that healthy human development depends on social connections. Chapter 3 provides numerous examples of the importance of social bonds, including the abnormal behavior of emotionally deprived Romanian orphans and the social exchanges required for language learning. Emotions elicit social reactions; infants are happier and healthier when other people (especially their mothers) are nearby, showing happiness in response.

Now we look closely at infant–caregiver bonds, beginning with the overall "fit" between baby and caregiver. Then we focus specifically on three processes of social development: synchrony, attachment, and social referencing.

Goodness of Fit

Many studies show that the interaction between environmental influences and in-herited traits shapes behavior, particularly in the first years of life. Whatever their child's temperament, parents need to find a **goodness of fit**—that is, a temperamen-tal adjustment that allows smooth infant–caregiver interaction. With a good fit, par-ents of difficult babies build a close relationship; parents of exuberant, curious infants learn to protect them from harm; parents of slow-to-warm-up toddlers give them time to adjust.

goodness of fit
A similarity of temperament and values that produces a smooth interaction be-tween an individual and his or her social context, including family, school, and community.

THE PARENTS' ADJUSTMENT All the theories described in the preceding section note the power of infant wishes, ideas, and needs. In the early months, it is up to parents to do most of the adjusting. This is evident in the example of Kevin and his infant daughter:

> Kevin is a very active, outgoing person who loves to try new things. Today he takes his 11-month-old daughter, Tyra, to the park for the first time. Tyra is playing alone in the sandbox, when a group of toddlers joins her. At first, Tyra smiles and eagerly watches them play. But as the toddlers become more active and noisy, Tyra's smiles turn quickly to tears.
>   She . . . reaches for Kevin, who picks her up and comforts her. But then Kevin goes a step further. After Tyra calms down, Kevin gently encourages her to play near the other children. He sits at her side, talking and playing with her. Soon Tyra is slowly creeping closer to the group of toddlers, curiously watching their moves.
>
> *[Lerner & Dombro, 2004, p. 42]*

Tyra needed Kevin's reassurance to allay her fears and encourage her to stay in the sandbox with the older children.

In general, anxious children (i.e., those who are high in the Big Five trait of neuroticism) are more affected by their parents' responsiveness than are easygoing children (Pauli-Pott et al., 2004). Ineffective or harsh parenting *combined with* a nega-tive temperament is likely to create an antisocial, destructive child (Cicchetti et al., 2007). Some children naturally cope with life's challenges; others do not.

ESPECIALLY FOR Nurses Parents come to you with their fussy 3-month-old. They say they have read that tempera-ment is "fixed" before birth, and they are worried that their child will always be difficult. What do you tell them? (see response, page 141) ➞

Strolling in the Park These three British fathers are sharing a bonding experience that is valuable for both themselves and their infants.

OBSERVATION QUIZ
Which of these three carriages is best for encouraging language develop-ment? (see answer, page 141) ➞

IT'S NOT ALL GENETIC In general, most develop-mentalists emphasize the interaction between inherited traits and parental behavior (Kagan & Fox, 2006). The discussion in Chapter 1 about the research on the MAOA gene and violence touched on this point: Parents must first understand their child and then pro-vide guidance so that inborn traits are expressed con-structively, not destructively. Thus, for example, a parent can help when "a shy child must control his or her fear and approach a stranger, and an impulsive child must constrain his or her desire and resist a temptation" (Derryberry et al., 2003, p. 1061).

Many developmentalists have long warned against blaming mothers for everything that goes wrong with their children. Now they caution against placing too much emphasis on genes, especially in infancy, because observations suggest that parenting style influences the

GETTY IMAGES

infant's behavior as much as or more than temperament does (Roisman & Fraley, 2006). What is needed is an awareness that both nature and nurture are involved.

Remember that inborn temperament is evident in brain activity in the first weeks of life, and it influences behavior from childhood through old age (Kagan & Fox, 2006). It is a mistake to emphasize parental influence too much or too little; child-rearing practices and genetic inheritance are both influential in the shaping of infants' behavior.

Synchrony

synchrony
A coordinated, rapid, and smooth exchange of responses between a caregiver and an infant.

Synchrony is a coordinated interaction between caregiver and infant, an exchange in which they respond to each other with split-second timing. Synchrony has been described as the meshing of a finely tuned machine (C. E. Snow, 1984), the emotional "attunement" of an improvised musical duet (Stern, 1985), and a smoothly flowing "waltz" (Barnard & Martell, 1995).

Learning Emotions Infants respond to their parents' expressions and actions. If the moments shown here are typical, one young man will be happy and outgoing and the other will be sad and quiet.

OBSERVATION QUIZ

For the pair at the top, where are their feet? (see answer, page 142) ➞

IN THE FIRST FEW MONTHS Synchrony between infant and parent becomes more frequent and more elaborate as time goes on; a 6-month-old is a more responsive social partner than a 3-month-old (Feldman, 2007). Parents and infants average about an hour a day in face-to-face play, although variations are apparent from baby to baby, from time period to time period, and from culture to culture.

Detailed research in the United States reveals the mutuality of the interaction: Adults rarely smile at newborns until the infants smile at them, at which point adults grin broadly and talk animatedly (Lavelli & Fogel, 2005). The elation that adults feel when their own infant smiles at them is evident not only in the adults' smiles but also in their brain activity, according to brain scans of 28 mothers looking at photos of their babies and of other babies the same age (Strathearn et al., 2008).

Each baby has a unique temperament and style, and parents learn to be sensitive to their particular infant (Feldman & Eidelman, 2005). Through synchrony, infants learn to read others' emotions and to develop the skills of social interaction, such as taking turns and paying attention.

Although infants imitate adults, synchrony usually begins with parents imitating infants (Lavelli & Fogel, 2005). When parents detect an emotion from an infant's facial expressions and body motions and then respond, the infant learns to connect an internal state with an external expression (Rochat, 2001). Such sensitive parenting is particularly apparent in Asian cultures, which place a high value on interpersonal sensitivity (Morelli & Rothbaum, 2007).

To see how synchrony develops, suppose that an infant is unhappy. An adult who mirrors the distress and then tries to solve the problem will teach that unhappiness is a valid emotion that can be relieved. An adult who always reacts to unhappiness by feeding the infant teaches the destructive lesson that food is the only source of comfort. But if an adult's response is more nuanced (differentiating hunger, pain, boredom, or fear and responding appropriately to each), then the infant will learn that there are varied reasons for unhappiness and many ways of responding.

WHEN SYNCHRONY DISAPPEARS Is synchrony needed for normal development? If no one plays with an infant, how will that infant develop? Experiments using the **still-face technique** have addressed these questions (Tronick, 1989; Tronick & Weinberg, 1997). An infant is placed facing his or her mother, who plays with the baby while two video cameras record each partner's reactions.

Frame-by-frame analysis typically reveals that mothers synchronize their responses to the infants' movements, usually with exaggerated tone and expression, and the babies reciprocate with smiles and waving arms. Then, in the still-face experiments, the mother erases all facial expression and stares with a "still face" for a minute or two. Sometimes by 2 months, and clearly by 6 months, babies are very upset by the still face.

This experiment has been done with mothers, fathers, and strangers. The babies are upset by the still face no matter who their partner is, but they are especially upset if their parents stop reacting. Many signs of stress are evident: Babies frown, fuss, drool, look away, kick, cry, or suck their fingers.

Interestingly, infants are much more upset when the parent presents a still face to them than when a parent leaves the room for a minute or two (Rochat, 2001). From a psychological perspective, this reaction is healthy: It shows that "by 2 to 3 months of age, infants have begun to expect that people will respond positively to their initiatives" (R. A. Thompson, 2006, p. 29).

Many research studies lead to the same conclusion: A parent's responsiveness to an infant aids development, measured not only psychosocially but also biologically—by heart rate, weight gain, and brain maturation (Moore & Calkins, 2004). Much depends on the particular parent. Some rarely play with their infants, which slows down development (A. C. Huston & Aronson, 2005). Infants' brains need social interaction—an essential, expected stimulant—to develop to their fullest.

Attachment

Toward the end of the first year, face-to-face play almost disappears. Once infants can move around and explore, they are no longer content to stay in one spot and follow an adult's facial expressions and vocalizations. Remember that, at about 12 months, most infants have begun to walk and talk, so the rhythms of their social interaction change (Jaffee et al., 2001). At this time another connection, called *attachment,* overtakes synchrony.

Attachment is a lasting emotional bond that one person has with another. Attachments begin to form in early infancy, are evident by 8 months, solidify by age 1, and influence a person's close relationships throughout life (see Table 4.3). In fact, attachment theory holds that adults' attachment to their parents, formed decades earlier in childhood, affects how they act with their own children. Babies learn how to relate to people, and those lessons echo lifelong (Grossmann et al., 2005; Kline, 2008; Sroufe et al., 2005).

When two people are attached, they respond to each other through *proximity-seeking behaviors* (e.g., when an infant approaches and follows a caregiver) and through *contact-maintaining behaviors* (e.g., touching, snuggling, and holding). A securely attached toddler is curious and eager to explore but maintains contact by occasionally looking back at the caregiver. A securely attached adult might phone home regularly or greet a parent with a warm hug.

Caregivers show attachment as well. They keep a watchful eye on their baby and respond to vocalizations, expressions, and gestures. For example, many mothers or fathers, awakening in the middle of the night, tiptoe to the crib to gaze fondly at their sleeping infant. During the day, many parents instinctively smooth their toddler's hair or caress their child's hand or cheek.

still-face technique
An experimental practice in which an adult keeps his or her face unmoving and expressionless in face-to-face interaction with an infant.

RESPONSE FOR Nurses (from page 139) It's too soon to tell. Temperament is not truly "fixed" but variable, especially in the first few months. Many "difficult" infants become happy, successful adolescents and adults. ●

attachment
According to Ainsworth, "an affectional tie" that an infant forms with a caregiver—a tie that binds them together in space and endures over time.

ANSWER TO OBSERVATION QUIZ
(from page 139) The one at left, which allows the father and baby to face each other. The models in which the baby faces forward give the baby more to look at, so you might think they would stimulate vocabulary building; but the "toward-facing" one permits more social interaction, which stimulates brain development—which, in turn, promotes language learning. ●

TABLE 4.3 AT ABOUT THIS TIME: Stages of Attachment

Age	Characteristics
Birth to 6 weeks	*Preattachment.* Newborns signal, via crying and body movements, that they need others. When people respond positively, the newborn is comforted and learns to seek more interaction. Newborns are also primed by brain patterns to recognize familiar voices and faces.
6 weeks to 8 months	*Attachment in the making.* Infants respond preferentially to familiar people by smiling, laughing, babbling. Their caregivers' voices, touch, expressions, and gestures are comforting, often overriding the impulse to cry. Trust (Erikson) develops.
8 months to 2 years	*Classic secure attachment.* Infants greet the primary caregiver, show separation anxiety when the caregiver leaves, play happily when the caregiver is present. Both infant and caregiver seek to be close to each other (proximity) and frequently look at each other (contact). In many caregiver–infant pairs, physical touch (patting, holding, caressing) is frequent.
2 to 6 years	*Attachment as launching pad.* Young children seek their caregiver's praise and reassurance as their social world expands. Interactive conversations and games (hide-and-seek, object play, reading, pretending) are common. Children expect caregivers to comfort and entertain.
6 to 12 years	*Mutual attachment.* Children seek to make their caregivers proud by learning what adults want them to learn, and adults reciprocate. In concrete operational thought (Piaget), specific accomplishments are valued by adults and children.
12 to 18 years	*New attachment figures.* Teenagers explore and make friendships on their own, using their working models of earlier attachments as a base. With more advanced, formal operational thinking (Piaget), physical contact is less important; shared ideals and goals are more influential.
18 years on	*Attachment revisited.* Adults develop relationships with others, especially romantic partnerships and parent–child relationships, that are influenced by earlier attachment patterns. Earlier caregivers continue to be supportive, and adults continue to seek their praise, but they are no longer the prime object of attachment. Past insecure attachments can be repaired, although this does not always happen.

Source: Adapted from Grobman, 2008.

Lifelong Bonds Although attachment is traditionally measured at about age 1 via the Strange Situation, it builds from the first days of life and remains apparent in adulthood.

ANSWER TO OBSERVATION QUIZ
(from page 140) The father uses his legs and feet to support his son at just the right distance for a great fatherly game of foot-kissing. ●

secure attachment
A relationship in which an infant obtains both comfort and confidence from the presence of his or her caregiver.

Over humanity's evolutionary history, various proximity-seeking and contact-maintaining behaviors have contributed to the survival of the species. Attachment keeps toddlers nearby, caregivers vigilant, and people of all ages secure.

SECURE AND INSECURE ATTACHMENT The concept of attachment was originally developed by John Bowlby (1969, 1973, 1988), a British developmentalist influenced by both psychoanalytic theory and ethology (the study of other animals). Inspired by Bowlby's work, Mary Ainsworth, then a young American graduate student, studied the relationship between parents and infants in Uganda (Ainsworth, 1973).

Ainsworth discovered that most infants develop special attachments to their caregivers, although there are cultural differences in expression and style (IJzendoorn et al., 2006). (Ugandan mothers almost never kiss their infants; many U.S. parents kiss their babies frequently.) In every culture, Ainsworth found some infants more securely attached than others. Scientists have confirmed this variability in many cultures (Cassidy & Shaver, 1999; Grossmann et al., 2005; Sroufe, 2005; R. A. Thompson, 2006).

Attachment is classified into four types, labeled A, B, C, and D (see Table 4.4). Infants with **secure attachment** (type B) feel comfortable and confident. They are comforted by closeness to the caregiver, which provides confidence to explore. The caregiver becomes a *base for exploration,* giving assurance that it is safe to venture forth. A toddler might, for example, scramble down from the caregiver's lap to play with a toy but periodically look back, vocalize a few syllables, and return for a hug.

TABLE 4.4 Patterns of Infant Attachment

Type	Name of Pattern	In Play Room	Mother Leaves	Mother Returns	Toddlers in Category (percent)
A	Insecure-avoidant	Child plays happily	Child continues playing	Child ignores her	10–20
B	Secure	Child plays happily	Child pauses, is not as happy	Child welcomes her, returns to play	50–70
C	Insecure-resistant/ambivalent	Child clings, is preoccupied with mother	Child is unhappy, may stop playing	Child is angry; may cry, hit mother, cling	10–20
D	Disorganized	Child is cautious	Child may stare or yell; looks scared, confused	Child acts oddly—may freeze, scream, hit self, throw things	5–10

By contrast, insecure attachment is characterized by fear, anxiety, anger, or indifference. Insecurely attached children have less confidence. Some play independently without maintaining contact with the caregiver; this is **insecure-avoidant attachment** (type A). By contrast, an insecure child might be unwilling to leave the caregiver's lap; this is **insecure-resistant/ambivalent attachment** (type C).

The fourth category (type D) is **disorganized attachment;** it has elements of the other types but is clearly different from them. Type D infants may shift from hitting to kissing their mothers, from staring blankly to crying hysterically, from pinching themselves to freezing in place.

About two-thirds of all infants are securely attached (type B). Their caregiver's presence gives them courage to explore. A caregiver's departure may cause distress; the caregiver's return elicits positive social contact (such as smiling or hugging) and then more playing. A balanced reaction—being concerned about the caregiver's departure but not overwhelmed by it—reflects secure attachment. Almost one-third of infants are insecure, either indifferent (type A) or unduly anxious (type C).

About 5 to 10 percent of infants fit into none of these categories and are classified as disorganized (type D). Children who are classified as type D may be prevented by their disorganization from developing an effective strategy for social interaction (even an avoidant or resistant one, type A or C). Instead they may become hostile and aggressive, difficult for anyone to relate to (Lyons-Ruth et al., 1999). (Many of the Romanian children who were adopted after age 2, as described in Chapter 2, were type D.)

MEASURING ATTACHMENT Ainsworth (1973) developed a now-classic laboratory procedure, called the **Strange Situation,** to measure attachment. In a well-equipped playroom, an infant is closely observed for eight episodes, each lasting three minutes.

First, the child and a caregiver are together. Then, according to a set sequence, a stranger or the caregiver enters or leaves the playroom. Infants' responses indicate which type of attachment they have formed to their caregivers. (Reactions to the caregiver indicate the type of attachment; reactions to the stranger are influenced more by temperament than by affection.) For research purposes, observers are carefully trained and are certified when they can clearly distinguish among attachment types. The key behaviors they focus on are the following:

- *Exploration of the toys.* A secure toddler plays happily.
- *Reaction to the caregiver's departure.* A secure toddler misses the caregiver.
- *Reaction to the caregiver's return.* A secure toddler welcomes the caregiver's reappearance.

insecure-avoidant attachment
A pattern of attachment in which an infant avoids connection with the caregiver, as when the infant seems not to care about the caregiver's presence, departure, or return.

insecure-resistant/ambivalent attachment
A pattern of attachment in which an infant's anxiety and uncertainty are evident, as when the infant becomes very upset at separation from the caregiver and both resists and seeks contact on reunion.

disorganized attachment
A type of attachment that is marked by an infant's inconsistent reactions to the caregiver's departure and return.

Strange Situation
A laboratory procedure for measuring attachment by evoking infants' reactions to the stress of various adults' comings and goings in an unfamiliar playroom.

(a)   (b)   (c)

ALL: COURTESY OF MARY AINSWORTH

The Attachment Experiment In this episode of the Strange Situation, Brian shows every sign of secure attachment. (a) He explores the playroom happily when his mother is present; (b) he cries when she leaves; and (c) he is readily comforted when she returns.

Attachment is not always measured by using the Strange Situation, especially when researchers want to study a large number of infants (Andreassen & West, 2007). Sometimes parents sort out 90 cards with questions about their children's characteristics, and sometimes they are interviewed extensively (according to a detailed protocol) about their relationships with their own parents.

CHANGES IN ATTACHMENT STATUS Early researchers expected secure attachment to "predict all the outcomes reasonably expected from a well-functioning personality" (R. A. Thompson & Raikes, 2003, p. 708). But this turned out not to be the case. Securely attached infants *are* more likely to become secure toddlers, socially competent preschoolers, academically skilled schoolchildren, and capable parents (R. A. Thompson, 2006). Many aspects of good parenting, including synchrony, generally correlate with secure attachment (see Table 4.5).

However, the type of attachment may change if family circumstances change. Temperament and age may also affect attachment. Many children shift in attachment

---

TABLE 4.5 General Predictors of Attachment Type

Secure attachment (type B) is more likely if:

- The parent is usually sensitive and responsive to the infant's needs.
- The infant–parent relationship is high in synchrony.
- The infant's temperament is "easy."
- The parents are not stressed about income, other children, or their marriage.
- The parents have a working model of secure attachment to their own parents.

Insecure attachment is more likely if:

- The parent mistreats the child. (Neglect increases type A; abuse increases types C and D.)
- The mother is mentally ill. (Paranoia increases type D; depression increases type C.)
- The parents are highly stressed about income, other children, or their marriage. (Parental stress increases types A and D.)
- The parents are intrusive and controlling. (Parental domination increases type A.)
- The parents are active alcoholics. (Alcoholic father increases type A; alcoholic mother increases type D.)
- The child's temperament is "difficult." (Difficult children tend to be type C.)
- The child's temperament is "slow to warm up." (This correlates with type A.)

status between one age and another (NICHD Early Child Care Research Network, 2001; Seifer et al., 2004), and personality does not always flow from the first attachments.

Social Referencing

Infants want to know adults' emotions. At about age 1, **social referencing** becomes evident as a child begins to look to another person for clarification or information, much as a student might consult a dictionary or other reference work. A glance of reassurance or words of caution, an expression of alarm, pleasure, or dismay—each becomes a social guide, telling toddlers how to react.

After age 1, when infants reach the stage of active exploration (Piaget) and the crisis of autonomy versus shame and doubt (Erikson), their need to consult others becomes especially urgent. As they move from one attractive object to another, toddlers search adult gazes and facial expressions for clues to appropriate behavior. They pay close attention to expressed emotions and watch carefully to detect intentions that explain other people's actions.

Social referencing has many practical applications. Consider mealtime. Caregivers the world over smack their lips, pretend to taste, and say "yum," encouraging toddlers to eat and enjoy their first taste of beets, liver, or spinach. For their part, toddlers become astute at reading expressions, insisting on eating only the foods that the adults *really* like. Through this process, children in some cultures develop a taste for raw fish or curried goat or smelly cheese—foods that children in other cultures refuse.

Most everyday instances of social referencing occur with mothers. Infants usually adopt their mother's attitude, as expressed in vocal tone and facial expression. The baby on the subway at the beginning of this chapter did not cry, probably because the mother was calm and confident as she handed the baby to me.

The fact that toddlers look to their parents for clues about how to react does not mean that infants are always obedient, especially in cultures where parents and children value independence. One such culture is that of the United States, where compliance and disobedience have been the focus of study.

In one U.S. experiment, most toddlers did not obey their mother's request (prompted by the researchers) to pick up dozens of toys that they had not scattered (Kochanska et al., 2001). Their refusal indicated that their self-awareness had led to pride and autonomy.

These same toddlers, however, were quite obedient when their mothers told them not to touch an attractive toy. The mothers used tone, expression, and words to make this prohibition clear. Because of social referencing, toddlers understood the message. Even when the mothers were out of sight, half of the 14-month-olds and virtually all of the 22-month-olds obeyed. Most (80 percent) of the older toddlers seemed to agree with the mothers' judgment, a trait called *committed compliance* (Kochanska et al., 2001).

Overall, mothers use a variety of expressions, vocalizations, and gestures to convey social information, and infants rely on them. For example, babies reflect their mother's anxiety about strangers (de Rosnay et al.,

social referencing
Seeking information about how to react to an unfamiliar or ambiguous object or event by observing someone else's expressions and reactions. That other person becomes a *social reference.*

Whose Smile to Believe? Logically, the doctor is the one to watch: She has the stethoscope, and she is closer. But this baby references her mother, as any securely attached 1-year-old would.

MICHAEL MALYSZKO / GETTY IMAGES

2006) and use their mother's cues to understand the difference between real and pretend eating (Nishida & Lillard, 2007).

Mothers are not the only or even necessarily the best social references. During toddlerhood, strangers are sometimes consulted more than mothers, especially about the suitability of toys that the mother has not seen (Stenberg & Hagekull, 2007; Walden & Kim, 2005).

FATHERS AS SOCIAL PARTNERS In most nations and ethnic groups, fathers spend much less time with infants than mothers do and are less involved parents (Parke & Buriel, 2006; Tudge, 2008). Indeed, when families around the world are compared, only Brazilian fathers are as actively engaged with their infants as mothers are (Tudge, 2008). Although fathers' own ideas of appropriate male behavior are one reason for this lack of involvement, mothers often act as gatekeepers, limiting fathers' interactions with their children in the stereotyped belief that child care is the special domain of mothers (Gaertner et al., 2007).

A related stereotype holds that Latino fathers are too *macho*—too assertively masculine—to be interested in child care. Several studies have refuted this view, however, showing that Hispanic American fathers tend to be more involved with daily child care than are fathers in other U.S. ethnic groups (Parke, 2002).

A study of more than 1,000 Latino 9-month-olds found "fathers with moderate to high levels of engagement" (Cabrera et al., 2006, p. 1203). Although this study analyzed many possible correlates of paternal involvement (including income, education, and age), only one significant predictor of the level of engagement was found: how happy the father was with the infant's mother. Happier husbands tend to be more involved fathers.

COMPARING FATHERS AND MOTHERS All the available evidence confirms that fathers can do much to enhance their children's social and emotional development. Fathers can read their infant's emotions and respond with synchrony, often provoking more laughter than the mothers do. Some research finds that fathers are particularly adept at helping children modulate their anger. For instance, teenagers are less likely to lash out at friends and authorities if, as infants, they experienced a warm, responsive relationship with their fathers (Trautmann-Villalba et al., 2006).

Infants may be equally securely attached to both parents, more attached to their mothers, or more attached to their fathers (Belsky et al., 2006). Close father–infant relationships can teach infants (especially boys) appropriate expressions of emotion (Boyce et al., 2006). The influence is mutual; close relationships with their infants reduce fathers' risk of depression (Borke et al., 2007; Bronte-Tinkew et al., 2007).

Some research finds that fathers encourage infants to explore, whereas mothers tend be more cautious and protective. According to several studies, "Mothers engage in more caregiving and comforting, and fathers in more high-intensity play" (Kochanska et al., 2008, p. 41).

When toddlers are about to explore, they often seek their father's approval, expecting fun from their fathers and comfort from their mothers (Lamb, 2000). In this, infants show social intelligence, because fathers play imaginative and exciting games. They move their infant's legs and arms in imitation of walking, kicking, or climbing; or play "airplane," zooming the baby through the air; or tap and tickle the baby's stomach. Mothers caress, murmur, read, or sing soothingly; combine play with caretaking; and use standard sequences such as peek-a-boo and patty-cake. In short, fathers are more proximal when it comes to stimulating body play.

Up, Up, and Away! The vigorous play typical of fathers is likely to help in the infant's mastery of motor skills and the development of muscle control. (Of course, fathers must be careful not to harm fragile bones and developing brains.)

CHROMOSOHM / SOHM / PHOTO RESEARCHERS, INC.

Infant Day Care

You have seen that social bonds are crucial for infants. Worldwide, most infants are cared for primarily by their mothers, with many of the rest cared for by relatives, typically grandmothers. On average, only about 15 percent of infants under age 2 receive care from a nonrelative who is both paid and trained to provide it (Melhuish & Petrogiannis, 2006).

INTERNATIONAL COMPARISONS The percentage of infants in day care varies markedly from nation to nation (Melhuish & Petrogiannis, 2006). Infant day care outside the home by strangers is common in France, Israel, and Sweden, where it is heavily subsidized by the government, but it is very scarce in India, Ethiopia, and most Latin American nations, where it is not subsidized.

In Canada, 70 percent of all children are cared for exclusively by their mothers in their first year, but in the United States, almost 80 percent are cared for by someone else (often the father) as well (S. M. Côté et al., 2008). One reason for this difference is that Canada provides financial support for new mothers, so more of them can afford to take time off from work to care for their babies (S. M. Côté et al., 2008).

Obviously, political and cultural values affect whether or not a mother provides exclusive care for her infant. People in some cultures believe that such exclusive care is beneficial, while those in other cultures prefer that infants have several caregivers. Which of these ethnotheories is correct? As you will soon learn, the effects of nonmaternal care are difficult to assess, partly because cultural and economic factors affect the quality of that care.

A large study in England found that fewer than half the infants were cared for exclusively by their mothers, but almost half of those in nonmaternal care (44 percent) were cared for by their grandmothers. Overall, this study found that infants in nonmaternal care were more likely to be emotionally immature later on—but that may be because the mothers of such infants tended to be young and poor. Youth and poverty correlate with children's behavioral problems no matter who the caregiver is (Fergusson et al., 2008).

It is not surprising that young, poor mothers relied on their own mothers for help with their babies; it is impossible to know how those children would have developed if they were cared for exclusively by their mothers—they might have been worse off, or they might have been better off.

Possible confounding factors occur whenever nonmaternal care is compared with maternal care. For obvious reasons, it would be unethical to force one mother of an infant to stay home and another to hold down a full-time job, so a valid comparison between an experimental group and a control group is impossible.

TYPES OF NONRELATIVE CARE More than half of all 1-year-olds in the United States are in "regularly scheduled" nonmaternal care (Loeb et al., 2004). Often a relative provides this care, which varies in quality and availability.

Another option is **family day care,** in which children are cared for in the home of a nonrelative. It is called "family" care because a relatively small group of young children of many ages are together, as siblings once were in large families. Family day care may be problematic for infants and toddlers because they get less attention than older children and are sometimes picked on by them (Kryzer et al., 2007).

A better option may be **center day care,** in which several paid adults care for many children in a place especially designed for the purpose. Most day-care centers group children by age, so infants and toddlers are separated from older children. Quality varies in such places, as do the laws that set standards.

In the United States, parents generally encounter a "mix of quality, price, type of care, and government subsidies" (Haskins, 2005, p. 168). Some center care is excellent

● **UNDERSTANDING THE NUMBERS**
How would you express the odds of a U.S. infant receiving nonmaternal care?

Answer A calculation of odds is always a comparison. Compared with Canadian infants, the odds are 80/30 = 2.7. Compared with a U.S. infant who receives maternal care exclusively, the odds are 80/20 = 4.0.

family day care
Child care that includes several children of various ages and usually occurs in the home of a woman who is paid to provide it.

center day care
Child care that occurs in a place especially designed for the purpose, where several paid adults care for many children. Usually the children are grouped by age, the day-care center is licensed, and providers are trained and certified in child development.

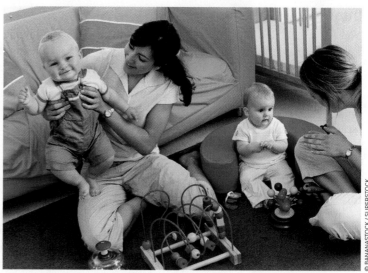

Fortunate Babies Center day care can be wonderful when it includes one-on-one care by trained professionals, as well as age-appropriate toys and furniture. Note that these caregivers are dressed for work—with bare feet.

OBSERVATION QUIZ

How old are these two babies? (see answer, page 150) →

(see Table 4.6), with adequate space, appropriate equipment, trained providers, and a ratio of two adults to five infants or better (de Schipper et al., 2006). Such care is hard to find, however. It is also quite expensive, so the families that use it are likely to have higher-than-average incomes. In some other nations where governments provide adequate funding, families at all income levels use center care.

THE EFFECTS OF INFANT DAY CARE The evidence is overwhelming that good preschool education (reviewed in Chapter 5) is beneficial for young children. However, when it comes to infant day care, "disagreements about the wisdom (indeed, the morality) of nonmaternal child care for the very young remain" (NICHD, 2005, p. xiv). Research that would resolve these disagreements is thwarted by the impossibility of randomly assigning infants to various kinds of care.

Nevertheless, it is apparent that the quality of day care varies because caregivers look after different numbers of infants and have received different types and amounts

---

TABLE 4.6 High-Quality Day Care: What to Look For

High-quality day care during infancy has five essential characteristics:

1. *Adequate attention to each infant.* This means a low caregiver-to-infant ratio (such as two reliable adults and five infants) and, probably even more important, a small group of infants. Infants need familiar, loving caregivers; continuity of care is crucial.

2. *Encouragement of language and sensorimotor development.* Infants should receive extensive language exposure through games, songs, conversations, and positive talk of all kinds, along with easily manipulated toys.

3. *Attention to health and safety.* Good signs are cleanliness routines (e.g., handwashing before meals), accident prevention (e.g., no small objects that could be swallowed), and safe areas to explore (e.g., a clean, padded area for movement).

4. *Well-trained and professional caregivers.* Ideally, every caregiver should have a degree or certificate in early-childhood education and should have worked with children for several years. Turnover should be low, morale high, and enthusiasm evident. Good caregivers love their children and their work.

5. *Warm and responsive caregivers.* Providers should engage the children in problem solving and discussions, rather than giving instructions. Quiet, obedient children may be an indication of unresponsive care.

For a more detailed evaluation of day care, see the checklist in NICHD, 2005.

of training (Waldfogel, 2006). Additional crucial variables are the responsiveness of mothers, grandmothers, and other caregivers and the temperaments of the infants involved.

A large study in Canada found that of the 30 percent of infants who were cared for by someone other than their mothers (usually relatives), boys from high-income families fared less well in nonmaternal care than other boys did (S. M. Côté et al., 2008). By age 4, they were slightly more likely to be aggressive and to have emotional problems (e.g., a teacher might note that a boy "seems unhappy").

In contrast, Canadian boys from low-income families actually benefited from nonmaternal care. This study found no differential effects of nonmaternal care in girls. The researchers insist that no policy implications can be derived from their findings, partly because care varied so much in quality, location, and provider (S. M. Côté et al., 2008).

In the United States, an ongoing longitudinal study by the Early Child Care Network of the National Institute of Child Health and Human Development (NICHD) has followed the development of more than 1,300 children from birth to age 11 (NICHD, 2005). It has found many cognitive benefits of infant day care, especially in language.

The social consequences are not as clear, but most analyses of the data found that secure attachment to the mother was as common among infants in center care as among infants cared for at home. Like other, smaller studies, the NICHD research confirms that infant day care, even for 40 hours a week before age 1, has much less influence on child development than does the warmth of the mother–infant relationship (NICHD, 2005).

The importance of the mother (even when she is employed full time) was evident in the NICHD study. Infant day care was correlated with later emotional problems *only* when the mother was insensitive *and* when the infant spent more than 20 hours a week in a poor-quality program, with too few caregivers who had too little training (NICHD, 2005).

This study found that boys were affected more than girls were. Boys who received extensive nonmaternal care became more quarrelsome and had more conflicts with their teachers in later years than did other boys (NICHD, 2003b). No study has found that children of employed mothers develop emotional or other problems *solely* because their mothers are working outside the home.

On balance, it seems that most children are likely to benefit from their mothers' employment (Goldberg et al., 2008), perhaps because mothers who work outside the home have higher income and self-esteem, which affects the quality of their mothering. Many employed mothers make infant care their top priority and devote more nonwork hours to it than to housework, self-care, and entertainment.

A time-use study found that mothers who worked full time outside the home spent almost as much time playing with their babies (14½ hours a week) as did mothers without outside jobs (16 hours a week) (A. C. Huston & Aronson, 2005). To make more time for their babies, the employed mothers spent half as much time on housework, less time with their husbands, and almost no time on leisure. The study concludes:

> There was no evidence that mothers' time at work interfered with the quality of their relationship with their infants, the quality of the home environment, or children's development. In fact, the results suggest the opposite. Mothers who spent more time at work provided slightly higher quality home environments.
>
> [A. C. Huston & Aronson, 2005, p. 479]

ESPECIALLY FOR Day-Care Providers A mother who brings her child to you for day care says that she knows she is harming her baby, but economic necessity compels her to work. What do you say? (see response, page 150) ➡

ANN HEISENFELT / AP PHOTO

Secure Attachment Kirstie and her 10-month-old daughter Mia enjoy a moment of synchrony in an infant day-care center sponsored by a family-friendly employer, General Mills. High-quality day care and high-quality home care are equally likely to foster secure attachment between mother and infant.

● **FOR DEEPER REFLECTION** Why is infant day care still controversial, since the evidence in favor of preschool education is so strong?

It is not surprising, given the importance of synchrony, attachment, and social referencing, that infants cared for at home by a depressed mother fare worse than they would in center care (Loeb et al., 2004). Many studies find that out-of-home day care is better than in-home care if an infant's family does not provide adequate stimulation and attention (Ramey et al., 2002; Votruba-Drzal et al., 2004). The infant's temperament, the parents' ethnotheories, and the family income affect any type of care the infant receives (Crockenberg, 2003).

ANSWER TO OBSERVATION QUIZ
(from page 148) Definitely less than a year old, and perhaps even younger than 6 months. Remember that the average baby sits unsupported at 6 months and stands alone at 10 months; the support behind the baby at right and the position of the feet of the baby at left suggest they are both quite young. ●

> ## KEY Points
>
> - Humans are social creatures and need each other; this is true for infants as well as for parents. Synchrony begins in the early months, as infants and caregivers interact face-to-face.
> - Attachment is an emotional bond between people. Secure attachment allows learning to progress more smoothly and efficiently; insecurely attached infants are less confident and may develop emotional impairments.
> - Social referencing teaches infants whether new things are fearsome or fun.
> - The quality of infant care may be pivotal for development, whether it comes from mothers, fathers, other relatives, or professional providers. No single type of day care has proven to be best.

Conclusions in Theory and in Practice

You have seen in this chapter that the first two years of life are filled with psychosocial interactions, which result from genes, maturation, culture, and caregivers. All theorists and researchers agree that the first two years are crucial for a person's development: Early emotional and social development is influenced by the parents' behavior, the quality of care, cultural patterns, and inborn traits.

It has not been proven whether one positive influence, such as a good day-care center, can fully compensate for another, negative influence, such as a depressed mother (although parental influence is always significant). Multicultural research has identified a wide variety of child-rearing practices in different societies. The data imply that no single event (such as toilet training, in Freud's theory) determines emotional health.

RESPONSE FOR Day-Care Providers
(from page 149): Reassure the mother that you will keep her baby safe and will help to develop the baby's mind and social skills by fostering synchrony and attachment. Also tell her that the quality of mother–infant interaction at home is more important than anything else for psychosocial development; mothers who are employed full time usually have wonderful, secure relationships with their infants. If the mother wishes, you can discuss ways in which she can be a more responsive mother. ●

On the basis of what you have learned, you could safely advise parents to play with their infants; respond to their physical and emotional needs; let babies explore; maintain a relationship; and expect every toddler to be sometimes angry, sometimes proud, sometimes fearful. Depending on infant temperament, parental actions and attitudes may or may not have a powerful effect on later development, but they certainly can make infants happier or sadder.

Synchrony, attachment, and social referencing are crucial to infant and toddler development. Beyond that, especially for individual children who have problems, we need to be more specific. Jacob, the boy whose emotional development was impaired (as you read earlier in this chapter), was not yet talking at age 3. Looking at Table 4.7, which shows the approximate ages at which infants typically develop various characteristics and achievements, you can see that even at 3 months Jacob's reactions to familiar people had been unusual. All infants need one or two people who are emotionally invested in them from the first days of their lives, and Jacob may have had no one. There was no indication of synchrony or secure attachment in the relationship between Jacob and his parents.

TABLE 4.7 AT ABOUT THIS TIME: Infancy

Approximate Age	Characteristic or Achievement
3 months	Rolls over Laughs Stays half-upright in stroller Uses two eyes together Grabs for object; if rattle in hand, can shake it Makes cooing noises Joyous recognition of familiar people
6 months	Sits up, without adult support (but sometimes using arms) Grabs and grasps objects with whole hand Babbles, listens, and responds Tries to crawl (on belly, not yet on all fours) Stands and bounces with support (on someone's lap, in a bouncer) Begins to show anger, fear, attachment
12 months	Stands without holding on Crawls well Takes a few unsteady steps Uses fingers, including pincer grasp (thumb and forefinger) Can feed self with fingers Speaks a few words (*mama, dada, baba*) Strong attachment to familiar caregivers Apparent fear of strangers, of unexpected noises and events
18 months	Walks well Runs (also falls) Tries to climb on furniture Speaks 50–100 words; most are nouns Responds to requests Likes to drop things, throw things, take things apart Recognizes self in mirror
24 months	Runs well Climbs up (down is harder) Uses simple tools (spoon, large marker) Combines words (usually noun–verb, sometimes noun–verb–noun) Can use fingers to unscrew tops, open doors Interested in new experiences and new children

An Eventful Time This table lists aspects of development that have been discussed in Chapters 3 and 4. Throughout infancy, temperament and experience affect when and how babies display the characteristics and achievements listed here. The list is meant as a rough guideline, not as a yardstick for indicating a child's progress in intelligence or any other trait.

After Jacob was diagnosed with pervasive developmental disorder, his parents consulted a psychiatrist who specialized in children with psychosocial problems (Greenspan & Wieder, 2003). He showed them how to relate to Jacob, saying, "I am going to teach you how to play with your son." They learned about "floor time," four hours a day set aside to get on their son's level. They were to imitate him, act as if they were part of the game, put their faces and bodies in front of his, create synchrony even though Jacob did not initiate it. The father reports:

> We rebuilt Jacob's connection to us and to the world—but on his terms. We were drilled to always follow his lead, to always build on his initiative. In a sense, we could only ask Jacob to join our world if we were willing to enter his. . . . He would drop rocks and we would catch them. He would want to put pennies in a bank and we would block the slot. He would want to run in a circle and we would get in his way. I remember a cold fall day when I was putting lime on our lawn. He dipped his hand in the powder and let it slip through his fingers. He loved the way it felt. I took the lawn spreader and ran to the other part of our yard. He ran after me. I let him have one dip and ran across the yard again. He dipped, I ran, he dipped, I ran. We did this until I could no longer move my arms.
>
> *[Jacob's father, 1997, p. 62]*

Jacob's case is extreme, but many infants and parents have difficulty establishing synchrony (Feldman, 2007). From the perspective of early psychosocial development, nothing could be more important than a connection like the one Jacob and his parents gradually established.

> In Jacob's case it worked. He said his first word at age 3, and by age 5 . . . he speaks for days at a time. He talks from the moment he wakes up to the moment he falls asleep, as if he is making up for lost time. He wants to know everything. "How does a live chicken become an eating chicken? Why are microbes so small? Why do policemen wear badges? Why are dinosaurs extinct? What is French? [A question I often ask myself.] Why do ghosts glow in the dark?" He is not satisfied with answers that do not ring true or that do not satisfy his standards of clarity. He will keep on asking until he gets it. Rebecca and I have become expert definition providers. Just last week, we were faced with the ultimate challenge: "Dad," he asked: "Is God real or not?" And then, just to make it a bit more challenging, he added: "How do miracles happen?"
>
> [*Jacob's father, 1997, p. 63*]

● **FOR DEEPER REFLECTION** According to the evidence presented in this chapter, what would have happened if Jacob had been institutionalized at age 3, as some advisers recommended?

Miracles do not always happen. Children with pervasive developmental disorder usually require special care throughout childhood; Jacob may continue to need extra attention. Nevertheless, almost all infants, almost all the time, develop strong relationships with their close family members. The power of early psychosocial development to influence the person's entire life is obvious to every developmentalist and, it is hoped, to every reader of this text.

SUMMARY

Emotional Development

1. Two emotions, contentment and distress, appear as soon as an infant is born. Anger emerges with restriction and frustration, between 4 and 8 months of age, and becomes stronger by age 1.

2. Fear of something specific, including fear of strangers and fear of separation, appears toward the end of the first year.

3. In the second year, social awareness produces more selective fear, anger, and joy. As infants become increasingly self-aware at about 18 months, emotions—specifically, pride, shame, and affection—emerge that encourage an interface between the self and others.

4. Synesthesia (the tendency of one part of the brain to stimulate another) is apparent early in life. Self-recognition (in the mirror/rouge test) emerges at about 18 months.

5. Stress impedes early brain and emotional development. The specifics about which infants suffer damage, and in what ways, are not yet known.

Theories of Infant Psychosocial Development

6. Freud hypothesized about the mother's impact on oral and anal pleasure; Erikson emphasized trust and autonomy.

7. Behaviorists focus on learning: Parents teach their babies many things, including when to be fearful or joyful. Cognitive theory holds that infants develop working models based on their experiences.

8. Systems theory explores the interactions among biology, child-rearing practices, and culture over time. Temperament and personality show the effects of such interactions.

9. Ethnotheories shape infant emotions and traits so that they fit well within the culture. Some cultures encourage proximal parenting (more physical touch); others promote distal parenting (more talk and object play).

The Development of Social Bonds

10. Parental practices guide a child's emotions, either inhibiting or reinforcing them. Ideally, a good fit develops between the parents' actions and the child's personality.

11. Sometimes by 2 months, and clearly by 6 months, infants become more responsive and social. Synchrony begins, with moment-by-moment interaction between caregiver and infant.

12. Attachment, measured by the baby's reaction to the caregiver's presence, departure, and return in the Strange Situation, is crucial. Some infants seem indifferent (type A—insecure-avoidant) or overly dependent (type C—insecure-resistant/ambivalent) instead of secure (type B). Disorganized attachment (type D) is the most worrisome form.

13. As they play, toddlers engage in social referencing, looking to other people's facial expressions to detect what is frightening and what is enjoyable. Fathers are wonderful playmates for infants, often serving as social references in infants' learning about emotions and exploration.

14. The impact of nonmaternal care depends on many factors. Psychosocial characteristics, including secure attachment, are influenced more by the mother's warmth than by the number of hours spent in nonmaternal care. Quality of care is crucial, no matter who provides that care.

KEY TERMS

social smile (p. 124)
stranger wariness (p. 125)
separation anxiety (p. 125)
self-awareness (p. 126)
trust versus mistrust (p. 131)
autonomy versus shame and doubt (p. 131)
social learning (p. 132)

working model (p. 133)
ethnotheory (p. 133)
temperament (p. 134)
Big Five (p. 135)
proximal parenting (p. 136)
distal parenting (p. 136)
goodness of fit (p. 139)
synchrony (p. 140)

still-face technique (p. 141)
attachment (p. 141)
secure attachment (p. 142)
insecure-avoidant attachment (p. 143)
insecure-resistant/ambivalent attachment (p. 143)

disorganized attachment (p. 143)
Strange Situation (p. 143)
social referencing (p. 145)
family day care (p. 147)
center day care (p. 147)

KEY QUESTIONS

1. How would a sensitive parent respond to an infant's distress?

2. How do emotions in the second year of life differ from emotions in the first year?

3. What is known and unknown about the impact of brain maturation on emotional development?

4. What are the similarities between the psychoanalytic and the behaviorist theories of infant development?

5. How and why have parental approaches to toilet training changed over the past 100 years?

6. How might synchrony affect the development of emotions in the first year?

7. Attachments are said to be lifelong. Describe an adult who is insecurely attached and explain how infant attachment could be relevant.

8. How are infants affected by the involvement (or noninvolvement) of their fathers?

9. What are the advantages and disadvantages of three kinds of nonmaternal infant care: relatives, family day care, and center day care?

APPLICATIONS

1. One cultural factor influencing infant development is how infants are carried from place to place. Ask four mothers whose infants were born in each of the past four decades how they transported them—front or back carriers, facing out or in, strollers or carriages, in car seats or on mother's laps, and so on. Why did they choose the mode(s) they chose? What are their opinions and yours on how that cultural practice might affect infants' development?

2. Observe synchrony for three minutes. Ideally, ask the parent of an infant under 8 months of age to play with the infant. If no

infant is available, observe a pair of lovers as they converse. Note the sequence and timing of every facial expression, sound, and gesture of both partners.

3. Telephone several day-care centers to try to assess the quality of care they provide. Ask about such factors as adult–child ratio, group size, and training for caregivers of children of various ages. Is there a minimum age? If so, why was that age chosen? Analyze the answers, using Table 4.6 as a guide.

The First Two Years

BODY GROWTH AND SKILLS

Rapid physical growth
Weight triples in the first year

2-year-olds are half their adult height

Gross motor skills
Reflexes at birth

Nature and nurture affect timing

Cephalocaudal (from head lifting to running)

BRAIN MATURATION

Cortex and neurons
Dendrites and axons grow with experience

Face recognition improves

Sensory areas develop
Hearing is most developed; vision least

Sleep patterns
Less REM sleep

Longer, deeper sleep

Sensory deprivation

Too much stress

"HOW DO MIRACLES HAPPEN?"
FROM HELPLESS REFLEXES TO TALKING, RUNNING, PLAYING

EARLY COGNITION

Piaget: Sensorimotor intelligence
From reflexes to mental combinations

Object permanence and deferred imitation

Information processing
Sensations lead to perceptions

Memory advances

Child-directed speech (baby talk)

Rapid language development
Early sounds, gestures

12 months: First words (holophrases)

18 months: Two-word sentences

No one talks to the baby

Theories of language learning
Reinforcement

Maturation:
  Language acquisition device (LAD)

Social learning

Hybrid: Age and context

HEALTH PRACTICES

Immunization
Smallpox eliminated

Polio, measles, mumps rare

Herd immunity

Nutrition
Breast is best

Other foods added at 6 months

Malnutrition

Sudden Infant Death Syndrome (SIDS)

EMOTIONS: MATURATION AND CULTURE

Smiling and laughing

Fear and anger
Social fears at age 1 (separation, strangers)
Anger at restraint and at specific people

Self-awareness (18 months)
Mirror recognition
Jealousy, embarrassment

Depressed mother

THEORIES OF EARLY EMOTIONS

Psychoanalytic
Freud:
  Oral and anal
Erikson: Trust and autonomy

Behaviorism
Reinforcement of personality patterns

Systems
Inborn temperament
Proximal and distal parenting

Cognitive
Working models
Ethnotheories guide adults

Too much emphasis on early parenting

Not enough emphasis on early parenting

SOCIAL CONNECTIONS: GOODNESS OF FIT

Synchrony
Mutual interaction

Social referencing
Adults guide responses

Nonresponsive parenting

Attachment
Secure: Parent as base for exploration
Insecure: Too dependent or too indifferent
Disorganized: Odd or inconsistent response

KEY
■ Major topic
■ Related topic
■ Potential problem

CHAPTER 5

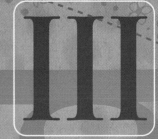

Early Childhood

From age 2 to 6, children spend most of their waking hours discovering, creating, laughing, and imagining as they acquire the skills they will need throughout life. They chase each other and attempt new challenges (developing their bodies); they play with sounds, words, and ideas (developing their minds); they invent games and dramatize fantasies (learning social skills and moral rules).

These years have been called the *preschool* (before school) *years,* but that has become a misnomer. School does not necessarily mean sitting at desks in rows. Many 2- to 6-year-olds are in a school of some sort, learning and playing.

These years have also been called the *play years.* The young child's delight in life seems magical—whether quietly tracking a beetle through the grass or riotously turning a bedroom into a shambles. Young children's minds seem playful, too; they explain that "a bald man has a barefoot head" or that "the sun shines so children can go outside to play." However, although young children do most of their learning as they play, playfulness is essential at every age.

Therefore, in these two chapters we use the more traditional term *early childhood* to refer to ages 2 to 6. Early childhood is a period of extraordinary growth, learning, and play—a joyful time not only for young children but also for anyone who knows them.

CHAPTER OUTLINE

EARLY CHILDHOOD
Body and Mind

In the early 1970s, when my daughter Bethany turned 3, I realized that she should no longer stay home with her younger sister all day. She was ready to make friends with other 3-year-olds, to paint and sculpt, and to advance her motor skills. Bethany was not ready for a traditional primary school (at 3, she would have been incapable of sitting quietly at a desk, practicing her penmanship), but she was ready for more formal education than she experienced at home.

I set out to visit various early-childhood programs, searching for the best one. Most were too impersonal, crowded, and standardized, unresponsive to the individuality of each child. I found one that seemed OK. Bethany and I were interviewed, and she was accepted. Then, as I was chatting with the director, Bethany took a comb from my handbag and sounded out "kuh, kuh, kuh, kome." I had been looking for a program that would appreciate Bethany's creativity, but at that moment I realized she also needed a program that would allow her to read. Most schools at that time either encouraged creativity or taught reading and math, not both.

I decided to unite with other idealistic young adults and start a better, more flexible preschool program. Bethany and Rachel both thrived in our school, and, yes, Bethany soon became both an avid reader and a creative artist.

As the director of our program, I learned a great deal about young children. Variability among our young students was dramatic. Some children were much more active, creative, or aggressive than others; some were painfully shy and others outright mean; some were very picky about what they ate, while others ate everything that was put before them. ●

- -

THIS CHAPTER DESCRIBES the many physical and intellectual accomplishments of children aged 2 to 6. As I discovered, and as the research confirms, learning is rapid and variability is marked—in eating, playing, and talking, as well as in many other characteristics.

The chapter also includes the crucial role of parents and communities in children's nutrition, brain growth, motor skills, speech, and other aspects of physical and cognitive development. It discusses various options for early-childhood education as well. Finally, we try to understand why and how families and communities sometimes fail young children. Neglect and abuse are far too common; some preventive efforts are successful.

MARCY MALOY / DIGITALVISION / GETTY IMAGES

Not Much Difference? The 6-year-old is only about a foot taller than her 2-year-old sister, and the width of their upper legs is almost the same. However, we perceive the older girl as much bigger than the younger one, because we notice proportions: The older girl's legs are almost twice as long, and they account for half her height.

Body Changes

Compared with cute and chubby 1-year-olds, 6-year-olds are quite mature. Their body proportions and motor skills are similar to those of adults.

Growth Patterns

During early childhood, children become slimmer as the lower body lengthens. Each year from age 2 through 6, well-nourished children add almost 3 inches (about 7 centimeters) in height and gain about 4½ pounds (2 kilograms).

A healthy 6-year-old:

- Weighs between 40 and 50 pounds (between 18 and 22 kilograms)
- Is at least 3½ feet tall (more than 100 centimeters)
- Looks lean, not chubby
- Has adultlike body proportions (legs constitute about half the total height)

The body mass index (BMI, the ratio of weight to height) is lower at age 5 than at any other age in the entire life span (Guillaume & Lissau, 2002). This is significant: Young children are meant to be relatively tall and thin, engaged in active play.

The child's center of gravity moves from the breastbone down to the belly button, enabling cartwheels and other motor skills that are beyond the toddler's ability. Indeed, 6-year-olds often can ride a bike, climb on cliffs, dive into deep water, and do many other things better than their parents. Later in this chapter, you will read about injury control and the need for adults to keep young children safe. But it is a child's poor judgment, not clumsiness resulting from poor balance or body proportions, that may lead to harm.

When comparing many ethnic groups that live in the same developed nation, statistics show that children of African descent tend to be tallest, followed by Europeans, Asians, and Latinos. However, size and shape differences are greater *within* groups than between groups. Height is especially variable among children of African heritage because they are more genetically diverse than are children whose ancestors came from other continents (Tishkoff et al., 2009).

Parents are understandably concerned when a child is unusually small. However, unless a medical deficiency leads to markedly slow growth, short children are as well adjusted socially as tall or average children (Sandberg et al., 2004). Although daily injections of growth hormones often add a few inches to height, pediatricians do not prescribe them unless laboratory tests confirm a severe deficiency (J. M. Lee & Menon, 2005).

If a child is genetically small, the parents should encourage everyone to respond to the child's level of maturity, not to his or her size. Certainly, no one should encourage growth by urging the child to overeat.

Nutrition

In past centuries, families protected children from famine by encouraging them to eat whenever food was available. Now such encouragement is destructive. Data from Brazil, for example, show that 40 years ago malnutrition was the primary food-related concern. In the twenty-first century, obesity is a more frequent problem (Monteiro et al., 2004).

Many parents do not realize that children—especially those who rarely run around outdoors—need far fewer calories per pound of body weight than infants do. Consequently, appetite tends to decrease in early childhood, causing parents to fret, threaten, and cajole their children into eating too much.

Children in low-income families are especially vulnerable to obesity because their cultures still guard against undernutrition and their parents may rely on fast foods, which are relatively cheap but high in calories and low in nutritional value. In the United States, Hispanic and Asian American immigrant grandparents are less often obese than the average grandparent, but their grandchildren are more often overweight than children with U.S.-born grandparents (L. M. Bates et al., 2008). Body weight increases as income falls, except in the very poorest countries. For example, the rate of overweight among low-income Brazilians is double the rate among wealthier ones (Monteiro et al., 2007).

In every nation, overfeeding is causing an epidemic of illnesses associated with obesity, such as heart disease and diabetes; poor nations have higher fatality rates from these diseases than do wealthier ones (Gluckman & Hanson, 2006a). An article in *Lancet* (the leading medical journal in England) has predicted that by 2020, more than 228 million adults worldwide will have diabetes as a result of unhealthy eating habits in childhood. This article suggests that "U.S. children could become the first generation in more than a century to have shorter life spans than their parents if current trends of excessive weight and obesity continue" (Devi, 2008, p. 105).

Public health experts encourage everyone to exercise regularly and to eat five to nine servings a day of fruits and vegetables. Few families do so. In order to avoid the health consequences of overweight, an increasing number of children in the United States take medicine to reduce blood pressure or to manage diabetes (see Table 5.1; Saul, 2008), another indication that overfeeding is becoming a major problem.

TABLE 5.1 Children with Prescriptions (per 1,000 Insured, Age 19 and Under)

Medication for . . .	2001	2004	2007	2001–2007 Change (percent)
Type 2 diabetes	0.48	0.78	1.20	+151.3
High blood pressure	7.03	7.76	8.32	+18.4
Cholesterol problems	0.62	0.67	0.70	+11.6

Source: Saul, 2008.

ESSENTIAL NUTRIENTS Many children's diets are deficient in iron, zinc, and calcium, but overconsuming even healthful items such as fruit juice and milk is discouraged. Doctors recommend no more than 6 ounces of juice and 24 ounces of milk per day and suggest that young children never drink cola or other sugary drinks (J. Collins et al., 2004).

Sweetened cereals and drinks are advertised as containing 100 percent of a day's recommended vitamins, but they also contain large quantities of sugar and may lack some nutrients that have not yet been identified. (Every few years, a new vitamin is discovered.) A varied diet of mostly fruits, grains, and vegetables, with modest amounts of protein (meat, fish, eggs) and dairy products (low-fat milk, yogurt), probably provides all dietary necessities (including fiber, fat, and unknown vitamins) and promotes health lifelong (Gluckman & Hanson, 2006a).

Unfortunately, many children want foods that are high in fat, salt, and sugar. Adults frequently give in, even rewarding children with candy. Traditions often reinforce these preferences. For example, birthday and holiday celebrations feature candy, cake, and other high-calorie, low-nutrition foods. In the United States, Halloween candy, Christmas candy, and Easter baskets are all outgrowths of Christian holidays that originally had nothing to do with such foods. Other nations and other religions have similar dietary customs.

No Spilled Milk This girl is demonstrating her mastery of the motor skills involved in pouring milk, to the evident admiration of her friend. The next skill will be drinking it—not a foregone conclusion, given the lactose intolerance of some children and the small appetites and notorious pickiness of children this age.

OBSERVATION QUIZ
What three things indicate that this attempt at pouring will probably be successful? (see answer, page 162) →

ORAL HEALTH Too much sugar and too little fiber rot the teeth. Tooth decay is the most common disease of young children in developed nations; it affects more than one-third of all children under age 6 in the United States (Brickhouse et al., 2008).

Primary "baby" teeth are replaced by permanent teeth between ages 6 and 10 (slightly earlier for girls than boys), but dental checkups should begin years earlier because decay in early childhood harms the permanent teeth (which are forming under the baby teeth). If severe, decay can cause malformation of the jaw, changing appearance and interfering with chewing and speaking lifelong.

Since malnutrition causes decay, gum bleeding, and delayed tooth growth, the state of a young child's mouth can alert adults to other health problems. National child health insurance covers oral health care in most developed nations (Brickhouse et al., 2008). The United States and Canada are exceptions, and many children in those countries never see a dentist because they have no private dental insurance. Parents may also avoid taking their children to the dentist because of memories of their own dental treatments. A study in San Francisco found that Chinese immigrants were particularly unlikely to obtain oral health exams for their children unless a problem had become obvious and painful (Hilton et al., 2007).

"JUST RIGHT" Another complication of early nutrition is that many young children are compulsive about daily routines, including meals. Some children insist on eating only certain foods, prepared and presented in a particular way. This rigidity, known as the "just-right" phenomenon, would be pathological in adults but is normal in children under age 6 (March et al., 2004). For example:

> Whereas parents may insist that the child eat his vegetables at dinner, the child may insist that the potatoes be placed only in a certain part of the plate and must not touch any other food; should the potatoes land outside of this area, the child may seem to experience a sense of near-contamination, setting off a tirade of fussiness for which many 2- and 3-year-olds are notorious.
>
> [*D. W. Evans et al., 1997*]

The just-right characteristic is evident in many aspects of young children's behavior. When 1,500 parents were surveyed about their 1- to 6-year-olds (D. W. Evans et al., 1997), their responses indicated that over 75 percent of the 3-year-olds (the peak age) evidenced some just-right tendency, in that they:

- Preferred to have things done in a particular order or in a certain way
- Had a strong preference to wear (or not wear) certain clothes
- Prepared for bedtime by engaging in a special activity, routine, or ritual
- Had strong preferences for certain foods

Most children will outgrow these behaviors (March et al., 2004). Meanwhile, the best response for parents may be patience. A young child's insistence on routine, on a preferred pair of shoes, or on a favorite cup can be tolerated until the child gets a little older. After all, many adults have preferred routines and improbable wishes themselves, although most keep them under control by employing some rational thought (D. W. Evans & Leckman, 2006).

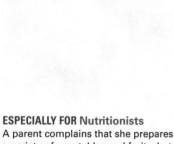

"I'm not hungry. I ate with Rover."

VAHAN SHIRVANIAN / CARTOONSTOCK

Motor Skills

Each month brings new abilities to young children as their brains and bodies mature. Unless something prevents them, they move in every way they can, developing all their gross and fine motor skills as they jump into lakes, unscrew bottle caps, crawl into holes, and do whatever else they can do—one reason adult supervision is needed.

PRACTICE AND MORE PRACTICE

Children develop all their motor skills spontaneously and diligently as they play. They run around, draw pictures, and create games by themselves and with others.

According to a study of children in Brazil, Kenya, and the United States (Tudge et al., 2006), young children spend most of their waking time in play. This is more than they spend in three other important activities (doing chores, learning lessons, or having conversations with adults) combined (see Figure 5.1).

By age 6, most North Americans ride tricycles; climb ladders; pump their legs on swings; and throw, catch, and kick balls. In some nations, 6-year-olds swim in the ocean, shoot wild animals, or climb mountains. Muscle growth, brain maturation, and guided practice advance every gross motor skill.

Fine motor skills, which involve small body movements (especially with hands and fingers), are harder to master. Pouring juice into a glass, cutting food with a knife and fork, and achieving anything more artful than a scribble with a pencil require muscular control, patience, and judgment that are beyond the ability of most young

The Joy of Climbing Would you delight in climbing on an unsteady rope swing, like this 6-year-old in Japan (and almost all his contemporaries worldwide)? Each age has special sources of pleasure.

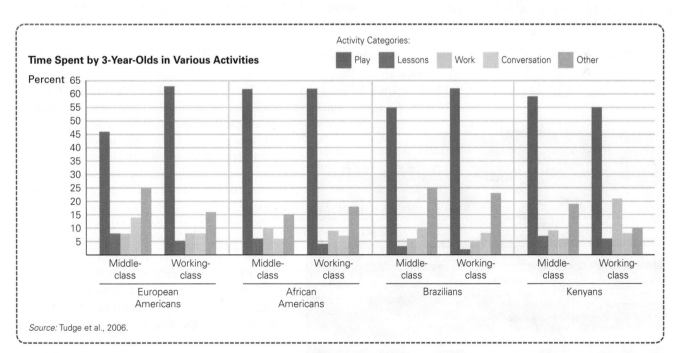

Time Spent by 3-Year-Olds in Various Activities

Activity Categories: Play | Lessons | Work | Conversation | Other

Source: Tudge et al., 2006.

FIGURE 5.1 Mostly Playing When researchers studied 3-year-olds in the United States, Brazil, and Kenya, they found that, on average, the children spent more than half their time playing. Note the low percentages of both middle- and working-class Brazilian children in the Lessons category, which included all intentional efforts to teach children something. There is a cultural explanation: Unlike parents in Kenya and the United States, most Brazilian parents believe that children of this age should not be in organized day care.

No Ears? (*a*) Elizabeth takes pride in drawing her family from memory. All have belly buttons and big smiles that reach their foreheads, but they have no arms or hair. (*b*) By age 6, this Virginia girl draws just one family member in detail—nostrils and mustache included.

(a)

(b)

LAURA DWIGHT

BLEND IMAGES / ALAMY

ESPECIALLY FOR Immigrant Parents You and your family eat with chopsticks at home, but you want your children to feel comfortable in Western culture. Should you change your family's eating customs? (see response, page 166) →

Exploring the Great Outdoors Two children climb over a rock outcrop in Shenandoah National Park in Virginia. Such outdoor play is important for the development of motor skills, even though many parents are tempted to try to keep their children safer by keeping them indoors.

JEFF GREENBERG / THE IMAGE WORKS

children. Again, each year adds practice and improves dexterity; many 6-year-olds are ready to read and write, not only using hand skills but also controlling eye movements—another fine motor skill.

ENVIRONMENTAL HAZARDS Environmental pollution sometimes interferes with the development of motor skills. A direct threat comes from toxins in the air, water, and food supply. All pollutants harm young, growing bodies more than they do older, developed ones. This is of particular concern for urban young children, who not only are more likely to breathe harmful substances but also have less opportunity to practice motor skills.

Much depends on local regulations. For example, Kolkata (Calcutta), India, a city of 14 million, has such extensive air pollution that childhood asthma rates are soaring and lung damage is prevalent. In Mumbai (Bombay), another Indian city, air pollution has been reduced and children's health improved through many laws, including one requiring that clean fuels be used in the city's huge fleet of buses (Bhattacharjee, 2008).

Crowded, violent streets not only impede development of gross motor skills but also add to the fear that comes naturally to young humans because of their immature brain development (more on that soon). Adults sometimes add to such fears. Gone are the days when parents told their children to go out and play, expecting them safely back when hunger, rain, or nightfall brought them home. Now parents—fearing strangers, automobiles, and stray animals—keep their children inside, perhaps watching television or playing video games and thus not developing gross motor skills.

The Need for Science Almost no research has been done on the long-term effects of children's exposure to air pollution and other environmental hazards. One team points out the need for "basic and applied research about the effects of pollutant exposures and ways to reduce children's pollutant burdens" (Dilworth-Bart & Moore, 2006, p. 264).

Most research on the dangers posed by various substances in the air and in food, milk, and water has been done on lower animals, not people. The animal studies raise the concern that hundreds of useful chemicals reduce growth and health of the body and particularly the brain, impeding balance, finger dexterity, and motivation.

A few substances—including lead in the water and air, pesticides in the soil or on clothing, bisphenol A (BPA) in plastic, and secondhand cigarette smoke—are known to impair young children's development. Even for these, it is not clear whether damage is universal. Perhaps high doses or genetic vulnerability must be present for damage to occur.

Lead Lead is one environmental hazard that *has* been thoroughly researched. Lead was widely used—as a pigment in paint and as an anti-knock additive in gasoline, for example—for many years. In the 1970s, it was proved that exposure to lead reduces intelligence and increases behavior problems in young children. In response, U.S. laws have banned the use of lead in paint and gasoline, and blood lead levels have dropped sharply. Some states (e.g., Colorado and Wyoming) report that the average level in children's blood is close to zero. In other states (e.g., Michigan and Ohio), however, average lead levels are still too high (MMWR, May 27, 2005; MMWR, December 22, 2000), probably because of residual lead from manufacturing.

Very high levels of lead (50 or more micrograms per deciliter of blood) can cause mental retardation and even death. However, experts do not agree about the threshold of danger or about all the consequences of exposure. As lead use is reduced, intelligence scores are rising in many nations, but there are dozens of possible explanations for that (Flynn, 2007). Crime rates among juveniles are falling in North America; the reduction of blood lead levels in young children may be the reason (Nevin, 2007) . . . or may not be.

Although more precision is needed, parents have nothing to lose by making sure their children consume enough calcium (which lowers lead levels); wiping window ledges clean (outdoor dust often contains lead); removing lead paint (sweet-tasting, and thus attractive to young children, and still present in some old buildings); and checking imported dishware, toys, and medicinal tonics for lead content (still permitted in some nations) (Dilworth-Bart & Moore, 2006).

RESPONSE FOR Nutritionists (from page 162) The nutritionally wise advice would be to offer only fruits, vegetables, and other nourishing, low-fat foods, counting on the child's eventual hunger to drive him or her to eat them. However, centuries of cultural custom make it almost impossible for parents to be wise in such cases. A physical checkup, with a blood test, may be warranted, to make sure the child is healthy. ●

KEY Points

- Children continue to grow rapidly during early childhood, adding more than 15 pounds and 10 inches from age 2 through 6.
- Many young children have strong preferences for what and how they eat, and many parents overfeed their children. Together, these factors lead to nutritional problems.
- Motor skills develop naturally as children enjoy active playmates and space to play, practicing the activities their culture encourages.
- Pollution in the environment affects early development in many ways; for example, lead and other toxins are harmful to the brain.

RESPONSE FOR Immigrant Parents
(from page 164) Children develop the
motor skills that they see and practice.
They will soon learn to use forks,
spoons, and knives. Do not abandon
chopsticks completely, because young
children can learn several ways of
doing things, and the ability to eat
with chopsticks is a social asset. ●

myelination
The process by which axons become
coated with myelin, a fatty substance
that speeds the transmission of nerve
impulses from neuron to neuron.

Brain Development

By age 2, a child's brain weighs 75 percent of what it will in adulthood, and extensive sprouting and then pruning of dendrites has already taken place. Yet some crucial neurological developments have yet to occur, not only in brain size (the brain reaches 90 percent of adult weight by age 6) but also in the speed, coordination, social awareness, and complexity of thinking (Kagan & Herschkowitz, 2005). (The major structures of the brain are diagrammed in Figure 5.2.)

These neurological advances are essential for our species. A study found that young human children were similar to chimpanzees in their understanding of the physical world (object permanence, tool use, and so on) but were far advanced in their understanding of the social world (communication, intentions) (Hermann et al., 2007). Brain development is the reason for the difference.

Speed of Thought

Some brain growth during early childhood is the result of continued proliferation of the communication pathways (dendrites and axons) already described in Chapter 3. However those messages are quicker than earlier, which has a marked effect on a child's thought and behavior.

MYELINATION The primary reason for faster thinking is new and extensive **myelination.** *Myelin* is a fatty coating on the axons that speeds signals between neurons.

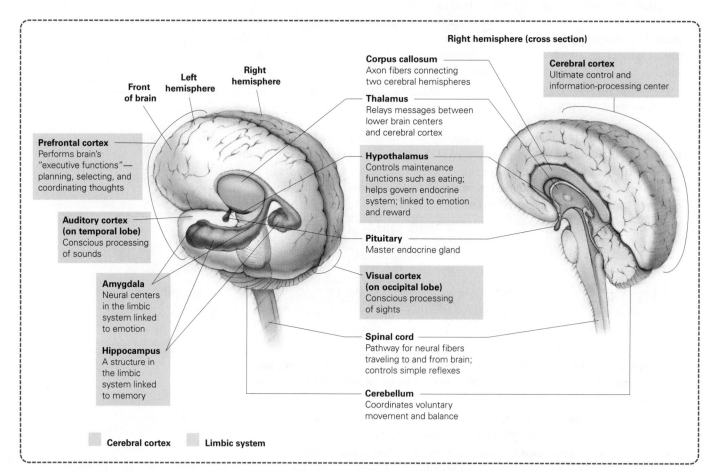

FIGURE 5.2 Connections A few of the dozens of named parts of the brain are shown here. Although each area has particular functions, the entire brain is interconnected. The processing of emotions, for example, occurs primarily in the limbic system, but many other brain areas are also involved.

Myelination continues for decades; reduction in myelin is one reason people's reactions tend to slow down as they get older (C. A. Nelson et al., 2006).

Although myelination is a lifelong process, its effects are most noticeable over the years of childhood. Because of inadequate myelination, the youngest children are slow at everything. Parents must patiently listen to them talk, help them dress, or watch them write. Less myelination means more time required for walking, eating, even crying.

A gradual increase in myelination makes 5-year-olds much quicker than 3-year-olds, who themselves are quicker than toddlers, who take so long to complete a task that they sometimes forget what they are doing even before they finish. Greater speed becomes more important when several thoughts must occur in rapid succession.

By age 6, most children can listen and then answer, catch a ball and then throw it, write the alphabet in sequence, count to 100 without repeating themselves, and so on. This process continues into adolescence. By age 16, many teenagers are lightning fast at playing video games, figuring out math problems, or responding to an insult.

LEFT AND RIGHT HEMISPHERES One part of the brain that grows and myelinates rapidly during early childhood is the **corpus callosum,** a band of nerve fibers that connects the left and right sides of the brain. Growth of the corpus callosum makes communication between the two brain hemispheres more efficient. Failure of the corpus callosum to develop normally results in serious disorders and is one of many possible causes of autism (see Chapter 7) (Mason et al., 2008).

Both sides of the body, and therefore both sides of the brain, are needed for almost every skill: The fork stabs the meat while the knife cuts it; one hand steadies the paper while the other writes; skating, skiing, and riding a bicycle require balance between left and right. Brain immaturity may be the reason that, for many young children, shoelaces get knotted, paper gets ripped, and bicycles tip over. A child's genes and age both influence the rate of maturation and myelination of the corpus callosum (Boles et al., 2008).

Left and Right Hands To understand the significance of left–right communication, remember that the two sides of the body are not identical. Each side is dominant for certain functions—a process called **lateralization** (literally, "sidedness"), which explains why everyone is either right- or left-handed. Infants usually use one hand more than the other for grabbing a spoon, a rattle, and so on, a preference that is at least partly genetic (Goymer, 2007).

For centuries, adults forced left-handed children to be right-handed. This caused frustration and conflict but often succeeded, for the young brain is influenced by experience. Such children ate and wrote with their right hands but sometimes used their left to hammer, or bat a ball, or wave in greeting. Not surprisingly, the corpus callosum of a left-handed person is often thicker than that of a right-handed person, since left-handers especially need coordination of both sides of the body (Cherbuin & Brinkman, 2006).

A disproportionate number of artists, musicians, and sports stars are left-handed, including Michelangelo, Seal, Jimi Hendrix, Paul McCartney, Larry Bird, and Sandy Koufax. Left-handed U.S. presidents include Ronald Reagan, Jimmy Carter, Bill Clinton, and Barack Obama.

ESPECIALLY FOR Early-Childhood Teachers You know you should be patient, but you feel your frustration rising when your young charges dawdle as they walk to the playground a block away. What should you do? (see response, page 168) →

corpus callosum
A long, thick band of nerve fibers that connects the left and right hemispheres of the brain and allows communication between them.

lateralization
Literally, sidedness, referring to the specialization in certain functions by each side of the brain, with one side dominant for each activity. The left side of the brain controls the right side of the body, and vice versa.

ELLEN B. SENISI / THE IMAGE WORKS

Signing His Artwork A large sheet of paper and a marker are excellent equipment for brain exercise in early childhood.

OBSERVATION QUIZ
How is this boy different from more than 90 percent of other 3-year-olds? (see answer, page 169) →

RESPONSE FOR Early-Childhood
Teachers (from page 167) One solution
is to remind yourself that the children's
brains are not yet myelinated enough
to enable them to quickly walk, talk, or
even button their jackets. Maturation
has a major effect, as you will observe
if you can schedule excursions in
September and again in November.
Progress, while still slow, will be a few
seconds faster in November than it
was in September. ●

perseveration
The tendency to persevere in, or stick
to, one thought or action for a long
time.

Left and Right Together Lateralization affects the entire body: We are all right- or left-footed, -eyed, and -eared. This does not mean that a person uses only one side of the body: Both feet coordinate to walk, run, climb, and so on. But imagine kicking a ball—one foot is preferred.

Through studies of people with brain damage as well as through brain imaging, neurologists have determined how the brain's hemispheres specialize: The left half of the brain controls the right side of the body, and, for most people, it also contains the areas dedicated to logical reasoning, detailed analysis, and language. The right half controls the left side of the body and contains the areas dedicated to emotional and creative impulses, including appreciation of music, art, and poetry. Thus, in general, the left side notices details and the right side grasps the big picture.

This distinction between the hemispheres is sometimes exaggerated. No one (except someone with severe brain damage) is exclusively left-brained or right-brained. Every cognitive skill requires both hemispheres, just as every gross motor skill requires both sides of the body (Hugdahl & Davidson, 2002). The corpus callosum, as well as the prefrontal cortex, helps the entire brain function as a whole.

The Prefrontal Cortex

Neurons have two kinds of impulses: those that activate and those that inhibit. Each impulse is signaled by biochemical messages from axon to dendrite. Both activation and inhibition are necessary for thoughtful adults, who neither hesitate too long nor leap too quickly. Indeed, at the other end of the life span, a major problem with some aging brains is loss of inhibition, which may lead to talkativeness or "off-target verbosity" (von Hippel, 2007). A balanced brain is most effective throughout life.

Many young children have not yet found the right balance because, as you learned in Chapter 3, a critical part of the brain, the *prefrontal cortex* (sometimes called the *frontal cortex* or *frontal lobe*), is immature. The prefrontal cortex is said to be the *executive* of the brain because all the other areas of the cortex are ruled by prefrontal decisions (Kolb & Whishaw, 2008). For example, the prefrontal cortex can think ahead to prevent anxiety from prevailing when a shy person meets someone new. Anxious children hide their heads or even run away; as adults, they may be brave enough to talk to a stranger.

Maturation of the prefrontal cortex gradually enables children to focus attention and curb impulsiveness. Before such maturation, many young children jump from task to task; they cannot stay quiet. Others act in the opposite way: In a phenomenon called **perseveration,** some children persevere in, or stick to, one thought or action, unable to quit. They repeat a phrase over and over (sometimes singsong), seemingly oblivious to the fact that communication is the primary purpose of language. Or they may burst into tears when told to stop what they are doing.

Impulsiveness and perseveration have the same underlying cause: immaturity of the prefrontal cortex. During early childhood, brain maturation (innate) and emotional regulation (learned) decrease both impulsiveness and perseveration. Children gradually become better able to pay attention, activating and inhibiting as needed (de Haan & Johnson, 2003).

From ages 2 to 6, maturation of the prefrontal cortex has several notable benefits:

- Sleep becomes more regular.
- Emotions become more nuanced and responsive.
- Temper tantrums subside.

Immaturity of the prefrontal cortex may be the underlying reason for a fascinating mistake that 3-year-olds make but 5-year-olds do not (Zelazo et al., 2003). In a series of experiments, children are given cards with the shapes of trucks and flowers, some red and some blue. They are asked to "play the shape game," putting trucks in one pile and flowers in another. Three-year-olds almost always do this correctly.

Then the children are asked to "play the color game," sorting the cards by color. Most 3-year-olds fail, sorting by shape again instead (A. Diamond & Kirkham, 2005; Zelazo et al., 2003). The same problem occurs if they sort first by color and then by shape: They get stuck on their initial sorting pattern. Older children correctly make the switch—something in the executive function of their brains has changed.

As with every aspect of brain maturation, experience and training have some impact. For instance, in one study, Korean preschoolers were better able to pay attention and resist perseveration than were comparable children in England (Oh & Lewis, 2008). When 3-year-olds were given the shape/color sorting task, 40 percent of the Koreans, but only 14 percent of the Britons, successfully shifted from sorting objects by shape to sorting by color.

The researchers explored many possible explanations for the advances among the Koreans. They inferred from the data that culture was the probable reason (Oh & Lewis, 2008). Korean children are taught to inhibit their impulses more than British children are, and that may encourage maturation of the prefrontal cortex. Note, however, that even with this cultural push, 60 percent of the Korean 3-year-olds made the usual mistake. Brain immaturity is universal; experience has some impact, but it is limited by maturation.

Emotions and the Brain

Now we turn to the *limbic system*, a term that refers to parts of the brain that are crucial in the expression and regulation of emotions. Although emotions are affected by many brain regions, the amygdala, the hippocampus, and the hypothalamus are specific areas of the limbic system that many neuroscientists consider to be pivotal in emotional expression.

The **amygdala** (from the Greek word for "almond," because it is about the shape and size of an almond) is a tiny structure deep in the brain that registers emotions, both positive and negative—especially fear (C. A. Nelson et al., 2006). Increased activity of the amygdala is one reason some young children have frightening nightmares or sudden terrors. Fear responses originating in the amygdala can overwhelm the functioning of the prefrontal cortex and disrupt reason.

The **hippocampus** is located right next to the amygdala. It is a central processor of memory, especially memory for locations (Andersen et al., 2007).

Together, the amygdala and hippocampus help people learn. When these parts of the limbic system are immature, some children are fearless when they should be cautious. The opposite reaction is also a sign of an immature brain: Some children are fearful when there is no objective reason to be, perhaps refusing to ride in an elevator or even to use an unfamiliar bathroom.

A third part of the limbic system, the **hypothalamus,** responds to signals from the amygdala (arousing) and the hippocampus (usually dampening) to produce hormones that activate other parts of the brain and body (see Figure 5.3). Ideally, the hypothalamus produces hormones in moderation (Tarullo & Gunnar, 2006). However, if excessive stress hormones flood the brain, part of the hippocampus may be destroyed, and permanent deficits in learning and memory may result (E. P. Davis et al., 2003). Many hormones are produced from the hypothalamus to the pituitary to the adrenal glands (HPA axis), so this disruption has lifelong consequences.

Now you can understand how, as mentioned in Chapter 3, prolonged stress may lead to emotional and cognitive impairment. The Romanian children who spent their first years in institutions were shown pictures of happy, sad, frightened, and angry faces while the activity of their brains was measured. Compared to Romanian

ANSWER TO OBSERVATION QUIZ
(from page 167) He is left-handed. ●

amygdala
A tiny brain structure that registers emotions, particularly fear and anxiety.

hippocampus
A brain structure that is a central processor of memory, especially memory for locations.

hypothalamus
A brain area that responds to the amygdala and the hippocampus to produce hormones that activate other parts of the brain and body.

ESPECIALLY FOR Neurologists Why do many experts think that identifying the limbic system as the regulator of emotions is an oversimplified explanation of brain function? (see response, page 170) →

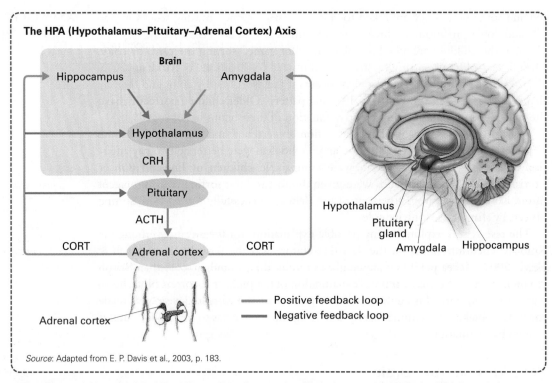

The HPA (Hypothalamus–Pituitary–Adrenal Cortex) Axis

Source: Adapted from E. P. Davis et al., 2003, p. 183.

FIGURE 5.3 A Hormonal Feedback Loop This diagram simplifies a hormonal linkage, the HPA (hypothalamus–pituitary–adrenal) axis. Both the hippocampus and the amygdala stimulate the hypothalamus to produce CRH (corticotropin-releasing hormone), which in turn signals the pituitary gland to produce ACTH (adrenocorticotropic hormone). ACTH then triggers the production of CORT (glucocorticoids) by the adrenal cortex (the outer layers of the adrenal glands, atop the kidneys). Fear may either build or disappear, depending on other factors, including how the various parts of the brain interpret that first alert from the amygdala.

children who lived with their parents, the orphans' limbic systems were less reactive and their brains were less lateralized (Parker & Nelson, 2005).

The relationships among stress, memory, and the limbic system are complex. In some circumstances, stress seems to facilitate memory. However, because developing brains are fragile, "prolonged physiological responses to stress and challenge put children at risk for a variety of problems in childhood, including physical and mental disorders, poor emotional regulation, and cognitive impairments" (Quas et al., 2004, p. 379).

KEY Points

- Brain development continues during early childhood; myelination of axons is crucial for speeding up thought.

- The corpus callosum connects the left and right hemispheres of the brain, allowing coordination of thinking and behavior.

- The prefrontal cortex is the executive of the brain, the site of planning and forethought. This part of the brain is crucial for learning in school; it continues to develop through adolescence.

- Several parts of the brain, including the amygdala, the hippocampus, and the hypothalamus, are said to be part of the limbic system, which aids the expression and control of emotions.

RESPONSE FOR Neurologists (from page 169) The more we discover about the brain, the more complex we realize it is. Each part has specific functions and is connected to every other part. ●

Thinking During Early Childhood

You have just learned that every year of early childhood brings more developed motor skills, further brain maturation, and better control of impulses. All these accelerate cognitive development. Now we look at some of the specifics of thinking in early childhood, beginning with the theories of Jean Piaget and Lev Vygotsky, both justly famous for their descriptions of early cognition.

Piaget: Preoperational Thought

Early childhood is the second of Piaget's four periods of cognition. His term for cognitive development between the ages of about 2 and 6 is **preoperational intelligence.** The word *preoperational* means "before (pre) logical operations (reasoning processes)" (Inhelder & Piaget, 1964).

This stage builds on the final period of sensorimotor intelligence (mental combinations), but now language allows much more elaborate thinking. To be specific, the child's verbal ability permits *symbolic thinking*. For example, the child uses the sound *dog* to symbolize the real animal. That symbolic thought allows the child to say "The dog is sleeping" to express a thought and convey meaning even when the dog is not currently seen, heard, or otherwise sensed.

Symbolic thinking frees the child from the limits of sensorimotor experiences. Thus, the major advance of preoperational thought is symbolic thinking, particularly via language. The main deficiency at this age is difficulty with logic, which Piaget described in detail and to which we turn now.

OBSTACLES TO LOGICAL OPERATIONS Piaget noted four characteristics of preoperational thought: centration, focus on appearance, static reasoning, and irreversibility. Each of these limits the child's thinking.

Centration is the tendency to focus on one aspect of a situation to the exclusion of others. Young children may, for example, insist that lions and tigers at the zoo cannot be cats because the children "center" on the house-pet aspect of the cats they know. Or a child may insist that Daddy is a father, not a brother, because the child centers on his or her personal experience. The latter example illustrates a particular type of centration, *ego-centration,* which Piaget called **egocentrism**—literally, self-centeredness.

Piaget did not equate egocentrism with selfishness. One 3-year-old, against his aunt's advice, bought a model car as a birthday present for his mother. His "behavior was not selfish or greedy; he carefully wrapped the present and gave it to his mother with an expression that clearly showed that he expected her to love it" (Crain, 2005, p. 108). His egocentrism made him believe that everyone thought as he did.

A second characteristic of preoperational thought is a **focus on appearance** to the exclusion of other attributes. A girl given a short haircut might look into a mirror and burst into tears because she thinks she has turned into a boy.

Third, preoperational children use **static reasoning,** the belief that the world is unchanging. They might look with disbelief at old photographs of their parents as children.

The fourth characteristic of preoperational thought is **irreversibility.** Preoperational thinkers fail to recognize that reversing a process sometimes restores whatever existed before. A 3-year-old might cry because her mother put lettuce on her hamburger. Overwhelmed by the desire to have things "just right," she might reject the hamburger after the lettuce is removed because she believes that what is done cannot be undone.

CONSERVATION AND LOGIC Piaget devised many experiments demonstrating the constraints on thinking that result from preoperational reasoning. A famous set of

preoperational intelligence
Piaget's term for cognitive development between the ages of about 2 and 6; it includes language and imagination (which involve symbolic thought), but logical, operational thinking is not yet possible.

● **FOR DEEPER REFLECTION** What could humans communicate without symbolic thought? (Remember that most gestures are symbols, which are part of language.)

centration
A characteristic of preoperational thought whereby a young child focuses (centers) on one idea, excluding all others.

egocentrism
Piaget's term for young children's tendency to think about the world entirely from their own personal perspective.

focus on appearance
A characteristic of preoperational thought whereby a young child ignores all attributes that are not apparent.

static reasoning
A characteristic of preoperational thought whereby a young child thinks that nothing changes. Whatever is now has always been and always will be.

irreversibility
A characteristic of preoperational thought whereby a young child thinks that nothing can be undone. A thing cannot be restored to the way it was before a change occurred.

ESPECIALLY FOR Nutritionists How can Piaget's theory help you encourage children to eat healthy foods? (see response, page 173) ➡

COURTESY OF KATHLEEN BERGER

Demonstration of Conservation My youngest daughter, Sarah, here at age 5¾, demonstrates Piaget's conservation-of-volume experiment. First, she examines both short glasses to be sure they contain the same amount of milk. Then, after the contents of one are poured into the tall glass and she is asked which has more, she points to the tall glass, just as Piaget would have expected. Later she added, "It looks like it has more because it's taller," indicating that some direct instruction might change her mind.

experiments involved **conservation,** the idea that something remains the same (is conserved) despite changes in its appearance.

Suppose two identical glasses contain the same amount of liquid. Then the liquid from one glass is poured into a glass that is taller and narrower. When preoperational children are asked if both glasses still contain the same amount, they say that the narrower glass has more.

All four characteristics of preoperational thought are evident in this mistake. Young children fail to understand conservation of liquids because they focus *(center)* on what they see *(appearance)*, noticing only the immediate *(static)* condition. It does not occur to them that they could reverse the process and re-create the liquid level of a moment earlier *(irreversibility)*. (See Figure 5.4 for other examples.)

Tests of Various Types of Conservation

Type of Conservation	Initial Presentation	Transformation	Question	Preoperational Child's Answer
Volume	Two equal glasses of liquid.	Pour one into a taller, narrower glass.	Which glass contains more?	The taller one.
Number	Two equal lines of checkers.	Increase spacing of checkers in one line.	Which line has more checkers?	The longer one.
Matter	Two equal balls of clay.	Squeeze one ball into a long, thin shape.	Which piece has more clay?	The long one.
Length	Two sticks of equal length.	Move one stick.	Which stick is longer?	The one that is farther to the right.

FIGURE 5.4 Conservation, Please According to Piaget, until children grasp the concept of conservation at (he believed) about age 6 or 7, they cannot understand that the transformations shown here do not change the total amount of liquid, checkers, clay, and wood.

ANIMISM IN PREOPERATIONAL THOUGHT A final aspect of preoperational thought is called **animism,** the belief that natural objects and phenomena are alive (Piaget, 1951). Animism arises naturally from egocentrism because children egocentrically assume that other creatures—and even things—are similar to themselves. Clouds, mountains, and trees are thought to have feelings, goals, and even souls. Many young children believe in animism, insisting that various spirits are active under certain circumstances (Subbotsky, 2000).

The connection between animism and symbolic thought is apparent when words are used to talk to animals or to give names to trees or clouds or rivers. Many children repeat certain phrases as incantations, as if the words hold magical power. Often stories for children include animals or inanimate objects that talk and help people. Children are not skeptical when they hear such stories.

Magical happenings and magical sayings are also common in young children's daily lives. Wishing on a star or an eyelash, saying "Cross my heart and hope to die," holding one's breath when passing a cemetery—these and many more such behaviors are frequent in early childhood.

It is easy for adults and older children to belittle children who believe that a tree has feelings or who whisper a wish to a star. It is also common for many Westerners to criticize animistic religions. However, a multicultural and multidirectional view of development, as explained in Chapter 1, suggests that this may be a mistake.

Many of the world's religions include beliefs that outsiders consider far-fetched and illogical. Yet talking animals are found in almost every religion, and certain names or curses are powerful. Given that, it seems ill advised to criticize children for having their own animism and for using symbolic thinking that adults do not share.

Indeed, a childish sympathy for animals and respect for nature are, according to some people, needed correctives to the technology and materialism of modern society (Harding, 2006). A child's insistence on a burial ceremony for a dead bird, or belief that a dog sympathizes with the child's lengthy tales of wishes and worries, might be healthier than a refusal to be moved by death or an inability to share emotions.

Vygotsky: Social Learning

For many years, the magical, illogical, and egocentric aspects of cognition dominated descriptions of early childhood. Vygotsky was the first leading developmentalist to highlight the other side of early cognition.

CHILDREN AS APPRENTICES Vygotsky believed that every aspect of children's cognitive development is embedded in the social context (Vygotsky, 1934/1987). Children are curious and observant. They seek answers to their questions about how machines work, why weather changes, and where the sky ends. They assume that adults know those answers.

Vygotsky saw every child as an **apprentice in thinking,** whose intellectual growth is stimulated and directed by mentors who are usually older and more skilled members of society. According to Vygotsky, children learn because their mentors (especially their teachers and parents) do the following:

- Present challenges (attainable but not too easy)
- Offer assistance (without taking over)
- Provide instruction (not as commands, but as suggestions)
- Encourage motivation (with praise and enthusiasm)

You learned in Chapter 1 that Vygotsky believed children learn to think via *guided participation* in their social experiences and explorations. A parent might guide a child to recognize a street sign or might ask a child to help stir a cake batter.

conservation
The principle that the amount of a substance remains the same (i.e., is conserved) when its appearance changes.

animism
The belief that natural objects and phenomena are alive.

RESPONSE FOR Nutritionists (from page 171) Take each of the four characteristics of preoperational thought into account. Because of egocentrism, having a special place and plate might assure the child that this food is exclusively his or hers. Since appearance is important, food should look tasty. Since static thinking dominates, if something healthy is added (e.g., grate carrots into the cake, add milk to the soup), do it before the food is given to the child. In the reversibility example in the text, the lettuce should be removed out of the child's sight and the "new" hamburger presented. ●

apprentice in thinking
Vygotsky's term for a person whose cognition is stimulated and directed by older and more skilled members of society.

The reality that children are curious and remember their experiences is evidence of impressive cognition in young children. The ability to learn may be a better indicator of intelligence than is a score on any test that measures accumulated knowledge. As Vygotsky (1935/1978) said: "What children can do with the assistance of others might be in some sense even more indicative of their mental development than what they can do alone" (p. 5).

SCAFFOLDING Vygotsky believed that for each developing individual, there is a **zone of proximal development (ZPD),** which includes all the skills the person can perform with assistance but cannot quite perform independently. The challenge for the mentor (parent, peer, or professional) is to find appropriate challenges for the learner. A mentor must first locate the learner's ZPD—the skills, knowledge, and concepts that the learner is close (i.e., proximal) to acquiring but cannot yet master without help.

zone of proximal development (ZPD)
Vygotsky's term for the skills—cognitive as well as physical—that a person can exercise only with assistance, not yet independently.

The mentor then engages the student, avoiding two opposite dangers: (1) boredom because the task is not challenging and (2) failure because the standards are set too high. Often a balanced intellectual engagement occurs in play, such as the imaginative role-playing that can occur when preschoolers are together (e.g., "Pretend I am the mommy and you are the baby") (Andresen, 2005). In that zone, boundaries can be pushed with less fear of criticism, as play allows flexibility in structuring a task. (In the context of play, "balanced" means give-and-take, not strict equality. Typically, as children play, each learns from the other.)

Mentors provide **scaffolding,** or temporary support, to enable learners to move through their zone and learn new skills. Caregivers scaffold when they teach children to look both ways before crossing a street (while holding the child's hand) or when they show children how to tie their shoes.

scaffolding
Temporary support that is tailored to a learner's needs and abilities and aimed at helping the learner master the next task in a given learning process.

Scaffolding is particularly important for experiences that are directly cognitive—that is, experiences that advance the mastery of words and ideas. When reading to 3-year-olds, for instance, most adults provide excellent scaffolding—explaining, pointing, listening, affirming—within the child's zone of development.

Parents often answer young children's questions not with a simple answer but with a response that builds vocabulary and understanding (Chouinard, 2007). If a child asks, "What is that?" the mother, instead of simply saying, "A truck," might say, "That is a kind of t-r-r . . ." (guiding the child to respond "truck") or "That is a garbage truck. What do you think it has inside?"

Remember that children pay particular attention to other children. They readily learn from an older child who is slightly more competent than they are—who can provide guidance within their ZPD. Such guidance often involves scaffolding, as was evident in a yearlong mentoring project that assigned third-graders to work on craft projects with preschoolers. One of the older children commented afterward, "I learned how little kids think" (quoted in Fair et al., 2005, p. 229).

Older siblings can be excellent mentors, partly because their speech is just ahead of the child's own language ability. In Chiapas, Mexico, 8-year-old Tonik taught his 2-year-old sister, Katal, how to wash a doll. After several minutes of demonstrating and describing, Tonik continues:

> **Tonik:** Pour it like this. *(Demonstrates)*
> **Tonik:** Sister, pour it. *(Hands glass)*
> **Tonik:** Look! Pour it.
> **Katal:** *(Pours, with some difficulty)*

Weaving Skills Baskets made in the Pacific island nation of Palau are known worldwide for their beauty and durability. The skills involved in weaving them are taught through scaffolding and apprenticeship.

TIM ROCK / LONELY PLANET

Tonik: Like that. *(Approval)*
Katal: *(Looks away)*
Tonik: It's finished now.

[quoted in Maynard, 2002, p. 977]

Note that when Katal loses interest and looks away, Tonik wisely declares the session finished. His response encourages Katal to participate in later apprenticeships. Motivation is crucial in early education—one reason why sensitive verbal encouragement is so powerful.

LANGUAGE AS A TOOL FOR COGNITION Vygotsky believed that talking, listening, reading, and writing are tools to advance thought. He held that language promotes thinking in two ways. First, **private speech** occurs when people talk to themselves, developing new ideas (Vygotsky, 1934/1987). Young children use private speech often, typically talking out loud to review, decide, and explain events to themselves (and, incidentally, to anyone else within earshot). Older preschoolers use private speech more selectively, sometimes in a whisper, as they tell themselves what to do next (Winsler et al., 2000). Adolescents and adults often write in order to think more clearly, to sort through conflicting values or priorities.

The second way in which Vygotsky said language advances cognition is through social exchanges. This **social mediation** function of speech occurs during both formal instruction (e.g., when teachers explain things) and casual conversation (e.g., when children tell each other what to do). Language is the link between brain potential and knowledge; people learn by using words.

Note that both Piaget and Vygotsky emphasize language development in the first years of life. The differences are subtle: Piaget considers language possible once symbolic thinking is attained, and Vygotsky believes that language itself promotes thought. No matter what the sequence, however, all observers of cognitive development in early childhood consider language and cognition to be closely connected.

ESPECIALLY FOR Driving Instructors Sometimes your students cry, curse, or quit. How would Vygotsky advise you to proceed? (see response, page 176) ➔

private speech
The internal dialogue that occurs when people talk to themselves (either silently or out loud).

social mediation
Human interaction that expands and advances understanding, often through words that one person uses to explain something to another.

A whole turkey

1 big bag full of a whole turkey (Get the kind with no feathers on, not the kind the Pilgrims ate.)
A giant lump of stuffin'
1 squash pie
1 mint pie
1 little fancy dish of sour berries
1 big fancy dish of a vegetable mix
20 dishes of all different candies; chocolate balls, cherry balls, good'n plenties and peanuts

Get up when the alarm says to and get busy fast. Unfold the turkey and open up the holes. Push in the stuffin' for a couple of hours. I think you get stuffin' from that Farm that makes it.

I know you have to pin the stuffin' to the turkey or I suppose it would get out. And get special pins or use big long nails.

Get the kitchen real hot, and from there on you just cook turkey. Sometimes you can call it a bird, but it's not.

Then you put the vegetables in the cooker—and first put one on top, and next put one on the bottom, and then one in the middle. That makes a vegetable mix. Put 2 red things of salt all in it and 2 red things of water also. Cook them to just ½ of warm.

Put candies all around the place and Linda will bring over the pies.

When the company comes put on your red apron.

Unfold the Turkey This recipe (from *Smashed Potatoes*, edited by Jane Martel) shows many characteristics of preschool thought, among them literal interpretation of words ("Sometimes you can call it a bird, but it's not") and an uncertain idea of time ("Push in the stuffin' for a couple of hours") and quantity ("A giant lump of stuffin'").

Children's Theories

Both Piaget and Vygotsky also realized that children try to comprehend their world and sometimes develop explanations of their own. Many current developmentalists study exactly how children explain what they experience, especially how they explain what other people do.

THEORY-THEORY One theory of early cognitive development begins with the hypothesis that all humans are driven to develop theories. Especially when something unexpected and random happens, many people search for a reason. They might connect a sudden downpour to God; to numerology; or to nature's way of punishing, rewarding, or reminding the people who experienced it.

The fact that humans seek reasons for experiences led to what is called **theory-theory,** the idea that children construct theories to explain everything they see and hear:

> More than any animal, we search for causal regularities in the world around us. We are perpetually driven to look for deeper explanations of our experience, and broader and more reliable predictions about it.... Children seem, quite literally, to be born with ... the desire to understand the world and the desire to discover how to behave in it.
>
> *[Gopnik, 2001, p. 66]*

Exactly how does this search transpire? In one study, Mexican American mothers kept detailed diaries of every question their 3- to 5-year-olds asked and how they themselves responded (Kelemen et al., 2005). Most of the questions were about human behavior and characteristics (see Figure 5.5)—for example:

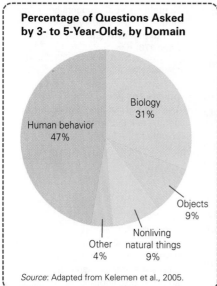

Percentage of Questions Asked by 3- to 5-Year-Olds, by Domain

Biology 31%

Human behavior 47%

Objects 9%

Nonliving natural things 9%

Other 4%

Source: Adapted from Kelemen et al., 2005.

FIGURE 5.5 Questions, Questions Parents found that most of their children's questions were about human behavior—especially the parents' behavior toward the child. Children seek to develop a theory to explain things, so the question "Why can't I have some candy?" is not satisfactorily answered by "It's almost dinnertime."

theory-theory
The idea that children attempt to explain everything they see and hear.

- "Why do you give my mother a kiss?"
- "Why is my brother bad?"
- "Why do women have breasts?"
- "Why are there Black kids?"

Fewer questions were about nonliving things or objects:

- "Why does it rain?"
- "Why is my daddy's car white?"

Many questions concerned the underlying purpose of various phenomena, although parents often did not respond in that way. An adult might interpret a child's one-word question "Why?" to mean simply "What causes *X* to happen?" when the child's intended meaning might be "I want to know more about *X*" (Leach, 1997).

As this finding reveals, parents often answer as if children were asking about scientific abstractions, rather than asking in an egocentric way. For example, when a child asks why women have breasts, a mother might talk about hormones and puberty, not about how that child was fed as a baby.

Some support for theory-theory came from a series of experiments that explored when and how 3-year-olds imitate other people (Williamson et al., 2008). They do not thoughtlessly imitate whatever they observe. Instead, they figure out the other person's intentions before deciding whether to copy or ignore what they see.

As an example of such reasoning, if an adult seems to do something by mistake, the child will not usually copy the mistake. But if an adult does something that seems deliberate (opening a drawer in an odd way or putting on a hat before eating a sandwich), the child is more likely to do the same thing.

RESPONSE FOR Driving Instructors (from page 175) Use guided participation and scaffold the instruction so your students are not overwhelmed. Be sure to provide lots of praise and days of practice. If emotion erupts, do not take it as an attack on you. ●

THEORY OF MIND Human mental processes—thoughts, emotions, beliefs, motives, and intentions—are among the most complicated and puzzling phenomena of life. Adults wonder why people fall in love, or vote as they do, or make foolish choices; children are puzzled about a playmate's unexpected anger or an aunt's too-wet kiss.

To know what goes on in another's mind, people develop what is sometimes called a *folk psychology,* a **theory of mind** that is based more on personal experience and common sense (or folk wisdom) than on science. Theory of mind begins when children become less egocentric and are able to understand that other people might have ideas and knowledge unlike their own. Theory of mind enables a person to comprehend the emotions of other people as well as to realize what other people may or may not know.

Many researchers have found that theory of mind typically appears rather suddenly (Wellman et al., 2001), in "an important intellectual change at about 4 years" (Perner, 2000, p. 396). At that point, children can play jokes on other people and also feel sorry for making someone else feel bad. Both are difficult for younger children.

"Holy Moly!" Three-year-olds almost always believe that what they know now is the same as what they once knew and what other people know. Another way of describing this is to say that they are "cursed" by their own knowledge, too egocentric to grasp other perspectives (Birch & Bloom, 2003).

Theory of mind was illustrated in a classic experiment in which an adult shows a 3-year-old a candy box and asks, "What is inside?" The child says, naturally, "Candy." But the child has been tricked:

> **Adult:** Let's open it and look inside.
> **Child:** Oh . . . holy moly . . . pencils!
> **Adult:** Now I'm going to put them back and close it up again. *(Does so)* Now . . . when you first saw the box, before we opened it, what did you think was inside it?
> **Child:** Pencils.
> **Adult:** Nicky [friend of the child] hasn't seen inside this box. When Nicky comes in and sees it . . . what will he think is inside it?
> **Child:** Pencils.

[adapted from Astington & Gopnik, 1988, p. 195]

Maturation and Learning Recently, developmentalists have asked what, precisely, strengthens theory of mind at about age 4. Is this change more a matter of nature or of nurture, of brain maturation or of experience?

Neurological maturation is influential. In one study, 68 children aged 2 to 5½ were presented with four standard theory-of-mind situations, including a Band-Aid box that really contained pencils (similar to the candy-box experiment just described) (Jenkins & Astington, 1996). In each situation, they were asked to perform a specific task. More than one-third of the children succeeded at all four tasks, and more than one-third failed at three or all four of the tasks. Maturity was the main factor: Five-year-olds were most likely to succeed on all tasks, 4-year-olds had middling success, and most 3-year-olds failed every time (Perner et al., 2002).

Further evidence that an understanding of other people's thoughts requires maturation comes from children with autism, whose brains function differently from those of other children. Such children may be gifted in some ways and normally mature in others, but they are nonetheless impaired in social understanding, particularly in theory of mind (García-Pérez et al., 2008).

However, maturation is not the entire explanation. Some influences on theory of mind *are* affected by context. Language ability is one factor. Children with greater verbal fluency (at any age) are more likely to have a theory of mind. This is partly the

theory of mind
A person's theory of what other people might be thinking. In order to have a theory of mind, children must realize that other people are not necessarily thinking the same thoughts that they themselves are. That realization is seldom achieved before age 4.

ESPECIALLY FOR Social Scientists
Can you think of any connection between Piaget's theory of preoperational thought and 3-year-olds' errors in this theory-of-mind task? (see response, page 179) ➔

Road Rage? From their expressions, it looks as if this brother and sister may crash their toy jeep and cry, each blaming the other for the mishap. But a benefit of such sibling interactions is that they can advance theory of mind by helping children realize that people do not always think the same way.

result of verbal experience, especially participation in mother–child conversations that involve thoughts and wishes (Ontai & Thompson, 2008).

A second influence on the acquisition of theory of mind is interaction with other children who have already developed the concept. Having older brothers and sisters may be pivotal. One researcher estimates that, in the development of theory of mind, "two older siblings are worth about a year of chronological age" (Perner, 2000, p. 383). As they argue, agree, compete, and cooperate with their older siblings, and as their older siblings teasingly try to fool them, children come to realize that not everyone thinks as they do. That is the seminal idea of theory of mind.

A third factor is the cultural exosystem. A study comparing theory of mind among young children in preschools in Canada, India, Peru, Samoa, and Thailand found that the Canadian 5-year-olds were slightly ahead and the Samoan 5-year-olds were slightly behind, but across cultures most 5-year-old children passed the false-belief tests (such as a culture-fair version of the experiment with pencils in the candy box) (see Figure 5.6). The researchers concluded that brain maturation was a prerequisite but that language, social interaction, and culture were also influential (Callaghan et al., 2005).

Similar conclusions were drawn from a meta-analysis comparing 254 studies in China and North America (involving about 5,000 children). The overall conclusion was that although culture mattered (the Hong Kong children tended to be slowest), there was a strong "universal, early development of theory of mind" (D. Liu et al., 2008, p. 527). Each child's logical ability and brain maturation are important (Piaget), but language, social interaction, and culture are mediators (Vygotsky) once the necessary neurological connections have formed.

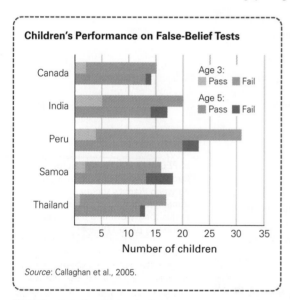

Children's Performance on False-Belief Tests

Source: Callaghan et al., 2005.

FIGURE 5.6 Few at Age 3, Most by Age 5 The advantage of cross-cultural research is that it can reveal universal patterns. Although the number of children in each group is small (from 31 3-year-olds in Peru to 13 5-year-olds in Thailand), the pattern is obvious. Something changes at about age 4 that enables most children to acquire theory of mind by age 5.

KEY Points

- Piaget believed that young children can think symbolically but not logically, which is why he referred to this period of cognitive development as preoperational.

- According to Piaget, limitations on preoperational thinking include egocentrism, a focus on appearance, and animism (the belief that natural objects are alive).

- Vygotsky emphasized the social and cultural aspects of cognition, stressing that mentors use language and guided participation as scaffolds to help learners advance within their zones of proximal development.

- Children develop theories to explain whatever they observe. By about age 4, theory of mind is evident, as children realize that other people have thoughts and ideas unlike their own.

Language

Language is pivotal to every kind of cognition in early childhood. Maturation and myelination, along with extensive social interaction, make early childhood the most productive years for language development and then for using words to think (an ability that is beyond the sensorimotor infant but then continues to be crucial for thought lifelong). Indeed, scientists once believed these years were a *critical period* for language, the *only* time when language could be mastered.

This critical-period hypothesis has been disproven. Language learning continues lifelong; many people become fluent in languages they began to learn after age 6 (Bialystok, 2001; Hakuta et al., 2003). Nonetheless, early childhood is a *sensitive period,* the best time to master vocabulary, grammar, and pronunciation. Young children are sometimes called "language sponges" because they soak up every drop of language they encounter. (The concepts of critical and sensitive periods were discussed in Chapter 1.)

Preschoolers normally talk a lot—to adults, to each other, to themselves, to their toys—unfazed by mispronunciation, misuse, or stuttering. This is a developmental asset. Language comes easily because young children are not self-conscious about what they say and how they talk. In other words, their underdeveloped theory of mind has cognitive advantages.

Vocabulary

Children learn new words rapidly. The average child knows about 500 words at age 2 and more than 10,000 at age 6. The *naming explosion* (explained in Chapter 3) becomes more general: Verbs, adjectives, adverbs, and conjunctions, as well as many more nouns, are mastered during early childhood.

How does this vocabulary explosion occur? After painstakingly learning one word at a time at age 1, children develop an interconnected set of categories for words, a kind of grid, or mental map. This neurological development (aided by myelination) makes speedy vocabulary acquisition possible through a process called **fast-mapping** (Woodward & Markman, 1998). Rather than figuring out an exact definition after hearing a word used in several contexts, children hear a word once and use fast-mapping to stick it into one of the categories in their mental language map. Generally, the more linguistic clues or categories children already have, the more rapid and accurate their fast-mapping is (Mintz, 2005).

Like more conventional mapping, language mapping is not always precise. Children quickly learn new animal names, for instance, because they are mapped in the brain close to already-known names. Thus, *baboon* is easier to learn if you already know *monkey*. Trips to the zoo facilitate fast-mapping, since zoos scaffold by placing similar animals together. Lack of precision is evident when a gorilla is called a chimpanzee or even a big monkey.

As with "big monkey," children use their available vocabulary to cover all the territory they want to talk about (Behrend et al., 2001). They use logic to try to figure out meaning—for instance, they might decide that butter comes from butterflies and birds grow from birdseed.

Knowing one word helps in learning another. Experimenters teaching the names of parts of objects found that children learned best if adults named the object that had the part, and then spoke of the part in the possessive (e.g., "See this butterfly? Look, this is its thorax"), rather than just providing the label ("See this? It is a thorax") (Saylor & Sabbagh, 2004).

RESPONSE FOR Social Scientists (from page 177) According to Piaget, preschool children focus on appearance and on static conditions (so they cannot mentally reverse a process). Furthermore, they are egocentric, believing that everyone shares their point of view. No wonder they believe that they had always known that the candy box held pencils and that a friend would know that, too. ●

fast-mapping
The speedy and sometimes imprecise way in which children learn new words by tentatively placing them in mental categories according to their perceived meaning.

A Shared Pleasure As they read stories to young children, many adults express exaggerated surprise, excitement, worry, and relief. They realize that words are better understood and remembered when they are connected to emotions.

Fast-mapping is evident even before age 2, and it accelerates; each word makes it easier to map other words (Gershkoff-Stowe & Hahn, 2007). The same may be true for new ideas. As an example, young children around the world vary markedly in math knowledge and comprehension. Compared with the typical North American 6-year-old, East Asian children are advanced and rural South American children are behind in math.

Experience (obtained through parents, preschool, or children's number games) is the usual explanation for these differences (Siegler & Ramani, 2008; Zhou et al., 2006). However, differences in the way a child's first language uses numbers may be significant.

Some of the world's 6,000 languages have few counting words; a language may have only the equivalents of *one, two,* and *many.* Adults who speak such languages are impaired at estimating quantity (P. Gordon, 2004). Other languages (e.g., Chinese) make counting easy, which may affect children's math readiness; in Chinese, for example, the words for eleven and twelve are the equivalent of ten-one and ten-two.

In every nation, young children have difficulty with words that imply comparisons (such as *tall* and *short, near* and *far, high* and *low, deep* and *shallow*) when meaning depends on context (Ryalls, 2000). A boy might splash in every puddle after being told to stay out of the deep ones because he knows about the deep end of a swimming pool—and no puddle is as deep as that.

Similarly, words expressing relationships of place and time—such as *here* and *there, yesterday* and *tomorrow*—are difficult. More than one pajama-clad child has awakened on Christmas morning and asked, "Is it tomorrow yet?" A girl who is told to "stay there" or "come here" may be puzzled about what she is expected to do.

Basic Grammar

In Chapter 3, we noted that the *grammar* of a language includes the structures, techniques, and rules that communicate meaning. Word order and word repetition, prefixes and suffixes, intonation and emphasis—all are part of grammar.

Grammar can be seen in children's early holophrases. By age 3, children understand and use grammar quite well. They know about word order (usually subject/verb/object), saying, "I eat the apple" and not any of the 23 other possible sequences of those four words. They use plurals; tenses (past, present, and future); and nominative, objective, and possessive pronouns (*I/me/mine* or *my*). English-learning children use articles (*the, a, an*) correctly, even though their proper use is quite complex.

Young children learn grammar so well that they may apply certain rules when they should not. This mistake, called **overregularization,** is especially likely to create trouble when a language includes many exceptions, as English does. An example involves a grammatical rule that most English-speaking toddlers know: Add *-s* to form the plural of a noun. A 24-month-old might say "more blocks." By age 4, that child might overregularize, talking about *foots, tooths, sheeps, mouses.*

A fascinating sign of early intelligence occurs when young children first say words correctly and then, when they are a little older and understand the rule, make overregularization mistakes. It takes many years for children to master all the grammatical structures, with appropriate exceptions, of their native language (Tomasello, 2006).

overregularization
The application of rules of grammar even when exceptions occur, making the language seem more "regular" than it actually is.

Student and Teachers Children at the Lawrence, Massachusetts, YWCA show Rashon McCloud of the Boston Celtics how they use a computer to learn reading. They are participating in an NBA-sponsored program called Read to Achieve.

RAY AMATI/NBAE / GETTY IMAGES

A VIEW FROM SCIENCE

Learning Two Languages

In today's world, bilingualism is an asset; some would say it is a necessity. Yet as they grow up, language-minority children (those who are not fluent in the dominant language of their nation) are disadvantaged. They are more likely to do poorly in school, to feel ashamed, and to become unemployed as adults (see Chapter 7). Learning the majority language is crucial, but when and how should this learning happen?

Before exploring how and when, consider why: What is the goal of having a second language? Is a nation better off if all its citizens speak one language, or should there be more than one official language, as in Switzerland, which has three, or Canada, which has two? Does it advance a child's intellectual ability if he or she speaks more than one language fluently?

Apparently so. A study that compared bilingual (Spanish and English) with monolingual (English-only) children found that the bilingual children were more advanced in nine measures of executive control, such as being able to make the switch on the color/shape sorting task described earlier (S. M. Carlson & Meltzoff, 2008). This study included only 29 children, too few to prove that brain development accelerates in bilingual children; but other research with bilingual Chinese–English and French–English children leads to the same conclusion (e.g., Bialystock & Martin, 2004). As the authors of the Spanish–English study point out, researchers have focused on the disabling effects of speaking two languages; research on the advantages of bilingualism is relatively new (S. M. Carlson & Meltzoff, 2008).

About 20 percent of children in the United States speak a language other than English at home. Most of them speak English "very well" by the time they reach school age (see Figure 5.7; U.S. Bureau of the Census, 2008). Those who do not are disadvantaged, perhaps pulling down the overall average for language-minority children.

Remarkably, soon after the naming explosion, young children can master two distinct sets of words and grammar, along with each language's characteristic pauses, pronunciations, intonations, and gestures (E. Bates et al., 2001; Mayberry & Nicoladis, 2000). This is true for children who speak the majority language at home and those who do not.

Neurological research finds that bilingual children under age 6 typically site both languages in the same area on the left side of their brains, yet manage to keep each language distinct. This separation allows bilingual speakers to activate one language and temporarily inhibit the other, experiencing no confusion when they speak to a monolingual person (Crinion et al., 2006).

By contrast, brain scans of people who learn a second language in adulthood typically reveal different activation sites for each language. A few fortunate adults who become

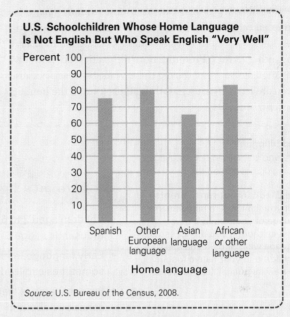

U.S. Schoolchildren Whose Home Language Is Not English But Who Speak English "Very Well"

Source: U.S. Bureau of the Census, 2008.

FIGURE 5.7 Mastering English: The Younger, the Better Immigrant children who attend school almost always master English within five years. Adolescents and adults who speak no English on arrival have a much harder time learning it. This chart shows Asian children to be less proficient in English because the majority of Chinese and Indian families in North America have only recently immigrated, so a larger proportion of those children have not yet had time to master the new language.

Smiling Faces . . . Sometimes Everyone in this group is an immigrant, born far from their current home in Burlington, Vermont. Jean Luc Dushime escaped the 1994 genocide in Rwanda, central Africa, when he was 14. He eventually adapted to his new language, climate, surroundings, and culture. Today he helps immigrant children make the same transition.

fluent in a second language after puberty show activation in the same brain areas for both languages; they tend to be unusually adept bilinguals (M. S. C. Thomas & Johnson, 2008).

Pronunciation difficulties are common in all young children. English-only 3-year-olds transpose sounds (*magazine* becomes *mazagine*), drop consonants (*truck* becomes *ruck*), and convert difficult sounds to easier ones (*father* becomes *fadder*), among other errors. Pronunciation difficulties do not slow down language learning during these years, however, because children are less self-conscious than adults (one of the benefits of egocentrism).

For that reason, bilingual children, especially, need to be "bathed in language," as some early-childhood educators express it. The emphasis is on oral language, hearing and speaking in every situation, just as a person taking a bath is surrounded by water (Otto, 2008).

Ideally, every young child will become a **balanced bilingual,** fluent in two languages, speaking each language so well that no audible hint suggests the other. Young children become balanced bilinguals if they have often heard and spoken two languages throughout childhood, conversing with people who speak the language well.

balanced bilingual
A person who is fluent in two languages, not favoring one over the other.

ESPECIALLY FOR Immigrant Parents
You want your children to be fluent in the language of your family's new country, even though you do not speak that language well. Should you speak to your children in your native tongue or in the new language? (see response, page 184) ➔

KEY Points

- Children aged 2 to 6 explode into speech, from about 100 words at age 2 to many thousands at age 6, using fast-mapping and basic grammar.

- Early language learning is aided by fast-mapping and grammar use, which sometimes can lead to mistakes such as overregularization.

- Pronunciation is learned painlessly, partly because young children are not self-conscious about making mistakes. Extensive listening and speaking lead to fluency.

- Children can readily learn two languages during these years, becoming balanced bilinguals if they are given abundant exposure to two languages.

Early-Childhood Education

A hundred years ago, children received no formal education until first grade, which is why it was called "first" and why younger children were called "preschoolers." Today, most 3- to 5-year-olds in developed nations are in school (see Figure 5.8 for U.S. trends), partly because, as research has now documented, early childhood is a time of "rapid development and great learning potential" (Hyson et al., 2006, p. 6).

Early-education institutions are given different names (*preschool, nursery school, day care, pre-primary, pre-K*), but names do not indicate the curriculum. We will consider three general types of early-education programs: child-centered, teacher-directed, and intervention programs.

Child-Centered Programs

Many programs are child-centered, or developmental, stressing children's natural inclination to learn through play rather than by following adult directions (Weikart, 1999). Many of these programs use a Piaget-inspired model that allows children to discover ideas at their own pace. The physical space and the materials—dress-up clothing, art supplies, puzzles, blocks of many sizes, and other toys—are organized to encourage self-paced exploration.

"We teach them that the world can be an unpredictable, dangerous, and sometimes frightening place, while being careful not to spoil their lovely innocence. It's tricky."

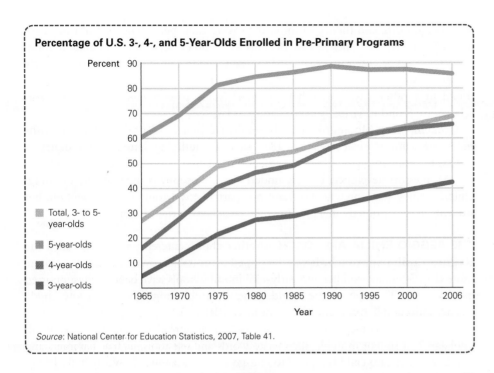

Percentage of U.S. 3-, 4-, and 5-Year-Olds Enrolled in Pre-Primary Programs

- Total, 3- to 5-year-olds
- 5-year-olds
- 4-year-olds
- 3-year-olds

Source: National Center for Education Statistics, 2007, Table 41.

FIGURE 5.8 Changing Times As research increasingly finds that preschool education provides a foundation for later learning, more and more young children are enrolled in educational programs.

OBSERVATION QUIZ

Which age group experienced the most dramatic increase in preschool attendance from 1965 to 1975? (see answer, page 185) →

Child-centered programs encourage artistic expression. Some educators describe all young children as artists and poets, gifted at seeing the world magically and imaginatively. Child-centered programs offer children many opportunities to tell stories, draw, paint, dance, build, and make music (Egan & Ling, 2002).

These programs also show the influence of Vygotsky, who thought that children learn through play with other children and through cultural practices that structure life. For example, to learn number skills, the curriculum includes math games (counting, keeping score), measurements (calendars, schedules), and counting (only three children in the blocks corner at one time, two volunteers to get the juice).

The focus on the child's interests does *not* mean that teachers are passive. Many teachers have extensive training in child development, so they are aware of the scaffolding needed to foster learning. Often they document specific goals and signs of progress for each child, making daily notes and assembling a portfolio of the child's creative work. In every child-centered program, teachers plan and prepare, yet they are always flexible, alert to each individual child's wishes and needs.

MONTESSORI SCHOOLS A hundred years ago, Maria Montessori opened schools for poor children in Rome. She believed that children need structured, individualized projects to give them a sense of accomplishment. At her schools, children proudly completed puzzles, used a sponge and water to clean a table, and drew shapes.

The various Montessori tasks (such as specially designed puzzles) were fashioned so that children can do them without adult help. Adults make suggestions and provide encouragement, but children are not forced, because pride in their work is crucial.

Like Piaget (who was her contemporary), Montessori (1936/1966) realized that children are not merely small adults: They learn from activities that adults might call play. Teachers therefore provide tasks that dovetail with the cognitive eagerness of the child. For example, because children have a need for order, for language learning, and for using all their senses, they happily learn from exercises that develop these skills. Connecting the smell of a lemon or a rose with the object itself might be a Montessori task.

In Milwaukee, Wisconsin, inner-city 5-year-olds who in 1997 and 2003 had been chosen by lottery for a Montessori program were found after a year to be better at

RESPONSE FOR Immigrant Parents
(from page 182) Children learn by listening, so it is important to speak with them often. You might prefer to read to your children, sing to them, and converse with them primarily in your native language and find a good preschool where they will learn the new language. The worst thing you could do would be to restrict speech in either tongue. ●

Reggio Emilia approach
A famous program of early-childhood education that originated in the town of Reggio Emilia, Italy; it encourages each child's creativity in a carefully designed setting.

prereading, math, and theory of mind than were their peers who had not been selected (Lillard & Else-Quest, 2006). Benefits were also evident for older children in this Milwaukee school, after five years of Montessori education. This study involved only 59 Montessori children and 53 children in a control group. Would the same results be found in another city, with other children? Many parents believe so: Montessori schools are found in virtually every nation today.

Contemporary Montessori schools emphasize individual pride and accomplishment, presenting literacy-related tasks (such as outlining letters and looking at books) to quite young children (Lillard, 2005). Many current tasks differ from those that Montessori developed, but the underlying philosophy is the same. Some things children enjoy (e.g., pretend play) are not part of the Montessori curriculum, but students never sit quietly in a group while a teacher instructs them.

THE REGGIO EMILIA APPROACH Another child-centered program is called the **Reggio Emilia approach.** It was developed in an Italian town of that name, where more than 50 infant–toddler and early-childhood schools have been built, supported by city funds. Throughout the world, Reggio Emilia programs have a low child/teacher ratio, ample space, and abundant materials.

Children are encouraged to master skills not usually introduced in American schools until age 7 or so. For example, they write words and use tools, such as hammers and knives. However, no child is *required* to engage in such learning (Edwards et al., 1998). There is no large-group instruction with formal lessons in, say, forming letters or cutting paper.

Children are considered "rich and powerful learners . . . competent, creative individuals" (Abbott & Nutbrown, 2001, pp. 24, 47), each with learning needs and artistic drive. Indeed, the varied perspectives and interests of each individual child are encouraged in Reggio Emilia schools (Dahlberg et al., 2007).

Appreciation of creativity and the arts is also evident in the physical design of the schools. Every Reggio Emilia establishment has a large central room where children gather, with floor-to-ceiling windows opening onto to a spacious, plant-filled playground. Big mirrors cover several surfaces (which is thought to foster individuality), and children's art is displayed on white walls and hung from high ceilings.

Another Place for Children High ceilings, uncrowded play space, varied options for art and music, a glass wall revealing trees and flowers—all these features reflect the Reggio Emilia approach to individualized, creative learning for young children. Such places are rare in nations other than Italy.

OBSERVATION QUIZ

How many children appear in this photograph, and how many are engaged in creative expression? (see answer, page 186) →

ATELIER—FROM "OPEN WINDOWS." © MUNICIPALITY OF REGGIO EMILIA INFANT-TODDLER CENTERS AND PRESCHOOLS, PUBLISHED BY REGGIO CHILDREN 1994.

One of the distinctive features of the curriculum is that one teacher is an artist, who helps all the children to produce works of art (Gandini et al., 2005). Another feature is that a small group of children become engaged in long-term projects of their choosing. Such projects foster the children's pride in their accomplishments (their finished products are displayed for everyone to admire) while teaching them to plan and work together.

Teacher-Directed Programs

Unlike Montessori and Reggio Emilia schools, some programs stress academic subjects taught by a teacher to an entire class. Children learn letters, numbers, shapes, and colors, as well as how to listen to the teacher and sit quietly. Teachers give praise and other reinforcements for good behavior.

In teacher-directed programs, there is a clear distinction between the serious work of schooling and the cozy play of home. As one German boy explained:

> So home is home and kindergarten is kindergarten. Here is my work and at home is off-time, understand? My mum says work is me learning something. Learning is when you drive your head, and off-time is when the head slows down.
>
> *[quoted in Griebel & Niesel, 2002, p. 67]*

The teachers' goal is to make all children "ready to learn" by the time they enter first grade. Some teacher-directed programs explicitly teach basic skills, including reading, writing, and arithmetic. At school and for homework, children practice forming letters, sounding out words, counting objects, and writing their names.

If a 4-year-old learns to read, that is seen as a success in a teacher-directed program. (By contrast, in a child-centered program, early reading might arouse suspicion that the child had too little time to play and to create.) Many teacher-directed programs were inspired by behaviorism, which emphasizes step-by-step learning and repetition, with rewards for performing well.

One advantage of teacher-directed programs is that they are much less expensive, since the child/adult ratio can be higher. Another advantage is that every child learns basic skills that will be needed in elementary school.

Intervention Programs

Developmental scientists, linking research findings and practical applications, recognize that early childhood is a prime learning period. Five-year-olds differ dramatically from one another in their ability to count, talk, and even listen—all indications of readiness for school.

The main reason for this school-readiness gap between the slower and faster kindergartners is thought to be early education. Some parents provide a wealth of learning opportunities, talking and playing with their children for many hours a day; others do not (B. Hart & Risley, 1995). The slower ones may be handicapped throughout their school years because they learned less during early childhood.

Many nations try to narrow this gap by offering pre-kindergarten programs. Some nations (e.g., China, France, Italy, and Sweden) make early-childhood education free for everyone. In other nations, public funding does not support any early education. In still others, offerings vary depending on the family's needs and place of residence.

ANSWER TO OBSERVATION QUIZ
(from page 183) Attendance by 4-year-olds increased from 15 percent to 40 percent. The discussion of Head Start that follows explains why. ●

Learning from One Another Every nation creates its own version of early education. In this scene at a nursery school in Kuala Lumpur, Malaysia, note the head coverings, uniforms, bare feet, and absence of boys. None of these elements would be found in most early-childhood-education classrooms in North America or Europe.

OBSERVATION QUIZ
What seemingly universal aspects of childhood are visible in this photograph? (see answer, page 187) →

PAUL CHESLEY / STONE / GETTY IMAGES

ANSWER TO OBSERVATION QUIZ
(from page 184) Eight children, and all of them are engaged in creative projects—if the boy standing at right is making music, not just noise, with that cymbal. ●

Project Head Start
The most widespread early-childhood-education program in the United States, begun in 1965 and funded by the federal government.

LAURA DWIGHT

Learning Is Fun The original purpose of the Head Start program was to boost disadvantaged children's academic skills. The most enduring benefits, however, turned out to be improved self-esteem and social skills, as is evident in these happy Head Start participants, all crowded together.

OBSERVATION QUIZ
How many of these children are in close physical contact without discomfort or disagreement? (see answer, page 188) →

For example, in the United States, Oklahoma provides free full-day kindergarten and preschool education for everyone. In most other states, a few hours of pre-K a day are funded for children from poor families or with special needs. Some public schools provide only half-day kindergarten, which saves money but seems foolish to developmentalists, who consider young children to be more prodigious learners than older children—yet it's the latter group that is required to have a full day of school.

HEAD START In the United States, the preeminent federal early-childhood-education program is **Project Head Start.** It began in 1965, as part of the federal government's War on Poverty, with half a million students. It now enrolls nearly 1 million children each year (Jacobson, 2007).

Since the beginning, Head Start has been controversial. A major problem is that initially there was no provision for evaluation of the program (D. A. Phillips & White, 2004). Partly for this reason, the findings on the effectiveness of Head Start have varied. At first, the program was thought to be highly successful at raising children's intelligence. Ten years later, early gains were said to fade. Now Head Start is considered beneficial but far from ideal.

For success to be measured, goals need to be set; but goals for Head Start have varied from place to place, from time to time, and from politician to politician. For some, the program's goal was to lift families out of poverty; thus, a major component was involvement of parents in their children's education, which included hiring parents as teachers. By contrast, other jurisdictions sought to make every young child a reader, so trained professionals emphasized vocabulary and letter recognition. Still other Head Start programs stressed health and included dental care and a special emphasis on nutrition. Some classrooms were child-centered and others teacher-directed; some Head Start directors considered parents part of the problem, while others regarded parents as allies (D. R. Powell, 2006).

Ongoing political controversies in the United States regarding solutions to poverty, the funding of government programs, and the education of young children have complicated Head Start's curricula and evaluation. Over the decades, early education has been proven to be beneficial, but the priorities and direction of Head Start programs change continually as the political winds shift (Zigler & Styfco, 2004).

Since 1996, an intervention program called Early Start has been added. This program is for children under age 3. As with Head Start, availability of Early Start varies from state to state.

EXPERIMENTAL INTERVENTION PROGRAMS The same social concerns that led to Head Start led to several other intensive programs that began at about the same time and have been well evaluated. Three projects in particular have excellent follow-up data: one in Michigan, called Perry or *High/Scope* (Schweinhart & Weikart, 1997; Schweinhart et al., 2005); one in North Carolina, called *Abecedarian* (F. A. Campbell et al., 2001); and one in Chicago, called *Child–Parent Centers* (A. J. Reynolds, 2000; A. J. Reynolds et al., 2004).

Like Head Start, these three federally funded programs began as part of the War on Poverty, enrolling young children from low-income families. All were designed according to principles of developmental science. For instance, they compared experimental groups with control groups and documented exactly what the teachers did and what the children learned.

All the evaluations of these three programs reached the same conclusion, which is now accepted by developmentalists: Good early education has many long-term benefits. Children in these programs scored higher on math and reading achievement tests by age 10 than did other children from the same backgrounds, schools, and neighborhoods. They were also significantly less likely to be placed in special classes for slow or disruptive children or to repeat a year of school.

Many benefits were social, rather than strictly cognitive. Adolescents who had been in these three programs tended to have higher aspirations and a greater sense of achievement. As young adults, they more often attended college, owned homes, had jobs, and stayed out of prison.

All three research projects found that providing direct cognitive training (not simply letting children play), with instruction in school-readiness skills, was useful and that each child's needs and talents should be considered. The curriculum was neither solely child-centered nor solely teacher-directed, but a combination of the two. In addition, parents were engaged with their child's learning.

These three programs were expensive (perhaps as much as $48,000 annually per child in 2009 dollars). However, many believe that the decreased need later on for special education and other social services makes such programs a wise investment in the long term.

Indeed, one economist calculates that, on average, governments eventually spend five times more (because of increased rates of special education, unemployment, and crime) for each child who does not attend an intensive preschool program (Lynch, 2004). As you remember from Chapter 1, such cost-benefit analysis is favored by developmentalists, who often find that an investment made in childhood pays dividends years later.

THE BEST KIND OF PROGRAM Generally, an educational, center-based program is better for young children than home care. Play with other children may help with brain development and social skills, and even the most devoted parenting cannot substitute for interaction with peers. Furthermore, good programs offer a wider variety of activities and projects than any parent could.

However, quality is crucial. High-quality home care is better than low-quality day care at a center (Clarke-Stewart & Allhusen, 2005). One critical issue is curriculum. Programs with an emphasis on learning may be best, as they offer extensive practice with language, motor skills, and numbers. Encouragement of creativity and individual initiative is also important.

Teachers must respond to each child as an individual, which is one reason that children suffer if caregivers change over the year, or if there are too many children and caregivers in the group. Six 2-year-olds and two caregivers are better than a dozen 2-year-olds and 4 caregivers, even though the child–adult ratio is the same. Obviously, parents have a natural advantage here; a child has the same parent day in and day out.

Partly for these reasons, many early-childhood educators in Europe, Asia, and the Americas believe that the Reggio Emilia approach is ideal. However, the architecture, professional teachers, and emphasis on individual learning make Reggio Emilia education expensive—perhaps $22,000 per year per student in 2009. These programs originated in Italy, which has a very low birth rate (the average couple has one child) and low military spending; that country's investment in early education is difficult for other nations to match.

ESPECIALLY FOR Teachers In trying to find a preschool program, what should parents look for? (see response, page 188) →

ANSWER TO OBSERVATION QUIZ
(from page 186) All five—not four
(look again at the right-hand side of
the photograph)! ●

RESPONSE FOR Teachers (from page
187) Tell parents to look at the people
more than the program. Parents
should see the children in action and
note whether the teachers show
warmth and respect for each child. ●

> ## KEY points
>
> - Child-centered early education, such as Montessori and Reggio Emilia programs, encourage each child to discover ideas, master skills, and be creative.
> - Teacher-directed programs help every child become ready for school, learning letters and numbers.
> - Early-intervention programs advance the well-being of children from low-income families. This is apparent in carefully researched programs; evidence about massive early-intervention efforts is less clear.
> - High-quality early education benefits all children, who improve particularly in language, self-confidence, and social skills.

Injuries and Maltreatment

Worldwide, the United Nations estimates that about 2 million children and adolescents die accidentally each year (Peden et al., 2008). Millions more are abused or neglected. Such harm is far from inevitable, however.

Accidents

Accidents are the leading cause of death worldwide for people under age 40. Rates are highest in developing nations, but the proportion of deaths by accident is highest in developed nations. In other words, a child's chance of dying accidentally is higher in poor nations than in wealthy ones, but so is that child's chance of dying from disease. In wealthy nations, it is rare for a child to die of disease, and that makes accidents the one cause of child death that is still far more common than need be.

Among 2- to 6-year-olds in the United States, four times more children die in accidents than die of cancer, which is the second most common cause of death (U.S. Bureau of the Census, 2008). Furthermore, during early childhood, nonfatal injuries result in more lasting damage, more hospitalization, and more pain than all diseases combined.

Preschoolers are particularly likely to swallow poison or to die from burning, suffocating, choking, or drowning. Ironically, small children are vulnerable to these accidents because of the developmental advances described earlier in this chapter. Their improved motor skills enable them to run, climb, and use dangerous objects (matches, bottles, guns), and their thinking is rapid and impulsive but not logical. Their curiosity is boundless; their impulses are uninhibited.

injury control/harm reduction
Practices that are aimed at anticipating, controlling, and preventing dangerous activities; these practices reflect the beliefs that accidents are not random and that injuries can be made less harmful if proper controls are in place.

HARM REDUCTION Experts prefer the term **injury control** or **harm reduction** rather than *accident prevention*. Minor mishaps are bound to occur, but the "accident paradigm" leads to the false idea that "injuries will occur despite our best efforts" (G. C. Benjamin, 2004, p. 521). (A paradigm is a general concept that frames other thoughts.) The accident paradigm is the belief that serious mishaps occur randomly, by chance. Not so.

Every young child sometimes scrapes a knee, bumps a forehead, or breaks a toe. Some are injured more often than others for genetic, gender, or contextual reasons. However, injuries can be controlled. Harm is limited if a child falls on a safety surface instead of on concrete, if a car seat protects the body, if a bicycle helmet cracks instead of a skull. Thanks to harm reduction, less than half as many 1- to 4-year-olds in the United States were fatally injured in 2005 as in 1980 (National Center for Health Statistics, 2007).

THREE LEVELS OF PREVENTION Injury control begins before any particular person is careless or encounters danger. There are three recognized levels of prevention:

- **Primary prevention** changes overall conditions to make injuries less likely.
- **Secondary prevention** averts harm to individuals in high-risk situations.
- **Tertiary prevention** limits damage after an injury occurs.

One way to distinguish these three types of prevention is by considering when they occur. Primary prevention is systemic, beginning long before harm occurs; for example, enclosures with locked gates keep unsupervised children out of swimming pools. Secondary prevention reduces the immediate danger in a high-risk situation, as when a young, impulsive child approaches a pool but a caregiver makes the child wear a life vest and swims nearby. Tertiary prevention happens after harm has occurred; for example, CPR administered by a trained passerby improves a drowning victim's chances of recovery. Some measures can be considered part of all three levels; for instance, having trained lifeguards at every pool can serve as primary, secondary, and tertiary prevention.

All three levels of prevention once protected my daughter Bethany. At age 2, she climbed onto the kitchen counter to grab, open, and swallow most of a bottle of baby aspirin. In so doing, she demonstrated the impressive memory and motor skills of young children, as well as their goal-directed intensity. (She also illustrated parental neglect—I was in the other room, feeding Rachel. Having two young children is a high-risk condition.)

Laws had limited the number of baby aspirin allowed per container (primary prevention), my pediatrician had told me to buy syrup of ipecac and keep it on hand for emergencies (secondary prevention), and I phoned Poison Control (tertiary prevention). The stranger on the phone asked several questions and then told me to give Bethany some ipecac so that she'd throw up the aspirin. I did and she did, and thus harm was averted.

A more general illustration comes from data on pedestrian deaths. Fewer people in the United States die after being hit by a motor vehicle than did 25 years ago (see Figure 5.9). How does each level of prevention contribute to this decline?

Primary prevention includes sidewalks, speed bumps, pedestrian overpasses, streetlights, and traffic circles (Retting et al., 2003; Tester et al., 2004). Other examples are

primary prevention
Actions that change overall background conditions to prevent some unwanted event or circumstance, such as injury, disease, or abuse.

secondary prevention
Actions that avert harm in a high-risk situation, such as stopping a car before it hits a pedestrian or installing traffic lights at dangerous intersections.

tertiary prevention
Actions, such as immediate and effective medical treatment, that are taken after an adverse event (such as illness, injury, or abuse) occurs and that are aimed at reducing the harm or preventing disability.

And If He Falls . . . None of these children are injured, so no tertiary prevention is needed. Photos (*b*) and (*c*) both illustrate secondary prevention, and, as shown in (*c*), crossing the street in a clearly marked crosswalk, under adult supervision, is safest for children. A five-point car seat (the safest kind) protects the Russian child in (*b*). In photo (*a*), the metal climbing equipment with large gaps and peeling paint is hazardous. Primary prevention suggests that this "attractive nuisance" be dismantled.

(a)

(b)

(c)

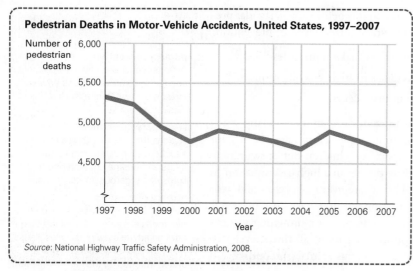

Pedestrian Deaths in Motor-Vehicle Accidents, United States, 1997–2007

Source: National Highway Traffic Safety Administration, 2008.

FIGURE 5.9 Stalled Safety? The biggest dip in pedestrian deaths in motor vehicle accidents occurred between 1997 and 2000.

● **UNDERSTANDING THE NUMBERS**
Have efforts to prevent motor vehicle accidents stalled in recent years?

Answer Not if you consider that this graph shows the annual numbers, not the rates, of such deaths. The absolute number of pedestrian deaths in 2007 (4,654) is only 2 percent less than in 2000 (4,763). However, during those years, the U.S. population increased (by about 7 percent), as did the number of miles driven by the average person (by about 12 percent). Rate is a better indicator than absolute number. In the case of pedestrian deaths, the rate was about 20 percent lower in 2007 than in 2000.

ESPECIALLY FOR Urban Planners
Describe a neighborhood park that would benefit 2- to 5-year-olds. (see response, page 192) ➡

child maltreatment
Intentional harm to or avoidable endangerment of anyone under 18 years of age.

child abuse
Deliberate action that is harmful to a child's physical, emotional, or sexual well-being.

child neglect
Failure to meet a child's basic physical, educational, or emotional needs.

redesigned cars (with better headlights, bumpers, and brakes) and improved driver competence (via stronger drunk-driving penalties and tougher licensing exams). Primary prevention may also occur if traffic is reduced because of congestion, driving costs, and improved mass transit.

Secondary prevention reduces danger in high-risk situations. For child pedestrians, this includes flashing lights on stopped school buses, school-crossing guards, and fences to keep children from running into streets. For teenagers, this includes later ages to qualify for a full driver's license. For everyone, salting icy roads, posting warning signs before blind curves, and installing walk signals at busy intersections are examples of secondary prevention.

Finally, *tertiary prevention* reduces damage after automobile crashes; examples include laws against hit-and-runs, speedy ambulances, improved emergency room procedures, and effective rehabilitation. Medical personnel remember the *golden hour*. Although there is nothing magical about 60 minutes in contrast to 59 or 61 minutes, the faster an injured person reaches a trauma center, the better the chance of survival (Bledsoe, 2002).

Child Maltreatment

The next time you hear about some horribly neglected or abused child, think of these words from a leading researcher in child maltreatment:

> Make no mistake—those who abuse children are fully responsible for their actions. However, creating an information system that perpetuates the message that offenders are the only ones to blame may be misleading. . . . We all contribute to the conditions that allow perpetrators to succeed.
>
> *[Daro, 2002, p. 1133]*

"We all contribute" in the sense that child maltreatment has multifaceted causes, involving not only parents but also neighbors, the community, and the culture. Moreover, although victims are never to blame for their maltreatment, certain characteristics make some children more vulnerable to abuse than others. Thus, infants are most at risk of being maltreated if they are difficult (fragile, needing frequent feeding, crying often) *and* if their mothers are depressed and do not feel in control of their lives or their infants *and* if the family is isolated and under financial stress (Bugental & Happaney, 2004).

MALTREATMENT NOTICED AND DEFINED Until about 1960, people thought maltreatment was rare and consisted of a sudden attack by a disturbed stranger. Today we know better, thanks to a pioneering study based on careful observation in one Boston hospital that reported on the *battered-child syndrome* (Kempe & Kempe, 1978). In this study, it became obvious that many children had been repeatedly abused by their caregivers. Later research revealed that neglect of a child is also maltreatment, often more damaging than outright abuse (Valentino et al., 2008).

More Inclusive Definitions **Child maltreatment** now refers to all intentional harm to, or avoidable endangerment of, anyone under 18 years of age. **Child abuse** is deliberate action that harms a child's physical, emotional, or sexual well-being; **child neglect** is failure to meet a child's basic physical, educational, or emotional needs.

Not all cases of maltreatment are noticed, not all that are noticed are reported, and not all that are reported are substantiated. **Substantiated maltreatment** is a reported case that has been investigated and verified (see Figure 5.10). The number of *substantiated* cases in the United States in 2005 was 900,000; among 2- to 5-year-olds, about 1 child in every 70 was maltreated (U.S. Department of Health and Human Services, 2008).

Overall, about two-thirds of reported cases are not substantiated, and many cases of maltreatment are not even reported. According to a survey of young adults in the United States, 1 in 4 said they had been physically abused ("slapped, hit, or kicked") by a parent or other adult caregiver, and 1 in 22 had been sexually abused ("touched or forced to touch someone in a sexual way") (Hussey et al., 2006). Almost never had their maltreatment been reported.

One reason for this high rate of reported abuse might be that the young adults in this survey were asked if they had *ever* been mistreated before sixth grade, while most other sources report rates per year. Another reason is that few children report their own abuse. Many adults do not realize that they had been maltreated until they reflect back on their childhood. The authors of this study think the rates they found are *underestimates!*

Warning Signs Because children may not know that they are being maltreated, it is up to adults to notice and report signs. Often the first sign is delayed development, such as slow growth, immature communication, lack of curiosity, or unusual social interactions. All these difficulties may be evident even at age 1 (Valentino et al., 2006). During early childhood, maltreated children may seem fearful, startled by noise, defensive and quick to attack, and confused between fantasy and reality.

Table 5.2 lists these and other signs of child maltreatment, both neglect and abuse. None of these signs are proof that a child has been abused, but whenever any of them occurs, it signifies trouble. Many nations, including the United States, require all professionals who deal with children (teachers, nurses, social workers, doctors, police officers) to report any suspected maltreatment.

Nobody Watching? Madelyn Gorman Toogood looks around to make sure no one is watching before she slaps and shakes her 4-year-old daughter, Martha, who is in a car seat inside the vehicle. A security camera recorded this incident in an Indiana department store parking lot. A week later, after the videotape was repeatedly broadcast nationwide, Toogood was recognized and arrested. The haunting question is: How much child abuse takes place that is not witnessed?

substantiated maltreatment
Harm or endangerment that has been reported, investigated, and verified.

ESPECIALLY FOR Nurses While weighing a 4-year-old, you notice several bruises on the child's legs. When you ask about them, the child says nothing and the parent says the child bumps into things. What should you do? (see response, page 193) →

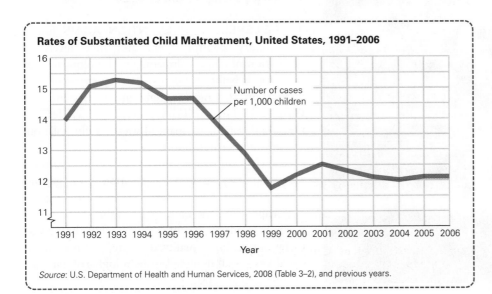

Rates of Substantiated Child Maltreatment, United States, 1991–2006

Number of cases per 1,000 children

Year

Source: U.S. Department of Health and Human Services, 2008 (Table 3–2), and previous years.

FIGURE 5.10 Still Far Too Many
The number of reported and substantiated cases of maltreatment of children under age 18 in the United States is too high, but there is some good news: The rate has declined significantly from the peak in 1993.

OBSERVATION QUIZ
The data point for 1999 is close to the bottom of the graph. Does that mean it is close to zero? (see answer, page 193) →

MISHAWAKA POLICE DEPARTMENT / GETTY IMAGES

RESPONSE FOR Urban Planners (from page 190) The adult idea of a park—a large, grassy open place—is not best for young children. For them, you would design an enclosed area, small enough and with adequate seating to allow caregivers to socialize while watching their children. The playground surface would have to be protective, with equipment that encourages both gross motor skills (such as climbing) and fine motor skills (such as sandbox play). Swings are not beneficial, since they do not develop many motor skills. Teenagers and dogs should have their own designated area, far from the youngest children. ●

TABLE 5.2 Signs of Maltreatment in Children Aged 2 to 10

Injuries that do not fit an "accidental" explanation: bruises on both sides of the face or body; burns with a clear line between burned and unburned skin; "falls" that result in cuts, not scrapes

Repeated injuries, especially broken bones not properly tended

Fantasy play with dominant themes of violence or sexual knowledge

Slow physical growth, especially with unusual appetite or lack of appetite

Ongoing physical complaints, such as stomachaches, headaches, genital pain, sleepiness

Reluctance to talk, to play, or to move, especially if development is slow

No close friendships; hostility toward others; bullying of smaller children

Hypervigilance, with quick, impulsive reactions, such as cringing, startling, or hitting

Frequent absences from school, changes of address, or new caregivers

Expressions of fear rather than joy on seeing the caregiver

Source: Adapted from Scannapieco & Connell-Carrick, 2005.

Abuse or Athletics? Four-year-old Budhia Singh ran 40 miles in 7 hours with adult marathoners. He says he likes to run, but his mother (a widow who allowed his trainer to "adopt" him because she could not feed him) has charged the trainer with physical abuse. The government of India has declared that Singh cannot race again until he is fully grown. If a child, the parent, and the community approve of some activity, can it still be maltreatment?

REUTERS / SANJIB MUKHERJEE

CONSEQUENCES OF MALTREATMENT The impact of any child-rearing practice is affected by the cultural context. Certain customs (such as circumcision, ear piercing, and spanking) are considered abusive in some cultures but not in others. The effects on children vary accordingly. Children suffer if they think their parents do not love them because they do not treat them according to their community's standards.

Although the degree of harm varies with community standards, severely maltreated children suffer physiologically, academically, and socially in every culture. The worst consequence is that maltreated children come to consider other people to be hostile and exploitative. That belief makes them fearful, aggressive, and lonely. The earlier their abuse starts and the longer it continues, the more trouble they have with peers and adults (Manly et al., 2001; Scannapieco & Connell-Carrick, 2005).

A life-span perspective reveals that these deficits may continue lifelong. Maltreated children may become bullies or victims or both. They tend to dissociate—that is, to disconnect their memories from their understanding of themselves (Valentino et al., 2008). When they grow up, they often abuse drugs or alcohol, enter unsupportive relationships, and become victims or aggressors themselves (M. G. Smith & Fong, 2004). They experience more emotional disorders and suicide attempts (Afifi et al., 2008).

THREE LEVELS OF PREVENTION, AGAIN Just as with injury control, there are three levels of prevention of child maltreatment. The ultimate goal is to stop it before it begins—*primary prevention* that focuses on the macrosystem and exosystem (see Chapter 1). Thus, primary prevention includes any measure that reduces financial stress, family isolation, and unwanted parenthood.

Secondary prevention involves spotting warning signs and keeping a risky situation from getting worse. For example, insecure attachment is a sign of a disrupted parent–child relationship that needs repair. Secondary prevention may include home visits by nurses, high-quality day care, and preventive social work—all designed to help high-risk families (Zielinski et al., 2009).

Tertiary prevention reduces harm when maltreatment has already occurred. Reporting and substantiating abuse are essential and should be followed immediately by helping the parents provide better care or removing the child from the home. All children need a caregiver they trust, in a safe and stable environment, whether they live with their biological parents, with a foster family, or with an adoptive family.

Whenever a child suffers maltreatment, tertiary prevention requires **permanency planning,** an effort to find a long-term solution to the problem. If the child remains with the parents, measures must be put in place to ensure that the family will provide good care. For example, parents may need to enter a drug treatment program, to learn better parenting skills, or to have daily home visits from a child-care specialist. If child-welfare authorities decide that removal from the home is the best solution, a permanent family must be found to nurture the child until adulthood (Waddell et al., 2004).

STEPHANIE MAZE / CORBIS

Tertiary Prevention Adoption has been these children's salvation, particularly for 9-year-old Leah, clinging to her mother. The mother, Joan, has five adopted children. Adoption is generally better than foster care for maltreated children because it is a permanent, stable arrangement.

FOSTER CARE In **foster care,** children are entrusted to another adult or family. In 2006, more than half a million children in the United States were officially in foster care, with three times as many unofficially taken in by relatives other than their parents. About half of the children officially in foster care were in **kinship care,** in which a relative—usually a grandparent—of the maltreated child becomes the foster caregiver (U.S. Department of Health and Human Services, 2004).

Although many children entering foster care have cognitive, physical, and social disabilities, they generally develop better in stable foster care (including kinship care) than with their original families if a supervising agency provides ongoing financial support and counseling (Kenrick et al., 2006; Oosterman et al., 2007). Stability is hard to come by: Foster children average three placements before a permanent home is found for them (Pew Commission on Foster Care, 2004). Each move increases the risk of a poor outcome (Oosterman et al., 2007). Adoption is usually the best permanent placement, but, for many reasons, it is the least common solution.

This chapter illustrates what I learned when I started a preschool for Bethany: Young children grow and develop well if given a chance—learning languages, developing motor skills, exploring their social world. However, adults—especially parents but other adults as well—create the conditions that allow children to grow happily and healthily. This theme is continued in the next chapter, which focuses particularly on the social contexts of early childhood.

permanency planning
An effort by child-welfare authorities to find a long-term living situation that will provide stability and support for a maltreated child. A goal is to avoid repeated changes of caregiver or school, which can be particularly harmful to the child.

foster care
A legal, publicly supported system in which a maltreated child is removed from the parents' custody and entrusted to another adult or family, which is reimbursed for expenses incurred in meeting the child's needs.

kinship care
A form of foster care in which a relative of a maltreated child, usually a grandparent, becomes the approved caregiver.

RESPONSE FOR Nurses (from page 191) Any suspicion of child maltreatment must be reported, and these bruises are suspicious. Someone in authority must find out what is happening so that the parent as well as the child can be helped. ●

ANSWER TO OBSERVATION QUIZ (from page 191) No. The number is actually 11.8 per 1,000. Note the little squiggle on the graph's vertical axis below the number 11. This means that numbers between 0 and 11 are not shown. ●

KEY Points

- Many young children are injured because of adults' lack of forethought.

- Each year, almost 1 million children in the United States experience substantiated maltreatment, which includes abuse and neglect.

- The source of maltreatment is often the family system and the cultural context, not a deranged stranger. The consequences affect victims lifelong.

- Three levels of prevention include primary prevention (laws and practices that protect everyone), secondary prevention (protective measures for high-risk situations), and tertiary prevention (reduction of harm after an injury or substantiated maltreatment has occurred).

SUMMARY

Body Changes

1. Children continue to gain weight and height during early childhood. Many become quite picky eaters. One reason this occurs is that many adults overfeed children, not realizing that young children are naturally quite thin.

2. Motor skills continue to develop, turning clumsy 2-year-olds into 6-year-olds able to move their bodies in whatever ways their culture values and they themselves have practiced. Both gross and fine motor skills develop in early childhood.

Brain Development

3. The brain continues to grow. Myelination is substantial, speeding messages from one part of the brain to another. The corpus callosum becomes thicker and functions much better. The prefrontal cortex, known as the executive of the brain, is strengthened as well.

4. Brain changes enable more reflective, coordinated thought and memory; better planning; and quicker responses. All brain functions are localized in one hemisphere or the other. Left–right specialization is apparent in the entire body.

5. The expression and regulation of emotions are fostered by several brain areas, including the amygdala, the hippocampus, and the hypothalamus. Abuse in childhood may cause overactivity in the amygdala and hippocampus, creating a flood of stress hormones that interfere with learning.

Thinking During Early Childhood

6. Piaget stressed the egocentric and illogical aspects of thought during early childhood. He called this stage preoperational thought, because young children often cannot yet use logical operations to think about their observations and experiences.

7. Young children, according to Piaget, sometimes focus on only one thing (centration) and see things only from their own viewpoint (egocentrism), remaining stuck on appearances and on current reality. They may believe that living spirits reside in inanimate objects, a belief called animism.

8. Vygotsky stressed the social aspects of childhood cognition, noting that children learn by participating in various experiences, guided by more knowledgeable adults or peers. That guidance assists learning within the zone of proximal development, which encompasses the knowledge and skills that the child has the potential to learn.

9. Children develop theories, especially to explain the purpose of life and their role in it. Among these theories is theory of mind—an understanding of what others may be thinking. Theory of mind is partly the result of brain maturation at around age 4, but language and experiences also have an impact.

Language

10. Language develops rapidly during early childhood, which is a sensitive period but not a critical one for language learning. Vocabulary increases dramatically, with thousands of words added between ages 2 and 6. In addition, basic grammar is mastered.

11. Many children learn to speak more than one language, gaining cognitive as well as social advantages. Ideally, children become balanced bilinguals, equally proficient in two languages, by age 6.

Early-Childhood Education

12. Organized educational programs during early childhood advance cognitive and social skills. Montessori and Reggio Emilia are two child-centered programs that began in Italy and now are offered in many nations. Behaviorist principles led to many specific practices of teacher-directed programs.

13. Longitudinal research on intervention programs has demonstrated that early-childhood education reduces the likelihood of later problems, both in school and in adult life.

14. Although many types of preschool programs are successful, the quality of early education matters. Children learn best if there is a clear curriculum and if the child/adult ratio is low. The training and continuity of early-childhood teachers are also important.

Injuries and Maltreatment

15. Injury control occurs on many levels, including long before and immediately after each harmful incident, with primary, secondary, and tertiary prevention. Close supervision is required to protect young children from their own eager, impulsive curiosity.

16. Child maltreatment typically results from ongoing abuse and neglect by a child's own parents. Each year almost 3 million cases of child maltreatment are reported in the United States, almost 1 million of which are substantiated.

17. Foster care, including kinship care, is sometimes necessary in cases of severe abuse or neglect. Permanency planning is required, because frequent changes are harmful to children.

KEY TERMS

myelination (p. 166)
corpus callosum (p. 167)
lateralization (p. 167)
perseveration (p. 168)
amygdala (p. 169)

hippocampus (p. 169)
hypothalamus (p. 169)
preoperational intelligence (p. 171)
centration (p. 171)

egocentrism (p. 171)
focus on appearance (p. 171)
static reasoning (p. 171)
irreversibility (p. 171)
conservation (p. 172)

animism (p. 173)
apprentice in thinking (p. 173)
zone of proximal development (ZPD) (p. 174)
scaffolding (p. 174)

private speech (p. 175)
social mediation (p. 175)
theory-theory (p. 176)
theory of mind (p. 177)
fast-mapping (p. 179)
overregularization (p. 180)

balanced bilingual (p. 182)
Reggio Emilia approach
(p. 184)
Project Head Start (p. 186)
injury control/harm reduction
(p. 188)

primary prevention (p. 189)
secondary prevention (p. 189)
tertiary prevention (p. 189)
child maltreatment (p. 190)
child abuse (p. 190)
child neglect (p. 190)

substantiated maltreatment
(p. 191)
permanency planning (p. 193)
foster care (p. 193)
kinship care (p. 193)

KEY QUESTIONS

1. How are growth rates, body proportions, and motor skills related during early childhood?

2. Does low family income tend to make young children eat more or less? Explain your answer.

3. How do emotions, and their expression, originate in the brain?

4. How would parents act differently toward their child according to whether they agreed with Piaget or with Vygotsky?

5. How do the ideas of Piaget and Vygotsky relate to theory of mind?

6. How do fast-mapping and brain development apply to children's learning of curse words?

7. What are the differences between child-centered and teacher-directed instruction?

8. Why do some cities and nations provide much better preschool education than others?

9. Why do public health workers prefer to speak of "injury control" instead of "accident prevention"?

10. What are the differences among the three kinds of prevention?

11. What are the advantages and disadvantages of kinship care?

APPLICATIONS

1. Keep a food diary for 24 hours, writing down what you eat, how much, when, how, and why. Then think about nutrition and eating habits in early childhood. Did your food habits originate in early childhood, in adolescence, or at some other time? Explain.

2. Go to a playground or other place where young children play. Note the motor skills that the children demonstrate, including abilities and inabilities, and keep track of age and sex. What differences do you see among the children?

3. Replicate one of Piaget's conservation experiments. The easiest one is conservation of liquids (illustrated in Figure 5.4). Work with a child under age 5 who tells you that two identically shaped glasses contain the same amount of liquid. Then carefully pour one glass of liquid into a taller, narrower glass. Ask the child which glass now contains more or if the glasses contain the same amount.

4. Think back on your childhood and the friends you had at that time. Was there any maltreatment? Considering what you have learned about prevention in this chapter, why or why not?

CHAPTER OUTLINE

EARLY CHILDHOOD
Psychosocial Development

M y daughter Bethany, at about age 5, challenged one of my students to a fight. "Girls don't fight," he said, laughing. "*Nobody* fights," I sternly corrected him. We were both teaching Bethany how to express emotions, a skill considered crucial for young children. She learned emotional regulation well; by age 6, she no longer threatened physical fights.

But I remember that incident because I am troubled by what I said. Although my words "Nobody fights" referred to both sexes, my statement could be seen as expressing an attitude typical of women, who are sometimes called the weaker sex. Was I keeping Bethany from becoming strong and brave? Should I have encouraged her to fight and asked my student to play-fight with her, as men do with young boys? Or maybe the opposite response was needed. Perhaps I should have kept quiet, allowing my student to teach Bethany proper gender norms. ●

EMOTIONAL CONTROL, aggression, parenting, moral development, and sex differences are all discussed in this chapter. Some aspects of these issues have been studied for decades, and experts agree on them. For instance, no developmentalist doubts that bullying should be stopped, that play teaches social understanding, or that parents should guide and discipline their children. However, many topics, including sex-role development, are still controversial. It is not surprising that I wonder whether my student's "Girls don't fight" was the right response.

Emotional Development

Learning when and how to express emotions—the preeminent psychosocial accomplishment between ages 2 and 6—is made possible as the emotional hot spots of the limbic system begin to connect to the prefrontal cortex, the decision-making area of the brain (N. Eisenberg et al., 2004). Children who master this **emotional regulation** become more capable in every aspect of their lives (Denham et al., 2003; Matsumoto, 2004).

Six-year-olds regulate and control their emotions in ways not yet known to exuberant, expressive, and often overwhelmed toddlers. Children learn they can be friendly to new acquaintances but not too friendly, angry about a confiscated

emotional regulation
The ability to control when and how emotions are expressed.

SEAN CAYTON /THE IMAGE WORKS

Close Connection Unfamiliar events often bring developmental tendencies to the surface, as with the curious boy and his worried brother, who are attending Colorado's Pikes Peak or Bust Rodeo breakfast. Their attentive mother keeps the livelier boy calm and reassures the shy one.

OBSERVATION QUIZ

Mother is obviously a secure base for both boys, who share the same family and half the same genes but are different ages: One is 2 and the other is 4. Can you tell which boy is younger? (see answer, page 201) ➡

toy but not explosive, frightened by a clown but not terrified. They learn to distract themselves and limit their impulses if need be. (All these abilities emerge during early childhood and continue to develop throughout life.) Now we explain some specific aspects of emotional regulation.

Initiative Versus Guilt

Taking initiative means, for example, saying something new, extending a skill, or beginning a project. Depending on the outcome (including the parents' response), children can feel either pride or guilt about their initiatives. Guilt makes them afraid to try new activities.

The tension between these opposite responses is captured by Erikson's term for this stage, **initiative versus guilt.** Usually parents encourage young children's natural enthusiasm, effort, and self-evaluation, which are typical during early childhood. If parents dismiss these emotional expressions (whether fear or excitement, anger or joy), children may not learn emotional regulation (A. S. Morris et al., 2007). Instead, they may feel ashamed and then guilty about the emotion.

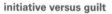

initiative versus guilt
Erikson's third psychosocial crisis, in which children undertake new skills and activities and feel guilty when they do not succeed at them.

self-esteem
A person's evaluation of his or her own worth, either in specifics (e.g., intelligence, attractiveness) or in general.

self-concept
A person's understanding of who he or she is, incorporating self-esteem, physical appearance, personality, and various personal traits, such as gender and size.

PRIDE IN ONESELF Ideally, what emerges from the acquisition of the skills and competencies described in Chapter 5 is **self-esteem**—a belief in one's own ability, a personal estimate of success and worthiness. Parents encourage and confirm their children's self-esteem by reminding them of their positive accomplishments (Reese et al., 2007): "Remember when you helped Daddy sweep the sidewalk? You made it very clean."

However, some parents are routinely critical of their children. Such parents foster low self-esteem, the belief that "the self is fundamentally flawed" (Harter, 2006, p. 529). Extremely harsh criticism amounts to emotional abuse, causing children to develop a low estimate of their own competence that lasts lifelong.

Erikson noted that children become more confident and independent, eager to begin new activities and adventures, as their self-esteem builds. The autonomy of 2-year-olds, often expressed as stubbornness, becomes the initiative of 5-year-olds, often seen in their self-motivated activities. Over these years, children form a **self-concept,** or an understanding of themselves, that encompasses not only self-esteem but also awareness of personal traits such as gender and size. Girls are happy to be girls, boys to be boys, and both are glad they are not babies. "Crybaby" becomes a major insult.

Erikson recognized that most young children have immodest self-concepts, holding themselves in high esteem. They believe they are strong, smart, and good-looking—and thus believe any goal is quite achievable. They think that whatever they are (their self-concept) is also good. For instance, they believe their nation and religion are best, and they feel sorry for children who do not belong to their country or faith.

Young children are confident that their good qualities will endure but that any bad qualities (even biological traits such as poor eyesight) will disappear with time (Lockhart et al., 2002). As one group of researchers explained:

> Young children seem to be irrepressibly optimistic about themselves. . . . Consider, for example, the shortest, most uncoordinated boy in a kindergarten class who pro-claims that he will be the next Michael Jordan.
>
> *[Lockhart et al., 2002, pp. 1408–1409]*

The new initiative that Erikson described is aided by a longer attention span, which is made possible by neurological maturity (as explained in Chapter 5). Young children can concentrate on a task through completion—an ability that is crucial for social competence (Murphy, 2007).

Feeling proud (but not unrealistically so) is the foundation for the child's ongoing practice of skills. A child may draw the same picture again and again or repeat a joke, a cartwheel, or any other behavior he or she is encouraged to perform. This practice leads to mastery, as 4-year-olds pour juice, zip pants, or climb trees.

Preschoolers predict that they can solve impossible puzzles, remember long lists of words, and control their dreams (Stipek et al., 1995; Woolley & Boerger, 2002). Such naive predictions, sometimes called *protective optimism*, help them try new things (Lockhart et al., 2002). This is one reason why, as you remember, young children are quick to learn languages: They do not realize that they are mispronouncing words.

Proud to Be Who They Are These two boys, riding in Chicago's Mexican Independence Day parade, seem to have found a good balance of emotional strengths: ethnic pride, friendship, and forward momentum.

GUILT AND SHAME Even without adult criticism, children are caught between their own fears and fantasies. As Erikson puts it, "The child indulges in fantasies of being a giant and a tiger, but in his dreams he runs in terror" (Erikson, 1963, p. 256). The psycho-analytic understanding of dreams is that they emerge from uncon-scious emotions that erupt when the conscious mind is quiet.

Notice that Erikson called the negative side of the crisis at this stage of development guilt, not shame. Generally, *guilt* refers to the self-blame that people experience (especially in dreams) when they do something wrong; *shame* refers to people's feeling that others blame them, disapprove of them, or are disappointed in them.

Erikson believed that as children become more self-aware, they feel guilt when they realize their own mistakes. Many peo-ple believe that guilt is a more mature emotion than shame because guilt comes from within the person (Kochanska et al., 2002; Tangney et al., 2007) whereas shame depends on others' awareness.

As an example of this distinction, some children feel ashamed of their ethnic background because they think others devalue it, but they do not feel guilty unless they have done something wrong. To counter shame, many parents of minority children (Mexican, African, or Indian American, among others) encourage ethnic pride (Parke & Buriel, 2006). Similarly, parents typically protect the self-esteem of any child who might encounter negative remarks based on gender, family origin, religion, or appearance.

KIM KARPELES / ALAMY

intrinsic motivation
A drive, or reason to pursue a goal, that comes from inside a person, such as the need to feel smart or competent.

extrinsic motivation
A drive, or reason to pursue a goal, that arises from the need to have one's achievements rewarded from outside, perhaps by receiving material possessions or another person's esteem.

ARIEL SKELLEY / CORBIS

Happy and Colorful No wonder this 5-year-old is proud—her picture is worth framing. High self-esteem is one of the strengths of being her age. Can you imagine a 9-year-old holding an equally colorful picture so proudly?

ESPECIALLY FOR Teachers One of your students tells you about playing, sleeping, and talking with an imaginary friend. Does this mean that that child is emotionally disturbed? (see response, page 202) →

ESPECIALLY FOR College Students Is extrinsic or intrinsic motivation more influential in your study efforts? (see response, page 202) →

Motivation

The idea that guilt comes from within and shame comes from other people echoes another distinction, between *intrinsic motivation* and *extrinsic motivation*. **Intrinsic motivation** is on display when people do something for their own gratification. Thus, a musician might play for the sheer delight of making music, even if no one else is listening. **Extrinsic motivation** comes from outside, manifested when people do something to gain praise (or some other reinforcement) from someone else. A musician might want payment or applause for performing.

Both intrinsic and extrinsic motivation are connected to emotional regulation. Children become motivated to control their emotions, or at least the expression of their emotions. No 5-year-old wants to cry in front of his friends; that inhibition begins extrinsically, but the emotional expression is soon internalized, as when a child never lets himself cry even when he is alone.

For the most part, preschool children are intrinsically motivated. They enjoy learning, playing, and practicing whether or not someone else wants them to. For instance, when they play a game, young children might not keep score; the fun is in playing, not winning.

IMAGINARY COMPANIONS Intrinsic motivation is apparent when children invent dialogues for their toys, concentrate on a work of art or architecture, and converse with *imaginary friends* (who exist only in the child's imagination). Imaginary friends are increasingly common from ages 2 through 6, as initiative builds. Children create such companions for their own private reasons (no one can create an imaginary friend for someone else), primarily to combat loneliness and to practice emotional expression and regulation.

For example, one girl had an imaginary friend named Elephant, "7 inches tall, grey color, black eyes, wears tank top and shorts . . . [who] plays with the child [but] sometimes is mean" (M. Taylor et al., 2004, p. 1178). By having an imaginary friend who is sometimes mean, this child can develop strategies to deal with mean people.

AN EXPERIMENT IN MOTIVATION In a classic experiment, preschool children were given markers and paper and assigned to one of three groups: (1) no award, (2) expected award (told *before* they drew anything that they would get a certificate), and (3) unexpected award (*after* they had drawn something, they heard "You were a big help" and got a certificate) (Lepper et al., 1973). Later, observers noted how often children in each group chose to draw on their own. Those who had received the expected award were less likely to draw than were those who got the unexpected award. The interpretation was that extrinsic motivation (condition 2) undercut intrinsic motivation.

This research triggered a flood of studies seeking to understand whether, when, and how positive reinforcement should be given. The consensus is that praising or paying a person after work has been done usually encourages that behavior to continue, as long as the reinforcement is based on accomplishment. However, if a substantial payment is promised in advance for something that the person already enjoys doing, the extrinsic reinforcement may backfire by diminishing intrinsic motivation (J. Cameron & Pierce, 2002; Deci et al., 1999).

CULTURE AND MOTIVES Cross-cultural research adds complexity to our understanding of emotional regulation. Of course, every culture wants children to be happy, self-controlled, and kind (not necessarily in that order). Beyond that, however, various cultures encourage children to modify different emotions. Here is a list of goals for emotional regulation that seem to be important in certain cultures (Hong et al., 2000; J. G. Miller, 2004; Stubben, 2001):

- Overcome fear (United States)
- Modify anger (Puerto Rico)
- Temper pride (China)
- Control aggression (Japan)
- Be patient and cooperative (Native American communities)

Families also vary in their priorities regarding which emotion most needs control and how that control is best achieved (Matsumoto, 2004). Since shame indicates social awareness, cultures and families that stress social sensitivity encourage shame and embarrassment. In some places, upholding one's family's reputation is crucial— so much so that a lack of shame is considered a sign of mental illness (A. Stein, 2006). Each child is motivated to express whatever emotions his or her culture values and to restrain those that are not appreciated.

Seeking Emotional Balance

Children who experience moderate levels of shame, guilt, and other emotions are considered emotionally healthy. Although symptoms and diagnoses are influenced by culture, lack of emotional regulation is universally accepted as an early sign of **psychopathology,** an illness or disorder (-*pathology*) of the mind (*psycho-*).

EXTERNALIZING AND INTERNALIZING PROBLEMS Emotional regulation is in part neurological, a matter of brain functioning. Because a child's ability to regulate emotions requires thinking before acting (deciding whether and how to display joy, anger, or fear), emotional regulation is the province of the prefrontal cortex, the executive area of the brain. As you remember from Chapter 5, the prefrontal cortex regulates those parts of the limbic system (especially the amygdala) where powerful emotions, such as fear and anxiety, form.

Without adequate control, emotions are overpowering, as is evident in infancy. Gradually, as the prefrontal cortex allows more thoughtful analysis, children begin to regulate their emotions. At about age 4 or 5, children become less likely to throw a temper tantrum, provoke a physical attack, or burst into giggles during prayer (Kagan & Hershkowitz, 2005).

Throughout early childhood, violent outbursts, uncontrollable crying, and terrifying phobias (irrational, crippling fears) continue to diminish. The capacity for self-control—such as not opening a present immediately if asked to wait or not expressing disappointment at an undesirable gift—becomes more evident (S. M. Carlson, 2003; Grolnick et al., 2006).

Lashing Out Some children are slow to control their emotions. They may have **externalizing problems,** meaning that their powerful feelings burst out. They may externalize a feeling of rage, for example, by lashing out at other people or breaking things. Such children are sometimes called *undercontrolled.*

Often the externalizing emotion that most needs control is anger because "dys-regulated anger may trigger aggressive, oppositional behavior" (Gilliom et al., 2002, p. 222). Without emotional regulation, an angry child might flail at another person or lie on the floor, screaming and kicking.

ANSWER TO OBSERVATION QUIZ
(from page 198) Size is not much help, since children grow slowly during these years and the heads of these two boys appear about the same size. However, emotional development is apparent. Most 2-year-olds, like the one at the right, still cling to their mothers; most 4-year-olds are sufficiently mature, secure, and curious to watch the excitement as they drink their juice. ●

psychopathology
An illness or disorder of the mind.

Who's Chicken? Genes and good parenting have made this boy neither too fearful nor too bold. Appropriate caution is probably the best approach to meeting a chicken.

externalizing problems
Difficulty with emotional regulation that involves expressing powerful feelings through uncontrolled physical or verbal outbursts, as by lashing out at other people or breaking things.

Such externalizing behavior is typical of a 2-year-old's temper tantrum, but most children master overwhelming anger as their brain matures. An angry 6-year-old usually has more self-control, perhaps pouting and cursing, but not hitting and screaming. (Whether or not the 6-year-old's curses are pathological depends on the culture and context.)

Holding In Other children have **internalizing problems:** They are fearful and withdrawn, internalizing their emotional distress by turning it inward. They are sometimes called *overcontrolled*. Again, with neurological maturity, extreme fears and shyness usually diminish.

The fears of a 2-year-old (e.g., of the bathtub drain, of an imaginary tornado, of a stranger with a missing finger) can be quite normal even if not rational. Those same fears in a 6-year-old can be pathological terror, again depending on the culture and on the child's experiences. Fear of a tornado, for instance, is not pathological when a child frequently hears tornado warnings or has lived through a tornado.

SEX DIFFERENCES IN EMOTIONAL REGULATION Girls are usually more advanced in emotional regulation, especially when it comes to externalizing emotions. However, they seem more likely than boys to have internalizing problems. By adolescence, undercontrolled boys may be delinquents and overcontrolled girls may be anxious or depressed (Pennington, 2002).

Fighting Versus Hugging Sex differences in emotional expression become apparent toward the end of early childhood and continue throughout development. For instance, in an experiment, 5-year-olds were given toy figures and then heard the beginnings of several stories (Zahn-Waxler et al., 2008). In one story, two children (named Mark and Scott for the boys, Mary and Sarah for the girls) were said to start yelling at each other. Each 5-year-old was asked to use his or her toys to show what happened next.

Many of the boys responded by acting out physical aggression, making the two figures hit and kick each other. By contrast, girls were less likely to attack and more likely to have the girls in the story talk about the problem or change the subject.

Later testing showed that the boys whose behavior problems got worse between ages 5 and 9 (as rated by their teachers and parents) had been the most aggressive with the toys at age 5. They had become even more so at age 7. Curiously, those girls whose behavior problems got worse over the first years of primary school were more likely than the boys and the other girls to engage in *reparative behavior*, such as having one girl hug the other and say, "I'm sorry." This behavior seems to indicate maturity, but it may in fact signify internalized anger that makes the girl feel guilty and apologetic. As the authors explain:

> Gender-role stereotypes or exaggerations of masculine qualities (e.g., impulsive, aggressive, uncaring) and feminine qualities (submissive, unassertive, socially sensitive) are reflected not only in the types of problems males and females tend to develop but also in different forms of expression.
>
> *[Zahn-Waxler et al., 2008, p. 114]*

These researchers suggest that, for both sexes, extreme stereotypical reactions—either externalizing or internalizing—predict future psychopathology.

Boy Brains, Girl Brains Male and female brains differ, although the precise impact of those differences on emotional regulation is controversial (Becker et al., 2008). Neurological and hormonal effects may make boys vulnerable to externalizing problems and girls vulnerable to internalizing ones. Such inclinations can be either moderated or exaggerated by the parents' behavior.

internalizing problems
Difficulty with emotional regulation that involves turning one's emotional distress inward, as by feeling excessively guilty, ashamed, or worthless.

RESPONSE FOR Teachers (from page 200) No. In fact, imaginary friends are quite common, especially among creative children. The child may be somewhat lonely, though; you could help him or her find a friend. ●

RESPONSE FOR College Students (from page 200) Both are important. Extrinsic motivation includes parental pressure and the need to get a good job after graduation. Intrinsic motivation includes the joy of learning, especially if you can express that learning in ways others recognize. Have you ever taken a course that was not required and was said to be difficult? That was intrinsic motivation. ●

Normally, children of both sexes learn to regulate their emotions appropriately and are quite similar in their ability to avoid either extreme of emotional imbalance. However, maternal stress, illness, or heavy drug use may cause neurological damage to a fetus. In infancy, such damage may occur if the baby is chronically malnourished, injured, or frightened. As explained in earlier chapters, extreme stress can kill some neurons and stop others from developing properly. The damage may affect a child's ability to regulate his or her emotions.

Psychopathology is not typical. Guided by their parents, most boys and girls develop some control over their emotions by age 6. However, when a child is vulnerable for any of the reasons mentioned above, and when the parents are not helpful, the specific psychopathology the child develops is influenced by the child's sex. At age 5, vulnerable boys are likely to throw things and vulnerable girls to sob uncontrollably.

Caregivers' Influence on Emotional Regulation

As just mentioned, although inborn brain patterns are important, the quality of early caregiving makes a difference in a child's ability to regulate emotions. Children of depressed parents are particularly vulnerable to difficulty with emotional control (Forbes et al., 2006). The reason is probably that depression is characterized by a lack of emotional reaction, which prevents the child from learning appropriate emotional expression.

By contrast, nurturing caregivers have many opportunities to guide impulsive children; those children can become *more* competent than less impulsive children (Hane & Fox, 2006; Quas et al., 2004). Indeed, genetically vulnerable children sometimes have an advantage, not a handicap. Several studies find that difficult infants become more competent, intellectually and emotionally, than does the average child in kindergarten if their upbringing is unusually patient, responsive, and warm.

Experiments with lower animals illustrate the power of caregiving. Highly stressed infant rats develop abnormal brain structures. However, if stressed rat pups are raised by nurturing mothers, their brains do not form the abnormalities because they are protected by hormones elicited by the caregiving—the frequent licking, nuzzling, grooming, and feeding (J. Kaufman & Charney, 2001). They become normal adult rats, unlike equally stressed pups that had less solicitous mothers.

Obviously, such experiments are unethical to perform with people, but it is evident that negligent and inconsistent caregiving (as happens with depressed mothers) makes the young children who receive it less capable, neurologically and emotionally, than the average child (Ashman et al., 2008). For example, one study found that 80 percent of maltreated 4- to 6-year-olds are "emotionally dysregulated," showing either indifference or extreme anger when strangers criticize their mothers (Maughan & Cicchetti, 2002).

This finding underscores the need to prevent child neglect and abuse, which were discussed in Chapter 5. Maltreatment in the early years causes more extreme internalizing or externalizing problems than maltreatment that begins later (Lopez et al., 2004; Manly et al., 2001). Fortunately, parents are more open to intervention when their children are very young, especially if the intervention builds on their strengths rather than simply telling them what they are doing wrong (Dishion et al., 2008).

Of course, many influences affect each child. Nurture and nature always interact, influencing the brain as well as behavior (Cicchetti & Curtis, 2007). The development of psychopathology in childhood is a complex process. Many different causes, both biological and psychosocial, sometimes lead to a particular disorder. The opposite occurs as well: Many disorders may result from a single cause. However, psychopathology is not the inevitable result of either inborn temperament or unresponsive caregiving.

Learning Emotional Regulation Like this girl in Hong Kong, all 2-year-olds burst into tears when something upsets them—a toy breaks, a pet refuses to play, or it's time to go home. Mothers who comfort them and help them calm down are teaching them to regulate their emotions.

● **FOR DEEPER REFLECTION** In your culture, which emotions most need regulation, and why?

This interaction is true for the emotions of every young child, all of whom sometimes seem uncontrollable and sometimes not. Parents are important, but they deserve neither all the blame nor all the credit. Scientists who studied 1,720 children from infancy to age 5 explain, "The fit between the child's temperament and the type of parenting the child experiences (rather than either factor alone) is predictive of children's behavioral trajectories" (Jaffee, 2007, p. 641). This theme will soon be explained in more detail.

KEY Points

- Erikson called the early-childhood stage *initiative versus guilt,* a time when most children are self-confident and motivated to try new activities.
- Emotional regulation, influenced by brain maturation and social guidance, gradually increases from age 2 to age 6.
- Psychopathology may be evident in either internalizing or externalizing extremes in the expression of emotions.
- Boys tend to be aggressive (externalizing) and girls anxious (internalizing), but children of both sexes usually learn to regulate their emotions as their brains mature and their parents nurture them.

Play

Developmentalists believe play is the most productive and enjoyable activity that children undertake (Elkind, 2007). Play is universal: Archeologists find toys that are many thousands of years old, and anthropologists report play in every part of the world.

The particular form of play changes with age and culture. Two-year-olds' social play is quite simple, such as bouncing a ball and trying to catch it—and becoming upset if another child does not cooperate. By contrast, most 5-year-olds know how to gain entry to a play group, to manage conflict through the use of humor, to take turns, and to select and keep friends and playmates—all signs that they have acquired theory of mind (see Chapter 5).

The difference between these 2-year-olds and 5-year-olds is partly the consequence of brain maturation but is also the outcome of many hours of social play. Children must learn how to make, and keep, friends (K. H. Rubin et al., 2005).

Peers and Parents

Young children play best with *peers,* people of about the same age and social status as themselves. Peers provide practice in emotional regulation, empathy, and social understanding (D. Cohen, 2006). For example, one child (about age 3) was new to peers and to preschool:

> She commanded another child, "Fall down. Go on, do what I say." When the other child stayed stalwartly on his feet, she pushed him over and was clearly amazed when he jumped up and said, "No pushing!"
>
> *[Leach, 1997, p. 474]*

This boy understood the rules of social play. The girl's amazement may have stemmed from having had her mother as her regular playmate—many mothers fall down on command. Fathers also follow orders. One father of a 3-year-old wrote:

Nora casts me in the role of mommy in her pretend play as often as daddy. "Baby" is common, as is "Prince Charming" and "mermaid." I'm her go-to guy when she needs someone to sit next to at dinner or someone to sit still for a new hairstyle. . . .

One day she asked me if I wanted to make valentines with her. Do I want to make valentines, Nora? Frankly? No. No, I don't. Before everyone judges me, realize that I was tired. I had made valentines with Nora every day for two weeks. Also it was November. Nora put on her serious face, looked me straight in the eye and said forcefully, "Dada, you can make a valentine for Grandma or a valentine for Nona. Those are your choices!"

[Ken, personal communication, 2008]

Developmentalists encourage parents of both sexes to play with their children. However, children usually prefer to play with each other rather than with their parents—and with good reason. Emotional regulation is best learned through interaction with other children.

Even the most patient parent is outmatched by another child when it comes to negotiating the rules of tag, wrestling on the grass, pretending to be a sick baby, fighting a dragon. Of course, children do not always cooperate with one another. Some play groups exclude a particular child, and some children quit if they cannot have their way. Generally, however, children learn to get along.

Cultural Differences in Play

All young children play, whether they are on Arctic ice or desert sand. But play varies by culture, gender, and age. That makes play an ideal circumstance for learning whatever social skills are required for adults in a particular society (Sutton-Smith, 1997). Chinese children fly kites, Alaskan natives tell dreams and stories, Lapp children pretend to be reindeer, and so on. Children's dramas reflect their culture as they play games that were created by previous generations (Kalliala, 2006; Roopnarine et al., 1994).

THE ECOLOGICAL CONTEXT The physical setting is one aspect of culture that shapes play. Some communities provide many toys and close supervision; in other places, children are left to play on their own with whatever they find.

Play Ball! In every nation, young children play with balls, but the specific games they play vary with the culture. Soccer is the favorite game in many countries, including Brazil, where these children are practicing their dribbling on Copacabana Beach in Rio de Janeiro.

The birth rate and economic conditions in some nations give children numerous siblings and neighbors as playmates. They learn to play without adults but with other children of both sexes and many ages. A play group's setting in Ua Pou, an island 2,000 miles southeast of Hawaii, is described as follows:

Children ranged from two to five years old. They played several hours a day without supervision while their siblings attended school nearby.

The play area was potentially dangerous. A strong surf broke on the boat ramp. The large rocks on the shore were strewn with broken glass. The valley walls were steep and slippery. Children played on a high bridge and high, sharp, lava-rock walls. Machetes, axes, and matches were occasionally left around and young children played with these. In spite of these dangers, accidents were rare and minor. . . .

Disputes were frequent but these dissipated after a few minutes. Children did not seek adults or older children to settle conflicts or direct their play.

[Martini, 1994]

By contrast, in the cities of developed nations, undeveloped space is scarce and families are small. Consequently, play usually occurs in child-care settings. Child-centered programs provide space, playmates, toys, and often teachers who believe that play encourages emotional and social learning (Clarke-Stewart & Allhusen, 2005).

CHANGING SOCIAL CIRCUMSTANCES As children grow older, their play becomes more social, although culture, temperament, sex, parents, and experience all influence play at every stage (K. H. Rubin et al., 2006). One cultural shift that began in technologically advanced nations has now spread worldwide: the increasing prevalence of television.

Recent studies of young children's play show that they use plots and characters that originated on the TV screen and that they display advanced (although confused) sexual awareness by age 6 (D. Cohen, 2006; Kalliala, 2006). (Knowledge of sexual activities is not necessarily a sign of child abuse, as was once believed; young children may become sexually aware by watching television.)

Types of Play Children in all cultures become more socially aware as they grow older. This progression was first noted by Mildred Parten (1932), who distinguished five kinds of play, each more interactive than the previous one:

1. *Solitary play:* A child plays alone, unaware of any other children playing nearby.
2. *Onlooker play:* A child watches other children play.
3. *Parallel play:* Children play with similar toys in similar ways, but not together.
4. *Associative play:* Children interact, observing each other and sharing material, but their play is not yet mutual and reciprocal.
5. *Cooperative play:* Children play together, creating and elaborating a joint activity or taking turns.

Children move up this sequence toward the more social forms of play as they approach age 6, when they become capable of playing games with turns and rules. Piaget (1932) thought that rule-based play was an early manifestation of morality, although not everyone agrees.

Modern Differences Parten's hierarchy of play did not account for the influence of the chronosystem and the exosystem (as described in Bronfenbrenner's bioecological-systems theory, discussed in Chapter 1). Parten studied children in the United States 75 years ago; today it is quite normal for U.S. 4-year-olds to prefer to play alone rather than with strangers (Henderson et al., 2004). Even 5-year-olds may not engage in cooperative play with unfamiliar peers, perhaps because the average U.S. family size has decreased and individualism has increased over the past few decades.

Although many children are less sociable than Parten depicted, many others seem more sociable at younger ages; these differences are especially apparent when culture and context are taken into account (Xu, 2008). In some twenty-first-century families and nations, children as young as 2 take turns, share, and otherwise engage in social play (D. Cohen, 2006). In China and many other nations, children are expected to play cooperatively by age 3, and most do so.

Active Play

Children need physical activity to develop both muscle strength and emotional control. Peers provide an audience, role models, and sometimes competition. For instance, running skills develop best when children chase or race each other, not when a child runs alone. Young children particularly enjoy active play—climbing, kicking, running, and tumbling (Case-Smith & Kuhaneck, 2008)—even when parents want them to be quiet. One 5-year-old boy came to his parents' bedroom every night to entertain them with an "action show," which involved elaborate jumps and acrobatics. And as soon as his 1-year-old brother was able to, he joined in (D. Cohen, 2006).

ROUGH-AND-TUMBLE PLAY The most common form of active play is called **rough-and-tumble play** because it looks quite rough and because the children seem to tumble over one another. The term was coined by British scientists who studied primates in East Africa (Blurton-Jones, 1976).

These researchers noticed that monkeys often chased, attacked, rolled in the dirt, and wrestled, without hurting one another. If a young monkey wanted to play, all it had to do was come close, catch the eye of a peer, and then run a few feet away, looking back. This invitation was almost always accepted, as the other monkey responded with a *play face* (the monkey equivalent of a friendly smile), not an angry one. Puppies, kittens, and young chimpanzees do the same.

When the scientists returned from Africa to their families in England, they saw that their children were like other animals—that human youngsters, like baby monkeys, enjoy rough-and-tumble play (Pellegrini & Smith, 2005). They chase, wrestle, and grab each other, developing games like tag, capture-the-flag, and cops-and-robbers.

Rough-and-tumble play is distinguished not only by a play face but also by many other expressions and gestures signifying that the child is "just pretending." Rough-and-tumble play appears in every nation of the world, particularly among young males (human and otherwise) when they are allowed to play freely (Berenbaum et al., 2008).

Some ecological conditions make rough-and-tumble play more likely, among them ample space and distant adults. (Even young monkeys avoid older monkeys as they chase each other.) Children are more likely to engage in rough-and-tumble play with friends than with strangers.

Although rough-and-tumble play is obviously physical, it is fun and constructive, not aggressive. It teaches children how to enter a relationship, assert themselves, and respond to someone else. Some psychologists think that it also helps the prefrontal cortex to develop—that roughhousing helps children learn to regulate their emotions as well as strengthen their bodies (Pellegrini et al., 2007).

During rough-and-tumble play, children are more likely to injure themselves by falling or bumping into something than they are to hurt one another. If adults are unsure whether they are observing a fight that should be stopped or a social activity that should continue, they should look for the play face. Children almost always smile, and often laugh, in rough-and-tumble play; they frown or scowl in real fights.

Rough-and-tumble play is an illustration of increasing brain maturation. Two-year-olds typically just chase and catch one another, but older children keep the play fair, long-lasting, and fun. In tag, for instance, older players set rules (which vary depending on availability of base, safety, and terrain) and then each child decides when and how far to venture. If one child is "It" for too long, another child (often a friend) makes it easy to be caught. Rough-and-tumble play also fosters caregiving, especially if a child is accidentally hurt (Reed & Brown, 2001).

DRAMA AND PRETENDING Another form of active play in early childhood is **sociodramatic play,** in which children act out various roles and plots, taking on "any identity, role, or activity that they choose. They can be mothers, babies, Cinderella, or Captain Hook. They can make tea or fly to the moon. Or they can fight, hurt others, or kill or imprison someone" (Dunn & Hughes, 2001, p. 491).

rough-and-tumble play
Play that mimics aggression through wrestling, chasing, or hitting, but in which there is no intent to harm.

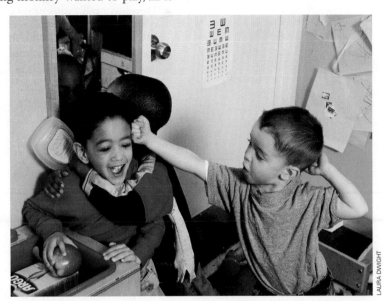

LAURA DWIGHT

Male Bonding Sometimes the only way to distinguish aggression from rough-and-tumble play is to look at the faces. The hitter is not scowling, the hittee is laughing, and the hugger is just joining in the fun. Another clue that this is rough-and-tumble play comes from gender and context. These boys are in a Head Start program, where they are learning social skills, such as how to avoid fighting.

sociodramatic play
Pretend play in which children act out various roles and themes in stories that they create.

Sociodramatic play enables children to do the following:

● Explore and rehearse the social roles enacted around them
● Test their ability to explain and to convince playmates of their ideas
● Practice regulating their emotions by pretending to be afraid, angry, brave, and so on
● Develop a self-concept in a nonthreatening context

Sociodramatic play builds on pretending and social interest, both of which emerge in toddlerhood. But preschool children do more than toddlers; they interact, combining their own imagination with that of their playmates.

The beginnings of sociodramatic play are illustrated by this pair, a 3-year-old girl and a 2-year-old boy. The girl wanted to be a baby, and she persuaded the boy to play a parent.

> **Boy:** Not good. You bad.
> **Girl:** Why?
> **Boy:** 'Cause you spill your milk.
> **Girl:** No. 'Cause I bit somebody.
> **Boy:** Yes, you did.
> **Girl:** Say, "Go to sleep. Put your head down."
> **Boy:** Put your head down.
> **Girl:** No.
> **Boy:** Yes.
> **Girl:** No.
> **Boy:** Yes. Okay, I will spank you. Bad boy. *(Spanks her, not hard)*
> **Girl:** No. My head is up. *(Giggles)* I want my teddy bear.
> **Boy:** No. Your teddy bear go away. *(At this point she asked if he was really going to take the teddy bear away.)*
>
> [*from Garvey, reported in D. Cohen, 2006, p. 72]*

Note that the girl not only directed the play but also played her part, sometimes accepting what the boy said and sometimes not. The boy took direction yet also made up his own dialogue ("Bad boy") and actions.

Compare their simple plot to the play of four older boys, about age 5, in a day-care center in Finland. Joni plays the role of the evil one who menaces the other boys; Tuomas directs the drama and acts in it as well.

Ladies and Babies A developmental difference is visible here between the 14-month-old's evident curiosity and the 4-year-old friends' pleasure in socio-dramatic play. The mother's reaction—joy at the children's imaginative play or irritation at the mess they've made—is less predictable.

FELICIA MARTINEZ / PHOTOEDIT, INC.

Tuomas: And now he [Joni] would take me and would hang me. . . . This would be the end of all of me.

Joni: Hands behind.

Tuomas: I can't help it. I have to. *(The two other boys follow his example.)*

Joni: I would put fire all around them. *(All three brave boys lie on the floor with hands tied behind their backs. Joni piles mattresses on them, and pretends to light a fire, which crackles closer and closer.)*

Tuomas: Everything is lost. *(One boy starts to laugh.)*

Petterl: Better not to laugh, soon we will all be dead. . . . I am saying my last words.

Tuomas: Now you can say your last wish. . . . And now I say I wish we can be terribly strong.

(At that point, the three boys suddenly gain extraordinary strength, pushing off the mattresses and extinguishing the fire. Good triumphs over evil, but not until the last moment because, as one boy explains, "Otherwise this playing is not exciting at all.")

[adapted from Kalliala, 2006, p. 83]

Good versus evil is a favorite theme of boys' sociodramatic play, which often includes superheroes, wild animals, and so on. In contrast, girls tend to develop domestic scenes. Such gender differences are found in many cultures. In the same day-care center where Joni piles mattresses on his playmates, the girls say their play is "more beautiful and peaceful . . . [but] boys play all kinds of violent games" (Kalliala, 2006, p. 110).

KEY𝔭**oints**

- Playing with other children aids development of emotional regulation.
- From age 2 to age 6, children's play becomes increasingly social and complex.
- Play is universal, although its particular forms vary by gender and culture.
- Rough-and-tumble play and sociodramatic play advance children's social understanding.

Challenges for Parents

We have seen that young children's emotions and actions are affected by many factors, including brain maturation, culture, and peers. Now we focus on another primary influence: parents. It could be said that the first challenge faced by parents is the need to decide on an approach to dealing with their children—that is, on a parenting style.

Parenting Styles

Every culture has specific beliefs about how children should be raised; these beliefs sometimes conflict with those held by other cultures. Parents in the same nation differ as well, partly because, as explained in Chapter 1, everyone is influenced by many cultures. For instance, in the United States, people are affected by the dominant culture as well as by their ethnic, regional, religious, and economic cultures—each of which favors particular child-rearing methods.

Thousands of researchers have studied the effects of various parenting styles on child development. Their conclusions vary. Given the diversity of styles and studies, it is remarkable that one scientist's observations of 100 preschool children in California continue to influence scholars around the world.

That scientist is Diana Baumrind (1967, 1971), who found that parents differed on four important dimensions:

- *Expressions of warmth.* Some parents are very affectionate; others are cold and critical.
- *Strategies for discipline.* Parents vary in whether and how they explain, criticize, persuade, ignore, and punish.
- *Communication.* Some parents listen patiently to their children; others demand silence.
- *Expectations for maturity.* Parents vary in the standards they set for their children regarding responsibility and self-control.

BAUMRIND'S THREE PATTERNS OF PARENTING On the basis of these dimensions and her research, Baumrind identified three parenting styles (see Table 6.1).

authoritarian parenting
An approach to child rearing that is characterized by high behavioral standards, strict punishment of misconduct, and little communication.

- **Authoritarian parenting.** The parents' word is law, not to be questioned. Misconduct brings strict punishment, usually physical (but not so harsh as to be considered abusive). Authoritarian parents have rules and high standards. They do not listen to children's opinions; discussion about emotions is rare. (One adult from such a family said that the question "How do you feel?" had only two possible answers: "Fine" and "Tired.") Authoritarian parents love their children, but they seem aloof, rarely showing affection.

permissive parenting
An approach to child rearing that is characterized by high nurturance and communication but little discipline, guidance, or control.

- **Permissive parenting.** Permissive parents make few demands, hiding any frustration they may feel. Discipline is lax, partly because they have low expectations for maturity. Instead, permissive parents are nurturing and accepting, listening to whatever their offspring say. They are supportive, but they do not feel responsible for shaping their children.

authoritative parenting
An approach to child rearing in which the parents set limits and enforce rules but are flexible and listen to their children.

- **Authoritative parenting.** Authoritative parents set limits and enforce rules, yet they are flexible and listen to their children. They may demand maturity, but they are usually forgiving (not punishing) if the child falls short. They consider themselves guides, not authorities (as authoritarian parents do) or friends (as permissive parents do).

neglectful/uninvolved parenting
An approach to child rearing in which the parents are indifferent toward their children and unaware of what is going on in their children's lives.

A fourth style, called **neglectful/uninvolved parenting,** is sometimes mistaken for the permissive style but is actually quite different (L. Steinberg, 2001). Neither permissive nor neglectful parents use physical punishment, but the similarity stops there. Neglectful parents do not know what their children are doing—they seem not to care. By contrast, permissive parents are involved in their children's lives, defending them from teachers' criticism, arranging play dates, and sacrificing to buy them particular toys. Some of this involvement is not helpful to the child's development, but it is far better than indifference.

TABLE 6.1 Characteristics of Parenting Styles Identified by Baumrind

| | Characteristics | | | Communication | |
Style	Warmth	Discipline	Expectations of Maturity	Parent to Child	Child to Parent
Authoritarian	Low	Strict, often physical	High	High	Low
Permissive	High	Rare	Low	Low	High
Authoritative	High	Moderate, with much discussion	Moderate	High	High

THE IMPLICATIONS OF PARENTING STYLE All children need parents who care about them. No matter what the parents' punishments, rules, and expectations are, "parental involvement plays an important role in the development of both social and cognitive competence" (Parke & Buriel, 2006, p. 437).

Children are always harmed by abusive or neglectful parenting. Authoritarian parents must not punish too often or too harshly, and permissive parents must not slide toward neglect. Beyond that, the following long-term effects of Baumrind's three parenting styles have been reported (Baumrind, 1991; L. Steinberg et al., 1994):

"He's just doing that to get attention."

Pay Attention Children develop best with lots of love and attention. They shouldn't have to ask for it!

- *Authoritarian* parents raise children who are likely to become conscientious, obedient, and quiet but not especially happy. Such children tend to feel guilty or depressed, internalizing their frustrations and blaming themselves when things don't go well. As adolescents, they sometimes rebel, leaving home before age 20.

- *Permissive* parents raise unhappy children who lack self-control, especially in the give-and-take of peer relationships. Inadequate emotional regulation makes them immature and impedes friendships, which is the main reason for their unhappiness. They tend to continue to live at home, still dependent, in early adulthood.

- *Authoritative* parents raise children who are successful, articulate, happy with themselves, and generous with others. Teachers and peers usually like these children, especially in societies in which individual initiative is valued.

Baumrind's three-part classification, although still influential, is generally regarded as too simplistic. Among the criticisms of it are the following (Bornstein, 2006; Galambos et al., 2003; Lamb & Lewis, 2005; Parke & Buriel, 2006):

- Her original sample had little economic, ethnic, or cultural diversity.
- She focused more on attitudes than on daily interactions.
- Some authoritarian parents are very loving toward their children.
- Some permissive parents guide their children intensely, but with words, not rules.
- She overlooked the child's contribution to the parent–child relationship.

The last item on this list is significant; a child's temperament matters (Kagan & Fox, 2006). If they do not consider the personality of the child, authoritarian parents might terrorize children who are innately fearful and anxious, or permissive parents might watch their impulsive children flail out of control.

A longitudinal study that followed a group of children from age 2 to age 5 found that children who were temperamentally reactive (that is, obviously distressed by frustration) became disruptive 5-year-olds if their parents were very strict with them. That confirmed the researchers' expectations. However, they were surprised to see that low-reactive 2-year-olds tended to become disruptive 5-year-olds if their parents were too lax (Degnan et al., 2008).

CULTURAL VARIATIONS The value of a systems approach to development is particularly obvious when parenting styles of various ethnic groups are compared, even within the same nation. Effective Chinese American, Caribbean American, and African American parents are often stricter than effective European American parents (R. K. Chao, 2001; N. E. Hill & Bush, 2001).

The punishment styles of non-European parents may make them appear authoritarian, but a great deal depends on the parents' attitude. In every nation that has been studied, specific discipline methods and family rules are less important than parental warmth, support, and concern. Children everywhere benefit if they believe that their parents appreciate them; by the same token, children everywhere suffer if they feel rejected and unwanted (Khaleque & Rohner, 2002; Maccoby, 2000).

Values, climate, history, and family income all affect child rearing (Matsumoto & Yoo, 2006). Authoritarian parenting is more common as income falls, perhaps because low-income families tend to have more children or because poor parents want obedient children who will not disrespect the police or their employers later on. Parents everywhere try to raise their children to adjust to the society and culture they know.

Partly for this reason, family patterns change with time and circumstance. A multicultural study of Canadian parents found that, contrary to predictions based on U.S. research, East Asian and Caribbean immigrant parents were *less* harsh with their children than the average Canadian parent, and teachers rated their children as less aggressive than the Canadian norm (Ho et al., 2008). Obviously, context and culture interact.

Given a systems perspective, developmentalists hesitate to recommend any particular parenting style. Circumstances, the child's temperament, and cultural values all influence the effectiveness of child-rearing practices (Bugental & Grusec, 2006; Dishion & Bullock, 2002; J. G. Miller, 2004).

This does not mean that developmentalists consider all parenting styles equally good—far from it. Signs of serious trouble are obvious in children's behavior, including overcontrol, undercontrol, lack of social play, and unprovoked aggression. Ineffective parenting is one possible cause of such troubles, but not the only one.

Children, Parents, and the Media

One reason parenting styles change is that new challenges confront each generation of parents. One current challenge is the ever-increasing influence of electronic media on children. All media—the Internet, video games, television, movies—can be harmful, especially when the content is violent (C. A. Anderson et al., 2007; Kearney & Pivec, 2007; Smyth, 2007).

Remember from Chapter 1 that scientists seek longitudinal, replicated, experimental research before they consider conclusions valid. Such multidisciplinary and multifaceted research is not yet available regarding young children and the newest media, such as computer games and cell phones. However, television's effects on children have been studied for 30 years. Most scientists believe that the conclusions regarding television probably apply to other media as well.

TELEVISION Watching television keeps young children entertained, allowing parents to go about their own activities. Not surprisingly, the typical young child watches television for three hours a day (see Table 6.2). One recent study reported that more than one-fourth of all children in the United States had a television in their bedrooms by age 3, a percentage that rises as children grow older (D. F. Roberts & Foehr, 2004) and undoubtedly is higher today.

Television may be a boon for parents, but it is harmful to development, according to U.S. experts. Six major organizations (the American Psychological Association, the American Academy of Pediatrics, the American Medical Association, the American Academy of Child and Adolescent Psychiatry, the American Academy of Family Physicians, and the American Psychiatric Association) implore parents to reduce or eliminate television watching, especially for children under age 6 (C. A. Anderson & Bushman, 2002).

● **UNDERSTANDING THE NUMBERS**

What percentage of the day does a U.S. child aged 2 to 4 typically spend watching television? (Remember that the average child that age sleeps about 12 hours a day.)

Answer More than 25 percent. All three groups of 2- to 4-year-olds watched TV more than 3 hours a day, and 3 hours represent 25 percent of the average child's 12 waking hours.

TABLE 6.2 Average Daily Exposure to Electronic Media

Age 2 to 4 Years	Hours per Day
White	3:18
Black	4:30
Hispanic	3:37
Age 5 to 7 Years	Hours per Day
White	3:17
Black	4:16
Hispanic	3:38

Source: Adapted from D. F. Roberts & Foehr, 2004.

Did you notice that all six organizations have *American* in their titles? That signals the need for a cultural caveat: Most research has focused on children and media in the United States. Readers need to ask themselves whether American television is so pervasive worldwide that the same conclusions apply in every nation.

THE SIGNIFICANCE OF CONTENT Many parents hope the media teach good values or enhance learning, but this does not usually happen. For example, one universal human value is that hurting other people is bad. Yet in commercial media, the "good guys" (whether in cartoons, police dramas, or video games) hit, shoot, kick, and kill as often as the "bad guys." Their violence is depicted as morally acceptable.

Given their cognitive immaturity (pre-logical, egocentric), young children may be more affected by what they watch than are adults. That may explain the results of extensive and carefully controlled studies: Children who watch televised violence become more violent themselves (C. A. Anderson et al., 2003; Gentile et al., 2007; B. J. Wilson, 2008). They are more likely to fight, break things, and—when they grow up—to use physical force on other people, with fists, knives, or guns.

Another widely held value is that every human should be equally respected. Yet racial and gender stereotypes are still evident (Mastro et al., 2008). In children's programs, heroes and leaders are male and White, except when all the characters are Black or (on Spanish channels) Latino. Females are often victims or girlfriends, not leaders—except in girl-oriented programs that boys rarely watch.

Consider the results of a longitudinal study that began with children at about age 5 and studied those same children in adolescence (D. R. Anderson et al., 2001). Children who watched only educational television tended to become good students. Many of the children who watched television violence became more aggressive, less creative, and lower-achieving adolescents. The most dramatic effects were found among the girls.

FAMILY TIME Many parents and older siblings are more engaged with electronic media than with one another. As a result, 2- to 6-year-olds follow their family's example and miss out on some learning that their brains are ready for. For instance, language development depends on one-to-one conversations (television is a poor language tutor), and emotional regulation depends on parental responsiveness.

In most families, parents and children have their own TVs, radios, and computers. Parents and children rarely use media together, playing the same game or watching the same program. Even when they do, they rarely converse. Many families have the television on during meals, further limiting interaction (D. F. Roberts & Foehr, 2004).

Researchers have found an odd correlation: The more television children watch, the angrier they are (D. F. Roberts & Foehr, 2004). Is this because television content makes them angry, or because the images affect their limbic systems, or because they miss the comfort and calm of their parents? The answer is not known.

Despite professionals' warnings, few parents can enforce a total prohibition on TV, video games, the Internet, and other electronic

"Why don't you get off the computer and watch some TV?"

Not Connected When they hand over the TV remote to their children, parents give up the opportunity—and the responsibility—for interacting as a family.

media. Parents can, however, limit their own and their children's screen time and instead play, read, and talk together. Too few children know a proven fact: An animated parent can be more entertaining than SpongeBob SquarePants.

> **KEY Points**
>
> - Diana Baumrind found that authoritative parenting (warm, with guidance) is better than either authoritarian (strict) or permissive (lenient) parenting.
> - Other researchers add that loving parents are beneficial regardless of which of these three parenting styles they use. Uninvolved parenting is worst of all.
> - Effective parenting and discipline vary, depending on temperament, culture, ethnicity, family income, and other factors.
> - Experts recommend that parents limit their young children's television viewing and spend more time talking and playing with them.

Moral Development

Children develop increasingly complex moral values, judgments, and behaviors as they mature. In early childhood, as you have seen, children try to please their parents and avoid punishment, to make friends and exclude enemies. The emotional development described in this chapter, and the theory of mind described in Chapter 5, are the foundation for the self-concept and social awareness that make morality possible.

Many parents and teachers consider morality even more important than any of the other early-childhood developments already described (strength, motor skills, intelligence, language, and so on). Perhaps for this reason, a debate rages over how children internalize standards of right and wrong, in the process developing virtues and avoiding vices. Conflicting perspectives about the origins of morality are evident in psychology, philosophy, theology, and sociology. They reflect the basic debate in the study of human development—that is, whether nature or nurture is responsible for a given outcome.

- The "nature" side of the debate suggests that morality is genetic, an outgrowth of natural bonding and attachment. That would explain why young children tend to help and defend their parents, no matter what the parents do. In an alternative view, infants are born selfish and wicked, needing discipline to set them straight.

- The "nurture" side contends that culture is crucial, as children learn the values of their community. That would explain why young children admire or ridicule peers who eat raw fish, or hamburgers, or crickets, depending on their cultural preferences. That would also explain why parents are held responsible when a child misbehaves.

● **FOR DEEPER REFLECTION** What is the origin of your most heartfelt moral principles? Why doesn't everyone else share your ideals?

We have repeatedly seen that both nature and nurture are always important and that developmentalists differ as to which is more important, how, and when (Killen & Smetana, 2007; Krebs, 2008; Turiel, 2006). To avoid taking sides prematurely, here we describe what is known about moral development from ages 2 to 6.

Two topics have attracted ample research: the early manifestation of prosocial and antisocial behavior (including aggression)—all of them rooted in either empathy or antipathy—and the implications of parental methods of discipline. We examine those topics here; later chapters discuss other moral issues.

Empathy and Antipathy

As children play with one another, they choose friends and reject enemies, showing the beginnings of love and hate. With increasing social experiences and decreasing egocentrism, they develop **empathy,** an understanding of other people's feelings and concerns, as well as **antipathy,** dislike or even hatred of another person.

Empathy is not the same as sympathy, which means feeling sorry *for* someone. Rather, empathy means feeling sorry *with* someone, experiencing the other person's pain or sadness. Research with mirror neurons (see Chapter 1) suggests that observing someone else doing something may activate the same areas in the brain of the observer as are active in the person being observed.

PROSOCIAL AND ANTISOCIAL BEHAVIOR Ideally, empathy leads to **prosocial behavior,** helpfulness and kindness offered without any obvious benefit for oneself. Expressing concern, offering to share food or a toy, and including a shy child in a game or conversation are examples of prosocial behavior, all evident in some young children. Furthermore, young children's prosocial behavior often naturally leads to developing friendships (K. H. Rubin et al., 2005). This innate prosocial urge is considered one foundation of morality.

Antipathy can lead to **antisocial behavior,** actions that deliberately harm another person (Caprara et al., 2001). Antisocial actions include verbal insults, social exclusion, and physical assaults. An antisocial 4-year-old might look another child in the eye, scowl, and then kick him hard without provocation. By age 4 or 5—as a result of brain maturation, theory of mind, emotional regulation, and interactions with caregivers—most children can be deliberately prosocial or antisocial.

Prosocial behavior generally increases from age 3 to 6 and beyond, and antisocial actions decline beginning at age 2 (N. Eisenberg et al., 2006; Tremblay & Nagin, 2005). Both are outgrowths of emotional understanding, although teaching empathy is difficult, according to a team of scientists who worked with 270 children in Head Start preschool programs (Izard et al., 2008). Moral emotions and moral behavior both increase during early childhood.

AGGRESSION The regulation of emotions, development of morality, and emergence of empathy and antipathy are nowhere more apparent than in the way children learn to deal with their aggressive impulses. The gradual control of aggression is evident in rough-and-tumble play; in the fantasies of domination and submission that are often acted out in sociodramatic play; and in the sharing of art supplies, construction materials, and wheeled vehicles (J. B. Peterson & Flanders, 2005). Through play, children learn moral behavior—specifically, how to defend friends, cooperate with playmates, and control their anger (Tremblay & Nagin, 2005).

Types of Aggression Researchers recognize four general types of aggression, described in Table 6.3. Not surprisingly, given the moral sensibilities of children, by age 5 children make moral judgments regarding which type of aggression is justified and which is not in a given situation (Etchu, 2007). They do not like mean playmates.

Instrumental aggression is very common among young children, who often seem to want something they do not have and try, without thinking, to get it. **Reactive aggression** is common as well; this type, particularly, becomes better controlled as emotional regulation increases. **Relational aggression** destroys another child's self-esteem and social networks and actually becomes more hurtful as children mature, since their increasing social awareness renders self-esteem and social networks more fragile.

The fourth and most ominous type is **bullying aggression.** It is fairly common in young children, but it should be stopped before they reach school age. As described

empathy
The ability to understand the emotions and concerns of another person, especially when they differ from one's own.

antipathy
Feelings of dislike or even hatred for another person.

prosocial behavior
Actions that are helpful and kind but that are of no obvious benefit to the person doing them.

antisocial behavior
Actions that are deliberately hurtful or destructive to another person.

instrumental aggression
Hurtful behavior that is intended to get something that another person has and to keep it.

reactive aggression
An impulsive retaliation for another person's intentional or accidental action, verbal or physical.

relational aggression
Nonphysical acts, such as insults or social rejection, aimed at harming the social connection between the victim and other people.

bullying aggression
Unprovoked, repeated physical or verbal attack, especially on victims who are unlikely to defend themselves.

TABLE 6.3 The Four Forms of Aggression

Type of Aggression	Definition	Comments
Instrumental aggression	Hurtful behavior that is aimed at gaining something (such as a toy, a place in line, or a turn on the swing) that someone else has	Often increases from age 2 to 6; involves objects more than people; quite normal; more egocentric than antisocial.
Reactive aggression	An impulsive retaliation for a hurt (intentional or accidental) that can be verbal or physical	Indicates a lack of emotional regulation, characteristic of 2-year-olds. A 5-year-old can usually stop and think before reacting.
Relational aggression	Nonphysical acts, such as insults or social rejection, aimed at harming the social connections between the victim and others	Involves a personal attack and thus is directly antisocial; can be very hurtful; more common as children become socially aware.
Bullying aggression	Unprovoked, repeated physical or verbal attack, especially on victims who are unlikely to defend themselves	In both bullies and victims, a sign of poor emotional regulation; adults should intervene before the school years. (Bullying is discussed in Chapter 8.)

in detail in Chapter 8, bullying aggression among older children is destructive for both victims and bullies. Young children do not like bullies, and they enforce the school rules (remember the boy who said, "No pushing"). In middle childhood and adolescence, adult intervention may actually make bullies behave even worse—another reason why moral behavior is best taught during early childhood.

Developmental Patterns of Aggression Not only bullying but all kinds of aggression follow a developmental pattern, becoming less common, but more hurtful, with time. Infants are very aggressive; they naturally pinch, slap, and even bite others. In Richard Tremblay's dramatic words, "The only reason babies do not kill each other is that we do not give them knives or guns" (quoted in Holden, 2000, p. 580). Fortunately, babies are weak and weaponless, so parents have time to teach self-control.

One of the first moral values that children learn is to not hurt others (Krebs, 2008). Almost all 2-year-olds are instrumentally and reactively aggressive, but such behavior usually diminishes with each passing year after that. A 5-year-old who still attacks his or her mother is showing a lack of emotional control, which may lead to attacks on peers and externalizing problems of all kinds later in life (Moss et al., 2004).

Early childhood offers an opportunity for adults to teach aggressive children emotional regulation. Generally, aggressive 5-year-olds who learn to temper their aggression by middle childhood also tend to do well academically and socially (NICHD Early Child Care Research Network, 2004b).

Parental Discipline

Many developmentalists believe that children's attachment to their parents, and then their responsiveness to others, is the beginning of morality. Humans protect, cooperate, and even sacrifice for one another because social groups evolved to encourage such prosocial behavior (Krebs, 2008). To foster moral values, parents need to establish strong and affectionate bonds with their infants, as explained in Chapter 4.

Beyond attachment, a particular concern for many developmentalists and parents is discipline. Ideally, parents anticipate misbehavior and guide their children toward patterns of behavior and internalized standards of morality that will help them lifelong. But especially in early childhood, parents cannot always anticipate and prevent problems, partly because children lack emotional control.

A study of mothers and 3-year-olds during stressful times found that children with secure attachments to their mothers had as many conflicts as the insecurely attached children. Overall, conflicts (including verbal disagreements) arose about every two minutes. The resolution of such conflicts differed, however (Laible et al., 2008). Here is one example:

> **Child:** I want my other shoes.
> **Mother:** You don't need your other shoes. You wear your Pooh sandals when we go for a walk.
> **Child:** Noooooo.
> **Mother:** [*Child's name*]! You don't need your other shoes!
> **Child:** *(Cries loudly)*
> **Mother:** No, you don't need your other shoes. You wear your Pooh sandals when we go for a walk.
> **Child:** Ahhhh. Want pretty dress. *(Crying)*
> **Mother:** Your pretty dress.
> **Child:** Yeah.
> **Mother:** You can wear them some other day.
> **Child:** Noooooo. *(Crying)*
>
> [*Laible et al., 2008, pp. 442–443*]

Sometimes, as here, child and mother each insist on getting her own way. However, in contrast to this example, the mothers of children who were securely attached were likely to compromise and explain.

Regarding discipline, children need to learn the standards of behavior within their particular culture, and parents also need to clarify their expectations for proper behavior. What is "rude" or "nasty" or "undisciplined" behavior in one community is often accepted, even encouraged, in another. Mothers and fathers and grandparents often disagree about what behavior is desirable: They need to discuss and compromise to avoid confusing the child.

Parents are often unaware of their expectations and ethnotheories, so it is no wonder that young children disagree, disappoint, and disobey (Bornstein, 2006; Bugental & Grusec, 2006). Children need explicit standards, followed up by guidelines and appropriate discipline. For instance, having breakfast at a restaurant, my friend told his 4-year-old son, Josiah, not to order a big meal because he would not be able to eat it all. Josiah insisted; his father relented. The boy ate only a little of his pancakes and bacon. My friend said, "See, you can't eat what you ordered," and finished the meal for him. While the father may have thought Josiah learned not to order so much food, what the boy actually learned was that his father would get him what he wanted if he was persistent enough in his demands.

Parents sometimes teach moral values—such as "Obey your elders"—that they themselves do not follow. When they are uncertain, children follow parents' examples more than their words; when adults disagree, children are inclined to obey the one who is more indulgent. A parental alliance is crucial, but parents often argue over child rearing instead of taking a common approach.

Although experts disagree about particulars, they agree that young children are naturally eager to please their parents. If a child disobeys, it may be that the parent's demand was beyond the child's ability: Young children cannot always control their bodies, their impulses, or their emotions. For instance, no child deliberately wets the bed, but some are punished for doing so. Cognitive immaturity also fosters conflict, as we now explain.

DISCIPLINE AND CHILDREN'S THINKING Many developmentalists have studied the relationship between young children's thinking and their behavior. Here are four reminders:

1. *Remember theory of mind.* Young children gradually come to understand things from other viewpoints. Encouraging empathy ("How would you feel if someone did that to you?") increases prosocial behavior, but it takes time to emerge.

ESPECIALLY FOR Parents of 3-Year-Olds How could a parent compromise with a child who wants to wear "other shoes"? (see response, page 218) ➡

ESPECIALLY FOR Political Scientists Many observers contend that children learn their political attitudes at home, from the way their parents treat them. Is this true? (see response, page 218) ➡

RESPONSE FOR Parents of 3-Year-Olds (from page 217) Remember, authoritative parents listen but do not usually give in. A parent could ask why the child did not want the Pooh sandals (ugly, too tight, old?) and explain why the "other shoes" were not appropriate (raining, save for special occasions, hard to walk in?). A promise for the future (e.g., "Let's save your other shoes and pretty dress for the birthday party tomorrow") might stop the "Noooo." ●

RESPONSE FOR Political Scientists (from page 217) There are many parenting styles, and it is difficult to determine each one's impact on children's personalities. At this point, attempts to connect early child rearing with later political outlook are speculative. ●

Angela at Play Research suggests that being spanked is a salient and memorable experience for young children, not because of the pain but because of the emotions. Children seek to do what they have learned; they know not only how to place their hands but also that an angry person does the hitting. The only part of the lesson they usually forget is what particular misdeed precipitated the punishment. Asked why she is spanking her doll, Angela will likely explain, "She was bad."

ESPECIALLY FOR Parents Suppose you agree that spanking is destructive, but you sometimes get so angry at your child's behavior that you hit him or her. Is your reaction appropriate? (see response, page 220) →

psychological control
A disciplinary technique that involves threatening to withdraw love and support and that relies on a child's feelings of guilt and gratitude to the parents.

time-out
A disciplinary technique in which a child is separated from other people and activities for a specified time.

2. *Remember emerging self-concept.* When the sense of self is developing, sharing becomes more difficult. Maturation makes sharing harder at age 3 than it was in babyhood.

3. *Remember fast-mapping.* Young children are eager to talk and think, but they say more than they really understand. Children who "just don't listen" may have listened but not understood. Explanations and discussion before and after misbehavior help children learn.

4. *Remember that young children are not logical.* Children confuse lies and wishes, and they may disconnect a misdeed from the punishment. If you were spanked, do you remember why?

None of this means that children should never be disciplined. Remember that children of permissive parents tend to be immature and unhappy. Morality may be innate, but standards of ethical behavior must be learned. In this process, parents need to consider their child's perspective, making sure the child does not conclude that the punishment results from the parents' anger, power, and rejection rather than from his or her own actions.

Parents do not necessarily think of the effects that punishment may have on children's moral development. For developmentalists, however, the long-term effects are crucial. Let us now consider what children learn when their parents punish them.

DAVID STRICKLER / MONKMEYER

PHYSICAL PUNISHMENT Children between ages 2 and 6 are slapped, spanked, or beaten more often than younger and older children. Many parents remember being spanked and see no harm in it, partly because people tend to believe that their own upbringing was adequate—unless it becomes patently obvious that it was not.

Some researchers believe that physical punishment is harmless; some do not (Gershoff, 2002; Larzelere & Kuhn, 2005). However, a developmental perspective reminds us of long-term consequences. Physical punishment succeeds at the moment it is administered—spanking stops a child's misbehavior—but longitudinal research finds that children who are physically punished are more likely to become bullies, delinquents, and ultimately abusive adults. They learn the moral value that "might makes right"—that power is to be sought and valued (Jaffee et al., 2004; Straus, 1994).

Of course, many children who are spanked do not become violent adults. Spanking increases the risk, but other factors (poverty and temperament, among others) are stronger influences on whether a child becomes a violent criminal. Nonetheless, many developmentalists wonder why parents would take any risk. Physical punishment increases obedience temporarily, especially when children are small, but increases the possibility of later aggression (Amato & Fowler, 2002; Gershoff, 2002).

OTHER FORMS OF PUNISHMENT Spanking is not the only punishment with unintended consequences. Another method of discipline is **psychological control,** which uses children's guilt and gratitude to control their behavior (Barber, 2002). This may also undermine children's self-esteem, making them feel unworthy.

A disciplinary technique often used in North America is the **time-out,** in which an adult requires the misbehaving child to sit quietly, without toys or playmates, for a short time (Barkin et al., 2007). The time must be brief; one minute for each year of the child's age is often suggested.

Some parents prefer *time-in,* when they remove the child from the play situation to talk about the misbehavior. Conversation helps children internalize standards, but this method takes time and patience. Since 3-year-olds confuse causes with consequences, they cannot answer an angry "Why did you do that?" or appreciate a lengthy explanation. Simple induction ("You made him sad") is appropriate for 3-year-olds. In general, time-in is recommended if the goal is moral development (Turiel, 2006).

CONSIDERING THE CONSEQUENCES Every method of discipline has consequences, and the effectiveness of a given method depends on temperament, culture, and the adult–child relationship. For example, time-out is effective *if* the child prefers to be with other people, but otherwise not.

One version of time-out for older children is suspension from school. However, if a child hates school, suspension amounts to reinforcement, not punishment. In fact, if a teacher is relieved when a particular child is absent, the teacher might unconsciously provoke the child to misbehave so as to get suspended. Both the child and the teacher are reinforced, not punished.

Adults have powerful emotions, memories, and stresses. That's why punishment of children is not a simple issue. One child who was disciplined for fighting protested, "Sometimes the fight just crawls out of me." Ideally, punishment won't "just crawl out" of the parent.

SHE USED TO HAVE 'TIME OUT' IN HER BEDROOM BUT WE FIND MAKING HER WATCH RERUNS OF THE 'ANTIQUES ROADSHOW' IS **FAR** MORE EFFECTIVE!

Cruel and Unusual? The PBS series *Antiques Roadshow* is popular among adults, but for a child whose sense of the finer things in life is still developing, it might be an apt punishment.

A VIEW FROM SCIENCE

Culture and Punishment

Worldwide, cultural differences in child discipline are apparent. For example, only half as many Canadian parents slap, pinch, or smack their children as parents in the United States (Oldershaw, 2002). The U.S. Supreme Court decided in 2004 that teachers and parents could use "reasonable force" to punish children (Bugental & Grusec, 2006), but physical punishment is illegal in many other developed nations, among them Austria, Croatia, Cyprus, Denmark, Finland, Germany, Israel, Italy, Norway, and Sweden.

Perhaps the United States has more authoritarian parents than those other nations do. However, cultural differences are evident by region and income within the United States (Giles-Sims & Lockhart, 2005). Parents in the southern states and parents in low-income families do more spanking than do parents in New England and in wealthier families.

Such cultural differences may lie behind a controversy that recently arose in the United States over a recommendation by some evangelical Christians that parents put a drop of hot sauce (which burns) on a child's tongue as punishment for forbidden speech. This method is included in a book on "creative correction" (Whelchel, 2000). Most evangelical parents as well as developmentalists consider this method abusive. Yet opinions are strongly divided: Comments (posted on Amazon.com in 2008) regarding this book were either highly favorable or highly unfavorable. One man wrote:

This lady is crazy. A sadistic monster. I wouldn't treat my dog like this, much less my kid. Tell me, how many kids did Jesus Hotsauce?

A woman who highly recommended the book wrote:

Like most moms, I want to have obedient, fun children. I was, however, struggling to find effective means to discipline the children when they strayed.

As for cross-cultural comparisons, Japanese mothers seem quite permissive. They almost never punish children younger than 6; instead, they use reasoning, empathy, and expressions of disappointment to control them.

However, while U.S. children in permissive families tend to be immature and unhappy, Japanese children usually develop well. The reason for this difference may be summed up in the word *amae,* which refers to the strong and affectionate bond that is typical of Japanese mother–child relationships (Rothbaum et al., 2000).

For many Japanese children, their mother's approval is so important that punishment is not needed. Six-year-olds who, to a Western eye, might appear overly dependent and affectionate toward their indulgent mothers, might seem quite normal in Japan.

In Finland, as well, physical punishment is rare. However, psychological control is common. One study began with an entire cohort (Aunola & Nurmi, 2004). Parents were asked about their child-rearing practices, including agreement or disagreement with four items that measured psychological control:

1. My child should be aware of how much I have done for him/her.

2. I let my child see how disappointed and shamed I am if he/she misbehaves.

3. My child should be aware of how much I sacrifice for him/her.

4. I expect my child to be grateful and appreciate all the advantages he/she has.

Over the next several years, the children's math achievement was measured. Those whose parents had ranked high in psychological control tended to have lower math scores; this correlation became more apparent as the children grew older. Surprisingly, math achievement suffered most if parents not only used psychological control but also were high in affection (e.g., frequently hugging their children) (Aunola & Nurmi, 2004).

Research in the United States also finds that parents' psychological control depresses children's achievement, creativity, and social acceptance. Contrary to the results in Finland, however, the U.S. data do not show that parental affection has a negative effect on children's math achievement (Barber, 2002). Why is that?

It may be that the particular mode of discipline is not as crucial as parents believe. Some research finds that if children know their parents are genuinely concerned with their welfare and are trying to do their best to raise them, the children will turn out fine.

Emphasis on parental attitudes more than on specifics of discipline is one interpretation of a study of African American mothers who spanked their children. If the mothers disapproved of spanking but did it anyway, their children were likely to become depressed. However, if the mothers thought that spanking was an appropriate punishment and thus did it partly as an expression of love and concern, their children were usually all right (McLoyd et al., 2007).

Can all the observations noted here lead to any general conclusions? One conclusion is that one must be careful about drawing such conclusions. A multicultural understanding of discipline and morals makes it difficult to judge any one disciplinary tactic as best. All children need parents who love and guide them, but it is not always clear exactly how parents should provide that guidance.

The Same Situation, Many Miles Apart: Which Boy Is Sadder? Of the two punishments shown here, which is harsher? The answer depends on temperament, culture, and circumstances.

RESPONSE FOR Parents (from page 218) No. The worst time to spank a child is when you are angry. You might seriously hurt the child, and the child will associate anger with violence. You would do better to learn to control your anger and develop other strategies for discipline and for prevention of misbehavior. ●

KEY Points

- Moral development is ongoing; social values are the result of both nature and nurture.

- Children teach one another to be kind and loyal friends and to control their aggressive impulses.

- Parents use many methods of discipline, each of which teaches moral lessons.

- Long-term consequences of physical punishment and psychological control suggest that these methods should be used sparingly, if at all.

Becoming Boys and Girls

Identity as either male or female is an important feature of a child's self-concept and a major source of self-esteem (with each gender believing that it is best) (Powlishta, 2004). The first question asked about a newborn, or even a sonogram, is "Boy or girl?" Parents select gender-distinct clothes, blankets, diapers, and pacifiers.

Children learn more about gender with every year of age (Ruble et al., 2006). Even 2-year-olds know whether they are boys or girls and apply gender labels (*Mrs., Mr., lady, man*) consistently. By age 4, children are convinced that certain toys (such as dolls or trucks) are appropriate for one gender but not the other.

Sex and Gender

Social scientists attempt to distinguish between **sex differences,** which are the biological differences between males and females, and **gender differences,** which are culturally prescribed roles and behaviors for males and females. In theory, this seems like a straightforward separation: A penis or vagina is a sex difference; pants or a skirt is a gender difference.

However, as with every nature–nurture distinction, the interaction between sex and gender sometimes makes it hard to separate the two (Hines, 2004). Young children are often quite confused about gender and sex. Some little girls think that they will grow a penis when they get older, and some little boys offer to buy their mother one at the store.

A child's uncertainty about the biological determination of sex was demonstrated by a 3-year-old who went with his father to see a neighbor's newborn kittens. Returning home, the child told his mother that there were three girl kittens and two boy kittens. "How do you know?" she asked. "Daddy picked them up and read what was written on their tummies," he replied.

In recent years, cultural acceptance of various types of sexual orientation has increased. Some people of all ages resist the either/or, masculine or feminine, categories. Most adults are heterosexual, but some are bisexual, homosexual, "mostly straight," or "mostly gay" (E. M. Thompson & Morgan, 2008).

Despite the shift toward increasing tolerance in the overall culture, the social construction that the two sexes are opposites is still strong. At around age 5, children become very aware of sex and gender differences; by age 8, they believe that their biological sex is a permanent trait, and they are usually happy they are male or female.

Indeed, developmentalists note that children's awareness of sex differences, and their preferences for same-sex playmates and stereotypical gender activities, *increase* from age 2 to age 8, which might not be expected (Golombok et al., 2008). How and why does this occur? To answer, we need to explore the origin of sex/gender differences.

Theories of Gender Differences

Experts as well as parents disagree about what proportion of observed male–female differences is biological (perhaps originating in hormones, brain structure, body shape) and what proportion is environmental (perhaps embedded in the culture or the family's traditions) (Leaper, 2002; Ruble et al., 2006). For

sex differences
Biological differences between males and females, in organs, hormones, and body shape.

gender differences
Differences in the roles and behaviors that are prescribed by a culture for males and females.

Two Trios at Play Sex differences are apparent by age 3, not only in haircuts and clothing but also in physical closeness (girls hold hands) and preferred activities (boys more readily take risks).

example, you read earlier that girls are often ahead of boys in emotional regulation. Is that difference connected to the 23rd pair of chromosomes, or does it arise from how parents treat their sons and daughters? A multidisciplinary approach to development finds evidence for both possibilities.

Neuroscientists tend to look for male–female brain differences, and they find many; sociologists tend to look for male–female family and cultural patterns, and they also find many. Historians, anthropologists, political scientists, and psychologists of every perspective have likewise identified genetic and environmental sources of male–female differences.

Many articles and books have been written about this complex and controversial topic. Here we simply consider one aspect of it: the explanations for sex and gender differences in early childhood that have been offered by the four major theories described in Chapter 1.

PSYCHOANALYTIC THEORY Freud (1938) called early childhood the **phallic stage** because he believed its focus is the *phallus,* or penis. At about 3 or 4 years of age, said Freud, boys become aware of their male sexual organ. They masturbate, fear castration, and develop sexual feelings toward their mothers. These feelings make them jealous of their fathers—so jealous, according to Freud, that, by age 5, every son wants to replace his dad.

Oedipus and Electra Freud called the universal wish of young boys to replace their fathers the **Oedipus complex,** named for Oedipus, son of a king in an ancient Greek drama. Abandoned as an infant and raised in a distant kingdom, Oedipus later returned to his birthplace and, not realizing who they were, killed his father and married his mother. When he discovered what he had done, Oedipus blinded himself in a spasm of guilt.

Freud believed that this drama has been replayed over the millennia because it evokes the love and hate that all boys feel about their parents. Every male feels guilty about incestuous and murderous impulses that are buried in his unconscious. Boys fear that their fathers will inflict terrible punishment if their secret wishes are discovered.

In self-defense, boys develop a powerful conscience called the **superego,** which is quick to judge and punish. According to psychoanalytic theory, a boy's fascination with superheroes, guns, and kung fu arises from his unconscious impulse to kill his father. An adult man's homosexuality, homophobia, or obsession with punishment can be explained by an imperfectly resolved phallic stage and an overwhelming superego. Later psychoanalytic theorists agree that morality originates from the clash between unconscious wishes and parental prohibitions in childhood (J. M. Hughes, 2007).

As for girls, Freud thought that their superegos were less developed, partly because they did not experience the powerful Oedipal conflict. However, according to one Freudian explanation, girls have an **Electra complex** (also named after a character in Greek drama). The Electra complex is similar to the Oedipus complex in that the little girl wants to eliminate the same-sex parent (her mother) and become intimate with the opposite-sex parent (her father). Freud also thought that girls experienced *penis envy,* wishing they were boys.

The outcome of the phallic stage for children of both sexes is **identification.** They identify with the same-sex parent by taking on that parent's behavior and attitudes. Guilt and fear push young boys to copy their father's mannerisms, opinions, actions, and so on, while girls copy their mother's. Because of their immaturity, both sexes exaggerate the male or female role, which explains why young boys want guns and young girls want frilly dresses. This leads to the sex differences in patterns of play that were mentioned earlier.

phallic stage
Freud's third stage of development, when the penis becomes the focus of concern and pleasure.

Oedipus complex
The unconscious desire of young boys to replace their fathers and win their mothers' exclusive love.

superego
In psychoanalytic theory, the judgmental part of the personality that internalizes the moral standards of the parents.

Electra complex
The unconscious desire of girls to replace their mothers and win their fathers' exclusive love.

identification
An attempt to defend one's self-concept by taking on the behaviors and attitudes of someone else.

More Recent Psychoanalytic Views Since the middle of the twentieth century, social scientists generally have agreed that Freud's explanation of sexual and moral development "flies in the face of sociological and historical evidence" (David et al., 2004, p. 139). Most women who are psychoanalysts consider penis envy a product of paternalism, not biology (Person & Ovesey, 1999).

Recently some of Freud's ideas have become more acceptable. My own criticism of Freud has softened because of my children. My family's first "Electra episode" occurred in a conversation I had with Bethany when she was about 4 years old:

> **Bethany:** When I grow up, I'm going to marry Daddy.
> **Mother:** But Daddy's married to me.
> **Bethany:** That's all right. When I grow up, you'll probably be dead.
> **Mother:** *(Determined to stick up for myself)* Daddy's older than me, so when I'm dead, he'll probably be dead, too.
> **Bethany:** That's OK. I'll marry him when he gets born again.

At this point, I couldn't think of a good reply, especially since I had no idea where she had heard about reincarnation. Bethany saw my face fall, and she took pity on me:

> **Bethany:** Don't worry, Mommy. After you get born again, you can be our baby.

The second episode was a conversation I had with Rachel when she was about 5:

> **Rachel:** When I get married, I'm going to marry Daddy.
> **Mother:** Daddy's already married to me.
> **Rachel:** *(With the joy of having discovered a wonderful solution)* Then we can have a double wedding!

Pillow Talk Elissa placed this artwork on my husband's pillow. My pillow, beside it, had a less colorful, less elaborate note—an afterthought. It read "Dear Mom, I love you too."

The third episode was considerably more graphic. It took the form of the "valentine," reproduced here, that was left on my husband's pillow by my daughter Elissa. Finally, when Sarah turned 5, she also expressed the desire to marry my husband. When I told her she couldn't, because he was married to me, her response revealed one more hazard of watching TV: "Oh, yes, a man can have two wives. I saw it on television."

I am not the only developmentalist to be taken aback by the words of her own children. Nancy Datan (1986) wrote about the Oedipal conflict: "I have a son who was once five years old. From that day to this, I have never thought Freud mistaken." Obviously, this does not prove that Freud was correct. I believe he was wrong on many counts. But Freud's description of the phallic stage seems less bizarre than it once did.

BEHAVIORISM In contrast to psychoanalytic theorists, behaviorists believe that virtually all roles are learned, resulting from nurture, not nature. To behaviorists, gender distinctions are the product of ongoing reinforcement and punishment.

Some research supports this theory. Parents, peers, and teachers all reward behavior that is "gender-appropriate" more than behavior that is "gender-inappropriate." For example, "adults compliment a girl when she wears a dress but not when she wears pants" (Ruble et al., 2006, p. 897).

According to *social learning theory*, children themselves notice the ways men and women behave and then internalize the standards they observe, becoming proud of themselves when they act like "little men" and "little ladies" (Bandura & Bussey, 2004; Bussey & Bandura, 1999).

Interestingly, male–female distinctions seem more significant to males than to females (Banerjee & Lintern, 2000; David et al., 2004). Fathers, more than mothers, expect their daughters to be feminine and their sons to be tough. Boys are more often criticized for being sissies than girls are for being tomboys. The result in adulthood is just what learning theory would predict: Women wear pants suits but men don't wear dresses; women take on traditionally male jobs more often than vice versa.

Behavioral theory explains why gender prejudice is particularly strong during early childhood: Those are the years when young children are most likely to see their parents and teachers in traditional gender roles. By adulthood, some of these prejudices are less strong.

As a consequence of developmental change, if a college man wants to teach young children or a college woman wants to be a police officer, their classmates will probably respect the choice. However, if a 4-year-old boy wants to become a nursery school teacher, his peers will laugh because their experience has been quite gender-segregated. As one professor reports:

> My son came home after 2 days of preschool to announce that he could not grow up to teach seminars (previously his lifelong ambition, because he knew from personal observation that everyone at seminars got to eat cookies) because only women could be teachers.
>
> *[Fagot, 1995, p. 173]*

Thus, as children learn to identify with their own sex, they are reinforced (particularly by fathers and by other children) for acting in gender-specific ways (Berenbaum et al., 2008). That is the behaviorist explanation for gender distinctions.

COGNITIVE THEORY Cognitive theory offers an alternative explanation for the strong gender identity that becomes apparent at about age 5. Remember that cognitive theorists focus on how children understand various ideas, forming their concepts on the basis of their experiences. These theorists conclude that children develop a **gender schema,** which is their concept of sex differences (Kohlberg et al., 1983; C. L. Martin et al., 2002; Renk et al., 2006).

The gender schema emerges because young children have many gender-related experiences but not much cognitive depth. They tend to see the world in simple terms, categorizing male and female as opposites, even when evidence contradicts such a view. Nuances, complexities, exceptions, and gradations about gender (as well as about everything else) are beyond the mental grasp of the preoperational child.

Young children categorize themselves and everyone else as either male or female, and then they think and behave in whatever way fits their either/or categories (M. Rhodes & Gelman, 2008). For that reason, cognitive theorists see "Jill's claim that she is a girl because she is wearing her new frilly socks as a genuine expression of her gender identity" (David et al., 2004, p. 147).

Similarly, a 3-year-old boy whose aunt called him *cute* insisted that he should be called *handsome* instead (Powlishta, 2004). Obviously, he had developed gender-based categories, deciding that certain words applied to girls but not to boys, and he wanted others to see him as he conceptualized himself.

Cognitive and social learning theories differ in that "while both theories explain how the social reality of sex differences is internalized, social learning theory proposes that society socializes children, while cognitive developmental theory proposes that children actively socialize themselves" (David et al., 2004, pp. 139–140).

gender schema
A child's cognitive concept or general belief about sex differences, which is based on his or her observations and experiences.

Trick or Treat? Any doubt about which of these children are girls and which are boys? No. Any question about whether such strict gender distinctions are appropriate at age 4? Maybe.

ARIEL SKELLEY / CORBIS

SYSTEMS THEORY As discussed in Chapter 1, systems theory attempts to understand the interaction between social systems and biological forces. Every culture has a system of gender distinctions, evident in dramatic stories, taboos, and terminology and often in sex-segregated schools and play activities. Children adopt whatever patterns their culture prescribes for their sex (Leaper & Smith, 2004).

To break through the restrictiveness of culture and to encourage individuals to define themselves primarily as humans, not as males or females, some parents and teachers have embraced the idea of androgyny. **Androgyny** is a balance, within one person, of traditionally masculine and feminine characteristics. To achieve androgyny, boys are encouraged to be nurturing and girls to be assertive so that both will develop less restrictive, gender-free self-concepts (Bem, 1993).

The idea of androgyny runs counter to systems theory because no single idea can undercut all the values, practices, and traditions of a society. In fact, young adults who are particularly androgynous are not usually those with higher self-esteem or a healthier self-concept (Ruble et al., 2006). Systems theory holds that parents cannot raise happily androgynous children unless their entire social context promotes androgyny in its ideas and practices—something no culture has done.

Modern systems theory incorporates the influence of biological forces. That is why, as Chapter 1 noted, Urie Bronfenbrenner changed the name of his approach from *ecological systems* to *bioecological systems,* to emphasize the impact of biology in the micro-, macro-, and exosystems. The systems perspective can be applied to some of the sex differences referred to in this chapter: Boys tend to externalize their troubles while girls tend to internalize, but whether such biological tendencies become pathological depends on family systems more than on gender.

The interaction of biological and social systems is evident throughout life. For instance, hormones are biological and stress is social. Yet stress increases testosterone production in males, making them ready for "fight or flight," but increases levels of oxytocin (another hormone) in females, making them likely to "tend and befriend" (S. E. Taylor, 2006). A similar systemic interaction was described earlier in this chapter: Under stress, young boys are likely to punch their rivals while girls tend to seek comfort and forgiveness from their friends.

All the evidence on sex differences from age 2 to age 8 now converges to incorporate all these theories of gender development. As one study explains:

> It is now generally agreed that sex differences in behavior result from an interplay among biological, psychological, and social mechanisms from early fetal development onward. . . . [B]iological influences would be expected to be maintained postnatally, the processes of differential reinforcement and modeling that characterize the classic social learning approach are apparent[,] . . . and the cognitive processes of gender concept formation and gender schematization occur during the preschool and middle school years.
>
> [Golombok et al., 2008, p. 1585]

Keep the mix of explanations in mind when remembering this entire chapter. For young children, emotions, friendships, parenting, morality, and sex differences are

androgyny
A balance within one person of traditionally masculine and feminine psychological characteristics.

Toy Guns for Boys, Cinderella for Girls Young boys throughout the world are the ones who aim toy guns, while young girls imagine themselves as a Disney Cinderella, waiting for her handsome prince. The question is why: Are these young monks in Laos and this girl in Mexico responding to biology or to culture?

BJORN SVENSSON / ALAMY

BLICKWINKEL / ALAMY

not as straightforward as they might seem. Many factors influence each developmental twist and turn, all interacting in complex ways. Yet the outcome is quite obvious: A 6-year-old is much more capable than he or she was only a few years earlier. The child is ready for middle childhood, which we discuss in the next pair of chapters.

KEY points

- Young children hold strong gender stereotypes and beliefs.
- Various theories present conflicting explanations for sex and gender differences.
- To explain gender differences, Freud described unconscious incestuous urges, behaviorists highlight social reinforcement, and cognitive theorists point to immature categorization.
- Systems theories offer the most complex and comprehensive explanations for gender differences. Genes and culture, parents and peers, ideas and customs all interact, affecting each child.

SUMMARY

Emotional Development

1. Regulation of emotions is crucial during the play years, when children learn emotional control. Emotional regulation is made possible by maturation of the brain, particularly of the prefrontal cortex, as well as by experiences with parents and peers.

2. In Erikson's psychosocial theory, the crisis of initiative versus guilt occurs during early childhood. Children normally feel pride and self-esteem, sometimes mixed with feelings of guilt. Shame is also evident, particularly in some cultures.

3. Both externalizing and internalizing problems indicate impaired self-control. Many severe emotional problems that indicate psychopathology are first evident during these years.

4. Boys more often manifest externalizing behaviors and girls internalizing behaviors. For both sexes, brain maturation and the quality of early caregiving affect emotional control.

Play

5. All young children enjoy playing—with other children of the same sex, if possible, alone or with parents if not.

6. The specifics of play vary by setting and culture. In contemporary cities, most children's social play occurs in day-care centers.

Challenges for Parents

7. Three classic styles of parenting have been identified, as follows: authoritarian, permissive, and authoritative. Generally, children are more successful and happy when their parents express warmth and set guidelines. Parenting that is rejecting and uninvolved is harmful.

8. Children are prime consumers of many kinds of media, usually for several hours a day, often without their parents' involvement. Content is crucial. The themes and characters of many television programs can lead to increased aggression.

Moral Development

9. The young child's sense of self and social awareness become the foundation for morality. This is evident in both prosocial and antisocial behavior.

10. Children develop standards for aggression. Unprovoked injury (bullying) is considered wrong by children as well as by adults. Parents' choice of punishment can have long-term consequences.

Becoming Boys and Girls

11. Even 2-year-olds correctly use sex-specific labels, and young children become aware of gender differences in clothes, toys, future careers, and playmates. Gender stereotypes, favoritism, and segregation increase throughout early childhood.

12. Freud emphasized that children are attracted to the opposite-sex parent and eventually seek to identify, or align themselves, with the same-sex parent. Behaviorists hold that gender-related behaviors are learned through reinforcement and punishment (especially for males) and social modeling.

13. Cognitive theorists note that simplistic preoperational thinking leads to developing a gender schema and therefore stereotypes.

14. A systems explanation notes that some sex differences result from hormones affecting brain formation. Experiences enhance or halt those neurological patterns, as the many aspects of culture and biology interact.

KEY TERMS

emotional regulation (p. 197)	rough-and-tumble play (p. 207)	prosocial behavior (p. 215)	sex differences (p. 221)
initiative versus guilt (p. 198)	sociodramatic play (p. 207)	antisocial behavior (p. 215)	gender differences (p. 221)
self-esteem (p. 198)	authoritarian parenting (p. 210)	instrumental aggression (p. 215)	phallic stage (p. 222)
self-concept (p. 198)	permissive parenting (p. 210)		Oedipus complex (p. 222)
intrinsic motivation (p. 200)	authoritative parenting (p. 210)	reactive aggression (p. 215)	superego (p. 222)
extrinsic motivation (p. 200)	neglectful/uninvolved	relational aggression (p. 215)	Electra complex (p. 222)
psychopathology (p. 201)	parenting (p. 210)	bullying aggression (p. 215)	identification (p. 222)
externalizing problems (p. 201)	empathy (p. 215)	psychological control (p. 218)	gender schema (p. 224)
internalizing problems (p. 202)	antipathy (p. 215)	time-out (p. 218)	androgyny (p. 225)

KEY QUESTIONS

1. How can adults help children develop self-esteem?

2. What is the connection between psychopathology and emotional regulation?

3. What do children learn from rough-and-tumble play? From sociodramatic play?

4. Describe the characteristics of the parenting style that seems to promote the happiest, most successful children. To what extent is this outcome culture-bound?

5. How does moral development relate to aggression and to discipline?

6. How do children change from ages 2 to 6 in their male and female roles and behaviors?

7. Describe the differences among three of the four theories about the origins of sex differences and gender roles.

8. List the similarities between two of the four theories about the origins of sex differences and gender roles.

APPLICATIONS

1. Ask three parents about punishment, including their preferred type, at what age, for what misdeeds, and by whom. Ask your three informants how they were punished as children and how that affected them. If your sources agree, find a parent (or a classmate) who has a different view.

2. Children's television programming is rife with stereotypes about ethnicity, gender, and morality. Watch an hour of children's TV, especially on a Saturday morning, and describe the content of both the programs and the commercials. Draw some conclusions about stereotyping in the material you watched, citing specific evidence (rather than merely reporting your impressions).

3. Gender indicators often go unnoticed. Go to a public place (park, restaurant, busy street) and spend at least 10 minutes recording examples of gender differentiation, such as articles of clothing, mannerisms, interaction patterns, and activities. Quantify what you see, such as baseball hats on eight males and two females or (better but more difficult) four male–female conversations, with gender differences in length and frequency of talking, interruptions, vocabulary, and so on.

Early Childhood (Ages 2 to 6)

BODY AND BRAIN

Steady growth
Lowest BMI of life span at age 5½
Gross and fine motor skills
New teeth

Nutrition
Small appetites
"Just-right" preferences

Environmental poisons (lead)

Brain development
75 to 90 percent of adult weight
Quicker responses (myelination)
Stronger fears (amygdala)
Coordination (prefrontal cortex, limbic system)
Lateralization (corpus callosum)

Perseveration

Maltreatment (abuse and neglect)

Injuries (leading cause of death)

"GIRLS DON'T FIGHT— OR DO THEY?"
TALKING, THINKING, AND PLAYING: GENDER, FAMILY, CULTURE

PARENTS AND PEERS

Patterns of parenting
Warmth, communication, and expectations
Baumrind: Authoritarian, authoritative, permissive styles

Ways of discipline
Physical (spanking)
Isolation (time out)
Psychological control (guilt, shame)

Sex roles and concepts
Freud: Phallic stage, Oedipus complex
Behaviorism: Reinforcement and social learning
Cognitive: Gender stereotypes

Play as a way of learning
From solitary to cooperative
Rough-and-tumble
Sociodramatic

Neglectful-uninvolved parenting

Learning from television

LEARNING AT HOME AND SCHOOL

First language
Explosion of vocabulary (fast-mapping)

Mastery of grammar

Pronunciation difficulty

Children not "bathed in language"

Children not in any school

Second language
Rapid learning

Balanced bilinguals

Early-childhood education
Child-centered programs (Reggio Emilia)

Teacher-directed programs (school "readiness")

Intervention programs (Head Start)

COGNITIVE DEVELOPMENT

Searching for theories and explanations

Vygotsky: Social learning
Apprenticeship in thinking: Mentors, scaffolding

Piaget: Preoperational intelligence
Symbolic thought

Lack of logic

Egocentrism

Culture clash

DEVELOPMENT OF EMOTIONS

Emotional regulation
Holding in and lashing out

Prosocial and antisocial behavior

Empathy and antipathy

Imaginary companions

Initiative versus guilt
Pride and self-esteem

Learning family values

Aggression
In response (reactive)

To get something (instrumental)

Bullying aggression

Shyness

KEY
- Major topic
- Related topic
- Potential problem

IV

Middle Childhood

If someone asked you to pick the best years of the entire life span, you might answer like a good developmentalist, saying that every age has joys and sorrows, gains and losses. But if you were pushed to choose just one, you might select puberty, which occurs sometime between ages 9 and 13, and defend your choice persuasively.

For many children, these healthy and productive years allow measured (not dramatic) growth; mastery of new athletic skills; acquisition of concepts, vocabulary, and intellectual abilities; a degree of independence from family. In the twenty-first century, children throughout the world attend school during these years and become skilled at reading and writing—thereby opening up new possibilities. Children typically appreciate their parents, make new friends, and are proud of themselves, not only in terms of their personal development but also in terms of their nationality, gender, and ethnicity. For the most part, they are too young for the hazards of addiction, sex, and other dangers.

All this is true for many, but not all. Some school-age children struggle with special educational needs; some live in dysfunctional families; some cope with poverty and homelessness; some contend with obesity, asthma, learning disabilities, or bullying. For them these years are the worst, not the best. The next two chapters celebrate the joys and acknowledge the difficulties of middle childhood.

CHAPTER OUTLINE

MIDDLE CHILDHOOD
Body and Mind

My family moved a thousand miles across the country when I was in the second grade, so I had to attend a new school. I spoke with a midwestern accent; the teacher criticized my math ability and my lack of awareness of school rules; I often had a runny nose (caused by allergies that no one had yet recognized). Fortunately, a classmate, Cynthia, was also new. She talked to me; I asked her to be my friend.

"We cannot be friends," she told me, "because I am a Democrat."

"So am I," I answered. (I knew my family believed in democracy.)

"No, you're not. You are a Republican," she replied and walked away.

I was stunned and sad. We never became friends. ●

THE AGES FROM 7 TO 11 are sometimes called the school years, since almost all children are enrolled in school at those ages. However, since many children older or younger than 7 to 11 are also in school, this time is more appropriately called **middle childhood.**

As you will learn, all school-age children have much in common. Most are quite healthy and grow steadily. In every nation, almost all are enrolled in schools where they learn eagerly and rapidly, following their teachers' lead. They prefer to befriend children of the same age and sex and are not interested in romance or even rebellion. Most of them care for themselves, sit quietly when required to do so, and get along with everyone.

Yet you will soon read that the way school-age children think causes them to misinterpret minor differences among themselves—in appearance, culture, clothes, language, or (as with Cynthia) political background. Institutions, especially families and schools, can provide critical encouragement and guidance to bring children together. I wish my teacher had helped Cynthia and me. I needed a friend.

In this chapter, you will learn about characteristics that almost all 7- to 11-year-olds share, in nutrition, thinking, language, and education. You will also read about differences in body weight, motor skills, intelligence, and special needs. How important these variations become depends on parents and schools, also described in this chapter.

I was lonely at my new school even though it was only in a different state, not a different nation. Children who move to other nations, especially when they don't speak that country's dominant language, can have many more difficulties—but it need not be so. Bilingual education is also discussed in this chapter.

middle childhood
The period between early childhood and early adolescence, approximately from ages 7 to 11.

Expert Eye–Hand Coordination The specifics of motor-skill development in middle childhood depend on the culture. These flute players are carrying on the European Baroque musical tradition that thrives among the poor, remote Guarayo people of Bolivia.

asthma
A chronic disease of the respiratory system in which inflammation narrows the airways from the nose and mouth to the lungs, causing difficulty in breathing. Signs and symptoms include wheezing, shortness of breath, chest tightness, and coughing.

A Healthy Time

The average 7- to 11-year-old gains about 2 inches (5 centimeters) and 5 pounds (about 2.2 kilograms) per year. Healthy 7-year-olds tend to be agile and to be neither too heavy nor too thin (Guillaume & Lissau, 2002). They move—leaping, twisting, racing, hopping—better than almost any older or younger child. After age 6, the rate of growth slows as muscles strengthen, allowing children to master any motor skill that doesn't require an adult-size body (Malina et al., 2004).

Most fatal diseases and accidents occur before or after middle childhood (see Figure 7.1). Three environmental factors favor survival: (1) Children have learned to be cautious, (2) parents have instilled some health habits, and (3) societies have provided immunization. A fourth protective factor, genetic inheritance, is suggested by the fact that even in past centuries, when infant mortality rates were high and immunization was not yet available, school-age children were quite hardy.

Once a family and community have invested resources in their offspring long enough for them to survive past babyhood, it makes evolutionary sense for children to continue to live at least until they give birth to the next generation. Thus, human genes guard against serious illness before puberty. This is one explanation for statistics on genetic diseases: They are most likely to be fatal in infancy or late adulthood and almost never appear during middle childhood.

Not every child grows as well or as much as their genes would allow. Children with stunted (unusually short) growth probably experienced malnutrition at younger ages. Children who have chronic illnesses also grow more slowly, but again those illnesses usually appeared years earlier. However, two particular physical conditions, asthma and obesity, merit discussion here because they often impair development in middle childhood.

Asthma

Asthma is a chronic inflammatory disorder of the airways that makes breathing difficult. In 2005 in the United States, 10 percent of all school-age children had at least one asthma attack. Asthma rates were higher among Puerto Rican, Hawaiian, and African American children than among those of Mexican, European, or Asian

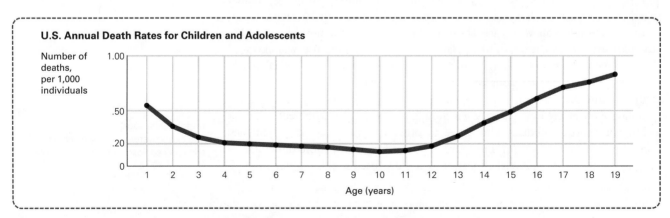

U.S. Annual Death Rates for Children and Adolescents

Number of deaths, per 1,000 individuals

Age (years)

FIGURE 7.1 Death at an Early Age? Almost Never! Schoolchildren are remarkably hardy, as measured in many ways. This chart shows that death rates for 7- to 11-year-olds are lower than those for children under 7 or over 11.

heritage (U.S. Bureau of the Census, 2008). The rates for all groups are about double what they were in 1980 and are increasing worldwide (Akinbami, 2006; Bousquet et al., 2007).

Asthma is rarely lethal in middle childhood; people who die of it are typically either very young or quite old. However, asthma is the leading cause of missed school as well as the most common medical condition to require ongoing treatment during middle childhood (Centers for Disease Control and Prevention, 2009). If the causes of asthma were better understood and if adequate preventive measures were in place, millions of the world's children would breathe easier.

CAUSES OF ASTHMA Scientists have found dozens of genes associated with asthma—so many that it is misleading to use genetic analysis as a predictor (Bossé & Hudson, 2007). Some children with suspect genes never develop the disease. Risk factors in a child's environment, however, play a crucial role in the onset of asthma, especially when they interact with a genetic vulnerability.

Numerous aspects of modern life—carpets, pets inside the home, airtight windows, less time spent outdoors—increase the chances of developing asthma (Tamay et al., 2007). Many allergens that trigger asthma attacks (e.g., pet dander, cigarette smoke, dust mites, cockroaches, mold) are more concentrated in today's well-insulated homes than in the drafty houses of a century ago.

Poverty and air quality both correlate with the incidence of asthma, and air pollution is increasing in many nations. For instance, in Mongolia, rates of asthma increase as more people move from sparsely populated rural areas to lives of poverty in the cities, where the air is contaminated by high levels of smoke and exhaust fumes (Viinanen et al., 2007).

Pride and Prejudice In some city schools, asthma is so common that using an inhaler is a sign of prestige, as suggested by the facial expressions of these two boys. The "prejudice" is more apparent beyond the walls of this school nurse's room, in a society that allows high rates of childhood asthma to occur.

Some experts suggest a *hygiene hypothesis* for the current increase in all allergies, from peanuts (an allergen for about 1 percent of U.S. children) to cockroach droppings (a trigger for asthma) (J. Couzin, 2007b; Sachs, 2007). The hypothesis is that young children are overprotected from viruses, bacteria, and allergens, preventing normal development of their immune systems. In other words, *too much* hygiene may be a problem.

PREVENTION OF ASTHMA The three levels of prevention discussed in Chapter 5 apply to every chronic health problem, including asthma. *Primary prevention* requires changes in the entire society. Better ventilation of schools and homes, fewer smokers, eradication of cockroaches, and more outdoor play areas would decrease childhood asthma. Reducing air pollution is a primary-prevention measure of proven effectiveness (Friedman et al., 2001; X. Pan et al., 2007).

Secondary prevention avoids onset among high-risk children. If asthma runs in the family or if a baby is vulnerable to an allergy, then breast-feeding and ridding homes of dust, pets, cockroaches, secondhand cigarette smoke, and other allergens can cut the rate of allergies and asthma in half (Elliott et al., 2007; Gdalevich et al., 2001).

Finally, *tertiary prevention* includes the prompt use of injections and inhalers by children who have asthma to reduce wheezing and prevent the need for overnight hospitalization (Glauber et al., 2001). The use of hypoallergenic materials (e.g., for mattress covers) can also reduce the frequency of asthma attacks, although not by much, probably because tertiary prevention at home usually does not begin until after the allergy is well established (MMWR, January 14, 2005).

Indeed, adequate tertiary prevention occurs for less than half the children in the United States. Some parents do not recognize the symptoms of asthma, take preventive measures, follow doctors' advice, or respond to early warning signs of illness. Consequently, they do not treat their children until a full-blown asthma attack is under way (Bokhour et al., 2008; Sales et al., 2008).

Obesity

body mass index (BMI)
The ratio of weight to height, calculated by dividing a person's body weight in kilograms by the square of his or her height in meters.

overweight
In an adult, having a BMI of 25 to 29. In a child, having a BMI above the 85th percentile, according to the U.S. Centers for Disease Control's 1980 standards for children of a given age.

obesity
In an adult, having a BMI of 30 or more. In a child, having a BMI above the 95th percentile, according to the U.S. Centers for Disease Control's 1980 standards for children of a given age.

Many 7- to 11-year-olds eat too much, exercise too little, and become overweight or obese as a result. Weight status is assessed by means of the **body mass index (BMI)**, the ratio of weight to height, calculated by dividing a person's weight in kilograms by the square of his or her height in meters. For children, **overweight** is defined as having a BMI above the 85th percentile of children the same age; **obesity** is defined as having a BMI above the 95th percentile. Those percentiles are based on measurements of a large sample of children taken in the United States in 1980. (Weight ranges for children are listed in Appendix A, page A-7. The criteria for overweight and obesity are different for adults and are discussed in Chapter 11.)

CURRENT RATES If the distribution of children's weight remained what it was, then, by definition, only 15 percent of children would be considered overweight and only 5 percent would be classified as obese today. But applying the old cutoff weights to the current generation leads us to realize that the rates of obesity and overweight have increased at every age (even infants), especially in middle childhood.

Although massive public-education efforts have slowed the rate of increase, the United States is still in the midst of an epidemic of childhood obesity. The proportion of obese 6- to 11-year-olds in the United States has increased nearly fourfold, from 5 percent to 19 percent, since the late 1960s (Ogden et al., 2008; see Figure 7.2). African American girls and Mexican American boys are at particular risk, but the average child of every age, family income, nationality, and cultural group is heavier today than his or her counterpart in 1970.

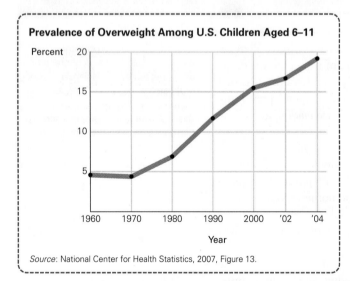

Prevalence of Overweight Among U.S. Children Aged 6–11

Source: National Center for Health Statistics, 2007, Figure 13.

FIGURE 7.2 Not Fat? Experts hesitate to call children "fat" or "obese," but no one doubts that today's school-age children weigh much more than earlier cohorts.

Most other nations are also experiencing an increase in overweight among children. Longitudinal data since 1948 from Ireland, for instance, finds that children of both sexes and every age are becoming heavier with every decade. The results are cumulative: By age 14, the average Irish child is about 50 pounds heavier than 14-year-olds were in 1948 (I. J. Perry et al., 2009).

Except in times of famine or war, poverty no longer automatically means underweight. Comparisons worldwide (even in China and India, where childhood obesity was once rare) find obesity "increasing at especially alarming rates in children" (Branca et al., 2007, p. 9).

With every year of middle childhood, the proportion of overweight children increases, as do their problems. Such children exercise less and have higher blood pressure than children of normal weight, and their school achievement and self-esteem decline. Even if they lose weight later, people who were obese in childhood face increased risks of diabetes, heart disease, and stroke in adulthood (S. L. Friedlander et al., 2003; Guillaume & Lissau, 2002).

CAUSES AND PREVENTION OF OBESITY Why is one child overweight, while another child the same age is of normal weight? Genes are part of the reason; they affect activity level, food preferences, body type, and metabolic rate. People who inherit from both parents a particular allele of what is called the FTO gene (as about

16 percent of all children of European ancestry do) are more likely to be obese (Frayling et al., 2007).

But genes never act alone: "Fat runs in families but so do frying pans, which makes it hard to know whether DNA or dripping is more to blame for today's plague of obesity" (S. Jones, 2006, p. 1879). Studies suggest dozens of familial and cultural culprits. For instance, children who watch more than two hours of television and drink more than two servings of soda ("pop") every day are more likely to be overweight than are those who do neither (Institute of Medicine, 2006).

Experimental research with genetically identical mice and cats shows that maternal nourishment during pregnancy is crucial. If a mouse is born unusually thin or fat, it is more likely to become an obese adult (Coe et al., 2008). Correlational data find the same pattern among humans: Low or high birthweight increases the risk of obesity (Gluckman & Hanson, 2006b).

This link is especially ominous for nations with many underweight or overweight pregnant women. In India, for instance, malnourished women have underweight infants who become overweight children—a "thin-to-fat" pattern that often leads to diabetes in adulthood (Yajnik, 2004). Mothers with diabetes tend to have overweight babies, which perpetuates the problem.

What is a parent to do? The simple solution, to put the overweight child on a diet, may boomerang. One study of 7- to 12-year-olds found that "restricting access to certain foods increases rather than decreases preference. Forcing a child to eat a food will decrease liking for that food" (Benton, 2004, p. 858). A more effective strategy is for parents to keep their own weight down by eating sensibly and exercising regularly and to encourage their child to do the same (Patrick et al., 2004).

Physical Activity

Active play benefits children in every way, especially by helping them maintain a healthy weight. Children often play joyfully, "fully and totally immersed" (Loland, 2002, p. 139). Much more than for younger children, the maturation of body and brain enables school-age children to join in sports. The benefits can last a lifetime:

● Better overall health, including less asthma
● Less obesity
● Appreciation of cooperation and fair play
● Improved problem-solving ability
● Respect for teammates and opponents of many ethnicities and nationalities

But there are hazards as well:

● Loss of self-esteem because of critical teammates or coaches
● Injuries (the infamous "Little League elbow" is one example)
● Prejudice (especially against the other sex)
● Increases in stress (evidenced by altered hormone levels, insomnia)

Where can children reap the benefits and avoid the hazards of active play? Three possibilities are neighborhoods, schools, and sports leagues.

NEIGHBORHOOD GAMES Neighborhood play is flexible; children improvise to meet their needs. Rules and boundaries ("Out of bounds is past the tree" or "the parked truck") are adapted to the context. Stickball, touch football, tag, hide-and-seek,

A Happy Meal A close look at this photograph reveals that this scene is a McDonald's in Switzerland—one of hundreds of fast-food chain branches in Europe, where many normal-weight 6-year-olds become overweight 12-year-olds.

ESPECIALLY FOR Parents Suppose that you always serve dinner with the television on, tuned to a news broadcast. Your hope is that your children will learn about the world as they eat. Can this practice be harmful? (see response, page 239) →

ESPECIALLY FOR Teachers A child in your class is overweight, but you are hesitant to say anything to the parents, who are also overweight, because you do not want to insult them. What should you do? (see response, page 239) →

jump rope, and dozens of other games that involve running and catching, or kicking and jumping, can go on forever—or at least until dark. The play is active, interactive, and inclusive—ideal for children.

Unfortunately, modern life has made informal neighborhood games increasingly scarce. Exploding urbanization means there are fewer open areas that are both fun and safe. For example, the population of Mexico City was 3 million in 1970 but had grown to 23 million in 2008. With so many more people crowded within the city limits, children in Mexico City have less space to play.

To make matters worse, many parents keep their children indoors because of "stranger danger"—although "there is a much greater chance that your child is going to be dangerously overweight from staying inside than that he is going to be abducted" (Layden, 2004, p. 96). Indoor activities (homework, television, and video games) compete with outdoor play in every nation.

EXERCISE IN SCHOOL Especially when opportunities for neighborhood play are scarce, physical education in school is an alternative. Dedicated and trained gym teachers know developmentally appropriate, cooperative games and exercises for children (Belka, 2004).

However, many children hate physical education because they spend most of their gym time waiting for a turn or watching other children. Actually, forces beyond their control have relieved them of the need to make excuses to miss gym. A study of 648 elementary schools found that only 6 percent had daily physical education (National Institute of Child Health Human Development Study of Early Child Care and Youth Development Network, 2003).

Schools have reduced physical education and cut teachers in order to meet academic standards (Trudeau & Shephard, 2008). This seems logical, but it is counterproductive. Paradoxically, up to an hour a day of active play is more likely to improve academic achievement than to impair it (S. A. Carlson et al., 2008).

ATHLETIC CLUBS AND LEAGUES Private or nonprofit clubs and organizations offer opportunities for children to play. Culture and family affect the specifics: Some children learn golf, others tennis, others boxing. Cricket and rugby are common in England and in former British colonies such as India, Australia, and Jamaica; baseball is widely played in Japan, the United States, Cuba, Panama, and the Dominican Republic; soccer is central in many European, African, and Latin American nations.

The best-known organized recreation program for children is Little League. Each year, 2.7 million children play baseball and softball on more than 200,000 teams in 80 countries. When it began in 1939, Little League had only three teams of boys aged 9 to 12. Now it includes girls, younger and older children, and 22,000 children with disabilities. For most children (but not necessarily for their parents and coaches), playing is more important than winning. One adult confesses:

> I was a lousy Little League player. Uncoordinated, small, and clueless are the accurate adjectives I'd use if someone asked politely. . . . What I did possess, though, was enthusiasm. Wearing the uniform—cheesy mesh cap, scratchy polyester shirt, old-school beltless pants, uncomfortable cleats and stirrups that never stayed up—gave me a sort of pride. It felt special and made me think that I was part of something important.
>
> [M. J. Ryan, 2005]

Being "part of something important" is a goal of every child, but that raises a significant problem with organized children's sports: Many children are left out (M. F. Collins, 2003). Not all parents can pay their children's fees, transport them to practices and games, and coach or cheer their children's teams. Children who are from poor families, who are not well coordinated, or who have

A Hand Up Neighborhood play is usually cooperative and free-form, but scenes like this one are becoming increasingly rare as the world's children have less access to open space and less time for unstructured play.

MOODBOARD / CORBIS

THE NEW YORKER COLLECTION 2001 PAT BYRNES FROM CARTOONBANK.COM. ALL RIGHTS RESERVED.

"Just remember, son, it doesn't matter whether you win or lose— unless you want Daddy's love."

disabilities are less likely to play in the neighborhood, to enjoy school recreation, or to belong to after-school sports leagues. Yet those are the very children who could benefit most; they need the strength, activity, and teamwork that active play provides.

ESPECIALLY FOR Physical Education Teachers A group of parents of fourth- and fifth-graders has asked for your help in persuading the school administration to sponsor a competitive sports team. How should you advise the group to proceed? (see response, page 241) ➜

KEYⓅoints

- Growth is steady in middle childhood, and health is usually good.
- Rates of asthma are increasing.
- Insufficient exercise and overeating are causing a worldwide epidemic of childhood obesity, which has lifelong consequences.
- Physical activity benefits children greatly, but opportunities for active play are diminishing.

RESPONSE FOR Parents (from page 237) Habitual TV watching correlates with obesity, so you may be damaging your children's health rather than improving their intellect. Your children would probably profit more if you were to make dinner a time for family conversation. ●

RESPONSE FOR Teachers (from page 237) Speak to the parents, not accusingly (because you know that genes and culture have a major influence on body weight), but helpfully. Alert them to the potential social and health problems their child's weight poses. Most parents are very concerned about their child's well-being and will work with you to improve the child's snacks and exercise level. ●

Theories About Cognition

School-age children have active minds and can learn almost anything: how to divide fractions, when to search the Internet, what to feed an orphaned kitten, how to navigate a boat. But they cannot learn everything; the adults in their lives must make choices about what to teach them. Not surprisingly, controversy swirls around teaching and learning during middle childhood. We begin with theories about the nature of cognition in these years.

Piaget and School-Age Children

In Piaget's view, the most important cognitive structure attained in middle childhood is **concrete operational thought,** the ability to reason logically about direct experiences and perceptions. Piaget thought that, sometime between ages 5 and 7, children begin to apply logic in *concrete* situations—that is, situations that deal with visible, tangible things (Inhelder & Piaget, 1964). Children become more systematic, objective, and educable thinkers.

concrete operational thought
Piaget's term for the ability to reason logically about direct experiences and perceptions.

CONCRETE OPERATIONS: TWO EXAMPLES Concrete thinking applies to every aspect of a child's life, from what they think love is (physical touch, specific caregiving tasks) to what kind of pants they wear (a particular style, a certain brand). Piaget studied concrete operations by asking children questions about dozens of topics and then analyzing their answers. We present two of the most famous examples of concrete thinking here.

Classification One crucial logical concept involved in concrete operational thought is **classification,** the organization of things into groups (or *categories* or *classes*) according to some property that they have in common. For example, a child's parents and siblings are classified as belonging to a group called *family.* Other common classes are *people, animals, food,* and *toys.*

Each class includes some elements and excludes others, and each is part of a hierarchy. Food, for instance, contains the subclasses of meat, grains, fruits, and so on. Most subclasses can be further divided: Meat includes poultry, beef, and pork, which again can be further subdivided. It is apparent to adults who have mastered classification, but not always to children, that items at the bottom of the hierarchy belong to every higher category (bacon is always pork, meat, and food) but that the process does not work in reverse (most foods are not bacon).

classification
The logical principle that things can be organized into groups (or categories or classes) according to some characteristic they have in common.

His Science Project Concrete operational 10-year-olds like Daniel, shown here with some of his family's dairy cows, can be logical about anything they see, hear, or touch. Daniel's science experiment, on the effect of music on milk production, won first place in a Georgia regional science fair.

Piaget developed many experiments to reveal children's understanding of classification. For example, an examiner shows a child a bunch of nine flowers—seven yellow daisies and two white roses (revised and published in Piaget et al., 1977/2001). The examiner makes sure the child understands *flowers, daisies,* and *roses* and asks the crucial question: "Are there more daisies or more flowers?" Until age 7, most children say, "More daisies." Then, the logical structures of concrete operational thought allow a better understanding of classification. By age 8, most children have a solid understanding of the categories of objects they can see (that is, concrete objects, not yet hypothetical ones) and they confidently answer, "More flowers than daisies."

Transitive Inference Another example of the ability to apply logic that appears at about age 7 involves making connections that are implied, not stated. Piaget studied *transitive inference,* the ability to figure out (infer) the unspoken link (transfer) between one fact and another.

As a test of transitive inference, a child is told, "John is taller than Jim. Jim is taller than David." Then the child is asked, "Who is taller, John or David?" Preoperational children are stumped. They cannot make this simple transitive inference, because they know only what they have been told directly. By contrast, school-age children can infer the relationship. Later research connects transitive inference to the maturation of the hypothalamus, which reaches a crucial level of development at about age 7, making mental logic possible (A. J. Greene et al., 2006; Heckers et al., 2004).

Transitive inference may be a prerequisite for another concrete operational concept called *seriation,* the idea that things can be arranged in a series. Seriation is crucial for understanding the number sequence. By age 5, most American children can count up to 100, but they cannot correctly estimate where any particular two-digit number would be placed on a line that starts at 0 and ends at 100 because seriation is beyond their comprehension at this stage. Generally, seriation is understood by age 8, allowing more advanced math operations (e.g., multiplication of two-digit numbers) to be understood (Meadows, 2006).

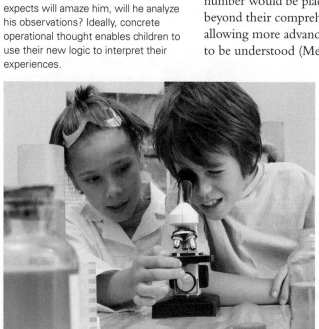

After "Gee Whiz!" After he sees the magnified image that his classmate expects will amaze him, will he analyze his observations? Ideally, concrete operational thought enables children to use their new logic to interpret their experiences.

THE SIGNIFICANCE OF PIAGET'S FINDINGS ABOUT LOGIC Contemporary developmentalists find that, in some ways, Piaget was mistaken. The research does *not* confirm a sudden shift between preoperational and concrete operational thought. Research does show that some children learn logic via math, not math after logic; that classification appears before middle childhood (Halford & Andrews, 2006; S. P. Nguyen & Murphy, 2003); and that transitive inference is more complex than Piaget imagined.

Nonetheless, Piaget discovered and explained something important. What develops during middle childhood is the ability to use mental categories and subcategories flexibly, inductively, and simultaneously (Meadows, 2006). This is apparent with more than just flowers and daisies; older children are more precise and flexible than younger ones in their classification, so they are better able to separate the essential from the irrelevant (Hayes & Younger, 2004).

The movement that Piaget described—away from egocentrism and toward a more flexible understanding—is illustrated by a study involving 5- and 9-year-olds. They were asked about two hypothetical boys: David, who thought chocolate ice cream was disgusting, and Daniel, who found it delicious. Most 5-year-olds (63 percent) thought David was wrong; many felt he was bad or stupid as well. By contrast, almost all 9-year-olds (94 percent) thought both boys could be right; very few were critical of David (Wainryb et al., 2004).

This study illustrates Piaget's essential idea: Older children are not limited by their own subjective preferences and egocentric assumptions. Their ability to apply logic to concrete experiences allows them to think more objectively.

RESPONSE FOR Physical Education Teachers (from page 239) Discuss with the parents their reasons for wanting the team. Children need physical activity, but some aspects of competitive sports are better suited to adults than to children. ●

Vygotsky and School-Age Children

Vygotsky agreed with one aspect of Piaget's theory—the assertion that educators need to consider the thought processes of the child and design their teaching accordingly. This kind of teaching was a marked improvement over the dull "meaningless acquisition" approach of many traditional schools, which rendered the child "helpless in the face of any sensible attempt to apply any of this acquired knowledge" (Vygotsky, 1934/1994, pp. 356–357).

However, whereas Piaget emphasized the child's discovery, Vygotsky regarded instruction as essential. As discussed in Chapter 5, he believed that peers, teachers, and the overall cultural context provide the bridge between children's developmental potential and the skills and knowledge they need. In guiding each child through his or her *zone of proximal development,* or almost-understood ideas, other people are crucial.

Remember that for Vygotsky, formal education is only one of many contexts for learning. Children are "apprentices in learning" as they play with each other, watch television, eat dinner with their families, and engage in other daily interactions. Language is integral as a mediator, a vehicle for understanding and learning. This differs from the view of Piaget, who tended to see early language as the *result* of cognitive change, not the instigator of it.

In short, Vygotsky's emphasis on the sociocultural context contrasts with Piaget's more maturational approach. Vygotsky believed that cultures (tools, customs, words, and mentors) teach people. A child who is surrounded by adults who read for pleasure, by well-stocked bookcases, and by daily newspaper deliveries is likely to read sooner than a child who encounters the printed word only at school.

CULTURAL VARIATIONS According to Vygotsky, each community offers distinct values and knowledge. In the cities of Brazil, for example, street children sell fruit, candy, and other products to earn their living. Many have never attended school and consequently score poorly on standard math achievement tests. This is no surprise to developmentalists, who have described many examples of slower academic proficiency in children who are unschooled (Rogoff et al., 2005).

However, most young Brazilian peddlers are adept at pricing their wares, making change, and giving discounts for large quantities—a set of operations that must be recalibrated almost every day. These children calculate "complex markup computations and adjust for inflation in these computations by using procedures that were widespread in their practice but not known to children in school" (Saxe, 1999, p. 255).

Thus, the knowledge reflected in these street children arises from three sources:

● The demands of the situation

● Learning from other sellers

● Daily experience

He Knows His Stuff Many child vendors, like this boy selling combs and other grooming aids on the streets of Manaus, Brazil, understand basic math and the give-and-take of social interaction; but, deprived of formal education, they know little or nothing about history and literature.

knowledge base
A body of knowledge in a particular area that makes it easier to master new information in that area.

This would not surprise Vygotsky. He would expect that street culture would teach children what they needed to know. He realized that, at every age, the more people know, the more they can learn and remember. That is, having an extensive **knowledge base,** a broad body of knowledge in a particular subject area, makes it easier to master new information in that area. Crucial for intellectual development is building on the knowledge base, applying "acquired knowledge" as Vygotsky said. Changing schools, and especially changing cultures, is difficult in middle childhood because the old knowledge base is no longer helpful.

A COMBINED APPROACH Today's educators and psychologists regard both Piaget and Vygotsky as insightful theorists, and international research confirms the merits of both their theories. Our understanding of how children learn depends on "a framework that was laid down by Piaget and embellished by Vygotsky" (C. Howe, 1998, p. 207).

In other words, Piaget's belief that children are eager and flexible learners, trying to understand the world in ways limited by their level of maturation, was extended by Vygotsky. Vygotsky realized that children learn from one another, from their culture, and from their teachers—as long as those mentors know the child's motivation, needs, and skills. In short, Piaget described universal changes; Vygotsky noted cultural forces.

ESPECIALLY FOR Teachers How might Piaget's and Vygotsky's ideas help in teaching geography to a class of third-graders? (see response, page 244) →

KEY Points

- During concrete operational thought (Piaget's third stage of development), children become more logical and less egocentric.
- Vygotsky emphasized the cultural context of learning, as peers and adults shape what children learn within their zones of proximal development.
- Both Piaget and Vygotsky describe children as active, eager learners.

Information Processing and the Brain

Many contemporary educators combine the insights of Piaget and Vygotsky and add a third element: the workings of the brain. They are inspired by **information-processing theory,** an approach to cognition that takes its name from computer functioning.

Computers receive and store vast quantities of information (numbers, letters, pixels, other coded symbols) and then use software programs to process that information. People, too, take in large amounts of information. They use mental processes to perform three functions: search for specific units of information when needed (as a search engine does), analyze (as software programs do), and express that analysis in a format that another person (or a networked computer) can interpret. By revealing the paths and links of each of these functions, scientists can understand the mechanisms of learning.

information-processing theory
A perspective that compares human thinking processes, by analogy, to computer analysis of data, including sensory input, connections, stored memories, and output.

The information-processing approach progresses from theories, models, and hypotheses to practical demonstrations (Munakata, 2006). Many studies in neuroscience follow an information-processing approach, tracing the thinking process from the activation of neurons to the expression of knowledge.

Brain Development

Recall from Chapter 5 that, in early childhood, emotional regulation, theory of mind, and left–right coordination emerge. The maturing corpus callosum connects the two hemispheres of the brain. The prefrontal cortex—the executive part of the brain—plans, monitors, and evaluates. These developments continue in middle childhood, resulting, "by 7 or 8 years of age, in a massively interconnected brain" (Kagan & Herschkowitz, 2005, p. 220). Advances in attention, automatization, and memory are the result.

ATTENTION Neurological advances allow children to process information in many areas of the brain at once, paying special heed to the most important elements. **Selective attention,** the ability to concentrate on some stimuli while ignoring others, is crucial for school competence (NICHD Early Child Care Research Network, 2003a). Selective attention is made possible at about age 7 by increases in myelination of axons and in the production of neurotransmitters (chemical messengers).

In the classroom, selective attention allows children to listen, take concise notes, and ignore distractions (all difficult at age 6, easier by age 10). In the din of the lunchroom, children can understand one another's gestures and expressions and respond quickly; on the ball field, children can pay attention to the trajectory of the batted ball. Throughout these years, advances in the "mental control processes that enable self-control" (Verté et al., 2005, p. 415) allow planning for the future, which is beyond the ability of a younger child.

School-age children not only notice various stimuli (one form of attention) but also choose how to respond when possibilities conflict (Rueda et al., 2007). That is selective attention: They ignore some sensations and focus on the task at hand. The information-processing approach not only flags attention as a critical start to the thinking process but also notes that some children need help to focus their thinking, such as a quiet work space at home and a well-structured classroom.

AUTOMATIZATION Another major advance in brain function during middle childhood is **automatization,** a process in which a sequence of thoughts and actions is repeated until it becomes automatic, or routine. This advance begins with quicker **reaction time,** the length of time it takes to respond to a stimulus. Myelination and repeated neuronal activity speed reactions and automatization.

At first, almost all behaviors under conscious control require careful and slow thought. After many repetitions, as sensations lead quickly to perceptions and neurons fire rapidly in sequence, actions become automatic and patterned. Less thinking is needed because firing one neuron sets off a chain reaction.

Think about the process of learning to read. At first, it takes great concentration; eyes (sometimes aided by a tracking finger) painstakingly focus to make out letters while the voice sounds out each one. This sequence leads to perception of syllables, then words. Eventually the sequence of reading becomes so automatic that an unintentional glance at a billboard suffices for a message to be read.

Automatization is apparent in every skill. Speaking a second language, reciting the multiplication tables, and writing one's name are haltingly, even painfully executed at first. With practice, more efficient information processing frees the brain for advanced reading, speaking, computation, and writing (Berninger & Richards, 2002).

In one study, the brains of children and adults were scanned as they tried to understand phrases that were obviously ironic. The children recognized the irony, but it took them considerable mental effort. Their scans showed activation of the prefrontal cortex. By adulthood, automatization had occurred and comprehension of irony was quick, requiring little deliberate mental effort. In the adults, the prefrontal cortex was relatively inactive (A. Wang et al., 2006).

selective attention
The ability to concentrate on some stimuli while ignoring others.

ELLEN SENISI / THE IMAGE WORKS

Finger Math Few schools teach children to count with their fingers, and some teachers forbid it. Yet concrete-operational children learn best when they begin with visible examples, as this wise 7-year-old and millions of others know.

automatization
A process in which repetition of a sequence of thoughts and actions makes the sequence routine, so that it no longer requires conscious thought.

reaction time
The time it takes to respond to a stimulus, either physically (with a reflexive movement such as an eye blink) or cognitively (with a thought).

Progress from initial effort at to mastery of automatization takes years, making repeated practice essential. Many children lose cognitive skills over the summer because a few months of vacation (with little or no reading) erases earlier academic learning (Alexander et al., 2007).

MEMORY One surprising neurological discovery in recent decades is that virtually every mental function activates many parts of the brain. For example, memory was once thought to be one thing, located in one part of the brain—specifically, the hippocampus (see Chapter 5). It is now apparent, however, that, in addition to the hippocampus, many parts of the brain as well as many strategies are involved with memory (Pressley & Hilden, 2006).

From Momentary Sensations to Enduring Memories One aspect of memory, called **sensory memory** (also called the *sensory register*), stores incoming stimuli for a split second to allow processing. To use terms explained in Chapter 3, *sensations* are retained momentarily so that some of them can become *perceptions*. This first step of sensory awareness is already quite efficient in early childhood and continues to improve slightly until about age 10.

Once sensations become perceptions, the brain selects meaningful perceptions to transfer to working memory for further analysis. It is in **working memory** (sometimes called *short-term memory*) that current, conscious mental activity occurs. Working memory improves steadily and significantly every year from age 4 to 15 (Gathercole et al., 2004). This improvement is possible in part because of increased myelination and dendrite formation in the prefrontal cortex.

Finally, some information is transferred to **long-term memory,** which stores it for minutes, hours, days, months, or years. The capacity of long-term memory—how much information can be crammed into one brain—is virtually limitless by the end of middle childhood. Together with sensory and working memory, long-term memory assists in organizing ideas and reactions.

Language helps solidify memories (R. Richardson & Hayne, 2007). Linguistic advances are one reason long-term memory improves markedly during the school years. In Chapter 14, you will learn that long-term memory is the most enduring of the three memory types in late adulthood. At that point, the senses fade, as does the sensory register, but long-term memories are strong. Likewise, reaction time slows in the elderly, but sequences that have been automatized continue—the oldest adults may walk slowly, but they have not forgotten how to walk.

Storage and Retrieval Memory *storage* (how much information is deposited in the brain) expands over childhood, but more important is *retrieval* (how readily stored material can be brought into working memory). As the prefrontal cortex matures, children are better able to use strategies to help them remember. Retrieval becomes more efficient and accurate.

To some extent, storage and retrieval are affected by biological factors. Another part of the brain, the hypothalamus (already explained in Chapter 5 for its role in the limbic system), produces hormones that affect memory. The hypothalamus can make a person's memory either quite accurate (especially for highly emotional events) or seriously impaired (especially when stress hormones flood the brain) (M. L. Howe et al., 2006).

Strategy Development

Crucial to all information-processing patterns is the overall strategy, or, in computer terms, the program that organizes the information that bombards the brain. For instance, for storage and retrieval, a person needs to know how to add information to the brain and how to produce it when needed.

---

sensory memory
The component of the information-processing system in which incoming stimulus information is stored for a split second to allow it to be processed. (Also called the *sensory register*.)

working memory
The component of the information-processing system in which current, conscious mental activity occurs. (Also called *short-term memory*.)

long-term memory
The component of the information-processing system in which virtually limitless amounts of information can be stored indefinitely.

RESPONSE FOR Teachers (from page 242) Here are two of the most obvious ways. (1) Use logic. Once children can grasp classification and class inclusion, they can understand cities within states, states within nations, and nations within continents. Organize your instruction to make logical categorization easier. (2) Make use of children's need for concrete and personal involvement. You might have the children learn first about their own location, then about the places where relatives and friends live, and finally about places beyond their personal experience (via books, photographs, videos, and guest speakers). ●

ESPECIALLY FOR Teachers How might your understanding of memory help you teach a 2,000-word vocabulary list to a class of fourth-graders? (see response, page 246) →

Knowledge of strategies is beyond many younger children, who sometimes remember details (what hat they were wearing) but forget the most important parts (where they were). If asked to remember 20 new vocabulary words for a test, for instance, kindergarten children would be at a loss, but fifth-graders usually have a strategy.

METACOGNITION **Metacognition** is "thinking about thinking," the ability to evaluate a cognitive task to determine how best to accomplish it and then to monitor and adjust one's performance of that task. It is one of the most impressive accomplishments of middle childhood. An essential part of metacognition is **metamemory,** the ability to understand how memory works in order to use it well.

Metacognition and metamemory continue to improve throughout a person's schooling. You probably know someone who spent hours studying for a test, only to realize that he or she had learned the wrong things; ideally, that experience led to improved metacognition. Similarly, college students ask each other thought-provoking questions and help each other with study techniques; that is metacognition.

Metacognition first becomes evident in middle childhood (Meadows, 2006). It begins to develop when children attain the ability to get past egocentrism (Piaget), and it can be enhanced with guidance from mentors (Vygotsky). The information-processing perspective is especially insightful about the importance of cognitive strategies because it has discovered both what they are and how to use them. All the components of information processing improve throughout middle childhood, aided by faster reaction time, selective attention, automatization, and the use of strategy (Ornstein et al., 2006). As a result, metacognition improves.

Neurological maturation underlies advances in metacognition and metamemory, and explicit teaching can speed the process. For that reason, classroom instruction often includes spelling rules such as "*i* before *e* except after *c.*" Children's metamemory improves when teachers ask students how they are planning to remember something, or query them about which aspects of a story are the most important, or suggest memorization strategies that they might use (Ornstein et al., 2006).

EXPERIMENTS IN LEARNING Extensive research into the intellectual abilities of contemporary children has found neither stagelike advances (Piaget) nor dramatic cultural influences (Vygotsky). Perhaps decades ago, when children were more isolated, both Piaget and Vygotsky were more accurate, but globalization seems to have diminished the applicability of their theories.

Most current research on cognition finds that children gradually accumulate skills and patterns that cascade into intellectual achievements (Meadows, 2006). Explicit teaching that adjusts to each child's comments and questions seems effective.

To illustrate the impact of instruction, one study sought to teach children that, to be valid, scientific experiments need to control the relevant variables and to measure each variable, one by one (Klahr & Nigam, 2004). The researchers showed 112 third- and fourth-graders an apparatus consisting of a downhill ramp connected to an uphill ramp (see Figure 7.3 on the next page). There were four variables: golf ball or rubber ball, steep or shallow downhill ramp, smooth or rough ramp surface, and long or short downhill run.

First, the children were asked to design four experiments on their own: two to determine the effect of distance and two to determine the effect of steepness on the distance a ball would travel. Only 8 of the 112 children designed experiments that controlled the variables. Unless the variables were controlled, the results would be confounded, or inappropriately combined. Thus, for example, a child might compare a trial with a steep ramp and a golf ball to a trial with a shallow ramp and a rubber ball.

metacognition
"Thinking about thinking"; the ability to evaluate a cognitive task in order to determine how best to accomplish it, and then to monitor and adjust one's performance on that task.

metamemory
The ability to understand how memory works in order to use it well. Metamemory is an essential element of metacognition.

● FOR DEEPER REFLECTION Are some kinds of learning best mastered through discovery?

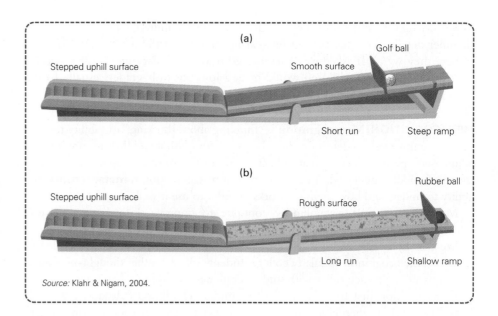

(a)

Stepped uphill surface   Smooth surface   Golf ball

Short run   Steep ramp

(b)

Stepped uphill surface   Rough surface   Rubber ball

Long run   Shallow ramp

Source: Klahr & Nigam, 2004.

FIGURE 7.3 Design for a Confounded Experiment On each of these two ramps, children could vary the steepness, surface, and length of the ramp, as well as the type of ball. The confounded experiment depicted here contrasts (a) a golf ball on a steep, smooth, short ramp with (b) a rubber ball on a shallow, rough, long ramp.

● **UNDERSTANDING THE NUMBERS**
Some children in both groups did equally well on their first assignment and, a week later, on their second one. Does this mean that both methods for learning about validity—discovery and direct instruction—were equally effective?

Answer No. Consider how few of the children in the discovery group learned on their own (12 of 52 = 23 percent) compared with the children in the direct-instruction group (40 of 52 = 77 percent). Thus—in this experiment, at least—a child's chance of learning was about three times better if a mentor explained and demonstrated the principles involved.

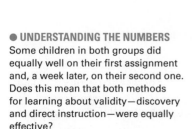

RESPONSE FOR Teachers (from page 244): Children this age can be taught strategies for remembering by making links between working memory and long-term memory. You might break down the vocabulary list into word clusters, grouped according to root words, connections to the children's existing knowledge, applications, or (as a last resort) first letters or rhymes. Active, social learning is useful; perhaps in groups the students could write a story each day that incorporates 15 new words. Each group could read its story aloud to the class. ●

The 104 children who did not demonstrate that they already had an understanding of validity in experiments were then divided into two groups. Half of them were allowed to create their own experiments; the other half received explicit instruction by watching an experimenter create pairs of demonstrations. The experimenter asked the children whether a demonstrated pair allowed them to "tell for sure" how a particular variable affected the distance traveled by the ball. After each answer, the experimenter explained the correct answer and emphasized the importance of testing a single variable at a time.

Then all 104 children were asked to design four experiments, as before. Far more children who received direct instruction (40 of 52) correctly isolated the variables than did children who explored on their own (12 of 52).

A week later, to assess whether the children had really learned the importance of controlling variables in an experiment, those children who seemed to understand were asked to examine two science posters created by 11-year-olds. The researcher requested suggestions to make the posters "good enough to enter in a state science fair." The 40 children who had been instructed were virtually as perceptive in their critiques of the posters as the 12 who had learned through discovery.

This study suggests that strategy can be taught—if the teacher actively engages the students. That is exactly what information processing would predict.

KEY Points

- Information-processing theory traces mental activity step by step, from input to output, as a computer might.
- During middle childhood, the brain becomes more selective in attention, more automatized in thinking sequences, and more efficient in memory.
- Memory begins with the input of information in the sensory register for a second; information proceeds to working memory and finally is stored in long-term memory.
- Crucial to information processing are learning strategies, which enable metacognition.

Learning in School

Everywhere children are expected to learn to read, write, and do math. Thirty years ago, many of the world's 7- to 11-year-olds (especially girls) were not in school; now most are (see Figure 7.4)

Every nation seeks a literate population. Now most young adults can read, unlike their elders. Beyond literacy, however, nations vary in how and what they teach. Even in nations that are geographically and culturally close to each other, curricula often differ. For example, every elementary school student in Australia spends at least two hours per week studying science, but this is true for only 23 percent in nearby New Zealand (T. D. Snyder et al., 2004).

The value of virtually every variation in the approach to education is not merely debatable; it is a matter of bitter dispute. We now focus on some of these raging controversies, shedding light on them by adding insights from developmentalists on how children learn.

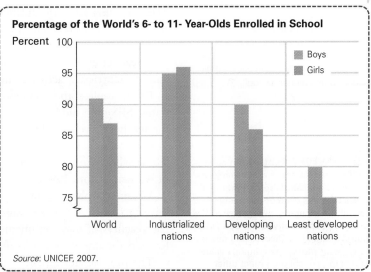

Percentage of the World's 6- to 11- Year-Olds Enrolled in School

Source: UNICEF, 2007.

FIGURE 7.4 Almost Everyone Most children are in school, even in the least developed nations, where many of them must walk miles to get there and parents must sacrifice to pay their school fees.

Teaching Values

Children develop their values during middle childhood, when they are less egocentric in their thinking. Consequently, every school teaches values—sometimes explicitly, as in religious instruction, and always implicitly, in a hidden curriculum.

RELIGIOUS INSTRUCTION In some nations, every public school teaches religion. For instance, Finnish schools give parents three choices: Lutheran, Christian Orthodox, or nonsectarian religious education (Marlow-Ferguson, 2002). In other nations, no public funds are provided to support religious instruction. For example, in the United States, most children (88 percent) attend public schools, which are forbidden by the Constitution to promote any religion.

Almost every nation has some private schools that are supported by religious groups, but their popularity varies by nations. In France, 16 percent of the children attend such schools, but in Japan only 1 percent do (Marlow-Ferguson, 2002).

In the United States, most children who attend private school (10 percent) or who are home-schooled (2 percent) learn specific religious content (Digest of Education Statistics, 2007). A developmental understanding of schoolchildren's cognition includes the awareness that children can learn whatever they are taught. Thus, if parents want their children to learn about religious tolerance and specific religious knowledge and practices, they need to make sure those values are taught somewhere —at school, at home, in a religious setting, or all three.

Among the other specifics taught in some schools are evolution and sex education, both ideas that most Americans want children to learn but some parents do not. Other issues involve discipline, multiculturalism, academic standards, and school prayer—all topics that cause some parents to avoid public schools and other parents to avoid private or religious schools.

Education for Girls These Iranian third-graders are acting out a poem they have memorized. They attend school in a UNICEF-supported Global Education pilot project.

SHEHZAD NOORANI / PETER ARNOLD, INC.

ESPECIALLY FOR Parents Suppose you and your school-age children move to a new community that is 50 miles from the nearest location that offers instruction in your faith or value system. Your neighbor says, "Don't worry, they don't have to make any moral decisions until they are teenagers." Is your neighbor correct? (see response, page 248) →

hidden curriculum
The unofficial, unstated, or implicit rules and priorities that influence the academic curriculum and every other aspect of learning in school.

RESPONSE FOR Parents (from page 247) No. In fact, these are prime years for moral education. You might travel those 50 miles once or twice a week or recruit other parents to organize a local program. Whatever you do, don't skip moral instruction. Discuss and demonstrate your moral and religious values, and help your children meet other children who share those values. ●

Connections Basic vocabulary is learned by age 4 or so, but the school years are best for acquiring expanded, derivative, and specialized vocabulary—especially if the child is actively connecting one word with another. With his father's encouragement, this boy in San Jose, California, will remember *Jupiter, Mars,* and the names of the other planets and maybe even *orbit, light-years,* and *solar system.*

RACHEL EPSTEIN / THE IMAGE WORKS

THE HIDDEN CURRICULUM In addition to formal curriculum mandates such as reading and algebra, there is a **hidden curriculum** consisting of the unrecognized lessons and values that children absorb at school. Sorting children by ability (tracking), teacher characteristics, discipline methods, sports contests, student government, and extracurricular activities are all part of the hidden curriculum.

For example, if the teachers differ from the children in ethnicity or socioeconomic status (SES), the hidden message may be that the children are not expected to reach the teacher's level of education. In the United States in the early twentieth century, primary school teachers were expected to be unmarried and sexually inactive women. Those who were wives (before 1940), or pregnant (before 1960), or homosexual men or women (before 1990) were excluded from employment in some school districts.

When schools were racially segregated, African American teachers were not allowed to teach European American students, although African American students had teachers of many ethnicities. Today in the United States, it is illegal to exclude teachers for any of these reasons.

The most obvious manifestation of the hidden curriculum currently is the physical setting. Some schools have spacious classrooms; wide hallways; personal computers; and large, grassy playgrounds. Others have crowded, poorly equipped classrooms and small, paved play yards. From their school settings, children learn how important their community thinks their education is. A former state commissioner of education explained:

> If you ask the children to attend school in conditions where plaster is crumbling, the roof is leaking and classes are being held in unlikely places because of overcrowded conditions, that says something to the child. . . . If, on the other hand, you send a child to a school in well-appointed [facilities], that sends the opposite message. That says this counts. You count. Do well.
>
> [Sobol, quoted in Campaign for Fiscal Equity v. State of New York, *2001]*

This statement reflects a developmental understanding of children at this age. School-age children are concrete thinkers, aware of what they see and hear and able to draw conclusions from their experiences. They are capable of receiving messages from the hidden curriculum as well as the overt one, so adults should be alert to the ideas and values they are transmitting through both these channels.

Underlying many debates about the hidden curriculum is a judgment regarding peer interaction. Does diversity of the student body—in income, ability, and background—benefit all children or hinder learning? Should the school encourage children to learn from one another, with small groups in classes, long lunch periods, and after-school activities? Consider these questions as you learn about the next topic, language.

Learning Language

As you remember, language advances rapidly during early childhood. By age 6, children know most of the basic vocabulary and grammar of their first language, and many speak a second or even a third language.

The process of language acquisition continues in middle childhood. Some school-age children learn as many as 20 new words a day and apply grammar rules they did not use before. Instead of simply picking up the speech they hear, school-age children are more flexible and logical than younger children in their knowledge and use of vocabulary, metaphors, prefixes and suffixes, and compound words.

For example, 2-year-olds know *egg*, but 10-year-olds also know *egg salad, egg-drop soup, eggless, eggplant, egghead*, as well as *walking on eggshells, egg on my face*, and *Last one in is a rotten egg*. The 10-year-olds understand that each of these expressions is logically connected to *egg* (a benefit of the knowledge base) but is also distinct from the dozen raw eggs in the refrigerator. They use each expression appropriately.

One of the most notable advances in middle childhood is the comprehension of metaphors, as in "Last one in is a rotten egg." Many adults do not realize that younger children (and people from other cultures) do not grasp such figures of speech. The humorist James Thurber (1999) remembered

> the enchanted private world of my early boyhood. . . . In this world, businessmen who phoned their wives to say they were tied up at the office sat roped to their swivel chairs, and probably gagged, unable to move or speak except somehow, miraculously, to telephone. . . . Then there was the man who left town under a cloud. Sometimes I saw him all wrapped up in the cloud and invisible. . . . At other times it floated, about the size of a sofa, above him wherever he went. . . . [I remember] the old lady who was always up in the air, the husband who did not seem able to put his foot down, the man who lost his head during a fire but was still able to run out of the house yelling.
>
> *[p. 40]*

Note that Thurber described the "private world of my early boyhood." One function of school is that other children make the world less private, allowing children to learn from one another. Children's natural tendency to talk suggests that they should certainly take advantage of that opportunity to learn from one another. The current redesign of elementary school classrooms, with movable chairs and tables instead of fixed desks, reflects this understanding.

CODE-SWITCHING Directly related to language learning is another capacity of the school-age child, the ability to switch from one manner of speaking, or language code, to another. Each language code differs in tone, pronunciation, gesture, sentence length, idiom, grammar, and vocabulary. Sometimes people switch from the *formal code* (used in academic contexts) to the *informal code* (used with friends). Many children use a third code in text messaging, with numbers (411), abbreviations (LOL), and emoticons (☺). Many English-speaking adults from the Deep South, Boston, or the Caribbean are able to speak with or without an accent. Almost always, they mastered both the local accent and the standard speech before they reached adolescence.

Some teachers insist that their students use the formal code in school. Others allow the informal code, using it themselves to help the children feel accepted. Research on information processing suggests that the formal code is better for teachers.

In middle childhood, children are adept at learning various codes. School is the place for them to learn the formal code, which allows them to communicate with people of all backgrounds. For that reason, teachers should probably teach the formal code, helping children learn to read, write, and speak it. The informal code is not rejected as wrong, but children will teach it (with nonstandard grammar and pronunciation) to one another.

SECOND-LANGUAGE LEARNING At the moment, the United States is embroiled in a related controversy: Should immigrant children be required to speak only Standard English in school right from the beginning, or should they be educated in their native language in the early grades? In the United States, 4 million students (10

ESPECIALLY FOR Parents You've had an exhausting day but are setting out to buy groceries. Your 7-year-old son wants to go with you. Should you explain that you are so tired that you want to make a quick solo trip to the supermarket this time? (see response, page 250) →

Can You Text Me? Few adults over 40 know how to "text" anyone, but many schoolchildren quickly become masters of text messaging. Their universal use of the informal texting code— terse, ungrammatical, symbol-laden— is evidence of their ability to learn rapidly from one another.

BRAND X PICTURES / JUPITER IMAGES

English-language learner (ELL)
A child who is learning English as a second language.

percent of the school population) are **English-language learners (ELLs).** (Previously, the commonly used term was *limited English proficiency,* or LEP.)

Almost every classroom includes at least one ELL child. Such children are vulnerable to two opposite hazards (C. E. Snow & Kang, 2006). On the one hand, many immigrant children make a *language shift* in U.S. primary schools, replacing their original language with English rather than becoming fluent in both languages (Tse, 2001). Partly to prevent this, some communities provide "heritage" language classes after school or on Saturdays. In the 1990s in the Los Angeles area, there were 80 Chinese heritage schools with 15,000 pupils (P. Liu, 2006).

On the other hand, many children never learn the school language well, which often leads to school failure and then to dropping out.

> Language minority children are at demonstrably greater risk than native speakers of experiencing academic difficulty . . . in the United States, . . . in the Netherlands, . . . in Great Britain, . . . and in Japan.
>
> [*C. E. Snow & Kang, 2006, p. 76*]

The lack of education obviously handicaps them in adulthood.

From a developmental perspective, both hazards can be avoided. Middle childhood is a good time to teach a second language. (Younger children often become bilingual just by listening, while school-age children benefit from more explicit instruction.) In middle childhood, as we have seen, children are eager to communicate, are logical, and have an ear (and brain) for nuances of code. The success of bilingual education in Canada, Israel, and many other nations proves that children can become fluent in two languages before puberty (at which point learning a new language becomes more difficult) (DeKeyser & Larson-Hall, 2005).

Ideally, all schoolchildren would learn to speak and write both the majority language and a second language. In the United States, that means everyone would speak English as well as their native language or some other language they learned before puberty.

When, how, to whom, and whether second-language instruction occurs varies markedly, sometimes from one school district to another (Hinkel, 2005). In the United States, some school districts offer *bilingual education* (teaching in two languages); others provide *ESL* (English as a second language) instruction; and others

RESPONSE FOR Parents (from page 249) Your son would understand your explanation, but you should take him along if you can do so without losing patience. You wouldn't ignore his need for food or medicine; don't ignore his need for learning. While shopping, you can teach vocabulary (does he know *pimientos, pepperoni, polenta?*), categories ("root vegetables," "freshwater fish"), and math (which size box of cereal is cheaper?). Explain in advance that you need him to help you find items and carry them and that he can choose only one item that you wouldn't normally buy. Seven-year-olds can understand rules, and they enjoy being helpful. ●

Together They Learn Thousands of children worldwide do not understand the language used in their schools because their families are refugees, asylum seekers, or immigrants. Ideally, teachers, like this one in London, use guided participation to individualize instruction as they help these children learn the new language. Note that both the teacher and the student point, listen, and speak.

GIDEON MENDEL / CORBIS

offer only *immersion,* in which children are taught exclusively in a language that is not spoken at home.

Although each of these methods sometimes succeeds and sometimes fails, the crucial elements may be more psychological than pedagogical. Any method will fail if the children are made to feel stupid and if their cultural background is not understood, as the following describes.

A VIEW FROM SCIENCE

Biculturalism Aids Bilingualism

Often in political debates about bilingual education, the issue is framed as purely linguistic, as if a language were disconnected from the culture that produced it (Gandara & Rumberger, 2009). This is contrary to the perspective of developmental scientists, who consider language an integral part of culture. Learning a new language is best accomplished if the teacher understands the entire family experience within a new cultural context (Suárez-Orozco & Carhill, 2008).

The cognitive advantages of bilingualism (described in Chapter 5) are connected to the benefits of biculturalism—to the realization that many human values, practices, and assumptions are cultural creations. Language learning itself may benefit from this understanding, as can be seen in the experience of one Canadian community.

According to school policy, Inuit children were taught in their native language by Inuit teachers for their first two years of school; then they were taught in French or English, the majority languages, by non-Inuits. Both groups of teachers realized that they were failing. Few Inuit children became fluent in a second language, and most dropped out long before graduation from high school.

Fortunately, the multidisciplinary approach to development (see Chapter 1) led to the discovery of an underlying problem. Anthropologists, trained in naturalistic observation of cultural differences, studied this school. They found that much more than a language shift occurred when the Inuit children moved from grade 2 to grade 3 (Eriks-Brophy & Crago, 2003). When the teachers changed from Inuit to non-Inuit, the way classes were conducted changed, too.

The Inuit teachers encouraged group learning and cooperation, almost never explicitly judging an individual student. By contrast, the non-Inuit third-grade teachers criticized behaviors that the second-grade teachers had encouraged, such as group cooperation (which the non-Inuit teachers called "talking out of turn"), helping each other ("cheating"), and attempts to answer ("mistakes").

A specific example illustrates this difference. A common pattern of instruction in North American schools is called *initiation/response/evaluation:* The teacher asks a question, a child responds, and the teacher states whether the response is correct or not. An analysis of 14 teachers in this Inuit school found that the initiation/response/evaluation routine dominated the instruction of the non-Inuit teachers (60 percent of the time) but not that of the Inuit teachers (18 percent) (Eriks-Brophy & Crago, 2003). For example, an Inuit teacher showed a picture and asked:

Teacher: This one. What is it?
Student: Tutuva [an insect].
Teacher: What is it?
Student: Tutuva.
Teacher: All of us, look carefully.
Student: Kituquianluti (*Another insect, this time correct. The teacher nodded and breathed in.*)

In contrast, a non-Inuit third-grade teacher asked:

Teacher: Richard, what is this?
Richard: It is an ear.
Teacher: Good.
Teacher: Rhoda, what is this?
Rhoda: Hair.
Teacher: No. What is this?

The Best of Both Worlds An Inupiat boy works at a computer keyboard in his classroom. His teachers want him and his classmates to benefit from both cultures—traditional and modern.

ALASKA STOCK IMAGES

Rhoda: Face.
Teacher: It is a face.
Rhoda: It is a face.
Teacher: Very good, Rhoda.

[quoted in Eriks-Brophy & Crago, 2003, pp. 406–407]

Note that the Inuit teacher never verbally evaluated the child (merely nodding and breathing in to signal correctness), but the second teacher did so at least three times ("Good," "No," "Very good"). No wonder the children became confused and discouraged. They were unprepared to make a cultural shift as well as a language one.

Such problems can emerge anywhere. Teaching methods are the outcome of cultural beliefs, a "social system that evolves over time" (Eriks-Brophy & Crago, 2003, p. 397), often hidden from the teachers themselves. Underlying the issues that parents seize on—such as discipline, reading instruction, and math scores—are deeper issues involving culture and values.

Every child wants to learn, every teacher wants to teach, and every family wants the best for its children. This makes hidden differences in curricula and teaching methods hard to reconcile. No one cares if a particular child eats goat, chitlins, or whale for dinner, but people everywhere care about what their own—and their neighbors'—children learn. They blame families, or maybe teachers, when children do poorly in school as a result of unnoticed cultural differences between teachers and students.

THE IMPACT OF SES ON LANGUAGE LEARNING Remember from Chapter 1 that ethnic and economic differences often overlap. Decades of research throughout the world have found a powerful connection among language development, ethnicity, and socioeconomic status (Plank & MacIver, 2003).

Compared with their peers, children from low-SES families tend to fall behind in talking, then in reading, and then in other subjects (C. E. Snow & Kang, 2006). Not only do children from low-income families have smaller vocabularies, but they use simpler grammar and shorter sentences (B. Hart & Risley, 1995; E. Hoff, 2003).

Information-processing theory has led scientists to search for specifics that might affect a child's ability to learn language, beyond the maturation emphasized by Piaget and the cultural influences noted by Vygotsky. Possibilities abound: ingestion of lead in old house paint, inadequate prenatal care, inexperienced teachers, a discouraging hidden curriculum, lack of a nourishing breakfast, overcrowded households, too few books at home, teenage parenthood, authoritarian child rearing. . . . All of these correlate with low SES, but none have been proved to be a major cause of poor language learning.

Exposure and Expectations Two factors, however, *do* appear to be influential. One is exposure to communication. Learning one code well—even a nonstandard code—makes it easier for children to learn another code. Deaf children need to learn sign language in infancy; immigrant children need to learn whatever language their parents speak. If a child can be exposed to two languages extensively in early childhood (as when one language is used in preschool and another at home), that is ideal.

The crucial factor is that the child's brain masters an expansive and nuanced communication system, with thousands of vocabulary words and hundreds of grammatical devices. Once that happens for one language, it is easier to accomplish for another.

In communicating with their children, many less educated parents rely on commands; parents with more education tend to use open-ended comments. In one study, researchers observed young children at home for three years, recording 30 hours of talk per family. Children in high-SES families heard about 2,000 words an hour; children in low-SES families heard only about 600 (B. Hart & Risley, 1995).

Extensive research has found a "powerful linkage" between adult linguistic input and later child output (Weizman & Snow, 2001, p. 276). The reasons for lack of adult input correlate with low income (financial stress, lack of time, single parenthood, neighborhood noise) but are not caused by it.

Remember that dendrites in the brain grow to accommodate a child's experiences, including experience with language. In this regard, it is noteworthy that the best preschool programs (see Chapter 5) emphasize language learning. Children in those programs who were from low-income families became much more verbal than their peers. Teachers know that the classrooms that help children develop their language abilities are filled with both teacher and child talk; language is an integral part of education via poems, reports, debates, and plays.

The second factor that has been associated with language learning is the expectations that adults have for a child. A major problem with labeling a child as mentally retarded is that adults expect less of children with IQs below 70. Lower expectations lead to less teaching and thus less learning. Teachers' and parents' expectations may be one reason some children master language quickly while others do not.

Children's own expectations are relevant as well. If a child believes that intelligence is *innate,* that each person is born with a certain level of intelligence, then he or she will not study hard or expect to improve. In contrast, if a child believes that knowledge is *incremental,* that education is the result of hard work and effort, then he or she will study diligently and expect to learn more (Blackwell et al., 2007).

● **FOR DEEPER REFLECTION** When do high expectations lead to a child's success, and when do they set a child up for failure?

Exceptions to the Pattern As with all generalities, this one has exceptions. Individuals do not necessarily follow the usual course for families of their linguistic or socioeconomic background. Some low-SES parents have high expectations for their children, providing extensive language practice and other aids to foster education. This may explain the "immigration paradox," the finding that children who have recently immigrated to the United States have higher reading scores (in English) in the early grades than do children who were born in the United States and whose ancestors came from the same nation as the recent immigrants (Palacios et al., 2008).

E. P. Jones, who won the 2004 Pulitzer Prize for his 2003 novel *The Known World,* illustrates the role that high parental expectations can play. He grew up in a very poor family, headed by a single mother who could not read or write. Jones writes:

> For as many Sundays as I can remember, perhaps even Sundays when I was in the womb, my mother has pointed across "I" street to Seaton [school] as we come and go to Mt. Carmel [church].
> "You gonna go there and learn about the whole world."
>
> *[1992/2003, p. 29]*

That excerpt is from a short story, but Jones says it is based on his own boyhood experiences. His mother always encouraged him to do well in school. As is evident in his writing, he did "learn about the whole world."

The Reading Wars

Reading is a complex activity. The ability to read with speedy, automatic comprehension is the cumulative result of many earlier steps—from looking at picture books (at age 2 or earlier) to learning how to figure out unknown technical words (at age 10 and beyond). Clashes over the best way to teach reading have led to "serious, sometimes acrimonious debate, fueling the well-named 'reading wars'" (Keogh, 2004, p. 93).

PHONICS VERSUS WHOLE-LANGUAGE READING INSTRUCTION Historically, schools used the **phonics approach** (from the root word for "sound"), in which children learn to read by learning letter–sound correspondences in order to decipher simple words. This approach seemed to be supported by behaviorism (see Chapter 1) and, more recently, by information-processing theory, which favors step-by-step instructions with frequent repetition.

phonics approach
Teaching reading by first teaching the sounds of each letter and of various letter combinations.

Reading with Comprehension (*left*) Reading and math scores in third-grader Monica's Illinois elementary school showed improvement under the standards set by the No Child Left Behind Act. The principal noted a cost for this success in less time spent on social studies and other subjects. (*right*) Some experts believe that children should have their own books and be able to read them wherever and however they want. This strategy seems to be working with Josue and Cristo, two 8-year-olds who were given books through their after-school program in Rochester, Washington.

whole-language approach
Teaching reading by encouraging early use of all language skills—talking and listening, reading and writing.

> From karla to My mom
> It's No fare
> that you mad
> me Lat my Lade
> bug Go Wat
> If I was your
> mom and I mad
> you tack your
> Lade bug I am
> Shir you wud
> be sad like me
> that lade bug
> mat of tan a orfan
> so you sod ov latme
> hav it ane wae

"You Wud Be Sad Like Me" Although Karla uses invented spelling, her arguments show that she is reasoning quite logically; her school-age mind is working quite well. (If you have trouble deciphering Karla's note, see the next page for a translation.)

The abstract, decontextualized memorization required in the phonics approach may be beyond the capacity of concrete operational thinkers. Piaget's theory—that children learn on their own as soon as their minds are ready—provided the rationale for another method of teaching reading, called the **whole-language approach.** This approach views literacy as the outcome of a person's natural motivation to use all language skills—talking and listening, reading and writing.

CALLING A TRUCE Research arising from every contemporary developmental theory has noted the uniqueness of each child as a beginning reader. Learning styles, past experiences, and motivation vary, as do language proficiency and maturation. In practical terms, this means that phonics may be essential for children who need help learning how to sound out new words. For them, targeted early instruction in letter–sound combinations may be crucial (Torgesen, 2004). Score one for phonics.

Yet for comprehension and memory, children need to make connections between concepts, not just between letters. Educators complain about a "fourth-grade slump," when many children have difficulty reading fluently with comprehension (Samuels, 2007). Phonics cannot help them with this; however, reading books that are challenging and interesting does help, as does writing about their own experiences and interests. Score one for whole-language instruction.

This tie points toward a truce in the reading wars. A focus on phonics need not undercut instruction that motivates children to read, write, and discuss with their classmates and their parents. For reading comprehension and fluency, phonetic awareness is a beginning, but other aspects of literacy are important as well (Muter et al., 2004). As the editors of a leading publication for teachers explain:

> In any debate on reading instruction that counterposes a focus on skills with a focus on enjoyment—or that pits phonological skills against the knowledge necessary to comprehend grade-level material—there is only one good answer: Kids need both.
>
> [*The Editors,* American Educator, *2004, p. 5]*

Fortunately, experts on the two sides in the reading wars have ended their bitter feud. Most developmentalists and many reading specialists now believe that there are many pathways in learning to read.

The Math Wars

Mathematics instruction has provoked even more controversy than instruction in reading, for at least three reasons:

1. Economic development depends on science and technology, and math is vital in both of those fields. In a time of worldwide economic recession, STEM (science, technology, engineering, mathematics) study is seen as crucial.

2. North American and western European students are weaker in math than are students from other nations, especially East Asian nations.

3. Many children hate math and feel intimidated by it. A 2009 Google search found 55,800 entries for "math phobia."

As a result, math education is widely seen as vital yet inadequate, and that makes it vulnerable to quick solutions suggested by angry adults. That is not the best way to develop a curriculum, but it is a good way to start a war.

According to one report, "U.S. mathematics instruction has been scorched in the pedagogical blaze known as the 'math wars'—a divide between those who see a need for a greater emphasis on basic skills in math and others who say students lack a broader, conceptual understanding of the subject" (Cavanagh, 2005, p. 1). This is similar to the debate over phonics versus whole-language reading instruction, or direct instruction versus discovery learning. Is there any chance of a truce?

"The path to becoming an astronaut is rougher than I thought."

OLD AND NEW MATH Historically, math was taught by rote; children memorized number facts, such as the multiplication tables, and filled page after page of workbooks. In reaction against this approach, many educators, inspired especially by Piaget and Vygotsky, sought to make math instruction more active and engaging— less a matter of memorization than of discovery (Ginsburg et al., 1998).

This newer approach is controversial. Many parents and educators still believe that children need to memorize number facts. Educators as well as mathematicians stress that math involves a particular set of rules, symbols, and processes that must be taught and that discovery can play only a limited role (Mervis, 2006).

A SEQUENCE OF SKILLS Following the information-processing approach, which looks at tiny increments in cognition, researchers have studied children day by day to understand how math understanding emerges (Siegler, 1996). Apparently, cognitive advances do *not* occur suddenly (in stages) and are *not* a matter of rote memory; rather, they occur in overlapping waves. Neither old nor new math is sufficient.

Strategies for manipulating numbers ebb and flow, gradually becoming standard. Children adding 5 and 3, for instance, first count one by one (often on their fingers, 1-2-3-4-5-6-7-8). Later they try a strategy called *min,* counting up from the higher number (5 + 6, 7, 8). Min is quicker, but a child might use min once or twice and then revert to counting one by one (as the wave ebbs). Eventually, the child uses min routinely. Finally, adding 5 + 3 = 8 is memorized and becomes automatic; children think they always knew it, forgetting the waves of earlier learning.

What can teachers do to help children learn math? Experts in TIMSS (an international math achievement test, discussed in the following section) videotaped 231 math classes in Japan, Germany, and the United States to analyze national differences (Stigler & Hiebert, 1999). The U.S. teachers presented math at a lower level than did their German and Japanese counterparts, with more definitions but less connection to what the students had already learned.

"From Karla to my mom. It's no fair that you made me let my lady bug go. What if I was your mom and I made you take your lady bug. I am sure you would be sad like me. That lady bug might have been an orphan. So you should have let me have it anyway."

Collaborative Learning Japanese children are learning mathematics in a more structured and socially interactive way than are their North Amerian counterparts

Math instruction was dull in the United States because "teachers seem to believe that learning terms and practicing skills is not very exciting" (p. 89). In contrast, the Japanese teachers were excited about math, working collaboratively and structuring lessons so that the children developed proofs and alternative solutions, alone and in groups. Teachers used social interaction (among groups of children and groups of teachers) and sequential curricula (daily, weekly, and yearly lessons built on previous knowledge).

Active learning is suggested by Piaget, social interaction by Vygotsky, and sequential learning by information-processing theory. The Japanese seem to incorporate all three approaches, and now that combination is endorsed by the National Council of Teachers of Mathematics (NCTM) in the United States. An example of sequential learning is that second-graders are to learn addition, subtraction, and place value; not until fourth grade are multiplication, fractions, and decimals taught (Mervis, 2006).

Other Issues in Education

As you see with the reading and math wars, the educational landscape is filled with controversies and assumptions. There are many more. For example, U.S. adults have become convinced that children learn from homework; now even kindergarten children often bring work home. Yet one researcher finds that homework undermines learning instead of advancing it (Kohn, 2006).

Similarly, although many parents choose to send their children to schools with small class sizes, the evidence about the effect of class size is mixed (Blatchford, 2003; Hanushek, 1999). Wide international variation is apparent, from a teacher/pupil ratio of 1 to 10 in Denmark to 1 to 30 in Turkey. Smaller is not necessarily better, as evidenced by Asian nations in which classes are large but students nonetheless tend to have high math and science scores (T. D. Snyder et al., 2006).

Data on class size thus "do not lend themselves to straightforward implications for policy" (NICHD Early Child Care Research Network, 2004a, p. 661). A famous study in Tennessee found that smaller classes in kindergarten benefited children for several years, but other interpretations are possible (J. D. Finn & Achilles, 1999). Longitudinal data show that children in those small Tennessee classes (averaging 15 students per teacher) are more likely to graduate from high school, which increases their lifetime earnings. This may increase government tax revenues and save on subsidies such as food stamps and medical care (Muenning & Woolf, 2007). But not everyone sees reduced class size as a good investment.

Other reforms, in addition to reducing class size, have been strongly advocated—and strongly opposed. These include raising teacher salaries; improving professional education; extending school hours; expanding the school year; increasing instruction time in sports and music; and increasing the amount of time set aside for silent reading. Also controversial are charter schools (publicly funded) that are exempted from some of the usual rules and voucher systems that enable parents to pay for their children to attend a private school of their choice.

Any or all of these measures might, or might not, help children learn. Valid, replicated, unbiased research on costs and benefits is thus far lacking (Duncan & Magnuson, 2007). One review about home schooling, charter schools, and vouchers points out "the difficulty of interpreting the research literature on this topic, most of which is biased and far from approaching balanced social science" (Boyd, 2007, p. 7). The need for "evidence-based" reforms is appreciated by developmentalists, as by all other scientists.

Measuring the Mind

Although all developmentalists agree that empirical evidence is needed to assess intellectual capacity and achievement, another major controversy concerns the form that evidence should take. Traditionally, mental processes have been measured via standardized tests. Each child's answers are compared with those of other children of the same age (to assess aptitude) or in the same school grade (to measure achievement). On the basis of children's scores, schools are compared with one another and nations are compared with other nations. As you will see, this is not as straightforward as it may appear (Kanaya & Ceci, 2007).

In theory, **aptitude** is the potential to master a particular skill or to learn a particular body of knowledge. The most important aptitude for school-age children is intellectual aptitude, or the ability to learn in school, which is usually measured by an **IQ test.**

In theory, aptitude leads to achievement, but achievement is distinct from aptitude. Achievement is what a person *has* learned, not what a person *might* learn. Students take **achievement tests** to measure what they know about a particular subject. If a child's achievement lags two years or more behind his or her aptitude, then some school districts would consider that child to have a learning disability.

The words *in theory* precede those definitions because, although aptitude and achievement tests are designed to measure different traits, the scores are strongly correlated, for individuals and for nations (Lynn & Mikk, 2007). Both also correlate with wealth—again, both for individuals and for nations (Lynn & Vanhanen, 2002).

aptitude
The potential to master a specific skill or to learn a certain body of knowledge.

IQ test
A test designed to measure intellectual aptitude, or ability to learn in school. Originally, intelligence was defined as mental age divided by chronological age, times 100—hence the term *intelligence quotient,* or *IQ.*

achievement test
A measure of mastery or proficiency in reading, mathematics, writing, science, or some other subject.

Measuring Aptitude

As you have just read, IQ tests are the traditional measure of schoolchildren's aptitude, since they predict how much a child is able to learn. Because IQ is supposed to be independent of achievement, licensed testers give these tests individually, to avoid the problem of a test-taker being unable to read or understand the questions. Any individual factors that might reduce a child's score, such as illness or hostility, is noted.

IQ is an abbreviation for "intelligence quotient." Originally, an IQ score was literally a quotient: Mental age (as indicated by how old children typically are when they achieve a particular test score) was divided by the tested child's actual chronological age, and the result was then multiplied by 100. (If people say that someone "thinks like an 8-year-old," they are alluding to mental age.)

CALCULATING IQ A child whose test performance equals the average performance of children who are exactly the child's age has a mental age equal to his or her chronological age. In that case, mental age divided by chronological age equals 1. Since $1 \times 100 = 100$, an IQ of 100 is exactly average.

The current method of calculating IQ is more complicated, but it is still assumed that aptitude for learning increases with every year until late adolescence, so dividing a child's score by the child's age equals the IQ. For instance, an 8-year-old who answered as well as a typical 10-year-old would score at $10/8 = 1.25 \times 100 = 125$ IQ. About two-thirds of people have an IQ between 85 and 115.

In adulthood, aptitude is assumed *not* to change year by year. Regardless of age, therefore, all adults take the same standardized test to measure IQ. As you will see in Chapter 12, this practice may penalize older adults, whose IQ scores are typically lower than those of younger adults.

Trial and Understanding This youngster completes one of the five performance tests of the Wechsler Intelligence Scale for Children (WISC). If her score is high, is that because of superior innate intelligence? ["Wechsler Adult Intelligence Scale" and "WAIS" are trademarks, in the U.S. and/or other countries, of Pearson Education, Inc. or its affiliate(s).]

IQ TESTS AND THE FLYNN EFFECT The first highly regarded IQ test was the *Stanford-Binet test*, now in its fifth edition (Roid, 2003). This test was originally developed by the French psychologist Alfred Binet to identify children who were mentally retarded, in the hope that they could be protected from being beaten, shamed, or otherwise punished because they did not learn as fast as other children.

An American named David Wechsler developed another set of IQ tests. There are Wechsler tests for preschoolers (the WPPSI, or Wechsler Preschool and Primary Scale of Intelligence), for adults (the WAIS, or Wechsler Adult Intelligence Scale), and for school-age children (the **WISC,** or **Wechsler Intelligence Scale for Children**), now in its fourth edition (D. Wechsler, 2003).

Like the Binet test, the Wechsler tests provide one overall IQ score, but they also have 10 subtests—including tests of vocabulary, general knowledge, memory, and spatial comprehension, each of which provides a score. The results of five of the subtests provide a verbal IQ (measured by vocabulary, math problems, and so on); the results of the other five yield a performance IQ (measured by puzzles, copying shapes, and so on).

Traditionally, experts (including Binet and Wechsler) thought IQ was genetic, with no plasticity. But over the past 100 years, average IQ scores worldwide have risen substantially—a phenomenon called the **Flynn effect,** after the scientist who first described it (Flynn, 2007; Rodgers & Wänström, 2007). Developmentalists believe that better health, smaller families, more schooling, and other environmental factors allow children to be quicker learners today than they were decades ago.

Wechsler Intelligence Scale for Children (WISC)
An IQ test designed for school-age children. The test assesses potential in many areas, including vocabulary, general knowledge, memory, and spatial comprehension.

Flynn effect
The rise in average IQ scores that has occurred over the decades in many nations.

mental retardation
Literally, slow, or late, thinking. In practice, people are considered mentally retarded if they score below 70 on an IQ test and if they are markedly behind their peers in the ability to meet the basic requirements of daily life.

GIFTED AND RETARDED LEARNING Children may receive special education if their IQ scores are either significantly higher or lower than average. A child with a high IQ (usually above 130) may be placed in *gifted-and-talented* classes. Policies and programs for gifted children vary from place to place. In the United States in 2004, 14 percent of children in Oklahoma, and fewer than 1 percent in Massachusetts, were in gifted classes (T. D. Snyder et al., 2008). High IQs are actually more common among children in Massachusetts than in Oklahoma, but adults—voters as well as legislators—have responded differently.

Thirty years ago, the definition of **mental retardation** was straightforward: Anyone with an IQ below 70 was considered retarded. The designation *mentally retarded* sometimes led parents and teachers to expect less than a child could actually do. Consequently, children with low IQ scores were not helped to reach their potential. Furthermore, the data showed that IQ scores could change with development. Currently, many experts believe that the category "mentally retarded" is misleading; only half as many children are considered mentally retarded today as 30 years ago.

The current definition of mental retardation stipulates that, to be designated as retarded, a person must not only score low on an IQ test but also be less able than peers to perform the basic *activities of daily life* (ADLs). If a 6-year-old with an IQ of

65 can dress herself, fix breakfast, walk to school, and greet her classmates by name, she is not considered retarded (Venn, 2004). (The concept of being able to perform ADLs is central to understanding intelligence in late adulthood, too; see Chapter 15.)

CRITICISMS OF TESTING A problem is now apparent with all major IQ tests: They reflect cultural bias. Every exam reflects the culture of those who write and administer it (Armour-Thomas & Gopaul-McNicol, 1998; Cianciolo & Sternberg, 2004). As two developmentalists comment:

> Like many other Western technological inventions (such as the printing press, the sewing machine, the bicycle, and the tractor), the intelligence test (popularly known as the IQ test) has been widely exported around the world. Like tractors, intelligence tests bring with them both ostensible utility and hidden implications.
>
> *[Serpell & Haynes, 2004, p. 166]*

In the United States, children of immigrant families or of non-European backgrounds score lower on IQ tests, but those scores do not accurately reflect their learning potential. Because their scores are lower, a higher proportion of such children are designated as mentally retarded (IQ below 70). Because of the way scores are calculated, if the overall average of an ethnic group is reduced by 10 points because of culturally unfair test questions, then about 12 percent of the group (not 2 percent, as is the case for the population as a whole) will score below 70 and be labeled as having mental retardation.

Some experts have tried to design a test that is equally fair for children from all cultures. For example, the Draw a Person test does not require the child to be able to read or write English. Still, every IQ test is subject to cultural bias.

Another question is whether there is just one intelligence (referred to as *g*, for general intelligence) or *multiple intelligences.* If humans do have multiple intelligences, then tests that produce a single IQ score do not provide a full assessment of intellectual capacity.

Robert Sternberg (1996) describes three distinct types of intelligence:

- *Academic,* measured by IQ and achievement tests
- *Creative,* evidenced by imaginative endeavors
- *Practical,* seen in everyday problem solving

Other psychologists stress *emotional intelligence,* including the abilities to regulate one's own emotions and to understand other people's feelings. They suspect that emotional intelligence may be more useful than the intelligence measured by IQ tests (Goleman, 1995; Salovey & Grewal, 2005). In reality, however, emotional intelligence (as popularized by Daniel Goleman in a book of that name) has not been validated by scientific research (Matthews et al., 2002).

The most comprehensive multiple-intelligence theory was proposed by Howard Gardner, who originally described the following seven intelligences: linguistic, logical-mathematical, musical, spatial, bodily-kinesthetic (movement), interpersonal (social understanding), and intrapersonal (self-understanding). He later added an eighth intelligence, naturalistic (understanding of nature, as in biology, zoology, or farming), and a ninth, existential (asking questions about life and death) (H. Gardner, 1983, 1999, 2006; H. Gardner & Moran, 2006).

According to Gardner, barring brain damage, everyone has at least some of all nine intelligences, but each of us shines in some intelligences and struggles in others. For example, a person might be gifted spatially but not linguistically (a visual artist who cannot describe her work) or might have interpersonal but not naturalistic intelligence (a gifted clinical psychologist whose houseplants wither). Personally, I am deficient in musical intelligence: I sing joyously but off key.

Demonstration of High IQ? If North American intelligence tests truly reflected all aspects of the mind, children would be considered mentally slow if they could not replicate the proper hand, arm, torso, and facial positions of a traditional dance, as this young Indonesian girl does brilliantly. She is obviously adept in kinesthetic and interpersonal intelligence. Given her culture, it would not be surprising if she were deficient in the logical-mathematical intelligence required to use the Internet effectively or to surpass an American peer in playing a video game.

© OWEN FRANKEN / STOCK, BOSTON

Gardner believes that the diversity of human intelligences is a social strength. Societies and schools function best if everyone cooperates, each doing what he or she does best and appreciating each other's contributions. In Gardner's words:

> A variety of potentials combining into different patterns allows a wider array of competencies and performances. . . . People, teams, and organizations can fine-tune their skills.
>
> [H. Gardner, 2006, p. 216]

According to advocates of multiple intelligences (including Sternberg, Goleman, and Gardner), standard IQ tests measure only part of brain potential. Other scientists are critical of the idea of multiple intelligences (e.g., Visser et al., 2006; Waterhouse, 2006). But almost all agree that education should be tailored to individual students' abilities, especially for children with special needs.

Measuring Achievement Within the United States

In the United States many political and educational leaders argue over the **No Child Left Behind (NCLB) Act** of 2001, a federal law that mandates annual standardized achievement tests for public school students. This law has been adjusted several times, but many school districts remain critical of it, partly because in the United States, local communities have always decided what children should learn.

One feature of No Child Left Behind is that each state can develop its own achievement tests to measure the success of its schools. Many suspect that some states are using tests that are unfair. This has led to a renewed call for a national or global measurement of achievement.

Another major complaint against No Child Left Behind is that it requires too much testing, based on the assumption that tests measure learning—an assumption many teachers dispute. Some learning (e.g., knowledge of creative strategies) is difficult to assess with test scores; other learning (e.g., knowledge of philosophical or justice issues) requires years of debate and questioning, beyond an immediate multiple-choice exam.

The **National Assessment of Educational Progress (NAEP)** is a nationwide set of tests in the United States; it is often referred to as "the nation's report card" (Pellegrino et al., 1999). The NAEP measures achievement in reading, mathematics, and other subjects. It is controversial for many reasons, among them the fact that it finds fewer children proficient in various skills than state tests show (see Figures 7.5 and 7.6). As one study points out:

> Local control of public schools is a hallowed tradition in American education and there has long been antipathy to the idea of a national test. . . . Some state educators say comparisons are unfair because NAEP is too rigorous and was designed to chart long-term trends, not to measure what states feel students should know.
>
> [Vu, 2007]

International Achievement Test Scores

Objective assessment of curricula might result from international, culture-neutral tests. Ideally, each nation would give the same test, under the same conditions, to a representative group of children of a particular age and grade in school.

Even-handed comparisons are impossible, however, because educational practices vary widely. For example, children in Scotland begin school at age 4 and thus had a three-year advantage over Russian children, who until recently began school at age 7 (Mullis et al., 2004). Furthermore, each nation favors some topics of study and kinds of assessment.

Whether because of classroom practices (the microsystem, in Bronfenbrenner's terms; see Chapter 1) or because of national values (the exosystem), children from

ESPECIALLY FOR Teachers What are the advantages and disadvantages of using Gardner's idea of multiple intelligences to guide your classroom curriculum? (see response, page 262) →

No Child Left Behind (NCLB) Act A U.S. law enacted in 2001 that was intended to increase accountability in education by requiring states to qualify for federal educational funding by administering standardized tests to measure school achievement.

National Assessment of Educational Progress (NAEP) An ongoing and nationally representative measure of U.S. children's achievement in reading, mathematics, and other subjects over time; nicknamed "the nation's report card."

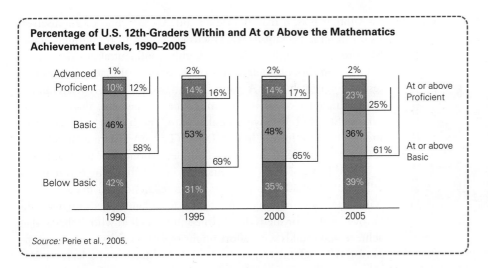

Percentage of U.S. 12th-Graders Within and At or Above the Mathematics Achievement Levels, 1990–2005

Source: Perie et al., 2005.

FIGURE 7.5 Better or Worse? Should a country's education policy emphasize helping more students become "proficient" or better in mathematics or trying to make sure that fewer students score "below basic"? The United States seems to be choosing the former policy, with more resources allocated to the schools where students score high in math achievement.

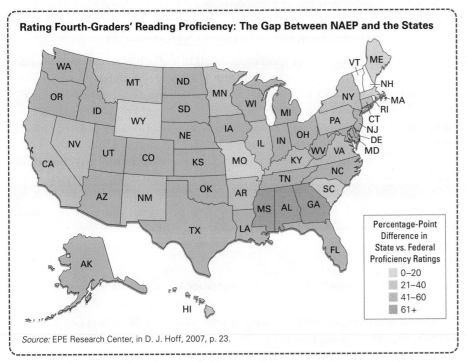

Rating Fourth-Graders' Reading Proficiency: The Gap Between NAEP and the States

Percentage-Point Difference in State vs. Federal Proficiency Ratings
- 0–20
- 21–40
- 41–60
- 61+

Source: EPE Research Center, in D. J. Hoff, 2007, p. 23.

FIGURE 7.6 Local Standards Each state sets its own level of proficiency, which helps states in which children score low on the NAEP obtain more federal money for education. That practice may undercut high standards for student learning.

many Western countries score high on an international test of reading, the **Progress in International Reading Literacy Study (PIRLS)**. In the 2006 study, most Canadian children did particularly well, and the United States ranked in the top half (Manzo, 2007).

However, another international test, the **Trends in Math and Science Study (TIMSS)**, has found that students in East Asia are far ahead of students in the rest of the world in math and science. One example comes from the fourth-grade math part of the TIMSS: The *average* 10-year-old in Singapore is ahead of the best (top 5 percent) 10-year-olds in the United States. Similarly, fourth-graders in Hong Kong, Japan, and Chinese Taipei (Taiwan) score markedly higher in both math and science than their counterparts in Western nations.

Many reasons for these differences have been offered, including the training and methods of the teachers, the respect for science and math in the culture, and the length of the school day and year (about 30 percent longer in Japan than in the United States).

Progress in International Reading Literacy Study (PIRLS)
Inaugurated in 2001, a planned five-year cycle of international trend studies in the reading ability of fourth-graders.

Trends in Math and Science Study (TIMSS)
An international assessment of the math and science skills of fourth- and eighth-graders. Although the TIMSS is very useful, different countries' scores are not always comparable because sample selection, test administration, and content validity are hard to keep uniform.

ESPECIALLY FOR Future Research Scientists What should you watch for in news reports about the TIMSS data? (see response, page 263) →

"Big deal, an A in math. That would be a D in any other country."

children with special needs
Children who, because of a physical or mental disability, require extra help in order to learn.

developmental psychopathology
The field that uses insights into typical development to understand and remediate developmental disorders, and vice versa.

RESPONSE FOR Teachers (from page 260) The advantages are that all the children learn more aspects of human knowledge and that many children can develop their talents. Art, music, and sports should be an integral part of education, not just a break from academics. The disadvantage is that they take time and attention away from reading and math, which might lead to less proficiency in those subjects on standard tests and thus to criticism from parents and supervisors. ●

She Knows the Answer Physical disabilities often mushroom into additional emotional and cognitive problems. However, a disability can be reduced to a minor complication if it is recognized and if appropriate compensation or remediation is made a part of the child's education. As she signs her answer, this deaf girl shows by her expression that she is ready to learn.

Another reason may be the attitude of the children themselves. The role of expectations was discussed earlier. In the United States, 51 percent of eighth-graders are highly confident about their math ability, even though their scores on international math achievement tests are relatively low. Among 46 nations, only Israel has children with a higher level of math confidence (59 percent) than does the United States (T. D. Snyder et al., 2006). The highest math achievement scores are from Chinese Taipei (Taiwan), where relatively few (26 percent) students are highly confident about their math ability.

The difference may lie in children's beliefs about the nature of intelligence. A child who believes that intelligence is a fixed quantity will never try something that might lead to failure, because it would "prove" that he or she is dumb. In contrast, a child who believes that achievement builds with effort might regard failure as a learning opportunity, a helpful way to find out what needs to be learned (another example of metacognition).

Developmental Psychopathology

Problems with measuring aptitude and achievement are multiplied when it comes to **children with special needs.** Such children require extra help in order to learn because of some physical or mental disability. In the United States, about one-sixth of all children are thought to have special needs—a much higher proportion than is found in other nations. Are those countries missing something, or does the United States overdiagnose?

A new field within human development called **developmental psychopathology** focuses on such questions. In developmental psychopathology, the typical course of development is used for comparison in order to understand various disorders, and vice versa. The goal is "to understand the nature, origins, and sequelae [consequences] of individual patterns of adaptation and maladaptation over time" (P. T. Davies & Cicchetti, 2004, p. 477). Several lessons from developmental psychopathology apply to everyone:

1. *Abnormality is normal.* Most people sometimes act oddly, and those with serious disabilities are, in many respects, like everyone else.

2. *Disability changes year by year.* Someone who is severely disabled at one stage may become quite capable later on, or vice versa.

TABLE 7.1 Education for Children with Special Needs: Some Important Terms

Term	Definition
Individual education plan (IEP)	Children with special needs are required to have an IEP, which specifies any special curricula or services they must receive.
Least restrictive environment (LRE)	Children with special needs are mandated to be educated in a regular classroom if possible. Segregated classes are a last resort.
Mainstreaming	The concept that all children should learn together, in the regular (mainstream) classroom. Teachers are supposed to accommodate special needs.
Inclusion	The policy of *including* children with special needs in the regular classroom. A special educator may provide help within the regular class.
Resource room	A room with books, teachers, and other materials for children with special needs.
Individuals with Disabilities Education Act (IDEA)	This U.S. law mandates educational services for children with special needs. It is updated every few years. The 2006 legislation stressed the need for early education (from birth on), periodic reevaluation, and parental access.

RESPONSE FOR Future Research Scientists (from page 261) The next set of results of the TIMSS was scheduled to be published in 2009. As someone who knows how to think like a scientist, see if the headlines accurately reflect the data. ●

Specialized Terms in Special-Needs Education Education of children with special needs is most beneficial when it begins early; but availability of programs varies within and among nations (Liptak et al., 2008). Furthermore, few parents know the terms that pertain to special educational needs. For U.S. parents, the definitions given in this table may help.

3. *Adulthood may be better or worse than childhood.* Prognosis is difficult. Many infants and children with serious disabilities that affect them psychologically (e.g., blindness) become happy and productive adults. Conversely, some conditions become more disabling at maturity, when interpersonal skills become more important.

4. *Diagnosis depends on the social context.* According to the widely used ***Diagnostic and Statistical Manual of Mental Disorders*** **(DSM-IV-TR),** "nuances of an individual's cultural frame of reference" must be considered before a diagnosis is rendered (American Psychiatric Association, 2000, p. xxxiv).

Many books and other resources are available for parents seeking to understand and educate children with special educational needs. As a beginning, Table 7.1 explains some terms, and here we discuss three of the many categories of disorders that developmental psychopathologists study: attention deficits, learning disabilities, and autistic spectrum disorders. An understanding of these conditions can lead to a better understanding of all children.

ATTENTION-DEFICIT/HYPERACTIVITY DISORDER As you have read, the ability to pay attention gradually improves with age. However, about 10 percent of children have an *attention-deficit disorder (ADD),* defined as extraordinary difficulty paying attention. At least half of them (5 percent of all children, more boys than girls) are also very active. This is **attention–deficit/hyperactivity disorder (ADHD).**

Children with ADHD have three problems: They are inattentive, impulsive, and overactive. For example, soon after sitting down to do homework, a child with ADHD might look up, ask questions, think about playing, get a drink, fidget, squirm, tap the table, jiggle his or her legs, and go to the bathroom—and then start the whole sequence again.

Often, other disorders are comorbid with ADHD, including "conduct disorder, depression, anxiety, Tourette syndrome, dyslexia, and bipolar disorder, . . . autism and schizophrenia" (Pennington, 2002, p. 163). (**Comorbidity** means that a person has two or more conditions at the same time.) Some comorbidities may predate ADHD

Diagnostic and Statistical Manual of Mental Disorders (DSM-IV-TR)
The American Psychiatric Association's official guide to the diagnosis (not treatment) of mental disorders. (IV-TR means "fourth edition, text revision." The fifth edition is scheduled to be published in 2011.)

attention-deficit/hyperactivity disorder (ADHD)
A condition in which a person is inattentive, impulsive, and overactive and thus has great difficulty concentrating for more than a few moments.

comorbidity
The presence of two or more unrelated disease conditions at the same time in the same person.

Use Your Hands A teacher helps a pupil work through a math problem. This boy has been diagnosed with mental retardation and ADHD. Note the position of her hands and his, helping him to focus his attention.

and have the same underlying cause, while others (such as conduct disorder or delinquency) may be consequences of untreated ADHD.

Many hypotheses about the cause of ADHD have been examined. The difficulty may be a slow-developing prefrontal cortex, an overactive limbic system, or an imbalance of neurotransmitters (Wolraich & Doffing, 2005). These could be genetic or the result of prenatal problems. Maternal smoking, parental permissiveness, exposure to lead, lack of rough-and-tumble play, and too much television have all been blamed.

Once the problem appears, artificial colorings and preservatives in food may make the symptoms worse. Recent research showed that when hyperactive children avoided food additives for two weeks and then drank beverages laced with additives, they became more impulsive (Eigenmann & Haenggeli, 2007).

Whatever the cause, children and adults with ADHD have extreme trouble paying attention (Barkley, 2006). Curiously, drugs that are stimulants for most adults, including amphetamines (e.g., Adderall) and methylphenidate (Ritalin), help some children become calmer and more attentive. However, the use of psychoactive drugs to treat children with psychological disorders is controversial, as the following explains.

A VIEW FROM SCIENCE

Overdosing and Underdosing Children with Psychoactive Drugs

In the United States, more than 3 million children and adolescents under age 18 take prescription drugs to regulate their emotions and behavior. This rate doubled between 1987 and 1996 (K. Brown, 2003; Zito et al., 2003). It is no longer increasing in the United States. Still, about 5 percent of 6- to 12-year-olds are currently taking stimulants (Vitiello et al., 2006; Zuvekas et al., 2006).

The most commonly prescribed drug is Ritalin for ADHD. At least 20 other psychoactive drugs (including Prozac, Zoloft, and Paxil) are also being used, sometimes for children as young as 2, for depression, anxiety, and many other conditions (L. C. Rubin, 2006). (Such drugs are called *psychoactive* because they affect the workings of the mind in order to change mood or behavior.) Few of these substances have been studied with children, who might respond better at higher or lower doses than those given to adults (K. Brown, 2003).

Many people fear that psychoactive drugs are being overprescribed (S. Rose, 2008). One writer contends:

> Squirming in a seat and talking out of turn are not "symptoms" and do not reflect a syndrome. [Such behaviors may be] caused by anything from normal childhood energy to boring classrooms or overstressed parents and teachers. We should not suppress these behaviors with drugs.
>
> [Breggin & Baughman, 2001, p. 595]

Most child psychologists fear that drugs are both underused and overused for children with ADHD (Angold et al., 2000; K. Brown, 2003; Willingham, 2004/2005). Some children who would benefit are never given medication; other children are given more medication than they need. Dosage is a concern because children's weight and metabolism change continuously, so that a dose that is right at age 5 might be too low at age 10. Overdosing is worse when brains and bodies are still developing, yet underdosing may cause a child to suffer a lifetime of loneliness and failure.

One group of researchers, seeking to find out whether drugs helped children with ADHD, began with small doses that were gradually increased until behavior improved without side effects. After several weeks at that dose, the children were given a *placebo,* a "sugar pill" that contained no medicine. (The children, parents, and teachers knew that this would occur but did not know when.) On the placebo, many children's behavior worsened, according to all observers. That convinced the scientists that the medication was effective (Hechtman et al., 2005).

Even if drugs help during middle childhood, some people fear that the children who use them will become dependent on drugs. Fortunately, longitudinal research comparing nonmedicated and medicated children with ADHD finds the opposite: Medicated children are less likely to abuse drugs later on (Faraone & Wilens, 2003; Mannuzza et al., 2008).

That is reassuring, but another set of findings is not. Far fewer children are diagnosed with ADHD in Europe than in North America. In the United States, rates of medication are highest among children from low-income, non-Hispanic, southern households (see Table 7.2) (Rowland et al., 2002; Zito et al., 2003). Boys overall are diagnosed and treated about three times more often than girls, but when girls have ADHD, it is more severe (Hinshaw et al., 2006).

These differences suggest that politics, economics, and culture influence diagnosis and treatment. In other words, the decision to treat ADHD may be a subjective, even arbitrary one—a possibility that, again, raises the concern that some children are under- or overmedicated.

Literally thousands of scientists in dozens of nations are responding to these concerns; many longitudinal studies are under way, and answers should appear soon. Millions of children need those answers.

TABLE 7.2 Rates of Diagnosis and Medication for ADHD

	Percent Diagnosed with ADHD	Percent of Those Diagnosed Taking Medication for ADHD
Girls	4.7	63
Boys	14.8	73
1st and 2nd grades	7.4	70
3rd, 4th, and 5th grades	12.2	72
Non-Hispanic White	10.8	76
Non-Hispanic Black	9.1	56
Hispanic	4.0	53

Source: Rowland et al., 2002.

LEARNING DISABILITIES Many people have a specific **learning disability** that leads to difficulty mastering a particular skill that most other people acquire easily. In contrast to ADHD, other learning disabilities do *not* usually result in lifelong impediments unless they are comorbid; the reason is that most children learn to compensate, finding ways to work around their deficiency, especially if they have adult help and parental support. During primary school, observant, skilled teachers (sometimes aided by good diagnostic tests) can help children overcome their disabilities. Winston Churchill, Albert Einstein, and Hans Christian Andersen all probably had learning disabilities. Learning disabilities are not likely to improve with medication, although other forms of therapy may be helpful (M. A. Barnes & Wade-Woolley, 2007).

If Gardner's theory of multiple intelligences is correct, no one is equally good at everything. Accordingly, some experts believe that children with learning disabilities are not much different from other children but are simply lower in one or more particular forms of intelligence (Kovas & Plomin, 2007).

One common learning disability is **dyslexia,** which refers to unusual difficulty with reading. No single test accurately diagnoses dyslexia—or any other learning disability (such as *dyscalculia,* difficulty with math, or *dysgraphia,* difficulty with handwriting)—because every academic achievement involves many skills (Sofie & Riccio, 2002) and dyslexia takes many different forms. In one common type, a child has trouble sounding out words but excels in other literacy skills, such as comprehension and memory of printed text.

Early theories hypothesized that visual difficulties—such as reversals of letters (reading *was* instead of *saw*) and mirror writing (*b* instead of *d*)—led to dyslexia, but current data find that speech and hearing problems are more often the origin (Pennington, 2002). If a 3-year-old does not talk clearly and does not experience a naming explosion (see Chapter 4), sometimes speech therapy prevents later dyslexia (Simpson, 2000).

AUTISTIC SPECTRUM DISORDERS About 1 in 150 8-year-olds (three times as many boys as girls) in the United States has been diagnosed with an **autistic spectrum disorder** (MMWR, February 9, 2007).

Symptoms and Causes Children with an autistic spectrum disorder have three symptoms: delayed language, impaired social responses, and unusual play. Underlying all three is a kind of emotional blindness (Scambler et al., 2007) that makes it difficult

ESPECIALLY FOR Health Workers
Parents ask that some medication be prescribed for their kindergarten child, who they say is much too active for them to handle. How do you respond? (see response, page 267) →

learning disability
A marked delay in a particular area of learning that is not caused by an apparent physical disability, by mental retardation, or by an unusually stressful home environment.

dyslexia
Unusual difficulty with reading; thought to be the result of some neurological underdevelopment.

autistic spectrum disorder
Any of several disorders characterized by impaired communication, inadequate social skills, and unusual patterns of play.

autism
A developmental disorder marked by an inability to relate to other people normally, extreme self-absorption, and an inability to acquire normal speech.

Asperger syndrome
An autistic spectrum disorder characterized by extreme attention to details and deficient social understanding.

FIGURE 7.7 Across State Lines
The large differences in rates of autism from one state to another is puzzling. It has been suggested, however, that the explanation for New Jersey's high ranking may include the greater awareness of autism, more meticulous record-keeping, and wider availability of school and community services in that state as compared to other states.

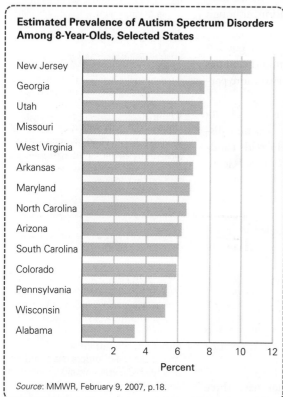

Estimated Prevalence of Autism Spectrum Disorders Among 8-Year-Olds, Selected States

Source: MMWR, February 9, 2007, p.18.

for the child to understand other people. Such children need help, especially with social skills, their most serious impairment.

Symptoms and their severity differ in individual children. Some children with classic **autism** (first described in 1943 as "extreme aloneness" by Leo Kanner) never talk, rarely smile, and play for hours with one object (such as a spinning top or a toy train). Others are diagnosed with **Asperger syndrome.** Their social interaction is impaired and they cannot be distracted from paying extreme attention to details, but they may be called "high functioning" because they are very intelligent in some ways (Dawson et al., 2007). Still other children are slow in all three areas (language, social interaction, and play) but not severely so.

Many studies confirm that "autism has a substantial genetic component" (Sutcliffe, 2008, p. 208). Indeed, there are dozens of genetic factors that make a person more likely to develop an autistic spectrum disorder. The problem may be a deficit in the brain's mirror neurons (Oberman & Ramachandran, 2007) that makes people with autism feel alien—like "an anthropologist on Mars," as Temple Grandin, an educator and writer with autism, expressed it (quoted in Sacks, 1995).

Some children with an autistic spectrum disorder show signs of it in early infancy (no social smile, for example) and continue to resist social contact. Others improve by age 3 (Chawarska et al., 2007). Still others (about one-fourth) start out developing normally and then deteriorate (MMWR, February 9, 2007). The most dramatic example of the latter pattern occurs in girls with *Rett syndrome.* Their brains develop slowly and thus are much smaller than those of other children the same age (Bienvenu, 2005).

In other children with autism, the problem may be too much neurological activity, not too little. Their heads are large, and parts of the brain (especially the limbic system) are unusually sensitive to noise, light, and other sensations (Schumann et al., 2004). Grandin described the effect of this hypersensitivity:

Every time you take the kid into Wal-Mart, he's screaming. Well, the reason for that is that the fluorescent lights are flickering and driving him crazy, the noise in there hurts his ears, the smells overpower his nose. Wal-Mart is like being inside the speaker at a rock and roll concert.

[Medscape Psychiatry and Mental Health, 2005]

Why the Increase? The number of children in the United States diagnosed with autism has increased dramatically since 1980 (Newschaffer et al., 2005). Moreover, the rates vary markedly from one state to another (see Figure 7.7). One possible explanation is twofold: The availability of special education has led to increased diagnosis, and the diagnosis itself has broadened. In Texas, the number of children with autism tripled in six years in the wealthiest school districts but did not change in poor ones, where fewer special education teachers were available (R. F. Palmer et al., 2005). This disparity in diagnosis based on SES has been confirmed by nationwide research (Liptak et al., 2008).

An organic, rather than educational, explanation for increases in autism has also been suggested. The claim is that some new teratogen is harming developing brains. Many parents suspected thimerosal, an antiseptic containing mercury, that was used in MMR (measles, mumps, rubella) immunizations. This charge has been disproved many times (Hornig et al., 2008). Thimerosal is no longer used, but the incidence of autism is rising. Many other possible chemical culprits (pesticides, cleaning chemicals, nail polish ingredients) have been suggested but have not yet been studied.

Insights for Everyone

Building on their strengths, children with special needs can become happy, successful adults. Winston Churchill became a world leader, Hans Christian Andersen a renowned storyteller, Temple Grandin a university professor. Many adults with undiagnosed ADHD find jobs in which they excel, from forest ranger to police officer, from taxi driver to CEO of a corporation. They still fidget when they must sit quietly, but only in middle childhood is everyone expected to sit at a desk for hours on end.

It may seem odd to end this chapter with a discussion of children with special needs. But remember that developmental psychopathology yields insights that enhance our understanding of all children. Throughout this chapter, you have read that normal children have problems (as I did with my allergies and loneliness), including asthma, obesity, selective attention, cultural differences, language deficits, inadequate family income, and many more.

Two themes are evident throughout this chapter. First, 7- to 11-year-olds are primed to grow and learn. Second, each child is different, with vulnerabilities as well as strengths.

PHANIE / PHOTO RESEARCHERS INC.

Precious Gifts Many children with autism are gifted artists. This boy attends a school in Montmoreau, France, that features workshops in which children with autism develop social, play, and learning skills.

KEY Points

- National and international tests of achievement reveal differences between states and nations. Culture and education interact, complicating interpretation of test results.

- The most common aptitude tests are IQ tests. The assumption that an IQ score measures general intelligence (*g*) is challenged by Robert Sternberg, Howard Gardner, and others, who believe that multiple intelligences exist.

- People with attention-deficit disorders, learning disabilities, and autistic spectrum disorders may be helped by early education, treatment, and maturation.

- Every child learns and grows in individual ways, affected by family, school, and culture as well as by developmental vulnerabilities.

RESPONSE FOR Health Workers (from page 265) Medication helps some hyperactive children, but not all. It might be useful for this child, but other forms of intervention should be tried first. Compliment the parents on their concern about their child, but refer them to an expert in early childhood for an evaluation and recommendations. Behavior-management techniques geared to the particular situation, not medication, will be the first strategy. ●

SUMMARY

A Healthy Time

1. Middle childhood is a time of steady growth and few serious illnesses. However, two health problems have reached the epidemic level: asthma and obesity. Both result from the combination of genetic and environmental contexts; both require all three levels of prevention.

2. Physical activity and outdoor play aid health in many ways, including reducing obesity and asthma. However, current environmental conditions and pollutants (from junk food to lead) make exercise less common and more hazardous.

Theories About Cognition

3. According to Piaget, children begin concrete operational thought at about age 6 or 7. Egocentrism diminishes and logic begins. School-age children can understand classification, conservation, identity, and reversibility, and they gradually master transitive inference.

4. Vygotsky stressed the social context of learning, including the specific teaching in school and home and the overall influence of culture. Mentors and students meet in the zone of proximal development.

Information Processing and the Brain

5. An information-processing approach examines each step of the thinking process, from input to output, with particular emphasis on brain functions that once were beyond the research of scientists. It is now apparent that brain development continues throughout childhood, with increasing myelination and automatization.

6. Memory improves with selective attention, as an expanded knowledge base allows much better working memory as well as long-term memory. Children become better at controlling and directing their thinking, using strategies for learning. Metacognition advances.

Learning in School

7. Nations and experts agree that education is critical during middle childhood, as children are ready to learn whatever their culture teaches. The vast majority of the world's children now attend primary school. Schools differ in what and how they teach, especially in the hidden curriculum.

8. Language learning is a crucial part of education in primary school, as children become adept at learning the formal code in the classroom and the informal code with their friends. Many children learn a second language and in the process learn a second culture.

9. The reading wars pitted advocates of phonics against advocates of the whole-language approach. Research finds that both phonological understanding and personal motivation are crucial to reading.

10. Math learned by rote and via social interaction are the two sides of the "math wars." Other controversies include which moral values are important, how big classes should be, and many other issues regarding school learning. More research is needed to understand what is most effective.

Measuring the Mind

11. IQ tests are designed to quantify intellectual aptitude. They also reflect the culture in which they were created. Achievement tests measure what a person has actually accomplished.

12. Critics contend that intelligence is actually manifested in multiple ways, which conventional IQ tests are too limited to measure. Among the multiple intelligences are creative and practical abilities, which are difficult to test.

13. International assessments are useful as comparisons, partly because few objective measures of learning are available. In the United States, the No Child Left Behind (NCLB) Act and the National Assessment of Educational Progress (NAEP) attempt to raise the standards of education, with mixed success.

14. Many children have special educational needs. One group comprises those with attention-deficit/hyperactivity disorder (ADHD), who manifest difficulty in three areas: inattention, impulsiveness, and overactivity. Medication often helps children with ADHD to settle down, but this treatment must be carefully monitored.

15. People with learning disabilities have trouble mastering a specific skill that other people learn easily. The most common learning disability during the school years is dyslexia, unusual difficulty with reading.

16. Children with autistic spectrum disorders typically show odd and delayed language ability, impaired interpersonal skills, and unusual play.

KEY TERMS

middle childhood (p. 233)
asthma (p. 234)
body mass index (BMI) (p. 236)
overweight (p. 236)
obesity (p. 236)
concrete operational thought (p. 239)
classification (p. 239)
knowledge base (p. 242)
information-processing theory (p. 242)
selective attention (p. 243)
automatization (p. 243)
reaction time (p. 243)
sensory memory (p. 244)

working memory (p. 244)
long-term memory (p. 244)
metacognition (p. 245)
metamemory (p. 245)
hidden curriculum (p. 248)
English-language learner (ELL) (p. 250)
phonics approach (p. 253)
whole-language approach (p. 254)
aptitude (p. 257)
IQ test (p. 257)
achievement test (p. 257)
Wechsler Intelligence Scale for Children (WISC) (p. 258)

Flynn effect (p. 258)
mental retardation (p. 258)
No Child Left Behind (NCLB) Act (p. 260)
National Assessment of Educational Progress (NAEP) (p. 260)
Progress in International Reading Literacy Study (PIRLS) (p. 261)
Trends in Math and Science Study (TIMSS) (p. 261)
children with special needs (p. 262)
developmental psychopathology (p. 262)

Diagnostic and Statistical Manual of Mental Disorders (DSM-IV-TR) (p. 263)
attention-deficit/hyperactivity disorder (ADHD) (p. 263)
comorbidity (p. 263)
learning disability (p. 265)
dyslexia (p. 265)
autistic spectrum disorder (p. 265)
autism (p. 266)
Asperger syndrome (p. 266)

KEY QUESTIONS

1. How does the physical growth of the school-age child compare with that of the younger child?

2. What measures to reduce obesity or asthma would benefit all children?

3. How does the development of logic help children understand the lessons they are likely to learn in school?

4. According to Vygotsky, if children never went to school, how would cognitive development occur?

5. How would an information-processing approach affect the curriculum in primary school?

6. What are the differences between language learning in early and middle childhood?

7. What are the benefits and dangers of teaching children who do not speak English in English-only classes?

8. Why are international tests of learning given, and what are some problems with such tests?

9. How might a hidden curriculum affect how well a child learns in school?

10. Why are disagreements about curriculum and method sometimes called *wars*, not merely differences of opinion? Give examples.

11. What are the benefits and misuses of aptitude and achievement tests?

12. What are the advantages and disadvantages of a child with ADHD being diagnosed before middle childhood?

13. How could an adult have a learning disability that was not spotted in childhood? What would the effects be?

14. What are the signs of autistic spectrum disorders, and why has this diagnosis increased in recent decades?

APPLICATIONS

1. Developmental psychologists believe that every teacher should be skilled at teaching children with a wide variety of needs. Does the teacher-training curriculum at your college or university reflect this goal? Give reasons for your opinions.

2. Visit a local elementary school and look for the hidden curriculum. For example, do the children line up? Why or why not, when and how? Does gender, age, ability, or talent affect the grouping of children or the selection of staff? What is the role of parents? For everything you observe, speculate about the underlying assumptions.

3. What do you remember about how you learned to read? Compare your memories with those of someone at least 10 years older and someone at least 5 years younger than you. What conclusions can you draw?

4. Internet sources vary in quality no matter what the topic, but this may be particularly true of Web sites designed for parents of children with special needs. Pick one childhood disability or disease and find several information sources on the Internet devoted to that condition. How might parents evaluate the information provided?

CHAPTER OUTLINE

MIDDLE CHILDHOOD
Psychosocial Development

T iffany, a student of mine, drove to a garage in New York City in 2007 to get a flat tire fixed.

As I pulled up, I saw a very short boy sitting at the garage door. I imagined him to be about 8 or 9 years old and wondered why he was sitting there by himself. He directed me to park, and summoned a man who looked at my tire and spoke to the boy in a language I did not understand. This little boy then lifted my car with a jack, removed all the bolts, and fixed the flat. I was in shock. When I paid the man (who was his father), I asked how long his son had been doing this. He said about three years.

[adapted from Tiffany, personal communication, March 15, 2008] ●

THE INTERNATIONAL LABOUR ORGANIZATION ESTIMATES that 218 million children throughout the world are employed, most at very low pay and some with work that destroys their health. It shocks many adults like Tiffany to learn that so many of the world's children are forced to work, in defiance of the United Nations' declaration that children have the right

to be protected from economic exploitation and from performing any work that is likely to be hazardous or to interfere with the child's education, or to be harmful to the child's health or physical, mental, spiritual, moral, or social development.

[United Nations Convention on the Rights of the Child]

Did this boy's work "interfere" with his education or harm his development? Maybe. Maybe not. Some contend that family poverty and unwise family planning underlie child labor, arguing that such deep-rooted causes mean that forbidding child labor is no solution (Basu & Pham, 1998). Others disagree, advocating international laws to stop the practice.

An understanding of child development sheds light on this issue. As with almost every aspect of middle childhood, details are crucial. All children need friends, families, and skills, but some peers are destructive, some families are harmful, and some skills should not be mastered. For the boy who changed Tiffany's tire, both sets of alternatives are possible.

This chapter explains some specifics regarding when and how a child's "physical, mental, spiritual, moral, or social development" is harmed. By the end of this

TUGELA RIDLEY / EPA / CORBIS

Caught in a Net Forced child labor, in which young bodies are exploited and young minds are neglected, is never beneficial. These boys are among the thousands who work in the fishing industry on Ghana's Lake Volta. Their impoverished parents gave them to fishermen, hoping that they would get some education and an apprenticeship in fishing. They are receiving neither; instead, they, like the fish they catch, are tangled in a net.

TABLE 8.1 AT ABOUT THIS TIME: Signs of Psychosocial Maturation Between Ages 6 and 11

Children are more likely to have specific chores to perform at home.

Children are more likely to have a weekly allowance.

Children are expected to tell time, and they have set times for various activities.

Children have more homework assignments, some over several days.

Children are less often punished physically, more often with disapproval or withdrawal of privileges.

Children try to conform to peer standards in such matters as clothing and language.

Children influence decisions about their after-school care, lessons, and activities.

Children use media (TV, computers, video games) without adult supervision.

Children are given new responsibility for younger children, pets, or, in some cultures, employment.

Children strive for more independence from parents.

---

chapter, you will know when child labor is harmful and when it is benign. We will also look at the influence of peer culture, bullying, self-esteem, poverty, divorce, and much else. We begin with the children themselves and then broaden our discussion to consider families, peers, and morality in middle childhood.

The Nature of the Child

As explained in the previous chapter, steady growth, brain maturation, and intellectual advances make middle childhood a time when children gain independence and autonomy (see Table 8.1). They acquire an "increasing ability to regulate themselves, to take responsibility, and to exercise self-control"—all strengths that make these years a time for positive growth (A. C. Huston & Ripke, 2006, p. 9).

One simple result is that school-age children can provide most of their own care. They can not only feed themselves but also make their own dinner, not only dress themselves but also pack their own suitcases for a trip, not only walk to school but also organize games during recess. They venture outdoors alone; boys in particular put some distance between themselves and home, as they engage in activities of which their parents are unaware and sometimes disapprove (Munroe & Romney, 2006). This budding independence fosters growth.

Industry and Inferiority

One characteristic of school-age children is that they "learn the skills to be increasingly autonomous and industrious" (Pagani et al., 2006, p. 133). Industrious children at this age busily and actively master whatever skills and abilities their culture values.

Think of learning to read and add—painstaking and boring efforts, with seemingly little reward. For instance, how exciting is it to slowly sound out, "Jane has a dog," or to write "3 + 4 = 7" for the hundredth time? Yet school-age children busily practice reading and math: They are intrinsically motivated to read a page, finish a worksheet, memorize a spelling word, color in a map, and so on. Similarly, they enjoy collecting, categorizing, and counting whatever they choose to accumulate—stamps, stickers, or sticks.

Celebrating Spring No matter where they live, 7- to 11-year-olds seek to understand and develop whatever skills are valued by their culture. They do so in active, industrious ways, as described in behaviorism as well as cognitive, psychoanalytic, and systems theories. This universal truth is illustrated here, as four friends in Assam, northeastern India, usher in spring with a Bihu celebration. Soon they will be given sweets and tea, which is the cultural validation of their energy, independence, and skill.

Some of their industry is applied not to skills or collections but to emotions. In Chapter 6, you learned that parents teach younger children to regulate their emotions. That continues during these years, but something else occurs as well, both at home and in school: Children themselves work on regulating their temper, shyness, honesty, and fear. They develop what is called **effortful control** in their conscious attempts to master social interactions and emotions (Kochanska & Knaack, 2003; Veenstra et al., 2008).

Effortful control does not always protect children from emotional imbalance, however. Schoolchildren are quick to feel inferior, ashamed about what they cannot do, even if their parents insist that they are wonderful. If a school focuses on only one or two of Gardner's nine intelligences (see Chapter 7), and few after-school options or reassurances from friends are available, many children judge themselves as deficient. Concerns about inferiority are evident in the schoolchild's ditty: "Nobody likes me. Everybody hates me. I think I'll go out and eat some worms." This lament has endured for generations because it captures, with humor that school-age children appreciate, the self-doubt that many of them feel.

ERIKSON ON THE SCHOOL-AGE CHILD In Erikson's fourth developmental crisis, **industry versus inferiority,** children try to master the skills that their culture values. They judge themselves as either *industrious* or *inferior*—that is, as competent or incompetent, productive or failing, winners or losers. Being productive is intrinsically joyous, and it fosters the self-control that defends against emotional problems (Bradley & Corwyn, 2005).

The tension between feeling productive and feeling useless was highlighted when Erikson described middle childhood as a time for devoted attention and perseverance in learning. The child "must forget past hopes and wishes, while his exuberant imagination is tamed and harnessed to the laws of impersonal things," becoming "ready to apply himself to given skills and tasks" (Erikson, 1963, pp. 258, 259).

FREUD ON LATENCY Sigmund Freud also stressed the child's achievements during these years. He called this period *latency,* a time when emotional drives are quiet and unconscious sexual conflicts are submerged. Latency is a "time for acquiring cognitive skills and assimilating cultural values as children expand their world to include

Yu-Gi-Oh The specifics vary tremendously—stamps, stickers, matchbooks, baseball cards, and many more—but the impulse to collect, organize, and trade certain items is characteristic of school-age children. For a few years, in south Florida and elsewhere, the coveted collector's item was Yu-Gi-Oh cards.

effortful control
The ability to regulate one's emotions and actions through effort, not simply through natural inclination.

industry versus inferiority
The fourth of Erikson's eight psychosocial crises, during which children attempt to master many skills, developing a sense of themselves as either industrious or inferior, competent or incompetent.

teachers, neighbors, peers, club leaders, and coaches. Sexual energy continues to flow, but it is channeled into social concerns" (P. H. Miller, 2002, p. 131).

Some experts complain that "middle childhood has been neglected at least since Freud relegated these years to the status of an uninteresting 'latency period'" (A. C. Huston & Ripke, 2006, p. 7). Current thinking is that, despite latency, these years are extremely important.

In one sense, at least, Freud was correct: Sexual impulses are quiet. This is true in every era and culture; even when children were betrothed before age 12 (rare today, but not unusual in earlier centuries), the young couple typically had little interaction. Everywhere, boys and girls usually choose to be with others of their own sex (Munroe & Romney, 2006). Indeed, many boys post signs that read "Girls stay out," and many girls proclaim that boys "stink" and are "stupid."

Puberty starts earlier today than it did in Freud's time (see Chapter 10), which means that latency ends earlier. The first sign of adolescence may be a 10-year-old phoning her first crush and hanging up as soon as he answers.

Self-Concept

The following self-description could have been written by many 10-year-olds:

> I'm in the fourth grade this year, and I'm pretty popular, at least with the girls. That's because I'm nice to people and can keep secrets. Mostly I am nice to my friends, although if I get in a bad mood I sometimes say something that can be a little mean. I try to control my temper, but when I don't, I'm ashamed of myself. I'm usually happy when I'm with my friends, but I get sad if there is no one to do things with.
>
> At school, I'm feeling pretty smart in certain subjects like Language Arts and Social Studies. I got As in these subjects on my last report card and was really proud of myself. But I'm feeling pretty dumb in Math and Science, especially when I see how well a lot of the other kids are doing.
>
> Even though I'm not doing well in those subjects, I still like myself as a person, because Math and Science just aren't that important to me. How I look and how popular I am are more important. I also like myself because I know my parents like me and so do other kids. That helps you like yourself.
>
> *[quoted in Harter, 1999, p. 48]*

This excerpt (from a book written by a scholar who studies development of the self-concept) captures the nature of school-age children. It includes several key concepts: *social comparison* ("especially when I see how well a lot of the other kids are doing"), *effortful control* ("I try to control my temper"), peer loyalty ("can keep secrets"), and the wish for approval ("I know my parents like me and so do other kids").

WHO KNOWS YOU BEST? The child's self-concept no longer mirrors the parents' perspective. Every developmental theory and every perceptive observer note that school-age children recognize themselves as individuals, distinct from what their parents and teachers think of them (A. C. Huston & Ripke, 2006).

One study confirming this independent outlook began by asking questions like, "Who knows best what you are thinking? . . . how tired you are? . . . your favorite foods?" (Burton & Mitchell, 2003). Unlike 3-year-olds—who might answer, "Mommy," and who rely on a parent to tell them, "Oh, you are tired, it's time for your nap"—school-age children become increasingly sure of their own minds. In this study, few (13 percent) of the 5-year-olds but most (73 percent) of the 10-year-olds thought that they knew themselves better than their parents or teachers did (Burton & Mitchell, 2003).

Because of concrete operational thinking, children engage in **social comparison,** judging themselves on the basis of what they see in other people. They become much

social comparison
The tendency to assess one's abilities, achievements, social status, and other attributes by measuring them against those of other people, especially one's peers.

more socially aware; thus, it becomes urgent for them to figure out if they are worse or better than their peers. Ideally, social comparison helps children value the abilities they have and abandon the imaginary, rosy self-evaluation of preschoolers.

However, increases in self-understanding and social awareness come at a price. Self-criticism and self-consciousness tend to rise from ages 6 to 12, and self-esteem dips (Merrell & Gimpel, 1998), especially for children who live with unusual stresses such as an abusive or alcoholic parent (Luthar & Zelazo, 2003). According to ratings by their parents, children's confidence plummets and their inhibition rises from about 18 months of age to 9 years (Janson & Mathiesen, 2008; see Figure 8.1).

Furthermore, as materialism rises toward the end of middle childhood, self-esteem dips (Chaplin & John, 2007). Babies and toddlers are unaware of the latest fashions: Their parents can dress them in faded hand-me-downs and they are quite happy. This is not true for schoolchildren, who notice styles and brands. Insecure 10-year-olds are especially likely to want the latest shoes, cell phones, and video games.

Parents' Ratings of Their Children's Levels of Confidence and Inhibition

Source: Janson & Mathiesen, 2008.

FIGURE 8.1 More Hesitant, Less Outgoing Although some continuity over time was apparent for each child, the overall trend was for children to become less sure of themselves and more shy with others. This particular study is part of an intensive longitudinal project in Norway, but the trends seem universal.

COMPLICATIONS OF UNREALISTIC SELF-ESTEEM Self-esteem is tricky (Heine, 2007). If it is unrealistically high, children may not realize they need to modify their impulses and emotions; thus, effortful control may decline and lower achievement may result (Baumeister et al., 2003). The same consequences may occur if a child is anxious and self-esteem is unrealistically low (Pomerantz & Rudolph, 2003).

Unrealistically high or low self-esteem also correlates with aggression (Sandstrom & Herlan, 2007). When children appreciate both themselves and other children (i.e., when self and peers both fare well in social comparisons), they tend to have more friends and to be prosocial, able to defend a friend if the need arises. In contrast, when children like themselves but not their peers, they are likely to have fewer friends, to show more aggression, and to be lonelier (Salmivalli et al., 2005).

In short, academic and social competence are aided by realistic self-evaluation, not by unrealistically high self-esteem (Baumeister et al., 2003). Ideally, as children begin to understand that they are simultaneously similar to and different from their peers, they learn to accept themselves. As one expert explains, "Children develop feelings of self-esteem, competence, and individuality during middle childhood as they begin comparing themselves with peers" (Ripke et al., 2006, p. 261).

Programs that teach anxious children to confide in friends as well as to understand their own emotions improve their self-concept; such programs have been successful not only in the United States but also in many other cultures (Siu, 2007). As detailed in Chapter 7, after-school activities, particularly team sports, can provide a foundation for friendship and realistic self-esteem, aiding self-concept and academic achievement (P. Morris & Kalil, 2006).

SELF-ESTEEM AS A SOCIAL CONSTRUCTION Cultural differences make self-esteem even more complex. Currently in the United States, high self-esteem is considered a positive trait. Probably because of that, U.S. college students think better of themselves than did the students of 30 years ago (Twenge & Campbell, 2001).

However, the importance of self-esteem may be a social construction, an idea that is held by many Americans who believe that high self-esteem improves a child's achievement. This construction is not universally held (Yamaguchi et al., 2007). For example, Australians say that "tall poppies" are cut down; the Japanese discourage social comparison aimed at making oneself feel superior (Toyama, 2001); and the people of Angola value modest children more than proud ones (Guest, 2007). As mentioned in the previous chapter, although Chinese children often excel at mathematics, only 1 percent said they were "very satisfied" with their performance in that subject (T. D. Snyder et al., 2004).

Self-esteem usually protects the fragile self-concepts of 6- to-11-year-olds, but it can be too high, too low, or culturally unacceptable. As with all social constructions, the social context makes a difference.

Resilience and Stress

Infants and young children depend on their immediate families for food, learning, and life itself. By school age, however, some children escape destructive family influences and find their own niche in the larger world. As one review explains, "Experiences in middle childhood can sustain, magnify or reverse the advantages or disadvantages children acquire in the preschool years" (A. C. Huston & Ripke, 2006, p. 2). Schoolchildren who seem unscathed by their troubled, stressful homes have been called *resilient* or even *invincible*.

resilience
The capacity to adapt well despite significant adversity and to overcome serious stress.

Resilience has been defined as "a dynamic process encompassing positive adaptation within the context of significant adversity" (Luthar et al., 2000, p. 543). Note three parts of this definition:

1. Resilience is *dynamic,* not a stable trait, which means a given person may be resilient at some periods but not at others. Resilience is more evident in middle childhood than earlier.

2. Resilience is a *positive adaptation* to stress. For example, if rejection by a parent leads a child to establish a closer relationship with another adult, perhaps a grandparent or the parent of a neighbor child, that child is resilient.

3. Adversity must be *significant*. Some adversities are comparatively minor (large class size, nearsightedness) and some are major (victimization, neglect). Resilient children overcome conditions that overwhelm many of their peers.

Researchers use the term *resilience* with great caution (see Table 8.2). As dynamic-systems theory reminds us, although some children seem to cope better than others, no one is impervious to the social context (Jenson & Fraser, 2006; Luthar et al., 2003). Some children with abusive or mentally ill parents or other sources of severe stress seem unaffected by their situations, but appearances may be deceiving.

CUMULATIVE STRESS Stresses accumulate. Many minor stresses (or *daily hassles*) can become major if they are ongoing. Almost every child can withstand one traumatic event, but several ongoing stresses make coping difficult (Jaffee et al., 2007). We will use the word *resilient* here, which does not actually mean that some children are impervious to stress; rather, resilient children cope surprisingly well.

An example comes from research on children living in a fly zone, who frequently hear the roar of airplanes overhead. If a child lives near an airport, he or she is subjected to the

TABLE 8.2 Dominant Ideas About Challenges and Coping in Children, 1965–Present

1965	All children have the same needs for healthy development.
1970	Some conditions or circumstances—such as "absent father," "teenage mother," "working mom," and "day care"—are harmful for every child.
1975	All children are *not* the same. Some children are resilient, coping easily with stressors that cause harm in other children.
1980	Nothing inevitably causes harm. Indeed, both maternal employment and preschool education, once thought to be risk factors, usually benefit children.
1985	Factors beyond the family, both in the child (low birthweight, prenatal alcohol exposure, aggressive temperament) and in the community (poverty, violence), are very risky for the child.
1990	Risk–benefit analysis finds that some children seem to be "invulnerable" to, or even to benefit from, circumstances that destroy others. (Some do well in school despite extreme poverty, for example.)
1995	No child is invincibly resilient. Risks are always harmful—if not in educational achievement, then in emotions.
2000	Risk–benefit analysis involves the interplay among all three domains (biosocial, cognitive, and psychosocial), including factors within the child (genes, intelligence, temperament), the family (function as well as structure), and the community (including neighborhood, school, church, and culture). Over the long term, most people overcome problems, but the problems are real.
2009	The focus is on strengths, not risks. Assets in the child (intelligence, personality), the family (secure attachment, warmth), the community (good schools, after-school programs), and the nation (income support, health care) must be nurtured.

Sources: Jenson & Fraser, 2006; Luthar, 2003; Luthar et al., 2000; Maton et al., 2004; McWhinnie et al., 2008.

stress of hearing that noise several times a day, but just for a minute at a time. A study of 2,844 children living near three airports found that the reading ability of some, but not all, was impaired. When a major airport shut down, average reading scores rose (Stansfeld et al., 2005).

Another example of the impact of cumulative stress comes from research on New Orleans children after Hurricane Katrina. Many experienced stress from several sources over the next several years (see Figure 8.2). Their rate of psychological problems was much higher than it had been before the hurricane (see Viadero, 2007).

A child's daily routines can be stressful, although details determine whether it is burdensome. For example, a mother's depression may have little effect on her child if an emotionally stable and available father buffers her influence; if the child's main caregiver is an energetic, optimistic grandmother; or if the mother herself functions well when she is with the child.

A warm and supportive adult–child relationship enables resilience (Huesmann et al., 2006). However, a mother's depression becomes a severe stress if no other adults are involved and the child must, day after day, wake up and prepare for school without help, supervise and discipline younger siblings, and keep friends at a distance.

Major stresses accumulate as well. For instance, the death of a beloved grandparent is a major stress, although the particular signs of stress vary with specifics. One 7-year-old boy seemed to take his grandmother's death in stride, even though two other grandparents (less involved with the boy) had died within the past two years. But he was unable to bounce back when his dog suddenly died. He refused, at first, to go back to school (K. R. Kaufman & Kaufman, 2006). It is not unusual for a child to seem resilient until some new event occurs and reveals the toll that has been taken by earlier demands on coping skills.

GATHERING STRENGTHS Some recent research has focused on strengths within the child and community that together enable a child to thrive in difficult circumstances. One such strength is the child's own working concept. In the example of the depressed mother above, a child might conclude that all the family problems are his or her own fault (a heavy burden) or, alternatively, that this difficult home life is only a temporary strain that will teach a potentially valuable lesson for the future.

Another key aspect of resilience is whether or not a stressed child can develop friends, activities, and skills. For some children, such competencies allow them to blossom once they are old enough to become less dependent on their parents.

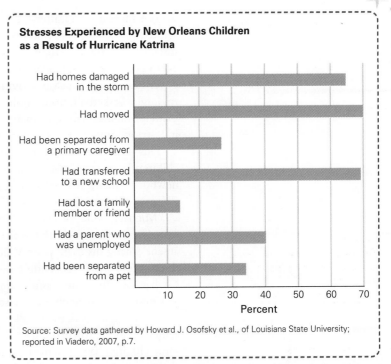

Stresses Experienced by New Orleans Children as a Result of Hurricane Katrina

(Bar chart, x-axis: Percent, from 10 to 70)

- Had homes damaged in the storm
- Had moved
- Had been separated from a primary caregiver
- Had transferred to a new school
- Had lost a family member or friend
- Had a parent who was unemployed
- Had been separated from a pet

Source: Survey data gathered by Howard J. Osofsky et al., of Louisiana State University; reported in Viadero, 2007, p.7.

FIGURE 8.2 Enough Stress for a Lifetime Many children experienced more than one kind of severe stress during Hurricane Katrina and its aftermath. That disaster inflicted more stress on the children of New Orleans than most adults ever experience in their lifetime, and its long-term impact will likely be dramatic.

Healing Time Children who survived Hurricane Katrina participate in a fire drill at their new charter school, Lafayette Academy in New Orleans. The resumption of school routines helped them overcome the stress they had experienced in the chaos of the deadly storm.

TIM MUELLER / THE NEW YORK TIMES / REDUX

School successes and after-school activities can be a lifeline. If parents cut off that outlet (by keeping the child home to babysit instead of allowing after-school play, for instance), healthy development will be blocked.

To encourage resilience, programs sponsored by the community, churches, and the government can develop activities that welcome all children—from 4-H clubs to midnight basketball, from choir to Little League. Then each child can choose from many possibilities, finding an area of competence and developing a self-concept as an industrious, not an inferior, person.

This possibility was demonstrated in a 40-year study in Hawaii that began with children born into poverty, often to parents who were alcoholic or mentally ill. As newborns, many had serious disabilities; experts predicted difficult lives for them (Werner & Smith, 2001).

"Michael," one of the children in the Hawaiian study, was born preterm to teenage parents, weighing less than 5 pounds. His family was poor, and his father was absent during his early years. When he was 8, Michael's mother abandoned him and three younger siblings, sending the four children to their father's parents. Surprisingly, Michael became a successful, happy, loving adult (Werner, 1979).

Other Hawaiian children also defied predictions. About one-third who were high-risk babies had, by middle childhood, found ways to cope with family stresses: achieving in school, making good friends, and finding adult mentors. By adolescence, some children had distanced themselves from their parents. As adults, they left family problems behind (many moved far away) and established their own healthy relationships (Werner & Smith, 1992, 2001).

For many of these children, education was an escape—first in primary school, then in high school, then in community college. An easygoing temperament and a high IQ also helped these and other troubled children (Curtis & Cicchetti, 2003). But being academically gifted is not essential for resilience. In the Hawaii study, "a realistic goal orientation, persistence, and 'learned creativity' enabled . . . a remarkable degree of personal, social, and occupational success," even for children with learning disabilities (Werner & Smith, 2001, p. 140).

SOCIAL SUPPORT AND RELIGIOUS FAITH A major factor that strengthens a child's ability to deal with stress is social support. Compared with the narrow, homebound lives of younger children, the expanding social world of school-age children opens up new possibilities (P. Morris & Kalil, 2006). A network of supportive relatives is a better buffer than having only one close parent (Y. Jackson & Warren, 2000). Grandparents, teachers, unrelated adults, peers, and even pets can help children cope with stress (B. K. Bryant & Donnellan, 2007).

Grandmother Knows Best About 20,000 grandmothers in Connecticut are caregivers for their grandchildren. This 15-year-old boy and his 17-year-old sister came to live with their grandmother in New Haven after their mother died several years ago. This type of family can help children cope with stress, especially when the grandmother is relatively young and has her own house, as is the case here.

B CHILD / AP PHOTO

Community institutions, including churches and libraries, can also be crucial sources of social support. One study concludes:

> When children attempt to seek out experiences that will help them overcome adversity, it is critical that resources, in the form of supportive adults or learning opportunities, be made available to them so that their own self-righting potential can be fulfilled.
>
> *[Kim-Cohen et al., 2004, p. 664]*

One experience that can help overcome adversity is found in the way some children gain social support from adults (both clergy and lay) in their faith community. Research shows that church involvement particularly helps African American children in communities where social stresses and racial prejudice abound (Akiba & García-

Coll, 2004). As the authors of one study explain, "The influences of religious importance and participation . . . are mediated through trusting interaction with adults, friends and parents who share similar views" (P. E. King & Furrow, 2004, p. 709).

The religious convictions of children are very diverse (Levesque, 2002); no particular set of beliefs seems essential. However, faith itself is psychologically protective; it helps children reinterpret their negative experiences.

Parents often provide religious guidance, but by middle childhood some children pray and attend religious services more often than their parents do. Adults may not realize that many children (by age 8 but not at age 4) believe that prayer is communication; children expect that prayer will make them feel better, especially when they are sad or angry (see Figure 8.3) (Bamford & Lagattuta, 2007).

Thus, religious beliefs become increasingly useful as school-age children cope with their problems. In accord with their self-righting impulses, children try to develop competencies. As two experts explain:

> Successful children remind us that children grow up in multiple contexts—in families, schools, peer groups, baseball teams, religious organizations, and many other groups—and each context is a potential source of protective factors as well as risks. These children demonstrate that children are protected not only by the self-righting nature of development, but also by the actions of adults, by their own actions, by the nurturing of their assets, by opportunities to succeed, and by the experience of success. The behavior of adults often plays a critical role in children's risks, resources, opportunities, and resilience.
>
> *[A. S. Masten & Coatsworth, 1998, p. 216]*

BILL ARON / PHOTOEDIT, INC.

Become Like a Child Although the particulars vary a great deal, school-age children's impulses toward industriousness, stability, and dedication place them among the most devout members of every religious faith.

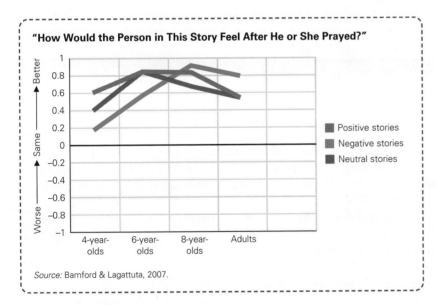

"How Would the Person in This Story Feel After He or She Prayed?"

Legend:
- Positive stories
- Negative stories
- Neutral stories

x-axis: 4-year-olds, 6-year-olds, 8-year-olds, Adults
y-axis: Worse (−1) / Same (0) / Better (1)

Source: Bamford & Lagattuta, 2007.

FIGURE 8.3 Help Me, God
The numbers on this graph are the averages when people were asked how characters in various scenarios would feel after praying. There were only three choices: better (= 1), same (= 0), or worse (= −1). As you can see, virtually all the 8-year-olds thought prayer would make a person feel better.

KEY Points

- According to Erikson, the crisis of industry versus inferiority allows children to master new skills and to absorb their culture's values, but it also generates self-doubt.

- School-age children develop a more realistic self-concept than younger children.

- Some children cope with difficult circumstances by becoming more independent, using school and after-school achievements, supportive adults, and religious beliefs to relieve their stress.

Families and Children

No one doubts that genes influence temperament and ability, that peers are vital, and that schools and cultures affect how children develop. Many people believe that parents also make a decided difference, but on this last belief some developmental researchers had doubts. They noted that genes, peers, and communities each make a major contribution to the child's habits, values, and skills. This allowed little room for child-rearing practices to have significant influence, especially after infancy (J. R. Harris, 1998, 2002; B. D. McLeod et al., 2007; T. G. O'Connor, 2002).

To measure whether parents influence children, researchers compare children of varying degrees of genetic similarity (monozygotic and dizygotic twins, full siblings, stepsiblings, adopted children) who are raised in the same or different homes (Reiss et al., 2000). The correlation among traits, genes, and environment is used to calculate how much of a trait is genetic and to estimate how much of the remaining, environmental portion comes from the parents (Canli, 2006; Lykken, 2006; Plomin et al., 2002; L. Wright, 1999).

Shared and Nonshared Environments

Analysis of the research finds that genes affect half or more of the variance for almost every trait, from political beliefs to emotional reactions. The data also show that the influence of *shared environment* (e.g., children raised by the same parents in the same home) shrinks with age, while the effect of *nonshared environment* (e.g., friends or schools) increases.

Not surprisingly, nonshared factors are increasingly significant in adulthood, when brothers and sisters establish their own lives. However, careful longitudinal research has revealed two unexpected findings:

1. Genetic influences persist lifelong and are more evident in adulthood than in infancy.

2. Nonshared environmental factors—particularly peers—are already more influential than are shared ones during middle childhood.

Adopted children seem powerfully influenced by their biological parents' genes. By middle childhood, their personality traits and intellectual abilities differ substantially from those of their nongenetic siblings raised in the same household (Wadsworth et al., 2006).

At first, these findings shocked some developmentalists, who suddenly wondered whether parents' actions were as influential as the traditionalists among them had thought. More recent studies, however, reassert the power of parents (Maccoby, 2000; Bornstein, 2006).

It is now apparent that the earlier analysis of shared and nonshared influences was correct but that the underlying assumption was wrong. Children raised in the same households by the same parents do *not* necessarily share the same environment. If the family moves, if parents divorce, or if someone loses a job, every family member is affected—but each is affected differently. The impact depends on age and gender.

In addition, many other influences—choice of school, neighborhood, or after-school activities—are the direct result of parental decisions but are not shared by siblings, partly because family income and community opportunities vary from year to year, preventing parents from making the same choices for each child (Simpkins et al., 2006). Thus, the fact that nonshared environment is powerful does not prove that parents have little impact. Instead, it indicates that parental impact varies from one child to another. Beyond structural differences, it is clear that most parents respond to each of their children differently (Suitor et al., 2008). Even identical twins can experience different family environments, as the following makes clear.

● FOR DEEPER REFLECTION Why would people want to believe that parenting is the crucial influence on children's behavior?

A VIEW FROM SCIENCE

"I Always Dressed One in Blue Stuff . . ."

An expert team of scientists compared 1,000 sets of monozygotic twins reared by their biological parents (Caspi et al., 2004). The team measured each child's temperament by asking the mothers and teachers to fill out a detailed, standardized checklist. They also assessed every mother's attitude toward each child. These ranged from very positive ("my ray of sunshine") to very negative ("I wish I never had her. . . . She's a cow, I hate her") (quoted in Caspi et al., 2004, p. 153).

Many mothers described temperamental differences between their twins, assuming these were innate. The mothers did not realize that their own actions may have created distinct personalities. For example, one mother spoke of her identical daughters:

> Susan can be very sweet. She loves babies . . . she can be insecure . . . she flutters and dances around. . . . There's not much between her ears. . . . She's exceptionally vain, more so than Ann. Ann loves any game involving a ball, very sporty, climbs trees, very much a tomboy. One is a serious tomboy and one's a serious girlie girl. Even when they were babies I always dressed one in blue stuff and one in pink stuff.

> *[quoted in Caspi et al., 2004, p. 156]*

Some mothers were much more cold and rejecting toward one twin than toward the other:

> He was in the hospital and everyone was all "poor Jeff, poor Jeff'" and I started thinking, "Well, what about me? I'm the one's just had twins. I'm the one's going through this, he's a seven-week-old baby and doesn't know a thing about it." . . . I sort of detached and plowed my emotions into Mike.

> *[quoted in Caspi et al., 2004, p. 156]*

After she was divorced, this mother blamed Jeff for favoring his father: "Jeff would do anything for Don but he wouldn't for me, and no matter what I did for either of them it wouldn't be right" (p. 157). She said Mike was much more lovable.

The researchers controlled for genes, gender, age, and personality differences in kindergarten (by measuring, among other things, antisocial behavior as indicated by the children's kindergarten teachers). They found that twins whose mothers were more negative toward them tended to *become* more antisocial than their co-twin. The rejected twins were found to be more likely to fight, steal, and hurt others at age 7 than at age 5 after all background factors were taken into account.

Mothers' attitudes and moods are especially influential. This is not to deny that many other *nonshared* factors—peers, teachers, and so on—are important. But the View from Science (above) confirms the popular belief: Parents matter. The assumption that parents and a home provide a shared environment for all their children is false. Parents often believe that they treat all their children the same, having no favorites, but objective observers and the children themselves often disagree (Suitor et al., 2008). As anyone with a brother or sister can attest, each sibling experiences a unique family.

ESPECIALLY FOR Scientists How would you determine whether or not parents treat all their children the same way? (see response, page 282) →

Family Function

The way a family works and cares for its members is called **family function.** The most important family function is to provide a safe haven of love and encouragement for every family member. Beyond that, people of various ages have special needs from their families: Infants need frequent caregiving and social interaction; teenagers need freedom and guidance; adults need peace and privacy; the aged need respect and appreciation. What do children in middle childhood need?

Children thrive if families function for them in five ways:

1. *Provide basic necessities.* Children aged 6 to 11 can eat, dress, wash, and sleep without help, but someone must provide food, clothing, and shelter.

2. *Encourage learning.* School-age children must master academic and social skills. Families can support and guide their education, via parent–teacher communication, homework help, trips to museums, and so on.

family function
The way a family works to meet the needs of its members. Children need families to provide basic material necessities, to encourage learning, to help them develop self-respect, to nurture friendships, and to foster harmony and stability.

KATHY MCLAUGHLIN /THE IMAGE WORKS

Meeting Her Need for Fit and Fashion A 10-year-old's rapidly growing feet frequently need new shoes, and peer pressure favors certain styles of footwear. Here, Rebekah's sisters wait and watch as their mother tries to find a boot that fits her and is fashionable.

OBSERVATION QUIZ

Why isn't a salesperson helping this family find boots? And, instead of shopping for boots for Rebekah in cold weather, why didn't the mother buy her a pair the previous spring, when they were on sale? (see answer, page 285) →

RESPONSE FOR Scientists (from page 281) Proof is very difficult when human interaction is the subject of investigation, since random assignment is impossible. Ideally, researchers would find identical twins being raised together and would then observe the parents' behavior over the years. ●

family structure
The legal and genetic relationships among relatives living in the same home; includes nuclear family, extended family, stepfamily, and so on.

nuclear family
A family that consists of a father, a mother, and their biological children under age 18.

3. *Instill self-respect.* As they become cognitively mature, school-age children are self-critical and socially aware. Families help them feel competent and capable.

4. *Nurture peer relationships.* School-age children need friends. Families can provide the time and opportunity to form friendships by arranging play dates and other social activities for them.

5. *Ensure harmony and stability.* School-age children need protective and predictable family routines; they are troubled by conflict and change.

Thus, families provide material and cognitive resources as well as emotional and social support. No family always functions perfectly, but some dysfunctions are worse at particular periods of the life span than others. For instance, divorce is always hard on everyone, but it is especially hard on children about to enter kindergarten or middle school because those children are already experiencing major transitions. The research finds that divorce can become too much to handle simultaneously with puberty and the start of middle school, an example of the stress accumulation described earlier. It is also true that some children are more affected by lack of harmony and stability in middle childhood because continuity is cherished during the concrete operational years.

Family Structure

Family structure refers to the legal and genetic connections among related people. When people refer to relatives "by marriage" (in-laws) and relatives "by blood," they are referring to family structure. Table 8.3 briefly describes common family structures, with specific percentages estimated for families with school-age children in the United States.

HOUSEHOLDS It is important to understand that a family, regardless of its structure, is not necessarily a household, and vice versa. As defined by the U.S. Bureau of the Census, a *household* is composed of people who live together in the same home. Most households consist of two or more people who are related to one another, but one person living alone can be a household, as can nonrelatives living together. In the

TABLE 8.3 Common Family Structures (with percentages of U.S. children aged 6–11 in each family type)

Two-Parent Families (67%)

Most human families have two parents. These families are of several kinds.

1. **Nuclear family** (56%) Named after the nucleus (the tightly connected core particles of an atom), the nuclear family consists of a husband and wife and their biological offspring. About half of all families with children are nuclear.

2. **Stepparent family** (9%) Divorced fathers (Stewart et al., 2003) are particularly likely to remarry. Usually his children from a previous marriage do not live with him, but if they do, they are in a stepparent family. Divorced mothers are less likely to remarry, but when they do, the children often live with her and their stepfather. Many children spend some time in a stepparent family, but relatively few spend their entire childhood in such families.
   Blended family A stepparent family that includes children born to several families, such as the biological children from the spouses' previous marriages and the biological children of the new couple. This type of family is a particularly difficult structure for school-age children.

3. **Adoptive family** (2%) Although as many as one-third of infertile married couples adopt children, fewer adoptable children are available than in earlier decades, which means that most adoptive families have only one or two children. A single parent is sometimes an adoptive parent, but this is unusual.

4. **Polygamous family** (0%) In some nations, it is common for one man to have several wives, each bearing his children.

One-Parent Families (28%)

One-parent families are increasingly common, but they tend to have fewer children than two-parent families.

1. **Single mother, never married** (10%) Many babies (about one-third of all U.S. newborns) are born to unmarried mothers, but most of these mothers intend to marry someday (K. Musick, 2002). Many of them do get married, either to their baby's father or to someone else. By school age, their children are often in two-parent families.

2. **Single mother—divorced, separated, or widowed** (13%) Although many marriages end in divorce (almost half in the United States, less in other nations), many divorcing couples have no children and many others remarry. Thus, only 13 percent of school-age children live with single, formerly married mothers.

3. **Single father, divorced or never married** (5%) About one in five divorced or unmarried fathers has physical custody of the children. This structure is the most rapidly increasing one in the United States, especially among divorced fathers who were actively involved in child rearing when they were married.

Other Family Types (5%)

Some children live in special versions of one- or two-parent families.

1. **Extended family** Many children live with a grandparent or other relatives as well as with one or both of their parents.

2. **Grandparents alone** For some school-age children, their one or two "parents" are their grandparents, because the biological parents are dead or otherwise unable to live with them. This family type is increasing, especially in Africa, where an epidemic of AIDS is killing many parents.

3. **Homosexual family** Some school-age children live in a homosexual family, usually when a custodial parent has a homosexual partner. Less often, a homosexual couple adopts children or a lesbian has a child. Varying laws and norms determine whether these are one- or two-parent families.

4. **Foster family** This family type is usually considered temporary, and the children are categorized by their original family structure. Otherwise, they are in one- or two-parent families depending on the structure of their foster family.

Source: Percentages are estimated from data in U.S. Bureau of the Census, 2007.

United States in 2005, 26 percent of households were single-person households and 6 percent were nonrelative households.

A *family household* includes a least one parent and at least one child under age 18. This structure accounts for about two-thirds of the households in the United States. In this chapter, we focus on a subset of family households—those that include a school-age child (almost one-third of all U.S. households; see Figure 8.4).

TWO-PARENT FAMILIES More than half of all school-age children live in two-parent homes as part of a **nuclear family** (a married couple and their biological offspring). Internationally, nuclear families are often headed by couples who live together but are not legally wed; instead, they are said to be *cohabiting*. Depending partly on local customs, such couples may be considered married.

The frequency of cohabitation varies by culture. For school-age children, the crucial factor is not the wedding certificate but the reality—whether or not they live with two parents who are committed to each other and to them. Several other types of households are usually counted in the two-parent category—adoptive parents, grandparents who raise children without parents, and biological parents married to stepparents.

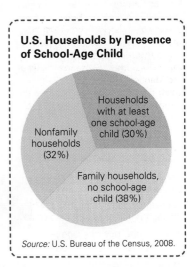

U.S. Households by Presence of School-Age Child

Households with at least one school-age child (30%)

Nonfamily households (32%)

Family households, no school-age child (38%)

Source: U.S. Bureau of the Census, 2008.

FIGURE 8.4 Family and Nonfamily Households Of the 68 percent of U.S. households that consist of families, a large proportion include one or more school-age children.

Nuclear Families The nuclear family has many advantages for children. Often people who marry and stay married have personal and financial strengths that also make them better parents. They tend to be wealthier, better educated, healthier, more flexible, and less hostile—even before marriage. Their personal assets, quite apart from the marriage, help the children.

Family Time Growing up in a nuclear family contributes to children's emotional regulation and sense of stability.

Furthermore, biological parents tend to be dedicated to their offspring, recognizing in the children something of their own characteristics. This dedication means that children growing up in nuclear families are likely to have someone to remind them to brush their teeth, to read to them at bedtime, to check their homework, and to plan for their college education.

Similar advantages occur, on average, for children who are adopted. As a result of parental dedication, adopted children tend to fare well in middle childhood. They are likely to have adequate self-esteem even when their adoptive parents are of another ethnicity (Juffer & van IJzendoorn, 2007).

A Texas Family Two-year-old Jackson's adoptive parents have been in a committed relationship for 13 years. Their home is in Dallas, where gay couples can adopt but cannot marry.

Families Headed by Gay Men or Lesbian Women Committed gay and lesbian couples make up less than 1 percent of all households in the United States. Many (exact numbers are unknown) have children, either because one of the partners was formerly married to a person of the other sex or because the couple has had a child via assisted reproduction or adoption.

The homosexual family seems to have strengths and weaknesses similar to those of the heterosexual family (Herek, 2006). By adolescence, children of homosexual parents have the same romantic impulses (usually heterosexual), school achievements, and psychosocial difficulties as children of heterosexual couples do (Wainright et al., 2004). Regardless of family type, children are more strongly affected by the quality of their relationships with their parents than by their parents' sexual interactions, the family structure, or the household status (Wainright & Patterson, 2008).

Stepfamilies Some stepfamilies are formed when a childless man or woman marries someone with children from another relationship. In this case, the success of the stepparent–stepchild relationship depends on the new adult finding a role that is not as intimate as that of the biological parents but that allows some involvement with the children. This is especially likely if the children are young (under age 3) and especially difficult if the children are teenagers. In middle childhood, much depends on the temperament of those involved.

A Comfortable Combination The blended family—husband, wife, and children from both spouses' previous marriages—often breeds resentment, depression, and rebellion in the children. That is apparently not the case for the family shown here, which provides cheerful evidence that any family structure is capable of functioning well.

A more complicated stepfamily structure is the **blended family,** in which both members of a newly married couple have offspring from earlier relationships. Blended families are often categorized in statistics as nuclear families, and they have a major asset of such families: They tend to be wealthier than single-parent families.

However, older children leave and new babies arrive more often in blended families than in nuclear families, and second marriages dissolve more often than do first marriages (Teachman, 2008a). The likelihood that children will thrive in blended families depends largely on the adults' economic and emotional security. Blended families are not necessarily better for children than are single-parent families, since emotional instability and added stress may outweigh the financial benefits.

SINGLE-PARENT FAMILIES In the United States, more than one-fourth (28 percent) of all school-age children live in a **single-parent family,** with one parent and no other adults. This is the dominant family structure among African Americans and in some other ethnic communities. Many children of all backgrounds spend some time in a single-parent family because of divorce or the death of a parent.

For many reasons, children in single-mother families "are at greatest risk," faring worse in school and in adult life than most other children (M. J. Carlson & Corcoran, 2001, p. 789). These households are often low-income and unstable; single-mother households move more often and add new adults more often than do other family types (Raley & Wildsmith, 2004).

Single-father families tend to have a slightly higher income, and single fathers tend to be slightly older than single mothers; both those characteristics help family functioning. However, single fathers as well as single mothers fill many roles—parent, wage earner, daughter or son (single parents are often dependent on their own parents), and lover (many single parents have new romantic relationships). Especially if they are the sole caregivers for several children, their many roles make it impossible to give each child ample attention.

MANY RELATIVES AT HOME The two-parent and single-parent family structures are sometimes contrasted with the **extended family,** in which children live not only with their parents but also with other relatives (usually grandparents, but often aunts, uncles, and cousins). Extended families are more common among low-income households, both in developed nations and in developing ones (where more families are poor). Expenses and responsibilities are more easily shared when many relatives live together. It usually benefits the children to have grandparents who have an ongoing relationship with them, as is often the case in extended families.

Distinctions among family types (i.e., between one-parent, two-parent, and extended families) are not as clear-cut as they might seem. Most households have close connections with other relatives who live nearby, share meals, provide emotional and financial support, and otherwise function as an extended family. In developing nations especially, many extended families actually have private living areas within the home for each couple and their children, as occurs in nuclear families (Georgas et al., 2006).

In some nations, the **polygamous family,** in which one man has two or more wives, is the family type for between 10 and 30 percent of the children. Overall, children do not fare as well in such families, primarily because income and fatherly attention per child is reduced (Omariba & Boyle, 2007). Polygamy is not legal in the United States (although it still sometimes occurs); therefore, reliable incidence data, or outcomes, are not published. Regardless of variations in laws or customs, however, the two-parent family that has frequent contact with other relatives is the most common structure worldwide (Georgas et al., 2006).

CULTURAL DIFFERENCES IN FAMILY STRUCTURE Every family type is affected by the culture within the community (Heuveline & Timberlake, 2004). For example, many French parents are not married, but couples share responsibilities and separate less often than do married adults in the United States. Thus, the cohabiting structure functions well for French children. However, in the United States, cohabiting couples split up more than married couples do. As a result, the cohabiting structure, on average, functions less well for U.S. schoolchildren (S. L. Brown, 2004).

blended family
A stepparent family that includes children born to several families, such as the biological children from the spouses' previous marriages and the biological children of the new couple.

single-parent family
A family that consists of only one parent and his or her children under age 18.

ESPECIALLY FOR Single Parents
You have heard that children raised in one-parent families will have difficulty in establishing intimate relationships as adolescents and adults. What can you do about this possibility?
(see response, page 287) →

extended family
A family consisting of parents, their children, and other relatives living in one household.

polygamous family
A family consisting of one man, several wives, and the biological children of the man and his wives.

ANSWER TO OBSERVATION QUIZ
(from page 282) The stacks of shoeboxes indicate that this is a discount store, which has no salespeople on the floor but is a good place for a mother of three to shop for boots. And if Rebekah had gotten new boots last spring, they probably wouldn't fit her now. ●

The effect of marriage and divorce on children's well-being also varies by ethnic group. In the United States, single parenthood is much more common, and more readily accepted, among African Americans than among other ethnic groups. As a result, there is less social stigma and more help from other relatives and friends of African American single parents than is the case in other groups (Cain & Combs-Orme, 2005; R. D. Taylor et al., 2008).

Compared with married couples in some other American ethnic groups, Hispanic and Asian American couples are less likely to divorce, and the husbands are typically quite concerned about their children's well-being. Children benefit from both of these factors.

However, if divorce does occur within Hispanic and Asian American families, the children may be more vulnerable than children of divorce in European American or African American families. If they have behavior problems, the father's involvement is less likely to be helpful in Hispanic and Asian families than in European or African American ones (E. Pan & Farrell, 2006).

Moreover, divorced Hispanic American fathers are less likely to stay involved with their children than are divorced fathers in other ethnic groups (V. King et al., 2004), and Asian American fathers are less likely to seek custody of the children. Single fathers in those two groups are relatively uncommon. In the United States, only 5 percent of Hispanic families and 3 percent of Asian families are headed by a single father (see Figure 8.5).

Among college students in the United States, children of divorced parents are more likely to want a close relationship with their fathers, but are less likely to have it, than students whose fathers are married to their mothers. According to one study, this seems to be true for more African Americans than Asian Americans (S. J. Schwartz & Finley, 2005). This research is tantalizing, but more is needed before we can draw conclusions about ethnicity, fathers, and divorce.

It is also important to remember that diverse family patterns exist within each ethnic group. Cuban families are different in many respects from Puerto Rican families, and Chinese families are unlike Cambodian families.

Furthermore, in any family structure, some children develop well and others do not. To learn how a family is affecting a child's development, it is "not enough to know that an individual lives in a particular family structure without also knowing what takes place within that structure" (Lansford et al., 2001, p. 850). Function, not structure, is the key aspect of a family's influence on a child.

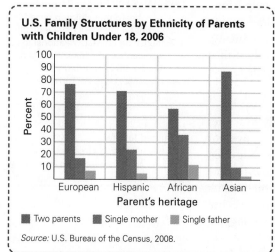

U.S. Family Structures by Ethnicity of Parents with Children Under 18, 2006

Source: U.S. Bureau of the Census, 2008.

FIGURE 8.5 Diverse Families The fact that family structure is affected partly by ethnicity has implications for everyone in the family. It is easier to be a single parent if there are others of the same background who are also single parents.

Family Trouble

Regardless of structure, any family can function well—or poorly. A family that does not support all its members is called *dysfunctional*. In every nation and with every type of family, three factors increase the likelihood that a family will be dysfunctional: low income, low stability, and low harmony (Teachman, 2008b). These three often occur together.

Imagine this scene: A 6-year-old spills his milk (as every 6-year-old sometimes does). In a well-functioning, financially stable family, the parents teach the child how to mop up a spill. Then they pour more milk, perhaps with a comment that encourages family harmony, such as, "Everyone has an accident sometimes."

What if the 6-year-old's parent is already overwhelmed by unemployment, overdue rent, a baby who needs changing, and an older child who wants money for a school trip? What if the last of the food stamps bought that milk and the mother is living with a man who is not the child's biological father?

Conflict almost inevitably erupts, with shouting, crying, and accusations (a sibling claiming, "He did it on purpose"; the 6-year-old saying, "You pushed me"; perhaps the man telling the mother, "You should teach him to be careful"); and then an argument between the adults ends with the man slamming the door as he walks out. As this example makes clear, poverty and instability can make anger spill over when the milk does.

LOW INCOME Family income correlates with function. Directly or indirectly, poverty makes it more difficult for parents to provide all five of the functions discussed earlier (Conger & Donellan, 2007; Gershoff et al., 2007; Yeung et al., 2002).

The Family-Stress Model To understand exactly how income affects child development, consider the *family-stress model,* which holds that the crucial question to ask about any risk factor (including poverty, divorce, job loss, eviction) is whether or not it increases the stress on a family.

In developed nations, poverty may not directly prevent children from having adequate food, clothing, and other necessities (function 1), since adults are usually able to secure at least the minimum needed, sometimes at the expense of time and self-respect. Especially if the poverty is temporary, the community is supportive, and the family's net worth (home ownership, investments, and so on) buffers the strain, low income in one particular year may not affect the child very much (Yeung & Conley, 2008).

Unfortunately, most poor families are chronically poor, and they live in communities with inadequate schools and violent streets. That increases the stress on the family and the child, making it difficult for the parents to provide the other four functions. Thus, for most poor families, ongoing economic hardship increases stress, which can make adults tense and hostile toward their partners and children (Conger et al., 2002; Parke et al., 2004). The family-stress model contends that the adults' stressful *reaction* to poverty is crucial in determining the effect on the children.

Reaction to wealth may be a problem, too, if it increases family stress. Children in high-income families have a disproportionate share of emotional disorders, which sometimes lead to adolescent delinquency and drug abuse. One reason may be parental pressure on the children to excel, a source of stress that undermines the child's self-respect, friendships, and peace of mind (functions 3, 4, and 5) (Luthar, 2003). Both very high- and very low-income families experience a higher percentage of teenage deaths from all causes than middle-income families do.

Many intervention programs aim to teach parents to be more encouraging and supportive of their children (McLoyd et al., 2006). In some families, however, this emphasis on parents' reaction to their children may be misplaced. For instance, poverty itself—with attendant problems such as inadequate child care, poor health, and the threat of homelessness—may be the root cause of both the stress and the reactions to stress. Whether parenting practices can supersede underlying causes, such as income-related stress, cultural norms, and past traumas, is a subject of debate among developmentalists.

Teaching Parents to Be Patient Do low-income parents, in particular, need to learn more about responsive parenting? Probably every parent, regardless of socioeconomic status (SES), could improve; but, although many low-income parents talk to their children too little and hit them too often, they may not benefit from parenting lessons.

An eight-year natural experiment began by assessing *psychopathology* (mental illness; see Chapter 6) among 1,420 schoolchildren, many of them American Indians. For children of every ethnicity, those from low-income households averaged four symptoms of mental disturbance, compared with only one symptom among the nonpoor (Costello et al., 2003).

RESPONSE FOR Single Parents (from page 285) Do not get married mainly to provide a second parent for your child. If you were to do so, things would probably get worse rather than better. Do make an effort to have friends of both sexes with whom your child can interact. ●

That poor children have more mental health problems than middle-class children from the same community is troubling, but it is not surprising. Much other research has noted a link between poverty and child psychopathology (McLoyd et al., 2006).

These researchers discovered something else, however. Midway through the eight-year study, profits from a new casino began paying each Native American adult about $6,000 per year. That lifted the families of about 200 children out of poverty. More important, this was not just a one-time boost. The families could become middle-class in net worth, not just in annual income, because the extra payments were to be made every year.

Remarkably, these children shed some of their emotional problems. To be specific, the incidence of externalizing behavior (such as impulsive aggression) among those 200 children fell to the same levels as that among the children whose families were middle-class when the study began (Costello et al., 2003). In this study, no targeted parental education was provided to help the children; reduction of poverty led to reduction of family stress, and that led to healthier children.

Other research also suggests that reducing a family's financial stress directly benefits the children (McLoyd et al., 2006). A family that includes several well-educated wage earners may have a family composition that is not typical (perhaps the household consists of a single parent, two grandparents, one child, and an unmarried sister of the grandfather). Nonetheless, a child in such a family would not lack material possessions or adult attention and would likely become well educated and happy.

Similarly, children who live with only one parent fare much better if the other parent pays adequate child support and helps with ongoing care (J. W. Graham & Beller, 2002). International data find that children of single parents do better in school if their parents receive government subsidies (as in Austria and Iceland) (Pong et al., 2003).

INSTABILITY Children in middle childhood prefer continuity. They may be upset if they are sent to a new school, if a new baby is born, or if an older sibling moves out. Adults might not realize that these transitions affect schoolchildren.

Let us look closely at one common reason for instability—moving to a new home. Many parents move to a better neighborhood, or even a new country, usually hoping to be happier. They expect the children to be happy, too, but that is not usually the case.

Children move often, but not by choice. To be specific, in the United States in 2006, 16 percent of all children aged 5 to 9 moved from one home to another—compared with only 4 percent of adults over age 65 (U.S. Bureau of the Census, 2008). Changing neighborhoods is particularly stressful in middle childhood. Unlike younger children, their self-awareness makes it harder to build new friendships; unlike teenagers, they cannot easily travel back to visit old friends.

The culture of children (to be discussed soon) differs from nation to nation, which makes it a particularly difficult adjustment for children who move to a new country (Suarez-Orozco et al., 2008). Virtues and values differ from one nation to another as well, further confusing young children (X. Chen & French, 2008).

Worldwide, disruptions correlate negatively with income: The poorest families may move several times a year, and the composition of the household may change each time. For example, a child might move into and out of a grandparent's house, an aunt's house, and a stepparent's house. Homeless or refugee children are hardest hit by such upheavals; they have high rates of moving, some siblings may be sent elsewhere, and cultural shifts may occur. Almost every physical and mental illness is more common for these children (R. J. Hamilton & Moore, 2004).

In Japanese Families Even middle-class children in stable marriages are upset by moving from one part of their nation to another. As shown by a study in Japan (Tanaka & Nakazawa, 2005), many companies there transfer junior employees repeatedly over several years. If the Japanese worker is a husband and father, his family is about equally likely to move with him or to stay put. School learning is not much disrupted because Japan has a sequential, standard curriculum nationwide.

Usually, children who live with their fathers do better, emotionally as well as academically, than children whose fathers are absent. For this reason, when researchers compared Japanese children who moved with their fathers to those who did not, they expected that the movers would benefit from the presence of their fathers. That is not what they found (Tanaka & Nakazawa, 2005). School-age children did better if they stayed put, without their fathers. (The mothers, however, were more stressed when they were temporarily single parents, an illustration of nonshared effects within the same family.)

In Military Families Similar problems occur with U.S. military families. Enlisted men and women have, on average, more income and education than civilians from the same backgrounds. Generally, the higher the SES of the parents, the better the family function. Thus, one might expect children of military families to do well. However, whenever a parent leaves, returns, or is transferred—which happens often in military families—children's lives are disrupted (Titus, 2007). As a result, these children (dubbed "military brats") have more emotional problems and lower school achievement than other children the same age. As one author explains:

> Military parents are continually leaving, returning, leaving again. School work suffers, more for boys than for girls, and . . . reports of depression and behavioral problems go up when a parent is deployed.
>
> *[Hall, 2008, p. 52]*

These difficulties might be attributed to the child's fear that the parent will die or be wounded, but the same problems appear in peacetime, when no danger is present. Adjustment to parental absence is difficult; so is adjustment to parental return.

Major Transitions Multiple, dramatic transitions affect children the most. Such instability occurs when parents divorce or remarry, which often means changes in children's place of residence, school, parent–child relationships, and caregivers.

Remember that stresses accumulate. Within a year of such multiple changes, many children quit school, leave home, use drugs, break the law, overeat, and/or have early sex (McLanahan et al., 2005). The specifics depend partly on the age of the child: 6-year-olds experiencing multiple transitions don't do drugs or have sex, but they may fight with their classmates, curse their teachers, and cry themselves to sleep.

HARMONY Closely related to stability is harmony, which is why those two characteristics are included together in item 5 on the list of family functions. Parents who habitually fight are also more likely to divorce, move, and otherwise disrupt the child's life (Buehler & Gerard, 2002; Khaleque & Rohner, 2002).

The need for harmony helps explain why children are the casualties in some families when divorced parents remarry, even though remarriage generally improves the family income (Hetherington & Kelly, 2002). Such families are fertile ground for jealousy, stress, and conflict because children must obey a new adult and sometimes share a room with an unrelated child. Some parents who formerly were very close to the child (maybe sharing too much!) now strive to please their new spouse, ignoring the child. Even in the best of such marriages, smooth parental alliances can take years to form, because the biological parent and the stepparent need time to coordinate their roles.

In any family, children's well-being declines if family members quarrel, especially if parents physically or verbally abuse each other. Children may suffer harm if an argument escalates into a fight, if one parent walks out and leaves the other distraught, or if divorcing parents argue over child custody. In contrast, children may learn valuable lessons from parental disagreements that result in compromise and reconciliation (Cummings et al., 2003).

SOCIAL-COGNITIVE CONNECTIONS In general, a child's interpretation of a family situation (poverty, divorce, and so on) determines how that situation affects him or her (Olson & Dweck, 2008). Some children consider the family they were born into a temporary hardship; they look forward to the day when they can break free and live on their own. Other children feel responsible for whatever happens. This is called *parentification,* as children assume a parental role and try to take care of everyone else in the family, including the adults (Byng-Hall, 2008).

Some parents push their children into distorted cognitions if they confide too much in a child by, for example, involving him or her in a marital dispute. Quarrels between grandparents and parents over child-rearing practices can also be harmful; this is one reason that children in the United States typically fare better when grandparents and parents live in separate homes (Cain & Combs-Orme, 2005). In middle childhood, children can use their cognitive skills to adjust to different rules and parenting styles (as when grandparents and parents have different standards); but when two adults whom they love argue about them, they have difficulty making sense of the situation.

An intriguing study of 8- to 11-year-olds assessed the impact of two related factors on children's stress levels: (1) conflict between parents and (2) each child's emotional reaction to the conflict (El-Sheikh & Harger, 2001). By far, the more important correlate with children's psychological and academic problems was not the severity of the marital discord but the children's feelings of self-blame or vulnerability.

The authors of this study conclude that, when children "do not perceive that marital conflict is threatening to them and do not blame themselves" for it (El-Sheikh & Harger, 2001, p. 883), they are much less troubled by it (see Figure 8.6). In general, children feel much less vulnerable if they feel they have some control over family circumstances; that provides a practical lesson for all families with potential troubles. The stress caused by low income, instability, or marital conflict will be diminished if a child can interpret the situation as something that he or she can affect in some way. It also helps if the child is given time to adjust.

For example, if income falls, the child can help decide what expenses can be cut—food, clothes, or something else. If the arrival of a newborn requires the older child to move to another room, that move could occur months before the birth, and the child could decorate the room. If the child must change schools, the transition could occur over the summer rather than in the middle of the school year. Everyone, of every age, copes better with stresses when offered some warning, some control, and the knowledge that there are other people who have the same problem.

Parental Conflict, Children's Self-Blame, and Level of Internalizing Behavior in Children

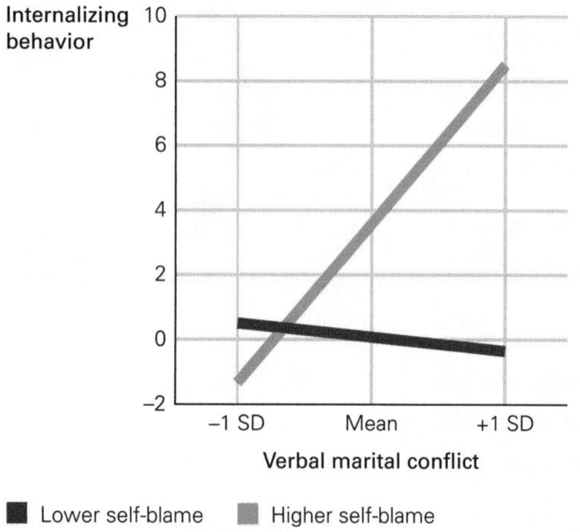

Source: El-Sheikh & Harger, 2001.

FIGURE 8.6 When Parents Fight and Children Blame Themselves
Husbands and wives who almost never disagree are below the first standard deviation (−1 SD) in verbal marital conflict. Couples who frequently have loud, screaming, cursing arguments are in the highest 15 percent (+1 SD). In such high-conflict households, children are not much affected—if they do not blame themselves for the situation. However, if children do blame themselves, they are likely to have internalizing problems, such as nightmares, stomachaches, panic attacks, and feelings of loneliness.

KEYⱣoints

- Families serve five crucial functions for school-age children: furnish basic necessities, encourage learning, instill self-respect, nurture friendships, and offer a peaceful refuge.

- The nuclear, two-parent family is the most common structure and often benefits the children by providing more income, stability, and adult attention.

- Single-parent families, extended families, grandparent families, blended families, and homosexual families are capable of raising successful, happy children.

- Low income, family conflict, and major life transitions interfere with these functions, no matter what the family structure happens to be.

The Peer Group

Getting along with peers is especially important during middle childhood, "central to living a full life and feeling good" (Borland, 1998, p. 28). Difficulties with peers can cause serious problems, and being well liked is protective, especially for children from conflicted, punishing, or otherwise stressful homes (Criss et al., 2002; K. H. Rubin et al., 2006).

Peer relationships change as children grow older. Younger children have friends and learn from them, but their egocentrism makes them less affected by acceptance or rejection. School-age children, in contrast, are well aware of their classmates' opinions, judgments, and accomplishments. They are stung by criticism, sometimes remembering an offhand remark for decades.

Peer relationships, unlike adult–child relationships, involve partners who negotiate, compromise, share, and defend themselves as equals. Adults sometimes command obedience, sometimes allow dominance, but always they are much older and bigger, with the values and experiences of their own cohort, not the child's. They are not on the same wavelength as children, and vice versa. For example, my aging mother told my daughter Rachel that she wanted to watch her dance but was too old to dance herself. Rachel replied, "Oh, Grandma, just dance and play with children and you will never get old." Sweet, but it revealed a wide generation gap.

The Culture of Children

Remember from Chapter 1 that culture includes habits and assumptions as well as more obvious manifestations such as clothing and food. Each age group has its own culture, but the culture of children is particularly noteworthy.

The **culture of children** includes the rules and behaviors that are passed down to younger children from slightly older ones; it includes not only fashions and gestures but also values and rituals. Jump-rope rhymes, insults, and superstitions are often part of the peer culture, and nursery games echo it. For instance, the chant "Ring around the rosy/Pocketful of posies/Ashes, ashes/We all fall down," originated with children coping with the idea of death (Kastenbaum, 2006). (*Rosy* is short for *rosary*.)

Throughout the world, the culture of children encourages independence from adult society. By age 10, if not before, peers pity those (especially boys) whose parents kiss them in public ("mama's boy"), tease children who please the teachers ("teacher's pet," "suck-up"), and despise those who betray other children to adults ("tattletale," "grasser," "snitch," "rat"). Keeping secrets from adults is part of the culture of children.

Clothing often signifies independence and peer-group allegiance. Many 9-year-olds refuse to wear clothes their parents buy, on the grounds that they are too loose, too tight, too long, too short, or wrong in color, style, or brand. A particular bookbag, lunchbox, or even notebook may be required.

Parents may encourage their children to form friendships with certain other children who are from "good" families (Dishion & Bullock, 2002). This attempt may succeed with young children, but not with older ones, who do not care about their friends' parents and may prefer peers who defy authority (J. Snyder et al., 2005). Choosing rebellious friends is sometimes harmless (passing a note during class), but sometimes not (shoplifting, spray-painting graffiti, smoking cigarettes).

The culture of children is not always benign, at least from an adult's perspective. For example, children may quickly learn a second language, but because communication with

culture of children
The particular habits, styles, and values that reflect the set of rules and rituals that characterize children as distinct from adult society.

How to Play Boys teach each other the rituals and rules of engagement. The bigger boy shown here could hurt the smaller one, but he won't; their culture forbids it in such situations.

BOB DAEMMRICH / THE IMAGE WORKS

The Rules of the Game These young monks in Myanmar (formerly Burma) are playing a board game that adults also play, but the children have some of their own refinements of the general rules. Children's peer groups often modify the norms of the dominant culture, as is evident in everything from superstitions to stickball.

KYUYA KAMAZAWA / HAGA /THE IMAGE WORKS

Friends and Culture Like children everywhere, these children—two 7-year-olds and one 10-year-old, of the Surma people in southern Ethiopia—model their appearance after that of slightly older children, in this case adolescents who apply elaborate body paint for courtship and stick-fighting rituals.

OBSERVATION QUIZ

Are they boys or girls? (see answer, page 294) ➡

CAROL BECKWITH & ANGELA FISHER / HAGA /THE IMAGE WORKS

peers is crucial, they may also be quick to learn and spout curses, accents, and slang if doing so signifies being in sync (or "up" or "down") with their friends. Children need the informal code explained in Chapter 7 to talk to each other; they may not realize that they need the formal code of their language as well.

Friendship

Although school-age children value acceptance by the entire peer group, personal friendship is even more important to them (Erwin, 1998; Ladd, 1999; Sandstrom & Zakriski, 2004). Gender differences persist in what children do together (girls talk more and share secrets, boys play more active games), but children of both sexes want and need best friends (Erwin, 1998; Underwood, 2004).

Indeed, if they had to choose between (1) being popular (widely accepted by peers) but friendless (lacking emotional closeness with peers) and (2) being unpopular but having close friends, most children would take the friends. That is a healthy choice: Friendship leads to psychosocial growth and provides a buffer against psychopathology. A longitudinal study of peer acceptance (popularity) and close friendship (mutual loyalty) beginning with fifth-graders found that, 12 years later, both popularity and friendship in the fifth grade affected social interactions and emotional health in adulthood but that having close friends was the more important influence of the two (Bagwell et al., 2001).

Another study found that children of all home backgrounds had about the same number of acquaintances, but those from violent homes were lonelier because they had fewer close friends. The researchers explained, "Skill at recruiting surface acquaintances or playmates is different . . . from the skill required to sustain close relationships" (McCloskey & Stuewig, 2001, p. 93).

Friendships become more intense and intimate as children grow older. This is not surprising, since social cognition (discussed below) and *effortful control* (described earlier in this chapter) improve with age. By age 10, most children know how to be a good friend. For example, when fifth-graders were asked how they would react if other children teased their friend, almost all of them said that they would ask their friend to do something fun with them and would provide reassurance that "things like that happen to everyone" (A. J. Rose & Asher, 2004).

Compared with 6-year-olds, when it comes to friendships, 10-year-olds do the following (K. H. Rubin et al., 2006):

- Demand more of their friends
- Change friends less often
- Become more upset when a friendship ends
- Find it harder to make new friends
- Seek friends who share their interests and values

By the end of middle childhood, close friendships are usually between children of the same sex, age, ethnicity, and SES. This occurs not because children become more prejudiced over the course of middle childhood (they do not) but because they seek friends who understand and agree with them (Aboud & Amato, 2001; Aboud & Mendelson, 1998; Powlishta, 2004).

POPULARITY AND REJECTION Some children are well liked; others are not. Often a child's popularity changes from year to year (Kupersmidt et al., 2004; Ladd, 2005). In a study conducted over six years, researchers asked 299 children which classmates they did or did not want as playmates. Overall, about one-third of the children were popular (often chosen), about half were average (sometimes chosen), and about one-sixth were unpopular (often rejected). Almost every child (89 percent) changed from one of these three clusters to another over the six years. Only 2 percent were unpopular every year, and only 6 percent were consistently popular (Brendgen et al., 2001).

Another longitudinal study found that, once children enter school, change in friendliness is not only possible but likely (Booth-LaForce & Oxford, 2008).

SHYNESS AND ARROGANCE Culture, age, and cohort influence which children are popular (X. Chen & French, 2008). In most communities in North America, shy children are not popular, but they are in China—or at least they were, according to a 1990 study in Shanghai (X. Chen et al., 1992). Then Chinese culture shifted as the government did. Assertiveness and individual expression became more valued. A new survey from the same Shanghai schools reported that shy children were no longer as respected and popular as their shy predecessors had been (X. Chen et al., 2005). The children were affected by their society: Compared with the children in the 1990 study, fewer children said they were shy in 2005.

Changes in popularity are also apparent as children get older. In the United States, among young children, the most popular ones are "kind, trustworthy, cooperative." As children grow older (by the sixth grade), a new group of popular children appears, those who are "athletic, cool, dominant, arrogant, and . . . aggressive." They are feared and respected, high in social status, although not necessarily sought as friends (Cillessen & Mayeux, 2004, p. 147).

SOCIAL AWARENESS **Social cognition** is the ability to understand human interactions. This ability begins in infancy (with *social referencing,* discussed in Chapter 4) and continues to develop in early childhood (as children cultivate a *theory of mind,* discussed in Chapter 5). In most cases, social cognition is well established by middle childhood. Children with impaired social cognition are likely to be rejected (Gifford-Smith & Rabiner, 2004; Ladd, 2005).

Understanding the social context (akin to emotional intelligence, discussed in Chapter 7) may be crucial for peer acceptance. One study found that 9 percent of children become increasingly withdrawn throughout primary school. Most of them had been insecurely attached infants who never learned to regulate their emotions because their parents were neglectful. They are increasingly rejected in school, probably because they are socially immature (Booth-LaForce & Oxford, 2008).

One extensive two-year study of social awareness began with 4½- to 8-year-olds. The researchers found that school-age children improve not only in social cognition but also in effortful control. As a result, the older children had fewer emotional problems than did the younger ones (N. Eisenberg et al., 2004).

Well-liked children generally assume that social slights, from a push to an unkind remark, are accidental (Dodge et al., 2006). Therefore, a social slight does not provoke fear, self-doubt, or anger in them, as it is likely to do in rejected children.

Further evidence of social cognition is found when a direct conflict occurs between children. Well-liked children think about the future of the relationship, seeking a compromise to maintain the friendship (A. J. Rose & Asher, 1999). These prosocial impulses and attitudes are a sign of social maturity, which is rare in rejected children (Gifford-Smith & Rabiner, 2004).

social cognition
The ability to understand social interactions, including the causes and consequences of human behavior.

Pity the Teacher The culture of children encourages pranks, jokes, and defiance of authorities at school. At the same time, as social cognition develops, many children secretly feel empathy for their teachers.

aggressive-rejected children
Children who are disliked by peers because of antagonistic, confrontational behavior.

withdrawn-rejected children
Children who are disliked by peers because of their timid, withdrawn, and anxious behavior.

REJECTED CHILDREN Over the years of middle childhood, three distinct types of unpopular children emerge:

- Some are *neglected,* not really rejected; they are ignored but not shunned.
- Others are **aggressive-rejected children**—disliked because they are antagonistic and confrontational.
- Still others are **withdrawn-rejected children**—disliked because they are timid, withdrawn, and anxious.

The first of these, the neglected children, may develop well, especially if they have a supportive family or outstanding talent (in music or the arts, say) (Sandstrom & Zakriski, 2004). If a child has even one close friend, either at school or in the neighborhood, being neglected by peers is not a major problem.

However, the other two types are actively rejected, often friendless; that hinders their development. Children of these two disliked types have much in common: They tend to misinterpret social situations, to lack emotional regulation, and to be mistreated at home (Pollak et al., 2000). All these factors make them more likely to be victims of bullying.

Loneliness Are the girls in the background whispering about the girl in the foreground loudly enough for her (but not the teacher) to hear? Perhaps this social situation is not what it appears to be, but almost every classroom has one or two rejected children, the targets of gossip, rumors, and social isolation.

bullying
Repeated, systematic efforts to inflict harm through physical, verbal, or social attack on a weaker person.

Bullies and Victims

Almost every adult remembers experiencing isolated attacks, occasional insults, and unexpected social slights in childhood. Fortunately, most adults also remember having good friends who kept these incidents from escalating into bullying.

NOT JUST ONCE OR TWICE **Bullying** is defined as repeated, systematic attacks intended to harm victims who are unable or unlikely to defend themselves and who have no protective social network. Bullying occurs in every nation, in every community, and in every kind of school—religious or secular, public or private, progressive or traditional, large or small. (Bullying occurs among adults as well, but that is not our topic here.)

Variation in the incidence and intensity of bullying is evident from one school to another but not from one *type* of school to another (e.g., urban or rural). This means that some schools have much less bullying than others that are similar in size, religious affiliation, and other characteristics.

Bullying may be *physical* (hitting, pinching, or kicking), *verbal* (teasing, taunting, or name-calling), or *relational* (designed to destroy peer acceptance). Some victims experience all three types, others just one type. In every case, the critical word in the definition is *repeated.* Victims endure shameful experiences again and again—being forced to hand over lunch money, laugh at insults, drink milk mixed with detergent, and so on, while others watch and never come to their defense.

Victimized children tend to be "cautious, sensitive, quiet . . . lonely and abandoned at school. As a rule, they do not have a single good friend in their class" (Olweus et al., 1999, p. 15). In multiethnic schools, bullies usually pick on members of their own group, which makes the victims feel more alone than they would if they could blame their rejection on ethnic prejudice.

Some people believe that victims of bullying are unusually ugly or impaired or odd, but that is not so. Victims may be teased because of something unusual about them—their red hair, their big feet, their glasses, their weird name—but actually every child is odd in some way. Bullies search for such an oddity, and then make it seem as if that is the reason for their attacks.

ANSWER TO OBSERVATION QUIZ
(from page 292) They are all girls. Boys would not be likely to stand so close together. Also, the two 7-year-olds have decorated their soon-to-be budding breasts. ●

In reality, victims are chosen because of their emotional vulnerability and social isolation. Most victims are withdrawn-rejected, but some are aggressive-rejected. The latter are called **bully-victims** (or *provocative victims*) (Unnever, 2005) because they invite retaliation by attacking others. Bully-victims are "the most strongly disliked members of the peer group," with neither friends nor sympathizers (Sandstrom & Zakriski, 2004, p. 110).

Most bullies are *not* rejected. They have a few admiring friends (henchmen). Unless they are bully-victims, they are socially perceptive—but they lack the empathy of prosocial children. Over the years of middle childhood, their social perception becomes apparent in their increasing skill at avoiding adult awareness (teachers often underestimate the bullying in their classes) and at finding victims who do not resist.

Gender differences are evident. Children usually bully others of their own sex. More boys are bullies and victims than girls. In the early grades, boy bullies are often bigger than their victims and tend to use force (physical aggression). Girl bullies are often sharp-tongued; they harass shyer, more soft-spoken girls, mocking, ridiculing, and spreading rumors (verbal aggression).

Both sexes use relational aggression, especially as they grow older, from age 6 up (Card et al., 2008). With maturation, all bullies use a wider variety of humiliating and hurtful tactics, including *cyberbullying* with computers and cell phones (discussed in Chapter 10).

CAUSES AND CONSEQUENCES OF BULLYING Bullying may originate with a genetic predisposition or a brain abnormality; some babies are already unusually angry and aggressive. However, most parents, teachers, and peers teach young children to restrain their aggressive impulses as part of developing emotional regulation and effortful control.

One study found that being somewhat aggressive in early childhood and then becoming less so with age is a healthy progression. Such children are no more likely to develop academic or emotional problems during middle childhood than are children who were very low in aggression during the preschool years. However, children who maintain a high level of aggression tend to have many problems by age 12 (S. B. Campbell et al., 2006).

bully-victim
Someone who attacks others and who is attacked as well. (Also called a *provocative victim* because he or she does things that elicit bullying, such as stealing a bully's pencil.)

Picking on Someone Your Own Sex
Bullies usually target victims of the same sex. Boy victims tend to be physically weaker than their tormentors, whereas girl victims tend to be socially out of step—unusually shy or self-conscious, or unfashionably dressed. In the photograph at right, notice that the bystanders seem very interested in the bullying episode, but no one is about to intervene.

The roots of bullying seem to be a combination of nature and nurture. Families that provide insecure attachment, stressful homes, ineffective discipline, or hostile siblings intensify children's aggression (Cairns & Cairns, 2001; Ladd, 2005).

The consequences echo for decades (Berger, 2007). Many victims develop low self-esteem and some explode violently. This is probably what happened in Columbine, Colorado, where two students shot to death 12 other students and a teacher in 1999 (Pittaro, 2007) before committing suicide; it was reported that both the shooters had been victims of bullying.

As they grow older, from age 5 to 15, many bullies become increasingly cruel, not just teasing but tormenting. Over time, both bullies and victims pay a price; they have a twisted understanding of social interaction that distorts their relationships with friends and lovers; they become increasingly depressed (Pepler et al., 2004).

Bystanders suffer as well. Children report that they like school less on the days that they observe bullying (Nishina & Juvonen, 2005). Perhaps their mirror neurons make them feel distress when they observe victimization, although children become less likely to defend victims as they grow older (Menesini et al., 1997). It is not known whether they do so because they are truly less sympathetic or because they fear becoming victims themselves if they intervene.

CAN BULLYING BE ELIMINATED? Bullying probably cannot be completely eliminated, but many victimized children find ways to cope with the attacks on them—ignoring, retaliating, defusing, or avoiding. A study of older children who were bullied in one year but not in the next indicated that finding new friends was crucial to the change (P. K. Smith et al., 2004). Friendships stop victimization, but the bullies might find new targets. If bullying cannot be eliminated altogether, can anything be done to decrease it?

Unsuccessful Efforts In many nations, efforts to stop bullying have been disappointing. In the northwestern United States, one extensive intervention decreased observed bullying but not reported bullying (Frey et al., 2005). Did this mean that the bullies learned to hide from adults? After another much-acclaimed effort at several schools in Texas, bullying actually *increased* (Rosenbluth et al., 2004). Putting troubled students together in a therapy group or a special school increases aggression as they try to outdo each other (Kupersmidt et al., 2004).

Many older children are more firmly stuck in their behavior patterns than younger children are; some efforts among high school students in Europe have backfired (Berger, 2007). Even in primary school, well-intentioned measures—such as letting children solve problems on their own or assigning guards to the school—may make the situation worse.

Teaching social cognition to victims seems sensible, but bullying arises from the school culture more than from any physical or cognitive characteristic of the victims. Many antibullying projects report discouraging results (J. D. Smith et al., 2004; P. K. Smith & Ananiadou, 2003).

It is not unusual for adults to believe that their intervention has had an impact, only to discover that the children do not agree. Solid scientific evidence is scarce. Although "a plethora of programs to prevent or reduce bully–victim problems have been marketed . . . few . . . have been empirically evaluated" (Ladd, 2005, p. 284).

Successful Efforts Successful reductions in bullying are more likely to occur when the intervention targets the entire school, including the teachers and bystanders. Dan Olweus, a pioneer in antibullying efforts, advocates a *whole-school strategy*—a dynamic-systems approach that involves every aspect of the school system. From a psychosocial perspective, this makes sense. As we have seen, school-age children are influenced by their relationships with peers and parents. Note that bullying itself is a relationship:

● **FOR DEEPER REFLECTION** The homicide rate is far lower among children at school than outside of school, yet many people think the reverse is true. Why?

A child cannot be a bully without a victim, and bullies often want other children to admire or at least respect them.

Forty years ago, no one seemed to think that bullying was widespread or serious. People said, "Boys will be boys" or "Names will never hurt me." Then, in the early 1980s, three victims of bullying in Norway killed themselves, and the government asked Olweus to survey all of Norway's 90,000 school-age children. His report startled the nation: Bullying was much more prevalent than they realized. Of all the children in grades 2 to 5, 14 percent said they were victims of bullying "now and then," and 10 percent admitted that they deliberately hurt other children (Olweus, 1993).

The Norwegian government asked Olweus to tackle the problem. He sent pamphlets to parents, showed videos to students, trained school staff, and increased supervision during recess. In each classroom, students discussed how to stop bullying and befriend lonely children. Bullies and their parents were counseled. Twenty months later, Olweus surveyed the children again. Bullying had been reduced by half (Olweus, 1992).

That success encouraged developmentalists in more than 20 nations, first in Australia, England, and Germany and then in dozens of other nations, including the United States and Canada. Hundreds of surveys have been reported, most of which have found rates of bullying higher than those in Norway. Many have attempted to reduce bullying. Unfortunately, other studies have failed to duplicate Olweus's success, even in Norway (Roland, 2000).

However, several efforts in various nations have reported some success. A recent review of 53 studies of efforts to deal with bullying in the United States reports that bullying is sometimes reduced when a whole school, or at least an entire grade, is targeted (Hahn et al., 2007).

The most dramatic recent success came from a multifaceted, eight-year effort that involved every school in one Finnish town. Victimization was reduced from 9 to 3 percent. Progress varied from year to year (multidirectional), including one year when the rate increased instead of decreasing (Koivisto, 2004).

A review of successful ways to halt bullying (Berger, 2007) finds the following:

- The whole school must be involved, not just the identified bullies.
- Intervention is more effective in the earlier grades.
- Evaluation of results is critical.

This final point merits special emphasis. Some programs make a difference, and some do not; some that seem sensible to adults are actually harmful. Only objective follow-up, months if not years after the intervention, can tell what works and what does not.

Only an Act? Fifth-grade boys play passengers on a school bus as they act out a scene in which three of them reject a fourth (at right). They are participating in a curriculum designed to increase empathy and reduce bullying.

● **UNDERSTANDING THE NUMBERS**
Express the results of this Finnish study, first to emphasize and then to minimize the reduction in victimization.

Answer To emphasize: Victimization was cut by two-thirds; it was three times higher before the project began than when it ended. To minimize: Before the project began, 93 percent of the children were not victims; eight years later, 97 percent were not victims—a reduction of less than 1 percent per year.

ESPECIALLY FOR Parents of an Accused Bully Another parent has told you that your child is a bully. Your child denies it and explains that the other child doesn't mind being teased. (see response, page 299) →

KEY points

- School-age children develop a culture of children, with customs that encourage them to be loyal to one another.
- All 6- to 11-year-olds want social acceptance and close, mutual friendships to protect against loneliness, depression, and victimization.
- Bullying occurs everywhere. The frequency and type of bullying are affected by the school, the culture, and the child's age and gender.
- Efforts to reduce bullying often fail; a whole-school approach seems most likely to be effective.

Morality in Middle Childhood

In middle childhood, children are quite capable of making moral judgments, differentiating universal principles from mere conventional norms (Turiel, 2008). That is one reason why middle childhood is a prime time for moral growth. One developmentalist explains that ages 6 to 11 are:

> years of eager, lively searching on the part of children . . . as they try to understand things, to figure them out, but also to weigh the rights and wrongs. . . . This is the time for growth of the moral imagination, fueled constantly by the willingness, the eagerness of children to put themselves in the shoes of others.
>
> *[Coles, 1997]*

The validity of that statement is suggested by a meta-analysis of dozens of studies: Generally, children are more likely to behave prosocially in middle childhood than earlier (N. Eisenberg & Fabes, 1998). They think in moral terms as well. Empirical research shows that, throughout middle childhood, children readily suggest moral arguments to distinguish right from wrong (Killen, 2007).

Peers and Culture

Many lines of research have shown that children develop their own standards of right and wrong, guided by peers, parents, and culture (Turiel, 2006). Some prosocial values are evident, perhaps originating in human genes and emotions. Among these are caring for close family members, cooperating with other children, and not hurting anyone directly (N. Eisenberg et al., 2006).

During the school years, children add to these general moral guidelines with ideas about when and how lying, cheating, stealing, and so on are acceptable. For instance, lies are wrong except to protect a friend, and each culture of children has particular rules that govern honesty. In my childhood culture, it was OK to lie if your fingers were crossed, but not if you swore on the Bible or said, "Hope to die if I tell a lie."

As children become more aware of themselves and others in middle childhood, they realize that values sometimes conflict. Concrete operational cognition, which gives them the ability to observe and to use logic, propels them to think about morality and to try to behave ethically (Turiel, 2006). As part of growing up, children become conscious of immorality in their peers (Abrams et al., 2008) and, later, in their parents, themselves, and their culture. As their understanding and experience increase, they note cultural differences. There are many:

> On the basis of the historical and ethnographic record, we know that different people in different times and places have found it quite natural to be spontaneously appalled, outraged, indignant, proud, disgusted, guilty and ashamed by all sorts of things [such as] Islam, Christianity, Judaism, capitalism, democracy, flag burning, miniskirts, long hair, no hair, alcohol consumption, meat eating, medical inoculation. . . .
>
> *[Shweder, 1994, p. 26]*

Young children initially endorse the morals of their own parents and own society, but if the culture of children conflicts with adult morality, they usually choose to align themselves with peers.

WHAT CHILDREN VALUE An example of developing morality is found in standards of inclusion and exclusion. One study found that 98 percent of a group of children believed that no child should be excluded from joining a club or team because of gender or race. This value was evident even when adult society was less tolerant. Many of the same children, however, justified excluding another child from a friendship circle. Children want to be fair to everyone, but they do not want to be friends with everyone (Killen et al., 2002).

In some ways, this is similar to the morality of adults. However, many adults have less tolerance for people of other religions than for people of the other sex. The opposite is likely for children. Indeed, gender stereotypes become more elaborate during the school years, when children prefer to play with children of their own sex and sometimes are quite critical of the opposite sex (Ruble et al., 2006). Gender segregation is strongly maintained (especially among the boys), but racial and ethnic segregation among children usually is not (Nesdale, 2004).

School-age children's sense of justice and fairness helps them recognize and reject prejudice when it affects a peer or affects them directly (C. S. Brown & Bigler, 2005; Killen, 2007). One study found that children, by age 10 but not by age 8, deliberately avoided racial categorizations, even when such categories were useful (Apfelbaum et al., 2008).

Interestingly, children think treating everyone fairly means treating everyone equally. Thus, a fair fight is between children who are about the same size and who follow certain rules (e.g., no throwing dirt in the eyes). Factors such as strength, confidence, and fighting experience are not taken into account.

PRIDE AND PREJUDICE Children identify with other children, no matter what their background. This was evident in a survey in England of school-age children's attitudes about refugees. A small intervention—reading and discussing stories about children who had been forced to leave their homeland—increased the children's friendliness toward and acceptance of immigrants (unlike some of their parents) (L. Cameron et al., 2006).

Some people think that pride in one's own group leads to prejudice against other groups, but this is not necessarily true—at least not for children. It is quite possible for them to be proud of their particular group (whether ethnic, national, or some other classification) without being prejudiced against children of other groups (Aboud, 2003). Children in multiethnic schools seem less prejudiced than children who attend ethnically homogeneous schools (Aboud, 2003; Killen et al., 2006).

Of course, children do not automatically become more tolerant as they mature. In some communities, middle childhood is a time of increasing prejudice because social cognition and concrete operational thought allow children to notice differences in race and religion that they were unaware of before. Personal experiences, in peer friendships and role-playing, can dispel the biased categorizations that often develop with social awareness (Pfeifer et al., 2007).

Friends are pivotal as children develop values regarding schoolwork, stealing, drugs, and almost everything else. Consider, for example, Yolanda and Paul, who are Mexican American children living in California. Yolanda was sometimes discouraged (she initially spoke no English):

> There's one friend . . . she's always been with me, in bad or good things. . . . She's always telling me, "Keep on going and your dreams are gonna come true."
>
> *[quoted in Nieto, 2000, p. 220]*

Paul thought about becoming a good student and a law-abiding young man, instead of being "just a mess-up," as he called himself.

> I think right now about going Christian, right? Just going Christian, trying to do good, you know? Stay away from drugs, everything. And every time it seems like I think about that, I think about the homeboys. And it's a trip because a lot of the homeboys are my family, too, you know?
>
> *[quoted in Nieto, 2000, p. 149]*

Yolanda's friend helped her, but Paul's friends kept him from "going Christian." As might be expected, Paul later left school and became a juvenile delinquent; Yolanda graduated from high school and began college.

RESPONSE FOR Parents of an Accused Bully (from page 297) The future is ominous if the charges are true. Your child's denial is a sign that there is a problem. (An innocent child would be worried about the misperception instead of categorically denying that any problem exists.) You might ask the teacher what the school is doing about bullying. Family counseling might help. Because bullies often have friends who egg them on, you may need to monitor your child's friendships and perhaps befriend the victim. Talk matters over with your child. Ignoring the situation might lead to heartache later on. ●

Advances in Moral Reasoning

Many forces drive children's growing interest in ethics. As you have seen, these include peer culture, personal experience, and emotion (particularly empathy, which becomes stronger as children's social cognition improves). Intellectual maturation is a fourth influential force, as we will now see.

Much of the developmental research on children's morality began with Piaget's descriptions of the rules used by children as they play (Piaget, 1932/1997). Piaget was intrigued by children's rules when they played marbles—for example, not only turn-taking and boundary-setting, but specific standards regarding winning or losing one's marbles. The culture of children fosters the rule-based thinking that is evident in all children's games.

KOHLBERG'S LEVELS OF MORALITY Building on Piaget's stages of development, Lawrence Kohlberg (1963) described stages of morality that stem from three levels of moral reasoning, with two stages at each level (see Table 8.4):

- **Preconventional moral reasoning** is egocentric, like preoperational thought.
- **Conventional moral reasoning** parallels concrete operational thought in that it relates to current, observable practices.
- **Postconventional moral reasoning** is like formal operational thought; it uses logic and abstractions, going beyond what is concretely observed in a particular society.

Kohlberg asked children and adolescents (and eventually adults) about different moral dilemmas. The story of a poor man named Heinz, whose wife was dying, serves as an example. A local druggist had the only cure for the wife's illness, an expensive drug that he sold for 10 times what it cost to make.

> Heinz went to everyone he knew to borrow the money, but he could only get together about half of what it cost. He told the druggist that his wife was dying and asked him to sell it cheaper or let him pay later. But the druggist said "no." The husband got desperate and broke into the man's store to steal the drug for his wife. Should the husband have done that? Why?
>
> *[Kohlberg, 1963, p. 19]*

That last word, *why,* is crucial. Kohlberg cares less about the answers a person gives than about the reasons for it. For instance, a person might say that the husband should steal the drug because he needs his wife (preconventional), or because people will blame him if he lets his wife die (conventional), or because preserving life is more important than obeying the law (postconventional). Each of these reasons indicates a different level of moral reasoning.

According to Kohlberg, intellectual maturation, as well as experience, advances moral

preconventional moral reasoning
Kohlberg's first level of moral reasoning, emphasizing rewards and punishments.

conventional moral reasoning
Kohlberg's second level of moral reasoning, emphasizing social rules.

postconventional moral reasoning
Kohlberg's third level of moral reasoning, emphasizing moral principles.

TABLE 8.4 Kohlberg's Three Levels and Six Stages of Moral Reasoning

Level I: Preconventional Moral Reasoning
The goal is to get rewards and avoid punishments; this is a self-centered level.

- *Stage One: Might makes right* (a punishment and obedience orientation). The most important value is to maintain the appearance of obedience to authority, avoiding punishment while still advancing self-interest. Don't get caught!

- *Stage Two: Look out for number one* (an instrumental and relativist orientation). Each person tries to take care of his or her own needs. The reason to be nice to other people is so that they will be nice to you.

Level II: Conventional Moral Reasoning
Emphasis is placed on social rules; this is a community-centered level.

- *Stage Three: "Good girl" and "nice boy."* Proper behavior is behavior that pleases other people. Social approval is more important than any specific reward.

- *Stage Four: "Law and order."* Proper behavior means being a dutiful citizen and obeying the laws set down by society, even when no police are nearby.

Level III: Postconventional Moral Reasoning
Emphasis is placed on moral principles; this level is centered on ideals.

- *Stage Five: Social contract.* Obey social rules because they benefit everyone and are established by mutual agreement. If the rules become destructive or if one party doesn't live up to the agreement, the contract is no longer binding. Under some circumstances, disobeying the law is moral.

- *Stage Six: Universal ethical principles.* General, universally valid principles, not individual situations (level I) or community practices (level II), determine right and wrong. Ethical values (such as "life is sacred") are established by individual reflection and may contradict egocentric (level I) or social and community (level II) values.

thinking. During middle childhood, children's answers shift from being primarily preconventional to being more conventional: Concrete thought and peer experiences help children move past level I (the first two stages) to level II (stages three and four).

CRITICISMS OF KOHLBERG Kohlberg has been criticized for ignoring culture and gender. Taking care of family members, even when it means sacrificing oneself, is more important in many cultures than Kohlberg seemed to recognize. His three levels could be labeled personal (instead of preconventional), communal (conventional), and worldwide (postconventional)—but family is not included.

In addition, the participants in Kohlberg's original research were all boys. That may have led him to devalue the importance of nurturance and relationships, which may be morally crucial for girls (Gilligan, 1982).

In one respect, however, Kohlberg was undeniably correct. Children use their reasoning power to justify their moral actions, and the more advanced they are in their thinking, the more closely their justifications match adult rationalizations.

This was shown in an experiment in which trios of children aged 8 to 18 had to decide how to divide a sum of money with another trio of children. Some groups chose to share equally; other groups were more selfish. There were no age differences in the actual decisions, but there were age differences in the arguments voiced. Older children suggested more complex rationales for their choices, both selfish and altruistic (Gummerum et al., 2008).

PROBLEMATIC IMPLICATIONS AND APPLICATIONS The discussion of children's morality and Kohlberg's levels raises a much broader issue: What is right and what is wrong? Adults disagree on the answer. A father consulted me about his son, who had stolen a coveted toy, hidden it in his lunchbox, and brought it home from school. The father was reluctant to punish his son for stealing because, as he said, "Charlie knows that I cheat on my income taxes."

A more general example of the effect that adults' moral behavior has on children comes from the development of a sense of civic responsibility. This civic sense is evident in adults who vote in elections, volunteer for nonprofit organizations, or get involved with neighborhood groups. Research on its origins suggests that it begins in middle childhood and is influenced more by the examples and discussions of parents and communities than by schools (D. E. Campbell, 2006).

Thus, adults can teach civic virtue by involving their school-age children in political debates, taking them along when they vote or help neighbors. However, in some nations almost every adult votes, and in other nations less than half the people do. Obviously, civic responsibility is not a prime moral value for every adult.

From a developmental perspective, it is apparent that 6- to 11-year-olds develop values, rules, and moral behavior. Peer relationships are one source of guidance for distinguishing right from wrong. Parents and society can have an impact, but moral values vary greatly from one adult to another and from one social group to another; as a result, children get mixed messages. No wonder children vary in their morality: Adults vary, too.

Finally, parents and peers may espouse clashing values. Three values tend to be universal among 6- to 11-year-olds: Protect your friends, don't tell adults what is happening, and don't be too different from your peers. The importance of these values to children sometimes prevents them from echoing their parents' values even when the adults try to teach them.

THE MORALITY OF CHILD LABOR Many nations forbid child labor, yet many adults believe that anyone who does not work is lazy. In view of these conflicting values, child labor is sometimes considered immoral and sometimes not.

Let us return to the young boy in the chapter-opening vignette who changed Tiffany's tire. Was his development harmed by his labor? Is his work immoral? Should there be a law against it?

This chapter emphasizes that each child needs to develop skills and knowledge that bolster self-esteem. Knowing how to change a tire seems quite useful in that regard. Furthermore, a good relationship with one's parents is beneficial, and the boy and his father seem to respect each other. The boy is also helping to support his family, which might improve family income and thus harmony and stability. A law forbidding him to help his father might undermine his family and his pride.

However, as this chapter emphasizes, children need peer friendships. Does the boy have time to play with friends? If he works whenever he is not in school, his labor may be detrimental. In that case, a law might protect him.

The only solid conclusion is that more information is required before we can judge whether the boy is being harmed. Just because a child is working with his father or, for that matter, just because a home has only one parent, a household is poor, or a child is unpopular, we cannot conclude that a child is in psychosocial trouble.

This chapter suggests that some generalities about self-esteem, family structures, or peer relationships are inaccurate when applied to a specific case. Each child is unique and each context has many nuances: We need to know much more about the tire changer and about every other schoolchild before we can decide whether what we see is "harmful to the child's health or physical, mental, spiritual, moral, or social development" (*United Nations Convention on the Rights of the Child*).

KEYpoints

- School-age children develop morals, which are affected by culture, parents, and peers.
- Kolhberg's six stages of moral thought suggest that the highest level of morality is a universal stance that goes beyond the norms of any particular nation.
- Children develop moral standards, which are based primarily on their experiences and on the peer culture.

SUMMARY

The Nature of the Child

1. All theories of development acknowledge that school-age children become more independent and capable in many ways. Erikson emphasized industry, when children are busy mastering various tasks; in psychoanalytic theory, Freud described latency, when psychosexual needs are quiet.

2. Children develop their self-concept during these years, basing it on a more realistic assessment of their competence than they had earlier. Many try to regulate their behavior with effortful control.

3. All children are affected by any family or peer problems they encounter. Depending partly on the child's interpretation, small stresses (daily hassles) may accumulate to create more difficulty than a major trauma.

4. Resilience is more likely to be found in children who have social support, independent activities, personal assets, and religious faith.

Families and Children

5. Families influence children in many ways, as do genes and peers. Each child in a family experiences different (nonshared) circumstances.

6. The five functions of a supportive family are: to satisfy children's physical needs; to encourage learning; to help with friendship; to instill self-respect; and to provide a safe, stable, and harmonious home.

7. The most common family structure worldwide is the nuclear family, a married husband and wife and their biological children. Other structures include single-parent, stepparent, blended, adoptive, homosexual, and grandparent families.

8. Generally, it seems better for children to have two parents rather than one, because a parental alliance can support their development. Single-parent families and blended families have higher rates of change in residence and family structure, which adds stress in middle childhood. However, structure matters less than function.

9. Children from impoverished families tend to have more emotional and behavioral problems because economic stress hinders effective parenting and stability. No matter what the family income, transitions are difficult and conflict is harmful.

The Peer Group

10. Peers are crucial for social development during middle childhood. Close friends are particularly helpful during these years.

11. Popular children may be cooperative and easy to get along with or may be competitive and aggressive. Much depends on the age and the culture of the children.

12. Rejected children may be neglected, aggressive, or withdrawn. Their social cognition, understanding the normal give-and-take of childhood, may be impaired.

13. Bullying is common among school-age children and has long-term consequences for bullies, victims, and perhaps bystanders. Although the origins of bullying may be at home, multifaceted, long-term, whole-school effort seems the best way to reduce bullying in school.

Morality in Middle Childhood

14. School-age children seek to understand right from wrong. Kohlberg described three levels of moral reasoning, from quite selfish to espousing principles for all humankind. One criticism of Kohlberg is that his perspective undervalued cultural differences.

15. Children's behavior reveals that they develop moral standards, often with the guidance of their peers. As with adults, morals vary by culture and between individuals.

KEY TERMS

effortful control (p. 273)
industry versus inferiority (p. 273)
social comparison (p. 274)
resilience (p. 276)
family function (p. 281)
family structure (p. 282)

nuclear family (p. 283)
blended family (p. 284)
single-parent family (p. 285)
extended family (p. 285)
polygamous family (p. 285)
culture of children (p. 291)
social cognition (p. 293)

aggressive-rejected children (p. 294)
withdrawn-rejected children (p. 294)
bullying (p. 294)
bully-victim (p. 295)

preconventional moral reasoning (p. 300)
conventional moral reasoning (p. 300)
postconventional moral reasoning (p. 300)

KEY QUESTIONS

1. How does a school-age child develop a sense of self?

2. What factors make it more likely that a child will cope successfully with major stress?

3. What is the difference between family function and family structure?

4. What are the advantages and disadvantages of a blended family?

5. Why is a safe, harmonious home particularly important during middle childhood?

6. Which of the five functions of family for school-age children is most difficult for single-parent households?

7. The culture of children strongly disapproves of tattletales. How does this affect bullies and victims?

8. Why might social rejection be especially devastating during middle childhood?

9. How might bullying be reduced?

10. What moral values are held most dearly by school-age children?

APPLICATIONS

1. Go someplace where school-age children congregate, such as a schoolyard, a park, or a community center, and use naturalistic observation for at least half an hour. Describe what popular, average, withdrawn, and rejected children do. Note at least one potential conflict (bullying, rough-and-tumble play, etc.). Describe the sequence and the outcome.

2. Focusing on verbal bullying, describe at least two times when someone said a hurtful thing to you and two times when you said

something that might have been hurtful to someone else. What are the differences between the two types of situations?

3. How would your childhood have been different if your family structure had been different, such as if you had (or had not) lived with your grandparents, if your parents had (or had not) gotten divorced, if you had (or had not) lived in a foster family?

Middle Childhood (Ages 7 to 11)

OVERALL HEALTH

Slower physical growth

Less disease and death

Active play

Decreasing physical activity

Increasing asthma

Increasing obesity

> **"PROTECTED FROM [HARM TO] PHYSICAL, MENTAL, SPIRITUAL, MORAL, OR SOCIAL DEVELOPMENT"**
> **MANY STRENGTHS: HEALTH, LEARNING, AND FRIENDS**

COGNITIVE ADVANCES

Vygotsky: Zone of proximal development (ZPD)
Cultural context
Instruction from peers and teachers

Piaget: Concrete operational thought
Logic
Discovery

Information processing
Memory
Attention, automatization, metacognition

LEARNING IN SCHOOL

Language learning
Metaphors and abstractions
Code-switching

"Wars"
Reading
Math
Morals

Measuring learning
Aptitude tests:
U.S. (NAEP) and international (TIMSS, PRLS)

Difficulty with concentration: ADD, ADHD

Dyslexia, other learning disabilities

Cultural bias

Autistic spectrum disorders

Overmedication

PEERS

Friends: crucial for well-being

Culture of children

Bullying: May be physical, verbal, or relational

Rejection: Child may become withdrawn, aggressive

PERSONAL STRENGTHS

Moral reasoning
Kohlberg: Stages of moral development

Active engagement
Erikson: Industry versus inferiority
Freud: Latency of sexual urges

Effortful control

Resilience

FAMILY FUNCTION AND STRUCTURE

Five family functions
Provide basic necessities
Encourage learning
Instill self-respect
Nurture friendships
Ensure harmony

Nine family structures
Nuclear
Extended
Grandparent
Single mother
Single father
Adoptive
Homosexual
Stepparent
Blended

Changes in location or structure (e.g., military families)

Poverty, economic stress

Conflict

KEY

 Major topic

 Related topic

Potential problem

Part V

Adolescence

Would you ride in a car with an unskilled driver? When my daughter Bethany had her learner's permit, I tried to convey confidence. Not until a terrified "Mom! Help!" did I grab the wheel to avoid hitting a subway kiosk. I should have helped sooner, but I didn't know when my help was needed. It is hard to know when children become adults, able to manage without their mothers.

Like every other adolescent, Bethany was neither child nor adult. A century ago, puberty began at age 15 or so. Soon after that, most girls married and most boys found work. In those conditions, adulthood came quickly after childhood.

It is said that *adolescence begins with biology and ends with culture.* If that is so, then adolescence once lasted a few months and now lasts more than a decade. Bodies mature earlier and social responsibilities begin later. Consequently, one observer has said that adolescence is like "starting turbo-charged engines with an unskilled driver" (Dahl, 2004, p. 17). Did I do that with Bethany?

In the next two chapters (covering ages 11 to 18), we begin with biology (the growth increases and other physical changes of puberty) and move toward culture (the social context). Understanding adolescence is more than an intellectual challenge: Those turbo-charged engines need skilled guidance. Get ready to grab the wheel.

CHAPTER OUTLINE

ADOLESCENCE
Body and Mind

Our eldest daughters, Bethany and Rachel, took public transportation to middle school with no problem. I expected the same of Elissa, our third daughter, who was almost always cooperative, outgoing, and happy. I rode the bus with her a few times, teaching her where to board, when to get off, and how to transfer. The first time she did it herself, I drove behind the bus—and saw her *not* get off at her stop. I zoomed ahead, yelling at her to exit. After many more trials, she finally succeeded on her own, still happy. I, however, was puzzled.

Other problems appeared. Elissa often lost her books, her homework, or her schedule. Her teachers praised her intelligence and personality, but the administrators concluded that she belonged in a special school. A series of tests diagnosed her as "severely spatially disorganized." Only then did Lissa begin to study conscientiously; only then did we help her with organizational skills, checking her homework and watching her pack her bookbag. Fortunately, she did brilliantly on her final exams. Her school allowed her to return for one more year of middle school, and six months later she was doing well. ●

ELISSA'S EXPERIENCES MADE ME REALIZE, first, that we all have vulnerabilities that might emerge when new stresses appear and, second, that parents do not necessarily know their children. As explained in detail in this chapter, the biological changes of puberty and the intellectual challenges of entering a new school may be significant stresses.

This chapter also describes various ways in which adolescents think about such stresses. They become able to reason logically and rationally, but they prefer to think egocentrically and intuitively. Lissa was an example: She did not take her difficulties seriously until she realized that she might need to leave her old friends and find new ones in the special school we visited, where most of the students were boys. About 1 adolescent in 5 has a more serious problem, such as engaging in early sex or using drugs.

Like most other people, Elissa managed to survive adolescence without major damage. She was valedictorian of her law school class and now is a wife and mother with a successful law career.

Puberty Begins

Puberty refers to the rapid physical growth and sexual maturation that end childhood, eventually producing a person of adult size, shape, and sexual potential. Puberty begins with a rush of hormones, usually between ages 8 and 14 (see Table 9.1).

For girls, the sequence of biological changes that take place during puberty is as follows: (1) growth of the nipples, (2) first pubic hairs, (3) height spurt, (4) first menstrual period (**menarche**), (5) final pubic-hair growth, and (6) full breast development. The average age of menarche is now 12½ years (Malina et al., 2004).

For boys, the usual sequence is as follows: (1) growth of the testes, (2) first pubic hairs, (3) enlargement of the penis, (4) first ejaculation of seminal fluid (**spermarche**), (5) height spurt, and (6) final pubic-hair growth (Biro et al., 2001; Herman-Giddens et al., 2001). The average age of spermarche is just under 13 years.

For both sexes, puberty is complete about four years after the first signs, although some individuals add height, fat, and muscle in their late teens.

Hormones

All these are the visible changes of puberty. Invisibly, the process begins with a marked increase in **hormones,** which are chemicals in the bloodstream. Hormones regulate hunger, sleep, moods, stress, sexual desire, immunity, reproduction, and many other bodily functions. At least 23 hormones affect human growth and maturation. Technically, those first straggly pubic hairs are "a late event" in puberty (J. L. Cameron, 2004, p. 116), the result of ongoing hormonal activity.

As you remember from Chapter 5, hormone production is regulated deep within the brain, where biochemical signals from the hypothalamus signal the **pituitary gland** (also in the brain) to produce hormones that signal the **adrenal glands** (located

TABLE 9.1 AT ABOUT THIS TIME: The Sequence of Puberty

Girls	Approximate Average Age*	Boys
Ovaries increase production of estrogen and progesterone[†]	9	
Uterus and vagina begin to grow larger	9½	Testes increase production of testosterone[†]
Breast "bud" stage	10	Testes and scrotum grow larger
Pubic hair begins to appear; weight spurt begins	11	
Peak height spurt	11½	Pubic hair begins to appear
Peak muscle and organ growth (also, hips become noticeably wider)	12	Penis growth begins
Menarche (first menstrual period)	12½	Spermarche (first ejaculation); weight spurt begins
First ovulation	13	Peak height spurt
Voice lowers	14	Peak muscle and organ growth (also, shoulders become noticeably broader)
Final pubic-hair pattern	15	Voice lowers; visible facial hair
Full breast growth	16	
	18	Final pubic-hair pattern

*Average ages are rough approximations, with many perfectly normal, healthy adolescents as much as three years ahead of or behind these ages.
[†]Estrogens and testosterone influence sexual characteristics, including reproduction. Charted here are the increases produced by the gonads (sex glands). The ovaries produce estrogens and the testes produce androgens, especially testosterone. Adrenal glands produce some of both kinds of hormones (not shown).

above the kidneys) to produce more hormones. This **HPA (hypothalamus–pituitary–adrenal) axis** is diagrammed in Figure 5.3 (page 170). It is the route for hormones that regulate puberty, as well as stress, growth, sleep, appetite, and sexual excitement.

Hormones interact with one another and with the HPA axis. Abnormalities of the HPA axis in adolescence are associated with severe attention-deficit disorder, eating disorders, anxiety, and depression; all of these conditions are connected to hormone imbalances and appear for the first time or worsen at puberty (T. C. Adam & Epel, 2007; Kallen et al., 2008; Randazzo et al., 2008).

SEX HORMONES At adolescence, the pituitary also activates the **gonads,** or sex glands (ovaries in females; testes, or testicles, in males). One hormone in particular, *GnRH* (gonadotropin-releasing hormone), causes the gonads to increase production of estrogens and androgens (female and male sex hormones, respectively), chiefly **estradiol** in girls and **testosterone** in boys.

The maturing adrenal glands also produce hormones in both sexes, but the gonads are responsible for the marked sex differences in hormones. To be specific, after decreasing in childhood, testosterone skyrockets in boys—rising to 20 times the prepubescent level or more (Roche & Sun, 2003). In girls, estradiol increases to about 8 times the childhood level (Malina et al., 2004).

The sex hormones affect the body's shape and functioning, including production of other hormones that regulate stress and immunity (E. A. Young et al., 2008). Estradiol and testosterone levels may also explain sex differences in psychopathology (Steiner & Young, 2008). These sex differences include the facts that males have twice the rate of schizophrenia as females, and females have twice the rate of depression as males. Boys are more likely to become delinquents, girls to develop eating disorders.

Gender differences in these psychological disorders could be affected by culture, but there is no doubt that the sex hormones affect the biology of the entire body. As the most dramatic effect, the activated gonads produce gametes (sperm and ova), whose maturation and release are heralded by spermarche or menarche. This signifies that the young person has the biological potential to become a parent. (Peak fertility is about four to six years later.)

The HPA axis leads from brain to body to behavior. We have already noted the brain (especially via the pituitary) and body (the sequence of puberty), but the third item in this sequence, the behavior changes, are often most unexpected, sudden, and unsettling. The behaviors triggered by hormones are responses to moodiness and lust, which overtake the relative emotional calm of the predictable, asexual child (J. L. Cameron, 2004; Susman & Rogol, 2004).

Not only do human thoughts and emotions result from hormones and other physiological and neurological processes, but they also *cause* them (Damasio, 2003). An adolescent's reactions to how other people respond to breasts, beards, and body shapes evoke thoughts and frustrations that, in turn, raise hormone levels.

BODY RHYTHMS As already described, the hypothalamus and the pituitary gland regulate hormones that affect stress, appetite, sleep, and so on, following the HPA axis. Beyond the sex hormones, another biological change affects adolescent emotions and impulses.

HPA (hypothalamus–pituitary–adrenal) axis
The sequence of a chain reaction of hormone production, originating in the hypothalamus and moving to the pituitary and then to the adrenal glands.

gonads
The paired sex glands (ovaries in females, testicles in males). The gonads produce hormones and gametes.

estradiol
A sex hormone, considered the chief estrogen. Females produce more estradiol than males do.

testosterone
A sex hormone, the best known of the androgens (male hormones); secreted in far greater amounts by males than by females.

MIKE KING / AP PHOTO

That's What Friends Are For
Jennifer's preparations for her prom include a pedicure and hairstyling, courtesy of her good friends Khushbu and Meredith. In every generation and society the world over, teenagers help their same-sex friends prepare for the display rituals involved in coming of age, but the specifics vary by cohort and culture.

ESPECIALLY FOR Parents of Teenagers Why would parents blame adolescent moods on hormones? (see response, page 312) →

DAVID LASSMAN / SYRACUSE NEWSPAPERS / THE IMAGE WORKS

Too Early It is 8:00 A.M. on their first day of high school, and these freshmen are having trouble staying awake for orientation in their homeroom.

In order to understand this change, you need to realize that the brain of every living creature responds to the environment with natural rhythms. One of these *biorhythms* is a day–night cycle of biological activity that occurs approximately every 24 hours—it is called the *circadian rhythm* (*circadian* means "about a day"). The rise and fall of the hormone melatonin and other body chemicals make sleep elusive at some moments and impossible to postpone at others.

Puberty alters biorhythms. Hormones from the pituitary often cause a "phase delay" in sleep–wake patterns, making many teens wide awake at midnight but half asleep all morning. By contrast, many adult brains are naturally alert in the morning and sleepy at night. As a result, social patterns set by adults may not accommodate adolescents. Many parents tell their teenagers to go to sleep before midnight to no avail and shake the same child awake for school.

Added to the adolescent day–night pattern, some people (especially males) are naturally more alert in the evening than in the morning, a genetic trait called *eveningness.* Exacerbated by the phase delay of puberty, eveningness puts adolescents at high risk for antisocial activities (Susman et al., 2007).

Another common effect of the adolescent phase delay is sleep disruption: "Even though there is evidence that sleep is important for learning and memory, teenagers are notoriously sleep deprived" (Ruder, 2008, p. 10). Uneven sleep schedules (more sleep on weekends, later bedtimes) decrease well-being just as overall sleep deprivation does (Fuligni & Hardway, 2006).

Sleep deprivation and irregular sleep schedules are associated with many other difficulties, such as falling asleep while driving, insomnia in the middle of the night, distressing dreams, and mood disorders (depression, conduct disorder, anxiety) (Carskadon, 2002; Fredriksen et al., 2004; Fuligni & Hardway, 2006).

Since sleep-deprived individuals cannot think or learn as well as they can when well rested, this research suggests an obvious need for a change in school schedules. As you will learn toward the end of this chapter, however, school policies are not always in accord with developmental understanding.

Influences on the Age of Puberty

A practical question for many parents, teachers, and children themselves is, "When will adolescence begin?" Age 11 or 12 is the most likely age of visible onset, but the rise in hormone levels that signals puberty is still considered normal in those as young as age 8 or as old as age 14. *Precocious puberty* (sexual development before age 8) occurs about once in 5,000 children, for unknown reasons (Cesario & Hughes, 2007). In most adolescents, genes, body fat, hormones, and stress all affect the age at which puberty begins (B. J. Ellis, 2004).

RESPONSE FOR Parents of Teenagers (from page 311) If something causes an adolescent to shout "I hate you," to slam doors, or to cry inconsolably, the parents may decide that hormones are the problem. This makes it easy to disclaim personal responsibility for the teenager's anger. However, research on stress and hormones suggests that this comforting attribution is too simplistic. ●

GENES About two-thirds of the variation in age of puberty is genetic (van den Berg & Boomsma, 2007). Monozygotic twins are more similar in onset of puberty than are same-sex dizygotic twins, who are more alike than half-sisters or half-brothers, who are more alike than nongenetic siblings of the same sex who are raised together (Ge et al., 2007).

Genes on the sex chromosomes have a marked effect on age of puberty. Girls generally develop ahead of boys. In a classroom of well-nourished fifth-graders, for instance, at least one girl (XX) has already developed breasts and has grown almost to full adult height. Not until age 18 or so will her last male classmate (XY) have sprouted facial hair and grown to adult height.

These dramatic sex differences are observable. On average, girls are about two years ahead of boys in height. However, when it comes to hormonal changes, girls are only a few months, not years, ahead of boys (S. M. Hughes & Gore, 2007). The discrepancy exists because the height spurt occurs about midway in female pubescence (before menarche) but is a late event for boys (after spermarche). Thus, the boy who has sexual thoughts about the taller girls in his class is not necessarily precocious; his hormones are merely ahead of his height.

Age of puberty varies among ethnic groups, probably because of genes. For instance, northern European girls are said to reach menarche at 13 years, 4 months, on average; southern European girls do so at an average age of 12 years, 5 months (Alsaker & Flammer, 2006). In the United States, African Americans tend to reach puberty earlier than European or Hispanic Americans do (see Figures 9.1 and 9.2). The average age of puberty for Asian Americans is several months later (Herman-Giddens et al., 2001; Malina et al., 2004).

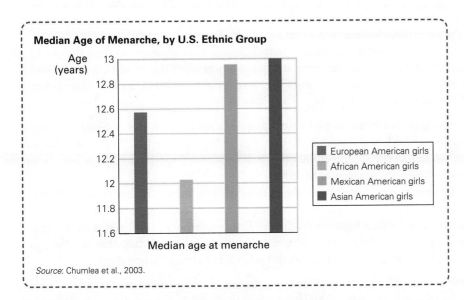

Median Age of Menarche, by U.S. Ethnic Group

Source: Chumlea et al., 2003.

FIGURE 9.1 Usually by Age 13 The median age of menarche (when half the girls have begun to menstruate) differs somewhat among ethnic groups in the United States. (The best signal of puberty is menarche in girls, but similar timing is apparent in boys of these ethnic groups.)

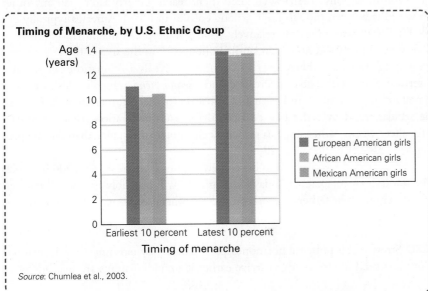

Timing of Menarche, by U.S. Ethnic Group

Source: Chumlea et al., 2003.

FIGURE 9.2 Almost Always by Age 14 This graph shows the age of menarche for the earliest and latest 10 percent of girls in three U.S. ethnic groups. Note that, especially for the slow developers (those in the 90th percentile), ethnic differences are very small.

OBSERVATION QUIZ

At first glance, ethnic differences seem dramatic in Figure 9.1 but minimal in Figure 9.2. Why is this first glance deceptive? (see answer, page 315) →

SKJOLD PHOTOGRAPHS / THE IMAGE WORKS

Both 12 The ancestors of these two Minnesota 12-year-olds came from northern Europe and West Africa. Their genes have dictated some differences between them, including the timing of puberty, but these differences are irrelevant to their friendship.

ESPECIALLY FOR Parents Worried About Early Puberty Suppose your cousin's 9-year-old daughter has just had her first period, and your cousin blames hormones in the food supply for this "precocious" puberty. Should you change your young daughter's diet? (see response, page 319) ➔

leptin
A hormone that affects appetite and is believed to be involved in the onset of puberty. Leptin levels increase during childhood and peak at around age 12.

ESPECIALLY FOR Doctors and Nurses When should hormones be given to an adolescent who is eager for puberty to arrive? (see response, page 319) ➔

BODY FAT AND HORMONES Children who have a relatively large proportion of body fat experience puberty sooner than do their thin contemporaries. This is true internationally. For example, puberty starts earlier in the cities of India and China than in the remote villages, probably because rural children are often hungry; it occurs fully a year earlier in Warsaw than in Polish villages, probably because the rural children are more active (Malina et al., 2004).

Some researchers believe that hormones in the food supply are one reason why puberty is occurring earlier than it did a century ago, and they blame additives in the food supply as the cause of precocious puberty. As evidence, they point to the steroids fed to cattle to increase their bulk, as well as to many other substances that children now consume (R. Y. Wang et al., 2005).

It is known that many environmental chemicals increase or decrease the production of testosterone and estrogen, and many others affect the appetite. It could be that hormones (both natural and artificial) cause weight gain, which then causes puberty (Ellison, 2002).

Leptin One hormone in particular has been implicated in the onset of puberty—**leptin,** which affects appetite. Leptin was only discovered in 1994 but is already known to increase during childhood, peaking at about age 12, with high levels at the onset of puberty (Rutters et al., 2008).

Curiously, leptin affects appetite in females more than in males (Geary & Lovejoy, 2008), and body fat is more closely connected to the onset of puberty in girls than in boys. An interaction between leptin and female hormones is suggested by the experience of many adolescent girls, whose appetites decrease when they are "in love" and increase at the end of their menstrual cycles (when estrogen dips).

Malnutrition In both sexes, chronic malnutrition delays puberty. Because of severe malnutrition in regions of Africa, children there reach puberty later than any other group worldwide, even though their genetic cousins in North America typically experience puberty when they are relatively young. Widespread malnutrition probably explains why puberty did not occur until about age 17 in the sixteenth century.

Examining data on puberty over the centuries reveals a dramatic example of a long-term statistical increase or decrease called a *secular trend,* which in this case is the tendency for improvements in health and nutrition to affect human growth. Because of the secular trend over the past two centuries, each generation has experienced puberty a few weeks earlier, and has grown a centimeter or so taller, than did the preceding one (Alsaker & Flammer, 2006).

The secular trend has stopped in developed nations (Roche & Sun, 2003), which may be good news for parents. Today's young men will probably not be tall enough to look down on their fathers, or girls on their mothers, as did young people in previous generations.

STRESS Stress affects pubertal hormones, paradoxically by *increasing* (not decreasing) their production. Puberty tends to arrive earlier if a child's parents are sick, addicted,

A VIEW FROM SCIENCE

Stress and Earlier Puberty

Why would stress trigger puberty? Logically, conflicted or stepfather families would benefit if the opposite happened— if teenagers looked and acted like children and could not reproduce. That would make them less emotional, and their appearance would evoke protection, not lust and rivalry. That would be particularly beneficial to the children and step-parents in conflicted families. Yet it is not what happens.

One study of 756 children, from infancy through adolescence, found that earlier puberty correlated with harsh parenting. Although parents were more likely to be harsh with their sons, the effects on puberty were evident only in their daughters, especially those girls who had been most distressed (in that they cried a lot) as infants (Belsky et al., 2007). Thus nurture, combined with nature, affected the onset of puberty.

Another study found that girls who fought with their mothers *and* who lived with an unrelated man (usually a stepfather) reached puberty earlier than their genes and body weight would predict. The longer a girl lived with a man who was not her brother or her father, the earlier menarche occurred (B. J. Ellis & Garber, 2000).

Animal research confirms the role of stress. Mice, rats, and opossums become pregnant at younger ages when they live in stressful circumstances (Warshofsky, 1999). Furthermore, female mice reach puberty and sexual receptivity at younger ages when reared near unrelated adult male mice (Caretta et al., 1995; Khan et al., 2008).

The timing of the stress may be crucial, according to studies of adopted children and of girls whose parents divorced. If a young girl's father is hostile, drug-addicted, or seriously depressed, and if he leaves the family before her hormonal changes begin, she is likely to begin puberty a year earlier than an older sister who had the same father but whose early life was not disrupted by divorce (Tither & Ellis, 2008).

Now let us see if any theory could explain why stress would trigger puberty and why this would affect girls more than boys. One explanation comes from evolutionary theory:

> Over the course of our natural selective history, ancestral females growing up in adverse family environments may have reliably increased their reproductive success by accelerating physical maturation and beginning sexual activity and reproduction at a relatively early age.
>
> [*B. J. Ellis & Garber, 2000, p. 486*]

In other words, in past stressful times, adolescent girls could replace themselves before they died, passing on family genes. This would not matter so much for boys, since men of any age could impregnate a woman. But pregnancy takes a toll on the female body, so it would make evolutionary sense for girls to give birth at a young age in societies characterized by conflict and stress. For survival of the species, it was better to have many teenage pregnancies.

Today, early sexuality and reproduction lead to social disruption, not social survival. However, the human genome has been shaped over millennia. The onset of puberty still seems to be affected by family and neighborhood circumstances (Romans et al., 2003).

---

or divorced or if his or her neighborhood is violent (B. J. Ellis, 2004). This surprising statement has been documented by many studies, as the View from Science explains.

Too Early, Too Late

For most adolescents, only one aspect of pubertal timing is important: their friends' schedules. Puberty can enhance or diminish a person's status, bringing joy or distress. No one wants to be early or late; early girls and late boys are particularly unhappy.

GIRLS Think about the early-maturing girl. If she has visible breasts at age 10, the boys in her class tease her; they are distressed by the sexual creature in their midst. She must fit her womanly body into a school chair designed for younger children, and she may hide her breasts in large T-shirts and bulky sweaters and refuse to undress for gym.

Early-maturing girls tend to have lower self-esteem, more depression, and poorer body image than later-maturing girls (Compian et al., 2004; Mendle et al., 2007). They even exercise much less than their classmates do (Davison et al., 2007).

ANSWER TO OBSERVATION QUIZ
(from page 313) The major reason is the vertical axis, which covers a total of 1½ years in Figure 9.1 and 14 years in Figure 9.2. ●

Getting Ready Her shape, hairstyle, eye makeup, and boa are those of a mature woman, but this girl is actually just 13 years old. Her emotional maturity is harder to gauge than her physical development.

JONATAN FERNSTROM / GETTY IMAGES

MIKA / ZEFA / CORBIS

The Emotional Message Cigarette smoking is much more common in Europe than in North America. This 15-year-old boy in Germany may be signaling his manhood with the cigarette behind his ear, and the girl, said to be just 9 years old, may be seeking to participate in his show of maturity by accepting a light.

OBSERVATION QUIZ

What aspects of this scene suggest that the boy is asserting his sexuality and that the girl is actually quite young? (see answer, page 319) ➜

Early-maturing girls often have boyfriends who are several years older than they are, which adds status and protects against loneliness but also brings emotional distress and sometimes drugs and alcohol (Ge et al., 2003; Weichold et al., 2003). Early-maturing girls are more likely to enter abusive relationships than other girls are (Schreck et al., 2007). For all these reasons, girls are better off if they begin puberty on time.

BOYS Cohort is crucial for boys. In previous generations, boys tended to benefit from early puberty. Early-maturing boys who were born around 1930 often became leaders in high school and beyond (M. C. Jones, 1965). They also tended to be more successful as adults (Taga et al., 2006).

Since about 1960, however, the problems with early male maturation have outweighed the benefits. Currently, early-maturing boys are more aggressive, lawbreaking, and alcohol-abusing than later-maturing boys (Biehl et al., 2007; Lynne et al., 2007). Early puberty correlates with sexual activity and teenage parenthood, which in turn correlate with depression and other psychosocial problems (B. B. Brown, 2004; Siebenbruner et al., 2007).

Late puberty may also be difficult, especially for boys. Slow-developing boys tend to be more anxious, depressed, and afraid of sex, according to research in Finland (Lindfors et al., 2007). Late puberty means being relatively thin and short, a social handicap for adolescent boys.

Late maturers of both sexes may be troubled by their lack of development. One study of more than 3,000 Australian adolescents found that late developers exhibited four times the rate of self-harm (cutting or poisoning themselves), an indication of serious depression (Patton et al., 2007).

Nutrition

As you read earlier, puberty itself is connected to nutrition. Beyond the necessary body fat to begin the process, proper nourishment is critical once the body starts to grow rapidly. Yet many adolescents are deficient in their intake of necessary vitamins or minerals.

Today's youth consume more calories (contributing to earlier puberty and more obesity), but they are less likely to eat a balanced diet than their parents or grandparents did—or even than they themselves did a few years earlier. In 2007, fewer high school seniors (19 percent) ate five or more servings of fruits and vegetables a day (MMWR, June 6, 2008) than did their counterparts a decade earlier (27 percent) (MMWR, August 14, 1998). A longitudinal study of individual Minnesota teenagers found that nutrition deteriorates with age (N. I. Larson et al., 2007).

DIET DEFICIENCIES Deficiencies of iron, calcium, zinc, and other minerals may be even more problematic during adolescence than vitamin deficiencies, since minerals are needed for bone and muscle growth. Some specifics illustrate the point. The recommended daily dose of iron is 15 milligrams, but less than half of all U.S. teenagers consume that much. Iron is found in green vegetables, eggs, and meat—foods that adolescents often spurn in favor of chips, sweets, and fries.

Menstruation depletes the body of iron, which combines with a widespread iron deficiency in their diets to make the incidence of anemia greater among adolescent girls than among females of any other age or among males (Belamarich & Ayoob, 2001). Iron deficiency also puts boys at risk: Worldwide, many boys do intense physical labor or sports, and muscles need iron to grow and strengthen (R. W. Blum & Nelson-Mmari, 2004). One symptom of anemia is tiredness, a common teenage complaint.

Calcium consumption among adolescents is also low. Although the daily recommended intake for teenagers is 1,300 milligrams, most consume about one-third of that. About half of adult bone mass is acquired from ages 10 to 20, yet few adolescents consume enough calcium to prevent osteoporosis (fragile bones), a major cause of disability, injury, and death in late adulthood—especially for people of European descent.

One reason for calcium deficiency is that milk drinking has declined. Most North American children once drank at least a quart (about 1 liter) a day, which provided 1,200 milligrams of calcium. In 2007, only 15 percent of U.S. ninth-graders drank even 24 ounces (¾ liter) of milk a day. Among twelfth-graders, the rates were 9 percent for girls and 19 percent for boys (MMWR, June 6, 2008). More aged women than men break their hips; this is one reason.

Choices Made Nutritional deficiencies result from the food choices that young adolescents are allowed, even enticed, to make. There is a direct link between nutritional deficiencies and the presence of vending machines in schools (Cullen & Zakeri, 2004). Fast-food establishments cluster around high schools. Some social scientists now advocate a "nudge" to encourage people to make better choices (Thaler & Sunstein, 2008).

Price is influential in food choices, especially for adolescents. At least experimentally, 10- to 14-year-olds choose healthy foods if they are cheaper than unhealthy ones (Epstein et al., 2006). However, milk and fruit juice are more expensive than fruit punch or soda. In New York City in 2008, a McDonald's salad cost four times as much as a hamburger.

Body Image Another reason for poor nutrition is anxiety about **body image**—that is, a person's idea of how his or her body looks. Since puberty alters the entire body, it is almost impossible for teenagers to welcome every change. Unfortunately, their perceptions are distorted; they tend to focus on and exaggerate the imperfections.

This viewpoint is connected to their new sexual interests. Girls diet partly because boys tend to prefer to date thin girls (Halpern et al., 2005). Boys want to look taller and stronger, a concern that increases from ages 12 to 17, partly because girls value well-developed muscles in males (D. Jones & Crawford, 2005).

In North America, the ideal body type and facial appearance are Anglo-Saxon. Children of ethnic minorities are bombarded by media images of celebrities and models whose faces and bodies look quite different from those their own genes have produced. Of course, few Anglo-Saxon youth achieve the ideal of beauty,

LEE SNIDER / THE IMAGE WORKS

Come Here Often? Teenagers worldwide (like this group in Yangshuo, China) are attracted by fast-food restaurants because the cheap food and public setting of such places make them ideal for snacking and socializing. However, the food—usually high in fat and low in nutrition—contributes to overweight and undernourishment in many of their young customers.

body image
A person's idea of how his or her body looks.

Does He Like What He Sees? During adolescence, all the facial features do not develop at the same rate, and the hair often becomes less manageable. If B. T. here is typical, he is not pleased with the appearance of his nose, lips, ears, or hair.

LAURA DWIGHT

either. No real woman has the proportions of a Barbie doll. Almost all young adolescents wish their bodies looked different.

EATING DISORDERS One result of the widespread dissatisfaction with body image among teenagers is that many of them—mostly girls—eat erratically or ingest drugs (especially diet pills) to lose weight. Meanwhile, many boys take steroids to increase muscle mass. The incidence of eating disorders increases dramatically at puberty and is correlated with distorted body image, obsession with food, and suicidal depression (Bulik et al., 2008; Hrabosky & Thomas, 2008).

Individual adolescents sometimes switch from one abnormal pattern to another—from obsessive dieting to overeating to overexercising and back again—without yet having any diagnosable disorder (Henig, 2004). Obesity was discussed in Chapter 7 and will be discussed again in Chapter 12; it is a lifelong problem, evident in adolescence as well. Now we describe two eating disorders that are particularly common in adolescence and emerging adulthood, anorexia and bulimia.

Anorexia Some individuals voluntarily undereat and overexercise, depriving their vital organs. They may suffer from **anorexia nervosa,** a disorder characterized by self-starvation. Between 5 and 20 percent of victims eventually die of organ failure or suicide. Anorexia nervosa is diagnosed when four symptoms are evident (American Psychiatric Association, 2000):

● Refusal to maintain a weight that is at least 85 percent of normal BMI

● Intense fear of weight gain

● Disturbed body perception and denial of the problem

● Absence of menstruation (in adolescent and adult females)

If someone's body mass index (BMI) is 18 or lower, or if she (or, less often, he) loses more than 10 percent of body weight within a month or two, anorexia is suspected.

Although anorexia may have existed in earlier centuries (think of the saints who refused all food), the disease was undiagnosed before about 1950, when some high-achieving, upper-class adults in the United States grew so emaciated that they died. Soon anorexia became evident among younger women (the rate increases notably at puberty and again at the end of adolescence), among men, and in every nation and ethnic group (Y. M. Chao et al., 2008). Genetic makeup can make it more likely that a person will develop anorexia: The risk increases if a young woman has a close relative, especially a monozygotic twin, with anorexia or severe depression.

Bulimia About three times as common as anorexia is **bulimia nervosa.** The person (again, usually female) with bulimia overeats compulsively (consuming thousands of calories within an hour or two) and then purges via induced vomiting or laxatives. Most people with bulimia are close to normal in weight and therefore unlikely to starve. However, they risk serious health problems, including damage to their gastrointestinal systems and cardiac arrest from electrolyte imbalance (Shannon, 2007).

Three things combine to warrant a clinical diagnosis of bulimia:

● Bingeing and purging at least once a week for three months

● Uncontrollable urges to overeat

● A distorted perception of body size

Between 1 and 3 percent of women in the United States are clinically bulimic during early adulthood (American Psychiatric Association, 2000).

LAUREN GREENFIELD / VII VIA AP

Guess Her Age Jennifer has gained some weight since she was first admitted to an eating-disorders clinic, but she still looks younger than her years. One hypothesis about anorexia is that it stems from an unconscious desire to avoid growing up. (Jennifer is 18 years old.)

anorexia nervosa
An eating disorder characterized by self-starvation. Affected individuals voluntarily undereat and often overexercise, depriving their vital organs of nutrition. Anorexia can be fatal.

bulimia nervosa
An eating disorder characterized by binge eating and subsequent purging, usually by induced vomiting and/or use of laxatives.

ORIGINS OF DISORDERED EATING Eating disorders may begin with the odd eating habits of many adolescents who try new diets, go without food for 24 hours (as 12 percent of U.S. high school students did in 2007), or take diet drugs (as 6 percent did) (MMWR, June 6, 2008). There may be a genetic threshold, with some dieters crossing over into anorexia while others do not.

Each episode of bingeing, purging, or fasting makes the next one easier. It is likely that a combination of causes leads to obesity, anorexia, and bulimia. This destructive combination has five elements: cultural ideals of thinness, social stress, increased appetite, hormones of puberty, and childhood habits that disconnect eating from hunger (Shannon, 2007).

> Parental control in child feeding may have unintended effects on . . . eating patterns [when it involves an] emphasis on "external" cues in eating and decreased opportunities for the child to experience *self*-control. . . . Parental pressure to eat may result in food dislike and refusal, and restriction may enhance children's . . . consumption of restricted foods.
>
> [*J. O. Fisher & Birch, 2001, p. 35*]

One family practice seems to reduce the risk of adolescent eating disorders: eating together during childhood (Franko et al., 2008). It is not known whether family cohesion is an underlying protective factor or whether family meals directly encourage good nutritional practices. Nonetheless, developmentalists agree that a sound nutritional foundation begins with childhood habits and family examples. Many people who were overweight or underweight as infants have no weight problems as adults, but the older an overweight or underweight child is, the more likely it is that he or she will have an eating disorder in adulthood.

RESPONSE FOR Parents Worried About Early Puberty (from page 314) Probably not. If she is overweight, her diet should change, but the hormone hypothesis is speculative. Genes are the main factor; she shares only one-eighth of her genes with her cousin. ●

RESPONSE FOR Doctors and Nurses (from page 314) In very rare cases, and only when all other possible solutions (including the passage of time) have not had the desired effect. Many normal adolescents are slow to develop, and hormones affect other hormones. ●

KEYPoints

- Puberty usually begins between ages 8 and 14 (typically at age 11 or 12) in response to hormones that begin deep within the brain, traveling from the hypothalamus to the pituitary.
- Hormones affect the emotions as well as the physique, with adolescent rage, lust, and despair caused by hormones as well as by social reactions to visible body changes.
- The timing of puberty is affected by genes, body fat, hormones, and stress.
- Good nutrition is especially important, but especially unlikely, during adolescence; excessive dieting sometimes leads to severe eating disorders, such as anorexia and bulimia.

ANSWER TO OBSERVATION QUIZ (from page 316) The boy has a lighter in his hand, but he is using a more intimate way of sharing a light; the girl is holding her cigarette awkwardly, unlike an experienced smoker. Although it is difficult to believe that she is only 9 (as the photographer states), her plastic bracelets, her tentative posture, her hand covering her mouth, and her timid expression all suggest that she is no older than 12. ●

The Transformations of Puberty

Every body part changes during puberty. For the sake of discussion, the transformation from a child into an adult may be divided into two parts: physical growth and sexual maturation.

Bigger and Stronger

The first set of changes during puberty is the **growth spurt**—a sudden, uneven increase in the size of almost every body part. Growth proceeds from the extremities to the core: Hands and feet grow before arms and legs; arms and legs before the torso.

growth spurt
The relatively sudden and rapid physical growth that occurs during puberty. Each body part increases in size on a schedule: A weight increase usually precedes a height increase, and growth of the limbs precedes growth of the torso.

A height spurt follows the increase in body fat, and then a muscle spurt occurs. Lungs triple in weight, and adolescents breathe more deeply and less rapidly. The heart doubles in size and beats more slowly, while blood pressure and volume rise (Malina et al., 2004). Physical endurance increases: Teenagers can run or dance for hours.

Note that height increases *before* muscles and the size of internal organs do, which means that athletic training should be tailored to an adolescent's size the previous year. Sports injuries are common at puberty, partly because young bones are more easily fractured than adult bones (until old age) (Roche & Sun, 2003).

Only one organ system, the lymphoid system (which includes the tonsils and adenoids), *decreases* in size, thus making teenagers less susceptible to respiratory ailments. Mild asthma, for example, often switches off at puberty (Busse & Lemanske, 2005), and teenagers have fewer colds than younger children do.

Another organ system, the skin, changes in marked ways, becoming oilier, sweatier, and more prone to acne. Hair also changes. During puberty, hair on the head and limbs (those dark leg hairs) becomes coarser and darker. New hair grows under arms, on faces, and over sex organs (this is called *pubic hair,* which, like the word *puberty,* comes from the Latin word *puber,* meaning "adult"). Visible facial and chest hair is sometimes considered a sign of manliness, although hairiness in either sex depends on genes as well as on hormones.

Sexual Maturation

The second set of changes turns boys into men and girls into women. This transformation is signaled by the appearance of sex characteristics and an increase in sexual thoughts and emotions.

primary sex characteristics
The parts of the body that are directly involved in reproduction, including the vagina, uterus, ovaries, testicles, and penis.

secondary sex characteristics
Physical traits that are not directly involved in reproduction but that indicate sexual maturity, such as a man's beard and a woman's breasts.

SEXUAL BODY CHANGES The term **primary sex characteristics** refers to organs involved in conception and pregnancy. During puberty, every sex organ (the ovaries, the uterus, the penis, and the testes) grows and matures in response to increased hormone production.

Over the same time period, **secondary sex characteristics** develop. These do not directly affect fertility (which is why they are called *secondary*). For example, during puberty, boys grow an average of 5 inches taller than girls and their shoulders widen; girls develop breasts and a wider pelvis and add, on average, twice as much body fat as boys (Roche & Sun, 2003). Breasts and hips are often considered signs of womanhood, but neither are required for conception; thus, they are secondary, not primary, sex characteristics.

Secondary sex characteristics are important psychologically, if not biologically. Consider breasts. Many adolescent girls buy "minimizer," "maximizer," "training," or "shaping" bras, hoping to make their breasts conform to an idealized body image. During the same years, many boys are horrified to notice a swelling around their nipples—a normal and temporary result of the erratic hormones of early puberty. If a boy's breast growth is very disturbing, drugs can reduce the swelling, although many doctors prefer to let time, rather than tamoxifen, deal with the problem (Derman et al., 2003).

Another secondary sex characteristic is a lower voice as the larynx grows. This change is more noticeable in boys, although girls' voices also become somewhat deeper.

SEXUAL ACTIVITY The primary and secondary sex characteristics just described are not the only manifestations of the sexual hormones. Fantasizing, flirting, hand-holding, staring, displaying, and touching all reflect gender, availability, and culture. Hormones trigger thoughts and emotions, and the social context shapes thoughts into enjoyable fantasies, shameful preoccupations, frightening impulses, or actual contact.

Some experts believe that boys are more influenced by hormones and girls by culture (Baumeister & Blackhart, 2007). Perhaps. When a relationship includes sexual intimacy, girls seem more concerned about commitment (Zani & Cicognani, 2006). However, these sex differences may be exaggerated.

Adolescents of both sexes are influenced by both biology and culture. The combination explains why some teenagers engage in sexual activities that teenagers in other nations, and even adults in their own society, would not (S. Moore & Rosenthal, 2006).

Our major discussion of sexual relationships appears in Chapter 10, on psychosocial development in adolescence. Here, we focus on two possible biological consequences of sexual activity—namely, pregnancy and infections—and on sexual abuse, which is directly related to the physical changes of puberty.

A 15-Year-Old A religious ceremony is part of the Quinceañera, a coming-of-age celebration for girls in Latino communities. The church ritual is usually followed by a lavish party. Traditionally, the Quinceañera meant that a girl was ready for marriage.

SEX TOO SOON Sex can, of course, be thrilling and affirming, a bonding experience that increases the love and affection shared between two people. However, compared to 100 years ago, adolescent sexual development is more hazardous, for five reasons:

1. Earlier puberty and weaker social taboos mean teens have sexual experiences at younger ages. Early sex correlates with depression and drug abuse.

2. Most contemporary teenage mothers have no husbands to help them, whereas many teenage mothers a century ago were married; in 2007 in the United States, 86 percent were unwed (B. E. Hamilton et al., 2009).

3. Raising a child has become more complex and expensive.

4. Mothers of teenagers are often employed and therefore less available as caregivers for their teenager's child.

5. Sexually transmitted infections are more widespread and dangerous.

Teenage Pregnancy Teenage births in the past 50 years have decreased markedly: The rate in 2006 was less than half the rate in 1960 in the United States (U.S. Bureau of the Census, 2008; see Figure 9.3). Today's teenagers are better informed, so they use contraception more often and have fewer abortions and fewer births.

Rates of teen births have declined even further in other nations, but problems remain. In some nations (notably those of sub-Saharan Africa), inadequate medical care makes pregnancy the leading cause of death for teenage girls (H. W. Reynolds et al., 2006). In regions where almost everyone is malnourished, three times as many maternal deaths from birth complications occur for mothers under age 20 as for mothers aged 20 to 35 (R. W. Blum & Nelson-Mmari, 2004).

In the United States, the pregnancy rate for girls aged 11 to 14 is less than 2 percent of the rate for 15- to 19-year-olds, but younger girls who do become pregnant have higher rates of every complication. These complications include spontaneous and induced abortion, high blood pressure, stillbirth, preterm birth, and low-birthweight babies. For the 6,000 babies born to women under age 15 in the United States each year, medical and educational problems of all sorts are common.

One reason for these complications of pregnancy is that the youngest teenagers are most likely to postpone getting prenatal care (Borkowski et al., 2007). Another reason is that their immature bodies are less ready for pregnancy. Then, after they give birth, they are less able to provide the responsive mothering that newborns need.

A Daughter's Promise At a "purity ball" in Colorado, a father reads the pledge signed by his 14-year-old daughter, in which she promises that she will abstain from sex until she marries. Young adolescents who take a virginity pledge are more likely than their peers to be celibate in high school. However, they are also more likely to become parents before they graduate from college.

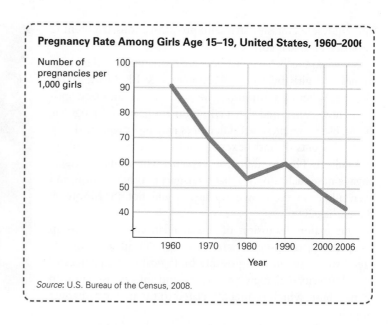

FIGURE 9.3 Fewer Teen Mothers
The birth rate among teenage girls in the United States has fallen dramatically since 1960. The reasons include the greater availability of legal abortion and the more frequent choice of education over motherhood. Girls age 18 and 19 give birth almost four times as often as 15- to 16-year-olds. Although the decline is encouraging, the United States still has a rate of teen pregnancy that is more than twice that of many other developed nations.

Pregnancy Rate Among Girls Age 15–19, United States, 1960–2006

Number of pregnancies per 1,000 girls

Source: U.S. Bureau of the Census, 2008.

In developed nations, among healthy 15- to 19-year-olds who become pregnant, complications at birth are minimal—typically, less than among women over age 35. However, the nutritional demands of pregnancy, added to the already poor nutrition of adolescent girls, increase the likelihood of health problems later on. Furthermore, for both mother and child, the average teenage birth reduces education, increases insecure attachment, and elevates the risk of every psychosocial problem for decades.

Sexually Transmitted Infections Unfortunately, the other major problem of teenage sexuality shows no signs of abating. A **sexually transmitted infection (STI)** (sometimes referred to as a sexually transmitted disease [STD] or venereal disease [VD]) is any infection transmitted through sexual contact. Worldwide, sexually active teenagers have higher rates of the most common STIs—gonorrhea, genital herpes, and chlamydia—than any other age group (World Health Organization, 2005). In the United States, young persons aged 15 to 24 constitute only one-fourth of the sexually active population but account for half of all sexually transmitted infections (MMWR, October 20, 2006).

sexually transmitted infection (STI)
A disease spread by sexual contact, including syphilis, gonorrhea, genital herpes, chlamydia, and HIV.

The youngest adolescents are particularly vulnerable. If a boy has sex before age 16, or a girl has sex before age 16 with an older partner, the chance of catching an infection is twice as high as it would have been if he or she had waited a few years (S. Ryan et al., 2008). One reason is biological. Fully developed women have some natural biological defenses against STIs; this is less true for pubescent girls, who are more likely to catch any STI they are exposed to, including AIDS (World Health Organization, 2005).

No Safer? Posters and even intense educational programs have little proven effect on the incidence of AIDS among adolescents. This poster was displayed outside an HIV testing center in Windhoek, Namibia, a country that has one of the highest HIV infection rates in the world.

In addition, for psychological reasons, young sexually active boys and girls are unlikely to seek immediate treatment of an STI or to alert their partners. Furthermore, many have sexual relationships with two or more people within a short time, thus hastening the spread of infection (see Figure 9.4).

An added complication, over and above the usual fears about confidentiality, occurs for homosexual adolescents. In some families and cultures, same-sex relationships are secret, even shameful. This makes it even more difficult for gay or lesbian teens to seek treatment than it is for their heterosexual peers.

There are hundreds of STIs (James, 2007). *Chlamydia* is the most frequently reported one; it often begins without symptoms, yet it can cause permanent infertility. A laboratory test can detect chlamydia, and it can be treated and cured, but many young people avoid doctors.

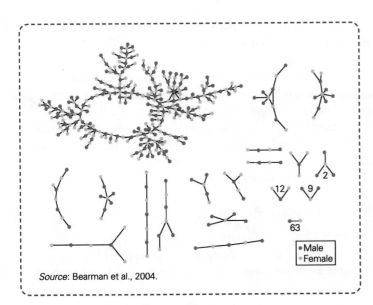

FIGURE 9.4 Romantic Networks: Your Partner Becomes My Partner
This is a diagram of the romances that students in one U.S. high school reported having during the preceding six months. Each dot represents a romantic relationship. Patterns that occurred more than once are indicated with a number. Thus, 63 couples were still together at the end of the six-month period. Those monogamous teenagers were in the minority; most of the other students were linked to two or more romantic partners. If one person in the busy circle of relationships at the upper left had an untreated infection, it could have been transmitted to 100 other people.

● Male
● Female

Source: Bearman et al., 2004.

Another common STI is *human papillomavirus* (HPV), which has no immediate consequences but, later in life, increases a female's risk of uterine cancer and death. Immunization before a girl's first intercourse makes contracting HPV much less likely, but many parents refuse to immunize their young daughters. Information about other STIs is provided in Appendix A, pages A-18–A-19, and the interested reader is encouraged to consult other publications, doctors, and reliable Web sites on the topic.

National differences in assumptions about, rates of, and policies regarding STIs are striking. In France, 91 percent of adolescents use contraception (usually a condom) at first intercourse (P.-A. Michaud et al., 2006); not coincidentally, every French high school is required to provide students with free, confidential medical care. In contrast, far fewer Italian, German, and U.S. teenagers use condoms. For instance, in the United States, only half of sexually active high school senior girls said they had used a condom during their most recent sexual encounter (MMWR, June 6, 2008).

Sexual Abuse Legally, **child sexual abuse** is any sexual activity between a juvenile and a person over age 18. Developmentalists are quite clear that this may include activities beyond physical contact, such as anything that sexually arouses an adult and shames, confuses, or excites a child. Sexual abuse can be very destructive of overall development, not only of sexual development. Virtually every adolescent problem, including early pregnancy, is more common in adolescents who are sexually abused.

The United Nations reports that millions of girls in their early teens are forced into marriage, genital surgery, or prostitution (often across national borders) each year (Pinheiro, 2006). Exact numbers are elusive. Almost every nation has laws against child sexual abuse, but these laws are rarely enforced, and sensationalism often crowds out efforts to prevent, monitor, and eliminate the problem (Davidson, 2005).

Analysis of substantiated (that is, reported, investigated, and verified) child sexual abuse in the United States confirms that, as elsewhere, the rate is higher among 12- to 15-year-olds than among younger children and older teens (U.S. Department of Health and Human Services, Administration on Children, Youth, and Families, 2006). Nearly 20,000 teens in that age bracket were victims of substantiated sexual abuse in the United States in 2007 (see Table 9.2). Girls are particularly vulnerable, although boys are also at risk.

In the United States, overall rates of sexual abuse are declining, perhaps because adolescents are becoming better informed (Finkelhor &

ESPECIALLY FOR Health Practitioners How might you encourage adolescents to seek treatment for STIs? (see response, page 325) ➡

child sexual abuse
Any erotic activity that arouses an adult and excites, shames, or confuses a child, whether or not the victim protests and whether or not genital contact is involved.

TABLE 9.2 Age and Sex Abuse: United States, 2007

Age	Number of Sex-Abuse Victims	Percent of Maltreatment That Is Sex Abuse
Less than 1 year	315	0.3%
1–3	3,249	2.2
4–7	13,137	7.4
8–11	13,459	9.5
12–15	19,848	14.5
16–17	6,084	13.5

Source: U.S. Department of Health and Human Services, Administration on Children, Youth, and Families, 2009.

Jones, 2004). However, many adolescents remain ignorant. Schools teach only the biology of sex and disease, peers brag and lie about their sexual exploits, and the teen media virtually never discuss healthy sexuality (Hust et al., 2008). That leaves youth to depend on their families—the worst possible source of information and protection for sexually abused adolescents, since most abusers are family members of the victims.

As with other types of child maltreatment, the consequences of sexual abuse extend far beyond the trauma of the moment. Young people who are sexually exploited tend to fear sexual relationships and to devalue themselves lifelong. Abusers often isolate adolescents from their peers and refuse to let them socialize, so they are never able to develop healthy friendships and romances.

● **FOR DEEPER REFLECTION** Why are negative words such as *dirty* and *nasty* often used when the subject is sex?

KEY ℘oints

- Every part of the body changes during puberty. One major set of changes is called the growth spurt, as weight, height, muscles, and the size of inner organs increase dramatically.

- Another set of changes is sexual, as the almost unisex body of a child takes on the shape and function of a man or woman.

- Primary sexual characteristics (needed for reproduction) as well as secondary sexual characteristics (dozens of male/female differences) develop during adolescence.

- With sexual maturity comes vulnerability to pregnancy and sexual abuse. Although less common than they once were, both can harm development lifelong, especially if they occur soon after puberty. Sexually transmitted infections are an increasing risk.

Cognitive Development

To the puzzlement of many developmentalists, adolescent thought combines brilliance and foolishness, lofty idealism and crass selfishness. Some theorists (e.g., Piaget) are rightly impressed with the abstract logic that many teenagers are able to use. Others (e.g., Elkind) note the destructive narrowness of early adolescent thinking. We begin with recent research from brain scans that has helped reconcile these opposite perspectives.

Neurological Development

As with the rest of the body, different parts of the brain grow at different rates (Blakemore, 2008). The limbic system (fear, emotional impulses) matures before the prefrontal cortex (planning ahead, emotional regulation). Myelination and maturation proceed from inside the brain to the cortex and from back to front (Sowell et al., 2007).

That means the instinctual and emotional areas develop before the reflective ones do, making adolescent brains the "turbo-charged engines with an unskilled driver," mentioned on page 307. Furthermore, the hormones of puberty affect the amygdala (part of the limbic system) more directly than the cortex, which is more affected by age and experience. Earlier puberty means emotional rushes, unchecked by caution.

PROBLEMS WITH ADOLESCENT BRAIN DEVELOPMENT As one expert in adolescent thinking points out, when emotions are intense, especially when one is with peers, the logical part of the brain shuts down. This shutdown is not reflected in questionnaires that require teenagers to respond to paper-and-pencil questions regarding hypothetical dilemmas. On those tests, teenagers think carefully and answer correctly. They know the risks of sex and drugs. However,

> the prospect of visiting a hypothetical girl from class cannot possibly carry the excitement about the possibility of surprising someone you have a crush on with a visit in the middle of the night. It is easier to put on a hypothetical condom during an act of hypothetical sex than it is to put on a real one when one is in the throes of passion. It is easier to just say no to a hypothetical beer than it is to a cold frosty one on a summer night.
>
> [L. Steinberg, 2004, p. 53]

Ideally, research on adolescent brains will lead to effective ways of protecting teens from their dangerous impulses (Monastersky, 2007). Meanwhile, scholars caution against letting incomplete brain development become an explanation for just about everything about teens that adults have found perplexing—from sleep patterns to risk taking and mood swings, "from teen-driving mishaps to recent school shootings" (Sowell at al. 2007, p. 55). However, there is no doubt that teenage "response inhibition, emotional regulation, and organization" are underdeveloped (Sowell et al., 2007, p. 59) because the prefrontal cortex is not yet mature.

The combination of the normal sequence of brain maturation (limbic system, then cortex) and the earlier onset of puberty (perhaps because of better nutrition or greater stress) means that, for many contemporary youths, emotions rule behavior (Blakemore, 2008; Compas, 2004). The limbic system, unchecked by the slower-maturing prefrontal cortex, makes strong, immediate sensations attractive to teens:

> [A]dolescents *like* intensity, excitement, and arousal. They are drawn to music videos that shock and bombard the senses. Teenagers flock to horror and slasher movies. They dominate queues waiting to ride the high-adrenaline rides at amusement parks. Adolescence is a time when sex, drugs, *very* loud music, and other high-stimulation experiences take on great appeal. It is a developmental period when an appetite for adventure, a predilection for risks, and a desire for novelty and thrills seem to reach naturally high levels.
>
> [Dahl, 2004, pp. 7–8; emphasis in original]

When stress, arousal, passion, sensory bombardment, drug intoxication, or deprivation is extreme, the adolescent brain is overtaken by impulses that might shame adults. As further explained in the section on drug abuse in Chapter 10, teenagers brag about being so drunk they were "wasted," "bombed," "smashed"—a state most adults try to avoid. Some teenagers choose to spend a night without sleep or a day without eating, or to exercise in pain. Hormones that instigate puberty have little effect on the neurological advances necessary for adult planning and reflection (L. Steinberg, 2008). The prefrontal cortex may not mature until years after the young person first has hormonal rushes, overwhelming sexual urges, and access to weapons.

BENEFITS OF ADOLESCENT BRAIN DEVELOPMENT It is easy to be critical of adolescent behavior and then to blame it on raging hormones, immature brains, or society at large. Yet remember that difference is not the same as deficit. Uneven brain growth in adolescence has benefits as well as hazards.

With increased myelination, reactions become lightning fast, and speed is valued in many aspects of modern life. For instance, adolescent athletes are potential superstars, unafraid to steal a base, tackle a fullback, and race when legs and lungs hurt.

RESPONSE FOR Health Practitioners (from page 323) Many adolescents are intensely concerned about privacy and fearful of adult interference. This means your first task is to convince the teenagers that you are nonjudgmental and that everything is confidential. ●

Twisted Memorial This wreck was once a Volvo, driven by a Colorado teenager who ignored an oncoming train's whistle at a rural crossing. The car was hurled 167 feet and burst into flames. The impact instantly killed the driver and five teenage passengers. They are among the statistics indicating that accidents, many of which result from unwise risk taking, kill 10 times more adolescents than diseases do.

ESPECIALLY FOR Parents Worried About Their Teenager's Risk Taking You remember the risky things you did at the same age, and you are alarmed by the possibility that your child will follow in your footsteps. What should you do? (see response, page 327) →

Sacred Thread Every religion has some ritual in which young people make a public commitment to their faith. These Hindu boys are receiving the *jenoi*, a sacred thread that they will wear all their lives. In this initiation ceremony, they shave their heads, wear new robes, and vow to pray three times a day and to study the Vedas, which are the scriptures of Hinduism.

Ideally, coaches supply wisdom and strategy to direct their young players' quick and brave impulses.

Adolescence increases the activity of the dopamine system, including neurotransmitters that trigger great pleasure. The joy of a first love, a first job, or even an A on a term paper is memorable, not to be dismissed. Before the brain becomes fully mature (at about age 25), formation of new connections between synapses occurs more readily, before another wave of pruning (like that at age 2) sets in. As one author explains it, "Young brains have both fast-growing synapses and sections that remain unconnected" (Ruder, 2008, p. 8). These new connections facilitate the acquisition of new ideas, words, memories, personality patterns, and dance steps (D. P. Keating, 2004).

Synaptic growth enhances moral development as well. Values acquired during adolescence are more likely to endure than those learned later, after brain connections are firmly established. This is an asset if values developed during adolescence are less self-centered than those of children or more culturally attuned than those of older generations.

In short, several aspects of adolescent brain development are positive. The fact that the prefrontal cortex is still developing "confers benefits as well as risks. It helps explain the creativity of adolescence and early adulthood, before the brain becomes set in its ways" (Monastersky, 2007, p. A17).

The emotional intensity of adolescents "intertwines with the highest levels of human endeavor: passion for ideas and ideals, passion for beauty, passion to create music and art" (Dahl, 2004, p. 21). As a practical application, those who care about the next generation must attend to the life lessons that adolescents are learning. Adults should provide "scaffolding and monitoring" until adolescents' brains can function well on their own (Dahl, quoted in Monastersky, 2007, p. A18).

Thinking About Oneself

During puberty, young people center many of their thoughts on themselves. They watch the physical transformations of puberty with anticipation, horror, and delight. Young adolescents wonder how others perceive them, and they think deeply (but not always realistically) about their future. One reason adolescents spend so much time talking on the phone, e-mailing, and texting is that they want to confer with close friends about every nuance of everything they have done, are doing, and plan to do next.

adolescent egocentrism
A characteristic of adolescent thinking that leads young people (ages 10 to 14) to focus on themselves to the exclusion of others.

EGOCENTRISM Young adolescents not only think intensely about themselves but also imagine what others may think about them. This **adolescent egocentrism** was first described by David Elkind (1967).

The difference between egocentrism during adolescence and the same trait during preoperational thought is that adolescents, unlike younger children, have a well-developed theory of mind (Artar, 2007). They know that other people are not necessarily thinking the same thing they are. However, their egocentrism distorts their understanding of what others may be thinking, especially about them.

As one teenager explained: "My mom thinks that she was right; she couldn't understand me and what I feel. . . . That's the cause of the quarrel actually" (quoted in Artar, 2007, p. 1217). Like many of her peers, this girl realized that her mother had her own thoughts, but she didn't recognize the limitations of her own thinking.

In their egocentrism, adolescents regard themselves as unique, special, and much more socially significant (that is, noticed by everyone) than they actually are. Accurately

DAVID M. GROSSMAN / THE IMAGE WORKS

Don't Start with Me . . . All six of these Brooklyn teenagers are affected by adolescent egocentrism. They share an intense concern about how they look to other people. It is not easy to appear unique and part of a group simultaneously.

OBSERVATION QUIZ

There are some obvious differences among these teens, but they have three visible characteristics in common. What are they? (see answer, page 329) →

imagining someone else's perspective is especially difficult when egocentrism rules (Lapsley, 1993). For example, it seems unlikely that adolescent girls are especially attracted to boys with pimples and braces, but Edgar thought so, according to his older sister:

> Now in the 8th grade, Edgar has this idea that all the girls are looking at him in school. He got his first pimple about three months ago. I told him to wash it with my face soap but he refused, saying, "Not until I go to school to show it off." He called the dentist, begging him to approve his braces now instead of waiting for a year. The perfect gifts for him have changed from action figures to a bottle of cologne, a chain, and a fitted baseball hat like the rappers wear.
>
> *[adapted from Eva, personal communication, 2007]*

Egocentrism also leads adolescents to interpret another's behavior as if it were related to themselves. A stranger's frown or a teacher's critique could make a teenager conclude that "no one likes me" and then to deduce that "I am unlovable" or even to claim that "I can't go out in public." More positive casual reactions—a smile from a sales clerk or an extra-big hug from a younger brother—could lead to the thought that "I am great" or "Everyone loves me," with similarly distorted self-perception.

Acute self-consciousness is probably more prevalent between ages 10 and 14 than earlier or later (Rankin et al., 2004). Young adolescents would rather not stand out from their peers, hoping instead to blend in. They also believe that other people are as egocentric as they are. As one girl said:

> I am a real worrier when it comes to other people's opinions. I care deeply about what they say, think and do. If people are very complimentary, it can give you a big confidence boost, but if people are always putting you down, you feel less confident and people can tell. A lot of advice that is given is "Do what you want and don't listen to anyone else," but I don't know one person who can do that.
>
> *[quoted in J. H. Bell & Bromnick, 2003, p. 213]*

IRRATIONAL BELIEFS Elkind gave names to several aspects of adolescent egocentrism. One is the **personal fable**, the belief that one is unique, destined to have a heroic, even legendary, life. This belief gives rise to the **invincibility fable**, in which

RESPONSE FOR Parents Worried About Their Teenager's Risk Taking (from page 325) You are right to be concerned, but you cannot keep your child locked up for the next decade or so. Since you know that some rebellion and irrationality are likely, try to minimize them by not boasting about your own youthful exploits, by reacting sternly to minor infractions to nip worse behavior in the bud, and by making allies of your child's teachers. ●

personal fable
An aspect of adolescent egocentrism characterized by an adolescent's belief that his or her thoughts, feelings, or experiences are unique, more wonderful or awful than anyone else's.

invincibility fable
An adolescent's egocentric conviction that he or she cannot be overcome or even harmed by anything that might defeat a normal mortal, such as unprotected sex, drug abuse, or high-speed driving.

NORBERT SCHWERIN / THE IMAGE WORKS

Not Me! A young woman jumps into the Pacific Ocean near Santa Cruz, California, while at a friend's birthday party. The jump is illegal, yet since 1975, 52 people have died taking that leap off these cliffs. Hundreds of young people each year decide that the thrill is worth the risk, aided by the invincibility fable and by what they think are sensible precautions. (Note that she is wearing shoes. Also note that the dog has apparently decided against risking a jump.)

imaginary audience
The other people who, in an adolescent's egocentric belief, are watching and taking note of his or her appearance, ideas, and behavior. This belief makes many teenagers self-conscious.

formal operational thought
In Piaget's theory, the fourth and final stage of cognitive development, characterized by more systematic logic and the ability to think about abstract ideas.

adolescents believe that, unlike other mortals, they cannot be hurt by drunk driving, unprotected sex, and so on. If they take risks and survive without harm, they feel special, not thankful.

For example, in every nation, people who volunteer for military service—knowing or even hoping that they will be sent into combat—are more likely to be under age 20 than over it. Young recruits take risks more often than older, more experienced soldiers do (Killgore et al., 2006). In the military as well as in civilian life, more young males than older males or females believe that they are invincible (Alberts et al., 2007).

Egocentrism also creates an **imaginary audience** in the minds of many adolescents, both male and female. They seem to believe that they are at center stage, with all eyes on them, and that others are as intensely interested in them as they themselves are. As a result, they are continually imagining how others might react to their appearance and behavior.

The imaginary audience can cause teenagers to enter a crowded room as if they are the most attractive human beings alive. They might put studs in their lips or blast music for all to hear, calling attention to themselves.

The reverse is also possible: Unlike Edgar, they might avoid scrutiny lest someone notice a blemish on their chin or make fun of their braces. Many a 12-year-old balks at going to school with a bad haircut or the wrong shoes. Many adolescents cringe from their imaginary audience, fearful that their peers will notice them. One girl remarked, "I would like to be able to fly if everyone else did; otherwise it would be rather conspicuous" (quoted in A. Steinberg, 1993). A 12-year-old boy said:

> I dress different now that I'm in middle school. . . . Now I really care [and] take time to think about it. So it bugs me when my mom yells at me for wearing jeans with holes or big shirts. It's a big deal to her if my clothes aren't clean. She thinks my teachers will think she's a bad mother or something.
>
> *[Daniel, quoted in R. Bell, 1998, p. 59]*

Note that this boy imagines that his mother is troubled by her own audience, which consists of his teachers. It is typical to begin with the imagined reactions of other people and end by judging the cluelessness of one's own parents.

Formal Operational Thought

In sorting through their life experiences, adolescents begin to develop logic that is no longer dependent on concrete experiences. They are now able to consider abstractions. Jean Piaget noticed and described this cognitive advance, which is signaled by the ability to reason on the basis of "assumptions that have no necessary relation to reality" (Piaget, 1950/1972, p. 148).

Piaget realized that cognitive processes, not just cognitive contents, can shift after childhood to a level called **formal operational thought.** To distinguish formal from concrete thinking, compare curricula in primary and secondary school:

- *Math.* Younger children multiply real numbers ($4 \times 3 \times 8$); adolescents can multiply unreal numbers, such as $(2x)(3y)$ or even $(25xy^2)(3zy^3)$.
- *Social studies.* Younger children study other cultures by experiencing aspects of daily life—drinking goat's milk or building an igloo, for instance; adolescents can grasp concepts like "gross national product" and "fertility rate" and can figure out how these phenomena might affect elections.

● *Science.* Younger students plant carrots and feed rabbits; adolescents understand that hydrogen and oxygen can combine to make water and can then test H_2O in the lab.

PIAGET'S EXPERIMENTS Piaget and his colleagues devised a number of tasks that demonstrate formal operational thought (Inhelder & Piaget, 1958). Successful completion of these tasks shows that "in contrast to concrete operational children, formal operational adolescents imagine all possible determinants . . . [and] systematically vary the factors one by one, observe the results correctly, keep track of the results, and draw the appropriate conclusions" (P. H. Miller, 2002).

In one experiment (diagrammed in Figure 9.5), children balance a scale by hooking weights onto the scale's arms. To master this task, a person must realize that the heaviness of the weights and their distance from the center interact reciprocally to affect balance. Therefore, a heavier weight close to the center can be counterbalanced with a lighter weight far from the center. For example, a 12-gram weight placed 2 centimeters to the left of the center might balance a 6-gram weight placed 4 centimeters to the right.

This concept was completely beyond the ability or interest of 3- to 5-year-olds. In Piaget's experiments, they randomly hung different weights on different hooks. By age 7, children realized that the scale could be balanced by putting the same amount of weight on each arm. However, they didn't know or care that the distance from the center was important. By age 10, at the end of the concrete operational stage, children thought about location, but they used trial and error, not logic. They succeeded with equal weights at equal distances and were pleased when they balanced different weights, but they did not figure out the formula.

Finally, by about age 13 or 14, some children hypothesized the reciprocal relationship between weight and distance, tested this hypothesis, and formulated the mathematical formula, solving the balance problem accurately and efficiently. Piaget attributed each of these advances to attainment of the next cognitive stage beyond concrete operations (Piaget & Inhelder, 1969).

ANSWER TO OBSERVATION QUIZ
(from page 327) They share gender, facial expressions, and hand positions. They are all boys; the presence of a girl or two would call for the boys to assume very different expressions and postures. Instead, they are all wearing impassive expressions, trying to look cool: No one is smiling, scowling, or clowning. Not one of them is touching another with his hands; although one boy is leaning on two friends' shoulders, he is careful to rest on his wrists, not his hands. ●

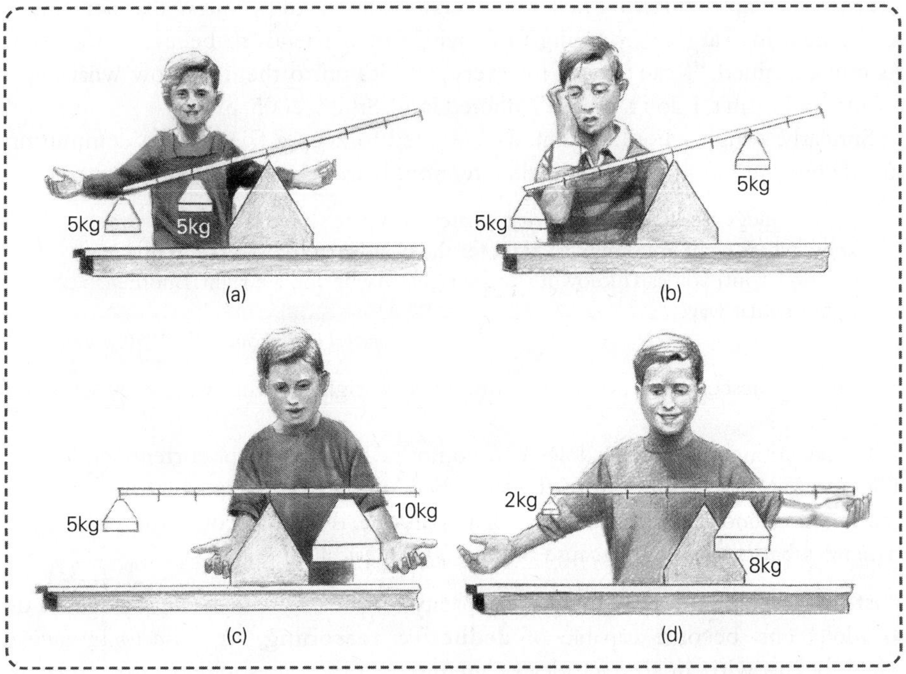

FIGURE 9.5 How to Balance a Scale Piaget's balance-scale test of formal reasoning, as it is attempted by *(a)* a 4-year-old, *(b)* a 7-year-old, *(c)* a 10-year-old, and *(d)* a 14-year-old. The key to balancing the scale is to understand the reciprocity of weight and distance; the realization of that principle requires formal operational thought.

HYPOTHETICAL-DEDUCTIVE THOUGHT One hallmark of formal operational thought is the capacity to think of possibility, not just reality. Adolescents "start with possible solutions and progress to determine which is the real solution" (Lutz & Sternberg, 1999, p. 283). "Here and now" is only one of many alternatives, including "there and then," "long, long ago," "nowhere," "not yet," and "never." As Piaget said:

> The adolescent . . . thinks beyond the present and forms theories about everything, delighting especially in considerations of that which is not.
>
> *[Piaget, 1950/1972, p. 148]*

hypothetical thought
Reasoning that includes propositions and possibilities that may not reflect reality.

AP PHOTO / LAS CRUCES SUN-NEWS, VLADIMIR CHALOUPKA

A Proud Teacher "Is it possible to train a cockroach?" This hypothetical question, an example of formal operational thought, was posed by 15-year-old Tristan Williams of New Mexico. In his award-winning science project, he succeeded in conditioning Madagascar cockroaches to hiss at the sight of a permanent marker. (His parents' logical reasoning about having 600 cockroaches living in their home is not known.)

Tiny Elephants Adolescents are therefore primed to engage in **hypothetical thought,** reasoning about *what-if* propositions that may or may not reflect reality. For example, consider this question:

> If dogs are bigger than elephants, and
> If mice are bigger than dogs,
> Are elephants smaller than mice?

Children younger than about age 10 answer no. They have seen elephants and mice, so the logic escapes them. Some adolescents answer yes. They understand what *if* means (Moshman, 2005).

Note that this is an advanced example of *transitive inference,* explained in Chapter 7. School-age children learn to do simple comparisons ("Jim is taller than David"), but they are confused when a comparison contradicts what they know. By contrast, some adolescents proudly say, "Yes, elephants are smaller than mice." Piaget said:

> *Possibility* no longer appears merely as an extension of an empirical situation or of action actually performed. Instead, it is *reality* that is now secondary to *possibility.*
>
> *[Inhelder & Piaget, 1958, p. 251; emphasis in original]*

Conviction and Criticism Hypothetical thought transforms a person's perceptions, although not necessarily for the better. Adolescents' reflection about serious issues becomes complicated because they consider many possibilities, sometimes sidetracking logical conclusions about the immediate issues (Moshman, 2005).

For example, a survey of U.S. teenagers' religious ideas found that most 13- to 17-year-olds considered themselves religious and thought that practicing their particular faith would help them avoid hell. However, they hesitated to follow that conviction to the next logical step by trying to convince their friends to believe as they did. As one explained, "I can't speak for everybody, it's up to them. I know what's best for me, and I can't, I don't, preach" (quoted in C. Smith, 2005, p. 147).

Similarly, a high school student who wanted to keep a friend from committing suicide hesitated to judge her friend's intentions because

> [T]o . . . judge [someone] means that whatever you are saying is right and you know what's right. You know it's right for them and you know it's right in every situation. [But] you can't know if you are right. Maybe you are right. But then, right in what way?
>
> *[quoted in Gilligan et al., 1990, p. 130]*

deductive reasoning
Reasoning from a general statement, premise, or principle, through logical steps, to figure out (deduce) specifics. (Sometimes called *top-down reasoning*.)

inductive reasoning
Reasoning from one or more specific experiences or facts to a general conclusion; may be less cognitively advanced than deduction. (Sometimes called *bottom-up reasoning*.)

Although adolescents are not always sure what is "right in what way," they see what is wrong.

Unlike younger children, adolescents do not necessarily accept current conditions. They criticize everything, from the way their mother cooks spaghetti to why the Gregorian calendar, not the Chinese or Jewish one, is used to count the years. They criticize what *is,* precisely because of their hypothetical thinking.

Abstract Thinking In developing the capacity to think hypothetically, by age 14 or so adolescents become capable of **deductive reasoning,** or *top-down reasoning,* which begins with an abstract idea or premise and then uses logic to draw specific conclusions (Galotti, 2002; D. P. Keating, 2004). By contrast, **inductive reasoning,** or *bottom-up reasoning,* predominates during the school years, as children accumulate facts and personal experiences (the knowledge base) to aid their thought.

In essence, a child's reasoning goes like this: "This creature waddles and quacks. Ducks waddle and quack. Therefore, this creature must be a duck." This reasoning is inductive: It progresses from particulars ("waddles" and "quacks") to a general conclusion ("It's a duck"). By contrast, deduction progresses from the general to the specific: "If it's a duck, it will waddle and quack" (see Figure 9.6).

ESPECIALLY FOR Natural Scientists
Some ideas that were once universally accepted, such as the belief that the sun moved around the Earth, have been disproved. Is it a failure of inductive or deductive reasoning that leads to false conclusions? (see response, page 333) →

Inductive reasoning
General conclusion
Observation   Ideas from authority
Past experiences

Deductive reasoning
General principle
Application   Test case
Example   Extension
Hypothetical case

FIGURE 9.6 Bottom Up or Top Down? Children, as concrete operational thinkers, are likely to draw conclusions on the basis of their own experiences and what they have been told. This is called inductive, or bottom-up, reasoning. Adolescents can think deductively, from the top down.

Intuitive, Emotional Thought

As many developmentalists over the past three decades have shown, the fact that adolescents *can* use hypothetical-deductive reasoning does not necessarily mean that they *do* use it (Kuhn & Franklin, 2006). Adolescents find it much easier and quicker to forget about logic and follow their impulses.

TWO MODES OF THINKING Advanced logical thought is counterbalanced by the increasing power of intuitive thinking. A **dual-process model** of adolescent cognition has been formulated. In this model, two processing networks exist in the brain and have been given various names: intuitive/analytic, implicit/explicit, creative/factual, contextualized/decontextualized, unconscious/conscious, gist/quantitative, emotional/intellectual, experiential/rational.

Although each pair of labels refers to the same duality, acknowledging that the mind is not one simple structure but has multiple functions and pathways (J. Evans, 2008), the emphasis of each pair differs. We focus here on the intuitive/analytic pair, which is often used to describe dual-process thinking in adolescence (Gerrard et al., 2008).

dual-process model
The notion that two networks exist within the human brain, one for emotional and one for analytical processing of stimuli.

Dual Processing Signs of both analysis and emotion are evident in these two girls at a school in south Texas. They are using wireless computers to study, perhaps analyzing information, formatting questions, and drawing logical conclusions. At the same time, intuitive thinking is also on display: The girls are sitting side by side for companionship and are dressed similarly, wearing shoes designed more for fashion than for walking.

intuitive thought
Thought that arises from an emotion or a hunch, beyond rational explanation, and is influenced by past experiences and cultural assumptions.

analytic thought
Thought that results from analysis, such as a systematic ranking of pros and cons, risks and consequences, possibilities and facts. Analytic thought depends on logic and rationality.

- **Intuitive thought** begins with a prior belief, past experience, or common assumption, rather than with a logical premise. Thoughts spring forth from memories and feelings. Intuitive cognition is quick and powerful; it feels "right."

- **Analytic thought** is the formal, logical, hypothetical-deductive thinking described by Piaget. It involves rational analysis of many factors whose interactions must be calculated, as in the scale-balancing problem. Analytic thinking requires a certain level of intellectual maturity, brain capacity, motivation, and practice.

Comparing Intuition and Analysis Paul Klaczynski has conducted many studies comparing the thinking of children, young adolescents, and older adolescents (usually 9-, 12-, and 15-year-olds). In one study (2001), he presented 19 logical problems, one of which read as follows:

> Timothy is very good-looking, strong, and does not smoke. He likes hanging around with his male friends, watching sports on TV, and driving his Ford Mustang convertible. He's very concerned with how he looks and with being in good shape. He is a high school senior now and is trying to get a college scholarship.
>
> *Based on this [description], rank each statement in terms of how likely it is to be true. . . . The most likely statement should get a 1. The least likely statement should get a 6.*

_____ Timothy has a girlfriend.
_____ Timothy is an athlete.
_____ Timothy is popular and an athlete.
_____ Timothy is a teacher's pet and has a girlfriend.
_____ Timothy is a teacher's pet.
_____ Timothy is popular.

PETER HVIZDAK / THE IMAGE WORKS

Her Whole Brain Chess players like this girl, who is competing in a Connecticut championship match, must be analytic, thinking several moves ahead. But sometimes an unexpected intuitive move unnerves the opposition and leads to victory.

In ranking these statements, most (73 percent) of the students made at least one analytic error. Their mistake was to rank a double statement (e.g., popular *and* an athlete) as more likely than a single statement included in it (popular *or* an athlete). A double statement cannot be more likely than either of its parts; therefore, those 73 percent were illogical and wrong.

This error is an example of intuitive thought: The adolescents jumped to the more inclusive statement, taking a quick, experiential leap rather than sticking to the logic. In this study, almost all were analytical and logical on some of the 19 problems but not on others. Klaczynski concluded that teenagers *can* use logic but that "most adolescents do not demonstrate a level of performance commensurate with their abilities" (2001, p. 854).

Preferred Conclusions What would motivate adolescents to use—or fail to use—their formal operational thinking? The students in the example above had learned the scientific method in school, and they knew that scientists use empirical evidence and deductive reasoning. But they did not always think like scientists. Why not?

Dozens of experiments and extensive theorizing have revealed some answers (A. Diamond & Kirkham, 2005; Klaczynski, 2005; Kuhn & Franklin, 2006). Essentially, logic is more difficult than intuition, and it does not always feel right. It sometimes leads people to doubt their comfortable, long-standing prejudices.

Once people (of any age) reach an emotional conclusion (sometimes called a "gut feeling"), they resist changing their minds, avoiding logic that might reveal their poor judgment. Egocentrism makes rational analysis even more difficult, as one psychologist discovered when her teenage son called late one night to be picked up from a party that had "gotten out of hand." The boy heard

his frustrated father lament "drinking and trouble—haven't you figured out the connection?" Despite the late hour and his shaky state, the teenager advanced a lengthy argument to the effect that his father had the causality all wrong and the trouble should be attributed to other covariates, among them bad luck.

[Kuhn & Franklin, 2006, p. 966]

RESPONSE FOR Natural Scientists (from page 331) Probably both. Our false assumptions are not logically tested, because we do not realize that they might need testing. ●

BETTER THINKING Sometimes adults believe that advanced thinking leads to more cautious behavior (as in the father's connection between trouble and alcohol in the excerpt above). Adults are particularly critical of the egocentrism that leads a teenager to risk future addiction by experimenting with drugs or to risk pregnancy and AIDS in order to avoid the awkwardness of using a condom.

But adults may themselves be egocentric in making such judgments and in assuming that adolescents share their values. Parents want healthy, long-living children, and they conclude that adolescents miscalculate or use faulty reasoning when they risk their lives. Adolescents, however, value social warmth and friendship. A 15-year-old who is offered a cigarette might make a rational decision to choose immediate social acceptance over the distant risk of lung cancer (Engels et al., 2006).

Intuitive thinking is quick and passionate—and therefore sometimes beneficial. As one expert explains, "Zeal in adolescents can fuel positive humanistic efforts to feed the poor and care for the sick, yet it can also lead to dogmatic attitudes, intolerance . . . passions captured by a negatively charismatic figure like Adolf Hitler or Osama bin Laden" (Dahl, 2004, p. 21).

At every age, sometimes the best thinking is "fast and frugal" (Gigerenzer et al., 1999). Weighing alternatives, and thinking of possibilities, may become paralyzing. The systematic, analytic thought that Piaget described may be slow and costly— wasting precious time when a young person should take action. Some of these actions would disturb adults if they knew about them, but many adults fondly remember their own adolescent risk taking: Their fond memories turn to fear only when they imagine their own children behaving in the same way.

KEYPoints

- Adolescent brain development is uneven, with growth of the limbic system outpacing advances in the prefrontal cortex. This imbalance may result in emotional impulses that are poorly moderated by reflection.

- Thinking reaches heightened self-consciousness at puberty, when adolescent egocentrism includes personal fables, feelings of invincibility, and imaginary audiences.

- Piaget's fourth and final stage of intelligence, formal operational thought, is characterized by abstract reasoning, deductive logic, and hypothetical thinking.

- The brain's dual-processing networks cause people to use analytical thinking sometimes and quick, intuitive reasoning at other times.

Teaching and Learning

Given the nature of the adolescent brain and mind, what and how should teenagers be taught? Many educators, developmentalists, political leaders, and parents want to know exactly what curricula and school structures are best for 11- to 18-year-olds. The research does not support any single answer. Various scientists, nations, and schools are trying many different strategies, some of which are based on opposite, but logical, hypotheses.

ANDREW LICHTENSTEIN / CORBIS

secondary education
The period after primary education (elementary or grade school) and before tertiary education (college). It usually occurs from about age 12 to age 18, although the age range varies somewhat by school and by nation.

middle school
A school for children in the grades between elementary and high school. Middle school usually begins with grade 5 or 6 and ends with grade 8.

A School Connection Middle schools are more likely to succeed when they combine high academic standards with consistent discipline and high motivation among both students and teachers. This public school in New York City's South Bronx is affiliated with the Knowledge Is Power Program, offering college preparation to students from low-income families.

Since definitive answers are elusive, we offer definitions, facts, issues, and possibilities. **Secondary education**—traditionally grades 7 through 12—describes the school years after elementary school (known as *primary education*) and before college or university (known as *tertiary education*). Adults with more education tend to be healthier and wealthier. Worldwide, "secondary education has [the] transformational ability to change lives for the better. . . . For young people all over the world, primary education is no longer enough" (World Bank, 2005, pp. xi–xii).

Partly because political leaders recognize that an educated population advances national wealth, the number of students in secondary schools is increasing rapidly. In 2006, an estimated 85 percent of the world's children received some secondary education: This included virtually all the 10- to 14-year-olds in the Americas, East Asia, and Europe; 70 percent in South Asia; and 40 percent in sub-Saharan Africa (UNESCO Institute for Statistics, 2009).

Middle School

In many nations, two levels of secondary education follow primary school. Traditionally, these two secondary levels were junior high schools for younger students (usually grades 7 and 8) and senior high schools for older children (usually grades 9 through 12). More recently, intermediate schools, or **middle schools,** have been established to educate children in grades 6, 7, and 8.

LESS LEARNING Middle school is a crucial time. "Long-term academic trajectories—the choice to stay in school or to drop out and the selection in high school of academic college-prep courses versus basic-level courses—are strongly influenced by experience in grades 6–8" (C. E. Snow et al., 2007, p. 72).

Nevertheless, during the middle school years, academic achievement often slows down and behavioral problems increase. Instead of being supportive of developing egos, middle schools may be "developmentally regressive" (Eccles, 2004, p. 141), forcing children to take a step backward. The first year of middle school has been called the "low ebb" of learning (Covington & Dray, 2002).

One reason for this decline is that students become less conscientious about their schoolwork, possibly distracted by their newly maturing bodies and their dawning interest in sex (Heaven & Ciarrochi, 2008). Another reason is that, even though bonding between students and teachers helps students learn and avoid risky behavior (Crosnoe et al., 2004), teachers and students are disconnected from one another, partly because each teacher has dozens, sometimes hundreds, of students (Eccles, 2004).

Students' relationships with one another also deteriorate in middle school, partly because they suddenly find themselves among hundreds of strangers, many older and bigger than they are. Relational aggression is admired, and it does not diminish the bully's self-esteem (A. J. Rose & Swenson, 2009).

Because new middle school students have many classmates they have never seen before, first impressions become especially significant. Unfortunately, this coincides with the various physiological changes that make each developing person acutely self-conscious.

Several studies find that aggressive and drug-using students in middle schools tend to be admired over those who are conscientious and studious. This is a marked difference from elementary school experience (J. P. Allen et al., 2005; Mayeux & Cillessen, 2007; A. J. Rose et al., 2004).

Concerns about being popular prevent students from emulating those who are studious—the so-called geeks and nerds. Many students at this age would rather sacrifice their academic standing than risk social exclusion. A study of math achievement in middle schools in three nations (Germany, Canada, and Israel) found that mathematically gifted girls were particularly likely to underachieve (Boehnke, 2008). Many boys consider academic success to be unattractive (C. E. Snow et al., 2007).

FEAR OF FAILURE To pinpoint the developmental mismatch between students' needs and the middle school environment, remember that egocentrism leads young people to feelings of shame or fantasies of stardom (performing for an imaginary audience). Antithetical to that, school schedules often require a change of rooms, teachers, and classmates every 40 minutes or so, making acclaim, recognition, and even friendship difficult.

When extracurricular activities become competitive, fragile egos may shun the glare of attention from coaches, advisers, or other students. Extracurricular activities that welcome all youth and catch their interest are scarce.

In middle school, grades often fall because teachers mark more harshly and students are less motivated to do their best. One way to avoid failing is to avoid trying; in such a situation, a low grade may be considered unimportant.

Young adolescents sometimes cope with stress by blaming their troubles on others—classmates, teachers, parents, governments. This tendency may help explain the results of a study in Los Angeles: Middle school students in more ethnically diverse schools felt safer and less lonely than did children in more homogeneous schools. The researchers suggest that students who feel attacked "can attribute their plight to the prejudice of other people" rather than to their own shortcomings (Juvonen et al., 2006, p. 398); thus, they feel more a part of their group.

Electronic Technology and Cognition

A mere two decades ago, no one knew about the World Wide Web, instant messaging, Facebook, blogs, iPods, Blackberries, or digital cameras. Yet today, teenagers are intimately acquainted with all of them, even creating new texting "languages" to communicate with one another. In 1995, only half of all U.S. public schools had Internet capacity; now just about all of them do (U.S. Bureau of the Census, 2008).

THE DIGITAL DIVIDE The **digital divide,** which refers to the gap between people who have computer access and those who do not, was bemoaned in the 1990s because it separated boys from girls and rich from poor (Dijk, 2005; Norris, 2001). Today in most developed nations, both of these gaps have narrowed.

Age is now the greatest divider between Internet users and nonusers. In 2005 (the year of the latest reliable statistics), the proportion of U.S. adolescents who used the Internet (78 percent) was the largest of any age group. The proportion of people over age 65 who used the Internet was lowest (20 percent) (T. D. Snyder et al., 2006).

Teenagers worldwide use the Internet for, among other things, obtaining information about sex that their schools and parents do not provide (Borzekowski & Rickert, 2001; Gray et al., 2005; Suzuki & Calzo, 2006). An international political project involving 3,000 adolescents from 129 developed and developing nations linked all of them via e-mail—some from home and others through nearby schools, libraries, or Internet cafés (see Figure 9.7 on page 337; Cassell et al., 2006). Internationally, those who live in rural areas, especially areas without electricity, are the only adolescents who are unlikely to use computers as a learning tool (Holderness, 2006).

BENEFITS AND HAZARDS OF ELECTRONIC TECHNOLOGY The Internet and other forms of electronic technology can accelerate learning, but what they have to teach may not always be beneficial.

ESPECIALLY FOR Middle School Teachers You think your lectures are interesting and you know you care about your students, yet many of them cut class, come late, or sleep through it. What do you do? (see response, page 336) →

digital divide
The gap between students who have access to computers and those who do not, often a gap between rich and poor. In the United States and most developed nations, this gap has now been bridged due to the prevalence of computers in schools.

RAJESH KUMAR SINGH / AP PHOTO

Middle School Slump? These students in rural India are the same age as middle school students in developed nations, but their enthusiasm for school has not waned. One reason is that they do not take education for granted; only a select few are able to stay in school beyond age 11. Another reason may be seen here: The government is trying to upgrade the curriculum by providing traveling, Internet-connected computers.

Educational Uses Computers are now widely seen as essential for education. This view may be exaggerated, in that international tests of math achievement find that children with and without computers do equally well. Nonetheless, it seems that using word processing improves reading and spatial skills (L. A. Jackson et al., 2006; B. J. Sternberg et al., 2007).

Some students use the Internet to short-circuit research assignments, but savvy teachers require them to evaluate their sources—an important cognitive skill. The Internet can enhance collaboration among students and can encourage a creative synthesis of visual, verbal, and mathematical education (Palfrey & Gasser, 2008). Educators have often hoped to foster cooperation and multidisciplinary learning; now they have a tool to do so.

However, most teen Internet use is not educational as narrowly defined. Instead, the main use is social, as adolescents keep in touch with friends—usually friends they know from school—via e-mail, texting, and cell phones (P. M. Greenfield et al., 2006). Many technological advances require social interaction. A decade ago, the few teenagers who spent hours online may have become more isolated as a result, but the situation is different today: "Most recent Internet studies have demonstrated that adolescents' online communication stimulates, rather than reduces, social connectedness and/or well-being" (Valkenburg & Peter, 2009, p. 2).

Adolescent cognitive growth benefits from shared experiences and opinions (Subrahmanyam et al., 2006). Online communication brings friends closer and deepens thinking. These effects are strongest in adolescents who find face-to-face intimacy difficult, such as many younger teenagers and boys "for whom shyness and self-consciousness are inherent to their developmental stage" (Valkenburg & Peter, 2009, p. 2). Disabled adolescents use the Internet as much as their able-bodied peers do (Lathouwers et al., 2009).

Often communication via the Internet bolsters fragile self-esteem. That may be lifesaving for teenagers who feel socially isolated because of their sexual orientation, ethnic group, or native language. Even those who are not isolated can learn from sources beyond their immediate circle and gain information they need (Tynes, 2007).

Potential Abuses Although some of the problems attributed to the Internet are not problems at all, Internet use does have some pitfalls. Adolescents sometimes share

RESPONSE FOR Middle School Teachers (from page 335) Students need both challenge and involvement; avoid lessons that are too easy or too passive. Create small groups; assign oral reports, debates, and role-plays; and so on. Remember that adolescents like to hear one another's thoughts and their own voices. ●

personal information online without thinking about the possible consequences (Palfrey & Glasser, 2008). When young people connect with strangers on the Internet, adults fear that they will fall victim to sexual predators. Certainly, some teenagers are harmed by people whom they first meet online, but the technology itself may simply be a new avenue for the kind of abuse that has always plagued the young.

Similar arguments are made about **cyberbullying,** when one person bullies another by spreading insults and rumors via e-mail, texting, or anonymous but widespread messages and photos sent to cell phones and computers (Li, 2007). One study found that 23 percent of secondary school students had experienced cyberbullying and 16 percent of them said they had engaged in it (Dehue et al., 2008), although few of their parents knew about it.

There are differences in opinion regarding cyberbullying. Some fear that the anonymity provided by electronic technology brings out the worst in people, who flame and insult online but would not do so in person (Kornblum, 2008). However, one expert on bullying believes that cyberbullying is similar to other forms, new in mode but not in intent or degree of harm (P. K. Smith et al., 2008).

Indeed, the same uncertainties surround many adolescent uses of technology. Let us take a detailed look at the Internet-related challenges posed by one behavior in particular: self-mutilation, or self-injury done primarily to relieve depression and guilt (Whitlock et al., 2006). "Cutting," as this practice is known, may be thought of as one of the challenges posed by the Internet. Currently, more than 400 Web sites are dedicated to it.

Cutting is addictive, particularly for adolescent girls (Yates, 2004). Analysis of a representative sample of 3,219 posts on various cutting Web sites found that most were positive and helpful, allowing self-injuring adolescents to "establish interpersonal intimacy . . . , [which is] especially difficult for young people struggling with intense shame, isolation, and distress" (Whitlock et al., 2006, p. 415). The most common theme of the messages was informal support (28 percent), while many other posts described formal treatment (7 percent, usually positively) and emotional triggers (20 percent) (Whitlock et al., 2006).

Less common were negative posts that provided suggestions for concealment of the marks caused by self-injury (9 percent) or information on techniques and paraphernalia (6 percent). Here is one chilling exchange:

> Poster 1: Does anyone know how to cut deep without having it sting and bleed too much?

> Poster 2: I use box cutter blades. You have to pull the skin really tight and press the blade down really hard. You can also use a tourniquet to make it bleed more.

> Poster 3: I've found that if you press your blade against the skin at the depth you want the cut to be and draw the blade really fast it doesn't hurt and there is blood galore. Be careful, though, 'cause you can go very deep without meaning to.

> [quoted in Whitlock et al., 2006, p. 413]

Hello . . . . I believe that Katia has spoken for most of us when she tells us how discouraged she is. I have heard it from many other people and have heard of stagnation in other discussion groups. I am very frustrated right now. The groups I am in aren't doing much. . . . It's awfully discouraging! But think of it from the perspective that we are all part of an incredible process, a process which has never before happened in the history of humanity. We are all children, essentially "dumped" into virtual rooms with a broad topic in mind, and the rest is ultimately up to us. It's difficult! The process, like any (life, school, work, a hike, everything) has its ups and downs. That sounds kind of trite—but it's true. And it's inevitable. And it is very valuable for us as human beings. Perhaps even more so than changing the world, we are learning and growing personally, which IS indirectly shaping the future. . . . Practically speaking, I have a suggestion as to how we all can move forward from this point, and get out of the "rut."

1. Every group, think clearly and put something together in writing asking the question, "What is our ultimate goal?" I think that putting a finger on all of the objectives both practical and philosophical will be a good starting point.

2. Then, start by making a timeline to carry out those objectives—dividing them, starting small and then building it up. For example, "In the first two weeks we need to figure out a general organizational flow for our project. The week following that, we need to go into finer details and figure out what sub-groups will exist. The 4th week, we need to figure out how people will be elected and how people will carry out the tasks in each group. Blah, blah, blah."

. . . And, through time and through perseverance, it will take off! I hope that we can all move forward and get back into the fun and excitement of our work and play. I am so privileged to know all of you. I feel happy and look forward to all the years we will have together. What are all your thoughts?

Source: Quoted in Cassell et al., 2006.

FIGURE 9.7 Discouraged, But . . . You might think that the logical analysis shown in this e-mail must come from a wise adult; but, no, the writer is 14 years old. He is in India, writing to adolescents he had not met in nations he had not visited. This project joined adolescents worldwide in a junior political summit.

cyberbullying
Bullying that occurs via Internet insults and rumors, texting, anonymous phone calls, and video embarrassment.

Similarly, there are hundreds of Web sites directed at young people that deal with such topics as self-starvation, homophobia, violent sex, and racism. Some of them attempt to help adolescents deal with their problems in these areas. Others, however, prey on adolescents' vulnerabilities.

The Internet attracts adolescents to addictions that are known to harm adults. Many addictions may be especially harmful if they form before the person has the maturity to recognize the problem. For example, online gambling is especially attractive to adolescents (Yen et al., 2008). For some, the Internet itself is addictive (K. Choi et al., 2009).

Remember that adolescent emotions and impulses tend to develop faster than reason and reflection do. Internet sources may condone actions that adolescents would otherwise not engage in. Some Web sites require that a user be over age 18, but many teens ignore that restriction. Technology is just a tool, but adolescents must be taught to use it with care (Valkenburg & Peter, 2009).

Entering a New School

The transition from one school to another often impairs a young person's ability to function and learn. Changing schools just when the growth spurt is occurring and sexual characteristics are developing is bound to create stress. Remember from Chapter 7 that minor stresses can become overwhelming if they accumulate.

> A number of disorders and symptoms of psychopathology, including depression, self-injury behavior, substance abuse, eating disorders, bipolar disorder, and schizophrenia have striking developmental patterns corresponding to transitions in early and late adolescence.
>
> *[A. S. Masten, 2004, p. 310]*

Of course, the transition to middle school or high school cannot be blamed for every disorder, since hormones, body shape, sexual impulses, family, and culture also contribute. All the same, genes that predispose a person to psychopathology and thrill seeking may activate at puberty, causing havoc for those who lack emotional regulation (E. F. Walker, 2002).

The first year in any new school (middle school, high school, or college) correlates with increased bullying, decreased achievement, depression, and eating disorders. Many schools have instituted special programs for first-year students.

One particularly effective way to ease the transition to a new school is to strengthen the young person's support network. Proactive involvement of students and families may help, especially if some classmates are from the same community (Holland et al., 2007).

A special program for Mexican American adolescents (who, as a group, often do worse in secondary school than their intellectual ability would predict) encouraged new middle school students to support one another and provided parents with suggestions to aid their children's learning. Students in this program were more likely to stay in school than were other, similar adolescents (N. A. Gonzales et al., 2004).

This finding raises the special case of immigrant adolescents who enter a new country as well as a new school, a double transition. Perhaps because they undergo puberty at the same time they are learning a new language, such newcomers are less likely to graduate on time than are immigrants who arrived in their new country at younger ages. In general, however, immigrants entering a new school are more likely to graduate than are native-born students who likewise change schools (A. E. Schwartz, 2009).

The experience of immigrant adolescents underscores the need for support when teenagers change schools. Immigrants have far higher success rates (measured by achievement tests as well as graduation rates) if they attend a "newcomer school," in which all the students are immigrants and a support network is available.

High School

As we have seen, adolescents can think abstractly, analytically, hypothetically, and logically—as well as personally, emotionally, intuitively, and experientially. The curriculum and teaching style of high school often require only logical thinking.

In theory and sometimes in practice, high schools promote students' analytic ability. This new ability enables students to use logic to override the "biases that not only preserve existing beliefs but also perpetuate stereotypes and inhibit development" (Klaczynski, 2005, p. 71).

The question is whether too much stress is placed on rational and abstract thought. Most academic subjects emphasize logic, often requiring students to make systematic deductions from laboratory experiments or historical documents. This is exactly what formal operational thinking enables adolescents to do. As a practical matter, however, the curriculum of the high school is often disconnected from the needs and requirements of three key groups: employers, colleges, and students themselves.

FOCUS ON THE COLLEGE-BOUND From a developmental perspective, the fact that high schools emphasize formal thinking makes sense, since by the later years of adolescence, many students are capable of attaining that level. Some nations are trying to raise their standards, partly so that more students will achieve the highest levels of thought. However, high school classes often assume that students have mastered formal thinking, instead of teaching them how to do it (Kuhn & Franklin, 2006).

The Same Situation, Many Miles Apart: Top Students The New York girls just won a classroom history contest, and the Kenyan boys are studying physics, a subject available only to the brightest African students.

OBSERVATION QUIZ

Although the two groups of winners are thousands of miles apart, there are three evident similarities between them. What are they? (see answer, page 341) →

In the United States, an increasing number of high school students are enrolled in classes that are designed to be more rigorous and that require them to pass externally scored exams—for example, the International Baccalaureate (IB) or the Advanced Placement (AP) exam. In 2006, more than 1 million students took at least one AP class. The hope is that such classes will lead to better thinking, or at least higher achievement, although this effect has not yet been proved (McNeil, 2007; Viadero, 2006).

Another manifestation of the trend toward more rigorous education is the greater number of requirements that all students must fulfill in order to receive an academic diploma. In many U.S. schools, no one is allowed to earn a vocational or general diploma unless the parents specifically request it (L. Olson, 2005). Many schools require two years of math beyond algebra, two years of laboratory science, three years of history, and four years of English. Some study of a language other than English is usually required as well, although the specific requirements vary a great deal.

In 2008, twenty-three U.S. states required students to pass a **high-stakes test** (in addition to passing a certain number of required courses) in order to graduate (*Education Week,* 2008). Any exam for which the consequences of failing are severe is

high-stakes test
An evaluation that is critical in determining success or failure. A single test that determines whether a student will graduate or be promoted is a high-stakes test.

called a *high-stakes test*. (Traditionally, such tests were used when adults sought professional licenses to go into practice as, for example, lawyers, doctors, and clinical psychologists.)

Some people consider high-stakes tests and rigorous course requirements for high school graduation to be good ways to raise academic standards; others believe that these changes destroy true learning. The fear is that teachers may be forced to "teach to the test," concentrating on rote memorization of factual information and ignoring both analysis and intuition (S. L. Nichols & Berliner, 2007).

Ironically, just when U.S. schools are instituting high-stakes tests and requiring more courses, many East Asian nations are moving in the opposite direction (Fujita, 2000). According to a report on Chinese education:

> [S]ome prominent government officials have grown concerned that too many students have become the sort of stressed-out, test-acing drone who fails to acquire the skills—creativity, flexibility, initiative, leadership—said to be necessary in the global marketplace.
>
> *[Hulbert, 2007, p. 36]*

The same concerns have led to changes in the British, Korean, and Japanese educational systems, although cultural differences remain (Okumoto, 2008). The trend in Japan is toward fewer academic requirements for high school, classes five days a week instead of six, and less "examination hell," as the high-stakes tests in many East Asian nations have been called. The science adviser to the prime minister of Japan recommends more flexibility in education in order to promote more innovation. He wants students to "study whatever they are interested in" rather than to narrow their learning so as to score high on one final test (Normile, 2007).

ESPECIALLY FOR High School Teachers You are much more interested in the nuances and controversies than in the basic facts of your subject, but you know that your students will take high-stakes tests on the basics and that their scores will have a major impact on their futures. What should you do? (see response, page 342) ➜

COLLEGE FOR ALL? In the United States, one result of pushing almost all high school students to pursue an academic curriculum is that more are prepared for college. Another result is that more students drop out of high school. Of those who do graduate, many do not seek any further education. This category includes about one-third of high school students in the United States and at least two-thirds in most other nations (UNESCO Institute for Statistics, 2009).

One solution to this problem is to arrange apprenticeships, whereby students work for various local businesses and earn credits toward graduation for what they learn. Germany was the innovator in such programs, with tens of thousands of high school students in apprenticeships during the 1980s. The students were guaranteed jobs if they did well. The German apprenticeship system was successful when manufacturers needed more workers. As unemployment rates among adult workers increased, however, many employers left the program and only the most motivated students succeeded (Grollmann & Rauner, 2007).

Furthermore, enrollment in apprenticeship programs often depends not on students' interests and talents but on family socioeconomic status (SES) and the local job market (Lehmann, 2004). This happens in every nation. According to one counselor in a Korean school designed for students who were not college-bound:

> Our students start to search for jobs when they become seniors. Most of the jobs that they end up getting are service jobs that do not require special skills. So they do not need to prepare for such jobs. . . . What they are required to have are only two things: diploma and good appearance.
>
> *[quoted in J-a. Choi, 2005, p. 273]*

Most students aspire to college and spurn vocational education in high school. That makes sense in the twenty-first century because more and more jobs require tertiary education. Employers provide specific training (usually much more detailed than the training any high school can offer) and hope that the newly hired employees will be able to read, think, write, and get along with other workers. Those may be the skills that high schools should focus on—skills that are hard to measure on a high-stakes test.

HIGH SCHOOL DROPOUTS Our discussion thus far has assumed that students want to graduate from high school. However, many students do not complete their high school education. Developed nations typically require students to be enrolled in school until they reach a certain age, usually between 14 and 18, with age 16 being the average. Whenever high-stakes tests are a requisite for graduation, there is a "potential unintended consequence" that more high school students will drop out (Christenson & Thurlow, 2004, p. 36).

To understand this phenomenon, you need to realize that dropout and graduation statistics are presented in many ways, often to make schools seem particularly good or bad. When reading such statistics, be wary of the intent of the presenter.

One method to measure dropouts is to compare the number of students in the ninth grade with the number who do, or do not, graduate four years later. This method finds low graduation rates because those who take five years to graduate, who leave school and return, who earn a GED (General Education Development, formerly General Education Diploma), and who transfer to another school system are all counted as nongraduates. Using this method, researchers found that about 28 percent of U.S. students who were ninth-graders in 2004 did not graduate in 2008 (*Education Week,* 2008). In some major cities, including Detroit, Milwaukee, Baltimore, Los Angeles, and Nashville, less than half of ninth-graders graduated four years later.

Other methods find fewer dropouts. The most favorable statistics count as dropouts only those who officially indicate that they are leaving school and not enrolling elsewhere. Even students who attend school only occasionally, fail most of their classes, or disappear are not considered dropouts.

Probably the most valid measure is the percentage of 18- to 24-year-olds who have not completed high school; they are called *status dropouts.* By that measure, over the past few decades, the percentage of dropouts has gradually decreased in the United States in every ethnic group, although rates continue to be twice as high for Hispanics as for any other group (see Figure 9.8).

● **UNDERSTANDING THE NUMBERS**
What percentage of U.S. ninth-graders who fail to graduate in four years eventually earn a high school diploma?

Answer The text notes that 28 percent do not graduate in four years, and Figure 9.8 shows that about 11 percent of emerging adults have not completed high school. That means at least 61 percent (17/28; the 17 is derived by subtracting 11 from 28) of "dropouts" (as measured by the first method described here) earn a diploma. The percentage is higher if many people take and pass the GED exams in adulthood or if many immigrants arrive as young adults without diplomas.

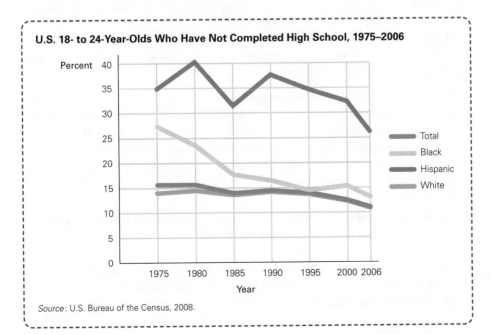

U.S. 18- to 24-Year-Olds Who Have Not Completed High School, 1975–2006

Source: U.S. Bureau of the Census, 2008.

FIGURE 9.8 Dropping Out of High School: Good News, Bad News The good news is that smaller percentages of young people, particularly African Americans, are leaving high school without graduating. The bad news is that too many young people—1 in every 9 young adults overall, and more than 1 in 4 Hispanics—still do not complete high school and are thus at a serious disadvantage in the workforce and in future health.

RESPONSE FOR High School Teachers (from page 000) It would be nice to follow your instincts, but the appropriate response depends partly on pressures within the school and on the expectations of the parents and administration. A comforting fact is that adolescents can think about and learn almost anything if they feel a personal connection to it. Look for ways to teach the facts your students need for the tests as the foundation for the exciting and innovative topics you want to teach. Everyone will learn more, and the tests will be less intimidating for your students. ●

STUDENT ENGAGEMENT Surprisingly, students who are capable of passing their classes are as likely to drop out as are those with learning disabilities. Family incomes, persistence, diligence, and motivation seem to play more crucial roles than intellectual ability when it comes to earning a high school diploma (Fredricks et al., 2004). Engagement may be in particularly short supply, according to a recent study of adolescents: Only one-fifth are actively involved in their schoolwork (Damon, 2008).

To be admired by their peers, some adolescents may appear to be detached from education. Attachment to school and assessment of self-competence typically decline in each consecutive year of high school, particularly among boys (Fredricks & Eccles, 2006; Porche et al., 2004; Wigfield et al., 1997).

One reason for disengagement may be that only formal operational thought is promoted in high school curricula, while egocentric and intuitive thought, which are more relational and social, are largely excluded. Schedules limit social interaction by allowing only a few minutes between classes, and school rules often prohibit students from gathering informally on school grounds before or after classes. Budget cutting often targets extracurricular activities first, and a lack of after-school programs undercuts students' attachment to school (Fredricks & Eccles, 2006).

Another reason for disengagement is that teachers are rarely chosen for their ability to keep students interested. Nor are they encouraged to do so, as I learned when I taught seventh-graders: I was praised when my students were working at their desks (quiet but bored), not when they were engaged in active discussion.

In general, high school teachers are hired for their expertise in one or more academic fields and are considered highly qualified if they studied that topic in college. They are formal operational thinkers, able to answer complex questions about the intricacies of theoretical physics, advanced calculus, and iambic pentameter.

However, some high school teachers believe it is not their role to deal effectively with the social needs of their students, especially students who are emotional and impulsive. Those students are usually sent to a guidance counselor or a dean, who may be responsible for hundreds of students and have no time to help the teacher learn how to engage disruptive students in learning.

Most high schools devalue egocentric, personal, and intuitive thought, to the point where some adolescents feel that they themselves are devalued. This is especially true of immigrant students, who are typically highly motivated to begin with but then disengage, according to a longitudinal study of five ethnic groups (Suarez-Orozco et al., 2008).

What can be done to encourage adolescents to be more engaged in their education? While there is no single, definitive answer to this question, there are many possible avenues to explore. These include the following:

● *Keeping high schools small.* Extensive research suggests that 200 to 400 is the ideal number of students to have in a high school, partly because there is more opportunity for almost every student to be involved in some sort of team or club. Nevertheless, two-thirds of high school students in the United States attend schools with enrollments of over 1,000 (T. D. Snyder et al., 2006). Big schools are more economical, but they do not necessarily increase learning and motivation (Eccles et al., 2003).

● *Encouraging extracurricular activities.* There are "developmental benefits of participation in extracurricular activities for many high school adolescents" (Fredricks & Eccles, 2006, p. 712). Athletic teams elicit positive emotions and school bonding, which explains why students on such teams (including those who are not star athletes) have a low incidence of depression, earn higher grades, and are less prone to using drugs or alcohol. Overall, adolescents who are active in school clubs and on athletic teams are more likely to graduate and go to college (Mahoney et al., 2005). The same is true of students who participate in activities sponsored by nonschool groups, including religious groups (Glanville et al., 2008).

- *Reducing harassment.* School violence is decreasing in the United States, but more students fear violence than before. Setting clear rules for student behavior, rewarding students for attendance, and organizing sporting events within (not just between) schools all reduce crime, according to a survey of Texas middle and high schools (Cheurprakobkit & Bartsch, 2005). The same study shows that measures that increase fear, such as installing metal detectors and handing out strict punishments, are more likely to increase violence than to decrease it. Primary prevention to improve the school climate is needed, because violence tends to be reduced by measures that (1) increase peer friendships, (2) strengthen teacher–student relationships, and (3) promote student involvement. Programs that teach conflict resolution have also had some success, perhaps because they make a point of accomplishing these three goals (e.g., Breunlin et al., 2002).

- *Changing the schedule.* Adolescents are often sleep deprived, partly because their schools start early in the day. Schools that have moved up their start time, from 7:00 or 8:00 A.M to 9:00 A.M., find livelier students (and fewer who fall asleep in class), higher grades, and less sickness.

- *Clustering students.* This means rearranging the schedule so that a small group of teachers shares the same group of students. The result is that the students and teachers can get to know each other better; such relationships seem crucial to attendance, achievement, and graduation.

This list is only a start. A review of adolescent education throughout the world finds that "no culture or nation has worked out a surefire educational psychology to guarantee that every one of the youth is motivated in school" (N. I. Larson & Wilson, 2004, p. 318). School administrators and teachers should recognize that the intellectual potential of adolescents needs challenge, guidance, and engagement. Once that is understood, further experimentation and research are needed in order to identify effective methods of meeting those needs.

KEY Points

- Middle schools tend to be less personal, less flexible, and more tightly regulated than elementary schools, all of which may contribute to declining student achievement.

- Transitions, such as the move into middle school, are difficult for children, especially when they are also coping with the demands of puberty and the self-centeredness of egocentrism.

- Electronic technology can improve learning and aid in the social interactions of students, which benefits their understanding. Cyberbullying and other destructive uses of the Internet are among the drawbacks.

- High school education can advance both analytic and intuitive thinking, but some students are disengaged and many leave without graduating.

SUMMARY

Puberty Begins

1. Puberty refers to the various changes that transform a child's body into an adult one. Biochemical signals from the hypothalamus to the pituitary gland to the adrenal glands (along the HPA axis) increase production of testosterone, estrogen, and various other hormones. These hormones cause the body to grow and change.

2. The visible changes of puberty normally occur anytime from about age 8 to about age 14; puberty more typically begins between ages 11 and 12. The young person's sex, genetic background, body fat, and level of family stress all contribute to this variation in timing.

3. Adolescents who do not reach puberty at about the same age as their friends experience additional stresses. Generally (depending on culture, community, and cohort), early-maturing girls have the most difficult time of all.

4. To sustain body growth, most adolescents consume large quantities of food, although they do not always make healthy choices. One reason for poor nutrition is the desire to lose (or, less often, gain) weight because of anxiety about body image.

5. Although eating disorders are not usually diagnosed until early adulthood, their precursors—overeating, undereating, excessive dieting—are evident during puberty. Many adolescents eat too much of the wrong foods or too little food overall.

The Transformations of Puberty

6. The growth spurt is an acceleration of growth in every part of the body. Peak weight increase usually precedes peak height, which is then followed by peak muscle growth.

7. Sexual characteristics emerge at puberty. The maturation of primary sex characteristics means that by age 13 or so, the young person may be capable of reproducing. Secondary sex characteristics include body shape, breasts, voice, body hair, and numerous other features that differentiate males from females.

8. Sexual activity is influenced more by culture than by physiology. This suggests that the hazards that sometimes occur early in adolescence—pregnancy, sexual abuse, and sexually transmitted infections—are affected as much by social practices as by puberty.

Cognitive Development

9. Various parts of the brain mature during puberty, each at its own rate. The neurological areas dedicated to emotional arousal (including the amygdala) mature ahead of the areas that regulate and rationalize emotional expression (the prefrontal cortex). Consequently, many adolescents seek intense emotional experiences, untempered by rational thought.

10. A form of thinking called adolescent egocentrism may appear, in which young adolescents become so absorbed in themselves that rational thinking is difficult.

11. *Formal operational thought* is Piaget's term for the last of his four periods of cognitive development. Adolescents are no longer earthbound and concrete in their thinking; they prefer to imagine the possible, the probable, and even the impossible, instead of focusing on what is real. They develop hypotheses and explore, using deductive reasoning.

12. Adolescents are increasingly capable of dual processing, or two forms of thought, which are called logical and experiential, or analytic and intuitive. Few teenagers always use logic, although they are capable of doing so. Emotional, intuitive thinking is quicker and more satisfying, and sometimes better, than analytic thought.

Teaching and Learning

13. In middle school, many students tend to be bored, difficult to teach, and hurtful to one another. One reason may be that middle schools are not structured to accommodate egocentrism or intuitive thinking.

14. Many forms of psychopathology increase at the transitions to middle school, to high school, and to college. Transitions may be particularly difficult in adolescence, when young people must also adjust to biological and social changes.

15. Adolescents use technology, particularly the Internet, more than people of any other age group. They reap many educational benefits from doing so, but there are hazards as well.

16. Education in high school seems to emphasize formal operational thinking. In the United States, the demand for accountability has led to more high-stakes testing. This may have unintended consequences, including a higher dropout rate.

KEY TERMS

puberty (p. 310)
menarche (p. 310)
spermarche (p. 310)
hormone (p. 310)
pituitary gland (p. 310)
adrenal glands (p. 310)
HPA (hypothalamus–pituitary–
 adrenal) axis (p. 311)
gonads (p. 311)
estradiol (p. 311)
testosterone (p. 311)

leptin (p. 314)
body image (p. 317)
anorexia nervosa (p. 318)
bulimia nervosa (p. 318)
growth spurt (p. 319)
primary sex characteristics
 (p. 320)
secondary sex characteristics
 (p. 320)
sexually transmitted infection
 (STI) (p. 322)

child sexual abuse (p. 323)
adolescent egocentrism
 (p. 326)
personal fable (p. 327)
invincibility fable (p. 327)
imaginary audience (p. 328)
formal operational thought
 (p. 328)
hypothetical thought (p. 330)
deductive reasoning (p. 330)
inductive reasoning (p. 331)

dual-process model (p. 331)
intuitive thought (p. 332)
analytic thought (p. 332)
secondary education (p. 334)
middle school (p. 334)
digital divide (p. 335)
cyberbullying (p. 337)
high-stakes test (p. 339)

KEY QUESTIONS

1. What aspects of puberty are under direct hormonal control?

2. For whom is experiencing puberty early or late especially difficult, and why?

3. Name two nutritional disorders and explain why adolescents are particularly vulnerable to them.

4. What are the differences between adolescent pregnancy in 1960 and today, both in the United States and worldwide?

5. Why does the limbic system develop before the prefrontal cortex, and what are the consequences?

6. What are the characteristics of formal operational thinking?

7. How might intuition and analysis lead to opposite conclusions?

8. What is it about middle schools and high schools that makes some people call them "developmentally regressive"?

9. What are the advantages and disadvantages of high-stakes testing?

10. What factors increase student engagement in secondary education?

APPLICATIONS

1. Visit a fifth-, sixth-, or seventh-grade class. Note variations in the size and maturity of the students. Do you see any patterns related to gender, ethnicity, body fat, or self-confidence?

2. Interview two to four of your friends who are in their late teens or early 20s about their memories of menarche or spermarche, including their memories of others' reactions. Analyze the connection between body changes and emotional reactions.

3. Talk to a teenager about politics, families, school, religion, or any other topic that might reveal the way that young person thinks. Do you hear any characteristics of adolescent cognition, such as egocentrism, intuitive thinking, or formal thought? Cite examples.

4. Think of a life-changing decision you have made. How did logic and emotion interact? What would have changed if you had given the matter more thought—or less?

CHAPTER OUTLINE

ADOLESCENCE
Psychosocial Development

Our eldest daughter wore the same pair of jeans to tenth grade, day after day. She washed them late each night by hand, and I put them in the dryer very early each morning. Martin, my husband, watched us with bewilderment masked by humor, asking, "Is this some weird female ritual?" Years later, she explained that if she had varied her clothing, her classmates would have thought that she cared about how she looked, and then they might have criticized her.

Our second daughter was 16 when she told me she had pierced her ears again. She wanted to wear more earrings at once than anyone in my generation. "Does this mean you'll take drugs?" I asked. She laughed at my naiveté, happy at my concern.

At age 15, our third daughter was diagnosed with Hodgkin disease, a form of cancer. Martin and I weighed divergent opinions from four physicians, each explaining why his or her treatment would minimize the risk of death. Our daughter had her own priorities: "I don't care what you choose, as long as I keep my hair." (Her hair fell out temporarily, but now her health is good.)

Our youngest, in her first year of middle school, refused to wear her jacket even on the coldest days, much to her teachers' and parents' dismay. Later she offered an explanation: She had wanted her peers to think she was tough.

What strikes me about these episodes now is that I was oblivious to my children's need for peer respect. I reacted as a mother, not as a wise developmentalist. Martin said, "I knew they would become teenagers, but I didn't realize we would become parents of teenagers." ●

AS DESCRIBED IN THIS CHAPTER, all adolescents want respect from their peers as they seek their own identity. Identity, however, is elusive, made more so by our contemporary social contexts. You will learn that religious, sexual, political, and vocational identities have all become more complicated as diversity and globalization have increased. This chapter also discusses the roles of peers and parents and their importance in development (as I witnessed with my own children).

Fortunately, although most adolescents experiment and rebel (many by trying drugs and breaking the law), relatively few succumb to the dangers that adults most fear, such as drug addiction, unwanted pregnancy, suicide, and jail. Instead, they are caught up in things that puzzle their parents but earn respect from their peers, as my daughters were.

This chapter describes the search for identity, the impact of social pressures and examples, and life's joys and hazards for 12- to 18-year-olds. We close with an extended example: drug and alcohol use during adolescence. The causes and consequences of substance abuse are not always what adults imagine.

Identity

identity versus role confusion
Erikson's term for the fifth stage of development, in which the person tries to figure out "Who am I?" but is confused as to which of many possible roles to adopt.

identity
A consistent definition of one's self as a unique individual, in terms of roles, attitudes, beliefs, and aspirations.

identity achievement
Erikson's term for the attainment of identity, or the point at which a person understands who he or she is as a unique individual, in accord with past experiences and future plans.

As Erik Erikson described it, life's fifth psychosocial crisis is **identity versus role confusion.** Many developmentalists agree with Erikson: Psychosocial development during adolescence is often understood as a search for a consistent understanding of oneself. Each young person wants to know, "Who am I?"

Unlike younger children, who believe they are whatever their parents and community say they are, adolescents strive to define themselves. The complexities of finding one's own **identity,** or sense of the self as a unique person, become the primary crisis of adolescence, as young people struggle to reconcile their individual identity with their connection to their heritage (Erikson, 1968).

According to Erikson, the ultimate goal that resolves this crisis is **identity achievement.** Identity is achieved when adolescents reconsider the goals and values set by their parents and culture, accepting some and rejecting others. With their new autonomy, they maintain continuity with their past in order to move toward their future (Chandler et al., 2003). They know who they are; they pursue their own goals.

As with all of Erikson's stages, the clash between the two extremes (here, identity versus role confusion) causes a crisis to be resolved. Erikson's insights inspired many other developmentalists—such as James Marcia (1966), who described three specific ways in which young people cope with this crisis as they strive for identity achievement: role confusion, foreclosure, and moratorium.

Over the past half-century, major psychosocial shifts have lengthened the duration of the identity crisis and added complications (J. E. Côté, 2006; Lichtwarck-Aschoff et al., 2008; Nurmi, 2004). As you will see in the next chapter, many emerging adults are still seeking identity achievement, so role confusion, foreclosure, and moratorium are still evident among them, too.

Not Yet Achieved

role confusion
A situation in which an adolescent does not seem to know or care what his or her identity is. (Also called *identity diffusion.*)

Role confusion is the opposite of identity achievement. It is characterized by a lack of commitment to any goals or values, with apathy and indifference regarding every possible role. Role confusion is sometimes called *identity diffusion,* to emphasize that some adolescents seem diffuse, unfocused, unconcerned about their future (T. M. Phillips & Pittman, 2007).

Even the usual social demands—such as putting away clothes, making friends, completing school assignments, and thinking about college or employment—are beyond adolescents in this identity status. Instead, they might escape by sleeping too much, watching mind-numbing television, turning from one romance to another. Their response to failure, criticism, demands, and deadlines is indifference—a shrug and, "Whatever."

foreclosure
Erikson's term for premature identity formation, which occurs when an adolescent adopts parents' or society's roles and values wholesale, without questioning or analysis.

Identity **foreclosure** occurs when, in order to halt the confusion, young people short-circuit their search by accepting traditional values without examining them (Marcia, 1966; Marcia et al., 1993). They might follow roles and customs handed down from their parents or culture, never exploring alternatives. Or they might adopt an oppositional, negative identity (as the preacher's kid becoming a rebel), again without any thoughtful questioning or individualizing of their path.

An example of foreclosure is a boy who has always anticipated following in his father's footsteps. If his father is a doctor, he might take advanced chemistry and biology in high school; if his father is a day laborer, he might drop out of school at age 16. In Erikson's day, some girls foreclosed by choosing early marriage and motherhood in order to avoid thinking about their own future. Even today, for some young people, foreclosure is a comfortable shelter, a way to avoid the stress of the identity crisis.

A better shelter is **moratorium,** a kind of time-out. Moratorium is considered a more mature response than foreclosure. Societies provide many moratoria that allow adolescents to postpone final identity achievement when they leave high school. The most obvious moratorium in North America is college, where a wide array of required general courses forestall the need to decide what to study or to set a career path.

Other avenues that allow postponement of identity toward the end of adolescence are joining the military or the Peace Corps; doing religious missionary work; and taking internships in government, academe, and industry. All these activities reduce the pressure to choose one identity, offering a ready rejoinder to any older relative who urges an 18-year-old to settle down.

Adolescents in moratorium try to do what is required as student, soldier, missionary, and so on, but they consider these roles temporary, not their final identity. A dynamic-systems approach to identity emphasizes that the identity search is a process, not a static condition.

Moratorium may be either an active or a passive period: Active adolescents question alternatives and explore options, as formal operational thinkers do, while passive adolescents welcome the reduced social pressure, happy with a respite from decision making (Crocetti et al., 2008; Lichtwarck-Aschoff et al., 2008).

moratorium
An adolescent's choice of a socially acceptable way to postpone making identity-achievement decisions. Going to college is a common example.

MITCH WOJNAROWICZ / THE IMAGE WORKS

Not Just a Uniform Adolescents in moratorium adopt temporary roles to postpone achieving their final identity. High school students like these may sign up for an ROTC (Reserve Officers Training Corps) class, but few of them go on to enlist in the U.S. Marine Corps.

Four Areas of Identity Achievement

Overall, many aspects of the search for identity have become more arduous than they were when Erikson first described them (Zimmer-Gembeck & Collins, 2003). Families, societies, and adolescents themselves have shifted. Fifty years ago, the drive to become independent and autonomous was thought to be the "key normative psychosocial task of adolescence" (Zimmer-Gembeck & Collins, 2003, p. 177).

Erikson (1968) highlighted four aspects of identity: religion, sex, politics, and vocation. Today, few developmentalists believe that achieving autonomy and identity in all four areas is likely by age 18. Terminology, timing, and emphasis have changed over the past half-century. However, these four domains are still significant.

RELIGIOUS IDENTITY The distinctions among role confusion, foreclosure, moratorium, and achievement are evident in religious identity, which few teenagers achieve. Some drift along, like one who said, "At the moment, religion's not that important. I guess when I get older it might become more so, but right now being with my friends and having fun and being a teenager is more important" (quoted in C. Smith, 2005, p. 159).

Many adolescents are in active moratorium regarding religion. They are willing to debate theological questions and are open to spiritual possibilities (Good & Willoughby, 2008).

Some suddenly convert to a religion that many adults consider a cult, a sign of foreclosure if the new religious group does not allow questioning. A more common

ROB HOWARD / CORBIS

A Religious Life These young adolescents in Ethiopia are studying to be monks. Their monastery is a haven in the midst of civil strife. Will the rituals and beliefs also provide them with a way to achieve identity?

gender identity
A person's acceptance of the roles and behaviors that society associates with the biological categories of male and female.

sexual orientation
A term that refers to whether a person is sexually and romantically attracted to others of the same sex, the opposite sex, or both sexes.

type of foreclosure is to stay in one's parents' faith, becoming extremely devout (again, without asking questions). That route was taken by 8 percent of the teenagers in a nationwide U.S. study. They often prayed, read scripture, and attended services (C. Smith, 2005).

To label such devotion *foreclosure* may be unfair, especially since many who choose that path rely on religion for guidance in values and practices, avoiding drugs and sex (Sinha et al., 2007). Some devout teenagers may have achieved a religious identity that will guide them throughout their lives. Time will tell.

Those who foreclosed prematurely on a religious identity might "lose" their faith, but those who achieved identity will deepen their commitment, exploring what their faith means for issues that few adolescents must confront (such as homelessness, immigration, and death). One indicator that identity has been achieved is that the person feels secure enough not to be threatened by conflicting tenets of other faiths.

GENDER IDENTITY A secure sexual identity also seems particularly difficult for many young people today, as well as for some of their elders. A half-century ago, Erikson and other psychoanalytic theorists thought of males and females as opposites (P. Y. Miller & Simon, 1980). They assumed that, although adolescents might be confused about sex, they would soon identify as men or women and adopt traditional roles (Erikson, 1968; A. Freud, 1958/2000).

In the past five decades, the multicultural perspective and historical circumstances have revealed the limitations of that assumption (R. A. Lippa, 2002). As you remember from Chapter 7, for social scientists *sex* and *sexual* refer to biological male and female characteristics, while *gender* refers to cultural and social customs that differentiate males and females (S. Tarrant, 2006). Accordingly, Erikson's term *sexual identity* has been replaced by **gender identity** (Denny & Pittman, 2007).

Gender identity refers primarily to a person's self-definition as male or female. It usually begins with biological sex and typically, but not always, leads to acceptance of a gender role and expression of a sexual orientation (Galambos, 2004). A *gender role* refers to behavior patterns that the culture considers appropriate only for men or only for women.

In traditional heterosexual marriages, for example, the division of gender roles meant that homemaker was the wife's role and breadwinner was the husband's. In the workplace, the female/male division of gender roles was evident in nurse/doctor, secretary/boss, stewardess/pilot, and so on. If teenagers balked at such prescribed roles, their reaction was assumed to be a temporary identity confusion that would soon be resolved when they attained sexual identity in adulthood.

The term **sexual orientation** refers to the direction of a person's erotic desires, awakened by the hormones of puberty. One meaning of *orient* is "to turn toward"; thus, sexual orientation refers to whether a person is romantically attracted to (turned on by) people of the other sex, the same sex, or both sexes. Sexual orientation and sexual impulses may be strong or weak and may be acted upon, unexpressed, or unconscious.

In Erikson's day, when social scientists wrote about sexual-identity achievement, they almost always assumed a heterosexual orientation. They realized that adolescents experience strong sexual drives as their hormone levels increase, and they observed that many teenagers are confused regarding when, how, and with whom to express those drives. Parents and societies guided adolescents, forbidding some sexual interactions and encouraging others.

A clash between biological impulses and parental wishes makes gender identity complicated for teenagers of every sexual orientation (Baumeister & Blackhart, 2007; Gilchrist & Sullivan, 2006). Some adolescents foreclose in that they exaggerate male or female roles (e.g., a teenage boy presents himself as a superstud or a teenage girl wears sexually suggestive clothes and makeup to her 8 A.M. class). Other adolescents seek a moratorium (avoiding all sexual contact), and still others move toward gender-identity achievement.

Many adolescents, as they search for a gender identity, switch from one identity to another. In one study, only a few (less than 2 percent) reported *exclusive* same-sex attraction at the first data collection, and only 11 percent of that small minority reported exclusive same-sex attraction a year later. Over the same year, others who did not originally identify themselves as homosexual later claimed that they were. Most of those who first reported exclusively same-sex attraction had changed to exclusive other-sex attraction, and one-third of those who changed reported no sexual attraction at all (Udry & Chantala, 2005).

Sometimes the gender-identity crisis becomes a pathological condition that is called *sexual identity disorder* in the *Diagnostic and Statistical Manual* (see Chapter 7; American Psychiatric Association, 2000). This label is controversial, an example of a difference-does-not-equal-deficit situation. Depending on the specifics as well as on the values of the society, an unusual sexual role may signify either psychological illness or healthy identity (Manners, 2009). (Patterns of sexual activity, beyond sexual orientation, are discussed later in this chapter.)

POLITICAL/ETHNIC IDENTITY A few decades ago, achieving a political identity was assumed to mean identifying with a political party. Today, most adolescent voters say that they choose to support the person, not the party. Even in a two-party nation such as the United States, most adolescents say they are Independent rather than Republican or Democrat.

That fluidity is one reason their votes are avidly sought but hard to secure. In 2008, the youth vote was decisive in electing President Barack Obama (a CNN exit poll of 18,000 voters found that 66 percent of the youngest voters chose Obama, compared with 48 percent of the older voters). But voting for a candidate is quite different from choosing a political affiliation, a choice that shows stronger generational differences.

Internationally as well, many adolescents seem oblivious to political parties. Their activities seem more closely related to ethnicity, religion, and even genes than to a political identity (J. H. Fowler et al., 2008; Kinder, 2006; Torney-Purta et al., 2001).

Typical of such obliviousness to politics is a young man from Pécs, Hungary. While he was growing up, his nation revolutionized its political and economic system, replacing a Communist government with a capitalistic one. As a teenager, he heard gunfire and saw warplanes from neighboring Yugoslavia, which was being split by civil war into three new nations. Yet he neither loved nor hated communism. He said, without irony, "There were no essential, important events in my life, only that I was born" (quoted in van Hoorn et al., 2000, p. 22).

The breakup of Yugoslavia, and this young man's statement, are examples of a shift since Erikson's time. Values and attitudes no longer spring primarily from allegiances to political parties. Instead, identity is increasingly influenced by ethnic loyalty—hence the often-used term *identity politics*.

Friendship, Romance, or Passion? Sexual identity is much more complex for today's adolescents than it once was. Behavior, clothing, and hairstyles are often ambiguous. Girls with shorn hair, boys with pierced ears, or same-sex couples embracing do not necessarily identify as homosexual.

The Same Situation, Many Miles Apart: Learning in School For these two groups of Muslim girls, the distance between their schools in Dearborn, Michigan (*left*), and Jammu, Kashmir (*right*), is more than geographical. The schools' hidden curricula teach different lessons about the roles of women.

OBSERVATION QUIZ

What three differences are evident? (see answer, page 354) ➡

For many adolescents, especially those who are a minority in their school, ethnic identity is pivotal to their overall identity (Phinney, 2006; Umaña-Taylor et al., 2006). In the United States, ethnic identity is central to many adolescents of African, Asian, and Hispanic descent, who struggle to reconcile their group's history, their parents' perspectives, and their own experiences. As they do so, they become more aware of, and more sensitive to, racial insults, according to a study of 12- to 18-year-olds of several ethnic groups (Seaton et al., 2008).

All adolescents struggle to find a political/ethnic identity while remaining connected to their family roots. For example, in 2008, only 15 percent of youth voted for the presidential candidate who was not supported by their parents. Achieving a political/ethnic identity is usually fostered by elders in the community and does not necessarily conflict with respect for people of other ethnicities or political affiliations; in fact, quite the opposite (Marks et al., 2007).

The need to establish ethnic identity arises in early adolescence and may peak at about age 15 (S. E. French et al., 2006; Pahl & Way, 2006). Then ethnic identity continues to evolve, partly because social and historical circumstances continue to change. One developmentalist contends that for members of ethnic minorities, "The need to explore the implications of their group membership may extend the identity exploration period throughout the 20s and often beyond" (Phinney, 2006, p. 118).

Ethnicity is particularly salient for many adolescents when it is connected with religion. Indeed, the previously mentioned split of Yugoslavia into three nations occurred because of ethnic/religious divisions; young men were prominent in all three warring groups. Achieving a political or ethnic identity also affects language, manners, dating patterns, clothing, values, and other personal characteristics (Trimble et al., 2003).

VOCATIONAL IDENTITY Vocational identity in the twenty-first century is rarely achieved until age 25 or later, for at least four reasons:

1. Few teenagers can find meaningful work (Csikszentmihalyi & Schneider, 2000) but instead have jobs that do not allow for creativity, initiative, or advancement.

2. It takes years to acquire the skills needed for many careers, so it is premature to select a vocation at age 16.

3. Most jobs are unlike those of a generation ago, so it is unwise for youth to foreclose on a vocation.

4. Most new jobs are in the service or knowledge sectors of the economy and no longer require physical strength (an asset of young workers). To be employable, adolescents spend years mastering literacy, logic, technology and human relations.

Parents still advise adolescents as to their careers, but sometimes that advice boils down to, "Don't do what I did." In one study, for example, a boy whose father was in construction said, "I look at how hard he works and I appreciate what he does, but he always tells me, 'No, you're not doing this!'" (quoted in Lehmann, 2004, p. 390).

In the same study, one mother advised her daughter "not to be dependent" and another to be "very careful"—in both cases to avoid following their mothers' example of early pregnancy (Lehmann, 2004, pp. 390, 388). Many adolescents learn from their parents what vocation *not* to choose; it takes time to decide what they *should* choose.

Some parents urge their teenagers to work part-time while they are still in school. However, working more than 20 hours a week during adolescence correlates with weaker identity formation, strained family relationships, lower academic achievement, and limited career success (Greenberger & Steinberg, 1986; Staff et al., 2004). Most wage-earning adolescents spend their money on drugs, clothes, cars, and entertainment.

Immigrant adolescents are less often employed (Perreira et al., 2007), which may be one reason they earn higher grades in high school. However, their parents may assume that they will go to work after graduation to help support the family, which may reduce the likelihood that they will go on to college (Konczal & Haller, 2008).

KEYPoints

- Erikson's fifth psychosocial crisis, identity versus role confusion, highlights adolescents' psychosocial need to achieve identity, to know who they are.
- Many adolescents experience confusion (diffusion), foreclosure, or moratorium before they achieve identity.
- Sexual identity now includes more diversity of gender roles than previously acknowledged.
- Contemporary teenagers strive to find their own ethnic identity amid the changing conflicts and aspirations they experience.
- Vocational identity requires skills and maturity that are beyond most adolescents.

Relationships with Elders and Peers

The changing seas of human development are never sailed alone. At every turn, a voyager's family, friends, and community provide sustenance, directions, ballast for stability, and a safe harbor when it is time to rest. Social forces also provide a reason to move ahead or change direction. In adolescence, a time when the winds of change blow particularly strong, adults and peers are valuable companions.

The Older Generation

Adolescence is often characterized as a period of waning adult influence during which young people distance themselves from the values and behaviors of their elders. There is some validity to this observation, but it does not always apply—and such distancing is not necessarily a good sign. In fact, when young people feel valued by their communities, trusted by teachers, and connected to parents or other adults, they are far less likely to abuse drugs, drop out of school, and take unnecessary risks (Benson, 2003; B. Stanton & Burns, 2003).

Many people besides parents can foster a young person's healthy development throughout puberty and adolescence (Levitt et al., 2005). Young people learn from music, from sports stars, from political leaders. More directly, extended-family members, teachers, church leaders, and parents of friends contribute to the social network (Parke & Buriel, 2006). "Supportive relationships with non-parent adults [are] key developmental assets predicting positive youth outcomes" (J. E. Rhodes & Roffman, 2003, p. 195).

AP PHOTO / THE PLAIN DEALER, DALE OMORI

You Don't Listen Adolescent girls are particularly likely to accuse their mothers of not understanding them. For their part, mothers' responses vary, from anger to support and guidance.

bickering
Petty, peevish arguing, usually repeated and ongoing.

CONFLICTS WITH PARENTS Although many adults are influential, the parent–adolescent relationship is pivotal (W. A. Collins & Laursen, 2004). Disputes are common, as the adolescent's drive for independence often clashes with the parents' customary control. The specifics depend on many factors, including the adolescent's age, gender, and culture.

Bickering Parent–adolescent conflict, especially between mothers and daughters, typically peaks in early adolescence and is more a sign of attachment than of distance (Scharf & Mayseless, 2007; Smetana et al., 2006). Usually, it manifests as **bickering**—repeated, petty arguments (more nagging than fighting) about routine, day-to-day concerns such as cleanliness, clothes, chores, and schedules (N. Eisenberg et al., 2008). Few parents can resist disapproving of dirty socks on the floor or a ring through a newly pierced eyebrow; few adolescents can calmly listen to parental concerns without reacting.

Some conflict may be inevitable, part of children's evolutionary impulse to become independent. One common conflict arises when parents want their children to be present at family occasions, while teenagers want to be with their friends. More generally, parents notice rebellion and jump to conclusions, fearing addiction, jail, disappearance. Usually, after a period of frequent bickering, parents grant more autonomy, and "friendship and positive affect [emotional state] typically rebound to preadolescent levels" (W. A. Collins & Laursen, 2004, p. 337).

Teenagers adjust as well. By age 18, increased emotional maturity and reduced egocentrism often allow them to appreciate their parents. But not always. If conflict smolders because of parental hostility, adolescents are likely to become disobedient and dishonest (Buehler, 2006). In such situations, the two generations may disengage.

Neglect In Chapter 6, you learned that uninvolved parenting is usually the worst style for raising young children. The same holds true for adolescents. Although teenagers may act as if they no longer need their parents, neglect can be very destructive.

Joy was from a European American family that had lived in the same rural area for decades. Her parents divorced when she was young, and her mother remarried. When she was 16, Joy's stepfather said confidently, "Teens all around here [are] doing booze and doing drugs. . . . But my Joy here ain't into that stuff" (C. Smith, 2005, p. 10). Neither parent knew that Joy was in far worse trouble than most "teens all around here." In fact, she was not only drinking alcohol but also smoking pot and having sex with her boyfriend. She reported that she:

> overdosed on a bunch of stuff once, pills or some prescription of my mom's—
> I took the whole bottle. It didn't work. I just went to sleep for a long time. . . .
> They never ever found out . . . pretty pitiful.

[quoted in C. Smith, 2005, p. 12]

As with Joy, even if teenagers seem oblivious, independent, or defiant, parents are still influential. This is true for all families, no matter what their socioeconomic status (SES), ethnicity, or location (B. B. Brown, 2005; R. A. Richardson, 2004).

One detailed study measured the self-esteem of low-income minority students in a large New York City high school. The researchers found that the school climate had little impact on self-esteem but that relationships with parents were significant. In the words of the study, "Parents are a primary presence in their children's emotional lives throughout adolescence" (M. L. Greene & Way, 2005, p. 171).

Independence and Culture Regarding parent–adolescent relationships, some cultures value family harmony above all else. Attempting to live up to that ideal, both generations avoid conflict; the adolescents suppress their own needs and wishes for the sake of keeping peace in the family.

Developmentalists do not agree about the effects of this suppression, however. It could be that adolescent rebellion is merely a *social construction,* assumed to be necessary by middle-class Westerners but destructive for many families (N. I. Larson & Wilson, 2004). Or it could be that bickering followed by independence is the foundation of a healthy adulthood.

There is no disagreement that culture influences family conflicts. For example, Japanese youth expect autonomy in their choice of what music to play, but they want their parents to help them with romance. In contrast, for U.S. adolescents, even a hint of parental interference in their love lives might make them bristle (Hasebe et al., 2004). In Chile, adolescents typically obey their parents' legitimate authority, even when they disagree (Darling et al., 2008). This is not necessarily the case for North American teens.

In every nation, family role models are influential. If older siblings are aggressive, are sexually active, or use drugs, teenagers are more likely to follow their siblings' example than to learn from their mistakes (Bank et al., 2004; G. H. Brody, 2004; East & Kiernan, 2001). Conflict with parents peaks earlier for younger siblings, another example of the power of observation of a family role model (Shanahan et al., 2007).

CLOSENESS WITHIN THE FAMILY Conflict is one dimension of the parent–child relationship, easy to notice but not necessarily the most important. More crucial may be closeness, which has four aspects:

1. Communication (do parents and teens talk openly with one another?)
2. Support (do they rely on one another?)
3. Connectedness (how emotionally close are they?)
4. Control (do parents encourage or limit adolescent autonomy?)

No developmentalist doubts that the first two, communication and support, are helpful —perhaps even essential—for emotional health. Patterns set during childhood continue lifelong.

Emotional Dependency Regarding connectedness and control, consequences vary and observers differ. Consider the experience of one of my students:

> I got pregnant when I was sixteen years old, and if it weren't for the support of my parents, I would probably not have my son. And if they hadn't taken care of him, I wouldn't have been able to finish high school or attend college. My parents also helped me overcome the shame that I felt when . . . my aunts, uncles, and especially my grandparents found out that I was pregnant.

> [I., personal communication, 2004]

"So I blame you for everything—whose fault is that?"

This young woman is grateful to her parents, but some observers might wonder whether her early motherhood allowed the parents too much psychological control, requiring her to remain dependent instead of seeking her own identity. A study of pregnant adolescents in the United States found that many (though not all) fared best if parents were supportive but did not take over the care of the child (Borkowski et al., 2007).

For my student, an added complexity is that her family had emigrated from South America: Cultural expectations affected their responses. Generally, adolescents are more dependent on their parents if they are female and from a minority ethnic group (Gnaulati & Heine, 2001). Again, this pattern could be considered either repressive or healthy, depending on the culture and the specific circumstances.

parental monitoring
Parents' ongoing awareness of what their children are doing, where, and with whom.

Do You Know Where Your Teenager Is? An important aspect of family closeness is **parental monitoring**—that is, parental knowledge about the child's whereabouts, activities, and companions. When monitoring is part of a warm, supportive relationship, the child is likely to become a confident, well-educated adult and to avoid drugs and risky sex (G. M. Barnes et al., 2006; Fletcher et al., 2004).

However, overly restrictive and controlling parenting correlates with depression and other disorders in teenagers, who may develop a habit of deceiving their parents. Worst of all may be *psychological control,* a disciplinary technique in which parents make a child feel guilty and impose gratefulness by threatening to withdraw love and support (see Chapter 6; B. K. Barber, 2002). Thus, it seems that, at least in the United States, adolescents need freedom in order to feel competent and loved. Parental monitoring itself may be harmful when it derives from harsh suspicion instead of from a warm connection with the adolescent (Smetana, 2008; Stattin & Kerr, 2000).

ESPECIALLY FOR Parents of a Teenager Your 13-year-old comes home after a sleepover at a friend's house with a new, weird hairstyle—perhaps cut or colored in a bizarre manner. What do you say and do? (see response, page 358) ➜

Early parenting practices continue to affect later behavior (N. Eisenberg et al., 2008). For example, one longitudinal study found a correlation between parenting style when children were in seventh grade and any problems they had (including law-breaking, unprotected sex, and drug use) in eleventh grade. These researchers wrote:

> When parents permit too much freedom, they may put their young adolescents at risk for a negative peer context, but they can also put their young adolescents at risk if they are perceived as being too intrusive.
>
> *[Goldstein et al., 2005, p. 409]*

Peer Support

Parental influence is notable in childhood and at puberty. During adolescence, peer influence becomes more prominent. From hanging out with a crowd to whispering with a confidant, peers add joy to life (M. Tarrant et al., 2006). As one high school boy said:

> A lot of times I wake up in the morning and I don't want to go to school, and then I'm like, you know, I have got this class and these friends are in it, and I am going to have fun. That is a big part of my day—my friends.
>
> *[quoted in Hamm & Faircloth, 2005, p. 72]*

clique
A group of adolescents made up of close friends who are loyal to one another while excluding outsiders.

crowd
A larger group of adolescents who have something in common but who are not necessarily friends.

CLIQUES AND CROWDS Adolescents organize themselves into cliques and crowds (W. A. Collins & Steinberg, 2006; Eckert, 1989), groups that help their members "bridge the gap between childhood and adulthood" (Bagwell et al., 2001, p. 26). A cluster of close friends who are loyal to one another and who exclude outsiders is called a **clique**. A **crowd** is a larger group of adolescents who share common interests, although they may not necessarily be friends. Cliques and crowds provide social control and social support.

Crowds may be based predominantly on race, ethnicity, or some personal affiliation. There may be a crowd made up of the brains, jocks, skaters, or burnouts. Allegiance to a crowd is much looser than to a clique. For example, a student could dress like those in a crowd (with trench coats, baggy pants, or sports shirts) but never drink alcohol, unlike most members of that crowd. By contrast, cliques are more influential because they are composed of close friends who are in frequent contact (Killeya-Jones et al., 2007).

CHOOSING FRIENDS For many teenagers, peers become "like family," "brothers and sisters" (Way et al., 2005). In violent neighborhoods, friends not only defend against attacks but also help one another avoid fights. One 16-year-old boy said about his friend:

> Well, with him when I'm in an argument with somebody that disrespected me and he just comes out and backs me up and says, "Yo, Chris, don't deal with that. Yo, let's just go on," you know, 'cause I could snap.
>
> *[quoted in Way et al., 2005, p. 48]*

"Snapping" is a potential danger for all adolescents, given their quick, intuitive reactions (described in Chapter 9). Having a friend who says, "Don't deal with that," protects them. As in this example, peers can be constructive (Audrey et al., 2006; B. B. Brown, 2004).

Parents fear that their adolescent children will be influenced by **peer pressure,** which usually means social pressure to conform to negative peer activities. That fear ignores the other possibility—that "friends generally encourage socially desirable behaviors" (Berndt & Murphy, 2002, p. 281). Members of a clique or crowd support one another in positive activities such as joining sports teams, studying for exams, not smoking cigarettes, and applying to college.

Contemporary adolescents often choose friends of the other sex. Adults sometimes worry that such friendships may lead to sex. Adults may also worry that close *same-sex* friendships will lead to homosexual activity. However, both of these worries are usually groundless. Teenagers have close, asexual friendships with peers of both sexes, in part because friends provide essential information and advice regarding romance (B. L. Barber, 2006; W. A. Collins & van Dulmen, 2006; Feiring, 1999).

Selection and Facilitation To understand the impact of peers, two concepts are helpful: *selection* and *facilitation*. Teenagers select friends whose values and interests they share, abandoning friends who follow other paths. Peer selection and rejection is an active process, as adolescents test each other in various ways—confiding secrets, lending money, and so on (Way & Hamm, 2005).

Peers facilitate both destructive and constructive behaviors in one another, making it easier to do both the wrong thing ("Let's all skip school on Friday") and the right thing ("Let's study together for that chemistry exam"). Peer facilitation helps individuals do things that they would be unlikely to do on their own.

Peer pressure is not always benign; young people *can* lead one another into trouble. Peers sometimes provide **deviancy training,** in which one person shows another how to rebel against social norms (Dishion et al., 2001). Especially if adolescents believe that the most popular, most admired peers are having sex, doing drugs, or ignoring homework, they become more likely to follow that example (Rodgers, 2003).

In short, selection and facilitation can work in any direction (Lacourse et al., 2003). One teenager joins a clique whose members smoke cigarettes and drink beer, and together they take the next step, perhaps passing around a joint at a party. Another teenager chooses friends who enjoy math puzzles, and, like Lindsay and her friends, all of them enroll in Advanced Placement (AP) calculus:

peer pressure
Encouragement to conform to one's friends or contemporaries in behavior, dress, and attitude; usually considered a negative force, as when adolescent peers encourage one another to defy adult authority.

deviancy training
Destructive peer support in which one person shows another how to rebel against authority or social norms.

RESPONSE FOR Parents of a Teenager (from page 356) Remember: Communicate, do not control. Let your child talk about the meaning of the hairstyle. Remind yourself that a hairstyle in itself is harmless. Don't say "What will people think?" or "Are you on drugs?" or anything that might give your child reason to stop communicating. ●

That is a hard class, but when you need help with calculus, you go to your friends. You may think no one could be excited about calculus, but I am. Having friends in class with you definitely makes school more enjoyable.

[quoted in Hamm & Faircloth, 2005, p. 72]

Thus, adolescents select and facilitate, choose and are chosen, encourage one another. Happy, energetic, successful adolescents have friends who are high-achieving, with no major emotional problems. The opposite also holds: Those who are drug users, sexually active, and alienated from school choose compatible friends and provide mutual support in continuing on that path (Crosnoe & Needham, 2004).

Playing "Chicken" An interesting experiment (M. Gardner & Steinberg, 2005) in peer facilitation compared the risk-taking behavior of three age groups: adolescents (ages 13 to 16), emerging adults (ages 18 to 22), and adults (over age 24). They all played a video driving game called *Chicken*. Every so often, the video screen would flash a yellow light, indicating that soon (in one to several seconds) the car would crash into a wall.

The participants had to decide when to brake. The goal was to keep driving as long as possible but to stop before crashing. Points were gained for longer travel times; a crash erased all the points from that round. The participants were randomly assigned to one of two conditions: playing alone or with two strangers of the same sex and age as themselves. When they played alone, adolescents, emerging adults, and adults all averaged one crash per 15-round session. That single crash was enough to make them wary.

Adults were just as cautious when playing with two onlookers as when alone. But when the adolescents were with peers, they became much bolder, crashing three times, on average (see Figure 10.1). They chose to lose points rather than to appear cautious (M. Gardner & Steinberg, 2005; L. Steinberg, 2007).

Facilitation is usually mutual, not a matter of a rebel leading an innocent astray (B. B. Brown & Klute, 2003). In the video game experiment, each person in a three-member group played 15 rounds while the other two players watched. Witnessing a crash did not diminish the bystanders' willingness to take risks when it was their turn (M. Gardner & Steinberg, 2005).

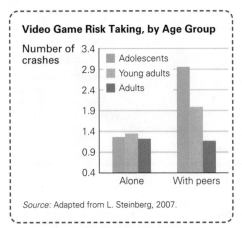

Video Game Risk Taking, by Age Group

Number of crashes

Adolescents / Young adults / Adults

Alone   With peers

Source: Adapted from L. Steinberg, 2007.

FIGURE 10.1 Admire Me Everyone wants to accumulate points in a game, earn high grades, and save money—unless one is a teenager and other teens are watching. Then a desire to obtain peer admiration by taking risks may overtake caution. At least in this game, teenage participants chose to lose points and increase crashes when other teens were present.

IMMIGRANT YOUTH Friends play a special role for immigrant adolescents. Many become model youth, with higher grades, fewer emotional problems, and more professional success than nonimmigrants of the same ethnicity (Portes & Fernández-Kelly, 2008; Vega et al., 2007). They do not usually join the cliques of the native-born, instead relying on friends who are also immigrants (Azmitia et al., 2006).

Parents Versus Peers Immigrant family members typically depend on their adolescents, who help out at home and mediate between the old and new cultures (see Figure 10.2) (Trickett & Jones, 2007; Tseng, 2004). Adolescents benefit from this arrangement, in that they gain respect within their families and experience community support, encouragement, and ethnic pride—all of which help them in a strange and sometimes hostile environment (Fuligni et al., 2005).

However, conflict can arise if the parents seek to maintain traditional practices that differ markedly from those of teenage culture in the new country (Suarez-Orozco & Suarez-Orozco, 2001). Conflict also seems to arise when the parents rely too much on their adolescents to translate and mediate between the original culture and the new one (Trickett & Jones, 2007). For one thing, these demands reduce the amount of time adolescents can spend socializing with peers.

All adolescents want to respect their parents and fit in with their peers—a sometimes impossible combination, made more difficult when the new and old cultures have different attitudes about the importance of friends (Bukowski & Adams, 2006).

ESPECIALLY FOR Teachers of Immigrants Your immigrant students' parents never come to open-school nights or answer the written notes you send home. What should you do? (see response, page 360) ➔

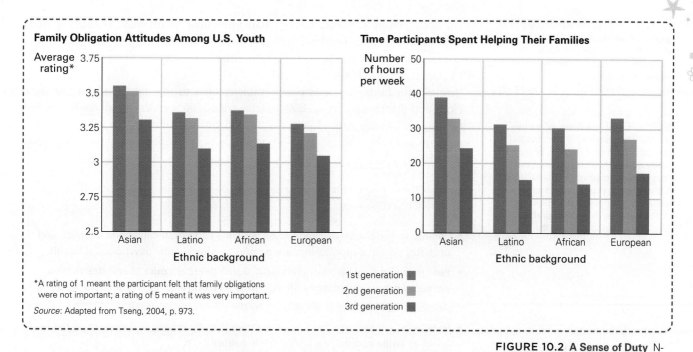

Family Obligation Attitudes Among U.S. Youth

Average rating*

Ethnic background

*A rating of 1 meant the participant felt that family obligations were not important; a rating of 5 meant it was very important.

Source: Adapted from Tseng, 2004, p. 973.

Time Participants Spent Helping Their Families

Number of hours per week

Ethnic background

1st generation
2nd generation
3rd generation

FIGURE 10.2 A Sense of Duty Nearly 1,000 U.S. college students from four ethnic groups were asked how important they thought family obligations were and how much time they spent each week helping their families (e.g., by doing household chores, translating for their parents, taking care of siblings, or working in the family business).

OBSERVATION QUIZ

How many hours a week does the average first-generation immigrant college student spend helping out at home? (see answer, page 361) →

A parent–peer clash can occur in any family, but it is particularly common when immigrant parents expect children to silently heed their elders, while adolescents expect to follow the North American practice of expressing their disagreement and making their own choices (W. A. Collins & Steinberg, 2006).

A Yemeni Girl in Michigan Friends may be crucial in helping adolescents and parents reconcile conflicting cultures, traditions, and desires. One example is Layla, whose family emigrated from Yemen and now lives near Detroit. At age 15, Layla was sent back to Yemen to marry her father's nephew. She later returned to her Michigan public high school and tried to keep her marriage secret (she wore no wedding ring).

Layla's high school was "both liberating and a sociocultural threat" (Sarroub, 2001, p. 390). In the school's *hidden curriculum* (see Chapter 7), teenagers were expected to speak their minds (receiving points for class participation), dress as they chose (no uniforms), and question adult authority (the student council). Equal education for both sexes is U.S. law, whereas "the gender gap in education in Yemen is among the highest in the world, with more than half of the women illiterate" (UNICEF, 2006).

As is true for many adolescents of all backgrounds, Layla's search for her own identity required her to combine traditional values with the dominant values in her current situation. She respected her parents and adhered to the tenets of the family's Islamic faith, but she rebelled against many aspects of her heritage.

For example, she was troubled that her father chewed *qaat* (a mild narcotic that is legal in Yemen), that he wanted her to wear traditional long dresses (she wore jeans instead), and that he did not endorse her plan to get a divorce and go to college. Layla especially resented that her brother thought he could tell her what to do.

> At times Layla was confused and unhappy at home. She ... preferred going to school where she could be with her Yemeni friends who understood her problems and with whom she could talk. "They make me feel, like, really happy. I have friends that have to deal with the same issues." ... Layla was often angry that girls in Yemen were taken out of school.... She thought that the boys had been given too much freedom, much more than the girls.
>
> [*Sarroub, 2001, pp. 408–409*]

Is the closeness of immigrant families helpful or harmful to adolescents? The answer probably depends on the specifics, including the issue, the culture, and the family

● **FOR DEEPER REFLECTION** Some people value friends more than family, while others put family first. Is this preference developmental, cultural, neither, or both?

RESPONSE FOR Teachers of Immigrants (from page 358) Perhaps the parents cannot read English, or work or family obligations may prevent them from coming to school in the evening. You might ask your students to set up home visits for you at a suitable time for the parents. Then go to praise their child more than to criticize. ●

dynamics (Trickett & Jones, 2007). Asian immigrant youth may particularly need friends, as they tend to have lower self-esteem, shoulder more family obligations, and encounter more discrimination from non-Asian peers (M. L. Greene & Way, 2005; M. L. Greene et al., 2006).

Just as with Layla, youth of every ethnicity tend to rely on friends of the same background (McPherson et al., 2001). Since friendship is crucial to all teens, it is not surprising that immigrant adolescents depend on one another. For all adolescents, immigrant and otherwise, peers help one another cope with puberty, parents, school, and romance.

KEY Points

- Parents and adolescents often bicker, yet family communication and support, and probably parental monitoring, are helpful to adolescents' psychosocial health.
- Peer pressure may be misunderstood. Some peers encourage self-destructive, antisocial behavior, but more often friends help one another in constructive ways.
- Adolescents choose and are chosen by their crowds and cliques.
- Immigrant adolescents are helped by their friends as they try to maintain family loyalties while succeeding in their new culture.

Sexuality

Probably no arena highlights the overlapping influences of parents, peers, and the wider community—as well as the interaction of body, mind, and culture—more clearly than sexuality. Much remains to be discovered about sexual activity during adolescence (B. B. Brown, 2006). Research ethics require parental permission before questions are asked of anyone younger than 18, and many parents refuse to let strangers ask their children about sex.

Nonetheless, some basics are known. The sex drive is strong and universal, triggered by androgens and estrogens, but sexual relationships vary in strength and expression. Some adolescents repress their sexual urges and others are obsessed by them. Some 15-year-olds are married and pregnant, while others have multiple partners and run from commitment. Still others are not only virginal but seem asexual.

Historical and cultural evidence confirm this variability. Traditionally, intense romantic attachments in adolescence were considered a threat to normal development because they disrupted bonding between families (Coontz, 2006). Arranged childhood marriages (often to uncles or cousins), placement of adolescents in monasteries or convents, chastity belts, shotgun weddings, polygamy—each of these reactions to adolescent sexuality has been considered desirable in some cultures and unnatural in others.

From Asexual to Active

Decades ago, Australian researcher Dexter Dunphy (1963) described the sequence of male–female relationships during childhood and adolescence:

1. Groups of friends, exclusively one sex or the other
2. A loose association of girls and boys, with public interactions within a crowd
3. Small mixed-sex groups of the advanced members of the crowd
4. Formation of couples, with private intimacies

Culture, ethnicity, gender, and SES affect the timing and manifestation of each of these steps, but research in many nations validates Dunphy's sequence (Cavanagh, 2007; Meier & Allen, 2008). Everywhere children (and even the young of many species) avoid members of the other sex early on but are attracted to them by the time they reach adulthood. This suggests that biology underlies these changes (Weisfeld, 1999).

Currently, with puberty beginning at about age 10 and marriage usually more than a decade later, each stage of the sequence lasts several years. Same-sex groups dominate in primary school. In middle school, boys and girls talk to the other sex but avoid one-on-one intimacy until later. Early, exclusive romance signifies trouble, not maturity (B. B. Brown, 2004).

Romance: Straight and Gay

The first romances appear in high school and rarely last more than a year. Girls claim a steady partner more often than boys do. Breakups are common; so are unreciprocated crushes. Both can be devastating, in part because often entire high school crowds are witnesses (P. Schwartz, 2006). Adolescents are crushed by rejection and sometimes contemplate revenge or suicide (H. E. Fisher, 2006). In such cases, friends can be a lifesaver.

Overall, healthy romances in later adolescence manifest a life replete with good relationships with parents and peers (Laursen & Mooney, 2007). That triple support network means that a fight with a parent, a slight from a peer, or the breakup of a romance is taken in stride because people in the other two arenas provide reassurance.

For homosexual adolescents, complications slow down the formation of friendships and romantic bonds. To begin with, many do not acknowledge their sexual orientation, sometimes not even to themselves.

Furthermore, national and peer cultures often make the homosexual young person feel ashamed. For example, in many Latino cultures, "adolescents who pursue same-sex sexuality are viewed by their communities as having fundamentally failed as men or women" (L. M. Diamond & Savin-Williams, 2003, p. 399). Many gay youth of every ethnicity date members of the other sex to hide their true orientation (B. B. Brown, 2006).

Past cohorts of gay youth had higher rates of clinical depression, drug abuse, and suicide than did their heterosexual peers. This may be less true for the current cohort (Savin-Williams & Diamond, 2004), although much depends on the local culture.

It is unclear how many youth are homosexual, heterosexual, bisexual, or asexual. In the mid-1990s, one large study of high school students in Massachusetts found only 1 in 200 who identified as gay or lesbian (Garofalo et al., 1999). Recently, a large Dutch study of high school students found that 1 in 12 said they were attracted to people of the same sex as themselves (Bos et al., 2008). The eightfold difference between these two studies may reflect culture or cohort.

Alternatively, the differences may result from the way the question was phrased. Perhaps youth are willing to acknowledge same-sex attraction but do not want to *identify* with any orientation, homosexual or heterosexual (Savin-Williams, 2005). This latter possibility is suggested by research on adults conducted in the United States in the mid-1990s. About 10 percent of the participants remembered and acknowledged having had same-sex encounters or desires when they were teenagers, yet most were heterosexual as adults (Laumann et al., 1994).

It could be that homosexual desires are part of sexual awakening for many adolescents (only a fraction of whom report it), or it could be that many bisexual or asexual teenagers later become exclusively heterosexual. Eleanor Maccoby (1998), an expert on gender issues, wrote that "a substantial number of people experiment with same-sex sexuality at some point in their lives, and a small minority settle into

The Same Situation, Many Miles Apart: Teenagers in Love No matter where in the world they are, teenage couples broadcast their love in universally recognized facial expressions and body positions. Samantha and Ryan (*top*), visiting New York City from suburban Philadelphia, are similar in many ways to the teen couple (*bottom*) in Chicute, Mozambique, even though their social contexts are dramatically different.

a lifelong pattern of homosexuality" (p. 191). No one knows how big that "substantial number" is.

Retrospectively, many homosexual men report that they became aware of their sexual orientation at about age 11 but told no one until about age 17 (Maguen et al., 2002). By contrast, most adolescents who later identify as lesbian are unaware or in denial of their sexual urges, perhaps because either biology or culture makes sexual self-knowledge more difficult for girls (Baumeister & Blackhart, 2007).

Similar secrecy, awakening, and sexual confusion may occur for all youth. Many teenagers believe they have found the love of their life, temporarily feeling so "in love" that they cannot eat, sleep, or think normally—but soon afterward, they wonder how they could have been so wrong. Many also worry that they are oversexed, undersexed, or deviant. Research on adult sexuality finds great diversity; few adolescents realize there are thousands, maybe millions, of people like themselves.

Sex Education

Consistent and reliable information and guidance about the joys and the hazards of sex are scarce. Oral sex is one example. Parents and teachers rarely mention it, the media are silent about it, adolescents often do it but do not discuss it (Brewster & Tillman, 2008). This lack of information leads many adolescents to believe that oral sex is "safe"—a dangerous assumption, since some serious infections can occur through oral as well as genital sexual contact (Kalmuss et al., 2003).

LEARNING FROM PEERS Adolescent sexual behavior is strongly influenced by peers, who may be the only sex educators a young person has. Many teens discuss details of romance and sex with other members of their clique, seeking their friends' approval (Laursen & Mooney, 2007). Often, the boys brag and the girls worry. Young couples teach each other.

Specifics of peer education depend on the group: All members of a clique may be virgins, or all may be sexually active. Among contemporary U.S. teens, some church-based crowds take a "virginity pledge," vowing to postpone sexual intercourse until marriage.

Virginity pledgers are an example of the benefits and problems of peer pressure (Brückner & Bearman, 2005). If a group considers itself a select minority, then virginity may become a distinguishing value for all group members, and fewer of them than of their classmates will become sexually active before age 18.

However, when high school crowds disperse at graduation, members who have taken a virginity pledge are less likely to use contraception and more likely to marry young than are their peers. Their rates of sexually transmitted infections (STIs) are similar to those of peers who never took the pledge (Brückner & Bearman, 2005). More become young parents, but fewer become single parents (K. A. Johnson & Rector, 2004).

Sexual experience is also strongly influenced by whether an adolescent is in an ongoing romantic relationship because young couples have the motivation and opportunity for intimacy. Physically attractive adolescents who experience early puberty are more likely to be part of a couple, which in turn makes them more likely to become sexually active, especially if they are girls who are gratified by the attention of older boys (L. J. Friedlander et al., 2007).

The lessons that adolescent partners teach one another are not always what adults would hope. For instance, ideally, before having sex, a teenage girl and boy would discuss what they could do to reduce the risks of pregnancy and STIs as well as how they would respond if either of those occurred. However, only about half of U.S. adolescent couples actually talk about those issues, much less come to a shared conclusion based on accurate information (S. Ryan et al., 2007).

LEARNING FROM PARENTS Parents, through monitoring, modeling, and conversation, are pivotal in every teenager's sexual decisions. Yet many parents underestimate their adolescent's need for information, waiting to talk about sex until their child is already in a romantic relationship. That may be too late (N. Eisenberg et al., 2006).

Many parents know little about their adolescents' sexual activity. For example, when parents of 12-year-old girls were asked if their daughter had hugged or kissed a boy "for a long time" or hung out with older boys (both signs that sex information is urgently needed), only 5 percent said yes—but 38 percent of the daughters said yes (O'Donnell et al., 2008). If a teenager gets pregnant, her parents are often shocked.

Religious parents often hesitate to talk about sex (except to warn against it), but religion is *not* the most significant correlate of parent–child conversations; gender and age are (Regnerus, 2005). Parents are more likely to talk about sex to daughters than to sons and to older adolescents (over 15) than to younger ones. This is unfortunate; pubescent boys are most likely to need—and to heed—the information they can get from sex education (Kirby, 2001; T. E. Mueller et al., 2008).

One specific problem is that parents underestimate adolescents' capacity to engage in responsible sex. One study found that few parents (23 percent of mothers, 33 percent of fathers) believed that teenagers were capable of using a condom correctly (M. E. Eisenberg et al., 2004). In fact, however, many parents could learn from their children: Proper condom use is higher among adolescents than among adults.

Parental example may be more important than conversation. Teens notice if their single parents seek sexual partners. For many reasons, adolescents who live with single or stepparents are more than twice as likely as teens who live with both biological parents to begin a sexual relationship sooner (R. W. Blum et al., 2000; B. J. Ellis et al., 2003).

LEARNING IN SCHOOL Aware that things have changed since they were teenagers, almost all parents want other adults to provide their adolescents with up-to-date sex education, especially about safe sex and contraception (Landry et al., 2003; Yarber et al., 2005). Developmentalists agree that sex education belongs in the schools as well as in parent–child conversations. Adolescents need to learn from trusted and experienced adults rather than misinforming one another.

Sex-education policies vary dramatically. Most European schools begin sex education early in primary school, teaching self-respect and personal responsibility. Many European middle schools teach about fertility, masturbation, and oral and anal sex. By contrast, in many Asian and African nations, sex education is absent from the school curriculum.

In the United States, the timing and content of sex education vary by state and community. Some high schools provide comprehensive sex education, offering free condoms and medical treatment; others offer nothing. Most programs focus on biology, not on human relationships.

Abstinence-Only Programs The U.S. government began a massive experiment in 1998, spending about $1 billion over 10 years to promote *abstinence-only* sex education in the nation's public schools. The goal was to persuade adolescents to prevent pregnancy and STIs by waiting until marriage before becoming sexually active. These programs emphasized the need for younger teens to feel confident in themselves, able to say no to sex.

No information about other methods of avoiding pregnancy and infection was provided in these programs because it was feared that such knowledge might encourage teens to become sexually active. The focus on abstaining from sex made sense to some adults, since many problems would disappear if teenagers never had sex. However, few teenagers were convinced.

"Smirking or Non-Smirking?"

Longitudinal evaluation revealed that the abstinence-only curriculum had little effect. To be specific, about half the students in both experimental (abstinence-only) and control groups had had sex by age 16. The number of partners and use of contraceptives were the same with and without the special curriculum (Trenholm et al., 2007). Students in the control groups knew slightly more on a written test about preventing disease and pregnancy, but this knowledge neither slowed down nor sped up their sexual initiation.

Starting Early One major problem with sex-education programs in the United States may be that they start in high school. That may seem sensible, since the average age of first intercourse in the United States is 16; but one-fourth of all U.S. students have had sex by the time they turn 14 (MMWR, June 6, 2008). Furthermore, the best time to learn about sex is *before* the hormones of puberty awaken sexual interest.

The most effective programs (1) begin before high school, (2) include assignments that require parent–child communication, (3) focus on behavior (not just on conveying information), (4) provide medical referrals on request, and (5) last for years (Kirby, 2002; T. E. Mueller et al., 2008; Weaver et al., 2006). Even when students have been exposed to a program with these five features, however, adolescent sexual activity depends more on family, peers, and community culture than on school classes, according to a nationwide study in the United Kingdom (E. Allen et al., 2007).

Nonetheless, some school programs make a difference. For example, in one Texas program, half of the ninth-graders—the experimental group—had sex education that included attitudes and behavior as well as information (Coyle et al., 2001). Three years later, the researchers found that students in both groups had begun to have sexual intercourse at the same ages. However, the experimental group had sex less frequently and used condoms more often. The evaluators wished that the program had started earlier because one-fourth of the ninth-grade students had already had sex.

Is ninth grade too soon for sex education for those who are not yet sexually active? Not according to one ninth-grade boy:

> I do look forward to it, if it's with a good girl, a good person. I'm going to make sure to wear protection, make sure she doesn't have a disease, make sure we know what to do if the protection doesn't work. Make sure we know the consequences of it, make sure she would know the consequences of what would happen if not everything went right.
>
> *[quoted in Michels et al., 2005, p. 594]*

This boy's use of "make sure" five times indicates that he had learned a great deal before he decided to have sex.

Sexual Behavior

Adolescent sexual activity varies widely from place to place and from era to era. The U.S. Youth Risk Behavior Survey found that more than twice as many high school students in Baltimore had had sex as those in San Francisco (67 percent compared with 26 percent) (MMWR, June 6, 2008). In 2007, more than half of all U.S. teenagers had had sexual intercourse by age 16, a lower rate than in 1990 but higher than in 2006 (see Figure 10.3).

The rate of teenage pregnancy in the United States has declined dramatically since 1960, as discussed in Chapter 9 (see Figure 9.3 on page 322). Nevertheless, that rate is still higher in the United States than in any other developed nation (about eight times the rate in Japan, twice the rate in Canada and Great Britain), not because American girls have more sex but because they use less contraception.

Today, 86 percent of new teenage mothers in the United States are unmarried, compared with only 13 percent in 1960 (U.S. Bureau of the Census, 1972, 2008). Although far fewer teenage girls worldwide became pregnant in the past decade than

ESPECIALLY FOR Sex Educators Suppose adults in your community never talk to their children about sex or puberty. Is that a mistake? (see response, page 366) ➤

in the preceding 10 years, those who do become pregnant are less likely to marry the fathers, less likely to have abortions, and less likely to choose adoption.

In almost every nation, contraception, particularly condom use among adolescent boys, has increased markedly since 1990 (Santelli et al., 2007). The U.S. Youth Risk Behavior Survey found that 76 percent of sexually active ninth-grade boys had used a condom during their most recent intercourse (MMWR, June 6, 2008). About 20 percent of U.S. teenage couples use the pill *and* condoms, to prevent both pregnancy and infection (Manlove et al., 2003).

Taken all together, the data on teenage sexual behavior lead to one conclusion: Although adolescent bodies and sex hormones are the same now as they have been for centuries, teenage responses to biological drives have changed dramatically. Public policies and social norms affect the most personal and private decisions.

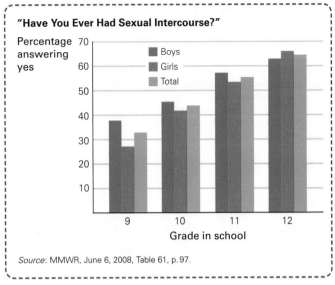

"Have You Ever Had Sexual Intercourse?"

Source: MMWR, June 6, 2008, Table 61, p. 97.

FIGURE 10.3 Is Everybody Doing It? No. About one-third of high school seniors and two-thirds of ninth-graders are still virgins. The data for this graph are from the Youth Risk Behavior Survey, a national survey that asks the same questions of thousands of U.S. students in the ninth through twelfth grades each year. In 2007, about 14,000 students in 150 public and private schools in 44 states were surveyed.

OBSERVATION QUIZ

How do boys' and girls' rates of sexual activity compare? (see answer, page 366) →

KEYPoints

- Many adolescents learn about sex from uninformed peers; U.S. youth begin having sexual intercourse at age 16, on average.

- Parents are influential role models, but many are slow to begin talking with their children about sex.

- Effective sex education should begin before students become sexually active.

- Sexual behavior varies a great deal by community and culture, as shown by fewer adolescent births and more contraception worldwide today than in earlier decades.

Sadness and Anger

Adolescence is usually a wonderful time. Compared with a few generations ago, pregnancy and early marriage are less common today, more teenagers are in school, and almost none die of disease. The pressure to establish an identity is still there, but modern teens have at least five extra years to achieve it. The editor of a leading academic journal calls adolescence more joyful than problem-filled (B. B. Brown, 2005). Most teenagers agree.

Nonetheless, for about 20 percent of adolescents, serious trouble plagues development. Most problems are comorbid, in that several disorders (morbidities) coexist in the same person. For instance, a sad teenager who uses illegal drugs before age 15 is vulnerable to depression, unwanted parenthood, and suicide. An angry adolescent who is a bully is also at higher risk of leaving school, being arrested, and dying by accident or homicide. Worldwide, accidents, suicides, and homicides are the three top causes of adolescent death, while all the deadly diseases are far less common during that time.

Distinguishing between the moodiness typical of every adolescent and the pathology typical of that troubled 20 percent is crucial. This section will help you differentiate.

RESPONSE FOR Sex Educators (from page 364) Yes, but forgive them. Ideally, parents should talk to their children about sex, presenting honest information and listening to the child's concerns. However, many parents find it very difficult to do this because they feel embarrassed and ignorant. You might schedule separate sessions for adults over 30, for emerging adults, and for adolescents. ●

clinical depression
Feelings of hopelessness, lethargy, and worthlessness that last two weeks or more.

rumination
Repeatedly thinking and talking about past experiences; can contribute to depression.

suicidal ideation
Thinking about suicide, usually with some serious emotional and intellectual or cognitive overtones.

ANSWER TO OBSERVATION QUIZ (from page 365) Girls tend to become sexually active a little later than boys, but by the end of high school, girls have surpassed boys (usually because of older partners). ●

Depression

The general trend from late childhood through adolescence is toward less self-confidence. Self-esteem for boys as well as girls dips at puberty (R. C. Barnett & Rivers, 2004; Jacobs et al., 2002). Often, but not always, lower self-esteem in early adolescence continues through high school. One reason is that young adolescents who dislike themselves often turn to drugs, early sex, and disordered eating, all of which further reduce esteem (Biro et al., 2006; Trzesniewski et al., 2006).

Signs of depression are common. Easiest to see are anger or tears, but missing school or refusing to answer the phone may also indicate depression. In the 2007 Youth Risk Behavior Survey of ninth- to twelfth-graders, more than one-third (36 percent) of the girls and one-fifth of the boys (21 percent) said that within the past year, they had felt so hopeless that they stopped doing some usual activities for two weeks or more (MMWR, June 6, 2008).

For some, the sobering self-awareness of early adolescence sinks to **clinical depression,** a deep sadness and hopelessness that halts regular activities for several weeks. Clinically depressed adolescents sleep too much, study too little, and sometimes cannot even shower or get dressed. Although as many boys as girls lose confidence at puberty, every study finds that more girls experience severe depression.

GENDER DIFFERENCES IN SERIOUS DEPRESSION The causes of depression include genetic vulnerability and a depressed mother who was the adolescent's primary caregiver in infancy (Cicchietti & Toth, 1998; L. Murray et al., 2006). These conditions predate adolescence and occur for both sexes, but something happens at puberty to push the most vulnerable into despair. Compared to children, twice as many adolescents experience clinical depression, which affects about 1 in every 5 teen girls (20 percent) and 1 in every 10 boys (10 percent) (Graber, 2004).

It is not known whether this gender disparity is biological, psychological, or social (Alloy & Abramson, 2007; Ge et al., 2001). Obviously hormones differ, but so do family, peer, and cultural pressures. A cognitive explanation has also been suggested: **Rumination**—talking about, remembering, and mentally replaying past unpleasant experiences—is more common among girls. Such recollections may result in a slide into depression (Nolen-Hoeksema et al., 2008).

Although rumination makes girls sad, it may also protect them from lonely, impulsive action. In fact, some people think that teenage boys are depressed as often as girls but are less likely to admit it. Instead, depressed boys shut out their friends and family, using drugs and violence instead of talk and tears. Data on suicide support this hypothesis.

SUICIDE Having serious, distressing thoughts about killing oneself is called **suicidal ideation,** and it is quite common in mid-adolescence (Rueter & Kwon, 2005). In the United States, 19 percent of all ninth- to twelfth-grade girls and 10 percent of the boys thought seriously about suicide in 2007 (MMWR, June 6, 2008). A decade earlier, suicidal ideation was even more common (27 percent overall) (MMWR, September 27, 1996).

However, although suicidal ideation is common, completed suicides are not. Adolescents are *less* likely to kill themselves than adults are. Many people mistakenly think suicide is more frequent in adolescence for four reasons:

1. The suicide rate for adolescents, low as it is, is higher than it was in the early 1960s (see Figure 10.4).
2. Statistics on "youth" often include emerging adults, whose suicide rates are higher than those of adolescents.
3. Adolescent suicides capture media attention.
4. Suicide *attempts* (*parasuicides,* discussed below) are relatively common in adolescence.

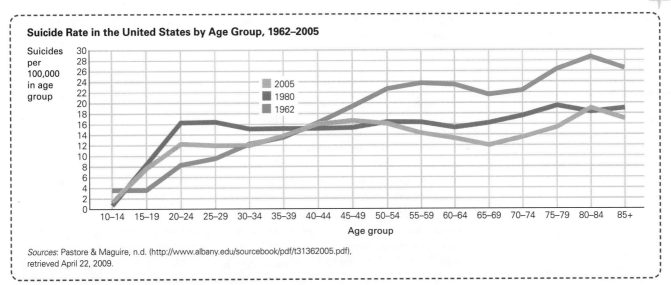

Suicide Rate in the United States by Age Group, 1962–2005

Suicides per 100,000 in age group

Legend:
- 2005
- 1980
- 1962

Age group: 10–14, 15–19, 20–24, 25–29, 30–34, 35–39, 40–44, 45–49, 50–54, 55–59, 60–64, 65–69, 70–74, 75–79, 80–84, 85+

Sources: Pastore & Maguire, n.d. (http://www.albany.edu/sourcebook/pdf/t31362005.pdf), retrieved April 22, 2009.

FIGURE 10.4 Much Depends on Age A historical look at U.S. suicide statistics reveals two trends, both of which were still apparent in 2005. First, older teenagers today are twice as likely to take their own lives as in 1960 but less likely to do so than in 1980. Second, suicide rates overall are down, but they continue to be highest among elderly people age 80 and older.

OBSERVATION QUIZ

In a typical cross-section of 1,000 U.S. 15- to 19-year-olds, how many committed suicide in 2005? (see answer, page 369) ➔

If one teenager commits suicide, parents and teachers should pay special attention to that adolescent's friends and schoolmates. Adolescents are particularly affected when they hear about a suicide, either via media reports or from peers (B. J. Insel & Gould, 2008). That makes them susceptible to **cluster suicides,** a term for several suicides within a group over a brief span of time—a few weeks or months.

cluster suicides
Several suicides committed by members of a group within a brief period of time.

Parasuicide Experts use the word **parasuicide** to describe any deliberate self-harm that could have been lethal but was not. They do not say "attempted suicide" or "failed suicide" because emotions and confusion typically disguise the seriousness of the person's, especially an adolescent's, intention to end his or her life. After surviving parasuicide, most adolescents wonder why they risked death, while the others wonder why they failed.

parasuicide
Any potentially lethal action against the self that does not result in death.

Internationally, rates of teenage parasuicide range between 6 and 20 percent. This range reflects cultural differences in data collection as well as in parasuicide itself. Everywhere, parasuicide is common; completed suicide is not. For example, among U.S. high school students, 9 percent of the girls and 4.5 percent of the boys said that they had tried to kill themselves in the past year (MMWR, June 6, 2008). Almost one-third of those attempts were treated by a doctor or nurse, an indication that they were serious. Yet the U.S. annual rate of completed suicide for ages 15 to 19 (in school or not) was about 8 per 100,000, or 0.008 percent. That is less than one completed suicide for every 1,000 parasuicides.

Nothing to Do Compared with most other Americans, these three adolescents are at higher risk of diabetes, alcoholism, unemployment, and suicide. They live on the Rosebud Sioux Reservation in South Dakota. The suicide rate among Native American teenagers is more than three times as high as the rate for U.S. adolescents overall.

Completed Suicide Although suicide in adolescence is rare, it is enormously tragic. Decades of a person's life are lost in an impulsive, foolish moment. If the risks were better known, they might be reduced and lives might be saved. At least four factors are known to increase the risk of teen suicide (Berman et al., 2006):

1. Availability of guns
2. Use of alcohol and other drugs
3. Lack of parental supervision
4. A culture that condones suicide

The first three factors suggest why the rate of youth suicide in North America and Europe has doubled since 1960: Adolescents have more guns, alcohol, and drugs and less supervision. That also suggests why rates have gone down in the past decade: Laws reducing gun possession and adolescent drinking have taken effect.

Regarding the fourth factor, cultural differences are evident. Rates are higher in eastern Europe and southern Africa than in western Europe and South America. Suicide rates among immigrants tend to be similar to, but somewhat higher than, rates in their native land (Belfer & Eisenbruch, 2007). In the United States, more teen suicides occur in the western states. The highest rate is in Montana, where 18 percent of the high school students say that they have made a suicide plan in the past year, compared with only 8 percent in Florida (MMWR, June 6, 2008).

When U.S. statistics on adolescent suicides are reported by ethnicity, the rate for one group—African American teenage boys—is increasing, not decreasing (although it is still below the rate for European American boys). Among the many cultural hypotheses: Young Black males have fewer employment opportunities, easier access to guns, less supervision, and a greater reluctance to seek help (Joe, 2003).

Gender Differences in Suicide Although many females experience depression and parasuicide, completed suicide is higher for males in every nation except China. For instance, the suicide rate among boys age 15 to 19 in the United States is four times higher than the rate for girls that age (National Center for Health Statistics, 2007).

The reasons are many. One is availability of lethal means; another is a male culture that shames those who attempt suicide but fail (Aseltine & DeMartino, 2004). Thus, males typically shoot themselves (an immediately lethal method), whereas females typically swallow pills or hang themselves (methods that allow time for intervention).

Access to deadly methods may explain why China has more female than male suicides. Few Chinese of either sex have guns. Ingestion of lethal pesticides (many illegal in the United States) is the most common method in China, and pesticides are equally available to both sexes.

Another explanation for gender differences in suicide is that girls tend to let their friends and families know that they are depressed, but boys do not. A psychologist wrote about a 17-year-old high school senior named Bill:

> A good student, hard working, some would say "driven," Bill has achieved well and is hoping to go to either Harvard or Stanford next year. He is also hopeful that his college career will lead him to medical school and a career as a surgeon like his father. Bill is a tall, handsome boy, attractive to girls but surprisingly shy among them. . . . [O]n the school football team . . . this past season Bill led all receivers in pass catches. . . . The elder of two sons, Bill has always been close to his parents, and a "good son." Perhaps for these reasons, he has been increasingly preoccupied as verbalized threats of separation and divorce become common in his parents' increasingly frequent conflicts. These worries he has kept largely to himself.
>
> [Berman et al., 2006, pp. 43–44]

Bill, perhaps following the masculine stereotype of being strong and independent, had no close friends to perceive the warning signs. Even his parents did not realize his trouble until

Bill's body was brought to the local medical examiner's office; he put his father's .22-caliber handgun to his head and ended his life in an instant.

[Berman et al., 2006, p. 44]

In retrospect, there had been danger signs. Bill had no close friends, male or female; his parents were fighting; he had foreclosed on his father's profession; he had a drive for perfection (Harvard or Stanford, football star); he had no older siblings to advise and comfort him. Moreover, Bill's shyness around girls might suggest that he was worried about his sexual orientation. The greatest danger was his access to his father's loaded gun; more people are killed by family-owned guns than by the intruders such guns are intended to thwart.

Drugs and Depression Some adolescents are said to self-medicate with drugs and alcohol to deal with their anxiety and low self-esteem. This is usually destructive, as explained at the end of this chapter. However, some drugs may reduce depression.

Since 1990, rates of adolescent suicide in the United States have fallen, especially among those with more income and education. One reason may be that fewer teenagers are desperately sad because more of them are being treated by doctors who prescribe the new wave of antidepressants (Gould, 2003).

A British study suggested that some antidepressants (especially Prozac) may increase suicidal ideation (not suicide). The U.S. Food and Drug Administration advises physicians prescribing antidepressants for adolescents to be alert to further depression in the first few months. Such caution is always warranted; many adolescents are impulsive.

However, untreated depression may be worse than potentially hazardous drug treatments. A meta-analysis of 27 controlled clinical trials (similar to experiments, except that the participants all have a particular illness or disorder) reported reassuring findings. For adolescents, antidepressants (especially when combined with cognitive-behavioral therapy) were more likely to reduce depression and anxiety than to increase suicidal ideation (Bridge et al., 2007).

Anger and Aggression

Angry outbursts are common in adolescence. Many adolescents slam doors, defy parents, and tell friends exactly how badly other teenagers (or parents, siblings, or teachers) have behaved. Some—particularly boys—"act out" by breaking laws. They steal, destroy property, or injure others.

Is such behavior normal? Most developmentalists who agree with psychoanalytic theory (see Chapter 1) answer yes (Austrian, 2008). A leading advocate of this view was Anna Freud (Sigmund's daughter, herself a prominent psychoanalyst). She called adolescent resistance to parental authority "welcome . . . beneficial . . . inevitable." She explained:

> We all know individual children who, as late as the ages of fourteen, fifteen or six-
> teen, show no such outer evidence of inner unrest. They remain, as they have been
> during the latency period, "good" children, wrapped up in their family relationships,
> considerate sons of their mothers, submissive to their fathers, in accord with the
> atmosphere, idea and ideal of their childhood background. Convenient as this may
> be, it signifies a delay of their normal development and is, as such, a sign to be
> taken seriously.
>
> *[A. Freud, 1958/2000, p. 263]*

Contrary to Freud, many psychologists, most teachers, and almost all parents are happy with well-behaved, considerate teenagers. For them, good behavior is not a sign of serious developmental problems at all.

Which view is valid? Both. Adolescents are individuals, and understanding individuality is crucial in helping each adolescent develop. Most teenagers obey the law

ANSWER TO OBSERVATION QUIZ
(from page 367) Statistically speaking, none. The rates are given per 100,000 in each age group. This means that fewer than 1 in 10,000 teens commit suicide in a year. ●

The Same Situation, Many Miles Apart: Following Tradition Adolescents worldwide flout adult conventions. Here, for instance, note the bracelet on one of the boys in a Los Angeles high school (*top*) and the dyed red hair (or is it a wig?) on one of the girls in a Tokyo park (*bottom*). As distinctive as each of these eight rebels is, all are following a tradition for their age group—just as their parents probably did when they were adolescents.

juvenile delinquent
A person under the age of 18 who breaks the law.

● **UNDERSTANDING THE NUMBERS**
How does the arrest risk of an Asian American teenage girl compare to that of an African American teenage boy?

Answer The ratio is about 1-to-21, since the ethnic risk is 1-to-7 (2 × 3.5) and the sex ratio is 1-to-3. (Of course, the text ratios are approximate, and many factors change over the years. The current risk in your community may be quite different.)

most of the time, and a law-abiding adolescence does not predict a later explosion or breakdown. According to the longitudinal study in New Zealand, first mentioned in Chapter 1, teenage boys who had never been arrested became men who earned degrees, "held high-status jobs, and expressed optimism about their own futures" (Moffitt, 2003, p. 61).

Dozens of other longitudinal studies that followed people from childhood through adulthood have now been completed (Offer et al., 2004). Their consensus is that increased anger during puberty is normal but that most adolescents express their anger in acceptable ways. They yell at their parents, curse at their peers, complain about school. For a minority, anger explodes, and they break something or hurt someone. That does not necessarily signal later problems.

However, a small proportion of adolescents (about 7 percent, more boys than girls) are steadily aggressive throughout childhood and early adolescence (Broidy et al., 2003). They are the ones to worry about; steady aggression is far more troubling in the long term than occasional outbursts.

BREAKING THE LAW Any lawbreaker under age 18 is a **juvenile delinquent.** Some laws apply only to juveniles (laws against drinking, buying cigarettes, and breaking curfews), while others apply to everyone (laws against stealing, raping, and killing). Although dealing with minor offenses may prevent major crimes (parents whose daughter hides a bottle of vodka under her bed or whose son breaks a window in anger should not ignore it), our focus here is on serious offenses.

Major crimes are more frequent during adolescence and emerging adulthood than at any other period of life, as arrest statistics in every nation attest. Confidential self-reports reveal that virtually everyone breaks the law at least once before age 20, and many of those infractions are considered serious: assault, car theft, robbery, rape.

The frequency of youthful lawbreaking was evident in one study of 1,559 urban seventh-graders of both sexes and many ethnicities, from parochial as well as public schools. In the past year, more than three-fourths had committed at least one offense (stolen something, damaged property, or hurt someone physically) (T. R. Nichols et al., 2006).

Only about one-fourth of young lawbreakers are caught, and many who are apprehended are not arrested (Dodge et al., 2006). The youngest teenagers are especially likely to be warned and released. Nonetheless, in the United States in 2007, more than 1 million 13- to 18-year-olds were arrested—about 5 percent of the total teen population.

Gender, income, and ethnic differences in juvenile arrest rates are dramatic; they are much more evident in official statistics than in self-reports (Dodge et al., 2006). In the United States, adolescent males are arrested three times as often as females; African Americans are arrested twice as often as European Americans, who are arrested three and a half times as often as Asian Americans (Owens-Sabir, 2007; Pastore & Maguire, 2005). (These statistics count most Hispanics as European Americans.) Rates of imprisonment at all ages (though usually reflecting crimes committed between ages 16 and 25) are even more striking: Seven times as many men as women are in jail (West & Sabol, 2008).

Other kinds of data show smaller gender differences in angry, aggressive behavior. Both genders include many antisocial people, as the following makes clear.

A VIEW FROM SCIENCE

A Feminist Looks at the Data

"Sugar and spice, and everything nice, that's what little girls are made of" was a rhyme I showed my mother soon after I learned to read, announcing, "That proves it." To my young mind, seeing those words in print proved that I was better than my older brother, who, like all little boys, was made of "snakes and snails and puppy dog tails." As my mother always told it, I have always been proud to be a girl, and then a woman.

However, as an adult scientist, I examine evidence carefully before drawing conclusions. A cursory glance at statistics suggests that adolescent girls *are* nicer than boys. For example, one large study found that, among U.S. high school seniors who graduated in 2003, 11 percent of the boys but only 4 percent of the girls had been arrested in the previous year. Among those who had often hurt someone badly enough that bandages or a doctor was needed, the male–female ratio was 10 to 1 (3 percent to 0.3 percent) (Pastore & Maguire, 2005). A careful review by three well-respected male developmental researchers finds that a greater percentage of boys than of girls exhibit antisocial behavior (Dodge et al., 2006).

But scientists know the difference between wishful thinking and data, between direct and indirect aggression. Several female scholars, as well as the three men just cited, suggest that although boys are more often in physical fights, girls engage in *relational aggression*—manifested in gossip, social exclusion, and the spreading of rumors—as often as boys do (Card et al., 2008; Crick et al., 2001; Underwood, 2003). Girls' antisocial impulses may be less noticeable, but they are not necessarily less hurtful, than boys'.

The study of high school seniors just cited found that 47 percent of the girls, but only 38 percent of the boys, had gotten into five or more arguments or fights with their parents that year (Pastore & Maguire, 2005). A study of seventh-graders found that more girls than boys reported getting angry and losing self-control (T. R. Nichols et al., 2006).

Female aggression continues into adulthood. Among heterosexual couples, women are more likely to curse, hit, and even injure their partners than are men (Archer, 2000; Moffitt et al., 2001). If that is true, why are reports of wife abuse more common than reports of husband abuse? Two reasons: (1) Men are generally stronger and thus more likely to seriously injure or even kill their partners in a dispute, and (2) most men hate to admit they have been hurt, especially by their wives, so they keep their injuries to themselves.

Females are less likely to express anger in public, physical ways. They stab with words, not knives. Adolescent girls caught in lawbreaking often talk their way out of an arrest, whereas boys are more likely to be defiant, often physically. In this, I like to think that girls are smart, not sneaky, since defiance leads to arrest, conviction, and prison.

Most parents teach their young children to be kind, most adolescents control their anger, most people become loving, responsible adults. Neither sex is "everything nice." As a scientist, I know that many men (including my brother) are kind and helpful and that some "snakes and snails" are in me. Gender differences are many, but individuals of both sexes are sometimes aggressive.

CAUSES OF CRIME Two clusters of factors, one from childhood (primarily brain-based) and one from adolescence (primarily contextual), predict who is likely to commit violent crimes. Usually the brain and the social context are both necessary to make someone a serious delinquent (Dupéré et al., 2007; Lahey et al., 2003).

Persistent Offenders The first of these two clusters signifies neurological problems. A short attention span, hyperactivity, inadequate emotional regulation, slow language development, low intelligence, certain alleles (such as low MAOA, as seen in Chapter 1), early and severe malnutrition, autistic tendencies, maternal smoking during fetal development, and severe child abuse—all of these correlate with later delinquency, although no single one of them necessarily produces it (Brennan et al., 2003).

Many of these factors are more common among boys than girls, which may be one reason for the gender difference in arrests. Neurological impairment of any kind increases the risk that a child will become a **life-course-persistent offender** (Moffitt et al., 2001), someone who breaks the law before and after adolescence as well as during it.

life-course-persistent offender
A person whose criminal activity typically begins in early adolescence and continues throughout life; a career criminal.

adolescence-limited offender
A person whose criminal activity stops by age 21.

Adolescence-Only Offenders The second cluster includes risk factors that are primarily psychosocial, not biological, and that are most damaging during adolescence. They include having deviant friends; having few connections to school; living in a crowded, violent, unstable neighborhood; not having a job; abusing drugs and alcohol; and having close relatives (especially older siblings) in jail.

These risks are more prevalent among low-income, urban adolescents, but many adolescents at all income levels experience them. Any teen with these problems risks becoming an **adolescence-limited offender,** someone whose criminal activity begins during adolescence but stops by adulthood (Moffitt, 1997, 2003).

Adolescence-limited offenders were not perfect as children, but unlike life-course-persistent offenders, they were not the worst-behaved in their class or the first to use drugs, have sex, or be arrested. They tend to break the law with their friends, facilitated by their chosen antisocial clique, while many life-course-persistent offenders are loners. Both types of offenders are more likely to be boys than girls, but some lawbreaking cliques emerge after the formation of mixed-gender groups. Consequently, the gender gap in arrests is narrower in late adolescence than earlier (Moffitt et al., 2001).

By mid-adolescence, the criminal records of adolescence-limited and life-course-persistent offenders look alike. However, if adolescence-limited delinquents can be protected from various snares (such as quitting school, time in prison, drug addiction, early parenthood), they may outgrow their criminal behavior (Moffitt, 2003). Outgrowing criminality is especially likely if delinquents are female, from harmonious two-parent families, alcohol- and drug-free, doing well in school, religious, and with parents who monitor their activity. None of these six factors is a guarantee, but each reduces risk.

Make no mistake: Adolescence-limited lawbreaking is neither inevitable nor insignificant. Antisocial behavior in adolescence is dangerous to young delinquents and to victims, who are usually other adolescents (Baum, 2005). But adolescence-limited delinquency is more plastic and less serious, from a life-span viewpoint, than it may seem to be at the time.

ESPECIALLY FOR Police Officers
You see some 15-year-olds drinking beer in a local park when they belong in school. What do you do? (see response, page 374) ➔

HUMAN RELATIONSHIPS AND CRIME PREVENTION One preventive and protective measure—human relationships—diminishes anger and prevents crime at every age (Heilbrun et al., 2005). Adolescents whose parents are active in their lives, or adults who have families of their own, have much lower rates of violent crime than do their more isolated contemporaries. Adolescents who feel connected to their teachers, or who are engaged in after-school activities, are less likely to break the law.

Of course, not every relationship is equally beneficial. Delinquents who learn from deviant peers are likely to be arrested again (Dishion et al., 1999; Leve & Chamberlain, 2005). Hostile and neglectful parents make serious lawbreaking more likely.

In an approach called *therapeutic foster care,* however, arrested adolescents are placed with foster parents who receive extra help, training, and financial support to establish a relationship with their foster child and his or her teachers. According to police records in Oregon, delinquents in therapeutic foster care are subsequently arrested only half as often as those with similar histories who are placed in traditional foster care or sent to reform school or prison (MMWR, July 2, 2004).

Family relationships are crucial throughout adolescence. Even teenagers in foster care, whose birth families typically are dysfunctional, still reach out to their relatives when they need support (M. E. Collins et al., 2008). Relatives may be helpful even if they were severely inadequate earlier in their teens' lives.

Every young person, delinquent or not, foster child or not, depressed or not, needs social support and tries to find it. Overall, close relationships with supportive adults and avoidance of deviant peers help rebellious youth (adolescence-limited offenders or not) stay within bounds (J. Barnes et al., 2006; Kumpfer & Alvarado, 2003).

Do You Know This Boy? Warren Messner fights back tears as he is sentenced in a Daytona Beach, Florida, courtroom for the 2005 beating murder of a homeless man. Messner is 16; he was sentenced to be imprisoned until he is 39. Like most teenage criminals, he was unhappy at school and broke the law with three other boys who also pleaded guilty.

Drug Use and Abuse

Adolescents use drugs and alcohol, although the law does not allow it. In the United States, according to the most recent Monitoring the Future study (a nationwide annual survey of U.S. high school students that began in 1975), 72 percent of high school seniors drank alcohol (more than a few sips) at least once in their lives, 46 percent tried smoking cigarettes, and 42 percent tried marijuana (Johnston et al., 2008).

Adolescents enjoy doing something forbidden, and their hormonal surges and cognitive immaturity (discussed in Chapter 9) may cause them to be particularly attracted to the sensations produced by certain drugs (Witt, 2007). For many adolescents, both their brains and bodies push them toward physical thrills and toward confusing human relationships. For some socially awkward teens, the "use of substances . . . provides a form of commerce with the social world" (Dishion & Owen, 2002, p. 489). As an example, one of my students said she smoked cigarettes because it gave her something to do with her hands!

Variations Among Adolescents

Most adolescents try *psychoactive drugs,* some of which are legal and some of which are not. To a developmentalist (but not to a police officer), cigarettes, alcohol, and many prescription medicines are all drugs that may be as addictive and damaging as illegal drugs like marijuana, cocaine, and heroin. The crucial factor is not the legality but the effect on development. In that context, age, culture, cohort, and gender are all influential.

AGE DIFFERENCES For almost every drug, use becomes more widespread from about age 10 to 25 and then decreases (although addiction to prescription drugs probably increases throughout adulthood). Drug use before age 18 is the best predictor of later drug abuse.

Inhalants (fumes from aerosol containers of spray paint or whipped cream, nail polish remover, lighter fluid, glue, cleaning fluid, and so on) are the only drug category used more by eighth-graders (16 percent) than twelfth-graders (11 percent) (Johnston et al., 2008). Middle school boys who live in quiet neighborhoods are particularly vulnerable.

One reason inhalants are attractive to young teens is that they are easy to obtain; they can be purchased at any drug, grocery, or hardware store. Another reason is that the youngest adolescents are least able, cognitively, to analyze risks, and their parents are unlikely to suspect a drug problem. Some young adolescents die from breathing toxic vapors, which can suddenly stop the heart or cut off all oxygen. Very few parents realize their child is in danger until it is too late.

RESPONSE FOR Police Officers (from page 372) Avoid both extremes: Don't let them think this situation is either harmless or serious. You might take them to the police station and call their parents. These adolescents are probably not life-course-persistent offenders; jailing them or grouping them with other lawbreakers might encourage more crime. ●

NATIONAL DIFFERENCES Nations have markedly different rates of adolescent drug use, even nations with common boundaries (Buelga et al., 2006). For example, one study found that among 15-year-olds, 9.4 percent of the Swiss are heavy users of marijuana, compared with only 3.3 percent of Italians. Canadian youth smoke more marijuana, but less tobacco, than U.S. youth do. Although marijuana is legal and widely available in the Netherlands, Dutch 15-year-olds have a very low rate of heavy use (2.8 percent) (Buelga et al., 2006).

In some nations, young adolescents drink alcohol more often than they use any other drug; in others, smoking is more common than drinking. In many places (especially eastern Europe), teenagers use both alcohol and tobacco at higher rates than in North America. In still other places (much of the Middle East), teenagers rarely use any drugs at all (Buelga et al., 2006; Eisner, 2002).

These variations are partly due to differing laws the world over. For example, in many Arab nations, alcohol is strictly forbidden; in many European nations, young children routinely drink wine and beer. In many Asian nations, anyone may smoke anywhere; in the United States, smoking is not allowed in most schools, hospitals, and public places. Canadian laws are stricter—cigarette advertising is outlawed.

COHORT DIFFERENCES Overall, drug use among adolescents has decreased in the United States since 1976 (as Figure 10.5 shows). Adolescent culture may have a greater effect on drug-taking behavior than laws do. As evidence, despite the law, most adolescents in the United States have experimented with drug use and say that they could find illegal drugs if they tried.

Nationwide, most U.S. adolescents are *not* regular drug users. For every drug, the number of high school seniors who report use within the past 30 days (44 percent for alcohol, 21 percent for cigarettes, and 19 percent for marijuana) is only about half the number who report ever having used that drug (Johnston et al., 2008). A significant minority (about 20 percent) never use any drugs, usually because of religious values, not because drugs are illegal or unavailable (C. Smith, 2005). Religious factors were more influential in previous decades and were a major reason for enacting Prohibition (no alcohol at all) in the United States in 1920.

FIGURE 10.5 Rise and Fall By asking the same questions year after year, the Monitoring the Future study shows notable historical effects. It is encouraging that something in society, not in the adolescent, makes drug use increase and decrease and that the most recent data show a decline. However, as Chapter 1 emphasized, survey research cannot prove what causes change.

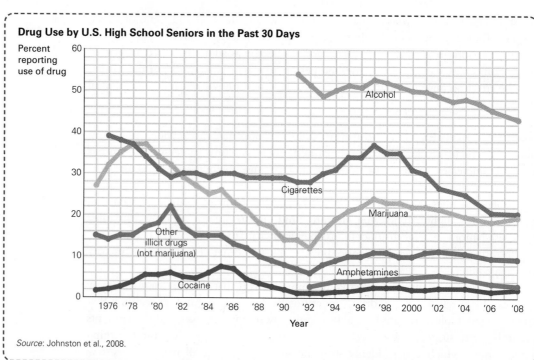

Drug Use by U.S. High School Seniors in the Past 30 Days

Source: Johnston et al., 2008.

Laws, customs, beliefs, and cohort interact and change from state to state. For instance, 28 percent of high school girls in West Virginia are smokers (defined as having smoked at least one cigarette in the past 30 days), compared with 14.6 percent of high school girls in Florida (MMWR, June 6, 2008). Both rates are much lower than they were 20 years ago. The United States is now the world leader in adolescent use of synthetic narcotics. During 2007, 10 percent of U.S. high school seniors used Vicodin and 5 percent used OxyContin (Johnston et al., 2008).

GENDER DIFFERENCES IN DRUG USE With some exceptions, adolescent boys use more drugs, and use them more often, than girls do. An international survey of 13- to 15-year-olds in 131 nations found that more boys are smokers (except in a few European nations), including three times as many boys as girls in Southeast Asia (Warren et al., 2006). According to another international survey of 31 nations, almost twice as many boys as girls have tried marijuana (26 to 15 percent) (ter Bogt et al., 2006).

Gender differences are reinforced by social constructions about proper male and female behavior. In Indonesia, for instance, 38 percent of the boys smoke cigarettes but only 5 percent of the girls do. One Indonesian boy explains, "If I don't smoke, I'm not a real man" (quoted in Ng et al., 2007).

Like every other aspect of adolescent behavior, drug use is affected by cohort shifts in gender norms. In the United States, before 1970, far more boys than girls were smokers, but then the rate among boys began to fall. By the 1990s, more girls than boys smoked. Recently, girls again have lower rates of smoking than boys (Johnston et al., 2008).

In the United States, occasional drug use (such as trying marijuana) is almost equally common in both sexes, except that girls seldom use steroids but use diet pills more often than boys do. However, heavy use of drugs (such as daily use of marijuana) is about twice as prevalent among boys (Johnston et al., 2008). Another gender difference relates to age: Among eighth-graders in the United States, drug use is unisex, but then drug use among boys increases faster than among girls (Johnston et al., 2008).

Harm from Drugs

For many teenagers, drug use signifies independence from social restrictions, enhances sensations, and fosters social connections. This—as well as the fact that drugs are widely used by adults—leads many adolescents to believe that adults exaggerate the evils of teen drug use. That may be, but developmentalists see much immediate and long-term harm when teenagers or preteens use psychoactive substances.

Abuse, addiction, and brain damage are among "the deleterious consequences of drug use [that] appear to be more pronounced in adolescents than in adults, a difference that has been linked to brain maturation" (Moffit et al., 2006, p. 12). Few adolescents notice when they move past use (experimenting) to *abuse* (experiencing harm) and then to *addiction* (needing the drug to avoid feeling ill).

TOBACCO An obvious negative effect of tobacco use is that it slows down growth. All psychoactive drugs impair digestion, nutrition, and appetite, but tobacco may be worst of all, partly because smokers use it so often. All kinds of tobacco (bidis, cigars, pipes, chewing tobacco) inhibit growth, making adolescent smokers shorter and heavier adults than they otherwise would be.

Tobacco reduces the appetite, which may interfere with nutrition that growing bodies need. Protein and vitamin deficiencies caused by tobacco are particularly serious in India, where undernutrition is chronic and tobacco use is widespread (Warren et al., 2006). Since internal organs continue to mature after the height spurt, teenagers who appear full-grown and who use tobacco or any other drug may still damage their developing hearts, lungs, brains, and reproductive systems.

ALCOHOL Alcohol is the most frequently abused drug among North American teenagers. Heavy drinking may permanently impair memory and self-control by damaging the hippocampus and the prefrontal cortex (S. A. Brown et al., 2000; De Bellis et al., 2005; A. M. White & Swartzwelder, 2004). Experiments with lower animals suggest that slower thinking as a result of alcohol use is particularly likely among adolescent drinkers (Sircar & Sircar, 2005).

Like many other drugs, alcohol allows momentary denial of problems; worries seem to disappear when a person is under the influence. When problems get worse because they have been ignored, more alcohol is needed—a vicious cycle that often leads to addiction. Denial is a problem for all alcoholics, but this is particularly true for teenagers who have not yet learned that they cannot drive, write, or even think straight after having several drinks.

MARIJUANA Similarly, many people (especially teenagers) are oblivious to the dangers of marijuana, partly because users seem more relaxed than inebriated. A girl named Johanna said:

> I started off using about every other weekend, and pretty soon it increased to three to four times a week. . . . I started skipping classes to get high. I quit soccer because my coach was a jerk. My grades dropped, but I blamed that on my not being into school. . . . Finally some of my friends cornered me and told me how much I had changed, and they said it started when I started smoking marijuana. They came with me to see the substance-abuse counselor at school.
>
> *[quoted in R. Bell, 1998, p. 199]*

If Johanna had not quit, her future would have been affected. Adolescents who regularly smoke marijuana are more likely to drop out of school, become teenage parents, and be unemployed (Chassin et al., 2004). Marijuana affects memory, language proficiency, and motivation (Lane et al., 2005)—all of which are especially crucial during adolescence.

Those are correlations, which, as you know, do not reveal causation. Is it possible that adolescents who are not particularly clever or ambitious choose to smoke marijuana, rather than vice versa? Is some third variable (such as hostile parents) the cause of both the academic problems and the drug use, rendering the correlation deceptive? This seemed plausible because researchers over the years have noted that drug-using adolescents distrust their parents, injure themselves, hate their schools, and break many laws.

This led to a hypothesis that the psychic strains of adolescence led to drug use. In fact, however, longitudinal research suggests that drug use *causes* more problems than it solves, often *preceding* anxiety disorders, depression, and rebellion (Chassin et al., 2004). Rather than lack of ambition leading to marijuana use, marijuana itself destroys ambition.

OCCASIONAL USE OF ANY DRUG Drug use is progressive. The first use usually occurs as part of a social gathering. Almost no teenager smokes or drinks alone for the first time. As a result, many adolescents believe that occasional use is harmless, just an expression of friendship or generational solidarity. Few adolescent drug users are addicts, and, for those who are, usually they and their friends are unaware of it.

If an adult cries wolf, suggesting that a teen who tries a drug has a severe drug problem or is addicted, the adult may lose credibility. Worse may be a lack of adult concern, however.

According to the Monitoring the Future study, 26 percent of high school seniors are binge drinkers (defined as consuming five or more alcoholic drinks in a row in the past two weeks), 12 percent are daily cigarette smokers, and 5 percent are daily marijuana users (Johnston et al., 2008). These figures are ominous, suggesting that addiction is the next step. The younger a person is when beginning drug use, the more likely addiction will occur (Merline et al., 2004). The best safeguard is to postpone that first drag or drink.

Occasional drug use presents another risk, which may be worse than addiction. Every psychoactive drug excites the limbic system and interferes with the prefrontal cortex. Drug users are thus more emotional (specifics vary, from ecstasy to terror, paranoia to rage) than they otherwise would be, as well as less reflective. Every hazard of adolescence—including car crashes, unsafe sex, and parasuicide—is more common among teens who have taken a psychoactive drug.

Preventing Drug Abuse: What Works?

With harmful drugs, as with many other aspects of life, each generation prefers to learn things for themselves. A common phenomenon is **generational forgetting,** the idea that each new generation forgets what the previous generation learned (Chassin et al., 2004; Johnston et al., 2008). One reason is that teenagers tend to distrust adults because their social contexts pertaining to drug use, sex, and education were different.

The most widely used drug prevention program in U.S. schools, Project DARE (Drug Abuse Resistance Education), features adults (usually police officers) telling students about the dangers of drugs. Perhaps because of generational forgetting, DARE has no impact on later drug use, according to several reliable studies (West & O'Neal, 2004).

Similarly, some antidrug advertisements using scare tactics (such as the one that showed eggs being broken into a hot frying pan while an announcer intoned, "This is your brain on drugs") may have the opposite effect from that intended, increasing rather than decreasing drug use. One reason may be that such advertisements make drugs seem exciting; another may be that adolescents recognize the exaggeration; a third may be that the ads give some teenagers ideas about ways to show defiance.

Solid research has been done on advertising campaigns against adolescent smoking. Apparently, antismoking announcements produced by cigarette companies (such as one that showed a clean-cut young person advising viewers to think before they started smoking) actually increase use (Block et al., 2002; Fishbein et al., 2002). Cigarette sponsorship of sports or entertainment events also encourages adolescent smoking.

You have read about similar results from other campaigns. Some antibullying efforts backfire in high school; some sex-education curricula have no effect. Parents are often told to educate their children about the harm from drugs, but many parents do not know about their children's drug use, so their educational efforts may be too late, too general, or too ignorant. For instance, in one U.S. study, less than 1 percent of parents of sixth-graders thought their children had ever had alcohol, but 22 percent of the children said they had (O'Donnell et al., 2008).

Mistrust of the older generation, added to loyalty to one's peers, leads not only to generational forgetting but also to a backlash. If adults say something is forbidden until age 21, that is often an incentive to try it!

This does not mean that trying to halt early drug use is hopeless. Massive ad campaigns in Florida and California have cut adolescent smoking almost in half, in part because the publicity appealed to the young (Wakefield et al., 2003). A particularly effective ad depicted young people dumping 1,200 body bags in front of the corporate headquarters of a tobacco company to highlight the number of smoking-related deaths that occur in the United States each day (Farrelly et al., 2005). The anti-corporation message, with dramatic black-and-white footage (as if a teen had shot it), had an impact.

Changing the social context is also helpful. Throughout the United States, higher prices, targeted warnings, and better law enforcement have led to a marked decline

generational forgetting
The idea that each new generation forgets what the previous generation learned. As used here, the term refers to knowledge about the harm drugs can do.

in cigarette smoking among younger adolescents. In 2007, only 7 percent of eighth-graders had smoked cigarettes in the past month, compared with 21 percent 10 years earlier (Johnston et al., 2008).

All the research suggests that parents continue to be influential in adolescence. When parents forbid smoking in their homes, fewer adolescents smoke (Messer et al., 2008); when parents are careful with their own drinking, fewer teenagers abuse alcohol (Van Zundert et al., 2006). The declining U.S. rates of teenage births and abortions, as well as all the variations in drug use just described, suggest that adolescent biology is far from destiny. Family and context are as influential during the teen years as before.

Perhaps parents and other adults simply need to be reminded of the joy and energy they felt during their teen years. Surely, they would wish the same for the next generation.

KEY points

- Most adolescents worldwide experiment with drugs, usually cigarettes and alcohol, although regular drug use is less common among teenagers than among young adults.

- Variations in adolescent drug use and abuse related to age, culture, cohort, and gender are evident.

- Drug use in adolescence is especially risky, as many drugs reduce learning and growth, as well as smooth the path to addiction and abuse.

- Generational forgetting is one reason each cohort has distinctive drug-use patterns.

SUMMARY

Identity

1. Adolescence is a time for self-discovery. According to Erikson, adolescents seek their own identity, sorting through the traditions of their families and cultures.

2. Many young adolescents foreclose on their options without exploring possibilities, experience role confusion, or reach moratorium. Identity achievement takes longer for contemporary adolescents than it did half a century ago, when Erikson first described it.

3. Identity achievement occurs in many domains, including religious identity, sexual identity (now often called gender identity), political identity (often replaced by ethnic identity), and vocational identity. Each of these is sought by adolescents, although few achieve a solid identity during these years.

Relationships with Elders and Peers

4. Parents continue to influence their growing children, despite bickering over minor issues. Ideally, from age 10 to 18, communication and warmth remain high within the family, while parental control decreases and adolescents develop autonomy.

5. There are cultural differences in the timing of conflicts and particulars of parental monitoring. Too much parental control, with psychological intrusiveness, is harmful, as is neglect. Parents need to grant some freedom and yet provide guidance—not an easy balance.

6. Peers can be beneficial or harmful, depending on particular friends, cliques, and crowds. Peer pressure is evident in adolescence. Adolescents select their friends, including friends of the other sex, who then facilitate constructive and/or destructive behavior.

7. Peers may be particularly crucial for immigrant adolescents, who often have a strong commitment to family values but who also try to adjust to new norms and customs. Most immigrant adolescents do well in school and help their families.

Sexuality

8. Like adults, adolescents experience diverse sexual needs and may be involved in short-term or long-term romances, depending in part on their peer culture. Homosexual youth are likely to take longer than their heterosexual peers to achieve a satisfying sexual identity.

9. Most parents want schools to teach adolescents about sex, although such education often comes later than the personal experiences of the teen. No curriculum (including abstinence-only programs) has affected the age at which adolescents become sexually active, although some reduce pregnancy and STIs.

10. The teenage birth rate has fallen, and the use of contraception has increased worldwide. When teenage births do occur, the mothers are much less likely to be married than was the case 50 years ago.

Sadness and Anger

11. Almost all adolescents become self-conscious and self-critical. A few become chronically sad and depressed. Many adolescents (especially girls) think about suicide, and some attempt it. Few adolescents actually kill themselves; most who do so are boys.

12. Almost all adolescents become more independent and angry as part of growing up, although most still respect their parents. Lawbreaking as well as momentary rage are common; boys are more likely to be arrested for violent offenses than are girls.

13. Adolescence-limited delinquents should be prevented from hurting themselves or others; their criminal behavior will disappear with maturation. Life-course-persistent offenders have

broken laws in childhood and continue to do so in adulthood; usually they have some neurological or learning difficulties that are lifelong.

Drug Use and Abuse

14. Most adolescents experiment with drugs, especially alcohol and tobacco, although such substances impair growth of the body and the brain. National culture has a powerful influence on which specific drugs are used, as well as on frequency of use.

15. Prevention and moderation of adolescent drug use and abuse are possible. Antidrug programs and messages need to be carefully designed to avoid a backlash or generational forgetting.

KEY TERMS

identity versus role confusion (p. 348)

identity (p. 348)

identity achievement (p. 348)

role confusion (p. 348)

foreclosure (p. 348)

moratorium (p. 349)

gender identity (p. 350)

sexual orientation (p. 350)

bickering (p. 354)

parental monitoring (p. 356)

clique (p. 356)

crowd (p. 356)

peer pressure (p. 357)

deviancy training (p. 357)

clinical depression (p. 366)

rumination (p. 366)

suicidal ideation (p. 366)

cluster suicides (p. 367)

parasuicide (p. 367)

juvenile delinquent (p. 370)

life-course-persistent offender (p. 371)

adolescence-limited offender (p. 372)

generational forgetting (p. 377)

KEY QUESTIONS

1. What are the differences between identity achievement and role confusion?

2. When would foreclosure or moratorium be beneficial to a teenager?

3. Give several examples of decisions a person must make in establishing gender identity.

4. Why and how do parents remain influential during their children's teen years?

5. How and when can peer pressure be helpful and how can it be harmful?

6. What is the usual developmental pattern of romances during adolescence?

7. How are homosexual youth similar to, and different from, heterosexual youth?

8. What is the effect of sex education from parents, peers, and teachers on adolescent sexual experience?

9. What gender differences are evident in depression, suicidal ideation, and suicide, and why?

10. What are the similarities and differences between adolescence-limited and life-course-persistent offenders?

11. What factors make serious delinquency more likely, and what factors decrease the risk?

12. What variations in adolescent drug use are evident? Why?

APPLICATIONS

1. Teenage cliques and crowds may be more important in large U.S. high schools than elsewhere. Interview people who spent their teenage years in U.S. schools of various sizes, or in another nation, about the peer relationships in their high schools. Describe and discuss any differences you find.

2. Locate a news article about a teenager who committed suicide. Can you find evidence in the article that there were warning signs that were ignored? Does the report inadvertently encourage cluster suicides?

3. Research suggests that most adolescents have broken the law but that few have been arrested or incarcerated. Ask 10 of your

fellow students whether they broke the law when they were under 18 and, if so, how often, in what ways, with what consequences. (Assure them of confidentiality.) What hypothesis arises about lawbreaking in your cohort?

4. Cultures have different standards for drug use among children, adolescents, and adults. Interview three people from different cultures (not necessarily from different nations; each occupation, generation, or religion can be said to have a culture) about their culture's drug-use standards. Ask your respondents to explain the reasons for any differences.

Adolescence (Ages 11 to 18)

PUBERTY

Hormones
HPA axis
Menarche and spermarche
Sexual thoughts and emotions

Age variations
Earlier for girls
Body fat
Genes and ethnicity
Stress

Emotions without reflection

Brain development
Limbic system before prefrontal cortex

Eating disorders (anorexia, bulimia)

Puberty early or late

"LIKE STARTING TURBO-CHARGED ENGINES WITH AN UNSKILLED DRIVER"
BETWEEN CHILDHOOD AND ADULTHOOD, EMOTION AND LOGIC

THINKING AND LEARNING

Piaget: Formal operational intelligence
The possible overtakes the actual
Deductive reasoning

Adolescent egocentrism
Fables and fantasies

Dual processing
Analysis versus emotion

Secondary education
Middle school: The low ebb
High school and high stakes

Disengagement

School dropouts

WHO AM I?

Identity versus role confusion

Foreclosure and moratorium

Gender: More than just male or female

Needing peers

Facilitation and selection

Same sex and other sex

Needing parents

Monitoring with warmth

Bickering and support

Peer pressure

Parents too intrusive

SEXUAL DEVELOPMENT

Primary sex characteristics

For reproduction

Secondary sex characteristics

Differentiate male and female

Romances

Not too early

Abstinence or safe sex

Sex education

Schools, parents, friends

Sexually transmitted diseases

Early pregnancy

Sexual abuse

DRUG USE AND ABUSE

Culture and context

Destroying body and brain

Alcohol most common

Generational forgetting

Addiction (with every drug)

Slow growth (esp. with tobacco)

Risky behavior (esp. with alcohol)

Reduced motivation (esp. with marijuana)

KEY

- Major topic
- Related topic
- Potential problem

- CHAPTER 11
- CHAPTER 12
- CHAPTER 13

Adulthood

Social scientists traditionally cite three roles as signifying adulthood: employee, spouse, and parent. Until recently, those roles were expected of young people, and usually coveted by them, once puberty was over. Today, however, many young adults avoid taking on those three classic roles that early—if they decide to take them on at all. That topic is thus postponed to Chapters 12 and 13.

We first look at Chapter 11 on emerging adulthood, which is said to last from age 18 to age 25. Note, however, that all three chapters reveal chronological age to be an imperfect guide to development. Some people take on adult roles by age 20, whereas others don't do so even by age 30; there are also some adults who are considered middle-aged at 35, whereas still others maintain their youthful energy at 60.

Globalization and today's ever-advancing technology make it possible for adolescents and young adults to put off fulfilling adult roles as long as they can, while they seek more education and independence than older generations in their community ever did. The same forces bring more flexibility throughout the adult years, as is evident not only in developed nations but also in almost every culture.

Over the many decades of adult life, bodies grow more mature; minds master new material and consolidate what is already known; and people work productively, nurture marriages, raise children, and care for aging parents. Adults experience disasters, windfalls, divorces, illnesses, recoveries, births, deaths, travel, job loss, promotion, poverty, wealth.

Thus, adulthood is a long sweep, punctuated by myriad events. As you know, those events are not random: Adults build on their maturation and experience within their social context, creating their own ecological niche, with chosen people, activities, communities, and habits. In the twenty-first century, age restrictions are less rigid and possibilities abound. Enjoy your access to the choices your grandparents never had the opportunity to make.

11

EMERGING ADULTHOOD
Body, Mind, and Social World

During my senior year in high school, I applied to three colleges. Each was carefully chosen after I read a thick book describing hundreds of institutions, discussed my future with my family, listed my priorities, and visited several campuses. On the morning I was to take the College Board Achievement Tests, I opened a letter from the only one of those three that did not require Achievement Test scores. That college (in California) accepted me, offering a small scholarship to boot.

I had never visited California. I knew no one at that institution, which was 3,000 miles from my home and from the boy who had given me his fraternity pin. At that point in my life, none of that mattered. I was thrilled that a college wanted me.

To my parents' dismay (my mother had envisioned me at a nearby women's college), I skipped the exam, withdrew my applications to the other two colleges, and flew west the following September. More adventures soon followed. By the time I was 25 years old, I had attended four colleges (I transferred back east after two years), changed majors three times, rejected marriage proposals from four young men, lived in 10 places, and started several jobs—none lasting more than 18 months. ●

MY BEHAVIOR WAS in marked contrast to that of my grandparents. By age 20, they had married, had a son, and bought the farm where they lived and worked until they died. I was, however, certainly typical of millions of other contemporary young people aged 18 to 25, who, thanks to advances in three major realms—globalization, technology, and medicine—spurred the creation of a new stage of the life span: **emerging adulthood.**

This new stage, also called *young adulthood* or *youth,* is distinguished by later marriage and parenthood (five or more years later than in 1950, on average), more education (most study past high school), financial dependence (many receive parental support), and vocational uncertainty (few have jobs they intend to keep until retirement). All this allows a new freedom, "a substantial amount of exploration and instability that are two of the defining characteristics of emerging adulthood" (Arnett, 2004, p. 39).

emerging adulthood
The period between the ages of 18 and 25, which is now widely thought of as a separate developmental stage. (Also called *young adulthood* or *youth.*)

This chapter describes the trends as well as the variations among emerging adults. Almost all have strong bodies but are susceptible to particular health hazards, as you will soon see. We also discuss cognitive development, focusing particularly on the impact of a college education. Relationships have changed, but the basic need for companionship remains, as our discussion of cohabitation and friendship reveal. By the end of this chapter, it will be clear why emerging adulthood is considered a new stage, evident worldwide, with implications for people of all nations and generations.

Cultural and National Differences

One of the most important questions to ask about emerging adulthood is whether it is relevant only for middle-class North Americans, as the U.S. data given above might imply. In fact, researchers find that emerging adulthood is a separate stage among all economic, ethnic, and national groups. The hallmarks of this stage mentioned above—later marriage, more education, prolonged financial dependence, and vocational instability—are increasingly evident among 18- to 25-year-olds in China, India, Brazil, Mexico, and South Africa as well as in North America, Europe, Australia, and East Asia.

However, people reaching adulthood experience different sociocultural and economic pressures, depending on their background. Individuals from poor families are less able to postpone parenting or to extend education for more than a year or two; with more financial support comes more freedom.

Strong and Healthy Bodies

Emerging adults are usually in good health. Traditionally, the years between ages 18 and 25 were a time for hard physical work and childbearing. However, thanks to the three macrosystems already mentioned—globalization, technology, and medicine—physical work and parenthood are no longer expected of every young adult in the twenty-first century. Employment almost never requires physical strength, and societies no longer depend on women to bear as many children as possible.

Of course, biology still allows hard work and childbearing if a young adult wishes to take on those traditional roles. Maturation and fertility begin in adolescence, as you read in Chapter 9. The current level of food availability means that in almost every nation, emerging adults have reached full height (girls usually by age 16, boys by age 18). For both sexes, muscle growth and fat accumulation continue into the early 20s, when women attain adult breast and hip size and men reach full shoulder width and upper-arm strength.

A higher proportion of the male body is muscle, not fat, which makes men stronger than women, on average. In general, emerging-adult men are better than any other age or gender group at running up a steep hill, lifting a heavy load, or gripping an object with maximum force.

All this has always been true. However, much has changed in the biological development of the typical young adult, especially as regards health and resistance to disease.

FEWER DISEASES Many chronic conditions that were common among young adults a century ago—malnutrition, parasite infestations, and tuberculosis among them—are now much more rare. Specifics vary (a Japanese 20-year-old usually lives to be 90, a Nigerian only 50), but every emerging adult can anticipate many more healthy years than was the case for previous generations (United Nations, 2007). Serious disease is uncommon until at least middle age, and chronic illnesses are less troubling. (Sexually transmitted infections are an exception that will be discussed later in this chapter.)

In a mammoth U.S. survey, 96.4 percent of emerging adults rated their health as good, very good, or excellent (National Center for Health Statistics, 2007). Similarly, 96 percent of U.S. 18- to 25-year-olds reported having no limitations due to chronic health conditions—the best rate of any age group (see Figure 11.1). Rates of disability vary among nations, but everywhere advances in immunization, clean water, and food distribution help make these years the healthiest.

By age 20, the immune system has developed well enough to fight off everything from the sniffles to cancer (Henson & Aspinall, 2003). Usually, blood pressure is normal, teeth develop no new cavities, heart rate is steady, the brain is fully grown, and lung capacity is as large as it will ever be. Cancer is so unusual at this time that most diagnostic tests—such as the PSA (for prostate cancer), mammogram (for breast cancer), and colonoscopy (for colon cancer)—are not recommended until after age 40 or 50.

Death from disease almost never occurs during emerging adulthood (see Table 11.1), and some chronic childhood diseases and allergies can be outgrown. For instance, childhood asthma disappears as often as it continues, according to longitudinal research in New Zealand (M. R. Sears et al., 2003). Even the common cold is less frequent.

DYNAMIC SYSTEMS Health is interdependent, which means that health or illness in one part of the body affects all the other parts. All the body systems, including the digestive, respiratory, circulatory, and sexual-reproductive systems, function optimally in emerging adulthood. Every aspect of these systems interacts with other body systems to keep a person healthy. Exercise, for instance, directly benefits the heart and also affects the entire body and mind.

A longitudinal study that began with 18- to 30-year-olds (called CARDIA, for Coronary Artery Risk Development in Young Adulthood) reported that the fittest young adults were four times less likely to have developed diabetes or high blood pressure 15 years later than the least fit (Carnethon et al., 2003). This finding illustrates dynamic systems: Inactivity allowed circulatory problems to begin, and that affected the whole person later on.

Fortunately, in every nation, most young adults lead active lives, which is one reason they are usually healthy. It is in their nature to run, climb stairs, hike, join intramural college and company teams, play neighborhood games, jog, sail, bicycle, dance, and so on (Biddle & Mutrie, 2001).

In 2000, a collaboration among 600 U.S. organizations and agencies produced a framework for national health called *Healthy People 2010*. It set out nationwide exercise goals, including recommendations that 25 percent of trips be walking (not driving) and that 50 percent of the adult population exercise (including walking) for half an hour a day at least five days a week. In 2005, an estimated 38 percent of 18- to 24-year-olds reached those exercise targets. This age group came closer than any older age group to achieving the goals (the rate for people over 65 was 22 percent) (National Center for Health Statistics, 2009).

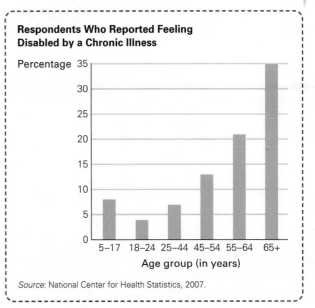

Respondents Who Reported Feeling Disabled by a Chronic Illness

Source: National Center for Health Statistics, 2007.

FIGURE 11.1 Nothing to Stop Me Residents of the United States (or their parents, in the case of young children) were asked if any chronic health problems—physical, mental, or emotional—impaired their ability to do what people their age usually did, such as attend school, go to work, and perform household tasks. Only 1 in 25 young adults said that they had any such disability, including depression, schizophrenia, blindness, mental retardation, heart disease, and AIDS.

TABLE 11.1
U.S. Deaths from the Top Four Diseases, by Age

Age Group	Annual Rate per 100,000
15–24	8
25–34	18
35–44	71
45–54	235
55–64	656
65–74	1,632
75–84	3,706
85+	8,981

Source: National Center for Health Statistics, 2007.

Young and Healthy Young adults rarely die of any disease, including the top four: heart disease, cancer, stroke, and obstructive pulmonary disease. These are *annual* rates, which means that for each person, the chance of death in that decade is 10 times the yearly rate. Thus, a 15-year-old has less than 1 chance in 10,000 of dying of disease before age 25; a 75-year-old has more than 1 chance in 3 of dying of disease before age 85.

homeostasis
The adjustment of all the body's systems to keep physiological functions in a state of equilibrium. As the body ages, it takes longer for these adjustments to occur, so it becomes harder for older bodies to adapt to stress.

HOMEOSTASIS To appreciate the interdependence of systems as well as the emerging adult's resistance to disease, it is useful to understand **homeostasis,** which refers to the body's natural adjustment to any disruptions. Bodies are designed to stay healthy and balanced, maintaining equilibrium (Widmaier et al., 2008). The pituitary regulates homeostatic responses via shifts in hormone levels (Timiras, 2003). Other body systems adjust as well. Homeostasis is quick and efficient during emerging adulthood, which is a major reason why young adults are less likely to be sick, fatigued, or obese than older adults.

All systems work at their peak in emerging adulthood, with rapid and dynamic adjustment to any stress. Young adults can run a marathon or skip sleep or catch the flu and bounce right back. The immune system itself is homeostatic, sometimes using fever, nausea, and lethargy to restore people to health, a process that occurs more quickly among young adults than among older ones.

Obvious examples of homeostasis occur when the weather changes. For instance, when temperatures rise, people sweat, move slowly, and want cold drinks—all of which help reduce their internal temperature. When temperatures fall, shivering flesh and chattering teeth increase internal body heat. Natural body heat varies with the individual, but emerging adults are generally warmer than older ones. (This explains why your mother may tell you to put on a sweater because she is cold or why one spouse wants more blankets on the bed than the other does.)

As another example, homeostasis is what keeps each person's body weight hovering around a certain *set point,* or settling point, by making the person eat when hungry and stop when full. The set point is affected by age, genes, diet, hormones, and exercise. Overeating or starvation disrupts homeostasis, but nature tries to keep every system balanced. As the body's overall salt, glucose, water, fat, and acid levels fluctuate, complex interactions among many internal organs and systems continually return the body to equilibrium.

Nutrition and exercise underlie health at every age. Emerging adults sometimes subvert their natural homeostasis because of their odd eating habits. Here we emphasize only that eating and exercising are part of the natural balance of systems, affecting the entire body, not merely its size and shape.

Homeostasis prevents young adults from realizing that they are aging or that they are harming themselves. For instance, unlike some older adult smokers, younger smokers do not cough after each cigarette. Because their lungs adjust readily to the smoke, they may be unaware that each cigarette increases their likelihood of eventually developing emphysema. Only when people stop using an addictive drug do their withdrawal symptoms (which become more prolonged with age) reveal past homeostasis.

Sex and Reproduction

The sexual-reproductive system is especially vigorous during emerging adulthood: The sex drive is powerful, infertility is rare, orgasm is frequent, and birth is easy, with fewer complications in the early 20s than at any other time. These factors all originate from homeostasis and other biological processes that allow a young woman to adjust easily to pregnancy and that allow a young man to be ready for sex again relatively soon after ejaculation.

Sexual-reproductive characteristics are produced by sex hormones, which peak in both sexes at about age 20 (Anis, 2007; J. Huang, 2007). For that reason, the optimal functioning of the sexual-reproductive system in emerging adulthood results more from *nature* than *nurture,* more from biology than culture, and is apparent in every nation. Of course, the social context powerfully influences these natural processes, reducing birth rates and encouraging sexual activity in emerging adults (and, unfortunately, exposing them to sexually transmitted infections), as we now describe.

FEWER BABIES Traditionally, a year or two after a young couple married, a baby would arrive. If that didn't occur, relatives wondered what was wrong. They were right to wonder: With frequent intercourse and without contraception, the average woman in her early 20s becomes pregnant within three months, sooner than older or younger women. Today, however, globalization, advanced technology, and modern medicine have combined to produce effective contraception, available in almost every nation. People are now able to have sex with less fear of unwanted pregnancy (Arnett, 2007a).

The same three forces have reduced infant mortality. As fewer infants die, people no longer need to begin childbearing before age 20 or to have four or more children simply to ensure that some of their children will survive. Even in the developing nation of Nepal, a lower birth rate correlated more closely with the rate of childhood immunization than with the availability of family-planning clinics (Brauner-Otto et al., 2007).

Remember that social constructions change more slowly than historical circumstances do. Centuries ago, large families were essential for survival of the species. The social construction was that large families were desirable, even blessed. Then, beginning in the early twentieth century, advances in public health reduced infant mortality. The implications of that reduction were not fully understood at first; large families remained the desired norm.

Because of that outdated social construction, births greatly exceeded deaths in the later twentieth century, and a global population explosion occurred. Having expanded very slowly for millennia, the world's population suddenly increased very rapidly, doubling from 3 billion in 1960 to more than 6 billion in 2000. Once the connection between overpopulation and poverty became widely recognized and contraception became effective, the social construction changed and the size of the average family shrank. The rate of population increase between 2000 and 2040 is projected to be less than half what it was in the preceding 40 years (United Nations, 2007).

New Policies and Practices In some nations, government policies have reduced the birth rate. The Chinese government decided that a lower birth rate was a cause, not merely a correlate, of economic development. Accordingly, toward the end of the twentieth century, China required many couples to postpone marriage and enacted a one-child-only policy. The result was that from 1950 to 1990, the average Chinese couple went from having six children to having fewer than two. Prosperity has followed: The Chinese economy has grown 10-fold over the past 35 years.

No other government has followed China's example. Nonetheless, couples everywhere are influenced by social concerns, and the birth rate worldwide has recently plummeted. I see this in my family; you can probably see it in yours as well.

Cohort Changes Early in our marriage (about 1970), Martin and I wanted a large family but worried about the world population explosion. So after having Bethany and Rachel, we waited six years. By that time, our closest friends had not yet had children and told us we could have an extra one or two to represent their share. We did (Elissa and Sarah), realizing that families as big as ours were unusual in our cohort. My grandparents had 19 children and 37 grandchildren; I have four children and only one grandchild. Generations matter.

For today's young adults, including my own children, the fertility rate is now below the **replacement rate** (about 2.1 births per woman). The term refers to the fact that the two parents are essentially replacing themselves, thus maintaining the population with no increases or decreases. In 2007, the birth rate of 90 nations was below replacement.

JUPITER IMAGES / BRAND X / ALAMY

Love Without Pregnancy Both government policy and modern contraception have changed the nature of loving relationships for young Chinese couples. This Shanghai couple may marry, they may have sex, and they may be together for 50 years or more, but they will probably have only one child.

● **UNDERSTANDING THE NUMBERS**
If the *rate* of increase of the world's population from 2000 to 2040 is half the rate of the previous 40 years, what will the world's population be in 2040?

Answer About 9 billion. The rate was double, or 2 times. Half the rate of increase would be 1½ times: 6 × 1½ = 9.

● **FOR DEEPER REFLECTION** How many children do you want and why? If this differs from your grandparents' choice, which generation is less selfish?

replacement rate
The number of births per woman that would be required to maintain a nation's (or the world's) population with no increases or decreases. The current replacement rate is considered to be about 2.1 births per woman.

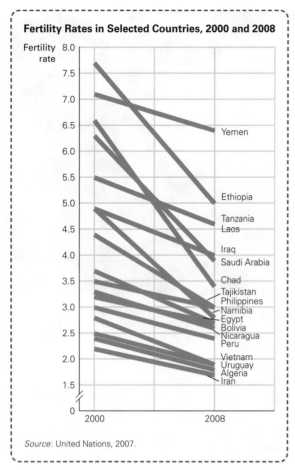

Fertility Rates in Selected Countries, 2000 and 2008

Source: United Nations, 2007.

FIGURE 11.2 Fewer Children Per Woman Since the end of the twentieth century, fertility rates in one-third of the world's nations, including all those in Europe, have been lower than the replacement rate. The most dramatic recent reductions have occurred in developing nations.

OBSERVATION QUIZ

The source for this graph was compiled in 2006 and published in 2007, but it includes data for 2008. How can this be? (see answer, page 392) →

Do They Talk? This couple in Schenectady, New York, are in a "long-term relationship," probably years from marriage. We hope they agree about what they would do if she got pregnant, or if he found someone else, or if either was offered a great job or university scholarship in another state. Few emerging-adult couples discuss such matters until they happen.

© ELLEN SINISI / THE IMAGE WORKS

Birth rates have declined the world over, with developing as well as developed nations recording lower fertility rates (see Figure 11.2). For example, in Egypt, the average woman had 7 offspring in 1960, 4 in 1990, and 3.7 in 2000; a rate of 1.9 is projected by 2050 (United Nations, 2007).

Smaller families correlate with healthier children, more education, improved economies, and longer lives. These factors have made emerging adulthood possible. All this change is welcomed not only by young adults, who enjoy their new freedom, but also by developmentalists, who want all people to fulfill their potential.

However, as with all other aspects of development, gains are accompanied by losses. Fewer births mean fewer young workers. For this reason, some nations now encourage births, via tax and child-care policies. Such encouragement has not been successful in Japan, which has low fertility (1.2 children per couple), long life expectancy (84 years), and many college graduates (52 percent at age 25). In a historical shift, Japan is encouraging immigration in order to ensure its labor supply.

MORE SEX Advances in contraception have not only reduced the birth rate; they have also increased the rate of sexual activity, especially among unmarried adults. Globally, emerging adults have fewer babies but engage in more sexual activity than older adults (married or not) do or than people their own age once did (Pew Research Center, 2007).

Emerging adults are not necessarily promiscuous, with a different partner each night. Instead, most have one steady partner, then another, then another—a pattern called *serial monogamy* (Gagnon et al., 2001; Laumann & Michael, 2001; Schmookler & Bursik, 2007). Contrary to the assumptions (and perhaps experiences) of the older generation, emerging-adult couples who are committed to each other have the most varied sex lives, as their intimacy and trust allow experimentation (Kaestle & Halpern, 2007).

Again, a historical perspective is useful. For most of human history, a powerful *double standard* prevailed: Men were expected to seek premarital sex to satisfy their biological urges, while women were expected to avoid it. Consequently, "good" girls were virgins when they married. The double standard affected marital sex as well. Some wives, employing one of the few available ways to prevent pregnancy, used headaches or other excuses to avoid having sex. Some cultures practiced female genital mutilation to keep women from experiencing sexual pleasure—another way to reduce pregnancy.

In developed nations, this double standard is disappearing among emerging adults. Rates of sexual activity for unmarried young women in North America and Europe are close to those for young men.

This increase in sexual activity has been accompanied by a striking change in attitudes. In the United States, a national poll found that a majority (53 percent) of people in their mid-20s believe that premarital sex is "not wrong at all," while only 18 percent of those over age 65 agree. Many emerging adults accept premarital sex as a way to postpone marriage, although most remain opposed to extramarital sex (T. W. Smith, 2005).

SEXUALLY TRANSMITTED INFECTIONS Sexually transmitted infections (STIs) have probably existed since the beginning of humankind. Laboratory tests confirm a syphilis epidemic in London five centuries ago (Hayden, 2003). Most experts believe that AIDS existed long before the first diagnosis was made. Until recently, however, most outbreaks of STIs were localized, not widespread.

Now half of all emerging adults in the United States have had at least one STI (Lefkowitz & Gillen, 2006). Serial monogamy means that soon after one sexual relationship ends, another usually begins. Ideally, emerging adults would wait at least six months between partners, in the meantime getting tested and treated for any STIs. Few of them do so, however, and the spread of STIs is one result (Foxman et al., 2006).

Globalization promotes international employment for many young adults, and modern technology allows rapid travel. As an unintended consequence, HIV and other STIs can spread easily and rapidly anywhere in the world (UNAIDS, 2008). In developing nations, increasing numbers of wives are being infected with HIV and other STIs by husbands who have extramarital sexual encounters while working far from home (Hirsch et al., 2007; Parikh, 2007). Globalization also affects sex workers, who now have patrons from many nations (James, 2007).

Young adults of both sexes are vectors (transmitters of disease) as well as victims (Cockerham, 2006). The consequences of the spread of STIs are felt by every generation. For example, millions of children are being raised by grandparents because their parents have died of AIDS.

> **ESPECIALLY FOR Nurses** When should you suspect that a patient has an untreated STI? (see response, page 393) →

Taking Risks

Emerging adulthood is marked by a greater willingness to take risks of all sorts, not just sexual ones. Young adults are innovators, adventurers, and explorers. They invent new things (Einstein developed his groundbreaking ideas about physics in his 20s, while he was working at a patent office), they volunteer to fight in wars and revolutions (note the typical ages of soldiers who die in combat or people who commit acts of terror), and they readily uproot themselves to search for greener pastures (most immigrants are young adults).

Emerging adults also seem inclined to risk their health and safety: They enjoy danger, drive without seat belts, carry guns, try addictive drugs. They jeopardize their health for reasons that they find compelling, but older adults consider them reckless (Teese & Bradley, 2008). Who is right? We consider some specifics.

EDGEWORK An affinity for risk taking is characteristic of **edgework**—that is, occupations, recreational activities, or other ventures that involve living on the edge, managing stress and fear (Lyng, 2005). The joy is in the intense concentration and mastery that are required; edgework is more compelling if failure can mean disaster.

Risky occupations—from firefighting to bond trading, from becoming a soldier to becoming an artist—attract young adults. The dot-com start-up companies that were prevalent in the United States in the early 1990s were staffed by young adults, who were less devastated than the older investors when many of those companies failed. The miners in South Africa tend to be under age 30. Bicycle messengers, who pedal furiously through congested urban areas to deliver documents, are almost always

> **edgework**
> Occupations, recreational activities, or other ventures that involve a degree of risk or danger. The prospect of "living on the edge" makes edgework compelling to some individuals.

CHRIS STOWERS / GETTY IMAGES

On the Edge Wearing no helmet, moving against traffic, and riding a racing bike among buses and trucks—these are a thrilling combination for bicycle messengers, almost all of whom are emerging-adult men.

extreme sports
Forms of recreation that include apparent risk of injury or death and that are attractive and thrilling as a result.

drug abuse
The ingestion of a drug to the extent that it impairs the user's biological or psychological well-being.

drug addiction
A condition of drug dependence in which the absence of the given drug from the individual's system produces a drive—physiological, biological, or both—to ingest more of the drug.

ANSWER TO OBSERVATION QUIZ
(from page 390) The 2008 data are projected, or estimated, on the basis of past trends. At least for the near term, fertility-rate projections (the average number of children born during a woman's lifetime) are quite accurate. The crucial element of these projections—how many children, on average, each woman has already borne—is known and will not change. ●

emerging adults. As one social scientist explains, "Their entire lives are wrapped inside a distinct messenger lifestyle that cherishes thrills and threats of dodging cars as they speed through the city" (Kidder, 2006).

Nonoccupational risks are also common. Entering college, starting a business, filming a movie, forming a band, moving far from home, falling in love—all these could be considered edgework.

The threat of death is part of the thrill of **extreme sports,** another area of edgework. For instance, freestyle motocross was "practically invented" in the mid-1990s by Brian Deegan and Mike Metzger when they were about 20 years old (M. Higgins, 2006). Motocross involves riding motorcycles over barriers and off ramps, including a 50-foot-high leap into "big air." As rider and cycle fall, points are gained by doing tricks, such as backward somersaults.

> As a result of their longevity, Deegan and Metzger [now in their early thirties] are considered legends, graybeard veterans in a much younger man's game. . . . One has lost a kidney and broken a leg and both wrists; the other has broken arms and legs and lost a testicle. Watching them perform, many observers wonder whether they have lost their minds.
>
> *[M. Higgins, 2006, p. D5]*

The contestants and spectators for extreme sports are almost all under age 30. Such sports (from parachute jumping to pond swooping) depend on technology and income that are unavailable in developing regions. Automobiles are common everywhere, however, and many young-adult drivers use them for edgework. Consequently, the automobile death rate is highest between ages 18 and 25 in every nation.

DRUG ABUSE Some drugs (such as crack cocaine and heroin) are used infrequently by high school seniors (less than 2 percent) and even more rarely by emerging adults (less than 1 percent). However, emerging adults are more likely than high school seniors to drink too much and to be addicted to cigarettes (see Figure 11.3; Johnston et al., 2007). In general, all forms of drug use increase during emerging adulthood.

Many emerging adults who use drugs begin to do so as part of their quest for independence and adventure. Other correlates of drug use are high socioeconomic status (SES), European American ethnicity, and good grades in high school (K. M. Jackson et al., 2008; Ludden & Eccles, 2007). Thus, the heavy drinkers and drug experimenters are also likely to be the most advantaged emerging adults.

It is important to distinguish among use, abuse, and addiction. Simply using a drug (as in drinking a glass of wine) does not amount to abuse if no harm is done. **Drug abuse** is the ingestion of a drug in a quantity or a manner that is harmful to physical, cognitive, or psychosocial well-being. Abuse often leads to frequent use (e.g., daily marijuana smoking) and high doses (e.g., *binge drinking,* defined as having five or more alcoholic drinks on one occasion) that impair the body, the mind, and/or social interaction.

Frequent use often leads to **drug addiction,** a condition in which the absence of the particular drug causes a craving to satisfy a physiological need (to stop the shakes, settle the stomach, sleep) or a psychological need (to quiet fears or lift depression). *Withdrawal symptoms*—the unpleasant, sometimes life-threatening physical reactions that occur when a person who has regularly been using a drug for a long time suddenly stops taking it—are a telltale sign of addiction.

College itself seems to elicit drug use, as does youth culture (H. R. White et al., 2006). For example, a longitudinal study at a large university found that almost all

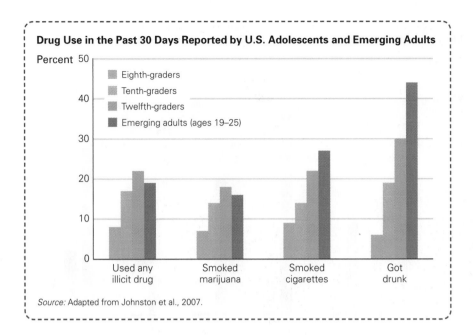

Drug Use in the Past 30 Days Reported by U.S. Adolescents and Emerging Adults

Percent

Legend:
- Eighth-graders
- Tenth-graders
- Twelfth-graders
- Emerging adults (ages 19–25)

Categories: Used any illicit drug, Smoked marijuana, Smoked cigarettes, Got drunk

Source: Adapted from Johnston et al., 2007.

FIGURE 11.3 Current Drug Use by Adolescents and Emerging Adults Most U.S. adolescents (60 percent) try illicit drugs, although few of them become chronic users. In contrast, emerging adults are more likely than adolescents to have used legal drugs—alcohol and cigarettes—recently.

students (83 percent), including more than one-third of former abstainers, drank excessive amounts of alcohol (13 drinks, on average) to celebrate their 21st birthday, the legal age for drinking in the United States. A substantial minority (10 percent) consumed 21 drinks—with glasses of beer, glasses of wine, and shots of liquor each counted as one (Rutledge et al., 2008). These "21-at-21" drinkers included as many women as men. Such binge drinking is always hazardous and sometimes fatal—another example of risk taking among emerging adults (Zernike, 2005).

As dynamic-systems theory would predict, youthful drug use may have long-term effects. A study of 6,000 young adults in Scotland found that two decades later, the rate of death among the heavy drinkers was double the average (C. L. Hart et al., 1999). Those emerging adults in Scotland who drank alcohol and suffered later are an example of a general trend: Emerging adults who are heavy drug users are less likely to earn a college degree, to find satisfactory employment, to sustain a romance, or to live to old age.

VIOLENT DEATH Drug abuse is particularly common among those who die violently. With one exception, every nation that keeps accurate statistics reports that accidents, homicides, and suicides are the three leading causes of death from age 15 to 35—killing more adolescents and emerging adults than all diseases combined.

Young men, particularly, are shot in the street, crash their car into a truck, drown while drunk, overdose on drugs, ski in a blizzard, drive over a cliff, and so on. The one exception is South Africa, where death from AIDS (itself the result of risky behavior) is the leading cause of death for emerging adults, killing as many young women as men.

In the United States, between the ages of 15 and 25, almost 1 male in every 100 dies violently, through suicide, homicide, or a motor-vehicle accident (see Figure 11.4 on page 394). The death rate among emerging-adult U.S. men is about 15,000 per year (U.S. Bureau of the Census, 2008).

DAVID YOUNG-WOLFF / PHOTOEDIT INC.

Higher Education College provides many benefits, but it also seems to encourage drug use. Everyone at this fraternity party appears to be using alcohol, and one young woman is drinking from a beer bong. Seeking admiration for drinking a lot in a short time is a sign that a person is at risk for alcoholism.

RESPONSE FOR Nurses (from page 391) Always. In this context, "suspect" refers to a healthy skepticism, not to prejudice or disapproval. Your attitude should be professional rather than judgmental, but be aware that education, gender, self-confidence, and income do not necessarily mean that a given patient is or is not free of a sexually transmitted infection. ●

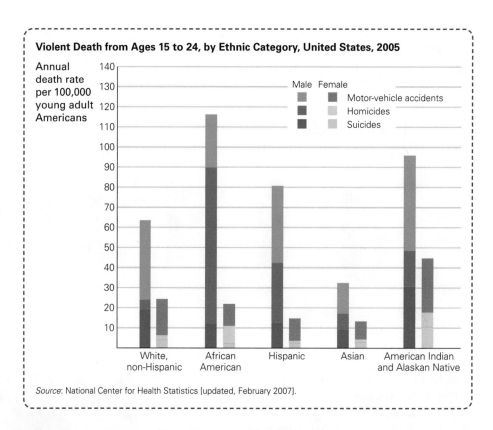

Violent Death from Ages 15 to 24, by Ethnic Category, United States, 2005

Source: National Center for Health Statistics [updated, February 2007].

FIGURE 11.4 A Dangerous Time for Young Americans This graph shows the rates of violent death by ethnic category among Americans aged 15 to 24. Ethnic differences have narrowed over the past decade, but they are still readily apparent. Emerging adulthood is the peak period for all forms of violent death except suicide, which has higher rates among older White males and older Asian females than among young adults.

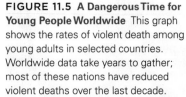

OBSERVATION QUIZ

In the United States, which group has the smallest gender disparity? Which has the largest? (see answer, page 396) ➡

FIGURE 11.5 A Dangerous Time for Young People Worldwide This graph shows the rates of violent death among young adults in selected countries. Worldwide data take years to gather; most of these nations have reduced violent deaths over the last decade.

Violent death rates among emerging adults in Canada, New Zealand, Mexico, and Australia are almost as high as in the United States (see Figure 11.5). The specific proportion of suicides, homicides, and accidents varies from country to country. Canada, for example, has far more suicides than homicides, whereas in the United States more young adults are killed by other young adults than by themselves.

The sex imbalance is universal: About 4 times as many young men as young women commit suicide or die in motor-vehicle accidents, and 6 times as many are murdered. One theory connects this sex imbalance to the sex drive, suggesting that

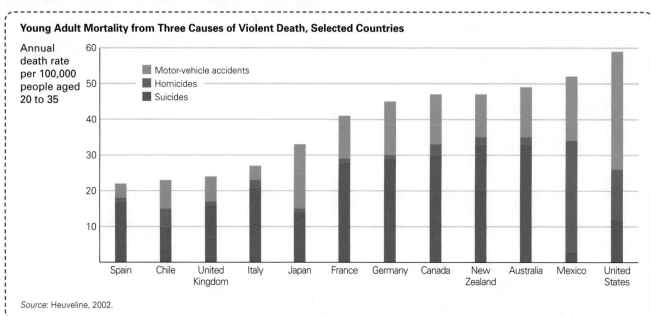

Young Adult Mortality from Three Causes of Violent Death, Selected Countries

Source: Heuveline, 2002.

men take risks to prove to potential mates that they are stronger and braver than other males, capable of producing superior offspring (Archer, 2004). Many other explanations for the sex difference are also plausible. Variation in the male/female ratio of violent death (in some nations, it is 3:1; in others, 10:1) raises questions about culture and sex roles. Perhaps the social construction that men are brave (or are they foolhardy?) and women are careful (or are they timid?) is stronger in some cultures than in others.

LAWS AND NORMS Since drug use meets some developmental needs of young adults (reduced anxiety, social bonding, increased adventure) but at a very high cost (addiction, death), many developmentalists have tried to find ways to keep drug use from becoming abuse.

Legislation is one strategy that some developmentalists advocate. Many nations have made some drugs illegal, although most nations allow alcohol and cigarettes at any age. This strategy is prominent in the United States, where the legal age for drinking was raised from 18 to 21 in 1984 and where it is illegal for adolescents to buy cigarettes. Some state legislators and college administrators advocate reducing the legal drinking age to 18 again, partly to avoid the widespread lawbreaking that prevents the most troubled youth from seeking help. Some also advocate legalization of other drugs, especially marijuana. Still others believe that the current laws are helpful and need to be stringently enforced.

Another approach to reducing drug use is to increase the supervision of emerging adults. Those who live with their parents or their spouses are less likely to abuse drugs. Should parents or societies encourage emerging adults to stay at home or to marry, contrary to current trends? This may be impossible or may have other, less desirable consequences (extended dependence, more divorces).

Third, a **social norms approach** has been suggested. An example of this approach is to survey college students regarding their alcohol use and then publicize the results. Usually, emerging adults learn that their peers drink less than they thought; thus, they reduce their own consumption. About half the colleges in the United States have surveyed students about alcohol use on their campuses, reported the results, and seen a decline in heavy drinking (Berkowitz, 2005; H. Wechsler et al., 2003).

This approach assumes that emerging adults (1) misperceive how many of their peers use drugs and (2) are sufficiently mature that they can apply factual information to their own lives. The first of these two assumptions is valid. College students do overestimate how much their peers drink, smoke, and use other drugs because they presume their loud, outgoing, and seemingly popular peers tend to take the most risks. They brag about being wasted or hung over, or about escaping arrest, not about staying home to study.

Moreover, drug users befriend heavy users, concluding that some people are worse off than they are. Furthermore, in large gatherings of emerging adults (at parties, concerts, sporting events), alcohol and other drugs are typically present. It is not unusual for emerging adults to overestimate how much their peers consume; this is proven to be true not only for alcohol and illegal drugs but even for cigarettes, according to a Canadian study in which smokers estimated the prevalence of smoking among their age group. Emerging adult smokers were particularly likely to guess high: 71 percent overestimated smoking prevalence by more than one-fifth (Cunningham & Selby, 2007).

What about the second assumption, that emerging adults can apply what they learn? The answer is not simple, since unlike cognitive development in childhood, adult cognition depends more on experience and education than on age (Dawson-Tunik et al., 2005). We now explore that aspect of emerging adulthood.

social norms approach
A method of reducing risky behavior among emerging adults that is based on their desire to follow social norms. This approach publicizes survey results to make emerging adults aware of the actual prevalence of various behaviors within their peer group.

● FOR DEEPER REFLECTION Could a law against a behavior ever cause an increase in that activity?

KEY Points

- Emerging adulthood (roughly ages 18 to 25) is a new period of development, characterized by later marriage and more education, as well as robust good health.

- Sexual impulses and reproductive health reach a peak during emerging adulthood, although the birth rate tends to be much lower today than in previous centuries. Many nations are below the replacement rate of 2.1 births per woman.

- During emerging adulthood, risk taking is prevalent, sometimes constructively and sometimes not. Edgework and violent death both increase, especially in men.

- Drug abuse and addiction increase during emerging adulthood; social norms are powerful influences on drug use.

Cognitive Maturity

As you remember, the adolescent limbic system develops before the prefrontal cortex matures. Consequently, adolescents are more likely than others to switch between two modes of thought: intuitive and logical. In emerging adulthood, these two modes gradually become better aligned. Crucial to the process are experiences, which sculpt brain connections that form new dendrites while unused neurons disappear.

Informed by Experience

The practical experiences of emerging adults require connections between emotions and logic. As one expert explains, emerging adulthood is a "crucial period of the life span" because "complex, critical, and relativizing thinking emerges only in the 20s" (Labouvie-Vief, 2006, p. 78). The word *relativizing* means considering things in relation to one another. Unlike egocentric adolescents, emerging adults contemplate the perspectives of many people and the lessons they have learned from experience, combining intuition and logic.

One study investigated age differences in the way people described themselves (see Figure 11.6; Labouvie-Vief, 2006). These self-descriptions were categorized as follows:

- *Self-protective* (high in self-involvement, low in self-doubt)
- *Dysregulated* (fragmented, overwhelmed by emotions or problems)
- *Complex* (valuing openness and independence above all)
- *Integrated* (able to regulate emotions and logic)

No one under age 20 had reached the advanced "integrated" stage, but some adults of every age had. The largest shift in self-description toward higher levels occurred between adolescence and emerging adulthood.

This data from verbal descriptions matches the evidence from brain scans. Adults are able to use their entire brains flexibly to deal with whatever practical concerns they might have. In other words, young adults can combine *subjective* and *objective* thought. Subjective thought arises from an individual's personal experiences and perceptions; objective thought follows abstract, impersonal logic.

WORKING TOGETHER One of the best aspects of the maturing mind occurs when emerging adults begin to realize that "there are multiple views of the same phenom-

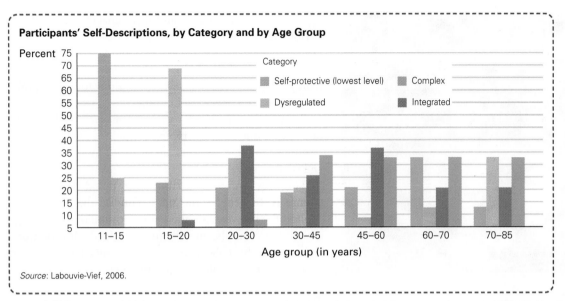

Participants' Self-Descriptions, by Category and by Age Group

Source: Labouvie-Vief, 2006.

FIGURE 11.6 Talk About Yourself
People gradually became less self-centered and less confused as they described themselves over the years of adulthood. Many adults, but no children or adolescents, achieved a level of self-acceptance at which emotions and reason were integrated.

enon" (P. B. Baltes et al., 1998, p. 1093). They show more cognitive flexibility, becoming less likely to insist that they are right and more likely to compromise, change, and take other perspectives into account. Consider this problem:

> Every card in a pack has a letter on one side and a number on the other. Imagine that you are presented with the following four cards, each of which has something on the back. Turn over only those cards that will confirm or disconfirm this proposition: *If a card has a vowel on one side, then it always has an even number on the other side.*
>
> E   7   K   4
>
> Which cards must be turned over?

The difficulty of this puzzle is "notorious" (Moshman, 2005, p. 36). Almost everyone wants to turn over the E and the 4; almost everyone is mistaken. In one experiment with college students working independently, 91 percent were wrong.

However, when groups of college students (who usually guess wrong) discussed the problem, 75 percent got it right. They avoided the 4 card (even if it has a consonant on the other side, the statement could be true) and selected the E and the 7 cards (if the 7 has a vowel on the other side, the proposition is false). In this instance, emerging adults could and did change their minds after listening to others (Moshman & Geil, 1998).

CONSIDERING NEW IDEAS Emerging adults show many signs of such cognitive flexibility in daily life. The very fact that emerging adults marry and become parents later than previous generations did suggests that, couple by couple, thinking processes are not tied to childhood experiences or traditional norms.

Another example of cognitive flexibility is one you have probably witnessed in your circle of friends. Specifically, college plans (courses to be taken, majors declared, careers sought, degrees earned) typically change several times between a student's first and last semesters, as advice from other students and professors, as well as personal experiences, provide new information (T. E. Miller et al., 2005).

Many of the social constructions of earlier generations change as a result of naturally evolving young-adult experiences. Women have been elected heads of state in Liberia, India, England, and many other countries, and a man whose father was Black has been elected president of the United States. Fifty years ago, almost no voters thought such victories could be possible. Emerging-adult voters in each of these nations were the most likely to overcome the cultural stereotypes.

United States? Canada? Guess Again!
These students attend the University of Cape Town in South Africa, where previous cohorts of Blacks and Whites would never have been allowed to socialize so freely. Such interactions foster learning.

stereotype threat
The fear that someone else will judge one's appearance or behavior negatively and thereby confirm that person's prejudiced attitudes.

The Threat of Bias If students fear that others expect them to do poorly in school because of their ethnicity or gender, they may not identify with academic achievement and do worse on exams than they otherwise would have.

OBSERVATION QUIZ
Which of these three college students taking an exam is least vulnerable to stereotype threat? (see answer, page 400) →

Such data on behavioral and attitudinal change could be attributed to many factors other than cognitive flexibility. However, research specifically examining adult cognition finds evidence of flexibility, in that adults are more likely than children to imagine several solutions for every problem and then to select the best one.

For instance, if adults of various ages are asked what to do about life issues, they typically think of several possible responses. Younger thinkers are likely to find one solution and stick to it.

This was found in a study that posed 15 common dilemmas. In general, the more familiar the problem to adults of whatever age, the more possibilities were suggested. For example, one dilemma involved a loss of motivation to finish a college degree. Emerging adults suggested an average of four solutions (Artistico et al., 2003).

STEREOTYPE THREAT Recent research has discovered a pernicious kind of self-prejudice called **stereotype threat.** People worry that someone else will judge them to be stupid, lazy, oversexed, or worse because of their race, sex, age, or some other innate characteristic (Steele, 1997). The mere *possibility* of being negatively stereotyped arouses anxiety that can disrupt cognition and distort emotional regulation (Inzlicht et al., 2006; Osborne, 2007). Stereotype threat can be crippling, but it also can be overcome.

Often when young people become aware of a possible prejudice because of their status as, say, an African American, a Jew, or a homosexual, their first reaction is to identify strongly with their group. As explained in Chapter 10, ethnic identity is stronger among people who are aware of others' prejudices.

Psychologically, such strong *identification* is healthier than *disidentification,* a deliberate refusal to identify with one's group ("I am not like other women"). It is also much healthier than *counteridentification,* which involves identifying with the majority and thereby believing the stereotype. However, strong identification does not indicate cognitive flexibility, which Piaget and many others consider a sign of intelligence.

Identification and thus stereotype threat are often evoked when circumstances remind the person of a prejudice other people might have about his or her group (J. Keller, 2007). For example, in one study, college students were given 20 difficult math problems to solve (Schmader, 2002). Half the participants simply took the test, but the other half were told that the exam might reveal sex differences. This likely reminded several female test-takers of the stereotype that women are deficient in math.

The results of this study showed that stereotype threat had been evoked for women who heard that sex differences would be assessed *and* who identified strongly with their sex. Their scores were lower than those of the men and those of the women who had not been reminded of the stereotype. Apparently, the threat triggered anxiety, which interfered with performance.

Stereotype threat is one explanation for a distressing fact: African American men generally have lower grades in school and are less likely to attend college than are their genetic peers, African American women. Although social and economic factors are part of the reason, a cognitive interpretation is also possible (Cokley, 2003; Sackett et al., 2004). If a young man fears that others expect him to be a good athlete but a poor scholar, his anxiety about that stereotype might make him disidentify with academic success and disengage from studying (Ogbu, 2003).

Stereotype threat affects people from many groups. In addition to those already cited (women and African American men), "caste-like minorities in industrial and nonindustrial nations throughout the world (e.g., the Maoris of New Zealand, the Baraku of Japan, the Harijans of India, the Oriental Jews of Israel, and the West Indians of Great Britain)" show evidence of stereotype threat (Steele, 1997, p. 623). So do older adults and even European men (Abrams et al., 2006; Cadinu et al., 2006).

Stereotype threat makes people of all ages doubt their ability, which reduces learning if their anxiety interferes with cognition. Fortunately, there is evidence that reducing stereotype threat is possible, particularly among emerging adults. Female and African American college students typically perform better when they attend institutions where almost everyone is from their group (Astin & Oseguera, 2002; Freeman & Thomas, 2002). One explanation is that if all the students have similar backgrounds, no one worries that the other students are judging on the basis of stereotypes.

Obviously, adults must also be able to function within communities of people of various backgrounds. There are some signs that emerging adults are sufficiently flexible that they can escape stereotypes and stereotype threats. Compared with older adults, they are less limited by familiar ideas and more able to learn something new (Klaczynski & Robinson, 2000; W. J. L. Thornton & Dumke, 2005). This became evident in another study on stereotype threat, explained in the following.

A VIEW FROM SCIENCE

Reducing Stereotype Threat

One of the problems with traditional concepts of intellectual ability is that many Americans believe IQ is innate. Some people are thought to be *born* smarter than others. If emerging adults can be convinced that they can improve their intellect through hard work, they may overcome handicaps caused by stereotype threat.

This possibility led to a hypothesis: Academic performance will increase if people *internalize* (believe wholeheartedly, not just intellectually) the belief that intelligence is plastic and can be changed. One group of scientists tested this hypothesis, building on two findings from prior research: (1) Stereotype threat regarding intellectual ability is powerful among African Americans, and (2) people are more likely to accept and internalize ideas when they express those ideas, a phenomenon called "saying is believing."

The researchers recruited students of African and European descent at Stanford University, where African Americans are a small minority (Aronson et al., 2002). After the students' attitudes and IQ scores were determined, they were randomly divided into three matched groups, similar to one another in terms of European to African American ratios, as well as attitude, IQ, and grade point average.

No intervention occurred for Group I, the control group. Students in Groups II and III experienced almost identical interventions, in three sessions. In the first session, they read a letter, supposedly from a struggling junior high school student, and wrote an encouraging response that included references to current research on intelligence.

Groups II and III differed only in the particular current research they learned about (via a video as well as printed text) and were asked to incorporate into their letters. Group II was told to emphasize that there are multiple intelligences (see Chapter 7); Group III was asked to explain that intelligence expands with effort and that new neurons may grow (e.g., Segalowitz & Schmidt, 2003). This later research undercuts the notion that racial differences in IQ are genetic; learning about it should reduce stereotype threat (although this was not made explicit to the students).

In the second session, the experimenter praised the letters and privately gave each Stanford student a thank-you note, ostensibly from the younger student. They were then asked to encourage other young students by preparing speeches, which were videotaped as first drafts. Later, at the third session, their speeches were taped again in a "final" version. All three sessions were designed to help them internalize the research about intelligence.

Months later, participants in Group III (but not in Groups I and II) were found to believe in the plasticity of intelligence. Their new belief had affected their studies: African Americans in Group III improved their attitudes about academic achievement, reported more joy in learning, and increased their average grades (see Table 11.2).

This experiment and hundreds of other studies have found that stereotype threat is powerful but that it can be reduced by relieving the anxiety that undercuts achievement, with each particular threat requiring a somewhat different intervention (Johns et al., 2008; J. R. Shapiro & Neuberg, 2007). Success is more common among younger adults than older ones. Thinking can change, and that affects learning and intellectual achievement.

TABLE 11.2 Attitudes and Grades in Academic Term Following Stereotype-Threat Experiment

	Group I (no intervention)		Group II (IQ is multiple)		Group III (IQ is malleable)	
	Blacks	Whites	Blacks	Whites	Blacks	Whites
Value placed on academics, from 1 (lowest) to 7 (highest)	3.5	5.7	3.9	5.7	4.8	5.6
Average grade	B	B+	B	B+	B+	A–

Source: Aronson et al., 2002.

Culture and Cognition

As the existence of stereotype threat suggests, cultural ideas and underlying assumptions can affect how people think about themselves and others. Research confirms this, particularly when it focuses on the cognitive strategies used by Asians compared with those used by Europeans and North Americans.

Several researchers believe that the influence of ancient Greek philosophy on Western culture has led Europeans to rely on analytic, absolutist logic. The justice system, for instance, assumes that someone is guilty or innocent, an aggressor or a victim, a winner or a loser. Children are taught to take sides in the battle between right and wrong, angels and demons, saints and sinners. By contrast, Confucianism and Taoism led the Chinese and other Asians to seek compromise, and Buddhism is called the "Middle Way."

Some researchers have demonstrated these different approaches by comparing how students solve problems. For instance, Asian and European American students were asked to respond to various situations, such as the following:

> Mary, Phoebe, and Julie all have daughters. Each mother has held a set of values that has guided her efforts to raise her daughter. Now the daughters have grown up, and each of them is rejecting many of her mother's values. How did it happen and what should they do?
>
> [K. Peng & Nisbett, 1999]

As part of this research, judges who did not know the respondents' ethnic backgrounds scored the answers as to whether they sought some middle ground or took sides. For example, a response like "Both mothers and daughters have failed to understand each other" considered both viewpoints, but "Mothers have to recognize that daughters have a right to their own values" did not (K. Peng & Nisbett, 1999). The Asian students' responses sought a middle ground.

Another series of studies compared three groups of students: a group in Seoul, Korea; a group of Americans born in Korea who had lived most of their lives in the United States; and a group of native-born European Americans. Participants were told:

> Suppose you are the police officer in charge of a case involving a graduate student who murdered a professor. . . . As a police officer, you must establish motive.
>
> [I. Choi et al., 2003]

ANSWER TO OBSERVATION QUIZ (from page 398) It depends on what is being tested and on the students' backgrounds. White males are generally least vulnerable, but if the test is about literature and if the male student believes that men are not as good as women at writing about poetry and fiction, his performance on the exam may be affected by that stereotype. ●

Participants indicated which of 97 possible items of information they would want to know. Some of the items were clearly relevant (e.g., whether the professor had publicly ridiculed the graduate student), and virtually every student in all three groups wanted to know these facts. Some other facts were clearly irrelevant (e.g., the graduate student's favorite color), and almost everyone left them out. Other items on the list were questionable (e.g., what the professor was doing that fateful night, how the professor was dressed).

Compared with both groups of Americans, the students born and raised in Korea asked for 15 more items, on average, including some questionable items that the American participants left out. The authors believe that students in Seoul had been taught by their culture to consider the entire context (I. Choi et al., 2003).

This research has wider implications. Emerging adults have the brain maturity to think flexibly and holistically, combining emotions and reasoning. How they actually think depends on past experiences and on their cultural contexts. When people disagree about interpretations or values, their backgrounds influence their thinking. Ideally, their cognitive maturity allows them to understand one another's perspective.

Cognitive Growth and Higher Education

Most contemporary students attend college primarily to secure their vocational and financial future, learning marketable skills that will be valuable in careers such as computer technology, business, and health care. General education is less important to them (Komives & Nuss, 2005). One of my 18-year-old students acknowledged that she was pursuing both goals:

> A higher education provides me with the ability to make adequate money so I can provide for my future. An education also provides me with the ability to be a mature thinker and to attain a better understanding of myself. . . . An education provides the means for a better job after college, which will support me and allow me to have a stable, comfortable retirement.
>
> *[E., personal communication]*

Her concern about retirement income may seem premature, but her hope that her education will help provide for her future is realistic. College is an investment: In 2006 in the United States, the average annual income of those with a BA degree was $56,788, compared with $31,071 for those with only a high school diploma. More education means more money: Those with a professional degree earned an annual average of $116,514 (U.S. Bureau of the Census, 2008).

College also correlates with better health: College graduates everywhere smoke less, eat better, exercise more, and live longer. Does something gained in college—perhaps knowledge, self-control, relief from depression, or better job prospects—affect health in positive ways? All these factors seem likely to contribute to better health, although researchers are not certain to what degree (N. E. Adler & Snibbe, 2003).

Another possibility is that the family backgrounds of emerging adults provide wealth and health advantages that affect adult life with or without college. Let's look closely at whether college itself affects cognition.

There is no doubt that tertiary education improves verbal and quantitative abilities, knowledge of specific subject areas, skills in various professions, reasoning, and reflection. According to one comprehensive review:

> Compared to freshmen, seniors have better oral and written communication skills, are better abstract reasoners or critical thinkers, are more skilled at using reason and evidence to address ill-structured problems for which there are no verifiably correct answers, have greater intellectual flexibility in that they are better able to understand more than one side of a complex issue, and can develop more sophisticated abstract frameworks to deal with complexity.
>
> *[Pascarella & Terenzini, 1991, p. 155]*

● **UNDERSTANDING THE NUMBERS**
Does the percent difference between the Koreans and the Americans indicate the cultural gap or the generational similarity between them?

Answer It depends on how you look at it. The Koreans' 15 additional items out of 97 may represent either a slightly more than 15 percent difference or a slightly more than 84 percent similarity.

CHANGES OVER TIME Thinking may become more reflective and expansive with each year of college (Clinchy, 1993; P. M. King & Kitchener, 1994; Perry, 1981). First-year students tend to believe that clear and perfect truths exist; they are distressed if their professors do not explain these truths. They gather knowledge as if facts were nuggets of gold, each one separate from other bits of knowledge and each one pure and true. One first-year student said he was like a squirrel, "gleaning little acorns of knowledge and burying them for later use" (Bozik, 2002, p. 145).

This initial phase is followed by a wholesale questioning of personal and social values, including doubts about the idea of truth itself. If a professor makes an assertion without extensive analysis and evidence, upper-level students are skeptical. No fact is taken at face value, much less stored intact for future use.

Finally, as graduation approaches, after considering many ideas, students become committed to certain values, even as they realize their opinions might change (Pascarella & Terenzini, 2005; Rest et al., 1999). Facts have become neither gold nor dross, but useful steps toward a greater understanding.

A further breakdown of the cognitive progression of college students was found by William Perry. In a classic study (Perry, 1970/1998), he described nine levels of cognitive progress over the four years leading to a BA degree, from a simplistic either/or dualism (right or wrong, success or failure) to a relativism that recognizes a multiplicity of perspectives (see Table 11.3). New questions and advanced thinking

TABLE 11.3 Perry's Scheme of Cognitive and Ethical Development During College

Freshmen	Position 1	Authorities know, and if we work hard, read every word, and learn Right Answers, all will be well.
Dualism modified	Transition	But what about those Others I hear about? And different opinions? And Uncertainties? Some of our own Authorities disagree with each other or don't seem to know, and some give us problems instead of Answers.
	Position 2	True Authorities must be Right, the others are frauds. We remain Right. Others must be different and Wrong. Good Authorities give us problems so we can learn to find the Right Answer by our own independent thought.
	Transition	But even Good Authorities admit they don't know all the answers *yet!*
	Position 3	Then some uncertainties and different opinions are real and legitimate *temporarily,* even for Authorities. They're working on them to get to the Truth.
	Transition	But there are *so many* things they don't know the Answers to! And they won't for a long time.
Relativism discovered	*Position 4a*	Where Authorities don't know the Right Answers, everyone has a right to his own opinion; no one is wrong!
	Transition	Then what right have They to grade us? About what?
	Position 4b	In certain courses Authorities are not asking for the Right Answer. They want us to *think* about things in a certain way, *supporting* opinion with data. That's what they grade us on.
	Position 5	Then *all* thinking must be like this, even for Them. Everything is relative but not equally valid. You have to understand how each context works. Theories are not Truth but metaphors to interpret data with. You have to think about your thinking.
	Transition	But if everything is relative, am I relative too? How can I know I'm making the Right Choice?
	Position 6	I see I'm going to have to make my own decisions in an uncertain world with no one to tell me I'm Right.
	Transition	I'm lost if I don't. When I decide on my career (or marriage or values), everything will straighten out.
Commitments in relativism developed	Position 7	Well, I've made my first Commitment!
	Transition	Why didn't that settle everything?
	Position 8	I've made several Commitments. I've got to balance them—how many, how deep? How certain, how tentative?
	Transition	Things are getting contradictory. I can't make logical sense out of life's dilemmas.
	Position 9	This is how life will be. I must be wholehearted while tentative, fight for my values yet respect others, believe my deepest values right yet be ready to learn. I see that I shall be retracing this whole journey over and over—but, I hope, more wisely.
Seniors		

Source: W. G. Perry, 1970/1998.

occur because of the combined influence of fellow students, professors, books, and class discussions.

CURRENT LEARNING IN COLLEGE You probably noticed that Perry's study was first published in 1981. The undergraduates he studied were Harvard students. There-fore, conclusions based on elite college students 30 years ago may no longer apply. As you know, brains adapt to experiences, and cultural values shape thinking. Since 1980, major changes have occurred in college education, including much greater diversity among students and professors as well as extensive changes in what is taught and why. Such changes may affect how students think.

A close look reveals the scope of these changes in western Europe and North America. In the first half of the twentieth century, fewer than 1 in every 20 young adults earned a college degree, and virtually all those graduates were of European descent. In developing nations, fewer than 1 in 1,000 graduated from college.

In contrast, rates of college attendance now vary from about one-half to one-fifth of all emerging adults in developed nations, including the nations of East Asia. In the United States, most graduates are still European American, but 27 percent are not—that's nearly twice the proportion 24 years earlier. In a reversal of the former gender breakdown, more girls than boys attend college now, and they plan on professional careers more often than boys do (Mello, 2008). In the United States, of those earning advanced degrees (i.e., master's, doctoral, or professional), 57 percent are women (*Chronicle of Higher Education,* 2006).

The number of international students in the United States has risen only slightly, to just under 4 percent, but the increase of college students in South America, Africa, and South Asia is dramatic. India is another example: When India became independ-ent from Great Britain in 1948, only 100,000 students attended college. By the early twenty-first century, India could boast 11 million college students (Bagla, 2008).

Today's students have different experiences, skills, and goals. Most are technologi-cally savvy, having spent more hours using computers than watching television or reading. The number of personal blogs, chat rooms, and Facebook and MySpace pages has exploded, as have music downloading, texting, online virtual worlds (e.g., *Second Life*), and interactive video games. Fewer college students now major in the liberal arts and more specialize in business and the professions (e.g., law and medi-cine). Most take on massive loans and are employed while still in college, to meet the expenses of higher education (see Figure 11.7).

In light of all these changes, does college still make students more mature, flexible thinkers? Most research indicates that the answer is yes (Pascarella & Terenzini, 2005). College is still mind-altering, "a transforming element in human development" (R. Benjamin, 2003, p. 11), especially for the mil-lions of students who are the first in their families to attend. Such students are sometimes at a disadvantage, partly because the hidden curriculum in college can be confusing, but many catch on and succeed (Pike & Kuh, 2005).

In fact, some researchers suggest that college may advance thinking even more than it once did: "Attending college may be a consciousness-raising experience for emerging adults because they en-counter new and varied people and perspectives" (Syed & Azmitia, 2008, p. 1013). Among 18-year-old high school graduates of similar backgrounds

● **UNDERSTANDING THE NUMBERS**
How would you express the increase in the number of India's college students in percentage terms?

Answer If the college population had doubled, it would be 200 percent of what it was. In fact, it increased 110 times, which is 11,000 percent of what it was.

FIGURE 11.7 Valuable, But Increas-ingly Unaffordable In the past 25 years, U.S. family income (up 147 per-cent since 1982) has kept pace with rising prices except in two important sectors: health care (up 251 percent) and college tuition and fees (up 439 percent).

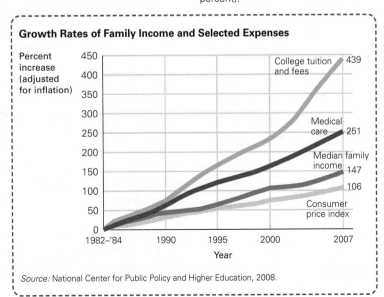

Growth Rates of Family Income and Selected Expenses

Percent increase (adjusted for inflation)

College tuition and fees 439
Medical care 251
Median family income 147
Consumer price index 106

Source: National Center for Public Policy and Higher Education, 2008.

and abilities, those who go straight into full-time employment rather than entering college achieve less and are less satisfied, definitely for the next few years and probably for life (Osgood et al., 2005; Schulenberg et al., 2005).

Furthermore, children of U.S. immigrants who attend college are more successful, economically and intellectually, than are those who do not. Even students who begin attending a community college and drop out fare better than do those with no college experience at all (Trillo, 2004). Obviously, colleges and students vary tremendously, and the college experience is sometimes transforming and sometimes not (Pascarella & Terenzini, 2005).

KEY points

- Experience as well as maturation advance cognition in emerging adulthood. Young adults are better able to combine emotions and rational analysis.
- Stereotype threat appears when emotional fears overwhelm cognition. This self-handicapping prejudice is common among many groups, but it may be overcome.
- Over the years of college, students gradually become less inclined to seek absolute truths from authorities and more inclined to draw their own conclusions.
- In every nation, the sheer number of college students has multiplied, and their goals and backgrounds have become more diverse. Despite all the changes, college education still seems to advance intellectual development during emerging adulthood.

Personality Patterns

Personality endures lifelong. As you remember from previous chapters, the origins of personality are genetic, and early childhood experience shapes the expression of genetic impulses. Yet personality is far from static after childhood, and new personality dimensions are particularly likely to appear in emerging adulthood.

Continuity and Change

The personality patterns of adults of every age are affected by the norms of their culture and by their social context. Emerging adults today are less anchored to their original families and neighborhoods than people of the same age in earlier generations; they make choices that are adventuresome breaks with their past, and they have not yet settled into a chosen family and lifestyle. It is thus not surprising that their personalities may change as a result.

Psychological research on personality traits of twins from ages 17 to 24 finds both genetic continuity and developmental improvements. In one longitudinal study, those 17-year-olds who saw life in positive terms maintained their outlook as time went on; those who were negative were likely to shift toward less worried, less anxious personalities (Blonigen et al., 2008).

Shifts toward positive development are also evident in another longitudinal study, which traced individuals who were extremely inhibited or aggressive at age 4. Those traits are definitely genetic and seem quite stable in primary school, but this study found changes taking place by emerging adulthood (Asendorpf et al., 2008).

The actual patterns of change were complex: Aggressiveness and inhibition do not disappear. To be specific, those who had been very aggressive had more conflicts with their parents and friends as emerging adults and were more likely to leave school and quit jobs. Two-thirds of them left high school before graduation, compared with one-third of their nonaggressive peers. By age 23, half of them had been arrested at least once. All these tendencies might be expected of people who were unusually aggressive.

Yet, unexpectedly, these aggressive young adults had as many friends as their more temperate peers did, and they rated themselves as quite conscientious. Most of their arrests were for minor offenses. Only one had been imprisoned, and only one other had been arrested several times. Most of them wanted more education: They had left school earlier because they had been discouraged by having to repeat grades when they were young. Most of them seemed on course to become productive adults, modifying their aggressive traits and putting their childhood problems behind them.

As for the emerging adults who had been inhibited as children, their prospects were excellent, as they were "cautious, reserved adults with few signs of internalizing problems" (Asendorpf et al., 2008, p. 1007). Perhaps because of their personality, they were slower than the average young adult to secure a job, choose a career, or find a romantic partner (at age 23, two-thirds had no current partner).

However, the inhibited participants were no more anxious or depressed than others of their cohort, and their self-esteem was equally good. They had many friends, whom they saw often. Their delayed employment and later marriage are increasingly typical for emerging adults, who like to keep their options open for a while before settling on one spouse, one career, one lifestyle. In other words, the personality trait (shyness) that was considered to be handicapping in childhood had become an asset by about age 20.

In this and other research, plasticity is evident. Personality is not fixed by age 5, or 15, or 20, as it was once thought to be. Emerging adults are open to new experiences (a reflection of their adventuresome spirit), and this receptiveness allows personality shifts. The trend is toward less depression and more joy, along with more insight into the self (Galambos et al., 2006; McAdams et al., 2006).

Going to college, leaving home, becoming independent, stopping drug abuse, moving to a new city, finding satisfying work and performing it well, making new friends—all these have the potential to change the life course. This does not mean that total change is possible: Some childhood experiences, genetic predispositions, and family burdens affect people lifelong. Furthermore, new experiences do not always result in desirable changes. But personality shifts are possible, especially during emerging adulthood.

Mental Health and Illness

Emerging adults usually feel quite pleased with themselves. In one U.S. study of 3,912 high school seniors who were followed until age 23 or 24, nine different trajectories were identified. Generally, transitions increased well-being; those in college and living away from home showed the largest increase (Schulenberg et al., 2005).

Two circumstances tended to slow down happiness: (1) becoming a single parent and/or (2) living with one's parents. Yet even the people who took one of those two paths tended to be happier than they had been in high school, although not as happy as their more independent peers. Over the emerging-adult years, self-esteem keeps rising (see Figure 11.8; Schulenberg et al., 2005). Similarly, 404 young adults in Canada, repeatedly questioned from ages 18 to 25, also reported rising self-esteem (Galambos et al., 2006).

This positive trend of increasing happiness between adolescence and adulthood has become more evident over recent decades, perhaps because young adults are more likely than adolescents to

FIGURE 11.8 Worthy People
This graph shows a steady increase in young adults' sense of well-being from age 18 to age 24, as measured by respondents' ratings of statements such as "I feel I am a person of worth." The ratings ranged from 1, indicating complete disagreement, to 5, indicating complete agreement. The average rating was already quite high at age 18, and it increased steadily over the years of emerging adulthood.

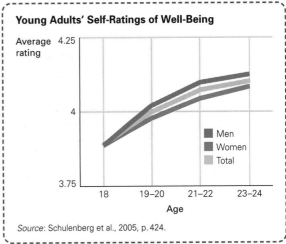

Young Adults' Self-Ratings of Well-Being

Source: Schulenberg et al., 2005, p. 424.

make their own life decisions (Twenge et al., 2008). Logically, the many stresses and transitions of emerging adulthood might be thought to reduce self-esteem, but the research seems to say otherwise.

Dealing with transitions successfully—especially leaving home, achieving identity, attending and then graduating from college, and securing a full-time job—correlates with well-being (Schulenberg et al., 2005), which allows young adults to be less self-centered and more caring of other people (N. Eisenberg et al., 2005; Padilla-Walker et al., 2008). Taking on one responsibility (such as a new job, residence, or relationship) makes it easier to take on another (Sneed et al., 2007).

PSYCHOPATHOLOGY Most emerging adults benefit from independence, but some are overwhelmed by the many choices and challenges they face. From ages 18 to 25, "young people are coming to grips with their lives" (Galambos et al., 2006, p. 360). Some lose their grip. Average well-being increases, but so does the incidence of *psychopathology,* or mental disorders (Mowbray et al., 2006; Schulenberg & Zarrett, 2006).

Worldwide, adults are more likely to have an episode of mental illness during emerging adulthood than during any later time. The specific incidence figures vary by nation as well as by the criteria used, but all observers agree that the late teens and early 20s are a particularly sensitive period (T. R. Insel & Fenton, 2005).

Vocational, financial, and interpersonal stresses cluster in early adulthood (Kessler et al., 2005). The **diathesis–stress model** "views psychopathology as the consequence of stress interacting with an underlying predisposition (biological, psychosocial, or sociocultural) to produce a specific disorder" (Hooley, 2004, p. 204). Thus, the stresses of emerging adulthood, especially without the social supports of family members and friends, may be too much if added to preexisting vulnerability.

Furthermore, some of the actions of emerging adults disrupt healthy emotions. Earlier in this chapter we discussed drug abuse, or, as clinicians call it, *substance use disorder.* Throughout life, and especially in the first years after adolescence, abuse of psychoactive drugs is a cause and a result of many disorders, of which depression is the most common (Y.-F. Chan et al., 2008).

SPECIFIC MENTAL DISORDERS Each particular psychopathology has a developmental trajectory, becoming more common at certain ages than at others. In addition to substance use disorders, specific other problems—including mood disorders, anxiety disorders, and schizophrenia—are more likely to appear in emerging adulthood.

Mood Disorders About one-quarter of mood disorders begin in adolescence, and another quarter begin in young adulthood. Before age 30, 15 percent of U.S. residents suffer from a mood disorder such as major depression, which is signaled by a "loss of interest or pleasure in nearly all activities" for two weeks or more. Other difficulties —in sleeping, concentrating, eating, carrying on friendships, and experiencing hope and meaning in life—are also symptoms of depression (American Psychiatric Association, 2000, p. 249). Women are about twice as likely as men to suffer from depression.

The origins of major depression are biochemical, involving imbalances in neurotransmitters and hormones, but the stresses common in adolescence and emerging adulthood (e.g., a romantic breakup, an unwanted birth, an arrest) can be triggers. Young adults with psychological problems are less likely to have supportive friendships, and that itself can contribute to depression (A. R. King & Terrance, 2006).

Many sufferers fail to get the treatment they need. Depressed emerging adults often distance themselves from anyone who might realize the depth of their despair and urge them to seek treatment. Furthermore, depressed people of all ages charac-

diathesis–stress model
The view that psychological disorders, such as schizophrenia, are produced by the interaction of a genetic vulnerability (the diathesis) and stressful environmental factors and life events.

teristically believe that nothing will help; they need encouragement from other people. Untreated mood disorders are one reason why suicides are twice as high in emerging adulthood as in adolescence.

Although effective treatment has been found for almost all types of depression (usually cognitive therapy plus medication), this disorder remains a leading cause of impairment and premature death worldwide. When the World Health Organization (WHO) estimates the productive years lost due to various chronic illnesses, depression is usually high on the list. In the words of the latest report on health worldwide:

> Depression is an important global public health problem due to both its relatively high lifetime prevalence and the significant disability that it causes. In 2002, depression accounted for 4.5% of the worldwide total burden of disease (in terms of disability-adjusted life years). It is also responsible for the greatest proportion of burden attributable to non-fatal health outcomes, accounting for almost 12% of total years lived with disability worldwide.
>
> *[United Nations, 2007, p. 8]*

(Disability is discussed in Chapter 12; our emphasis here is on depression as a major health problem in every nation.)

Anxiety Disorders Anxiety disorders occur in about one-fourth of all emerging adults in the United States. These include post-traumatic stress disorder (PTSD), obsessive-compulsive disorder (OCD), panic attacks, and eating disorders (described in Chapter 9). The manifestations of anxiety disorders are influenced by age, cultural context, and economic pressure.

As an example of cultural influence on mental illness, a new anxiety disorder has appeared in Japan within the last 20 years (Furlong, 2008; Watts, 2002). It is called *hikikomori*, or "pull away," and may affect more than 100,000 young adults. The sufferer stays in his (or, less often, her) room almost all the time for six months or more. Typically, a person with *hikikomori* is intensely anxious about the social and academic pressures of high school and college and has parents who "fear that their children won't survive without them" (M. Jones, 2005, p. 51).

It is easy to see why emerging adulthood might cause anxiety. Pressures to succeed academically, vocationally, and romantically can overwhelm young adults who are already prone to worry. Parental pressure, explicit or implicit, can make the anxiety worse (Luthar, 2003). So can a depressed job market (Furlong, 2008).

Schizophrenia About 1 percent of all adults experience at least one episode of schizophrenia. They have irrational, disorganized, and bizarre thoughts, delusions, hallucinations, and emotions (American Psychiatric Association, 2000). Schizophrenia is present in every nation, but age, gender, culture, and context affect the incidence, severity, and symptoms (Cantor-Graae & Selten, 2005; Kirkbride et al., 2006).

There is no doubt that schizophrenia is partly genetic. A child who has a biological parent with schizophrenia has about 1 chance in 8 of developing the disorder. Other factors beyond heredity increase the rate, including anoxia at birth, malnutrition while the brain is developing (St. Clair et al., 2005), and social pressure. Among young-adult immigrants to the United States who have no family members to ease their stress, the rate of schizophrenia triples (Cantor-Graae & Selten, 2005; C. Morgan et al., 2007).

Particularly interesting to developmentalists is the relationship among age, gender, and schizophrenia. Almost never does a first episode occur before age 10 or after age 35. Instead, the diagnosis is most common from ages 18 to 24; young males are particularly vulnerable (Kirkbride et al., 2006). Does something in the bodies, minds, or social surroundings of young men trigger schizophrenia? The diathesis–stress model suggests that the answer is yes, yes, and yes—that is, all three are factors in the onset of schizophrenia.

> ### KEYPoints
>
> - Personality patterns are evident lifelong, in part because genes and early childhood are influential. Nonetheless, emerging adults may modify some traits and develop others that were not evident in earlier years.
>
> - For most people, emerging adulthood is a happy time, as the various transitions increase a sense of well-being.
>
> - The diathesis–stress model of psychological disorders suggests that genetic vulnerability, past experiences, and current stresses combine to cause serious psychological problems in some people.
>
> - A minority of emerging adults are disabled by severe depression, anxiety disorders, and schizophrenia.

Identity and Intimacy

When Erik Erikson first described his eight stages of development, most developmentalists believed that identity was usually achieved before age 18 and that intimacy soon followed. Now it is apparent that many people take much longer to find their identity and that intimacy needs are often interspersed with identity ones.

Identity Achieved

The search for identity (see Chapter 10) still begins at puberty, but it continues much longer; most emerging adults are still seeking to determine who they are (Azmitia et al., 2008; J. E. Côté, 2006; R. O. Kroger, 2006). Erikson believed that, at each stage, the outcome of earlier crises provides the foundation of each new era. This is evident in emerging adulthood (see Table 11.4); childhood affects adult development.

Worldwide, emerging adults ponder their religious commitments, gender roles, political loyalties, and career options, trying to reconcile hopes for the future with

Past as Prologue In elaborating his eight stages of development, Erikson associated each stage with a particular virtue and a type of psychopathology, as shown here. He also thought that earlier crises could reemerge, taking a specific form at each stage. Here are some possible problems (not directly from Erikson) that could occur in emerging adulthood if earlier crises were not resolved.

TABLE 11.4 Erikson's Eight Stages of Development

Stage	Virtue/Pathology	Possible in Emerging Adulthood If Not Successfully Resolved
Trust vs. mistrust	Hope/withdrawal	Suspicious of others, making close relationships difficult
Autonomy vs. shame and doubt	Will/compulsion	Obsessively driven, single-minded, not socially responsive
Initiative vs. guilt	Purpose/inhibition	Fearful, regretful (e.g., very homesick in college)
Industry vs. inferiority	Competence/inertia	Self-critical of any endeavor, procrastinating, perfectionistic
Identity vs. role diffusion	Fidelity/repudiation	Uncertain and negative about values, lifestyle, friendships
Intimacy vs. isolation	Love/exclusivity	Anxious about close relationships, jealous, lonely
Generativity vs. stagnation	Care/rejectivity	[In the future] Fear of failure
Integrity vs. despair	Wisdom/disdain	[In the future] No "mindfulness," no life plan

Source: Erikson, 1982.

beliefs acquired in the past. Although none of these identities are necessarily set by age 18, as noted in Chapter 10, the social context of the twenty-first century has made two of them, ethnic and vocational identity, particularly elusive during adolescence.

ETHNIC IDENTITY In the United States and Canada, about half of the 18- to 25-year-olds are either children of immigrants or are native-born adults whose ancestors were African, Asian, Latino, or Indian (sometimes called Native American in the United States and called Aboriginal or First Nations in Canada). For them, ethnicity is a significant aspect of identity (Phinney, 2006). Most such individuals identify with very specific ethnic groups. For example, unlike adolescents, who might say they are simply Asian Americans, emerging adults are more likely to specify that they are Vietnamese, Bangladeshi, or Korean Americans (Dion, 2006).

Similarly, people who are descendants of American slaves no longer call themselves colored or Negro, but African American or Carib-American. Not surprisingly, the first individuals to self-identify as African American were usually emerging adults. Ethnicity is salient for many emerging adults, who are more likely to be proud, or at least accepting, of their ethnic background than are adolescents (Worrell, 2008).

More than any other age group, emerging adults have friends with diverse backgrounds. They become more aware of history, customs, and prejudices. By providing a context, their experiences shape the specifics of their ethnic identity because "without a context, identity formation and self-development cannot occur" (Trimble et al., 2003, p. 267).

Many European Americans, realizing the importance of ethnicity for their immigrant friends, become more conscious of their own background and religion. They might go beyond identifying themselves simply as Catholic or Jewish and say that they are Ukrainian Catholic or Russian Jewish.

Although everyone struggles to forge an identity, this is particularly difficult for immigrants because combining past and future means reconciling their parents' background with their new social context. Conflicts often arise, not only in choice of vocation or partner (as can happen with any emerging adult) but also in something more basic—"the assumption that these choices should be made independently by the young adult daughter or son" (Dion, 2006, p. 303). Young immigrants are often expected to be proud of their ethnic roots, and many are, but they are also expected by their peers to make independent choices about their future careers and mates. Many clash with their parents as they do so.

Ethnic identity may affect choices in language, manners, romance, employment, neighborhood, religion, clothing, and values. Some aspects of this identification are easier than others (Trimble et al., 2003), but ethnic identity is always complex:

- It is reciprocal, both a personal choice and a response to others.
- It depends on context, so it changes with time and circumstances.
- It is multifaceted: Emerging adults choose to accept some attributes and reject others.

The changing contexts of life require ethnic identity to be reestablished at each phase. Thus, a person might adhere to one aspect of ethnic identity in adolescence, another in emerging adulthood, and still another as a parent. Young people whose parents belong to different ethnic groups must deal with added complexity. Contrary

AP/WIDE WORLD PHOTOS

A Woman Now Two young girls participate in the traditional coming-of-age ceremony in Japan. Their kimonos and hairstyles are elaborate and traditional, as is the sake (rice wine) they drink. This is part of the ceremony signifying passage from girlhood to womanhood.

OBSERVATION QUIZ
At what age do you think this event occurs—15, 16, 18, or 20? (see answer, page 410) ➔

ANSWER TO OBSERVATION QUIZ
(from page 409) The most obvious
clue—that the girls look like teenagers—
is misleading. If you remembered that
the social clock is somewhat slower
in developed nations and that Asian
adolescents mature relatively late, you
might have guessed, accurately, that the
girls are 20 years old. This is five years
later than the Quinceañera, the similar
occasion for Latinas, and four years
later than the European American
"sweet sixteen." ●

to what one might guess, by emerging adulthood, many self-identify with whichever group experiences more prejudice (Herman, 2004).

Consider Kevin Johnson, son of a European American father and a Mexican American mother. As a high school student, he thought of himself as Anglo. But in a book called *How Did You Get to Be Mexican?*, he explains that as an emerging adult, he chose to identify with the Mexican half of his heritage, criticizing his mother for not teaching him Spanish. He married a Mexican American, gave his children Spanish names, and sent them to bilingual schools (K. R. Johnson, 1999). Nevertheless, he went to a Massachusetts college and decided to live in California (not Mexico).

Like Johnson, adults choose which facets of their ethnic identity to adopt and express. In adolescence, many second-generation immigrants criticize their parents for speaking their original language and for restricting their teenagers' dating choices (Ghuman, 2003; Portes & Rumbaut, 2001). In adulthood, however, some of those same individuals adopt traditional values and practices.

For this reason, college classes in ethnic studies include many emerging adults who want to learn about their culture. Fellow students as well as classes help solidify identity. College is a useful context for discovering and developing a self-concept, including an ethnic identity (Syed & Azmitia, 2008).

Because ethnicity is multifaceted and changing, no young adult conforms to his or her ethnic heritage precisely; all emerging adults reassess their national and religious identities as well. Meanwhile, every culture in the world keeps developing. Some former immigrants visit their "home" country and find that they are strangers (Long & Oxfeld, 2004).

Thus, in the globalization of the twenty-first century, when people seek their ethnic identity, combining past and future is a complex but crucial task. One's background cannot be ignored, but it must not become a retreat. As powerfully expressed by one young adult:

> Questioning their identity, as inevitable as that experience is, is not enough. To have passed through the ambiguities, contradictions, and frustration of cultural schizophrenia is to have passed only the first test in the process. . . . We need to embody our own history. *El pueblo que pierde su memoria pierde su destino:* The people who forgets its past, forfeits its future.
>
> [Gaspar de Alba, 2003, pp. 211–212]

VOCATIONAL IDENTITY Establishing a vocational identity is considered part of adulthood not only by developmental psychologists influenced by Erikson but also by emerging adults themselves (Arnett, 2004). For many, that is one reason they go to college: It is considered an important step toward a career (see Table 11.5).

A correlation between college education and income has always been apparent, as explained earlier in this chapter. The connection between college and career is even stronger today as unskilled work becomes less common and more knowledge-based jobs are created. The correlation between college and income is not perfect (1 percent of those in the top one-fifth income bracket are not high school graduates), but it is very high (77 percent in that top bracket have at least a bachelor's degree) (Swanson, 2007).

Most emerging adults (75 percent) are employed while they are in college, but, whether in college or not, most young adults move from job to job, not considering any of them a career based on vocational identity. Between ages 18 and 27, the average U.S. worker has eight jobs (U.S. Bureau of the Census, 2006).

TABLE 11.5 Top Six "Very Important" Reasons for Deciding to Attend College*

To learn more about things that matter to me	78 percent
To be able to get a better job	72 percent
To be able to make more money	71 percent
To get training for a specific career	69 percent
To gain a general education and appreciation of ideas	65 percent
To prepare myself for graduate or professional school	58 percent

*Based on a national survey of students entering four-year colleges in the United States in Fall 2005.

Source: *Chronicle of Higher Education*, August 25, 2006.

Charles, a college graduate, is typical. He has worked for the same advertising agency for a year but still thinks of himself as a "temp," able to leave the company at any moment to pursue his career in music. He explains:

> I'm single. I don't have a car or a house or a mortgage or a significant other that's pulling me in another direction, or kids or anything. I'm highly portable, and I can basically do what I want as long as I can support myself.
>
> *[quoted in Arnett, 2004, p. 37]*

A Wannabe Not all professions are glamorous, but many young people dream of rising to the top of their chosen field.

Many developmentalists wonder if vocational identity is an illusion in the twenty-first century. Hiring and firing seem disconnected from the worker's training or need for a steady job, especially for those workers who are young (Vaupel & Loichinger, 2006). Perhaps adults of all ages should see employment the way Charles and many other young adults do, as a way to earn money while they satisfy their creative, self-expressive impulses elsewhere. Although many societies, pension plans, and work schedules are structured as if every worker was steady, dedicated, and full-time, this may be an outdated social construction.

> Some young adults assume that they will find a vocational niche that is perfect for their aspirations and talents. They have high expectations for work. They expect to find a job that will be an expression of their identity.... With such high expectations ... some of them are likely to find that the actual job they end up in for the long term falls considerably short.
>
> *[Arnett, 2004, pp. 143, 163]*

Intimacy

The reality that people need each other was forcefully noted by Erikson, who described his eight stages as *psychosocial,* not psychosexual (as his mentor Freud did), psychological, or sociological (as many other developmentalists do). Erikson's sixth psychosocial stage, *intimacy versus isolation,* particularly emphasizes that humans are social creatures. He explains:

> The young adult, emerging from the search for and the insistence on identity, is eager and willing to fuse his identity with others. He is ready for intimacy, that is, the capacity to commit himself to concrete affiliations and partnerships and to develop the ethical strength to abide by such commitments, even though they call for significant sacrifices and compromises.
>
> *[Erikson, 1963, p. 263]*

All intimate relationships have much in common—not only in the psychological needs they satisfy but also in the behaviors they require (Reis & Collins, 2004). Intimacy progresses from attraction to close connection to ongoing commitment. As Erikson noted, each relationship demands some personal sacrifice, including vulnerability that brings deeper self-understanding and shatters the isolation caused by too much self-protection.

The human need for other people is evident to every social scientist. From the moment of birth, people depend on one another. Yet many emerging adults seem to break away from social ties: They become independent from their parents, and they do not want to marry or have children. Does this mean they are isolated, lonely, and "suffering, selfish slackers" (Arnett, 2007b, p. 23)?

These are myths (Arnett, 2007b). Although Erikson was right in saying that people need "concrete affiliations and partnerships," emerging adults have found new ways to establish intimacy with friends, lovers, and families. Marriage and parenthood, as emerging adults are discovering, are only two of several paths to intimacy.

FRIENDSHIPS Throughout life, friends defend against stress and provide joy (Bukowski et al., 1996; Krause, 2006). They are chosen for the very qualities that make them good companions, trustworthy confidants, and reliable sources of support (e.g., understanding, tolerance, loyalty, affection, humor). Unlike family members, friends are earned; they choose us. Friends, new and old, are particularly crucial during emerging adulthood.

Traditionally, young men and women preferred friends of their own sex and engaged in sex-specific activities with them. Male friendships centered on shared activities such as sports, cars, and contests (sometimes fighting with words, not weapons). Women's friendships were more intimate and emotional, involving self-disclosing talk about health, romances, and relatives.

These male–female distinctions are less apparent among contemporary emerging adults. For instance, most have one or two cross-sex friendships and several more nonsexual same-sex relationships (Lenton & Webber, 2006). The common contexts of emerging adulthood today—colleges and universities, large corporations and international travel, residences far from one's original neighborhood—all foster multiple acquaintances and friends of both sexes.

Most single young adults have larger and more supportive friendship networks than newly married young adults once did. Typically, they use online connections not to distance themselves, as some of the older generation feared, but to extend and deepen their friendships that began face-to-face (Subrahmanyam et al., 2008). This is a gain in intimacy.

ROMANCE Would you marry someone you didn't love if he or she had all the other qualities you seek? Most emerging adults respond with a resounding *NO!,* but some young adults (especially women) in developing nations say yes (Hatfield & Rapson, 2006). Relationships are universally crucial, but culture and cohort guide their expression.

The Dimensions of Love Love is not a simple emotion, not something universally recognized as the glue that holds a relationship together. In a classic analysis, Robert Sternberg (1988b) described three distinct aspects of love—passion, intimacy, and commitment. Sternberg believes that the relative presence or absence of these three components gives rise to seven different forms of love (see Table 11.6).

Early in a relationship, *passion* is evident in "falling in love," an intense physical, cognitive, and emotional onslaught characterized by excitement, ecstasy, and euphoria. The entire body and mind, hormones and neurons, are activated (Aron et al., 2005).

Passion has been the dominant aspect of love for young adults in recent years, displayed in film and poetry. There is some evidence that passion is fueled by novelty. Siblings rarely are attracted to each other sexually; they know each other too well. In India, future brides who have lived in the groom's household since they were children have fewer offspring than do those who first met their future spouse after puberty (Lieberman, 2006).

Intimacy is knowing someone well, sharing secrets as well as sex. This phase of a relationship is reciprocal, with each partner gradually revealing more of himself or herself.

Commitment takes time. It grows gradually through decisions to be together, mutual caregiving, kept secrets, shared possessions, and forgiveness (Fincham et al., 2007). Maintaining a committed relationship over the years takes dedication and work (Dindia & Emmers-Sommer, 2006).

Commitment is affected by the social context. One intriguing study in Sweden suggests that couples living

TABLE 11.6 Sternberg's Seven Forms of Love

	Present in the Relationship?		
Form of Love	Passion	Intimacy	Commitment
Liking	No	Yes	No
Infatuation	Yes	No	No
Empty love	No	No	Yes
Romantic love	Yes	Yes	No
Fatuous love	Yes	No	Yes
Companionate love	No	Yes	Yes
Consummate love	Yes	Yes	Yes

Source: Sternberg, 1988b.

in detached houses (with yards between them) break up more often than couples in attached dwellings (such as apartments). Perhaps "single-family housing might have deleterious effects on couple stability due to the isolating lack of social support for couples staying together" (Lauster, 2008, p. 901). In other words, suburban couples may be too far from their neighbors to be helped by them when conflicts arise.

For both men and women, children add stress but also make separation less likely. Social forces also affect commitment; in-laws may either strengthen or weaken a couple's long-term relationship. Jokes about in-laws often have the ring of truth.

The power of the social context helps to explain why few arranged marriages end, even when the couple moves to another nation where divorce is easy. Arranged marriages begin with commitment; intimacy and passion may follow. Families "make great efforts . . . to keep the couple together" (Georgas et al., 2006, p. 19), providing practical support (such as child care), emotional encouragement, and conflict resolution. Domestic violence may occur in arranged marriages (as well as in love marriages), but often a bride's father or brother will intervene if her husband is too demanding.

The Western ideal of consummate love is characterized by all three components: passion, intimacy, and commitment. This ideal combines "the view of love promulgated in the movies . . . [and the] more prosaic conceptions of love rooted in daily and long-lived experience" (Gerstel, 2002, p. 555). For developmental reasons, this ideal is difficult to achieve. Passion seems to be sparked by unfamiliarity, uncertainty, and risk, all of which are diminished by the growing familiarity and security that contribute to intimacy as well as by the time needed to demonstrate commitment.

With time, passion may fade, intimacy may grow, and commitment may develop. This pattern occurs for all types of couples—married, unmarried, and remarried; heterosexual and homosexual; young and old (Ganong & Coleman, 1994; Kurdek, 1992). The divorce rate decreases with every year of marriage.

Contemporary Lovers As mentioned above, passion has been crucial for love and marriage in Western nations. Teenagers "fall in love" and parents are forbidden to interfere with a young adult's choice of a partner. However, the modern sequence of passion/intimacy/commitment (via dating, engagement, and marriage) has not necessarily led to successful relationships.

Moonstruck joy can become bittersweet once the two people involved have been together for months or years. As one observer explains, "Falling in love is absolutely no way of getting to know someone" (Sullivan, 1999, p. 225). Many young adults may be reluctant to marry precisely because they realize the truth of this observation. Those who do marry young are more likely to divorce (Rodrigues et al., 2006).

It seems a mistake to assume that passion will lead to commitment. Indeed, according to some research, lust and affection arise from different parts of the brain (L.M. Diamond, 2004). As one author explains, "Sex and love drift in and out of each other's territories and their foggy frontiers cannot be rigidly staked out. . . . Although lust does not contain love, love contains lust" (Sullivan, 1999, pp. 95–96).

Establishing an intimate nonsexual relationship, and later moving toward a sexual one, may be wiser than the reverse—sex first and friendship later (Furman & Hand, 2006). Emerging adults refer to "friends with benefits," implying that sexual passion is less significant (an extra benefit, not the core attraction) than the friendship.

Sexual interactions can occur between people who are not friends. Couples sometimes *hook up,* having a sexual encounter with neither intimacy nor commitment. Hookups are more common among first-year college students than among those about to graduate because older students have learned that, as one put it, "If you hook up with someone it probably is just a hookup and nothing is going to come of it" (quoted in Bogle, 2008, p. 38).

● **FOR DEEPER REFLECTION** Genes are said to affect everything, including human behavior, but can someone be genetically inclined to choose passion over commitment?

AP / WIDE WORLD PHOTOS

Mail-Order Bride He was looking for a woman with green eyes and reddish hair but without strong religious convictions, and he posted these criteria on a social-networking Web site. That led to an e-mail courtship and eventually marriage to "the girl of my dreams."

cohabit
To live with an unrelated person—typically a romantic partner—to whom one is not married.

The desire for physical intimacy without emotional commitment may be stronger in young men than in young women. If that is true, the reasons could be either hormonal (especially due to testosterone) or cultural (women want men to stay with them if children are born). Interestingly, emerging adults of both sexes say that if they want a serious relationship with someone, they are less likely to hook up with them, preferring to get to know them first (Bogle, 2008).

Given the national, international, and historical differences, there is no one pattern that is guaranteed to lead to a happy relationship. Emerging adults reject the patterns of the past: "Finding a love partner in your teens and continuing in that relationship with that person through your early twenties, culminating in marriage, is now viewed as unhealthy, a mistake, a path likely to lead to disaster" (Arnett, 2004, p. 73).

Cohabitation Most young adults in the United States, England, and northern Europe **cohabit** (live with someone not related, typically a romantic partner) rather than marry before age 25. Such couples may share expenses and routines as well as a bed, although they often shy away from a joint bank account and long-term commitment. The Add Health study found that about 60 percent of their sample had cohabited by age 24 (Schoen et al., 2007).

Contrary to widespread belief, cohabitation does not preclude the problems that may arise after a wedding. In fact, the opposite is more likely (Cohan & Kleinbaum, 2002; Kamp Dush & Amato, 2005). Domestic violence and excessive drinking are more likely to occur among young adults who cohabit than among those who marry, and married couples are *more* likely to divorce if they have lived together before marriage. Ending a cohabiting relationship is stressful in much the same way that divorce is, although typically the stress of divorce is more intense and long-lasting (Blekesaune, 2008).

It seems that cohabitation solves some problems for emerging adults, but it does not remedy a major developmental difficulty of our era—divorce. Divorce is common (ending 45 percent of U.S. marriages) and difficult, not only for the partners but also for their families—their parents as well as their children. Developmentalists are working to understand these consequences in the hope of helping to alleviate them (Amato, 2000; Furstenburg & Cherlin, 1991), a topic further discussed in Chapter 13.

Anything Wrong with this Picture? The beaming man is a proud and responsive father, old enough to take his responsibilities seriously. A close look at his 22-month-old daughter suggests that he is doing a good job: She is delighted at the game he is playing with the ball, and he has moved his tall body way down, to be exactly at face level with her. Another fact also makes bonding easier: She is the biological child of these two young adults. So in terms of child and adult development, everything is right with this family picture—but some people might be troubled by one detail: Neither parent has a wedding ring. They have never married.

RICHARD LORD / THE IMAGE WORKS

FAMILY CONNECTIONS It is hard to overestimate the importance of the family throughout the life span. Families are "our most important individual support system" (Schaie, 2002, p. 318). Although made up of individuals, a family is much more than the persons who belong to it.

In dynamic synergy, children grow, adults find support, and every member is part of a family ethos that gives meaning to, and provides models for, personal aspirations and decisions. All members of each family have *linked lives,* meaning that the experiences and needs of family members at one stage of life are affected by those of members at other stages (Macmillan & Copher, 2005).

Emerging adults are supposedly independent, leaving their childhood home and parents behind. That is the story line, but it is not quite true. Parents continue to be crucial influences after age 18—more so now than in the past, since fewer emerging adults today have established their own families, secured high-paying jobs, or achieved a definitive understanding of their identity and goals.

Given the linked lives of family members, it is useful to consider the life circumstances that are typical for parents of emerging adults. Because of demographic changes over the past few decades, most middle-aged parents have just one or two children, who were born within a few years of each other. The parents can thus attend to the needs of their emerging adults, since they have no young children. Their concern is intensified by several factors: Their young-adult children are usually not married, not parents, and almost never vocationally secure (long gone are the days when the young took over the family business or farm).

Financially, many parents of emerging adults are relatively well off. Usually, both parents are employed and have some seniority in their jobs. Households headed by someone aged 45 to 54 report more income than those headed by someone older or younger (U.S. Bureau of the Census, 2008). Parents of emerging adults are not yet distracted by their own health or retirement concerns: Most can expect to live for decades longer, which is another reason they want their adult children to be successful.

As a result of all these factors, many parents help their adult children. Specifics vary from nation to nation. Almost all unmarried young adults in Italy and Japan live with their parents, as do half of those in England (Manzi et al., 2006). Fewer adult children live with their parents in the United States, but many parents underwrite their young-adult children's rent (Pew Research Center, 2007).

In the United States, almost three-fourths of emerging adults receive cash from their parents. One respected team writes:

> Our best estimate implies that on average parents provide roughly $38,000 in material assistance—housing, food, educational expenses, or direct cash assistance—during the transition to adulthood. This averages over $2,200 in each year from ages eighteen to thirty-four, although assistance diminishes with age.
>
> *[Schoeni & Ross, 2005, p. 414]*

Most emerging adults are also given help with daily tasks such as laundry, moving, household repairs, and, if needed, free pet care and child care. All this helps to make their achievement (higher education, better jobs) possible (Schoeni & Ross, 2005).

Lack of family financial support is a problem for some emerging adults. College is costly; living expenses must be covered, and even with government subsidies, many

CHRIS ROUTE / ALAMY

CHARLOTTE THEGE / PETER ARNOLD, INC.

The Same Situation, Many Miles Apart: Happy Young Women The British woman *(top)* and the Kenyan woman *(bottom)* are both developing just as their families and cultures had hoped they would. The major difference is that 23-year-old Kim is not yet married to Dave, while her contemporary already has a husband, son, and daughter.

young adults from low-income families cannot afford higher education. In every nation, college graduation rates decrease as family income falls (OECD, 2008).

A particular problem is evident for children who are in foster care: At age 18, they are considered adults, able to take their place in society. Given all that is now known about emerging adulthood, this is far too soon (Avery & Freundlich, 2009).

As we think about the experiences of emerging adults overall, it is apparent that this stage has many pitfalls as well as benefits. These years may be crucial, as "decisions made during the transition to adulthood have a particularly long-lasting influence on the remainder of the life course because they set individuals on paths that are sometimes difficult to change" (A. Thornton et al., 2007, p. 13).

Fortunately, most emerging adults, like humans of all ages, have strengths as well as liabilities. Many survive risks, overcome substance abuse, combat loneliness, and deal with other problems through further education, social support, and maturation. Most find it liberating to postpone marriage, prevent parenthood, and avoid climbing the career ladder until their identity is firmly established and their education complete. Then they are ready for the commitment and responsibility of adulthood, described in the next chapters.

KEY Points

- Identity achievement is often not attained until adulthood.

- Two aspects of identity often take time to achieve: ethnic identity and vocational identity. Many people do not select a career or find a job they like until age 25 or later.

- Intimacy needs are strong during emerging adulthood. Friendships, romances, and family all help young adults meet these needs.

- Far fewer emerging adults marry today than in earlier decades. Cohabitation has become much more common.

SUMMARY

Cultural and National Differences

1. Emerging adulthood is a new period of development, characterized by later marriage and more education. Age variations are apparent; nonetheless, ages 18 to 25 can be described as a distinct period worldwide.

2. All the body systems function optimally during these years; death from disease is rare. Homeostasis helps emerging adults feel strong and recover quickly from infections and injuries.

3. The sexual-reproductive system functions especially well during emerging adulthood, the time of peak fertility. However, most people this age do not yet want to become parents. Sexual activity before marriage is accepted by most young adults.

4. One consequence of changing sexual mores is an increase in sexually transmitted infections; they are much more common now than in earlier generations because many young adults have several sexual relationships.

5. Risk taking increases during emerging adulthood, with edgework particularly attractive to young men, who are more likely to die violently than are young women.

6. Drug and alcohol abuse increases during emerging adulthood; these years are the most common period for addiction. However, most emerging adults are not drug abusers: knowledge of this fact may deter drug abuse,

Cognitive Maturity

7. One hallmark of adult thought is the ability to combine emotions and rational analysis. This ability is particularly useful in responding to emotionally arousing situations, as when childhood prejudices or stereotype threats are still present.

8. Stereotype threat can affect people of all ages and cultures, but it is particularly likely to slow down cognition when a person worries that other people might be biased in their assessment of his or her abilities.

9. Many more students of all backgrounds and nationalities attend college currently than in former decades. Despite many cohort differences, college students not only gain skills and future career advances but also become less inclined to seek absolutes from authorities and more inclined to make their own decisions.

Personality Patterns

10. Personality patterns change in emerging adulthood, but continuity is also apparent. Many emerging adults find an appropriate combination of education, friendship, and achievement that improves their self-esteem.

11. The rates of some forms of psychopathology, including substance abuse, anxiety disorders, depression, and schizophrenia, rise during emerging adulthood. As the diathesis–stress model of mental illness predicts, the seeds of these disorders are planted early in life, but the stress of young adulthood may produce mental health disorders.

Identity and Intimacy

12. The process of identity achievement continues from adolescence through emerging adulthood. In a diverse, modern society,

ethnic and vocational identities are particularly difficult to achieve. Most young adults seek an identity that differs from that of their heritage, and take much longer to settle on a career than their parents did.

13. Close friendships are common during emerging adulthood, typically including some opposite-sex as well as same-sex friendships. Romantic love is complex, involving passion, intimacy, and commitment. Many emerging adults have a series of sexual relationships, hooking up and cohabiting before establishing an intimate partnership in marriage.

14. Family support is needed lifelong. In emerging adulthood, this often means that parents pay college costs and contribute in other ways to their young-adult children's independence. Total separation from family is unusual and impairs young adults' achievement. Everywhere, members of families have linked lives.

KEY TERMS

emerging adulthood (p. 385)
homeostasis (p. 388)
replacement rate (p. 389)

edgework (p. 391)
extreme sports (p. 392)
drug abuse (p. 392)

drug addiction (p. 392)
social norms approach (p. 395)
stereotype threat (p. 398)

diathesis–stress model (p. 406)
cohabit (p. 414)

KEY QUESTIONS

1. What age range does emerging adulthood encompass, and what social conventions tend to characterize this period?

2. What are the sex differences in the rate of violent deaths, and to what degree are they the result of nature or nurture?

3. How do social norms affect the incidence of health problems, including drug use, in early adulthood?

4. How is adult thinking different from adolescent thinking?

5. According to research, how does college education affect the way people think?

6. Why is vocational identity more complex for today's young adults than it was when Erikson developed his theory?

7. When, how, and why do people develop an ethnic identity?

8. What are the three main ways in which young adults meet their need for intimacy?

9. How does cohabitation affect marriage?

10. What is the role of nonmarital relationships during emerging adulthood?

11. How does the family of origin (primarily the parents) affect the well-being of emerging adults?

APPLICATIONS

1. Describe an incident during your emerging adulthood when taking a risk could have led to disaster. What were your feelings at the time? What would you do if you knew that a child of yours was about to do the same thing?

2. Describe the daily patterns of someone you know who has unhealthy habits related to eating, exercise, drug abuse, risk taking, or some other aspect of lifestyle. What would it take for that person to change his or her habits? Consider the impact of time, experience, medical advice, and fear.

3. One way to study cognitive development during college is to study yourself and your classmates. Compare thoughts and decisions at the beginning of college and at graduation. Remembering that case studies are provocative but not definitive, identify some hypotheses about college and intellectual growth.

4. Talk with several people over age 30 about their work history. Are they doing what they expected when they were younger? Are they settled in their vocation and job? Pay attention to their age when they decided on their jobs. Was age 25 a turning point?

ADULTHOOD
Body and Mind

12

Jenny was in her early 30s, a star student in my human development class. She told the class that she was divorced, raising her two children and two orphaned nephews in the South Bronx. She talked eloquently about free activities for her children—public parks, museums, the zoo, Fresh Air camp. We were awed by her creativity and energy.

One day Jenny came to my office to speak privately. She said that she was four weeks pregnant. The father, Billy, was a married man who told her he would not leave his wife but would pay for an abortion. She thought she should terminate the pregnancy, but she wanted to talk to me first.

She was about to graduate with honors and had found a job that would enable her to move out of her dangerous neighborhood. She told me other facts: Her son needed special education; she was a carrier for sickle-cell anemia; her crowded apartment was not "babyproof," since her youngest child was 7; she thought she was too old to have another infant.

After a long talk she thanked me, although I had only asked questions and listened.

Then came the surprise: "I'll have the baby," she said. "Men come and go, but children are always with you." ●

ADULTHOOD COVERS four decades, from age 25 to 65. Despite feeling "too old" to have another baby, Jenny was far from middle-aged, but her concerns about childbearing are common among adults of all ages. This chapter explains the issues behind the choices each adult makes about sex and reproduction.

We also discuss the physiological changes of adulthood—changes in strength, appearance, and body functioning. Many people are concerned about aging long before they are senior citizens; you will learn about some aspects of vision, hearing, and disease that concern many adults.

Then we describe adult cognition, noting how intelligence—as measured by IQ tests and as defined in various ways—is affected by aging as well as by other influences. Many adults become selective experts as they spend years mastering a specific task or topic. You will learn more about the characteristics and consequences of such specialized knowledge. At the end of this chapter, we return to Jenny, who may have been more expert than I knew.

The Aging Process

We begin with the facts of aging. This may seem depressing if you are only in your 20s, but physical aging is not discouraging to most adults who experience it. The reason is that, usually, they are in good health, able to do almost everything at age 65 that they did at age 25. Even in the sexual-reproductive system, the one organ system that shows significant aging, some age-related changes are welcome.

Senescence

senescence
A gradual physical decline that is related to aging and during which the body becomes less strong and efficient.

Everyone ages, at his or her own rate. When growth stops, **senescence,** a gradual physical decline over time, begins. Every natural substance in the blood, every organ of the body, every bone and cell is affected by aging—some more than others. The rate of senescence is influenced by many factors, not just the passage of time (Masoro, 2006).

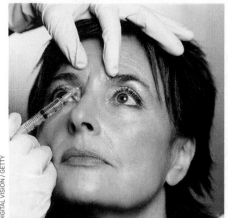

No Wrinkles An injection of Botox to plump the skin beneath her eyebrows is what this woman decided she needs, although she is quite beautiful and shows no signs of aging.

PHYSICAL APPEARANCE Outward signs of senescence appear long before old age. The first visible changes are in the skin. Collagen, the connective tissue of the body, decreases by about 1 percent per year, starting in early adulthood (M. L. Timiras, 2003). As a result, by age 30 the skin is already becoming thinner and less flexible, and wrinkles become visible, particularly around the eyes.

Especially on the face (most exposed to sun, rain, heat, cold, and pollution), the skin loses "firmness and elasticity, leading to the formation of sagging areas such as the infamous double chin" (Whitbourne, 2008, p. 88). This is barely noticeable in young adulthood, but if you know a typical pair of siblings, one 18 and the other 28, you can tell which one is older by the appearance of the skin. By age 60, all faces are wrinkled, some much more than others.

Hair usually turns gray and gets thinner; "middle-age spread" appears in the stomach; pockets of fat settle on the abdomen, the upper arms, the buttocks, and the chin (Whitbourne et al., 2002). All the muscles weaken, not only because of disuse but also because the number of muscle fibers diminishes with age (McCarter, 2006).

Many of these changes occur more slowly in people who exercise wisely and regularly, but senescence begins for everyone when growth stops at the end of adolescence. The change is most evident in athletic contests that require strength, agility, and speed: Gymnasts, boxers, and basketball players are among the athletes who benefit from youth but already experience slowdowns by age 20.

By late middle age, people get shorter. Back muscles, connective tissue, and bones lose density, making the vertebrae in the spine shrink. People lose about an inch of height (2 to 3 centimeters) by age 65. That loss occurs not in the leg bones but in the trunk, as the cushioning between spinal disks becomes compressed (Tilling et al., 2006)—another reason that waists widen during adulthood.

SENSE ORGANS Not only does the rate of senescence vary from person to person and organ to organ, but each part of each organ is on its own timetable. This is notable in the organs associated with the five senses, all of which become less acute with each decade; some functions fade faster than others.

Changes in the eyes are perhaps the most obvious example of the varied rates of senescence within one organ. Peripheral vision (at the sides) narrows faster than frontal vision;

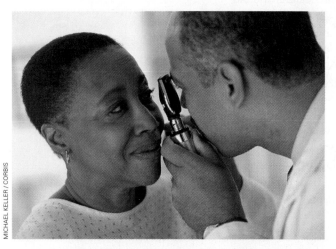

Healthy Eyes Annual examinations of the lens and retina are crucial for all middle-aged adults, especially those who are of African heritage.

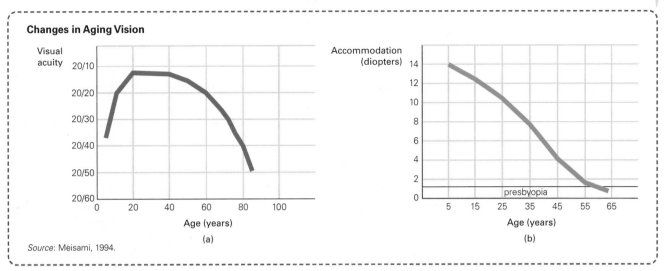

Changes in Aging Vision

Visual acuity (left graph, y-axis: 20/10, 20/20, 20/30, 20/40, 20/50, 20/60; x-axis: Age (years) 0, 20, 40, 60, 80, 100)

(a)

Accommodation (diopters) (right graph, y-axis: 14, 12, 10, 8, 6, 4, 2, 0; x-axis: Age (years) 5, 15, 25, 35, 45, 55, 65; line labeled presbyopia)

(b)

Source: Meisami, 1994.

color vision shifts from vivid to faded more quickly than does black and white. Difficulty seeing objects at a distance, or *nearsightedness,* increases gradually beginning in one's 20s (see Figure 12.1).

By middle age, it becomes harder to focus on objects that are very close (called *far-sightedness*) because the lens of the eye is less elastic and the cornea flattens (Schieber, 2006). This explains why 40-year-olds tend to hold reading matter twice as far away from their eyes (it is in focus at that distance) as 20-year-olds do and why many older adults use bifocals (Meisami et al., 2003). Younger adults with vision problems are usually either nearsighted *or* farsighted; most older adults are both.

Losses also occur in hearing, which is most acute at about age 10. Some adults hear much better than others, and typically not until about age 60 is **presbycusis** (literally, "aging hearing") diagnosed. One practical measure of presbycusis is the "whisper test." A person is asked to repeat something whispered by someone unseen who is 3 feet away (Pirozzo et al., 2003). Almost all emerging adults pass this test, as do two-thirds of people age 50, but only half of those over 65 do.

FIGURE 12.1 Age-Related Declines in Vision Every aspect of bodily functioning follows its own rate of senescence. Vision is a prime example. (*a*) Sharpness of distance vision, as measured by the ability to see an object at 20 feet, reaches a peak at about age 20 and declines gradually until old age. (*b*) By contrast, ability to focus on a small point about 12 inches in front of the eyes declines from childhood on; at about age 60, the typical person becomes officially farsighted.

presbycusis
A loss of hearing that is associated with senescence and that usually does not become apparent until after age 60.

Hard Rocking, Hard of Hearing
Les Claypool is an example of the dangers posed by prolonged exposure to loud noise. Night after night of high-decibel rocking with his band, Primus, has damaged his hearing. When this photo was taken in 1999, Claypool was not only performing but also protecting his remaining hearing. He is active with HEAR—Hearing Education and Awareness for Rockers.

VAUGHN YOUTZ / LIAISON

The Sexual-Reproductive System

Although senescence affects every body part, most 60-year-olds are able to do almost everything they could do 30 years earlier, albeit more slowly. Few are appalled by their wrinkled faces and diminished arm muscles. The one major exception to these generalities is the ability to reproduce, which late middle age makes virtually impossible for women and difficult for men.

When childbearing was crucial for survival of the species, this loss of fertility was devastating for couples who did not yet have several children. Now, in contrast, loss of fertility may be welcomed, not feared.

SEXUAL RESPONSIVENESS Sexual arousal occurs more slowly with age, and orgasm takes longer. For some couples, those slowdowns may be counterbalanced by reduced anxiety and better communication. Distress at slower responsiveness seems more associated with anxiety, interpersonal relationships, and expectations than with aging itself (Duplassie & Daniluk, 2006; L. Siegel & Siegel, 2007).

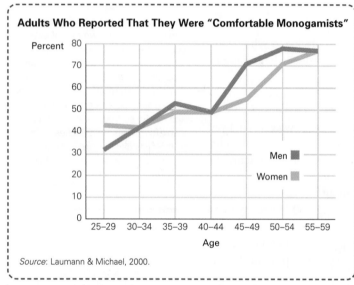

Adults Who Reported That They Were "Comfortable Monogamists"

Source: Laumann & Michael, 2000.

FIGURE 12.2 Sexually Satisfied with Monogamy In a cross section of more than 2,000 adults in the United States, most were "comfortable monogamists," a category for those who were happy with their one partner, with whom they usually had sex once or twice a week. Note that the percentages in this category were quite similar for men and women. The other categories differed by gender. For example, women could be "enthusiastic cohabiters," a category that included 25 percent of the women aged 25 to 39 and 10 percent of those aged 40 to 59. Men could be "enthusiastic polygamists," a category that included 10 percent of the 25- to 39-year-old men and 4 percent of those aged 40 to 59. Almost no women were polygamists, but about one-third of the men were called "venturesome cohabiters."

According to a study of Chicago couples conducted in the early 1990s, adults of all ages enjoy "very high levels of emotional satisfaction and physical pleasure from sex within their relationships" (Laumann & Michael, 2000, p. 250). That study found that men and women were most likely to report that they were "extremely satisfied" with sex if they were in a committed, monogamous relationship, a circumstance that was more likely to be true as they grew older (see Figure 12.2; Laumann & Michael, 2000).

That cohort not only witnessed the onset of better contraception but also had much higher rates of surgical sterilization than did earlier cohorts. In 1995 in the United States, half of all sexually active women older than 35 had been surgically sterilized. That meant they could enjoy sex without fear of pregnancy (most already had children).

Contemporary adults not only have fewer children but are more comfortable with nonsurgical contraception. Couples now are less troubled by age-related slowdowns if they are satisfied with their partner (J. A. Higgins & Hirsch, 2008).

FERTILITY ISSUES For couples who have not had as many children as they wish, aging adds to their regret. Infertility is most common in nations where medical care is scarce and sexually transmitted infections (STIs) are common. In the United States, about 15 percent of all couples are infertile (unable to conceive after trying for at least a year), partly because many postpone childbearing (Inhorn & van Balen, 2002). When couples in their 40s try to conceive, about half are infertile and the other half risk various complications.

As explained in Chapter 11, fertility peaks in the early 20s. From a biological (not psychological) perspective, women should try to conceive before age 30 and men before age 40. If they are unsuccessful, then medical interventions may help them conceive, but success is most likely if the couple is relatively young (Bhasin, 2007).

Causes of Infertility A common reason for male infertility is a low sperm count. Conception is most likely if a man ejaculates more than 20 million sperm per milliliter of semen, two-thirds of them mobile and viable, because each sperm's journey through the cervix and uterus is aided by its millions of fellow travelers. In fact, a new and surprisingly effective method of male contraception is a drug that reduces the sperm count to under 3 million (P. Y. Liu et al., 2006).

Daily, about 100 million sperm reach maturity after a developmental process that lasts about 75 days. Anything that impairs body functioning (e.g., fever, radiation, prescription drugs, time in a sauna, excessive stress, environmental toxins, drug abuse, alcoholism, cigarette smoking) over that 75-day period can reduce sperm number, shape, and motility (activity), thus making conception less likely.

Age also reduces sperm count. Low sperm count is probably the reason that men take five times as many months to impregnate a woman when they are over 45 as when they are under 25 (Hassan & Killick, 2003). (This study controlled for frequency of sex and age of the woman.)

As with men, female fertility is affected by anything that impairs physical functioning—not only diseases but also smoking, extreme dieting, and obesity. One specific disease may cause infertility, although the woman may not even be aware of it: Pelvic inflammatory disease can block a woman's fallopian tubes, preventing the sperm from reaching an ovum. Age impedes every step of reproduction—ovulation, implantation, fetal growth, and birth.

Assisted Reproductive Technology (ART) In the past 40 years, advances in medicine have solved about half of all fertility problems. Surgery can repair the male or female reproductive systems, and, if repair is impossible, *assisted reproductive technology* (ART) overcomes obstacles such as a low sperm count and blocked fallopian tubes, as explained in Chapter 2.

The most common ART method is **in vitro fertilization (IVF),** in which ova are surgically removed and fertilized in a laboratory (*in vitro* as contrasted with *in vivo*). Zygotes thus created divide until the eight- or sixteen-cell stage and then are implanted in the woman's uterus.

Currently, a typical IVF cycle also uses *intra-cytoplasmic sperm injection* (ICSI), whereby one sperm is inserted into one ovum. This avoids the possibility that a viable ovum will not be fertilized and solves the problem of low sperm count. It can also be used when a man is HIV-positive and his wife is HIV-negative. Such couples use condoms for sexual intercourse, but sperm are collected and washed in the laboratory to rid them of the virus before one is inserted into an ovum (Kato et al., 2006).

Only about one-third of all IVF cycles produce a pregnancy, since implantation does not always occur. Nonetheless, since 1978, when the world's first "test-tube baby" was born in England, IVF has produced more than a million babies from almost all nations, currently including 1 percent of all U.S. newborns (MMWR, June 8, 2007).

Complications and birth defects increase with IVF, especially when several zygotes are implanted at once (A. P. MacKay et al., 2006; Shevell et al., 2005). Low-birthweight twins or triplets are born in almost half of all IVF pregnancies in the United States (MMWR, June 8, 2007).

Although IVF helps many couples become parents, infertility remains a psychological burden for many adults. One woman's response captures the feeling of many, although certainly not all:

> I just cannot imagine ever feeling good about anything again. I do not even know if my husband will stay with me when he realizes that children are not an option for us. My guess is he will find someone else who will be able to give him a baby. Since I cannot do that, I cannot imagine that he would be happy with me. I am not happy with me.
>
> *[quoted in Deveraux & Hammerman, 1998]*

Of the 15 percent of couples who are infertile, some are not helped by medical means, which makes their distress greater. Others find the process (in clinics, not

● **UNDERSTANDING THE NUMBERS**
You read in Chapter 11 that at peak fertility, a newly married woman in her early 20s typically becomes pregnant within three months. That assumes that her husband is about her age. How long would pregnancy take, on average, if her husband is 50 years old?
Answer A year or more.

in vitro fertilization (IVF)
A technique in which ova (egg cells) are surgically removed from a woman and fertilized with sperm in a laboratory. After the original fertilized cells (the zygotes) have divided several times, they are inserted into the woman's uterus.

A Happy 67-Year-Old Mother This Romanian woman gave birth after in vitro fertilization. Other nations would not allow IVF at her age, but every nation has new fathers who are that age or older.

● **FOR DEEPER REFLECTION** Would you like to have twins? Is your answer based primarily on culture, personality, or statistics?

menopause
The time in middle age, usually around age 50, when a woman's menstrual periods cease completely and the production of estrogen, progesterone, and testosterone drops considerably. Strictly speaking, menopause is dated to one year after a woman's last menstrual period.

Could This Be a Grandmother? Yes. Most middle-aged women are strong and competent, like this grandmother cutting wood in rural Italy.

hormone replacement therapy (HRT)
Treatment to compensate for hormone reduction at menopause or following surgical removal of the ovaries. Such treatment, which usually involves estrogen and progesterone, minimizes menopausal symptoms and diminishes the risk of osteoporosis in later adulthood.

bedrooms) depressing and the babies (often twins) more demanding than anticipated. Naturally occurring pregnancies result in demanding infants as well, but greater expectations may lead to more disappointment. This is a problem for the parents, not for the children produced through ART, who usually develop as well as other children (Wagenaar et al., 2008).

MENOPAUSE During adulthood, the level of sex hormones circulating in the bloodstream declines—suddenly in women, gradually in men. As a result, sexual desire, frequency of intercourse, and odds of reproduction decrease. The specifics differ for women and men.

Women in Middle Age For women, sometime between ages 42 and 58 (the average age is 51), ovulation and menstruation stop because of a marked drop in production of several hormones (Wise, 2006). This is **menopause.** If a woman has a *hysterectomy* (surgical removal of the uterus) that includes removal of her ovaries, then sudden, premature menopause occurs. In the United States, one in four women, usually between ages 35 and 55, undergo this operation for various medical or personal reasons (M. K. Whiteman et al., 2008).

Removing the ovaries produces menopausal symptoms—most commonly, disturbances of body temperature, including hot flashes (feeling hot), hot flushes (looking hot), and cold sweats (feeling chilled) (Gold et al., 2006). Natural menopause produces the same feelings, but not suddenly and not in everyone. Symptoms vary by genes and ethnicity—with no marked disturbances for 40 percent of Asian Americans, 25 percent of European and Hispanic Americans, and 15 percent of African Americans.

The psychological consequences vary more than the physiological ones do. Some menopausal women find new zest, while others become depressed (L. S. Cohen et al., 2006). The historical Western notion that menopausal women "temporarily lose their minds" (Neugarten & Neugarten, 1986) contrasts with the traditional view among Hindi women in India that menopause represents liberation (Menon, 2001).

Estrogen Added Over the past 30 years, in **hormone replacement therapy (HRT),** millions of post-menopausal women took hormone supplements, usually estrogen combined with progesterone. Some did so to alleviate symptoms of menopause; others, to prevent osteoporosis (fragile bones), heart disease, strokes, or dementia. Correlational studies found that these diseases occurred less often among women who took hormones.

Researchers now believe that the true correlation was between low disease rates and higher income and better education. In fact, in controlled longitudinal studies in the United States, the Women's Health Initiative found that taking estrogen for 10 years or more *increased* heart disease, stroke, and breast cancer and did not prevent dementia (U.S. Preventive Services Task Force, 2002).

Estrogen replacement does reduce hot flashes and decrease osteoporosis, but women who want those benefits need to weigh the costs just as carefully. Surprisingly, culture seems more influential than a cost-benefit analysis on a woman's decision about taking estrogen. Many U.S. women are now more anxious about hormone replacement than the research warrants (Powledge, 2007) and have thus stopped or outright rejected hormone replacement therapy.

In contrast, many older women in Europe still take estrogen (Gompel & Plu-Bureau, 2007). The European form of estrogen differs from the one used in the Women's Health Initiative study; moreover, other factors, such as diet and exercise, make heart disease and dementia less common in Europe (Rosano et al., 2003).

Men in Middle Age Do men undergo anything like menopause? Some say yes, suggesting that the word **andropause** should be used to signify the lower testosterone levels of older men, which reduce sexual desire, erections, and muscle mass. Even with erection-inducing drugs such as Viagra and Levitra, sexual desire and speed of orgasm decline with age, as do many other physiological and cognitive functions.

But most experts think that the term *andropause* (or *male menopause*) is misleading, because it implies a sudden drop in reproductive ability or hormones, as happens in women. That does not occur in men (L. Siegel & Siegel, 2007). Men continue to produce sperm throughout their lives.

It may be sexual inactivity and anxiety more than age that reduces testosterone—a phenomenon similar to menopause but with a psychological, not physiological, cause. As one review explains, "Retirement, financial problems, unresolved anger, and dwindling social relationships can wreak havoc on some men's sense of masculinity and virility" (L. Siegel & Siegel, 2007, p. 239).

To combat the natural decline in testosterone, some men have turned to hormone replacement. Some women also take smaller amounts of testosterone to increase their sexual desire. But a longitudinal study with both sexes comparing testosterone with a placebo found no benefits (sexual or otherwise) from testosterone (Nair et al., 2006).

A few men naturally have very low testosterone levels, putting them at risk for many disabilities if they are not given supplemental hormones (Morales, 2008). Age-related lower testosterone, however, is no more pathological than menopause is. As one physician writes, most men would be better off learning about "the health benefits of physical activity . . . . [T]ell them to take the $1,200 they'll spend on testosterone per year and join a health club; buy a Stairmaster—they'll have money left over for their new clothes" (Casey, 2008, p. 48).

Researchers are understandably cautious; supplemental doses of hormones may be harmful for both men and women (Bhasin, 2007; Moffat, 2005). Disease prevention and better health depend much more on habits of life than on drugs.

andropause
A term coined to signify a drop in testosterone levels in older men, which normally results in a reduction in sexual desire, erections, and muscle mass. Also known as *male menopause*.

Naturally Happy Middle age seems to sit lightly on these married organic farmers in Virginia.

KEY Points

- Senescence is the process of aging. All parts of the body experience senescence once puberty is over and growth stops.

- The muscles, the five senses, and other physical systems become weaker with age, beginning by age 20 (or earlier); each part of the body follows a particular schedule.

- Sexual responsiveness is reduced with age, but the nature of a person's sexual relationship may be more important than physical changes.

- Fertility decreases with age as hormone levels decline—rapidly for women at menopause and more slowly for men. Replacing those hormones by taking supplements may involve health risks.

ESPECIALLY FOR Young Men A young man who impregnates a woman is often proud of his manhood. Is this reaction valid? (see response, page 426) →

RESPONSE FOR Young Men (from page 425) The answer depends on a person's definition of what a man is. No developmentalist would define a man as someone who has a high sperm count. ●

Poor Health Habits and Senescence

Age-related declines are accelerated by years of engaging in self-destructive behavior or living in an unhealthy community, high in stress and pollution. Susceptibility to almost all diseases and chronic conditions that are normally associated with aging—from arthritis to varicose veins—is powerfully affected by the routines of daily life (Abeles, 2007; Crews, 2003).

For instance, although all the senses diminish with age, every loud noise—traffic, music, construction—damages the eardrums to some extent. Some sources of noise can be avoided, but many young adults (especially men) work with jackhammers without protection or listen to music at ear-splitting levels. The resulting damage causes hearing deficits that become evident later on.

As another example, the decreasing sexual interest and reduced fertility that accompany aging are affected by the relationship between partners, the treatment of STIs, and the availability of contraception. These factors are more psychosocial than biological and are heavily influenced by culture and national policy.

As for birth control, scientific evidence of its benefits and side effects is less persuasive than local beliefs. More than half the people who use contraception in India rely on sterilization, more than half in Cuba use the intrauterine device (IUD), and more than half in Algeria (but very few in Japan) use the pill (T. M. Sullivan et al., 2006). Because medical contraception is unavailable to most couples in Bangladesh, they rely on early abortion to control family size (Gipson & Hindin, 2008).

Now we explore three health habits that accelerate senescence: drug abuse, overeating, and inactivity.

Drug Abuse

Drug abuse, especially of illegal drugs, decreases over adulthood, primarily because of maturity and marriage. Of the illegal drugs, marijuana is the most frequently used (about 8 percent of those aged 25 to 34 use it) and impairs not only cognition but also oral health. More than one-fourth of people in their early 30s who smoke marijuana more than once a week have serious gum disease (Thomson et al., 2008). Despite the popularity of marijuana, by far the most commonly abused drugs in adulthood are tobacco and alcohol; they are our focus here.

TOBACCO Notable declines in cigarette smoking have occurred in the United States over the past 50 years. In 1970, half of adult men and one-third of women smoked, but by 2007 only 24 percent of men and 19 percent of women did (see Figure 12.3; U.S. Bureau of the Census, 2008). Smoking rates have also fallen in Mexico and Canada (Franco-Marina et al., 2006; Shields, 2007).

Worldwide trends are less encouraging. Almost half the men and women in Germany, Denmark, Poland, Holland, Switzerland, and Spain are smokers. In developing nations, rates of smoking are rising: More than half the men and more than one-tenth of the women now smoke. Variations are dramatic from nation to nation. For instance, smoking is allowed in most Pakistani homes (92 percent) but in few Guatemalan ones (17 percent) (Bloch et al., 2008). Smoking-related cancers throughout the world are increasing (J. Mackay & Eriksen, 2002; Mascie-Taylor & Karim, 2003). The rate of lung cancer deaths in China, where 350 million adults now smoke, almost tripled from 1975 to 2005 (Xin, 2008).

Although cigarettes are available everywhere, variations among nations, cohorts, and the sexes are evidence that smoking is affected by social norms, laws, and advertising. Norms have changed: 50 years ago cigarettes were free for everyone in the U.S. armed forces and some doctors endorsed cigarettes in advertisements. For developmental health, the decline in smoking in North America is heartening; the hope is that other nations will follow that example.

Guess His Age A man puffs on a bidi, a flavored cigarette, in Bangalore, India. He looks elderly but is actually middle-aged. He is at risk of being among the 1 million Indians who die each year of smoking-related causes.

AP PHOTO / AIJAZ RAHI

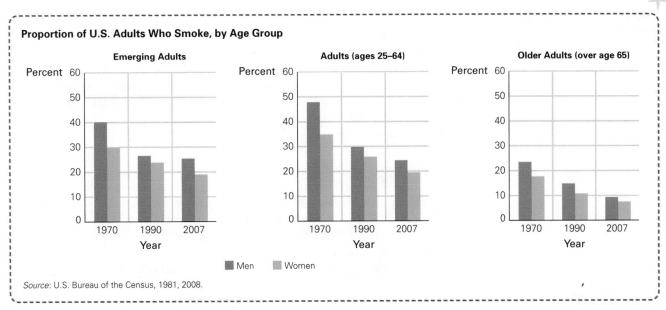

Proportion of U.S. Adults Who Smoke, by Age Group

Source: U.S. Bureau of the Census, 1981, 2008.

FIGURE 12.3 Quitters Win This figure shows the well-known historical declines in the number of people who start smoking and also shows that many adults quit. Half of all men aged 25 to 64 in 1970 smoked; 35 years later, almost all were over age 65 and almost all had quit. (Of course some had died, but most of that cohort were still alive and smoke-free.)

OBSERVATION QUIZ

Are the two sexes growing closer together or farther apart in rates of smoking in the United States? (see answer, page 428) →

ALCOHOL The harm from cigarettes is dose-related: Each additional puff, each additional day of smoking, each breath of secondhand smoke makes cancer, heart disease, strokes, and emphysema more likely. No such linear harm results from drinking alcohol. In fact, alcohol can be beneficial: People who drink wine, beer, or spirits *in moderation*—no more than two drinks a day—live longer than abstainers.

The primary reason is that alcohol reduces coronary heart disease and strokes. It increases HDL (high-density lipoprotein), the "good" form of cholesterol, and reduces LDL (low-density lipoprotein), the "bad" cholesterol that causes clogged arteries and blood clots. It also lowers blood pressure (Panagiotakos et al., 2007; Wannamethee & Shaper, 1999).

However, moderation is impossible for some people. Alcoholics find it easier to drink nothing than to have one, and only one, drink a day. As explained in Chapter 11, heavy drinking increases the risk of violent death. It is also implicated in 60 diseases, including not only damage to the liver but also cancer of the breast, stomach, and throat (Hampton, 2005).

There are stark international variations in alcohol abuse. It is extremely rare in Muslim nations where alcohol is illegal, but it causes about half the deaths of Russian men under age 60 (Leon et al., 2007). About 20 percent of U.S. adults had five or more drinks on a single occasion in the past year; such *binge drinking* signals a problem (National Center for Health Statistics, 2007).

Some experts think that "alcohol causes a disproportionate burden of harm in poorer countries" (Gonzalez, quoted in Grimm, 2008, p. 863) because prevention and treatment strategies have not been fully established in many less developed nations. There is no doubt about it: Alcohol in moderation may be healthy, but lack of moderation is often deadly.

Overeating

Eating fruits and vegetables is beneficial, yet many adults choose high-calorie, low-nutrient foods instead. Few U.S. adults (only 27 percent) eat three daily servings of vegetables, a rate lower than that five years ago (MMWR, March 16, 2007).

Too many high-calorie foods combined with too little activity impair health, especially when the combination leads to obesity—as it does for more than 10 percent of all adults worldwide (Wisse et al., 2007). Excess weight increases the risk of every chronic disease, including diabetes. As an editorial in the *Journal of the American*

Medical Association warned, "Obesity is a worldwide epidemic and will be followed by a worldwide epidemic of diabetes" (Bray, 2003, p. 1853).

The United States is the world leader for both epidemics. Of all U.S. adults, 66 percent are overweight (with a body mass index, or BMI, above 25); of those, 33 percent are obese (with a BMI of 30 or more) and 5 percent are morbidly obese (with a BMI of 40 or more) (National Center for Health Statistics, 2008). (BMI is discussed in Chapter 7, and a BMI chart for adults is given in Table 12.1.)

Even if a person eats and exercises as much as ever, metabolism decreases by one-third between ages 20 and 60. To maintain the same weight, adults need to eat less and move more each year. Few adults do so.

It has been known for decades that body weight is partly determined by genetics, but recent research has found two alleles that correlate with both diabetes and weight (Frayling et al., 2007; Herbert et al., 2006). The *increase* in rates of obesity cannot be blamed on genes, however, because genes change little from one generation to the next. Culture must be at fault.

Some cultural influences are apparent, since few nations have as many overweight adults as the United States. The typical U.S. family consumes a diet that is meat-based, high in fat, and low in fiber. In contrast, the "Mediterranean" diet common in Italy and Greece features lots of fiber, fish, and heart-healthy olive oil. The Chinese eat more vegetables and less meat; the French gather at the table to talk as well as to eat, thus consuming smaller portions (Rozin et al., 2003).

Calculating Adult BMI One objective assessment of appropriate weight is the amount of body fat as represented by the body mass index (BMI). A person's BMI is calculated by dividing his or her weight (in kilograms) by height (in meters) squared. Since most U.S. readers do not know their weight and height in the metric system, this table calculates BMI for them. A healthy BMI is between 19 and 25. A very muscular person may be healthy at a BMI of 26 or even 27, because muscle and bone weigh more than fat.

TABLE 12.1 Body Mass Index (BMI)

To find your BMI, locate your height in the first column, then look across that row. Your BMI appears at the top of the column that contains your weight.

BMI	19	20	21	22	23	24	25	26	27	28	29	30	35	40
Height (in feet and inches)							Weight (in pounds)							
4'10"	91	96	100	105	110	115	119	124	129	134	138	143	167	191
4'11"	94	99	104	109	114	119	124	128	133	138	143	148	173	198
5'0"	97	102	107	112	118	123	128	133	138	143	148	153	179	204
5'1"	100	106	111	116	122	127	132	137	143	148	153	158	185	211
5'2"	104	109	115	120	126	131	136	142	147	153	158	164	191	218
5'3"	107	113	118	124	130	135	141	146	152	158	163	169	197	225
5'4"	110	116	122	128	134	140	145	151	157	163	169	174	204	232
5'5"	114	120	126	132	138	144	150	156	162	168	174	180	210	240
5'6"	118	124	130	136	142	148	155	161	167	173	179	186	216	247
5'7"	121	127	134	140	146	153	159	166	172	178	185	191	223	255
5'8"	125	131	138	144	151	158	164	171	177	184	190	197	230	262
5'9"	128	135	142	149	155	162	169	176	182	189	196	203	236	270
5'10"	132	139	146	153	160	167	174	181	188	195	202	207	243	278
5'11"	136	143	150	157	165	172	179	186	193	200	208	215	250	286
6'0"	140	147	154	162	169	177	184	191	199	206	213	221	258	294
6'1"	144	151	159	166	174	182	189	197	204	212	219	227	265	302
6'2"	148	155	163	171	179	186	194	202	210	218	225	233	272	311
6'3"	152	160	168	176	184	192	200	208	216	224	232	240	279	319
6'4"	156	164	172	180	189	197	205	213	221	230	238	246	287	328
			Normal					Overweight				Obese		

Source: National Heart, Lung, and Blood Institute, n.d.

Regional differences are evident within nations as well. For example, the rate of obesity among adults aged 25 to 65 in Mississippi is almost double that in Colorado (MMWR, July 18, 2008).

Recognition of such differences is evident in a report on the decline in fruit and vegetable consumption among U.S. adults, which concluded that "nutritional interventions should go beyond increasing individual awareness and target the family, local community, and overall society" (MMWR, March 16, 2007, p. 217). Each person chooses what to eat, but that choice is affected by the actions of other people, by food and restaurant advertisements, and by food availability.

Inactivity

Regular physical activity at every stage of life protects against serious illness, even if a person has other undesirable health habits, such as smoking and overeating. Exercise reduces blood pressure; strengthens the heart and lungs; and makes depression, osteoporosis, heart disease, arthritis, and even some cancers less likely. Health benefits from exercise are substantial for men and women, old and young, former sports stars and those who never joined a team.

By contrast, sitting for long hours correlates with almost every unhealthy condition, especially heart disease and diabetes, both of which carry additional health hazards (Hu et al., 2003). Even a little movement—gardening, light housework, walking up the stairs or to the bus—helps. Walking briskly for 30 minutes a day, five days a week, is better. More intense exercise (e.g., swimming, jogging, bicycling) is ideal. It is possible to exercise too much, but almost no adults aged 25 to 65 do so.

The close connection between exercise and health, both physical and mental, is well known. This is not merely a correlation but a cause: People who are more fit are likely to resist disease and to feel healthier as they age (Carnethon et al., 2003; Shirom et al., 2008). In reality, however, rates of exercise decrease with age, as adults take on marriage, parenthood, and career responsibilities.

Personal friendships and public policies can prevent this decline in exercise. To be specific:

- *Friendship.* People exercise more if their friends do. Adults benefit from meeting friends for a jog instead of a beer or for a game of tennis instead of a movie. Husbands and wives affect each other's habits of exercise, drug use, and nutrition both directly and indirectly (Falba & Sindelar, 2008).

- *Communities.* Adults exercise more in neighborhoods with walking and biking paths, ample fields and parks, and subsidized pools and gyms. Most communities have no such places, but some do: Germany and the Netherlands have tripled their bike paths, banished cars from many streets, and added two years to their adult citizens' average life span (Pucher & Dijkstra, 2003). Exercise-friendly communities reduce their residents' obesity, hypertension, and depression (R. J. Jackson, 2003; McElroy, 2002).

Developmentalists have learned that the link between cognition and behavior is fragile. Adults know they should exercise; they make resolutions, buy special equipment, and join gyms. However, changing habits is a complex proposition; social scientists are seeking ways to encourage exercise among adults (Conner, 2008).

Preventive health care, including regular exercise, is particularly urgent in the United States. One reason is that rates of healthy diet and exercise are lower than in other nations. Another is that the cost of treating disease in the United States is the highest in the world—an estimated $7,000 per resident per year (Kuttner, 2008).

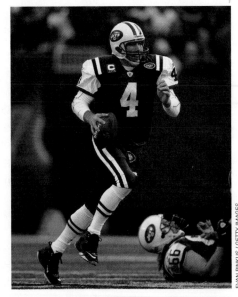

Body and Mind By keeping himself fit both physically and mentally, star quarterback Brett Favre has sustained an unusually long career in professional football. After 16 years with the Green Bay Packers and one year with the New York Jets, he signed a two-year contract with the Minnesota Vikings in 2009, at age 39.

Getting Somewhere To help employers reduce their health-care costs and to encourage employees to keep fit, a noted manufacturer of office furniture offers a work station that combines a treadmill and a computer.

EVAN PINKUS / GETTY IMAGES

TIMOTHY A. CLARY / AFP / GETTY IMAGES

ESPECIALLY FOR Doctors and Nurses If you had to choose between recommending various screening tests and recommending various lifestyle changes to a 35-year-old, which would you do? (see response, page 432) →

> ## KEY points
>
> - Sound health habits can slow down the aging process.
>
> - The dangers of cigarettes are linear, with each exposure increasing the harm. Moderate alcohol use can be beneficial to the heart, but alcohol abuse can be deadly.
>
> - Good nutrition underlies health; the fact that many adults are overweight or obese poses a danger to their health.
>
> - Exercise is protective, but adults tend to move less with age. Friends and communities can encourage exercise, although not all of them do so.

Measuring Health

Most of the U.S. expenditure on health goes to preventing death among people who are already sick rather than protecting health among people who are well. Yet health is much more than not dying. There are at least four distinct measures of health: mortality, morbidity, disability, and vitality.

Mortality and Morbidity

Death is the ultimate loss of health. This basic indicator, **mortality,** is usually expressed as the annual number of deaths per 1,000 population. The rate is often adjusted for age: A nation with few old people would be expected to have few deaths, so that country's age-adjusted rate is higher than the actual number of people who died per 1,000.

The age-adjusted mortality rate among people in the United States in 2004 was 8.0. The figure for various age, gender, and racial groups in the United States ranged from about 0.1 (1 in 10,000 deaths per year for Asian American girls aged 5 to 14) to 153 (about 1 in 6 deaths per year for European American men over age 85) (U.S. Bureau of the Census, 2007).

Mortality statistics are compiled from death certificates, which indicate age, sex, and immediate cause of death. This practice allows valid international and historical comparisons because deaths have been counted and recorded for decades—sometimes even for centuries. Japan has the world's lowest age-adjusted mortality rate (about 5 per 1,000) and Sierra Leone, the highest (about 35 per 1,000); both of these rates are markedly lower than a few decades ago.

Another measure of health is **morbidity** (from the Latin word for "disease"), which refers to illnesses of all kinds—acute, chronic, and fatal. Morbidity statistics are based on surveys in which people are asked to identify any diseases they have and doctors are asked to report on illnesses among a sample of their patients.

Morbidity does not necessarily correlate with mortality. For example, in many African nations, a parasite causes "river blindness," destroying energy and eyesight in millions but not directly causing death (Basáñez, 2006). In the United States, almost half of older women have osteoarthritis; none die of it.

Disability and Vitality

Health is not only the absence of death and disease (mortality and morbidity) but also the ability to enjoy life, as indicated by disability and vitality.

Disability refers to difficulty in performing normal activities of daily life because of a "physical, mental, or emotional condition" (U.S. Bureau of the Census, 2008). Limitation in functioning (not severity of disease) is the hallmark of disability. Disability

---

mortality
Death. As a measure of health, mortality usually refers to the number of deaths each year per 1,000 members of a given population.

● UNDERSTANDING THE NUMBERS
How does the age-adjusted death rate in the United States (0.8 percent) compare with that of Japan (0.5 percent) and Sierra Leone (3.5 percent)?

Answer The U.S. rate is 60 percent higher (3 additional deaths per 1,000) than Japan's but less than one-fourth the rate (27 fewer deaths per 1,000) in Sierra Leone.

morbidity
Disease. As a measure of health, morbidity refers to the rate of diseases of all kinds—physical and emotional, acute (sudden), chronic (ongoing), and fatal—in a given population.

disability
Long-term difficulty in performing normal activities of daily life because of some physical, emotional, or mental condition.

does not necessarily equal morbidity: In the United States, of the people who are disabled, 27 percent consider their health very good or excellent, as do 60 percent of those who are not disabled (MMWR, October 3, 2008).

Normal activities, and hence ability, vary by social context. For example, people who cannot walk 200 feet without resting could be said to have a disability if their job requires walking (a mail carrier) but not if they sit at work (a post office clerk).

Disability hurts a society more than mortality or morbidity does, because disabled persons are less able to contribute to the general welfare. Measures to reduce disability (e.g., public areas that include wheelchair ramps) are one reason the disability rate has decreased in the United States (Murabito et al., 2008). To be specific, 10 percent of U.S. adults aged 25 to 65 were disabled in 2005 compared with 12 percent in 1960.

The fourth measure of health, **vitality,** refers to how healthy and energetic—physically, intellectually, and socially—an individual feels. Vitality is *joie de vivre,* the zest for living, the love of life (Gigante, 2007). A person can feel terrific despite having a serious disease with disability. For example, in a Japanese study of people who had cancer and were in pain, some (not most) were high in vitality (Fujimori et al., 2006). Vitality is affected by personality and social affirmation more than by biological functioning.

Disabled But Vital Therapists find that the most serious consequence of losing a limb is losing the will to live. This young man not only learned to cope with crutches after losing a leg but also regained his spirit: He ran all 26.2 miles (42 kilometers) of the New York City Marathon.

vitality
A measure of health that refers to how healthy and energetic—physically, emotionally, and socially—an individual actually feels.

Variations in Health

Gender, socioeconomic status (SES), and culture affect lifestyle patterns and health choices. Consequently, gender, SES, and heritage influence mortality, morbidity, disability, and vitality, sometimes in unexpected ways.

GENDER DIFFERENCES Mortality is lower for women. Worldwide, women live five years longer than men, with marked national variations. On average, men die 14 years earlier than women in Russia, 5 years earlier in the United States, and 2 years earlier in Nigeria. Worldwide, old women outnumber old men (by 2 to 1 in the United States at age 85) not because more old men die but because more younger men and boys die. The sex ratio favors boys at birth, is about equal at age 20, and tilts toward women from then on.

This gender difference in mortality might be biological—the second X chromosome or extra estrogen could protect women from some illnesses (Crews, 2003). Or it might be cultural, since women tend to have more friends and take better care of themselves. One public health expert wrote:

> Men are socialized to project strength, individuality, autonomy, dominance, stoicism, and physical aggression, and to avoid demonstrations of emotion or vulnerability that could be construed as weakness. These [characteristics] . . . combine to increase health risks.
>
> *[D. R. Williams, 2003, p. 726]*

On other measures of health, women may suffer more. Both sexes notice superficial signs of aging in women more than in men. Vitality may be reduced if a 50-year-old

RESPONSE FOR Doctors and Nurses
(from page 430) Obviously, much
depends on the specific patient. Overall, however, far more people develop
disease or die because of years of
poor health habits than because of
various illnesses not spotted in time.
With some exceptions, age 35 is too
early to detect incipient cancers or
circulatory problems, but it's prime
time for stopping cigarette smoking,
curbing alcohol abuse, and improving
exercise and diet. ●

woman feels "past her prime." Women have higher rates of depression than men. Indeed, for every chronic disease except heart disease in middle age, women have higher rates of morbidity (Cleary et al., 2004). Women are more often disabled as well: A higher percentage of women cannot run, lift, or see as well as they would like (although fewer women than men have trouble hearing).

SOCIOECONOMIC STATUS AND HEALTH Money and education protect health in every nation. Well-educated, financially secure adults live longer and avoid morbidity and disability more than their fellow citizens.

According to an economist who analyzed historical U.S. data, after age 35 the life span increases by 1.7 years for each year of education (Lleras-Muney, 2005). The reason may be that education teaches healthy habits. Obesity and cigarette smoking in the United States are almost twice as common among adults with the least education compared to those with post-college degrees.

A related explanation is that education leads to higher income, which allows better medical care as well as a home distant from areas of high pollution and violence. Or education may merely be a marker for intelligence. A longitudinal study of an entire cohort in Scotland found that IQ scores in childhood were more protective of health throughout adulthood than was almost any other factor (Deary et al., 2008).

For whatever reason, differences can be dramatic. The 10 million Americans with the highest SES (and the best health care) outlive—by about 30 years—the 10 million with the lowest SES, who live in rundown areas (C. J. L. Murray et al., 2006).

SES is protective between nations as well as within them. Rich nations have lower rates of disease, injury, and death than poor nations. For example, a baby born in 2005 in East Asia can expect to live to age 73; in Southeast Asia, to 63; and in sub-Saharan Africa, to 48 (World Health Organization, 2006).

Some rich nations do better than others, however. The United States has a lower life expectancy and a higher morbidity rate than several poorer nations (i.e., nations with a lower gross domestic product per capita)—among them, Spain, Portugal, Ireland, and Greece (Burd-Sharps et al., 2008).

CULTURE AND HEALTH Within and between nations, economic and health disparities often follow ethnic and geographic divisions (Marmot & Fuhrer, 2004). In the United States, among Hispanics, Cuban Americans live years longer than Puerto Rican Americans; among Asians, Japanese Americans live longer than Filipino Americans; among European Americans, city dwellers live longer than rural residents. No matter what their ethnicity is, people who live in the Northwest are healthier than those who live in the Southeast.

Certain diseases, particularly lung and breast cancer, were once called *diseases of affluence* because they were more common among the rich than the poor (Krieger, 2002, 2003). These diseases were also more common in wealthier ethnic groups: European Americans had higher death rates from those cancers than did African Americans. The reason was thought to be more genetic than cultural—but no longer. When smoking became cheaper (between 1920 and 1950) and cancer better diagnosed, the so-called diseases of affluence became more common among African Americans, and cultural rather than genetic or economic reasons were suggested.

In truth, making a distinction among income, education, genes, and culture is very difficult because, as you remember from Chapter 1, all these factors overlap. For instance, currently African American women are more likely to die of breast cancer than women of other U.S. ethnic groups, but medical researchers are

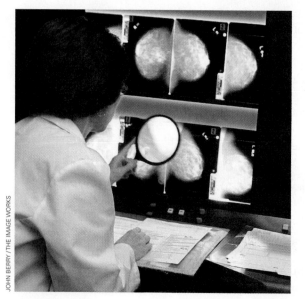

Looking for Trouble A radiologist examines mammograms for breast abnormalities, such as tiny lumps that cannot be felt but may be malignant. The National Cancer Institute recommends a screening mammogram every one to two years for women who are 40 or older or who have certain risk factors for breast cancer.

JOHN BERRY /THE IMAGE WORKS

not sure why. The reason could be genetic, it could be quality of health care, it could be cultural eating habits, or it could be cultural fear of diagnosis and treatment (J. Couzin, 2007a).

Data on immigrants to the United States further complicate the relationship between culture and health. By almost every measure, immigrants are healthier than the native-born. For example, see Figure 12.4, which shows the relationship between U.S. or foreign birth and one measure of heart attack risk (Lutsey et al., 2008).

The most extensive research on the health of immigrants has involved people of Mexican background living in the United States. The data are decisive: Those born in Mexico are usually very poor, Spanish-speaking, and of low education, yet they are healthier and more vital than the average U.S.-born Mexican American.

The same trends are apparent in all immigrant groups. Children and grandchildren of immigrants tend to surpass their elders in education, income, and English fluency, but with higher SES and more exposure to American culture come higher rates of obesity and of virtually every illness (Barger & Gallo, 2008; Bates et al., 2008).

One suggested explanation for this paradox is that healthy people of high SES are more likely to emigrate; then their good health protects them as they struggle in their new nation. In other words, they bring their "social capital" with them, which continues to sustain them even though they may be at the bottom of the social ladder in the United States. However, the data suggest that something beyond this "healthy migrant" theory is at work (Bates et al., 2008). Something within the U.S. culture may impair health.

Overall, although health and wealth are positively correlated, the relationship is not always found when cultural differences are included. Sometimes more wealth leads to more sickness rather than less.

> There is a complex causal web involving socioeconomic determinants such as income, education, employment, ... environmental factors such as tobacco use, physical activity, diet, ... [and] physiological factors such as cholesterol levels, blood pressure, and genes that influences mortality and disability.
>
> [C. Michaud et al., 2001, p. 537]

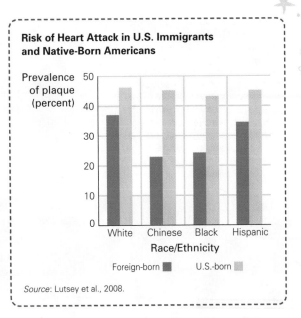

Risk of Heart Attack in U.S. Immigrants and Native-Born Americans

Source: Lutsey et al., 2008.

FIGURE 12.4 Immigrants Are Healthier Members of all these ethnic groups who were born in the United States are more likely to have arterial plaque than are their counterparts who were born elsewhere and emigrated to the United States. Plaque is a buildup of fatty substances (including cholesterol) that constricts blood flow inside an artery, increasing the risk of heart attack.

● **FOR DEEPER REFLECTION** Why are first-generation immigrants healthier than their descendants in the United States?

Blue Skies Ahead Turkey is one of the nations where children still die at high rates, but some adults live long, happy, and active lives. The social context, illustrated by this man riding a donkey, is the reason.

All Equally Sick? These photographs were used in a study that assessed physicians' biases in recommending treatment (Schulman et al., 1999). These supposed "heart patients" were described as identical in occupation, symptoms, and every other respect except age, race, and sex. However, the participating physicians who looked at the photos and the fictitious medical charts that accompanied them did not make identical recommendations. The appropriate treatment for the supposed symptoms would be catheterization, but for the younger, White, or male patients, catheterization was recommended 90, 91, and 91 percent of the time, respectively; for the older, female, or Black patients, 86, 85, and 85 percent of the time, respectively. Are you surprised that the bias differences were less than 10 percent? Or are you surprised that physician bias existed at all?

● **FOR DEEPER REFLECTION** Is health primarily a matter of personal choice, cultural values, or social policies?

Certainly for individuals, the factors already mentioned—drug use, nutrition, exercise—affect health. This is useful knowledge, especially for people from groups that are less healthy. For instance, adults of American Indian descent have, on average, the lowest SES and shortest life span among U.S. citizens, but 10,000 American Indians are over 90 years old. Many of them are still quite able and vital, and few—if any—are obese, inactive, or addicted to drugs. There is a lesson here for everyone: The personal choices that we make may enable us to defy demographic predictions.

KEY Points

- Health can be measured in at least four ways. Mortality, or death rate, is the easiest way to compare nations and cohorts: People are expected to live decades longer in the twenty-first century than in the twentieth, and decades longer in wealthy nations and neighborhoods than in poor ones.

- Morbidity measures chronic illness, which is more common in women than in men.

- Disability is indicated by difficulty performing daily tasks. It varies by social circumstances and demands, and it affects a society more than any other measure of health.

- Vitality is the joy of life. It is sought by everyone, affected by culture, and does not necessarily correlate with the other three measures of health.

Cognition in Adulthood

Awareness of the crucial impact of personal choices brings us to cognition over the years of adulthood. Do adults grow smarter or dumber with age? As you will see, the answer depends on how the evidence about aging and the brain is interpreted.

The Aging Brain

Like every other part of the body, the brain slows down with age. Neurons fire more slowly, and messages sent from the axon of one neuron are not picked up as quickly by the dendrite of another neuron. Furthermore, the total size of the brain decreases. Already by middle adulthood, there are fewer neurons and synapses (Buckner et al., 2006).

DIFFICULTY WITH MULTITASKING Overall, because of these brain changes, reactions take longer. Complex memory tasks (e.g., repeating a series of eight numbers, then adding the first four, deleting the fifth one, subtracting the next two, and multiplying the new total by the last one—all in your head) become impossible.

Multitasking becomes more difficult with every passing decade (Reuter-Lorenz & Sylvester, 2005). For example, although driving while talking on a cell phone is dangerous for everyone, this is particularly true for older drivers because the brain focuses on the conversation, making it difficult to perceive what the eyes see (Strayer & Drews, 2007). Some jurisdictions require drivers to use hands-free phones, but these misguided laws have not reduced traffic accidents resulting from cell phone use; the brain is the problem, not the hands. Some say that passenger conversation is equally distracting, but in fact years of practice have taught experienced drivers and adult passengers (not young children) when to stop talking and focus on the road (S. G. Charlton, 2009).

For many tasks, aging makes it harder to process two things at once; distractions become more difficult to ignore (Park & Gutchess, 2005). Some distractions are obvious (a noisy overheard conversation), but others are hidden, such as emotional stress.

Exactly what is distracting, and to whom, depends on many factors. For instance, one study of cognitive processing and racial prejudice found that White (but not Black) participants were distracted by reading about overt, or open, prejudice, whereas Black (but not White) participants were affected by reading about covert, or hidden, prejudice (Salvatore & Shelton, 2007).

THE NEED FOR SLEEP Regular sleep is increasingly essential for proper brain functioning. Skipping a night's sleep slows down thinking of all kinds, particularly memory (M. P. Walker & Stickgold, 2006). This was proven with hospital interns, who used to be on call for up to 48 hours at a time, snatching only catnaps when possible (Lockley et al., 2004). The lack of sleep caused them to make many errors, which eventually led to new regulations (not always enforced) requiring that doctors-in-training be on duty no more than 24 hours at a time and that they have at least 10 hours of rest between assignments.

Sleep deprivation and drugs can make a person appear to be awake when brain scans indicate that he or she is actually asleep. In such situations, confused thoughts and dangerous actions often result (Gunn & Gunn, 2007). Senescence makes these problems worse; disrupted sleep is characteristic of aging (as well as of diseases of all kinds) (Foley et al., 2004).

SERIOUS BRAIN CONFUSION As we will discuss soon, most adults think quite well and even improve in some cognitive abilities as they age. However, beginning in the 30s, brain power shows a "shallow decline," which becomes steeper at about age 60

ESPECIALLY FOR Drivers A number of states have passed laws requiring that hands-free headphones be worn by people who use cell phones while driving. Do those measures cut down on accidents? (see response, page 436) →

RESPONSE FOR Drivers (from page 435) No. Car accidents occur when the mind is distracted, not the hands. ●

(Dangour et al., 2007, p. 54). Adults compensate with various strategies, using more parts of their brain when challenged. As a result, brain declines are rarely noticeable until late adulthood, except on fMRI or PET brain scans (Buckner et al., 2006; Reuter-Lorenz & Sylvester, 2005).

A few individuals (less than 1 percent under age 65) experience much greater brain loss, both in reduced connections between neurons and in total brain volume. They "encounter a catastrophic rate of cognitive decline, passing through . . . the dementia threshold" (Dangour et al., 2007, p. 54).

When dementia does occur before old age, it rarely comes as a complete surprise. A younger person who develops dementia may have inherited a dominant gene for Alzheimer disease; may have Down syndrome or another serious genetic condition; may have suffered major brain damage through trauma (such as being hit repeatedly on the head); or may have had a massive stroke (which can cause extensive damage by interrupting blood flow to the brain).

Several lifestyle factors also make brain loss more common.

- *Drug abuse.* Consuming large quantities of alcohol over decades puts a person at risk for a disease called Wernike-Korsakoff syndrome ("wet brain"), signified by irreversible brain damage. Memory, especially of personal experiences, is particularly shaky (Borsutzky et al., 2008). Smoking cigarettes also causes cognitive decline over the years of adulthood (Nooyens et al., 2008). Other psychoactive drugs (including prescription pain relievers) also damage the brain. One reason might be severe vitamin deficiency: Many drugs interfere with vitamin absorption and reduce appetite (Stacey & Sullivan, 2004).

- *Excessive stress.* Stress hormones disrupt thought processes. Though usually temporary, this disruption may lead to depression, an overactive immune system, and harm to the brain if stress is ongoing (Pace et al., 2006).

- *Poor circulation.* Everything that protects the circulatory system—such as exercise, a healthy diet, and low blood pressure—also protects the brain. Hypertension (high blood pressure) impairs cognition, beginning in middle age (Elias et al., 2004).

- *Viruses.* Although the blood–brain barrier keeps most viruses out of the brain, some viruses and infections cross this barrier. The most dramatic example is HIV, which can attack the brain, causing personality changes and dementia. Several other viruses (e.g., the prion that causes mad cow disease) destroy the brain.

Overall, past education, current intellectual activity, exercise, and overall health all promote brain function. To think your best, keep moving and learning.

Research on Age and Intelligence

For most of the twentieth century, almost everyone—scientists and the general public alike—assumed that there is such a thing as "intelligence" and that some people are smarter than others because they have more of it. Charles Spearman (1927) famously proposed that there is a single entity, **general intelligence,** which he called *g.*

general intelligence (g)
A construct based on the idea that intelligence is one basic trait that involves all cognitive abilities, which people possess in varying amounts.

Spearman contended that, although *g* cannot be measured directly, it can be inferred from various abilities, such as vocabulary, memory, and reasoning. Therefore, a person could be assigned one overall IQ score, based on carefully standardized tests of intelligence, and that score would indicate whether the person was a genius, average, or retarded, as explained in Chapter 7.

The idea that *g* exists continues to be influential (Jensen, 1998; R. J. Sternberg & Grigorenko, 2002). Many scientists are trying to find one common factor—perhaps genes, early brain development, or some specific aspect of health—that undergirds IQ. Much research has focused on changes in IQ scores over the life span.

CROSS-SECTIONAL RESEARCH For the first half of the twentieth century, psychologists were convinced that intelligence rises in childhood, peaks in adolescence, and then gradually declines. This belief seemed to be confirmed by the evidence. For instance, the U.S. Army tested the aptitude of all literate draftees during World War I. When the scores of men of various ages were compared, intellectual ability peaked at about age 18, stayed at that level until the mid-20s, and then began to decline (Yerkes, 1923).

Similar results came from a classic study of 1,191 individuals, aged 10 to 60, from 19 New England villages. Most of them had lived in the same village all their lives, as had all their relatives, which meant that the scientists could test people of various ages who shared genes and experiences. The IQ scores of these New Englanders peaked between ages 18 and 21 and then gradually fell, with the average 55-year-old scoring the same as the average 14-year-old (H. E. Jones & Conrad, 1933).

NATIONAL ARCHIVES

Smart Enough for the Trenches? These young men were drafted to fight in World War I. Younger men (about age 17 or 18) did better on the military's intelligence tests than did slightly older ones.

OBSERVATION QUIZ
Beyond the test itself, what conditions of the testing favored the teenaged men? (see answer, page 439) →

LONGITUDINAL RESEARCH Like all other researchers, Nancy Bayley knew that "the invariable findings had indicated that most intellectual functions decrease after about 21 years of age" (Bayley, 1966, p. 117). But in the 1950s, when she retested adults who had first taken IQ tests as gifted children in 1921, she found that their scores *increased* after age 20 (Bayley & Oden, 1955).

Did their high childhood intelligence protect these people from the usual age-related declines? To explore this possibility, Bayley then retested 36-year-olds who had not been particularly bright children. These individuals had been selected in infancy as representative of the population of Berkeley, California, and had taken IQ tests every few years. Far from peaking at age 21, most of them kept improving on tests of vocabulary, comprehension, and information (Bayley, 1966).

Why did this research contradict previous conclusions? As you remember from Chapter 1, each cohort has unique life experiences. People born early in the twentieth century developed cognitive skills that differed from those developed by people born decades later. Over the century, more people attended high school and college, and everyone was exposed to new sources of information from newspapers and radio (and, later, television and the Internet). These advances allowed adults to continue learning, improving their intellect.

Developmentalists now realize that earlier cross-sectional research comparing adults of various ages did not take into account the fact that older adults who left school by eighth grade might not have fully developed their intellect, especially as IQ tests measure it. Therefore, while cross-sectional research would find each generation scoring higher than the previous one, longitudinal data would show that the older adults were still learning.

Comparing 18-year-olds with 50-year-olds might lead to the mistaken conclusion that people become less intelligent after age 18. As best we know, intellectual potential has not changed over the decades. The difference seems to be that younger generations are able to develop more of their potential than members of older generations could.

The *Flynn effect*, first mentioned in Chapter 7, refers to the fact that younger cohorts outscore older ones on IQ tests (Flynn, 2007). In fact, the norms of IQ tests have been raised several times; a young adult who scores at the level that classified adults as intellectually gifted 100 years ago would be classified as merely average today. Developmentalists are convinced that changes in the environment (more education, improved nutrition, smaller family size, fewer infections), not changes in innate intelligence, are the reason for the better performance of younger cohorts.

CROSS-SEQUENTIAL RESEARCH Longitudinal research is better than cross-sectional research, but it is not perfect. One problem is that repeated testing allows practice, which leads to greater learning. Furthermore, people who drop out of longitudinal studies tend to have lower IQ scores (Sliwinski et al., 2003). Thus, longitudinal research may find average IQ scores increasing partly because the people who remain to be retested are those who get higher scores.

As you learned in Chapter 1, cross-sequential research combines both cross-sectional and longitudinal designs. In 1956, as a doctoral student, K. Warner Schaie tested 500 adults, aged 20 to 50, on five primary mental abilities that were considered the basis of intelligence: (1) verbal meaning (comprehension), (2) spatial orientation, (3) inductive reasoning, (4) number ability, and (5) word fluency (rapid associations).

Schaie then had a brilliant idea: He would retest his initial sample 7 years later *and* he would test a new group who were the same age that his earlier sample had been at their first test. He did this again and again, every 7 years for 56 years, retesting each group and adding a new cohort (Schaie, 2005).

Schaie compared the scores of the retested individuals with their own earlier scores (a longitudinal analysis) and with the scores of a new group at that age. In this way, he found a more accurate view of the development of intelligence over adulthood than was possible from either longitudinal or cross-sectional research alone.

The results of Schaie's ongoing project, known as the **Seattle Longitudinal Study,** confirmed and extended what others had found: People improve in most mental abilities during adulthood. As Figure 12.5 shows, each particular ability has a distinct pattern for each gender. Note the gradual rise and the eventual decline of all abilities, with young men better at spatial orientation and numbers and women later excelling at verbal skills.

Seattle Longitudinal Study
The first cross-sequential study of adult intelligence. K. Warner Schaie began this study in 1956; the most recent testing was conducted in 2005.

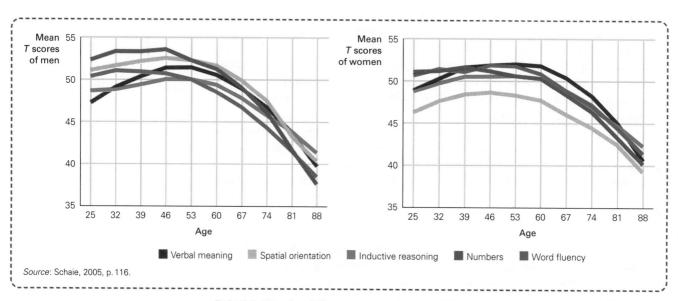

Source: Schaie, 2005, p. 116.

FIGURE 12.5 Age Differences in Intellectual Abilities Cross-sectional data on intellectual abilities at various ages would show much steeper declines. Longitudinal research, in contrast, would show more notable rises. Because Schaie's research is cross-sequential, the trajectories it depicts are more revealing: None of the average scores for the five abilities at any age are above 55 or below 35. Because the methodology takes into account the cohort and historical effects, the age-related differences from ages 25 to 60 are very small.

Other researchers from many nations have replicated these basic trends. For example, Paul Baltes (2003) tested hundreds of Germans and found that not until they reached age 80 did every cognitive ability decline. Thus, overall intelligence in adulthood (before age 65) does not usually drop (H. F. Lee et al., 2008; M. Martin & Zimprich, 2005).

One correlate of high adult IQ in the Seattle Longitudinal Study was intellectual complexity at work and in personal life. Such complexity peaked between ages 39 and 53 and was more apparent for adults born after 1940. Another correlate of high scores was social status, which peaked at age 46. These midlife peaks are among the reasons IQ typically increases throughout adulthood.

Schaie adds that "individual decline prior to 60 years of age is almost inevitably a symptom or precursor of pathological age changes" (Schaie, 2005, p. 418). In other words, most adults at some time between age 40 and 60 reach their highest intellectual ability; those who show substantial decline are probably ill in some way.

ANSWER TO OBSERVATION QUIZ
(from page 437) Sitting on the floor with no back support, with a test paper at a distance on your lap, and with someone standing over you holding a stopwatch—all are enough to rattle anyone, especially people over 18. ●

KEY points

- The brain reacts somewhat more slowly in each decade of adulthood, but the losses are so small that they are rarely noticed.
- Cross-sectional research suggested that IQ reached a peak at about age 18; longitudinal research found many intellectual gains through adulthood.
- Cross-sequential research combines several research methods and finds more varied development of intellectual ability. For example, vocabulary continues to increase with age.
- The Seattle Longitudinal Study, now spanning almost 60 years, finds many cohort differences in IQ scores, as societies change their emphasis on various intellectual skills.

Components of Intelligence

Responding to these data, developmentalists seek reasons for gains and losses in adult cognition. Some search for one factor that underlies intelligence, such as speed of working memory. The data have not confirmed the existence of any single g factor (Rabbitt et al., 2003).

Since every aspect of brain functioning is affected by health, emotions, and experience, it may be impossible to prove that one particular ability underlies all IQ changes. Finding such proof is especially unlikely during adulthood, when not only do conscious choices in lifestyle have an impact but the brain itself "has the apparent ability to reorganize in the face of the neural insults of aging in what is an apparently compensatory manner" (Park & Payer, 2006, p. 138).

Rather than seeking one, and only one, common factor as the foundation for intelligence, many researchers prefer to cluster related intellectual abilities (more than 100 abilities have been identified). An early attempt at clustering resulted in the identification of the five primary mental abilities that Schaie tested. More recent researchers have found two, or three, or nine clusters, as you will now see. Each cluster is somewhat distinct, not merely an expression of g.

Two Clusters: Fluid and Crystallized

In the 1960s, leading personality researcher Raymond Cattell teamed up with a promising PhD student, John Horn, to study the results of intelligence tests. They

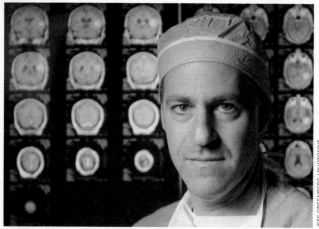

Not Brain Surgery? Yes, it is! Both these adults need to combine fluid and crystallized intelligence, insight and intuition, logic and experience. One *(left)* is in fact a neurosurgeon, studying brain scans before picking up his scalpel. The other *(right)* is a court reporter for a TV station, jotting down notes during a lunch recess before delivering her on-camera report on a trial.

concluded that adult intelligence is best understood when grouped into two categories, which they called *fluid* and *crystallized*.

As the name implies, **fluid intelligence** is like water, flowing until it reaches its own level, no matter where that happens to be. Quick and flexible, fluid intelligence enables a person to learn anything, including unfamiliar things that are not connected to what is already known. Fluid intelligence is the product of basic mental abilities, such as inductive reasoning, abstract analysis, reaction speed, and working memory. The kind of question that tests fluid intelligence among Western adults might be as follows:

> What comes next in each of these two series?*
> 4 9 1 6 2 5 3
> V X Z B D

Researchers often use puzzles to measure fluid intelligence, awarding bonus points for speedy solutions (as many IQ tests do). Immediate recall—of nonsense words, of numbers, of a sentence just read—indicates fluid intelligence because working memory is considered crucial in fluid ability.

Crystallized intelligence is the accumulation of facts, information, and knowledge as a result of education and experience. The size of vocabulary, the knowledge of chemical formulas, and long-term memory for dates in history all indicate crystallized intelligence. Tests that measure crystallized intelligence might include questions like the following:

> Who would hold a harpoon?
> What is the formula for calculating the area of a circle?
> What was Sri Lanka called in 1950?

Although such questions seem to measure achievement more than aptitude, intelligent people remember more information. Knowledge of vocabulary, for example, is a mainstay of IQ tests and is a crystallized ability.

To reflect the total picture of a person's intellectual potential, Cattell and Horn believe that both fluid and crystallized intelligence must be measured. Scores on items measuring fluid intelligence decrease with age, whereas crystallized intelligence

fluid intelligence
Those types of basic intelligence that make learning of all sorts quick and thorough. Abilities such as working memory, abstract thought, and speed of thinking are usually considered aspects of fluid intelligence.

crystallized intelligence
Those types of intellectual ability that reflect accumulated learning. Vocabulary and general information are examples.

---

*The correct answers are 6 and F.

scores increase (J. L. Horn & Masunaga, 2000). These two clusters, changing in opposite directions, make total IQ scores fairly steady from ages 30 to 70, even though many particular abilities rise or fall.

Thus, intelligence is age-sensitive. As you read earlier, brain slowdown begins at age 20 or so, decreasing fluid intelligence. Meanwhile, crystallized intelligence rises, masking the decline in fluid intelligence. Not until massive declines in fluid intelligence begin to overtake crystallized intelligence does overall IQ drop (Lindenberger, 2001).

Three Clusters: Analytic, Creative, and Practical

Remember from Chapter 7 that Robert Sternberg (1988a, 2003, 2006) proposed three types of intelligence: *analytic, creative,* and *practical.* Analytic intelligence is valued in higher education but might lead intellectuals to disagree with popular culture; creative individuals might be appreciated by the young because they resist authority but would not be tolerated in authoritarian regimes; practical intelligence might be underrated in normal times but valued (as "street smarts") if survival is threatened.

Schools and colleges value analytic intelligence, but not every community agrees. Sternberg cites an example from rural Kenya, where illness was often fatal. Smart children learned which herbs could cure which diseases; they did not necessarily excel in school.

> Knowledge of these natural herbal medicines was negatively correlated both with school achievement in English and with scores on conventional tests of crystallized abilities. . . . [C]hildren who spend a great deal of time on school-based learning may be viewed as rather foolish.
>
> [R. J. Sternberg et al., 2000, p. 19]

Think about how Sternberg's three forms of intelligence come into play over the life span:

- Analytic intelligence is valuable in high school and college, as students are expected to remember and analyze various ideas.

- Creative intelligence allows people to find "a better match to one's skills, values, or desires" (R. J. Sternberg, 2002, p. 456). Emerging adults appreciate the adventuresome spirit (they are the prime consumers of creative films, music, and technology), but creativity is less appreciated after age 25, when young adults are expected to settle down. Historically, creative adults have been scorned, ignored, or even killed.

- Practical intelligence is useful as people age and need to manage their daily lives.

The value of practical intelligence becomes apparent as we consider adult cognition. Few adults need to know that Ceylon was renamed Sri Lanka or how to deduce the next element in a number sequence (analytic intelligence) or to imagine better ways to play music, structure local government, or write a poem (creative intelligence).

Instead, adults need to solve real-world challenges: maintaining a home; advancing a career; managing finances; analyzing information from media, mail, and the Internet; responding to the emotions of their family, neighbors, and colleagues. Practical intelligence can be very useful (C. A. Berg & Klaczynski, 2002). In the

Quick and Smart Rotate the cubes until they match the picture: The faster you succeed at this task, the higher your IQ. Is this item on the WAIS (Wechsler Adult Intelligence Scale) equally valid for a midlife woman and an emerging-adult man? ["Wechsler Adult Intelligence Scale" and "WAIS" are trademarks, in the US and/or other countries, of Pearson Education, Inc. or its affiliate(s).]

Listening Quietly This elementary school teacher appears to be explaining academic work to one of her students, a boy who seems attentive and quiet.

OBSERVATION QUIZ

If this situation is typical in this classroom, what kind of intelligence is valued? (see answer, page 442) →

ANSWER TO OBSERVATION QUIZ
(from page 441) Solely analytic learning. Neither practical nor creative intelligence is fostered by a student working quietly at her desk (the girl at right) or the boy asking the teacher for private instruction. Fortunately, there are signs that this moment is not typical; notice the teacher's sweater, earrings, lipstick, and, especially, the apple on her desk. ●

ESPECIALLY FOR Prospective Parents In terms of the intellectual challenge, what type of intelligence is most needed for effective parenthood? (see response, page 444) ➡

Seattle Longitudinal Study, scores on tests of practical intelligence improved or stayed steady until people were well into late adulthood (Schaie, 2005).

Nine Clusters: Cultural Variations

Recall from Chapter 7 that Howard Gardner (1983, 1998, 2006) now believes that there are nine distinct intelligences: linguistic, logical-mathematical, musical, spatial, bodily-kinesthetic, naturalistic, social understanding (interpersonal intelligence), self-understanding (intrapersonal intelligence), and existential. The particular kind of intelligence that is most valued depends partly on age and culture, which means that the social context encourages some forms of intelligence and devalues others.

Gardner's theory of nine intelligences is particularly beneficial for cross-cultural understanding. Each nation values some of these nine but not others. For instance, agricultural nations might cultivate naturalistic intelligence, whereas people in nations with few farmers but overcrowded cities might need social understanding. I have colleagues who laughingly announce that their plants die, that they have two left feet, or that they cannot carry a tune. They would not be laughing if they lived in Indonesia, where farming, dancing, and singing are valued skills.

This example highlights a problem: At every stage of life, and in every culture, certain intellectual abilities are considered useful and others not. Consequently, schools and families teach children some skills and discourage or even punish others. Since contexts change for everyone over time, especially for children raised in one culture who live as adults in another, people can mistakenly judge others to be "stupid" because their form of intelligence is not appreciated in a particular context.

Fortunately, adults can awaken their neglected potential under certain circumstances. In the Seattle Longitudinal Study, some 60-year-olds declined markedly in spatial or reasoning skills. They then had five one-hour sessions of training in those skills. Forty percent improved to the level they had achieved 14 years earlier. When retested 7 years later, they had maintained their levels of improvement (Schaie, 2005).

A more familiar example may be found within families. Parents learn from their adult children as well as from their relatives who live elsewhere. My own children have taught me about digital cameras and current movies and revived my dormant interest in knitting and midwestern politics.

One overall conclusion that can be drawn from the array of existing intellectual tests and abilities is that cultural assumptions affect concepts of intelligence and the construction of IQ tests. If a culture values youth, then abilities that favor the young (quick reaction time, capacious short-term memory, fluid intelligence) become central to IQ tests.

KEY𝒫oints

- Researchers have identified various clusters of intellectual abilities. According to Cattell, there are two such clusters: Fluid abilities decrease in adulthood, making it harder for adults to learn new things, but crystallized abilities increase, making it easier for adults to connect facts.

- In Sternberg's three clusters, analytic intelligence is valued in educational settings, creativity is valued by young adults but may be hazardous later on, and practical intelligence is needed throughout adulthood.

- Each culture stresses a different set of Gardner's nine types of intelligence. Everyone has all nine to some extent, but each person develops only some of them.

Selective Gains and Losses

As we have just seen, research on age trends in cognitive abilities focuses on general trends, as if factors beyond individual control (such as aging and culture) were crucial. There is merit in that focus: Obviously, time cannot be stopped, and each of us is immersed in our culture—we could not function otherwise.

However, a realistic understanding of adulthood recognizes both gains and losses, as well as the fact that individuals differ in the particular gains and losses they experience and even more in how they react to them. As one team of developmentalists states, "Physical fitness, health, sensory acuity, multi-tasking ability, and functional brain efficacy decrease throughout adulthood, [yet] . . . individuals might continue to gain, for example, in social status, material belongings, knowledge, and professional expertise" (Lindenberger et al., 2008, p. 60).

Given this mix of gains and losses, every adult needs to decide how to maximize gain and minimize loss. Some of the biases embedded in IQ tests, such as the high value placed on quick thinking, may be less important the older an adult is.

Optimization

Paul and Margaret Baltes (1990) developed a theory called **selective optimization with compensation,** which holds that people seek to develop in the best way they can. Each person compensates for physical and cognitive losses, becoming more proficient at activities they want to do well.

Selective optimization with compensation applies to every aspect of life, from choosing friends to playing baseball. For example, as people grow older, their circles of friends become smaller but their friendships become more intense because they seek intimacy without the effort of wider socialization (Schaie & Carstensen, 2006). To take another example, the speedy reactions of the young may explain why younger baseball players steal more bases and older athletes prefer golf. Every adult practices some abilities and ignores others (Wellman, 2003).

Many researchers in Europe and North America have tested the theory of selective optimization with compensation by studying adolescents, adults, and the elderly. It is evident that people of all ages adjust their goals and habits to accomplish what they want, compensating for weaknesses and finding success (Freund, 2008).

Every ability can be either enhanced or ignored. An "old dog" can learn, but learning "new tricks" requires motivation and practice. Each person selects certain

selective optimization with compensation The theory, developed by Paul and Margaret Baltes, that people try to maintain a balance in their lives by looking for the best way to compensate for physical and cognitive losses and to become more proficient in activities they can already do well.

DAVIS BARBER / PHOTOEDIT

Handicapped Learner? This woman is using a computer in her ESL (English as a Second Language) class.

OBSERVATION QUIZ

Do you see any evidence that this is a good way for her to learn a new language? (see answer, page 445) ➤

aspects of intelligence to optimize, neglecting the rest. If those neglected aspects happen to be the ones measured by IQ tests, then scores will fall, although the person may be as smart as ever.

Expertise

Another way to express this idea is to say that everyone develops expertise. Each person becomes a **selective expert**, specializing in activities that are personally meaningful, whether they involve car repair, gourmet cooking, diagnosis of illness, or fly fishing. As people develop expertise in some areas, they pay less attention to other areas.

For example, each adult tunes out most channels on the TV, ignores some realms of human experience, and has no interest in attending particular events. Meanwhile, other people wait in line for hours to buy a particular product, to hear a favorite singer, to attend the very event that others avoid.

Culture and context guide expertise, as is evident in tests of cognition. Adults born 60 years ago are better than recent cohorts at math calculations and at writing letters with distinctive, legible handwriting. As children, they memorized the multiplication tables and practiced penmanship; as adults they maintain those skills. Contemporary schools guide children to make other choices. Computer skills, for instance, are taught, but penmanship is not.

Although sometimes people use the word *expert* to signify an extraordinarily talented and skilled individual, to developmentalists the term means more—and less—than that (Ericsson, 1996). Experts are more skilled, proficient, and knowledgeable at a particular task than the average person, especially a novice (literally, "a new person") who has not practiced that skill.

Experts do not necessarily have extraordinary intellectual ability, and their expertise is not merely a matter of more knowledge (Wellman, 2003). At a certain point, the accumulation of knowledge, practice, and experience becomes transformative, putting the expert in a different league from the novice. The quality, not just quantity, of cognition advances.

THE CHARACTERISTICS OF EXPERT THOUGHT Expert thought is *intuitive, automatic, strategic,* and *flexible.*

Expertise Is Intuitive Novices follow formal procedures and rules. Experts rely more on their past experiences and on immediate contexts; their actions are therefore more intuitive and less stereotypic. For example, when they look at X-rays, expert physicians interpret them more accurately than do young doctors, though they cannot always verbalize how they reached their diagnosis.

The role of experience and intuition is particularly apparent in medicine, since expertise requires a combination of specialized knowledge and individualization. Although the practice of medicine may seem straightforward, expert doctors and nurses are aware of many complications and dangers:

> Hospitals are filled with varieties of knives and poisons. Every time a medication is prescribed, there is potential for an unintended side effect. In surgery, collateral damage is inherent. External tissue must be cut to allow internal access so that a diseased organ may be removed, or some other manipulation may be performed to return the patient to better health.
>
> *[Dominguez, 2001, p. 287]*

In one study, surgeons all saw the same videotape of a gallbladder operation and were asked to talk about it. The experienced surgeons anticipated and noted problems twice as often as the surgical residents (who also had removed gallbladders) (Dominguez, 2001).

The fictional detective Sherlock Holmes is an example of expertise. Many of Arthur Conan Doyle's stories feature scenes in which Holmes tells his colleague, Dr. Watson, about his astonishing intuitions. For instance, in *The Adventure of the Blue Carbuncle*, Holmes hands Watson a hat. Watson says, "I can see nothing." Holmes retorts:

> On the contrary, Watson, you can see everything. You fail, however, to reason from what you see. You are too timid in drawing your inferences. . . .
>
> There are a few inferences which are very distinct, and a few others which represent at least a strong balance of probability. That the man was highly intellectual is of course obvious upon the face of it, and also that he was fairly well-to-do within the last three years, although he has now fallen upon evil days. He had foresight, but has less now than formerly [he had bought a device to prevent the hat from blowing away, but Holmes could see that the elastic was broken and had not been replaced], pointing to a moral retrogression, which, when taken with the decline of his fortunes, seems to indicate some evil influence, probably drink. . . .
>
> He . . . is middle-aged, has grizzled hair which he has had cut within the last few days, and which he anoints with lime-cream.
>
> *[cited in Didierjean & Gobet, 2008, p. 111]*

Most people are more like Watson than like Holmes. A contemporary, nonfictional example comes from bird-watchers. Very few people spend their free time in unfamiliar places at dawn, hoping to glimpse a particular flying creature. Yet expert birders can hear a bird call and intuitively distinguish it from another—an example of expert auditory knowledge (Chartrand et al., 2008).

Another example of expert intuition is *chicken-sexing*, the ability to tell whether a newborn chicken is male or female. As David Myers (2002) explains:

> Poultry owners once had to wait five to six weeks before the appearance of adult feathers enabled them to separate cockerels (males) from pullets (hens). Egg producers wanted to buy and feed only pullets, so they were intrigued to hear that some Japanese had developed an uncanny ability to sex day-old chicks. . . . Hatcheries elsewhere then gave some of their workers apprenticeships under the Japanese. . . . After months of training and experience, the best Americans and Australians could almost match the Japanese, by sexing 800 to 1,000 chicks per hour with 99 percent accuracy. But don't ask them how they do it. The sex difference, as any chicken sexer can tell you, is too subtle to explain.
>
> *[p. 55]*

Expertise Is Automatic Many elements of expert performance are automatic; that is, the complex action and thought that they involve seem routine, as if they were performed instinctively. Experts process incoming information more quickly and analyze it more efficiently than nonexperts; then they act in well-rehearsed ways that appear unconscious.

In fact, some of the automatic actions of experts are no longer accessible to the conscious mind. For example, adults are much better at tying their shoelaces than children are (adults can do it efficiently in the dark) but much worse at describing how they do it (P. McLeod et al., 2005).

The unconscious nature of automatic actions is apparent if you are an experienced driver and have attempted to teach someone else to drive. Excellent drivers who are inexperienced instructors find it hard to recognize or verbalize aspects of driving that have become automatic, such as noticing pedestrians and cyclists on the far side of the road, or feeling the gears shift on a hill, or hearing tires lose traction on a bit of sand. Yet such factors differentiate the expert from the novice.

This explains why, despite powerful motivation, quicker reactions, and better vision, teenagers have far more car accidents than middle-aged drivers. Sometimes

ANSWER TO OBSERVATION QUIZ
(from page 443) Individual learning styles differ, but there are three signs that this may be an effective method of language instruction: The equipment is new; both oral and auditory exercises are part of the curriculum; and she and each of her fellow students can learn at their own pace. ●

teenage drivers deliberately take risks, of course, but more often they simply misjudge and misperceive conditions that a more experienced driver would automatically notice.

Automatic processing is thought to be a crucial reason that expert chess and Go players are much better than novices. They see a configuration of game pieces and automatically encode it as a whole, rather than analyzing it bit by bit. Interestingly, one study of expert Go players (aged 23–76) found that, for experts, recognition memory of Go pieces did not show age-related deficits, although recall memory usually diminishes with age and the memory of the less expert Go players declined (Masunaga & Horn, 2001).

A study of expert chess players (aged 17–81) found some age-related declines, but expertise was much more important than age. This was particularly apparent for speedy recognition that a player's king was threatened. Even though standard tests of memory and speed showed a decline among older chess experts, they were still quick to defend their king (Jastrzembski et al., 2006).

Automaticity can lead to mistakes if the quick automatic response is not the best one. In chess, some players quickly see a good move and fail to see a better one that is unusual. Many good players make this mistake, called *Einstellung* ("setting, getting stuck"), but the true experts almost never automatically miss a better move (Bilalić et al., 2008).

Expertise Is Strategic Experts have more and better strategies, especially when problems are unexpected (Ormerod, 2005). Indeed, planning ahead strategically may be critical to expertise. For example, expert team leaders (in business, the military, and so on) build trust and communication during slow times so that, under stress, no team member will disobey or misinterpret commands.

Of course, strategies need to be updated as situations change and people gain knowledge. The monthly fire drill required by some schools, the standard lecture given by some professors, and the pat safety instructions read by airline attendants before each flight are increasingly less effective than they were originally. I recently heard a flight attendant precede his standard talk with, "For those of you who have not ridden in an automobile since 1960, this is how you buckle a seat belt." That day, I actually listened to the safety instructions.

Superior strategies sometimes require that personal, emotional reactions be overcome. The most expert football players are not the biggest, strongest, or quickest but the ones who react with less emotion and more awareness of the other players (Gygax et al., 2008). Those diabetics who successfully control their insulin levels are the most analytical, neither denying nor panicking when the unexpected occurs (K. D. Lippa et al., 2008).

The superior strategies of the expert permit selective optimization with compensation. Many developmentalists regard the capacity to accommodate to changes over time (compensation) as essential to successful aging (M. M. Baltes & Carstensen, 2003; Rowe & Kahn, 1998). People need to compensate for any slippage in their fluid abilities.

Such compensation was evident in a study of airplane pilots, who were allowed to take notes on directions given by air traffic controllers in a flight simulation (Morrow et al., 2003). Experienced pilots took more accurate and complete notes. They used better graphic symbols (such as arrows) than did pilots who were trained in air traffic instructions but did not have much flight experience. In other words, although non-experts had paper, pencil, and a suggestion to take notes, they did not use those tools as well as the experts did.

In actual flights, too, older pilots take more notes than younger ones do because they have mastered this strategy, perhaps to compensate for their slower working memory. Probably as a result, these researchers found no differences in the ability to repeat complex instructions and conditions among experienced pilots of three age groups: 22–40, 50–59, and 60–76 (Morrow et al., 2003). In many studies, people who are not experts show age-related deficits—even the experienced pilots showed deficits in areas not related to flying—but experts of all ages often maintain their proficiency at their occupation.

Expertise Is Flexible Finally, perhaps because they are intuitive, automatic, and strategic, experts are also more flexible. The expert artist, musician, or scientist is creative and curious, deliberately experimenting and enjoying the challenge when things do not go according to plan.

Consider the expert surgeon, who seeks complex cases and prefers unusual patients over typical ones because operating on them might bring sudden, unexpected complications. Compared with the novice, the expert surgeon not only is more likely to notice telltale signs (an unexpected lesion, an oddly shaped organ, a rise or drop in a vital sign) that may signal a problem but also is more flexible, more willing to deviate from standard textbook procedures if they prove ineffective (Patel et al., 1999).

In the same way, experts in all walks of life adapt to individual cases and exceptions —like an expert chef who adjusts ingredients, temperature, technique, and timing as a dish develops and seldom follows a recipe exactly. Interestingly, a study of forensic scientists, who must find telltale clues from a mishmash of relevant and irrelevant evidence, reported that the most expert were more methodical as well as more flexible, using more strategies to study the most relevant objects (Schraagen & Leijenhorst, 2001).

Most people think they can detect whether someone is telling the truth, but actually the layperson's judgment is as likely to be wrong as right (Bond, 2008). Likewise, polygraphs (lie detector machines) are notoriously inaccurate, especially with practiced liars. However, experts who are highly motivated and experienced at ferreting out the truth—as are some police officers, corrections officers, and forensic psychologists (not academic psychologists)—do far better than chance (O'Sullivan, 2008).

One study pitted expert lie detectors against expert liars (felons who had served their time). Only two of the judges did extremely well, almost always knowing who was lying and who was not. Both of them were Native American women who worked for the Bureau of Indian Affairs, and both relied more on nonverbal clues than on verbal ones.

Crucial to lie detection is the need to put aside stereotypes, since each case is unique and thus prejudices might cloud judgment. The two Native Americans were not swayed by racial or gender bias, pro or con. Perhaps something in American Indian culture made them particularly sensitive, able to think more flexibly and less stereotypically when assessing honesty.

Make No Mistake Humans are not always expert at judging other humans. Juries have convicted some defendants who were later proved to be innocent and acquitted others who were actually guilty. If this lab technician is an expert at her work, and if the genetic evidence she is testing was carefully collected, DNA test results can provide objective proof of guilt or innocence.

EXPERTISE AND AGE The relationship between expertise and age is not lockstep; some extraordinary talents are inborn, already evident in young children. Someone who lacks musical talent can never become an expert musician, a person with poor coordination can never become a top athlete, and so on.

Talent alone is not enough, however. Lengthy practice (for at least 10 years, according to some researchers) is needed to develop and maintain expertise (Kneebone et al., 2004; D. J. Palmer et al., 2005). With "intense, well-focused practice to attain expertise . . ., there may be no aging decline of abilities in the domain of that expertise" (Masunaga & Horn, 2001, p. 309).

The relationship between expertise and age depends partly on which particular kind of expertise is required. For example, in one study, participants aged 17 to 79

Voilà! This chemist is thinking intensely and watching carefully for a result that will merit an excited *"Voilà!"* ("There it is!") He is in France, so we can guess his linguistic expertise; but unless we are also experienced chemists, we would not recognize an important result if it happened. Expertise is astonishingly selective.

were asked to identify nine common tunes (such as "Happy Birthday" and "Old MacDonald Had a Farm") when notes from midsong were first played very slowly and then gradually faster until the listener identified the tune. The listeners were grouped according to their musical experience, from virtually none to 10 or more years of training and performing.

In this slow-to-fast phase of the experiment, responses correlated with expertise but not with age. Those individuals who had played more music themselves were quicker to recognize songs played very slowly (Andrews et al., 1998). In other words, at every age, experts were equally proficient and much faster than novices.

In another phase of this study, the songs were played very fast at first and then gradually slowed down. In this condition, age made a difference. Although the older experts still did better than the novices, they were slower to recognize the tunes than were the younger experts (Andrews et al., 1998).

Remember that speed is one part of fluid intelligence, and this harks back to the question raised a few pages ago: What abilities should be assessed on IQ tests? Perhaps "all measures of intelligence measure a form of developing expertise" (R. J. Sternberg, 2002, p. 452). The specific items should reflect the kind of expertise that is valued—which is easier said than done.

Is there such a thing as moral expertise, a sensitivity to right and wrong that increases with age as religious thinking matures? Some researchers think so; others think not (Rossano, 2008). The following explores this issue.

A VIEW FROM SCIENCE

Moral Expertise and Age: Stages of Faith

How should morality be defined and measured? One scholar, James Fowler (1981, 1986), believes that theological discussions and religious guidelines are designed to increase moral action and that devout adults learn to question their actions and apply moral standards to what they do. If this is so, then the development of faith over adulthood should lead to more advanced moral thinking as people age. Fowler developed a sequence of six stages of faith, building on the work of Piaget and Kohlberg:

- *Stage 1: Intuitive-projective faith.* Faith is magical, illogical, imaginative, and filled with fantasy, especially about the power of God and the mysteries of birth and death. It is typical of children ages 3 to 7.

- *Stage 2: Mythic-literal faith.* Individuals take the myths and stories of religion literally, believing simplistically in the power of symbols. God is seen as rewarding those who follow His laws and punishing those who do not. Stage 2 is typical from ages 7 to 11, but it also characterizes some

adults. Fowler cites a woman who says extra prayers at every opportunity, to put them "in the bank."

- *Stage 3: Synthetic-conventional faith.* Faith is conventional, reflecting concern about other people and favoring "what feels right" over what makes intellectual sense. Fowler quotes a man whose personal rules include "being truthful with my family. Not trying to cheat them out of anything. . . . I'm not saying that God or anybody else set my rules. I really don't know. It's what I feel is right."

- *Stage 4: Individual-reflective faith.* Faith is characterized by intellectual detachment from the values of the culture and from the approval of other people. Emerging adults are often in this stage, as they question the authority of parents, teachers, and other powerful figures and rely instead on their own understanding of the world. By adulthood, faith becomes an active commitment.

- *Stage 5: Conjunctive faith.* Faith incorporates both powerful unconscious ideas (such as the power of prayer and

AP PHOTO / GENE J. PUSKAR

LUDOVIC CAREME / CORBIS

The Same Situation, Many Miles Apart:
Expressions of Faith Both these photographs
depict Christian worship services, one in Mount
Union, Pennsylvania *(above)*, and the other in
Lagos, Nigeria *(left)*. In any group of worshippers,
some may be at Fowler's first stages of faith and
some may be in the final one. The difference
depends on their experiences and maturation,
not on their devotion to particular elements of
creed or ritual.

the love of God) and rational, conscious values (such as
the sanctity of life). People are flexible, accepting contra-
dictions. Fowler says that this cosmic perspective is seldom
achieved before middle age.

● *Stage 6: Universalizing faith.* People at this stage have a
powerful vision of universal compassion, justice, and love
that compels them to live their lives in a way that many
other people consider to be either saintly or foolish. A
transforming experience is often the gateway to stage 6,
as happened to Moses, Muhammad, the Buddha, St. Paul,
and, more recently, to Mohandas Gandhi, Martin Luther
King Jr., and Mother Teresa. Stage 6 is rarely achieved.

If Fowler is correct, faith, like other aspects of cognition,
progresses from a simple, self-centered, one-sided perspective

to a more complex, altruistic (unselfish), and many-sided
view. In Fowler's scheme, moral thinking develops as faith
matures, finally arriving at the moral self-sacrifice that is
characteristic of people who achieve stage 6.

Although not everyone agrees with Fowler's particular
stages, the role of religion in human development is now
widely accepted, especially when people are confronted
with "unsettling life situations" (Day & Naedts, 1999; W. R.
Miller & Thoresen, 2003). Apparently, faith is one way people
combat stress, overcome adversity, and analyze challenges.

This process continues over the years of adulthood. Young
adults are least likely to attend religious services or to pray
(Wilhelm et al., 2007), and older adults are not only more
likely to be religious but also more likely to adhere to moral
values.

Like almost all forms of thinking and analyzing, faith and
morals change with time and experience. Whether this is
progress, expertise, or regression depends on one's definitions
of those terms. Here it is not possible to present definitive
conclusions or even insightful research, since basic definitions
are not yet agreed upon. It is for future scientists to discover
the relationships among adult development, cognition, and
moral expertise.

OLDER WORKERS: EXPERTS OR HAS-BEENS? Experienced adults often use selective optimization with compensation (Freund, 2008). This is particularly apparent in the everyday workplace (Sterns & Huyck, 2001). The best employees may be the older ones—if they are trained and motivated to do their best (Smedley & Whitten, 2006).

Complicated work requires more cognitive practice and expertise than does routine work; as a result, it may have intellectual benefits for the workers themselves. In the Seattle Longitudinal Study, the cognitive complexity of the occupations of more than 500 workers was measured, including the complexities involved in social interactions, in object use, and in analyzing data. All three kinds of occupational challenges maintained the workers' intellectual prowess (Schaie, 2005).

A classic study of age and employment focused on a familiar occupation, waitressing. Waiting on tables demands many skills—among them, communication, memory for orders, knowledge of routines, time management, and the ability to smooth social interactions with customers and coworkers—as well as physical stamina. Young waitresses have advantages in strength, speed, and memory. Can older waitresses compensate?

Marion Perlmutter and her colleagues sought to answer this question. They identified the skills required for successful waitressing and then measured those skills in 64 waitresses who varied in age from 19 to 60 and in work experience from 2 months to 31 years (Perlmutter et al., 1990).

The women were assessed on memory, strength, dexterity, knowledge of the technical and organizational requirements of the job, and social skills. They were also observed during different times of the workday, including rush and slack periods. Perlmutter wanted to know whether younger and older employees differed in job performance—and, if so, whether the cause was physical and cognitive skills, work experience, or both.

The researchers were surprised to discover that years of experience had little impact on work-related physical or cognitive skills. Apparently, expertise at waiting on tables takes far less than 10 years to attain. However, the employees' age (independent of their experience) made a significant difference (Perlmutter et al., 1990). Younger women, as expected, had better physical skills and memory abilities, and they were quicker in calculating customers' checks. Nevertheless, older women outperformed their younger counterparts in the number of customers served, especially during rush periods.

One restaurant owner learned this the hard way, saying:

> A pretty girl is an asset to any business, but we tried them and they fell apart on us.... They could not keep up the pace of our fast and furious lunch hours.... Our clients want good service; if they want sex appeal, they go elsewhere.
>
> *[quoted in Perlmutter et al., 1990, p. 189]*

The researchers noted that many restaurant managers

> consistently reported that older workers chunk tasks to save steps by combining orders for several customers at several tables and/or by employing time management strategies such as preparing checks while waiting for food delivery.... Although younger experienced food servers may have the knowledge and skills necessary for such organization and chunking, they do not seem to use the skills as often, perhaps because they do not believe they need to.
>
> *[Perlmutter et al., 1990, pp. 189–190]*

Thus, older waitresses developed strategies to compensate for their declining job-related abilities. The researchers concluded that "adaptive competence in adulthood represents functional improvements that probably are common, particularly in the workplace" (Perlmutter et al., 1990, p. 196).

HUMAN RELATIONS EXPERTISE Probably the most important skill for people of every age is the ability to understand the emotional as well as practical needs of other people in order to help them function well. Think of an expert coach, therapist, or judge. All of them gain something from their life experience.

To return to Jenny, whose story began this chapter, she decided to continue her pregnancy. Her decision to have the baby meant postponing her job, her education, and her move from the South Bronx.

In the end, though, her choice turned out well. Billy's wife hired a detective, who found out about Jenny. The wife gave Billy an ultimatum: Never see Jenny again or file for divorce. Two years later, the divorce became final and Billy married Jenny. They moved to Florida, found good jobs, bought a house with a pool, and together raised their unplanned child—a daughter who has now graduated from college. Jenny's son, who had special education needs, thrived as well: He is a psychology professor. Both parents are now retired and happy together.

None of this means that everyone, or even anyone, should follow Jenny's path. Each person's experience is different, and some choices turn out to be foolish. What strikes me now is that Jenny knew more about her relationship with Billy than she conveyed to me. She analyzed her options as an adult, not as a teenager, who might have acted impulsively. She realized that she should seek me out, since she had learned that talking would help her think. Choosing the baby over the romance was intuitive and strategic; it was one reason Billy married her.

Jenny's choice was wise, even expert. My own expertise about her life was limited, but my years of teaching students of many backgrounds have taught me to listen. There is more to this story, and it reflects the benefits of adulthood. Jenny and I have kept in touch, still learning from each other.

KEY points

- Over the years of adulthood, gains as well as losses are evident.
- In selective optimization with compensation, people learn to maximize their potential and work around any deficits.
- Expertise is developed by everyone in the areas they choose, which may not be the areas measured by IQ tests or appreciated by most people in a society.
- Expert thinking is unlike ordinary thought in that it is more intuitive, automatic, strategic, and flexible.

SUMMARY

The Aging Process

1. With each year of life from puberty onward, signs of senescence (a gradual physical decline associated with aging) become more apparent. All the organs as well as the external appearance change gradually during every decade of adult life.

2. The rate of senescence is most apparent in the sense organs. Vision becomes less sharp with age, with farsightedness increasing. Hearing also becomes less acute.

3. Traditionally, the most troubling changes were in the sexual-reproductive system. Fertility problems become more common with increased age (although in vitro fertilization, or IVF, and other forms of assisted reproductive technology, or ART, solve some of these), and sexual responsiveness slows down.

4. At menopause, ovulation ceases, and levels of estrogen are markedly reduced. Hormone production also declines in men. For both sexes, hormone replacement therapy (HRT) should be used cautiously, if at all.

Poor Health Habits and Senescence

5. Adults in North America are smoking cigarettes much less than they once did, and rates of lung cancer and other diseases are falling, largely for that reason. Alcohol abuse remains a major health problem, however.

6. Good health habits include avoiding drugs, exercising regularly, and avoiding weight gain. Cigarette smoking has been markedly reduced in the United States but is increasing in many developing nations. A worldwide "epidemic of obesity" is apparent, and, especially in developed nations, adults exercise less as they grow older.

Measuring Health

7. Variations in health can be measured in terms of mortality, morbidity, disability, and vitality. Although death and disease are easier to quantify in terms of the health of a population, disability and vitality may be more significant.

8. Aging and health status vary by gender, SES, and culture. Social, economic, and psychological factors may be even more influential than genetic or ethnic differences.

Cognition in Adulthood

9. Longitudinal research has found that each person tends to increase in IQ, particularly in vocabulary and general knowledge, until age 60 or so. Flynn found that average IQ scores have increased over the past century.

10. K. Warner Schaie found that some primary abilities decline with age while others (such as vocabulary) increase. Education, vocation, and family, as well as age, seem to affect these abilities.

Components of Intelligence

11. Crystallized intelligence, which is based on accumulated knowledge, increases with time, while fluid, flexible reasoning skills decline with age.

12. Sternberg proposed three fundamental forms of intelligence: analytic, creative, and practical. Of these, practical intelligence may improve with age.

13. Gardner identified nine kinds of intelligence. Each person's genetic heritage and culture influence which of these intelligences are valued and thus more highly developed.

Selective Gains and Losses

14. As people grow older, they select certain aspects of their lives to focus on, optimizing and compensating if need be. Thus, people become experts in whatever intellectual skills they choose to develop, while abilities that are not exercised may fade.

15. In addition to being more experienced, experts are more intuitive. Furthermore, their cognitive processes are automatic, they use more and better strategies to perform whatever task is required, and they are more flexible.

KEY TERMS

senescence (p. 420)
presbycusis (p. 421)
in vitro fertilization (IVF) (p. 423)
menopause (p. 424)

hormone replacement therapy (HRT) (p. 424)
andropause (p. 425)
mortality (p. 430)
morbidity (p. 430)

disability (p. 430)
vitality (p. 431)
general intelligence (g) (p. 436)
Seattle Longitudinal Study (p. 438)

fluid intelligence (p. 440)
crystallized intelligence (p. 440)
selective optimization with compensation (p. 443)
selective expert (p. 444)

KEY QUESTIONS

1. What age-related changes in appearance typically occur during adulthood?

2. How do vision and hearing change during adulthood?

3. What are some of the factors that diminish fertility?

4. Why might a woman welcome menopause?

5. What changes in tobacco use have occurred, where, and with what consequences?

6. How does obesity affect health?

7. What are the four measures of health, and what does each signify?

8. Why does health vary between and within SES and ethnic groups?

9. Why do cross-sectional and longitudinal studies of intelligence reach different conclusions?

10. How is fluid intelligence different from crystallized intelligence?

11. How do Sternberg's three fundamental forms of intelligence—analytic, creative, and practical—vary with age?

12. What are the four characteristics of expertise?

13. How do people compensate for the losses that come with age?

APPLICATIONS

1. Guess the ages of five people you know, and then ask them how old they are. Analyze the clues you used for your guesses and the people's reactions to your question.

2. Attend a gathering for people who want to stop a bad habit or start a good one, such as an open meeting of Alcoholics Anonymous or another 12-step program, an introductory session of Weight Watchers or Smoke Enders, or a meeting of prospective gym members. Analyze who attended, what you learned, and what your reactions were.

3. The importance of context and culture is illustrated by the things that people think are basic knowledge. Write four questions that you think are hard but fair as measures of general intelligence and ask someone else to do the same. Then give your test to the other person and answer the four questions that person has prepared for you. What did you learn from the results?

4. Skill at video games is sometimes thought to reflect intelligence. Go to a public place where people play such games and interview people who play them. What abilities do they think video games require? Analyze their responses in terms of experience, age, and expertise.

CHAPTER OUTLINE

ADULTHOOD
Psychosocial Development

13

I once invited two long-married couples to our home for dinner. "George and I will be arriving separately," one of the wives told me. "No problem," I assured her. "I guess one of you will be coming directly from work."

"No, we are coming from our homes. We are divorced."

I was taken aback. I had had no idea that their marriage was in trouble.

"I'm so sorry. Should I have invited only one of you?"

"Don't be sorry. We are happier and good friends."

I was stunned. I thought divorce meant a failed marriage, a broken home, and at least one bitter spouse. Not so. The dinner party was a success, with lots of laughter. ●

I AM NOT THE ONLY ONE WHOSE ASSUMPTIONS do not fit the current realities of adult development. As explained in this chapter, the *midlife crisis,* the *sandwich generation,* and the *empty nest* are myths. Divorce, remarriage, and single adulthood are not always what people once assumed.

Overall, age boundaries are less distinct than they were in the past or than they still are in childhood. You will see that some topics that could be in this chapter (e.g., choosing friends, cohabitation) are discussed primarily in Chapter 11 and others (grandparenthood, retirement) are addressed in Chapter 15. This does not mean that they do not occur during the four decades that are our focus here. Indeed, almost any adult experience can occur anytime from age 15 to 115.

This chapter focuses on personality, marriage, parenthood, divorce, caregiving, and employment—each of which is sometimes joyous and sometimes not. When pressure from these aspects of life builds up, the burden of stress increases—and this heavy allostatic load sometimes has devastating consequences, as is also explained. We begin with normative development between ages 25 and 65.

Ages and Stages

Certain psychosocial needs and circumstances characterize the adult years, but always remember that boundaries are fluid. As you will see, that fluidity is recognized even by theorists who describe stages that usually occur in adulthood.

Erikson's Stages

Often when developmentalists describe adulthood, they begin with Erik Erikson. As you learned in Chapter 1, Erikson originally envisioned eight stages of development, which occur in sequence from birth through old age. He knew that development continues in adulthood: Three of his stages cover the years after adolescence.

> Erikson stands alone as the one thinker who changed our minds about what it means to live as a person who has arrived at a chronologically mature position and yet continues to grow, to change, and to develop.
>
> *[Hoare, 2002, p. 3]*

ESPECIALLY FOR People Under 20 Will future "decade" birthdays—30, 40, 50, and so on—be major turning points in your life? (see response, page 454) ➜

Later in his life, Erikson stressed that stages and ages do not occur in lockstep. People of many ages can be in his fifth stage, *identity versus role diffusion*, or in any of his three adult stages—called *intimacy versus isolation, generativity versus stagnation*, and *integrity versus despair* (Hoare, 2002; McAdams, 2006) (see Table 13.1).

Erikson himself reassessed his eighth and final stage when he reached old age. He wrote that "the demand to develop integrity and wisdom in old age seems to be somewhat unfair, especially when made by middle-aged theorists—as, indeed, we then were" (Erikson, 1984, p. 160). He decided that the psychosocial virtues of late adulthood could and often did develop much earlier (Hoare, 2002).

TABLE 13.1 Erikson's Stages of Adulthood

Unlike Freud or other early theorists who thought adults simply worked through the legacy of their childhood, half of Erikson's eight stages described psychosocial needs after puberty. His most famous book, *Childhood and Society* (1963), devoted only two pages to each adult stage, but published and unpublished elaborations in later works led to a much richer depiction (Hoare, 2002).

Identity Versus Role Diffusion
Although the identity crisis was originally set for adolescence, Erikson realized that identity concerns could be lifelong. Identity combines values and traditions from childhood with the current social context. Since contexts keep evolving, many adults reassess all four types of identity (sexual/gender, vocational/work, religious/spiritual, and political/ethnic).

Intimacy Versus Isolation
Adults seek intimacy—a close, reciprocal connection with another human being. Intimacy is mutual, not self-absorbed, which means that adults need to devote time and energy to one another. This process begins in emerging adulthood and continues lifelong. Isolation is especially likely when divorce or death disrupts established intimate relationships.

Generativity Versus Stagnation
Adults need to care for the next generation, either by raising their own children or by mentoring, teaching, and helping younger people. Erikson's first description of this stage focused on parenthood, but later he included other ways to achieve generativity. Adults extend the legacy of their culture and their generation with ongoing care, creativity, and sacrifice.

Integrity Versus Despair
When Erikson himself was in his 70s, he decided that integrity, with the goal of combating prejudice and helping all humanity, was too important to be left to the elderly. He also thought that each person's entire life could be directed toward connecting a personal journey with the historical and cultural purpose of human society, the ultimate achievement of integrity.

Maslow's Stages

Another theorist explicitly declined to link chronological age and adult development. Abraham Maslow (1954) described five stages, which occur in sequence. This *hierarchy of needs* must be climbed from the bottom up (see Figure 13.1).

Maslow declared that people do not necessarily move to a higher stage after a certain amount of time. Instead, movement occurs when people have satisfied their needs at one level and are ready for the next step.

As an example of this progression, people who are in the third stage (*love and belonging*, similar to Erikson's intimacy versus isolation) seek to be loved and accepted by those who are close to them. Romantic partners, immediate family members, and best friends are all possible sources of such love.

People who do not receive acceptance and affection might stay stuck at that level. They need love but never feel satisfied or fulfilled by the affection they get.

However, adults who do experience abundant love are ready to move to the next level, *success and esteem*. Their primary psychological need at this stage is to be respected by many people and to be recognized as successful by other members of their profession, community, or some other group. They do not abandon their immediate family (spouse, children, parents); the love of those people is assured. Thus, they are able to seek esteem in the wider world.

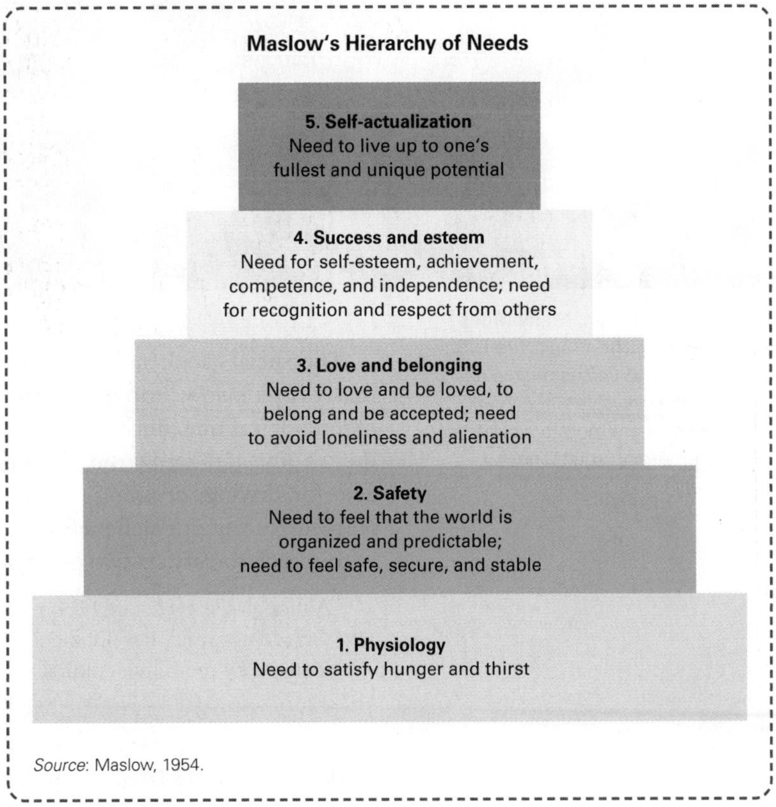

Maslow's Hierarchy of Needs

5. Self-actualization
Need to live up to one's fullest and unique potential

4. Success and esteem
Need for self-esteem, achievement, competence, and independence; need for recognition and respect from others

3. Love and belonging
Need to love and be loved, to belong and be accepted; need to avoid loneliness and alienation

2. Safety
Need to feel that the world is organized and predictable; need to feel safe, secure, and stable

1. Physiology
Need to satisfy hunger and thirst

Source: Maslow, 1954.

FIGURE 13.1 Moving Up, Not Looking Back Maslow's hierarchy is like a ladder: Once a person stands firmly on a higher rung, the lower rungs are no longer needed. Thus, someone who has arrived at step 4 might devalue security (step 2) and be willing to take risks to gain success.

In his later years, Maslow, like Erikson, reassessed his final level, *self-actualization*. He suggested another level after that, called *self-transcendence* (Koltko-Rivera, 2006)—a level not usually attained until late in life (described in Chapter 15).

Remember, however, that age boundaries are fluid: An adult might reach the final stages before old age or might remain at the bottom steps of the hierarchy. Childhood experiences, especially a lack of praise and encouragement from parents, could cause an adult to remain lonely and self-critical. Poverty, too, makes it more difficult to achieve higher-order needs—including self-actualization—since basic needs might go unsatisfied.

The Social Clock

As you can see, half a century ago, major theorists and researchers in development already realized that the chronological clock is a poor predictor of adulthood. The accumulation of birthdays merely measures the passage of time, not the rate of *senescence* (the process of getting older).

Yet, although they have abandoned a strict age-based view of development, scholars in sociology and anthropology have noted that time cannot be completely ignored. Many adults check their developmental timing against a **social clock,** an internalized timetable based on social norms and expectations (Neugarten & Neugarten, 1986). These norms set the ideal ages for men or women to finish school, marry, establish a career, and have children (S. Greene, 2003; Keith, 1990; Settersten & Hagestad, 1996).

social clock
A developmental timetable based not on biological maturation but on social norms, which set the stages of life and the behaviors considered appropriate to each of them. For example, "middle age" begins when a culture believes it does, rather than at a certain age in all cultures.

The Same Situation, Many Miles Apart: Beating the Clock The U.S. college graduate *(left)* is middle-aged, and the Israeli skydiver *(right)* is 80. Their activities are more typically done by emerging adults, not by older people.

The social clock reflects social standards. To say that a woman is "too old to marry" or a man is "too old to become a father" is to refer to the social clock, not the chronological one, since even at age 90 women can marry and men can father children. Some ages set by the social clock are enacted into law, in the form of minimal ages for driving, drinking, voting, getting married, signing a mortgage, and being entitled to retirement benefits. Age norms for accomplishments are set by people within each society. As two psychologists explain:

> Although life cycles are becoming more fluid, people are still . . . judged harshly if they do not reach developmental milestones on the timetable set by the social clock (defined by prevailing cultural norms).
>
> *[DePaulo & Morris, 2005]*

A SHIFTING TIMETABLE The social clock is less restrictive now that age boundaries have relaxed. Historical and cultural conditions have changed. For instance, a century ago, women expected to have their first baby before age 20; in developed nations today, most women begin motherhood much later (Bornstein & Putnick, 2007). The median age of first-time mothers is over 30 in many nations, including Spain and Australia (C. Lee & Gramotnev, 2007).

To take another example, almost all college students 50 years ago were aged 18 to 22. By contrast, in the United States in 2005, 37 percent of all enrolled students were age 25 or older—most of them part-time. Some students earn their bachelor's degrees at age 60 or older (Chronicle of Higher Education, 2007).

Lowered Expectations It was once realistic, a "secular trend," for adults to expect to be better off than their parents had been, but hard times have reduced the socioeconomic status of many adults.

As a third indication of the loosening of the social clock's restrictions, retirement age has become more variable. Historically, most people retired at age 65. Then, in the last half of the twentieth century, retirement began to occur at younger ages and continues to do so. Currently, some people retire at age 50 while others are still working at age 80, responding more to economic conditions and individual circumstances than to the social clock.

Not only do culture and cohort affect the social clock, but so does socioeconomic status (SES). The lower a person's SES, the faster the clock ticks; therefore, life's turning points occur at younger ages. In developing nations, many impoverished women *finish* childbearing by age 30. Indeed, the average age for marriage of a recent cohort of women in India was 16; most were surgically sterilized before age 30, usually after several births (Padmadas et al., 2004).

NOT AS WELL OFF AS OUR PARENTS WERE AT OUR AGE

Dana Fradon

THE MIDLIFE CRISIS If the social timetable is so variable, why is the **midlife crisis** frequently referred to in the popular media? This is a time of anxiety and radical change that supposedly begins like clockwork as age 40 approaches. The idea of the midlife crisis was popularized more than 30 years ago by writer Gail Sheehy (1976), who called it "the age 40 crucible," and by psychologist Daniel Levinson (1978), who wrote that midlife men experienced

> tumultuous struggles within the self and with the external world. . . . Every aspect of their lives comes into question, and they are horrified by much that is revealed. They are full of recriminations against themselves and others.
>
> *[p. 199]*

The midlife crisis continues to be referenced in popular movies and books. A 2009 Google search found more than 5 million citations for "midlife crisis." An article in the *Wall Street Journal* claimed that many successful middle-aged men experience this crisis (Clements, 2005), and a popular book aimed at wives is titled *How to Survive Your Husband's Midlife Crisis* (Courter & Gaudette, 2003).

No Evidence Despite this public recognition, no large study has found any evidence for the midlife crisis. Current life-cycle theorists sometimes describe transitions of middle age but never normative crises (Austrian, 2008).

Of course, adults leave jobs and abandon spouses, but these life changes occur at many ages and vary by personality more than by birthday. Some adults never quit their jobs or seek divorce; others do so repeatedly. A midlife crisis is *not* typical for either men or women.

How could earlier developmentalists have been so badly misled? In retrospect, considering cohort, culture, and income, the mistake is easy to understand.

Limits of Research Middle-class men who reached age 40 in the early 1970s were the cohort that provided the data for Levinson and Sheehy. Those men were affected by historic upheavals in their own families, in which teenagers became radically rebellious (the 1960s generation) and wives suddenly became assertive (the first wave of modern feminism). Those phenomena were more common in middle-class than in lower-class families.

Many of those men began marriages and careers in their early 20s (as most of that cohort did), expecting grateful children, wives, and coworkers. For them, middle age raised self-doubts and recriminations, creating an existential anxiety that came to be called a *crisis*. But that crisis was the result of personal and historical experiences, not chronological age.

Furthermore, Levinson's research was based on only 40 men living in New England, with the data analyzed by a multidisciplinary group of men who were also middle-aged. Such a limited sample would no longer be considered sufficient. Sheehy was not trained as a scientist, and her research base was even smaller: She supplemented her reading of research reports by Levinson and other psychologists with interviews of a handful of people. The work of these two authors captured the popular imagination, but neither of them used the replicated, multimethod, longitudinal research designs that are the bedrock of developmental science today.

Personality Throughout Adulthood

Unlike the social clock or stage theories, which emphasize transitions, personality theory emphasizes continuity. Personality, originating from temperament and early experiences (see Chapter 4), provides coherence and identity, allowing people to know themselves and to be known by others over the years (Cloninger, 2003).

Genes, parental practices, culture, and adult circumstances all contribute to personality. Of these four, genes are probably the most influential, according to longitudinal

midlife crisis
A period of unusual anxiety, radical self-reexamination, and sudden transformation that is widely associated with middle age but that actually has more to do with developmental history than with chronological age.

RESPONSE FOR People Under 20 (from page 456) Probably not. While many younger people associate certain ages with particular attitudes or accomplishments, few people find those ages significant when they actually live through them. ●

studies of monozygotic and dizygotic twins and other research (Pedersen et al., 2005). Since genes do not change from conception through death, it is not surprising that every study finds substantial continuity in personality.

THE BIG FIVE As already mentioned in Chapter 4, longitudinal, cross-sectional, and multicultural research has identified five clusters of personality traits—called the *Big Five*—that generally remain quite stable throughout life (Digman, 1990; McCrae & Costa, 2003; B. W. Roberts et al., 2006). As a reminder, the Big Five traits are:

● Openness: imaginative, curious, artistic, creative, open to new experiences
● Conscientiousness: organized, deliberate, conforming, self-disciplined
● Extroversion: outgoing, assertive, active
● Agreeableness: kind, helpful, easygoing, generous
● Neuroticism: anxious, moody, self-punishing, critical

The Big Five (arranged above so that their first letters spell the word *ocean,* as a memory aid) correlate with almost every aspect of adulthood. That includes not only career choices and health habits but also education (conscientious people are more likely to graduate from college), marriage (extroverts are more likely to get married), and divorce (which correlates with neuroticism) (Duckworth et al., 2007; Pedersen et al., 2005).

CHOOSING A LIFESTYLE In adulthood, people choose their particular social context, or **ecological niche.** Adults select vocations, mates, and neighborhoods, and they settle into chosen routines and surroundings. Two researchers quipped, "Ask not how life's experiences change personality; ask instead how personality shapes lives" (McCrae & Costa, 2003, p. 235).

The idea of a chosen ecological niche may explain why, far from being a time of midlife crisis, ages 30 to 50 are marked by more stability of personality than are other periods of life, according to at least one research team (B. W. Roberts et al., 2006). Before age 30, many adults marry, divorce, quit jobs, move, and explore hidden aspects of

ecological niche
The particular lifestyle and social context that adults settle into because it is compatible with their individual personality needs and interests.

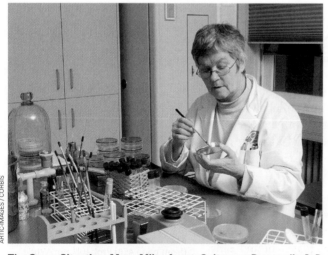
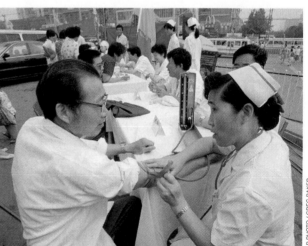

The Same Situation, Many Miles Apart: Culture or Personality? Personality is more evident here than is culture, according to research on the ecological niche. The women in both of these photographs studied biology, but the more introverted one in Iceland *(left)* prefers to analyze samples of fish tissue on her own, while the more extroverted one in China *(right)* takes blood pressure readings in a city square.

their personality; after age 30, they make fewer changes of that kind. Consequently, their personality does not change any further until old age.

Although temperament begins with genes that push people toward one ecological niche or another, adult traits are not immutable. For example, marriage to a warm, supportive spouse affects the personality. Typically, those high in neuroticism do not find such a mate, but if they do, they become less neurotic (Rönkä et al., 2002). By contrast, neuroticism increases if a person experiences a hostile workplace, ill health, or poverty.

If life circumstances are dramatically altered—perhaps by divorce or widowhood, recovery from addiction, emigration, treated depression, a sudden disabling disease—people may behave in new ways (Mroczek et al., 2006). Often, however, new events bring out old personality patterns (McCrae & Costa, 2003; B. W. Roberts & Caspi, 2003).

Young Stephen King

Researchers have particularly studied happiness over adulthood. People who experience things that might make them overjoyed (e.g., winning a million dollars) or depressed (e.g., losing a leg) soon revert to the level of happiness they had before the windfall or tragedy. Personality trumps experience (Gilbert, 2006).

Although stability is more evident than change, the average person experiences some minor personality shifts over the 40 years of adulthood. A massive study of midlife (called MIDUS) found that, of the Big Five, agreeableness and conscientiousness increased slightly while openness, extroversion, and neuroticism decreased (Lachman & Bertrand, 2001).

Other research confirms this finding, adding that extroversion decreases (Allemand et al., 2008; Pulkkinen et al., 2005; Schaie, 2005) (see Figure 13.2). Still another study of 14,000 adults in England and 20,000 in Germany found that conscientiousness peaks at about age 44, then decreases slightly, especially among the British (Donnellan & Lucas, 2008).

These changes do not contradict the conclusion that personality is quite stable. Extroverts at age 20 are still extro-

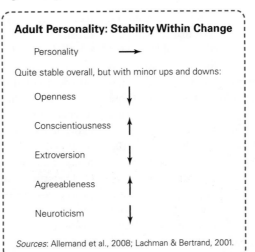

Adult Personality: Stability Within Change

Personality   →

Quite stable overall, but with minor ups and downs:

Openness   ↓

Conscientiousness   ↑

Extroversion   ↓

Agreeableness   ↑

Neuroticism   ↓

Sources: Allemand et al., 2008; Lachman & Bertrand, 2001.

FIGURE 13.2 Trends, Not Rules Overall stability, and some marked individual variation, is the main story for the Big Five over the decades of adulthood. In addition, each of the traits tends to shift slightly, as depicted here.

verts at age 60 when compared with other 60-year-olds. The shift means that, on average, they are slightly less extroverted than they were 40 years earlier.

The overall stability of personality may also be vulnerable to the influence of culture. It seems evident that traits that are pathological within a particular society (such as extreme neuroticism in most cultures) are likely to become less extreme as people grow older (L. A. Clark, 2009). It is possible—but has not been proven—that less notable modifications occur if a particular cultural setting encourages or discourages certain traits. The following examines that possibility.

ESPECIALLY FOR Immigrants and Children of Immigrants Poverty and persecution are the main reasons some people leave their home for another country, but personality is also influential. Which of the Big Five personality traits do you think is most characteristic of immigrants? (see response, page 464) →

A VIEW FROM SCIENCE

Culture and Personality

Two opposite hypotheses offer plausible explanations of the relationship between culture and personality. The first hypothesis is that personality is powerfully shaped by culture, so that, say, a Mexican's personality would be quite different from a Canadian's because of their national contexts. The opposite hypothesis is that personality is innate, fixed at birth and impervious to social pressures. Science finds that both ideas are too simplistic.

On the one hand, evidence for the innateness hypothesis comes from the fact that the same Big Five traits are found in adults of many nations; and everywhere, similar age-related trends are apparent. Surprisingly, national political upheavals have little impact on overall personality among citizens caught up in the turmoil.

An example of the small effect of national events is illustrated in the experience of people living in East and West Germany who were surveyed from 1960 until 2000—a period of radical political disruption during which the communist East and the capitalist West became one country again. Over these years, the basic personality patterns of Germans changed little (Bode, 2003). Other research has also found that personality variations are greater among individuals within a nation than between two nations' averages (McCrae & Allik, 2002; Schmitt et al., 2007).

On the other hand, some research has shown that culture does affect personality. The culture of one nation may encourage a trait that is seldom found in members of other cultures. For example, some social scientists believe that a sixth personality dimension called *dependence on others* should be added to the Big Five because it is significant for Asian cultures and is not captured by the standard five. Social dependence is evident among people in Western cultures, too, but it is more common in Korea, Japan, and China, perhaps because those cultures encourage it (Hofstede, 2007; Suh et al., 2008).

Consider another example. In the United States, the Big Five scores differ slightly for people living in different states. According to an Internet survey of 619,397 Americans, New Yorkers are highest in openness, New Mexicans are highest in conscientiousness, North Dakotans are highest in both extroversion and agreeableness, and West Virginians are highest in neuroticism. Lowest in each of these five are, in order, the residents of North Dakota, Alaska, Maryland, Alaska (again), and Utah (Rentfrow et al., 2008).

This research was based on self-reports collected via the Internet, which is not a random sample—a problem the scientists themselves pointed out. To validate their research, they compared the Internet responses to census data and concluded that the respondents were representative in ethnic, gender, and geographical categories but that there were too few low-income respondents. Further supporting the validity of the research is the fact that the data correlated with other measures. For example, states high in agreeableness tend to have less crime and longer life expectancy.

Of course, not everyone in these states fits the profile, but social norms, institutions, and the geographical setting might influence everyone's personality. Residents of Utah, for instance, grow up among many Mormons (no drugs, large families, good health) and awesome mountains. Those surroundings might make them less anxious, more serene, and thus low in neuroticism.

An alternative explanation is that people whose personalities clash with the culture of their community might move to a state where they feel more at home. A North Dakotan who, unlike his neighbors, was high in openness might feel stifled and relocate to New York.

Patterns of migration in Finland suggest that personality is indeed one factor that could affect a move. A longitudinal study, beginning when participants were children and continuing through decades of adulthood, traced migration within Finland as well as migration to Sweden (Jokela et al., 2008; Silvertoinen et al., 2008). After controlling for factors that made a move more likely (for instance, emerging adults often leave home; adults who have become parents usually stay put), the researchers found that people with an outgoing personality (high in extroversion, or sociability) were more likely to move, especially from an isolated rural area to an urban one. Thus, personality came first and the geographical setting followed.

Consider again the possible sixth trait, dependence on others. It could be cultural, in that children growing up in East Asia might develop the trait because their parents, teachers, and community encourage it. Or it could be genetic, if East Asians over the centuries who were innately strong in social dependence were more likely to survive and hence transmit their genes to the next generation.

The same could be true for traits in most people in the various parts of the United States. Certain traits may benefit people in certain communities, and their offspring would have those traits more than children in other communities. Most people spend their adulthood in the same state where they were born, so over the years, certain personality patterns would become more common in one state or another.

Scientists confirm that people differ in personality and that adults tend to find a spouse, neighbors, and employment that match their inclinations. Whether or not culture nudges people to develop traits that are not inborn remains an open question.

JOSE LUIS PELAEZ, INC. / CORBIS

PETER HORREE / ALAMY

The Same Situation, Many Miles Apart: Caregiving Dads Fathers are often caregivers for their young children, as shown here in Indonesia *(left)* and the United States *(right)*. Most developmentalists think that men have always nurtured their children, although in modern times employed mothers, plastic bottles, and sturdy baby carriers are among the specifics that have changed.

OBSERVATION QUIZ
Is the man on the right really sleeping? (see answer, page 465) →

UNISEX PERSONALITY Are there gender differences in personality? Most people think so. Within nations and internationally, men tend to *express* aggression (more physical fights) and women to *express* nurturance (more child care). Similarly, men take risks, while women are more cautious. That makes men higher in extroversion and openness, women higher in conscientiousness and agreeableness.

These sex differences may be innate, perhaps related to hormones. But it is also possible that men and women *think* they should act in a certain way, being brave and reckless (the men) or patient and sweet (the women) even when they do not want to be. Personality traits vary between individuals far more than between the sexes.

Evidence of *gender divergence,* or differentiation over time, is found on questionnaires assessing the Big Five. However, male and female behavior is more similar than the questionnaire results would suggest. Some developmentalists believe that over the course of adulthood, the two sexes become more alike—a phenomenon called **gender convergence** (Gutmann, 1994).

In a study that began with children who were then followed for 30 years (Pulkkinen et al., 2005), the boys' and the girls' behavior was divergent but, by age 42, the men had become less aggressive and more conforming; the opposite was true for the women. Perhaps because of the culture of youth, which encourages quite different traits in males and in females, scores on these two personality traits diverged in adolescence but were almost identical by middle age.

That was only one study in one nation. Overall, the developmental research on sex differences in personality provides a mixed and complicated picture (Gauthier & Furstenberg, 2005; van der Meer, 2006). In some ways, especially in drug use and employment, gender convergence has increased over the past 50 years as restrictions on women have lifted. This suggests that past sex differences were cultural, not innate. Yet in every modern nation, women still spend more time than men doing housework and providing child care.

gender convergence
A tendency for men and women to become more similar as they move through middle age.

From Warrior to Peacemaker Ariel Sharon joined the Haganah (a Jewish underground military organization) when he was 14, earning a reputation as a brave commando. He served in the Israeli army until he was 45. Elected prime minister in 2001 at age 62, he became known as a champion of peace. He is shown here praying at the Western Wall in Jerusalem.

AP PHOTO / DAVID GUTTENFELDER

● **FOR DEEPER REFLECTION** Do men and women become more similar in personality over the years of adulthood, or do the sex differences that are evident in adolescence remain lifelong?

ANSWER FOR Immigrants and Children of Immigrants (from page 461) Extroversion and neuroticism, according to one study (Silventoinen et al., 2008). Because these traits decrease over adulthood, fewer older adults migrate. ●

This remaining divergence could be biological or cultural. Why are mothers more likely than fathers to spoon-feed babies, brush children's hair, tend to their sick offspring, and so on? Is it because of expectations or personality? Scientists disagree about how, when, and for whom gender divergence or convergence emerges.

> ### KEYｐoints
>
> - Age boundaries in adulthood are fluid; the social clock is less heeded now than it was in earlier generations.
> - Erikson and Maslow both described stages (Erikson: identity, intimacy, generativity, and integrity; Maslow: basic physiological needs, safety, love, respect, and self-actualization), but neither theorist set age boundaries.
> - Personality characteristics tend to be quite stable in adulthood, although some slight age-related trends are apparent. Conscientiousness peaks in middle age.
> - Personality traits are affected by genes and early child rearing, and possibly by geography, culture, and gender.

Intimacy

Intimacy needs are lifelong. As you remember from Chapter 11, adults meet their need for social connection through their relationships with relatives, friends, coworkers, and romantic partners. Specifics vary: Some adults are distant from their parents but close to partners and friends; others rely on family members but not on nonrelatives.

social convoy
Collectively, the family members, friends, acquaintances, and even strangers who move through life with an individual.

Such relationships make each person part of a **social convoy,** a group of people who "provide a protective layer of social relations to guide, encourage, and socialize individuals as they go through life" (Antonucci et al., 2001, p. 572). Members of a social convoy are not necessarily from the same cohort (people born at about the same time) and may not be family members. Even a stranger can become part of a social convoy, if he or she is supportive of a person's life journey.

Thus, social support in adulthood can come from anyone, including relatives (distant cousins as well as members of nuclear families), neighbors, classmates, and acquaintances such as familiar store clerks, bankers, and police officers.

The term *convoy* originally referred to a group of travelers in hostile territory, such as the pioneers in ox-drawn wagons headed for California or soldiers marching across unfamiliar terrain. Individuals were strengthened by being part of the convoy, buoyed by sharing the same difficult conditions with others and better able to defend themselves against attacks.

As people move through life, their social convoy metaphorically functions as those earlier convoys did (Crosnoe & Elder, 2002). The social-convoy perspective applies in childhood and adolescence, since many people other than parents protect and guide each child (Levitt, 2005), but it becomes most apparent as people move through adulthood. Current changes in the historical context, including the trends toward greater globalization, longevity, and diversity, make the sources of intimacy increasingly important (Antonucci et al., 2007).

Friends

Friends are typically the most crucial members of the social convoy, partly because they are chosen for the very traits that make them reliable fellow travelers. They are usually about the same age, with similar experiences and values; thus, they are often able to provide practical help and useful advice when serious problems—death of a family member, personal illness, loss of a job—arise.

Perhaps equally important, friends in everyday life provide companionship, information, and laughter—helping each adult figure out how to get a child to eat his carrots, whether to remodel or replace the kitchen cabinets, when to ask for a raise, and, as time goes on, how to deal with grandchildren, menopause, and retirement.

A comprehensive research study (Fingerman et al., 2004) found that friendships tend to improve with age. Most adolescents and emerging adults rate their friendships as close, but a significant minority consider them ambivalent or problematic. By adulthood, almost all friendships are close, few are ambivalent, and almost none are problematic. (Ironically, the same study found that many adults consider their relationship to their spouse ambivalent or problematic.)

For many North Americans and Europeans, friends are essential, but this idea may not be universal. A study of adults in Germany and Hong Kong found that, over time, the number of close companions was about the same in both cultures, but the Germans tended to feel closer to their friends and the Chinese closer to their family members (Fung et al., 2008). Of course, a family member may also be a friend. Especially in countries where most adults have many siblings and cousins, it is not unusual for some of these relatives to be close companions.

Family Bonds

A close friend is often referred to as being "like a sister" or "my brother." Such terms reflect the assumption that family connections are intimate. Especially when family bonds are similar to friendship bonds, relatives are mainstays of the social convoy.

RELATIONSHIPS BETWEEN ADULT CHILDREN AND THEIR PARENTS Although most adults in modern societies leave their parents' homes to establish their own households, physical separation does not necessarily weaken family ties. In fact, relationships between parents and adult children are more likely to deteriorate if they live together (Ward & Spitze, 2007). (Intergenerational living may signify that either the parents or the children are unable to live independently.)

Living together, in and of itself, is a poor measure of family closeness. In rural Thailand, the greatest influence on whether a young married couple lives with the wife's parents (the traditional custom) or establishes their own household is not affection but income. Thai families establish separate households if they can afford to do so (Piotrowski, 2008). Noteworthy is that the main source of extra income for these Thai families is money voluntarily sent by adult children who work far from home. Thus, out of family loyalty, some adult children support independent households for other adult children, a practice that could be considered a sign of closeness, not distance.

In every culture, when adult children have serious financial, legal, or marital problems, their parents usually try to be supportive. However, the parent–child relationship is smoothest when both generations are independent and doing well. Friction is particularly evident when an adult child has problems and the middle-aged parent has no spouse to buffer his or her distress (E. A. Greenfield & Marks, 2006).

Generally, parents are proud of their adult children, not disappointed in them. Throughout North America and Europe, adult parents seem happy to contribute to the well-being of their adult children by providing money and time, especially when such support is not desperately needed (Albertini, 2007; Antonucci et al., 2007).

A DEVELOPMENTAL VIEW OF FAMILY CLOSENESS Over the years of adulthood, parents and adult children typically increase in closeness, forgiveness, and pride as both generations gain maturity (Connidis, 2001). Today's adults relate well to their

ANSWER TO OBSERVATION QUIZ
(from page 463) Probably not, as some clues indicate the photograph is posed. Look at the angle of the bottle, the age of the baby (old enough to hold the bottle himself), and the father's hand—securely holding on to his son. ●

Like Parent, Like Child Even when a child becomes bigger than a parent, as is evident with this Mexican son and California daughter, parents and adult children continue to admire each other.

parents, even when the latter are over age 65, partly because older adults are usually healthy, active, and independent.

Some closeness is cultural. In North America, Europe, and Australia, older adults cherish their independence and dread burdening their children. Even frail parents seek to maintain independence, feeling that they will have failed in life if they have to move in with their children. By contrast, in China and in some other nations where dependence on others is a desirable personality trait, intergenerational living is not thought of as a burden and does not necessarily reduce affection (Harvey & Yoshino, 2006).

Specifics of family bonds depend on many factors, including childhood attachments, cultural norms, and the financial and practical resources of each generation. One cultural norm is **familism,** the belief that family members should sacrifice personal freedom and success to care for one another. Familism (in Spanish, *familismo*) is particularly strong among Mexican Americans, for whom family solidarity cushions the strains of poverty, parenthood, and prejudice (Behnke et al., 2008).

In general, familism leads relatives to help one another, even if the person who needs help is drug-addicted, abusive, or wanted by the police. In some families, it is considered a betrayal for a family member to report a relative who is abusing his or her children. In such a case, instead of calling the authorities, the relative is expected to take over child care from the parent who is suspected of maltreatment.

A contrasting value is individuality. In families whose adult members are expected to be self-supporting and law-abiding, relatives who violate social standards are not protected from the social consequences.

Family members can disagree in their interpretations of familism. One of my students shot someone (he said it was justified) and then hid in his cousin's house. To his shock and resentment, she turned him in to the police. A famous case was that of the Unibomber, Theodore Kaczynski, who mailed letter bombs that killed 3 people and wounded 23 others. He escaped detection for 17 years until his younger brother became suspicious and alerted the police.

familism
The belief that family members should support one another, sacrificing individual freedom and success, if necessary, in order to preserve family unity.

These are dramatic examples, but often adults who are sick, addicted, unemployed, or single parents expect to be supported and protected by their relatives, who may resent the drag on their own success. In many nations, immigrants and members of minority groups are likely to live in three-generation households, dependent on one another not only for practical reasons but also because of a strong cultural endorsement of familism.

ADULT SIBLINGS Not only do parents and children usually become mutually supportive in adulthood, but siblings often do as well. Although only about one-third of U.S. adolescents consider themselves close to their siblings, two-thirds of adults do, as do almost all the oldest adults (Fingerman et al., 2004; see Figure 13.3).

Adult siblings help one another cope with children, marriage, and elderly relatives. For many adults, siblings become friends, providing both practical support (especially between brothers) and emotional support (especially between sisters) (Voorpostel & van der Lippe, 2007). A

● **FOR DEEPER REFLECTION** When family values conflict with personal success (such as the debate over whether a young adult should go to work or go to college), what is the best way to decide?

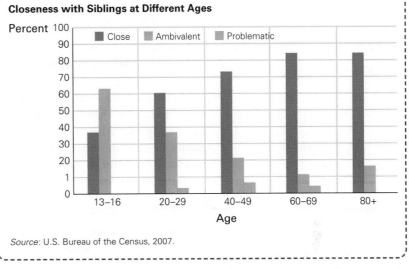

Closeness with Siblings at Different Ages

Source: U.S. Bureau of the Census, 2007.

middle-aged woman who lived thousands of miles from her four siblings said:

> I have a good relationship with my brothers.... Every time I come, they are very warm and loving, and I stayed with my brother for a week.... Sisters is another story. Sisters are best friends. Sisters is like forever. When I have a problem, I phone my sisters. When I'm feeling down, I phone my sisters. And they always pick me up.
>
> [quoted in Connidis, 2007, p. 488]

FIGURE 13.3 From Rival to Friend Adolescents are not usually close to their siblings, but that often changes with time. By late adulthood, brothers and sisters usually consider each other among their best friends.

Sibling bonds are particularly likely to develop during adulthood among children who grew up in large families with major stressors like extreme poverty, a bitter divorce, or repeated racial or religious discrimination. They share childhood memories of surviving despite those difficulties. In those families, adolescents usually criticize one another, emerging adults seek independence, and then older adults connect with the brother or sister they formerly avoided.

Family closeness can sometimes be destructive, however. Some adults wisely keep their distance from their blood relatives. They may instead become **fictive kin** in another family, that is, someone who is accepted and treated like a family member.

Fictive kin are usually introduced to a family by a friend who considers them like a brother or sister; gradually, they are accepted by the other family members. Especially if adults are rejected by their original family (perhaps because of their sexual orientation) or if they are far from home (perhaps immigrants), being adopted by a new family is a lifeline (Ebaugh & Curry, 2000; Muraco, 2006). Adults need kin, fictive or otherwise.

fictive kin
A term used to describe someone who becomes accepted as part of a family to which he or she has no blood relation.

Committed Partners

As detailed earlier, people in every nation take longer than previous generations did to publicly commit to one long-term sexual partner. Nonetheless, although specifics differ (marriage at age 20 is late in some cultures and too young in others), adults everywhere seek committed sexual partnerships to help meet their needs for intimacy as well as to raise children, share resources, and provide care when needed.

Although adults marry later in life than earlier generations did, this change is more a shift in timing than a rejection of intimacy. As explained in Chapter 11, many young adults cohabit, living together before or instead of marrying. Currently, less than 15 percent of U.S. residents marry before age 25, but by age 40, 85 percent have married (U.S. Bureau of the Census, 2008). Furthermore, of those unmarried 40-year-olds, some will eventually marry; about one-third avoid a wedding but are committed to a partner they have lived with for years.

Less than 10 percent of contemporary U.S. adults will never make a marriage-like commitment. In some other nations, less than 2 percent stay single lifelong. Not only culture but also cohort is influential. Of U.S. residents who were born before 1940, 96 percent married, usually before age 25 (U.S. Bureau of the Census, 2008).

MARRIAGE AND HAPPINESS From a developmental perspective, marriage is a useful institution. Adults thrive if another person is committed to their well-being; children benefit when they have two parents who are legally as well as emotionally dedicated to them; societies are stronger if individuals sort themselves into families.

From an individual perspective, the consequences are more mixed. Generally speaking, married people are a little happier, healthier, and richer than never-married ones—but not by much.

A 16-nation survey 20 years ago found one nation (Portugal) where single people were happier than married ones, another (France) where both groups were equally content, and several where married adults were slightly more likely to be "very happy" than never-married adults. The largest differences were in the United States, where more married than single adults were "very happy" (37 versus 26 percent) (Inglehart, 1990). One large longitudinal study of married adults found that

> there were as many people who ended up less happy than they started as there were people who ended up happier than they started (a fact that is particularly striking given that we restricted the sample to people who stayed married).
>
> [Lucas et al., 2003, p. 536]

Thus, most adults marry and expect ongoing happiness because of it, but some will be disappointed (Coontz, 2005). Those who never marry can be quite happy as well (DePaulo, 2006).

Cohort Effects Some people say that modern life has destroyed marriage; others say the opposite. Neither seems entirely true.

Comparing recent marriages with those of previous decades reveals that husbands now do more housework (making them less happy but their wives happier) and more wives are employed (easing financial pressure on the husbands but reducing time spent together). Both spouses tend to be more independent than in the past, when mutual dependency helped to keep couples together. These changes balance out: Overall, marital satisfaction is as high as it used to be (Amato et al., 2007).

Duration Effects Not surprisingly, a meta-analysis of 93 studies found that personal well-being is affected by the quality of the marriage as well as vice versa, especially for people married eight years or longer (Proulx et al., 2007). Domestic violence is more likely early in a relationship than later on (Kim et al., 2008). The long-term quality of a marriage is affected by many factors, including the childhood experiences of both spouses (Overbeek et al., 2007), cohabitation before marriage (decreasing happiness), and the partners' personalities.

The sheer passage of time also makes a difference. For instance, the honeymoon period tends to be happy, but then frustration increases because conflicts arise. Marriages tend to gradually become better by late adulthood (Scarf, 2008). Although

The Same Situation, Many Miles Apart: More Than Yesterday Some older couples worldwide experience greater joy in being together than when they were younger. These married couples are nurtured by their relationship, one on a farm in Mexico *(left)* and the other in St. Paul, Minnesota *(right)*.

marriages tend to be happiest soon after the wedding. Over the decades, fluctuations are rarely dramatic: An abusive partnership may be better ended than endured, and most marriages that are blissful in late adulthood were always pretty good.

Children do not necessarily improve marital satisfaction, although they make divorce less likely. Couples who have children tend to be happier when the children are grown. Marital happiness typically dips at the first child's birth and again when children reach puberty (Kluwer & Johnson, 2007; S. D. Whiteman et al., 2007). (See Table 13.2.)

Contrary to outdated impressions, the **empty nest** (the time when parents are alone again after their children have moved out and launched their own lives) often improves a relationship (Gorchoff et al., 2008). Simply spending time together without the interruptions and stresses of child rearing reminds the couple why they chose each other in the first place; furthermore, pubescent children—a common irritant—are out of the picture.

Another common problem, inadequate income, is also alleviated somewhat, as time goes on. Most child-related costs are no longer a major drain on the couple, and often both spouses are employed at higher salaries than when they were first married.

As the years go by, old arguments are settled as well. Most long-married people stay together because they love and trust each other, not simply because they are

empty nest
The time in the lives of parents when their children have left the family home to pursue their own lives.

TABLE 13.2 AT ABOUT THIS TIME: Marital Happiness over the Years

Interval After Wedding	Characterization
First 6 months	Honeymoon period—happiest of all.
6 months to 5 years	Happiness dips; divorce is common; usual time for birth of first child.
5 to 10 years	Happiness holds steady.
10 to 20 years	Happiness dips as children reach puberty.
20 to 30 years	Happiness rises when children leave the nest.
30 to 50 years	Happiness is high and steady, barring serious health problems.

Not Hard and Fast As always, the phrase "At about this time" is meant to indicate that the time periods given here are very general. For one thing, levels of happiness do not usually dip and rise in marriages without children as much as they do in marriages with children. For another, many couples experience unique circumstances, especially involving employment, that affect their happiness with their relationship.

ESPECIALLY FOR Young Couples
Suppose you are one-half of a turbulent relationship in which moments of intimacy alternate with episodes of abuse. Should you break up? (see response, page 473) ➔

stuck (Previti & Amato, 2003). Several leading researchers cite evidence that some troubled marriages rebound, with spouses becoming happy again as they learn to understand and forgive each other (Fincham et al., 2007).

However, such generalities can obscure specifics. Economic stress causes marital friction no matter how many years a couple has been together (Conger et al., 1999), and contextual factors can undermine a couple's willingness to communicate and compromise (Karney & Bradbury, 2005). A long-standing relationship might crumble, especially with major financial and relationship stresses (such as demanding in-laws or an extramarital affair).

Some long-term marriages are blissful; others are horrible. Marriage has never been magical: It does not necessarily make adults happier or children more successful (Acs, 2007; Foster & Kalil, 2007). As you remember from the discussion of family structure in Chapter 8, correlation is not causation, and there are happy adults and successful children in all kinds of families.

HOMOSEXUAL PARTNERS Almost everything just described applies to homosexual partners as well as to heterosexual ones (Herek, 2006). Some same-sex couples are faithful and supportive of each other; their emotional well-being benefits from their relationship. Others are conflicted, with problems of finances, communication, and domestic abuse resembling those of heterosexual marriages.

Political and cultural contexts for homosexual couples are changing markedly. As of this writing, six nations (Belgium, Canada, Cuba, Nepal, the Netherlands, and Spain) and six U.S. states (Connecticut, Iowa, Maine, Massachusetts, New Hampshire, and Vermont) recognize same-sex marriage. Many other nations and U.S. states are ambivalent about it, and most countries, as well 30 states, explicitly outlaw homosexual marriage. (These numbers are likely to change at any time.)

Because of these recent developments, data from decades ago may no longer be relevant. However, up-to-date research with a large, randomly selected sample of gay and lesbian couples is not yet available, and many smaller studies are designed or cited to prove that gay marriage is, or is not, a good idea.

It is not even known how many committed same-sex couples there are. According to the U.S. Bureau of the Census (2008), only 0.7 percent of U.S. households are headed by an unmarried homosexual couple. All gay and lesbian groups, and most social scientists, consider this an underestimate because many such couples are reluctant to proclaim their status.

Before 2000, the United States census defined an *unmarried couple* as a "cohabiting man and woman." Now *unmarried partners* are allowed to specify male/female, male/male, or female/female. The data (see Table 13.3) show a 31 percent increase in the number of homosexual couples between 2000 and 2006, probably because more homosexual couples are declaring themselves officially.

How Many Homosexual Couples?
The 31 percent increase is probably the result of more same-sex couples being willing to declare themselves in official U.S. statistics. The 7 percent jump among heterosexuals may indicate increased willingness to publicly acknowledge their status, or it may reflect a genuine shift in the number of committed couples who do not want to marry. However, since the homosexual increase is four times as high as the heterosexual one, many undeclared gay and lesbian cohabitants in 2000 were probably braver in 2006.

TABLE 13.3 Unmarried-Partner Households in the United States, 2000 and 2006*

	Male/Female	Male/Male	Female/Female	Total Homosexual Couples
2000	4,881,377	301,026	293,365	594,391
2006	5,237,595	417,044	362,823	779,867
Increase from 2000 to 2006: Number and Percent				
	356,218 (7%)	116,018 (39%)	69,458 (24%)	185,476 (31%)

*Officially declared.
Source: U.S. Bureau of the Census, 2002, 2008.

One recently published study (based on a 1978 survey) of more than 1,000 each of four kinds of couples—gay, lesbian, cohabiting heterosexual, and married heterosexual—found that the couples were similar in most important ways (Kurdek, 2006). Other research on homosexual couples also finds more similarities than differences between them and heterosexuals (Herek, 2006).

All four types of couples were similar in overall satisfaction with their relationships. One of the few differences was that, compared to the other three groups, married heterosexuals with children were less equitable in household labor; most of the wives did far more than half the housework (Kurdek, 2006). In those relationships, both spouses were quite satisfied, probably because the major influence on relationship satisfaction is a person's expectations, which are inevitably based on the social norms of the time.

The greatest difference among the child-free couples was not in the couples themselves but in their parents (Kurdek, 2006). Fathers were less likely to treat the mates of their homosexual children "like family" than they did the mates of their married heterosexual children. Parental acceptance of cohabiting heterosexual partners was halfway between the two.

Another interesting difference was that same-sex couples scored higher than the other couples on contact with friends. Apparently, they were more likely to meet their intimacy needs with their friends than with their relatives.

Divorce

Throughout this text, developmental events that seem isolated, personal, and transitory are shown to be interconnected, socially mediated, and subject to enduring consequences. Divorce is a prime example. Marriages never improve or end in a vacuum; they are influenced by the social and political context (Fine & Harvey, 2006). (See Table 13.4.)

Adults are affected (for better or for worse) by divorce in ways they never anticipated. Generally, those in very distressed marriages are happier after divorce, while those in merely distant marriages (most U.S. divorces) are less happy than they thought they would be (Amato & Hohmann-Marriott, 2007).

Divorce reduces income, severs friendships (many couples have only other couples as friends), and weakens family ties. Family problems arise not only with children (usually custodial parents become stricter and noncustodial parents feel excluded) but also with other relatives (C. Anderson, 2003; V. King, 2003). Many divorced people think they have failed, either as a spouse or in choosing a partner.

Each of these effects also occurs when a cohabiting relationship ends but is worse when a marriage ends (perhaps because marriage connections are more public and legal). Each is particularly devastating if the couple have been together a long time.

The consequences of divorce last for decades. Income, family welfare, and self-esteem are lower among the formerly married than among people of the same age who are still married or who have always been single. Children of divorce often develop academic or social problems, either immediately or later on, adding to their parents' stress (Amato & Cheadle, 2005).

The data show that adults who were divorced decades ago tend to be less happy than their never-married peers. Although some research finds that women suffer from divorce more than men do (their income, particularly, is lower), aging divorced fathers are often lonely, alienated from their adult children and grandchildren (Lin, 2008a).

This research on divorce is sobering. As with all of adult development, the shifting social context may have improved life for the formerly married, and some people escape the usual patterns. Nonetheless, for adult development, divorce is never pain-free.

TABLE 13.4 Factors That Make Divorce More Likely

Before Marriage

Parents were divorced

Either partner is under age 21

Family is opposed

Cohabitation before marriage

Previous divorce of either partner

Large discrepancy in age, background, interests, values (heterogamy)

During Marriage

Divergent plans and practices regarding childbearing and child rearing

Financial stress, unemployment

Substance abuse

Communication difficulties

Lack of time together

Emotional or physical abuse

Relatives who do not support the relationship

In the Culture

High divorce rate in cohort

Weak religious values

Laws that make divorce easier

Approval of remarriage

Acceptance of single parenthood

Sources: Fine & Harvey, 2006; Gottman et al., 2002; R. A. Thompson & Wyatt, 1999; Wolfinger, 2005.

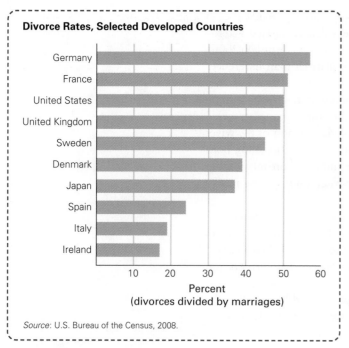

Divorce Rates, Selected Developed Countries

Percent
(divorces divided by marriages)

Source: U.S. Bureau of the Census, 2008.

FIGURE 13.4 Many Troubled Couples Divorce rates are high in most developed countries. One consoling fact is that in the United States, the first nation that saw its divorce rate skyrocket, the rate has held steady for the past 15 years.

OBSERVATION QUIZ

What do the two nations with the lowest divorce rates have in common? (see answer, page 474) ➞

● **UNDERSTANDING THE NUMBERS**

Can you figure out how a society could have a 50 percent divorce rate when less than one-third of the adults ever get divorced?

Answer There are many possibilities. For example:

Imagine a society with 100 adults.

80 percent of them marry = 40 marriages

40 percent divorce = 16 divorces (32 people, less than one-third)

Half of those 32 divorced people marry one another = 8 marriages

Seven of those 8 marriages end = 7 divorces

Four of those 14 divorced people remarry = 2 marriages

Both of those remarriages end = 2 divorces

Total: 50 marriages (40 + 8 + 2) and 25 divorces (16 + 7 + 2) = 50 percent divorce rate, even though 68 percent of the adults never divorced.

CONTEXTUAL VARIATIONS The power of the social context is evident in variations in divorce rates and consequences. Over the past two decades, every nation has seen fewer marriages and more divorces. Even in Ireland and Italy, where once almost everyone married and no one divorced, now about one in every six marriages ends (see Figure 13.4). In the United States, divorce rates have stabilized but are high: Almost one out of two marriages ends in divorce. (This does not mean, however, that half of all adults will divorce, because an increasing number of individuals never marry and others are divorced several times.)

Although divorce is always stressful for adults and children, it is also sometimes beneficial, again depending on the social context. According to research in 39 nations, adults whose parents fought constantly but stayed married report less happiness than adults whose equally conflicted parents got divorced (Gohm et al., 1998).

African American Couples Much depends on the community and other relatives, who may either support or inadvertently punish the survivors of divorce. This helps explain a curious phenomenon: About 70 percent of African American marriages end in divorce or separation, but the children of such relationships are less troubled (as shown, for instance, by failing in school) by divorce than are European American children whose parents divorce (Fomby & Cherlin, 2007).

Another statistic about African American marriages also suggests the power of circumstances: Married African Americans in the U.S. Army are much less likely to divorce than are civilians. This is not true for other ethnic groups (Teachman & Tedrow, 2008). Clearly, ethnicity and social circumstances interact, but it is not obvious exactly how.

Teenage Marriages As already stressed, cohort effects are crucial. This is apparent in teenage marriage. A hundred years ago, people who married before age 20 tended to be happier than those who married later in their lives. The opposite is true now. Married teenagers are likely to become depressed and aggressive, with reduced chances of higher education, professional employment, successful children, and satisfying relationships (Coleman et al., 2007; Glick et al., 2006).

Today, even pregnant teenagers rarely marry. This fact has lowered the divorce rate, which increased beginning in about 1970, decreased slightly in about 2000, and now has stabilized at slightly less than 50 percent.

REMARRIAGE Divorce is most likely to occur within the first five years after a wedding. Usually, former partners reestablish former friendships and resume dating. Often they marry again, especially if they are young men. Women with children are less likely to remarry, but when they do, their new husbands often have children from a previous marriage (Goldscheider & Sassler, 2006). About half of all U.S. marriages are remarriages for at least one of the partners.

Initially, remarriage brings intimacy, health, and financial security. For remarried fathers, bonds with their new stepchildren or with a new baby may replace strained relationships with their children from the earlier marriage (Hofferth & Anderson, 2003). Divorce usually increases depression and loneliness; remarriage brings relief. Most remarried adults are quite happy after the wedding (Blekesaune, 2008).

However, such happiness may not endure. Remember that personality tends to change only slightly over the life span; many people who were chronically unhappy in their first marriage may become unhappy in their second as well. In fact, second marriages end in divorce more often than do first marriages, partly because stepchildren add unexpected stresses (Coleman et al., 2007; Hetherington & Kelly, 2002).

Lewis Terman's 1921 research on gifted children has now produced longitudinal data on marriages that lasted 50 years. One finding is that adults who never married or who had only one marriage were notably healthier and more successful than were participants who married, divorced, and remarried (Tucker et al., 1996).

As with homosexual partnerships and divorce, the social context of remarriage is changing. As remarriages become more common, these strains may be reduced.

RESPONSE FOR Young Couples (from page 470) There is no simple answer, but you should bear in mind that, while abuse usually decreases with age, breakups become more difficult with every year, especially if children are involved. ●

KEY Points

- Intimacy is a universal need that is met in many ways—through friendship, family bonds, and romantic partnerships. Friends buffer against stress.
- Throughout life, family support typically flows from older members to younger ones. Siblings may become more important to each other as time goes by.
- Marriage provides companionship, child-rearing help, and emotional support. Some adults (about 10 percent) never have a long-term romantic partnership but find other ways to meet their intimacy needs.
- Divorce disrupts family ties and friendships. Remarriage may also be problematic, especially if children are involved.

Generativity

According to Erikson, after the stage of *intimacy versus isolation* comes *generativity versus stagnation,* when adults seek to be productive in a caring way. Without generativity, adults experience "a pervading sense of stagnation and personal impoverishment" (Erikson, 1963, p. 267).

Generativity is more likely to come with maturity, but, as already emphasized, chronological age is neither necessary nor sufficient for generative caring and giving (Sheldon & Kasser, 2001). Those who are generative at any age tend to believe their good fortune (more evident with maturity) leads them to help others (McAdams, 2006).

Adults satisfy their need to be generative in many ways, including creativity, caregiving, and employment. Of these three, the link between creativity and generativity has been least studied, although (as we will see in the next chapter) creative expression is recognized as an avenue for self-expression.

We now explore what has been learned about the two other generative activities: caregiving, particularly caring for children, and employment, particularly work that allows personal growth while producing goods or services that help others prosper.

Caregiving

Erikson wrote that a mature adult "needs to be needed" (Erikson, 1963, p. 266). Some caregiving involves meeting another person's physical needs—feeding, cleaning, and so on—but much of it has to do with fulfilling another person's psychological needs. As one study concludes:

> The time and energy required to provide emotional support to others must be reconceptualized as an important aspect of the *work* that takes place in families. . . . Caregiving, in whatever form, does not just emanate from within, but must be managed, focused, and directed so as to have the intended effect on the care recipient.

> *[Erickson, 2005, p. 349]*

kinkeeper
A caregiver who takes responsibility for maintaining communication among family members.

PHOTODISC

Four Generations of Caregiving
These four women, from the great-grandmother to her 17-year-old great-granddaughter, all care for one another. Help flows to whoever needs it, not necessarily to the oldest or youngest.

ANSWER TO OBSERVATION QUIZ
(from page 472) The populations of both Ireland and Italy are predominantly Roman Catholic, but that is also true of France and Spain. The probable reason for the low divorce rates in Ireland and Italy is that the laws of both those nations make divorce very difficult to obtain. ●

Thus, caregiving includes responding to the emotions of people who need a confidant, a cheerleader, a counselor, a close friend. Parents and children care for one another, as do partners. Often neighbors, friends, and more distant relatives are caregivers as well.

Most families include a **kinkeeper,** a caregiver who takes responsibility for maintaining communication among family members. The kinkeeper gathers everyone for holidays; spreads the word about anyone's illness, relocation, or accomplishments; and reminds family members of one another's birthdays and anniversaries. Guided by their kinkeeper, all the family members become generative.

Fifty years ago, kinkeepers were almost always women, usually the mother or grandmother of a large family. Now families are smaller and gender equity is more apparent, so some men and young women are kinkeepers—although most kinkeepers are still older women. This role may seem burdensome, but caregiving provides both satisfaction and power. The best caregivers share the work, and that sharing is itself a sign of generativity.

CARING FOR BIOLOGICAL CHILDREN As Erikson points out, although generativity can take many forms, its chief form is "establishing and guiding the next generation," usually through parenthood (Erikson, 1963, p. 267). Thus, adults pass along their values as they decide how to respond to the hundreds of requests and unspoken needs of each child each day.

Parenting has been discussed many times in this text, with a primary focus on its impact on children. Now we concentrate on the adult half of this interaction—its impact on the parents themselves. Bearing and rearing children are labor-intensive expressions of generativity, although they are not always recognized as such.

Erikson says, "The fashionable insistence on dramatizing the dependence of children on adults often blinds us to the dependence of the older generation on the younger one" (1963, p. 266). This dependence seems capable of being satisfied as much by having one child as by having several (H.-P. Kohler, 2005). As this fact becomes more widely recognized, birth rates continue to fall: The birth rate is below the replacement rate (about two children per couple) in 90 nations.

Every parent is tested and transformed by the dynamic experience of raising children. As experienced parents know, just when an adult thinks he or she has mastered the art of parenting, the child advances to the next stage and the adult is required to make major adjustments.

Over the decades, new babies arrive and older children grow up, the financial burdens of child care change, family income almost never seems adequate, seldom is every child thriving. Illness or disability may suddenly require extra care. If parents have only one child, often they are intensely focused on that child, and some aspect of development awakens concern. Most parents manage to cope with all these demands, and this resilience is evidence of their generativity.

CARING FOR NONBIOLOGICAL CHILDREN As described in Chapter 8, children can develop well in any family structure—nuclear or extended; heterosexual or homosexual; single-parent, two-parent, or grandparent. Can adults also thrive in any kind of parenting relationship?

Roughly one-third of all North American adults become stepparents, adoptive parents, or foster parents. These nonbiological parents face great challenges, but they also have abundant opportunities for generativity.

The Parent-Child Bond One major challenge is the mistaken notion that the only "real" parents are the biological ones. This belief is a social construction that hinders a secure attachment between parents and their nonbiological children.

Many adopted or foster children remain attached to their birth parents, part of the normal human affection for familiar caregivers. However, if their birth parents were abusive, these children's early attachment can be problematic.

A worse situation occurs if children are not attached to anyone (as can happen when they spend years in an institution). They are mistrustful of all adults and fearful of becoming too dependent. Even in the best institutions, few 1-year-olds are securely attached (St. Petersburg–USA Orphanage Research Team, 2008). As one team wrote about children who were growing up in an institution where they received good physical care but little emotional interaction:

> They look at other children or strangers as if they were objects, staring blankly and examining a person as something to be explored or studied. . . .
>
> Older children tend to play in isolation. . . . Toddlers stare and older children are often indiscriminately friendly, running up to a stranger and hugging him or her repeatedly.
>
> *[St. Petersburg–USA Orphanage Research Team, 2008, p. 26]*

Secure attachment is further hampered if both adult and child know that their connection can be severed for reasons unrelated to caregiving quality or relationship strength. Such separations often occur with foster children (Pew Commission on Children in Foster Care, 2004).

Foster parents face the dilemma of "whether to 'love' the children or maintain a cool, aloof posture with minimal sensitive or responsive interactions" (St. Petersburg–USA Orphanage Research Team, 2008, p. 15). A loving bond is better for both the foster parent and the child, and separation is harmful to both. The indifferent attitude of many foster children and institutionalized children is as understandable as it is tragic, and it discourages a generative response.

Stepfamilies The average age of new stepchildren is 9 years, which means that usually they are strongly connected to their biological parents. This helps the child but hinders the stepparents.

Stepmothers may hope to heal a broken family through love and understanding, whereas stepfathers may think their new children will welcome a benevolent disciplinarian. Neither of these expectations is realistic. Some stepparents go to the other extreme, remaining distant from the children. One reason they do so may be that they know their connection to their stepchildren depends on the strength of their relationship with their spouse, the biological parent.

Young stepchildren often get hurt, sick, lost, or disruptive, and teenage stepchildren may get pregnant, drunk, or arrested. If adults overreact or are indifferent to such situations, the two generations become further alienated (Coleman et al., 2007). The temperament of the adults and the nature of the marriage affect whether a family will weather such storms (Ganong & Coleman, 2004).

Ties to the biological parents (custodial or not) seem to be more predictive of how well a child functions than is the quality of the relationship with the stepparent (V. King, 2007; M. E. Scott et al., 2007). Generativity, with patient, authoritative parenting, is needed. With time, most stepparents find satisfaction in their role (Ganong & Coleman, 2004).

Adoption Adoptive parents have several advantages: They are legally connected to their children for life, the biological parents are usually absent, and they desperately wanted the child. Strong bonds can develop, especially when the children are adopted as infants.

Nevertheless, during adolescence, these bonds may stretch and loosen. Some adoptive children become intensely rebellious. As you remember, this can happen with biological teenagers as well, but it is more common among adoptees, who may reject family control as they seek to be reunited with their birth parents (J. K. Kohler et al., 2002).

As mentioned in earlier chapters, the scarcity of adoptable children in North America and western Europe has led more couples in those areas to adopt children from eastern Europe, Asia, and South America. If those children are adopted after 12 months of age, they may have emotional and learning problems that cause difficulties for their parents as well as themselves (Juffer & Van IJzendoorn, 2005).

Adoptive parents who undergo the complications of international adoption are usually intensely dedicated to their children, as are parents of domestic adoptees of a different background. From the parents' perspective, a child's different ethnicity is an insignificant factor.

However, when the children become adults themselves, a complication arises: They need to reconcile their appreciation of their adoptive parents with their pride in their ethnic identity (Trenka et al., 2006). On their part, some adoptive parents are surprised to recognize prejudice in themselves, their communities, and their children (Register, 2005).

Despite such complications, most adopting adults cherish their parenting experience, typically seeking to adopt a second child within a few years of the arrival of the first. As Erikson realized, adults want to be needed, and many adoptees offer their parents an opportunity to be useful every day.

Other Adult-Child Relationships Nonparents (grandparents, teachers, neighbors, aunts, and uncles) may also develop close relationships with children and cherish their generative roles. As one man explained his relationship with his nephew:

> I find I just like talking with him. He needs to express his ideas . . . and I think anything that develops companionship . . . really I don't mind.
>
> *[quoted in Milardo, 2005, p. 1230]*

Perhaps even more than biological parenthood, alternative routes to child rearing can make adults more humble, less self-absorbed, and more aware of the problems facing children everywhere. When this occurs, adults become true exemplars of generativity, as Erikson and others (1986) described it, through caring for others.

Not Lonely When they were 2, 4, and 6 years old, these boys went to live with their grandparents in Virginia. The family is attending a picnic for grandparents who have become surrogate parents for their grandchildren. Events like this fill a need: Many such grandparents feel isolated from their peers.

OBSERVATION QUIZ

This family is typical of grandparent–grandchild families in age and sex. Can you guess how? (see answer, page 478) ➜

WAYNE SCARBERRY / AP / WIDE WORLD PHOTOS

CARING FOR AGING PARENTS In the United States in the twenty-first century:

- Most adults, including two-thirds of middle-aged women, are employed full-time.
- People live longer; most adults have many older relatives.
- Families are smaller (fewer than two children per family, on average).

These three demographic trends mean that fewer adults are available to care for elderly family members and that there are more older adults. It is not unusual for an adult couple to have, between them, twelve parents and grandparents—more than that if there are stepparents or great-grandparents involved as well. It is also not unusual for that couple to have only one or two siblings (or sometimes none at all) who can help with elder care.

Siblings Caring for Their Parents Siblings' relationships can be strained if a parent becomes frail and needs care. One sibling usually becomes the chief caregiver. The inequity of that situation may be resented by everyone, caregiver or not.

For example, in one family, the caregiving sister described one of her two siblings as "real immature . . . a little slow" and the other as "very irresponsible," adding that "when it came right down to having to bathe and having to take care of physical tasks, neither of them would be able to handle it" (quoted in Ingersoll-Dayton et al., 2003, p. 209). A brother in another family resented his caregiving sister: "My sister reminds me all the time that she's taking care of [our parents]. They're actually pretty self-sufficient" (quoted in Ingersoll-Dayton et al., 2003, pp. 208–209).

The reality of linked lives (Chapter 11) means that everyone in the family—caregiver or not, sibling or parent—is strained when a family member becomes ill or disabled (Amirkhanyan & Wolf, 2006). Fortunately, however, most adults never need to deal with that strain because most elders never need full-time care from their adult children. Usually elders care for other elders, as explained in Chapter 15.

The "Sandwich" Generation Because of their position in the generational hierarchy, many middle-aged adults feel an obligation to help both the older and younger generations. They are called the **sandwich generation** (Zal, 1992/2001), a term that evokes an image of a layer of filling pressed between two slices of bread. This analogy suggests that the middle generation is squeezed between younger and older relatives. This sandwich metaphor is vivid, but it gives a false impression (Grundy & Henretta, 2006).

It is true that many adults are concerned about the well-being of their aging parents and grandparents as well as of their children. It is *not* true, however, that most adults are significantly burdened by family obligations. Indeed, the older generation more often helps the younger one, financially as well as emotionally. One U.S. study of married adults aged 51 to 61 with living parents found that less than 20 percent gave significant income or time to aid their parents (Shuey & Hardy, 2003).

Similarly, a longitudinal study of adults in England found that only a minority became family caregivers (Henz, 2006). When adults who were employed professionals began caring for an older family member, they did not usually leave their jobs. Instead, they found someone else—another relative or a paid caregiver—to do most of the caregiving tasks.

Those adults who quit work to become full-time caregivers were, for the most part, less committed to their jobs, which often were part-time and routine (not generative). They also were unlikely to have dependent children or a needy spouse and thus were not sandwiched by their caregiving because one "slice of bread" was missing (Henz, 2006).

Selective Caregiving Interestingly, care for elderly parents does not flow equally to all parents of a married couple. A detailed breakdown found that in the United States,

sandwich generation
The generation of middle-aged people who are supposedly "squeezed" by the needs of the younger and older members of their families. In reality, some adults do feel pressured by these obligations, but most are not burdened by them, either because they enjoy fulfilling them or because they choose to take on only some of them or none of them.

TABLE 13.5 Contacts and Help Provided by Middle-Aged Couples to Parents and In-Laws

	Phone Calls per Month	Visits per Month	Minutes of Help per Week
Wife to own parents	11	6	120
Husband to wife's parents	8	5	70
Total to wife's parents	19	11	190
Husband to own parents	7	4	100
Wife to husband's parents	5	4	58
Total to husband's parents	12	8	158

Source: E. Lee et al., 2003.

both husbands and wives tend to tilt toward the wife's parents in providing care (E. Lee et al., 2003; see Table 13.5). In some other nations, such as China, it is the husband's parents who are more likely to receive support (Lin et al., 2003; Zhan et al., 2006).

An adult's personality and belief in familism are more influential than the needs of the care recipient in determining whether the adult will become a full-time caregiver (Grundy & Henretta, 2006). The U.S. study already mentioned, in which less than 20 percent of married adults were major caregivers for a parent, also found that those same 20 percent more often actively supported their own adult children. The researchers suggest that a personality trait (generosity) is the probable explanation (Shuey & Hardy, 2003).

Caregiving is beneficial because people feel useful when they help one another. A study that examined the attitudes of young adults toward family conflict found that those who were more forgiving and caring were also those whose physiological responses indicated healthier cardiovascular systems (Lawler et al., 2003). Another study found that older adults, aged 50 to 75, were *less* likely to be depressed if they were providing support for their adult children than if they were not (Byers et al., 2008).

Overall, although caregivers are sometimes overwhelmed (as already described in Chapter 7 on child maltreatment), more often caregiving is part of a satisfying relationship in which caregivers are gratified; those who feel overburdened are elderly themselves. Caregiving is further described in Chapter 15.

Employment

Besides family caregiving, the other major avenue for generativity is employment. The interaction between adult development and paid work is not well understood (Bianchi et al., 2005). Most of the research has focused on productivity and career choice. Social scientists need to put "thinking about working into the broader fabric of psychological theory and practice" (Blustein, 2006, p. xiv).

However, psychological theory does not completely overlook employment. Erikson in his *generativity versus stagnation* and Maslow in his *success and esteem* recognized the importance of accomplishments in adulthood. Many other theorists also recognize employment in research on instrumental needs (as contrasted with emotional needs) and achievement-striving (as contrasted with affiliation). It seems that adults want to accomplish something over the course of their lives, not simply to be loved and appreciated.

As is evident from the words *generativity, esteem, instrumental,* and *achievement,* adults have many psychosocial needs that employment can fulfill. The converse is also true:

● **FOR DEEPER REFLECTION** How might caregiving benefit the giver but harm the recipient?

ANSWER TO OBSERVATION QUIZ
(from page 476) The grandparents are relatively young, and the grandchildren are boys, as is the case for most such surrogate parents and children. ●

Unemployment is associated with higher rates of child abuse, alcoholism, depression, and many other social problems (Freisthler et al., 2006).

WAGES AND BENEFITS Salary is sometimes considered a mark of self-worth. Some adults are happy to be earning more than their parents or resentful of being paid less than other workers, quite apart from their basic material needs. In other words, even if a worker has a salary sufficient to pay for food, clothing, and shelter, he or she might resent it if another worker is paid more for doing the same task.

Beginning with Thorstein Veblen (1899/2008), sociologists have described *conspicuous consumption,* in which people buy things—such as expensive cars, hip sunglasses, and MP3 players—primarily for the purpose of showing them off to others. A recent study found that people tend to buy more when they are depressed; money is a mood-changer, and people still display their wealth as a way of asserting their worth (Cryder et al., 2008).

Given this human characteristic, it is not surprising that raises and bonuses increase motivation and that salary cuts have emotional, not just financial, effects. Surprisingly, the absolute amount of income (whether a person earns $30,000 or $33,000 or $40,000 a year, for instance) is less significant to most people than how their income compares to that of others in their profession or neighborhood, or to their own salary a year or two ago.

One finding from research on emotions is that even though average income has doubled, overall happiness within the United States has not risen in the past 50 years. Worldwide, the rich are not necessarily happier than the poor. Extreme poverty correlates with unhappiness, but most people of all incomes are mildly happy and some people at every income level are depressed (E. Diener & Biswas-Diener, 2008).

One reason may be **relative deprivation,** the idea that people compare themselves to others in their group and are satisfied if they are no worse off than the group norm. Thus, relatively poor people who know only other poor people may be quite happy; they are content with what they have, as long as it is enough for food and shelter. However, if people cannot afford to buy what their neighbors have—for instance, a flat-screen television, an extra bathroom, or a new car—they may feel deprived.

Relative deprivation is apparent internationally. One study found it even in Nepal, one of the world's poorest nations (Fafchamps & Shilpi, 2008). In England, workers were less happy and more likely to quit if they thought the salary ranking within their company was unfair, especially if the higher ranks were paid much more than the lower ones (G. D. A. Brown et al., 2008). In the United States, many are offended by extremely high salaries of corporate executives.

The sense of unfairness is innate and universal, encoded in the human brain (Hsu et al., 2008). Of course, the specifics vary by context. For example, Americans might covet a flat-screen television, whereas in poor nations a luxury might be meat for dinner or a pair of new shoes.

Relative deprivation also is evident within professions. This was shown by a study of nurses who were proud to be nurses until a governmental reorganization of the medical delivery system resulted in new demands being placed on them (de la Sablonnière & Tougas, 2008). Although all the nurses had to do more work without an increase in salary, their perceptions differed. Those who identified strongly with their profession had a greater sense of deprivation.

Generally, in times of rapid social change, people work best if they believe their goals are being advanced, even if they do not personally benefit. For example, a nurse who is stressed by new treatment protocols and additional paperwork might not feel deprived if those changes lead to healthier patients and more respect for nurses.

Knowledge of relative deprivation is also useful in understanding attitudes regarding health insurance, which U.S. workers receive primarily through their employers.

relative deprivation
The idea that people compare themselves to others in their group and are satisfied if they are no worse off than the group norm.

About one-third of U.S. adults are uninsured. Globalization has made more Americans aware of the Canadian and European health care systems, which provide care for everyone; as a result, pressure for the United States to switch to a similarly all-inclusive system has been growing.

WORKING FOR MORE THAN MONEY Work is obviously a major concern for economists, who focus primarily on the financial aspects of employment. However, to understand human development, we must focus on the generative aspects of work—and there are many. Work provides a structure for daily life, a setting for human interaction, a source of social status and fulfillment (Wethington, 2002). In addition, work meets generativity needs by allowing people to do the following:

● Develop and use their personal skills

● Express their creative energy

● Aid and advise coworkers, as a mentor or friend

● Support the education and health of their families

● Contribute to the community by providing goods or services

The pleasure of "a job well done" is universal, as is the joy of having supportive supervisors and friendly coworkers. Job satisfaction correlates more strongly with challenge, creativity, productivity, and relationships among employees than with high pay or easy work (Pfeffer, 2007).

Abusive supervisors and hostile coworkers reduce employee motivation and effectiveness. Workers quit their jobs more often because of unpleasant social interactions at the workplace than because of dissatisfaction with wages or benefits (Le Blanc & Barling, 2004).

These facts highlight the distinction between the **extrinsic rewards of work,** which are the tangible benefits such as salary, health insurance, and pension, and the **intrinsic rewards of work,** which are the intangible gratifications of actually doing the job. Intrinsic rewards are more important to developmentalists and, surprisingly, to many workers.

Extrinsic rewards tend to be more important at first, when young people enter the workforce and begin to establish their careers. Then, in a developmental shift, the "intrinsic rewards of work—satisfaction, relationships with coworkers, and a sense of participation in meaningful activity—become more important as an individual ages" (Sterns & Huyck, 2001, p. 452).

The power of intrinsic rewards explains why older employees display, on average, less absenteeism, less lateness, and more job commitment than do younger workers (Landy & Conte, 2007). A crucial factor may be that, in many jobs, older workers have more control over what they do at work, and when and how they do it. This autonomy reduces strain and increases their dedication and vitality.

In a demonstration of this effect, one study began with 972 men who went back to work after having had a mild heart attack. Their work was categorized as high strain (with many psychological demands but little personal control), low strain (fewer demands but more control), or mixed (moderate demands and some control). After controlling for age, high blood pressure, and 24 other factors that make heart attacks more likely, the researchers found that new heart problems (including death) were twice as common among those with high work strain (Aboa-Éboulé et al., 2007).

CHANGES IN WORKING CONDITIONS Obviously, work is changing in many ways—some good for developing persons, some not. As a result of globalization, each nation exports what it does best (and cheapest) and imports what it needs. Specialization, interdependency, and international trade are increasing.

---

extrinsic rewards of work
The tangible benefits, usually in the form of compensation (e.g., salary, health insurance, pension), that one receives for doing a job.

intrinsic rewards of work
The intangible gratifications (e.g., job satisfaction, self-esteem, pride) that come from within oneself as a result of doing a job.

ESPECIALLY FOR Entrepreneurs
Suppose you are starting a business. In what ways would middle-aged adults be helpful to you? (see response, page 000) ➡

The Global Market These women sorting cashews *(left)* and the men working on an offshore oil rig *(right)* are participants in globalization— a phenomenon that has changed the economies of every nation and every family in the world. Radical changes coexist with traditional inequities. For instance, the women here are said to have easy, unskilled work, which is the reason they are paid less than 10 percent of the men's wages.

Advanced nations are shifting from industry-based economies to information and service economies; poorer nations are shifting from subsistence agriculture to industry. Multinational corporations are replacing small, local businesses. Financial entrepreneurs seek to coordinate all this growth, investing to maximize profit.

These changes may affect human development by causing a clash between the best interests of workers and employers. For adults to attain intimacy and generativity, employees' psychological and physical health is more important than profit. Yet owners, investors, and managers judge success on whether "the bottom line" shows a profit, not on whether the workplace fosters caregiving, creativity, comradeship, and esteem (Bianchi et al., 2005).

We will now discuss three new features of the workplace, exploring their implications for human development: diversity among employees, frequent job changes, and nonstandard work schedules.

Diversity of the Workforce Developmentalists welcome employee diversity in background, gender, and ethnicity. Equal-opportunity policies make it more likely that all job seekers will find work that allows them to develop their potential.

Discrimination is still evident, but increasingly employers hire the job applicants who are most likely to perform best, regardless of their background. In the United States, as in many other developed nations, almost half the civilian labor force is female and almost one-fourth is of non-European ancestry—a marked change over a relatively short period of time (see Figure 13.5 on page 482).

Some occupations continue to be segregated by sex or ethnicity, but to a lesser extent than before. For example, in the United States, only 8 percent of nurses are men and only 5 percent of firefighters are women, but both these percentages are almost triple what they were 30 years ago (U.S. Bureau of the Census, 2008).

In a diverse workplace, functioning effectively and happily is a developmental need for everyone. Younger adults have an advantage here, since often they have studied and socialized with people of various backgrounds. Older people have their own

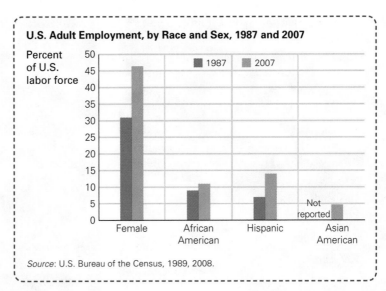

FIGURE 13.5 Closer to Equality
In just 20 years, women and minorities achieved a significantly greater presence in the U.S. workforce. Today, each group's representation in the workforce is almost equal to its percentage of the population. Equality in pay and promotion remains elusive.

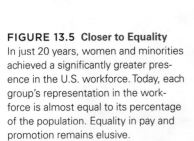

U.S. Adult Employment, by Race and Sex, 1987 and 2007

Source: U.S. Bureau of the Census, 1989, 2008.

mentor
A skilled and knowledgeable person who advises or guides an inexperienced person.

advantage if their life experience has enabled them to shed their adolescent egocentrism. Much depends on the context: The feeling of relative deprivation correlates with ethnic prejudice, probably because people who think their group is unfairly treated seek some other group to blame (Pettigrew et al., 2008).

Human resource counselors seek to identify personal skills and traits that predict how well a prospective employee will work with others of various backgrounds (D. Chan, 2005). A job candidate's personality (openness, agreeableness) is more important in this regard than his or her age.

Diversity in employees' backgrounds presents a challenge for employers as well as for workers. Not everyone has the same expectations, needs, and desires. Differences in these areas increase the need for **mentors,** who can help new employees understand what is expected. Good mentoring is a difficult but gratifying form of generativity (Eby et al., 2006).

On the employer's part, working conditions must be adjusted to accommodate the diversity of the workforce. This involves much more than reconsidering the cafeteria menu and the holiday schedule. The social scientist's understanding of culture is helpful here, since culture includes very basic values, routines, and assumptions, not just superficial differences.

For example, one study found that U.S. employees are most stressed when they have little control over their work or when they have direct confrontations with their supervisors, whereas employees in China are most stressed by the possibility of negative job evaluations and indirect conflicts (C. Liu et al., 2007). Women may be discouraged by working conditions (such as sexual jokes or lack of child care) that men do not notice.

For job satisfaction, culture and gender matter, but other aspects of work matter more (X. Huang & Van de Vliert, 2004). Everyone—employers, coworkers, and social scientists—needs to listen with an open mind to workers of other backgrounds, who may not want or need what traditional workers expect.

Frequent Job Changes One recent change in the labor market that impedes generativity is an increased frequency of hiring and firing. Between ages 25 and 42, the average worker in the United States has five separate employers (U.S. Bureau of the Census, 2008). Some of these job changes are involuntary, resulting from companies' decisions to downsize, eliminate positions, relocate certain divisions, outsource work, cancel contracts, merge, and hire temporary employees. In other circumstances, frequent job changes are voluntary, stemming from workers' ambition or restlessness.

RESPONSE FOR Entrepreneurs (from page 480) As employees and as customers. Middle-aged workers are steady, with few absences and good "people skills," and they like to work. In addition, household income is likely to be higher at about age 50 than at any other time, so middle-aged adults will probably be able to afford your products or services. ●

No matter what the origin, whenever social connections are broken, people suffer. The human costs of job change are confirmed by longitudinal research: People who frequently changed jobs by age 36 were three times more likely to have various health problems by age 42 (Kinnunen et al., 2005). This study controlled for cigarette smoking and excessive drinking. If it had not, the contrast would have been even greater, since poor health habits correlate with job instability.

Older workers find job changes particularly difficult, for at least three reasons:

1. Seniority brings higher salaries, more respect, and greater expertise; workers who leave lose their seniority and can no longer benefit from these advantages.

2. Many skills required for new jobs were not taught 20 years ago, so older workers who lose their jobs have more trouble finding another position.

3. Relocation is more difficult for older workers.

This last factor is crucial. Imagine that you are a middle-aged adult who loves living in Michigan, where unemployment is three times as high as in Idaho. Would you move 2,000 miles away from your family, church, and community to take a job in Boise, Idaho? If you were unemployed and in debt, and a new job was guaranteed, you might. But then, would it be fair to expect your spouse and children to leave their jobs, schools, and social networks and move with you?

Such difficulties are magnified for immigrants, who make up about 15 percent of the U.S. adult workforce and more than 20 percent of Canada's. Not only must they learn their new country's language, culture, and job skills, but they may also encounter hostility at work or in the community.

Many immigrants seek housing as well as social support from other immigrants from their homeland. But by limiting their social contacts in this way, they isolate themselves from the larger community; as a result, their adjustment to their new lives becomes more difficult. If they have had to leave their families behind in their native country, immigrants are vulnerable to loneliness, sexually transmitted infections, and many other problems (Hirsch et al., 2007).

Nonstandard Work Schedules Another recent change in employment patterns is the proliferation of work schedules beyond the traditional 9-to-5, Monday-through-Friday one. In the United States, only about half of all employees work on the traditional schedule (U.S. Bureau of the Census, 2008). In Europe, the proportion of employees on nonstandard work schedules varies from 25 percent in Sweden to 40 percent in Italy (see Figure 13.6; Presser et al., 2008).

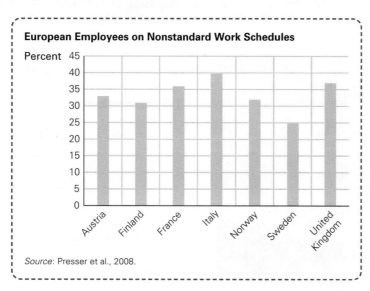

Source: Presser et al., 2008.

FIGURE 13.6 In Whose Favor? The traditional work schedule—Monday to Friday, 9:00 A.M. to 5:00 P.M.—is best for workers and their families. Employers and consumers, however, would prefer to have workers on the job on weekends and during evening and night shifts. European nations tilt toward the standard schedule. In the United States, about half of all workers have nonstandard schedules. In developing nations, most workers have nonstandard hours.

One crucial variable for job satisfaction is whether employees choose their own hours. Workers who can volunteer for overtime and who are paid for their extra time are usually satisfied with their jobs; workers who are required to do overtime, even if they are paid for it, tend to be less satisfied with their jobs (Beckers et al., 2008).

In a recent innovation called **flextime,** flexible schedules allow workers to balance personal and occupational responsibilities. They work the same number of hours as they would under a traditional schedule, but they have more leeway in deciding when to put in those hours. This allows them to take a sick child to the doctor, attend a parent–teacher conference, or meet other personal obligations (Landy & Conte, 2007).

However, flextime is usually offered to senior office workers rather than to people in manufacturing, construction, or service jobs—even though a disproportionate number of young parents are employed in such jobs. Whether or not a worker has a nonstandard or flextime schedule depends much more on the industry than on the worker's parental status (Presser et al., 2008).

In theory, part-time work is also desirable for people like college students, young mothers, and those who want to work two jobs. But the reality does not conform to the theory. In many nations (except the Netherlands, where half the workers are part-time), part-time work is usually underpaid and offers no benefits. Thus, workers avoid it if possible.

About one-third of all working couples who have young children and nonstandard schedules save on child care by having one parent at home while the other is at work. This arrangement, too, has its drawbacks (Presser, 2005). Night work and other nonstandard work schedules correlate with personal, marital, and child-rearing difficulties (K. D. Davis et al., 2008; Joshi & Bogen, 2007; Perry-Jenkins et al., 2007). In addition, health problems increase among workers with nonstandard schedules. One woman probably spoke for many when she said:

> Right now I feel torn between a rock and a hard place—my husband and I work opposite shifts, so we do not have to put our children in day care, . . . [but] opposite shifts are putting a strain on our marriage. . . . It is very stressful.
>
> *[quoted in Glass, 1998]*

Shift work creates a practical problem as well: Adult body rhythms do not allow a person to sleep deeply whenever they want to, day or night. Sleep-deprived adults are often cranky, impatient, and muddle-headed, especially with children. They are more often sick and in pain as well.

For the optimal biosocial development of individuals and families, a regular schedule (even if it always includes odd hours) is better than an irregular one, and a steady job is better than one that involves intense overtime alternating with periods of no work (Presser, 2005). Obviously, developmentalists do not determine corporate policy.

Telecommuting—working at home while keeping in touch with the office via computer, phone, and fax—enables parents to be near their preschool children during the day. It can also be convenient: A telecommuter can interrupt work at any time to answer the door, help a child with homework, or do a load of laundry. Employers like it because it requires less office space, and public officials like it because it reduces rush hour traffic.

However, one study found that while telecommuters "experience the benefits of greater family

flextime

An arrangement in which work schedules are flexible so that employees can balance personal and occupational responsibilities.

telecommuting

Working at home and keeping in touch with the office via computer, telephone, and fax.

No Distractions Like me, this man telecommutes, doing a large proportion of his work at home. He seems to find it easy to concentrate on his task while his daughter reads quietly nearby. For many reasons, I need a home office with a door that closes.

enrichment," the demands of family life can increase the worker's stress by interfering with work efficiency (Golden et al., 2006, p. 1348). Furthermore, telecommuters who live alone miss many of the intrinsic rewards of work, such as the friendships and social interactions that occur when people work together.

Thus, telecommuting, like other nontraditional work, has "an upside and a down-side" (Golden et al., 2006, p. 1348). To a great extent, job satisfaction depends on the particular job, the home situation, and the worker's ability to balance intimacy and generativity needs (Voydanoff, 2007).

Chosen schedules (optional overtime, flexible hours) increase worker motivation, happiness, and health (Grzywacz et al., 2008; E. J. Hill et al., 2008). Although some employers consider the needs of developing persons as they schedule work, most do not (Breaugh & Frye, 2008).

> ### KEY Points
>
> - Adults seek to be generative, which includes creativity, caregiving, and satisfying employment.
> - Raising children is difficult but rewarding. Each stage of a child's development, and each type of biological and nonbiological parenthood, challenges adults to be generative.
> - In addition to providing a livelihood, work has intrinsic rewards that, from a developmental perspective, are crucial.
> - Work-related factors such as diversity of employees, frequent job changes, and nonstandard schedules are extremely important in adult development.

Coping with Stress

The final topic for this chapter is coping with stress, which may originate in any aspect of adult development—physical, cognitive, or social. Every adult encounters many stresses between ages 25 and 65.

Examples and Definitions

If you read this chapter with your own experiences in mind, you understood that there is no one who always has a close circle of friends; an affectionate bond with parents and siblings; a blissful marriage; children and elders who appreciate the care they receive; work that is fairly compensated; and coworkers who are companions, mentors, and protégés. Even in the best of adult lives, disturbances occur.

Furthermore, some physical or cognitive problems appear during these years. The problem might be merely the need for glasses or minor aches and pains, or it might be a cancer scare or notable memory loss. In short, stress is inevitable; the crucial question is how an adult responds to it.

We must begin our discussion of stress by clarifying two terms: *stressor* and *allostatic load*. A distinction can be made between a *stress* (which *might* cause a person to feel physical or mental pressure, tension, or strain) and a **stressor** (which actually *does* have an adverse effect on a person). Many stresses are stressors for one person but not another. An insult might be quickly forgotten or might linger; a long walk on a cold day might be either an invigorating outing or a brutal stressor.

stressor
Any situation, event, experience, or other stimulus that causes a person to feel stressed.

Traditionally, each stressor was considered separately, contrary to the dynamic-systems approach (described in Chapter 1). Now extensive research shows that the accumulated interaction of many stressors is pivotal; too great a buildup of stress has the potential to cause a physical or emotional breakdown.

allostatic load
The total, combined burden of stress and disease that an individual must cope with.

Allostatic load is the term for the total burden (load) on a person's body from all the stressors experienced, both physical (such as obesity) and psychological (such as divorce) (Chida & Hamer, 2008). *Allostasis* is the ability to maintain stability through change; it is connected to homeostasis. To measure allostatic load, a combination of 10 or more biological markers are assessed (including blood pressure, various hormones, and blood glucose level). All stressors have an impact, and this combination of measurements reveals it.

The idea underlying allostatic load has appeared many times in previous chapters, although it has not been named as such. A cascade of adverse circumstances and harmful substances may cause problems in prenatal development (alcohol and nicotine are more teratogenic in combination than alone), in childhood (divorce is harder on a child who is entering a new school), and in adolescence (a teenager who drops out of school is also more likely to become depressed, to use drugs, and to get pregnant).

Allostatic load is even more significant in adulthood, in part because the buffers of youth (a growing body, parental protection) are gone. Almost any adult can cope with one or two problems, such as criticism from a supervisor or an occasional bout of insomnia. However, each additional problem increases vulnerability. That same remark or sleepless night may be the final straw, causing an emotional or physical breakdown.

A Cascade of Stressors

Some stressors, such as serious illness or unexpected job loss, are major. Others are minor but ongoing hassles, such as traffic on the daily commute or the added work of raising twins. The hypothalamus reacts to stressors by triggering the release of hormones (mainly cortisol and adrenaline) that protect the body by helping it adapt, maintain homeostasis, and overcome the problem.

However, physiological reactions take a toll, and past stressors make it more likely that a new stressor will have an impact. For example, that criticism from a supervisor might be magnified by the fact that it echoes parental criticism endured decades earlier. An occasional traffic jam or crowded train is no problem, but a difficult daily commute to work can undermine health (G. W. Evans & Wener, 2006; Gottholmseder et al., 2008). Repeated stress responses cause physical damage as hormonal reactions eventually tax tissues and organs, accelerating disease processes.

Furthermore, each stressor makes the others worse. A simple example comes from marriage. Having several sources of strain in a marriage at once—say, money troubles *plus* drug abuse *plus* in-law conflicts—reduces marital satisfaction faster than would be predicted by simply adding up the effects of each strain (Rauer et al., 2008). In turn, having marital problems affects work performance, consistency of parenting, and physical health.

Although the measurements of allostatic load are biological and the verifiable consequence is disease, every aspect of development—body, mind, and social world—is a potential cause, a possible defense, and a notable outcome of excessive stress. Stressors make the immune system less efficient, weaken the working memory, and fray the temper. Thus, a woman dealing with a stressor in one aspect of life, such as her mother's illness, is likely to catch a cold, forget her keys, and pick a fight with her husband.

Physiological measures of stress reflect past events as well as current stressors, including diseases that have been overcome or discord, hunger, and neighborhood violence that were experienced in childhood. A large allostatic load first causes minor health problems (e.g., recurrent indigestion) and then increases the risk of major disease (e.g., cancer or heart disease), premature aging (in appearance as well as strength), and death (Geronimus et al., 2006).

AGE EFFECTS This progression from a stomachache to a heart attack is apparent over the years of adulthood (Crimmins et al., 2003). For example, U.S. veterans who, as healthy young men, fought in World War II, Korea, or Vietnam were assessed in middle age. The veterans who had symptoms of post-traumatic stress disorder (PTSD) (e.g., sleep problems, flashbacks, startle reactions) but no evidence of heart disease were followed for 11 to 16 years. By then, they were far more likely to have had heart attacks than were other veterans, also followed longitudinally, who had similar combat experiences but who did not develop PTSD (Kubzansky et al., 2007).

To better understand the effect of chronic stressors, it is useful to understand another concept, **organ reserve.** Each part of the body is designed to have an extra capacity, or reserve, for withstanding unusual events. For example, the organ reserve of the lungs allows a person to obtain enough oxygen when climbing a mountain at high altitudes. Even though senescence begins at about age 20, it is not usually noticed until much later because the gradual declines in organ strength begin in the reserve, not in the daily output. Only in unusual conditions, such as mountain climbing, does age become relevant.

Research on stressors and allostatic load suggests that humans have a wide-ranging *recovery reserve* that is activated in emergencies. Recovery reserve includes organ reserves and homoeostasis, which trigger responses in both the mind and the body.

The selective optimization with compensation described in Chapter 12 works for health as well as cognition: When an older person must deal with a crisis at work, he or she uses recovery reserve to meet the challenge, typically performing as well as a younger person. Age can become a factor *after* the crisis, however, as the older worker may need extra time to unwind.

Age differences are apparent in strategies for coping with stress. Younger adults tend to use **problem-focused coping,** attacking the issue directly. For example, if their work situation is difficult, they might complain to their boss, transfer to another location, quit their job, or find some other way to eliminate the problem. If their romantic relationship is troubled, they might discuss necessary changes with their partner or plan a breakup.

Older adults are more likely to use **emotion-focused coping,** changing their feelings about a situation rather than changing the situation itself. For example, in a stressful work context, they might remind themselves that the boss's opinions are uninformed or they might rely on a good relationship with a coworker, joking and complaining but not taking direct action. If something about their marriage is frustrating, older adults might focus on their partner's good qualities and ignore the annoying ones.

GENDER DIFFERENCES Gender also affects how a person responds to stress and thus affects allostatic load (Aldwin, 2007). Among dual-earner families, men are more likely to let work stress interfere with their mood, becoming a stressor; women, in contrast, are more troubled by marital stress. This is a tendency, not a universal difference: Both men and women are affected by both kinds of stress (Saxbe et al., 2008).

Biologically, the two sexes respond differently to stress. Men are inclined to be problem-focused, reacting in a "fight-or-flight" manner. Their sympathetic nervous system (faster heart rate, increased adrenaline) prepares them for attack or escape. Their testosterone level rises when they attack a problem and decreases if they fail.

organ reserve
The capacity of human organs to allow the body to cope with unusual stress.

problem-focused coping
A strategy often used by younger adults to deal with stress in which they tackle a stressful issue directly.

emotion-focused coping
A strategy often used by older adults to deal with stress in which they change their feelings about the stressor rather than changing the stressor itself.

KATHLEEN MCLAUGHLIN / THE IMAGE WORKS

Stress or Stressor Facing a desk overflowing with income tax forms and checks is stressful, and this woman is new to the job—she began it less than a year ago. Will she quit? Probably not. She is mature enough to establish priorities and to cope with any unreasonable demands from her supervisor.

On the other hand, women are more emotion-focused, likely to "tend and befriend"—that is, to seek the company of other people when they are under pressure. Their bodies produce oxytocin, a hormone that leads them to seek confidential and caring interactions (S. E. Taylor, 2006; S. E. Taylor et al., 2000).

This gender difference in coping explains why a woman might get upset if a man doesn't want to talk about his problems and why a man might get upset if a woman just wants to talk instead of taking action. Both problem- and emotion-focused coping can be effective in overcoming stresses; individuals need to learn from one another that every man and woman should sometimes fight and sometimes befriend.

TALK AND THOUGHT Virtually every study finds that social support is crucial in reducing allostatic load. People seek companionship, connecting with sympathetic friends and relatives when a sudden tragedy occurs. Social support reduces the body's production of cortisol, a major stress hormone, and thus reduces allostatic load.

Intimacy helps with both physical and psychological health (Krause, 2006). Women may have an advantage here, in that they are more involved in receiving and giving care. In a study of working conditions and severe depression, both sexes were twice as likely to become depressed if they lacked social support, but the men were more troubled and lonelier when work strain occurred (Robertson Blackmore et al., 2007).

A person's interpretation of the situation is a major reason why some stresses become stressors and others do not. As you learned in the discussions of stress in childhood (Chapter 8) and of stereotype threat (Chapter 11), a person's thoughts about an event affect how he or she responds to it. In adulthood, past experiences continue to guide perceptions, affecting whether a particular event will become a stressor.

The power of past experiences to affect cognition was shown by an experiment in which African American and European American students read transcripts of discussions among hiring teams who were supposedly analyzing job applicants (Salvatore & Shelton, 2007). Sometimes the applicants were judged on their merits regardless of race; sometimes the judgments were clearly racist; and sometimes a minority applicant was rejected with reasons that seemed plausible though not entirely convincing.

After reading the transcripts, the participants took a test that required mental concentration. The performance of the European Americans was impaired after they read the blatantly racist responses but not after they read the more subtle ones. The opposite was true for the African Americans—their intellectual sharpness was not affected by the clearly racist responses but was hindered by the ambiguous ones.

The experimenters believe that this result shows that the African Americans were not surprised by overt racism, so mentally processing the racist transcripts did not require much mental energy. However, more subtle prejudice did trouble them because considerable mental effort was required for them to decide whether racism was a factor.

The importance of interpretation is also evident in research on work/family strain. Many social scientists, as well as the general public, once assumed that mothers who worked outside the home would experience stress from *role overload* as they tried to be both good parents and good employees. Most recent research finds that dual roles do not usually create stressors, primarily because women gain additional support and pride from working, and those benefits buffer any stress they might encounter (R. C. Barnett & Rivers, 2004; Hill et al., 2008).

As you might expect, a crucial factor is the working mother's interpretation of her role as mother and worker. If she believes that her children are better served by having an employed mother, then the children will probably do well, especially if she also spends time with them when she is not working. In fact, the research on maternal employment finds that the attitude and behavior of the mother and father are crucial in the children's achievement and happiness (Harrison & Ungerer, 2002; A. C. Huston et al., 2002).

Earlier, we noted a recent study's finding that, although the division of household work between two committed partners varied widely, the partners were usually quite satisfied if they thought the division was fair. This was true of both heterosexual and homosexual couples, although married women did much more than half the housework (Kurdek, 2006). As another research team wrote, "Despite huge imbalances in the distribution of household labor, scholars have been surprised by the relatively low prevalence of perception of injustice on the part of women" (M. Braun et al., 2008, p. 1145).

In a study of 25 nations, women's perceptions of equity in household work were much less influenced by the actual amount of work they did than by their ideology regarding how much work they should do. Women in Portugal felt most fairly treated, even though their husbands did less housework than did husbands in some other nations. Equal work is not universally appreciated; fairness is (M. Braun et al., 2008).

This point about perception of fairness pertains to every topic in this chapter. Whatever values are expressed and whatever decisions are made regarding children, marriage, elder care, or employment, if a person has considered the issues, made a choice, and followed up with action, the situation is unlikely to become a stressor. To return to the theme stated at the beginning of this chapter, variations in adult norms and social clocks are widespread; no one pattern seems ideal.

To close our discussion of adulthood and to preview the next stage, late adulthood, consider what Erikson wrote: "Although aware of the relativity of all the various life styles which have given meaning to human striving, the possessor of integrity is ready to defend the dignity of his own life style" (Erikson, 1963, p. 268). Thus, the ability to appreciate the diversity of lifestyles while maintaining one's chosen ways to achieve intimacy and generativity is the mark of integrity, the final goal of adulthood.

KEY points

- Stress is frequent in adulthood. Some situations become stressors, increasing the allostatic load.
- Each person's body, mind, and social world interact to create stressors, to defend against them, and sometimes to suffer because of them.

SUMMARY

Ages and Stages

1. Adult development is remarkably diverse, yet it appears to be characterized by two basic needs, intimacy and generativity. First, adults seek intimacy, which is achieved through friendships, family attachments, and romantic partnerships.

2. Traditional patterns of development following specific tasks at specific ages have been replaced by more varied and flexible patterns. The social clock still influences behavior, but less profoundly than it once did. The midlife crisis does not usually occur.

3. Personality traits are a source of continuity. The Big Five traits —openness, conscientiousness, extroversion, agreeableness, and neuroticism—are often stable in adulthood. The two sexes may become more similar to each other as people age.

4. Each person selects an ecological niche of career, partner, and social context which reinforces personality patterns. Culture and social roles also influence personality.

Intimacy

5. Everyone has a social convoy of other people with whom to travel through life. Friends are crucial for buffering stress and sharing secrets.

6. Siblings typically become closer over the years of adulthood, and adult children and their parents continue to help each other in practical and emotional ways.

7. Almost all adults find a partner to share life with, usually raising children together. Some marriages improve with time; others do not.

8. Homosexual partnerships are similar in most ways to heterosexual ones. Single people fare well if they have close friends. Social contexts are crucial for all kinds of relationships.

9. Divorce is difficult for every family member. Remarriage solves some of the problems of divorced adults (particularly involving finances and intimacy), but such new family relationships are often complicated, with divorce more likely than in a first marriage.

Generativity

10. Adults seek to feel generative, achieving, successful, instrumental—all words used to describe a major psychosocial need. This need is met through creativity, employment, and caregiving.

11. Caring for partners, parents, children, and others is a major expression of generativity. Often one family member becomes the chief kinkeeper and caregiver, usually by choice. The sandwich generation metaphor is misleading.

12. Many adults care for children who are not their biological offspring. Step-, foster-, and adoptive parenting can be both challenging and satisfying. Aunts and uncles also can be generative for the next generation.

13. Employment brings many rewards to both men and women, including intrinsic benefits such as pride and friendship. Changes in employment patterns—including job switches, shift work, and diversity of coworkers—affect other aspects of adult development.

Coping with Stress

14. Adults experience many stresses as they seek to meet their intimacy and generativity needs. They use various coping measures, both problem-focused and emotion-focused, depending on the particular issue as well as on the person's age.

15. A combination of stressors increases allostatic load and reduces health. Social support and judgments of fairness protect against illness and distress.

KEY TERMS

social clock (p. 457)
midlife crisis (p. 459)
ecological niche (p. 460)
gender convergence (p. 463)
social convoy (p. 464)
familism (p. 466)
fictive kin (p. 467)

empty nest (p. 469)
kinkeeper (p. 474)
sandwich generation (p. 477)
relative deprivation (p. 479)
extrinsic rewards of work
  (p. 480)

intrinsic rewards of work
  (p. 480)
mentor (p. 482)
flextime (p. 484)
telecommuting (p. 484)
stressor (p. 485)

allostatic load (p. 486)
organ reserve (p. 487)
problem-focused coping
  (p. 487)
emotion-focused coping
  (p. 487)

KEY QUESTIONS

1. Describe the two basic needs of adulthood.

2. How does the social clock affect life choices for both high-income and low-income adults?

3. Explain how the midlife crisis, the empty nest, and gender convergence might reflect cohort rather than maturational changes.

4. Compare the various sources of intimacy.

5. What are the psychological and social factors that make divorce better or worse for an adult?

6. How are family relationships affected by the passage of time?

7. Compare the advantages and disadvantages of biological and nonbiological parenthood.

8. Women are more often kinkeepers and caregivers than are men. How is this role both a blessing and a burden?

9. Pick one of the changes in work over the past decades and explain how it has affected family life and adults' development.

10. Who benefits and who suffers from the increased diversity of the workplace?

APPLICATIONS

1. Describe a relationship that you know of in which a middle-aged person and a younger adult learned from each other.

2. Did your parents' marital and employment status affect you? How would you have fared if they had chosen other marriage or work paths?

3. Think about becoming a foster or adoptive parent yourself. What would you see as the personal benefits and costs?

4. Ask several people how their personalities have changed in the past decade. The research suggests that changes are usually minor. Is that what you found?

Adulthood: Ages 18–65

BODY

Protective health
Peak strength in early adulthood
Homeostasis
Organ reserve
Exercise

Sexual development
Sex without marriage
Sexually transmitted infections
Declining fertility
Declining hormones

Senescence and illness
Obesity increases
Hearing: Less acute
Vision: More farsighted

Violent death in early adulthood

Disability, morbidity, mortality in middle age

Cumulative stress (allostatic load)

No preventive health care (low SES)

"THE NEED TO BE NEEDED"
ADULTS FIND IDENTITY, INTIMACY, AND GENERATIVITY

THINKING AND LEARNING

Combining emotions and logic
Multiple perspectives and flexibility
Experience as a teacher
Tertiary education: Advances from college

Intelligence
Fluid intelligence decreases
Crystallized intelligence increases
Selective expertise

Stereotype threat

Information processing
Sensations lead to perceptions
Memory advances

College not accessible (too expensive, lack of family support)

GENERATIVITY

Employment
Diversity: Opportunities
  for women and minorities
Status and productivity
Social connections

Raising children
Biological offspring
Adopted, step-, and
  foster children

Caregiving
Kinkeepers

**Myth: Sandwich
generation**

**Nonstandard
work schedules**

Unemployment

PERSONALITY

Emerging adulthood
Risk taking:
  Drug experimentation
Edgework:
  Brave and foolish

Big Five traits
Stability over time
Ecological niche
  (chosen)
Some change
  (less neuroticism)
Gender convergence

Myth: Midlife crisis

**Depression,
anxiety,
schizophrenia**

INTIMACY

Romance
Cohabitation
and marriage
Same sex and
other sex
Passion and
commitment

Family connections
With parents
With siblings
With grown children

Friendship
Cultural variations
Social convoy

Divorce

Remarriage

**Myth: Empty
nest syndrome**

KEY

■ Major topic
■ Related topic
■ Potential problem

part VII

Late Adulthood

What emotions do you think you will experience as you read about development in late adulthood? Given the myths that abound about old age, you might expect to feel discomfort, depression, resignation, and sorrow. At moments as you read the next two chapters, such reactions are appropriate.

However, your most frequent reaction may be surprise. For example, you will learn in Chapter 14 that thousands of centenarians are active, alert, and happy and that severe intellectual decline in late adulthood ("senility") is unusual. Chapter 15 describes relationships between the generations, and among elders themselves, that are often quite satisfying. In fact, elders are more positive about their lives, marriages, and other social relationships than are many younger adults.

Generally, late adulthood continues earlier patterns rather than breaking from them. Older adults reap the benefits of lifelong health habits, education, close friendships, family connections, and work. Instead of resigning themselves to lonely isolation, most older adults are social and independent.

This period of life, more than any other, is a magnet for misinformation and prejudice. Why? Think about the answer whenever you are surprised by the facts and research findings presented in the next two chapters.

CHAPTER OUTLINE

LATE ADULTHOOD
Body and Mind

" "How does it feel to be 90?" I asked my mother on her birthday.

"OK, but 89 felt better."

My father chuckled. "She's amazing. She comes out with these zingers."

They looked old, but their humor was as intact as their love for each other.

My friends asked, "How are their minds?"

Thinking of my mother's wit, I answered, "Good."

"Isn't that wonderful!" my friends sometimes replied.

I wanted to shout, "No! Not wonderful!" and lecture about aging bodies and minds. But the picture was too complicated for a simple denial. My parents moved slowly, in pain, and told me stories I had already heard. Not wonderful. But I knew that my friends were really asking about senility. Like most elderly people, my parents were not what people would consider senile. ●

LATE ADULTHOOD IS COMPLEX, as many signs of aging appear: Bones get brittle, hearing fades, everything slows down. Yet there are surprising strengths, including wit and wisdom. For some of my friends and many other people, prejudice makes it hard to recognize the complexities of elderly adults' strengths and limitations. This chapter explains both.

Ageism

What proportion of the population of the United States is over age 65? Of those, how many are in nursing homes or hospitals? How about in the entire world? (Make a note of your answers. These questions will be answered soon.)

Two leading *gerontologists* (social scientists who study the biological, psychological, and sociological aspects of aging) noted:

> The "typical" old person is often viewed as uninterested in (and incapable of) sex, on the road to (if not arrived at) senility, conservative and rigid. The stereotype would have us believe that old people are tired and cranky, passive, without energy, weak, and dependent on others.
>
> *[Schaie & Willis, 1996, p. 17]*

This stereotype is false. It arises from **ageism,** the tendency to categorize and judge people solely on the basis of their chronological age. "Ageism is a social disease, much like racism and sexism" in that it considers people as part of a category and not as individuals, creating "needless fear, waste, illness, and misery" (Palmore, 2005, p. 90).

ageism
A form of prejudice in which people are categorized and judged solely on the basis of their chronological age.

Good Game All the players in this senior baseball league are men over age 65. Older athletes are not as quick as younger ones, but they excel at sportsmanship.

ESPECIALLY FOR Young Adults
Should you always speak louder and slower when talking to a senior citizen? (see response, page 501) ➡

Partly because ageism has been identified and its harmful effects made known, and partly because the baby boomers—the large cohort of active adults born between 1946 and 1964—are now entering late adulthood, stereotypes about the elderly are not as widely held as they once were. Nonetheless, ageism lurks in the attitudes of everyone, including the elderly themselves.

One manifestation of ageism is **elderspeak**, the condescending way many younger people talk to the elderly. Like child-directed speech (discussed in Chapter 3), elderspeak is characterized by simple and short sentences, exaggerated emphasis, slower speech, higher pitch, louder volume, and frequent repetition (Burke & Shafto, 2007). People who use elderspeak are likely to enunciate artificially, or to call an older person "honey" or "dear," or to use a nickname instead of a surname ("Sammy," not "Mr. White").

Service providers (such as social workers and nurses) who know only the age, not the person, often use elderspeak (B. P. O'Connor & St. Pierre, 2004). Indeed, people of all ages are kinder to, and less critical of, those whom they perceive to be old (Fingerman et al., 2008).

Some older adults react to such condescension with anger or, worse, self-doubt. The effects are insidious, seeping into the older person's feelings of competence and undermining self-esteem. The result may be a downward spiral, as self-doubt allows the rates of senility, morbidity, and mortality to increase (Bugental & Hehman, 2007).

Believing the Stereotypes About Old Age

Thus, ageism becomes a self-fulfilling prophecy that undercuts health and intellect (Golub & Langer, 2007). Adults who have ageist ideas are likely to be less capable decades later when they themselves are old (Levy & Leifheit-Limson, 2009).

Perhaps the worst part is that many older people agree with ageist stereotypes. Most people over age 70 think they are doing well compared with other people their age—who, they believe, have worse problems and are too self-absorbed (Cruikshank, 2003; Townsend et al., 2006).

AN IMAGINED THREAT *Stereotype threat,* or anxiety about the possibility that other people have prejudiced beliefs (discussed in Chapter 11), can be as debilitating for the aged as for other stereotyped groups (Chasteen et al., 2005). If the elderly fear they are losing their minds because they believe that old age inevitably brings dementia, that fear itself may undermine their cognitive competence (Hess et al., 2009).

Those older people who think their contemporaries are impaired by age often fear that they themselves may be judged harshly. Responses to that stereotype threat include dyeing hair, undergoing plastic surgery, dressing in youthful clothes, and moving quickly to look agile (or spry), especially when anxiety makes them think slowly and remember less.

Does ageism really bother the elderly? Some ageism seems benevolent. For instance, older people send sentimental cards to one another and report more positive social relationships (Fingerman et al., 2008). But kindness can be demeaning if it implies that a person is less capable than he or she used to be or than other people are.

THREE RESEARCH EXAMPLES One study measured perceptions of discrimination (such as people acting as if the participants were not smart) in older African American and European American residents of Chicago (L. L. Barnes et al., 2008).

elderspeak
A condescending way of speaking to older adults that resembles baby talk, with simple and short sentences, exaggerated emphasis, repetition, and a slower rate and a higher pitch than normal speech.

The researchers were surprised to find that Whites seemed more negatively affected by discrimination than Blacks did.

They reasoned that ageism was the problem: Those who had not experienced much prejudice when they were younger were unprepared for ageism and had trouble coping with it. In this study, the ultimate negative consequence was mortality: European Americans (but not African Americans) who reported more prejudice were also more likely to die within the next five years (L. L. Barnes et al., 2008).

The influence of stereotyping was apparent in a second study. This one included members of two groups that might be less exposed to ageism: residents of China, where the old are traditionally venerated, and deaf people in North America, whose disability prevents them from hearing elderspeak (Levy & Langer, 1994).

Memory tests were given to old and young adults from these two groups and from a third group, hearing North Americans. As expected, in all three groups the elderly people scored lower than the younger adults. As you will read soon, some memory loss in late adulthood is not unusual.

However, measuring memory loss itself was not the purpose of this study. Instead, the researchers wondered whether the gap between younger and older adults would be affected by ageism. It was. The gap in memory scores between younger and older hearing North Americans was twice as wide as the gap between older and younger deaf North Americans and five times wider than the gap among the Chinese.

Similar trends have been found in a third study, in which the cognitive scores of elderly Chinese immigrants to Canada were tallied. The aged immigrants who had arrived in recent years had higher scores, perhaps because they were less affected by North American ageism than were the more acculturated Chinese Canadians who had emigrated decades before (Yoon et al., 2000).

Ageism can prevent depressed elderly people from seeking help (the suicide rate is highest among elderly men) and can prevent those with heart problems from getting treatment (heart disease is the leading killer of older women). It can also keep doctors, family members, and social workers from intervening to assist elderly people when problems arise.

Young-Old, Old-Old, and Oldest-Old

Ageism lumps everyone over age 60 together, ignoring the many differences among them. One distinction—among the *young-old,* the *old-old,* and the *oldest-old*—is based not exclusively on age but also on health and well-being.

The **young-old** are the largest group (about 70 percent in the United States) of older adults. They are usually healthy, active, financially secure, and independent. Many leaders in politics, business, and entertainment are young-old, although they may be perceived as younger than they are. One example is Dolly Parton, country singer, songwriter ("Jolene"), and actress (*9 to 5*), who in her 60s (she was born in 1946) remains a popular entertainer.

The **old-old** (about 20 percent) suffer notable losses in body, mind, or social support, although they maintain their independence, caring for other people as well as themselves. The **oldest-old** (10 percent) are dependent, at risk for illness and injury, unable to live safely alone. In North America, about half of them live with a spouse or adult child; the other half are in nursing homes or hospitals.

In general, the young-old are aged 60 to 75, the old-old are aged 75 to 85, and the oldest-old are 85 and over. However, age is not the determining factor in these groupings: Health, vigor, and financial security are crucial. For that reason, some of the young-old are in their 80s, and a few of the oldest-old are only 65. The same three categories can be applied to people in every nation, although in the poorest regions of the world, people tend to become oldest-old before age 80 and are almost never in nursing homes.

young-old
Healthy, vigorous, financially secure older adults (generally, those aged 60 to 75) who are well integrated into the lives of their families and communities.

old-old
Older adults (generally, those aged 75 to 85) who suffer from physical, mental, or social deficits.

oldest-old
Elderly adults (generally, those over age 85) who are dependent on others for almost everything, requiring supportive services such as nursing-home care and hospital stays.

● **FOR DEEPER REFLECTION** For younger adults, when are attempts at kindness likely to be experienced as demeaning or condescending?

AP PHOTO / KEVORK DJANSEZIAN

At Age 60 As one of 12 children, Dolly Parton grew up "dirt poor" in Tennessee; as a young-old woman, she is still a very popular singer, songwriter, and actress. Her Imagination Library program distributes more than 2.5 million free books to children every year. She maintains her image as a full-figured blonde bombshell via extensive cosmetic surgery, quipping, "It takes a lot of money to look this cheap."

The Same Situation, Many Miles Apart: Keep Smiling Good humor seems to be a cause of longevity, and vice versa. This is as true among the elderly in nations where few reach old age, such as Afghanistan *(left)*, as it is in countries where the aged outnumber the young, such as Germany *(right)*.

● UNDERSTANDING THE NUMBERS
In 2050 in the United States, among every 100 people, how many will be under and how many over age 65?

Answer Although the absolute numbers are increasing rapidly, the proportions are rising more slowly. In 2050, the aged will still be outnumbered: 80 people in every 100 will be under 65 and only 20 will be over that age.

population pyramid
A graphic representation of population as a series of stacked bars in which each age cohort is represented by one bar, with the youngest cohort at the bottom.

Some gerontologists prefer labels that do not refer to age: *optimal* (also called *successful*) *aging, usual aging,* and *impaired aging* (Aldwin & Gilmer, 2003; D. H. Powell, 1994; Rowe & Kahn, 1998). Focusing on the successful may be a benign manifestation of ageism; focusing on the impaired may be blatantly ageist. In every case, measures of biological and social aging are much better indicators of successful, usual, or impaired aging than is chronological age (Crimmins et al., 2008).

THE ELDERLY: BURDEN OR BLESSING? Whether an older adult is a burden or blessing to the rest of society depends on whether he or she is young-old, old-old, or oldest-old. A hundred years ago, it was assumed that every old person was among the oldest-old, always a burden but not a common one. The reason was that, at the time, most people aged more quickly and died at younger ages. Consequently, the world had 20 times more people under age 18 than over age 60.

In a major shift, now a few nations (notably Japan) have more people over age 65 than under 18. The United Nations (2007) predicts that, by 2050, dozens of nations will follow Japan's example. This shift is sometimes portrayed as a looming burden for younger adults, based on the false assumption that the aged are all dependent.

However, the size of the elderly population will remain relatively small: Today, only about 1 in 8 people in the United States (13 percent) and 1 in 12 people worldwide (8 percent) are over age 65. Increases—to 20 percent for the United States and 16 percent for the world—are expected by 2050 (United Nations, 2007; U.S. Bureau of the Census, 2008). Note that younger adults far outnumber older ones. As you will now see, most older adults are quite independent.

A Pyramid Becomes a Square A look back at Figure 1.9 (page 31) will remind you that demographers often depict a given population as a series of stacked bars, one bar for each age cohort. The bar representing the youngest cohort is at the bottom, and the bar for the oldest cohort is at the top. Historically, the result has been a shape called a **population pyramid,** with the *y* (vertical) axis being age and the *x* (horizontal) axis being the number of people of that particular generation. Like a wedding cake, this diagram has usually been widest at the base (since there were far more children than older people), with each higher level narrower than the one beneath it.

There were three reasons for this traditional pyramidal shape: (1) Far more children were born than the replacement rate; (2) before modern sanitation and nutrition, about half of all children died before age 5; and (3) middle-aged people rarely survived adult diseases like cancer and heart attacks. After age 50 or so, each five-year cohort was about 20 percent smaller than the next-younger group.

Unusual world events caused a deviation from the wedding-cake pattern. For example, the Great Depression and World War II reduced the birth rate from about 1925 to 1945. Then postwar prosperity increased marriage, home ownership, and births. A "baby boom" between 1946 and 1964 created a bulge in the pyramid.

In the past half-century, improved sanitation and better medical care have meant that more children survive and fewer middle-aged adults die. A sudden population increase resulted. Many demographers feared an ongoing population explosion that would result in mass starvation; Earth would become so crowded that each person would have only a few feet of living space (Ehrlich, 1968).

That fear has not been realized. Birth rates have fallen so low that some experts now warn of a new population problem—not enough babies, which will mean too few adults to care for the elders (Booth & Crouter, 2005). The demographic stacks for Germany, Italy, and Japan are already almost square. The median age in Japan is 43, which means that half the population is older than that, while half is younger.

The population of some nations still forms a pyramid shape. In Afghanistan, Iraq, Uganda, and Sudan, contraception is rare, medical care is scarce, and violence kills many adults. In those countries, more than 30 percent of the population are under age 15 and less than 3 percent are over age 65. However, even in the poorest nations, where once almost no one lived past 65, now 1 person in 35 does; where families once averaged 8 children, the average is now fewer than 5 (United Nations, 2007).

Dependence and Independence Every society is blessed with independent, productive people, and every society is burdened with dependents who need some support. Traditionally, it was assumed that those aged 15 to 64 were contributing members of society, while those under age 15 and over 64 were dependent. That led to the concept of the **dependency ratio,** a calculation of the number of self-supporting people (aged 15 to 64) in a given population compared to the number of dependents, young and old.

In most industrialized countries, the current dependency ratio—about 2-to-1, or two independent adults for every one dependent (a child or an elder)—is better than it has ever been. That's because the birth rate was unusually low from 1930 to 1945 (so that there are fewer old people now) and after 1970 (so that there are fewer children now). By contrast, in poorer nations, the birth rate is still high and there are many young children. In Uganda, for instance, the dependency ratio is about 1-to-1, and the median age is 15.

What will happen if the members of the baby-boom generation live to 100 and if the emerging adult generation is not self-sufficient until age 25? If only the middle third of the population is working, the dependency ratio could flip from the current 2-to-1 to 1-to-2.

This worries some social scientists and demographers worldwide (Lloyd-Sherlock, 2004; A. Walker, 2004). A major concern is in the poorest nations, where the fastest increases in the elderly population will occur (United Nations, 2007). For example, China in 2008 had a dependency ratio of about 2.5-to-1, with more than 1 billion working adults—one reason for the recent economic boom. Currently, many middle-aged Chinese couples have only one child and one grandchild. Chinese demographers ask, "Who will care for the elderly?" (Zhang & Goza, 2006), a concern echoed in almost every nation.

Caregivers or Care Receivers? Some of this concern is based on the false premise that all older people are dependents who need care. In fact, they probably give more care than they receive.

Elders play important social roles as "caregivers, guardians, leaders, stabilizing centers, teachers . . . culture bearers" (Carey, 2003, p. 231). Most are young-old—fiercely independent, providing for themselves, and serving as caregivers of the young and of the oldest-old. They are more likely than younger adults to vote, pray, participate in

RESPONSE FOR Young Adults (from page 498) No. Some seniors hear quite well, and they would resent it. ●

dependency ratio
A calculation of the number of self-sufficient, productive adults compared with the number of dependents (children and the elderly) in a given population.

Determined to Vote Older voters tend to have stronger political opinions, more party loyalty, and higher voting rates than younger adults. This Punjabi woman takes an active interest in politics, even though she must depend on her son to carry her to the polling place.

compression of morbidity
A shortening of the time a person spends ill or infirm before death; accomplished by postponing illness.

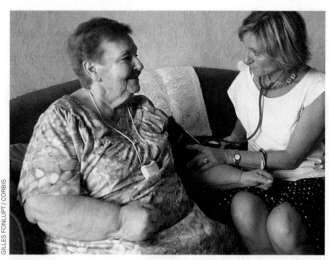

GILLES FONLUPT / CORBIS

Reducing Risk The woman at left has some lifestyle factors, especially her excessive weight, that increase her risk of illness. On the plus side, however, she evidently has a cheerful attitude and sees her doctor regularly.

OBSERVATION QUIZ

Can you spot another sign that this patient is making an effort to protect her health? (see answer, page 505) →

JOSEF POLLEROSS / THE IMAGE WORKS

Current Events If you had to choose between staying informed about current events and being able to see well without glasses, which one would you pick? Most elderly people can no longer see well without glasses, but, like this man reading a newspaper in Cairo, Egypt, older adults tend to be more knowledgeable than people half their age.

civic groups, and donate time and money to various causes as well as to their own descendants (Lloyd-Sherlock, 2004; Longino, 2005).

Only the oldest-old need ongoing care. In the United States and Canada, less than half of them—about 4 percent of the over-65 population—are in nursing homes or hospitals. When responding to the question at the beginning of this chapter, did you write that more than 4 percent of the aged are in nursing homes or hospitals? If so, you made a common mistake: Many college students guess more than 20 percent (Palmore et al., 2005), as do many caregivers of the elderly (Rust & Kwong See, 2007).

A SHORT TIME FOR ILLNESS One reason that most older adults remain self-sufficient is called **compression of morbidity,** a shortening (compression) of the time a person is seriously ill (morbid) before death. Morbidity has been compressed over the past few decades, thanks to improvements in lifestyle, medicine, and technological aids that allow people who have serious conditions (such as arthritis, heart disease, and deafness) to be more independent than in former times (Murabito et al., 2008). If a North American lives to be 95, he or she is likely to be independent (not old-old) almost all of those years.

Compression of morbidity is a social blessing. A healthy person is intellectually alert and socially active. Today's elderly live with less pain, more mobility, better vision, stronger teeth, sharper hearing, clearer thinking, and greater vitality than their grandparents did.

Ageism and the Aging Senses

To say that morbidity is compressed is not to deny that senescence is pervasive and inevitable. This is obvious in appearance (skin gets wrinkled, bodies change shape) and in the senses, all of which are slower and less sharp every year (Meisami et al., 2003).

Only 10 percent of people over age 65 see well without glasses. Taste, smell, touch, and hearing are also impaired. Men are particularly likely to have impaired hearing, either because of something connected to the Y chromosome or because men are more likely to have been exposed to noisy machinery, gunfire, loud music, and the like. By age 90, the average man in North America is almost deaf, hearing only 20 percent of what he once did (Aldwin & Gilmer, 2003).

TECHNOLOGY AND SENSORY DEFICITS Technology can compensate for almost all sensory loss. For common visual problems, brighter lights and bifocals or two pairs of glasses are needed (Madden & Whiting, 2004). Cataracts, glaucoma, and macular degeneration (see Table 14.1) are more serious, but they can be avoided or mitigated if diagnosed early (Houde, 2007). Elaborate visual aids (canes that sense when an object is near, infrared lenses that light the darkness, service animals, computers that "speak" written words) allow even the legally blind to be independent.

For auditory problems, small and sensitive hearing aids have replaced the larger devices of the past. Nevertheless, many people with hearing loss hesitate to get aids, fearing that the devices would make them look old.

This is unfortunate, since missing out on bits of conversation cuts down on communication and precipitates many other social losses. Younger people tend to yell or use elderspeak, both of which are demeaning. Elderly people are less vulnerable to stereotype threat if they have positive interactions with the younger generations; severe hearing loss precludes this (Abrams et al., 2006).

TABLE 14.1 Visual Impairments Common Among the Elderly

- *Cataracts* involve a thickening of the lens, causing vision to become cloudy, opaque, and distorted. As early as age 50, about 10 percent of adults have such clouding, with 3 percent experiencing a partial loss of vision. By age 70, 30 percent have some visual loss because of cataracts. These losses are initially treatable with eyeglasses and then with outpatient surgery, which removes and replaces the cloudy lens.

- *Glaucoma* is devastating if not detected. About 1 percent of those in their 70s and 10 percent in their 90s have glaucoma, a buildup of fluid within the eye. The pressure that results from excess fluid damages the optic nerve, causing the visual field to narrow and ultimately causing sudden blindness. Until then, the person has no symptoms, but an ophthalmologist or optometrist can detect signs and relieve the problem with eye drops or laser surgery. Glaucoma is partly genetic; it occurs at younger ages among African Americans and people with diabetes.

- *Macular degeneration* is deterioration of the retina and is the most common cause of blindness. It affects about 1 in 25 people in their 60s and 1 in 6 over age 80. It is diagnosed early via eye exams or by noticing spotty vision (such as reading with some letters missing). Macular degeneration is progressive, becoming severe five years after it starts (Mukesh et al., 2004). Medication (ranibizumab) can restore some vision if treatment begins early enough (P. J. Rosenfeld et al., 2006).

THE SOCIETY AND SENSORY LOSS Overall, a passive acceptance of sensory loss increases morbidity of all kinds, from depression to heart disease (Horowitz & Stuen, 2003). Thus, ageism affects everyone of every age, not only the older man who refuses a hearing aid or the older woman who stays home because she cannot see well outdoors.

It is easy to blame the elderly for letting their disabilities handicap them. But even when the technology is available, it is not easy to get the individualized, personal attention required for effective remediation.

For instance, ordering hearing aids online or by mail order is a waste. It takes several one-on-one appointments to be properly fitted and weeks to learn how to use hearing

(a)

(b)

(c)

(d)

ALL: PHOTODISC / GETTY IMAGES

Through Different Eyes
These photographs depict the same scene as it would be perceived by a person with (a) normal vision, (b) cataracts, (c) glaucoma, or (d) macular degeneration. Thinking about how difficult it would be to find your own car if you had one of these disorders may help you remember to have your vision checked regularly.

Taking Her Ears for a Walk This profoundly deaf woman is greatly helped by Murphy, who is trained to get her attention whenever the telephone or doorbell rings or the smoke alarm goes off. Murphy's assistance enables her to remain in her home in Brainerd, Minnesota.

aids. Similarly, annual visits to an eye doctor require making and keeping appointments, transportation, waiting, taking tests, and enduring drops that blur vision—and perhaps surgery or at least filling a new prescription for glasses or medication. Without encouragement, many of the elderly just adjust to sensory loss.

Furthermore, ageism is inherent in the design of everything from airplane seats to shoes. Older adults need younger advocates to help them avoid or remediate disabilities as well as to spot the social problems that need to be changed. Remembering that context is crucial, if a relative has a hearing problem, for instance, younger people can arrange for conversations to occur in settings where lip reading is easy—such as a well-lit living room, not a noisy, dimly lit restaurant with background music.

Many disabilities would disappear if the environment were better designed, as advocates and developmentalists realize. Possibilities include longer traffic lights for pedestrians who must walk slowly and doorbells that alert the hearing-impaired by turning on an indicator light (Satariano, 2006).

Here is a practical application of what you have learned. Instead of honking at slow elderly drivers, younger adults can demand visible signs, well-marked lanes, better car mirrors, and other devices to make driving easier and safer. Driving exams need to be required periodically for everyone, since some of the elderly should stop driving, but age itself is not the reason. In sum, many of the disabilities of late adulthood are far from inevitable; they are socially created and socially removable.

KEY Points

- Ageism is a common but destructive prejudice, evident in the patronizing tones of elderspeak.

- More people are now living longer than in earlier generations. Currently, 13 percent in the United States and 8 percent worldwide are elderly.

- Most elderly people are young-old, able to remain self-sufficient and independent. Only the oldest-old need full-time care, either at home or in an institution.

- All the senses become less acute with age, but compression of morbidity is possible if people recognize problems and use various means to limit disability.

Health and Sickness

As you remember from Chapter 11, *senescence* is the aging process, which begins in adolescence. Gerontologists distinguish between **primary aging,** the universal changes of senescence, and **secondary aging,** the consequences of particular chronic diseases (Masoro, 2006).

Primary and Secondary Aging: Cardiovascular Disease

As you might imagine, the distinction between primary and secondary aging is blurry. Most diseases involve aspects of both types of aging (Masoro, 2006). As an example, consider **cardiovascular disease (CVD),** which involves the heart (*cardio*) and circulatory system (*vascular*). Cardiovascular disease is usually thought of as secondary aging because it is more risk-related than age-related (Supiano, 2006).

The *Cardiovascular Health Study* began with more than 5,000 people over age 65 in the United States without coronary (heart) problems. Six years later, some of those 5,000 participants had developed heart disease, but most had not. The likelihood of CVD was related less to age than to six risk factors, all affected by health habits and

primary aging
The universal and irreversible physical changes that occur to all living creatures as they grow older.

secondary aging
The specific physical illnesses or conditions that become more common with aging but result from poor health habits, genetic vulnerability, and other influences that vary from person to person.

cardiovascular disease (CVD)
Illness that involves the heart and the circulatory system.

genes. Those risk factors were: diabetes, smoking, abdominal fat, high blood pressure, lack of exercise, and high cholesterol (Fried et al., 1998).

But a primary aging component was evident: All six risks are more common with age. Consider high blood pressure (also called *hypertension*). Lifestyle (e.g., salt, excess weight) has a marked effect, as do social context (e.g., socioeconomic status, racial discrimination) and genes. Yet beyond such secondary factors, there is no doubt that primary aging is relevant.

In one study, a group of 65-year-old women with normal blood pressure were followed for 20 years (Vasan et al., 2002). By age 85, nearly 90 percent of them had high blood pressure. Almost all of the 10 percent who avoided high blood pressure had an unusually healthy lifestyle, a social context that involved very few stressors, and a healthy family history. Even those factors were not always protective, however: Some of the 90 percent with hypertension were also quite healthy and had no family history of it, yet their blood pressure rose as they aged.

Thus, cardiovascular disease is considered secondary aging because not everyone develops it. However, although CVD correlates with hypertension, which is also considered secondary aging, both are related to primary aging as well in that the circulatory system becomes less efficient with every passing decade (Supiano, 2006).

No single factor (including age, hypertension, inactivity, and smoking) makes CVD inevitable. Some people with heart disease have never had high blood pressure and are relatively young (Lawes et al., 2008). Nonetheless, the links among aging, risk, and CVD are undeniable.

The blurriness of the line between primary and secondary aging arises because the mere passage of time does not cause disease, but almost all the biological changes that come with time (primary aging) increase vulnerability to disease (secondary aging). A 90-year-old is 1,000 times more likely to die of cardiovascular disease than is a 30-year-old, even if both have identical genes, social contexts, and health habits. Age matters.

The distinction between primary and secondary aging reminds us that no specific disease is inevitable. Indeed, less than half those over age 65 have cardiovascular disease, diabetes, or dementia, the three most common serious diseases of the aged. But almost everyone has, or will have, at least one of these three by age 90. Statistics reveal that risk factors and diseases of the aged are not distributed randomly: If a person has one risk factor, it is likely that he or she has several (e.g., Power et al., 2008).

The combination of primary and secondary aging causes many illnesses. One study of a large group of U.S. adults over age 65 found that 16 percent had no disease, 22 percent had one, and 62 percent had two or more (G. Anderson & Horvath, 2004). Protecting health and treating disease are both crucial with aging.

Staying Healthy

Health habits have been stressed many times in previous chapters. Here we discuss them as they apply specifically to the aging body.

NUTRITION As people age, their bodies become less efficient at digesting food and using nutrients. Merely to maintain a steady weight, people need fewer calories as they grow older. Because adequate nourishment needs to be packed into less food, a varied and healthful diet is especially important in late adulthood, for the mind as well as the body. Indeed, deficits of B vitamins, particularly B_{12} and folic acid, lead to impaired cognition (Durga et al., 2007).

Problems may arise when people take drugs that affect nutrition. Aspirin (taken daily by many who have arthritis or who are trying to reduce their risk of stroke or heart attack) increases the need for vitamin C. Antibiotics impair the body's absorption

ANSWER TO OBSERVATION QUIZ
(from page 502) She is wearing a medical alert pendant, which enables her to summon help if she should fall or become ill. Not visible in the photograph is the fact that this doctor has practiced in Marseille, France, for 14 years; continuity in health care is life-prolonging. ●

of iron, calcium, and vitamin K. Antacids reduce the body's ability to absorb protein. Oil-based laxatives deplete vitamins A and D. Caffeine reduces the water in the body. Even multivitamins can do more harm than good—if they include too much iron, for instance.

The research on vitamin pills leads to conflicting conclusions. One expert writes:

> The use of various dietary supplements, including vitamins, to prevent or delay disease or aging rests for the most part on epidemiological associations. It does appear from this data that a diet rich in vitamins is associated with a tendency for improved health. However, the results from controlled trials are dismal.
>
> [D. R. Thomas, 2009, p. 27]

Why "dismal"? The author explains that people who take vitamins are also likely all their lives to keep their weight down, exercise daily, avoid smoking, and obtain good medical care. He suspects that they are healthier for all those reasons, not because of the vitamins.

Aging brings additional nutritional demands but less efficient digestion. As you can see in Figure 14.1, the basic requirements are similar at every age, but the quantities should be reduced so that the elderly avoid overeating while still obtaining adequate nutrition.

As at younger ages, undereating is also a potential problem. If older people are depressed or worried about their income, their teeth, or their digestion, they may not eat enough (Brocker & Schneider, 2009).

Furthermore, although dehydration causes physical and cognitive problems, many elders do not drink enough. One reason is that the awareness of thirst is reduced. In addition, the kidneys and bladder are less efficient, so many drink less to avoid incontinence or nighttime waking.

EXERCISE Like nutrition, exercise may be especially important later in life. For example, elders benefit more from lifting weights than younger adults do because they are more likely to be out of shape and "strength training has the greatest impact on the most debilitated subjects" (Rice & Cunningham, 2002, p. 138).

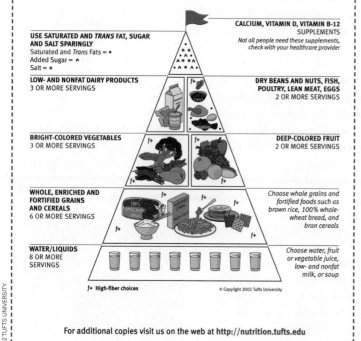

FIGURE 14.1 Modified for Seniors Nutritionists at Tufts University in Massachusetts prepared this food pyramid, which is a modification of the U.S. Department of Agriculture's food pyramid for younger adults. One notable difference appears in the bottom row. Homeostasis for hydration (thirst) is diminished in late adulthood, so many older people should be sure to drink at least eight glasses of fluid each day.

Unfortunately, older people exercise less, not more, than younger adults do. One reason is that most exercise classes, team sports, and even bicycles are designed for the young. Another reason is that, as muscles stiffen and atrophy, range of motion diminishes, making it harder to kick from the knee, swing the arms, and turn the torso (Masoro, 1999).

Despite such limitations, older people should continue to exercise. Movement of any kind—climbing stairs, gardening, even setting the table—is better than sitting still (Manini et al., 2006). Regular exercise is a proven way to compress morbidity: One study found that moderate exercise added an average of two disability-free years (Nusselder et al., 2008). Other research is less specific, but every study that compares active and inactive adults finds that the former are healthier, for a longer time.

Of course, accommodation to disability may be needed. The general strategy here is *selective optimization with compensation* (discussed in Chapter 12). For example, walking may replace running and dancing may become more sedate.

Fear of falling is "a common and modifiable cause of excess disability" (Lach, 2002–2003, p. 37). *Excess* disability means more disability than is warranted. Falls are a major hazard for the elderly, partly because *osteoporosis* (fragile bones) can mean that a tumble that bruises a younger person will break the hip of an older one. Falls are the leading cause of accidental death after age 60 (Stevens, 2002–2003).

Few falls are lethal, but even minor falls frighten elderly people. Some react not by wearing better shoes or avoiding slippery surfaces, but by walking less. This occurred for one-third of the elderly participants who fell in a Dutch study (Stel et al., 2004). Only 6 percent had serious injuries. The other 94 percent who had less severe falls (no broken hips) were as likely to reduce their walking as the 6 percent—some of whom returned to their usual activity when they could.

Thus, attitude and action are more influential than injury, yet diminished movement increases the risk of every illness (Satariano, 2006). Specific exercises (e.g., tai chi for balance and weight machines for leg strength) and specific contextual factors (e.g., no area rugs or uneven sidewalks) decrease the risk of falling. As with sensory losses, the burden of prevention should not be borne by the elders alone—but that is not the case.

DRUG USE Most people stop abusing drugs before middle age. Active addicts rarely survive to old age. Those two facts suggest that drug addiction is not a problem for the elderly—but that is not the case.

In fact, addiction—typically to alcohol or legally prescribed medications—may begin in late adulthood. It then continues because ageism prevents an elderly person's children, doctors, and others from realizing that a problem has developed:

> A 70-year-old widow named Audrey . . . was covered with large black bruises and burns from her kitchen stove. Audrey no longer had an appetite, so she ate little and was emaciated. One night she passed out in her driveway and scraped her face. The next morning, her neighbor found her face down on the pavement in her nightgown.
>
> Audrey couldn't be trusted with the grandchildren anymore, so family visits were fewer and farther between. She rarely showered and spent most days sitting in a chair alternating between drinking, sleeping, and watching television. She stopped calling friends, and social invitations had long since ceased.
>
> Audrey obtained prescriptions for Valium, a tranquilizer, and Placidyl, a sleep inducer. Both medications, which are addictive and have more adverse effects in patients over age 60, should only be used for short periods of time. Audrey had taken both medications for years at three to four times the prescribed dosage. She mixed them with large quantities of alcohol. She was a full-fledged addict. . . .
>
> Her children . . . became desensitized to the seriousness of her problem—until it progressed to a dangerously advanced stage. Luckily for Audrey, she was referred to a new doctor who recognized her addiction. . . . Once Audrey was in treatment and weaned off the alcohol and drugs, she bloomed. Audrey's memory improved; her appetite returned; she regained her energy; and she started walking, swimming and exercising every day. Now, a decade later, Audrey plays an important role in her grandchildren's lives, gardens, and she lives creatively and with meaning.

> [Colleran & Jay, 2003, p. 11]

Alcohol is particularly troublesome for elders, whose metabolism, less efficient liver functioning, and increased likelihood of living alone are risk factors for alcoholism. Historical moral prohibitions lead some of the elderly to proud abstinence and others

His Daily Bread An older man rides his bicycle home in Fecamp, France, after buying a loaf of fresh bread.

OBSERVATION QUIZ

What three things are evident that contribute to good health? (see response, page 509) ➞

Moving Along Her stiffening joints have made a walker necessary, but this elderly woman in Gujarat, India, is maintaining her mobility by walking every day.

to rebellious excesses. In fact, moderation is best: One or two glasses of wine or beer a day, not more, benefit the heart and may postpone dementia (Mukamal et al., 2006).

Younger family members should be aware that an unsteady gait, confused thinking, and slurred speech are not typical of older adults. They are signs that something is seriously wrong. It is ageist to ignore such symptoms.

Living a Long Life

Although life seems long to those who are young, many of the elderly worry that their time is short. Actually, if a person has already reached an advanced age in good health, chances are he or she will live for many more years.

maximum life span
The oldest possible age to which members of a species can live, under ideal circumstances. For humans, that age is approximately 122 years.

average life expectancy
The number of years that the average person in a particular population is likely to live.

MAXIMUMS AND AVERAGES Genes bestow on every species a **maximum life span,** defined as the oldest possible age to which a member of that species can live. Maximum life span is said to be 13 years for rabbits, 55 years for chimpanzees, 122 years for humans, and 180 years for giant tortoises (W. R. Clark, 1999; Finch, 1999).

These variations among species imply that the maximum life span is genetic, which (as you remember) means that genes are part of the story but not all of it. The oldest of the old may have genes that allow a long life, but every living creature has some genes that lead to senescence and death, and no person, even those without any disease, has lived past 122 (Perls, 2008).

Maximum life span is much longer than **average life expectancy,** which is the number of years that the average person in a particular population is likely to live. In ancient times, humans had an average life expectancy of about 20 years, because, although a few lived to be 80, most newborns died. In 1900 in developed nations, the average life span was about 50 years, primarily because more infants survived. Since the middle of the twentieth century, immunization, sanitation, medical care, safe water, and antibiotics have further extended the average life span, primarily because more adults live past middle age (Finch, 2007).

In the United States today, average life expectancy at birth is about 75 years for men and 81 years for women (U.S. Bureau of the Census, 2008). Those who are already 65 years old (and thus no longer at risk of early death) can expect to live to 84; those who are already 80 live to 90, on average.

Although the maximum life span is the same for the entire human race, the average life expectancy varies markedly from nation to nation. Among the 40 nations

Celebrating a Dozen Decades Only a few people in the world have lived much beyond 100 years. Two of those oldest of the old are shown here. (*left*) Jeanne Calment of France celebrates her 121st birthday; she died at 122 in 1997. (*right*) Maria do Carmo Jeronimo of Brazil celebrates her 125th. Jeronimo was born in slavery and had no reliable birth records; she died in 2000, supposedly aged 129. Several other people are known to have lived to 122, and that age seems to be the upper limit for the human species. Even with the best medical care, most people die before age 80.

LIONEL CIRONNEAU / AP /WIDE WORLD PHOTOS

DIEGO GIUDICE / AP /WIDE WORLD PHOTOS

(a)   (b)

(c)   (d)

ALL: JOHN LAUNOIS / BLACK STAR

Longevity Three remote regions of the world are renowned for the longevity of their people (although verified birth certificates are unavailable). In Vilcabamba, Ecuador, (*a*) 87-year-old Jose Maria Roa stands on the mud from which he will make adobe for a new house. In Abkhazia in the Republic of Georgia, companionship is an important part of late life, as shown by (*b*) Selekh Butka, 113, posing with his wife, Marusya, 101, and (*c*) Ougula Lodara talking with two "younger" friends. Finally, (*d*) Galum Mohammad Shad, at 100, builds a house in the Hunza area of Pakistan.

that keep accurate statistics, half report that their population dies later, on average, than people in the United States (United Nations, 2007).

A few humans inherit alleles that allow them to live much longer than the average life expectancy. However, the maximum life span is literally a maximum: Each species not only has a distinct genetic form and brain but also a distinct program of death genes. For that reason, no rabbit lives to age 30, and no human lives to 130.

ANTI-AGING Some people have sought a "fountain of youth," or at least a way to slow aging, and some hope to return from death. Thousands of people have arranged to have their bodies frozen at subzero temperatures, to be brought back when science has discovered how to revive dead people. But few scientists believe this is possible or that *anti-aging* (efforts to stop aging) can succeed.

Gerontologist Leonard Hayflick (2004) calls anti-aging an oxymoron, a term that contradicts itself (like "alone together" or "jumbo shrimp"). He believes that aging is a natural process built into the DNA of each species.

Remember the four measures of health explained in Chapter 12? According to Hayflick, societies can compress morbidity and avoid premature mortality. The other two indicators of health involve more choice: Individuals can avoid or mitigate disability and increase vitality. However, no society or individual can halt senescence. Humans can "add life to years" but cannot "add years to life."

Living a long and happy life may itself seem an oxymoron to young adults, who associate aging with illness, pain, and depression. They notice people who are frail (the old-old), and they are not upset that the average U.S. life span is shorter than that in many other nations.

ANSWER TO OBSERVATION QUIZ
(from page 507) Exercise, good nutrition (freshly baked bread provides fiber and nutrients), and usefulness (picking up the bread every day is a valuable activity in the French family). ●

centenarian
A person who has lived 100 years or more.

Francisco Ayala at 100 Ayala wrote his first novel at age 18. Eighty-one years later, he noted that he had always maintained his "curiosity and fundamental skepticism." Ayala left his native Spain after the civil war that brought a fascist regime to power in the 1930s. He taught in Argentina and the United States for 25 years. Since age 60, he has been writing and lecturing in his homeland, winning every Spanish literary prize.

ESPECIALLY FOR Biologists What are some immediate practical uses for research on the causes of aging? (see response, page 512) →

Thus, many young adults are not worried that less than 1 percent of the U.S. population are **centenarians** (people 100 years or older). They may be more worried that their age group is increasing more rapidly than any other. In contrast, people over age 60 are concerned that most Americans do not survive past 80. Many of the elderly hope to reach 100.

Young adults need to be reminded that ageism makes people notice exceptions rather than general truths. Surprisingly, researchers who study centenarians find that some are active and in good health, hoping to live several more years. Furthermore, although many people older than 100 are impaired, most of them, with or without disabilities, are content, even happy (Jopp & Rott, 2006; Perls, 2008). According to every study of centenarians, the idea that older people are suffering, sad, and irritable is contrary to the evidence.

Nonetheless, most scientists agree with Hayflick that anti-aging is delusional (H.-Y. Huang et al., 2006). Some go farther: They fear that trying to stop senescence not only wastes time and money but also undermines health. As a leading physician wrote:

I consider the fixation on anti-aging and life extension to be a distraction from the important goal of healthy aging. That is, we should concentrate on making positive lifestyle choices now—eating better, exercising more, getting enough sleep, even improving our mental state—so that we can enjoy not just a longer life but a healthier one. Such a life would also end in due course, but the decline would be rapid. The scientific term for this is *compression of morbidity*, literally squeezing the period of disability and decline at the end of life into as short a period as possible. Live long and well, then have a rapid drop-off at the end.

[Weil, 2007, p. 41]

It is not surprising that many older people want to extend their lives and, indeed, try to do so. As an Australian scientist said at a conference on anti-aging: "We're talking while the horse has already bolted, the stable is empty," because "sixty-one percent of Australians and probably a larger percentage of Americans are already" taking supplements, hoping for longer life (Dransfield, quoted in Reiter, 2007). The following explores anti-aging efforts.

A VIEW FROM SCIENCE

Trying to Live Past the Maximum

Many people are willing to spend a fortune to live longer. At least a dozen companies and hundreds of researchers are searching for the pill, the machine, or the genetic fix that will extend life. Some researchers believe governments should devote extensive resources to "hasten the defeat of aging" (De Grey & Rae, 2007, p. 7).

Genetic engineering is one possibility for increasing the life span. As one team explains, "A large number of genes have been isolated and identified that influence aging and longevity in nematodes, fruit flies and rodents" (Singh et al., 2007, p. 4504). In humans as well, several alleles are called *longevity genes*; people who inherit them live to 90, 100, or even more (R. N. Butler et al., 2003). Genes that bolster the

immune system and defend against stressors may limit the cellular damage caused by aging (Singh et al., 2007).

However, transferring such knowledge from population studies or mouse experiments to aging humans is problematic. For example, one group found a gene (called UCP-2) in the mouse brain that regulates temperature. They changed the expression of that gene, lowering the core body temperature. The result: longer mouse life (Conti et al., 2006).

On the basis of this research with mice, some scientists suggest that humans might live longer if their body temperature were lowered from its "normal" level of 98.6°F (37°C). However, many scientists warn that tampering with one allele may cause a host of unanticipated problems. A skeptical scientist asks anti-aging enthusiasts to consider "why this temperature has been selected by evolution as normal for humans. . . . One would certainly want to know the consequences of . . . abnormally low body temperature before pursuing it as a way to increase life span" (Saper, 2006, p. 774).

Several other genetic changes have extended mouse life. But altering human genes, or adding stem cells, or changing human biochemistry is much more complex than it might appear. Some genetic therapy for severely ill children and young adults caused cancerous tumors; a vaccination against one cause of senility was successful with mice but triggered brain inflammation in humans (R. A. Miller, 2005).

Because altering or adding human genes is such a drastic measure, with unknown consequences, many scientists search instead for drugs to reduce the toxins that accumulate with age. For instance, antioxidants (such as vitamins C and E) might halt damage from *oxygen free radicals,* molecules that attack other cells. Unfortunately, "the search for anti-oxidant drugs that slow aging and extend life span in mammals has produced much frustration and a lamentable absence of authentic anti-aging pills" (R. A. Miller, 2005, p. 1875).

Frustration and lament continue. Recently, another supplement has shown promise—*resveratrol,* a chemical in red grape skins (and thus in red wine) that may prevent primary aging (Markus & Morris, 2008; Orallo, 2008). For rodents, fish, and worms, resveratrol decreases the rate of heart disease, cancer, and dementia. Studies with humans are just beginning; the scientists involved are hopeful but skeptical; some take the drug, some do not (Wade, 2006).

Ironically, one anti-aging measure has proven results, but few humans—scientists or not—try it. That is **calorie restriction,** drastically reducing food consumption while maintaining adequate intake of vitamins, minerals, and other nutrients. Calories are typically limited to about 1,000 a day (less than half of what adults usually consume).

In dozens of experiments—first with mice and fruit flies and more recently with dogs, monkeys, and chimpanzees—animals that were given only half their usual calories lived much longer than their brothers and sisters who ate normally. Some of them exceeded what was thought to be the maximum life span for their species.

Animals on such restricted diets develop far fewer diseases of aging (Sinclair & Howitz, 2006). For humans, one team found that volunteers who limited their calories successfully slowed their aging only if protein was also cut back (Fontana et al., 2008).

Several thousand North Americans belong to the Calorie Restriction Society. They eat only about 1,000 calories a

calorie restriction
The practice of limiting dietary energy intake, while still consuming sufficient quantities of vitamins, minerals, and other important nutrients, for the purpose of improving health and slowing down the aging process.

112/63, 6 Feet, 135 Pounds These numbers are this man's blood pressure, height, and weight after six years on a calorie-restricted diet. So far, so good—he is now 36 years old.

JIM WILSON / THE NEW YORK TIMES

day, none from fat or sugar. One member is Michael Rae, from the city of Calgary in Alberta, Canada, who said to a reporter:

> Aging is a horror and it's got to stop right now. People are popping antioxidants, getting face lifts, and injecting Botox, but none of that is working. At the moment, C.R. [calorie restriction] is the only tool we have to stay younger longer.
>
> *[quoted in Hochman, 2002, p. 5]*

The reporter noted that Mr. Rae "is 6 feet tall, weighs just 115 pounds, and is often very hungry."

Another scientist wrote:

> The only proven method of life extension for mammals is caloric restriction in infancy, which is impractical for human purposes. Search for a Fountain of Youth has always been a delusion.
>
> *[H. R. Moody, 2001–2002, p. 34]*

It is not surprising that scientists are wary of anti-aging efforts. In the history of every academic discipline, some measures, substances, and inventions that initially seemed promising (such as asbestos, DDT, and lead) have later proven to be more harmful than helpful. Among such efforts cited in this book are the implantation of multiple zygotes to overcome infertility, abstinence education to prevent teen pregnancy, DARE to reduce adolescent drug use, and hormone replacement therapy to stave off heart disease.

Weil (2007) warns: "Granted, eating right and exercising more aren't as easy as . . . popping a resveratrol supplement, but then, the best things in life rarely are" (p. 41).

RESPONSE FOR Biologists (from page 510) Although ageism and ambivalence limit the funding of research on the causes of aging, the applications include prevention of AIDS, cancer, senility, and physical damage from pollution—all urgent social priorities. ●

KEY points

- Primary aging consists of the inevitable and universal physical changes that accompany aging.
- Secondary aging involves diseases that occur as a result of genetic vulnerability, poor health habits, and environmental toxins.
- Good nutrition and regular exercise are particularly important in late adulthood.
- Every species has a maximum life span and an average life expectancy. The latter varies a great deal, depending on health habits and environmental conditions.

Thinking in Late Adulthood

You have already read that development in later adulthood may be "usual," "impaired," or "optimal." All three variations are evident in cognition. The impaired are those with severe problems in memory and reasoning; the optimal are those who are remarkably wise. Most older people are neither senile nor wise, yet their thinking is affected by senescence. To understand the specifics of cognition in the elderly, we begin by exploring what happens to the brain.

The Aging Brain

New neurons form and dendrites grow in adulthood—a fact that surprised many developmentalists who thought brain growth stopped in childhood (Yang et al., 2006). However, growth is slow. Just like the legs, the heart, and every other part of the body, the brain becomes less efficient as people grow older.

BRAIN SLOWDOWN There are many reasons why the brain slows down. Senescence reduces production of neurotransmitters—glutamate, acetylcholine, serotonin, and especially dopamine—that allow a nerve impulse to jump quickly across the synapse from one neuron to another (Bäckman & Farde, 2005). Neural fluid decreases, myelination thins, and cerebral blood circulates more slowly.

Speed is crucial for many aspects of cognition, not only for memory but also for sensation, perception, and strategy. As their brains slow down, older people need more time to perceive new sensations because their minds are still processing prior sensations. Their conclusions are less logical because slower thinking makes it difficult to hold in mind and analyze large quantities of information simultaneously.

Some experts believe that speed is the *g* mentioned in Chapter 7, the intellectual ability that is the foundation of all other aspects of intelligence (Salthouse, 2000). Evidence for this includes the fact that deterioration in cognitive ability correlates with slower walking as well as with almost every kind of physical disability (Kuo et al., 2007). However, although all scientists agree that reduced speed is a component of late-life cognition, some consider other factors to be important as well (Dixon et al., 2007).

VARIATION IN BRAIN EFFICIENCY As is the case with every other organ, brain senescence varies markedly from individual to individual. In a longitudinal study of 900 people in their 70s, 80s, and 90s, there were "both greater-than-expected deterioration as well as less-than-expected deterioration (including improvement)" (Christensen et al., 1999, p. 366). Another group of researchers agreed that "in some people cognition declines precipitously, but in many others cognition declines only slightly or not at all, or improves slightly" (R. S. Wilson et al., 2002, p. 179).

Among the suggested reasons for the variation in brain senescence are gender, education, and experience. In addition, elders' assessment of whether their everyday activities are restricted by their health also seems to affect the brain, although the specifics of how this occurs are not yet known (Wahlin et al., 2006).

BRAIN SHRINKAGE In addition to slower responses, the aging of the brain is quantifiable in another way: It gets smaller. Some areas shrink more than others, among them the hypothalamus (crucial for memory) and the prefrontal cortex (necessary for planning, inhibiting unwanted responses, and coordinating thoughts) (Kramer et al., 2006).

Many scientists believe that the crucial function of the prefrontal cortex is to inhibit speech and action, and thus a significant problem for the elderly is lack of inhibition. Prefrontal shrinkage may explain why some of the elderly say too much, with "off-target verbosity," to inattentive listeners (von Hippel, 2007).

The relationship among past education, current mental exercise, and intellectual functioning in late adulthood is complicated (Alley et al., 2007). Some scientists find that schooling slows the rate of brain shrinkage. Others disagree, suggesting instead that, because good health aids brain circulation and correlates with education, it may seem as if education protects the brain when it is actually good health that does so. Another theory is that education strengthens inhibition, the ability to say no or keep quiet, and this learned inhibition masks impairment when the prefrontal cortex shrinks.

USING MORE PARTS OF THE BRAIN A curious finding from PET and fMRI scans is that, compared with younger adults, older adults use more parts of their brains, including both hemispheres, to solve problems. This may be selective compensation: Older adults may find that using only one brain region is inadequate for complex thinking, so they automatically use more parts.

In this way, intellectual output may be unimpaired, even though the process of thinking has changed (Daselaar & Cabeza, 2005). As one team explains, "The brain has the apparent ability to reorganize in the face of neural insults of aging in what is an apparently compensatory manner" (Park & Payer, 2006, p. 138).

A second, less upbeat explanation is that since control processes become weaker with age, the brain "de-differentiates," or stops using a focused region for each function, as younger brains do. Inhibition fails, attention wanders, and thinking becomes diffuse (Nielson et al., 2002). Still, such diffusion may be an adaptation that combines intellectual and emotional skills. As such, it would be "strategic diversity" that helps to optimize cognition (Lindenberger & von Oertzen, 2006, p. 310).

A recent study of multitasking, memory, and brain activation confirmed that older adults use more of their brains than younger ones do. However, these researchers reported a crucial difference among the elders: which particular parts of their brains were activated. Older adults who were better at working memory and at multitasking used their prefrontal cortex; those who were worse did not (Goffaux et al., 2008).

As you can see, neurological research on older brains is intriguing, but there is much yet to be discovered. Now we look at what is already known about late-life cognition.

The Usual: Information Processing After Age 65

Both recent brain research and thousands of more conventional studies over many decades find that minds work differently in late adulthood than earlier. One way to understand this is via the information-processing approach, separating cognition into four steps: input (sensing), storage (memory), programming (control processes), and output.

● **FOR DEEPER REFLECTION** The elderly are frequently criticized for talking too much, but that judgment comes from younger people. Is "off-target" talkativeness ever beneficial?

INPUT (SENSING) Information processing starts with input— that is, with stimuli taken in by the senses in order to be perceived by the brain. As you have just read, no sense is as sharp at age 61 as at age 16. Reduced sensory input impairs cognition (Anstey et al., 2003; Wingfield et al., 2005). Some information, such as the details of a road sign 300 feet away or the words of a conversation in a noisy place, never reaches sensory memory because the older person's senses never detect the stimuli.

Sensory deficits may be subtle; most older people believe they see and hear whatever is important. However, this is not the case. For example, in one study, more than 200 adults (half young, half old) were shown 10 video clips of men lying or telling the truth about whether they had stolen money. The older adults thought they could detect liars, but they were less accurate than the younger people were (Stanley & Blanchard-Fields, 2008). One practical implication is that older people may be more likely to believe a con artist.

These researchers tried to determine exactly why the older adults did less well. They discovered that the main deficit was the inability to notice subtle facial indicators of fear or shame (Stanley & Blanchard-Fields, 2008). Thus, it was input, not processing, that contributed to their inaccuracy.

From Ten-Hut to Plant-Tending This man needed all his senses when he was on active duty as a colonel in the U.S. Marine Corps. Now, nearing age 90, he is partially deaf and has problems with balance. These sensory impairments don't keep him from enjoying the sights, smells, and textures of the plants he tends at a senior center's greenhouse in Louisiana.

Likewise, another study examined gaze-following in people of varied ages (Slessor et al., 2008). Older adults were less adept at knowing where someone was looking. Since humans understand a social partner's emotions better if they know when that person is glancing away and what captures attention (Emery, 2000), this difficulty may put older people at a disadvantage in social interactions.

The brain automatically fills in missed sights and sounds; as a result, vital information may be distorted or lost without the person realizing it. Several researchers have wondered whether elderly people's underlying problem with sensory input is (1) in the brain (the input is not processed correctly) or (2) directly in the senses (the input never reaches the brain). The probable answer is both (Glass, 2007).

STORAGE (MEMORY) The second step of information processing is memory, a particularly sensitive topic since memory loss can be the first symptom of dementia. Remember stereotype threat: If older people suspect their memories are fading, anxiety itself impairs memory, a phenomenon more apparent among those with more education (Hess et al., 2009).

Actually, research finds that some aspects of memory remain strong throughout late adulthood while others do not. For example, memory for vocabulary (semantic memory) is good, but memory for events (episodic memory) declines. Source amnesia— forgetting the source of a specific fact, idea, or snippet of conversation—is common (Craik & Salthouse, 2000).

Working Memory You learned in Chapter 7 that *working memory,* or *short-term memory,* includes the information that the brain holds at a given moment, allowing processing and new ideas based on recent information. The brain slowdown already described means that older individuals take longer to perceive and process the sensations they experience; thus, working memory is reduced.

This would explain why vocabulary recognition is the final ability to show decline: Speed is not a factor in deciding if *chartreuse* is a color or a dwelling. However, speed is crucial in repeating a list of six digits backwards (a common test of working memory) because a slow-thinking person may have already lost the memory of the first digits when it is time to repeat them.

AP PHOTO /THE NEWS-STAR, ARELY CASTILLO

For the same reason, older people are notably less adept at multitasking, which requires screening out distractions and inhibiting irrelevant thoughts while focusing on two or more relevant tasks. A slower brain, with diminished working memory, cannot handle too much at once.

By contrast, when older people can take their time and concentrate, their working memory seems as good as ever (Verhaeghen et al., 2003). Such concentration may crowd out other mental tasks that a younger person could do simultaneously. In the laboratory, for instance, when an older adult is asked to interpret what they are reading while walking on a treadmill, both abilities slow down.

Ecological Validity This raises a crucial point. Researchers need to take extra care in assessing the memory of older adults because motivation, anxiety, and context are crucial. Almost invariably, the more realistic the testing circumstances (as when people are quizzed at home instead of in a university laboratory), the better an older person remembers.

Ecological validity is the idea that memory should be measured in everyday tasks and circumstances, not as laboratory tests assess it. Ecological validity is important at every age (Spooner & Pachana, 2006) but particularly for the elderly, who are handicapped in many ways by traditional practices (Marsiske & Margrett, 2006).

For example, older adults are at their best in the morning, just when adolescents are half asleep. It would be inaccurate to compare the two groups in late afternoon, as some researchers have done. Similarly, since older adults are slower, it is invalid to use a timed test to measure accuracy.

In daily life, older adults use routines, pacing, strategies, and cues to "help ameliorate, and sometimes eliminate, age-related memory impairment" (Moscovitch et al., 2001). Consequently, compared with college students, older adults score lower on fill-in-the-blanks tests of newly learned material (as might be given in a college class) or in recalling nonsense syllables (a traditional memory test), but they are better at remembering to send birthday cards, to take their vitamins, and even to brush their teeth.

Awareness of the need for ecological validity has helped scientists restructure research on working memory, finding fewer deficits than originally thought. However, valid research on long-term memory is especially hard to design.

Many older adults can recount memories of their distant childhood, which might be evidence for intact long-term memory. But recent research on people of many ages finds that such memories can be false. When listening to Grandpa describe his boyhood home, how does a grandchild assess accuracy?

Some researchers test long-term memory via verifiable public events, such as presidential elections and space flights, finding "replicable findings of age-related decline, stability and even in some cases increase" (Zacks & Hasher, 2006, p. 162). One question often used to measure adult memory in the United States is "Who is the current president of the United States . . . and who was the president before that, and before that?" Many older adults name presidents quite well. However, political awareness may increase over time faster than long-term memory decreases. Again, ecological validity is an issue.

PROGRAMMING (CONTROL PROCESSES) If late-life cognitive difficulties involved only senses and memory, then eyeglasses, hearing aids, PDAs, and written lists would correct them. But older adults are also "impaired in controlled cognitive processes" (Jacoby et al., 2001, p. 250), and those problems are not easy to fix.

ecological validity
The idea that memory should be measured as people actually experience it, not as laboratory tests assess it.

ESPECIALLY FOR Students If you want to remember something you learn in class for the rest of your life, what should you do? (see response, page 516) →

COURTESY OF KATHLEEN BERGER

Recognition At every age, recognition memory is much better than recall. Chances are that few of my high school classmates could describe how I looked back then, but all of them could point out my picture among the hundreds of photos in our yearbook.

control processes
The part of the information-processing system that consists of methods for regulating the analysis and flow of information. Useful control processes include memory and retrieval strategies, selective attention, and rules or strategies for problem solving.

Control processes are the various methods used to regulate the analysis and flow of information. They include memory and retrieval strategies, selective attention, and rules or strategies for problem solving. Control processes usually depend on the prefrontal cortex, which, as you just learned, shrinks with age (Raz, 2005).

Perhaps as a result, younger adults are more able to gather and consider relevant information (Cicirelli, 2006). For this reason, the elderly often stick to preconceived ideas rather than consider new evidence and change their minds (Pierce et al., 2004). Similarly, their source amnesia (already mentioned) can lead to an unhappy consequence: They may believe a rumor or a prejudiced statement because they forget that it came from an untrustworthy source (Jacoby & Rhodes, 2006).

In general, the elderly rely on prior knowledge, general principles, familiarity, and rules of thumb in their decision making (Jacoby & Rhodes, 2006). This is called a *top-down strategy,* which involves using deductive rather than inductive reasoning. Top-down thinking is not necessarily wrong, but it is limited.

One control process is retrieval, which some developmentalists believe to be crucial in that memory problems for older adults involve recall, not storage. An older person may be quite accurate when he says, "I know it, I just can't remember it."

That something is amiss with retrieval is one explanation for the fact that older adults have extensive vocabularies (measured by a written test) but reduced verbal fluency when they write or talk. Similarly, compared with younger adults, the elderly have more tip-of-the-tongue forgetfulness, less accurate memory for familiar names, and poorer spelling (Burke & Shafto, 2004).

In a study that illustrates the need for better control strategies, adults of varying ages were given props with which they could perform 30 odd and memorable actions, such as kissing an artificial frog or stepping into a large plastic bag (Thomas & Bulevich, 2006). Fifteen of these actions they were told to do (and they did them) and 15 they were told to *imagine* doing. Two weeks later, each participant read a list of 45 actions (15 done, 15 imagined, and 15 new) and was asked which were performed, imagined, or new. Half the participants just read the list; the other half were told to use particular memory strategies.

Among the half who were list-readers, the young far surpassed the old: The younger adults assigned 78 percent of the items to the correct categories, whereas the older adults got only 52 percent correct. As for the half who were told memory strategies, the younger adults still got 78 percent correct, but the older ones benefited, getting 66 percent right (Thomas & Bulevich, 2006). Thus, retrieval strategies might be more helpful to the old than to the young.

Don't Forget As a retrieval strategy, this Maryland shop owner posts dozens of reminders for herself on the wall.

COGNITIVE OUTPUT The final step in information processing is output. In the Seattle Longitudinal Study (described in Chapter 12), the measured output of all five primary mental abilities—verbal meaning, spatial orientation, inductive reasoning, number ability, and word fluency—all declined beginning at about age 60. This was particularly notable in the subtests affected by spatial perception and processing speed (Schaie, 2005).

Thus, the usual path of cognition in late adulthood is gradual decline, at least in output. However, there are two important modifiers of the generality: health and training.

Health is a better predictor of cognition than age, as is apparent in studies of older adults who are tested repeatedly until they die. Those who will die soon (whether

RESPONSE FOR Students (from page 515) Learn it very well now, and you will probably remember it in 50 years, with a little review. ●

they are 75 or 105) may experience "terminal decline," a faster loss of cognitive ability in the final years of their lives (Rabbitt et al., 2008). Those who have many more decades to live experience much less decline, if any.

The second finding is that training can improve cognitive ability, even for the very old. This has long been shown in studies of specific abilities (such as training to improve scores on the primary mental abilities) but also seems true for cognition overall (Marsiske & Margrett, 2006; Willis et al., 2006). The saying "You can't teach an old dog new tricks" certainly does not apply to all older people.

New Tricks With a grandchild as a patient tutor, this woman, like many other older people, is delighted to learn how to use a laptop computer.

The Impaired: Dementia

The generalizations you just read challenge another assumption, that senility is typical. Actually, *senile* simply means "old," but senility is defined as a severe impairment of the mind. The implication is that old age inevitably brings intellectual failure—an ageist and false idea.

Dementia is a more precise term than *senility* for irreversible, pathological loss of brain functioning caused by organic brain damage or disease. The word *dementia* literally means "out of mind," referring to severely impaired judgment, memory, or problem-solving ability. Dementia is diagnosed when a person of any age has chronic "multiple cognitive deficits . . . sufficiently severe to cause impairment in occupational or social functioning" (American Psychiatric Association, 2000, p. 148).

Memory loss is one significant aspect of dementia, but people with dementia have other cognitive problems as well. They may easily get lost, even in their neighborhood, or may be confused about how to use common objects like a telephone or toothbrush, or may have emotional reactions that are unlike their usual personality.

dementia
Irreversible loss of intellectual functioning caused by organic brain damage or disease. Dementia becomes more common with age, but it is abnormal and pathological even in the very old.

THE PREVALENCE OF DEMENTIA In one nationwide assessment, researchers selected a representative sample of elderly people from every part of the United States, examined each one, and spoke with someone who knew them well (usually an immediate relative). They combined this information with test results, medical records, and clinical judgment and found that 14 percent of those who were over age 70 had some form of dementia (see Table 14.2; Plassman et al., 2007).

Internationally, rates of dementia among the elderly vary by nation, from about 2 percent to 25 percent, primarily because of differences in assessment techniques and definitions rather than because of actual frequency (Bondi et al., 2009). Valid cross-cultural studies that use the same objective criteria to differentiate dementia from mild cognitive impairment are not yet available.

TABLE 14.2 Prevalence of Dementia Among the Elderly, by Age, United States, 2002

Age	All Dementia (%)	Alzheimer Disease (%)	Vascular Dementia (%)
70–79	5	2.3	1
80–89	24.2	18.2	4.1
90+	37.4	29.7	6.2
Overall (70+)	13.9	9.7	2.4

Source: Plassman et al., 2007.

Not Everyone Gets It Most elderly people never experience dementia. Among people in their 70s, only 1 person in 20 does, and most of those who reach 90 or 100 are not demented. Presented another way, the prevalence data sound more dire: Almost 4 million people in the United States have dementia.

Since the U.S. study used many sources of information, 14 percent is probably quite accurate. Although the researchers did not survey people under age 70, only about 1 percent of people in their 60s have dementia, and even fewer people under age 60 have it. Thus, it is probably valid to estimate the total number of U.S. residents with dementia at about 4 million—less than 2 percent of the entire population. That proportion will increase as the baby boomers age unless hopes for prevention are realized.

DISTINGUISHING BETWEEN DEMENTIA AND MILD COGNITIVE IMPAIRMENT
Not everyone with memory loss has dementia. Some experience what is called *mild cognitive impairment.* Older adults who cannot remember names or places as well as they once did might be mildly impaired, but they are not considered demented because they are still able to function. About half of them will become demented, but some stabilize with mild impairment and others regain their cognitive abilities (Lopez et al., 2007).

Thus, mild impairment does not qualify as dementia, although it may lead to it. Differential diagnosis of mild impairment and the many forms of dementia is challenging; the following descriptions are a beginning.

ALZHEIMER DISEASE
The most feared as well as the most frequent type of dementia is **Alzheimer disease (AD),** also called *senile dementia of the Alzheimer type* (SDAT) (Weiner & Lipton, 2009). Alzheimer disease accounts for about half of all cases of dementia worldwide, affecting an estimated 20 million people (Goedert & Spillantini, 2006). It is characterized by the proliferation of *plaques* and *tangles* that form in the cerebral cortex. These abnormalities destroy the ability of neurons to communicate with one another, eventually causing the brain to stop functioning.

Plaques are clumps of a protein called *beta-amyloid,* found in the tissues surrounding the neurons; tangles are twisted masses of threads made of a protein called *tau* within the neurons. A normal brain contains some beta-amyloid and tau, but in AD these plaques and tangles proliferate, especially in the hippocampus (the brain structure that is crucial for memory). Forgetfulness is usually the first, and the dominant, symptom of AD, with short-term memory the first to disappear.

Genes Involved in Alzheimer Disease Alzheimer disease is partly genetic. It is unusual for AD to develop in middle age, but if it does occur, genes are the direct cause. A middle-aged person with Alzheimer disease either has trisomy-21 (Down syndrome) or has inherited one of three genes: APP (amyloid precursor protein), presenilin 1, or presenilin 2. The disease in middle age progresses quickly, reaching the last phase within three to five years.

Most cases of AD begin much later, at age 75 or so. Many genes have some impact, including SORL1 and ApoE4 (that is, allele 4 of the ApoE gene) (Marx, 2007). People who inherit one copy of ApoE4 (as about one-fifth of all U.S. residents do) have about a 50/50 chance of developing AD by their 80s. Those who inherit the gene from both parents almost always develop the disease if they live long enough, although many die before dementia is diagnosed because ApoE4 can also cause cardiovascular disease (Plassman et al., 2007).

Genetic tests for AD in late adulthood are rarely used before symptoms appear because they might evoke false fear or deceptive reassurance. People with no known genetic risk may develop AD, and people with an ApoE4 gene may never do so.

Stages of Alzheimer Disease In the beginning stages of AD, forgetfulness is far greater than the normal age-related slowness. The affected person is particularly likely to forget names and places and to become disoriented in his or her own neighborhood. Personality may change as well.

Alzheimer disease (AD)
The most common cause of dementia, characterized by gradual deterioration of memory and personality and marked by the formation of plaques of beta-amyloid protein and tangles of tau protein in the brain. Also called *senile dementia of the Alzheimer type (SDAT).*

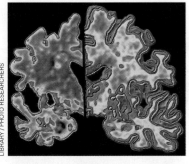

The AD Brain This computer graphic shows a vertical slice through a brain ravaged by Alzheimer disease *(left)* compared with a similar slice of a normal brain *(right).* The diseased brain is shrunken as the result of the degeneration of neurons. Not viewable in this cross section are tangles of protein filaments within the nerve cells as well as plaques that contain decaying dendrites and axons.

ESPECIALLY FOR Genetic Counselors
Would you order a test for ApoE4 if someone asked for it? (see response, page 520) ➜

Every year, symptoms worsen. Eventually, memory loss becomes dangerous. A person might leave the house and wander about, not knowing how to get back home, or might forget to turn off the stove and be confused when the house fills with smoke. More mundane problems also occur: A man might not eat or shower because he forgot when he last did so; a woman might invite someone over and then be surprised when the guest arrives.

In the final stage, people with AD need full-time care. Their sentences are short and simple; ultimately, they stop talking altogether. They no longer read, instead staring blankly at the TV or into space. At the end, identity and personality are gone; they recognize no one. When former president Ronald Reagan was at this late stage, a longtime friend who visited him was asked, "Did he recognize you?" The friend answered, "Worse than that—I didn't recognize him." Death comes 10 to 15 years after the first signs appear.

I Love You, Dad This man, who is in the last stage of Alzheimer disease, no longer remembers his daughter, but she obviously has fond memories of his fatherly affection.

VASCULAR DEMENTIA The second most common cause of dementia is a stroke (a temporary obstruction of a blood vessel in the brain) or a series of strokes, called *TIAs* (transient ischemic attacks, or ministrokes). The interruption in blood flow reduces oxygen in the affected area of the brain, and that destroys brain tissue. As part of the brain dies, immediate symptoms (blurred vision, weak or paralyzed limbs, slurred speech, and mental confusion) appear.

In a TIA, symptoms disappear quickly—in hours or even minutes—and may be so slight that no one (even the victim) notices. Nevertheless, brain damage has occurred. Repeated TIAs produce **vascular dementia (VaD),** also called *multi-infarct dementia.*

In North America and Europe, VaD is the primary diagnosis in 10 to 15 percent of people with dementia and is often a factor in AD. In Japan and China, VaD is more common than Alzheimer disease (De la Torre et al., 2002); this is also the case for the very old who live in North America. Centenarians who have dementia usually, on autopsy, are found to have more vascular damage than plaques and tangles.

vascular dementia (VaD)
A form of dementia characterized by sporadic, and progressive, loss of intellectual functioning caused by repeated infarcts, or temporary obstructions of blood vessels, which prevent sufficient blood from reaching the brain. Also called *multi-infarct dementia.*

OTHER DEMENTIAS **Frontal lobe dementia,** or *frontotemporal lobar degeneration* (Pick disease is the most common form), may cause 13 percent of all dementias in the United States (Levenson & Miller, 2007). Parts of the brain that regulate emotion and social behavior (the amygdala and the frontal lobes) deteriorate, with personality changes rather than memory loss being the main symptom (Bondi et al., 2009). Examples are a loving mother who rejects her children or a businessman who invests in a scheme he would have avoided earlier.

frontal lobe dementia
A form of dementia characterized by personality changes caused by deterioration of the frontal lobes and the amygdala. Also called *frontotemporal lobar degeneration.*

In some ways, frontal lobe dementia is worse than Alzheimer disease or vascular dementia in that it causes human compassion and self-awareness to fade in a person who seems otherwise normal. This brain disease usually begins before age 60 and progresses rapidly, leading to death in about five years.

Many other dementias begin with impaired motor control (shaking when picking up a coffee cup, falling when trying to walk), not with impaired thinking. The most common of these is *Parkinson disease,* which does not always lead to dementia but is the cause of about 3 percent of all cases (Aarsland et al., 2005). Parkinson disease starts with rigidity or tremor of the muscles as neurons that produce dopamine degenerate, affecting movement long before cognition. Younger adults with Parkinson disease have sufficient cognitive reserve to avoid dementia for years; older people develop dementia sooner (Starkstein & Merello, 2002).

RESPONSE FOR Genetic Counselors
(from page 518) A general guideline
for genetic counselors is to provide
clients with whatever information they
seek; but because of both the uncertainty and the devastation of Alzheimer
disease, the ApoE4 test is not available
at present. This may change (as was
the case with the test for HIV) if early
methods of prevention and treatment
become more effective. ●

Another 3 percent of all dementias in the United States are *Lewy body dementia*, named after round deposits of protein (Lewy bodies) in the neurons (Zaccai et al., 2005). Lewy bodies are present in Parkinson disease, but in Lewy body dementia they are numerous and dispersed throughout the brain. Motor movements and cognition are both impacted, although the effects are less severe than the motor deficits of Parkinson disease or the memory loss of Alzheimer disease (Bondi et al., 2009). The main symptom is loss of inhibition.

Our focus in this chapter is on late adulthood, but we should briefly mention that dementia can begin before age 65. Among the causes of adult dementia are Huntington disease; multiple sclerosis; severe head injury; and the last stages of syphilis, AIDS, and bovine spongiform encephalitis (BSE, or mad cow disease). The exact timing and symptoms vary; comorbid conditions produce quicker and more severe dementia.

PREVENTION OF IMPAIRMENT Slowing down senescence postpones dementia. For example, the underlying cause of the blood-vessel obstructions that lead to vascular dementia is arteriosclerosis (hardening of the arteries). Measures to improve circulation or to prevent hypertension and diabetes reduce arteriosclerosis and thus prevent dementia.

Indeed, some research has found that regular physical exercise reduces the incidence of all forms of dementia by half (Marx, 2005), especially if it also prevents overweight. One large study found that people who were obese in middle age were almost twice as likely to develop dementia by their 70s as were people of normal weight (Whitmer et al., 2005).

Exercise is particularly helpful in preventing vascular dementia, since successful stroke prevention precludes the damage of ministrokes. Other dementias may also be helped by exercise, because "some brain-cellular changes seen in normal aging can be slowed or reversed with exercise" (Woodlee & Schallert, 2006, p. 203). Because brain plasticity continues throughout life, exercise may build brain capacity, not merely prevent loss (Kramer & Erickson, 2007).

The other major preventive measure is to avoid the pathogens that cause dementia. For instance, testing beef for mad cow disease, using condoms to protect against AIDS, treating syphilis with antibiotics—all these have reduced dementia.

However, the most feared cause, Alzheimer disease, remains a challenge. Thousands of scientists seek to halt the production of beta-amyloid or tau, stopping AD before it starts (Marx, 2007; Roberson & Mucke, 2006). Some drugs do so in mice, but studies with human participants have many hurdles to overcome before true prevention is available. Among professionals, though, hope is beginning to replace despair, because

> researchers have made tremendous progress toward understanding the molecular events that appear to trigger the illness, and they are now exploring a variety of strategies for slowing or halting these destructive processes. Perhaps one of these treatments, or a combination of them, could impede the degeneration of neurons enough to stop Alzheimer's disease in its tracks.
>
> *[Wolfe, 2006, p. 73]*

For a developmentalist, it is thrilling to read research seeking cures for dementia. Many discoveries are recent, and breakthroughs seem likely. However, it is sobering to track the many possible treatments—including hormones, aspirin, coffee, antioxidants, and statins—that have gone nowhere (Zandi et al., 2005).

Some people hope to prevent dementia by keeping their minds alert, such as by doing crossword puzzles or reading newspapers. Sadly, there is no solid evidence that this prevents Alzheimer disease. Similarly, many toxins—lead, aluminum, copper, and pesticides among them—that were once hypothesized to cause AD are no longer thought to do so.

As you will now see, the treatment of dementia also gives rise to both hope and discouragement.

TREATMENT OF DEMENTIA The first step in treating dementia is to care for the overall health of the person. Many chronic conditions like high blood pressure, diabetes, arteriosclerosis, and emphysema impair cognition by disrupting the flow of oxygen to the brain (Caplan & Schooler, 2003; Elias et al., 2004). If a person with dementia has any one of these, symptoms worsen.

The next step is to get a proper diagnosis. Most scientists agree that earlier and more accurate diagnoses, years before obvious symptoms appear, can lead to treatment that slows the decline of brain functioning. Regarding diagnosis, there is progress—even a decade ago many people thought senility, dementia, and Alzheimer disease were synonyms. Currently, many physicians are learning about prefrontal dementias and other forms that they never studied in medical school.

Yet early diagnosis is notoriously difficult (Bondi et al., 2009). Mild cognitive impairment is an early sign of AD, but only about half the people with this symptom become demented. If you knew two elderly people who were mildly impaired, would you begin treatment for both, knowing that only one of them has the disease?

Perhaps you would seek definitive diagnosis, looking at behavior, test results, and factors in blood and brain fluid (Aluise et al., 2008). Yet no sign thus far identified is definitive, and testing is expensive, time-consuming, and anxiety-producing. Only an autopsy reveals to a pathologist the plaques and tangles, or the dead brain tissue, or the unusual neurons that prove the presence of AD or vascular or Lewy body dementia.

Nevertheless, an accurate diagnosis is urgent because treatment may be helpful. This is especially true for VaD because rehabilitation can overcome much brain damage, and diet, drugs, and exercise can prevent another TIA.

For Alzheimer disease, several drugs, especially cholinesterase inhibitors (e.g., donepezil) and memantine, allow years of close-to-normal functioning (Kaduszkiewicz et al., 2005; Kavirajan & Schneider, 2007). Other drugs are helpful for Parkinson disease, and surgery sometimes restores lost movement control (Deuschl et al., 2006). Unfortunately, treatment of Parkinson disease may increase impulsive behavior, such as gambling and sexual acting out. Obviously, treatment needs to be carefully targeted (Frank et al., 2007).

This leads to the most pressing requirement: the need for professionals who are trained and dedicated, able to provide individualized medical and psychological care for the patient and the family, who shoulder most of the burden of caring for people with dementia. (Caregiving is further discussed in Chapter 15).

REVERSIBLE DEMENTIA As you just read, it is pivotal to understand which form of dementia an impaired person has, but diagnosis is even more crucial when a person is mistakenly thought to have dementia. True dementias destroy parts of the brain and thus cannot be cured, but many older people are assumed to be losing their minds when in fact a reversible problem is at fault.

Mental Illness The most common such problem is depression. When an older person repeatedly complains about losing his or her mind, or despairs at every memory lapse, that is a sign of a treatable mental illness. Remember that older people tend to be quite content with their lives; constant sadness or anxiety is not normal.

Ironically, people with untreated anxiety or depression may exaggerate minor memory losses or refuse to talk. Quite the opposite reaction occurs

Waiting for a Bath This woman is in a Tokyo facility that provides baths for physically or cognitively impaired elderly people—not just as a hygienic necessity, but also as a soothing, sensual experience.

OBSERVATION QUIZ
Should someone take that doll away? (see answer, page 522) →

KAREN KASMAUSKI / CORBIS

with Alzheimer disease, when victims are surprised that they cannot answer questions, or with Lewy body or frontal lobe dementia, when people talk without thinking.

Specifics of memory are also clues to mental illness. People with dementia might forget what they just said, heard, or did but be able to describe in detail something that happened long ago. The opposite is true for many people with emotional disorders, who are impaired in episodic memory (months or years ago) but not in short-term memory.

Polypharmacy Other causes of reversible dementia include inadequate nutrition, dehydration, brain tumors, physical illness, and overmedication (Milosevic et al., 2007). We focus on the last of these now.

At home as well as in the hospital, most elderly people take numerous drugs—not only prescribed but also over-the-counter drugs and herbal remedies—a situation known as *polypharmacy* (Hajjar et al., 2007). This is a common cause of reversible dementia, a condition that few professionals and family members recognize. Audrey, the widow who was addicted to Valium, Placidyl, and alcohol, was a classic case (see page 507).

And the Print Is Too Small Patients, physicians, and pharmacists have reason to be confused about the eight or more drugs that the average elderly person takes. Very few patients take their medicines exactly as prescribed. Moreover, in addition to prescription drugs, most elderly people also take over-the-counter medications, vitamins, and herbal remedies, as well as drinking caffeinated beverages or alcohol. It is no wonder that drug interactions cause drowsiness, unsteadiness, and confusion in about half of all elderly persons.

TONY FREEMAN / PHOTOEDIT, INC.

One reason doctors sometimes overmedicate patients is that recommended doses are determined by clinical trials with younger adults. Their metabolism and digestive systems rid their bodies of excess drugs sooner than is true for the elderly.

Furthermore, people of every age forget when they are supposed to take which drugs (before, during, or after meals? after dinner or at bedtime?). This problem is multiplied when many drugs are needed. Even when medications are taken as prescribed, drug interactions can produce confusion and psychotic behavior.

Cognitive side effects (such as confusion and depression) can occur with almost any drug, including most that reduce blood pressure, combat Parkinson disease, and relieve pain (C. G. Davies & Thorn, 2002). Many of the elderly need surgery, but anesthesia in an unfamiliar setting often triggers hallucinations. If an elderly patient is discharged to a nursing home, overmedication and confusion may continue.

The solution to polypharmacy seems simple: Eliminate problematic drugs. But doing so requires careful analysis of drug harm, benefits, and interactions. If a patient is treated by many physicians (as most of the oldest-old are), each doctor may be unaware of the effects of the drugs prescribed by the others. The elderly themselves may find some drugs too expensive and may make harmful substitutions. Once again, caregivers who know a person's entire history and context may be vital in helping prevent dementia.

The Optimal: New Cognitive Development

You have learned that most older adults maintain adequate intellectual power. Some losses—in rapid responses, for instance—are quite manageable in daily life, and only a few of the elderly become senile. But one principle of the life-span perspective is that gains as well as losses occur throughout life. Are there cognitive gains in late adulthood?

Yes. As you will now learn, new skills, enhanced creativity, and perhaps wisdom are possible.

ANSWER TO OBSERVATION QUIZ (from page 521) No. Note that the woman is holding the doll close, with both hands and her chin. The photograph makes a valid point about the universal need for emotional comfort. ●

NEW LEARNING Several developmentalists have attempted to teach older people new skills. In the Seattle Longitudinal Study, some groups of people who had lost some spatial understanding (one of the five basic abilities) were given instruction and practice and regained the skill level they had had 14 years earlier (Schaie, 2005). This gain was limited, however; it did not spill over to the other four abilities.

Heartened by this limited success, many researchers have tried to teach skills that transfer from the initial task to a new one (C. S. Green & Bavelier, 2008). In one such attempt, a team of researchers taught older adults to play video games, which was an entirely new skill for almost all of them (Basak et al., 2008). After they played, not only did they score higher on the games but they scored higher on other tests. To be specific, the participants' working memory, task-switching prowess, and control processes improved—all abilities that usually fade with age.

Remember from Chapter 12 that expertise is selective; people become proficient in what they choose to practice. Most elderly people leave video games to the teenagers; none would be likely to challenge a grandchild to play Grand Theft Auto, for instance. However, this research suggests that older adults might productively take on projects that require new learning, not only for the sake of the project itself but also for the opportunity to stretch their minds.

ERIKSON AND MASLOW Both Erik Erikson and Abraham Maslow were particularly interested in the perspective of the elderly, interviewing older people in depth to understand their views. Erikson's final book, *Vital Involvement in Old Age* (Erikson et al., 1986), written when he was in his 90s, was based on responses from other 90-year-olds—the cohort who had been studied since they were babies in Berkeley, California.

Erikson found that older people gained interest in the arts, in children, and in human experience as a whole. He said they are "social witnesses," aware of the interdependence of the generations as well as of all of human experience. He called his eighth stage *integrity* (discussed in Chapter 15), when life comes together in a "resynthesis of all the resilience and strengths already developed" (Erikson et al., 1986, p. 40).

Maslow maintained that older adults are more likely than younger people to reach the highest stage of development, **self-actualization.** Remember that Maslow rejected a rigid age-based sequence of life stages, refusing to confine self-actualization to the old. He thought some youth might already be self-actualizers and that some elders are still at earlier steps of his hierarchy of needs, seeking love or success, for instance. However, he also believed that, with every decade, people are likely to move up his hierarchy. This means that more of the old than the young reach the final stage.

The stage of self-actualization is characterized by aesthetic, creative, philosophical, and spiritual understanding (Maslow, 1970). A self-actualized person might have a deeper spirituality than ever, or might be especially appreciative of nature, or might find life amusing, laughing often at him- or herself.

AESTHETIC SENSE AND CREATIVITY For many, "old age can be a time of emotional sensory awareness and enjoyment" (R. N. Butler et al., 1998, p. 65). For that reason, some of the elderly take up gardening, birdwatching, sculpting, painting, or making music, even if they have never done so before.

A great example of late creative development is Anna Moses, who was a farm wife in upstate New York. For most of her life, she expressed her

self-actualization
The final stage in Maslow's hierarchy of needs, characterized by aesthetic, creative, philosophical, and spiritual understanding.

It Pleases Me In young adulthood and middle age, many people feel that they must meet social expectations and conform to community values. With a strong hand, a vivid imagination, and bold colors, the elderly are finally free to express themselves as they never did before.

artistic impulses by stitching quilts and embroidering in winter, when farm work was slow. At age 75, arthritis made needlework impossible, so she took to "dabbling in oil."

Four years later, three of her paintings, displayed in a local drugstore, caught the eye of a New York City art dealer. He bought them, drove to her house, and bought 15 more. The following year, at age 80, "Grandma Moses" had a one-woman show in New York, receiving international recognition for her unique "primitive" style. She continued to paint, her work having "developed and changed considerably over the course of her twenty-year career" (Cardinal, 2001). Anna Moses died at age 101.

Other people have been well-known artists all their lives. For many, old age is a time of renewed inspiration (Lindauer, 2003). Famous examples abound: Michelangelo painted the awe-inspiring frescoes in the Sistine Chapel at age 75; Verdi composed the opera *Falstaff* when he was 80; Frank Lloyd Wright completed the design of New York City's Guggenheim Museum, an innovative architectural masterpiece, when he was 91.

In a study of extraordinarily creative people, almost none of them felt that their ability, their goals, or the quality of their work had been much impaired with age. The researcher observed, "In their seventies, eighties, and nineties, they may lack the fiery ambition of earlier years, but they are just as focused, efficient, and committed as before . . . perhaps more so" (Csikszentmihalyi, 1996, p. 503).

life review
An examination of one's own part in life, which often takes the form of stories written or spoken by elderly people who want to share them with younger ones.

THE LIFE REVIEW Erikson recognized that many older people become more reflective and philosophical, thinking about their own history, putting their lives in perspective, assessing their accomplishments and failures (Birren & Schroots, 2006). One outcome of such reflection may be a **life review,** an elderly person's examination of the part he or she has played in life, connecting the past with the future by writing or telling his or her story. A person's relationship to prior generations, to humanity, to God, and to life is reconsidered; memories are revived, reinterpreted, and finally reintegrated (Kotre, 1995).

The life review is more social than solitary. Elderly people want to tell their stories to others, and often their tales are not solely about themselves but also about their family, cohort, or ethnic group. Such stories tend to be richer in interesting details than those told by younger adults (Pratt & Robins, 1991). A leading gerontologist says that we must listen:

> We have been taught that this nostalgia represents living in the past and a preoccupation with self and that it is generally boring, meaningless, and time-consuming. Yet as a natural healing process it represents one of the underlying human capacities on which all psychotherapy depends. The life review should be recognized as a necessary and healthy process in daily life as well as a useful tool in the mental health care of older people.
>
> *[R. N. Butler et al., 1998, p. 91]*

WISDOM The idea that older people are wise is a "hoped-for antidote to views that have cast the process of aging in terms of intellectual deficit and regression" (Labouvie-Vief, 1990, p. 52). The belief that old age brings wisdom, like the opposite idea that aging always means senility, may be false (Brugman, 2006). The truth lies somewhere in between. As seen many times in this chapter, elderly individuals vary in all aspects of life, including wisdom, at least as much as younger adults do, if not more so.

One summary of wisdom describes it as an "expert knowledge system dealing with the conduct and understanding of life" (P. B. Baltes & Smith, 2008, p. 58). Several factors just mentioned, including the life review (perspective on living), the ability to put aside one's personal needs (as in self-actualization), and a self-reflective honesty (as in integrity) are considered part of wisdom. For all these reasons, some of the elderly have a head start in becoming wise.

Whether a person is *perceived* as wise depends on the society that judges the person's thoughts or actions. Wisdom is a social virtue, one that involves recognizing and responding to enduring cultural values and the current social conditions (Staudinger & Werner, 2003). For that reason, some younger adults may be wise about dilemmas that are more relevant to their life stage (such as whether a teenager should marry).

Yet philosophers, psychologists, and the general public connect wisdom with old age. Although no one has developed an empirical test of wisdom that is accepted by the scientific community, nonetheless this popular consensus seems to be grounded in observation. As two psychologists who have developed a test of wisdom explain:

> Wisdom is one domain in which some older individuals excel. . . . [They have] a combination of psychosocial characteristics and life history factors, including openness to experience, generativity, cognitive style, contact with excellent mentors, and some exposure to structured and critical life experiences.
>
> *[P. B. Baltes & Smith, 2008, p. 60]*

These researchers posed life dilemmas to adults of various ages and asked others to judge whether the responses were wise or not. They contend that wisdom is rare at any age, but, unlike physical strength and cognitive quickness, wisdom does not fade with maturity. Thus, some older people are wise, not only in thought but in deed.

Similarly, the author of a longitudinal study of 814 people concludes that wisdom is not reserved for the old, although humor, perspective, and altruism increase over the decades, gradually making a person wiser. He then writes:

> To be wise about wisdom we need to accept that wisdom does—and wisdom does not—increase with age. Age facilitates a widening social radius and more balanced ways of coping with adversity, but thus far no one can prove that wisdom is great in old age. Perhaps we are wisest when we keep our discussion of wisdom simple and when we confine ourselves to words of one and two syllables. Winston Churchill, that master of wise simplicity and simple wisdom, reminds us, "We are all happier in many ways when we are old than when we are young. The young sow wild oats. The old grow sage."
>
> *[Vaillant, 2002, p. 256]*

KEY Points

- Some aspects of cognition slow down with age, particularly working memory, as reactions slow and the need to concentrate increases.

- Memory and other control processes for regulating the flow and analysis of information become less effective with age. Perhaps in compensation, more parts of the brain are used when an elderly person must concentrate on an intellectual task.

- Dementia is often characterized by memory loss. This is particularly the case with Alzheimer disease. Other common forms of dementia include vascular dementia, frontal lobe dementia, Lewy body dementia, and Parkinson disease.

- Many people become more responsive to nature, more creative, and more reflective (e.g., conducting a life review) as they grow older. Some—not all— elderly people are unusually wise.

Ageism

1. Ageism stereotypes people based on age, often manifest in prejudice about the elderly. Ageism is apparent in elderspeak and in fears of the social burden of increasing numbers of people who are old. In truth, most elderly people are quite independent.

2. Gerontologists sometimes distinguish among the young-old, the old-old, and the oldest-old, according to each age group's relative degree of dependency. Compression of morbidity leads to fewer years of old-old age.

3. The senses become less acute with age. Compensation is possible with technology, caregiver and professional support, and social change.

Health and Sickness

4. Primary aging happens to everyone. Although the particulars of secondary aging depend on past health habits and genes, everyone eventually experiences an increase in morbidity, disability, and risk of mortality.

5. The number of centenarians is rising; many of these oldest-old are quite healthy and happy. The personality and attitudes of the very old suggest that long-term survival may be welcomed more than feared.

6. Most anti-aging measures are unproven, although exercise is beneficial for everyone. Calorie restriction has been successful with many mammals.

Thinking in Late Adulthood

7. Brain scans and measurements show that speed of processing slows down, parts of the brain shrink, and more areas of the brain are activated in older people.

8. Although thinking processes become slower and less sharp once a person reaches late adulthood, there is much variation. Some input may not reach the sensory memory; working memory declines; control processes (especially retrieval strategies) are less effective with age.

9. Stereotype threat is one reason older adults perform less well than younger adults on tests of cognitive functioning. Another problem is that some measures of cognition lack ecological validity. In daily life, few elderly are troubled by reduced cognition.

10. In the United States, 14 percent of the elderly suffer from dementia, half of them due to Alzheimer disease. Another common problem is vascular dementia, which is caused by mini-strokes, in which impairment of blood circulation destroys portions of brain tissue.

11. Other causes of dementia include Lewy bodies in the brain, frontal lobe dementia, Parkinson disease, and various viruses.

12. Exercise, diet, and other health practices protect the brain throughout life, reducing the incidence or onset of dementia, especially vascular dementia. Some medical interventions treat dementia. Accurate diagnosis and individualized care are needed.

13. Although Alzheimer disease is incurable, progressive, and eventually fatal, hope springs from research that seeks many ways to stop it.

14. Dementia is sometimes falsely diagnosed when people suffer from mental disorders or practice polypharmacy. Caregivers are crucial in knowing the context of an older person's life.

15. Many people become more responsive to nature, creative, spiritual, and philosophical as they grow older. The life review allows older people to remember earlier experiences and put their entire lives into perspective, achieving integrity or self-actualization.

16. Wisdom does not necessarily come with age, but some elderly people are unusually wise or insightful.

KEY TERMS

ageism (p. 497)
elderspeak (p. 498)
young-old (p. 499)
old-old (p. 499)
oldest-old (p. 499)
population pyramid (p. 500)
dependency ratio (p. 501)

compression of morbidity (p. 502)
primary aging (p. 504)
secondary aging (p. 504)
cardiovascular disease (CVD) (p. 504)
maximum life span (p. 508)

average life expectancy (p. 508)
centenarian (p. 510)
calorie restriction (p. 511)
ecological validity (p. 515)
control processes (p. 516)
dementia (p. 517)

Alzheimer disease (AD) (p. 518)
vascular dementia (VaD) (p. 519)
frontal lobe dementia (p. 519)
self-actualization (p. 523)
life review (p. 524)

KEY QUESTIONS

1. How is ageism comparable to racism or sexism?

2. Why is the increasing number of older people less problematic than it was once thought to be?

3. What is the difference between primary aging and secondary aging?

4. What changes occur in the sense organs in old age, and how can their effects be minimized?

5. What changes in the brain occur with age?

6. How is each part of the information-processing system—the sensory register, working memory, and control processes—affected by age?

7. How does ecological validity affect the research on long-term memory?

8. What are the similarities and differences between Alzheimer disease and vascular dementia?

9. Why is accurate diagnosis important when older people have cognitive difficulties?

10. What are the purpose and the result of the life review?

11. What is wisdom, and how does it relate to aging?

APPLICATIONS

1. Analyze Web sites that have information about aging for evidence of ageism, anti-aging measures, and exaggeration of longevity.

2. Compensating for sensory losses is difficult because it involves learning new habits. To better understand the experience, reduce your hearing or vision for a day by wearing earplugs or dark glasses that let in only bright lights. (Use caution and common sense: Don't drive a car while wearing earplugs or cross streets while wearing dark glasses.) Report on your emotions, the responses of others, and your conclusions.

3. Ask five people of various ages if they want to live to age 100, and analyze their responses. Would they be willing to eat half as much, exercise much more, experience weekly dialysis, or undergo other procedures in order to extend life?

4. Many factors affect intellectual sharpness. Recall an occasion when you felt stupid and an occasion when you felt smart. What do the contexts of the two experiences suggest about memory tests for the elderly?

CHAPTER OUTLINE

LATE ADULTHOOD
Psychosocial Development

G ilbert and Sadie are centenarians, more than 100 years old. They have been married for 80 years and retired for 40. They live together in their own home, with no outside helpers. They often talk about their offspring, who are already old themselves. Gilbert is proud of Sadie's agility:

> "She gets out of bed—I timed her this morning, just for fun. I got up first, but while I was in the bathroom, she gets up, she comes out here first and puts the coffee on. Got back and washed up and got dressed and just twelve minutes after she got out of bed—just twelve minutes this morning—I had her right on the watch."
>
> Sadie chuckles. "I don't have any secrets anymore."
>
> "So then you have breakfast together?" I ask.
>
> "Oh, yes!"
>
> "And then read the paper?"
>
> "After we get the dishes washed, we sit down and read the paper for a couple of hours."
>
> *[N. Ellis, 2002, pp. 107–108]* ●

FEW OF THE OLDEST-OLD LIVE AS WELL AS GILBERT AND SADIE: Many are widowed; most no longer live independently. But Gilbert and Sadie are not unusual in taking comfort in their families, pleasure in their daily routines, and interest in current events. Like them, many other elderly people are socially embedded, physically active, and mentally alert. It is ageist to assume otherwise.

In this chapter, we describe the variability and complexity of development in later life. Activities of daily life often include working and socializing, as well as self-care. In long-lasting marriages, both partners help each other stay active. We also examine the conditions for the minority of elderly people who are frail and unable to perform the activities of daily life. Most of them are well cared for, but frail elders are vulnerable to abuse from family members and others.

Theories of Late Adulthood

It is probably true that development is more diverse in late adulthood than at any other age: Some elderly people run marathons and lead nations, while others are no longer able to move or think. Many social scientists have tried to understand these variations as well as the general course of old age.

Some theories of late adulthood have been called *self theories* because they focus on individuals' perceptions of themselves and their ability to meet challenges to their identity. Other theories are called *stratification theories* because they describe the ways in which societies place people on a particular life path.

Self Theories

It can be said that people become more truly themselves as they grow old. The essential self is protected and fulfilled, despite all the changes that may occur. Thus, self theories emphasize "the ways people negotiate challenges to the self" (Sneed & Whitbourne, 2005, p. 380). Such negotiation is particularly crucial when older adults are confronted with multiple challenges like illness, retirement, and the death of loved ones.

A central idea of **self theories** is that each person ultimately depends on himself or herself. As one woman explained:

> I actually think I value my sense of self more importantly than my family or relationships or health or wealth or wisdom. I do see myself as on my own, ultimately. . . . Statistics certainly show that older women are likely to end up being alone, so I really do value my own self when it comes right down to things in the end.
>
> *[quoted in J. Kroger, 2007, p. 203]*

self theories
Theories of late adulthood that emphasize the core self, or the search to maintain one's integrity and identity.

integrity versus despair
The final stage of Erik Erikson's developmental sequence, in which older adults seek to integrate their unique experiences with their vision of community.

INTEGRITY The most comprehensive self theory came from Erik Erikson. His eighth and final stage of development is called **integrity versus despair,** a period when older adults seek to integrate their unique experiences with their vision of community (Erikson et al., 1986). The word *integrity* is often used to mean honesty, but it also means a feeling of being whole, not scattered, comfortable with oneself. *Integrity* comes from the same root word as *integer,* a math term meaning a whole number, not a fraction.

As an example of how integrity is achieved, many older people develop pride and contentment with their personal story: They are proud of their past, even when their memories involve skipping school, sneaking drugs, escaping arrest, or being punished by their parents. Psychologists sometimes call this the *"sucker or saint" phenomenon*—that is, people's tendency to recount their experiences as signs of their nobility (for endurance or rebellion), not their foolishness (for victimization or law breaking) (Jordan & Monin, 2008). As Erikson explains it, such distortion is far better than losing hope, "feeling that the time is now short, too short for the attempt to start another life" (Erikson, 1963, p. 269).

Elderly people typically realize that their life is no longer measured in years since birth but in years before death. For many, close family members become more important when life is seen as short (Carstensen, 2006). Within this perspective, they continue to try to understand themselves, but they focus less on the possibilities ahead of them than on the way they will be remembered.

On the Same Page This school volunteer, working with "high-risk" children, pays close attention to the picture that has captured the boy's interest. The ability to care for others is one sign of integrity, as older adults realize all the "high risks" they have personally overcome.

AP / WIDE WORLD PHOTOS

As at every crisis described by Erikson, tension occurs between the two opposing aspects of development. Past crises, particularly identity versus role confusion, reemerge when the usual pillars of the self-concept (such as one's job or physical appearance) crumble. One 70-year-old said, "I know who I've been, but who am I now?" (quoted in J. Kroger, 2007, p. 201).

That tension helps advance the person toward a fuller understanding. In this last stage,

> life brings many, quite realistic reasons for experiencing despair: aspects of the present that cause unremitting pain; aspects of a future that are uncertain and frightening. And, of course, there remains inescapable death, that one aspect of the future which is both wholly certain and wholly unknowable. Thus, some despair must be acknowledged and integrated as a component of old age.
>
> *[Erikson et al., 1986, p. 72]*

Ideally, the reality of death brings a "life-affirming involvement" in the present—with oneself, one's children, one's grandchildren, and all of humanity (Erikson et al., 1986). As many others have found, awareness of death can be self-liberating instead of frightening; this topic is explored in the Epilogue.

HOLDING ON TO ONE'S SELF Most older people consider their personalities and attitudes to have remained quite stable over their life span, even as they recognize the physical changes of their bodies (Fischer et al., 2008). One 103-year-old woman observed, "My core has stayed the same. Everything else has changed" (quoted in Troll & Skaff, 1997, p. 166). A nursing home resident,

> when asked whether she had changed much over the years, extracted a photo from a stack in her dresser drawer, one taken when she was in her early twenties, and said, "That's me, but I changed a little." She had indeed changed. She was now neither curvaceous nor animated, but was physically distorted from crippling arthritis and sullen from pain. To herself, however, she was still the same person she had always been.
>
> *[Tobin, 1996]*

A Reason for Hoarding When older adults are asked to select a "cherished object," most pick ordinary and inexpensive things that have great personal meaning (Sherman & Dacher, 2005). Objects and places become more precious in late adulthood than they were earlier, as a way to hold on to identity (J. Kroger, 2007; Whitmore, 2001).

The tendency to cling to familiar places and possessions may be problematic if it leads to *compulsive hoarding*. This urge to accumulate old papers, pieces of furniture, and mementos becomes increasingly common with age (Thobaden, 2006).

Many older people resist moving from a drafty and dangerous dwelling into a smaller, safer place, not because they do not recognize the social and health benefits of the move but because they fear that parting with familiar places may mean that they will lose themselves. Preserving the self is crucial to them, even if it shortens life.

Keeping Traditions The same impulse explains why many of the old strive to maintain the cultural and religious values of their youth. For instance, grandparents may painstakingly teach a grandchild a language that is rarely used in their current community or encourage the child to repeat rituals and prayers they grew up with.

In cultures that emphasize youth and novelty, the elderly worry that their old values may be lost. This is apparent in the United States among immigrants who were raised never to question their elders as U.S. children do. Older people from India, living with their offspring in New Jersey, reported to researchers that their grandchildren were disrespectful and that "Indian culture is ignored, compartmentalized, and debased in America" (Kalavar & van Willigen, 2005, p. 228).

continuity theory
The theory that each person experiences the changes of late adulthood and behaves toward others in a way that is consistent with his or her behavior in earlier periods of life.

CONTINUITY THEORY Some gerontologists, seeking to stress that the self remains the same throughout life, developed **continuity theory,** which "assumes that a primary goal of adult development is adaptive change, not homeostatic equilibrium" (Atchley, 1999). Continuity is apparent even while people adapt to whatever circumstances they find themselves in, although superficially it may seem as if the person changes.

In this perspective, each innovation is a new expression of the old self (Nimrod & Kleiber, 2007). Thus, an intellectually curious person who had dropped out of high school in adolescence might earn a college degree in old age; an extrovert who was the center of the family might, if the spouse dies and children have moved away, suddenly join a political group. Elderly women whose husbands are terminally ill temporarily become less socially active as they tend their husbands and then become more sociable after their husbands die (Utz et al., 2002).

One source of continuity is temperament. Reinforced by the ecological niches that individuals have carved out for themselves, the Big Five personality traits (see Chapter 13) are maintained throughout old age as in younger years, shifting somewhat but always oriented toward the same life goals (D. B. Cook et al., 2005). Therefore, a person's reactions to potentially disruptive problems reflect continuity, as do attitudes toward all other topics—drugs, sex, money, neatness, privacy, health, government.

The life story of a woman who became a teacher because she liked to help others is an example of continuity. When she retired, she did volunteer work and then, when she could no longer walk, she welcomed high school students who interviewed her at home. Finally, physical impairment forced her to enter a nursing home, where the entire staff and all the other residents became more sociable because of her. Her former students visited her often, although the home was several miles away from the town where she had taught (Atchley, 1999).

Resilience Nelson Mandela celebrates his 90th birthday, smiling despite his lifelong—and ultimately successful—struggle against South Africa's racist political system. His life serves as evidence for self theory, for the positivity effect, and for miracles.

positivity effect
The tendency for elderly people to perceive, prefer, and remember positive images and experiences more than negative ones.

THE POSITIVITY EFFECT As you remember, some people cope successfully with the changes of late adulthood through *selective optimization with compensation*. This concept is central to self theories. Individuals set their personal goals, assess their own abilities, and figure out how to accomplish what they want to achieve despite limitations and declines. For some people, simply maintaining their identity correlates with well-being (Ebner et al., 2006).

One example of selective optimization is known as the **positivity effect.** Elderly people are more likely to perceive, prefer, and remember positive images and experiences than negative ones (Carstensen et al., 2006). Selective memory is a way to compensate for whatever troubles occur; unpleasant experiences are reinterpreted as inconsequential.

Research has found that the positivity effect has both cognitive and social aspects. For example, in a laboratory experiment to test memory, people were shown a batch of photographs. They were then shown another batch (some duplicates, some new) and were asked which of those photographs they had seen before. Compared with younger adults (aged 18–28), the older adults (aged 64–80) were more likely to remember the positive photos (such as a baby seal) than the negative ones (such as a snake) (Mikels et al., 2006).

Another study compared the responses of older and younger adults to confrontation. Almost 1,000 people over age 65 were asked how often they experienced 12 types of unpleasant social exchanges (Sorkin & Rook, 2006). More than one-third (39 percent) of the older people reported no negative interactions. Of those who remembered unpleasant encounters, 60 percent said that their primary goal after the event was to maintain goodwill. Only a few sought to change the other person's behavior (see Figure 15.1). The goal of achieving harmony led to effective strategies, such as compromise rather than assertion:

Participants whose primary coping goal was to preserve goodwill reported the highest levels of perceived success and the least intense and shortest duration of distress. In contrast, participants whose . . . goal was to change the other person reported the lowest levels of perceived success and the most intense and longest lasting distress.

[Sorkin & Rook, 2006, p. 723]

In many ways, the positivity effect enhances life in late adulthood. Despite impairments, older adults generally are happy with themselves. However, the positivity effect is deeper than an overall rosy glow. Older adults notice the negative, too. Laboratory experiments show that the positivity effect does not always emerge; it depends on the situation (Fernandes et al., 2008).

Nonetheless, self-perception normally tilts toward integrity rather than despair. Most people realize they could have chosen other paths through life, especially if they lived in other cultures, but they also appreciate their particular self. As Erikson put it, the older person

knows that an individual life is the accidental coincidence of but one life cycle with but one segment of history and that for him all human integrity stands or falls with the one style of integrity of which he partakes. . . . In such a final consolation, death loses its sting.

[Erikson, 1963, p. 268]

Research on what people hope for themselves (the ideal self) and how they perceive themselves (the real self) finds that, with age, the two selves come closer together (George, 2006). This may explain much of the contentment that older adults generally feel (Cheng, 2004). As self theory contends, self-acceptance leads to happiness.

Stratification Theories

There is another major set of theories regarding late adulthood that emphasize the relationship between society and old age. Instead of stressing how people become more and more themselves with age, these **stratification theories** focus on the society's impact on each individual—an impact felt because societies place each person in a category or role. Those roles are difficult to break away from because societies stratify each group.

According to stratification theories, social forces and cultural influences limit choice and direct life at every stage. The effects over the years accumulate to make one older person's life quite different from another's (O'Rand, 2006).

Individual factors—including quality of marriage and friendship, personality, and cognitive capacity—affect each person's position in his or her society. Nonetheless, stratification theories note significant social restrictions imposed by stratification categories such as age, gender, and ethnicity. An American who is old, female, and non-European may be in "triple jeopardy," likely to be poor, sick, and frail (Cruikshank, 2003). Stratification works the other way, too: Low socioeconomic status (SES) itself stratifies people (Schieman & Plickert, 2007).

STRATIFICATION BY AGE Industrialized nations segregate elderly people, gradually shunting them out of the mainstream of society as they grow older (Achenbaum, 2005). According to stratification theory, segregation by age harms everyone because it

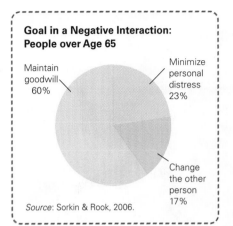

Goal in a Negative Interaction: People over Age 65

Maintain goodwill 60%

Minimize personal distress 23%

Change the other person 17%

Source: Sorkin & Rook, 2006.

FIGURE 15.1 Keep the Peace When someone does something mean or unpleasant, what is your goal in your interaction with that person? If your goal is to maintain goodwill, as was the case for a majority of older adults studied, you are likely to be quicker to forgive and forget.

Not Completely Identical These 90-year-old monozygotic twins have the same genes, but, judging from their faces, life has not treated them the same way. Continuity of self in late adulthood reflects earlier experiences, not just genes.

stratification theories Theories that emphasize that social forces, particularly those related to a person's social stratum, or social category, limit individual choices and affect a person's ability to function in late adulthood as past stratification continues to limit life in various ways.

STEPHANIE MAZE / CORBIS

Silver on Display In the foreground is Layla Eneboldsen, enjoying the company of three other elderly people who live with her. Since more than 90 percent of the elderly in the United States are White (and mostly female), like this group of friends, and since the furniture, lights, and artwork date from 60 years ago, this might seem to be a scene from the 1940s in the United States. In fact, this is twenty-first-century Denmark.

disengagement theory
The view that aging makes a person's social sphere increasingly narrow, resulting in role relinquishment, withdrawal, and passivity.

activity theory
The view that elderly people want and need to remain active in a variety of social spheres—with relatives, friends, and community groups—and become withdrawn only unwillingly, as a result of ageism.

"creates socialization deficits for members of all age groups" (Hagestad & Dannefer, 2001, p. 13). A "socialization deficit" is a lack of needed social experiences: Younger as well as older people have a narrow perspective on life if they interact only with people their own age.

Disengagement Theory The most controversial version of age-stratification theory is **disengagement theory** (Cumming & Henry, 1961). According to this theory, as people age, traditional roles become unavailable or unimportant, the social circle shrinks, coworkers stop asking for help, and adult children turn away to focus on their own children.

Age stratification is mutual, according to disengagement theory. Children want to be with other children, adults with other adults, and older adults with one another or by themselves. Thus, younger people disengage from the old, who themselves voluntarily disengage from the activities of younger adults. They relinquish past roles, withdrawing from life's action. If they can afford it, they move to senior residences where no young people are allowed.

Activity Theory Disengagement theory provoked a storm of protest because people feared it justified ageism. Many gerontologists insisted that older people need new involvements. Some developed an opposite theory, called **activity theory**, which holds that the elderly seek to remain actively involved with relatives, friends, and community groups. If the elderly disengage and withdraw, activity theorists contend, they do so unwillingly (J. R. Kelly, 1993; Rosow, 1985).

Research supports both theories. Many of the elderly disengage, but most studies find that happier and healthier elders are quite active, filling various roles (worker, wife, husband, mother, father, neighbor, worker) (Lampinen et al., 2006; Rowe & Kahn, 1998). Indeed, literally being active—bustling around the house, climbing stairs, walking to work—lengthens life and increases satisfaction (Manini et al., 2006).

Some research finds that the elderly themselves seek to be active. A longitudinal study of 77- to 98-year-olds in Sweden found that quality of life was directly related to having many leisure activities. Over a 10-year period, one-third of those studied added activities rather than cutting back; some participants substituted new activities if old ones were no longer available (Silverstein & Parker, 2002). The inactive people were the least happy.

STRATIFICATION BY GENDER Feminist theory draws attention to stratification on the basis of gender. From the newborn's pink or blue blanket to the color of an elderly resident's bedspread in a nursing home, gender is signaled to everyone. Society guides and pressures males and females into divergent paths. For women, especially, this kind of stratification may result in a diminished old age.

The ongoing implications of gender differences were revealed by a study of retirement and caregiving among older married couples. Both men and women provided care if their spouse needed it, but they did it in opposite ways: Women quit their jobs, whereas men worked longer. To be specific, employed women whose husbands needed care were five times more likely to retire than were other older women who were not caregivers. By contrast, when employed husbands had a sick wife, they retired only half as often as other men did (Dentinger & Clarkberg, 2002).

The responses of both husbands and wives make sense in terms of caregiving: The men who kept working could afford household help, and the women who quit working had time to provide care. Both responses result from past stratification: Men are more likely to have had jobs with better pay and benefits, while women are socialized to be caregivers. However, the female strategy is more likely than the male one to lead to poverty and social isolation—as in this example, where gender expectations and past experiences put elderly women in jeopardy.

Irrational, gender-based fear may also limit women's independence. For example, adult children persuade their elderly mothers more than their fathers to stop traveling or living alone, arguing that the women would be unsafe otherwise. However, only 2 percent of violent crime victims are women over age 65. The rate of victimization for older men is slightly higher, at about 5 percent (P. Klaus, 2005). There is ageism here as well: If avoiding travel protects against crime, then it is emerging adults (who are much more likely to be victims), not the elderly, who should stay home.

Many of the oldest-old women married men older than they were and outlived them. Especially if they lived in rural areas (as most Americans did until about 1950), they relied on their husbands to drive, to manage money, and to keep up with politics. Such accumulated, lifelong stratification may lead to poverty, frailty, and dependence.

STRATIFICATION BY ETHNICITY Like age and gender, ethnic background affects every aspect of development, including education, health, place of residence, and employment. Stratification theory suggests that these factors accumulate over the years, creating large discrepancies in income by old age (see Figure 15.2).

One example of such a discrepancy is home ownership, a major source of financial security for many seniors. Far fewer old African Americans than European Americans own homes, because past racial stratification prevented them from moving into certain neighborhoods or obtaining fair mortgages.

Similarly, health disparities are evident lifelong (Kelley-Moore & Ferraro, 2004). In the United States, on average, a Black woman who has reached age 65 (and thus has escaped earlier mortality differentials) has 15 more years to live, but a 65-year-old White woman has 17 more years (U.S. Bureau of the Census, 2008).

A particular form of ethnic stratification affects immigrant elders. Many expect to move in with their adult children, as is traditional in most African, Eastern European, and Asian nations. However, in many modern developed nations, not only are expectations different, but stratification is reflected in housing designs, employment patterns, and cultural values. It is logistically difficult for three generations of a family to live together.

Consider the fate of an elderly man born in Russia. He was placed by his U.S.-born son in an assisted-living center for senior citizens. The man hated the place and left. He rented a room from an 85-year-old Russian widow, to whom he became attached. But when the landlady became frail and the elderly man began taking care of her, his son moved him out. Once again, the father was on his own and unhappy. He said:

> Would I like to live with my kids? Of course. But I know that's impossible. They don't want me. . . . not that they don't love me. I understand that. In the old days, a hundred years ago, old people stayed at home.
>
> *[quoted in Koch, 2000, p. 53]*

As a result of this cultural divide, the man's life was described as one of "lonely independence . . . a quintessentially American tragedy" (Koch, 2000, p. 55).

This is a reminder that, while different societies have different forms and degrees of stratification, complications inevitably arise when people raised in one system are thrust into another. This is true currently for millions of people who, after escaping

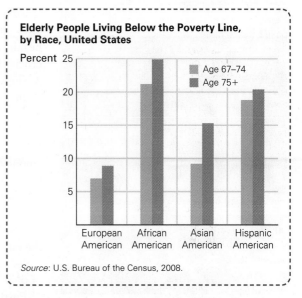

Elderly People Living Below the Poverty Line, by Race, United States

Source: U.S. Bureau of the Census, 2008.

FIGURE 15.2 Ethnic Gaps in Poverty Other data show that, overall, those under age 25 are more likely to be poor than elders are but that ethnic discrepancies in income are much greater among the old. This is what theories of cumulative stratification would predict.

● **UNDERSTANDING THE NUMBERS**
Do racial gaps in poverty increase or decrease as elderly people grow older?

Answer It varies according to ethnicity. Ethnic disparities in income increase for Asians but decrease for Hispanics. The percent gap between African Americans and European Americans in poverty increases (from 14 to 16 percent), but the ratio shrinks (from about 1-to-3 to about 1-to-2.7).

persecution and starvation in their homeland, find themselves in a new culture; it is also true whenever a nation's political and economic situation changes radically, as in South Africa, Iraq, and East Germany (Westerhof & Keyes, 2006).

BETTER TO BE OLD, FEMALE, AND NON-WHITE? Most critics of stratification theory focus on age stratification, although, as you will soon see, gender and ethnic stratification may also be less widespread, or less devastating, than is sometimes portrayed. One leading gerontologist suggests that both disengagement theory and activity theory may be too extreme:

> Staff members working with old people . . . reported having very mixed feelings when trying to "activate" certain old people. They maintained that activity is good, but they nevertheless confessed feeling that they were doing something wrong when they try to drag certain older people to various forms of arranged social activity or activity therapy.
>
> *[Tornstam, 2005, p. 34]*

A similar cautionary note comes from research in China. Among the young-old, activity correlated with health, particularly if activities involved social interactions. But among the oldest-old, activity did not correlate with longevity: Sometimes disengagement was more closely associated with health (R. Sun & Liu, 2008). Research in Israel found that relationships were crucial, but neither activity nor disengagement predicted well-being (Litwin & Shiovitz-Ezra, 2006).

In some ways, being an older non-White woman does not signify triple jeopardy at all. Because women tend lifelong to be caregivers and kinkeepers, they are better able than men to cope with those roles and to derive social satisfaction from them. Religion and family connections seem stronger among members of some minority ethnic groups, especially among older female members, and may be beneficial in later life (Idler, 2006).

Another advantage for elderly females is that grown children tend to be more nurturing toward their aging mothers than toward their aging fathers. It seems that old men are more often lonely than old women are. Indeed, the rate of suicide is eight times higher among elderly males than elderly females and twice as high among older Whites than older Blacks (U.S. Bureau of the Census, 2008).

Furthermore, older women and older minority-group members seem to benefit from close relationships with others of their sex or ethnicity. They choose churches, senior activities, or friendship groups whose members are similar to them. Perhaps it is both ageist and racist to believe that they do so because they are excluded from more mixed groups.

Thus, the relationship between stratification and the triple jeopardy of age, gender, and ethnicity is complex. It is simplistic to draw the sweeping conclusions that the elderly should be active, or that they should behave like people of other ages, or that gender and ethnic differences are always harmful to women and minorities.

The crucial variable in the well-being of the elderly may be income, not gender or ethnicity (Achenbaum, 2006–2007). Sexist and racist practices are always harmful, of course, but when income is held constant, female, non-White elders seem happier than male, White ones (Schieman & Plickert, 2007).

There is no question that health and income disparities unfairly make poverty more common among elderly women and minorities, but research finds that, at least among the poor, old age is more depressing for people of the majority group. One suggested explanation is that they never learned to cope with loss of privilege, so they are unprepared for age discrimination (Schieman & Plickert, 2007).

SONDA DAWES / THE IMAGE WORKS

Dig Deeper A glance at this woman at her outdoor pump might evoke sympathy. Her home's lack of plumbing suggests that she is experiencing late adulthood in poverty, in a rural community that probably offers few social services. Her race and gender put her at additional risk of problems as she ages. However, a deeper understanding might reveal many strengths: religious faith, strong family ties, and gritty survival skills.

ESPECIALLY FOR Social Scientists The various social science disciplines tend to favor different theories of aging. Can you tell which theories would be more acceptable to psychologists and which to sociologists? (see response, page 538) ➡

KEY points

- Many theories attempt to organize and explain development in late adulthood. As at other stages, these theories are useful and provocative but not always correct.

- Self theories emphasize that each person becomes more himself or herself in old age. Erikson's final stage of development, integrity versus despair, can be one culmination of self-affirmation.

- Stratification theories emphasize the power of social groupings, in which one category of person is treated differently from another. Disengagement theory and activity theory reach opposite conclusions, but both focus on age stratification.

- Although some consequences of gender and ethnic stratification are negative (e.g., impact on income), others may be beneficial (e.g., strength of family connections).

Activities in Late Adulthood

It is ageist to think that older people are inactive. In fact, their activities are intense and varied. This might come as a surprise to younger adults, who see few elders at sports events, political rallies, or midnight concerts. However, the elderly are engaged with life in other ways, as we now describe.

Work

As explained in Chapter 13, work provides many psychological benefits besides the practical benefit of income. Research on late adulthood finds that many of these benefits can be obtained from volunteer work as well.

PAID EMPLOYMENT Developmentalists are aware of "a growing body of research that points to the positive physical and psychological impacts, for women as well as men, of employment" (Moen & Spencer, 2006, p. 135). Work provides social support and status, boosting self-esteem. For many people, employment allows generativity and is evidence of "productivity, effectiveness, and independence," all cherished Western values (Tornstam, 2005, p. 23).

This is not to ignore the importance of income. Some of those who keep working in late adulthood do so because they need the money: Many elderly people live on pensions, Social Security, and investments, but substantial numbers of them keep

The Same Situation, Many Miles Apart: Sustained by Mother Nature These elderly men are similar in that they both benefit from the growth of plants.

OBSERVATION QUIZ

What are two important differences between these men? (see answer, page 538) ➔

working. In 2007 in the United States, 21 percent of the men and 13 percent of the women over age 65 were in the labor force (U.S. Bureau of the Census, 2008). Those rates have risen since 2000 and are expected to keep rising as other sources of income shrink in the economic downturn that began in 2007.

Besides needing the money, some employees over age 65 stay on the job because they appreciate the social recognition and self-fulfillment that work brings. Elder participation in the labor force is higher among nonunionized low-wage workers (who probably need the income) and among professionals at the top of their game (who may enjoy the recognition) than among those in between.

For younger adults, paid employment is central to well-being: Depression, drug abuse, and family stress all correlate with unemployment (Galambos et al., 2006). Extending those findings to older adults who leave the labor market, many social scientists warned about "the presumed traumatic aspects of retirement" (Tornstam, 2005, p. 19). This worry may have arisen from ageism, as you will see.

NOT WORKING The generalization that work is important for well-being is based on surveys of adults of both sexes and every age. Remember, however, that summaries do not reflect reality for everyone surveyed.

It is psychologically devastating to be fired from a job or to be unable to find work. This is especially true for married men aged 30 to 55. However, some other people—such as emerging adults who have not yet started the career they want or married mothers whose chosen work is to care for their young children—are less depressed. They may find unemployment easier than working.

This variability explains a paradox found among older adults. Many people once believed that older adults were healthier and happier when they were employed than when they were unemployed and that retirement led to illness and death (Burgess, 1960). Accordingly, in the 1980s, U.S. legislators outlawed mandatory retirement (except in special occupations, such as that of jet pilot).

The paradox is revealed by the finding that since 1980, when older workers were no longer required to quit their jobs at age 65, the average age of retirement has *decreased*. Rather than preferring to work until they die, many older adults retire as soon as they can (Hardy, 2006). Only when retirement is precipitated by poor health or fading competence does it correlate with illness (A. Shapiro & Yarborough-Hayes, 2008).

In more than a dozen European nations where adequate pensions are offered to employees in their 50s, half the workers retire before age 60 (A. Walker, 2004). In the United States, Social Security payments increase for people who wait until age 70 to stop working; nonetheless, most people stop working years before that. If income is adequate, retirement in every nation is more likely to make older adults happy rather than sad.

Indeed, an unexpected social problem has resulted from the retirement of workers at relatively young ages. Some professions (including nursing, policing, and teaching) have too few experienced workers over age 50.

Of course, just as employment does not always bring joy, retirees are not always happy. Planning is often inadequate, and married couples may disagree as to who should retire, when retirement should begin, and how their lives should be restructured (Moen et al., 2005).

One particular problem is financial. This is especially true if adults calculate costs based on past expense. They may not realize that people who reach age 65 are likely to live for several more decades, or that inflation reduces buying power over time, or that Medicare does not cover all health care expenses. Furthermore, after long-postponed projects (anything from traveling to China to painting the porch) are completed, former goals need "expanding, reducing, concentrating and diffusing" (Nimrod, 2007, p. 91).

VOLUNTEER WORK Volunteering offers some of the advantages of paid employment (generativity, social connections). The benefits are many, for the individual (better health, less depression) as well as for society (help in providing health, education, and other social services).

Several successful programs that connect members of a community depend on older volunteers (e.g., Foster Grandparents and OASIS [Online Asperger Syndrome Information and Support] Person to Person). No wonder "gerontologists have been strongly attracted to the idea that active engagement [volunteering and political activity] in society is related to well-being in later life" (Morrow-Howell & Freedman, 2006–2007, p. 6).

Is the connection between well-being and volunteering merely an "idea"? No; empirical data reveal that it is much more. Cross-sectional research finds a strong link between good health and volunteering. As with any correlation, it is not obvious which came first: Healthy elders are more likely to be volunteers, as well as vice versa. However, many signs indicate that volunteering itself aids well-being.

Steady volunteers are less likely than other elderly people to become depressed or sick (Herzog et al., 2002; Luoh & Herzog, 2002; Sugihara et al., 2008). Benefits are particularly evident when older volunteers are useful, socially involved, and appreciated (George, 2006; Okun et al., 2007; F. Tang, 2006). Advantages are clearest when volunteering occurs in moderation—for 2 hours a week, not 20, and for one organization, not several (M. A. Musick et al., 1999; Windsor et al., 2008).

Who Volunteers? As continuity theory would predict, volunteer work attracts older people who feel strongly committed to their community. Many have volunteered earlier in adulthood and seek to continue. They appreciate the chance to serve their neighbors and to be "mentors, guides, and repositories of experience" for younger people (Settersten, 2002, p. 65).

The rate of volunteering varies by culture; the elderly in Nordic nations (e.g., Sweden and Norway) volunteer far more often than those in Mediterranean nations (e.g., Italy and Greece). One reason is that northern Europeans are healthier, but differences persist even when illness is taken into account (Erlinghagen & Hank, 2006).

Still, the data reveal two areas of concern. First, contrary to what most people imagine, older, retired people are less likely to volunteer than are middle-aged, employed people. Three-fourths of people over 65 do no volunteer work (see Figure 15.3).

Second, less than half of all adults of any age volunteer. Several observers consider this a sign of social isolation: People may feel so disconnected from their communities that they allow their personal interests to overshadow broader concerns (Bellah et al., 2007; Putnam, 2000).

Why Not More Volunteers? Some gerontolotists wonder if the push for more volunteering is a way for public institutions to avoid hiring paid workers to do needed tasks

Mutual Help Senior citizens are steady volunteers at this Tokyo day-care center. Small children benefit from personal attention as they learn new skills. The elders benefit from social interaction with the children.

KAREN KASMAUSKI / CORBIS

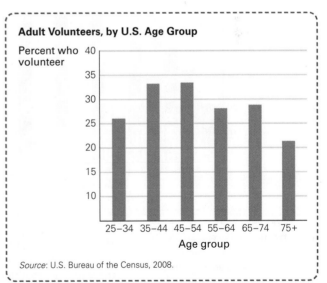

Adult Volunteers, by U.S. Age Group

Percent who volunteer

Source: U.S. Bureau of the Census, 2008.

FIGURE 15.3 Giving Their Time These statistics count only hours spent in formal volunteer work, usually for a church or hospital. In addition, many older adults informally provide free services to friends and family members. Almost every grandparent babysits; many elders care for older relatives (spouses, siblings, parents). If these services are counted, the percentage who volunteer is much higher (N. G. Choi et al., 2007).

ESPECIALLY FOR Social Workers
Your agency needs more personnel but does not have money to hire anyone. Should you go to your local senior-citizen center and recruit volunteers? (see response, page 542) →

(Minkler & Holstein, 2008). However, most wish that volunteering were more common among the elderly and have offered four possible explanations for the lack of participation:

1. *Social culture.* Ageism may discourage meaningful volunteering. Many volunteer opportunities are geared toward the young, who are attracted to intense, short-term experiences. A few weeks of building a house during spring break or a few years of working in a rural community with the Peace Corps are obviously not experiences designed for older volunteers (Morrow-Howell & Freedman, 2006–2007).

2. *Organizations.* Institutions lack recruitment, training, and implementation strategies for attracting older volunteers. For instance, although most primary school students would benefit from a personal mentor, schools have barriers (e.g., health exams, background checks, long flights of stairs) that discourage elders, and few schools provide space, time, and training for tutors.

3. *The elderly themselves.* Perhaps older adults are too self-absorbed, more concerned with their own needs and those of their families than with the needs of strangers or of society in general. This narrow outlook is suggested by another statistic: About half of the elders who volunteer do so within their own religious organizations. Moreover, only 1 in 6 volunteer to work with youth, compared with about 1 in 3 younger adults (U.S. Bureau of Labor Statistics, 2008).

4. *The researchers.* The problem may lie not with the people but with the science. Surveys of volunteer work ignore most daily caregiving and informal helping. Babysitting, caring for an ill spouse, shopping for an infirm neighbor—perhaps if such activities were included, the data would reveal higher rates of volunteering in late adulthood.

● **FOR DEEPER REFLECTION** Do you think more elderly people should do volunteer work? Which of the four explanations for lack of volunteering by the elderly do you think is most valid? (Note: Liberals and conservatives are likely to give quite different answers.)

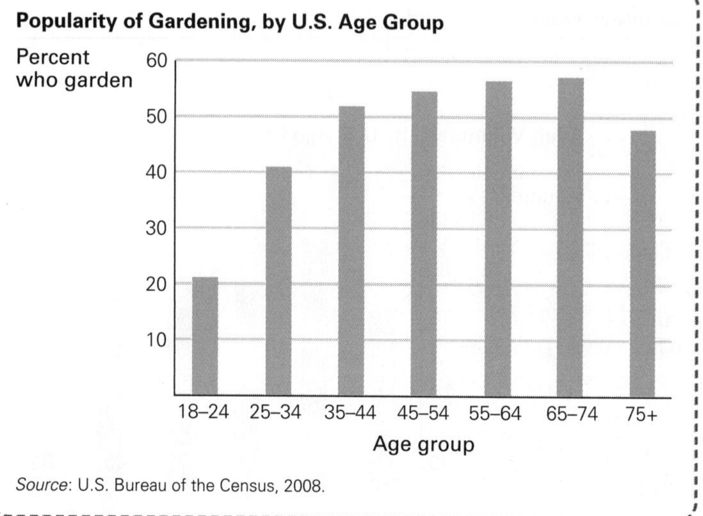

Home, Sweet Home

One of the favorite activities of many retirees is caring for their own homes. Typically, both men and women do more housework after retirement (Kleiber, 1999; Szinovacz, 2000). They also do yard work, redecorate, build shelves, rearrange furniture.

Gardening becomes more popular: More than half the elderly in the United States cultivate a garden each year (see Figure 15.4). As with paid employment, the complexity of hobbies and home-repair activities correlates with lower rates of dementia (E. Kröger et al., 2008).

In keeping up with household tasks and maintaining their property, many older people demonstrate that they prefer to **age in place.** They want to stay in the same dwelling where they lived as younger adults, adjusting but not leaving when health fades. If they must move, they prefer to stay near their old neighborhood, perhaps in a smaller apartment in a building with an elevator, but not in a different city or state.

The preference for aging in place is evident in statistics. Overall, 14.4 percent of U.S. residents are age 65 or over. But the distribution varies by state: About 18 percent of the populations of Maine, West Virginia, and North Dakota are age 65 or over; elderly people make up smaller percentages of the population in sunny California (13 percent), Georgia (11.6), and Texas (11.7) (U.S. Bureau of the Census, 2008). These figures indicate that some of the elderly would rather stay in familiar surroundings where winters are cold than move to warmer but unfamiliar climes.

Popularity of Gardening, by U.S. Age Group

Source: U.S. Bureau of the Census, 2008.

FIGURE 15.4 Dirty Fingernails
Almost three times as many 60-year-olds as 20-year-olds are gardeners. What is it about dirt, growth, and time that makes gardening an increasingly popular hobby as people age?

aging in place
Remaining in the same home and community in later life, adjusting but not leaving when health fades.

Sometimes a neighborhood or an apartment complex becomes a **naturally occurring retirement community (NORC)** when young adults who moved in decades earlier never leave. Many elderly people in NORCs are content to live alone. They stay on after their children move away and their partners die, in part because they are familiar with their community (C. C. Cook et al., 2007).

An important reason for both aging in place and NORCs is the social convoy, the result of years of close relationships (see Chapter 13). For example, one reason the elderly enjoy home repair, housework, and gardening is that family members or visitors appreciate the new curtains, the polished door, the blooming rosebush.

To age in place successfully, elderly people need many community services (K. Black, 2008). If a person is living alone in dilapidated housing, especially in a rural or high-crime urban community, simply pointing out the danger is not enough. Someone needs to help them move out or remodel. Aging in place does not mean that seniors need to be left alone; it means that care should come to them (Golant, 2008).

Continuing Education

About one out of five U.S. adults age 66 and older was enrolled in some kind of continuing education in 2005 (U.S. Bureau of the Census, 2008). Most elderly students (76 percent in one report) are motivated primarily by a desire for personal or social improvement through, for instance, mastering a hobby, managing income, exploring their roots, or understanding their grandchildren (Jeanneret, 1995).

In some ways, late adulthood is an ideal time for learning (Russell, 2008). Many older students have a strong intellectual curiosity as well as a wish to understand the deeper meaning of history, literature, philosophy, and other subjects. This approach to education is quite different from that of younger adults, who want skills that will be useful on the job.

However, many adult education programs do not consider the special characteristics of the elderly (L.-K. Chen et al., 2008). For example, older students' vocabulary may be strong but their short-term memory is weak; respect for teachers is evident, but computers are confusing; crystallized abilities are sharp, but fluid ones are not (Dellenbach & Zimprich, 2008). Of course, any generalizations (including these) will sometimes be wrong, since diversity of ability, interests, and background overtakes similarities in age (L.-K. Chen et al., 2008).

Some educational programs *are* designed for the elderly. One U.S. example is Elderhostel, which started in New England in 1975 with 220 students. Now, more than 160,000 people age 55 and over enroll in Elderhostel courses each year. Most courses are primarily academic, taken on college campuses while the regular students are on vacation. Some require more active involvement. For example, a 2009 Elderhostel course in Belize involved snorkeling and sand analysis as well as classroom lectures on the ecology of coral reefs.

Many other nations also encourage late-life education. At least a dozen European countries have *Universities of the Third Age,* which are college programs dedicated to older learners (Achenbaum, 2005). In China, free courses in calligraphy, traditional arts, exercise, and health are provided as part of the "Five Guarantees"—a government policy promising that "older people should be supported, have medical care, contribute to society, be engaged in lifelong learning, and have a happy life" (D. Peng & Phillips, 2004, p. 114). As elsewhere, policies diverge from practice in China, but at least the intention is to provide lifelong education.

Religious Involvement

Older adults are less likely to attend religious services than are the middle-aged, but faith increases with age, as do praying and other religious practices (Ingersoll-Dayton et al., 2002). Many studies (both cross-sectional and longitudinal) show that religious

naturally occurring retirement community (NORC)
A neighborhood or apartment complex whose population is mostly retired people who moved to the location as younger adults and never left.

ESPECIALLY FOR Religious Leaders
Why might the elderly have strong faith but poor church attendance? (see response, page 543) →

beliefs and practices of all kinds are positively correlated with physical and emotional health (Idler, 2006).

Social scientists have studied the reasons for the connection between religion and well-being. They have found many: (1) Faith encourages a healthier lifestyle (less drug use, for instance); (2) attendance at services fosters social relationships; and (3) belief in a divine plan decreases stress by fostering reinterpretation of past problems, by reducing fear of death, and by answering the question, "What is life about?" (Atchley, 2009).

Religious identity and religious institutions are especially important for older members of minority groups, many of whom feel a stronger commitment to their religious heritage than to their national or cultural background. For example, although Westerners may note only the national origin of Nigerians or Iraqis or Turks, elderly people in those groups may focus on their Muslim, or Christian, or Jewish faith (Gelfand, 2003). They identify more closely with a particular branch of their religion than with their nation—as is evident in Iraq, with its sharp distinctions between the Shiite and Sunni branches of Islam.

Religious institutions fulfill many needs, and a nearby house of worship is one reason American elders prefer to age in place. Particularly for older African Americans, their churches may be a cherished spiritual home, providing practical activities (choir, study, meals) as well as close, supportive friends. Many churches also have social service programs (e.g., feeding the homeless, counseling drug abusers, sponsoring after-school activities). Such programs give members a convenient way to "do the Lord's work" while obtaining the benefits of volunteering mentioned earlier (Carlton-LaNey, 2006–2007).

Religious faith may explain an oddity of mortality statistics. In the United States, suicide is far more common among elderly European American men than among the oldest African American women, by a ratio of about 50-to-1. Indeed, that ratio may be an underestimate, as so few elderly African American women kill themselves that the rate is almost zero (R. L. Walker & Hunter, 2008). A possible explanation is that African American women's religious faith, which is often very strong, makes them less depressed about their daily lives.

For all elderly people, no matter what their particular faith, psychological health depends on feeling that they are part of a long, continuous line of spiritual traditions that were handed down by their ancestors and will be carried on by their descendants. At least one gerontologist believes that an "increasing feeling of cosmic communion" comes with age, that older people are better able to see beyond their own immediate needs and to care about other people, ask enduring questions, and emphasize spiritual needs (Tornstam, 2005, p. 41). Every religion helps elders deal with these concerns (Idler, 2006).

Political Activism

Younger adults might be forgiven if they think that elderly people are not politically active. Fewer older people turn out for massive rallies, and only about 2 percent volunteer in political campaigns. Nor do they vote as a bloc. In Europe as well as in the United States, the elderly do not seem to be actively involved in politics (U.S. Bureau of the Census, 2008; A. Walker, 2006).

By other measures, however, the elderly are more politically active than people of any other age. More of them write letters to their elected representatives, vote, and identify with a political party.

Still Politically Active The man with the microphone is Floyd Red Crow Westerman, a Lakota Sioux who is an actor (in *Dances with Wolves*, among many other films) and director. Many members of his cohort fought in Vietnam. Disapproval of the war in Iraq was greater among his generation than among both older and younger cohorts.

DAVID YOUNG-WOLFF / PHOTOEDIT, INC.

TABLE 15.1 Voter Registration in Nonpresidential Election Years, by Age Group

Age group	Voters Registered in Election Year (%)		
	1974	1990	2006
18–20	36	35	37
21–24	45	43	45
25–34	55	56	50
35–44	67	66	59
45–64	74	71	70
65+	71	77	75

Source: U.S. Bureau of the Census, 2008.

Participation Varies According to Age, Not History Adults steadily increase their political involvement as they grow older. This table compares voter registration for off-year (nonpresidential) elections to avoid the effects of the temporary excitement that affects some generations more than others during presidential campaigns. Note that age, not cohort, is the driving force: People are about twice as likely to be registered when they are over age 65 than under 21.

Over the past 20 years in off-year (nonpresidential) U.S. elections, an average of 60 percent of those over age 65 voted, compared with 15 percent of those age 18 to 20 (U.S. Bureau of the Census, 2008). This difference seems more a result of age than cohort: As Table 15.1 shows, the number of people of a given age who are registered to vote in nonpresidential elections remains quite steady over time.

Like Sadie and Gilbert at the beginning of this chapter, the elderly are more likely than younger adults to keep up with the news. For example, the Pew Research Center for People and the Press periodically asks U.S. residents questions on current events. In 2008, elders (age 65 and over) beat the youngest (age 18–30) by a ratio of about 3-to-2 in knowing who was the Speaker of the U.S. House of Representatives (Nancy Pelosi) or what nation Nicolas Sarkozy led (France) (Pew Research Center, 2008).

AARP (originally the American Association of Retired Persons), the largest organized interest group in the world, advocates for the elderly. In 2008, AARP had close to 40 million members, many of whom were baby boomers (members must be over 50 but need not be retired). About 8 percent of AARP's budget goes to research and action regarding politics (Binstock, 2006–2007).

AARP's political influence is thought to be one reason that the U.S. Social Security program is called "the third rail" of domestic politics, after the high-voltage electrical conductor that delivers power to trains and will electrocute a person who touches it. The idea is that advocating changes in Social Security may be fatal to a politician's career—even though most experts believe that reform is needed.

Many government policies affect the elderly, especially those regarding housing, pensions, prescription drugs, and medical costs. However, members of this age group do not necessarily vote their own economic interests. Some are swayed by opposite perspectives on various issues, including global warming, military conflicts, and public education. For example, the elderly tend to support public spending for schools and often vote to commit their own tax dollars to educate children who are not theirs.

There is one exception to this generous outlook: Elders who are recent arrivals in a community are less likely to approve the issuance of bonds for public education (Berkman & Plutzer, 2004). It seems that elders who age in place are more likely to support neighborhood children than are those who do not know the families in their community.

As this example indicates, the political opinions of the elderly reflect national trends and their own personal history more than their chronological age (A. Walker, 2006). The idea that the political or economic concerns of the elderly clash with those of the young is not confirmed by the data: Many older people are passionate about the well-being of future generations who are not their direct descendants.

AARP
A U.S. organization of people aged 50 and older that advocates for the elderly. It was originally called the American Association of Retired Persons, but now only the initials AARP are used, since members need not be retired.

RESPONSE FOR Religious Leaders (from page 541) There are many possible answers, including the specifics of getting to church (transportation, stairs), physical comfort in church (acoustics, temperature), and content (unfamiliar hymns and language). ●

In fact, the idea of "gray power" may be a myth, designed to reduce support among younger people for programs to support health care for the elderly (A. Walker, 2006, p. 349). Given that ageism fluctuates from hostile to benign—and is often far from reality—it is not surprising that political perceptions of the elderly zigzag from compassion to fury, as "older persons [are] attacked as too powerful and, at the same time, as a burdensome responsibility" (Schulz & Binstock, 2008, p. 8). As you know, neither of these accusations is true.

KEY Points

- Older adults who keep working, whether as paid employees or as unpaid volunteers, tend to feel productive and socially connected. Most who retire enjoy their newfound leisure time.

- If having a job is an economic necessity, if retirement is mandated, or if volunteering is overwhelming or underappreciated, older adults do not benefit from being retired.

- Elders prefer to grow older in the same communities in which they spent the earlier years of adulthood. Often their religious involvement within their community is one reason for this preference.

- Elders like to learn and to be politically active; they vote more and are better informed about current events than are younger adults.

Friends and Relatives

Each of the domains just described—work, home, education, religion, and politics—involves some, but not all, of the aged. Now we turn to the one realm that involves everyone: companionship. Humans are social animals, dependent on one another for survival and drawn to one another for joy. This is as true in late life as in infancy.

Remember from Chapter 13 that every person travels the life course in the company of other people, who make up the social convoy (Antonucci et al., 2007). Bonds formed over a lifetime allow people to share triumphs and tragedies with others who understand their past victories and defeats. Siblings, old friends, and spouses are ideal convoy members, but anyone (celebrities, neighbors, acquaintances) can be part of a person's social convoy, especially in late adulthood.

Long-Term Partnerships

Spouses buffer each other against the problems of old age, thus extending life. This was one conclusion from a meta-analysis of dozens of studies with a combined total of 250,000 participants (Manzoli et al., 2007). Married older adults are healthier, wealthier, and happier than unmarried people their age.

Homosexuals also benefit from having an intimate partner who is committed to their well-being lifelong (Herek, 2006). Elderly divorced people are lower in health and happiness than are those who are still married, although some argue that income and personality are the reasons, not marital status (Manzoli et al., 2007). The evidence about widows, widowers, and single people is more nuanced, as we will soon see.

It is clear that personal happiness increases with the length as well as the quality of the marriage or intimate relationship—an association that is more apparent in longitudinal than in cross-sectional research (Proulx et al., 2007; Scarf, 2008). A lifetime of shared experiences—living together, raising children, and dealing with

The Same Situation, Many Miles Apart: Partners Whether in the living room of their home in the United States (*left*) or at a senior center in the Philippines (*right*), elderly people are more likely to smile when they are with one another than when they are alone.

OBSERVATION QUIZ

What does the clothing of the people in these photographs indicate about their economic status? (see answer, page 547) →

financial and emotional crises—brings partners closer in memories and values, as "spouses . . . increasingly internalize each other's ideas about appropriate behavior" (T. L. Huston, 2000, p. 314).

In general, older couples have learned how to disagree. I know a politically active couple in their 60s who seem happily married, are the proud parents of two young adults, yet vote for opposing candidates. That puzzled me until the wife explained: "We sit together on the fence, seeing both perspectives, and then, when it is time to get off the fence and vote, Bob and I fall on opposite sides."

I always knew who would fall on which side, but to this couple, both the discussion and the final choice were productive. Their long-term affection kept disagreements from becoming fights. Most other long-married couples deal with their disputes in the same way.

MUTUAL RESPECT One of the amazing aspects of long-term relationships is how interdependent the partners become over time, as we saw with Sadie and Gilbert at the opening of this chapter. In one U.S. study of long-lasting marriages, 86 percent of the partners surveyed thought their relationship was about equal in give-and-take (Gurung et al., 2003). Similar results were found in a comparison of various European nations. Objectively, wives were less equal in some nations than others, but subjectively they felt fairly treated (M. Braun et al., 2008).

Outsiders might judge many long-term marriages as unequal, since one or the other spouse usually provided most of the money, or needed most of the care, or did most of the housework. Yet such disparities do not seem to bother the partners or affect their judgments of equity.

Another aspect of long marriages also suggests mutual respect. Generally, older spouses accept each other's frailties, assisting with the partner's physical and psychological needs. Elders who are disabled (have difficulty walking, bathing, and performing other activities of daily

Shared Laughter One characteristic of long-married couples is that they often mirror each other's moods. Thanks to the positivity effect, the mood is often one of joy.

life) are less depressed and anxious if they are in a close marital relationship (Mancini & Bonanno, 2006). A couple can achieve selective optimization with compensation: The one who is bedbound but alert can keep track of what the mobile but confused one is supposed to do, for instance.

Besides caregiving, sexual intimacy is another major aspect of long-lasting marriages. Younger adults, and many researchers, tend to measure sexual activity by frequency of orgasm; by that measure, sexual activity decreases with each decade. But intercourse may not be the best measure for the elderly. Many older couples' sexual behavior has changed, but sex remains important (Johnson, 2007). One couple had this to say about their sex life:

Husband: We have sex less frequently now, but it's satisfying to me. Now that we are both home, we could spend all our time in bed. But it's still more amorous when we go away. When we travel, it's like a second honeymoon.

Wife: Sex has been important in our marriage, but not the most important. The most important thing has been our personal relationship, our fondness, respect, and friendship.

[quoted in Wallerstein & Blakeslee, 1995, p. 318]

THE IMPACT OF RETIREMENT In addition to relinquishing the work role, retirees must usually adjust the marriage interaction, now that they will be spending more time at home with their spouse. The transition is much harder for men in some professions (policemen, physicians) than in others, as many of them have done little work around the house (Davey & Szinovacz, 2004). This increased interaction sometimes precipitates relationship conflicts.

In past generations, the problem was that the husbands not only earned the income but also planned how to spend it, ignoring their wives' wishes and needs (Dennis, 2007). A man's travel plans, leisure pursuits, and mere presence at home could be unsettling to his wife. For current generations, it is much more common for planning to be mutual. When both spouses are employed, it seems best for them to retire together (D. B. Smith & Moen, 2004); if they do not, trouble is more likely.

In a study of 790 retirees, aged 57 to 67, usually neither spouse was employed and most were quite happy (Szinovacz & Davey, 2005). However, in cases in which a husband retired but his wife did not *and* she made most of the family decisions, only 25 percent of the husbands said they were "very satisfied" with retirement. This was in marked contrast to the men whose wives were not working *or* who felt that they made most family decisions. Almost all of them (80 percent) were "very satisfied."

Retired wives followed the same pattern (Szinovacz & Davey, 2005). They were very satisfied *unless* their husbands were employed and dominant. Apparently, older adults have two main sources of satisfaction: work and home. They are dissatisfied if they do not have control over either of those two spheres.

DEATH OF A SPOUSE Another common event that long-married older adults must face is the death of their spouse. Adjustment to being widowed is especially difficult during the first two years after the death (Hagedoorn et al., 2006). Because women tend to marry older men, the average married woman experiences 4 to 10 years of widowhood and the average man, none.

Problems for the Widows Among the current cohort of older women, many have centered their lives on being a wife, mother, caregiver, and homemaker. As a result, the death of a husband means more than loss of a mate; it also means a reduction in status, income, social activities, and identity as someone's wife.

Alone, But Not Lonely Ten million women in the United States are widows. Most, like this woman, are over age 60 and live alone. Many, though not all, are financially secure and well adjusted to their newly independent way of life.

MARKO HAGERTY / THE IMAGE BANK / GETTY IMAGES

With time, many older widows come to enjoy their independence. Few seek another man. A prospective study found that 18 months after the death of their husbands, only 19 percent of older widows were interested in remarrying and only 9 percent were currently dating (Carr, 2004). For companionship and emotional support, widows usually rely on women friends (who are often widows as well) and grown children, and they typically expand their social connections after a husband's death (Utz et al., 2002).

Problems for the Widowers Widowers are more vulnerable. They are less comforted by their families (Ha et al., 2006), and they have fewer men friends who have lost a partner. In addition, men typically find it difficult to seek and accept help. For both sexes, but particularly for men, the death of a spouse often precipitates a move to a nursing home (Nihtilä & Martikainen, 2008).

For all these reasons, elderly widowers are more likely than widows to be physically ill and socially isolated. Their risk of suicide has been found to increase, not only in the United States but also in Taiwan (H.-l. Liu et al., 2006), Denmark (Erlangsen et al., 2004), and every other nation that reports suicide data by age and marital status.

Although few elderly widowers seek to remarry, they are far more likely to do so than widows are, for two reasons: (1) They tend to be lonelier than the women and thus more strongly motivated to seek companionship; and (2) the sex ratio is in their favor, giving them more potential partners to choose from. For widowers, but not for widows, interest in dating and remarriage dating is particularly likely if they do not have many friends (Carr, 2004). For the man's mental as well as physical health, remarriage is usually beneficial.

Relationships with Younger Generations

In past centuries, most adults died before their grandchildren were born (Uhlenberg, 1996). Today, some families span five generations, consisting of elders and their children, grandchildren, great-grandchildren, and great-great-grandchildren. The result is "longer years of 'shared lives' across generations" (Bengston, 2001, p. 6).

Since the average couple now has fewer children, the *beanpole family*, with multiple generations but only a few members in each one, is becoming more common (see Figure 15.5). Some members of the youngest generation have no cousins, brothers, or sisters but a dozen or more elderly relatives. Intergenerational relationships will become more important when most grandparents have only one or two grandchildren (Bengston, 2001; Silverstein, 2006).

Although elderly people's relationships with members of younger generations are usually positive, they can also include tension and conflict. Few older adults stop parenting simply because their children are grown. As one 82-year-old woman put it: "No matter how old a mother is, she watches her middle-aged children for signs of improvement" (Scott-Maxwell, 1968). Adult children also imagine parental disapproval, even if it is not outwardly expressed.

ADULT CHILDREN Family members throughout life tend to support one another. Feelings of *familism* prompt siblings, cousins, and even more distant relatives to seek out one another

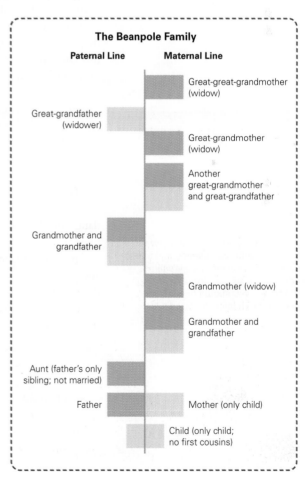

FIGURE 15.5 Many Households, Few Members The traditional nuclear family consists of two parents and their children living together. Today, as couples have fewer children, the beanpole family is becoming more common. This kind of family has many generations, each typically living in its own household, with only a few members in each generation.

as adulthood unfolds. The closest nonromantic relationship, beginning in infancy and continuing past death, is the parent–child one.

Obligation to Care **Filial responsibility** is the obligation of adult children to care for their aging parents. Members of the younger generation in every culture feel responsible for their parents.

When parents need material goods, their adult children often sacrifice to provide them, but emotional support is more crucial and more complex, sometimes increasing when financial help is not needed (Silverstein, 2006). Some elders resent exactly the same supportive behaviors that other elders expect from their children, such as visiting frequently, giving presents, cleaning the refrigerator, calling the doctor, or even paying the telephone bill.

A longitudinal study of attitudes found no evidence that recent changes in family structure (including divorce) reduce the sense of filial responsibility (Gans & Silverstein, 2006). In fact, younger cohorts (born in the 1950s and 1960s) endorsed *more* responsibility toward older generations, "regardless of the sacrifices involved," than did earlier cohorts (born in the 1930s and 1940s).

Amazingly, belief in filial responsibility was weaker among the elderly, who were most likely to need care. After midlife and especially after the death of their own parents, members of the older generation were *less* likely to express the view that children should provide substantial care for their parents.

The authors of this study conclude that, as adults become more likely to receive than to give intergenerational care, "reappraisals are likely the result of altruism (growing relevance as a potential receiver) or role loss (growing irrelevance as a provider)" (Gans & Silverstein, 2006, p. 974). This observation echoes an idea introduced in Chapter 13: Adults like to be needed, not to be needy.

Culture is crucial in determining what specific type of support people expect and who they think should provide it. As already stressed, a major goal among adults in the United States is to be self-sufficient. The old would rather take care of their own needs, but if that is not possible, they would rather rely on a spouse than on a child. Adult children may be more willing to offer support than their parents are to receive it.

This is not true in most Asian nations, where parents depend on sons, not daughters, for support in their old age. (This cultural preference does much to explain why more female than male fetuses are aborted and why many more infant Asian girls than boys are available for adoption.) Often the first-born son encourages his elderly parents to move in with him. Indeed, a study in rural China found increased rates of depression among the elderly people whose daughters-in-law (married to their sons) did not take care of them but whose daughters did (Cong & Silverstein, 2008).

Tensions Between Older and Younger Adults As noted in Chapter 13, a good relationship with successful grown children enhances a parent's well-being, especially when both generations do whatever the other generation expects. By contrast, a poor relationship makes life worse for everyone (E. A. Greenfeld & Marks, 2006; Koropeckyj-Cox, 2002). Ironically, conflict is more likely in emotionally close relationships than in distant ones (Van Gaalen & Dykstra, 2006), especially when either generation becomes dependent on the other (Birditt et al., 2009).

The mother–daughter relationship is most likely to be both close and conflicted, at least in the United States. For example, in one study of 48 mother–daughter pairs (average ages 76 and 44, respectively), 75 percent of the mothers and almost 60 percent of the adult daughters identified the other as one of the three most important persons in their lives. Yet 83 percent of the mothers and 100 percent of the daughters acknowledged having recently been "irritated, hurt, or annoyed" by the other.

filial responsibility
The obligation of adult children to care for their aging parents.

● **FOR DEEPER REFLECTION** How do you think your age, gender, and ethnic background will affect your willingness to receive care from your children, if you should need it when you approach late adulthood?

The mothers usually blamed someone else for the tension ("Her husband kept on turning up the radio every time I turned it down"), while the daughters were likely to blame their mother ("She tells me how to discipline my kids") (quoted in Fingerman, 1996). The mothers are more concerned with protecting the family image in their own minds, so they do not want to blame their child (Giarrusso et al., 2006).

Extensive research has found that relationships between parents and adult children are affected by many factors (Hareven, 2001; Van Gaalen & Dykstra, 2006):

- Assistance arises from need and from the ability to provide.
- Frequency of contact is related to geographical proximity, not affection.
- Love is influenced by the interaction remembered from childhood.
- Sons feel stronger obligation; daughters feel stronger affection.

Although all family members are supportive across the generations, members of each generation tend to overestimate how much they contribute (Lin, 2008b; Mandemakers & Dykstra, 2008). Contrary to popular perceptions, financial assistance and emotional support typically flow more from the older generation down instead of from the younger generation up, although much depends on who needs what (Silverstein, 2006). Not unless an elder becomes frail is he or she more likely to receive family assistance than to give it. (Caring for the frail elderly is discussed later.)

GRANDCHILDREN Most (85 percent) elders over age 65 are grandparents, but what that means to them varies a great deal. Their personality, ethnicity, national background, and past family interactions all influence the nature of the grandparent–grandchild relationship, as do the age and the personality of the child (M. M. Mueller & Elder, 2003).

As described earlier, a dramatic housing shift has occurred that alters the grandparent–grandchild relationship. Whereas a century ago, grandparents almost always lived with at least one of their grandchildren, now most do not. Among families that are new to North America, extended families are more common, partly because grandparents who reached adulthood abroad are not comfortable with the idea of living on their own in the new culture. However, whether their elders were immigrants or not, when children born in North America become old, they prefer to live apart from their adult children, but nearby.

This change in living arrangements does not necessarily weaken the grandparent–grandchild connection, but it does make it more voluntary and more varied (Thiele & Whelan, 2008). The existence of a good relationship between elderly parents and their grown children makes a good relationship more likely between grandparents and grandchildren. Fathers are particularly influential in the grandfathers' relationships with grandchildren; mothers affect the grandmothers' relationships (Monserud, 2008).

In the United States, contemporary grandparents follow one of four approaches to dealing with their grandchildren (Szinovacz, 1998). The first three were identified 25 years ago, when the implications of family members living apart from one another were first recognized, in a now-classic book titled *The New American Grandparent: A Place in the Family, a Life Apart* (Cherlin & Furstenberg, 1986). The fourth approach has been recognized more recently, now that a notable minority of grandparents (about 10 percent) live with their grandchildren and about half of them provide parental care.

- *Remote grandparents* (sometimes called *distant grandparents*) are emotionally distant from their grandchildren. They are esteemed elders who are honored, respected, and obeyed, expecting to get help whenever they need it.

"*They grow up too fast.*"

- *Companionate grandparents* (sometimes called *"fun-loving" grandparents*) entertain and "spoil" their grandchildren—especially in ways, or for reasons, that the parents would not.
- *Involved grandparents* are active in the day-to-day lives of their grandchildren. They live near them, see them daily, and provide substantial care.
- *Surrogate parents* raise their grandchildren, usually because the parents are unable or unwilling to do so.

Although remote grandparenting was once the norm and is still common in some nations (Maehara & Takemura, 2007), it is rare in the West. Many American men imagine that they will be remote, leaving playfulness to their wives, but most become less distant when they actually interact with their grandchildren (Roberto et al., 2001).

Currently, most grandparents of both sexes are companionate, partly because all three generations expect them to be beloved older companions rather than authority figures (Hayslip & Patrick, 2003). Grandparents themselves enjoy their independence from the demands of child rearing. If grandparents become intrusive, parents tend to be forgiving, not appreciative (Pratt et al., 2008).

As one expert describes it, the older generation stands by until needed, like a family version of the National Guard:

> Although remaining silent and unobserved for the most part, grandparents (and great-grandparents) muster up and march out when an emergency arises regarding younger generation members' well-being.
>
> *[Bengston, 2001, p. 7]*

Most are proud of their grandchildren and care about their well-being but keep their distance if possible. They provide babysitting and financial help but not advice or discipline. Their involvement leads to generativity and joy (Thiele & Whelan, 2008).

Such generative distance is not possible for grandparents who become surrogate parents, taking over parenting when the biological parents cannot do so because of imprisonment, addiction, absence, or death. Difficult grandchildren (such as drug-affected infants and rebellious school-age boys) are more likely to be sent to live with grandparents.

Social workers often prefer grandparents when seeking kinship foster care (see Chapter 7) for maltreated children. This may be best for the children, but not always for the grandparents.

The most vulnerable grandparents (disproportionately non–White and low-income) are pushed into surrogate parenting (Dunifon & Kowaleski-Jones, 2007). Grandparents who are responsible full time for grandchildren have more illness, depression, and marital problems than other elders do. This is true in Europe as well as in North America, although the frequency of this family form depends on local and national culture (Hank & Buber, 2009; S. J. Kelley & Whitley, 2003; Solomon & Marx, 2000). Not surprisingly, few surrogate parents welcome their role. As one explains:

> I don't know if God thought I did a poor job and wanted to give me a second chance, or thought I did well enough to be given the task one more time. My daughter tells me she cannot handle the children anymore, but maybe I won't be able to manage them either.
>
> *[quoted in Strom & Strom, 2000, p. 291]*

When a married couple take over care of their grandchildren, employed grandfathers postpone retirement and grandmothers are likely to quit work (Y. Wang & Marcotte, 2007). Single grandfathers who become surrogate parents usually stop working. None of these outcomes increase the elders' satisfaction. Furthermore, recent research has found that when the relationship between older parents and their adult children is troubled (as it often is in such cases), the grandchildren suffer as well.

A VIEW FROM SCIENCE

Not Always Grand

It is a myth that grandparents always enjoy their grandchildren and vice versa. Another assumption is that the more time grandparents spend with grandchildren, the better. Those are among the reasons that social workers prefer grandparents for kinship care (as just noted) and judges protect the visitation rights of grandparents, even when parents are adequate and do not want the grandparents around (T. J. Stein, 2007).

The data suggest that sometimes all three generations benefit from grandparenting, sometimes not (Thiele & Whelan, 2008). For example, researchers compared groups of 5- to 15-year olds to test their hypothesis that the children who lived with their grandparents would have higher academic achievements than those who did not, because the grandparents would provide stability, homework help, and encouragement (Dunifon & Kowaleski-Jones, 2007). However, this was not always the case.

The researchers looked at ethnic backgrounds and family structures, reporting that European American children did better when living with both older generations, but this was not true for all children. Specifically, the math scores of African American children were highest when they lived

with single mothers and no other adult, next highest when they lived with mothers and grandmothers, and lowest when they lived with mothers and an unrelated man. Perhaps in some families, three generations living together signifies poverty and stress (Dunifon & Kowaleski-Jones, 2007).

Another study examined depression and self-esteem in emerging adults who had single parents. Some of them had a good relationship with their grandparents and some did not (Ruiz & Silverstein, 2007). The researchers again expected the grandparent relationship to be crucial, but surprisingly, the child–parent relationship was the pivotal one. A close relationship with a grandparent meant less depression only when the emerging adult had a good relationship with his or her mother.

This finding was confirmed by another aspect of this study. In second marriages, the mothers often became less supportive of their children (they were more involved with their new spouse), and the grandparents became more distant as well. The result was that young adults under these conditions withdrew from both older generations and became more depressed (see Figure 15.6; Ruiz & Silverstein, 2007).

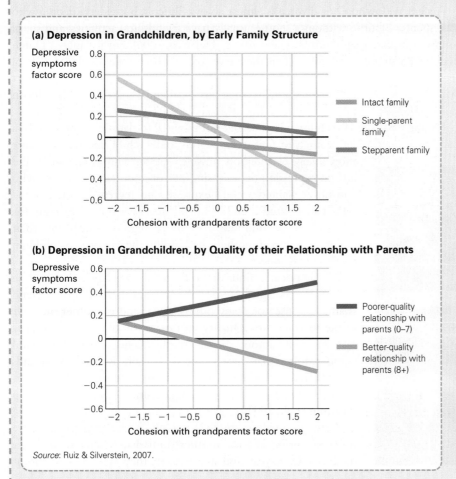

(a) Depression in Grandchildren, by Early Family Structure

Depressive symptoms factor score

— Intact family
— Single-parent family
— Stepparent family

Cohesion with grandparents factor score

(b) Depression in Grandchildren, by Quality of their Relationship with Parents

Depressive symptoms factor score

— Poorer-quality relationship with parents (0–7)
— Better-quality relationship with parents (8+)

Cohesion with grandparents factor score

Source: Ruiz & Silverstein, 2007.

FIGURE 15.6 One Puzzling Curve In these graphs, the vertical axis represents depressive symptoms, so curves that slope downward indicate that closeness to grandparents reduces depression in grandchildren. However, as part (b) shows, when the relationship with parents is poor, the relationship with grandparents also suffers, and depression is more likely.

It is apparent from these studies and from other research that grandparents can provide security and joy for their grandchildren, but not all of them do so. As the discussion of family structure and family function in Chapter 8 explained, the crucial variable is what actually occurs in their interaction, not simply the amount of contact they have.

The fact that grandparenting is not always wonderful should not obscure the usual situation: Most grandparents enjoy their role, gain generativity from it, and are appreciated by younger family members (C. L. Kemp, 2005; Thiele & Whelan, 2008).

Indeed, international college students, despite being thousands of miles away from their grandparents, often express warmth, respect, and affection for at least one of the grandparents (usually their maternal grandmother) back home (A. C. Taylor et al., 2005). In most conditions, grandparenting benefits all three generations.

The animal kingdom may help us see the bigger picture. Wild elephants normally live in multigenerational herds. In one region of Africa, elephant poachers killed most of the oldest generation—until strict laws put an end to the poaching. When the younger elephants became adults, many were infertile and most had higher levels of stress than elephants normally do (Gobush et al., 2008). Like humans, elephants benefit from having grandparents around.

Friendship

Of people currently over age 65 in the United States, only 4 percent (1.4 million) have never married, making this oldest generation the most-married cohort in history (U.S. Bureau of the Census, 2008). The next cohort will include far fewer married people. Many middle-aged adults, married and unmarried, have no children. Will they be lonely and lack social support?

Probably not. Members of the current oldest generation who never married are usually quite content. In future generations, as the number of unmarried elderly adults increases, the size of their social networks is likely to increase as well.

Recent widowhood or divorce is almost always difficult, but elderly people who have spent a lifetime without a spouse usually have friendships, activities, and social connections that keep them busy and happy (DePaulo, 2006). For instance, a Dutch study of 85 single elders found that their level of well-being was similar to that of people in long-term equitable marriages. The never-married older adults were happier than either recent widows or the married adults in unequal marriages (Hagedoorn et al., 2006).

Having a partner and children is good but not essential for late-life happiness. In a study that asked older women to rank their regrets, older, child-free women were more likely to mention missing out on education, career, and artistic expression than missing out on motherhood. Those who had never wanted a child expressed no regrets, although some who had wanted a child but did not have one were regretful. Ironically, older mothers had more regrets concerning their children than nonmothers had about the absence of children (Jeffries & Konnert, 2002).

All the research finds that older adults need at least one close companion. For many (especially husbands), this intimate friend is also a spouse; for many others, the friend is another member of the social convoy. Quality (not quantity) of friendship is crucial, especially among the oldest-old (Krause, 2006). Successful aging requires that people not be socially isolated. As friends and relatives die, elders become more supportive of the ones who remain, increasingly calling, visiting, and offering help (Gurung et al., 2003).

A study of widows found that adult children typically became more nurturing of their mother immediately after their father died; but by a year and a half later, they were less solicitous

Good to See You Again Older men, like younger ones, appreciate one another's friendship but seldom get together just to talk. These Delaware farmers met again at a melon auction and took the opportunity to get caught up on their families, their aches and pains, and the price of watermelon.

KEVIN FLEMMING / CORBIS

Together by Choice Elderly women outnumber elderly men in China by a very wide margin. Chinese cultural traditions include respect for the aged, group spirit, and self-efficacy. These six women in a public park in Guangzhou seek out one another for daily conversation.

(Zettel & Rook, 2004). The widows who fared best had friends before the death and increased their contact with them afterward. Many also revived old friendships or sought new ones: This strategy had not yet improved their mental health at the time of the study, although the researchers suggested that after months or years, benefits might be observed (Zettel & Rook, 2004).

KEY Points

- In late adulthood, the social convoy continues to provide emotional and psychological support as well as practical help.
- People in long-term partnerships typically live longer, healthier, and happier lives because of their mutual dependence.
- For people in late adulthood, relationships with adult children and with grandchildren are usually mutually supportive, although the older generation is more likely to help the younger ones than vice versa.
- Friends are needed and wanted in late adulthood, particularly by elderly people who do not have a living spouse or children.

The Frail Elderly

Remember that aging can be *usual, impaired,* or *optimal.* Thus far, we have focused on the usual and optimal—on those elderly people who are active and enjoy the support of friends and family. Now we look at the **frail elderly**, those who are infirm, very ill, or cognitively impaired. Usually the frail elderly are the oldest-old, not only over age 85 but also severely disabled.

Most older adults become frail if they live long enough, although *compression of morbidity* (explained in Chapter 14) means that the period of frailty may be short. Frailty is most common in the months preceding death, which means that some 90-year-olds are not yet frail.

frail elderly
People over age 65, and often over age 85, who are physically infirm, very ill, or cognitively disabled.

Mobility Is Crucial The best help is the kind that permits self-sufficiency. This man's legs can no longer carry him everywhere, but his motorized wheelchair (with room for his furry companion) lets him get around on his own, without having to depend on other people for transportation. Thus, although he is not strong, he is also not frail.

activities of daily life (ADLs)
Actions that are important to independent living, typically identified as five tasks of self-care: eating, bathing, toileting, dressing, and transferring from a bed to a chair. The inability to perform any of these tasks is a sign of frailty.

instrumental activities of daily life (IADLs)
Actions (for example, paying bills and driving a car) that are important to independent living and that require some intellectual competence and forethought. The ability to perform these tasks may be even more critical to self-sufficiency than ADL ability.

Activities of Daily Life

The crucial indicator of frailty is the inability to safely and adequately perform the physical and cognitive tasks of self-care needed to maintain independence. Gerontologists often refer to these tasks in terms of five physical **activities of daily life (ADLs)**—namely, eating, bathing, toileting, dressing, and transferring from a bed to a chair.

In the aftermath of illnesses and operations, doctors and nurses consider the patient's ability to perform these five ADLs to be the crucial sign of recovery. ADL capability is affected by age as well as health status and pain level (e.g., Osnes et al., 2004). Medical personnel strive to help all elderly persons perform their ADLs, providing occupational therapy or special equipment (such as a higher toilet seat) if needed.

Equally important may be the **instrumental activities of daily life (IADLs),** which require intellectual competence and forethought (Stone, 2006). It is more difficult to measure competence at IADLs because they vary from culture to culture. In developed nations, IADLs include shopping for groceries, paying bills, driving a car, taking medications as prescribed, and keeping appointments (see Table 15.2). In rural areas of other nations, feeding the chickens, cultivating the garden, mending clothes, getting water from the well, and baking bread might be IADLs.

Everywhere, the inability to perform IADLs makes people frail, even if they can perform all five ADLs (Stone, 2006). Ideally, compression of morbidity and good medical care will reduce the amount of time during which the average elderly person needs help with either ADLs or IADLs (Willis et al., 2006).

There are cultural differences in care for the frail elderly, as already mentioned. Many Asian and African cultures emphasize family responsibility and respect for the aged. India passed a law in 2007 making it a crime to neglect one's elderly parents.

However, gerontologists have criticized government policies that place too much reliance on family obligation, noting that some families are overburdened while

TABLE 15.2 Instrumental Activities of Daily Life

Domain	Exemplar Task
Managing medications	Determining how many doses of cough medicine can be taken in a 24-hour period Completing a patient medical history form
Shopping for necessities	Ordering merchandise from an online catalog Comparison of brands of a product
Managing one's finances	Comparison of Medigap insurance plans Completing income tax returns
Using transportation	Computing taxi rates versus bus rates Interpreting driver's right-of-way laws
Using the telephone	Determining amount to pay from a phone bill Determining emergency phone information
Maintaining one's household	Following instructions for operating a household appliance Comprehending appliance warranty
Meal preparation and nutrition	Evaluating nutritional information on food label Following recipe directions

Source: Adapted from Willis, 1996.

Another Test The items in the right-hand column are adapted from a questionnaire to assess IADL competence. As you can see, managing daily life is not easy, but most of the elderly do it.

others have no frail elders (Aboderin, 2004; Ogawa, 2004; Phillipson, 2006). They contend that the entire society, not only the relatives, should protect these elders, since appropriate caregiving requires temperament and skills that some families lack. Elder abuse (discussed later) may arise when people try to provide care that is beyond their ability.

Sometimes elders themselves are blamed for running out of money and being frail:

> By suggesting that the great majority of those elders in wheelchairs could indeed have been on cross-country skis had they but made the right choices and practiced the right behaviors can burden rather than liberate older people. . . . Concepts such as successful aging are marked by important and unacknowledged class, race, and gender concerns that result in further marginalizing the already marginalized.
>
> *[Holstein & Minkler, 2003, p. 794]*

Governments, families, and aging individuals sometimes blame one another for frailty. The responsibility actually rests with all three. To take a simple example, a person whose leg muscles are weakening might make choices that lead toward, or away from, frailty. He or she might start strength training, purchase a walker, avoid stairs, or become bedbound.

Those are personal choices, but relatives and public policies can make each option more or less attractive. Family members as well as friendly volunteers could walk with the elderly person on pathways that the local government has built to be safe and pleasant. Someone could help that elderly person buy a sturdy walker, and public funds could underwrite the purchase. Thus, all three—the elder, the family, and the community—could prevent or at least postpone frailty.

Caring for the Frail Elderly

The caregiver of a frail elderly person is usually the spouse, who is also elderly. If an impaired person has no living partner, often a sibling or an adult daughter provides care. Nursing homes are usually considered as a last resort.

THE DEMANDS OF FAMILY CARE Family caregivers experience substantial stress. Their health may suffer, and their risk of depression increases, especially if the care receiver has dementia (Pinquart & Sörensen, 2003; Roth et al., 2008). After listing the problems and frustrations of caring for someone who is mentally incapacitated but physically strong, the authors of one overview note:

> The effects of these stresses on family caregivers can be catastrophic. . . . They may include increased levels of depression and anxiety as well as higher use of psycho-tropic medicine such as tranquilizers, poorer self-reported health, compromised immune function, and increased mortality.
>
> *[Gitlin et al., 2003, p. 362]*

Not all caregivers feel overwhelmed. Sometimes they feel fulfilled because they believe they are repaying past debts and because everyone, including the care receiver, expresses appreciation. In fact, when caregivers feel increasingly supported by family, they experience less emotional stress as time goes on, even as the frail person's needs increase (Roth et al., 2005).

The designated caregiver of a frail elderly person is chosen less for practical reasons (e.g., the relative with the most patience, time, and skill) than for cultural ones. In the United States, the spouse is the usual caregiver, perhaps helped by the eldest daughter. In some European nations, most of the care is provided through a social safety net of senior day-care centers, seniors' homes, and skilled nurses. In some cultures, an older person who is dying is taken to a hospital to extend life; in other cultures, such intervention is seen as interference with the natural order.

In Asian nations, a son and his wife feel responsible for elder care. In a study of South Koreans, for instance, 80 percent of those with dementia were cared for by daughters-in-law and only 7 percent by spouses. In contrast, among Americans of Korean descent with dementia, 19 percent were cared for by daughters-in-law and 40 percent by spouses (Youn et al., 1999).

In every culture, the physical need for care is less crucial than the psychological needs of the elderly person, which are embedded in cultural expectations and assumptions. Some people are much more willing to accept help from a paid stranger than from a son or a daughter; others have the opposite preference.

Some cultures admire caregivers; others isolate them. That may explain why some research finds that caregiving African Americans are less depressed than caregivers of other ethnicities (Roth et al., 2008).

Nonetheless, even in ideal circumstances with community support, family caregiving can present problems:

● If one adult child is the primary caregiver, other siblings tend to feel relief or jealousy. The caregiver wants the other brothers and sisters to do more; they resist being told what to do—understandable but problematic reactions.

● Care receivers and caregivers often disagree about schedules, menus, doctor visits, and so on. Resentments on both sides disrupt mutual affection and appreciation.

● Public agencies rarely provide services unless an emergency arises.

This last item is of particular concern to developmentalists, who see frailty as a likely event that should be anticipated and postponed and who see caregiver exhaustion and elder abuse as problems to be prevented. In many nations, public policy and cultural values result in "a system that places inappropriate burdens of elder care upon the family" (Seki, 2001, p. 101). One cause of this burden is the widespread horror of nursing homes, even though many of them provide excellent care (as will soon be discussed). Some elderly people regard going into a nursing home as a fate worse than death; some cultures consider placing an elderly relative into a nursing home to be a mark of shame for the family.

Developmentalists, concerned about the well-being of people of all ages, advocate more help for families who choose to care for frail elders (see Fortinsky et al., 2007; Stone, 2006). The most important need is some relief from full responsibility, includ-

Morning, Afternoon, Evening, Bedtime Less than half of all adults follow doctors' orders about medication. For seniors, this negligence can lead to dementia or even death. Family caregiving usually begins with IADLs, as with this daughter, who is sorting her mother's 16 medications into a tray that is marked to help the older woman remember when to take them.

OBSERVATION QUIZ

Do this mother and daughter live together? (see answer, page 558) →

DENNIS MACDONALD / PHOTO EDIT

ing more free time (via professional providers of respite care or family members who take over on a regular schedule) and better medical attention (usually with visiting nurses who provide medical and psychological care for both caregiver and care receiver). Such measures can make home care tolerable, even fulfilling, for caregivers.

ELDER ABUSE When caregiving results in resentment and social isolation, the risk of depression, poor health, and abuse (of either the frail person or the caregiver) escalates. Most family members provide adequate care despite the stress. However, abuse of the elderly person is likely if the caregiver suffers from emotional problems or substance abuse (Brandl et al., 2006). Maltreatment ranges from direct physical attack to ongoing emotional neglect.

Analysis of elder abuse is complicated because three distinct elements contribute to the problem: the victim, the abuser, and the community (R. M. Gordon & Brill, 2001). Thus, abuse is likely when the care receiver is a feeble person who suffers severe memory loss, when the caregiver is a drug-addicted relative, or when care occurs in an isolated place where visitors are few and far between. If any one of those three conditions is absent, abuse is less likely.

Even in the Best Families The question of elder abuse became front-page news in the last months of Brooke Astor's life. The wealthy philanthropist and socialite is shown here at age 95; she died in 2007 at age 105. Her grandson accused his father, her only child, of plundering her fortune and neglecting her care. At this writing, the truth of the accusation is being argued in court.

Ironically, although relatives are less prepared to cope with difficult patients than professionals are, they typically provide round-the-clock care with little outside help or supervision. Some caregivers believe that such abusive measures as overmedication, locked doors, and physical restraints are their only options. Extensive public and personal safety nets for the frail are needed to prevent maltreatment (Mellor & Brownell, 2006).

The typical case of elder maltreatment begins benignly, as an outgrowth of caregiving. For example, an elder may provide money to a younger relative, who gradually spends the elder's assets until nothing is left to meet expenses; or a family member may be pressured to care for an increasingly frail relative, only to become so overwhelmed and isolated that neglect occurs; or a husband may feel resentment when he unexpectedly must take on the full-time care of his wife, who no longer recognizes him; or an underpaid and undertrained housekeeper must deal with an irrational elder.

Benign beginnings make elder abuse difficult to identify, and family members are reluctant to notify authorities. Sometimes the caregiver becomes the victim, cursed or even attacked by the confused elderly person. As with other forms of abuse, the dependency of the victim makes prosecution difficult (Mellor & Brownell, 2006). This problem gets worse when a family's pride, secrecy, and suspicion keep outsiders away.

Most research finds that about 5 percent of elders say they are abused and that up to one-fourth of all elders are vulnerable but do not report abuse (Cooper et al., 2008). Because elders who are mistreated by family members are ashamed to admit it, the actual rate is probably close to that one-fourth. Accurate measurement is complicated by lack of consensus regarding standards of care: Some elders feel abused, but caregivers disagree.

LONG-TERM CARE Many elders and their relatives, horrified by headlines and photographs of abuse in nursing homes, are convinced that those institutions should be

ANSWER TO OBSERVATION QUIZ
(from page 556) Probably not. Clues
include the small (not family-size)
refrigerator, the mother's medical-alert
pendant, and the fact that the daughter is organizing medications for an
entire week (as indicated by the large
number of compartments in the tray),
not just a single day. ●

**ESPECIALLY FOR Those Uncertain
About Future Careers** Would you
like to work in a nursing home? (see
response, page 560) ➤

avoided no matter what. And some institutions are dehumanizing. One 61-year-old
woman with cerebral palsy, who spent time in a nursing home, said:

> I would rather die than have to exist in such a place where residents are neglected,
> ignored, patronized, infantilized, demeaned; where the environment is chaotic,
> noisy, cold, clinical, even psychotic.
>
> *[quoted in W. H. Thomas, 2007, p. 159]*

Fortunately, outright abuse is now rare in nursing homes. Laws forbid the use of
physical restraints except temporarily in specific, extraordinary circumstances. Some
nursing homes provide individualized, humane care, allowing residents to decide
what to eat, where to walk, whether or not to have a pet (W. H. Thomas, 2007).

In North America and particularly in western Europe, good nursing-home care
is available for those who can afford it and know what to look for. Among the signs
of a humane setting are provisions for independence, individual choice, and privacy.
As with day care for young children, continuity of care is crucial: An institution with
a high rate of staff turnover is to be avoided.

Training and workload of the staff, especially of the aides who provide the most
frequent and most personal care, are also crucial: Such simple tasks as helping a frail
person out of bed can be done clumsily, painfully, or skillfully. The difference depends
partly on experience and partly on time; with a sufficient number of well-trained
and well-paid staff, care can be excellent. Currently, however, most frontline workers
have little training as well as low pay (Stone, 2006).

Quality care is labor-intensive and expensive; the average nursing home cost in
the United States in 2005 was $75,000 a year; some facilities charged more than
$200,000. In an AARP survey, only 8 percent of middle-aged adults guessed within
20 percent of the actual cost of nursing-home care in their community (L. L. Barrett,
2006). Most thought that Medicare or Medicaid covered such care—another mis-
conception (Feng et al., 2008).

In the United States, the trend over the past 20 years has been toward fewer
nursing-home residents (currently about 1.5 million people nationwide), and those
few are very frail and confused, needing assistance with both ADLs and IADLs

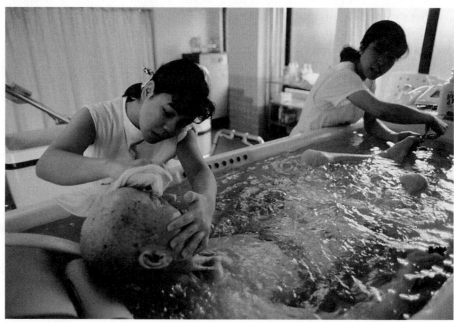

Help with an ADL A frail elderly man
who can no longer bathe himself (one
of the basic activities of daily living)
is assisted by trained attendants in a
model home for the aged in Tokyo.

(Stone, 2006). Although most elders are independent and community-dwelling at any given time, half of all North Americans will need nursing-home care at some point, usually for less than a month as they recuperate from hospitalization. It is projected that 1 in 8 will need such care for over a year, and a few will need it for 10 years or more (Stone, 2006).

Alternative Care Most elder-care arrangements—home care, aging in place, and NORCs—are less costly and more individualized than nursing homes. One common form in the United States is called **assisted living**, an arrangement that combines some of the privacy and independence of home life with some of the medical supervision of a nursing home (Imamoglu, 2007).

An assisted-living home might provide a private room for each person, allowing pets and furnishings just as in a traditional home. Services may include one communal meal per day, special bus trips and activities, and optional arrangements for household cleaning and minor repairs. Usually, medical assistance is readily available—from daily supervision of medication to emergency help, with a doctor and ambulance provided when necessary.

Assisted-living facilities range from group homes for three or four elderly people to large apartment or townhouse developments for hundreds of residents (Stone, 2006). Each state in the United States has its own standards for assisted-living facilities, but many such places are unlicensed. International variation is also wide: Some regions of the world (northern Europe) have many more residential options for older residents than do others (sub-Saharan Africa).

Skilled gerontologists consider it essential to help each resident retain independence, control over his or her decisions, and self-respect (R. D. Hill et al., 2002). Their efforts have resulted in new laws, which provide for limitations on the use of restraints and privacy requirements, and better practices, such as more self-management and social choices (J. E. Allen, 2007). Both correlate with physical and mental well-being as well as a longer, happier life.

The Best of Care We close with an example of family care and nursing-home care at their best. A young adult named Rob related that his 98-year-old great-grandmother "began to fail. We had no idea why and thought, well, maybe she is growing old" (quoted in L. P. Adler, 1995, p. 242). All three younger generations of the family conferred and reluctantly decided that it was time to move the matriarch from her suburban home, where she had lived for decades, into a nearby nursing home.

Fortunately, this nursing home encouraged independence and did not assume that decline is always a sign of "final failing." The doctors there discovered that the woman's heart pacemaker was not working properly. Rob tells what happened next:

> We were very concerned to have her undergo surgery at her age, but we finally agreed. . . . Soon she was back to being herself, a strong, spirited, energetic, independent woman. It was the pacemaker that was wearing out, not Great-grandmother.
>
> [quoted in L. P. Adler, 1995, p. 242]

This story contains a lesson repeated throughout this book. When a toddler does not talk, or a preschooler grabs a toy, or a teenager gets drunk, or an emerging adult takes dangerous risks, or an older person seems to be failing, one might conclude that such problems are normal for that particular age. There is some truth in that: Each of these behaviors is more common at those stages.

But just because people act their age, we should not withhold protection and guidance. Each of those behaviors should alert caregivers, who can encourage talking, sharing, moderation, caution, or self-care. The life-span perspective holds that, at every age, people can be "strong, spirited, and energetic" if all of us do our part.

assisted living
A living arrangement for elderly people that combines privacy and independence with medical supervision.

RESPONSE FOR Those Uncertain About Future Careers (from page 558) Why not? The demand for good workers will obviously increase as the population ages, and the working conditions will improve. An important problem is that the quality of nursing homes varies, so you need to make sure you work in one whose policies incorporate the view that the elderly can be quite capable, social, and independent. ●

KEY points

- Some elderly people become frail, unable to perform the activities of daily life (such as bathing and dressing) or the instrumental activities of daily life (such as taking medication and paying bills).

- If an elderly person needs full-time care, usually the spouse or another family member provides it.

- Caregiving of a frail elder, performed by an isolated and untrained family member, is stressful and sometimes leads to ill health in the caregiver and abuse of the care receiver.

- Alternate provisions for elder care, including assisted-living settings and nursing homes, are sometimes preferable to family care.

SUMMARY

Theories of Late Adulthood

1. Several self theories hold that adults make personal choices in ways that allow them to become fully themselves. Erikson believed that individuals seek integrity that connects them to the human community; research finds substantial continuity in personality traits as well as the existence of the positivity effect and appreciation of self and others.

2. Stratification theories maintain that social forces—such as ageism, racism, and sexism—limit personal choices throughout the life span. One such theory blames stratification for the disengagement of older adults, but that view is opposed by activity theory, which holds that older people wish to be active.

Activities in Late Adulthood

3. At every age, employment can provide social and personal satisfaction, as well as needed income. However, retirement may be welcomed by the elderly.

4. Some retired people continue their education, perform volunteer work, or become politically active. These activities enhance the health and well-being of the elderly and benefit the larger society.

5. More common among retirees are an increase in religious activity (but not church attendance) and a wish to "age in place." Many of the elderly engage in home improvement or redecoration, preferring to stay in their own homes.

Friends and Relatives

6. A spouse is the most important member of a person's social convoy. Older adults in long-standing marriages tend to be satis-

fied with their relationships and to safeguard each other's health. As a result, married elders tend to live longer, happier, and healthier lives than unmarried ones.

7. The death of a spouse is always difficult. Wives are more likely to experience this loss, and, partly because many of their women friends have the same experiences, women are more likely than men to adjust to the death of a partner.

8. Relationships with adult children and grandchildren are usually mutually supportive. Most of the elderly prefer to maintain their independence, living alone, but some become surrogate parents, raising their grandchildren. This surrogate parenting benefits many family members and society as a whole, but it adds to the stress of the older generation.

The Frail Elderly

9. Most elderly people are self-sufficient, but some eventually become frail. They need help with their activities of daily life, either with physical tasks (such as eating and bathing) or with instrumental ones (such as paying bills and arranging transportation).

10. Care of the frail elderly is usually undertaken by adult children or spouses, who are often elderly themselves. Most families have a strong sense of filial responsibility, although elder abuse may occur when the stress of care is great and social support is lacking.

11. Nursing homes, assisted living, and professional home care are of varying quality and availability. Each of these arrangements can provide necessary and beneficial care, but good care for the frail elderly cannot be taken for granted.

KEY TERMS

self theories (p. 530)
integrity versus despair (p. 530)
continuity theory (p. 532)
positivity effect (p. 532)
stratification theories (p. 533)

disengagement theory (p. 534)
activity theory (p. 534)
aging in place (p. 540)
naturally occurring retirement
  community (NORC) (p. 541)

AARP (p. 543)
filial responsibility (p. 548)
frail elderly (p. 553)
activities of daily life
  (ADLs) (p. 554)

instrumental activities of daily
  life (IADLs) (p. 554)
assisted living (p. 559)

KEY QUESTIONS

1. What are the similarities and differences between self theories and stratification theories?

2. How important is work in late adulthood?

3. What kinds of activities do most older people undertake after they retire?

4. What changes typically occur in long-term marriages in late adulthood?

5. Compare the roles of friends and family in late adulthood.

6. How and why does the death of a spouse affect men and women differently?

7. What factors affect the ability to perform ADLs and IADLs?

8. Why do there seem to be more frail elderly people today than there used to be?

9. What problems might arise in caring for a frail elderly person?

10. What are the advantages and disadvantages of nursing-home care?

APPLICATIONS

1. Attitudes about disabilities are influential. Visit the disability office on your campus, asking both staff and students what they see as the effects of attitude on the performance of students. How do your findings relate to the elderly?

2. People of different ages, cultures, and experiences vary in their values regarding family caregiving, including the need for safety, privacy, independence, and professional help. Find four people whose backgrounds (age, ethnicity, SES) differ. Ask their opinions, and analyze the results.

3. Visit a nursing home or assisted-living residence in your community. Record details about the physical setting, the social interactions of the residents, and the activities of the staff. Would you like to work or live in this place? Why or why not?

Late Adulthood (Age 65 and Older)

AGEISM

Ignores variations (young-old, old-old, oldest-old)

Similar to racism and sexism

Patronizing speech

Stereotype threat

Acceptance of sensory losses

Acceptance of emotional disorders

"I KNOW WHO I'VE BEEN, BUT WHO AM I NOW?"
MOST ELDERLY PEOPLE ARE INDEPENDENT, AWARE, AND NOT DISABLED

HEALTH AND FRAILTY

Primary aging for everyone

Dependence and frailty
Activities of daily life (ADLs)
Instrumental activities of daily life (IADLs)
Nursing homes (less than 5 percent of elderly)

Sensory losses: Need for glasses, hearing aids, etc.

Reluctance to use technology

Poor quality of care

COGNITIVE VARIATIONS

The usual
Some sensory loss
Some brain slowdown
Some memory decline

The optimal
Life review
Creativity
Wisdom

The impaired: Dementia
Alzheimer: Progressive memory loss
Vascular: Many small strokes
Frontal lobe: Loss of inhibition
Depression

Untreated depression

Overuse of drugs

THE SAME, ONLY BETTER

Integrity and continuity

Work (paid and unpaid)

Aging in place (NORCs)

Deeper religious beliefs (beyond the self)

Education and politics (not for everyone)

Disengagement

Not enough volunteering

Stratification

SOCIAL RELATIONSHIPS

Long-term marriages
Mutual love and care
Adjustments needed

With adult children
Filial care varies by culture

With grandchildren
Usually beneficial to both generations
Surrogate parenting—sometimes difficult

Death of spouse
Women: Lose income and status
Men: Lose social network

Elder abuse: Hidden, secretive

Caregiver stress and illness

KEY
Major topic
Related topic
Potential problem

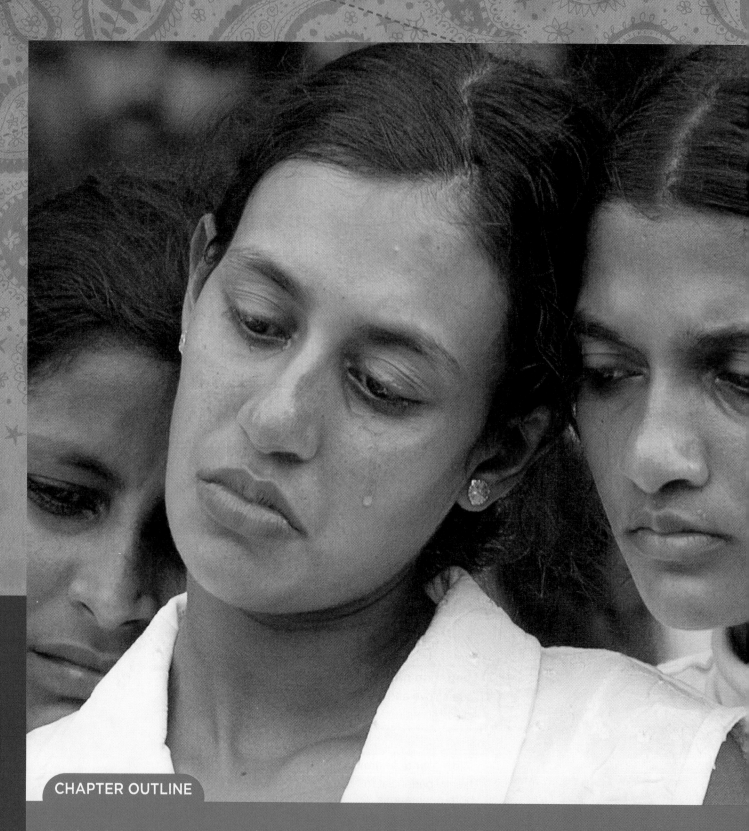

EPILOGUE
Death and Dying

On September 11, 2001, I left lower Manhattan at 7:00 A.M. to teach in the Bronx. Two hours later, my students told me about the attack on the World Trade Center. I thought first about my family: Three daughters were far away; when I phoned the fourth one, in Brooklyn, she assured me that she was safe. My husband, Martin, worked near the towers, but I remembered that he had an 8:00 A.M. appointment uptown.

When I finally got home (after walking for miles) that night, Martin told me he had walked toward his office after his appointment, undaunted by crowds running the other way. Finally, the police stopped him. Apparently his first impulse was to maintain normal life, not unlike my impulse to take care of my family.

Martin died 16 months later. The immediate cause was an infection, which was exacerbated by steroids, which he took because they helped him breathe, which he needed because he had lung cancer, which occurred because the toxins in the smoke from the burning towers, added to 50 years of smoking cigarettes, destroyed his lungs. For that, I blame myself; I never got him to quit smoking.

I blame the U.S. military, too, because they gave him free cigarettes when he was a 17-year-old volunteer. And I blame culture because boys smoked to act like men. I also blame Hitler, who was already dead when Martin enlisted, but Martin had grown up wanting to kill him.

In mourning, I am not rational: My search for causes—steroids, 9/11, pollution, addiction, me, the military, machismo, Hitler—arises from emotions of anger, guilt, and sorrow, not from an acceptance of death as a natural and inevitable part of the life span. As you will read, people react to death in many ways; I am not the only irrational mourner. ●

THIS CHAPTER DISCUSSES MANY THEMES. Dying is a process that begins with personal choices (smoking cigarettes) and social contexts (the toxic smoke from the destroyed buildings), and it often involves both immediate family and oblivious strangers—all of whom have widely varied emotions and rituals. Death has many signs and causes; bereavement takes many forms. Sometimes blame is elusive, dying is difficult to recognize, and death is hard to accept. Reactions and rituals surrounding death reflect history and culture; vast diversity is apparent.

Thanatology is the study of death and dying, especially of the social and emotional aspects. Perhaps surprisingly, thanatology is not morbid or gloomy.

thanatology
The study of death and dying, especially of the social and emotional aspects.

Rather, it reveals the reality of *hope* in death, *acceptance* of dying, and *reaffirmation* of life. This chapter describes some of the truths that thanatologists have learned.

Whether a particular death will be a "good" or "bad" one is influenced not only by the dying person but also by the medical profession, family and friends, and society itself. Mourners experience many forms of grief—including absent, repressed, complicated, and extended grief—which, again, may be considered good or bad. Always, culture and customs matter. Following the example of thanatologists, we begin with hope.

Death and Hope

Hope is not the usual response to death. Yet death is often considered a beginning, not an end; a community event, not a personal one; welcomed, not dreaded. A life-span perspective allows us to see that death is viewed through many cultural prisms. A culture's attitude toward death is affected by historical changes (see Table EP.1) as well as by the ages of the person who dies and the one who mourns.

Understanding Death Throughout the Life Span

In order to understand what death means to people, we begin with developmental differences. The meaning assigned to death—either a person's own death or the death of another—depends partly on cognitive maturation and personal experience. As humans age, death becomes more likely, understanding deepens, and hope becomes stronger.

DEATH IN CHILDHOOD Some adults think children are oblivious to death; others believe children are aware of death and should therefore participate in the rituals accompanying death, just as adults do. You know from your study of childhood cognition that neither view is correct.

Not Forgotten Archeologists have determined that remembrance of the dead is one of the oldest rituals of humankind. Each generation and circumstance evokes different rituals. Here, in one of the most recent and tragic circumstances, a worker at the Cotlands Baby Sanctuary of South Africa places the ashes of a young child who died of AIDS into a wall of remembrance in a cemetery. The baby had been found abandoned after both its parents died of AIDS.

DENIS FARRELL / AP / WIDE WORLD PHOTOS

TABLE EP.1 How Death Has Changed in the Past 100 Years

Death occurs later. A century ago, the average life span worldwide was less than 40 years (though it was 47 in the rapidly industrializing United States). Half of the world's babies died before age 5. Now newborns are expected to live to age 78; in many nations, elderly people age 85 and over are the fastest-growing age group.

Dying takes longer. In the early 1900s, death was usually fast and unstoppable; once the brain, the heart, or other vital organs failed, the rest of the body quickly followed. Now death can often be postponed through medical intervention: Hearts can beat for years after the brain stops functioning, respirators can replace lungs, and dialysis can do the work of failing kidneys. As a result, dying is often a lengthy process.

Death often occurs in hospitals. A hundred years ago, death almost always occurred at home, with the dying person surrounded by familiar faces. Now many deaths occur in hospitals, surrounded by medical personnel and technology.

The main causes of death have changed. People of all ages once died of infectious diseases (tuberculosis, typhoid, smallpox), and many women and infants died in childbirth. Now disease deaths before age 50 are rare, and almost all newborns (99 percent) and their mothers (99.99 percent) live, unless the infant is very frail or medical care of the mother is grossly inadequate.

And after death . . . People once knew about life after death. Some believed in heaven and hell; others, in reincarnation; others, in the spirit world. Many prayers were repeated—some on behalf of the souls of the deceased, some for remembrance, some to the dead asking for protection. Believers were certain that their prayers were heard. Today's young adults are aware of cultural and religious diversity, which makes them question what earlier generations believed, raising doubts that never occurred to their ancestors.

Source: Adapted from Kastenbaum, 2006; data from U.S. Bureau of the Census, 2007 and earlier editions.

Children as young as 2 years of age have some understanding of death, but their perspective differs from that of older family members. If a child has lost a loved one, adults should listen with full attention, neither ignoring the child's concerns nor expecting mourning (Kenyon, 2001). Children are more impulsive than deliberate (remember that the brain matures very gradually) and may seem happy one day and morbidly sad the next. Children do not "get over" the death of a parent, nor do they dwell on it.

A child who is fatally ill typically fears that death will mean being abandoned by beloved and familiar people (Wolchik et al., 2008). Consequently, parents are advised to stay with a dying child day and night, holding, reading, singing, and assuring that he or she will not be alone. Frequent and caring contact is more important than logic.

A child who loses a friend, a relative, or a pet typically demonstrates sadness, loneliness, and other signs of mourning, but adults cannot be certain how a particular child might react. Thus, one 7-year-old boy who lost three grandparents and an uncle within two years was especially upset when his dog, Twick, died.

This boy's parents, each grieving for a dead mother, were taken aback by the depth of the boy's emotions and regretted that they had not taken their son to the veterinarian's office to see the dog before it died. The boy refused to go back to school, saying, "I wanted to see him one more time. . . . You don't understand. . . . I play with Twick every day" (quoted in K. R. Kaufman & Kaufman, 2006, pp. 65–66).

Because the loss of companionship is a young child's prime concern, it is not helpful to say that Grandma is sleeping, that God wanted his or her sister in heaven, that Grandpa went on a trip, or that the dog can be replaced. The child may take such explanations literally, thinking that someone should wake up Grandma, complain to God, or tell Grandpa to come home. Even a 2-year-old knows that a new puppy is not the same dog.

As children become older and more concrete operational thinkers, they seek specific facts. In a study of 4- to 8-year-olds, those who knew more about the reality of a loved one's death were less anxious about death and dying (Slaughter & Griffiths, 2007).

A Florida study provided evidence that children understand death differently than adults do (Bering & Bjorklund, 2004). Children (aged 3–12 years) and adults saw a puppet skit about a sick mouse that was eaten by an alligator. When questioned afterward, the adults and nearly all the children acknowledged that the mouse was dead and would never be alive again. However, most of the younger children did not understand what it meant to be dead. They thought the dead mouse still felt sick.

This study was replicated in Spain (Bering et al., 2005). Children from Spanish public and religious schools also thought the dead mouse still felt sick, lonely, and so on, and those in Catholic schools were more likely to believe that the dead mouse could still hear voices and taste food. In this research, not only the children but also many adults believed that the dead mouse still loved his mother (see Figure EP.1).

DEATH IN ADOLESCENCE AND EMERGING ADULTHOOD "Live fast, die young, and leave a good-looking corpse." This widely repeated saying was used in the title of a biography of actor James Dean, who died in an automobile accident at age 24.

FIGURE EP.1 Love Endures Even the youngest children knew that the mouse was dead, but most of them believed that it still had feelings, needs, and wishes. For children, death does not stop life. These researchers also surveyed 20 college students, 13 of whom (65 percent) thought that love for one's mother continues after one's death. (In this series of studies, not every age group was asked every question, which explains why only two sets of responses are shown for two of the questions here.)

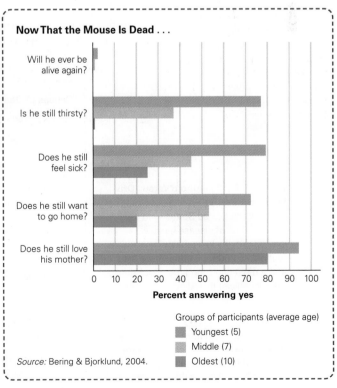

Now That the Mouse Is Dead . . .

Will he ever be alive again?

Is he still thirsty?

Does he still feel sick?

Does he still want to go home?

Does he still love his mother?

Percent answering yes

Groups of participants (average age)
- Youngest (5)
- Middle (7)
- Oldest (10)

Source: Bering & Bjorklund, 2004.

At what age would a person be most likely to agree with this advice? Age 25 and under, of course. Worldwide, teenagers seem to have little fear of death. They take risks, place a high value on appearance, and seek thrills (Chikako, 2004; Gullone & King, 1997). Adolescents typically predict that they will die at an early age (de Bruin et al., 2007); but over the years of high school, according to one study in Japan, they become less anxious about death (Chikako, 2004).

This reduced anxiety might be significant in understanding why adolescents and emerging adults tend to be such risk takers: Thinking about one's own death may increase dangerous behavior as anxiety decreases. For example, college students who heard about the death risks of binge drinking were more willing to binge, not less so (Jessop & Wade, 2008). It may be that, generally, young people who think they will die before midlife are more likely to use drugs and less likely to buckle seat belts or to back away from confrontations.

Especially when people age 15 to 24 have access to guns and cars, this developmental tendency toward risk taking can be deadly (see Figure EP.2). One reason why adolescents and emerging adults die in suicides, homicides, and accidents (especially when drunk) may be that they romanticize death. That makes young people vulnerable to cluster suicides, foolish dares, fatal gang fights, and drunk driving—all of which are much more common under age 25 than over.

DEATH IN ADULTHOOD A major shift in attitudes occurs when adults become responsible for work and family. Death is no longer romanticized; it is to be avoided instead—or at least postponed. Many adults quit taking addictive drugs, start wearing seat belts, and adopt other precautions.

A study of death anxiety over the years found that anxiety increased from one's teens to one's 20s and then gradually decreased—except for a momentary rise at age 50 for women. The authors think that different reproductive concerns (with young adults hoping to bear children and menopausal women realizing they can no longer become pregnant) may be the reason for the difference in anxiety levels (Russac et al., 2007).

To defend themselves against the fear of aging and untimely death, adults do not readily accept the death of others—even when those others are ready to die. Thus, when Dylan Thomas was about age 30, he wrote his most famous poem, addressed to

FIGURE EP.2 Typhoid Versus Driving into a Tree In 1905, most young adults in the United States who died were victims of diseases, usually infectious ones like tuberculosis and typhoid. In 2005, 25 times more died in the most common type of accident (motor vehicle) than died of the most common lethal disease (leukemia).

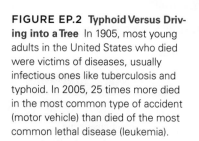

OBSERVATION QUIZ

Do these two pie charts show that 16 times more 15- to 24-year-olds were victims of homicide in 2005 than in 1907? (see answer, page 571) →

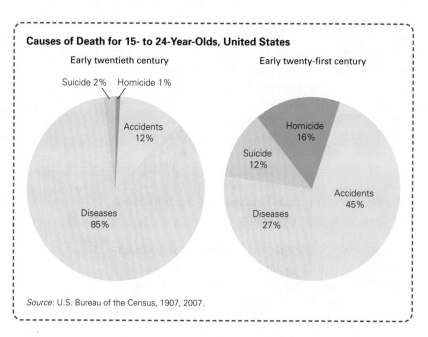

Causes of Death for 15- to 24-Year-Olds, United States

Early twentieth century

Suicide 2%   Homicide 1%

Accidents 12%

Diseases 85%

Early twenty-first century

Homicide 16%

Suicide 12%

Accidents 45%

Diseases 27%

Source: U.S. Bureau of the Census, 1907, 2007.

his dying father: "Do not go gentle into that good night. / Rage, rage against the dying of the light" (D. Thomas, 1957).

When adults hear about another's death, their reaction is closely connected to the person's age. Death in the prime of life is much harder to accept (especially for people who are that age themselves) than is death in late adulthood.

As an example of the power of age, consider the public reaction to the deaths of two U.S. presidents, Ronald Reagan and John Fitzgerald Kennedy. Reagan was probably the more popular of the two; he was president for eight years (Kennedy held office for only three) and was elected twice by a far wider margin. Yet Kennedy's violent death at age 46 continues to evoke far more public sorrow than did Reagan's death from disease at age 93.

Likewise, reactions to one's own terminal illness differ depending on developmental stage. From ages 25 to 60, terminally ill adults worry about leaving something undone or leaving family members—especially children—alone.

One such adult was Randy Pausch, a 47-year-old professor and the father of three young children. Ten months before he died of cancer in 2008, he delivered a famous "last lecture," detailing his childhood dreams and saluting those who would continue his work. After advising his students to follow their own dreams, he concluded "This talk is not for you, it's for my kids."

Moral Dilemmas Attitudes about death are often irrational and are sometimes contrary to beliefs or moral principles, especially in adulthood. Rationally, people should work to change social factors that increase the risk of death—such as air pollution, unhealthy foods, and unsafe transportation. Instead, many people react more strongly to events that only rarely cause death, such as anthrax outbreaks and avalanches.

Often, when people hear about someone's death, they want to know specifics in order to convince themselves that the person was not like them. This is easy if the person was much older, but if not, the impulse is to blame the person for not taking better care of him- or herself. Because few people are to blame for their own deaths, adults tend to fear unusual events that seem to be random, such as a freak accident, a bystander's murder, or a mysterious poison.

We tend to ignore common behaviors (especially our own) that can shorten lives, such as smoking cigarettes, eating a poor diet, and having unsafe sex. In studying this book, you probably have a reaction similar to mine as I write it: Those risky behaviors I exhibit myself do tend to get less of my attention than the behaviors I avoid altogether.

As a general example, statistics reveal that more people die *each day* of heart disease in the United States than died in the attacks of September 11, but that statistic has little impact on public policy or private behavior. Intensified airport security measures seem protective, yet people eat food that clogs their arteries and drive everywhere instead of taking an occasional walk. Not logical, but very human.

That people do not follow their values when thinking about death is one explanation for a classic moral puzzle sometimes called the *trolley car dilemma* (Thompson, 1986). When adults are asked whether they would pull a switch that would kill one innocent person but save five others, almost everyone would save the five, saying that is the right and moral choice. But if asked whether they would push someone off a footbridge to stop a trolley car that otherwise would kill five, most people say they would not.

"For My Kids" Randy Pausch was a brilliant, innovative scientist who specialized in virtual-reality research at Pittsburgh's Carnegie Mellon University. When he was diagnosed with terminal pancreatic cancer, he gave a talk that became famous worldwide as "The Last Lecture," titled "Really Achieving Your Childhood Dreams." He devoted the final 10 months of his life to his family—his wife Jai and their children, Chlöe, Dylan, and Logan.

Brain activation shown on fMRIs in response to the trolley car and other dilemmas confirms that life-or-death choices are not necessarily rational (J. D. Greene et al., 2001). Specifics matter in ways not predicted by general moral principles.

terror management theory (TMT) The idea that people adopt cultural values and moral principles in order to cope with their fear of death. This system of beliefs protects individuals from anxiety about their mortality and bolsters their self-esteem, so they react harshly when other people go against any of the moral principles involved.

Managing Terror To understand some of these irrational emotions regarding death, social scientists have developed **terror management theory (TMT).** This theory became prominent after September 11, when psychologists noted that remembering those horrific events led some people to become depressed, others to get drunk, and others to become extremely anxious about flying or about entering tall buildings (Pyszczynski et al., 2003).

It is apparent that, when adults think about death, they may become illogical. Consequently, "a health promotion message that equates smoking with death may ironically have the exact opposite effect"; it may increase smoking in people who want to protect their pride and self-esteem (Goldenberg & Arndt, 2008, p. 1049).

Other research in many nations finds that when adults think about death, they "strive to maintain self-esteem and faith in their cultural worldviews, at least in part to protect themselves from death-related anxiety" (Maxfield et al., 2007, p. 342). They are more likely to accept stereotypes and to be intolerant of people of other ethnicities. Some even blame people who are severely injured through no fault of their own (Hirschberger, 2006; Renkema et al., 2008). Most people would consider these responses low on the hierarchy of Kohlberg's stages of morality (see Chapter 8).

DEATH IN LATE ADULTHOOD In late adulthood, attitudes about death shift once more. Anxiety decreases and hope rises. Life-threatening illnesses decrease satisfaction less among the elderly than among the middle-aged (Wurm et al., 2008). Some older people are quite happy even when they know their remaining time is short. The irrational and seemingly immoral reactions that help people manage terror, as just explained, are less evident (see Figure EP.3; Maxfield et al., 2007).

This shift is a beneficial one. Indeed, many developmentalists believe that one sign of mental health among older adults is acceptance of their own mortality (e.g., M. M. Baltes & Carstensen, 2003; Erikson et al., 1986; Schindler et al., 2006) and altruistic concern about those who will live on after them.

As evidence of the change in attitude, older people write their wills, designate health care proxies, read scriptures, reconcile with estranged family members, and, in general, tie up all the loose ends that most young adults avoid dealing with (Kastenbaum, 2006). Sometimes grown children are troubled when their elderly parents take a spe-

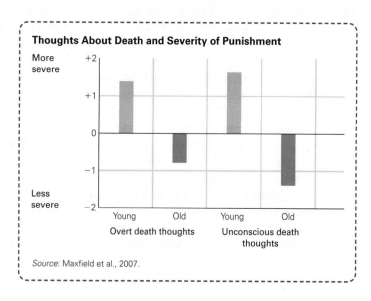

FIGURE EP.3 A Toothache Worse Than Death? Young (average age 21) and old (average age 74) adults were divided into three groups. One group wrote about death (so that they had overt thoughts about it), another did a puzzle with some words about death (so that their thoughts about death were unconscious), and the third wrote about dental pain (so that they served as the control group). Then they all judged how harshly people should be punished for various moral transgressions, using a scale of severity from 1 to 15. The groups who wrote about dental pain are represented by the zero point on this graph, meaning that they were not influenced by thoughts of death in making their ratings. Compared with those groups, the older groups who thought about death were less punitive, but the younger adults were more so. The difference in the ratings of the young and old groups was more pronounced if their thoughts about death were unconscious than if they were overt.

cific action, such as allocating heirlooms, choosing funeral music, or buying a burial plot, but such actions are developmentally appropriate toward the end of life.

This acceptance of death does not mean that the elderly give up on living. On the contrary, most try to maintain their health and independence. However, they adjust their priorities. In an intriguing series of studies, people were presented with the following scenario:

> Imagine that in carrying out the activities of everyday life, you find that you have half an hour of free time, with no pressing commitments. You have decided that you'd like to spend this time with another person. Assuming that the following three persons are available to you, which of them would you choose to spend that time with?
>
> ● A member of your immediate family
> ● The author of a book you have just read
> ● An acquaintance with whom you seem to have much in common

Older adults, more than younger ones, choose the family member. The likely explanation is that such conversations become more important when death seems imminent. This explanation is supported by a study in which the same question was asked of middle-aged gay men before the discovery of effective treatment for HIV. One group of men had AIDS and expected to die within a few years, a second group was HIV-positive but had no symptoms, and a third group was HIV-negative. Compared with the others, the men with AIDS were more likely to choose time with family (Carstensen & Fredrickson, 1998).

Another study of these three choices began with 329 people who had recently been diagnosed with cancer and another group of 170 people (matched for age and education) who had no serious illness (Pinquart & Silbereisen, 2006). The most marked difference was between those with or without cancer, regardless of age (see Figure EP.4).

Religions and Hope

People who think they might die soon are more likely than others to believe in life after death. This is one reason why the aged in the United States tend to be more religious than the young. It may also explain why people in nations with more deaths among the young tend to be more devout (Idler, 2006).

Virtually every one of the hundreds of world religions provides rites and customs to honor the dead and comfort the living. Specifics differ. As one review notes, "Rituals in the world's religions, especially those for the major tragic and significant events of bereavement and death, have a bewildering diversity" (Idler, 2006, p. 285).

Some specifics make the point. According to many sects of Hinduism, a person should die on the floor, surrounded by family, who neither eat nor wash until the funeral pyre is extinguished. Among some (not all) Christian denominations, funerals include food, drink, music, and dancing. In many Muslim cultures, the dead person is bathed by the next of kin; among the Navajo, no one touches the dead person.

Not everyone in each of these religions observes these customs; every religion has marked regional and individual variations. Nonetheless, those who care for the dying and their families need extraordinary sensitivity to cultural traditions, which might be quite different from their personal values (Schim et al., 2006).

ANSWER TO OBSERVATION QUIZ
(from page 568) No. The charts show the proportion of deaths, not the absolute number. ●

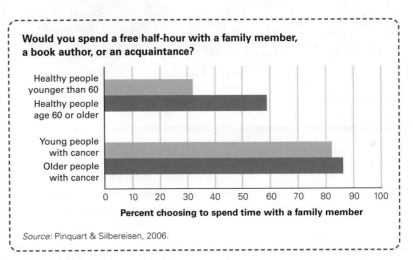

Would you spend a free half-hour with a family member, a book author, or an acquaintance?

Healthy people younger than 60

Healthy people age 60 or older

Young people with cancer

Older people with cancer

0 10 20 30 40 50 60 70 80 90 100

Percent choosing to spend time with a family member

Source: Pinquart & Silbereisen, 2006.

FIGURE EP.4 Turning to Family as Death Approaches Both young and old people diagnosed with cancer (one-fourth of whom died within five years) were found to be more likely to prefer to spend a free half-hour having a conversation with a family member rather than with an interesting person whom they did not know well. A larger difference was found between older and younger adults who did not have a serious disease: The healthy younger people were less likely to say they'd prefer to spend the time with a family member rather than with an interesting acquaintance.

The Same Situation, Many Miles Apart: Final Rest or Gateway to Heaven
Many differences are obvious between a Roman Catholic burial in Mbongolwane, South Africa *(left)*, and a Buddhist funeral procession before cremation in Bali, Indonesia *(right)*. In both places, however, friends and neighbors gather to honor the dead person and to comfort his or her family members.

In all religions and cultures, death is regarded as a passage, not an endpoint; a reason for people to come together, not a time when differences are magnified. In every tradition, throughout history and currently, religion provides hope at death (C. Kemp & Bhungalia, 2002; Shushan, 2009). For example, the ancient Greeks developed many myths about those who died; the ancient Egyptians wrote the *Book of the Dead,* constructed magnificent pyramids as royal tombs, and preserved mummies for eternal life; the ancient Maya held elaborate funerals for dead rulers.

Religious and spiritual concerns become particularly important for everyone at death (Idler, 2006). Many elderly people seek to return to their religious roots through devotion to traditional rituals, deeper spirituality, or an actual journey. Many dying adults ask that their bodies or ashes be returned to their birthplace, sometimes thousands of miles away.

In one study, seriously ill Hindus who had immigrated to Canada spoke nostalgically about their origins in India (Fry, 1999). Contrary to assumptions about acculturation, the more time an Indian immigrant had spent in Canada, the more he or she wanted a Hindu funeral (see Figure EP.5). One woman who had lived in Canada for 22 years said:

> I long to die among my relatives in the old country. . . . I miss the music, the chantings, the smells and sounds and the ringing of the temple bells in my hometown. I worry whether my own Hindu God will take me back or reject me because I am not a pure Hindu any more and have not been in communion with the elders of the Hindu faith for the years and years I have spent in Canada.
>
> *[quoted in Fry, 1999, p. 310]*

This impulse to return to one's cultural origins is evident in other research as well. For instance, adults were asked what they would want for their last meal if they knew they were to die soon. Many chose foods that bespoke their cultural origins, although those foods were not what they ate in daily life (Friese & Hofmann, 2008).

Spiritual beliefs and a connection to religious community give people the hope that is desperately needed at death. This hope provides a sense "that individual lives cannot be reduced to insignificance, that they can and do make a difference worth making, that the world is better for their existing" (Attig, 2003, pp. 62–63).

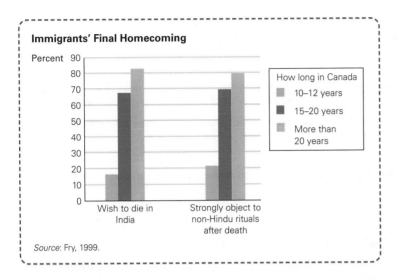

Immigrants' Final Homecoming

Percent

Source: Fry, 1999.

FIGURE EP.5 Strong Homeland and Religious Impulses Open-ended interviews with seriously ill Indians who had immigrated to Canada found that the longer they had been away, the more important India and Hinduism became as they thought about their deaths.

Even coming close to death is often an occasion for religious affirmation. This is most obvious in what is called a **near-death experience,** in which a person almost dies but survives and reports having left his or her body and moved toward a bright white light while feeling peacefulness and joy. The following classic report is typical:

> I was in a coma for approximately a week. . . . I felt as though I were lifted right up, just as though I didn't have a physical body at all. A brilliant white light appeared. . . . The most wonderful feelings came over me—feelings of peace, tranquility, a vanishing of all worries.
>
> *[quoted in R. A. Moody, 1975, p. 56]*

Near-death experiences often include religious elements (angels have been seen, celestial music heard), and survivors often adopt a more spiritual, less materialistic view of life (Vaillant, 2008). To some, near-death experiences prove that there is a heaven (Piper & Murphey, 2004). Scientists are more skeptical, claiming that

> there is no evidence that what happens when a person really dies and "stays dead" has any relationship to the experience reported by those who have recovered from a life-threatening episode. In fact, it is difficult to imagine how there could ever be such evidence.
>
> *[Kastenbaum, 2006, p. 448]*

near-death experience
An episode in which a person comes close to dying but survives and reports having left his or her body and having moved toward a bright white light while feeling peacefulness and joy.

ED KASHI / IPN / AURORA PHOTOS

The Same Faith in Another Country
An open coffin, pictures of saints, and burning candles are traditional features of many Christian funerals worldwide, including this Ukrainian Orthodox ceremony.

good death
A death that is peaceful, quick, and painless and that occurs after a long life, in the company of family and friends, and in familiar surroundings.

Dying and Acceptance

People in all religious and cultural contexts hope for a **good death** (Abramovitch, 2005)—one that is:

- At the end of a long life
- Peaceful
- Quick
- In familiar surroundings
- With family and friends present
- Without pain, confusion, or discomfort

A *bad death* (one that lacks these six characteristics) is dreaded, particularly by the elderly. Many of them have seen people die in hospitals, semiconscious and alone throughout their last days.

Attending to the Needs of the Dying

In some ways, modern medicine has made a good death more likely. The first item on the list has become the norm: Death usually occurs at the end of a long life. Young people still get sick, but surgery, drugs, radiation, and rehabilitation mean that, in developed countries, they go to the hospital, are treated, and then return home.

However, modern hospitals have also made a bad death more likely. When a cure is impossible, physical and emotional care may deteriorate. Fewer people die at home, surrounded by friends. As reported by leading thanatologist Robert Kastenbaum, when hospital patients are known to be dying, doctors spend less time with them, medication is inadequate, visitors are kept away, and nurses respond more slowly to the call button:

> Nurses were surprised and upset when told of this differential response pattern . . . and resolved to . . . respond promptly to terminally ill patients. After a few weeks, however, the original pattern reinstated itself. As much as they wanted to treat all patients equally, the nurses found it difficult to avoid being influenced by their society's fear of contact with dying people.
>
> *[Kastenbaum, 2006, p. 113]*

Fortunately, three recent trends make a good death more likely: honest talk, the hospice, and palliative care.

HONEST CONVERSATION In about 1960, researcher Elisabeth Kübler-Ross (1969, 1975) asked the administrator of a large Chicago hospital for permission to speak with dying patients. He informed her that no one in the hospital was dying! Eventually, she found a few terminally ill patients, who, to everyone's surprise, wanted to talk.

Stages of Dying From ongoing interviews, Kübler-Ross identified emotions experienced by dying people, which she divided into a sequence of five stages:

1. Denial ("I am not really dying.")
2. Anger ("I blame my doctors, or my family, or God for my death.")
3. Bargaining ("I will be good from now on if I can live.")
4. Depression ("I don't care about anything; nothing matters anymore.")
5. Acceptance ("I accept my death as part of life.")

Another set of stages of dying is based on Abraham Maslow's hierarchy of needs, discussed in Chapter 13 (Zalenski & Raspa, 2006).

1. Physiological needs (freedom from pain)
2. Safety (no abandonment)
3. Love and acceptance (from close family and friends)
4. Respect (from caregivers)
5. Self-actualization (spiritual transcendence)

Other researchers have *not* found sequential stages in dying people's approach to death. Kübler-Ross's stages of denial, anger, and depression disappear and reappear; bargaining is brief because it is fruitless; acceptance may never occur. Regarding Maslow, comfort, safety, love, and respect are important throughout the dying process, and transcendence does not require completion of Maslow's first four stages.

Nevertheless, both lists remind caregivers that each dying person has emotions and needs that may be unlike those of another dying person—or even unlike that same person's emotions and needs a few days or weeks earlier. Most important, the emotions of the dying may not be what family, medical personnel, and others might expect.

Telling the Truth As Kübler-Ross and others have discovered, most dying people want to spend time with loved ones and to talk honestly with medical and religious professionals. Human relationships are crucial: People continue to need each other (Planalp & Trost, 2008). Dying patients do not want to be cut off from daily life; they want to hear what their relatives and friends are doing and how they are feeling.

One consequence of Kübler-Ross's research is that the patient's right to be told the truth about his or her impending death is now widely accepted in Western hospitals. It is considered unethical to withhold information if the patient asks for it.

Kübler-Ross also stressed that each person responds to death in his or her own way; this means that some people do not want the whole truth. In some cultures, telling people they are dying is thought to destroy hope. Indeed, maintaining human relationships via long, honest, intimate conversations may be counter to some religious beliefs (Baugher, 2008). To determine the appropriate approach, hospital personnel need to respond to each dying person as an individual, not merely as someone who must understand that death is near.

THE HOSPICE In 1950s London, Cecily Saunders opened the first modern **hospice,** where terminally ill people could spend their last days in comfort (Saunders, 1978). Thousands of other such places have since opened throughout the world. Some dying people are helped by hospice workers at home, so that they die in familiar surroundings with friends and family nearby.

Hospice caregivers provide skilled treatment to relieve pain and discomfort, including massage, bathing, and so on. They avoid measures to delay death; their focus is to make dying easier. There are two principles for hospice care:

● **FOR DEEPER REFLECTION** Even if they know nothing else about thanatology, many people remember Kübler-Ross's sequence of stages of dying. Research has not validated this theory, yet it remains popular. Why?

hospice
An institution or program in which terminally ill patients receive palliative care.

1. Each patient's autonomy and decisions are respected. For example, pain medication is given when requested, not on a schedule.

2. Family members and friends are counseled before the death, shown how to provide care, and helped after the death.

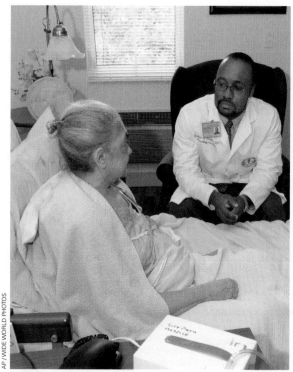

AP / WIDE WORLD PHOTOS

To Meet a Need The idea of hospice care has traveled far from its birthplace in London. Dr. Theodore Turnquest, shown here speaking with a patient in Lifepath Hospice House in Florida, plans to open the first hospice in his native country, the Bahamas.

palliative care
Care designed not to treat an illness but to provide physical and emotional comfort to the patient and support and guidance to his or her family.

double effect
An ethical situation in which an action (such as administering opiates) has both a positive effect, which is intended (relieving a terminally ill person's pain), and a negative effect, which is foreseen but not intended (hastening death by suppressing respiration).

ESPECIALLY FOR Relatives of a Person Who Is Dying Why would a healthy person want the attention of hospice caregivers? (see response, page 578) ➡

When the hospice patient remains at home (as occurs about half the time), relatives provide most of the care. When a person is in a hospice facility, a relative or a close friend is encouraged (and sometimes required) to be with the patient day and night.

Hospice staff members consider the needs of the caregivers, both before and after the death, to be as important as those of the person who is dying. In fact, thanks partly to hospice work, it is now recognized that long-time caregivers undergo major adjustments after death (Orzeck & Silverman, 2008).

Likewise, the needs of the hospice staff members themselves are also considered. Their level of hope and acceptance affects their care of the dying person and the caregivers (Running et al., 2008).

Unfortunately, many dying people never begin hospice care or enter it only in the last days before death. The reasons for this delay are detailed in Table EP.2. One report says that half of all hospice patients receive less than three weeks of specialized care before they die; that is too short a time for all the individualized medical and emotional needs of a dying person to be assessed and satisfied (J. E. Brody, 2007). A report from Britain reveals that only 10 percent of patients die in a hospice and that many of the rest do not receive good medical attention at home or in a hospital (R. Charlton, 2007).

In the United States, the number of patients in hospice care doubled from 1992 to 2000 (Han et al., 2006) and doubled again from 2000 to 2005 (to 1.2 million). Probably more than half of all dying North Americans (of all ethnic groups and income levels) receive hospice care. A dying person is more likely to receive hospice care in some places than in others (more in California than in Mississippi, for instance, and more in western Europe than in sub-Saharan Africa).

PALLIATIVE MEDICINE The same "bad death" conditions that inspired the hospice movement have led to the creation of a new field of medicine called **palliative care**, which consists of measures designed to relieve pain and suffering (Hallenbeck, 2003). Some people fear pain more than any other aspect of dying. Powerful painkillers were once prescribed sparingly, so as to prevent patients from becoming addicted—until policy makers realized that no social harm results if a dying person becomes dependent on a drug.

Morphine and other opiates have what is called a **double effect:** They relieve pain (a positive effect), but they also slow down respiration (a negative effect). A painkiller that not only reduces pain but slows breathing, so that death occurs more quickly than it otherwise would have, is considered acceptable in law, ethics, and medical practice. In England, for instance, it is illegal to cause the death of a terminally ill patient, even one who asks to die, but a survey found that a double effect is associated with one-third of English deaths (Seale, 2006).

Choices and Controversies

Because listening to the wishes of the dying and providing hospice and palliative care are now widely accepted by doctors and nurses, a good death is more likely today than it was 50 years ago. But new controversies have emerged in the wake of dramatic

---

TABLE EP.2 Barriers to Entering Hospice Care

- Hospice patients must be terminally ill, with death anticipated within six months, but such predictions are difficult to make. For example, in one study of noncancer patients, physician predictions were 90 percent accurate for those who died within a week but only 13 percent accurate when death was predicted in three to six weeks (usually the patients died sooner) (Brandt et al., 2006).

- Patients and caregivers must accept death. Traditionally, entering a hospice meant the end of curative treatment (chemotherapy, dialysis, and so on). This is no longer true (Abelson, 2007; Sulmasy, 2006). About 12 percent of patients live longer than expected, and about 2 to 3 percent are discharged (J. W. Finn, 2005). Nonetheless, many people avoid hospice because they want to keep hope alive.

- Hospice care is expensive, especially if curative therapy continues. Many skilled workers—doctors, nurses, psychologists, social workers, clergy, music therapists, and so on—provide individualized care day and night.

- Availability varies. Hospice care is more common in England than in mainland Europe and is a luxury in poor nations. In the United States, western states have more hospices than southern states do. Even in one region (northern California) and among clients of one insurance company (Kaiser), the likelihood that people with terminal cancer will enter hospice depends on exactly where they live (N. L. Keating et al., 2006)

---

medical advances: Breathing can now be continued with respirators, a heart that has stopped can be restarted, and nutrition can be provided to a comatose person via a stomach tube.

Choices regarding such measures are made in almost every life-threatening condition in hospitals. Treatments are avoided, started, or stopped, with either life-prolonging or death-hastening effects (B. Rosenfeld, 2004). Vehement disagreements about appropriate care arise, not only between national governments (as evidenced by radically different laws regulating health care) but also within them, among family members, religious advisers, and doctors (Engelhardt, 2005; Prado, 2008; R. Young, 2007). Culture, beliefs, and past experiences all influence every choice made in end-of-life care.

WHEN IS A PERSON DEAD? Modern medical interventions sustain many people who would once have succumbed to serious illness or injury. Now that such life-support measures are widely available, how do people know when death has occurred? Answers change as medicine does.

In the late 1970s, a group of Harvard physicians decided that the determining factor was brain function. They concluded that when brain waves ceased, brain death occurred and the person was dead. This definition was accepted by a U.S. presidential commission in 1981 and is now used worldwide. However, in recent years, many people have raised objections (Kellehear, 2008; Truog, 2007).

What if some primitive brain activity continues, even though the person is in a vegetative state? In such a situation, the definition of death is controversial (see Table EP.3 for descriptions of various states). Some researchers have attempted to distinguish between people who are in a permanent vegetative state (and thus will never regain the ability to think) and those who are in a coma and could recover.

In this research, a family member calls the name of the comatose person while an MRI measures brain activity (Di et al., 2007). If any activation (other than simply registering the sound) occurs, the

---

TABLE EP.3 Dead or Not? Yes, No, and Maybe

Brain death: Prolonged cessation of all brain activity with complete absence of voluntary movements; no spontaneous breathing; no response to pain, noise, and other stimuli. Brain waves have ceased; the EEG is flat; *the person is dead.*

Locked-in syndrome: The person cannot move, except for the eyes, but brain waves are still apparent; *the person is not dead.*

Coma: A state of deep unconsciousness from which the person cannot be aroused. Some people awaken spontaneously from a coma; others enter a vegetative state; *the person is not dead.*

Vegetative state: A state of deep unconsciousness in which all cognitive functions are absent, although eyes may open, sounds may be emitted, and breathing may continue; *the person is not yet dead.* This state can be *transient,* with recovery possible, *persistent,* or *permanent.* No one has ever recovered after two years; most who recover (about 15 percent) improve within three weeks (Preston & Kelly, 2006). After time has elapsed, the person may, effectively, be dead.

RESPONSE FOR Relatives of a Person Who Is Dying (from page 576)
Death affects the entire family, including children and grandchildren. I learned this myself when my mother was dying. A hospice nurse not only gave her pain medication (which made it easier for me to be with her) but also counseled me. At the nurse's suggestion, I asked for forgiveness. My mother indicated that there was nothing to forgive. We both felt a peace that would have eluded us without hospice care. ●

passive euthanasia
A situation in which a seriously ill person is allowed to die naturally, through the cessation of medical intervention.

DNR (do not resuscitate)
A written order from a physician (sometimes initiated by a patient's advance directive or by a health care proxy's request) that no attempt should be made to revive a patient if he or she suffers cardiac or respiratory arrest.

active euthanasia
A situation in which someone takes action to bring about another person's death, with the intention of ending that person's suffering.

physician-assisted suicide
A form of active euthanasia in which a doctor provides the means for someone to end his or her own life.

person is thought to be minimally conscious, not vegetative and thus not dead. This specific research is preliminary, but many scientists seek to define death more precisely than was possible 30 years ago.

HASTENING OR POSTPONING DEATH As you can see, powerful emotions are connected to dying. Many elderly people fear being kept alive too long when death is near, and many younger people fear dying too soon. In many cases, modern medical measures can bring death sooner or stave it off for a while.

Longer Life You learned earlier that the human life course has been radically altered in the past century: The average person lived twice as long in 2010 as in 1910. Among the measures that may postpone death are various drugs and surgery, as well as other interventions such as respirators to facilitate breathing, shocks to restart the heart, stomach tubes to provide nutrition, and antibiotics to halt infections. These measures have saved the lives of many people, sometimes allowing them to live on for decades.

A historical view shows that many adults under age 50 once died of causes that now kill relatively few adults in developed nations, such as complications of childbirth and epidemic diseases. In the past two decades, neonatal surgery, radiation, and thousands of protective drugs are saving millions of lives each year. Some forms of cancer (e.g., Hodgkins disease, breast cancer, and skin cancer), once fatal, are now almost always curable if diagnosed early.

Allowing Death The medical profession is justly proud of its successes. However, some people believe that these successes have given rise to circumstances that allow doctors to ignore the importance of patients' quality of life and the role of patients' choice.

In **passive euthanasia,** a person is allowed to die. The chart of a patient may include **DNR (do not resuscitate)** instructions, which direct the medical staff not to restore breathing or restart the heart if breathing or pulsating stop. A DNR usually reflects the expressed wishes of the patient or health care proxy (discussed below).

Passive euthanasia is legal everywhere and is relatively frequent (Löfmark et al., 2008), although a distinction is sometimes made between removing life-support equipment and not beginning medical intervention. Both have the same result, but many emergency personnel start artificial respiration and stimulate hearts without noticing a DNR. If the patient is revived as a result, the issue of passive euthanasia then becomes more complex.

Active euthanasia involves directly causing a person's death, as by giving the person a lethal drug. Some physicians perform active euthanasia when confronted with suffering they cannot relieve, an illness they cannot cure, and a patient who wants to die. It is legal under some circumstances in the Netherlands, Belgium, Luxembourg, and Switzerland, but it is illegal (yet rarely prosecuted) in most other nations.

Many see a major moral distinction between active and passive euthanasia, although the final result is the same (McLachlan, 2008; Prado, 2008). A survey of physicians in the United States found that while a majority (69 percent) objected to active euthanasia, fewer than 1 in 5 (18 percent) objected to sedation that had a double effect; even fewer (5 percent) objected to withdrawing life support when a patient was brain-dead (Curlin et al., 2008). A similar survey of seven other nations found wide variations within and among them, with some physicians saying they would never perform active euthanasia and others reporting that they had done so (Löfmark et al., 2008).

Between passive and active euthanasia there is another action: Someone may provide the means for a patient to end his or her own life. Opposite and adamant opinions about this action can be found among physicians, politicians, and laypeople.

Some people advocate **physician-assisted suicide,** in which a doctor provides medication that enables a person to take his or her own life. The state of Oregon legalized physician-assisted suicide in 1994, explicitly asserting that such a death should not be considered suicide, but rather "death with dignity."

Acceptance of this practice, by any name, varies markedly by culture (Prado, 2008). In Eastern nations, suicides can be noble, as when Buddhist monks publicly burned themselves to death to protest the war in Vietnam or when people choose to die for their nation or for their personal honor. Interestingly, however, in the United States, physicians who are Asian are *less* likely to condone physician-assisted suicide than are non-Asian physicians (Curlin et al., 2008).

The debate about euthanasia and physician-assisted suicide is especially heated in England as a result of several headline-making lawsuits brought by terminally ill British citizens who were determined to die. In England, as pain has become better controlled, the essential issue has become personal choice: Does an individual have a legal "right to die" or not (Finlay, 2009)?

Watching Her Die Diane Pretty suffered from motor neuron disease, a degenerative condition that destroyed her ability to move but did not affect her mind. She wanted her husband, Michael, to be legally allowed to help her die, but her petitions to the British courts and then to the European Court of Human Rights were denied. She died 13 days after this photograph of the couple was taken.

The Netherlands The Netherlands (Holland) has permitted both active euthanasia and physician-assisted suicide since 1980 and made the law more explicit in 2002. A doctor must approve and report every such death. Only half the patients who ask for help in dying receive it (one-fourth die before receiving medical approval and one-fourth are denied or dissuaded) (Jansen-van der Weide et al., 2005).

Many healthy people and medical professionals in other nations think the main reason for hastening death is to stop intense pain. One physician complained, "It is criminal the way my colleagues fail to treat pain. . . . Physician-assisted suicide . . . is a problem of physical ignorance and abandonment" (quoted in Curry et al., 2002).

In fact, however, pain is not the primary motivation reported by patients in the Netherlands who wish to die. If patients ask for help in dying, many physicians first increase pain medication. Some patients then withdraw their request. Those who persist are likely to fear loss of dignity, cognition, or control. They are firm and clear in wanting help in dying.

Most Dutch physicians believe that hospice and palliative care have improved in the Netherlands since active euthanasia became legal and regulated, although they also feel that palliative care cannot control all pain (Georges et al., 2006). In 2005, less than 2 percent of deaths in the Netherlands involved medical help, either active euthanasia (1.7 percent) or physician-assisted suicide (0.1 percent). An additional 7.1 percent occurred with sedation, sometimes the result of a double effect (van der Heide et al., 2007).

Oregon Oregon voters approved physician-assisted "death with dignity" (but not other forms of active euthanasia) in 1994 and again in 1997. The first such legal deaths occurred in 1998. The law requires that certain conditions be met:

● The dying person must be an adult and an Oregon resident.
● The dying person must request the lethal drugs twice orally and once in writing.
● Fifteen days must elapse between the first request and prescription of the lethal drugs.
● Two physicians must confirm that the person is terminally ill, has less than six months to live, and is competent (i.e., not mentally impaired or depressed).

The law also requires record-keeping and annual reporting. About one-third of the requests are approved, and more than one-third of those who are approved never take the drugs. Instead, they have the deadly drugs as reassurance, but they prefer to die naturally.

TABLE EP.4 Reasons Oregon Residents Gave for Requesting Physician Assistance in Dying, 1998–2005

Reason	Patients Giving Reason (%)
Loss of autonomy	86
Less able to enjoy life	85
Loss of dignity	83
Loss of control over body	57
Burden on others	37
Pain	22

Source: Oregon Department of Human Services, 2006.

slippery slope
The argument that a given action will start a chain of events that will culminate in an undesirable outcome.

● **UNDERSTANDING THE NUMBERS** Is the rate of physician-assisted suicide higher in the Netherlands or in Oregon?

Answer The rate is low in both places, but it is higher in the Netherlands—17 physician-assisted deaths per 1,000 deaths, compared with about 4 per 1,000 in Oregon.

advance directive
A document that contains an individual's instructions for end-of-life medical care, written before such care is needed.

living will
A document that indicates what kinds of medical intervention an individual wants or does not want if he or she becomes incapable of expressing those wishes.

health care proxy
A person chosen by another person to make medical decisions if the second person becomes unable to do so.

Between 1998 and 2007, about 90,000 people in Oregon died of a terminal illness. Only 341 of them obtained prescriptions for lethal drugs and used them to die. As Table EP.4 shows, people requested the drugs primarily for psychological, not biological, reasons. In 2007, 85 Oregonians obtained prescriptions for drugs that could kill them. Of those, 26 died naturally and 13 were still alive at year's end (Oregon Department of Human Services, 2008).

Many people fear that legalizing euthanasia or physician-assisted suicide will create a **slippery slope** (Lindsay, 2008; B. Rosenfeld, 2004; R. Young, 2007). They wonder if hastening death when terminally ill people request it will cause a society to slide into killing sick people who are *not* ready to die—especially the old and the poor.

Data from Oregon may assuage this fear. People who obtained help in dying tend to be advantaged, not disadvantaged. Of the 46 people who died this way in Oregon in 2007, all had health insurance, most (98 percent) were White, and most were well educated (69 percent had attended college). Some argue that it is less slippery to have strict laws than to allow such deaths to occur illegally, as happens in most nations (Magnusson, 2004).

Worldwide, most voters and lawmakers are not convinced by the data from Oregon or the Netherlands. Proposals to legalize physician-assisted suicide have been defeated in five U.S. states and in several nations (e.g., by Great Britain's House of Lords in 2006). However, in the state of Washington, just north of Oregon, 58 percent of the voters approved a Death with Dignity law in November 2008, and in 2009, Luxembourg joined the Netherlands in allowing active euthanasia.

Advance Directives

Many states have attempted to increase personal choice about death, even as they stop short of legalizing medical assistance to bring it about. For example, a massive effort in Hawaii to inform people about end-of-life issues resulted in *less* support for physician-assisted suicide but *more* support for **advance directives**—an individual's instructions regarding end-of-life medical care, written before such care is needed (K. L. Braun et al., 2005).

At least in Hawaii, once people understood the processes and complications of dying, they realized they could control many aspects of their deaths. That control is often exerted through creating a living will and assigning a health care proxy.

LIVING WILLS AND HEALTH CARE PROXIES A **living will** indicates what kinds of medical intervention a person wants or does not want if unable to express any preferences. (If the person is conscious, hospital personnel often ask about procedures, so a living will need not be referred to.) Living wills include phrases such as "incurable," "reasonable chance of recovery," and "extraordinary measures." Therein lies a problem: Doctors and family members may disagree about what such phrases mean.

Accordingly, people may designate a **health care proxy,** someone who can make specific medical decisions if the person becomes incapable of doing so. Only about 25 percent of all North Americans (mostly older adults) have arranged to have both a living will and a health care proxy, although they are recommended for everyone (Preston & Kelly, 2006).

Even with a living will and a health care proxy, the care provided may not always be what a person wants. For one thing, the person who is designated as a proxy often finds it difficult to choose death for a loved one. Even husbands and wives who have been married for years do not necessarily know each other's wishes; husbands are

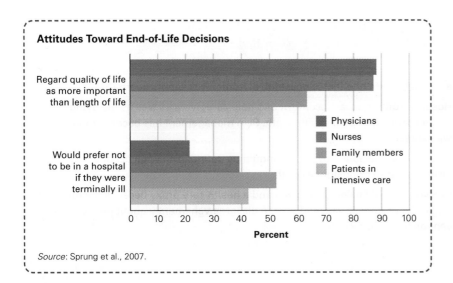

Attitudes Toward End-of-Life Decisions

Regard quality of life as more important than length of life

Would prefer not to be in a hospital if they were terminally ill

- Physicians
- Nurses
- Family members
- Patients in intensive care

0 10 20 30 40 50 60 70 80 90 100
Percent

Source: Sprung et al., 2007.

FIGURE EP.6 Interesting Discrepancies Responding to a survey taken in six European nations' intensive-care units (ICUs), higher percentages of ICU doctors and nurses than of ICU patients and their families said they considered quality of life more important than a long life.

more likely to believe they know but are less likely to be accurate (Zettel-Watson et al., 2008).

Furthermore, doctors and nurses may object to the specifics of an advance directive, yet they must take the final action. For example, as already mentioned, if breathing suddenly fails, many emergency personnel automatically begin artificial respiration. Conversely, many medical people think the stomach tube is overused, as it prolongs life but does not cure. Most laypeople, however, do not consider artificial feeding to be an "extraordinary measure" (Orentlicher & Callahan, 2004).

The discrepancy among the views of doctors, patients, and families was evident in a survey conducted in six European nations. Doctors were more likely than family members to choose quality of life over length of life (see Figure EP.6; Sprung et al., 2007). Some dying people want to end life sooner, or prolong life longer, than others.

THE NEED FOR ADVANCE DIRECTIVES: THE TERRI SCHIAVO CASE Theresa Marie Schiavo was 26 years old in 1990 when her heart suddenly stopped and anoxia destroyed some brain cells. Emergency personnel restarted her heart, but she was in a deep coma. Like most people her age, Terri had no advance directive, so a court designated Michael, her husband of six years, as her health care proxy.

Eleven years after Terri's collapse, Michael accepted her doctors' repeated diagnosis that Terri was in a persistent vegetative state. He petitioned to have her feeding tube removed. The court agreed, noting the testimony of witnesses who said that Terri had told them that she never wanted to be on life support. Terri's parents appealed and lost.

The Florida legislature then passed "Terri's Law," requiring that the tube be reinserted. It was, but Florida courts soon ruled that Terri's Law was unconstitutional. After three more years of legal wrangling, the U.S. Supreme Court ruled that the lower courts were correct. At that point, every North American newspaper and TV station was following the case. Congress passed a law requiring that artificial feeding be continued, but that law, too, was overturned. The stomach tube was removed, and Terri died on March 31, 2005—although some maintained that she had really died 15 years earlier.

Partly because of the conflicts between her husband and her parents, and between appointed judges and elected legislatures, Terri's case was widely publicized. Thousands of other family members, judges, and medical personnel have struggled privately with similar issues. Advance directives are intended to help people avoid such anguish.

ESPECIALLY FOR People Without Advance Directives Why do very few young adults have living wills? (see response, page 582) →

RESPONSE FOR People Without Advance Directives (from page 581) Young adults tend to avoid thinking realistically about their own deaths. This attitude is emotional, not rational. The actual task of preparing the documents is easy (the forms can be downloaded; no lawyer is needed). Young adults have no trouble doing other future-oriented things, such as getting a tetanus shot or enrolling in a pension plan. ●

KEY Points

- Modern medical care has postponed death but does not necessarily make for a "good" death, one that is peaceful, at home, with family nearby.
- Hospice workers ease discomfort and help caregivers as well as the dying person cope emotionally with death. Pain management has become more widespread.
- Controversies include how death should be defined and what actions may be taken to hasten or postpone death.
- Everyone should have a living will and a health care proxy because the range of medical measures is vast and people disagree vehemently about medical intervention for the dying.

Bereavement

In her book *The Year of Magical Thinking,* Joan Didion (2005), a highly respected author known for her honesty and logic, confesses that after her husband died suddenly of a heart attack, she decided not to give away his shoes. She reasoned that he would need them if he came back. With similar illogic, when someone dies, the bereaved often wonder why the world seems to continue as it did before.

Normal Grief

The death of a loved one typically arouses powerful emotions in surviving relatives and friends, including anger and shock, sadness and depression. Denial—as in Didion's initial refusal to accept that her husband would not return—alternates with deep waves of sadness and feelings of loss. Humans may be bewildered when they find themselves more overwhelmed by one death than by the deaths of thousands. As one woman said:

> Although I'm 62 I still miss my mother.... Since 9/11 it has been even harder. People make me feel ashamed. After all, they're right when they say to me, "Look at all the youngsters who were killed; their lives were just beginning. Your mother lived a full life, what more do you want?"
>
> [quoted in Schachter, 2003, p. 20]

bereavement
The sense of loss following a death.

grief
The powerful sorrow that an individual feels at the death of another.

GRIEF, MOURNING, AND BEREAVEMENT As we consider how people react to a death, some distinctions are in order. **Bereavement** is the sense of loss following a death. Grief and mourning are both aspects of bereavement, but they are quite different from each other.

Grief is the powerful sorrow that an individual feels at the death of another. It is a highly personal emotion, an anguish that overtakes daily life. It is manifest in uncontrollable crying, sleeplessness, and irrational and delusional thoughts—the "magical thinking" of Didion's title:

mourning
The ceremonies and behaviors that a religion or culture prescribes for people to employ in expressing their bereavement after a death.

> Grief has no distance. Grief comes in waves, paroxysms, sudden apprehensions that weaken the knees and blind the eyes and obliterate the dailiness of life.... I see now that my insistence on spending that first night alone was more complicated than it seemed, a primitive instinct.... There was a level on which I believed that what had happened remained reversible. That is why I needed to be alone.... I needed to be alone so that he could come back. This was the beginning of my year of magical thinking.
>
> [Didion, 2005, pp. 27, 32, 33]

A. RAMEY / PHOTOEDIT, INC.

The Flowers of Youth In many cultural traditions, mourners bring a token of their presence to funeral rites. Such items as pebbles, stuffed animals, notes, candles, and flowers are left at gravesites throughout the world. These young women are placing flowers on the coffin of a friend who was killed in a drive-by shooting.

Mourning is the public and ritualistic expression of bereavement. It is manifested in ceremonies and behaviors that a religion or culture prescribes to honor the dead. These may include special clothing, food, prayers, and informal shrines at the place where someone died, as well as the gestures of friends, who may send cards, bring food, and stay near the bereaved family.

Mourning is needed because the grief-stricken are vulnerable not only to irrational thoughts but also to self-destructive acts. Health, physical as well as mental, dips in the recently bereaved, and the rate of suicide increases (Ajdacic-Gross et al., 2008; Elwert & Christakis, 2008).

After natural or human-caused disasters, including hurricanes and wars, many people die of causes not directly attributable to the disaster. They are victims of the indifference of others or their own diminished self-care. Grief splinters people into jumbled pieces, making them vulnerable to many hazards. Mourning reassembles them, making them whole again and able to rejoin the larger community, as they are helped to recover.

Mourning customs are designed to move grief toward reaffirmation (Harlow, 2005). For this reason, eulogies emphasize the dead person's good qualities; people who did not personally know the deceased person attend wakes, funerals, or memorial services to help the survivors. If the dead person was a public figure, mourners could include thousands, even millions. They express their sorrow to one another, weep as they watch memorials on television, and promise themselves to affirm the best of that person as they ignore whatever criticisms they might have had.

Mourning is often time-limited by cultural custom or religious tradition. Examples include the week of sitting shiva at home in Judaism and the three days of active sorrow among some groups of Muslims.

Memories often return on the anniversary of a death, so mourning includes annual rituals such as visiting a grave or lighting a candle. Having a specific time, prayer, and place for remembering the dead (such as a home altar in China or a gravesite in places where burial is customary) helps bereaved people express their grief without being overwhelmed by it.

"Gone Too Soon" The public memorial services for Michael Jackson, such as this one at New York's Apollo Theater, emphasized his accomplishments as an entertainer and his generosity to others, not the sensational and scandalous aspects of his life: Only kind words about the dead person are considered appropriate.

© LUCAS JACKSON / REUTERS / CORBIS

No Peace Without Justice Jasmine Hightower sobs at a makeshift memorial in the Newark, New Jersey, schoolyard where her older sister, Iofemi, and two other college students were fatally shot during a random robbery that ended in murder in 2007. (A fourth victim was seriously wounded but survived.) Tears and the comfort of relatives and friends can help people cope with such sudden and senseless deaths. It may also be helpful to locate the blame and seek justice: Six young men with gang associations were soon arrested for these murders.

OBSERVATION QUIZ

What is the significance of the objects in the hand of the family member at left? (see answer, page 586) ➜

PLACING BLAME AND SEEKING MEANING A common impulse after death is for the survivors to assess blame, such as for medical measures not taken, laws not enforced, unhealthy habits not changed. The bereaved sometimes blame the dead person, sometimes themselves, and sometimes distant others. For public tragedies, nations may blame one another. Blame is not necessarily rational; for instance, outrage at the assassination of Archduke Francis Ferdinand of Austria by a Serbian terrorist in 1914 provoked a conflict between the governments of Austria and Serbia that led to the four years of World War I.

As you remember, denial and anger appear first on Kübler-Ross's list of reactions to death; ideally, people move on to acceptance of the deeper meaning. The need to find meaning may be crucial to the reaffirmation that follows grief. In some cases, this search starts with preserving memories: Displaying photographs and personal effects and telling anecdotes about the dead person are central to many memorial services.

Mourners may also be helped by strangers who have experienced a similar loss, especially when friends are unlikely to understand. This explains why groups have been organized for parents of murdered children, mothers whose adolescents were killed by drunk drivers, widows of firefighters who died at the World Trade Center, relatives of passengers who died in the same plane crash, and so on.

Sometimes "meaning becomes grounded in action" to honor the dead (Armour, 2003, p. 538). Organizations devoted to causes such as fighting cancer and banning handguns find their most dedicated supporters among people who have lost a loved one to that particular circumstance. Often when someone dies, the close family designates a charity that is somehow connected to the deceased, inviting other mourners to make contributions.

An example of action that allayed grief is one mother who carried a bag with the personal effects of her murdered son. She showed them, item by item, to young gang members, telling them:

> "This is all I had left of my son. A pair of tennis shoes and a pair of underwear that had no blood on them. He loved this little chain he had on. And you see it's broken up, with a shot?". . . These groups of young kids are sitting there . . . . Driving home from that group, I just get warm, like affirmation.
>
> [quoted in Armour, 2003, p. 532]

Thus, the normal grief reaction is intense and irrational at first but gradually eases, as time, social support, and traditions help first with the initial outpouring of emotion and then with the search for meaning and reaffirmation. The individual may engage in *grief work,* experiencing and expressing strong emotions and then moving toward wholeness, which includes recognizing the larger story of human life and death.

Complicated Grief

In recent times, mourning has become more private, less emotional, and less religious. As a result, new complications in the grieving process have emerged. Emblematic of this change are funeral trends in the United States: Whereas older generations prefer burial after a traditional funeral, younger generations are likely to prefer small memorial services after cremation (Hayslip et al., 1999).

NO MOURNING ALLOWED As mourning rituals diminish, many bereavement counselors have noted specific problems that may become pathological. One is **absent grief,** in which a bereaved person does not seem to mourn at all. This may be a first reaction, as some people cannot face the reality of the death, but if it continues, absent grief can trigger physical or psychological symptoms—for instance, trouble breathing or walking, sudden panic attacks, or depression. If such disabilities seem to appear for no reason, the underlying cause might be a death that was never mourned.

Absent grief may be more common in modern society than it was earlier. People who live and work where no one knows their personal lives have no community or recognized customs to help them grieve. Indeed, for workers at large corporations or students in universities, grief becomes "an unwelcome intrusion (or violent intercession) into the normal efficient running of everyday life" (M. Anderson, 2001, p. 141). This leads to isolation—exactly the opposite of what bereaved people need.

Modern life also increases the incidence of **disenfranchised grief,** when people who feel grief are not allowed to mourn publicly because of cultural customs or social restrictions. Unmarried lovers (of the same or opposite sex), former wives or husbands, young children, and close friends at work may be excluded (perhaps by the relatives, either deliberately or through ignorance) from saying goodbye to the dying person, viewing the corpse, or participating in the aftermath of death.

Typically, only a current spouse or close blood relative decides funeral arrangements, disposal of the body, and other matters. This made sense when all adults were closely connected to their relatives, but it may result in "gagged grief and beleaguered bereavement" when, for instance, a long-time but unmarried partner is excluded (L. Green & Grant, 2008, p. 275).

INTERRUPTED MOURNING Another possible problem is **incomplete grief.** Murders and suicides often trigger police investigations and press reports, which interfere with the grief process. An autopsy complicates grieving for those who believe that the body will rise again or that the soul does not leave the body immediately. The inability to recover a body, as happens for soldiers who are missing in action or some victims of a major flood or fire, impedes mourning and hence halts a bereaved person's progress toward reaffirmation.

absent grief
A situation in which overly private people cut themselves off from the community and customs that allow and expect grief; can lead to social isolation.

disenfranchised grief
A situation in which certain people, although they are bereaved, are prevented from mourning publicly by cultural customs or social restrictions.

incomplete grief
A situation in which circumstances, such as a police investigation or an autopsy, interfere with the process of grieving.

AP PHOTO / JOHN MOORE

Empty Boots The body of a young army corporal killed near Baghdad has been shipped home to his family in Mississippi for a funeral and burial, but his fellow soldiers in Iraq also need to express their grief. The custom is to hold an informal memorial service, placing the dead soldier's boots, helmet, and rifle in the middle of a circle of mourners, who weep, pray, and reminisce.

ANSWER TO OBSERVATION QUIZ
(from page 584) The young woman is holding an inhaler for relief of severe asthma symptoms. Asthma and other chronic conditions, such as heart disease and depression, are often made worse by grief. Relatives and friends should be alert to the need to offer health protection as well as comfort to a mourner who has a chronic illness. ●

Sometimes events interrupt the responses of the community. The bereaved need attention to their particular loss, and the grief process may be incomplete if mourning is cut short or if other people are distracted from their role in recovery. When death occurs on a major holiday, immediately after another death or disaster, or during wartime, it is harder for the survivors to grieve.

One widow whose husband died of cancer on September 10, 2001, complained, "People who attended the funeral talked only about the terrorist attack of September 11, and my husband wasn't given the respect he deserved" (quoted in Schachter, 2003, p. 20). Although she expressed concern for her husband, it is apparent that she herself needed sympathy.

Diversity of Reactions

Bereaved people depend on the customs and attitudes of their community, as well as on their social network, to guide them through their irrational thoughts and grief. Particulars depend on the specific culture. For example, mourners who keep the dead person's possessions, talk to the deceased, and frequently review memories are notably *less* well adjusted 18 months after the death if they are in the United States but *better* adjusted if they are in China (Lalande & Bonanno, 2006).

Childhood experiences also affect bereavement. Adults whose parents died when they were children are more distraught by death. Attachment history may be important (Hansson & Stroebe, 2007). Older adults who were securely attached may be more likely to experience normal grief; those whose attachment was insecure-avoidant may have absent grief; and those who were insecure-resistant may become stuck, unable to find meaning in the living and dying of someone they love and thus perhaps unable to reaffirm their own lives.

RESEARCH ON GRIEF Reaffirmation does not mean forgetting the dead person; many *continuing bonds* are evident years after death. There is a

> lack of empirical support for the presumed necessity of working through loss [which] has prompted a reversal of the historical trend in bereavement theory; moving away from the traditional focus on severing the attachment bond.
>
> *[Field & Friedrichs, 2006]*

As this quotation implies, bereavement theory once held that everyone should do grief work and then move on, realizing that the dead person is gone forever. It was thought that if this did not happen, pathological grief could result, with the person either not grieving enough (absent grief) or grieving too long (incomplete grief). Current research finds a much wider variety of reactions.

It is easy to see why some earlier studies overestimated the frequency of pathological grief. For obvious reasons, scientists often began their research on mourning with mourners—that is, with people who had recently experienced the death of a loved one. Furthermore, they often studied people who needed psychological help. Some experienced absent grief; others felt disenfranchised grief; some were overcome by unremitting sadness many months after the loss; others could not find meaning in a violent, sudden, unexpected death.

Such mourners are *not* typical. Almost everyone experiences several deaths over their lifetime, of parents and grandparents, of a spouse or close friend. Most feel sadness at first but then resume their customary activities, functioning as well a few months later as they had before. And "only a small subset, usually about 10 to 15 percent, exhibit extreme or complicated grief" (Bonanno & Lilienfeld, 2008).

The variety of grief reactions was evident in a longitudinal study that began by interviewing and assessing married older adults who lived in greater Detroit. Over several years, 319 became widows or widowers. Most (205) were reinterviewed at 6 and 18 months after the death and some (92) were seen again several years later (Boerner et al., 2004, 2005).

General trends were evident. Almost all the widows and widowers idealized their past marriages. Their recollections after death were rosier than the descriptions they had given of their relationships when their spouse was still alive. Another trend was that many thought of their spouse several times each day immediately after the death; with time, such thoughts became less frequent.

Reactions to the spouse's death were clustered into five categories:

1. Fifty percent were resilient. They were sad at first, but by 6 months later they were about as happy and productive as they had been before the death.

2. Eleven percent experienced normal grief, with increased depression for 6 months after the death but recovery by 18 months.

3. Eighteen percent were *less* depressed after the death than before, perhaps because they had been caregivers for their seriously ill partners.

4. Eleven percent were slow to recover, functioning poorly even at 18 months. By four years after the death, however, they functioned almost as well as they had before the death.

5. Ten percent were depressed at every assessment, before as well as after the death. If this research had begun only after the death, it might seem that the loss caused depression. However, the pre-loss assessment suggests that these people were chronically depressed, not stuck in grief.

PRACTICAL APPLICATIONS This research might help someone who is grieving or who knows someone in mourning. The first step is simply to be aware that powerful, complicated, and unexpected emotions are likely: A friend should listen and sympathize, never implying that the person is too grief-stricken or not grief-stricken enough.

The bereaved person *might or might not* want to visit the grave, light a candle, cherish a memento, pray, or sob. Those who have been taught to bear grief stoically may be doubly distressed if a friend advises them to cry but they cannot. Conversely, those whose cultures expect loud wailing may resent it if they are urged to hush.

ESPECIALLY FOR Educators How might a teacher help a young child cope with death? (see response, page 588) ➡

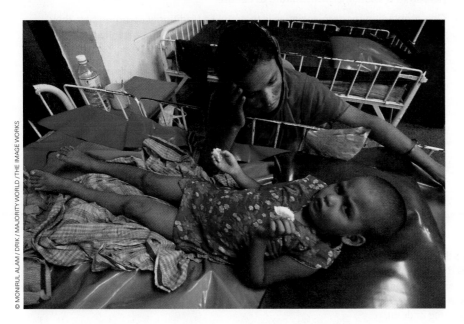

Life in the Balance The death of a young child is especially devastating to families. This girl is in a hospital in Bangladesh; she is suffering from cholera, which kills more than 2,000 children a year worldwide, most of them in areas with unsafe water supplies.

OBSERVATION QUIZ

Is this girl likely to die? (see answer, page 588) ➡

Even absent grief—in which the bereaved refuses to do any of these things—might be appropriate. So might the opposite reaction, when people want to talk about their loss, gathering sympathy, ascribing blame, and finding meaning. If emotions can be expressed in action—joining a bereavement group; protesting some government policy; planting a garden; walking, running, or biking to raise money for some cause—that may help.

Remember the 7-year-old boy whose grandparents, uncle, and dog (Twick) died? The boy wrote a memorial poem for the dog, which his parents framed and hung in the living room. This helped the boy (K. R. Kaufman & Kaufman, 2006).

No matter what rituals are followed or what pattern is evident in human reactions to death, the result may give the living a deeper appreciation of themselves as well as of the value of human relationships. In fact, a theme frequently sounded by those who work with the dying and the bereaved is that the lessons of death may lead to a greater appreciation of life, especially of the value of intimate, caring relationships.

George Vaillant is a psychiatrist who has studied the lives of a group of men from the time they were Harvard students through old age. He writes about funerals: "With tears of remembrance running down our cheeks, we are reunited with our remembrance of past love. . . . Remembered love lives triumphantly today" (Vaillant, 2008, p. 133).

It is fitting to end this Epilogue, and this book, with a reminder of the creative work of living. As first described in Chapter 1, the study of human development is a science, with topics to be researched, understood, and explained. But the process of living is an art as well as a science, with strands of love and sorrow woven into each person's unique tapestry. Dying, when it is accepted; death, when it leads to hope; grief, when it is allowed expression; and mourning, when it fosters reaffirmation—all give added meaning to birth, growth, development, and human relationships.

RESPONSE FOR Educators (from page 587) Death has varied meanings, so a teacher needs to take care not to contradict the child's cultural background. In general, however, specific expressions of mourning are useful, and acting as if the death did not happen is destructive. ●

ANSWER TO OBSERVATION QUIZ (from page 587) No. She is in a hospital, where she can receive the oral rehydration that saves almost every cholera patient. She has two additional advantages: an attentive mother and no signs of malnutrition. ●

KEY𝔭oints

- Rituals help the living come to terms with both mourning (the public process) and grief (the private emotion).

- Grief is not rational or predictable; grief and mourning vary a great deal from person to person and from culture to culture.

- One problem in modern societies is that, unlike traditional communities, they do not allow some of the bereaved the time and social support they need for mourning.

- Reactions to death are varied; other people need to be especially responsive to whatever needs a grieving person may have. Most bereaved people recover within a year.

SUMMARY

Death and Hope

1. Death has various meanings, depending partly on the age of the person involved and whether that person is dying or mourning. For example, young children are more concerned about being separated from those they see every day; adults are concerned about their own life plans; older adults are more accepting of death.

Dying and Acceptance

2. People who are dying need to be treated with honesty and respect. Their emotions may change over time. Some may move from denial to acceptance, although stages of dying vary much more than originally proposed.

3. Hospice nurses and other workers meet the biological and psychological needs of fatally ill people and their families. This can occur at home or at a place called a hospice.

4. Palliative care relieves pain and other uncomfortable aspects of dying, in modern hospitals as well as in hospices. Such care makes a good death much more possible.

5. The range of medical measures is vast, not only saving lives but also prolonging dying.

6. The issue of whether or not euthanasia or physician-assisted suicide is advisable or legal remains controversial. Nations and states have quite different laws and practices.

7. Since 1980, death has been defined as occurring when brain waves stop. However, the need for a more precise, updated definition is apparent.

Bereavement

8. Variations in grief and mourning are so great that it now seems there is no single best way to cope with death. Mourning rituals are cultural or religious expressions that aid survivors and the entire community.

9. Grief may be irrational and complicated, absent or disenfranchised. Most people find meaning in death that eventually helps them live a fuller life, although a feeling of having an ongoing bond with the deceased is no longer thought to be pathological.

KEY TERMS

thanatology (p. 565)

terror management theory (TMT) (p. 570)

near-death experience (p. 573)

good death (p. 574)

hospice (p. 575)

palliative care (p. 576)

double effect (p. 576)

passive euthanasia (p. 578)

DNR (do not resuscitate) (p. 578)

active euthanasia (p. 578)

physician-assisted suicide (p. 578)

slippery slope (p. 580)

advance directive (p. 580)

living will (p. 580)

health care proxy (p. 580)

bereavement (p. 582)

grief (p. 582)

mourning (p. 583)

absent grief (p. 585)

disenfranchised grief (p. 585)

incomplete grief (p. 585)

KEY QUESTIONS

1. How is a contemporary death different from a death a century ago?

2. How do dying people tend to feel about family members?

3. What is the relationship between religion and dying?

4. How does a near-death experience relate to developmental science?

5. Why did Kübler-Ross initially have trouble interviewing dying people?

6. What determines whether a dying person will receive hospice care?

7. What is the difference between passive and active euthanasia?

8. How is it determined that a person is dead?

9. Why do relatively few people in Oregon die by means of physician-assisted suicide?

10. What are the differences among bereavement, grief, and mourning?

APPLICATIONS

1. Death is sometimes said to be hidden, even taboo. Ask 10 people if they have ever been with someone who was dying. Note not only the yes and no answers but also the details and reactions. For instance, how many of the deaths occurred in hospitals?

2. Find quotes about death in *Bartlett's Familiar Quotations* or a similar collection. Do you see any historical or cultural patterns of acceptance, denial, or fear?

3. Every aspect of dying is controversial in modern society. Do an Internet search for a key term such as *euthanasia* or *grief*. Analyze the information and the underlying assumptions. What is your opinion, and why?

4. People of varying ages have different attitudes toward death. Ask people of different ages (ideally, one young person under 20, one adult under 60, and one older person) what thoughts they have about their own death. What differences do you find?

Appendix A

Supplemental Charts, Graphs, and Tables

Often, examining specific data is useful, even fascinating, to developmental researchers. The particular numbers reveal trends and nuances not apparent from a more general view. For instance, many people mistakenly believe that the incidence of Down syndrome babies rises sharply for mothers over 35, or that the tiniest newborns usually survive. Each chart, graph, or table in this appendix contains information not generally known.

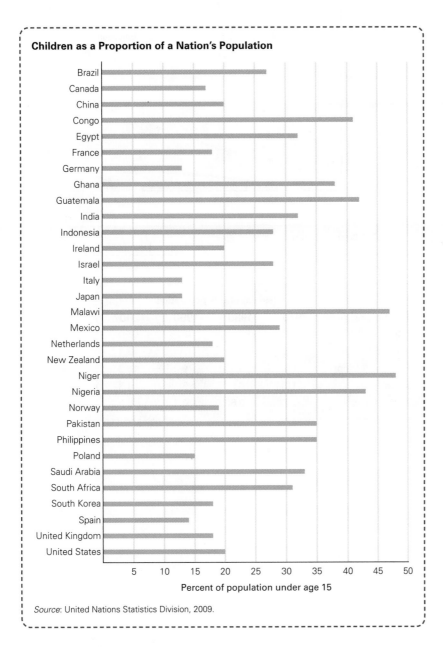

Children as a Proportion of a Nation's Population

Percent of population under age 15

Source: United Nations Statistics Division, 2009.

More Children, Worse Schools?
(Chapter 1)

Nations that have high birth rates also have high death rates, short life spans, and more illiteracy. A systems approach suggests that these variables are connected: For example, the Montessori and Reggio Emilia early-childhood education programs, said to be the best in the world, originated in Italy; Italy has the lowest proportion of children under 15.

Ethnic Composition of the U.S. Population (Chapter 1)

There are many ways to present data. A graph often makes change seem more dramatic than a table does.

OBSERVATION QUIZ

Which ethnic group is growing most rapidly? (see answer, page A-4) ⟶

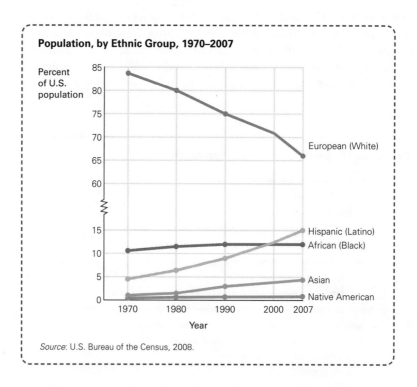

Population, by Ethnic Group, 1970–2007

Source: U.S. Bureau of the Census, 2008.

Ethnic origin	Percent of U.S. population			
	1970	1980	1990	2007
European (White)	83.7	80	75	66.0
African (Black)	10.6	11.5	12	12.4
Hispanic (Latino)	4.5	6.4	9	15.0
Asian	1.0	1.5	3	4.3
Native American	0.4	0.6	0.7	0.9

The Genetics of Blood Types (Chapter 2)

Blood types A and B are dominant traits, and type O is recessive. The percentages given in the first column of this chart represent the odds that a child born to the parents with the various combinations of genotypes will have the genotype given in the second column.

Genotypes of Parents*	Genotype of Offspring	Phenotype	Can Donate Blood to (Phenotype)	Can Receive Blood from (Phenotype)
AA + AA (100%) AA + AB (50%) AA + AO (50%) AB + AB (25%) AB + AO (25%) AO + AO (25%)	AA (inherits one A from each parent)	A	A or AB	A or O
AA + OO (100%) AB + OO (50%) AO + AO (50%) AO + OO (50%) AB + AO (25%) AB + BO (25%)	AO	A	A or AB	A or O
BB + BB (100%) AB + BB (50%) BB + BO (50%) AB + AB (25%) AB + BO (25%) BO + BO (25%)	BB	B	B or AB	B or O
BB + OO (100%) AB + OO (50%) BO + BO (50%) BO + OO (50%) AB + AO (25%) AB + BO (25%)	BO	B	B or AB	B or O
AA + BB (100%) AA + AB (50%) AA + BO (50%) AB + AB (50%) AB + BB (50%) AO + BB (50%) AB + BO (25%) AO + BO (25%)	AB	AB	AB only	A, B, AB, O ("universal recipient")
OO + OO (100%) AO + OO (50%) BO + OO (50%) AO + AO (25%) AO + BO (25%) BO + BO (25%)	OO	O	A, B, AB, O ("universal donor")	O only

*Blood type is not a sex-linked trait, so any of these pairs can be either mother-plus-father or father-plus-mother.
Source: Adapted from Hartl & Jones, 1999.

Odds of Down Syndrome by Maternal Age and Gestational Age (Chapter 2)

The odds of any given fetus, at the end of the first trimester, having three chromosomes at the 21st site (trisomy 21) and thus having Down syndrome are shown in the 10-weeks column. The data in this chart show the chances of Down syndrome before widespread pre-natal testing and induced abortion. Many Down syndrome fetuses are spontaneously aborted. There is no year when the odds suddenly increase (age 35 is an arbitrary cut-off). Other chromosomal abnormalities in fetuses also increase with mother's age, but the rate of spontaneous abortion is higher, so births of babies with chromosomal defects is not the norm, even for women over age 45.

Age (yrs)	Gestation (weeks) 10	Gestation (weeks) 35	Live Births
20	1/804	1/1,464	1/1,527
21	1/793	1/1,445	1/1,507
22	1/780	1/1,421	1/1,482
23	1/762	1/1,389	1/1,448
24	1/740	1/1,348	1/1,406
25	1/712	1/1,297	1/1,352
26	1/677	1/1,233	1/1,286
27	1/635	1/1,157	1/1,206
28	1/586	1/1,068	1/1,113
29	1/531	1/967	1/1,008
30	1/471	1/858	1/895
31	1/409	1/745	1/776
32	1/347	1/632	1/659
33	1/288	1/525	1/547
34	1/235	1/427	1/446
35	1/187	1/342	1/356
36	1/148	1/269	1/280
37	1/115	1/209	1/218
38	1/88	1/160	1/167
39	1/67	1/122	1/128
40	1/51	1/93	1/97
41	1/38	1/70	1/73
42	1/29	1/52	1/55
43	1/21	1/39	1/41
44	1/16	1/29	1/30

Source: Snijders & Nicolaides, 1996.

Saving Young Lives: Childhood Immunizations (Chapter 3)

Recommended Immunization Schedule for Persons Aged 0–6 Years, United States, 2009*

Vaccine ▼　　　　　　　　Age ▶	Birth	1 month	2 months	4 months	6 months	12 months	15 months	18 months	19–23 months	2–3 years	4–6 years
Hepatitis B	Hep B	Hep B			Hep B						
Rotavirus			RV	RV	RV						
Diphtheria, Tetanus, and Pertussis			DTaP	DTaP	DTaP		DTaP				DTaP
Haemophilus influenzae type b			Hib	Hib	*Hib*	Hib					
Pneumococcal			PCV	PCV	PCV	PCV				PPSV	
Inactivated Poliovirus			IPV	IPV	IPV						IPV
Influenza					Influenza (Yearly)						
Measles, Mumps, Rubella						MMR					MMR
Varicella						Varicella					Varicella
Hepatitis A						HepA (2 doses)				HepA Series	
Meningococcal										MCV	

*This chart summarizes the recommended ages or (as represented by the gold bars) age ranges for routine administration of currently licensed vaccines for children from birth to 6 years of age. For details about the schedules (including catchup schedules) for administering these vaccines, and for specific recommendations about immunizing children in certain high-risk groups, see www.cdc.gov/vaccines/recs/schedules and consult a doctor or other health-care professional.

Source: Centers for Disease Control and Prevention, 2009, August 11.

ANSWER TO OBSERVATION QUIZ
(from page A-2) Asian Americans, whose share of the U.S. population has quadrupled in the past 30 years. Latinos are increasing most rapidly in numbers, but not in proportion. ●

First Sounds and First Words: Similarities Among Many Languages (Chapter 3)

	Baby's word for:	
Language	Mother	Father
English	mama, mommy	dada, daddy
Spanish	mama	papa
French	maman, mama	papa
Italian	mamma	babbo, papa
Latvian	mama	te-te
Syrian Arabic	mama	baba
Bantu	ba-mama	taata
Swahili	mama	baba
Sanskrit	nana	tata
Hebrew	ema	abba
Korean	oma	apa

Which Mothers Breast-feed? (Chapter 4)

Differentiating excellent from destructive mothering is not easy, once the child's basic needs for food and protection are met. However, as the Jacob example in Chapter 4 makes clear, psychosocial development depends on responsive parent–infant relationships. Breast-feeding is one sign of intimacy between mother and infant.

Regions of the world differ dramatically in rates of breast-feeding, with the highest worldwide in Southeast Asia, where half of all 2-year-olds are still breast-fed. In the United States, factors that affect the likelihood of breast-feeding are ethnicity, maternal age, marital status, and education.

Provisional Breast-feeding Rates by Sociodemographic Factors, Among Children Born in 2006

	Ever breast-feeding	Breast-feeding at 6 months	Breast-feeding at 12 months
U.S. overall	73.9%	43.4%	22.7%
Race/ethnicity			
Native American	69.9	38.5	21.8
Asian or Pacific islander	83.1	55.1	35.1
Hispanic or Latino	82.1	48.5	27.2
African American (non-Hispanic)	56.5	27.5	12.3
European (non-Hispanic)	73.8	44.3	22.6
Birth order			
First born	73.6	45.4	23.8
Not first born	74.4	41.0	21.5
Mother's age			
Less than 20	55.6	24.0	7.8
20–29	69.2	34.1	17.3
30+	78.0	50.4	27.0
Mother's education			
Less than high school	68.3	38.0	21.1
High school graduate	64.9	33.3	16.6
Some college	75.3	41.9	21.8
College graduate	86.3	58.5	30.8
Mother's marital status			
Married	79.9	50.4	26.6
Unmarried*	60.6	27.6	14.0

*Unmarried includes never married, widowed, separated, and divorced.
Source: Adapted from CDC's National Immunization Survey, www.cdc.gov/breastfeeding/data/NIS_data/index.htm, retrieved September 3, 2009.

Height Gains from Birth to Age 18 (Chapter 5)

The range of height (on this page) and weight (see page A-7) of children in the United States. The columns labeled "50th" (the fiftieth percentile) show the average; the columns labeled "90th" (the ninetieth percentile) show the size of children taller and heavier than 90 percent of their contemporaries; and the columns labeled "10th" (the tenth percentile) show the size of children who are taller than only 10 percent of their peers. Note that girls are slightly shorter, on average, than boys.

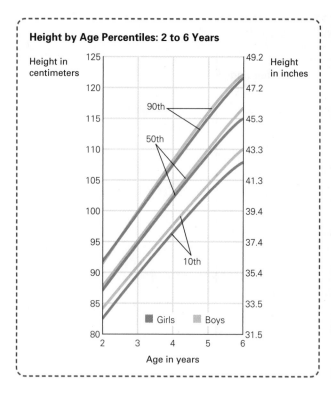

Height by Age Percentiles: 2 to 6 Years

Same Data, Different Form

The columns of numbers in the table at the right provide detailed and precise information about height ranges for every year of childhood. The illustration above shows the same information in graphic form for ages 2–6. The same is done for weight ranges on page A-7. Ages 2–6 are singled out because that is the period during which a child's eating habits are set. Which form of data presentation do you think is easier to understand?

Length in Centimeters (and Inches)

AGE	Boys: percentiles			Girls: percentiles		
	10th	50th	90th	10th	50th	90th
Birth	47.5 (18¾)	50.5 (20)	53.5 (21)	46.5 (18¼)	49.9 (19¾)	52.0 (20½)
1 month	51.3 (20¼)	54.6 (21½)	57.7 (22¾)	50.2 (19¾)	53.5 (21)	56.1 (22)
3 months	57.7 (22¾)	61.1 (24)	64.5 (25½)	56.2 (22¼)	59.5 (23½)	62.7 (24¾)
6 months	64.4 (25¼)	67.8 (26¾)	71.3 (28)	62.6 (24¾)	65.9 (26)	69.4 (27¼)
9 months	69.1 (27¼)	72.3 (28½)	75.9 (30)	67.0 (26½)	70.4 (27¾)	74.0 (29¼)
12 months	72.8 (28¾)	76.1 (30)	79.8 (31½)	70.8 (27¾)	74.3 (29¼)	78.0 (30¾)
18 months	78.7 (31)	82.4 (32½)	86.6 (34)	77.2 (30½)	80.9 (31¾)	85.0 (33½)
24 months	83.5 (32¾)	87.6 (34½)	92.2 (36¼)	82.5 (32½)	86.5 (34)	90.8 (35¾)
3 years	90.3 (35½)	94.9 (37¼)	100.1 (39½)	89.3 (35¼)	94.1 (37)	99.0 (39)
4 years	97.3 (38¼)	102.9 (40½)	108.2 (42½)	96.4 (38)	101.6 (40)	106.6 (42)
5 years	103.7 (40¾)	109.9 (43¼)	115.4 (45½)	102.7 (40½)	108.4 (42¾)	113.8 (44¾)
6 years	109.6 (43¼)	116.1 (45¾)	121.9 (48)	108.4 (42¾)	114.6 (45)	120.8 (47½)
7 years	115.0 (45¼)	121.7 (48)	127.9 (50¼)	113.6 (44¾)	120.6 (47½)	127.6 (50¼)
8 years	120.2 (47¼)	127.0 (50)	133.6 (52½)	118.7 (46¾)	126.4 (49¾)	134.2 (52¾)
9 years	125.2 (49¼)	132.2 (52)	139.4 (55)	123.9 (48¾)	132.2 (52)	140.7 (55½)
10 years	130.1 (51¼)	137.5 (54¼)	145.5 (57¼)	129.5 (51)	138.3 (54½)	147.2 (58)
11 years	135.1 (53¼)	143.33 (56½)	152.1 (60)	135.6 (53½)	144.8 (57)	153.7 (60½)
12 years	140.3 (55¼)	149.7 (59)	159.4 (62¾)	142.3 (56)	151.5 (59¾)	160.0 (63)
13 years	145.8 (57½)	156.5 (61½)	167.0 (65¾)	148.0 (58¼)	157.1 (61¾)	165.3 (65)
14 years	151.8 (59¾)	63.1 (64¼)	173.8 (68½)	151.5 (59¾)	160.4 (63¼)	168.7 (66½)
15 years	158.2 (62¼)	169.0 (66½)	178.9 (70½)	153.2 (60¼)	161.8 (63¾)	170.5 (67¼)
16 years	163.9 (64½)	173.5 (68¼)	182.4 (71¾)	154.1 (60¾)	162.4 (64)	171.1 (67¼)
17 years	167.7 (66)	176.2 (69¼)	184.4 (72½)	155.1 (61)	163.1 (64¼)	171.2 (67½)
18 years	168.7 (66½)	176.8 (69½)	185.3 (73)	156.0 (61½)	163.7 (64½)	171.0 (67½

Source: These data are those of the National Center for Health Statistics (NCHS), Health Resources Administration, DHHS. They were based on studies of The Fels Research Institute, Yellow Springs, Ohio. These data were first made available with the help of William M. Moore, M.D., of Ross Laboratories, who supplied the conversion from metric measurements to approximate inches and pounds. This help is gratefully acknowledged.

Weight Gains from Birth to Age 18 (Chapter 5)

These height and weight charts present rough guidelines; a child might differ from these norms and be quite healthy and normal. However, if a particular child shows a discrepancy between height and weight (for instance, at the 90th percentile in height but only the 20th percentile in weight) or is much larger or smaller than most children the same age, a pediatrician should see if disease, malnutrition, or genetic abnormality is part of the reason.

Weight by Age Percentiles: 2 to 6 Years

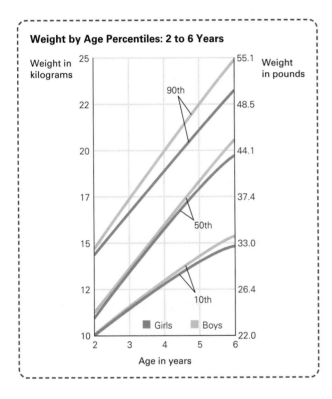

Comparisons

Notice that the height trajectories for boys and girls on page A-6 are much closer together than the weight trajectories shown above. By age 18, the height range amounts to only about 6 inches, but there is a difference of about 65 pounds between the 10th and the 90th percentiles.

● **FOR DEEPER REFLECTION**

How can this discrepancy between height and weight ranges be explained?

Weight in Kilograms (and Pounds)

| AGE | Boys: percentiles | | | Girls: percentiles | | |
	10th	50th	90th	10th	50th	90th
Birth	2.78 (6¼)	3.27 (7¼)	3.82 (8½)	2.58 (5¾)	3.23 (7)	3.64 (8)
1 month	3.43 (7½)	4.29 (9½)	5.14 (11¼)	3.22 (7)	3.98 (8¾)	4.65 (10¼)
3 months	4.78 (10½)	5.98 (13¼)	7.14 (15¾)	4.47 (9¾)	5.40 (12)	6.39 (14)
6 months	6.61 (14½)	7.85 (17¼)	9.10 (20)	6.12 (13½)	7.21 (16)	8.38 (18½)
9 months	7.95 (17½)	9.18 (20¼)	10.49 (23¼)	7.34 (16¼)	8.56 (18¾)	9.83 (21¾)
12 months	8.84 (19½)	10.15 (22½)	11.54 (25½)	8.19 (18)	9.53 (21)	10.87 (24)
18 months	9.92 (21¾)	11.47 (25¼)	13.05 (28¾)	9.30 (20½)	10.82 (23¾)	12.30 (27)
24 months	10.85 (24)	12.59 (27¾)	14.29 (31½)	10.26 (22½)	11.90 (26¼)	13.57 (30)
3 years	12.58 (27¾)	14.62 (32¼)	16.95 (37¼)	12.26 (27)	14.10 (31)	16.54 (36½)
4 years	14.24 (31½)	16.69 (36¾)	19.32 (42½)	13.84 (30½)	15.96 (35¼)	18.93 (41¾)
5 years	15.96 (35¼)	18.67 (41¼)	21.70 (47¾)	15.26 (33¾)	17.66 (39)	21.23 (46¾)
6 years	17.72 (39)	20.69 (45½)	24.31 (53½)	16.72 (36¾)	19.52 (43)	23.89 (52¾)
7 years	19.53 (43)	22.85 (50¼)	27.36 (60¼)	18.39 (40½)	21.84 (48¼)	27.39 (60½)
8 years	21.39 (47¼)	25.30 (55¾)	31.06 (68½)	20.45 (45)	24.84 (54¾)	32.04 (70¾)
9 years	23.33 (51½)	28.13 (62)	35.57 (78½)	22.92 (50½)	28.46 (62¾)	37.60 (83)
10 years	25.52 (56¼)	31.44 (69¼)	40.80 (90)	25.76 (56¾)	32.55 (71¾)	43.70 (96¼)
11 years	28.17 (62)	35.30 (77¾)	46.57 (102¾)	28.97 (63¾)	36.95 (81½)	49.96 (110¼)
12 years	31.46 (69¼)	39.78 (87¾)	52.73 (116¼)	32.53 (71¼)	41.53 (91½)	55.99 (123½)
13 years	35.60 (78½)	44.95 (99)	59.12 (130¼)	36.35 (80¼)	46.10 (101¾)	61.45 (135½)
14 years	40.64 (89½)	50.77 (112)	65.57 (144½)	40.11 (88½)	50.28 (110¾)	66.04 (145½)
15 years	46.06 (101½)	56.71 (125)	71.91 (158½)	43.38 (95¾)	53.68 (118¼)	69.64 (153¼)
16 years	51.16 (112¾)	62.10 (137)	77.97 (172)	45.78 (101)	55.89 (123¼)	71.68 (158)
17 years	55.28 (121¾)	66.31 (146¼)	83.58 (184¼)	47.04 (103¾)	56.69 (125)	72.38 (159½)
18 years	57.89 (127½)	68.88 (151¾)	88.41 (195)	47.47 (104¾)	56.62 (124¾)	72.25 (159¼)

Source: Data are those of the National Center for Health Statistics, Health Resources Administration, DHHS, collected in its Health Examination Surveys.

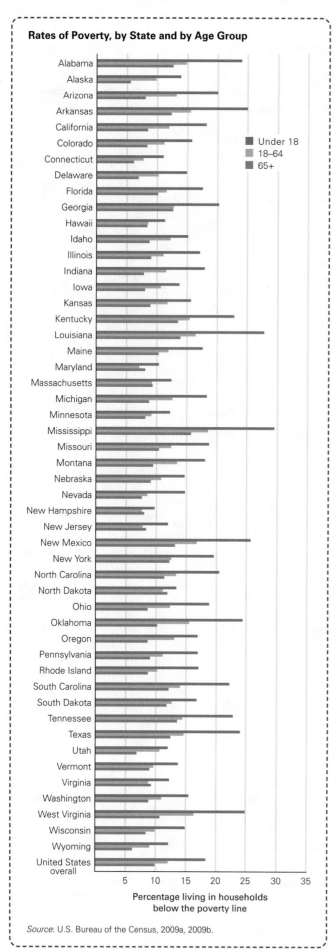

Rates of Poverty, by State and by Age Group

Legend:
- Under 18
- 18–64
- 65+

Percentage living in households below the poverty line

Source: U.S. Bureau of the Census, 2009a, 2009b.

Children Are the Poorest Americans (Chapter 6)

It probably comes as no surprise that the rate of poverty is twice as high in some states as in others. What is surprising is how much the rates vary between age groups within the same state.

OBSERVATION QUIZ

In which nine states is the proportion of poor children more than twice as high as the proportion of poor people over age 65? (see answer, page A-10) →

DSM-IV-TR Criteria for Attention-Deficit/Hyperactivity Disorder (ADHD)
(Chapter 7)
Many other childhood disorders have some of the same symptoms given here for ADHD.
Differentiating one problem from another is the main purpose of DSM-IV-TR. That is no easy
task, which is one reason the book is now in its fourth major revision and is more than 900
pages long. Those pages include not only the type of diagnostic criteria shown here but also
discussions of prevalence, age and gender statistics, cultural aspects, and prognosis for
about 400 disorders or subtypes, 40 of which appear primarily in childhood.

Diagnostic Criteria for Attention-Deficit/Hyperactivity Disorder

A. Either (1) or (2):

(1) Six (or more) of the following symptoms of **inattention** have persisted for at
least 6 months to a degree that is maladaptive and inconsistent with developmental level:

INATTENTION

(a) often fails to give close attention to details or makes careless mistakes in
schoolwork, work, or other activities
(b) often has difficulty sustaining attention in tasks or play activities
(c) often does not seem to listen when spoken to directly
(d) often does not follow through on instructions and fails to finish schoolwork, chores, or duties in the workplace (not due to oppositional behavior
or failure to understand instructions)
(e) often has difficulty organizing tasks and activities
(f) often avoids, dislikes, or is reluctant to engage in tasks that require sustained
mental effort (such as schoolwork or homework)
(g) often loses things necessary for tasks or activities (e.g., toys, school assignments, pencils, books, or tools)
(h) is often easily distracted by extraneous stimuli
(i) is often forgetful in daily activities

(2) Six (or more) of the following symptoms of **hyperactivity-impulsivity** have
persisted for at least 6 months to a degree that is maladaptive and inconsistent
with developmental level:

HYPERACTIVITY

(a) often fidgets with hands or feet or squirms in seat
(b) often leaves seat in classroom or in other situations in which remaining
seated is expected
(c) often runs about or climbs excessively in situations in which it is inappropriate (in adolescents or adults, may be limited to subjective feelings of
restlessness)
(d) often has difficulty playing or engaging in leisure activities quietly
(e) is often "on the go" or often acts as if "driven by a motor"
(f) often talks excessively

IMPULSIVITY

(g) often blurts out answers before questions have been completed

(h) often has difficulty awaiting turn

(i) often interrupts or intrudes on others (e.g., butts into conversations or games)

B. Some hyperactive-impulsive or inattentive symptoms that caused impairment were present before age 7 years.

C. Some impairment from the symptoms is present in two or more settings (e.g., at school [or work] and at home).

D. There must be clear evidence of clinically significant impairment in social, academic, or occupational functioning.

Changes in the Average Weekly Amount of Time Spent by 6- to 11-Year-Olds in Various Activities (Chapter 8)

Facts are the bedrock of science, but facts can be presented in many ways, with many interpretations. Your opinions about these facts reflect your values, which may be quite different from those of the parents and teachers of these children.

	Average Amount of Time Spent in Activity, per Week, United States			
Activity	In 1981	In 1997	In 2004	Change in Time Spent Since 1981
School	25 hrs, 17 min.	33 hrs, 52 min.	33 hrs, 33 min.	+8 hrs, 16 min.
Organized sports	3 hrs, 5 min.	4 hrs, 56 min.	2 hrs, 28 min.	−32 min.
Studying	1 hr, 46 min.	2 hrs, 50 min.	3 hrs, 25 min.	+1 hr, 21 min.
Reading	57 min.	1 hr, 15 min.	1 hr, 28 min.	+31 min.
Being outdoors	1 hr, 17 min.	39 min.	56 min.	−21 min.
Playing	12 hrs, 52 min.	10 hrs, 5 min.	10 hrs, 25 min.	−2 hrs, 27 min.
Watching TV	15 hrs, 34 min.	13 hrs, 7 min.	14 hrs, 19 min.	−1 hr, 15 min.

Percentage Change in Time Spent in Activity, 1981–2004

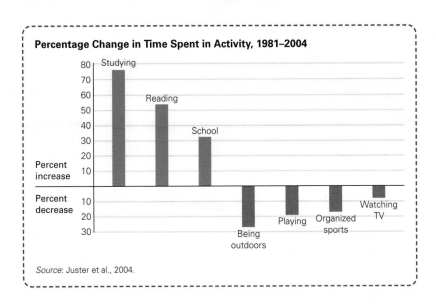

Source: Juster et al., 2004.

Who Is Raising the Children? (Chapter 8)

Most children still live in households with a male/female couple, who may be the children's married or unmarried biological parents, grandparents, stepparents, foster parents, or adoptive parents. However, the proportion of households headed by single parents has risen—by 500 percent for single fathers and by almost 200 percent for single mothers. (In 2008, 52 percent of U.S. households had *no* children under age 18.)

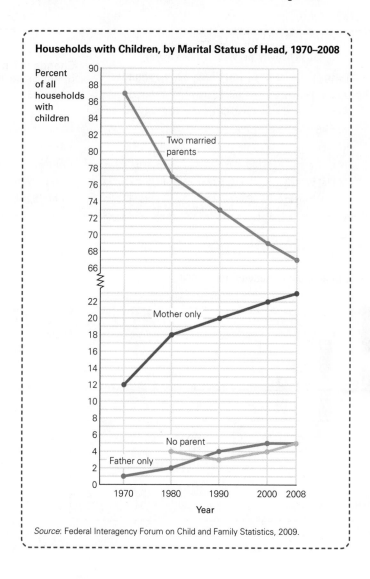

Households with Children, by Marital Status of Head, 1970–2008

Source: Federal Interagency Forum on Child and Family Statistics, 2009.

Smoking Behavior Among U.S. High School Students, 1991–2007 (Chapter 9)

The data in these two tables reveal many trends. For example, do you see that African American adolescents are much less likely to smoke than Hispanics or European Americans, but that this racial advantage is decreasing? Are you surprised to see that White females smoke more than White males?

Percentage of High School Students Who Reported Smoking Cigarettes

Smoking Behavior	1991	1995	1999	2003	2007
Lifetime (ever smoked)	70.1	71.3	70.4	58.4	50.3
Current (smoked at least once in past 30 days)	27.5	34.8	34.8	21.9	20.0
Current frequent (smoked 20 or more times in past 30 days)	12.7	16.1	16.8	9.7	8.1

Percentage of High School Students Who Reported Current Smoking, by Sex, Ethnicity, and Grade

Characteristic	1991	1995	1999	2003	2007
Sex					
Female	27.3	34.3	34.9	21.9	18.7
Male	27.6	35.4	34.7	21.8	21.3
Ethnicity					
White, non-Hispanic	30.9	38.3	38.6	24.9	23.2
Female	*31.7*	*39.8*	*39.1*	*26.6*	*22.5*
Male	*30.2*	*37.0*	*38.2*	*23.3*	*23.8*
Black, non-Hispanic	12.6	19.2	19.7	15.1	11.6
Female	*11.3*	*12.2*	*17.7*	*10.8*	*8.4*
Male	*14.1*	*27.8*	*21.8*	*19.3*	*14.9*
Hispanic	25.3	34.0	32.7	18.4	16.7
Female	*22.9*	*32.9*	*31.5*	*17.7*	*14.6*
Male	*27.9*	*34.9*	*34.0*	*19.1*	*18.7*
Grade					
9th	23.2	31.2	27.6	17.4	14.3
10th	25.2	33.1	34.7	21.8	19.6
11th	31.6	35.9	36.0	23.6	26.5
12th	30.1	38.2	42.8	26.2	20.0

Source: MMWR, 2008, June 6.

Major Sexually Transmitted Infections: Some Basics (Chapter 9)
These and other STIs, if left untreated, may lead to serious reproductive and other health problems or even, as with HIV/AIDS and syphilis, to death. STIs can be avoided by consistently using condoms, having sex only in a relationship with an uninfected partner, or abstaining from sex.

Sexually Transmitted Infection (and Cause)	Symptoms	Treatment
Chlamydia (bacterium)	The most frequently reported bacterial STI in the United States. In women, abnormal vaginal discharge or burning sensation when urinating; may be followed by pain in low abdomen or low back, nausea, fever, pain during intercourse, or bleeding between menstrual periods. In men, discharge from penis or burning sensation when urinating.	Antibiotics
Genital HPV infection (virus)	One of the most common STIs in the world. Causes no symptoms or health problems in most people, but certain types may cause genital warts and others can cause cervical cancer in women and other cancers of the genitals in both sexes.	A vaccine is now available and is recommended for 11- and 12-year-old girls who are not yet sexually active.
Genital herpes (virus)	Blisters on or around the genitals or rectum that break and leave sores, which may take 2 to 4 weeks to heal; some people may experience fever, swollen glands, and other flu-like symptoms. Later outbreaks are usually less severe and shorter. Many people never have sores and may take years to realize they are infected. May lead to potentially fatal infections in babies and makes infected person more susceptible to HIV infection.	There is no vaccine or cure, but antiviral medications can shorten and prevent outbreaks.
Gonorrhea (bacterium)	Some men and most women have no symptoms. In men, a burning sensation when urinating; a white, yellow, or green discharge from the penis; painful or swollen testicles. In women, symptoms—pain or burning during urination, increased vaginal discharge, vaginal bleeding between periods—may be so mild or nonspecific that they are mistaken for a bladder or vaginal infection. May cause pelvic inflammatory disease (PID) in women and infertility in both sexes. Infected person can more easily contract HIV.	Antibiotics
Pelvic inflammatory disease (PID) (various bacteria)	A common and serious complication in women who have certain other STIs, especially chlamydia and gonorrhea. Pain in lower abdomen, fever, unusual vaginal discharge that may have a foul odor, painful intercourse, painful urination, irregular menstrual bleeding, and (rarely) pain in the right upper abdomen. May lead to blocked fallopian tubes, causing infertility.	Administration of at least two antibiotics that are effective against a wide range of infectious agents. In severe cases, surgery.

Sexually Transmitted Infection (and Cause)	Symptoms	Treatment
HIV/AIDS (virus)	Infection with the human immunodeficiency virus (HIV) eventually leads to acquired immune deficiency syndrome (AIDS). Infection with other STIs increases a person's likelihood of both acquiring and transmitting HIV. Soon after exposure, some people have flu-like symptoms: fever, headache, tiredness, swollen lymph glands. Months or years later, when the virus has weakened the immune system, the person may experience lack of energy, weight loss, frequent fevers and sweats, yeast infections, skin rashes, short-term memory loss. Symptoms of full-blown AIDS include certain cancers (Kaposi sarcoma and lymphomas), seizures, vision loss, and coma. A leading cause of death among young adults in many nations.	There is no vaccine or cure, but antiretroviral drugs can slow the growth of the virus; antibiotics can cure some secondary infections, and various treatments are available to relieve painful or unpleasant symptoms.
Syphilis (bacterium)	Symptoms may not appear for years. *Primary stage:* One or more sores (*chancres*) a few days or weeks after exposure. *Secondary stage:* Skin rash, lesions of mucous membranes, fever, swollen lymph glands, sore throat, patchy hair loss, headaches, weight loss, muscle aches, fatigue. *Latent stage:* Primary and secondary symptoms disappear, but infection remains in the body. *Late stage (10 to 20 years after first infection):* Damage to brain, nerves, eyes, heart, blood vessels, liver, bones, and joints, progressing to difficulty coordinating muscle movements, paralysis, numbness, blindness, dementia.	Penicillin injections will kill the syphilis bacterium and prevent further damage but cannot repair damage already done.
Trichomoniasis (*Trichomonas vaginalis*, a single-celled protozoan parasite)	Most men have no symptoms, but some may temporarily have an irritation inside the penis, mild discharge, or slight burning after urination or ejaculation. Women may have a frothy, yellow-green, strong-smelling vaginal discharge and may experience discomfort during intercourse and urination; irritation and itching of the genital area; and, rarely, lower abdominal pain.	A single oral dose of metronidazole or tinidazole

Source: Centers for Disease Control and Prevention, 2009, July 14.

Sexual Behaviors of U.S. High School Students, 2005 (Chapter 10)

These percentages, as high as they may seem, are actually lower than they were in the early 1990s. (States not listed did not participate fully in the survey.) The data in this table reflect responses from students in the 9th to 12th grades. When only high school seniors are surveyed, the percentages are higher. In every state, more than half of all high school seniors say they have had sexual intercourse, and about 20 percent have had four or more sex partners.

State	Ever had sexual intercourse (%)			Had first sexual intercourse before age 13 (%)			Has had four or more sex partners during lifetime (%)			Is currently sexually active (%)		
	Female	Male	Total	Female	Male	Total	Female	Male	Total	Female	Male	Total
Alabama	46.8	54.6	**50.6**	4.9	12.8	**8.8**	9.5	21.1	**15.1**	37.7	38.0	**38.0**
Arizona	42.8	42.9	**42.8**	3.6	7.9	**5.7**	10.5	16.5	**13.5**	32.9	27.4	**30.2**
Arkansas	53.6	54.3	**54.0**	5.5	12.7	**9.2**	15.8	21.0	**18.3**	42.3	38.8	**40.6**
Colorado	37.2	41.3	**39.3**	2.3	7.0	**4.7**	8.7	13.9	**11.3**	29.3	29.4	**29.5**
Delaware	51.3	58.6	**55.1**	4.5	16.9	**10.8**	15.7	22.1	**19.1**	39.8	38.6	**39.2**
Florida	47.1	53.5	**50.5**	4.0	13.6	**8.8**	11.5	21.1	**16.3**	35.3	36.7	**36.2**
Hawaii	37.6	33.7	**35.7**	4.4	5.8	**5.1**	7.9	10.0	**9.0**	29.4	18.7	**24.1**
Idaho	39.5	37.4	**38.5**	4.2	9.0	**6.7**	—	—	**—**	—	—	**—**
Iowa	44.0	43.0	**43.5**	3.0	5.4	**4.2**	11.8	13.7	**12.7**	34.5	31.2	**32.8**
Kansas	44.3	45.3	**44.8**	2.8	7.9	**5.5**	11.7	14.7	**13.3**	36.3	30.0	**33.3**
Kentucky	44.6	48.0	**46.3**	4.1	11.5	**7.9**	10.6	16.6	**13.6**	34.5	32.5	**33.5**
Maine	46.4	43.0	**44.8**	3.0	6.1	**4.5**	10.6	13.4	**11.9**	36.9	30.1	**33.5**
Massachusetts	42.9	47.9	**45.4**	2.2	8.1	**5.2**	10.5	14.5	**12.6**	35.4	32.7	**34.1**
Michigan	41.2	43.2	**42.2**	3.9	8.5	**6.2**	9.6	14.1	**11.8**	31.1	27.7	**29.4**
Missouri	47.1	46.3	**46.7**	3.5	8.4	**5.9**	11.3	16.7	**14.0**	34.7	31.5	**33.2**
Montana	42.6	44.4	**43.6**	2.8	7.0	**5.1**	12.5	13.3	**13.1**	32.4	30.0	**31.2**
Nebraska	40.9	40.6	**40.8**	3.3	5.5	**4.4**	12.2	11.7	**11.9**	29.6	30.2	**29.9**
Nevada	39.6	48.5	**44.1**	3.8	11.5	**7.7**	11.5	18.7	**15.2**	30.6	30.8	**30.8**
New York	39.3	44.6	**42.0**	3.0	8.6	**5.8**	8.6	16.3	**12.5**	29.2	29.0	**29.2**
North Carolina	47.6	54.3	**50.8**	5.0	11.2	**8.1**	13.9	20.6	**17.2**	35.3	39.1	**37.1**
North Dakota	40.7	41.6	**41.2**	1.7	4.7	**3.3**	10.7	12.0	**11.3**	33.3	31.4	**32.4**
Ohio	46.5	49.0	**47.8**	3.5	7.2	**5.3**	15.1	18.5	**16.9**	35.5	37.2	**36.4**
Oklahoma	48.2	50.2	**49.3**	4.0	8.9	**6.5**	14.3	21.2	**17.8**	37.0	35.4	**36.3**
Rhode Island	44.9	48.3	**46.7**	2.3	9.4	**5.9**	9.3	16.8	**13.0**	36.4	36.6	**36.5**
South Carolina	49.7	55.1	**52.3**	4.8	13.9	**4.7**	14.5	23.5	**18.8**	38.2	36.7	**37.5**
South Dakota	47.1	41.4	**44.3**	3.6	8.0	**5.8**	16.9	11.5	**14.2**	33.7	28.7	**31.2**
Tennessee	55.6	53.7	**54.7**	5.8	11.2	**8.5**	14.7	19.1	**17.0**	41.1	35.3	**38.2**
Texas	49.6	55.2	**52.5**	4.0	10.7	**7.4**	13.1	19.5	**16.3**	37.5	37.6	**37.6**
West Virginia	51.1	53.8	**52.5**	3.7	11.0	**7.3**	11.0	18.5	**14.8**	41.1	37.3	**39.3**
Wisconsin	40.3	40.2	**40.3**	2.6	5.0	**3.9**	9.9	10.9	**10.4**	31.8	27.3	**29.5**
Wyoming	47.4	46.9	**47.1**	3.7	6.6	**5.2**	15.2	15.9	**15.5**	37.6	32.0	**34.7**
U.S. median	**44.9**	**46.3**	**44.8**	**3.6**	**8.4**	**5.8**	**11.3**	**16.3**	**13.6**	**35.3**	**31.4**	**33.3**

Source: National Center for Chronic Disease Prevention and Health Promotion, Youth Risk Behavior Surveillance System, *MMWR*, June 9, 2006.

Too Young for Motherhood? (Chapter 11)

These numbers show dramatic shifts in family planning, with teenage births continuing to fall and births after age 30 rising again. These data come from the United States, but the same trends are apparent in almost every nation. Can you tell when contraception became widely available?

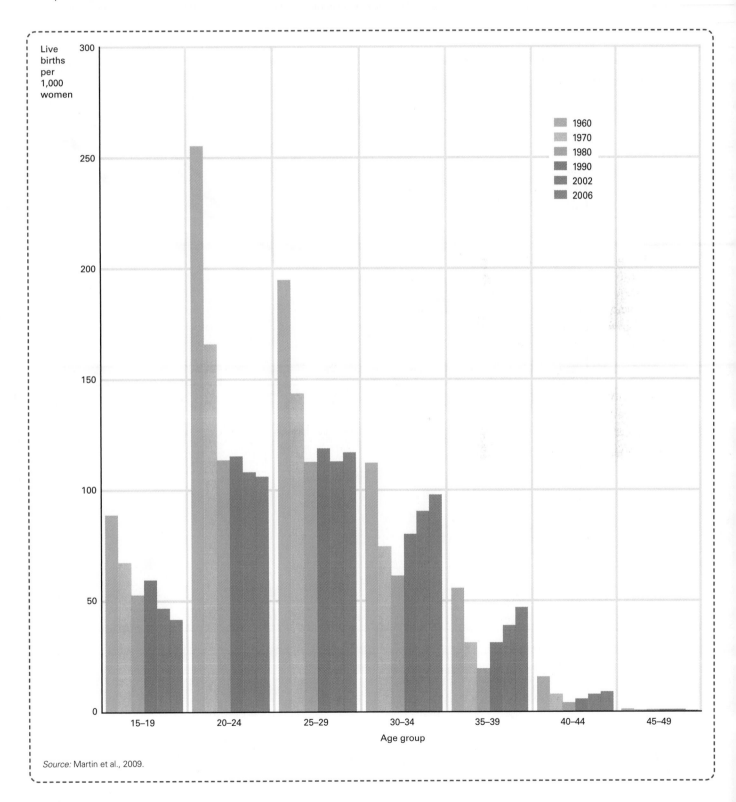

Source: Martin et al., 2009.

Education Affects Income (Chapter 11)

Although there is some debate about the cognitive benefits of college education, there is no doubt about the financial benefits. No matter what a person's ethnicity or gender is, an associate's degree more than doubles his or her income compared to that of someone who has not completed high school. These data are for the United States; similar trends, often with steeper increases, are found in other nations.

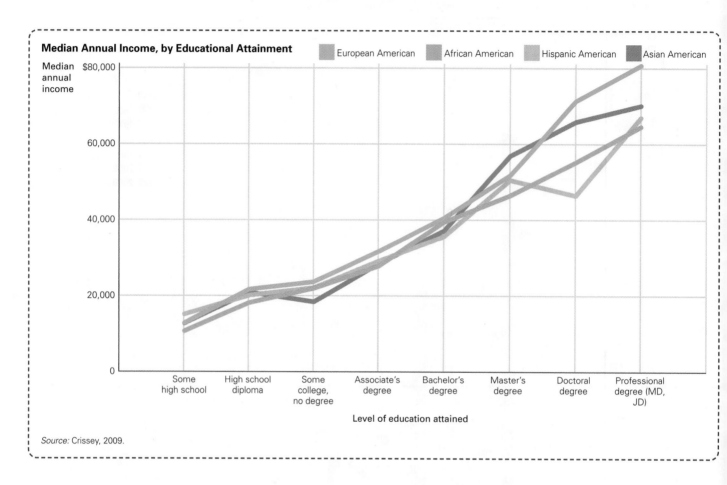

Median Annual Income, by Educational Attainment

Legend: European American, African American, Hispanic American, Asian American

Source: Crissey, 2009.

Obesity in the United States (Chapter 12)

About a third of all adults in the United States have a BMI of 30 or higher, which is not just overweight but seriously too heavy. Other data show that another third are overweight, again with increases over the past decades.

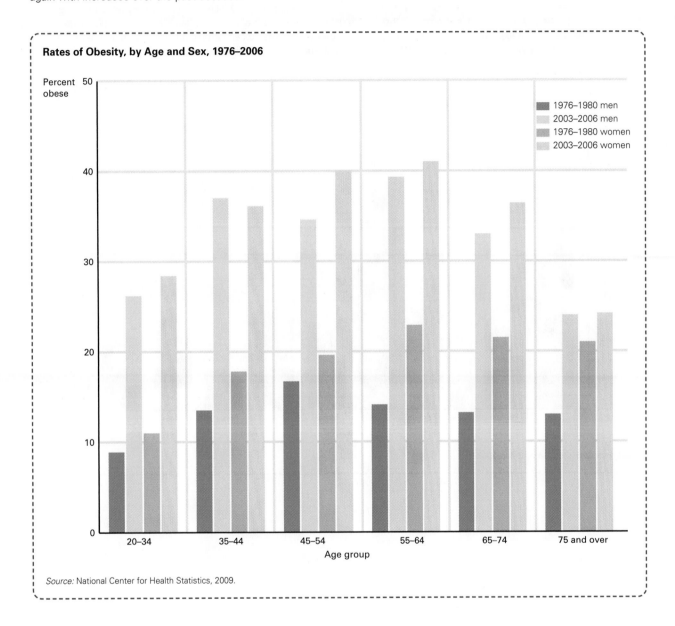

Rates of Obesity, by Age and Sex, 1976–2006

Source: National Center for Health Statistics, 2009.

Dying of Lung Cancer: It's Not Just Genes and Gender (Chapter 12)

For lung cancer as well as most other diseases, the male death rate is markedly higher than the female death rate in the United States. Moreover, the death rate for African Americans is almost twice the average, and for Asian Americans it is almost half the average. Genes and gender do not explain these discrepancies, however. As you can see, White women are at greater risk than Hispanic or Native American men, and the rate for Black men went down as the rate for some other groups rose. (These are "age-adjusted" rates, which means that they reflect the fact that more Asians reach old age and fewer Native Americans do. In other words, the sex and ethnic differences shown here are real—not artifacts of the age distribution.)

Lung Cancer Death Rates, by Ethnicity and Gender

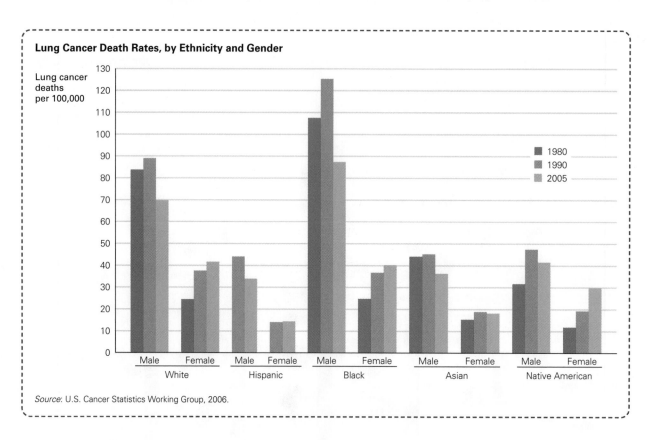

Source: U.S. Cancer Statistics Working Group, 2006.

Continuing Education (Chapter 12)

This chart shows the percentage of adults (aged 24–64) involved in job-related training.

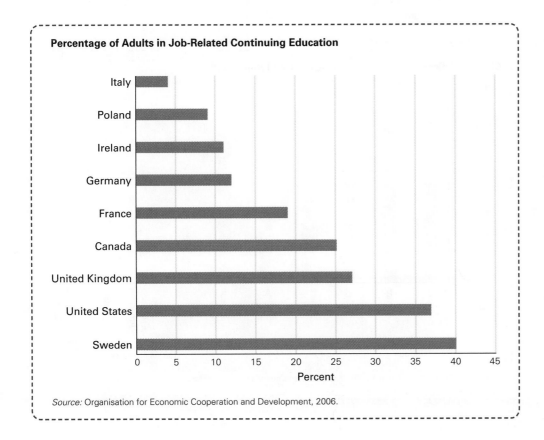

Percentage of Adults in Job-Related Continuing Education

Source: Organisation for Economic Cooperation and Development, 2006.

Grandparents Parenting Grandchildren (Chapter 13)

In 2007, 3.6 percent of U.S. households included grandparents living with grandchildren. In 40 percent of those households, 2.5 million grandparents were directly responsible for the care of their grandchildren.

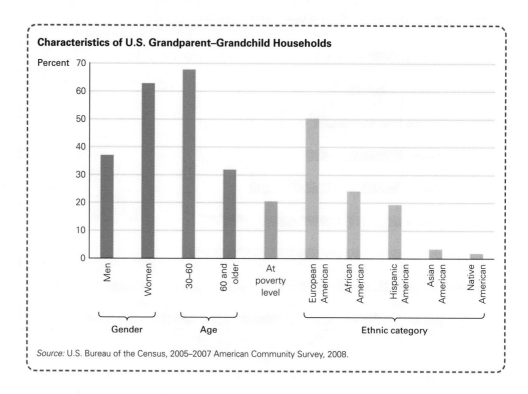

Characteristics of U.S. Grandparent–Grandchild Households

Source: U.S. Bureau of the Census, 2005–2007 American Community Survey, 2008.

Trouble with Personal Care (Chapter 14)

As you see, with age people become more likely to need help with daily activities, such as taking a shower, getting dressed, and even getting out of bed. What is not shown is who provides that help. Usually it is a husband or wife, sometimes a grown child (who often is elderly), and, only for the oldest and least capable, the aides in a nursing home.

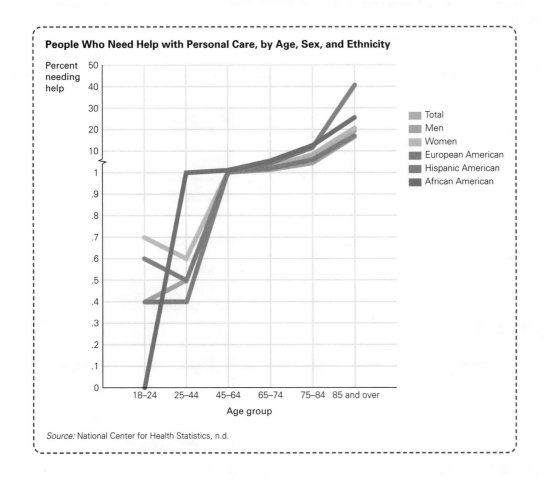

People Who Need Help with Personal Care, by Age, Sex, and Ethnicity

Legend:
- Total
- Men
- Women
- European American
- Hispanic American
- African American

Y-axis: Percent needing help

X-axis: Age group — 18–24, 25–44, 45–64, 65–74, 75–84, 85 and over

Source: National Center for Health Statistics, n.d.

Suicide Rates Around the World (Chapter 15)

In almost every nation, unmarried older men are most likely to kill themselves. The major exception is China. China's sexism is one explanation, but the difference may be simply accessible poison. Usually people kill themselves with guns, and men have more guns than women. In China, swallowing pesticides is the most common means, and lethal pesticides are readily available to every rural woman.

Aging Around the World (Chapter 15)

Almost always, the nations with the fewest older people have the most children, and generally, the more older people a nation has the wealthier the nation is.

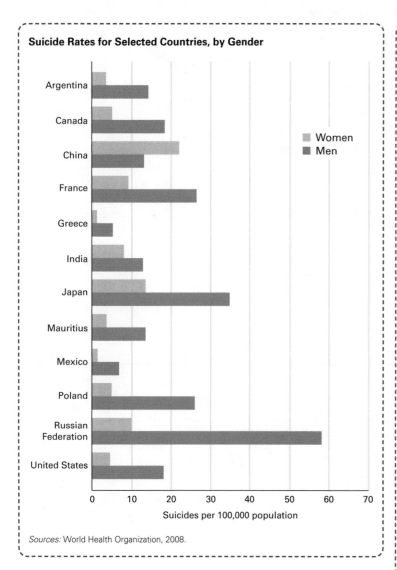

Suicide Rates for Selected Countries, by Gender

Suicides per 100,000 population

Sources: World Health Organization, 2008.

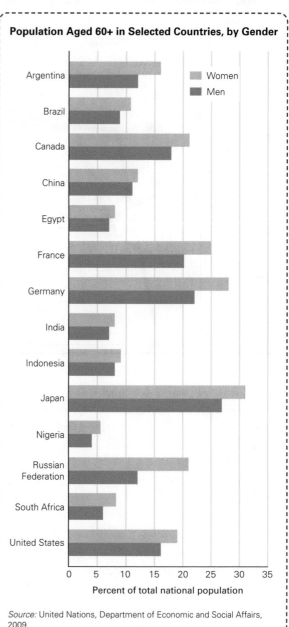

Population Aged 60+ in Selected Countries, by Gender

Percent of total national population

Source: United Nations, Department of Economic and Social Affairs, 2009.

Appendix B
More About
Research Methods

This appendix explains how to learn about any topic. It is crucial that you distinguish valid conclusions from wishful thinking. Such learning begins with your personal experience.

Make It Personal

Think about your life, observe your behavior, and watch the people around you. Pay careful attention to details of expression, emotion, and behavior. The more you see, the more fascinated, curious, and reflective you will become. Ask questions and listen carefully and respectfully to what other people say regarding development.

Whenever you ask specific questions as part of an assignment, **remember that observing ethical standards (see Chapter 1) comes first.** *Before* you interview anyone, inform the person of your purpose and assure him or her of confidentiality. Promise not to identify the person in your report (use a pseudonym) and do not repeat any personal details that emerge in the interview to anyone (friends or strangers). Your instructor will provide further ethical guidance. If you might publish what you've learned, get in touch with your college's Institutional Research Board (IRB).

Read the Research

No matter how deeply you think about your own experiences, and no matter how intently you listen to others whose background is unlike yours, you also need to read scholarly published work in order to fully understand any topic that interests you. Be skeptical about magazine or newspaper reports; some are bound to be simplified, exaggerated, or biased.

Professional Journals and Books

Part of the process of science is that conclusions are not considered solid until they are corroborated in many studies, which means that you should consult several sources on any topic. Four **journals in human development** are:

- *Developmental Psychology* (published by the American Psychological Association)
- *Child Development* (Society for Research in Child Development)
- *Developmental Review* (Elsevier)
- *Human Development* (Karger)

These journals differ in the types of articles and studies they publish, but all are well respected and *peer-reviewed,* which means that other scholars review each article submitted and recommend that it be accepted, rejected, or revised. Every article includes references to other recent work.

Beyond these four are literally thousands of other professional journals, each with a particular perspective or topic. To judge them, look for journals that are peer-reviewed. Also consider the following details: the background of the author (research funded by corporations tends to favor their products); the nature of the publisher (professional organizations, as in the first two journals above, protect their reputations); how long the journal has been published (the volume number tells you that). Some interesting work does not meet these criteria, but these are guides to quality.

Many **books** cover some aspect of development. Single-author books are likely to present only one viewpoint. That view may be insightful, but it is limited. You might consult a *handbook,* which is a book that includes many authors and many topics. Two good handbooks in development, both now in their sixth editions (a sign that past scholars have found them useful) are:

- *Handbook of Child Psychology* (2006, Damon & Lerner, eds.), four volumes, published by Wiley
- *Handbook of Aging* (2006), three volumes (biology, psychology, and social sciences), published by Academic Press

Again, dozens of good handbooks are available, many of which focus on a particular age or topic.

The Internet

The **Internet** is a mixed blessing, useful to every novice and experienced researcher but dangerous as well. Every library worldwide and most homes in North America, western Europe, and East Asia have computers that provide access to journals and other information. Ask for help from the librarians; many are highly skilled. In addition, other students, friends, and even strangers can be helpful.

Virtually everything is on the Internet, not only massive national and international statistics but also very personal accounts. Photos, charts, quizzes, ongoing experiments, newspapers from around the world, videos, and much more are available at the click of a mouse. Every journal has a Web site, with tables of contents, abstracts, and sometimes full texts (an abstract gives the key findings; for the full text, you may need to consult the library's copy of the print version).

Unfortunately, you can spend many frustrating hours sifting through information that is useless, trash, or tangential. *Directories* (which list general topics or areas and then move you step by step in the direction you choose) and *search engines* (which give you all the sites that use a particular word or words) can help you select appropriate information. Each directory or search engine provides somewhat different lists; none provides only the most comprehensive and accurate sites. With experience and help, you will find the best sites for you, but you will also encounter some junk no matter how experienced you are.

Anybody can put anything on the Web, regardless of its truth or fairness, so evaluate with a very critical eye everything you find. Make sure you have several divergent sources for every "fact" you find; consider who provided the information and why. Every controversial issue has sites that forcefully advocate opposite viewpoints, sometimes with biased statistics and narrow perspectives.

Here are seven Internet sites that are quite reliable:

- *www.worthpublishers.com/berger* Includes links to Web sites, quizzes, PowerPoint slides, and activities keyed to every chapter of the textbook.
- *embryo.soad.umich.edu* The Multidimensional Human Embryo. Presents MRI images of a human embryo at various stages of development, accompanied by brief explanations.

- *www.cdipage.com* Child Development Institute. A useful site, with links and articles on child development and information on common childhood psychological disorders.
- *ericeece.org* ERIC Clearinghouse. Provides links to many education-related sites and includes brief descriptions of each.
- *site.educ.indiana.edu/cafs* Adolescence Directory online (ADOL) is an electronic guide to information on adolescent issues. It is a service of the Center for Adolescent and Family Studies at Indiana University.
- *www.nih.gov.nia/* National Institute on Aging. Includes information about current research on aging.
- *www.cdc.gov/nchs/hus.htm* The National Center for Health Statistics issues an annual report on health trends, called *Health, United States.*

Every source—you, your interviewees, journals, books, and the Internet—is helpful. Do not depend on any particular one. Especially if you use the Web, also check print resources. Avoid plagiarism and prejudice by citing every source and noting objectivity, validity, and credibility. Your own analysis, opinions, words, and conclusions are crucial.

Additional Terms and Concepts

As emphasized throughout this text, the study of development is a science. Social scientists spend years in graduate school, studying methods and statistics. Chapter 1 touches on some of these matters (observation and experiments; correlation and statistical significance; independent and dependent variables; experimental and control groups; cross-sectional, longitudinal, and cross-sequential research), but there is much more. A few additional aspects of research are presented here, to help you evaluate research wherever you find it.

Who Participates?

The entire group of people about whom a scientist wants to learn is called the **population.** Generally, a research population is quite large—not usually the world's entire population of almost 9 billion, but perhaps all the 4 million babies born in the United States last year, or all the 25 million Japanese currently over age 65.

The particular individuals who are studied in a specific research project are called the **participants.** They are used as a **sample** of the larger group. Ideally, a large number of people are used as a **representative sample,** that is, a sample who reflect the entire population. Every peer-reviewed published study reports details on the sample.

Selection of the sample is crucial. Volunteers, or people with telephones, or people treated with some particular condition, are not a *random sample,* in which everyone in that population is equally likely to be selected. To avoid *selection bias,* some studies are *prospective,* beginning with an entire cluster (for instance, every baby born on a particular day) and then tracing the development of some particular characteristic.

For example, prospective studies find the antecedents of heart disease, or child abuse, or high school dropout rates—all of which are much harder to find if the study is *retrospective,* beginning with those who had heart attacks, experienced abuse, or left school. Thus, although retrospective research finds that most high school dropouts say they disliked school, prospective research finds that some who like school still decide to drop out and then later say they hated school, while others dislike school but stay to graduate. Prospective research discovers how many students are in these last two categories; retrospective research on people who have already dropped out does not.

population
The entire group of individuals who are of particular concern in a scientific study, such as all the children of the world or all newborns who weigh less than 3 pounds.

participants
The people who are studied in a research project.

sample
A group of individuals drawn from a specified population. A sample might be the low-birthweight babies born in four particular hospitals that are representative of all hospitals.

representative sample
A group of research participants who reflect the relevant characteristics of the larger population whose attributes are under study.

Research Design

Every researcher begins not only by formulating a hypothesis but also by learning what other scientists have discovered about the topic in question and what methods might be useful and ethical in designing research. Often they include measures to guard against inadvertently finding only the results they expect. For example, the people who actually gather the data may not know the purpose of the research. Scientists say that these data gatherers are **blind** to the hypothesized outcome. Participants are sometimes "blind" as well, because otherwise they might, for instance, respond the way they think they should.

Another crucial aspect of research design is to define exactly what is to be studied. Researchers establish an **operational definition** of whatever phenomenon they will be examining, defining each variable by describing specific, observable behavior. This is essential in quantitative research (see Chapter 1), but it is also useful in qualitative research. For example, if a researcher wants to know when babies begin to walk, does *walking* include steps taken while holding on? Is one unsteady step enough? Some parents say yes, but the usual operational definition of walking is "takes at least three steps without holding on." This operational definition allows comparisons worldwide, making it possible to discover, for example, that well-fed African babies tend to walk earlier than well-fed European babies.

Operational definitions are difficult but essential when personality traits are studied. How should *aggression* or *sharing* or *shyness* be defined? Lack of an operational definition leads to contradictory results. For instance, some say that infant day care makes children more aggressive, but others say it makes them less passive. Similarly, as explained in the Epilogue, the operational definition of death is the subject of heated disputes. For any scientist, operational definitions are crucial.

Reporting Results

You already know that results should be reported in sufficient detail so that another scientist can analyze the conclusions and replicate the research. Various methods, populations, and research designs may produce divergent conclusions. For that reason, handbooks, some journals, and some articles are called *reviews:* They summarize past research. Often, when studies are similar in operational definitions and methods, the review is a **meta-analysis,** combining the findings of many studies to present an overall conclusion.

Chapter 1 describes some statistical measures. One of them is *statistical significance,* which indicates whether or not a particular result could have occurred by chance.

Another statistic that is often crucial is **effect size,** a way of measuring how much impact one variable has on another. Effect size ranges from 0 (no effect) to 1 (total transformation, never found in actual studies). Effect size may be particularly important when the sample size is large, because a large sample often leads to highly "significant" results (unlikely to have occurred by chance) that have only a tiny effect on the variable of interest.

Hundreds of statistical measures are used by developmentalists. Often the same data can be presented in many ways: Some scientists examine statistical analysis intently before they accept conclusions as valid. A specific example involved methods to improve students' writing ability between grades 4 and 12. A meta-analysis found that many methods of writing instruction have a significant impact, but effect size is much larger for some methods (teaching strategies and summarizing) than for others (prewriting exercises and studying models). For teachers, this statistic is crucial, for they want to know what has a big effect, not merely what is better than chance (significant).

---

blind
The condition of data gatherers (and sometimes participants as well) who are deliberately kept ignorant of the purpose of the research so that they cannot unintentionally bias the results.

operational definition
A description of the specific, observable behavior that will constitute the variable that is to be studied, so that any reader will know whether that behavior occurred or not. Operational definitions may be arbitrary (e.g., an IQ score at or above 130 is operationally defined as "gifted"), but they must be precise.

meta-analysis
A technique of combining results of many studies to come to an overall conclusion. Meta-analysis is powerful, in that small samples can be added together to lead to significant conclusions, although variations from study to study sometimes make combining them impossible.

effect size
A way to indicate, statistically, how much of an impact the independent variable had on the dependent variable.

To read examples of meta-analysis and effect size, you might look at the following:

- Gentile, Brittany, Grabe, Shelly, Dolan-Pascoe, Brenda, Wells, Brooke E., Maitino, Alissa, & Twenge, Jean M. (2009). Gender differences in domain-specific self-esteem: A meta-analysis. *Review of General Psychology, 13,* 34–45. [This article offers not only meta-analysis and effect sizes of gender differences in self-esteem but also separate analyses by age, cohort, and domain. For instance, adult men in studies after 1980 seem to be happier with their appearance than women are.]

- Graham, Steve, & Perin, Dolores. (2007). A meta-analysis of writing instruction for adolescent students. *Journal of Educational Psychology, 99,* 445–476. [This article, mentioned above, contains many interesting details, including operational definitions and specific effect sizes.]

- Grissom, Robert J., & Kim, John J. (2005). *Effect Sizes for Research: A Broad Practical Approach.* Mahwah, NJ: Erlbaum. [This book provides many specifics about this statistical measure.]

- Olatunji, Bunmi O., Cisler, Josh M., & Tolin, David F. (2007). Quality of life in the anxiety disorders: A meta-analytic review. *Clinical Psychology Review, 2,* 572–581. [This review concludes that anxiety disorders reduce the quality of life, but some of them, such as post-traumatic stress disorder, have a greater negative effect than others.]

- Oosterman, Mirjam, Schuengel, Carlo, & Slot, N. Wim. (2007). Disruptions in foster care: A review and meta-analysis. *Children and Youth Services Review, 29,* 53–76. [This review finds that a child with behavior problems is likely to experience more changes in placement, but kinship care is unexpectedly stable.]

- Poropat, Arthur E. (2009). A meta-analysis of the five-factor model of personality and academic performance. *Psychological Bulletin, 135,* 322–338. [The relationship between the Big Five and school grades in primary, secondary, and tertiary education. One of the five, conscientiousness, seems most influential.]

- Simon, Viktória, Czobor, Pál, Bálint, Sára, Bitter, István, & Mészáros, Ágnes. (2009). Prevalence and correlates of adult attention-deficit hyperactivity disorder: Meta-analysis. *British Journal of Psychiatry, 194,* 204–211. [As in this study, meta-analysis often considers reports from many nations and criticizes cultural bias in definitions or subjectivity. This is useful for young scientists, who learn that even established research may be criticized and reinterpreted.]

- Zimmerman, Ryan D., & Darnold, Todd C. (2009). The impact of job performance on employee turnover intentions and the voluntary turnover process: A meta-analysis and path model. *Personnel Review, 38(2):* 142–158. [A "path model" considers the sequence of events, a good developmental approach. This review reports that workers who are poor performers tend to quit suddenly, while good performers may also intend to quit but do so only after planning.]

GLOSSARY

A

AARP A U.S. organization of people aged 50 and older that advocates for the elderly. It was originally called the American Association of Retired Persons, but now only the initials AARP are used, since members need not be retired.

absent grief A situation in which overly private people cut themselves off from the community and customs that allow and expect grief; can lead to social isolation.

accommodation Piaget's term for a type of adaptation in which old ideas are restructured to include, or accommodate, new experiences.

achievement test A measure of mastery or proficiency in reading, mathematics, writing, science, or some other subject.

active euthanasia A situation in which someone takes action to bring about another person's death, with the intention of ending that person's suffering.

activities of daily life (ADLs) Actions that are important to independent living, typically identified as five tasks of self-care: eating, bathing, toileting, dressing, and transferring from a bed to a chair. The inability to perform any of these tasks is a sign of frailty.

activity theory The view that elderly people want and need to remain active in a variety of social spheres—with relatives, friends, and community groups—and become withdrawn only unwillingly, as a result of ageism.

additive gene A gene that adds something to some aspect of the phenotype. Its contribution depends on additions from the other genes, which may come from either the same or the other parent.

adolescence-limited offender A person whose criminal activity stops by age 21.

adolescent egocentrism A characteristic of adolescent thinking that leads young people (ages 10 to 14) to focus on themselves to the exclusion of others.

adrenal glands Two glands, located above the kidneys, that produce hormones (including the "stress hormones" epinephrine [adrenaline] and norepinephrine).

advance directive A document that contains an individual's instructions for end-of-life medical care, written before such care is needed.

age of viability The age (about 22 weeks after conception) at which a fetus may survive outside the mother's uterus if specialized medical care is available.

ageism A form of prejudice in which people are categorized and judged solely on the basis of their chronological age.

aggressive-rejected children Children who are disliked by peers because of antagonistic, confrontational behavior.

aging in place Remaining in the same home and community in later life, adjusting but not leaving when health fades.

allele Any of the possible forms in which a gene for a particular trait can occur.

allostatic load The total, combined burden of stress and disease that an individual must cope with.

Alzheimer disease (AD) The most common cause of dementia, characterized by gradual deterioration of memory and personality and marked by the formation of plaques of beta-amyloid protein and tangles of tau protein in the brain. Also called *senile dementia of the Alzheimer type (SDAT)*.

amygdala A tiny brain structure that registers emotions, particularly fear and anxiety.

analytic thought Thought that results from analysis, such as a systematic ranking of pros and cons, risks and consequences, possibilities and facts. Analytic thought depends on logic and rationality.

androgyny A balance within one person of traditionally masculine and feminine psychological characteristics.

andropause A term coined to signify a drop in testosterone levels in older men, which normally results in a reduction in sexual desire, erections, and muscle mass. Also known as *male menopause*.

animism The belief that natural objects and phenomena are alive.

anorexia nervosa An eating disorder characterized by self-starvation. Affected individuals voluntarily undereat and often overexercise, depriving their vital organs of nutrition. Anorexia can be fatal.

antipathy Feelings of dislike or even hatred for another person.

antisocial behavior Actions that are deliberately hurtful or destructive to another person.

Apgar scale A quick assessment of a newborn's body functioning. The baby's heart rate, respiratory effort, muscle tone, color, and reflexes are given a score of 0, 1, or 2 twice—at one minute and five minutes after birth—and each time the total of all five scores is compared with the ideal score of 10 (which is rarely attained).

apprentice in thinking Vygotsky's term for a person whose cognition is stimulated and directed by older and more skilled members of society.

aptitude The potential to master a specific skill or to learn a certain body of knowledge.

Asperger syndrome An autistic spectrum disorder characterized by extreme attention to details and deficient social understanding.

assimilation Piaget's term for a type of adaptation in which new experiences are interpreted to fit into, or assimilate with, old ideas.

assisted living A living arrangement for elderly people that combines privacy and independence with medical supervision.

asthma A chronic disease of the respiratory system in which inflammation narrows the airways from the nose and mouth to the lungs, causing difficulty in breathing. Signs and symptoms include wheezing, shortness of breath, chest tightness, and coughing.

attachment According to Ainsworth, "an affectional tie" that an infant forms with a caregiver—a tie that binds them together in space and endures over time.

attention-deficit/hyperactivity disorder (ADHD) A condition in which a person is inattentive, impulsive, and overactive and thus has great difficulty concentrating for more than a few moments.

authoritarian parenting An approach to child rearing that is characterized by high behavioral standards, strict punishment of misconduct, and little communication.

authoritative parenting An approach to child rearing in which the parents set limits and enforce rules but are flexible and listen to their children.

autism A developmental disorder marked by an inability to relate to other people normally, extreme self-absorption, and an inability to acquire normal speech.

autistic spectrum disorder Any of several disorders characterized by impaired communication, inadequate social skills, and unusual patterns of play.

automatization A process in which repetition of a sequence of thoughts and actions makes the sequence routine, so that it no longer requires conscious thought.

autonomy versus shame and doubt Erikson's second crisis of psychosocial development. Toddlers either succeed or fail in gaining a sense of self-rule over their actions and their bodies.

average life expectancy The number of years that the average person in a particular population is likely to live.

axon A fiber that extends from a neuron and transmits electrochemical impulses from that neuron to the dendrites of other neurons.

B

babbling The extended repetition of certain syllables, such as *ba-ba-ba,* that begins when babies are between 6 and 9 months old.

balanced bilingual A person who is fluent in two languages, not favoring one over the other.

behaviorism A theory of human development that studies observable behavior. Behaviorism is also called *learning theory,* because it describes the laws and processes by which behavior is learned.

bereavement The sense of loss following a death.

bickering Petty, peevish arguing, usually repeated and ongoing.

Big Five The five basic clusters of personality traits that remain quite stable throughout life: openness, conscientiousness, extroversion, agreeableness, and neuroticism.

binocular vision The ability to focus the two eyes in a coordinated manner in order to see one image.

blended family A stepparent family that includes children born to several families, such as the biological children from the spouses' previous marriages and the biological children of the new couple.

body image A person's idea of how his or her body looks.

body mass index (BMI) The ratio of weight to height, calculated by dividing a person's body weight in kilograms by the square of his or her height in meters.

bulimia nervosa An eating disorder characterized by binge eating and subsequent purging, usually by induced vomiting and/or use of laxatives.

bullying Repeated, systematic efforts to inflict harm through physical, verbal, or social attack on a weaker person.

bullying aggression Unprovoked, repeated physical or verbal attack, especially on victims who are unlikely to defend themselves.

bully-victim Someone who attacks others and who is attacked as well. (Also called a *provocative victim* because he or she does things that elicit bullying, such as stealing a bully's pencil.)

C

calorie restriction The practice of limiting dietary energy intake, while still consuming sufficient quantities of vitamins, minerals, and other important nutrients, for the purpose of improving health and slowing down the aging process.

cardiovascular disease (CVD) Illness that involves the heart and the circulatory system.

carrier A person whose genotype includes a gene that is not expressed in the phenotype. Such an unexpressed gene occurs in half the carrier's gametes and thus is passed on to half the carrier's children, who will most likely be carriers, too. Generally, the characteristic appears in the phenotype only when such a gene is inherited from both parents.

centenarian A person who has lived 100 years or more.

center day care Child care that occurs in a place especially designed for the purpose, where several paid adults care for many children. Usually the children are grouped by age, the day-care center is licensed, and providers are trained and certified in child development.

centration A characteristic of preoperational thought whereby a young child focuses (centers) on one idea, excluding all others.

cesarean section (c-section) A surgical birth, in which incisions through the mother's abdomen and uterus allow the fetus to be removed quickly, instead of being delivered through the vagina.

child abuse Deliberate action that is harmful to a child's physical, emotional, or sexual well-being.

child maltreatment Intentional harm to or avoidable endangerment of anyone under 18 years of age.

child neglect Failure to meet a child's basic physical, educational, or emotional needs.

child sexual abuse Any erotic activity that arouses an adult and excites, shames, or confuses a child, whether or not the victim protests and whether or not genital contact is involved.

child-directed speech The high-pitched, simplified, and repetitive way adults speak to infants. (Also called *baby talk* or *motherese*.)

children with special needs Children who, because of a physical or mental disability, require extra help in order to learn.

chromosome One of the 46 molecules of DNA (in 23 pairs) that each cell of the human body contains and that, together, contain all the genes. Other species have more or fewer chromosomes.

classical conditioning A learning process in which a meaningful stimulus (such as the smell of food to a hungry animal) gradually comes to be connected with a neutral stimulus (such as a particular sound) that had no special meaning before the learning process began. (Also called *respondent conditioning*.)

classification The logical principle that things can be organized into groups (or categories or classes) according to some characteristic they have in common.

clinical depression Feelings of hopelessness, lethargy, and worthlessness that last two weeks or more.

clique A group of adolescents made up of close friends who are loyal to one another while excluding outsiders.

cluster suicides Several suicides committed by members of a group within a brief period of time.

cognitive theory A theory of human development that focuses on changes in how people think over time. According to this theory, our thoughts shape our attitudes, beliefs, and behaviors.

cohabit To live with an unrelated person—typically a romantic partner—to whom one is not married.

cohort A group defined by the shared age of its members, who, because they were born at about the same time, move through life together, experiencing the same historical events and cultural shifts.

comorbidity The presence of two or more unrelated disease conditions at the same time in the same person.

compression of morbidity A shortening of the time a person spends ill or infirm before death; accomplished by postponing illness.

concrete operational thought Piaget's term for the ability to reason logically about direct experiences and perceptions.

conditioning According to behaviorism, the processes by which responses become linked to particular stimuli and learning takes place. The word *conditioning* is used to emphasize the importance of repeated practice, as when an athlete *conditions* his or her body to perform well by training for a long time.

conservation The principle that the amount of a substance remains the same (i.e., is conserved) when its appearance changes.

continuity theory The theory that each person experiences the changes of late adulthood and behaves toward others in a way that is consistent with his or her behavior in earlier periods of life.

control processes The part of the information-processing system that consists of methods for regulating the analysis and flow of information. Useful control processes include memory and retrieval strategies, selective attention, and rules or strategies for problem solving.

conventional moral reasoning Kohlberg's second level of moral reasoning, emphasizing social rules.

corpus callosum A long, thick band of nerve fibers that connects the left and right hemispheres of the brain and allows communication between them.

correlation A number that indicates the degree of relationship between two variables, expressed in terms of the likelihood that one variable will (or will not) occur when the other variable does (or does not). A correlation indicates only that two variables are related, not that one variable causes the other to occur.

cortex The outer layers of the brain in humans and other mammals. Most thinking, feeling, and sensing involve the cortex. (Sometimes called the *neocortex*.)

co-sleeping A custom in which parents and their children (usually infants) sleep together in the same bed. (Also called *bed-sharing*.)

critical period A time when a particular type of developmental growth (in body or behavior) must happen if it is ever going to happen.

cross-sectional research A research design that compares groups of people who differ in age but are similar in other important characteristics.

cross-sequential research A hybrid research design in which researchers first study several groups of people of different ages (a cross-sectional approach) and then follow those groups over the years (a longitudinal approach). (Also called *cohort-sequential research* or *time-sequential research*.)

crowd A larger group of adolescents who have something in common but who are not necessarily friends.

crystallized intelligence Those types of intellectual ability that reflect accumulated learning. Vocabulary and general information are examples.

culture of children The particular habits, styles, and values that reflect the set of rules and rituals that characterize children as distinct from adult society.

cyberbullying Bullying that occurs via Internet insults and rumors, texting, anonymous phone calls, and video embarrassment.

D

deductive reasoning Reasoning from a general statement, premise, or principle, through logical steps, to figure out (deduce) specifics. (Sometimes called *top-down reasoning*.)

dementia Irreversible loss of intellectual functioning caused by organic brain damage or disease. Dementia becomes more common with age, but it is abnormal and pathological even in the very old.

dendrite A fiber that extends from a neuron and receives electrochemical impulses transmitted from other neurons via their axons.

dependency ratio A calculation of the number of self-sufficient, productive adults compared with the number of dependents (children and the elderly) in a given population.

dependent variable In an experiment, the variable that may change as a result of whatever new condition or situation the experimenter adds. In other words, the dependent variable *depends* on the independent variable.

developmental psychopathology The field that uses insights into typical development to understand and remediate developmental disorders, and vice versa.

developmental theory A group of ideas, assumptions, and generalizations that interpret and illuminate the thousands of observations that have been made about human growth. A developmental theory provides a framework for explaining the patterns and problems of development.

deviancy training Destructive peer support in which one person shows another how to rebel against authority or social norms.

Diagnostic and Statistical Manual of Mental Disorders **(DSM-IV-TR)** The American Psychiatric Association's official guide to the diagnosis (not treatment) of mental disorders. (IV-TR means "fourth edition, text revision." The fifth edition is scheduled to be published in 2011.)

diathesis–stress model The view that psychological disorders, such as schizophrenia, are produced by the interaction of a genetic vulnerability (the diathesis) and stressful environmental factors and life events.

difference-equals-deficit error The mistaken belief that a deviation from some norm is necessarily inferior to behavior or characteristics that meet the standard.

digital divide The gap between students who have access to computers and those who do not, often a gap between rich and poor. In the United States and most developed nations, this gap has now been bridged due to the prevalence of computers in schools.

disability Long-term difficulty in performing normal activities of daily life because of some physical, emotional, or mental condition.

disenfranchised grief A situation in which certain people, although they are bereaved, are prevented from mourning publicly by cultural customs or social restrictions.

disengagement theory The view that aging makes a person's social sphere increasingly narrow, resulting in role relinquishment, withdrawal, and passivity.

disorganized attachment A type of attachment that is marked by an infant's inconsistent reactions to the caregiver's departure and return.

distal parenting Caregiving practices that involve remaining distant from the baby, providing toys, food, and face-to-face communication with minimal holding and touching.

dizygotic twins Twins who are formed when two separate ova are fertilized by two separate sperm at roughly the same time. (Also called *fraternal twins*.)

DNA (deoxyribonucleic acid) The molecule that contains the chemical instructions for cells to manufacture various proteins.

DNR (do not resuscitate) A written order from a physician (sometimes initiated by a patient's advance directive or by a health care proxy's request) that no attempt should be made to revive a patient if he or she suffers cardiac or respiratory arrest.

dominant–recessive pattern The interaction of a pair of alleles in such a way that the phenotype reveals the influence of one allele (the dominant gene) more than that of the other (the recessive gene).

double effect An ethical situation in which an action (such as administering opiates) has both a positive effect, which is intended (relieving a terminally ill person's pain), and a negative effect, which is foreseen but not intended (hastening death by suppressing respiration).

doula A woman who helps with the birth process. Traditionally in Latin America, a doula was the only professional who attended childbirths. Now doulas are likely to work alongside a hospital's medical staff to help mothers through labor and delivery.

Down syndrome A condition in which a person has 47 chromosomes instead of the usual 46, with three rather than two chromosomes at the 21st position. People with Down syndrome typically have distinctive characteristics, including unusual facial features (thick tongue, round face, slanted eyes), heart abnormalities, and language difficulties. (Also called *trisomy-21*.)

drug abuse The ingestion of a drug to the extent that it impairs the user's biological or psychological well-being.

drug addiction A condition of drug dependence in which the absence of the given drug from the individual's system produces a drive—physiological, biological, or both—to ingest more of the drug.

dual-process model The notion that two networks exist within the human brain, one for emotional and one for analytical processing of stimuli.

dynamic-systems theory A view of human development as an ongoing, ever-changing interaction between the physical and emotional being and between the person and every aspect of his or her environment, including the family and society.

dyslexia Unusual difficulty with reading; thought to be the result of some neurological underdevelopment.

E

ecological niche The particular lifestyle and social context that adults settle into because it is compatible with their individual personality needs and interests.

ecological validity The idea that memory should be measured as people actually experience it, not as laboratory tests assess it.

ecological-systems approach The view that in the study of human development, the person should be considered in all the contexts and interactions that constitute a life. (Later renamed *bioecological theory*.)

edgework Occupations, recreational activities, or other ventures that involve a degree of risk or danger. The prospect of "living on the edge" makes edgework compelling to some individuals.

effortful control The ability to regulate one's emotions and actions through effort, not simply through natural inclination.

egocentrism Piaget's term for young children's tendency to think about the world entirely from their own personal perspective.

elderspeak A condescending way of speaking to older adults that resembles baby talk, with simple and short sentences, exaggerated emphasis, repetition, and a slower rate and a higher pitch than normal speech.

Electra complex The unconscious desire of girls to replace their mothers and win their fathers' exclusive love.

embryo The name for a developing human organism from about the third through the eighth week after conception.

embryonic period The stage of prenatal development from approximately the third through the eighth week after conception, during which the basic forms of all body structures, including internal organs, develop.

emerging adulthood The period between the ages of 18 and 25, which is now widely thought of as a separate developmental stage. (Also called *young adulthood* or *youth*.)

emotional regulation The ability to control when and how emotions are expressed.

emotion-focused coping A strategy often used by older adults to deal with stress in which they change their feelings about the stressor rather than changing the stressor itself.

empathy The ability to understand the emotions and concerns of another person, especially when they differ from one's own.

empty nest The time in the lives of parents when their children have left the family home to pursue their own lives.

English-language learner (ELL) A child who is learning English as a second language.

epigenetic Referring to the effects of environmental forces on the expression of an individual's, or a species', genetic inheritance.

estradiol A sex hormone, considered the chief estrogen. Females produce more estradiol than males do.

ethnic group People whose ancestors were born in the same region and who often share a language, culture, and religion.

ethnotheory A theory that underlies the values and practices of a culture but is not usually apparent to the people within the culture.

experiment A research method in which the researcher tries to determine the cause-and-effect relationship between two variables by manipulating one (called the *independent variable*) and then observing and recording the ensuing changes in the other (called the *dependent variable*).

extended family A family consisting of parents, their children, and other relatives living in one household.

externalizing problems Difficulty with emotional regulation that involves expressing powerful feelings through uncontrolled physical or verbal outbursts, as by lashing out at other people or breaking things.

extreme sports Forms of recreation that include apparent risk of injury or death and that are attractive and thrilling as a result.

extremely low birthweight (ELBW) A body weight at birth of less than 2 pounds, 3 ounces (1,000 grams).

extrinsic motivation A drive, or reason to pursue a goal, that arises from the need to have one's achievements rewarded from outside, perhaps by receiving material possessions or another person's esteem.

extrinsic rewards of work The tangible benefits, usually in the form of compensation (e.g., salary, health insurance, pension), that one receives for doing a job.

F

familism The belief that family members should support one another, sacrificing individual freedom and success, if necessary, in order to preserve family unity.

family day care Child care that includes several children of various ages and usually occurs in the home of a woman who is paid to provide it.

family function The way a family works to meet the needs of its members. Children need families to provide basic material necessities, to encourage learning, to help them develop self-respect, to nurture friendships, and to foster harmony and stability.

family structure The legal and genetic relationships among relatives living in the same home; includes nuclear family, extended family, stepfamily, and so on.

fast-mapping The speedy and sometimes imprecise way in which children learn new words by tentatively placing them in mental categories according to their perceived meaning.

fetal alcohol syndrome (FAS) A cluster of birth defects, including abnormal facial characteristics, slow physical growth, and retarded mental development, that may occur in the child of a woman who drinks alcohol while pregnant.

fetal period The stage of prenatal development from the ninth week after conception until birth, during which the organs grow in size and mature in functioning.

fetus The name for a developing human organism from the start of the ninth week after conception until birth.

fictive kin A term used to describe someone who becomes accepted as part of a family to which he or she has no blood relation.

filial responsibility The obligation of adult children to care for their aging parents.

fine motor skills Physical abilities involving small body movements, especially of the hands and fingers, such as drawing and picking up a coin. (The word *fine* here means "small.")

flextime An arrangement in which work schedules are flexible so that employees can balance personal and occupational responsibilities.

fluid intelligence Those types of basic intelligence that make learning of all sorts quick and thorough. Abilities such as working memory, abstract thought, and speed of thinking are usually considered aspects of fluid intelligence.

Flynn effect The rise in average IQ scores that has occurred over the decades in many nations.

focus on appearance A characteristic of preoperational thought whereby a young child ignores all attributes that are not apparent.

foreclosure Erikson's term for premature identity formation, which occurs when an adolescent adopts parents' or society's roles and values wholesale, without questioning or analysis.

formal operational thought In Piaget's theory, the fourth and final stage of cognitive development, characterized by more systematic logic and the ability to think about abstract ideas.

foster care A legal, publicly supported system in which a maltreated child is removed from the parents' custody and entrusted to another adult or family, which is reimbursed for expenses incurred in meeting the child's needs.

fragile X syndrome A genetic disorder in which part of the X chromosome seems to be attached to the rest of it by a very thin string of molecules. The cause is a single gene that has more than 200 repetitions of one triplet.

frail elderly People over age 65, and often over age 85, who are physically infirm, very ill, or cognitively impaired.

frontal lobe dementia A form of dementia characterized by personality changes caused by deterioration of the frontal lobes and the amygdala. Also called *frontotemporal lobar degeneration*.

G

gamete A reproductive cell; that is, a sperm or ovum that can produce a new individual if it combines with a gamete from the other sex to form a zygote.

gender convergence A tendency for men and women to become more similar as they move through middle age.

gender differences Differences in the roles and behaviors that are prescribed by a culture for males and females.

gender identity A person's acceptance of the roles and behaviors that society associates with the biological categories of male and female.

gender schema A child's cognitive concept or general belief about sex differences, which is based on his or her observations and experiences.

gene A section of a chromosome and the basic unit for the transmission of heredity, consisting of a string of chemicals that are instructions for the cell to manufacture certain proteins.

general intelligence (*g*) A construct based on the idea that intelligence is one basic trait that involves all cognitive abilities, which people possess in varying amounts.

generational forgetting The idea that each new generation forgets what the previous generation learned. As used here, the term refers to knowledge about the harm drugs can do.

genetic counseling Consultation and testing by trained experts that enable individuals to learn about their genetic heritage, including harmful conditions that they might pass along to any children they may conceive.

genome The full set of genes that are the instructions to make an individual member of a certain species.

genotype An organism's entire genetic inheritance, or genetic potential.

germinal period The first two weeks of prenatal development after conception, characterized by rapid cell division and the beginning of cell differentiation.

gonads The paired sex glands (ovaries in females, testicles in males). The gonads produce hormones and gametes.

good death A death that is peaceful, quick, and painless and that occurs after a long life, in the company of family and friends, and in familiar surroundings.

goodness of fit A similarity of temperament and values that produces a smooth interaction between an individual and his or her social context, including family, school, and community.

grief The powerful sorrow that an individual feels at the death of another.

gross motor skills Physical abilities involving large body movements, such as walking and jumping. (The word *gross* here means "big.")

growth spurt The relatively sudden and rapid physical growth that occurs during puberty. Each body part increases in size on a schedule: A weight increase usually precedes a height increase, and growth of the limbs precedes growth of the torso.

H

head-sparing A biological mechanism that protects the brain when malnutrition disrupts body growth. The brain is the last part of the body to be damaged by malnutrition.

health care proxy A person chosen by another person to make medical decisions if the second person becomes unable to do so.

heritability A statistic that indicates what percentage of the variation in a particular trait within a particular population, in a particular context and era, can be traced to genes.

hidden curriculum The unofficial, unstated, or implicit rules and priorities that influence the academic curriculum and every other aspect of learning in school.

high-stakes test An evaluation that is critical in determining success or failure. If a single test determines whether a student will graduate or be promoted, that is a high-stakes test.

hippocampus A brain structure that is a central processor of memory, especially memory for locations.

holophrase A single word that is used to express a complete, meaningful thought.

homeostasis The adjustment of all the body's systems to keep physiological functions in a state of equilibrium. As the body ages, it takes longer for these adjustments to occur, so it becomes harder for older bodies to adapt to stress.

hormone An organic chemical substance that is produced by one body tissue and conveyed via the bloodstream to another to affect some physiological function. Various hormones influence thoughts, urges, emotions, and behavior.

hormone replacement therapy (HRT) Treatment to compensate for hormone reduction at menopause or following surgical removal of the ovaries. Such treatment, which usually involves estrogen and progesterone, minimizes menopausal symptoms and diminishes the risk of osteoporosis in later adulthood.

hospice An institution or program in which terminally ill patients receive palliative care.

HPA (hypothalamus-pituitary-adrenal) axis The sequence of a chain reaction of hormone production, originating in the hypothalamus and moving to the pituitary and then to the adrenal glands.

hypothalamus A brain area that responds to the amygdala and the hippocampus to produce hormones that activate other parts of the brain and body.

hypothetical thought Reasoning that includes propositions and possibilities that may not reflect reality.

I

identification An attempt to defend one's self-concept by taking on the behaviors and attitudes of someone else.

identity A consistent definition of one's self as a unique individual, in terms of roles, attitudes, beliefs, and aspirations.

identity achievement Erikson's term for the attainment of identity, or the point at which a person understands who he or she is as a unique individual, in accord with past experiences and future plans.

identity versus role confusion Erikson's term for the fifth stage of development, in which the person tries to figure out "Who am I?" but is confused as to which of many possible roles to adopt.

imaginary audience The other people who, in an adolescent's egocentric belief, are watching and taking note of his or her appearance, ideas, and behavior. This belief makes many teenagers self-conscious.

immunization A process that stimulates the body's immune system to defend against attack by a particular contagious disease. Immunization may be accomplished either naturally (by having the disease) or through vaccination (often by having an injection). (Also called *inoculation* or *vaccination*.)

implantation The process, beginning about 10 days after conception, in which the developing organism burrows into the placenta that lines the uterus, where it can be nourished and protected as it continues to develop.

in vitro fertilization (IVF) A technique in which ova (egg cells) are surgically removed from a woman and fertilized with sperm in a laboratory. After the original fertilized cells (the zygotes) have divided several times, they are inserted into the woman's uterus.

incomplete grief A situation in which circumstances, such as a police investigation or an autopsy, interfere with the process of grieving.

independent variable In an experiment, the variable that is introduced to see what effect it has on the dependent variable. (Also called *experimental variable*.)

inductive reasoning Reasoning from one or more specific experiences or facts to a general conclusion; may be less cognitively advanced than deduction. (Sometimes called *bottom-up reasoning*.)

industry versus inferiority The fourth of Erikson's eight psychosocial crises, during which children attempt to master many skills, developing a sense of themselves as either industrious or inferior, competent or incompetent.

information-processing theory A perspective that compares human thinking processes, by analogy, to computer analysis of data, including sensory input, connections, stored memories, and output.

initiative versus guilt Erikson's third psychosocial crisis, in which children undertake new skills and activities and feel guilty when they do not succeed at them.

injury control/harm reduction Practices that are aimed at anticipating, controlling, and preventing dangerous activities; these practices reflect the beliefs that accidents are not random and that injuries can be made less harmful if proper controls are in place.

insecure-avoidant attachment A pattern of attachment in which an infant avoids connection with the caregiver, as when the infant seems not to care about the caregiver's presence, departure, or return.

insecure-resistant/ambivalent attachment A pattern of attachment in which an infant's anxiety and uncertainty are evident, as when the infant becomes very upset at separation from the caregiver and both resists and seeks contact on reunion.

instrumental activities of daily life (IADLs) Actions (for example, paying bills and driving a car) that are important to independent living and that require some intellectual competence and forethought. The ability to perform these tasks may be even more critical to self-sufficiency than ADL ability.

instrumental aggression Hurtful behavior that is intended to get something that another person has and to keep it.

integrity versus despair The final stage of Erik Erikson's developmental sequence, in which older adults seek to integrate their unique experiences with their vision of community.

internalizing problems Difficulty with emotional regulation that involves turning one's emotional distress inward, as by feeling excessively guilty, ashamed, or worthless.

intrinsic motivation A drive, or reason to pursue a goal, that comes from inside a person, such as the need to feel smart or competent.

intrinsic rewards of work The intangible gratifications (e.g., job satisfaction, self-esteem, pride) that come from within oneself as a result of doing a job.

intuitive thought Thought that arises from an emotion or a hunch, beyond rational explanation, and is influenced by past experiences and cultural assumptions.

invincibility fable An adolescent's egocentric conviction that he or she cannot be overcome or even harmed by anything that might defeat a normal mortal, such as unprotected sex, drug abuse, or high-speed driving.

IQ test A test designed to measure intellectual aptitude, or ability to learn in school. Originally, intelligence was defined as mental age divided by chronological age, times 100—hence the term *intelligence quotient*, or *IQ*.

irreversibility A characteristic of preoperational thought whereby a young child thinks that nothing can be undone. A thing cannot be restored to the way it was before a change occurred.

J

juvenile delinquent A person under the age of 18 who breaks the law.

K

kangaroo care A child-care technique in which the mother of a low-birthweight infant spends at least an hour a day holding the baby between her breasts, like a kangaroo that carries her immature newborn in a pouch on her abdomen.

kinkeeper A caregiver who takes responsibility for maintaining communication among family members.

kinship care A form of foster care in which a relative of a maltreated child, usually a grandparent, becomes the approved caregiver.

knowledge base A body of knowledge in a particular area that makes it easier to master new information in that area.

L

language acquisition device (LAD) Chomsky's term for a hypothesized mental structure that enables humans to learn language, including the basic aspects of grammar, vocabulary, and intonation.

lateralization Literally, sidedness, referring to the specialization in certain functions by each side of the brain, with one side dominant for each activity. The left side of the brain controls the right side of the body, and vice versa.

learning disability A marked delay in a particular area of learning that is not caused by an apparent physical disability, by mental retardation, or by an unusually stressful home environment.

leptin A hormone that affects appetite and is believed to be involved in the onset of puberty. Leptin levels increase during childhood and peak at around age 12.

life review An examination of one's own part in life, which often takes the form of stories written or spoken by elderly people who want to share them with younger ones.

life-course-persistent offender A person whose criminal activity typically begins in early adolescence and continues throughout life; a career criminal.

life-span perspective An approach to the study of human development that takes into account all phases of life, not just childhood or adulthood.

"little scientist" The stage-five toddler (age 12 to 18 months) who experiments without anticipating the results, using trial and error in active and creative exploration.

living will A document that indicates what kinds of medical intervention an individual wants or does not want if he or she becomes incapable of expressing those wishes.

longitudinal research A research design in which the same individuals are followed over time and their development is repeatedly assessed.

long-term memory The component of the information-processing system in which virtually limitless amounts of information can be stored indefinitely.

low birthweight (LBW) A body weight at birth of less than 5½ pounds (2,500 grams).

M

maximum life span The oldest possible age to which members of a species can live, under ideal circumstances. For humans, that age is approximately 122 years.

menarche A girl's first menstrual period, signaling that she has begun ovulation. Pregnancy is biologically possible, but ovulation and menstruation are often irregular for years after menarche.

menopause The time in middle age, usually around age 50, when a woman's menstrual periods cease completely and the production of estrogen, progesterone, and testosterone drops considerably. Strictly speaking, menopause is dated to one year after a woman's last menstrual period.

mental retardation Literally, slow, or late, thinking. In practice, people are considered mentally retarded if they score below 70 on an IQ test and if they are markedly behind their peers in the ability to meet the basic requirements of daily life.

mentor A skilled and knowledgeable person who advises or guides an inexperienced person.

metacognition "Thinking about thinking"; the ability to evaluate a cognitive task in order to determine how best to accomplish it, and then to monitor and adjust one's performance on that task.

metamemory The ability to understand how memory works in order to use it well. Metamemory is an essential element of metacognition.

middle childhood The period between early childhood and early adolescence, approximately from ages 7 to 11.

middle school A school for children in the grades between elementary and high school. Middle school usually begins with grade 5 or 6 and ends with grade 8.

midlife crisis A period of unusual anxiety, radical self-reexamination, and sudden transformation that is widely associated with middle age but that actually has more to do with developmental history than with chronological age.

mirror neurons Cells in an observer's brain that respond to an action performed by someone else in the same way they would if the observer had actually performed that action.

monozygotic twins Twins who originate from one zygote that splits apart very early in development. (Also called *identical twins.*)

moratorium An adolescent's choice of a socially acceptable way to postpone making identity-achievement decisions. Going to college is a common example.

morbidity Disease. As a measure of health, morbidity refers to the rate of diseases of all kinds—physical and emotional, acute (sudden), chronic (ongoing), and fatal—in a given population.

mortality Death. As a measure of health, mortality usually refers to the number of deaths each year per 1,000 members of a given population.

mourning The ceremonies and behaviors that a religion or culture prescribes for people to employ in expressing their bereavement after a death.

multifactorial Referring to a trait that is affected by many factors, both genetic and environmental.

myelination The process by which axons become coated with myelin, a fatty substance that speeds the transmission of nerve impulses from neuron to neuron.

N

naming explosion A sudden increase in an infant's vocabulary, especially in the number of nouns, that begins at about 18 months of age.

National Assessment of Educational Progress (NAEP) An ongoing and nationally representative measure of U.S. children's achievement in reading, mathematics, and other subjects over time; nicknamed "the nation's report card."

naturally occurring retirement community (NORC) A neighborhood or apartment building whose population is mostly retired people who moved to the location as younger adults and never left.

nature A general term for the traits, capacities, and limitations that each individual inherits genetically from his or her parents at the moment of conception.

near-death experience An episode in which a person comes close to dying but survives and reports having left his or her body and having moved toward a bright white light while feeling peacefulness and joy.

neglectful/uninvolved parenting An approach to child rearing in which the parents are indifferent toward their children and unaware of what is going on in their children's lives.

neuron One of billions of nerve cells in the central nervous system, especially in the brain.

neurotransmitter A brain chemical that carries information from the axon of a sending neuron to the dendrites of a receiving neuron.

No Child Left Behind Act A U.S. law enacted in 2001 that was intended to increase accountability in education by requiring states to qualify for federal educational funding by administering standardized tests to measure school achievement.

norm An average, or standard, measurement, calculated from the measurements of many individuals within a specific group or population.

nuclear family A family that consists of a father, a mother, and their biological children under age 18.

nurture A general term for all the environmental influences that affect development after an individual is conceived.

O

obesity In an adult, having a BMI of 30 or more. In a child, having a BMI above the 95th percentile, according to the U.S. Centers for Disease Control's 1980 standards for children of a given age.

object permanence The realization that objects (including people) still exist when they can no longer be seen, touched, or heard.

Oedipus complex The unconscious desire of young boys to replace their fathers and win their mothers' exclusive love.

oldest-old Elderly adults (generally, those over age 85) who are dependent on others for almost everything, requiring supportive services such as nursing-home care and hospital stays.

old-old Older adults (generally, those aged 75 to 85) who suffer from physical, mental, or social deficits.

operant conditioning The learning process in which a particular action is followed either by something desired (which makes the person or animal more likely to repeat the action) or by something unwanted (which makes the action less likely to be repeated). (Also called *instrumental conditioning.*)

organ reserve The capacity of human organs to allow the body to cope with unusual stress.

overregularization The application of rules of grammar even when exceptions occur, making the language seem more "regular" than it actually is.

overweight In an adult, having a BMI of 25 to 29. In a child, having a BMI above the 85th percentile, according to the U.S. Centers for Disease Control's 1980 standards for children of a given age.

P

palliative care Care designed not to treat an illness but to provide physical and emotional comfort to the patient and support and guidance to his or her family.

parasuicide Any potentially lethal action against the self that does not result in death.

parent–infant bond The strong, loving connection that forms as parents hold, examine, and feed their newborn.

parental monitoring Parents' ongoing awareness of what their children are doing, where, and with whom.

passive euthanasia A situation in which a seriously ill person is allowed to die naturally, through the cessation of medical interventions.

peer pressure Encouragement to conform to one's friends or contemporaries in behavior, dress, and attitude; usually considered a negative force, as when adolescent peers encourage one another to defy adult authority.

perception The mental processing of sensory information when the brain interprets a sensation.

permanency planning An effort by child-welfare authorities to find a long-term living situation that will provide stability and support for a maltreated child. A goal is to avoid repeated changes of caregiver or school, which can be particularly harmful to the child.

permissive parenting An approach to child rearing that is characterized by high nurturance and communication but little discipline, guidance, or control.

perseveration The tendency to persevere in, or stick to, one thought or action for a long time.

personal fable An aspect of adolescent egocentrism characterized by an adolescent's belief that his or her thoughts, feelings, of experiences are unique, more wonderful or awful than anyone else's.

phallic stage Freud's third stage of development, when the penis becomes the focus of concern and pleasure.

phenotype The observable characteristics of a person, including appearance, personality, intelligence, and all other traits.

phenylketonuria (PKU) A genetic disorder in which a child's body is unable to metabolize an amino acid called phenylalanine. The resulting buildup of phenylalanine in body fluids causes brain damage, progressive mental retardation, and other symptoms.

phonics approach Teaching reading by first teaching the sounds of each letter and of various letter combinations.

physician-assisted suicide A form of active euthanasia in which a doctor provides the means for someone to end his or her own life.

pituitary gland A gland in the brain that responds to a signal from the hypothalamus by producing many hormones, including those that regulate growth and control other glands, among them the adrenal and sex glands.

placenta The organ that surrounds the developing embryo and fetus, sustaining life via the umbilical cord. The placenta is attached to the wall of the pregnant woman's uterus.

polygamous family A family consisting of one man, several wives, and the biological children of the man and his wives.

polygenic Referring to a trait that is influenced by many genes.

population pyramid A graphic representation of population as a series of stacked bars in which each age cohort is represented by one bar, with the youngest cohort at the bottom.

positivity effect The tendency for elderly people to perceive, prefer, and remember positive images and experiences more than negative ones.

postconventional moral reasoning Kohlberg's third level of moral reasoning, emphasizing moral principles.

postpartum depression The sadness and inadequacy felt by some new mothers in the days and weeks after giving birth.

preconventional moral reasoning Kohlberg's first level of moral reasoning, emphasizing rewards and punishments.

prefrontal cortex The area of the cortex at the front of the brain that specializes in anticipation, planning, and impulse control.

preoperational intelligence Piaget's term for cognitive development between the ages of about 2 and 6; it includes language and imagination (which involve symbolic thought), but logical, operational thinking is not yet possible.

presbycusis A loss of hearing that is associated with senescence and that usually does not become apparent until after age 60.

preterm birth A birth that occurs 3 or more weeks before the full 38 weeks of the typical pregnancy have elapsed—that is, at 35 or fewer weeks after conception.

primary aging The universal and irreversible physical changes that occur to all living creatures as they grow older.

primary prevention Actions that change overall background conditions to prevent some unwanted event or circumstance, such as injury, disease, or abuse.

primary sex characteristics The parts of the body that are directly involved in reproduction, including the vagina, uterus, ovaries, testicles, and penis.

private speech The internal dialogue that occurs when people talk to themselves (either silently or out loud).

problem-focused coping A strategy often used by younger adults to deal with stress in which they tackle a stressful issue directly.

Progress in International Reading Literacy Study (PIRLS) Inaugurated in 2001, a planned five-year cycle of international trend studies in the reading ability of fourth-graders.

Project Head Start The most widespread early-childhood-education program in the United States, begun in 1965 and funded by the federal government.

prosocial behavior Actions that are helpful and kind but that are of no obvious benefit to the person doing them.

proximal parenting Caregiving practices that involve being physically close to the baby, with frequent holding and touching.

psychoanalytic theory A theory of human development that holds that irrational, unconscious drives and motives, often originating in childhood, underlie human behavior.

psychological control A disciplinary technique that involves threatening to withdraw love and support and that relies on a child's feelings of guilt and gratitude to the parents.

psychopathology An illness or disorder of the mind.

puberty The time between the first onrush of hormones and full adult physical development. Puberty usually lasts three to five years. Many more years are required to achieve psychosocial maturity.

Q

qualitative research Research that considers qualities instead of quantities. Descriptions of particular conditions and participants' expressed ideas are often part of qualitative studies.

quantitative research Research that provides data that can be expressed with numbers, such as ranks or scales.

R

reaction time The time it takes to respond to a stimulus, either physically (with a reflexive movement such as an eye blink) or cognitively (with a thought).

reactive aggression An impulsive retaliation for another person's intentional or accidental action, verbal or physical.

reflex An unlearned, involuntary action or movement emitted in response to a particular stimulus. A reflex is an automatic response that is built into the nervous system and occurs without conscious thought.

Reggio Emilia approach A famous program of early-childhood education that originated in the town of Reggio Emilia, Italy; it encourages each child's creativity in a carefully designed setting.

regulator gene A gene that controls the interactions of other genes, controlling their expression, duplication, and transcription.

reinforcement A technique for conditioning behavior in which that behavior is followed by something desired, such as food for a hungry animal or a welcoming smile for a lonely person.

relational aggression Nonphysical acts, such as insults or social rejection, aimed at harming the social connection between the victim and other people.

relative deprivation The idea that people compare themselves to others in their group and are satisfied if they are no worse off than the group norm.

REM (rapid eye movement) sleep A stage of sleep characterized by flickering eyes behind closed lids, dreaming, and rapid brain waves.

reminder session A perceptual experience that is intended to help a person recollect an idea, a thing, or an experience, without testing whether the person remembers it at the moment.

replacement rate The number of births per woman that would be required to maintain a nation's (or the world's) population with no increases or decreases. The current replacement rate is considered to be about 2.1 births per woman.

replication The repetition of a study, using different participants.

resilience The capacity to adapt well despite significant adversity and to overcome serious stress.

role confusion A situation in which an adolescent does not seem to know or care what his or her identity is. (Also called *identity diffusion*.)

rough-and-tumble play Play that mimics aggression through wrestling, chasing, or hitting, but in which there is no intent to harm.

rumination Repeatedly thinking and talking about past experiences; can contribute to depression.

S

sandwich generation The generation of middle-aged people who are supposedly "squeezed" by the needs of the younger and older members of their families. In reality, some adults do feel pressured by these obligations, but most are not burdened by them, either because they enjoy fulfilling them or because they choose to take on only some of them or none of them.

scaffolding Temporary support that is tailored to a learner's needs and abilities and aimed at helping the learner master the next task in a given learning process.

science of human development The science that seeks to understand how and why people of all ages and circumstances change or remain the same over time.

scientific method A way to answer questions that requires empirical research and data-based conclusions.

scientific observation A method of testing a hypothesis by unobtrusively watching and recording participants' behavior in a systematic and objective manner—in a natural setting, in a laboratory, or in searches of archival data.

Seattle Longitudinal Study The first cross-sequential study of adult intelligence. K. Warner Schaie began this study in 1956; the most recent testing was conducted in 2005.

secondary aging The specific physical illnesses or conditions that become more common with aging but result from poor health habits, genetic vulnerability, and other influences that vary from person to person.

secondary education The period after primary education (elementary or grade school) and before tertiary education (college). It usually occurs from about age 12 to age 18, although the age range varies somewhat by school and by nation.

secondary prevention Actions that avert harm in a high-risk situation, such as stopping a car before it hits a pedestrian or installing traffic lights at dangerous intersections.

secondary sex characteristics Physical traits that are not directly involved in reproduction but that indicate sexual maturity, such as a man's beard and a woman's breasts.

secure attachment A relationship in which an infant obtains both comfort and confidence from the presence of his or her caregiver.

selective attention The ability to concentrate on some stimuli while ignoring others.

selective expert Someone who is notably more skilled and knowledgeable than the average person about whichever activities are personally meaningful.

selective optimization with compensation The theory, developed by Paul and Margaret Baltes, that people try to maintain a balance in their lives by looking for the best way to compensate for physical and cognitive losses and to become more proficient in activities they can already do well.

self theories Theories of late adulthood that emphasize the core self, or the search to maintain one's integrity and identity.

self-actualization The final stage in Maslow's hierarchy of needs, characterized by aesthetic, creative, philosophical, and spiritual understanding.

self-awareness A person's realization that he or she is a distinct individual whose body, mind, and actions are separate from those of other people.

self-concept A person's understanding of who he or she is, incorporating self-esteem, physical appearance, personality, and various personal traits, such as gender and size.

self-esteem A person's evaluation of his or her own worth, either in specifics (e.g., intelligence, attractiveness) or in general.

senescence A gradual physical decline that is related to aging and during which the body becomes less strong and efficient.

sensation The response of a sensory system (eyes, ears, skin, tongue, nose) when it detects a stimulus.

sensitive period A time when a certain type of development is most likely to happen and happens most easily, although it may still happen later with more difficulty. For example, early childhood is considered a sensitive period for language learning.

sensorimotor intelligence Piaget's term for the way infants think—by using their senses and motor skills—during the first period of cognitive development.

sensory memory The component of the information-processing system in which incoming stimulus information is stored for a split second to allow it to be processed. (Also called the *sensory register*.)

separation anxiety An infant's distress when a familiar caregiver leaves, most obvious between 9 and 14 months.

sex differences Biological differences between males and females, in organs, hormones, and body shape.

sexual orientation A term that refers to whether a person is sexually and romantically attracted to others of the same sex, the opposite sex, or both sexes.

sexually transmitted infection (STI) A disease spread by sexual contact, including syphilis, gonorrhea, genital herpes, chlamydia, and HIV.

shaken baby syndrome A life-threatening injury that occurs when an infant is forcefully shaken back and forth, a motion that ruptures blood vessels in the brain and breaks neural connections.

single-parent family A family that consists of only one parent and his or her biological children under age 18.

slippery slope The argument that a given action will start a chain of events that will culminate in an undesirable outcome.

small for gestational age (SGA) Having a body weight at birth that is significantly lower than expected, given the time since conception. For example, a 5-pound (2,265-gram) newborn is considered SGA if born on time but not SGA if born two months early. (Also called *small-for-dates*.)

social clock A developmental timetable based not on biological maturation but on social norms, which set the stages of life and the behaviors considered appropriate to each of them. For example, "middle age" begins when a culture believes it does, rather than at a certain age in all cultures.

social cognition The ability to understand social interactions, including the causes and consequences of human behavior.

social comparison The tendency to assess one's abilities, achievements, social status, and other attributes by measuring them against those of other people, especially one's peers.

social construction An idea that is based on shared perceptions, not on objective reality. Many age-related terms, such as *childhood, adolescence, yuppie,* and *senior citizen,* are social constructions.

social convoy Collectively, the family members, friends, acquaintances, and even strangers who move through life with an individual.

social learning The acquisition of behavior patterns by observing the behavior of others.

social learning theory An extension of behaviorism that emphasizes the influence that other people have over a person's behavior. The theory's basic principle is that even without specific reinforcement, every individual learns many things through observation and imitation of other people.

social mediation Human interaction that expands and advances understanding, often through words that one person uses to explain something to another.

social norms approach A method of reducing risky behavior among emerging adults that is based on their desire to follow social norms. This approach publicizes survey results to make emerging adults aware of the actual prevalence of various behaviors within their peer group.

social referencing Seeking information about how to react to an unfamiliar or ambiguous object or event by observing someone else's expressions and reactions. That other person becomes a *social reference.*

social smile A smile evoked by a human face, normally first evident in infants about 6 weeks after birth.

sociodramatic play Pretend play in which children act out various roles and themes in stories that they create.

socioeconomic status (SES) A person's position in society as determined by income, wealth, occupation, education, and place of residence. (Sometimes called *social class.*)

sonogram An image of an unborn fetus (or an internal organ) produced by scanning it with high-frequency sound waves. (Also called *ultrasound.*)

spermarche A boy's first ejaculation of sperm. Erections can occur as early as infancy, but ejaculation signals sperm production. Spermache occurs during sleep (in a "wet dream") or via direct stimulation.

static reasoning A characteristic of preoperational thought whereby a young child thinks that nothing changes. Whatever is now has always been and always will be.

stereotype threat The fear that someone else will judge one's appearance or behavior negatively and thereby confirm that person's prejudiced attitudes.

still-face technique An experimental practice in which an adult keeps his or her face unmoving and expressionless in face-to-face interaction with an infant.

Strange Situation A laboratory procedure for measuring attachment by evoking infants' reactions to the stress of various adults' comings and goings in an unfamiliar playroom.

stranger wariness An infant's expression of concern—a quiet stare when clinging to a familiar person, or a look of sadness—when a stranger appears.

stratification theories Theories that emphasize that social forces, particularly those related to a person's social stratum, or social category, limit individual choices and affect a person's ability to function in late adulthood as past stratification continues to limit life in various ways.

stressor Any situation, event, experience, or other stimulus that causes a person to feel stressed.

substantiated maltreatment Harm or endangerment that has been reported, investigated, and verified.

sudden infant death syndrome (SIDS) A situation in which a seemingly healthy infant, at least 2 months of age, suddenly stops breathing and dies unexpectedly while asleep.

suicidal ideation Thinking about suicide, usually with some serious emotional and intellectual or cognitive overtones.

superego In psychoanalytic theory, the judgmental part of the personality that internalizes the moral standards of the parents.

survey A research method in which information is collected from a large number of people by interviews, written questionnaires, or some other means.

synapse The intersection between the axon of one neuron and the dendrites of other neurons.

synchrony A coordinated, rapid, and smooth exchange of responses between a caregiver and an infant.

T

telecommuting Working at home and keeping in touch with the office via computer, telephone, and fax.

temperament Inborn differences between one person and another in emotions, activity, and self-regulation. Temperament is epigenetic, originating in the genes but affected by child-rearing practices.

teratogens Agents and conditions, including viruses, drugs, and chemicals, that can impair prenatal development and result in birth defects or even death.

terror management theory (TMT) The idea that people adopt cultural values and moral principles in order to cope with their fear of death. This system of beliefs protects individuals from anxiety about their mortality and bolsters their self-esteem, so they react harshly when other people go against any of the moral principles involved.

tertiary prevention Actions, such as immediate and effective medical treatment, that are taken after an adverse event (such as illness, injury, or abuse) occurs and that are aimed at reducing the harm or preventing disability.

testosterone A sex hormone, the best known of the androgens (male hormones); secreted in far greater amounts by males than by females.

thanatology The study of death and dying, especially of the social and emotional aspects.

theory of mind A person's theory of what other people might be thinking. In order to have a theory of mind, children must realize that other people are not necessarily thinking the same thoughts that they themselves are. That realization is seldom possible before age 4.

theory-theory The idea that children attempt to explain everything they see and hear by constructing theories.

threshold effect A situation in which a certain teratogen is relatively harmless in small doses but becomes harmful once exposure reaches a certain level (the threshold).

time-out A disciplinary technique in which a child is separated from other people and activities for a specified time.

Trends in Math and Science Study (TIMSS) An international assessment of the math and science skills of fourth- and eighth-graders. Although the TIMSS is very useful, different countries' scores are not always comparable because sample selection, test administration, and content validity are hard to keep uniform.

trust versus mistrust Erikson's first crisis of psychosocial development. Infants learn basic trust if the world is a secure place where their basic needs (for food, comfort, attention, and so on) are met.

V

vascular dementia (VaD) A form of dementia characterized by sporadic, and progressive, loss of intellectual functioning caused by repeated infarcts, or temporary obstructions of blood vessels, which prevent sufficient blood from reaching the brain. Also called *multi-infarct dementia*.

very low birthweight (VLBW) A body weight at birth of less than 3 pounds, 5 ounces (1,500 grams).

visual cliff An experimental apparatus that gives an illusion of a sudden dropoff between one horizontal surface and another.

vitality A measure of health that refers to how healthy and energetic—physically, emotionally, and socially—an individual actually feels.

W

Wechsler Intelligence Scale for Children (WISC) An IQ test designed for school-age children. The test assesses potential in many areas, including vocabulary, general knowledge, memory, and spatial comprehension.

whole-language approach Teaching reading by encouraging early use of all language skills—talking and listening, reading and writing.

withdrawn-rejected children Children who are disliked by peers because of their timid, withdrawn, and anxious behavior.

working memory The component of the information-processing system in which current, conscious mental activity occurs. (Also called *short-term memory*.)

working model In cognitive theory, a set of assumptions that the individual uses to organize perceptions and experiences. For example, a person might assume that other people are trustworthy and be surprised by evidence that this working model of human behavior is erroneous.

X

XX A 23rd chromosome pair that consists of two X-shaped chromosomes, one each from the mother and the father. XX zygotes become females.

XY A 23rd chromosome pair that consists of an X-shaped chromosome from the mother and a Y-shaped chromosome from the father. XY zygotes become males.

Y

young-old Healthy, vigorous, financially secure older adults (generally, those aged 60 to 75) who are well integrated into the lives of their families and communities.

Z

zone of proximal development (ZPD) Vygotsky's term for the skills—cognitive as well as physical—that a person can exercise only with assistance, not yet independently.

zygote The single cell that is formed from the fusing of two gametes, a sperm and an ovum.

REFERENCES

Aarsland, Dag, Zaccai, Julia, & Brayne, Carol. (2005). A systematic review of prevalence studies of dementia in Parkinson's disease. *Movement Disorders, 20,* 1255–1263.

Abbott, Lesley, & Nutbrown, Cathy (Eds.). (2001). *Experiencing Reggio Emilia: Implications for pre-school provision.* Philadelphia: Open University Press.

Abeles, Ronald P. (2007). Foreword. In Carolyn M. Aldwin, Crystal L. Park, & Avron Spiro III (Eds.), *Handbook of health psychology and aging* (pp. ix–xii). New York: Guilford Press.

Abelson, Reed. (2007, February 10). A chance to pick hospice, and still hope to live. *New York Times,* pp. A1, C4.

Aboa-Éboulé, Corine, Brisson, Chantal, Maunsell, Elizabeth, Mâsse, Benoît, Bourbonnais, Renée, Vézina, Michel, et al. (2007). Job strain and risk of acute recurrent coronary heart disease events. *Journal of the American Medical Association, 298,* 1652–1660.

Aboderin, Isabella. (2004). Intergenerational family support and old age economic security in sub-Saharan Africa: The importance of understanding shifts, processes and expectations. An example from Ghana. In Peter Lloyd-Sherlock (Ed.), *Living longer: Ageing, development and social protection* (pp. 210–229). London: Zed Books.

Aboud, Frances E. (2003). The formation of in-group favoritism and out-group prejudice in young children: Are they distinct attitudes? *Developmental Psychology, 39,* 48–60.

Aboud, Frances E., & Amato, Maria. (2001). Developmental and socialization influences on intergroup bias. In Rupert Brown & Samuel L. Gaertner (Eds.), *Blackwell handbook of social psychology: Intergroup processes* (pp. 65–85). Malden, MA: Blackwell.

Aboud, Frances E., & Mendelson, Morton J. (1998). Determinants of friendship selection and quality: Developmental perspectives. In William M. Bukowski, Andrew F. Newcomb, & Willard W. Hartup (Eds.), *The company they keep: Friendship in childhood and adolescence* (pp. 87–112). New York: Cambridge University Press.

Abramovitch, Henry. (2005). Where are the dead? Bad death, the missing, and the inability to mourn. In Samuel Heilman (Ed.), *Death, bereavement, and mourning* (pp. 53–67). New Brunswick, NJ: Transaction.

Abrams, Dominic, Eller, Anja, & Bryant, Jacqueline. (2006). An age apart: The effects of intergenerational contact and stereotype threat on performance and intergroup bias. *Psychology and Aging, 21,* 691–702.

Abrams, Dominic, Rutland, Adam, Ferrell, Jennifer M., & Pelletier, Joseph. (2008). Children's judgments of disloyal and immoral peer behavior: Subjective group dynamics in minimal intergroup contexts. *Child Development, 79,* 444–461.

Accardo, Pasquale. (2006). Who's training whom? *The Journal of Pediatrics, 149,* 151–152.

Achenbaum, W. Andrew. (2006-2007). A history of civic engagement of older people. *Generations, 30*(4), 18–23.

Acs, Gregory. (2007). Can we promote child well-being by promoting marriage? *Journal of Marriage and Family, 69,* 1326–1344.

Adam, Emma K., Klimes-Dougan, Bonnie, & Gunnar, Megan R. (2007). Social regulation of the adrenocortical response to stress in infants, children, and adolescents: Implications for psychopathology and education. In Donna Coch, Geraldine Dawson, & Kurt W. Fischer (Eds.), *Human behavior, learning, and the developing brain: Atypical development* (pp. 264–304). New York: Guilford Press.

Adam, Tanja C., & Epel, Elissa S. (2007). Stress, eating and the reward system. *Physiology & Behavior, 91,* 449–458.

Adamson, Lauren B., & Bakeman, Roger. (2006). Development of displaced speech in early mother–child conversations. *Child Development, 77,* 186–200.

Adenzato, Mauro, & Garbarini, Francesca. (2006). The *as if* in cognitive science, neuroscience and anthropology: A journey among robots, blacksmiths and neurons. *Theory & Psychology, 16,* 747–759.

Adler, Lynn Peters. (1995). *Centenarians: The bonus years.* Santa Fe, NM: Health Press.

Adler, Nancy E., & Snibbe, Alana Conner. (2003). The role of psychosocial processes in explaining the gradient between socioeconomic status and health. *Current Directions in Psychological Science, 12,* 119–123.

Adolph, Karen E., & Berger, Sarah E. (2005). Physical and motor development. In Marc H. Bornstein & Michael E. Lamb (Eds.), *Developmental science: An advanced textbook* (5th ed., pp. 223–281). Mahwah, NJ: Erlbaum.

Adolph, Karen E., & Berger, Sarah E. (2006). Motor development. In William Damon & Richard M. Lerner (Series Eds.) & Deanna Kuhn & Robert S. Siegler (Vol. Eds.), *Handbook of child psychology: Vol. 2. Cognition, perception, and language* (6th ed., pp. 161–213). Hoboken, NJ: Wiley.

Adolph, Karen E., Vereijken, Beatrix, & Denny, Mark A. (1998). Learning to crawl. *Child Development, 69,* 1299–1312.

Adolph, Karen E., Vereijken, Beatrix, & Shrout, Patrick E. (2003). What changes in infant walking and why. *Child Development, 74,* 475–497.

Afifi, Tracie O., Enns, Murray W., Cox, Brian J., Asmundson, Gordon J. G., Stein, Murray B., & Sareen, Jitender. (2008). Population attributable fractions of psychiatric disorders and suicide ideation and attempts associated with adverse childhood experiences. *American Journal of Public Health, 98,* 946–952.

Ahmed, Saifuddin, Koenig, Michael A., & Stephenson, Rob. (2006). Effects of domestic violence on perinatal and early-childhood mortality: Evidence from North India. *American Journal of Public Health, 96,* 1423–1428.

Ainsworth, Mary D. Salter. (1973). The development of infant-mother attachment. In Bettye M. Caldwell & Henry N. Ricciuti (Eds.), *Review of child development research* (Vol. 3, pp. 1–94). Chicago: University of Chicago Press.

Ajdacic-Gross, Vladeta, Ring, Mariann, Gadola, Erika, Lauber, Christoph, Bopp, Matthias, Gutzwiller, Felix, et al. (2008). Suicide after bereavement: An overlooked problem. *Psychological Medicine, 38,* 673–676.

Akiba, Daisuke, & García Coll, Cynthia. (2004). Effective interventions with children of color and their families: A contextual developmental approach. In Timothy B. Smith (Ed.), *Practicing multiculturalism: Affirming diversity in counseling and psychology* (pp. 123–144). Boston: Pearson/Allyn and Bacon.

Akinbami, Lara J. (2006). *The state of childhood asthma, United States, 1980–2005.* National Center for Health Statistics. Retrieved September 11, 2009, from http://www.cdc.gov/nchs/data/ad/ad381.pdf

Alasuutari, Pertti, Bickman, Leonard, & Brannen, Julia (Eds.). (2008). *The SAGE handbook of social research methods.* Los Angeles: SAGE.

Albertini, Marco, Kohli, Martin, & Vogel, Claudia. (2007). Intergenerational transfers of time and money in European families: Common patterns—Different regimes? *Journal of European Social Policy, 17,* 319–334.

Alberts, Amy, Elkind, David, & Ginsberg, Stephen. (2007). The personal fable and risk-taking in early adolescence. *Journal of Youth and Adolescence, 36,* 71–76.

Aldwin, Carolyn M. (2007). *Stress, coping, and development: An integrative perspective* (2nd ed.). New York: Guilford Press.

Aldwin, Carolyn M., & Gilmer, Diane F. (2003). *Health, illness, and optimal aging: Biological and psychosocial perspectives.* Thousand Oaks, CA: Sage.

Alexander, Karl L., Entwisle, Doris R., & Olson, Linda Steffel. (2007). Lasting consequences of the summer learning gap. *American Sociological Review, 72,* 167–180.

Allemand, Mathias, Zimprich, Daniel, & Martin, Mike. (2008). Long-term correlated change in personality traits in old age. *Psychology and Aging, 23,* 545–557.

Allen, Arthur. (2007). *Vaccine: The controversial story of medicine's greatest lifesaver.* New York: W. W. Norton.

Allen, Elizabeth, Bonell, Chris, Strange, Vicki, Copas, Andrew, Stephenson, Judith, Johnson, Anne, et al. (2007). Does the UK government's teenage pregnancy strategy deal with the correct risk factors? Findings from a secondary analysis of data from a randomised trial of sex education and their implications for policy. *Journal of Epidemiology & Community Health, 61,* 20–27.

Allen, James E. (2007). *Nursing home administration* (5th ed.). New York: Springer.

Allen, Joseph P., Porter, Maryfrances R., McFarland, F. Christy, Marsh, Penny, & McElhaney, Kathleen Boykin. (2005). The two faces of adolescents' success with peers: Adolescent popularity, social adaptation, and deviant behavior. *Child Development, 76,* 747–760.

Alley, Dawn, Suthers, Kristen, & Crimmins, Eileen. (2007). Education and cognitive decline in older Americans: Results from the AHEAD sample. *Research on Aging, 29,* 73–94.

Alloy, Lauren B., & Abramson, Lyn Y. (2007). The adolescent surge in depression and emergence of gender differences: A biocognitive vulnerability-stress model in developmental context. In Daniel Romer & Elaine F. Walker (Eds.), *Adolescent psychopathology and the developing brain: Integrating brain and prevention science* (pp. 284–313). New York: Oxford University Press.

Alsaker, Françoise D., & Flammer, August. (2006). Pubertal development. In Sandy Jackson & Luc Goossens (Eds.), *Handbook of adolescent development* (pp. 30–50). Hove, East Sussex, UK: Psychology Press.

Aluise, Christopher D., Sowell, Rena A., & Butterfield, D. Allan. (2008). Peptides and proteins in plasma and cerebrospinal fluid as biomarkers for the prediction, diagnosis, and monitoring of therapeutic efficacy of Alzheimer's disease. *Biochimica et Biophysica Acta (BBA)/Molecular Basis of Disease, 1782,* 549–558.

Amato, Paul R. (2000). The consequences of divorce for adults and children. *Journal of Marriage and the Family, 62,* 1269–1287.

Amato, Paul R., & Afifi, Tamara D. (2006). Feeling caught between parents: Adult children's relations with parents and subjective well-being. *Journal of Marriage and Family, 68,* 222–235.

Amato, Paul R., Booth, Alan, Johnson, David R., & Rogers, Stacy J. (2007). *Alone together: How marriage in America is changing.* Cambridge, MA: Harvard University Press.

Amato, Paul R., & Cheadle, Jacob. (2005). The long reach of divorce: Divorce and child well-being across three generations. *Journal of Marriage and Family, 67,* 191–206.

Amato, Paul R., & Fowler, Frieda. (2002). Parenting practices, child adjustment, and family diversity. *Journal of Marriage and Family, 64,* 703–716.

Amato, Paul R., & Hohmann-Marriott, Bryndl. (2007). A comparison of high- and low-distress marriages that end in divorce. *Journal of Marriage and Family, 69,* 621–638.

American Psychiatric Association (APA). (2000). *Diagnostic and statistical manual of mental disorders: DSM-IV-TR* (4th ed.). Washington, DC: Author.

Amirkhanyan, Anna A., & Wolf, Douglas A. (2006). Parent care and the stress process: Findings from panel data. *Journals of Gerontology: Series B: Psychological Sciences and Social Sciences, 61,* S248–S255.

Andersen, Per, Morris, Richard, Amaral, David, Bliss, Tim, & O'Keefe, John (Eds.). (2007). *The hippocampus book.* New York: Oxford University Press.

Anderson, Carol. (2003). The diversity, strength, and challenges of single-parent households. In Froma Walsh (Ed.), *Normal family processes: Growing diversity and complexity* (3rd ed., pp. 121–152). New York: Guilford Press.

Anderson, Craig A., Berkowitz, Leonard, Donnerstein, Edward, Huesmann, L. Rowell, Johnson, James D., Linz, Daniel, et al. (2003). The influence of media violence on youth. *Psychological Science in the Public Interest, 4,* 81–110.

Anderson, Craig A., & Bushman, Brad J. (2002). Human aggression. *Annual Review of Psychology, 53,* 27–51.

Anderson, Craig A., Gentile, Douglas A., & Buckley, Katherine E. (2007). *Violent video game effects on children and adolescents: Theory, research, and public policy.* New York: Oxford University Press.

Anderson, Daniel R., Huston, Aletha C., Schmitt, Kelly L., Linebarger, Deborah L., & Wright, John C. (2001). Early childhood television viewing and adolescent behavior: The recontact study. *Monographs of the Society for Research in Child Development, 66*(1, Serial No. 264).

Anderson, Gerard, & Horvath, Jane. (2004). The growing burden of chronic disease in America. *Public Health Reports, 119,* 263–270.

Anderson, Mark, Johnson, Daniel, & Batal, Holly. (2005). *Sudden infant death syndrome and prenatal maternal smoking: Rising attributed risk in the Back to Sleep era.* Retrieved September 10, 2009, from http://www.biomedcentral.com/1741-7015/3/4

Anderson, Michael. (2001). 'You have to get inside the person' or making grief private: Image and metaphor in the therapeutic reconstruction of bereavement. In Jenny Hockey, Jeanne Katz, & Neil Small (Eds.), *Grief, mourning, and death ritual* (pp. 135–143). Buckingham, England: Open University Press.

Anderson, Ross, & Moore, Tyler. (2006, October 27). The economics of information security. *Science, 314,* 610–613.

Andreassen, Carol, & West, Jerry. (2007). Measuring socioemotional functioning in a national birth cohort study. *Infant Mental Health Journal, 28,* 627–646.

Andresen, Helga. (2005). Role play and language development in the preschool years. *Culture & Psychology, 11,* 387–414.

Andrews, Melinda W., Dowling, W. Jay, Bartlett, James C., & Halpern, Andrea R. (1998). Identification of speeded and slowed familiar melodies by younger, middle-aged, and older musicians and nonmusicians. *Psychology & Aging, 13,* 462–471.

Angold, Adrian, Erkanli, Alaattin, Egger, Helen L., & Costello, E. Jane. (2000). Stimulant treatment for children: A community perspective. *Journal of the American Academy of Child & Adolescent Psychiatry, 39,* 975–984.

Anis, Tarek. (2007). Hormones involved in male sexual function. In Annette Fuglsang Owens & Mitchell S. Tepper (Eds.), *Sexual health: Vol. 2. Physical foundations* (pp. 79–113). Westport, CT: Praeger/Greenwood.

Anstey, Kaarin J., Hofer, Scott M., & Luszcz, Mary A. (2003). A latent growth curve analysis of late-life sensory and cognitive function over 8 years: Evidence for specific and common factors underlying change. *Psychology & Aging, 18,* 714–726.

Antonucci, Toni C., Akiyama, Hiroko, & Merline, Alicia. (2001). Dynamics of social relationships in midlife. In Margie E. Lachman (Ed.), *Handbook of midlife development* (pp. 571–598). New York: Wiley.

Antonucci, Toni C., Jackson, James S., & Biggs, Simon. (2007). Intergenerational relations: Theory, research, and policy. *Journal of Social Issues, 63,* 679–693.

Apfelbaum, Evan P., Pauker, Kristin, Ambady, Nalini, Sommers, Samuel R., & Norton, Michael I. (2008). Learning (not) to talk about race: When older children underperform in social categorization. *Developmental Psychology, 44,* 1513–1518.

Apgar, Virginia. (1953). A proposal for a new method of evaluation of the newborn infant. *Current Researches in Anesthesia and Analgesia, 32,* 260–267.

Archer, John. (2000). Sex differences in aggression between heterosexual partners: A meta-analytic review. *Psychological Bulletin, 126,* 651–680.

Archer, John. (2004). Sex differences in aggression in real-world settings: A meta-analytic review. *Review of General Psychology, 8,* 291–322.

Armour, Marilyn. (2003). Meaning making in the aftermath of homicide. *Death Studies, 27,* 519–540.

Armour-Thomas, Eleanor, & Gopaul-McNicol, Sharon-Ann. (1998). *Assessing intelligence: Applying a bio-cultural model.* Thousand Oaks, CA: Sage.

Armson, B. Anthony. (2007). Is planned cesarean childbirth a safe alternative? *Canadian Medical Association Journal, 176,* 475–476.

Arnett, Jeffrey Jensen. (2004). *Emerging adulthood: The winding road from the late teens through the twenties.* New York: Oxford University Press.

Arnett, Jeffrey Jensen. (2007a). Socialization in emerging adulthood: From the family to the wider world, from socialization to self-socialization. In Joan E. Grusec & Paul D. Hastings (Eds.), *Handbook of socialization: Theory and research* (pp. 208–231). New York: Guilford Press.

Arnett, Jeffrey Jensen. (2007b). Suffering, selfish slackers? Myths and reality about emerging adults. *Journal of Youth and Adolescence, 36,* 23–29.

Aron, Arthur, Fisher, Helen, Mashek, Debra J., Strong, Greg, Li, Haifang, & Brown, Lucy L. (2005). Reward, motivation, and emotion systems associated with early-stage intense romantic love. *Journal of Neurophysiology, 94,* 327–337.

Aronson, Joshua, Fried, Carrie B., & Good, Catherine. (2002). Reducing the effects of stereotype threat on African American college students by shaping theories of intelligence. *Journal of Experimental Social Psychology, 38,* 113–125.

Artar, Müge. (2007). Adolescent egocentrism and theory of mind: In the context of family relations. *Social Behavior and Personality, 35,* 1211–1220.

Artistico, Daniele, Cervone, Daniel, & Pezzuti, Lina. (2003). Perceived self-efficacy and everyday problem solving among young and older adults. *Psychology & Aging, 18,* 68–79.

Aseltine, Robert H., Jr., & DeMartino, Robert. (2004). An outcome evaluation of the SOS suicide prevention program. *American Journal of Public Health, 94,* 446–451.

Asendorpf, Jens B., Denissen, Jaap J. A., & van Aken, Marcel A. G. (2008). Inhibited and aggressive preschool children at 23 years of age: Personality and social transitions into adulthood. *Developmental Psychology, 44,* 997–1011.

Ashman, Sharon B., & Dawson, Geraldine. (2002). Maternal depression, infant psychobiological development, and risk for depression. In Sherryl H. Goodman & Ian H. Gotlib (Eds.), *Children of depressed parents: Mechanisms of risk and implications for treatment* (pp. 37–58). Washington, DC: American Psychological Association.

Ashman, Sharon B., Dawson, Geraldine, & Panagiotides, Heracles. (2008). Trajectories of maternal depression over 7 years: Relations with child psychophysiology and behavior and role of contextual risks. *Development and Psychopathology, 20*, 55–77.

Astin, Alexander W., & Oseguera, Leticia. (2004). The declining "equity" of American higher education. *Review of Higher Education: Journal of the Association for the Study of Higher Education, 27*, 321–341.

Astington, Janet Wilde, & Gopnik, Alison. (1988). Knowing you've changed your mind: Children's understanding of representational change. In Janet W. Astington, Paul L. Harris, & David R. Olson (Eds.), *Developing theories of mind* (pp. 193–206). New York: Cambridge University Press.

Atchley, Robert C. (1999). *Continuity and adaptation in aging: Creating positive experiences.* Baltimore: Johns Hopkins University Press.

Atchley, Robert C. (2009). *Spirituality and aging.* Baltimore: Johns Hopkins University Press.

Atkinson, Janette, & Braddick, Oliver. (2003). Neurobiological models of normal and abnormal visual development. In Michelle De Haan & Mark H. Johnson (Eds.), *The cognitive neuroscience of development* (pp. 43–71). New York: Psychology Press.

Attig, Thomas. (2003). Respecting the spirituality of the dying and bereaved. In Inge Corless, Barbara B. Germino, & Mary A. Pittman (Eds.), *Dying, death, and bereavement: A challenge for living* (2nd ed., pp. 61–75). New York: Springer.

Audrey, Suzanne, Holliday, Jo, & Campbell, Rona. (2006). It's good to talk: Adolescent perspectives of an informal, peer-led intervention to reduce smoking. *Social Science & Medicine, 63*, 320–334.

Aunola, Kaisa, & Nurmi, Jari-Erik. (2004). Maternal affection moderates the impact of psychological control on a child's mathematical performance. *Developmental Psychology, 40*, 965–978.

Austrian, Sonia G. (2008). *Developmental theories through the life cycle* (2nd ed.). New York: Columbia University Press.

Avery, Rosemary J., & Freundlich, Madelyn. (2009). You're all grown up now: Termination of foster care support at age 18. *Journal of Adolescence, 32*, 247–257.

Azmitia, Margarita, Ittel, Angela, & Brenk, Charlotte. (2006). Latino-heritage adolescents' friendships. In Xinyin Chen, Doran C. French, & Barry H. Schneider (Eds.), *Peer relationships in cultural context* (pp. 426–451). New York: Cambridge University Press.

Azmitia, Margarita, Syed, Moin, & Radmacher, Kimberly Ann. (Eds.). (2008). On the intersection of personal and social identities: Introduction and evidence from a longitudinal study of emerging adults. *New Directions for Child and Adolescent Development, 120*, 1–16.

Azrin, Nathan H., & Foxx, Richard M. (1974). *Toilet training in less than a day.* New York: Simon and Schuster.

Bäckman, Lars, & Farde, Lars. (2005). The role of dopamine systems in cognitive aging. In Roberto Cabeza, Lars Nyberg, & Denise Park (Eds.), *Cognitive neuroscience of aging: Linking cognitive and cerebral aging* (pp. 58–84). New York: Oxford University Press.

Bagla, Pallava. (2008, June 13). India's education bonanza instills hope—and concern. *Science, 320*, 1415.

Bagwell, Catherine L., Schmidt, Michelle E., Newcomb, Andrew F., & Bukowski, William M. (2001). Friendship and peer rejection as predictors of adult adjustment. In William Damon (Series Ed.) & Douglas W. Nangle & Cynthia A. Erdley (Vol. Eds.), *New directions for child and adolescent development: No. 91. The role of friendship in psychological adjustment* (pp. 25–49). San Francisco: Jossey-Bass.

Baillargeon, Renée, & DeVos, Julie. (1991). Object permanence in young infants: Further evidence. *Child Development, 62*, 1227–1246.

Baldwin, Dare A. (1993). Infants' ability to consult the speaker for clues to word reference. *Journal of Child Language, 20*, 395–418.

Baltes, Margret M., & Carstensen, Laura L. (2003). The process of successful aging: Selection, optimization and compensation. In Ursula M. Staudinger & Ulman Lindenberger (Eds.), *Understanding human development: Dialogues with lifespan psychology* (pp. 81–104). Dordrecht, The Netherlands: Kluwer.

Baltes, Paul B. (2003). On the incomplete architechture of human ontogeny: Selection, optimization and compensation as foundation of developmental theory. In Ursula M. Staudinger & Ulman Lindenberger (Eds.), *Understanding human development: Dialogues with lifespan psychology* (pp. 17–43). Dordrecht, The Netherlands: Kluwer.

Baltes, Paul B., & Baltes, Margret M. (1990). Psychological perspectives on successful aging: The model of selective optimization with compensation. In Paul B. Baltes & Margret M. Baltes (Eds.), *Successful aging: Perspectives from the behavioral sciences* (pp. 1–34). New York: Cambridge University Press.

Baltes, Paul B., Lindenberger, Ulman, & Staudinger, Ursula M. (1998). Life-span theory in developmental psychology. In William Damon (Series Ed.) & Richard M. Lerner (Vol. Ed.), *Handbook of child psychology: Vol. 1. Theoretical models of human development* (5th ed., pp. 1029–1144). New York: Wiley.

Baltes, Paul B., Lindenberger, Ulman, & Staudinger, Ursula M. (2006). Life-span theory in developmental psychology. In William Damon & Richard M. Lerner (Series Eds.) & Richard M. Lerner (Vol. Ed.), *Handbook of child psychology: Vol. 1. Theoretical models of human development* (6th ed., pp. 569–664). Hoboken, NJ: Wiley.

Baltes, Paul B., & Smith, Jacqui. (2008). The fascination of wisdom: Its nature, ontogeny, and function. *Perspectives on Psychological Science, 3*, 56–64.

Bamford, Christi, & Lagattuta, Kristin H. (2007, April). *Children really do "talk to god": What children know about prayer and its emotional contexts.* Poster session presented at the Society for Research in Child Development, Boston, MA.

Bandura, Albert. (1977). *Social learning theory.* Englewood Cliffs, NJ: Prentice Hall.

Bandura, Albert. (2006). Toward a psychology of human agency. *Perspectives on Psychological Science, 1*, 164–180.

Bandura, Albert, Barbaranelli, Claudio, Caprara, Gian Vittorio, & Pastorelli, Concetta. (2001). Self-efficacy beliefs as shapers of children's aspirations and career trajectories. *Child Development, 72*, 187–206.

Bandura, Albert, & Bussey, Kay. (2004). On broadening the cognitive, motivational, and sociostructural scope of theorizing about gender development and functioning: Comment on Martin, Ruble, and Szkrybalo (2002). *Psychological Bulletin, 130,* 691–701.

Banerjee, Robin, & Lintern, Vicki. (2000). Boys will be boys: The effect of social evaluation concerns on gender-typing. *Social Development, 9,* 397–408.

Bank, Lew, Burraston, Bert, & Snyder, Jim. (2004). Sibling conflict and ineffective parenting as predictors of adolescent boys' antisocial behavior and peer difficulties: Additive and interactional effects. *Journal of Research on Adolescence, 14,* 99–125.

Barber, Bonnie L. (2006). To have loved and lost . . . Adolescent romantic relationships and rejection. In Ann C. Crouter & Alan Booth (Eds.), *Romance and sex in adolescence and emerging adulthood: Risks and opportunities* (pp. 29–40). Mahwah, NJ: Erlbaum.

Barber, Brian K. (Ed.). (2002). *Intrusive parenting: How psychological control affects children and adolescents.* Washington, DC: American Psychological Association.

Barger, Steven D., & Gallo, Linda C. (2008). Ability of ethnic self-identification to partition modifiable health risk among U.S. residents of Mexican ancestry. *American Journal of Public Health, 98,* 1971–1978.

Barkin, Shari, Scheindlin, Benjamin, Ip, Edward H., Richardson, Irma, & Finch, Stacia. (2007). Determinants of parental discipline practices: A national sample from primary care practices. *Clinical Pediatrics, 46,* 64–69.

Barkley, Russell A. (2006). *Attention-deficit hyperactivity disorder: A handbook for diagnosis and treatment* (3rd ed.). New York: Guilford Press.

Barnard, Kathryn E., & Martell, Louise K. (1995). Mothering. In Marc H. Bornstein (Ed.), *Handbook of parenting: Vol. 3. Status and social conditions of parenting* (pp. 3–26). Hillsdale, NJ: Erlbaum.

Barnes, Grace M., Hoffman, Joseph H., Welte, John W., Farrell, Michael P., & Dintcheff, Barbara A. (2006). Effects of parental monitoring and peer deviance on substance use and delinquency. *Journal of Marriage and Family, 68,* 1084–1104.

Barnes, Jacqueline, Katz, Ilan Barry, Korbin, Jill E., & O'Brien, Margaret. (2006). *Children and families in communities: Theory, research, policy and practice.* Hoboken, NJ: Wiley.

Barnes, Lisa L., de Leon, Carlos F. Mendes, Lewis, Tené T., Bienias, Julia L., Wilson, Robert S., & Evans, Denis A. (2008). Perceived discrimination and mortality in a population-based study of older adults. *American Journal of Public Health, 98,* 1241–1247.

Barnes, Marcia A., & Wade-Woolley, Lesly. (2007). Where there's a will there are ways to close the achievement gap for children with learning difficulties. *Orbit, 37*(1), 9–13.

Barnett, Kylie J., Finucane, Ciara, Asher, Julian E., Bargary, Gary, Corvin, Aiden P., Newell, Fiona N., et al. (2008). Familial patterns and the origins of individual differences in synaesthesia. *Cognition, 106,* 871–893.

Barnett, Rosalind C., & Rivers, Caryl. (2004). *Same difference: How gender myths are hurting our relationships, our children, and our jobs.* New York: Basic Books.

Barrett, Karen Caplovitz. (2005). The origins of social emotions and self-regulation in toddlerhood: New evidence. *Cognition & Emotion, 19,* 953–979.

Barrett, Linda L. (2006). *The costs of long-term care: Public perceptions versus reality in 2006.* Washington, DC: AARP.

Barros, Fernando C., Victora, Cesar G., Barros, Aluisio J. D., Santos, Ina S., Albernaz, Elaine, Matijasevich, Alicia, et al. (2005). The challenge of reducing neonatal mortality in middle-income countries: Findings from three Brazilian birth cohorts in 1982, 1993, and 2004. *Lancet, 365,* 847–854.

Baruch, Susannah, Kaufman, David, & Hudson, Kathy L. (2008). Genetic testing of embryos: Practices and perspectives of US in vitro fertilization clinics. *Fertility and Sterility, 89,* 1053–1058.

Basak, Chandramallika, Boot, Walter R., Voss, Michelle W., & Kramer, Arthur F. (2008). Can training in a real-time strategy video game attenuate cognitive decline in older adults? *Psychology and Aging, 23,* 765–777.

Basáñez, María-Gloria, Pion, Sébastien D. S., Churcher, Thomas S., Breitling, Lutz P., Little, Mark P., & Boussinesq, Michel. (2006). River blindness: A success story under threat? *PLoS Medicine, 3,* e371.

Basu, Kaushik, & Pham, Hoang Van. (1998). The economics of child labor. *American Economic Review, 88,* 412–427.

Bates, Elizabeth, Devescovi, Antonella, & Wulfeck, Beverly. (2001). Psycholinguistics: A cross-language perspective. *Annual Review of Psychology, 52,* 369–396.

Bates, Lisa M., Acevedo-Garcia, Dolores, Alegria, Margarita, & Krieger, Nancy. (2008). Immigration and generational trends in body mass index and obesity in the United States: Results of the National Latino and Asian American Survey, 2002–2003. *American Journal of Public Health, 98,* 70–77.

Bateson, Patrick. (2005, February 4). Desirable scientific conduct. *Science, 307,* 645.

Bauer, Patricia J., & Dow, Gina Annunziato. (1994). Episodic memory in 16- and 20-month-old children: Specifics are generalized but not forgotten. *Developmental Psychology, 30,* 403–417.

Baugher, John Eric. (2008). Facing death: Buddhist and western hospice approaches. *Symbolic Interaction, 31,* 259–284.

Baum, Katrina. (2005). *Juvenile victimization and offending, 1993–2003* (NCJ 209468). Washington, DC: U.S. Department of Justice, Office of Justice Programs.

Baumeister, Roy F., & Blackhart, Ginnette C. (2007). Three perspectives on gender differences in adolescent sexual development. In Rutger C. M. E. Engels, Margaret Kerr, & Håkan Stattin (Eds.), *Friends, lovers, and groups: Key relationships in adolescence* (pp. 93–104). Hoboken, NJ: Wiley.

Baumeister, Roy F., Campbell, Jennifer D., Krueger, Joachim I., & Vohs, Kathleen D. (2003). Does high self-esteem cause better performance, interpersonal success, happiness, or healthier lifestyles? *Psychological Science in the Public Interest, 4,* 1–44.

Baumrind, Diana. (1967). Child care practices anteceding three patterns of preschool behavior. *Genetic Psychology Monographs, 75,* 43–88.

Baumrind, Diana. (1971). Current patterns of parental authority. *Developmental Psychology, 4*(1, Pt. 2), 1–103.

Baumrind, Diana. (1991). The influence of parenting style on adolescent competence and substance use. *Journal of Early Adolescence, 11,* 56–95.

Bayley, Nancy. (1966). Learning in adulthood: The role of intelligence. In Herbert J. Klausmeier & Chester William Harris (Eds.), *Analyses of concept learning* (pp. 117–138). New York: Academic Press.

Bayley, Nancy, & Oden, Melita H. (1955). The maintenance of intellectual ability in gifted adults. *Journal of Gerontology Series B, 10,* 91–107.

Bearman, Peter S., Moody, James, & Stovel, Katherine. (2004). Chains of affection: The structure of adolescent romantic and sexual networks. *American Journal of Sociology, 110,* 44–91.

Becker, Jill B., Berkley, Karen J., Geary, Nori, Hampson, Elizabeth, Herman, James P., & Young, Elizabeth (Eds.). (2008). *Sex differences in the brain: From genes to behavior.* New York: Oxford University Press.

Beckers, Debby G. J., van der Linden, Dimitri, Smulders, Peter G. W., Kompier, Michiel A. J., Taris, Toon W., & Geurts, Sabine A. E. (2008). Voluntary or involuntary? Control over overtime and rewards for overtime in relation to fatigue and work satisfaction. *Work & Stress, 22,* 33–50.

Behne, Tanya, Carpenter, Malinda, Call, Josep, & Tomasello, Michael. (2005). Unwilling versus unable: Infants' understanding of intentional action. *Developmental Psychology, 41,* 328–337.

Behnke, Andrew O., MacDermid, Shelley M., Coltrane, Scott L., Parke, Ross D., Duffy, Sharon, & Widaman, Keith F. (2008). Family cohesion in the lives of Mexican American and European American parents. *Journal of Marriage and Family, 70,* 1045–1059.

Behrend, Douglas A., Scofield, Jason, & Kleinknecht, Erica E. (2001). Beyond fast mapping: Young children's extensions of novel words and novel facts. *Developmental Psychology, 37,* 698–705.

Beilin, Lawrence, & Huang, Rae-Chi. (2008). Childhood obesity, hypertension, the metabolic syndrome and adult cardiovascular disease. *Clinical and Experimental Pharmacology and Physiology, 35,* 409–411.

Belamarich, Peter, & Ayoob, Keith-Thomas. (2001). Keeping teenage vegetarians healthy and in the know. *Contemporary Pediatrics, 10,* 89–108.

Belfer, Myron L., & Eisenbruch, Maurice. (2007). International child and adolescent mental health. In Andrés Martin, Fred R. Volkmar, & Melvin Lewis (Eds.), *Lewis's child and adolescent psychiatry: A comprehensive textbook* (4th ed., pp. 87–98). Philadelphia: Lippincott Williams & Wilkins.

Belfield, Clive R., Nores, Milagros, Barnett, Steve, & Schweinhart, Lawrence. (2006). The High/Scope Perry Preschool Program: Cost benefit analysis using data from the age-40 followup. *Journal of Human Resources, 41,* 162–190.

Belizán, José M., Althabe, Fernando, Barros, Fernando C., & Alexander, Sophie. (1999). Rates and implications of caesarean sections in Latin America: Ecological study. *British Medical Journal, 319,* 1397–1402.

Belka, David. (2004). Substituting skill learning for traditional games in early childhood. *Teaching Elementary Physical Education, 15,* 25–27.

Bell, Joanna H., & Bromnick, Rachel D. (2003). The social reality of the imaginary audience: A ground theory approach. *Adolescence, 38,* 205–219.

Bell, Ruth. (1998). *Changing bodies, changing lives: A book for teens on sex and relationships* (Expanded 3rd ed.). New York: Times Books.

Bellah, Robert Neelly, Madsen, Richard, Sullivan, William M., Swidler, Ann, & Tipton, Steven M. (2007). *Habits of the heart: Individualism and commitment in American life* (3rd ed.). Berkeley, CA: University of California Press.

Belsky, Jay, Bakermans-Kranenburg, Marian J., & van IJzendoorn, Marinus H. (2007). For better and for worse: Differential susceptibility to environmental influences. *Current Directions in Psychological Science, 16,* 300–304.

Belsky, Jay, Melhuish, Edward, Barnes, Jacqueline, Leyland, Alastair H, & Romaniuk, Helena. (2006). Effects of Sure Start local programmes on children and families: Early findings from a quasi-experimental, cross sectional study. *British Medical Journal, 332,* 1476.

Bem, Sandra Lipsitz. (1993). *The lenses of gender: Transforming the debate on sexual inequality.* New Haven, CT: Yale University Press.

Benacerraf, Beryl R. (2007). *Ultrasound of fetal syndromes* (2nd ed.). Philadelphia: Churchill Livingstone/Elsevier.

Bengtson, Vern L. (2001). Beyond the nuclear family: The increasing importance of multigenerational bonds (The Burgess Award Lecture). *Journal of Marriage and Family, 63,* 1–16.

Benjamin, Georges C. (2004). The solution is injury prevention. *American Journal of Public Health, 94,* 521.

Benjamin, Roger. (2003). *The coming transformation of the American university.* New York: Council for Aid to Education/An Independent Subsidiary of RAND.

Benson, Peter L. (2003). Developmental assets and asset-building community: Conceptual and empirical foundations. In Richard M. Lerner & Peter L. Benson (Eds.), *Developmental assets and asset-building communities: Implications for research, policy, and practice* (pp. 19–43). New York: Kluwer/Plenum.

Bentley, Gillian R., & Mascie-Taylor, C. G. Nicholas. (2000). Introduction. In Gillian R. Bentley & C. G. Nicholas Mascie-Taylor (Eds.), *Infertility in the modern world: Present and future prospects* (pp. 1–13). Cambridge, England: Cambridge University Press.

Benton, David. (2004). Role of parents in the determination of the food preferences of children and the development of obesity. *International Journal of Obesity & Related Metabolic Disorders, 28,* 858–869.

Berenbaum, Sheri A., Martin, Carol Lynn, Hanish, Laura D., Briggs, Phillip T., & Fabes, Richard A. (2008). Sex differences in children's play. In Jill B. Becker, Karen J. Berkley, Nori Geary, Elizabeth Hampson, James P. Herman, & Elizabeth Young (Eds.), *Sex differences in the brain: From genes to behavior* (pp. 275–290). New York: Oxford University Press.

Berg, Cynthia A., & Klaczynski, Paul A. (2002). Contextual variability in the expression and meaning of intelligence. In Robert J. Sternberg & Elena L. Grigorenko (Eds.), *The general factor of intelligence: How general is it?* (pp. 381–412). Mahwah, NJ: Erlbaum.

Berg, Sandra J., & Wynne-Edwards, Katherine E. (2002). Salivary hormone concentrations in mothers and fathers becoming parents are not correlated. *Hormones & Behavior, 42,* 424–436.

Berger, Kathleen Stassen. (2007). Update on bullying at school: Science forgotten? *Developmental Review, 27,* 90–126.

Bering, Jesse M., & Bjorklund, David F. (2004). The natural emergence of reasoning about the afterlife as a developmental regularity. *Developmental Psychology, 40,* 217–233.

Bering, Jesse M., Blasi, Carlos Hernández, & Bjorklund, David F. (2005). The development of 'afterlife' beliefs in religiously and secularly schooled children. *British Journal of Developmental Psychology, 23,* 587–607.

Berkman, Michael B., & Plutzer, Eric. (2004). Gray peril or loyal support? The effects of the elderly on educational expenditures. *Social Science Quarterly, 85,* 1178–1192.

Berkowitz, Alan D. (2005). An overview of the social norms approach. In Linda Costigan Lederman & Lea Stewart (Eds.), *Changing the culture of college drinking: A socially situated health communication campaign* (pp. 193–214). Cresskill, NJ: Hampton Press.

Berman, Alan L., Jobes, David A., & Silverman, Morton M. (2006). *Adolescent suicide: Assessment and intervention* (2nd ed.). Washington, DC: American Psychological Association.

Berndt, Thomas J., & Murphy, Lonna M. (2002). Influences of friends and friendships: Myths, truths, and research recommendations. In Robert V. Kail (Ed.), *Advances in child development and behavior* (Vol. 30, pp. 275–310). San Diego, CA: Academic Press.

Berninger, Virginia Wise, & Richards, Todd L. (2002). *Brain literacy for educators and psychologists.* Amsterdam: Academic Press.

Bhasin, Shalender. (2007). Approach to the infertile man. *Journal of Clinical Endocrinology & Metabolism, 92,* 1995–2004.

Bhattacharjee, Yudhijit. (2008, February 8). Choking on fumes, Kolkata faces a noxious future. *Science, 319,* 749.

Bialystok, Ellen. (2001). *Bilingualism in development: Language, literacy, and cognition.* New York: Cambridge University Press.

Bialystok, Ellen, & Martin, Michelle M. (2004). Attention and inhibition in bilingual children: Evidence from the dimensional change card sort task. *Developmental Science, 7,* 325–339.

Bianchi, Suzanne M., Casper, Lynne M., & King, Rosalind Berkowitz (Eds.). (2005). *Work, family, health, and well-being.* Mahwah, NJ: Erlbaum.

Biddle, Stuart, & Mutrie, Nanette. (2001). *Psychology of physical activity: Determinants, well-being, and interventions.* London: Routledge.

Biehl, Michael C., Natsuaki, Misaki N., & Ge, Xiaojia. (2007). The influence of pubertal timing on alcohol use and heavy drinking trajectories. *Journal of Youth and Adolescence, 36,* 153–167.

Bienvenu, Thierry. (2005). Rett syndrome. In Merlin Gene Butler & F. John Meaney (Eds.), *Genetics of developmental disabilities* (pp. 477–519). Boca Raton, FL: Taylor & Francis.

Bilalić, Merim, McLeod, Peter, & Gobet, Fernand. (2008). Inflexibility of experts—Reality or myth? Quantifying the Einstellung effect in chess masters. *Cognitive Psychology, 56,* 73–102.

Binstock, Robert. (2006–2007). Older people and political engagement: From avid voters to 'cooled-out marks.' *Generations, 30*(4), 24–30.

Birch, Susan A. J., & Bloom, Paul. (2003). Children are cursed: An asymmetric bias in mental-state attribution. *Psychological Science, 14,* 283–286.

Birditt, Kira S., Miller, Laura M., Fingerman, Karen L., & Lefkowitz, Eva S. (2009). Tensions in the parent and adult child relationship: Links to solidarity and ambivalence. *Psychology and Aging, 24,* 287–295.

Birdsong, David. (2006). Age and second language acquisition and processing: A selective overview. *Language Learning, 56*(Suppl. 1), 9–49.

Birney, Damian P., Citron-Pousty, Jill H., Lutz, Donna J., & Sternberg, Robert J. (2005). The development of cognitive and intellectual abilities. In Marc H. Bornstein & Michael E. Lamb (Eds.), *Developmental science: An advanced textbook* (5th ed., pp. 327–358). Mahwah, NJ: Erlbaum.

Biro, Frank M., McMahon, Robert P., Striegel-Moore, Ruth, Crawford, Patricia B., Obarzanek, Eva, Morrison, John A., et al. (2001). Impact of timing of pubertal maturation on growth in black and white female adolescents: The National Heart, Lung, and Blood Institute Growth and Health Study. *Journal of Pediatrics, 138,* 636–643.

Biro, Frank M., Striegel-Moore, Ruth H., Franko, Debra L., Padgett, Justina, & Bean, Judy A. (2006). Self-esteem in adolescent females. *Journal of Adolescent Health, 39,* 501–507.

Birren, James E., & Schroots, Johannes J. F. (2006). Autobiographical memory and the narrative self over the life span. In James E. Birren & K. Warner Schaie (Eds.), *Handbook of the psychology of aging* (6th ed., pp. 477–498). Amsterdam: Elsevier.

Black, Corri, Kaye, James A., & Jick, Hershel. (2005). Cesarean delivery in the United Kingdom: Time trends in the General Practice Research Database. *Obstetrics & Gynecology, 106,* 151–155.

Black, Kathy. (2008). Health and aging-in-place: Implications for community practice. *Journal of Community Practice, 16,* 79–95.

Blackwell, Lisa S., Trzesniewski, Kali H., & Dweck, Carol Sorich. (2007). Implicit theories of intelligence predict achievement across an adolescent transition: A longitudinal study and an intervention. *Child Development, 78,* 246–263.

Blair, Peter S., & Ball, Helen L. (2004). The prevalence and characteristics associated with parent–infant bed-sharing in England. *Archives of Disease in Childhood, 89,* 1106–1110.

Blakemore, Sarah-Jayne. (2008). Development of the social brain during adolescence. *The Quarterly Journal of Experimental Psychology, 61,* 40–49.

Blatchford, Peter. (2003). *The class size debate: Is small better?* Maidenhead, Berkshire, England: Open University.

Bledsoe, Bryan E. (2002). The golden hour: Fact or fiction? *Emergency Medical Services, 31,* 105.

Blekesaune, Morten. (2008). Partnership transitions and mental distress: Investigating temporal order. *Journal of Marriage and Family, 70,* 879–890.

Bloch, Michele, Althabe, Fernando, Onyamboko, Marie, Kaseba-Sata, Christine, Castilla, Eduardo E., Freire, Salvio, et al. (2008). Tobacco use and secondhand smoke exposure during pregnancy: An investigative survey of women in 9 developing nations. *American Journal of Public Health, 98,* 1833–1840.

Block, Lauren G., Morwitz, Vicki G., Putsis, William P., Jr., & Sen, Subrata K. (2002). Assessing the impact of antidrug advertising on adolescent drug consumption: Results from a behavioral economic model. *American Journal of Public Health, 92,* 1346–1351.

Blonigen, Daniel M., Carlson, Marie D., Hicks, Brian M., Krueger, Robert F., & Iacono, William G. (2008). Stability and change in personality traits from late adolescence to early adulthood: A longitudinal twin study. *Journal of Personality, 76,* 229–266.

Bloom, Lois. (1993). *The transition from infancy to language: Acquiring the power of expression.* New York: Cambridge University Press.

Bloom, Lois. (1998). Language acquisition in its developmental context. In William Damon (Series Ed.) & Deanna Kuhn & Robert S. Siegler (Vol. Eds.), *Handbook of child psychology: Vol. 2. Cognition, perception, and language* (5th ed., pp. 309–370). New York: Wiley.

Blum, Deborah. (2002). *Love at Goon Park: Harry Harlow and the science of affection.* Cambridge, MA: Perseus.

Blum, Nathan J., Taubman, Bruce, & Nemeth, Nicole. (2003). Relationship between age at initiation of toilet training and duration of training: A prospective study. *Pediatrics, 111*(4, Pt. 1), 810–814.

Blum, Robert W., Beuhring, Trisha, Shew, Marcia L., Bearinger, Linda H., Sieving, Renee E., & Resnick, Michael D. (2000). The effects of race/ethnicity, income, and family structure on adolescent risk behaviors. *American Journal of Public Health, 90,* 1879–1884.

Blum, Robert Wm., & Nelson-Mmari, Kristin. (2004). Adolescent health from an international perspective. In Richard M. Lerner & Laurence D. Steinberg (Eds.), *Handbook of adolescent psychology* (2nd ed., pp. 553–586). Hoboken, NJ: Wiley.

Blurton-Jones, Nicholas G. (1976). Rough-and-tumble play among nursery school children. In Jerome S. Bruner, Alison Jolly, & Kathy Sylva (Eds.), *Play: Its role in development and evolution* (pp. 352–363). New York: Basic Books.

Blustein, David Larry. (2006). *The psychology of working: A new perspective for career development, counseling, and public policy.* Mahwah, NJ: Erlbaum.

Bode, Christina. (2003). *Individuality and relatedness in middle and late adulthood: A study of women and men in the Netherlands, East-, and West-Germany.* Enschede, The Netherlands: PrintPartners Ipskamp.

Boehnke, Klaus. (2008). Peer pressure: A cause of scholastic underachievement? A cross-cultural study of mathematical achievement among German, Canadian, and Israeli middle school students. *Social Psychology of Education, 11,* 149–160.

Boerner, Kathrin, Schulz, Richard, & Horowitz, Amy. (2004). Positive aspects of caregiving and adaptation to bereavement. *Psychology and Aging, 19,* 668–675.

Boerner, Kathrin, Wortman, Camille B., & Bonanno, George A. (2005). Resilient or at risk? A 4-year study of older adults who initially showed high or low distress following conjugal loss. *Journals of Gerontology: Series B: Psychological Sciences and Social Sciences, 60,* P67–P73.

Bogle, Kathleen A. (2008). *Hooking up: Sex, dating, and relationships on campus.* New York: New York University Press.

Bokhour, Barbara G., Cohn, Ellen S., Cortés, Dharma E., Yinusa-Nyahkoon, Leanne S., Hook, Julie M., Smith,

Lauren A., et al. (2008). Patterns of concordance and non-concordance with clinician recommendations and parents' explanatory models in children with asthma. *Patient Education and Counseling, 70,* 376–385.

Boles, David B., Barth, Joan M., & Merrill, Edward C. (2008). Asymmetry and performance: Toward a neurodevelopmental theory. *Brain and Cognition, 66,* 124–139.

Bonanno, George A., & Lilienfeld, Scott O. (2008). Let's be realistic: When grief counseling is effective and when it's not. *Professional Psychology: Research and Practice, 39,* 377–378.

Bond, Gary D. (2008). Deception detection expertise. *Law and Human Behavior, 32,* 339–351.

Bondi, Mark W., Salmon, David P., & Kaszniak, Alfred W. (2009). The neuropsychology of dementia. In Igor Grant & Kenneth M. Adams (Eds.), *Neuropsychological assessment of neuropsychiatric and neuromedical disorders* (3rd ed., pp. 159–198). New York: Oxford University Press.

Booth, Alan, & Crouter, Ann C. (2005). *The new population problem: Why families in developed countries are shrinking and what it means.* Mahwah, NJ: Erlbaum.

Booth-LaForce, Cathryn, & Oxford, Monica L. (2008). Trajectories of social withdrawal from grades 1 to 6: Prediction from early parenting, attachment, and temperament. *Developmental Psychology, 44,* 1298–1313.

Borke, Jörn, Lamm, Bettina, Eickhorst, Andreas, & Keller, Heidi. (2007). Father–infant interaction, paternal ideas about early child care, and their consequences for the development of children's self-recognition. *Journal of Genetic Psychology, 168,* 365–379.

Borkowski, John G., Farris, Jaelyn Renee, Whitman, Thomas L., Carothers, Shannon S., Weed, Keri, & Keogh, Deborah A. (2007). *Risk and resilience: Adolescent mothers and their children grow up.* Mahwah, NJ: Erlbaum.

Borland, Moira. (1998). *Middle childhood: The perspectives of children and parents.* London: Jessica Kingsley.

Bornstein, Marc H. (2006). Parenting science and practice. In William Damon & Richard M. Lerner (Series Eds.) & K. Ann Renninger & Irving E. Sigel (Vol. Eds.), *Handbook of child psychology: Vol. 4. Child psychology in practice* (6th ed., pp. 893–949). Hoboken, NJ: Wiley.

Bornstein, Marc H., Arterberry, Martha E., & Mash, Clay. (2005). Perceptual development. In Marc H. Bornstein & Michael E. Lamb (Eds.), *Developmental science: An advanced textbook* (5th ed., pp. 283–325). Mahwah, NJ: Erlbaum.

Bornstein, Marc H., Cote, Linda R., Maital, Sharone, Painter, Kathleen, Park, Sung-Yun, Pascual, Liliana, et al. (2004). Cross-linguistic analysis of vocabulary in young children: Spanish, Dutch, French, Hebrew, Italian, Korean, and American English. *Child Development, 75,* 1115–1139.

Bornstein, Marc H., & Lamb, Michael E. (2005). *Developmental science: An advanced textbook* (5th ed.). Mahwah, NJ: Erlbaum.

Bornstein, Marc H., & Putnick, Diane L. (2007). Chronological age, cognitions, and practices in European American mothers: A multivariate study of parenting. *Developmental Psychology, 43,* 850–864.

Borsutzky, Sabine, Fujiwara, Esther, Brand, Matthias, & Markowitsch, Hans J. (2008). Confabulations in alcoholic Korsakoff patients. *Neuropsychologia, 46,* 3133–3143.

Borzekowski, Dina L. G., & Rickert, Vaughn I. (2001). Adolescents, the internet, and health: Issues of access and content. *Journal of Applied Developmental Psychology, 22,* 49–59.

Bos, Henny M. W., Sandfort, Theo G. M., de Bruyn, Eddy H., & Hakvoort, Esther M. (2008). Same-sex attraction, social relationships, psychosocial functioning, and school performance in early adolescence. *Developmental Psychology, 44,* 59–68.

Bossé, Yohan, & Hudson, Thomas J. (2007). Toward a comprehensive set of asthma susceptibility genes. *Annual Review of Medicine, 58,* 171–184.

Bousquet, Jean, Dahl, Ronald, & Khaltaev, Nikolai. (2007). Global alliance against chronic respiratory diseases. *Allergy, 62,* 216–223.

Bowlby, John. (1969). *Attachment and loss: Vol. 1. Attachment.* New York: Basic Books.

Bowlby, John. (1973). *Attachment and loss: Vol. 2. Separation: Anxiety and anger.* New York: Basic Books.

Bowlby, John. (1988). *A secure base: Clinical applications of attachment theory.* London: Routledge.

Boyce, W. Thomas, Essex, Marilyn J., Alkon, Abbey, Goldsmith, H. Hill, Kraemer, Helena C., & Kupfer, David J. (2006). Early father involvement moderates biobehavioral susceptibility to mental health problems in middle childhood. *Journal of the American Academy of Child and Adolescent Psychiatry, 45,* 1510–1520.

Boyd, William L. (2007). The politics of privatization in American education. *Educational Policy, 21,* 7–14.

Bozik, Mary. (2002). The college student as learner: Insight gained through metaphor analysis. *College Student Journal, 36,* 142–151.

Bradley, Robert H., & Corwyn, Robert F. (2005). Productive activity and the prevention of behavior problems. *Developmental Psychology, 41,* 89–98.

Branca, Francesco, Nikogosian, Haik, & Lobstein, Tim (Eds.). (2007). *The challenge of obesity in the WHO European Region and the strategies for response.* Copenhagen, Denmark: WHO Regional Office for Europe.

Brandl, Bonnie. (2000). Power and control: Understanding domestic abuse in later life. *Generations, 24*(2), 39–45.

Brandt, Hella E., Ooms, Marcel E., Ribbe, Miel W., Wal, Gerrit van der, & Deliens, Luc. (2006). Predicted survival vs. actual survival in terminally ill noncancer patients in Dutch nursing homes. *Journal of Pain and Symptom Management, 32,* 560–566.

Braun, Kathryn L., Zir, Ana, Crocker, Joanna, & Seely, Marilyn R. (2005). Kokua Mau: A statewide effort to improve end-of-life care. *Journal of Palliative Medicine, 8,* 313–323.

Braun, Michael, Lewin-Epstein, Noah, Stier, Haya, & Baumgärtner, Miriam K. (2008). Perceived equity in the gendered division of household labor. *Journal of Marriage and Family, 70,* 1145–1156.

Brauner-Otto, Sarah, Axinn, William G., & Ghimire, Dirgha J. (2007). The spread of health services and fertility transition. *Demography, 44,* 747–770.

Bray, George A. (2003). Low-carbohydrate diets and realities of weight loss. *Journal of the American Medical Association, 289,* 1853–1855.

Brazelton, T. Berry, & Sparrow, Joshua D. (2006). *Touchpoints: Birth to 3: Your child's emotional and behavioral development* (2nd ed.). Cambridge, MA: Da Capo Press.

Breaugh, James, & Frye, N. Kathleen. (2008). Work-family conflict: The importance of family-friendly employment practices and family-supportive supervisors. *Journal of Business and Psychology, 22,* 345–353.

Breggin, Peter R., & Baughman, Fred A., Jr. (2001, January 26). Questioning the treatment for ADHD [Letter to the editor]. *Science, 291,* 595.

Brendgen, Mara, Vitaro, Frank, Bukowski, William M., Doyle, Anna Beth, & Markiewicz, Dorothy. (2001). Developmental profiles of peer social preference over the course of elementary school: Associations with trajectories of externalizing and internalizing behavior. *Developmental Psychology, 37,* 308–320.

Brennan, Patricia A., Grekin, Emily R., & Mednick, Sarnoff A. (2003). Prenatal and perinatal influences on conduct disorder and serious delinquency. In Benjamin B. Lahey, Terrie E. Moffitt, & Avshalom Caspi (Eds.), *Causes of conduct disorder and juvenile delinquency* (pp. 319–341). New York: Guilford Press.

Bretherton, Inge, & Munholland, Kristine A. (1999). Internal working models in attachment relationships: A construct revisited. In Jude Cassidy & Phillip R. Shaver (Eds.), *Handbook of attachment: Theory, research, and clinical applications* (pp. 89–111). New York: Guilford Press.

Breunlin, Douglas C., Bryant-Edwards, Tara L., Hetherington, Joshua S., & Cimmarusti, Rocco A. (2002). Conflict resolution training as an alternative to suspension for violent behavior. *Journal of Educational Research, 95,* 349–357.

Brewster, Karin L., & Tillman, Kathryn Harker. (2008). Who's doing it? Patterns and predictors of youths' oral sexual experiences. *Journal of Adolescent Health, 42,* 73–80.

Brickhouse, Tegwyn H., Rozier, R. Gary, & Slade, Gary D. (2008). Effects of enrollment in Medicaid versus the State Children's Health Insurance Program on kindergarten children's untreated dental caries. *American Journal of Public Health, 98,* 876–881.

Bridge, Jeffrey A., Iyengar, Satish, Salary, Cheryl B., Barbe, Remy P., Birmaher, Boris, Pincus, Harold Alan, et al. (2007). Clinical response and risk for reported suicidal ideation and suicide attempts in pediatric antidepressant treatment: A meta-analysis of randomized controlled trials. *Journal of the American Medical Association, 297,* 1683–1696.

Briley, Mike, & Sulser, Fridolin (Eds.). (2001). *Molecular genetics of mental disorders: The place of molecular genetics in basic mechanisms and clinical applications in mental disorders.* London: Martin Dunitz.

Brocker, Patrice, & Schneider, Stéphane M. (2009). Undernutrition and refeeding in elderly subjects. In Ronald R. Watson (Ed.), *Handbook of nutrition in the aged* (4th ed., pp. 29–44). Boca Raton, FL: CRC Press.

Brody, Gene H. (2004). Siblings' direct and indirect contributions to child development. *Current Directions in Psychological Science, 13,* 124–126.

Brody, Jane E. (2007, January 23). A humorist illuminates the blessings of hospice. *New York Times,* p. F7.

Broidy, Lisa M., Nagin, Daniel S., Tremblay, Richard E., Bates, John E., Brame, Bobby, Dodge, Kenneth A., et al. (2003). Developmental trajectories of childhood disruptive behaviors and adolescent delinquency: A six-site, cross-national study. *Developmental Psychology, 39,* 222–245.

Bronfenbrenner, Urie, & Morris, Pamela A. (2006). The bioecological model of human development. In William Damon & Richard M. Lerner (Series Eds.) & Richard M. Lerner (Vol. Ed.), *Handbook of child psychology: Vol. 1. Theoretical models of human development* (6th ed., pp. 793–828). Hoboken, NJ: Wiley.

Bronte-Tinkew, Jacinta, Moore, Kristin A., Matthews, Gregory, & Carrano, Jennifer. (2007). Symptoms of major depression in a sample of fathers of infants: Sociodemographic correlates and links to father involvement. *Journal of Family Issues, 28,* 61–99.

Brown, B. Bradford. (2004). Adolescents' relationships with peers. In Richard M. Lerner & Laurence D. Steinberg (Eds.), *Handbook of adolescent psychology* (2nd ed., pp. 363–394). Hoboken, NJ: Wiley.

Brown, B. Bradford. (2005). Moving forward with research on adolescence: Some reflections on the state of JRA and the state of the field. *Journal of Research on Adolescence, 15,* 657–673.

Brown, B. Bradford. (2006). A few "course corrections" to Collins & van Dulmen's "The course of true love." In Ann C. Crouter & Alan Booth (Eds.), *Romance and sex in adolescence and emerging adulthood: Risks and opportunities* (pp. 113–123). Mahwah, NJ: Erlbaum.

Brown, B. Bradford, & Klute, Christa. (2003). Friendships, cliques, and crowds. In Gerald R. Adams & Michael D. Berzonsky (Eds.), *Blackwell handbook of adolescence* (pp. 330–348). Malden, MA: Blackwell.

Brown, Christia Spears, & Bigler, Rebecca S. (2005). Children's perceptions of discrimination: A developmental model. *Child Development, 76,* 533–553.

Brown, Gordon D. A., Gardner, Jonathan, Oswald, Andrew J., & Qian, Jing. (2008). Does wage rank affect employees' wellbeing? *Industrial Relations, 47,* 355–389.

Brown, Kathryn. (2003, March 14). The medication merry-go-round. *Science, 299,* 1646–1649.

Brown, Sandra A., Tapert, Susan F., Granholm, Eric, & Delis, Dean C. (2000). Neurocognitive functioning of adolescents: Effects of protracted alcohol use. *Alcoholism: Clinical and Experimental Research, 24,* 164–171.

Brown, Susan L. (2004). Family structure and child well-being: The significance of parental cohabitation. *Journal of Marriage and Family, 66,* 351–367.

Brückner, Hannah, & Bearman, Peter. (2005). After the promise: The STD consequences of adolescent virginity pledges. *Journal of Adolescent Health, 36,* 271–278.

Brugman, Gerard M. (2006). Wisdom and aging. In James E. Birren & K. Warner Schaie (Eds.), *Handbook of the psychology of aging* (6th ed., pp. 445–475). Amsterdam: Elsevier.

Bryant, Brenda K., & Donnellan, M. Brent. (2007). The relation between socio-economic status concerns and angry peer conflict resolution is moderated by pet provisions of support. *Anthrozoös, 20,* 213–223.

Bryant, Gregory A., & Barrett, H. Clark. (2007). Recognizing intentions in infant-directed speech: Evidence for universals. *Psychological Science, 18,* 746–751.

Buccino, Giovanni, & Amore, Mario. (2008). Mirror neurons and the understanding of behavioural symptoms in psychiatric disorders. *Current Opinion in Psychiatry, 21,* 281–285.

Buccino, Giovanni, Binkofski, Ferdinand, & Riggio, Lucia. (2004). The mirror neuron system and action recognition. *Brain and Language, 89,* 370–376.

Buckner, Randy, Head, Denise, & Lustig, Cindy. (2006). Brain changes in aging: A lifespan perspective. In Ellen Bialystok & Fergus I. M. Craik (Eds.), *Lifespan cognition: Mechanisms of change* (pp. 27–42). Oxford, UK: Oxford University Press.

Buehler, Cheryl. (2006). Parents and peers in relation to early adolescent problem behavior. *Journal of Marriage and Family, 68,* 109–124.

Buehler, Cheryl, & Gerard, Jean M. (2002). Marital conflict, ineffective parenting, and children's and adolescents' maladjustment. *Journal of Marriage and Family, 64,* 78–92.

Buelga, Sofia, Ravenna, Marcella, Musitu, Gonzalo, & Lila, Marisol. (2006). Epidemiology and psychosocial risk factors associated with adolescent drug consumption. In Sandy Jackson & Luc Goossens (Eds.), *Handbook of adolescent development* (pp. 337–364). Hove, East Sussex, UK: Psychology Press.

Bugental, Daphne Blunt, & Grusec, Joan E. (2006). Socialization theory. In William Damon & Richard M. Lerner (Series Eds.) & Nancy Eisenberg (Vol. Ed.), *Handbook of child psychology: Vol. 3. Social, emotional, and personality development* (6th ed., pp. 366–428). Hoboken, NJ: Wiley.

Bugental, Daphne Blunt, & Happaney, Keith. (2004). Predicting infant maltreatment in low-income families: The interactive effects of maternal attributions and child status at birth. *Developmental Psychology, 40,* 234–243.

Bugental, Daphne Blunt, & Hehman, Jessica A. (2007). Ageism: A review of research and policy implications. *Social Issues and Policy Review, 1,* 173–216.

Bukowski, William M., & Adams, Ryan. (2006). Peers and culture: Details, local knowledge, and essentials. In Xinyin Chen, Doran C. French, & Barry H. Schneider (Eds.), *Peer relationships in cultural context* (pp. 481–486). New York: Cambridge University Press.

Bukowski, William M., Newcomb, Andrew F., & Hartup, Willard W. (Eds.). (1996). *The company they keep: Friendship in childhood and adolescence.* New York: Cambridge University Press.

Bulik, Cynthia M., Thornton, Laura, Pinheiro, Andréa Poyastro, Plotnicov, Katherine, Klump, Kelly L., Brandt, Harry, et al. (2008). Suicide attempts in anorexia nervosa. *Psychosomatic Medicine, 70,* 378–383.

Burd-Sharps, Sarah, Lewis, Kristen, & Martins, Eduardo Borges. (2008). *The measure of America: American human development report, 2008–2009.* New York: Columbia University Press.

Burgess, Ernest Watson. (1960). *Aging in Western societies.* Chicago: University of Chicago Press.

Burke, Deborah M., & Shafto, Meredith A. (2004). Aging and language production. *Current Directions in Psychological Science, 13,* 21–24.

Burke, Deborah M., & Shafto, Meredith A. (2007). Language and aging. In Fergus I. M. Craik & Timothy A. Salthouse (Eds.), *The handbook of aging and cognition* (3rd ed., pp. 373–443). New York: Psychology Press.

Burton, Sarah, & Mitchell, Peter. (2003). Judging who knows best about yourself: Developmental change in citing the self across middle childhood. *Child Development, 74,* 426–443.

Busse, William W., & Lemanske, Robert F. (Eds.). (2005). *Lung biology in health and disease: Vol. 195. Asthma prevention.* Boca Raton, FL: Taylor & Francis.

Bussey, Kay, & Bandura, Albert. (1999). Social cognitive theory of gender development and differentiation. *Psychological Review, 106,* 676–713.

Butler, Merlin Gene, & Meaney, F. John. (2005). *Genetics of developmental disabilities.* Boca Raton, FL: Taylor & Francis.

Butler, Robert N., Austad, Steven N., Barzilai, Nir, Braun, Andreas, Helfand, Stephen, Larsen, Pamela L., et al. (2003). Longevity genes: From primitive organisms to humans. *Journals of Gerontology Series A: Biological Sciences and Medical Science, 58,* B581–584.

Butler, Robert N., Lewis, Myrna I., & Sunderland, Trey. (1998). *Aging and mental health: Positive psychosocial and biomedical approaches* (5th ed.). Boston: Allyn & Bacon.

Byers, Amy L., Levy, Becca R., Allore, Heather G., Bruce, Martha L., & Kasl, Stanislav V. (2008). When parents matter to their adult children: Filial reliance associated with parents' depressive symptoms. *The Journals of Gerontology Series B: Psychological Sciences and Social Sciences, 63,* P33–40.

Byng-Hall, John. (2008). The significance of children fulfilling parental roles: Implications for family therapy. *Journal of Family Therapy, 30,* 147–162.

Cabrera, Natasha J., Shannon, Jacqueline D., West, Jerry, & Brooks-Gunn, Jeanne. (2006). Parental interactions with Latino infants: Variation by country of origin and English proficiency. *Child Development, 77,* 1190–1207.

Cadinu, Mara, Maass, Anne, Lombardo, Mery, & Frigerio, Sara. (2006). Stereotype threat: The moderating role of locus of control beliefs. *European Journal of Social Psychology, 36,* 183–197.

Cain, Daphne S., & Combs-Orme, Terri. (2005). Family structure effects on parenting stress and practices in the African American family. *Journal of Sociology & Social Welfare, 32,* 19–40.

Cairns, Robert B., & Cairns, Beverley D. (2001). Aggression and attachment: The folly of separatism. In Arthur C. Bohart & Deborah J. Stipek (Eds.), *Constructive & destructive behavior: Implications for family, school, & society* (pp. 21–47). Washington, DC: American Psychological Association.

Cairns, Robert B., & Cairns, Beverley D. (2006). The making of developmental psychology. In William Damon & Richard M. Lerner (Series Eds.) & Richard M. Lerner (Vol. Ed.), *Handbook of child psychology: Vol. 1. Theoretical models of human development* (6th ed., pp. 89–165). Hoboken, NJ: Wiley.

Calevo, Maria Grazia, Mezzano, P., Zullino, Emma, Padovani, P., & Serra, Emma. (2007). Ligurian experience on neonatal hearing screening: Clinical and epidemiological aspects. *Acta Pædiatrica, 96,* 1592–1599.

Calhoun, Faye, & Warren, Kenneth. (2007). Fetal alcohol syndrome: Historical perspectives. *Neuroscience & Biobehavioral Reviews, 31,* 168–171.

Callaghan, Tara, Rochat, Philippe, Lillard, Angeline, Claux, Mary Louise, Odden, Hal, Itakura, Shoji, et al. (2005). Synchrony in the onset of mental-state reasoning: Evidence from five cultures. *Psychological Science, 16,* 378–384.

Calvert, Karin. (2003). Patterns of childrearing in America. In Willem Koops & Michael Zuckerman (Eds.), *Beyond the century of the child: Cultural history and developmental psychology* (pp. 62–81). Baltimore: University of Pennsylvania Press.

Cameron, Judy, & Pierce, W. David. (2002). *Rewards and intrinsic motivation: Resolving the controversy.* Westport, CT: Bergin & Garvey.

Cameron, Judy L. (2004). Interrelationships between hormones, behavior, and affect during adolescence: Understanding hormonal, physical, and brain changes occurring in association with pubertal activation of the reproductive axis. Introduction to Part III. In Ronald E. Dahl & Linda Patia Spear (Eds.), *Adolescent brain development: Vulnerabilities and opportunities* (Vol. 1021, pp. 110–123). New York: New York Academy of Sciences.

Cameron, Lindsey, Rutland, Adam, Brown, Rupert, & Douch, Rebecca. (2006). Changing children's intergroup attitudes toward refugees: Testing different models of extended contact. *Child Development, 77,* 1208–1219.

Campaign for Fiscal Equity v. State of New York, 719 N.Y.S.2d 475 (2001).

Campbell, David E. (2006). *Why we vote: How schools and communities shape our civic life.* Princeton, NJ: Princeton University Press.

Campbell, Frances A., Pungello, Elizabeth P., Miller-Johnson, Shari, Burchinal, Margaret, & Ramey, Craig T. (2001). The development of cognitive and academic abilities: Growth curves from an early childhood educational experiment. *Developmental Psychology, 37,* 231–242.

Campbell, Susan B., Spieker, Susan, Burchinal, Margaret, Poe, Michele D., & NICHD Early Child Care Research Network. (2006). Trajectories of aggression from toddlerhood to age 9 predict academic and social functioning through age 12. *Journal of Child Psychology and Psychiatry, 47,* 791–800.

Camras, Linda A., Bakeman, Roger, Chen, Yinghe, Norris, Katherine, & Cain, Thomas R. (2006). Culture, ethnicity, and children's facial expressions: A study of European American, mainland Chinese, Chinese American, and adopted Chinese girls. *Emotion, 6,* 103–114.

Canadian Psychological Association. (2000). *Canadian code of ethics for psychologists* (3rd ed.). Ottawa, Ontario, Canada: Author.

Canli, Turhan. (2006). *Biology of personality and individual differences.* New York: Guilford Press.

Cantor-Graae, Elizabeth, & Selten, Jean-Paul. (2005). Schizophrenia and migration: A meta-analysis and review. *American Journal of Psychiatry, 162,* 12–24.

Caplan, Leslie J., & Schooler, Carmi. (2003). The roles of fatalism, self-confidence, and intellectual resources in the disablement process in older adults. *Psychology & Aging, 18,* 551–561.

Caprara, Gian Vittorio, Barbaranelli, Claudio, & Pastorelli, Concetta. (2001). Prosocial behavior and aggression in childhood and pre-adolescence. In Arthur C. Bohart & Deborah J. Stipek (Eds.), *Constructive & destructive behavior: Implications for family, school, & society* (pp. 187–203). Washington, DC: American Psychological Association.

Card, Noel A., Isaacs, Jenny, & Hodges, Ernest V. E. (2008). Multiple contextual levels of risk for peer victimization: A review with implications for prevention and intervention efforts. In Thomas W. Miller (Ed.), *School violence and primary prevention* (pp. 125–153). New York: Springer.

Cardinal, Roger. (2001). The sense of time and place. In Jane Kallir, *Grandma Moses in the 21st century* (pp. 79–102). Alexandria, VA: Art Services International.

Caretta, Carla Mucignat, Caretta, Antonio, & Cavaggioni, Andrea. (1995). Pheromonally accelerated puberty is enhanced by previous experience of the same stimulus. *Physiology & Behavior, 57,* 901–903.

Carey, James R. (2003). *Longevity: The biology and demography of life span.* Princeton, NJ: Princeton University Press.

Carlson, Marcia J., & Corcoran, Mary E. (2001). Family structure and children's behavioral and cognitive outcomes. *Journal of Marriage and Family, 63,* 779–792.

Carlson, Stephanie M. (2003). Executive function in context: Development, measurement, theory and experience. *Monographs of the Society for Research in Child Development, 68*(3, Serial No. 274), 138–151.

Carlson, Stephanie M., & Meltzoff, Andrew N. (2008). Bilingual experience and executive functioning in young children. *Developmental Science, 11,* 282–298.

Carlson, Susan A., Fulton, Janet E., Lee, Sarah M., Maynard, L. Michele, Brown, David R., Kohl, Harold W., III, et al. (2008). Physical education and academic achievement in elementary school: Data from the Early Childhood Longitudinal Study. *American Journal of Public Health, 98,* 721–727.

Carlton-LaNey, Iris. (2006–2007). 'Doing the lord's work': African American elders' civic engagement. *Generations, 30*(4), 47–50.

Carnethon, Mercedes R., Gidding, Samuel S., Nehgme, Rodrigo, Sidney, Stephen, Jacobs, David R., Jr., & Liu, Kiang. (2003). Cardiorespiratory fitness in young adulthood and the development of cardiovascular disease risk factors. *Journal of the American Medical Association, 290,* 3092–3100.

Carr, Deborah. (2004). The desire to date and remarry among older widows and widowers. *Journal of Marriage and Family, 66,* 1051–1068.

Carskadon, Mary A. (2002b). Risks of driving while sleepy in adolescents and young adults. In Mary A. Carskadon (Ed.), *Adolescent sleep patterns: Biological, social, and psychological influences* (pp. 148–158). New York: Cambridge University Press.

Carstensen, Laura L., & Fredrickson, Barbara L. (1998). Influence of HIV status and age on cognitive representations of others. *Health Psychology, 17,* 494–503.

Carstensen, Laura L., Mikels, Joseph A., & Mather, Mara. (2006). Aging and the intersection of cognition, motivation, and emotion. In James E. Birren & K. Warner Schaie (Eds.), *Hand-book of the psychology of aging* (6th ed., pp. 343–362). Amsterdam: Elsevier.

Case-Smith, Jane, & Kuhaneck, Heather Miller. (2008). Play preferences of typically developing children and children with developmental delays between ages 3 and 7 years. *OTJR: Occupation, Participation and Health, 28,* 19–29.

Casey, Richard. (2008). The use of hormonal therapy in "andropause": The con side. *Canadian Urological Association Journal, 2,* 47–48.

Caspi, Avshalom, McClay, Joseph, Moffitt, Terrie, Mill, Jonathan, Martin, Judy, Craig, Ian W., et al. (2002, August 2). Role of genotype in the cycle of violence in maltreated children. *Science, 297,* 851–854.

Caspi, Avshalom, Moffitt, Terrie E., Morgan, Julia, Rutter, Michael, Taylor, Alan, Arseneault, Louise, et al. (2004). Maternal expressed emotion predicts children's antisocial behavior problems: Using monozygotic-twin differences to identify environmental effects on behavioral development. *Developmental Psychology, 40,* 149–161.

Caspi, Avshalom, & Shiner, Rebecca L. (2006). Personality development. In William Damon & Richard M. Lerner (Series Eds.) & Nancy Eisenberg (Vol. Ed.), *Handbook of child psychology: Vol. 3. Social, emotional, and personality development* (Vol. 6, pp. 300–365). Hoboken, NJ: Wiley.

Cassell, Justine, Huffaker, David, Tversky, Dona, & Ferriman, Kim. (2006). The language of online leadership: Gender and youth engagement on the internet. *Developmental Psychology, 42,* 436–449.

Cassidy, Jude, & Shaver, Phillip R. (Eds.). (1999). *Handbook of attachment: Theory, research, and clinical applications.* New York: Guilford Press.

Cavanagh, Sean. (2005, January 5). Poor math scores on world stage trouble U.S. *Education Week, 24*(16), 1, 18.

Cavanagh, Sean. (2007, November 13). Top-achieving nations beat U.S. states in math and science. *Education Week, 27.*

CBS News. (2005, Feb 8). *World's smallest baby goes home: Cellphone-sized baby is discharged from hospital.* Retrieved September 9, 2009, from http://www.cbsnews.com/stories/2005/02/08/health/main672488.shtml

Centers for Disease Control and Prevention. (2008). *Breastfeeding among U.S. children born 1999–2005, CDC National Immunization Survey.* Retrieved July 30, 2009, from http://www.cdc.gov/breastfeeding/data/NIS_data/2005/socio-demographic_any.htm

Centers for Disease Control and Prevention. (2009, September 1). *Vaccines & immunizations.* Retrieved September 9, 2009, from http://www.cdc.gov/vaccines/

Centers for Disease Control and Prevention. (2009). *America breathing easier.* Chamblee, GA: CDC National Asthma Control Program.

Centers for Disease Control and Prevention. (2009, August 11). *2009 Child & adolescent immunization schedules.* Retrieved August 27, 2009, from http://cdc.gov/vaccines/recs/schedules/child-schedule.htm

Centers for Disease Control and Prevention. (2009). *Sexually transmitted diseases: Health communication: Fact sheets.* Retrieved

July 14, 2009, from http://www.cdc.gov/std/healthcomm/fact_sheets.htm

Cesario, Sandra K., & Hughes, Lisa A. (2007). Precocious puberty: A comprehensive review of literature. *Journal of Obstetric, Gynecologic, & Neonatal Nursing, 36,* 263–274.

Chan, David. (2005). Current directions in personnel selection research. *Current Directions in Psychological Science, 14,* 220–223.

Chan, Ya-Fen, Dennis, Michael L., & Funk, Rodney R. (2008). Prevalence and comorbidity of major internalizing and externalizing problems among adolescents and adults presenting to substance abuse treatment. *Journal of Substance Abuse Treatment, 34,* 14–24.

Chandler, Michael J., Lalonde, Christopher E., Sokol, Bryan W., & Hallett, Darcy. (2003). Personal persistence, identity development, and suicide: A study of Native and non-Native North American adolescents. *Monographs of the Society for Research in Child Development, 68*(2, Serial No. 273), vii–130.

Chao, Ruth K. (2001). Extending research on the consequences of parenting style for Chinese Americans and European Americans. *Child Development, 72,* 1832–1843.

Chao, Y. May, Pisetsky, Emily M., Dierker, Lisa C., Dohm, Faith-Anne, Rosselli, Francine, May, Alexis M., et al. (2008). Ethnic differences in weight control practices among U.S. adolescents from 1995 to 2005. *International Journal of Eating Disorders, 41,* 124–133.

Chaplin, Lan Nguyen, & John, Deborah Roedder. (2007). Growing up in a material world: Age differences in materialism in children and adolescents. *Journal of Consumer Research, 34,* 480–493.

Charlton, Rodger. (2007). The demise of palliative care. *The British Journal of General Practice, 57,* 247.

Charlton, Samuel G. (2009). Driving while conversing: Cell phones that distract and passengers who react. *Accident Analysis & Prevention, 41,* 160–173.

Chartrand, Jean-Pierre, Peretz, Isabelle, & Belin, Pascal. (2008). Auditory recognition expertise and domain specificity. *Brain Research, 1220,* 191–198.

Chassin, Laurie, Hussong, Andrea, Barrera, Manuel, Jr., Molina, Brooke S. G., Trim, Ryan, & Ritter, Jennifer. (2004). Adolescent substance use. In Richard M. Lerner & Laurence D. Steinberg (Eds.), *Handbook of adolescent psychology* (2nd ed., pp. 665–696). Hoboken, NJ: Wiley.

Chasteen, Alison L., Bhattacharyya, Sudipa, Horhota, Michelle, Tam, Raymond, & Hasher, Lynn. (2005). How feelings of stereotype threat influence older adults' memory performance. *Experimental Aging Research, 31,* 235–260.

Chawarska, Katarzyna, Klin, Ami, Paul, Rhea, & Volkmar, Fred. (2007). Autism spectrum disorder in the second year: Stability and change in syndrome expression. *Journal of Child Psychology and Psychiatry, 48,* 128–138.

Chen, Li-Kuang, Young Sek Kim, Moon, Paul, & Merriam, Sharan B. (2008). A review and critique of the portrayal of older adult learners in adult education journals, 1980–2006. *Adult Education Quarterly, 59,* 3–21.

Chen, Xinyin, Cen, Guozhen, Li, Dan, & He, Yunfeng. (2005). Social functioning and adjustment in Chinese children: The imprint of historical time. *Child Development, 76,* 182–195.

Chen, Xinyin, & French, Doran C. (2008). Children's social competence in cultural context. *Annual Review of Psychology, 59,* 591–616.

Chen, Xinyin, Rubin, Kenneth H., & Sun, Yuerong. (1992). Social reputation and peer relationships in Chinese and Canadian children: A cross-cultural study. *Child Development, 63,* 1336–1343.

Cheng, Sheung-Tak. (2004). Age and subjective well-being revisited: A discrepancy perspective. *Psychology and Aging, 19,* 409–415.

Cherbuin, Nicolas, & Brinkman, Cobie. (2006). Hemispheric interactions are different in left-handed individuals. *Neuropsychology, 20,* 700–707.

Cherlin, Andrew J., & Furstenberg, Frank F. (1986). *The new American grandparent: A place in the family, a life apart.* New York: Basic Books.

Chess, Stella, Thomas, Alexander, & Birch, Herbert G. (1965). *Your child is a person: A psychological approach to parenthood without guilt.* Oxford, England: Viking Press.

Cheurprakobkit, Sutham, & Bartsch, Robert A. (2005). Security measures on school crime in Texas middle and high schools. *Educational Research, 47,* 235–250.

Chida, Yoichi, & Hamer, Mark. (2008). Chronic psychosocial factors and acute physiological responses to laboratory-induced stress in healthy populations: A quantitative review of 30 years of investigations. *Psychological Bulletin, 134,* 829–885.

Chikako, Tange. (2004). [Changes in attitudes toward death in early and middle adolescence]. *Japanese Journal of Developmental Psychology, 15,* 65–76.

Chisholm, Kim. (1998). A three year follow-up of attachment and indiscriminate friendliness in children adopted from Romanian orphanages. *Child Development, 69,* 1092–1106.

Choi, Incheol, Dalal, Reeshad, Kim-Prieto, Chu, & Park, Hyekyung. (2003). Culture and judgment of causal relevance. *Journal of Personality & Social Psychology, 84,* 46–59.

Choi, Jung-ah. (2005). New generation's career aspirations and new ways of marginalization in a postindustrial economy. *British Journal of Sociology of Education, 26,* 269–283.

Choi, Kwisook, Son, Hyunsook, Park, Myunghee, Han, Jinkyu, Kim, Kitai, Lee, Byungkoo, et al. (2009). Internet overuse and excessive daytime sleepiness in adolescents. *Psychiatry and Clinical Neurosciences, 63,* 455–462.

Choi, Namkee G., Burr, Jeffrey A., Mutchler, Jan E., & Caro, Francis G. (2007). Formal and informal volunteer activity and spousal caregiving among older adults. *Research on Aging, 29,* 99–124.

Chomsky, Noam. (1968). *Language and mind.* New York: Harcourt Brace & World.

Chomsky, Noam. (1980). *Rules and representations.* New York: Columbia University Press.

Chouinard, Michelle M. (2007). Children's questions: A mechanism for cognitive development. *Monographs of the Society for Research in Child Development, 72*(1, Serial No. 286), vii–112.

Christensen, Helen, Mackinnon, Andrew J., Korten, Ailsa E., Jorm, Anthony F., Henderson, A. Scott, Jacomb,

Patricia A., et al. (1999). An analysis of diversity in the cognitive performance of elderly community dwellers: Individual differences in change scores as a function of age. *Psychology & Aging, 14,* 365–379.

Christenson, Sandra L., & Thurlow, Martha L. (2004). School dropouts: Prevention considerations, interventions, and challenges. *Current Directions in Psychological Science, 13,* 36–39.

Chronicle of Higher Education. (2006, August 25). *Almanac of higher education 2006-7.* Washington, DC: Author.

Chronicle of Higher Education. (2007). *Almanac of higher education 2007-8.* Washington, DC: Author.

Chumlea, William Cameron, Schubert, Christine M., Roche, Alex F., Kulin, Howard E., Lee, Peter A., Himes, John H., et al. (2003). Age at menarche and racial comparisons in U.S. girls. *Pediatrics, 111,* 110–113.

Cianciolo, Anna T., & Sternberg, Robert J. (2004). *Intelligence: A brief history.* Malden, MA: Blackwell.

Cicchetti, Dante, & Curtis, W. John. (2007). Multilevel perspectives on pathways to resilient functioning. *Development and Psychopathology, 19,* 627–629.

Cicchetti, Dante, Rogosch, Fred A., & Sturge-Apple, Melissa L. (2007). Interactions of child maltreatment and serotonin transporter and monoamine oxidase A polymorphisms: Depressive symptomatology among adolescents from low socioeconomic status backgrounds. *Development and Psychopathology, 19,* 1161–1180.

Cicchetti, Dante, & Toth, Sheree L. (1998). Perspectives on research and practice in developmental psychopathology. In William Damon (Series Ed.) & Irving E. Sigel & K. Ann Renninger (Vol. Eds.), *Handbook of child psychology: Vol. 4. Child psychology in practice* (5th ed., pp. 479–483). New York: Wiley.

Cicirelli, Victor G. (2006). Caregiving decision making by older mothers and adult children: Process and expected outcome. *Psychology and Aging, 21,* 209–221.

Cillessen, Antonius H. N., & Mayeux, Lara. (2004). From censure to reinforcement: Developmental changes in the association between aggression and social status. *Child Development, 75,* 147–163.

Clark, Lee Anna. (2009). Stability and change in personality disorder. *Current Directions in Psychological Science, 18,* 27–31.

Clark, William R. (1999). *A means to an end: The biological basis of aging and death.* New York: Oxford University Press.

Clarke-Stewart, Alison, & Allhusen, Virginia D. (2005). *What we know about childcare.* Cambridge, MA: Harvard University Press.

Cleary, Paul D., Zaborski, Lawrence B., & Ayanian, John Z. (2004). Sex differences in health over the course of midlife. In Orville Gilbert Brim, Carol D. Ryff, & Ronald C. Kessler (Eds.), *How healthy are we? A national study of well-being at midlife* (pp. 37–63). Chicago: University of Chicago Press.

Clements, Jonathan. (2005, October 5). *Rich, successful— and miserable: New research probes mid-life angst.* Retrieved August 5, 2009, from http://online.wsj.com/public/article/SB112846380547659946.html

Clinchy, Blythe McVicker. (1993). Ways of knowing and ways of being: Epistemological and moral development in undergraduate women. In Andrew Garrod (Ed.), *Approaches to moral development: New research and emerging themes* (pp. 180–200). New York: Teachers College Press.

Cloninger, C. Robert. (2003). Completing the psychobiological architecture of human personality development: Temperament, character and coherence. In Ursula M. Staudinger & Ulman Lindenberger (Eds.), *Understanding human development: Dialogues with lifespan psychology* (pp. 159–181). Dordrecht, The Netherlands: Kluwer.

Cockerham, William C. (2006). *Society of risk-takers: Living life on the edge.* New York: Worth.

Coe, Benjamin L., Kirkpatrick, James R., Taylor, Alan, & vom Saal, Frederick S. (2008). A new 'crowded uterine horn' mouse model for examining the relationship between foetal growth and adult obesity. *Basic & Clinical Pharmacology & Toxicology, 102,* 162–167.

Cohan, Catherine L., & Kleinbaum, Stacey. (2002). Toward a greater understanding of the cohabitation effect: Premarital cohabitation and marital communication. *Journal of Marriage and Family, 64,* 180–192.

Cohen, David. (2006). *The development of play* (3rd ed.). New York: Routledge.

Cohen, Jon. (2007a, March 9). Hope on new AIDS drugs, but breast-feeding strategy backfires. *Science, 315,* 1357.

Cohen, Jon. (2007b, September 7). DNA duplications and deletions help determine health. *Science, 317,* 1315–1317.

Cohen, Lee S., Soares, Claudio N., Vitonis, Allison F., Otto, Michael W., & Harlow, Bernard L. (2006). Risk for new onset of depression during the menopausal transition. *Archives of General Psychiatry, 63,* 385–390.

Cohen, Leslie B., & Cashon, Cara H. (2006). Infant cognition. In William Damon & Richard M. Lerner (Series Eds.) & Deanna Kuhn & Robert S. Siegler (Vol. Eds.), *Handbook of child psychology: Vol. 2. Cognition, perception, and language* (6th ed., pp. 214–251). Hoboken, NJ: Wiley.

Cokley, Kevin O. (2003). What do we know about the motivation of African American students? Challenging the "anti-intellectual" myth. *Harvard Educational Review, 73,* 524–558.

Cole, Michael. (2005). Culture in development. In Marc H. Bornstein & Michael E. Lamb (Eds.), *Developmental science: An advanced textbook* (5th ed., pp. 45–101). Mahwah, NJ: Erlbaum.

Coleman, Marilyn, Ganong, Lawrence H., & Warzinik, Kelly. (2007). *Family life in 20th-century America.* Westport, CT: Greenwood Press.

Coles, Robert. (1997). *The moral intelligence of children: How to raise a moral child.* New York: Random House.

Colleran, Carol, & Jay, Debra. (2003). Surviving addiction: Audrey's story. *Aging Today, 24*(1).

Collins, Juliet, Johnson, Susan L., & Krebs, Nancy F. (2004, October 1). Screen for and treat overweight in 2- to 5-year-olds? Yes! *Contemporary Pediatrics, 21,* 60–67.

Collins, Mary Elizabeth, Paris, Ruth, & Ward, Rolanda L. (2008). The permanence of family ties: Implications for youth transitioning from foster care. *American Journal of Orthopsychiatry, 78,* 54–62.

Collins, Michael F. (with Kay, Tess). (2003). *Sport and social exclusion*. London: Routledge.

Collins, W. Andrew, & Laursen, Brett. (2004). Parent–adolescent relationships and influences. In Richard M. Lerner & Laurence D. Steinberg (Eds.), *Handbook of adolescent psychology* (2nd ed., pp. 331–361). Hoboken, NJ: Wiley.

Collins, W. Andrew, & Steinberg, Laurence. (2006). Adolescent development in interpersonal context. In William Damon & Richard M. Lerner (Series Eds.) & Nancy Eisenberg (Vol. Ed.), *Handbook of child psychology: Vol. 3. Social, emotional, and personality development* (6th ed., pp. 1003–1067). Hoboken, NJ: Wiley.

Collins, W. Andrew, & van Dulmen, Manfred. (2006). "The course of true love(s) . . .": Origins and pathways in the development of romantic relationships. In Ann C. Crouter & Alan Booth (Eds.), *Romance and sex in adolescence and emerging adulthood: Risks and opportunities* (pp. 63–86). Mahwah, NJ: Erlbaum.

Compas, Bruce E. (2004). Processes of risk and resilience during adolescence: Linking contexts and individuals. In Richard M. Lerner & Laurence D. Steinberg (Eds.), *Handbook of adolescent psychology* (2nd ed., pp. 263–296). Hoboken, NJ: Wiley.

Compian, Laura, Gowen, L. Kris, & Hayward, Chris. (2004). Peripubertal girls' romantic and platonic involvement with boys: Associations with body image and depression symptoms. *Journal of Research on Adolescence, 14,* 23–47.

Conboy, Barbara T., & Thal, Donna J. (2006). Ties between the lexicon and grammar: Cross-sectional and longitudinal studies of bilingual toddlers. *Child Development, 77,* 712–735.

Cong, Zhen, & Silverstein, Merril. (2008). Intergenerational support and depression among elders in rural China: Do daughters-in-law matter? *Journal of Marriage and Family, 70,* 599–612.

Conger, Rand D., & Donnellan, M. Brent. (2007). An interactionist perspective on the socioeconomic context of human development. *Annual Review of Psychology, 58,* 175–199.

Conger, Rand D., Rueter, Martha A., & Elder, Glen H. (1999). Couple resilience to economic pressure. *Journal of Personality & Social Psychology, 76,* 54–71.

Conger, Rand D., Wallace, Lora Ebert, Sun, Yumei, Simons, Ronald L., McLoyd, Vonnie C., & Brody, Gene H. (2002). Economic pressure in African American families: A replication and extension of the family stress model. *Developmental Psychology, 38,* 179–193.

Conner, Mark. (2008). Initiation and maintenance of health behaviors. *Applied Psychology, 57,* 42–50.

Connidis, Ingrid Arnet. (2001). *Family ties & aging*. Thousand Oaks, CA: Sage.

Conti, Bruno, Sanchez-Alavez, Manuel, Winsky-Sommerer, Raphaelle, Morale, Maria Concetta, Lucero, Jacinta, Brownell, Sara, et al. (2006, November 3). Transgenic mice with a reduced core body temperature have an increased life span. *Science, 314,* 825–828.

Cook, Christine C., Martin, Peter, Yearns, Mary, & Damhorst, Mary Lynn. (2007). Attachment to "place" and coping with losses in changed communities: A paradox for aging adults. *Family & Consumer Sciences Research Journal, 35,* 201–214.

Cook, Diane B., Casillas, Alex, Robbins, Steven B., & Dougherty, Linda M. (2005). Goal continuity and the "Big Five" as predictors of older adult marital adjustment. *Personality and Individual Differences, 38,* 519–531.

Cook, Susan Wagner, Mitchell, Zachary, & Goldin-Meadow, Susan. (2008). Gesturing makes learning last. *Cognition, 106,* 1047–1058.

Coontz, Stephanie. (2005). *Marriage, a history: From obedience to intimacy or how love conquered marriage*. New York: Viking.

Coontz, Stephanie. (2006). Romance and sex in adolescence and emerging adulthood. In Ann C. Crouter & Alan Booth (Eds.), *Romance and sex in adolescence and emerging adulthood: Risks and opportunities* (pp. 87–91). Mahwah, NJ: Erlbaum.

Cooper, Claudia, Selwood, Amber, & Livingston, Gill. (2008). The prevalence of elder abuse and neglect: A systematic review. *Age and Ageing, 37,* 151–160.

Coovadia, H. M., & Wittenberg, D. F. (Eds.). (2004). *Paediatrics and child health: A manual for health professionals in developing countries* (5th ed.). New York: Oxford University Press.

Costello, E. Jane, Compton, Scott N., Keeler, Gordon, & Angold, Adrian. (2003). Relationships between poverty and psychopathology: A natural experiment. *Journal of the American Medical Association, 290,* 2023–2029.

Côté, James E. (2006). Emerging adulthood as an institutionalized moratorium: Risks and benefits to identity formation. In Jeffrey Jensen Arnett & Jennifer Lynn Tanner (Eds.), *Emerging adults in America: Coming of age in the 21st century* (pp. 85–116). Washington, DC: American Psychological Association.

Côté, Sylvana M., Borge, Anne I., Geoffroy, Marie-Claude, Rutter, Michael, & Tremblay, Richard E. (2008). Nonmaternal care in infancy and emotional/behavioral difficulties at 4 years old: Moderation by family risk characteristics. *Developmental Psychology, 44,* 155–168.

Courage, Mary L., Reynolds, Greg D., & Richards, John E. (2006). Infants' attention to patterned stimuli: Developmental change from 3 to 12 months of age. *Child Development, 77,* 680–695.

Courter, Gay, & Gaudette, Pat. (2003). *How to survive your husband's midlife crisis: Strategies and stories from the midlife wives club*. New York: Perigee.

Couzin, Jennifer. (2007a, February 2). Probing the roots of race and cancer. *Science, 315,* 592–594.

Couzin, Jennifer. (2007b, November 2). Testing the line between too much and too little. *Science, 318,* 740–741.

Covington, Martin V., & Dray, Elizabeth. (2002). The developmental course of achievement motivation: A need-based approach. In Allan Wigfield & Jacquelynne S. Eccles (Eds.), *Development of achievement motivation* (pp. 33–56). San Diego, CA: Academic Press.

Cowan, Nelson (Ed.). (1997). *The development of memory in childhood*. Hove, East Sussex, UK: Psychology Press.

Coward, Fiona. (2008, March 14). Standing on the shoulders of giants. *Science, 319,* 1493–1495.

Coyle, Karin, Basen-Engquist, Karen, Kirby, Douglas, Parcel, Guy, Banspach, Stephen, Collins, Janet, et al. (2001). Safer choices: Reducing teen pregnancy, HIV, and STDs. *Public Health Reports, 116*(Suppl. 1), 82–93.

Craik, Fergus I. M., & Salthouse, Timothy A. (2000). *The handbook of aging and cognition* (2nd ed.). Mahwah, NJ: Erlbaum.

Crain, William C. (2005). *Theories of development: Concepts and applications* (5th ed.). Upper Saddle River, NJ: Prentice Hall.

Crews, Douglas E. (2003). *Human senescence: Evolutionary and biocultural perspectives.* New York: Cambridge University Press.

Crick, Nicki R., Nelson, David A., Morales, Julie R., Cullerton-Sen, Crystal, Casas, Juan F., & Hickman, Susan E. (2001). Relational victimization in childhood and adolescence: I hurt you through the grapevine. In Jaana Juvonen & Sandra Graham (Eds.), *Peer harassment in school: The plight of the vulnerable and victimized* (pp. 196–214). New York: Guilford Press.

Crimmins, Eileen, Vasunilashorn, Sarinnapha, Kim, Jung Ki, & Alley, Dawn. (2008). Biomarkers related to aging in human populations. *Advances in Clinical Chemistry, 46,* 161–216.

Crimmins, Eileen M., Johnston, Melanie, Hayward, Mark, & Seeman, Teresa. (2003). Age differences in allostatic load: An index of physiological dysregulation. *Experimental Gerontology, 38,* 731–734.

Crinion, Jenny, Turner, R., Grogan, Alice, Hanakawa, Takashi, Noppeney, Uta, Devlin, Joseph T., et al. (2006, June 9). Language control in the bilingual brain. *Science, 312,* 1537–1540.

Criss, Michael M., Pettit, Gregory S., Bates, John E., Dodge, Kenneth A., & Lapp, Amie L. (2002). Family adversity, positive peer relationships, and children's externalizing behavior: A longitudinal perspective on risk and resilience. *Child Development, 73,* 1220–1237.

Crissey, Sarah R. (2009, January). *Educational attainment in the United States: 2007: Population characteristics* (P20-560). Washington, DC: U.S. Bureau of the Census.

Crocetti, Elisabetta, Rubini, Monica, Luyckx, Koen, & Meeus, Wim. (2008). Identity formation in early and middle adolescents from various ethnic groups: From three dimensions to five statuses. *Journal of Youth and Adolescence, 37,* 983–996.

Crockenberg, Susan C. (2003). Rescuing the baby from the bathwater: How gender and temperament (may) influence how child care affects child development. *Child Development, 74,* 1034–1038.

Crosnoe, Robert, & Elder, Glen H., Jr. (2002). Successful adaptation in the later years: A life course approach to aging. *Social Psychology Quarterly, 65,* 309–328.

Crosnoe, Robert, Johnson, Monica Kirkpatrick, & Elder, Glen H., Jr. (2004). Intergenerational bonding in school: The behavioral and contextual correlates of student–teacher relationships. *Sociology of Education, 77,* 60–81.

Crosnoe, Robert, & Needham, Belinda. (2004). Holism, contextual variability, and the study of friendships in adolescent development. *Child Development, 75,* 264–279.

Crow, James F. (2003, August 1). There's something curious about paternal-age effects. *Science, 301,* 606–607.

Cruikshank, Margaret. (2003). *Learning to be old: Gender, culture, and aging.* Lanham, MD: Rowman & Littlefield.

Cryder, Cynthia E., Lerner, Jennifer S., Gross, James J., & Dahl, Ronald E. (2008). Misery is not miserly: Sad and self-focused individuals spend more. *Psychological Science, 19,* 525–530.

Csikszentmihalyi, Mihaly. (1996). *Creativity: Flow and the psychology of discovery and invention.* New York: HarperCollins.

Csikszentmihalyi, Mihaly, & Schneider, Barbara. (2000). *Becoming adult: How teenagers prepare for the world of work.* New York: Basic Books.

Cullen, Karen Weber, & Zakeri, Issa. (2004). Fruits, vegetables, milk, and sweetened beverages consumption and access to a la carte/snack bar meals at school. *American Journal of Public Health, 94,* 463–467.

Cumming, Elaine, & Henry, William Earl. (1961). *Growing old: The process of disengagement.* New York: Basic Books.

Cummings, E. Mark, Goeke-Morey, Marcie C., & Papp, Lauren M. (2003). Children's responses to everyday marital conflict tactics in the home. *Child Development, 74,* 1918–1929.

Cunningham, John A., & Selby, Peter L. (2007). Implications of the normative fallacy in young adult smokers aged 19–24 years. *American Journal of Public Health, 97,* 1399–1400.

Curlin, Farr A., Nwodim, Chinyere, Vance, Jennifer L., Chin, Marshall H., & Lantos, John D. (2008). To die, to sleep: US physicians' religious and other objections to physician-assisted suicide, terminal sedation, and withdrawal of life support. *American Journal of Hospice and Palliative Medicine, 25,* 112–120.

Curry, Leslie, Schwartz, Harold I., Gruman, Cindy, & Blank, Karen. (2002). Could adequate palliative care obviate assisted suicide? *Death Studies, 26,* 757–774.

Curtis, W. John, & Cicchetti, Dante. (2003). Moving research on resilience into the 21st century: Theoretical and methodological considerations in examining the biological contributors to resilience. *Development & Psychopathology, 15,* 773–810.

Curtis, W. John, & Nelson, Charles A. (2003). Toward building a better brain: Neurobehavioral outcomes, mechanisms, and processes of environmental enrichment. In Suniya S. Luthar (Ed.), *Resilience and vulnerability: Adaptation in the context of childhood adversities* (pp. 463–488). New York: Cambridge University Press.

Dahl, Ronald E. (2004). Adolescent brain development: A period of vulnerabilities and opportunities. Keynote address. In Ronald E. Dahl & Linda Patia Spear (Eds.), *Adolescent brain development: Vulnerabilities and opportunities* (Vol. 1021, pp. 1–22). New York: New York Academy of Sciences.

Dahlberg, Gunilla, Moss, Peter, & Pence, Alan R. (2007). *Beyond quality in early childhood education and care: Languages of evaluation* (2nd ed.). New York: Routledge.

Damasio, Antonio R. (2003). *Looking for Spinoza: Joy, sorrow, and the feeling brain.* Orlando, FL: Harcourt.

Damon, William. (2008). *The path to purpose: Helping our children find their calling in life.* New York: Free Press.

Damon, William, & Lerner, Richard M. (Eds.). (2006). *Handbook of child psychology* (6th ed., Vol. 1–4). Hoboken, NJ: Wiley.

Dangour, Alan D., Fletcher, Astrid E., & Grundy, Emily M. D. (2007). *Ageing well: Nutrition, health, and social interventions.* Boca Raton, FL: CRC Press/Taylor & Francis.

Darling, Nancy, Cumsille, Patricio, & Martinez, M. Loreto. (2008). Individual differences in adolescents' beliefs about the legitimacy of parental authority and their own obligation to obey: A longitudinal investigation. *Child Development, 79,* 1103–1118.

Daro, Deborah. (2002). Public perception of child sexual abuse: Who is to blame? *Child Abuse & Neglect, 26,* 1131–1133.

Daselaar, Sander, & Cabeza, Roberto. (2005). Age-related changes in hemispheric organization. In Roberto Cabeza, Lars Nyberg, & Denise Park (Eds.), *Cognitive neuroscience of aging: Linking cognitive and cerebral aging* (pp. 325–353). New York: Oxford University Press.

Dasen, Pierre R. (2003). Theoretical frameworks in cross-cultural developmental psychology: An attempt at integration. In T. S. Saraswati (Ed.), *Cross-cultural perspectives in human development: Theory, research, and applications* (pp. 128–165). New Delhi, India: Sage.

Datan, Nancy. (1986). Oedipal conflict, platonic love: Centrifugal forces in intergenerational relations. In Nancy Datan, Anita L. Greene, & Hayne W. Reese (Eds.), *Life-span developmental psychology: Intergenerational relations* (pp. 29–50). Hillsdale, NJ: Erlbaum.

Daulaire, Nils, Leidl, Pat, Mackin, Laurel, Murphy, Colleen, & Stark, Laura. (2002). *Promises to keep: The toll of unintended pregnancies on women's lives in the developing world.* Washington, DC: Global Health Council.

Davey, Adam, & Szinovacz, Maximiliane E. (2004). Dimensions of marital quality and retirement. *Journal of Family Issues, 25,* 431–464.

David, Barbara, Grace, Diane, & Ryan, Michelle K. (2004). The gender wars: A self-categorization perspective on the development of gender identity. In Mark Bennett & Fabio Sani (Eds.), *The development of the social self* (pp. 135–157). Hove, East Sussex, England: Psychology Press.

Davidson, Julia O'Connell. (2005). *Children in the global sex trade.* Malden, MA: Polity.

Davies, Chris G., & Thorn, Brian L. (2002). Psychopharmacology with older adults in residential care. In Robert D. Hill, Brian L. Thorn, John Bowling, & Anthony Morrison (Eds.), *Geriatric residential care* (pp. 161–181). Mahwah, NJ: Erlbaum.

Davies, Patrick T., & Cicchetti, Dante. (2004). Toward an integration of family systems and developmental psychopathology approaches. *Development & Psychopathology, 16,* 477–481.

Davis, Elysia Poggi, Parker, Susan Whitmore, Tottenham, Nim, & Gunnar, Megan R. (2003). Emotion, cognition, and the hypothalamic-pituitary-adrenocortical axis: A developmental perspective. In Michelle de Haan & Mark H. Johnson (Eds.), *The cognitive neuroscience of development* (pp. 181–206). New York: Psychology Press.

Davis, Kelly D., Goodman, W. Benjamin, Pirretti, Amy E., & Almeida, David M. (2008). Nonstandard work schedules, perceived family well-being, and daily stressors. *Journal of Marriage and Family, 70,* 991–1003.

Davison, Kirsten Krahnstoever, Werder, Jessica L., Trost, Stewart G., Baker, Birgitta L., & Birch, Leann L. (2007). Why are early maturing girls less active? Links between pubertal development, psychological well-being, and physical activity among girls at ages 11 and 13. *Social Science & Medicine, 64,* 2391–2404.

Dawson, Michelle, Soulières, Isabelle, Gernsbacher, Morton Ann, & Mottron, Laurent. (2007). The level and nature of autistic intelligence. *Psychological Science, 18,* 657–662.

Dawson-Tunik, Theo L., Commons, Michael, Wilson, Mark, & Fischer, Kurt W. (2005). The shape of development. *European Journal of Developmental Psychology, 2,* 163–195.

Day, James, & Naedts, Myriam H. L. (1999). Constructivist and post-constructivist perspectives on moral and religious judgement research. In Ralph L. Mosher, Deborah J. Youngman, & James M. Day (Eds.), *Human development across the lifespan: Educational and psychological applications* (pp. 239–264). Westport, CT: Praeger.

De Bellis, Michael D., Narasimhan, Anandhi, Thatcher, Dawn L., Keshavan, Matcheri S., Soloff, Paul, & Clark, Duncan B. (2005). Prefrontal cortex, thalamus, and cerebellar volumes in adolescents and young adults with adolescent-onset alcohol use disorders and comorbid mental disorders. *Alcoholism: Clinical and Experimental Research, 29,* 1590–1600.

de Bruin, Wändi Bruine, Parker, Andrew M., & Fischhoff, Baruch. (2007). Can adolescents predict significant life events? *The Journal of Adolescent Health, 41,* 208–210.

De Grey, Aubrey D. N. J., & Rae, Michael. (2007). *Ending aging: The rejuvenation breakthroughs that could reverse human aging in our lifetime.* New York: St. Martin's Press.

de Haan, Michelle, & Johnson, Mark H. (2003). Mechanisms and theories of brain development. In Michelle De Haan & Mark H. Johnson (Eds.), *The cognitive neuroscience of development* (pp. 1–18). Hove, East Sussex, England: Psychology Press.

de la Sablonnière, Roxane, & Tougas, Francine. (2008). Relative deprivation and social identity in times of dramatic social change: The case of nurses. *Journal of Applied Social Psychology, 38,* 2293–2314.

De la Torre, Jack C., Kalaria, Raj, Nakajima, Kenji, & Nagata, Ken (Eds.). (2002). *Annals of the New York Academy of Sciences: Vol. 977. Alzheimer's disease: Vascular etiology and pathology.* New York: New York Academy of Sciences.

De Lee, Joseph Bolivar. (1938). *The principles and practice of obstetrics* (7th ed.). Philadelphia: Saunders.

de Rosnay, Marc, Cooper, Peter J., Tsigaras, Nicolas, & Murray, Lynne. (2006). Transmission of social anxiety from mother to infant: An experimental study using a social referencing paradigm. *Behaviour Research and Therapy, 44,* 1165–1175.

de Schipper, Elles J., Riksen-Walraven, J. Marianne, & Geurts, Sabine A. E. (2006). Effects of child–caregiver ratio on the interactions between caregivers and children in child-care centers: An experimental study. *Child Development, 77,* 861–874.

Deary, Ian J., Batty, G. David, Pattie, Alison, & Gale, Catharine R. (2008). More intelligent, more dependable children live longer: A 55-year longitudinal study of a representative sample of the Scottish nation. *Psychological Science, 19,* 874–880.

Deci, Edward L., Koestner, Richard, & Ryan, Richard M. (1999). A meta-analytic review of experiments examining the effects of extrinsic rewards on intrinsic motivation. *Psychological Bulletin, 125,* 627–668.

Degnan, Kathryn A., Calkins, Susan D., Keane, Susan P., & Hill-Soderlund, Ashley L. (2008). Profiles of disruptive behavior across early childhood: Contributions of frustration reactivity, physiological regulation, and maternal behavior. *Child Development, 79,* 1357–1376.

Dehue, Francine, Bolman, Catherine, & Völlink, Trijntje. (2008). Cyberbullying: Youngsters' experiences and parental perception. *CyberPsychology & Behavior, 11,* 217–223.

DeKeyser, Robert, & Larson-Hall, Jenifer. (2005). What does the critical period really mean? In Judith F. Kroll & Annette M. B. de Groot (Eds.), *Handbook of bilingualism: Psycholinguistic approaches* (pp. 88–108). Oxford, UK: Oxford University Press.

Dellenbach, Myriam, & Zimprich, Daniel. (2008). Typical intellectual engagement and cognition in old age. *Aging, Neuropsychology, and Cognition, 15,* 208–231.

Denham, Susanne A., Blair, Kimberly A., DeMulder, Elizabeth, Levitas, Jennifer, Sawyer, Katherine, Auerbach-Major, Sharon, et al. (2003). Preschool emotional competence: Pathway to social competence. *Child Development, 74,* 238–256.

Dennis, Helen. (2007). Retirement planning among couples: Observations and recommendations. *Generations, 31*(3), 60–62.

Denny, Dallas, & Pittman, Cathy. (2007). Gender identity: From dualism to diversity. In Mitchell S. Tepper & Annette Fuglsang Owens (Eds.), *Sexual health: Vol. 1. Psychological foundations* (pp. 205–229). Westport, CT: Praeger/Greenwood.

Dentinger, Emma, & Clarkberg, Marin. (2002). Informal caregiving and retirement timing among men and women: Gender and caregiving relationships in late midlife. *Journal of Family Issues, 23,* 857–879.

DePaulo, Bella M. (2006). *Singled out: How singles are stereotyped, stigmatized, and ignored and still live happily ever after.* New York: St. Martin's Press.

DePaulo, Bella M., & Morris, Wendy L. (2005). Singles in society and in science. *Psychological Inquiry, 16,* 57–83.

Derman, Orhan, Kanbur, Nuray Öksöz, & Kutluk, Tezer. (2003). Tamoxifen treatment for pubertal gynecomastia. *International Journal of Adolescent Medicine and Health, 15,* 359–363.

Derryberry, Douglas, Reed, Marjorie A., & Pilkenton-Taylor, Carolyn. (2003). Temperament and coping: Advantages of an individual differences perspective. *Development & Psychopathology, 15,* 1049–1066.

Deuschl, Günther, Schade-Brittinger, Carmen, Krack, Paul, Volkmann, Jens, Schäfer, Helmut, Bötzel, Kai, et al. (2006). A randomized trial of deep-brain stimulation for Parkinson's disease. *New England Journal of Medicine, 355,* 896–908.

Deveraux, Lara L., & Hammerman, Ann Jackoway. (1998). *Infertility and identity: New strategies for treatment.* San Francisco: Jossey-Bass.

Devi, Sharmila. (2008). Progress on childhood obesity patchy in the USA. *Lancet, 371,* 105–106.

Di, Haibo, Yu, Senming, Weng, Xuchu, Laureys, Steven, Yu, Dan, Li, Jinqing, et al. (2007). Cerebral response to patient's own name in the vegetative and minimally conscious states. *Neurology, 68,* 895–899.

Diamond, Adele, & Amso, Dima. (2008). Contributions of neuroscience to our understanding of cognitive development. *Current Directions in Psychological Science, 17,* 136–141.

Diamond, Adele, & Kirkham, Natasha. (2005). Not quite as grown-up as we like to think: Parallels between cognition in childhood and adulthood. *Psychological Science, 16,* 291–297.

Diamond, David M., Dunwiddie, Thomas V., & Rose, G. M. (1988). Characteristics of hippocampal primed burst potentiation in vitro and in the awake rat. *Journal of Neuroscience, 8,* 4079–4088.

Diamond, Lisa M. (2004). Emerging perspectives on distinctions between romantic love and sexual desire. *Current Directions in Psychological Science, 13,* 116–119.

Diamond, Lisa M., & Savin-Williams, Ritch C. (2003). The intimate relationships of sexual-minority youths. In Gerald R. Adams & Michael D. Berzonsky (Eds.), *Blackwell handbook of adolescence* (pp. 393–412). Malden, MA: Blackwell.

Didierjean, André, & Gobet, Fernand. (2008). Sherlock Holmes: An expert's view of expertise. *British Journal of Psychology, 99,* 109–125.

Didion, Joan. (2005). *The year of magical thinking.* New York: Knopf.

Diener, Ed, & Biswas-Diener, Robert. (2008). *Happiness: Unlocking the mysteries of psychological wealth.* Malden, MA: Blackwell.

Diener, Marissa. (2000). Gift from the gods: A Balinese guide to early child rearing. In Judy S. DeLoache & Alma Gottlieb (Eds.), *A world of babies: Imagined childcare guides for seven societies* (pp. 96–116). New York: Cambridge University Press.

DiGirolamo, Ann, Thompson, Nancy, Martorell, Reynaldo, Fein, Sara, & Grummer-Strawn, Laurence. (2005). Intention or experience? Predictors of continued breastfeeding. *Health Education & Behavior, 32,* 208–226.

Digman, John M. (1990). Personality structure: Emergence of the five-factor model. *Annual Review of Psychology, 41,* 417–440.

Dijk, Jan A. G. M. van. (2005). *The deepening divide: Inequality in the information society.* Thousand Oaks, CA: Sage.

Dijksterhuis, Ap, & Nordgren, Loran F. (2006). A theory of unconscious thought. *Perspectives on Psychological Science, 1,* 95–109.

Dilworth-Bart, Janean E., & Moore, Colleen F. (2006). Mercy mercy me: Social injustice and the prevention of environmental pollutant exposures among ethnic minority and poor children. *Child Development, 77,* 247–265.

Dindia, Kathryn, & Emmers-Sommer, Tara M. (2006). What partners do to maintain their close relationships. In Patricia Noller & Judith A. Feeney (Eds.), *Close relationships: Functions, forms and processes* (pp. 305–324). Hove, England: Psychology Press.

Dion, Karen Kisiel. (2006). On the development of identity: Perspectives from immigrant families. In Ramaswami Mahalingam (Ed.), *Cultural psychology of immigrants* (pp. 299–314). Mahwah, NJ: Erlbaum

Dionne, Ginette, Dale, Philip S., Boivin, Michel, & Plomin, Robert. (2003). Genetic evidence for bidirectional effects of early lexical and grammatical development. *Child Development, 74,* 394–412.

Dishion, Thomas J., & Bullock, Bernadette Marie. (2002). Parenting and adolescent problem behavior: An ecological analysis of the nurturance hypothesis. In John G. Borkowski, Sharon Landesman Ramey, & Marie Bristol-Power (Eds.), *Parenting and the child's world: Influences on academic, intellectual, and social-emotional development* (pp. 231–249). Mahwah, NJ: Erlbaum.

Dishion, Thomas J., McCord, Joan, & Poulin, François. (1999). When interventions harm: Peer groups and problem behavior. *American Psychologist, 54,* 755–764.

Dishion, Thomas J., & Owen, Lee D. (2002). A longitudinal analysis of friendships and substance use: Bidirectional influence from adolescence to adulthood. *Developmental Psychology, 38,* 480–491.

Dishion, Thomas J., Poulin, François, & Burraston, Bert. (2001). Peer group dynamics associated with iatrogenic effects in group interventions with high-risk young adolescents. In William Damon (Series Ed.) & Douglas W. Nangle & Cynthia A. Erdley (Vol. Eds.), *New directions for child and adolescent development: No. 91. The role of friendship in psychological adjustment* (pp. 79–92). San Francisco: Jossey-Bass.

Dishion, Thomas J., Shaw, Daniel, Connell, Arin, Gardner, Frances, Weaver, Chelsea, & Wilson, Melvin. (2008). The family check-up with high-risk indigent families: Preventing problem behavior by increasing parents' positive behavior support in early childhood. *Child Development, 79,* 1395–1414.

Dixon, Roger A., Garrett, Douglas D., Lentz, Tanya L., MacDonald, Stuart W. S., Strauss, Esther, & Hultsch, David F. (2007). Neurocognitive markers of cognitive impairment: Exploring the roles of speed and inconsistency. *Neuropsychology, 21,* 381–399.

Dodge, Kenneth A., Coie, John D., & Lynam, Donald R. (2006). Aggression and antisocial behavior in youth. In William Damon & Richard M. Lerner (Series Eds.) & Nancy Eisenberg (Vol. Ed.), *Handbook of child psychology: Vol. 3. Social, emotional, and personality development* (6th ed., pp. 719–788). New York: Wiley.

Dominguez, Cynthia O. (2001). Expertise in laparoscopic surgery: Anticipation and affordances. In Eduardo Salas & Gary Klein (Eds.), *Linking expertise and naturalistic decision making* (pp. 287–301). Mahwah, NJ: Erlbaum.

Donnellan, M. Brent, & Lucas, Richard E. (2008). Age differences in the Big Five across the life span: Evidence from two national samples. *Psychology and Aging, 23,* 558–566.

Doumbo, Ogobara K. (2005, February 4). It takes a village: Medical research and ethics in Mali. *Science, 307,* 679–681.

Dowling, John E. (2004). *The great brain debate: Nature or nurture?* Washington, DC: Joseph Henry Press.

Downs, Danielle Symons, & Hausenblas, Heather A. (2007). Pregnant women's third trimester exercise behaviors, body mass index, and pregnancy outcomes. *Psychology & Health, 22,* 545–559.

Duckworth, Angela L., Peterson, Christopher, Matthews, Michael D., & Kelly, Dennis R. (2007). Grit: Perseverance and passion for long-term goals. *Journal of Personality and Social Psychology, 92,* 1087–1101.

Dugger, Celia W. (2006, April 30). Mothers of Nepal vanquish a killer of children. *New York Times,* pp. A1, A16.

Duncan, Greg J., & Magnuson, Katherine. (2007). Penny wise and effect size foolish. *Child Development Perspectives, 1,* 46–51.

Dunifon, Rachel, & Kowaleski-Jones, Lori. (2007). The influence of grandparents in single-mother families. *Journal of Marriage and Family, 69,* 465–481.

Dunn, Judy, & Hughes, Claire. (2001). "I got some swords and you're dead!": Violent fantasy, antisocial behavior, friendship, and moral sensibility in young children. *Child Development, 72,* 491–505.

Dunphy, Dexter C. (1963). The social structure of urban adolescent peer groups. *Sociometry, 26,* 230–246.

Dupéré, Véronique, Lacourse, Éric, Willms, J. Douglas, Vitaro, Frank, & Tremblay, Richard E. (2007). Affiliation to youth gangs during adolescence: The interaction between childhood psychopathic tendencies and neighborhood disadvantage. *Journal of Abnormal Child Psychology, 35,* 1035–1045.

Duplassie, Danielle, & Daniluk, Judith C. (2007). Sexuality: Young and middle adulthood. In Mitchell S. Tepper & Annette Fuglsang Owens (Eds.), *Sexual health: Vol. 1. Psychological foundations* (pp. 263–289). Westport, CT: Praeger/Greenwood.

Durga, Jane, Boxtel, Martin P. J. van, Schouten, Evert G., Kok, Frans J., Jolles, Jelle, Katan, Martijn B., et al. (2007). Effect of 3-year folic acid supplementation on cognitive function in older adults in the FACIT trial: A randomised, double blind, controlled trial. *Lancet, 369,* 208–216.

East, Patricia L., & Kiernan, Elizabeth A. (2001). Risks among youths who have multiple sisters who were adolescent parents. *Family Planning Perspectives, 33,* 75–80.

Ebaugh, Helen Rose, & Curry, Mary. (2000). Fictive kin as social capital in new immigrant communities. *Sociological Perspectives, 43,* 189–209.

Ebner, Natalie C., Freund, Alexandra M., & Baltes, Paul B. (2006). Developmental changes in personal goal orientation from young to late adulthood: From striving for gains to maintenance and prevention of losses. *Psychology and Aging, 21,* 664–678.

Eby, Lillian T., Durley, Jaime R., Evans, Sarah C., & Ragins, Belle Rose. (2006). The relationship between short-term mentoring benefits and long-term mentor outcomes. *Journal of Vocational Behavior, 69,* 424–444.

Eccles, Jacquelynne S. (2004). Schools, academic motivation, and stage–environment fit. In Richard M. Lerner & Laurence D. Steinberg (Eds.), *Handbook of adolescent psychology* (2nd ed., pp. 125–153). Hoboken, NJ: Wiley.

Eccles, Jacquelynne S., Barber, Bonnie L., Stone, Margaret, & Hunt, James. (2003). Extracurricular activities and adolescent development. *Journal of Social Issues, 59,* 865–889.

Eckert, Penelope. (1989). *Jocks and burnouts: Social categories and identity in the high school.* New York: Teachers College Press.

Eddleman, Keith A., Malone, Fergal D., Sullivan, Lisa, Dukes, Kim, Berkowitz, Richard L., Kharbutli, Yara, et al. (2006). Pregnancy loss rates after midtrimester amniocentesis. *Obstetrics & Gynecology, 108,* 1067–1072.

Editors, The. (2004). Preventing early reading failure. *American Educator, 28,* 5.

Education Week. (2008). *Diplomas count 2008: School to college: Can state P-16 councils ease the transition?* Retrieved September 13, 2009, from http://www.edweek.org/ew/toc/2008/06/05/index.html

Edwards, Carolyn, Gandini, Lella, & Forman, George (Eds.). (1998). *The hundred languages of children: The Reggio Emilia approach—Advanced reflections* (2nd ed.). Greenwich, CT: Ablex.

Egan, Kieran, & Ling, Michael. (2002). We began as poets: Conceptual tools and the arts in early childhood. In Liora Bresler & Christine Marme Thompson (Eds.), *The arts in children's lives: Context, culture, and curriculum* (pp. 93–100). Dordrecht, The Netherlands: Kluwer.

Ehrlich, Paul R. (1968). *The population bomb.* New York: Ballantine Books.

Eigenmann, Philippe A., & Haenggeli, Charles A. (2007). Food colourings, preservatives, and hyperactivity. *Lancet, 370,* 1524–1525.

Eisenberg, Marla E., Bearinger, Linda H., Sieving, Renee E., Swain, Carolyne, & Resnick, Michael D. (2004). Parents' beliefs about condoms and oral contraceptives: Are they medically accurate? *Perspectives on Sexual and Reproductive Health, 36,* 50–57.

Eisenberg, Nancy, Cumberland, Amanda, Guthrie, Ivanna K., Murphy, Bridget C., & Shepard, Stephanie A. (2005). Age changes in prosocial responding and moral reasoning in adolescence and early adulthood. *Journal of Research on Adolescence, 15,* 235–260.

Eisenberg, Nancy, & Fabes, Richard A. (1998). Prosocial development. In William Damon (Series Ed.) & Nancy Eisenberg (Vol. Ed.), *Handbook of child psychology: Vol. 3. Social, emotional, and personality development* (5th ed., pp. 701–778). New York: Wiley.

Eisenberg, Nancy, Fabes, Richard A., & Spinrad, Tracy L. (2006). Prosocial development. In William Damon & Richard M. Lerner (Series Eds.) & Nancy Eisenberg (Vol. Ed.), *Handbook of child psychology: Vol. 3. Social, emotional, and personality development* (6th ed., pp. 646–718). Hoboken, NJ: Wiley.

Eisenberg, Nancy, Hofer, Claire, Spinrad, Tracy L., Gershoff, Elizabeth T., Valiente, Carlos, Losoya, Sandra, et al. (2008). Understanding mother–adolescent conflict discussions: Concurrent and across-time prediction from youths' dispositions and parenting. *Monographs of the Society for Research in Child Development, 73*(2, Serial No. 290), vii–viii, 1–160.

Eisenberg, Nancy, Spinrad, Tracy L., Fabes, Richard A., Reiser, Mark, Cumberland, Amanda, Shepard, Stephanie A., et al. (2004). The relations of effortful control and impulsivity to children's resiliency and adjustment. *Child Development, 75,* 25–46.

Eisner, Manuel. (2002). Crime, problem drinking, and drug use: Patterns of problem behavior in cross-national perspective. *Annals of the American Academy of Political & Social Science, 580,* 201–225.

Ekberg, Merryn. (2007). Maximizing the benefits and minimizing the risks associated with prenatal genetic testing. *Health, Risk & Society, 9,* 67–81.

El-Sheikh, Mona, & Harger, JoAnn. (2001). Appraisals of marital conflict and children's adjustment, health, and physiological reactivity. *Developmental Psychology, 37,* 875–885.

Elder, Glen H., Jr., & Shanahan, Michael J. (2006). The life course and human development. In William Damon & Richard M. Lerner (Series Eds.) & Richard M. Lerner (Vol. Ed.), *Handbook of child psychology: Vol. 1. Theoretical models of human development* (6th ed., pp. 665–715). Hoboken, NJ: Wiley.

Elias, Merrill F., Robbins, Michael A., Budge, Marc M., Elias, Penelope K., Hermann, Barbara A., & Dore, Gregory A. (2004). Studies of aging, hypertension and cognitive functioning: With contributions from the Maine-Syracuse Study.

In Paul T. Costa & Ilene C. Siegler (Eds.), *Recent advances in psychology and aging* (Vol. 15, pp. 89–132). Amsterdam: Elsevier.

Elkind, David. (1967). Egocentrism in adolescence. *Child Development, 38,* 1025–1034.

Elkind, David. (2007). *The power of play: How spontaneous, imaginative activities lead to happier, healthier children.* Cambridge, MA: Da Capo Press.

Elliott, Leslie, Arbes, Samuel J., Jr., Harvey, Eric S., Lee, Robert C., Salo, Päivi M., Cohn, Richard D., et al. (2007). Dust weight and asthma prevalence in the National Survey of Lead and Allergens in Housing (NSLAH). *Environmental Health Perspectives, 115,* 215–220.

Ellis, Bruce J. (2004). Timing of pubertal maturation in girls: An integrated life history approach. *Psychological Bulletin, 130,* 920–958.

Ellis, Bruce J., Bates, John E., Dodge, Kenneth A., Fergusson, David M., Horwood, L. John, Pettit, Gregory S., et al. (2003). Does father absence place daughters at special risk for early sexual activity and teenage pregnancy? *Child Development, 74,* 801–821.

Ellis, Bruce J., & Bjorklund, David F. (2005). *Origins of the social mind: Evolutionary psychology and child development.* New York: Guilford Press.

Ellis, Bruce J., & Garber, Judy. (2000). Psychosocial antecedents of variation in girls' pubertal timing: Maternal depression, stepfather presence, and marital and family stress. *Child Development, 71,* 485–501.

Ellis, Neenah. (2002). *If I live to be 100: Lessons from the centenarians.* New York: Crown.

Ellison, Peter Thorpe. (2002). Puberty. In Noël Cameron (Ed.), *Human growth and development* (pp. 65–84). San Diego, CA: Academic Press.

Elwert, Felix, & Christakis, Nicholas A. (2008). The effect of widowhood on mortality by the causes of death of both spouses. *American Journal of Public Health, 98,* 2092–2098.

Emery, Nathan J. (2000). The eyes have it: The neuroethology, function and evolution of social gaze. *Neuroscience and Biobehavioral Reviews, 24,* 581–604.

Engelhardt, H. Tristram, Jr. (1998). Critical care: Why there is no global bioethics. *The Journal of Medicine and Philosophy, 23,* 643–651.

Engels, Rutger C. M. E., Scholte, Ron H. J., van Lieshout, Cornelis F. M., de Kemp, Raymond, & Overbeek, Geertjan. (2006). Peer group reputation and smoking and alcohol consumption in early adolescence. *Addictive Behaviors, 31,* 440–449.

Enoch, Mary-Anne. (2006). Genetic and environmental influences on the development of alcoholism: Resilience vs. risk. In Barry M. Lester, Ann Masten, & Bruce McEwen (Eds.), *Resilience in children* (Vol. 1094, pp. 193–201). New York: New York Academy of Sciences.

Epstein, Leonard H., Handley, Elizabeth A., Dearing, Kelly K., Cho, David D., Roemmich, James N., Paluch, Rocco A., et al. (2006). Purchases of food in youth: Influence of price and income. *Psychological Science, 17,* 82–89.

Erickson, Rebecca J. (2005). Why emotion work matters: Sex, gender, and the division of household labor. *Journal of Marriage and Family, 67,* 337–351.

Ericsson, K. Anders. (1996). The acquisition of expert performance: An introduction to some of the issues. In Karl Anders Ericsson (Ed.), *The road to excellence: The acquisition of expert performance in the arts and sciences, sports, and games* (pp. 1–50). Hillsdale, NJ: Erlbaum.

Eriks-Brophy, Alice, & Crago, Martha. (2003). Variation in instructional discourse features: Cultural or linguistic? Evidence from Inuit and Non-Inuit teachers of Nunavik. *Anthropology & Education Quarterly, 34,* 396–419.

Erikson, Erik H. (1963). *Childhood and society* (2nd ed.). New York: Norton.

Erikson, Erik H. (1968). *Identity: Youth and crisis.* New York: Norton.

Erikson, Erik H. (1982). *The life cycle completed: A review.* New York: Norton.

Erikson, Erik H. (1984). Reflections on the last stage—And the first. *The Psychoanalytic Study of the Child, 39,* 155–165.

Erikson, Erik H., Erikson, Joan M., & Kivnick, Helen Q. (1986). *Vital involvement in old age.* New York: Norton.

Eriksson, Birgitta Sandén, & Pehrsson, Gunnel. (2005). Emotional reactions of parents after the birth of an infant with extremely low birth weight. *Journal of Child Health Care, 9,* 122–136.

Erlandsson, Kerstin, Dsilna, Ann, Fagerberg, Ingegerd, & Christensson, Kyllike. (2007). Skin-to-skin care with the father after cesarean birth and its effect on newborn crying and prefeeding behavior. *Birth: Issues in Perinatal Care, 34,* 105–114.

Erlangsen, Annette, Jeune, Bernard, Bille-Brahe, Unni, & Vaupel, James W. (2004). Loss of partner and suicide risks among oldest old: A population-based register study. *Age and Ageing, 33,* 378–383.

Erlinghagen, Marcel, & Hank, Karsten. (2006). The participation of older Europeans in volunteer work. *Ageing & Society, 26,* 567–584.

Erwin, Phil. (1998). *Friendship in childhood and adolescence.* London: Routledge.

Etchu, Koji. (2007). Social context and preschoolers' judgments about aggressive behavior: Social domain theory. *Japanese Journal of Educational Psychology, 55,* 219–230.

Evans, David W., & Leckman, James F. (2006). Origins of obsessive-compulsive disorder: Developmental and evolutionary perspectives. In Dante Cicchetti & Donald J. Cohen (Eds.), *Developmental psychopathology: Vol. 3. Risk, disorder, and adaptation* (2nd ed., pp. 404–435). Hoboken, NJ: Wiley.

Evans, David W., Leckman, James F., Carter, Alice, Reznick, J. Steven, Henshaw, Desiree, King, Robert A., et al. (1997). Ritual, habit, and perfectionism: The prevalence and development of compulsive-like behavior in normal young children. *Child Development, 68,* 58–68.

Evans, Gary W., & Wener, Richard E. (2006). Rail commuting duration and passenger stress. *Health Psychology, 25,* 408–412.

Evans, Jonathan St. B. T. (2008). Dual-processing accounts of reasoning, judgment, and social cognition. *Annual Review of Psychology, 59,* 255–278.

Eyer, Diane E. (1992). *Mother–infant bonding: A scientific fiction.* New Haven, CT: Yale University Press.

Fafchamps, Marcel, & Shilpi, Forhad. (2008). Subjective welfare, isolation, and relative consumption. *Journal of Development Economics, 86,* 43–60.

Fagan, Joseph F., Holland, Cynthia R., & Wheeler, Karyn. (2007). The prediction, from infancy, of adult IQ and achievement. *Intelligence, 35,* 225–231.

Fagot, Beverly I. (1995). Parenting boys and girls. In Marc H. Bornstein (Ed.), *Handbook of parenting: Vol. 1. Children and parenting* (pp. 163–183). Hillsdale, NJ: Erlbaum.

Fair, Cynthia, Vandermaas-Peeler, Maureen, Beaudry, Regan, & Dew, Jennifer. (2005). 'I learned how little kids think': Third-graders' scaffolding of craft activities with preschoolers. *Early Child Development and Care, 175,* 229–241.

Falba, Tracy A., & Sindelar, Jody L. (2008). Spousal concordance in health behavior change. *Health Services Research, 43,* 96–116.

Faraone, Stephen V., & Wilens, Timothy. (2003). Does stimulant treatment lead to substance use disorders? *Journal of Clinical Psychiatry, 64,* 9–13.

Farbrother, Jane E., & Guggenheim, Jeremy A. (2001). Myopia genetics: The family study of myopia. *Optometry Today, 41,* 41–44.

Farrelly, Matthew C., Davis, Kevin C., Haviland, M. Lyndon, Messeri, Peter, & Healton, Cheryl G. (2005). Evidence of a dose-response relationship between "truth" antismoking ads and youth smoking prevalence. *American Journal of Public Health, 95,* 425–431.

Federal Interagency Forum on Child and Family Statistics. (2009). *Family structure and children's living arrangements.* Retrieved September 17, 2009, from http://www.childstats.gov/americaschildren/famsoc1.asp

Feinberg, Andrew P. (2008). Epigenetics at the epicenter of modern medicine. *Journal of the American Medical Association, 299,* 1345–1350.

Feiring, Candice. (1999). Other-sex friendship networks and the development of romantic relationships in adolescence. *Journal of Youth & Adolescence, 28,* 495–512.

Feldman, Ruth. (2007). Parent–infant synchrony and the construction of shared timing; Physiological precursors, developmental outcomes, and risk conditions. *Journal of Child Psychology and Psychiatry, 48,* 329–354.

Feldman, Ruth, & Eidelman, Arthur I. (2005). Does a triplet birth pose a special risk for infant development? Assessing cognitive development in relation to intrauterine growth and mother–infant interaction across the first 2 years. *Pediatrics, 115,* 443–452.

Feldman, Ruth, Weller, Aron, Sirota, Lea, & Eidelman, Arthur I. (2002). Skin-to-skin contact (kangaroo care) promotes self-regulation in premature infants: Sleep–wake cyclicity, arousal modulation, and sustained exploration. *Developmental Psychology, 38,* 194–207.

Feng, Zhanlian, Grabowski, David C., Intrator, Orna, Zinn, Jacqueline, & Mor, Vincent. (2008). Medicaid payment rates, case-mix reimbursement, and nursing home staffing—1996–2004. *Medical Care, 46,* 33–40.

Fenson, Larry, Bates, Elizabeth, Dale, Philip, Goodman, Judith, Reznick, J. Steven, & Thal, Donna. (2000). Measuring variability in early child language: Don't shoot the messenger. *Child Development, 71,* 323–328.

Fergusson, Emma, Maughan, Barbara, & Golding, Jean. (2008). Which children receive grandparental care and what effect does it have? *Journal of Child Psychology and Psychiatry, 49,* 161–169.

Fernandes, Myra, Ross, Michael, Wiegand, Melanie, & Schryer, Emily. (2008). Are the memories of older adults positively biased? *Psychology and Aging, 23,* 297–306.

Field, Nigel P., & Friedrichs, Michael. (2004). Continuing bonds in coping with the death of a husband. *Death Studies, 28,* 597–620.

Finch, Caleb E. (1999). Longevity without senescence: Possible examples. In Jean-Marie Robine, Bernard Forette, Claudio Franceschi, & Michel Allard (Eds.), *The paradoxes of longevity* (pp. 1–9). New York: Springer.

Finch, Caleb Ellicott. (2007). *The biology of human longevity: Inflammation, nutrition, and aging in the evolution of life spans.* Burlington, MA: Academic Press.

Fincham, Frank D., Stanley, Scott M., & Beach, Steven R. H. (2007). Transformative processes in marriage: An analysis of emerging trends. *Journal of Marriage and Family, 69,* 275–292.

Fine, Mark A., & Harvey, John H. (2006). *Handbook of divorce and relationship dissolution.* Mahwah, NJ: Erlbaum.

Fingerman, Karen L. (1996). Sources of tension in the aging mother and adult daughter relationship. *Psychology & Aging, 11,* 591–606.

Fingerman, Karen L., Hay, Elizabeth L., & Birditt, Kira S. (2004). The best of ties, the worst of ties: Close, problematic, and ambivalent social relationships. *Journal of Marriage and Family, 66,* 792–808.

Fingerman, Karen L., Miller, Laura, & Charles, Susan. (2008). Saving the best for last: How adults treat social partners of different ages. *Psychology and Aging, 23,* 399–409.

Finkelhor, David, & Jones, Lisa M. (2004). *Explanations for the decline in child sexual abuse cases.* Office of Juvenile Justice and Delinquency Prevention. Retrieved July 19, 2009, from http://www.ncjrs.gov/html/ojjdp/199298/contents.html

Finlay, Ilora. (2009). Dying and choosing. *Lancet, 373,* 1840–1841.

Finn, Jeremy D., & Achilles, Charles M. (1999). Tennessee's class size study: Findings, implications, misconceptions. *Educational Evaluation and Policy Analysis, 21,* 97–109.

Finn, John W. (2005). Stories of Pearl: Surviving end-of-life care. In Donald E. Gelfand, Richard Raspa, Sherylyn H. Briller, & Stephanie Myers Schim (Eds.), *End-of-life stories: Crossing disciplinary boundaries* (pp. 134–147). New York: Springer.

Fischer, Regina Santamäki, Norberg, Astrid, & Lundman, Berit. (2008). Embracing opposites: Meanings of growing old as narrated by people aged 85. *International Journal of Aging and Human Development, 67,* 259–271.

Fishbein, Martin, Hall-Jamieson, Kathleen, Zimmer, Eric, von Haeften, Ina, & Nabi, Robin. (2002). Avoiding the boomerang: Testing the relative effectiveness of antidrug public service announcements before a national campaign. *American Journal of Public Health, 92,* 238–245.

Fisher, Helen E. (2006). Broken hearts: The nature and risks of romantic rejection. In Ann C. Crouter & Alan Booth (Eds.), *Romance and sex in adolescence and emerging adulthood: Risks and opportunities* (pp. 3–28). Mahwah, NJ: Erlbaum.

Fisher, Jennifer O., & Birch, Leann L. (2001). Early experience with food and eating: Implications for the development of eating disorders. In J. Kevin Thompson & Linda Smolak (Eds.), *Body image, eating disorders, and obesity in youth: Assessment, prevention, and treatment* (pp. 23–39). Washington, DC: American Psychological Association.

Fletcher, Anne C., Steinberg, Laurence, & Williams-Wheeler, Meeshay. (2004). Parental influences on adolescent problem behavior: Revisiting Stattin and Kerr. *Child Development, 75,* 781–796.

Floor, Penelope, & Akhtar, Nameera. (2006). Can 18-month-old infants learn words by listening in on conversations? *Infancy, 9,* 327–339.

Flynn, James R. (2007). *What is intelligence? Beyond the Flynn effect.* New York: Cambridge University Press.

Foley, Daniel, Ancoli-Israel, Sonia, Britz, Patricia, & Walsh, James. (2004). Sleep disturbances and chronic disease in older adults: Results of the 2003 National Sleep Foundation Sleep in America Survey. *Journal of Psychosomatic Research, 56,* 497–502.

Fomby, Paula, & Cherlin, Andrew J. (2007). Family instability and child well-being. *American Sociological Review, 72,* 181–204.

Fontana, Luigi, Weiss, Edward P., Villareal, Dennis T., Klein, Samuel, & Holloszy, John O. (2008). Long-term effects of calorie or protein restriction on serum IGF-1 and IGFBP-3 concentration in humans. *Aging Cell, 7,* 681–687.

Forbes, Erika E., Fox, Nathan A., Cohn, Jeffrey F., Galles, Steven F., & Kovacs, Maria. (2006). Children's affect regulation during a disappointment: Psychophysiological responses and relation to parent history of depression. *Biological Psychology, 71,* 264–277.

Fortinsky, Richard H., Tennen, Howard, Frank, Natalie, & Affleck, Glenn. (2007). Health and psychological consequences of caregiving. In Carolyn M. Aldwin, Crystal L. Park, & Avron Spiro III (Eds.), *Handbook of health psychology and aging* (pp. 227–249). New York: Guilford Press.

Foster, E. Michael, & Kalil, Ariel. (2007). Living arrangements and children's development in low-income White, Black, and Latino families. *Child Development, 78,* 1657–1674.

Fowler, James H., Baker, Laura A., & Dawes, Christopher T. (2008). Genetic variation in political participation. *American Political Science Review, 102,* 233–248.

Fowler, James W. (1981). *Stages of faith: The psychology of human development and the quest for meaning.* San Francisco: Harper & Row.

Fowler, James W. (1986). Faith and the structuring of meaning. In Craig Dykstra & Sharon Parks (Eds.), *Faith development and Fowler* (pp. 15–42). Birmingham, AL: Religious Education Press.

Fox, Nathan A., Henderson, Heather A., Rubin, Kenneth H., Calkins, Susan D., & Schmidt, Louis A. (2001). Continuity and discontinuity of behavioral inhibition and exuberance: Psychophysiological and behavioral influences across the first four years of life. *Child Development, 72,* 1–21.

Foxman, Betsy, Newman, Mark, Percha, Bethany, Holmes, King K., & Aral, Sevgi O. (2006). Measures of sexual partnerships: Lengths, gaps, overlaps, and sexually transmitted infection. *Sexually Transmitted Diseases, 33,* 209–214.

Franco-Marina, Francisco, Caloca, Jaime Villalba, Corcho-Berdugo, Alexander, & Grupo interinstitucional de cáncer pulmonar. (2006). Role of active and passive smoking on lung cancer etiology in Mexico City. *Salud Pública de México, 48*(Suppl. 1), s75–s82.

Frank, Michael J., Samanta, Johan, Moustafa, Ahmed A., & Sherman, Scott J. (2007, November 23). Hold your horses: Impulsivity, deep brain stimulation, and medication in parkinsonism. *Science, 318,* 1309–1312.

Frankenburg, William K., Dodds, Josiah, Archer, Philip, Shapiro, Howard, & Bresnick, Beverly. (1992). The Denver II: A major revision and restandardization of the Denver Developmental Screening Test. *Pediatrics, 89,* 91–97.

Franko, Debra L., Thompson, Douglas, Affenito, Sandra G., Barton, Bruce A., & Striegel-Moore, Ruth H. (2008). What mediates the relationship between family meals and adolescent health issues. *Health Psychology, 27*(Suppl. 2), S109–S117.

Frayling, Timothy M., Timpson, Nicholas J., Weedon, Michael N., Zeggini, Eleftheria, Freathy, Rachel M., Lindgren, Cecilia M., et al. (2007, May 11). A common variant in the FTO gene is associated with body mass index and predisposes to childhood and adult obesity. *Science, 316,* 889–894.

Fredricks, Jennifer A., Blumenfeld, Phyllis C., & Paris, Alison H. (2004). School engagement: Potential of the concept, state of the evidence. *Review of Educational Research, 74,* 59–109.

Fredricks, Jennifer A., & Eccles, Jacquelynne S. (2006). Is extracurricular participation associated with beneficial outcomes? Concurrent and longitudinal relations. *Developmental Psychology, 42,* 698–713.

Fredriksen, Katia, Rhodes, Jean, Reddy, Ranjini, & Way, Niobe. (2004). Sleepless in Chicago: Tracking the effects of adolescent sleep loss during the middle school years. *Child Development, 75,* 84–95.

Freeman, Kassie, & Thomas, Gail E. (2002). Black colleges and college choice: Characteristics of students who choose HBCUs. *Review of Higher Education, 25,* 349–358.

Freisthler, Bridget, Merritt, Darcey H., & LaScala, Elizabeth A. (2006). Understanding the ecology of child maltreatment: A review of the literature and directions for future research. *Child Maltreatment, 11,* 263–280.

French, Howard W. (2005, February 17). As girls 'vanish,' Chinese city battles tide of abortions. *New York Times,* p. A4.

French, Sabine Elizabeth, Seidman, Edward, Allen, LaRue, & Aber, J. Lawrence. (2006). The development of ethnic identity during adolescence. *Developmental Psychology, 42,* 1–10.

Freud, Anna. (2000). Adolescence. In James B. McCarthy (Ed.), *Adolescent development and psychopathology* (Vol. 13, pp. 29–52). Lanham, MD: University Press of America. (Reprinted from *Psychoanalytic Study of the Child,* pp. 255–278, 1958, New Haven, CT: Yale University Press)

Freud, Sigmund. (1935). *A general introduction to psychoanalysis* (Joan Riviere, Trans.). New York: Liveright.

Freud, Sigmund. (1938). *The basic writings of Sigmund Freud* (A. A. Brill, Ed. & Trans.). New York: Modern Library.

Freud, Sigmund. (1964). An outline of psycho-analysis. In James Strachey (Ed. & Trans.), *The standard edition of the complete psychological works of Sigmund Freud* (Vol. 23, pp. 144–207). London: Hogarth Press. (Original work published 1940)

Freund, Alexandra M. (2008). Successful aging as management of resources: The role of selection, optimization, and compensation. *Research in Human Development, 5,* 94–106.

Frey, Karin S., Hirschstein, Miriam K., Snell, Jennie L., Van Schoiack-Edstrom, Leihua, MacKenzie, Elizabeth P., & Broderick, Carole J. (2005). Reducing playground bullying and supporting beliefs: An experimental trial of the Steps to Respect program. *Developmental Psychology, 41,* 479–491.

Fried, Linda P., Kronmal, Richard A., Newman, Anne B., Bild, Diane E., Mittelmark, Maurice B., Polak, Joseph F., et al. (1998). Risk factors for 5-year mortality in older adults: The Cardiovascular Health Study. *Journal of the American Medical Association, 279,* 585–592.

Friedlander, Laura J., Connolly, Jennifer A., Pepler, Debra J., & Craig, Wendy M. (2007). Biological, familial, and peer influences on dating in early adolescence. *Archives of Sexual Behavior, 36,* 821–830.

Friedlander, Samuel L., Larkin, Emma K., Rosen, Carol L., Palermo, Tonya M., & Redline, Susan. (2003). Decreased quality of life associated with obesity in school-aged children. *Archives of Pediatrics & Adolescent Medicine, 157,* 1206–1211.

Friedman, Michael S., Powell, Kenneth E., Hutwagner, Lori, Graham, LeRoy M., & Teague, W. Gerald. (2001). Impact of changes in transportation and commuting behaviors during the 1996 Summer Olympic Games in Atlanta on air quality and childhood asthma. *Journal of the American Medical Association, 285,* 897–905.

Fries, Alison B. Wismer, & Pollak, Seth D. (2007). Emotion processing and the developing brain. In Donna Coch, Kurt W. Fischer, & Geraldine Dawson (Eds.), *Human behavior, learning, and the developing brain. Typical development* (pp. 329–361). New York: Guilford Press.

Friese, Malte, & Hofmann, Wilhelm. (2008). What would you have as a last supper? Thoughts about death influence evaluation and consumption of food products. *Journal of Experimental Social Psychology, 44,* 1388–1394.

Fry, Prem S. (1999). The sociocultural meaning of dying with dignity: An exploratory study of the perceptions of a group of Asian Indian elderly persons. In Brian de Vries (Ed.), *End of life issues: Interdisciplinary and multidimensional perspectives* (pp. 297–318). New York: Springer.

Fujimori, Maiko, Kobayakawa, Makoto, Nakaya, Naoki, Nagai, Kanji, Nishiwaki, Yutaka, Inagaki, Masatoshi, et al.

(2006). Psychometric properties of the Japanese version of the Quality of Life-Cancer Survivors Instrument. *Quality of Life Research, 15,* 1633–1638.

Fujita, Hidenori. (2000). Education reform and education politics in Japan. *The American Sociologist, 31*(3), 42–57.

Fuligni, Andrew J., & Hardway, Christina. (2006). Daily variation in adolescents' sleep, activities, and psychological well-being. *Journal of Research on Adolescence, 16,* 353–378.

Fuligni, Andrew J., Witkow, Melissa, & Garcia, Carla. (2005). Ethnic identity and the academic adjustment of adolescents from Mexican, Chinese, and European backgrounds. *Developmental Psychology, 41,* 799–811.

Fung, Helene H., Stoeber, Franziska S., Yeung, Dannii Yuen-lan, & Lang, Frieder R. (2008). Cultural specificity of socioemotional selectivity: Age differences in social network composition among Germans and Hong Kong Chinese. *Journals of Gerontology Series B: Psychological Sciences and Social Sciences, 63,* 156–164.

Furlong, Andy. (2008). The Japanese *hikikomori* phenomenon: Acute social withdrawal among young people. *Sociological Review, 56,* 309–325.

Furman, Wyndol, & Hand, Laura Shaffer. (2006). The slippery nature of romantic relationships: Issues in definition and differentiation. In Ann C. Crouter & Alan Booth (Eds.), *Romance and sex in adolescence and emerging adulthood: Risks and opportunities* (pp. 171–178). Mahwah, NJ: Erlbaum.

Furstenberg, Frank F., & Cherlin, Andrew J. (1991). *Divided families: What happens to children when parents part.* Cambridge, MA: Harvard University Press.

Gaertner, Bridget M., Spinrad, Tracy L., Eisenberg, Nancy, & Greving, Karissa A. (2007). Parental childrearing attitudes as correlates of father involvement during infancy. *Journal of Marriage and Family, 69,* 962–976.

Gagnon, John H., Giami, Alain, Michaels, Stuart, & de Colomby, Patrick. (2001). A comparative study of the couple in the social organization of sexuality in France and the United States. *Journal of Sex Research, 38,* 24–34.

Galambos, Nancy L. (2004). Gender and gender role development in adolescence. In Richard M. Lerner & Laurence D. Steinberg (Eds.), *Handbook of adolescent psychology* (2nd ed., pp. 233–262). Hoboken, NJ: Wiley.

Galambos, Nancy L., Barker, Erin T., & Almeida, David M. (2003). Parents do matter: Trajectories of change in externalizing and internalizing problems in early adolescence. *Child Development, 74,* 578–594.

Galambos, Nancy L., Barker, Erin T., & Krahn, Harvey J. (2006). Depression, self-esteem, and anger in emerging adulthood: Seven-year trajectories. *Developmental Psychology, 42,* 350–365.

Gall, Stanley (Ed.). (1996). *Multiple pregnancy and delivery.* St. Louis, MO: Mosby.

Gallup, Gordon G., Anderson, James R., & Shillito, Daniel J. (2002). The mirror test. In Marc Bekoff, Colin Allen, & Gordon M. Burghardt (Eds.), *The cognitive animal: Empirical and theoretical perspectives on animal cognition* (pp. 325–333). Cambridge, MA: MIT Press.

Galotti, Kathleen M. (2002). *Making decisions that matter: How people face important life choices.* Mahwah, NJ: Erlbaum.

Gandara, Patricia, & Rumberger, Russell W. (2009). Immigration, language, and education: How does language policy structure opportunity? *Teachers College Record, 111,* 750–782.

Gandini, Lella, Hill, Lynn, Cadwell, Louise, & Schwall, Charles (Eds.). (2005). *In the spirit of the studio: Learning from the atelier of Reggio Emilia.* New York: Teachers College Press.

Ganong, Lawrence H., & Coleman, Marilyn. (1994). *Remarried family relationships.* Thousand Oaks, CA: Sage.

Gans, Daphna, & Silverstein, Merril. (2006). Norms of filial responsibility for aging parents across time and generations. *Journal of Marriage and Family, 68,* 961–976.

García-Pérez, Rosa M., Hobson, R. Peter, & Lee, Anthony. (2008). Narrative role-taking in autism. *Journal of Autism and Developmental Disorders, 38,* 156–168.

Gardner, Howard. (1983). *Frames of mind: The theory of multiple intelligences.* New York: Basic Books.

Gardner, Howard. (1999). Are there additional intelligences? The case for naturalist, spiritual, and existential intelligences. In Jeffrey Kane (Ed.), *Education, information, and transformation: Essays on learning and thinking* (pp. 111–131). Upper Saddle River, NJ: Merrill.

Gardner, Howard. (2006). *Multiple intelligences: New horizons in theory and practice* (Completely rev. and updated ed.). New York: Basic Books.

Gardner, Howard, & Moran, Seana. (2006). The science of multiple intelligences theory: A response to Lynn Waterhouse. *Educational Psychologist, 41,* 227–232.

Gardner, Howard E. (1998). Extraordinary cognitive achievements (ECA): A symbol systems approach. In William Damon (Series Ed.) & Richard M. Lerner (Vol. Ed.), *Handbook of child psychology: Volume 1: Theoretical models of human development* (5th ed., pp. 415–466). Hoboken, NJ: Wiley.

Gardner, Margo, & Steinberg, Laurence. (2005). Peer influence on risk taking, risk preference, and risky decision making in adolescence and adulthood: An experimental study. *Developmental Psychology, 41,* 625–635.

Garofalo, Robert, Wolf, R. Cameron, Wissow, Lawrence S., Woods, Elizabeth R., & Goodman, Elizabeth. (1999). Sexual orientation and risk of suicide attempts among a representative sample of youth. *Archives of Pediatrics & Adolescent Medicine, 153,* 487–493.

Gaspar de Alba, Alicia. (2003). Rights of passage: From cultural schizophrenia to border consciousness in Cheech Marin's Born in East L.A. In Alicia Gaspar de Alba (Ed.), *Velvet barrios: Popular culture & Chicana/o sexualities.* Basingstoke, England: Palgrave Macmillan.

Gathercole, Susan E., Pickering, Susan J., Ambridge, Benjamin, & Wearing, Hannah. (2004). The structure of working memory from 4 to 15 years of age. *Developmental Psychology, 40,* 177–190.

Gauthier, Anne H., & Furstenberg, Frank F., Jr. (2005). Historical trends in the patterns of time use among young adults in developed countries. In Richard A. Settersten, Frank F. Furstenberg,

& Rubén G. Rumbaut (Eds.), *On the frontier of adulthood: Theory, research, and public policy* (pp. 150–176). Chicago: University of Chicago Press.

Gdalevich, Michael, Mimouni, Daniel, & Mimouni, Marc. (2001). Breast-feeding and the risk of bronchial asthma in childhood: A systematic review with meta-analysis of prospective studies. *Journal of Pediatrics, 139,* 261–266.

Ge, Xiaojia, Conger, Rand D., & Elder, Glen H., Jr. (2001). Pubertal transition, stressful life events, and the emergence of gender differences in adolescent depressive symptoms. *Developmental Psychology, 37,* 404–417.

Ge, Xiaojia, Kim, Irene J., Brody, Gene H., Conger, Rand D., Simons, Ronald L., Gibbons, Frederick X., et al. (2003). It's about timing and change: Pubertal transition effects on symptoms of major depression among African American youths. *Developmental Psychology, 39,* 430–439.

Ge, Xiaojia, Natsuaki, Misaki N., Neiderhiser, Jenae M., & Reiss, David. (2007). Genetic and environmental influences on pubertal timing: Results from two national sibling studies. *Journal of Research on Adolescence, 17,* 767–788.

Geary, Nori, & Lovejoy, Jennifer. (2008). Sex differences in energy metabolism, obesity, and eating behavior. In Jill B. Becker, Karen J. Berkley, Nori Geary, Elizabeth Hampson, James P. Herman, & Elizabeth Young (Eds.), *Sex differences in the brain: From genes to behavior* (pp. 253–274). New York: Oxford University Press.

Gelfand, Donald E. (2003). *Aging and ethnicity: Knowledge and services* (2nd ed.). New York: Springer.

Gentile, Douglas A., Saleem, Muniba, & Anderson, Craig A. (2007). Public policy and the effects of media violence on children. *Social Issues and Policy Review, 1,* 15–61.

Gentner, Dedre, & Boroditsky, Lera. (2001). Individuation, relativity, and early word learning. In Melissa Bowerman & Stephen C. Levinson (Eds.), *Language acquisition and conceptual development* (pp. 215–256). Cambridge, UK: Cambridge University Press.

Georgas, James, Berry, John W., van de Vijver, Fons J. R., Kagitçibasi, Çigdem, & Poortinga, Ype H. (2006). *Families across cultures: A 30-nation psychological study.* Cambridge, UK: Cambridge University Press.

George, Linda K. (2006). Perceived quality of life. In Robert H. Binstock & Linda K. George (Eds.), *Handbook of aging and the social sciences* (6th ed., pp. 320–336). Amsterdam: Elsevier.

Georges, Jean-Jacques, Onwuteaka-Philipsen, Bregje D., Van Der Heide, Agnes, Van Der Wal, Gerrit, & Van Der Maas, Paul J. (2006). Physicians' opinions on palliative care and euthanasia in The Netherlands. *Journal of Palliative Medicine, 9,* 1137–1144.

Georgieff, Michael K., & Rao, Raghavendra. (2001). The role of nutrition in cognitive development. In Charles A. Nelson & Monica Luciana (Eds.), *Handbook of developmental cognitive neuroscience* (pp. 149–158). Cambridge, MA: MIT Press.

Geronimus, Arline T., Hicken, Margaret, Keene, Danya, & Bound, John. (2006). "Weathering" and age patterns of allostatic load scores among Blacks and Whites in the United States. *American Journal of Public Health, 96,* 826–833.

Gerrard, Meg, Gibbons, Frederick X., Houlihan, Amy E., Stock, Michelle L., & Pomery, Elizabeth A. (2008). A dual-process approach to health risk decision making: The prototype willingness model. *Developmental Review, 28,* 29–61.

Gershkoff-Stowe, Lisa, & Hahn, Erin R. (2007). Fast mapping skills in the developing lexicon. *Journal of Speech, Language, and Hearing Research, 50,* 682–696.

Gershoff, Elizabeth Thompson. (2002). Corporal punishment by parents and associated child behaviors and experiences: A meta-analytic and theoretical review. *Psychological Bulletin, 128,* 539–579.

Gershoff, Elizabeth T., Aber, J. Lawrence, Raver, C. Cybele, & Lennon, Mary Clare. (2007). Income is not enough: Incorporating material hardship into models of income associations with parenting and child development. *Child Development, 78,* 70–95.

Gerstel, Naomi Ruth. (2002). Book reviews [Review of the book *Talk of love: How culture matters*]. *Journal of Marriage and Family, 64,* 549–556.

Ghuman, Paul A. Singh. (2003). *Double loyalties: South Asian adolescents in the West.* Cardiff, United Kingdom: University of Wales Press.

Giarrusso, Roseann, Silverstein, Merril, Gans, Daphna, & Bengtson, Vern L. (2005). Ageing parents and adult children: New perspectives on intergenerational relationships. In Malcolm Lewis Johnson, Vern L. Bengtson, Peter G. Coleman, & Thomas B. L. Kirkwood (Eds.), *The Cambridge handbook of age and ageing* (pp. 413–421). New York: Cambridge University Press.

Gibson, Eleanor J., & Walk, Richard D. (1960). The "visual cliff." *Scientific American, 202*(4), 64–71.

Gifford-Smith, Mary E., & Rabiner, David L. (2004). Social information processing and children's social adjustment. In Janis B. Kupersmidt & Kenneth A. Dodge (Eds.), *Children's peer relations: From development to intervention* (pp. 61–79). Washington, DC: American Psychological Association.

Gigante, Denise. (2007). Zeitgeist. *European Romantic Review, 18,* 265–272.

Gigerenzer, Gerd, Todd, Peter M., & ABC Research Group. (1999). *Simple heuristics that make us smart.* New York: Oxford University Press.

Gilbert, Daniel. (2006). *Stumbling on happiness.* New York: Knopf.

Gilchrist, Heidi, & Sullivan, Gerard. (2006). The role of gender and sexual relations for young people in identity construction and youth suicide. *Culture, Health & Sexuality, 8,* 195–209.

Giles-Sims, Jean, & Lockhart, Charles. (2005). Culturally shaped patterns of disciplining children. *Journal of Family Issues, 26,* 196–218.

Gilligan, Carol. (1982). *In a different voice: Psychological theory and women's development.* Cambridge, MA: Harvard University Press.

Gilligan, Carol, Murphy, John Michael, & Tappan, Mark B. (1990). Moral development beyond adolescence. In Charles N. Alexander & Ellen J. Langer (Eds.), *Higher stages of human development: Perspectives on adult growth* (pp. 208–225). London: Oxford University Press.

Gilliom, Miles, Shaw, Daniel S., Beck, Joy E., Schonberg, Michael A., & Lukon, JoElla L. (2002). Anger regulation in disadvantaged preschool boys: Strategies, antecedents, and the development of self-control. *Developmental Psychology, 38,* 222–235.

Ginsburg, Herbert P., Klein, Alice, & Starkey, Prentice. (1998). The development of children's mathematical thinking: Connecting research with practice. In William Damon (Series Ed.) & Irving E. Sigel & K. Ann Renninger (Vol. Eds.), *Handbook of child psychology: Vol. 4. Child psychology in practice* (5th ed., pp. 401–476). New York: Wiley.

Gipson, Jessica D., & Hindin, Michelle J. (2008). "Having another child would be a life or death situation for her": Understanding pregnancy termination among couples in rural Bangladesh. *American Journal of Public Health, 98,* 1827–1832.

Gitlin, Laura N., Belle, Steven H., Burgio, Louis D., Czaja, Sara J., Mahoney, Diane, Gallagher-Thompson, Dolores, et al. (2003). Effect of multicomponent interventions on caregiver burden and depression: The REACH multisite initiative at 6-month follow-up. *Psychology & Aging, 18,* 361–374.

Glanville, Jennifer L., Sikkink, David, & Hernández, Edwin I. (2008). Religious involvement and educational outcomes: The role of social capital and extracurricular participation. *Sociological Quarterly, 49,* 105–137.

Glass, Jennifer. (1998). Gender liberation, economic squeeze, or fear of strangers: Why fathers provide infant care in dual-earner families. *Journal of Marriage and the Family, 60,* 821–834.

Glass, Jennifer M. (2007). Visual function and cognitive aging: Differential role of contrast sensitivity in verbal versus spatial tasks. *Psychology and Aging, 22,* 233–238.

Glauber, James H., Farber, Harold J., & Homer, Charles J. (2001). Asthma clinical pathways: Toward what end? *Pediatrics, 107,* 590–592.

Glick, Jennifer E., Ruf, Stacey D., White, Michael J., & Goldscheider, Frances. (2006). Educational engagement and early family formation: Differences by ethnicity and generation. *Social Forces, 84,* 1391–1415.

Gluckman, Peter D., & Hanson, Mark A. (2006a). *Developmental origins of health and disease.* Cambridge, England: Cambridge University Press.

Gluckman, Peter D., & Hanson, Mark A. (2006b). *Mismatch: Why our world no longer fits our bodies.* Oxford, England: Oxford University Press.

Gnaulati, Enrico, & Heine, Barb J. (2001). Separation-individuation in late adolescence: An investigation of gender and ethnic differences. *Journal of Psychology: Interdisciplinary and Applied, 135,* 59–70.

Gobush, Kathleen S., Mutayoba, Benezeth M., & Wasser, Samuel K. (2008). Long-term impacts of poaching on relatedness, stress physiology, and reproductive output of adult female African elephants. *Conservation Biology, 22,* 1590–1599.

Goedert, Michel, & Spillantini, Maria Grazia. (2006, November 3). A century of Alzheimer's disease. *Science, 314,* 777–781.

Goffaux, Philippe, Phillips, Natalie A., Sinai, Marco, & Pushkar, Dolores. (2008). Neurophysiological measures of task-set switching: Effects of working memory and aging. *Journals of Gerontology Series B: Psychological Sciences and Social Sciences, 63,* P57–66.

Gohm, Carol L., Oishi, Shigehiro, Darlington, Janet, & Diener, Ed. (1998). Culture, parental conflict, parental marital status, and the subjective well-being of young adults. *Journal of Marriage and the Family, 60,* 319–334.

Golant, Stephen M. (2007). Low-income elderly homeowners in very old dwellings: The need for public policy debate. *Journal of Aging and Social Policy, 20,* 1–28.

Gold, Ellen B., Colvin, Alicia, Avis, Nancy, Bromberger, Joyce, Greendale, Gail A., Powell, Lynda, et al. (2006). Longitudinal analysis of the association between vasomotor symptoms and race/ethnicity across the menopausal transition: Study of women's health across the nation. *American Journal of Public Health, 96,* 1226–1235.

Goldberg, Wendy A., Prause, JoAnn, Lucas-Thompson, Rachel, & Himsel, Amy. (2008). Maternal employment and children's achievement in context: A meta-analysis of four decades of research. *Psychological Bulletin, 134,* 77–108.

Golden, Timothy D., Veiga, John F., & Simsek, Zeki. (2006). Telecommuting's differential impact on work–family conflict: Is there no place like home? *Journal of Applied Psychology, 91,* 1340–1350.

Goldenberg, Jamie L., & Arndt, Jamie. (2008). The implications of death for health: A terror management health model for behavioral health promotion. *Psychological Review, 115,* 1032–1053.

Goldin-Meadow, Susan. (2006). Nonverbal communication: The hand's role in talking and thinking. In William Damon & Richard M. Lerner (Series Eds.) & Deanna Kuhn & Robert S. Siegler (Vol. Eds.), *Handbook of child psychology: Vol. 2. Cognition, perception, and language* (6th ed., pp. 336–369). Hoboken, NJ: Wiley.

Goldin-Meadow, Susan, & Mayberry, Rachel I. (2001). How do profoundly deaf children learn to read? *Learning Disabilities Research & Practice, 16,* 222–229.

Goldscheider, Frances, & Sassler, Sharon. (2006). Creating stepfamilies: Integrating children into the study of union formation. *Journal of Marriage and Family, 68,* 275–291.

Goldstein, Sara E., Davis-Kean, Pamela E., & Eccles, Jacquelynne S. (2005). Parents, peers, and problem behavior: A longitudinal investigation of the impact of relationship perceptions and characteristics on the development of adolescent problem behavior. *Developmental Psychology, 41,* 401–413.

Goldston, David B., Molock, Sherry Davis, Whitbeck, Leslie B., Murakami, Jessica L., Zayas, Luis H., & Hall, Gordon C. Nagayama. (2008). Cultural considerations in adolescent suicide prevention and psychosocial treatment. *American Psychologist, 63,* 14–31.

Goleman, Daniel. (1995). *Emotional intelligence.* New York: Bantam Books.

Golombok, Susan, Rust, John, Zervoulis, Karyofyllis, Croudace, Tim, Golding, Jean, & Hines, Melissa. (2008). Developmental trajectories of sex-typed behavior in boys and girls: A longitudinal general population study of children aged 2.5–8 years. *Child Development, 79,* 1583–1593.

Golub, Sarit A., & Langer, Ellen J. (2007). Challenging assumptions about adult development: Implications for the health of older adults. In Carolyn M. Aldwin, Crystal L. Park, & Avron Spiro III (Eds.), *Handbook of health psychology and aging* (pp. 9–29). New York: Guilford Press.

Gompel, Anne, & Plu-Bureau, Geneviève. (2007). Hormone replacement therapy and breast cancer. The European view. *European Clinics in Obstetrics and Gynaecology, 3,* 7–15.

Gonzales, Nancy A., Dumka, Larry E., Deardorff, Julianna, Carter, Sara Jacobs, & McCray, Adam. (2004). Preventing poor mental health and school dropout of Mexican American adolescents following the transition to junior high school. *Journal of Adolescent Research, 19,* 113–131.

Gonzalez, Enrique, Kulkarni, Hemant, Bolivar, Hector, Mangano, Andrea, Sanchez, Racquel, Catano, Gabriel, et al. (2005, March 4). The influence of CCL3L1 gene-containing segmental duplications on HIV-1/AIDS susceptibility. *Science, 307,* 1434–1440.

Good, Marie, & Willoughby, Teena. (2008). Adolescence as a sensitive period for spiritual development. *Child Development Perspectives, 2,* 32–37.

Goodwyn, Susan W., Acredolo, Linda P., & Brown, Catherine A. (2000). Impact of symbolic gesturing on early language development. *Journal of Nonverbal Behavior, 24,* 81–103.

Gopnik, Alison. (2001). Theories, language, and culture: Whorf without wincing. In Melissa Bowerman & Stephen C. Levinson (Eds.), *Language acquisition and conceptual development* (pp. 45–69). Cambridge, UK: Cambridge University Press.

Gorchoff, Sara M., John, Oliver P., & Helson, Ravenna. (2008). Contextualizing change in marital satisfaction during middle age: An 18-year longitudinal study. *Psychological Science, 19,* 1194–1200.

Gordis, Elana B., Granger, Douglas A., Susman, Elizabeth J., & Trickett, Penelope K. (2008). Salivary alpha amylase-cortisol asymmetry in maltreated youth. *Hormones and Behavior, 53,* 96–103.

Gordon, Peter. (2004, August 19). Numerical cognition without words: Evidence from Amazonia. *Science, 306,* 496–499.

Gordon, Robert M., & Brill, Deborah. (2001). The abuse and neglect of the elderly. In David N. Weisstub, David C. Thomasma, Serge Gauthier, & George F. Tomossy (Eds.), *Aging: Caring for our elders* (pp. 203–218). Dordrecht, The Netherlands: Kluwer.

Goss, David A. (2002). More evidence that near work contributes to myopia development. *Indiana Journal of Optometry, 5,* 11–13.

Gotlib, Ian H., & Hamilton, J. Paul. (2008). Neuroimaging and depression: Current status and unresolved issues. *Current Directions in Psychological Science, 17,* 159–163.

Gotlib, Ian H., & Hammen, Constance L. (2002). *Handbook of depression.* New York: Guilford Press.

Gottesman, Irving I., & Hanson, Daniel R. (2005). Human development: Biological and genetic processes. *Annual Review of Psychology, 56,* 263–286.

Gottholmseder, Georg, Nowotny, Klaus, Pruckner, Gerald J., & Theurl, Engelbert. (2009). Stress perception and commuting. *Health Economics, 18,* 559–576.

Gottlieb, Alma. (2000). Luring your child into this life: A Beng path for infant care. In Judy S. DeLoache & Alma Gottlieb (Eds.), *A world of babies: Imagined childcare guides for seven societies* (pp. 55–90). New York: Cambridge University Press.

Gottlieb, Alma. (2003). Probabilistic epigenesis of development. In Jaan Valsiner & Kevin J. Connolly (Eds.), *Handbook of developmental psychology* (pp. 3–17). Thousand Oaks, CA: Sage.

Gottlieb, Gilbert. (1992). *Individual development and evolution: The genesis of novel behavior.* New York: Oxford University Press.

Gottlieb, Gilbert. (2002). *Individual development and evolution: The genesis of novel behavior.* Mahwah, NJ: Erlbaum. (Original work published 1992)

Gottman, John Mordechai, Murray, James D., Swanson, Catherine, Tyson, Rebecca, & Swanson, Kristin R. (2002). *The mathematics of marriage: Dynamic nonlinear models.* Cambridge, MA: MIT Press.

Gould, Madelyn. (2003). Suicide risk among adolescents. In Daniel Romer (Ed.), *Reducing adolescent risk: Toward an integrated approach* (pp. 303–320). Thousand Oaks, CA: Sage.

Goymer, Patrick. (2007). Genes know their left from their right. *Nature Reviews Genetics, 8,* 652.

Graber, Julia A. (2004). Internalizing problems during adolescence. In Richard M. Lerner & Laurence D. Steinberg (Eds.), *Handbook of adolescent psychology* (2nd ed., pp. 587–626). Hoboken, NJ: Wiley.

Gradin, Maria, Eriksson, Mats, Holmqvist, Gunilla, Holstein, Åsa, & Schollin, Jens. (2002). Pain reduction at venipuncture in newborns: Oral glucose compared with local anesthetic cream. *Pediatrics, 110,* 1053–1057.

Graham, John W., & Beller, Andrea H. (2002). Nonresident fathers and their children: Child support and visitation from an economic perspective. In Catherine S. Tamis-LeMonda & Natasha Cabrera (Eds.), *Handbook of father involvement: Multidisciplinary perspectives* (pp. 431–453). Mahwah, NJ: Erlbaum.

Gray, Nicola J., Klein, Jonathan D., Noyce, Peter R., Sesselberg, Tracy S., & Cantrill, Judith A. (2005). Health information-seeking behaviour in adolescence: The place of the internet. *Social Science & Medicine, 60,* 1467–1478.

Green, C. Shawn, & Bavelier, Daphne. (2008). Exercising your brain: A review of human brain plasticity and training-induced learning. *Psychology and Aging, 23,* 692–701.

Green, Lorraine, & Grant, Victoria. (2008). "Gagged grief and beleaguered bereavements?" An analysis of multidisciplinary theory and research relating to same sex partnership bereavement. *Sexualities, 11,* 275–300.

Green, Nancy S., Dolan, Siobhan M., & Murray, Thomas H. (2006). Newborn screening: Complexities in universal genetic testing. *American Journal of Public Health, 96,* 1955–1959.

Greenberger, Ellen, & Steinberg, Laurence D. (1986). *When teenagers work: The psychological and social costs of adolescent employment.* New York: Basic Books.

Greene, Anthony J., Gross, William L., Elsinger, Catherine L., & Rao, Stephen M. (2006). An fMRI analysis of the human hippocampus: Inference, context, and task awareness. *Journal of Cognitive Neuroscience, 18,* 1156–1173.

Greene, Joshua D., Sommerville, R. Brian, Nystrom, Leigh E., Darley, John M., & Cohen, Jonathan D. (2001, September 14). An fMRI investigation of emotional engagement in moral judgment. *Science, 293,* 2105–2108.

Greene, Melissa L., & Way, Niobe. (2005). Self-esteem trajectories among ethnic minority adolescents: A growth curve analysis of the patterns and predictors of change. *Journal of Research on Adolescence, 15,* 151–178.

Greene, Melissa L., Way, Niobe, & Pahl, Kerstin. (2006). Trajectories of perceived adult and peer discrimination among Black, Latino, and Asian American adolescents: Patterns and psychological correlates. *Developmental Psychology, 42,* 218–238.

Greene, Sheila. (2003). *The psychological development of girls and women: Rethinking change in time.* New York: Routledge.

Greenfield, Emily A., & Marks, Nadine F. (2006). Linked lives: Adult children's problems and their parents' psychological and relational well-being. *Journal of Marriage and Family, 68,* 442–454.

Greenfield, Patricia M., Gross, Elisheva F., Subrahmanyam, Kaveri, Suzuki, Lalita K., & Tynes, Brendesha. (2006). Teens on the Internet: Interpersonal connection, identity, and information. In Robert Kraut, Malcolm Brynin, & Sara Kiesler (Eds.), *Computers, phones, and the Internet: Domesticating information technology* (pp. 185–200). New York: Oxford University Press.

Greenhalgh, Susan. (2008). *Just one child: Science and policy in Deng's China.* Berkeley, CA: University of California Press.

Greenough, William T., & Volkmar, Fred R. (1973). Pattern of dendritic branching in occipital cortex of rats reared in complex environments. *Experimental Neurology, 40,* 491–504.

Greenspan, Stanley I., & Wieder, Serena. (2006). *Engaging autism: Using the floortime approach to help children relate, communicate, and think.* Cambridge, MA: Da Capo Lifelong Books.

Griebel, Wilfried, & Niesel, Renate. (2002). Co-constructing transition into kindergarten and school by children, parents, and teachers. In Hilary Fabian & Aline-Wendy Dunlop (Eds.), *Transitions in the early years: Debating continuity and progression for young children in early education* (pp. 64–75). New York: RoutledgeFalmer.

Grimm, David. (2008, May 16). Staggering toward a global strategy on alcohol abuse. *Science, 320,* 862–863.

Grobman, Kevin H. (2008). *Learning & teaching developmental psychology: Attachment theory, infancy, & infant memory development.* Retrieved June 17, 2009, from http://www.devpsy.org/questions/attachment_theory_memory.html

Grollmann, Philipp, & Rauner, Felix. (2007). Exploring innovative apprenticeship: Quality and costs. *Education & Training, 49,* 431–446.

Grolnick, Wendy S., McMenamy, Jannette M., & Kurowski, Carolyn O. (2006). Emotional self-regulation in infancy and toddlerhood. In Lawrence Balter & Catherine S. Tamis-LeMonda (Eds.), *Child psychology: A handbook of contemporary issues* (2nd ed., pp. 3–25). New York: Psychology Press.

Gros-Louis, Julie, West, Meredith J., Goldstein, Michael H., & King, Andrew P. (2006). Mothers provide differential feedback to infants' prelinguistic sounds. *International Journal of Behavioral Development, 30,* 509–516.

Grossmann, Klaus E., Grossmann, Karin, & Waters, Everett (Eds.). (2005). *Attachment from infancy to adulthood: The major longitudinal studies.* New York: Guilford Press.

Grosvenor, Theodore. (2003). Why is there an epidemic of myopia? *Clinical and Experimental Optometry, 86,* 273–275.

Grundy, Emily, & Henretta, John C. (2006). Between elderly parents and adult children: A new look at the intergenerational care provided by the 'sandwich generation.' *Ageing & Society, 26,* 707–722.

Grzywacz, Joseph, Carlson, Dawn, & Shulkin, Sandee. (2008). Schedule flexibility and stress: Linking formal flexible arrangements and perceived flexibility to employee health. *Community, Work & Family, 11,* 199–214.

Guerin, Diana Wright, Gottfried, Allen W., Oliver, Pamella H., & Thomas, Craig W. (2003). *Temperament: Infancy through adolescence: The Fullerton Longitudinal Study.* New York: Kluwer Academic/Plenum.

Guest, Andrew M. (2007). Cultures of childhood and psychosocial characteristics: Self-esteem and social comparison in two distinct communities. *Ethos, 35,* 1–32.

Guillaume, Michele, & Lissau, Inge. (2002). Epidemiology. In Walter Burniat, Tim J. Cole, Inge Lissau, & Elizabeth M. E. Poskitt (Eds.), *Child and adolescent obesity: Causes and consequences, prevention and management* (pp. 28–49). New York: Cambridge University Press.

Gullone, Eleonora, & King, Neville J. (1997). Three-year-follow-up of normal fear in children and adolescents aged 7 to 18 years. *British Journal of Developmental Psychology, 15,* 97–111.

Gummerum, Michaela, Keller, Monika, Takezawa, Masanori, & Mata, Jutta. (2008). To give or not to give: Children's and adolescents' sharing and moral negotiations in economic decision situations. *Child Development, 79,* 562–576.

Gunn, Shelly R., & Gunn, W. Stewart. (2007). Are we in the dark about sleepwalking's dangers? In Cynthia A. Read (Ed.), *Cerebrum 2007: Emerging ideas in brain science* (pp. 71–84). Washington, DC: Dana Press.

Guo, Sufang, Padmadas, Sabu S., Zhao, Fengmin, Brown, James J., & Stones, R. William. (2007). Delivery settings and caesarean section rates in China. *Bulletin of the World Health Organization, 85,* 755–762.

Gurung, Regan A. R., Taylor, Shelley E., & Seeman, Teresa E. (2003). Accounting for changes in social support among married older adults: Insights from the MacArthur Studies of Successful Aging. *Psychology & Aging, 18,* 487–496.

Gustafson, Kathryn E., Bonner, Melanie J., Hardy, Kristina K., & Thompson, Robert J., Jr. (2006). Biopsychosocial and developmental issues in sickle cell disease. In Ronald T. Brown (Ed.), *Comprehensive handbook of childhood cancer and sickle cell disease: A biopsychosocial approach* (pp. 431–448). New York: Oxford University Press.

Gutmann, David. (1994). *Reclaimed powers: Men and women in later life* (2nd ed.). Evanston, IL: Northwestern University Press.

Gygax, Pascal M., Wagner-Egger, Pascal, Parris, Ben, Seiler, Roland, & Hauert, Claude-Alain. (2008). A psycholinguistic investigation of football players' mental representations of game situations: Does expertise count? *Swiss Journal of*

Psychology/Schweizerische Zeitschrift für Psychologie/Revue Suisse de Psychologie, 67, 85–95.

Ha, Jung-Hwa, Carr, Deborah, Utz, Rebecca L., & Nesse, Randolph. (2006). Older adults' perceptions of intergenerational support after widowhood: How do men and women differ? *Journal of Family Issues, 27,* 3–30.

Hack, Maureen, Flannery, Daniel J., Schluchter, Mark, Cartar, Lydia, Borawski, Elaine, & Klein, Nancy. (2002). Outcomes in young adulthood for very-low-birth-weight infants. *New England Journal of Medicine, 346,* 149–157.

Hagedoorn, Mariët, Van Yperen, Nico W., Coyne, James C., van Jaarsveld, Cornelia H. M., Ranchor, Adelita V., van Sonderen, Eric, et al. (2006). Does marriage protect older people from distress? The role of equity and recency of bereavement. *Psychology and Aging, 21,* 611–620.

Hagerman, Randi Jenssen. (2002). The physical and behavioral phenotype. In Randi Jenssen Hagerman & Paul J. Hagerman (Eds.), *Fragile X syndrome: Diagnosis, treatment, and research* (3rd ed., pp. 3–109). Baltimore: Johns Hopkins University Press.

Hagestad, Gunhild O., & Dannefer, Dale. (2001). Concepts and theories of aging: Beyond microfication in social science approaches. In Robert H. Binstock (Ed.), *Handbook of aging and the social sciences* (5th ed., pp. 3–21). San Diego, CA: Academic Press.

Hahn, Robert, Fuqua-Whitley, Dawna, Wethington, Holly, Lowy, Jessica, Crosby, Alex, Fullilove, Mindy, et al. (2007). Effectiveness of universal school-based programs to prevent violent and aggressive behavior: A systematic review. *American Journal of Preventive Medicine, 33,* S114–S129.

Hajjar, Emily R., Cafiero, Angela C., & Hanlon, Joseph T. (2007). Polypharmacy in elderly patients. *American Journal of Geriatric Pharmacotherapy, 5,* 345–351.

Hakuta, Kenji, Bialystok, Ellen, & Wiley, Edward. (2003). Critical evidence: A test of the critical-period hypothesis for second-language acquisition. *Psychological Science, 14,* 31–38.

Halford, Graeme S., & Andrews, Glenda. (2006). Reasoning and problem solving. In William Damon & Richard M. Lerner (Series Eds.) & Deanna Kuhn & Robert S. Siegler (Vol. Eds.), *Handbook of child psychology: Vol. 2. Cognition, perception, and language* (6th ed., pp. 557–608). Hoboken, NJ: Wiley.

Hall, Lynn K. (2008). *Counseling military families: What mental health professionals need to know.* New York: Taylor and Francis.

Hallenbeck, James. (2003). *Palliative care perspectives.* New York: Oxford University Press.

Halpern, Carolyn Tucker, King, Rosalind Berkowitz, Oslak, Selene G., & Udry, J. Richard. (2005). Body mass index, dieting, romance, and sexual activity in adolescent girls: Relationships over time. *Journal of Research on Adolescence, 15,* 535–559.

Hamerton, John L., & Evans, Jane A. (2005). Sex chromosome anomalies. In Merlin Gene Butler & F. John Meaney (Eds.), *Genetics of developmental disabilities* (pp. 585–650). Boca Raton, FL: Taylor & Francis.

Hamilton, Brady E., Martin, Joyce A., & Sutton, Paul P. (2004, November 23). Births: Preliminary data for 2003. *National Vital Statistics Reports, 53*(9), 1–17.

Hamilton, Brady E., Martin, Joyce A., & Ventura, Stephanie J. (2009). Births: Preliminary data for 2007. *National Vital Statistics Reports, 57*(12), 1–23.

Hamilton, Richard J., & Moore, Dennis (Eds.). (2004). *Educational interventions for refugee children: Theoretical perspectives and implementing best practice.* London: RoutledgeFalmer.

Hamm, Jill V., & Faircloth, Beverly S. (2005). The role of friendship in adolescents' sense of school belonging. *New Directions for Child and Adolescent Development, 107,* 61–78.

Hammond, Christopher J., Andrew, Toby, Mak, Ying Tat, & Spector, Tim D. (2004). A susceptibility locus for myopia in the normal population is linked to the PAX6 gene region on chromosome 11: A genomewide scan of dizygotic twins. *American Journal of Human Genetics, 75,* 294–304.

Hampton, Tracy. (2005). Alcohol and cancer. *Journal of the American Medical Association, 294,* 1481.

Han, Beth, Remsburg, Robin E., & Iwashyna, Theodore J. (2006). Differences in hospice use between Black and White patients during the period 1992 through 2000. *Medical Care, 44,* 731–737.

Hane, Amie Ashley, & Fox, Nathan A. (2006). Ordinary variations in maternal caregiving influence human infants' stress reactivity. *Psychological Science, 17,* 550–556.

Hank, Karsten, & Buber, Isabella. (2009). Grandparents caring for their grandchildren: Findings from the 2004 Survey of Health, Ageing, and Retirement in Europe. *Journal of Family Issues, 30,* 53–73.

Hansson, Robert O., & Stroebe, Margaret S. (2007). *Bereavement in late life: Coping, adaptation, and developmental influences.* Washington, DC: American Psychological Association.

Hanushek, Eric A. (1999). The evidence on class size. In Susan E. Mayer & Paul E. Peterson (Eds.), *Earning and learning: How schools matter* (pp. 131–168). Washington, DC: Brookings Institution Press/Russell Sage Foundation.

Harding, Stephan. (2006). *Animate earth: Science, intuition and Gaia.* Totnes, Devon, UK: Green Books.

Hardy, Melissa. (2006). Older workers. In Robert H. Binstock & Linda K. George (Eds.), *Handbook of aging and the social sciences* (6th ed., pp. 201–218). Amsterdam: Elsevier.

Hareven, Tamara K. (2001). Historical perspectives on aging and family relations. In Robert H. Binstock (Ed.), *Handbook of aging and the social sciences* (5th ed., pp. 141–159). San Diego, CA: Academic Press.

Harjes, Carlos E., Rocheford, Torbert R., Bai, Ling, Brutnell, Thomas P., Kandianis, Catherine Bermudez, Sowinski, Stephen G., et al. (2008, January 18). Natural genetic variation in lycopene epsilon cyclase tapped for maize biofortification. *Science, 319,* 330–333.

Harlow, Ilana. (2005). Shaping sorrow: Creative aspects of public and private mourning. In Samuel Heilman (Ed.), *Death, bereavement, and mourning* (pp. 33–52). New Brunswick, NJ: Transaction.

Harris, James C. (2003). Social neuroscience, empathy, brain integration, and neurodevelopmental disorders. *Physiology & Behavior, 79,* 525–531.

Harris, Judith Rich. (1998). *The nurture assumption: Why children turn out the way they do.* New York: Free Press.

Harris, Judith Rich. (2002). Beyond the nurture assumption: Testing hypotheses about the child's environment. In John G. Borkowski, Sharon Landesman Ramey, & Marie Bristol-Power (Eds.), *Parenting and the child's world: Influences on academic, intellectual, and social-emotional development* (pp. 3–20). Mahwah, NJ: Erlbaum.

Harrison, Linda J., & Ungerer, Judy A. (2002). Maternal employment and infant–mother attachment security at 12 months postpartum. *Developmental Psychology, 38,* 758–773.

Hart, Betty, & Risley, Todd R. (1995). *Meaningful differences in the everyday experience of young American children.* Baltimore: Brookes.

Hart, Carole L., Smith, George Davey, Hole, David J., & Hawthorne, Victor M. (1999). Alcohol consumption and mortality from all causes, coronary heart disease, and stroke: Results from a prospective cohort study of Scottish men with 21 years of follow up. *British Medical Journal, 318,* 1725–1729.

Harter, Susan. (1998). The development of self-representations. In William Damon (Series Ed.) & Nancy Eisenberg (Vol. Ed.), *Handbook of child psychology: Vol. 3. Social, emotional and personality development* (5th ed., pp. 553–618). New York: Wiley.

Harter, Susan. (1999). *The construction of the self: A developmental perspective.* New York: Guilford Press.

Harter, Susan. (2006). The self. In William Damon & Richard M. Lerner (Series Eds.) & Nancy Eisenberg (Vol. Ed.), *Handbook of child psychology: Vol. 3. Social, emotional, and personality development* (6th ed., pp. 505–570). Hoboken, NJ: Wiley.

Hartl, Daniel L., & Jones, Elizabeth W. (1999). *Essential genetics* (2nd ed.). Sudbury, MA: Jones and Bartlett.

Hartmann, Donald P., & Pelzel, Kelly E. (2005). Design, measurement, and analysis in developmental research. In Marc H. Bornstein & Michael E. Lamb (Eds.), *Developmental science: An advanced textbook* (5th ed., pp. 103–184). Mahwah, NJ: Erlbaum.

Harvey, Carol D. H., & Yoshino, Satomi. (2006). Social policy for family caregivers of elderly: A Canadian, Japanese, and Australian comparison. *Marriage & Family Review, 39,* 143–158.

Hasebe, Yuki, Nucci, Larry, & Nucci, Maria S. (2004). Parental control of the personal domain and adolescent symptoms of psychopathology: A cross-national study in the United States and Japan. *Child Development, 75,* 815–828.

Haskins, Ron. (2005). Child development and child-care policy: Modest impacts. In David B. Pillemer & Sheldon Harold White (Eds.), *Developmental psychology and social change: Research, history, and policy* (pp. 140–170). New York: Cambridge University Press.

Hassan, Mohamed A. M., & Killick, Stephen R. (2003). Effect of male age on fertility: Evidence for the decline in male fertility with increasing age. *Fertility and Sterility, 79*(Suppl. 3), 1520–1527.

Hassold, Terry J., & Patterson, David (Eds.). (1999). *Down syndrome: A promising future, together.* New York: Wiley-Liss.

Hatfield, Elaine, & Rapson, Richard L. (2006). Passionate love, sexual desire, and mate selection: Cross-cultural and historical perspectives. In Patricia Noller & Judith A. Feeney (Eds.), *Close relationships: Functions, forms and processes* (pp. 227–243). Hove, England: Psychology Press/Taylor & Francis.

Hayden, Deborah. (2003). *Pox: Genius, madness, and the mysteries of syphilis.* New York: Basic Books.

Haydon, Jo. (2007). *Genetics in practice: A clinical approach for healthcare practitioners.* Hoboken, NJ: Wiley.

Hayes, Brett K., & Younger, Katherine. (2004). Category-use effects in children. *Child Development, 75,* 1719–1732.

Hayflick, Leonard. (2004). "Anti-aging" is an oxymoron. *Journals of Gerontology: Series A: Biological Sciences and Medical Sciences, 59A,* 573–578.

Hayslip, Bert, & Patrick, Julie Hicks. (2003). Custodial grandparenting viewed from within a life-span perpective. In Bert Hayslip, Jr. & Julie Hicks Patrick (Eds.), *Working with custodial grandparents* (pp. 3–11). New York: Springer.

Hayslip, Bert, Jr., Servaty, Heather L., & Guarnaccia, Charles A. (1999). Age cohort differences in perceptions of funerals. In Brian de Vries (Ed.), *End of life issues: Interdisciplinary and multidimensional perspectives* (pp. 23–36). New York: Springer.

Heath, Andrew C., Madden, Pamela A. F., Bucholz, Kathleen K., Nelson, Elliot C., Todorov, Alexandre, Price, Rumi Kato, et al. (2003). Genetic and environmental risks of dependence on alcohol, tobacco, and other drugs. In Robert Plomin, John C. DeFries, Ian W. Craig, & Peter McGuffin (Eds.), *Behavioral genetics in the postgenomic era* (pp. 309–334). Washington, DC: American Psychological Association.

Heathcock, Jill C., Lobo, Michele, & Galloway, James C. (2008). Movement training advances the emergence of reaching in infants born at less than 33 weeks of gestational age: A randomized clinical trial. *Physical Therapy, 88,* 310–322.

Heaven, Patrick C. L., & Ciarrochi, Joseph. (2008). Parental styles, conscientiousness, and academic performance in high school: A three-wave longitudinal study. *Personality and Social Psychology Bulletin, 34,* 451–461.

Hechtman, Lily, Abikoff, Howard B., & Jensen, Peter S. (2005). Multimodal therapy and stimulants in the treatment of children with attention-deficit/hyperactivity disorder. In Euthymia D. Hibbs & Peter S. Jensen (Eds.), *Psychosocial treatments for child and adolescent disorders: Empirically based strategies for clinical practice* (2nd ed., pp. 411–437). Washington, DC: American Psychological Association.

Heckers, Stephan, Zalesak, Martin, Weiss, Anthony P., Ditman, Tali, & Titone, Debra. (2004). Hippocampal activation during transitive inference in humans. *Hippocampus, 14,* 153–162.

Heilbrun, Kirk, Goldstein, Naomi E. Sevin, & Redding, Richard E. (Eds.). (2005). *Juvenile delinquency: Prevention, assessment, and intervention.* New York: Oxford University Press.

Heine, Steven J. (2007). Culture and motivation: What motivates people to act in the ways that they do? In Shinobu Kitayama & Dov Cohen (Eds.), *Handbook of cultural psychology* (pp. 714–733). New York: Guilford Press.

Hemminki, Kari, Sundquist, Jan, & Lorenzo Bermejo, Justo. (2008). Familial risks for cancer as the basis for evidence-based clinical referral and counseling. *The Oncologist, 13,* 239–247.

Henderson, Heather A., Marshall, Peter J., Fox, Nathan A., & Rubin, Kenneth H. (2004). Psychophysiological and behavioral evidence for varying forms and functions of nonsocial behavior in preschoolers. *Child Development, 75,* 251–263.

Henig, Robin Marantz. (2004, November 30). Sorry. Your eating disorder doesn't meet our criteria. *New York Times Magazine,* pp. 32–37.

Henson, Sian M., & Aspinall, Richard J. (2003). Ageing and the immune response. In Richard J. Aspinall (Ed.), *Aging of organs and systems* (pp. 225–242). Boston: Kluwer Academic.

Henz, Ursula. (2006). Informal caregiving at working age: Effects of job characteristics and family configuration. *Journal of Marriage and Family, 68,* 411–429.

Herbert, Alan, Gerry, Norman P., McQueen, Matthew B., Heid, Iris M., Pfeufer, Arne, Illig, Thomas, et al. (2006, April 14). A common genetic variant is associated with adult and childhood obesity. *Science, 312,* 279–283.

Herek, Gregory M. (2006). Legal recognition of same-sex relationships in the United States: A social science perspective. *American Psychologist, 61,* 607–621.

Herman, Melissa. (2004). Forced to choose: Some determinants of racial identification in multiracial adolescents. *Child Development, 75,* 730–748.

Herman-Giddens, Marcia E., Wang, Lily, & Koch, Gary. (2001). Secondary sexual characteristics in boys: Estimates from the National Health and Nutrition Examination Survey III, 1988–1994. *Archives of Pediatrics & Adolescent Medicine, 155,* 1022–1028.

Hernandez-Reif, Maria, Diego, Miguel, & Field, Tiffany. (2007). Preterm infants show reduced stress behaviors and activity after 5 days of massage therapy. *Infant Behavior & Development, 30,* 557–561.

Herrmann, Esther, Call, Josep, Hernàndez-Lloreda, María Victoria, Hare, Brian, & Tomasello, Michael. (2007, September 7). Humans have evolved specialized skills of social cognition: The cultural intelligence hypothesis. *Science, 317,* 1360–1366.

Herschensohn, Julia Rogers. (2007). *Language development and age.* New York: Cambridge University Press.

Hertenstein, Matthew J., & Campos, Joseph J. (2001). Emotion regulation via maternal touch. *Infancy, 2,* 549–566.

Herzog, A. Regula, Ofstedal, Mary Beth, & Wheeler, Laura M. (2002). Social engagement and its relationship to health. *Clinics in Geriatric Medicine, 18,* 593–609.

Hess, Thomas, Hinson, Joey, & Hodges, Elizabeth. (2009). Moderators of and mechanisms underlying stereotype threat effects on older adults' memory performance. *Experimental Aging Research, 35,* 153–177.

Hetherington, E. Mavis, & Kelly, John. (2002). *For better or for worse: Divorce reconsidered.* New York: Norton.

Heuveline, Patrick. (2002). An international comparison of adolescent and young adult mortality. *Annals of the American Academy of Political and Social Science, 580,* 172–200.

Heuveline, Patrick, & Timberlake, Jeffrey M. (2004). The role of cohabitation in family formation: The United States in comparative perspective. *Journal of Marriage and Family, 66,* 1214–1230.

Higgins, Jenny A., & Hirsch, Jennifer S. (2008). Pleasure, power, and inequality: Incorporating sexuality into research on contraceptive use. *American Journal of Public Health, 98,* 1803–1813.

Higgins, Matt. (2006, August 5). Risk of injury is simply an element of motocross. *New York Times,* p. D5.

Hill, E. Jeffrey, Jacob, Jenet, Shannon, Laurie, Brennan, Robert, Blanchard, Victoria, & Martinengo, Giuseppe. (2008). Exploring the relationship of workplace flexibility, gender, and life stage to family-to-work conflict, and stress and burnout. *Community, Work & Family, 11,* 165–181.

Hill, Nancy E., & Bush, Kevin R. (2001). Relationships between parenting environment and children's mental health among African American and European American mothers and children. *Journal of Marriage and Family, 63,* 954–966.

Hill, Robert D., Thorn, Brian L., Bowling, John, & Morrison, Anthony (Eds.). (2002). *Geriatric residential care.* Mahwah, NJ: Erlbaum.

Hillier, Dawn. (2003). *Childbirth in the global village: Implications for midwifery education and practice.* New York: Routledge.

Hilton, Irene V., Stephen, Samantha, Barker, Judith C., & Weintraub, Jane A. (2007). Cultural factors and children's oral health care: A qualitative study of carers of young children. *Community Dentistry and Oral Epidemiology, 35,* 429–438.

Hinds, David A., Stuve, Laura L., Nilsen, Geoffrey B., Halperin, Eran, Eskin, Eleazar, Ballinger, Dennis G., et al. (2005, February 18). Whole-genome patterns of common DNA variation in three human populations. *Science, 307,* 1072–1079.

Hines, Melissa. (2004). *Brain gender.* Oxford, England: Oxford University Press.

Hinkel, Eli. (2005). *Handbook of research in second language teaching and learning.* Mahwah, NJ: Erlbaum.

Hinshaw, Stephen P., Owens, Elizabeth B., Sami, Nilofar, & Fargeon, Samantha. (2006). Prospective follow-up of girls with attention-deficit/hyperactivity disorder into adolescence: Evidence for continuing cross-domain impairment. *Journal of Consulting and Clinical Psychology, 74,* 489–499.

Hirsch, Jennifer S., Meneses, Sergio, Thompson, Brenda, Negroni, Mirka, Pelcastre, Blanca, & del Rio, Carlos. (2007). The inevitability of infidelity: Sexual reputation, social geographies, and marital HIV risk in rural Mexico. *American Journal of Public Health, 97,* 986–996.

Hirschberger, Gilad. (2006). Terror management and attributions of blame to innocent victims: Reconciling compassionate and defensive responses. *Journal of Personality and Social Psychology, 91,* 832–844.

Ho, Caroline, Bluestein, Deborah N., & Jenkins, Jennifer M. (2008). Cultural differences in the relationship between parenting and children's behavior. *Developmental Psychology, 44,* 507–522.

Hoare, Carol Hren. (2002). *Erikson on development in adulthood: New insights from the unpublished papers.* New York: Oxford University Press.

Hochman, David. (2003, November 23). Food for holiday thought: Eat less, live to 140? *New York Times*, p. A9.

Hoehl, Stefanie, Reid, Vincent, Mooney, Jeanette, & Striano, Tricia. (2008). What are you looking at? Infants' neural processing of an adult's object-directed eye gaze. *Developmental Science, 11,* 10–16.

Hoff, David J. (2007). Not all agree on meaning of NCLB proficiency. *Education Week, 26*(33), 1, 23.

Hoff, Erika. (2003). The specificity of environmental influence: Socioeconomic status affects early vocabulary development via maternal speech. *Child Development, 74,* 1368–1378.

Hofferth, Sandra L., & Anderson, Kermyt G. (2003). Are all dads equal? Biology versus marriage as a basis for paternal investment. *Journal of Marriage and Family, 65,* 213–232.

Hofstede, Geert. (2007). A European in Asia. *Asian Journal of Social Psychology, 10,* 16–21.

Holden, Constance. (2000, July 28). The violence of the lambs. *Science, 289,* 580–581.

Holderness, Bill. (2006). Toward bridging digital divides in rural (South) Africa. In David Buckingham & Rebekah Willett (Eds.), *Digital generations: Children, young people, and new media* (pp. 251–272). Mahwah, NJ: Erlbaum.

Holland, Janet, Reynolds, Tracey, & Weller, Susie. (2007). Transitions, networks and communities: The significance of social capital in the lives of children and young people. *Journal of Youth Studies, 10,* 97–116.

Hollich, George J., Hirsh-Pasek, Kathy, Golinkoff, Roberta Michnick, Brand, Rebecca J., Brown, Ellie, Chung, He Len, et al. (2000). Breaking the language barrier: An emergentist coalition model for the origins of word learning. *Monographs of the Society for Research in Child Development, 65*(3, Serial No. 262), v–123.

Holstein, Martha B., & Minkler, Meredith. (2003). Self, society, and the "new gerontology." *Gerontologist, 43,* 787–796.

Hong, Ying-yi, Morris, Michael W., Chiu, Chi-yue, & Benet-Martinez, Veronica. (2000). Multicultural minds: A dynamic constructivist approach to culture and cognition. *American Psychologist, 55,* 709–720.

Hooley, Jill M. (2004). Do psychiatric patients do better clinically if they live with certain kinds of families? *Current Directions in Psychological Science, 13,* 202–205.

Horn, Ivor B., Brenner, Ruth, Rao, Malla, & Cheng, Tina L. (2006). Beliefs about the appropriate age for initiating toilet training: Are there racial and socioeconomic differences? *The Journal of Pediatrics, 149,* 165–168.

Horn, John L., & Masunaga, Hiromi. (2000). New directions for research into aging and intelligence: The development of expertise. In Timothy J. Perfect & Elizabeth A. Maylor (Eds.), *Models of cognitive aging* (pp. 125–159). London: Oxford University Press.

Hornig, Mady, Briese, Thomas, Buie, Timothy, Bauman, Margaret L., Lauwers, Gregory, Siemetzki, Ulrike, et al. (2008). Lack of association between measles virus vaccine and autism with enteropathy: A case-control study. *PLoS ONE, 3*(9), e3140.

Horowitz, Amy, & Stuen, Cynthia. (2003). Introduction: Aging and the senses. *Generations, 27*(1), 6–7.

Houde, Susan Crocker. (2007). *Vision loss in older adults: Nursing assessment and care management.* New York: Springer.

Howe, Christine. (1998). *Conceptual structure in childhood and adolescence: The case of everyday physics.* London: Routledge.

Howe, Mark L., Cicchetti, Dante, & Toth, Sheree L. (2006). Children's basic memory processes, stress, and maltreatment. *Development and Psychopathology, 18,* 759–769.

Hrabosky, Joshua I., & Thomas, Jennifer J. (2008). Elucidating the relationship between obesity and depression: Recommendations for future research. *Clinical Psychology: Science and Practice, 15,* 28–34.

Hsu, Ming, Anen, Cedric, & Quartz, Steven R. (2008, May 23). The right and the good: Distributive justice and neural encoding of equity and efficiency. *Science, 320,* 1092–1095.

Hu, Frank B., Li, Tricia Y., Colditz, Graham A., Willett, Walter C., & Manson, JoAnn E. (2003). Television watching and other sedentary behaviors in relation to risk of obesity and type 2 diabetes mellitus in women. *Journal of the American Medical Association, 289,* 1785–1791.

Huang, Han-Yao, Caballero, Benjamin, Chang, Stephanie, Alberg, Anthony J., Semba, Richard D., Schneyer, Christine R., et al. (2006). The efficacy and safety of multivitamin and mineral supplement use to prevent cancer and chronic disease in adults: A systematic review for a National Institutes of Health State-of-the-Science Conference. *Annals of Internal Medicine, 145,* 372–385.

Huang, Jannet. (2007). Hormones and female sexuality. In Annette Fuglsang Owens & Mitchell S. Tepper (Eds.), *Sexual health: Vol. 2. Physical foundations* (pp. 43–78). Westport, CT: Praeger/Greenwood.

Huang, Xu, & Van de Vliert, Evert. (2004). Job level and national culture as joint roots of job satisfaction. *Applied Psychology: an International Review, 53,* 329–348.

Hubbard, Raymond, & Lindsay, R. Murray. (2008). Why *p* values are not a useful measure of evidence in statistical significance testing. *Theory and Psychology, 18,* 69–88.

Hubel, David H., & Wiesel, Torsten N. (2005). *Brain and visual perception: The story of a 25-year collaboration.* New York: Oxford University Press.

Huesmann, L. Rowell, Dubow, Eric F., Eron, Leonard D., & Boxer, Paul. (2006). Middle childhood family-contextual and personal factors as predictors of adult outcomes. In Aletha C. Huston & Marika N. Ripke (Eds.), *Developmental contexts in middle childhood: Bridges to adolescence and adulthood* (pp. 62–86). New York: Cambridge University Press.

Hugdahl, Kenneth, & Davidson, Richard J. (Eds.). (2002). *The asymmetrical brain.* Cambridge, MA: MIT Press.

Hughes, Judith M. (2007). *Guilt and its vicissitudes: Psychoanalytic reflections on morality.* New York: Routledge.

Hughes, Sonya M., & Gore, Andrea C. (2007). How the brain controls puberty, and implications for sex and ethnic differences. *Family & Community Health, 30*(Suppl. 1), S112–S114.

Hulbert, Ann. (2007, April 1). Re-education. *New York Times Magazine,* p. 34ff.

Husain, Nusrat, Bevc, Irene, Husain, M., Chaudhry, Imram B., Atif, N., & Rahman, A. (2006). Prevalence and social correlates of postnatal depression in a low income country. *Archives of Women's Mental Health, 9,* 197–202.

Hussey, Jon M., Chang, Jen Jen, & Kotch, Jonathan B. (2006). Child maltreatment in the United States: Prevalence, risk factors, and adolescent health consequences. *Pediatrics, 118,* 933–942.

Hust, Stacey J. T., Brown, Jane D., & L'Engle, Kelly Ladin. (2008). Boys will be boys and girls better be prepared: An analysis of the rare sexual health messages in young adolescents' media. *Mass Communication and Society, 11,* 3–23.

Huston, Aletha C., & Aronson, Stacey Rosenkrantz. (2005). Mothers' time with infant and time in employment as predictors of mother–child relationships and children's early development. *Child Development, 76,* 467–482.

Huston, Aletha C., Chang, Young Eun, & Gennetian, Lisa. (2002). Family and individual predictors of child care use by low-income families in different policy contexts. *Early Childhood Research Quarterly, 17,* 441–469.

Huston, Aletha C., & Ripke, Marika N. (2006). Middle childhood: Contexts of development. In Aletha C. Huston & Marika N. Ripke (Eds.), *Developmental contexts in middle childhood: Bridges to adolescence and adulthood* (pp. 1–22). New York: Cambridge University Press.

Huston, Ted L. (2000). The social ecology of marriage and other intimate unions. *Journal of Marriage and the Family, 62,* 298–319.

Hyson, Marilou, Copple, Carol, & Jones, Jacqueline. (2006). Early childhood development and education. In William Damon & Richard M. Lerner (Series Eds.) & K. Ann Renninger & Irving E. Sigel (Vol. Eds.), *Handbook of child psychology: Vol. 4. Child psychology in practice* (6th ed., pp. 3–47). Hoboken, NJ: Wiley.

Iacoboni, Marco. (2009). Imitation, empathy, and mirror neurons. *Annual Review of Psychology, 60,* 653–670.

Idler, Ellen. (2006). Religion and aging. In Robert H. Binstock & Linda K. George (Eds.), *Handbook of aging and the social sciences* (6th ed., pp. 277–300). Amsterdam: Elsevier.

IJzendoorn, Marinus H. Van, Bakermans-Kranenburg, Marian J., & Sagi-Schwartz, Abraham. (2006). Attachment across diverse sociocultural contexts: The limits of universality. In Kenneth H. Rubin & Ock Boon Chung (Eds.), *Parenting beliefs, behaviors, and parent–child relations: A cross-cultural perspective* (pp. 107–142). New York: Psychology Press.

Imamoglu, Çagri. (2007). Assisted living as a new place schema: A comparison with homes and nursing homes. *Environment and Behavior, 39,* 246–268.

Ingersoll-Dayton, Berit, Krause, Neal, & Morgan, David. (2002). Religious trajectories and transitions over the life course. *International Journal of Aging & Human Development, 55,* 51–70.

Ingersoll-Dayton, Berit, Neal, Margaret B., Ha, Jung-Hwa, & Hammer, Leslie B. (2003). Redressing inequity in parent care among siblings. *Journal of Marriage and Family, 65,* 201–212.

Inglehart, Ronald. (1990). *Culture shift in advanced industrial society.* Princeton, NJ: Princeton University Press.

Inhelder, Bärbel, & Piaget, Jean. (1958). *The growth of logical thinking from childhood to adolescence: An essay on the construction of formal operational structures.* New York: Basic Books.

Inhelder, Bärbel, & Piaget, Jean. (1964). *The early growth of logic in the child.* New York: Harper & Row.

Inhorn, Marcia Claire, & van Balen, Frank (Eds.). (2002). *Infertility around the globe: New thinking on childlessness, gender, and reproductive technologies.* Berkeley, CA: University of California Press.

Insel, Beverly J., & Gould, Madelyn S. (2008). Impact of modeling on adolescent suicidal behavior. *Psychiatric Clinics of North America, 31,* 293–316.

Insel, Thomas R., & Fenton, Wayne S. (2005). Psychiatric epidemiology: It's not just about counting anymore. *Archives of General Psychiatry, 62,* 590–592.

Institute of Medicine, Committee on Food Marketing and the Diets of Children and Youth. (2006). *Food marketing to children and youth: Threat or opportunity?* Washington, DC: National Academies Press.

Inzlicht, Michael, McKay, Linda, & Aronson, Joshua. (2006). Stigma as ego depletion: How being the target of prejudice affects self-control. *Psychological Science, 17,* 262–269.

Irwin, Scott, Galvez, Roberto, Weiler, Ivan Jeanne, Beckel-Mitchener, Andrea, & Greenough, William. (2002). Brain structure and the functions of FMR1 protein. In Randi Jenssen Hagerman & Paul J. Hagerman (Eds.), *Fragile X syndrome: Diagnosis, treatment, and research* (3rd ed., pp. 191–205). Baltimore: Johns Hopkins University Press.

Iverson, Jana M., & Fagan, Mary K. (2004). Infant vocal-motor coordination: Precursor to the gesture-speech system? *Child Development, 75,* 1053–1066.

Izard, Carroll E., Fine, Sarah, Mostow, Allison, Trentacosta, Christopher, & Campbell, Jan. (2002). Emotion processes in normal and abnormal development and preventive intervention. *Development & Psychopathology, 14,* 761–787.

Izard, Carroll E., King, Kristen A., Trentacosta, Christopher J., Morgan, Judith K., Laurenceau, Jean-Philippe, Krauthamer-Ewing, E. Stephanie, et al. (2008). Accelerating the development of emotion competence in Head Start children: Effects on adaptive and maladaptive behavior. *Development and Psychopathology, 20,* 369–397.

Jackson, Kristina M., Sher, Kenneth J., & Schulenberg, John E. (2008). Conjoint developmental trajectories of young adult substance use. *Alcoholism: Clinical and Experimental Research, 32,* 723–737.

Jackson, Linda A., von Eye, Alexander, Biocca, Frank A., Barbatsis, Gretchen, Zhao, Yong, & Fitzgerald, Hiram E. (2006). Does home internet use influence the academic performance of low-income children? *Developmental Psychology, 42,* 429–435.

Jackson, Richard J. (2003). The impact of the built environment on health: An emerging field. *American Journal of Public Health, 93,* 1382–1384.

Jackson, Yo, & Warren, Jared S. (2000). Appraisal, social support, and life events: Predicting outcome behavior in school-age children. *Child Development, 71,* 1441–1457.

Jacob's father. (1997). Jacob's story: A miracle of the heart. *Zero to Three, 17,* 59–64.

Jacobs, Janis E., Lanza, Stephanie, Osgood, D. Wayne, Eccles, Jacquelynne S., & Wigfield, Allan. (2002). Changes in children's self-competence and values: Gender and domain differences across grades one though twelve. *Child Development, 73*, 509–527.

Jacobson, Linda. (2007, April 25). For Head Start, a marathon run. *Education Week, 26*, 28–31.

Jacoby, Larry L., Marsh, Elizabeth J., & Dolan, Patrick O. (2001). Forms of bias: Age-related differences in memory and cognition. In Moshe Naveh-Benjamin, Morris Moscovitch, & Henry L. Roediger (Eds.), *Perspectives on human memory and cognitive aging: Essays in honour of Fergus Craik* (pp. 240–252). New York: Psychology Press.

Jacoby, Larry L., & Rhodes, Matthew G. (2006). False remembering in the aged. *Current Directions in Psychological Science, 15*, 49–53.

Jaffe, Eric. (2004). Mickey Mantle's greatest error: Yankee star's false belief may have cost him years. *Observer, 17*(9), 37.

Jaffee, Sara, Caspi, Avshalom, Moffitt, Terrie E., Belsky, Jay, & Silva, Phil. (2001). Why are children born to teen mothers at risk for adverse outcomes in young adulthood? Results from a 20-year longitudinal study. *Development & Psychopathology, 13*, 377–397.

Jaffee, Sara R. (2007). Sensitive, stimulating caregiving predicts cognitive and behavioral resilience in neurodevelopmentally at-risk infants. *Development and Psychopathology, 19*, 631–647.

Jaffee, Sara R., Caspi, Avshalom, Moffitt, Terrie E., Polo-Tomas, Monica, Price, Thomas S., & Taylor, Alan. (2004). The limits of child effects: Evidence for genetically mediated child effects on corporal punishment but not on physical maltreatment. *Developmental Psychology, 40*, 1047–1058.

Jaffee, Sara R., Caspi, Avshalom, Moffitt, Terrie E., Polo-Tomás, Monica, & Taylor, Alan. (2007). Individual, family, and neighborhood factors distinguish resilient from non-resilient maltreated children: A cumulative stressors model. *Child Abuse & Neglect, 31*, 231–253.

James, Raven. (2007). Sexually transmitted infections. In Annette Fuglsang Owens & Mitchell S. Tepper (Eds.), *Sexual health: Vol. 4. State-of-the-art treatments and research* (pp. 235–267). Westport, CT: Praeger/Greenwood.

Jansen-van der Weide, Marijke C., Onwuteaka-Philipsen, Bregje D., & van der Wal, Gerrit. (2005). Granted, undecided, withdrawn, and refused requests for euthanasia and physician-assisted suicide. *Archives of Internal Medicine, 165*, 1698–1704.

Janson, Harald, & Mathiesen, Kristin S. (2008). Temperament profiles from infancy to middle childhood: Development and associations with behavior problems. *Developmental Psychology, 44*, 1314–1328.

Jansson, Ulla-Britt, Hanson, M., Sillen, Ulla, & Hellstrom, Anna-Lena. (2005). Voiding pattern and acquisition of bladder control from birth to age 6 years—A longitudinal study. *Journal of Urology, 174*, 289–293.

Jastrzembski, Tiffany S., Charness, Neil, & Vasyukova, Catherine. (2006). Expertise and age effects on knowledge activation in chess. *Psychology and Aging, 21*, 401–405.

Jeanneret, Rene. (1995). The role of a preparation for retirement in the improvement of the quality of life for elderly people. In Eino Heikkinen, Jorma Kuusinen, & Isto Ruoppila (Eds.), *Preparation for aging* (pp. 55–62). New York: Plenum Press.

Jeffries, Sherryl, & Konnert, Candace. (2002). Regret and psychological well-being among voluntarily and involuntarily childless women and mothers. *International Journal of Aging & Human Development, 54*, 89–106.

Jenkins, Jennifer M., & Astington, Janet Wilde. (1996). Cognitive factors and family structure associated with theory of mind development in young children. *Developmental Psychology, 32*, 70–78.

Jensen, Arthur Robert. (1998). *The g factor: The science of mental ability.* Westport, CT: Praeger.

Jenson, Jeffrey M., & Fraser, Mark W. (2006). *Social policy for children & families: A risk and resilience perspective.* Thousand Oaks, CA: Sage.

Jessop, Donna C., & Wade, Jennifer. (2008). Fear appeals and binge drinking: A terror management theory perspective. *British Journal of Health Psychology, 13*, 773–788.

Joe, Sean. (2003). Implications of focusing on black youth self-destructive behaviors instead of suicide when designing preventative interventions. In Daniel Romer (Ed.), *Reducing adolescent risk: Toward an integrated approach* (pp. 325–332). Thousand Oaks, CA: Sage.

Joh, Amy S., & Adolph, Karen E. (2006). Learning from falling. *Child Development, 77*, 89–102.

Johns, Michael, Inzlicht, Michael, & Schmader, Toni. (2008). Stereotype threat and executive resource depletion: Examining the influence of emotion regulation. *Journal of Experimental Psychology: General, 137*, 691–705.

Johnson, Dana E. (2000). Medical and developmental sequelae of early childhood institutionalization in Eastern European adoptees. In Charles A. Nelson (Ed.), *The Minnesota symposia on child psychology: Vol. 31. The effects of early adversity on neurobehavioral development* (pp. 113–162). Mahwah, NJ: Erlbaum.

Johnson, Kevin R. (1999). *How did you get to be Mexican? A white/brown man's search for identity.* Philadelphia: Temple University Press.

Johnson, Kirk A., & Rector, Robert. (2004). *Adolescents who take virginity pledges have lower rates of out-of-wedlock births.* The Heritage Foundation. Retrieved September 13, 2009, from http://www.heritage.org/Research/Family/upload/63285_1.pdf

Johnson, Mark H. (2005). Developmental neuroscience, psychophysiology and genetics. In Marc H. Bornstein & Michael E. Lamb (Eds.), *Developmental science: An advanced textbook* (5th ed., pp. 187–222). Mahwah, NJ: Erlbaum.

Johnson, Mark H. (2007). The social brain in infancy: A developmental cognitive neuroscience approach. In Donna Coch, Kurt W. Fischer, & Geraldine Dawson (Eds.), *Human behavior, learning, and the developing brain. Typical development* (pp. 115–137). New York: Guilford Press.

Johnson, Mary. (2007). Our guest editors talk about couples in later life. *Generations, 31*(3), 4–5.

Johnston, Lloyd D., O'Malley, Patrick M., Bachman, Jerald G., & Schulenberg, John E. (2007). *Monitoring the Future*

national survey results on drug use, 1975–2006. Volume I: Secondary school students (NIH Publication No. 07-6205). Bethesda, MD: National Institute on Drug Abuse.

Johnston, Lloyd D., O'Malley, Patrick M., Bachman, Jerald G., & Schulenberg, John E. (2008). *Monitoring the Future national survey results on adolescent drug use: Overview of key findings, 2007* (NIH Publication No. 08-6418). Bethesda, MD: National Institute on Drug Abuse.

Jokela, Markus, Elovainio, Marko, Kivimäki, Mika, & Keltikangas-Järvinen, Liisa. (2008). Temperament and migration patterns in Finland. *Psychological Science, 19,* 831–837.

Jones, Diane, & Crawford, Joy. (2005). Adolescent boys and body image: Weight and muscularity concerns as dual pathways to body dissatisfaction. *Journal of Youth and Adolescence, 34,* 629–636.

Jones, Edward P. (2003). *Lost in the city: Stories.* New York: Amistad. (Original work published 1992)

Jones, Harold Ellis, & Conrad, Herbert S. (1933). The growth and decline of intelligence: A study of a homogeneous group between the ages of ten and sixty. *Genetic Psychology Monographs, 13,* 223–298.

Jones, Ian. (2006). Why do women experience mood disorders following childbirth? *British Journal of Midwifery, 14,* 654–657.

Jones, Maggie. (2006, January 15). Shutting themselves in. *New York Times Magazine,* pp. 46–51.

Jones, Mary Cover. (1965). Psychological correlates of somatic development. *Child Development, 36,* 899–911.

Jones, Steve. (2006, December 22). Prosperous people, penurious genes. *Science, 314,* 1879.

Jopp, Daniela, & Rott, Christoph. (2006). Adaptation in very old age: Exploring the role of resources, beliefs, and attitudes for centenarians' happiness. *Psychology and Aging, 21,* 266–280.

Jordan, Alexander H., & Monin, Benoît. (2008). From sucker to saint: Moralization in response to self-threat. *Psychological Science, 19,* 809–815.

Joshi, Pamela, & Bogen, Karen. (2007). Nonstandard schedules and young children's behavioral outcomes among working low-income families. *Journal of Marriage and Family, 69,* 139–156.

Juffer, Femmie, & van IJzendoorn, Marinus H. (2005). Behavior problems and mental health referrals of international adoptees: A meta-analysis. *Journal of the American Medical Association, 293,* 2501–2515.

Juffer, Femmie, & van IJzendoorn, Marinus H. (2007). Adoptees do not lack self-esteem: A meta-analysis of studies on self-esteem of transracial, international, and domestic adoptees. *Psychological Bulletin, 133,* 1067–1083.

Jukelevics, Nicette. (2008). *Understanding the dangers of cesarean birth: Making informed decisions.* Westport, CT: Praeger.

Juster, F. Thomas, Ono, Hiromi, & Stafford, Frank P. (2004). *Changing times of American youth: 1981–2003.* Ann Arbor, MI: Institute for Social Research, University of Michigan.

Juvonen, Jaana, Nishina, Adrienne, & Graham, Sandra. (2006). Ethnic diversity and perceptions of safety in urban middle schools. *Psychological Science, 17,* 393–400.

Kaduszkiewicz, Hanna, Zimmermann, Thomas, Beck-Bornholdt, Hans-Peter, & van den Bussche, Hendrik. (2005). Cholinesterase inhibitors for patients with Alzheimer's disease: Systematic review of randomised clinical trials. *British Medical Journal, 331,* 321–327.

Kaestle, Christine Elizabeth, & Halpern, Carolyn Tucker. (2007). What's love got to do with it? Sexual behaviors of opposite-sex couples through emerging adulthood. *Perspectives on Sexual and Reproductive Health, 39,* 134–140.

Kagan, Jerome. (2002). *Surprise, uncertainty, and mental structures.* Cambridge, MA: Harvard University Press.

Kagan, Jerome. (2007). A trio of concerns. *Perspectives on Psychological Science, 2,* 361–376.

Kagan, Jerome, & Fox, Nathan A. (2006). Biology, culture, and temperamental biases. In William Damon & Richard M. Lerner (Series Eds.) & Nancy Eisenberg (Vol. Ed.), *Handbook of child psychology: Vol. 3. Social, emotional, and personality development* (6th ed., pp. 167–225). Hoboken, NJ: Wiley.

Kagan, Jerome, & Herschkowitz, Norbert (with Herschkowitz, Elinore Chapman). (2005). *A young mind in a growing brain.* Mahwah, NJ: Erlbaum.

Kagan, Jerome, & Snidman, Nancy C. (2004). *The long shadow of temperament.* Cambridge, MA: Belknap Press.

Kalavar, Jyotsna, & van Willigen, John. (2005). Older Asian Indians resettled in America: Narratives about households, culture and generation. *Journal of Cross-Cultural Gerontology, 20,* 213–230.

Kallen, Victor L., Tulen, Joke H. M., Utens, Elisabeth M. W. J., Treffers, Philip D. A., De Jong, Frank H, & Ferdinand, Robert F. (2008). Associations between HPA axis functioning and level of anxiety in children and adolescents with an anxiety disorder. *Depression and Anxiety, 25,* 131–141.

Kalliala, Marjatta. (2006). *Play culture in a changing world.* Maidenhead, England: Open University Press.

Kalmuss, Debra, Davidson, Andrew, Cohall, Alwyn, Laraque, Danielle, & Cassell, Carol. (2003). Preventing sexual risk behaviors and pregnancy among teenagers: Linking research and programs. *Perspectives on Sexual and Reproductive Health, 35,* 87–93.

Kamlin, C. Omar F., O'Donnell, Colm P. F., Davis, Peter G., & Morley, Colin J. (2006). Oxygen saturation in healthy infants immediately after birth. *Journal of Pediatrics, 148,* 585–589.

Kamp Dush, Claire M., & Amato, Paul R. (2005). Consequences of relationship status and quality for subjective well-being. *Journal of Social and Personal Relationships, 22,* 607–627.

Kanaya, Tomoe, & Ceci, Stephen J. (2007). Are all IQ scores created equal? The differential costs of IQ cutoff scores for at-risk children. *Child Development Perspectives, 1,* 52–56.

Kanner, Leo. (1943). Autistic disturbances of affective contact. *Nervous Child, 2,* 217–250.

Kapornai, Krisztina, & Vetró, Ágnes. (2008). Depression in children. *Current Opinion in Psychiatry, 21,* 1–7.

Karney, Benjamin R., & Bradbury, Thomas N. (2005). Contextual influences on marriage: Implications for policy and intervention. *Current Directions in Psychological Science, 14,* 171–174.

Kastenbaum, Robert. (2006). *Death, society, and human experience* (9th ed.). Boston: Allyn and Bacon.

Kato, Shingo, Hanabusa, Hideji, Kaneko, Satoru, Takakuwa, Koichi, Suzuki, Mina, Kuji, Naoaki, et al. (2006). Complete removal of HIV-1 RNA and proviral DNA from semen by the swim-up method: Assisted reproduction technique using spermatozoa free from HIV-1. *Aids, 20,* 967–973.

Kaufman, Joan, & Charney, Dennis. (2001). Effects of early stress on brain structure and function: Implications for understanding the relationship between child maltreatment and depression. *Development & Psychopathology, 13,* 451–471.

Kaufman, Kenneth R., & Kaufman, Nathaniel D. (2006). And then the dog died. *Death Studies, 30,* 61–76.

Kavirajan, Harish, & Schneider, Lon S. (2007). Efficacy and adverse effects of cholinesterase inhibitors and memantine in vascular dementia: A meta-analysis of randomised controlled trials. *Lancet Neurology, 6,* 782–792.

Kearney, Paul, & Pivec, Maja. (2007). Sex, lies and video games. *British Journal of Educational Technology, 38,* 489–501.

Keating, Daniel P. (2004). Cognitive and brain development. In Richard M. Lerner & Laurence D. Steinberg (Eds.), *Handbook of adolescent psychology* (2nd ed., pp. 45–84). Hoboken, NJ: Wiley.

Keating, Nancy L., Herrinton, Lisa J., Zaslavsky, Alan M., Liu, Liyan, & Ayanian, John Z. (2006). Variations in hospice use among cancer patients. *Journal of the National Cancer Institute, 98,* 1053–1059.

Kedar, Yarden, Casasola, Marianella, & Lust, Barbara. (2006). Getting there faster: 18- and 24-month-old infants' use of function words to determine reference. *Child Development, 77,* 325–338.

Keith, Jennie. (1990). Age in social and cultural context: Anthropological perspectives. In Robert H. Binstock & Linda K. George (Eds.), *Handbook of aging and the social sciences* (3rd ed., pp. 91–111). San Diego, CA: Academic Press.

Kelemen, Deborah, Callanan, Maureen A., Casler, Krista, & Perez-Granados, Deanne R. (2005). Why things happen: Teleological explanation in parent–child conversation. *Developmental Psychology, 41,* 251–264.

Kellehear, Allan. (2008). Dying as a social relationship: A sociological review of debates on the determination of death. *Social Science & Medicine, 66,* 1533–1544.

Keller, Heidi, Lamm, Bettina, Abels, Monika, Yovsi, Relindis, Borke, Jörn, Jensen, Henning, et al. (2006). Cultural models, socialization goals, and parenting ethnotheories: A multicultural analysis. *Journal of Cross-Cultural Psychology, 37,* 155–172.

Keller, Heidi, Yovsi, Relindis, Borke, Joern, Kartner, Joscha, Jensen, Henning, & Papaligoura, Zaira. (2004). Developmental consequences of early parenting experiences: Self-recognition and self-regulation in three cultural communities. *Child Development, 75,* 1745–1760.

Keller, Johannes. (2007). Stereotype threat in classroom settings: The interactive effect of domain identification, task difficulty and stereotype threat on female students' maths performance. *British Journal of Educational Psychology, 77,* 323–338.

Kelley, Sue A., Brownell, Celia A., & Campbell, Susan B. (2000). Mastery motivation and self-evaluative affect in toddlers: Longitudinal relations with maternal behavior. *Child Development, 71,* 1061–1071.

Kelley, Susan J., & Whitley, Deborah M. (2003). Psychological distress and physical health problems in grandparents raising grandchildren: Development of an empirically-based intervention model. In Bert Hayslip, Jr. & Julie Hicks Patrick (Eds.), *Working with custodial grandparents* (pp. 127–144). New York: Springer.

Kelley-Moore, Jessica A., & Ferraro, Kenneth F. (2004). The Black/White disability gap: Persistent inequality in later life? *Journals of Gerontology Series B: Psychological Sciences and Social Sciences, 59,* S34–43.

Kelly, John R. (1993). *Activity and aging: Staying involved in later life.* Newbury Park, CA: Sage.

Kelly, Michelle M. (2006). The medically complex premature infant in primary care. *Journal of Pediatric Health Care, 20,* 367–373.

Kemp, Candace L. (2005). Dimensions of grandparent–adult grandchild relationships: From family ties to intergenerational friendships. *Canadian Journal on Aging, 24,* 161–177.

Kemp, Charles, & Bhungalia, Sonal. (2002). Culture and the end of life: A review of major world religions. *Journal of Hospice & Palliative Nursing, 4,* 235–242.

Kempe, Ruth S., & Kempe, C. Henry. (1978). *Child abuse.* Cambridge, MA: Harvard University Press.

Kempner, Joanna, Perlis, Clifford S., & Merz, Jon F. (2005, February 11). Forbidden knowledge. *Science, 307,* 854.

Kennedy, Colin R., McCann, Donna C., Campbell, Michael J., Law, Catherine M., Mullee, Mark, Petrou, Stavros, et al. (2006). Language ability after early detection of permanent childhood hearing impairment. *New England Journal of Medicine, 354,* 2131–2141.

Kenrick, Jenny, Lindsey, Caroline, & Tollemache, Lorraine (Eds.). (2006). *Creating new families: Therapeutic approaches to fostering, adoption, and kinship care.* London: Karnac Books.

Kenyon, Brenda L. (2001). Current research in children's conceptions of death: A critical review. *Omega: Journal of Death and Dying, 43,* 63–91.

Keogh, Barbara K. (2004). The importance of longitudinal research for early intervention practices. In Peggy D. McCardle & Vinita Chhabra (Eds.), *The voice of evidence in reading research* (pp. 81–102). Baltimore: Brookes.

Kessler, Ronald C., Berglund, Patricia, Demler, Olga, Jin, Robert, & Walters, Ellen E. (2005). Lifetime prevalence and age-of-onset distributions of DSM-IV disorders in the National Comorbidity Survey Replication. *Archives of General Psychiatry, 62,* 593–602.

Khaleque, Abdul, & Rohner, Ronald P. (2002). Perceived parental acceptance–rejection and psychological adjustment: A meta-analysis of cross-cultural and intracultural studies. *Journal of Marriage and Family, 64,* 54–64.

Khan, Ayesha, Bellefontaine, Nicole, & deCatanzaro, Denys. (2008). Onset of sexual maturation in female mice as measured in behavior and fertility: Interactions of exposure to males, phytoestrogen content of diet, and ano-genital distance. *Physiology & Behavior, 93,* 588–594.

Khawaja, Marwan, Jurdi, Rozzet, & Kabakian-Khasholian, Tamar. (2004). Rising trends in cesarean section rates in Egypt. *Birth: Issues in Perinatal Care, 31,* 12–16.

Kidder, Jeffrey L. (2006). "It's the job that I love": Bike messengers and edgework. *Sociological Forum, 21,* 31–54.

Killen, Melanie. (2007). Children's social and moral reasoning about exclusion. *Current Directions in Psychological Science, 16,* 32–36.

Killen, Melanie, Lee-Kim, Jennie, McGlothlin, Heidi, & Stangor, Charles. (2002). How children and adolescents evaluate gender and racial exclusion. *Monographs of the Society for Research in Child Development, 67*(4, Serial No. 271).

Killen, Melanie, Margie, Nancy Geyelin, & Sinno, Stefanie. (2006). Morality in the context of intergroup relationships. In Melanie Killen & Judith G. Smetana (Eds.), *Handbook of moral development* (pp. 155–183). Mahwah, NJ: Erlbaum.

Killen, Melanie, & Smetana, Judith. (2007). The biology of morality: Human development and moral neuroscience. *Human Development, 50,* 241–243.

Killeya-Jones, Ley A., Costanzo, Philip R., Malone, Patrick, Quinlan, Nicole Polanichka, & Miller-Johnson, Shari. (2007). Norm-narrowing and self- and other-perceived aggression in early-adolescent same-sex and mixed-sex cliques. *Journal of School Psychology, 45,* 549–565.

Killgore, William D. S., Vo, Alexander H., Castro, Carl A., & Hoge, Charles W. (2006). Assessing risk propensity in American soldiers: Preliminary reliability and validity of the Evaluation of Risks (EVAR) scale-English version. *Military Medicine, 171,* 233–239.

Kim, Hyoun K., Laurent, Heidemarie K., Capaldi, Deborah M., & Feingold, Alan. (2008). Men's aggression toward women: A 10-year panel study. *Journal of Marriage and Family, 70,* 1169–1187.

Kim-Cohen, Julia, Moffitt, Terrie E., Caspi, Avshalom, & Taylor, Alan. (2004). Genetic and environmental processes in young children's resilience and vulnerability to socioeconomic deprivation. *Child Development, 75,* 651–668.

Kinder, Donald R. (2006, June 30). Politics and the life cycle. *Science, 312,* 1905–1908.

King, Alan R., & Terrance, Cheryl. (2006). Relationships between personality disorder attributes and friendship qualities among college students. *Journal of Social and Personal Relationships, 23,* 5–20.

King, Pamela Ebstyne, & Furrow, James L. (2004). Religion as a resource for positive youth development: Religion, social capital, and moral outcomes. *Developmental Psychology, 40,* 703–713.

King, Patricia M., & Kitchener, Karen S. (1994). *Developing reflective judgment: Understanding and promoting intellectual growth and critical thinking in adolescents and adults.* San Francisco: Jossey-Bass.

King, Valarie. (2003). The legacy of a grandparent's divorce: Consequences for ties between grandparents and grandchildren. *Journal of Marriage and Family, 65,* 170–183.

King, Valarie. (2007). When children have two mothers: Relationships with nonresident mothers, stepmothers, and fathers. *Journal of Marriage and Family, 69,* 1178–1193.

King, Valarie, Harris, Kathleen Mullan, & Heard, Holly E. (2004). Racial and ethnic diversity in nonresident father involvement. *Journal of Marriage and Family, 66,* 1–21.

Kinnunen, Marja-Liisa, Kaprio, Jaakko, & Pulkkinen, Lea. (2005). Allostatic load of men and women in early middle age. *Journal of Individual Differences, 26,* 20–28.

Kirby, Douglas. (2001). *Emerging answers: Research findings on programs to reduce teen pregnancy.* Washington, DC: The National Campaign To Prevent Teen Pregnancy.

Kirby, Douglas. (2002). Effective approaches to reducing adolescent unprotected sex, pregnancy, and childbearing. *Journal of Sex Research, 39,* 51–57.

Kirkbride, James B., Fearon, Paul, Morgan, Craig, Dazzan, Paola, Morgan, Kevin, Tarrant, Jane, et al. (2006). Heterogeneity in incidence rates of schizophrenia and other psychotic syndromes: Findings from the 3-center AESOP study. *Archives of General Psychiatry, 63,* 250–258.

Kitzinger, Sheila. (2001). *Rediscovering birth.* New York: Simon & Schuster.

Klaczynski, Paul A. (2001). Analytic and heuristic processing influences on adolescent reasoning and decision-making. *Child Development, 72,* 844–861.

Klaczynski, Paul A. (2005). Metacognition and cognitive variability: A dual-process model of decision making and its development. In Janis E. Jacobs & Paul A. Klaczynski (Eds.), *The development of judgment and decision making in children and adolescents* (pp. 39–76). Mahwah, NJ: Erlbaum.

Klaczynski, Paul A., & Robinson, Billi. (2000). Personal theories, intellectual ability, and epistemological beliefs: Adult age differences in everyday reasoning biases. *Psychology and Aging, 15,* 400–416.

Klahr, David, & Nigam, Milena. (2004). The equivalence of learning paths in early science instruction: Effects of direct instruction and discovery learning. *Psychological Science, 15,* 661–667.

Klassen, Terry P., Kiddoo, Darcie, Lang, Mia E., Friesen, Carol, Russell, Kelly, Spooner, Carol, et al. (2006). *The effectiveness of different methods of toilet training for bowel and bladder control* (AHRQ Publication No. 07-E003). Rockville, MD: Agency for Healthcare Research and Quality.

Klaus, Marshall H., & Kennell, John H. (1976). *Maternal–infant bonding: The impact of early separation or loss on family development.* St. Louis, MO: Mosby.

Klaus, Patsy. (2005). *Crimes against persons age 65 or older, 1993–2002* (NCJ 206154). Washington, DC: Bureau of Justice Statistics.

Kleiber, Douglas A. (1999). *Leisure experience and human development: A dialectical interpretation.* New York: Basic Books.

Kline, Kathleen Kovner. (2008). *Authoritative communities: The scientific case for nurturing the whole child.* New York: Springer.

Klug, William, Cummings, Michael, Spencer, Charlotte, & Palladino, Michael. (2008). *Concepts of genetics* (9th ed.). San Francisco: Pearson/Benjamin Cummings.

Kluwer, Esther S., & Johnson, Matthew D. (2007). Conflict frequency and relationship quality across the transition to parenthood. *Journal of Marriage and Family, 69,* 1089–1106.

Kneebone, Roger L., Scott, William, Darzi, Ara, & Horrocks, Michael. (2004). Simulation and clinical practice: Strengthening the relationship. *Medical Education, 38,* 1095–1102.

Kobler, John. (1993). *Ardent spirits: The rise and fall of prohibition.* New York: Da Capo Press. (Original work published 1973)

Koch, Tom. (2000). *Age speaks for itself: Silent voices of the elderly.* Westport, CT: Praeger.

Kochanska, Grazyna, Aksan, Nazan, Prisco, Theresa R., & Adams, Erin E. (2008). Mother–child and father–child mutually responsive orientation in the first 2 years and children's outcomes at preschool age: Mechanisms of influence. *Child Development, 79,* 30–44.

Kochanska, Grazyna, Coy, Katherine C., & Murray, Kathleen T. (2001). The development of self-regulation in the first four years of life. *Child Development, 72,* 1091–1111.

Kochanska, Grazyna, Gross, Jami N., Lin, Mei-Hua, & Nichols, Kate E. (2002). Guilt in young children: Development, determinants, and relations with a broader system of standards. *Child Development, 73,* 461–482.

Kochanska, Grazyna, & Knaack, Amy. (2003). Effortful control as a personality characteristic of young children: Antecedents, correlates, and consequences. *Journal of Personality, 71,* 1087–1112.

Kohlberg, Lawrence. (1963). The development of children's orientations toward a moral order: I. Sequence in the development of moral thought. *Vita Humana, 6,* 11–33.

Kohlberg, Lawrence, Levine, Charles, & Hewer, Alexandra. (1983). *Moral stages: A current formulation and a response to critics.* New York: Karger.

Kohler, Hans-Peter. (2005). Attitudes and low fertility: Reflections based on Danish twin data. In Alane Booth & Ann C. Crouter (Eds.), *The new population problem: Why families in developed countries are shrinking and what it means* (pp. 99–113). Mahwah, NJ: Erlbaum.

Kohler, Julie K., Grotevant, Harold D., & McRoy, Ruth G. (2002). Adopted adolescents' preoccupation with adoption: The impact on adoptive family relationships. *Journal of Marriage and Family, 64,* 93–104.

Kohn, Alfie. (2006). *The homework myth.* Cambridge, MA: Da Capo Lifelong Books.

Koivisto, Maila. (2004). A follow-up survey of anti-bullying interventions in the comprehensive schools of Kempele in 1990–98. In Peter K. Smith, Debra Pepler, & Ken Rigby (Eds.), *Bullying in schools: How successful can interventions be?* (pp. 235–249). New York: Cambridge University Press.

Kolb, Bryan, & Whishaw, Ian Q. (2008). *Fundamentals of human neuropsychology* (6th ed.). New York: Worth.

Koltko-Rivera, Mark E. (2006). Rediscovering the later version of Maslow's hierarchy of needs: Self-transcendence and opportunities for theory, research, and unification. *Review of General Psychology, 10,* 302–317.

Komives, Susan R., & Nuss, Elizabeth M. (2005). Life after college. In Thomas E. Miller, Barbara E. Bender, & John H. Schuh (Eds.), *Promoting reasonable expectations: Aligning student and institutional views of the college experience* (pp. 140–174). San Francisco: Jossey-Bass.

Konczal, Lisa, & Haller, William. (2008). Fit to miss, but matched to hatch: Success factors among the second generation's disadvantaged in South Florida. *The Annals of the American Academy of Political and Social Science, 620,* 161–176.

Konner, Melvin. (2007). Evolutionary foundations of cultural psychology. In Shinobu Kitayama & Dov Cohen (Eds.), *Handbook of cultural psychology* (pp. 77–105). New York: Guilford Press.

Kornblum, Janet. (2008, July 15). Cyberbullying grows bigger and meaner with photos, video. *USA Today.*

Koropeckyj-Cox, Tanya. (2002). Beyond parental status: Psychological well-being in middle and old age. *Journal of Marriage and Family, 64,* 957–971.

Kotre, John N. (1995). *White gloves: How we create ourselves through memory.* New York: Free Press.

Kovas, Yulia, & Plomin, Robert. (2007). Learning abilities and disabilities: Generalist genes, specialist environments. *Current Directions in Psychological Science, 16,* 284–288.

Kramer, Arthur F., & Erickson, Kirk I. (2007). Capitalizing on cortical plasticity: Influence of physical activity on cognition and brain function. *Trends in Cognitive Sciences, 11,* 342–348.

Kramer, Arthur F., Fabiani, Monica, & Colcombe, Stanley J. (2006). Contributions of cognitive neuroscience to the understanding of behavior and aging. In James E. Birren & K. Warner Schaie (Eds.), *Handbook of the psychology of aging* (6th ed., pp. 57–83). Amsterdam: Elsevier.

Krause, Neal. (2006). Social relationships in late life. In Robert H. Binstock & Linda K. George (Eds.), *Handbook of aging and the social sciences* (6th ed., pp. 181–200). Amsterdam: Elsevier.

Krcmar, Marina, Grela, Bernard, & Lin, Kirsten. (2007). Can toddlers learn vocabulary from television? An experimental approach. *Media Psychology, 10,* 41–63.

Krebs, Dennis L. (2008). Morality: An evolutionary account. *Perspectives on Psychological Science, 3,* 149–172.

Krentz, Ursula C., & Corina, David P. (2008). Preference for language in early infancy: The human language bias is not speech specific. *Developmental Science, 11,* 1–9.

Krieger, Nancy. (2002). Is breast cancer a disease of affluence, poverty, or both? The case of African American women. *American Journal of Public Health, 92,* 611–613.

Krieger, Nancy. (2003). Does racism harm health? Did child abuse exist before 1962? On explicit questions, critical science, and current controversies: An ecosocial perspective. *American Journal of Public Health, 93,* 194–199.

Kröger, Edeltraut, Andel, Ross, Lindsay, Joan, Benounissa, Zohra, Verreault, René, & Laurin, Danielle. (2008). Is complexity of work associated with risk of dementia? The Canadian Study of Health and Aging. *American Journal of Epidemiology, 167,* 820–830.

Kroger, Jane. (2007). *Identity development: Adolescence through adulthood* (2nd ed.). Thousand Oaks, CA: Sage.

Kroger, Rolf O. (2006). *Review of the development of a postmodern self: A computer-assisted comparative analysis of personal documents:*

PsycCRITIQUES. (Reprinted from *Contemporary Psychology: APA Review of Books, 1989, 34*(1), 84)

Kryzer, Erin M., Kovan, Nikki, Phillips, Deborah A., Domagall, Lindsey A., & Gunnar, Megan R. (2007). Toddlers' and preschoolers' experience in family day care: Age differences and behavioral correlates. *Early Childhood Research Quarterly, 22,* 451–466.

Kübler-Ross, Elisabeth. (1969). *On death and dying.* New York: Macmillan.

Kübler-Ross, Elisabeth. (1975). *Death: The final stage of growth.* Englewood Cliffs, NJ: Prentice-Hall.

Kubzansky, Laura D., Koenen, Karestan C., Spiro, Avron, III, Vokonas, Pantel S., & Sparrow, David. (2007). Prospective study of posttraumatic stress disorder symptoms and coronary heart disease in the Normative Aging Study. *Archives of General Psychiatry, 64,* 109–116.

Kuhn, Deanna, & Franklin, Sam. (2006). The second decade: What develops (and how). In William Damon & Richard M. Lerner (Series Eds.) & Deanna Kuhn & Robert Siegler (Vol. Eds.), *Handbook of child psychology: Vol. 2. Cognition, perception, and language* (6th ed., pp. 953–993). Hoboken, NJ: Wiley.

Kumpfer, Karol L., & Alvarado, Rose. (2003). Family-strengthening approaches for the prevention of youth problem behaviors. *American Psychologist, 58,* 457–465.

Kuo, Hsu-Ko, Leveille, Suzanne G., Yu, Yau-Hua, & Milber, William P. (2007). Cognitive function, habitual gait speed, and late-life disability in the National Health and Nutrition Examination Survey (NHANES) 1999–2002. *Gerontology, 53,* 102–110.

Kupersmidt, Janis B., Coie, John D., & Howell, James C. (2004). *Resilience in children exposed to negative peer influences.* Washington, DC: American Psychological Association.

Kurdek, Lawrence A. (1992). Relationship stability and relationship satisfaction in cohabiting gay and lesbian couples: A prospective longitudinal test of the contextual and interdependence models. *Journal of Social & Personal Relationships, 9,* 125–142.

Kurdek, Lawrence A. (2006). Differences between partners from heterosexual, gay, and lesbian cohabiting couples. *Journal of Marriage and Family, 68,* 509–528.

Kuttner, Robert. (2008). Market-based failure—A second opinion on U.S. health care costs. *New England Journal of Medicine, 358,* 549–551.

Labouvie-Vief, Gisela. (1990). Wisdom as integrated thought: Historical and developmental perspectives. In Robert J. Sternberg (Ed.), *Wisdom: Its nature, origins, and development* (pp. 52–83). Cambridge, England: Cambridge University Press.

Labouvie-Vief, Gisela. (2006). Emerging structures of adult thought. In Jeffrey Jensen Arnett & Jennifer Lynn Tanner (Eds.), *Emerging adults in America: Coming of age in the 21st century* (pp. 59–84). Washington, DC: American Psychological Association.

Lach, Helen W. (2002–2003). Fear of falling: An emerging public health problem. *Generations, 26*(4), 33–37.

Lachman, Margie E., & Bertrand, Rosanna M. (2001). Personality and the self in midlife. In Margie E. Lachman (Ed.), *Handbook of midlife development* (pp. 279–309). New York: Wiley.

Lacourse, Eric, Nagin, Daniel, Tremblay, Richard E., Vitaro, Frank, & Claes, Michel. (2003). Developmental trajectories of boys' delinquent group membership and facilitation of violent behaviors during adolescence. *Development & Psychopathology, 15,* 183–197.

Ladd, Gary W. (1999). Peer relationships and social competence during early and middle childhood. *Annual Review of Psychology, 50,* 333–359.

Ladd, Gary W. (2005). *Children's peer relations and social competence: A century of progress.* New Haven, CT: Yale University Press.

Lahey, Benjamin B., Moffitt, Terrie E., & Caspi, Avshalom (Eds.). (2003). *Causes of conduct disorder and juvenile delinquency.* New York: Guilford Press.

Laible, Deborah, Panfile, Tia, & Makariev, Drika. (2008). The quality and frequency of mother–toddler conflict: Links with attachment and temperament. *Child Development, 79,* 426–443.

Lalande, Kathleen M., & Bonanno, George A. (2006). Culture and continuing bonds: A prospective comparison of bereavement in the United States and the People's Republic of China. *Death Studies, 30,* 303–324.

Lamb, Michael E. (1982). Maternal employment and child development: A review. In Michael E. Lamb (Ed.), *Nontraditional families: Parenting and child development* (pp. 45–69). Hillsdale, NJ: Erlbaum.

Lamb, Michael E. (2000). The history of research on father involvement: An overview. In H. Elizabeth Peters, Gary W. Peterson, Suzanne K. Steinmetz, & Randal D. Day (Eds.), *Fatherhood: Research, interventions, and policies* (pp. 23–42). New York: Haworth Press.

Lamb, Michael E., & Lewis, Charlie. (2005). The role of parent–child relationships in child development. In Marc H. Bornstein & Michael E. Lamb (Eds.), *Developmental science: An advanced textbook* (5th ed., pp. 429–468). Mahwah, NJ: Erlbaum.

Lamm, Bettina, Keller, Heidi, Yovsi, Relindis D., & Chaudhary, Nandita. (2008). Grandmaternal and maternal ethnotheories about early child care. *Journal of Family Psychology, 22,* 80–88.

Lampinen, Päivi, Heikkinen, Riitta-Liisa, Kauppinen, Markku, & Heikkinen, Eino. (2006). Activity as a predictor of mental well-being among older adults. *Aging & Mental Health, 10,* 454–466.

Landon, Mark B., Hauth, John C., Leveno, Kenneth J., Spong, Catherine Y., Leindecker, Sharon, Varner, Michael W., et al. (2004). Maternal and perinatal outcomes associated with a trial of labor after prior cesarean delivery. *New England Journal of Medicine, 351,* 2581–2589.

Landry, David J., Darroch, Jacqueline E., Singh, Susheela, & Higgins, Jenny. (2003). Factors associated with the content of sex education in U.S. public secondary schools. *Perspectives on Sexual and Reproductive Health, 35,* 261–269.

Landy, Frank J., & Conte, Jeffrey M. (2007). *Work in the 21st century: An introduction to industrial and organizational psychology* (2nd ed.). Malden, MA: Blackwell.

Lane, Scott D., Cherek, Don R., Pietras, Cynthia J., & Steinberg, Joel L. (2005). Performance of heavy marijuana-smoking adolescents on a laboratory measure of motivation. *Addictive Behaviors, 30,* 815–828.

Lansford, Jennifer E., Ceballo, Rosario, Abbey, Antonia, & Stewart, Abigail J. (2001). Does family structure matter? A comparison of adoptive, two-parent biological, single-mother, stepfather, and stepmother households. *Journal of Marriage and Family, 63,* 840–851.

Lapsley, Daniel K. (1993). Toward an integrated theory of adolescent ego development: The "new look" at adolescent egocentrism. *American Journal of Orthopsychiatry, 63,* 562–571.

Lara, Marielena, Gamboa, Cristina, Kahramanian, M. Iya, Morales, Leo S., & Hayes-Bautista, David E. (2005). Acculturation and Latino health in the United States: A review of the literature and its sociopolitical context. *Annual Review of Public Health, 26,* 367–397.

Larson, Nicole I., Neumark-Sztainer, Dianne, Hannan, Peter J., & Story, Mary. (2007). Trends in adolescent fruit and vegetable consumption, 1999–2004: Project EAT. *American Journal of Preventive Medicine, 32,* 147–150.

Larson, Nicole I., & Wilson, Suzanne. (2004). Adolescence across place and time: Globalization and the changing pathways to adulthood. In Richard M. Lerner & Laurence D. Steinberg (Eds.), *Handbook of adolescent psychology* (2nd ed., pp. 299–330). Hoboken, NJ: Wiley.

Larzelere, Robert E., & Kuhn, Brett R. (2005). Comparing child outcomes of physical punishment and alternative disciplinary tactics: A meta-analysis. *Clinical Child and Family Psychology Review, 8,* 1–37.

Lathouwers, Karen, de Moor, Jan, & Didden, Robert. (2009). Access to and use of Internet by adolescents who have a physical disability: A comparative study. *Research in Developmental Disabilities, 30,* 702–711.

Laumann, Edward O., Gagnon, John H., Michael, Robert T., & Michaels, Stuart. (1994). *The social organization of sexuality: Sexual practices in the United States.* Chicago: University of Chicago Press.

Laumann, Edward O., & Michael, Robert T. (Eds.). (2000). *Sex, love, and health in America: Private choices and public policies.* Chicago: University of Chicago Press.

Laumann, Edward O., & Michael, Robert T. (2001). Setting the scene. In Edward O. Laumann & Robert T. Michael (Eds.), *Sex, love, and health in America: Private choices and public policies* (pp. 1–38). Chicago: University of Chicago Press.

Laursen, Brett, & Mooney, Karen S. (2007). Individual differences in adolescent dating and adjustment. In Rutger C. M. E. Engels, Margaret Kerr, & Håkan Stattin (Eds.), *Friends, lovers, and groups: Key relationships in adolescence* (pp. 81–92). Hoboken, NJ: Wiley.

Lauster, Nathanael T. (2008). Better homes and families: Housing markets and young couple stability in Sweden. *Journal of Marriage and Family, 70,* 891–903.

Lavelli, Manuela, & Fogel, Alan. (2005). Developmental changes in the relationship between the infant's attention and emotion during early face-to-face communication: The 2-month transition. *Developmental Psychology, 41,* 265–280.

Lawes, Carlene M. M., Vander Hoorn, Stephen, & Rodgers, Anthony. (2008). Global burden of blood-pressure-related disease, 2001. *Lancet, 371,* 1513–1518.

Lawhon, Gretchen, & Hedlund, Rodd E. (2008). Newborn individualized developmental care and assessment program training and education. *Journal of Perinatal & Neonatal Nursing, 22,* 133–144.

Lawler, Kathleen A., Younger, Jarred W., Piferi, Rachel L., Billington, Eric, Jobe, Rebecca, Edmondson, Kim, et al. (2003). A change of heart: Cardiovascular correlates of forgiveness in response to interpersonal conflict. *Journal of Behavioral Medicine, 26,* 373–393.

Layden, Tim. (2004, November 15). Get out and play! *Sports Illustrated, 101,* 80–93.

Leach, Penelope. (1997). *Your baby & child: From birth to age five* (3rd ed.). New York: Knopf.

Leaper, Campbell. (2002). Parenting girls and boys. In Marc H. Bornstein (Ed.), *Handbook of parenting: Vol. 1. Children and parenting* (2nd ed., pp. 189–225). Mahwah, NJ: Erlbaum.

Leaper, Campbell, & Smith, Tara E. (2004). A meta-analytic review of gender variations in children's language use: Talkativeness, affiliative speech, and assertive speech. *Developmental Psychology, 40,* 993–1027.

LeBlanc, Manon Mireille, & Barling, Julian. (2004). Workplace aggression. *Current Directions in Psychological Science, 13,* 9–12.

Lee, Christina, & Gramotnev, Helen. (2007). Life transitions and mental health in a national cohort of young Australian women. *Developmental Psychology, 43,* 877–888.

Lee, Eunju, Spitze, Glenna, & Logan, John R. (2003). Social support to parents-in-law: The interplay of gender and kin hierarchies. *Journal of Marriage and Family, 65,* 396–403.

Lee, Hoyee Flora, Gorsuch, Richard L., Saklofske, Donald H., & Patterson, Colleen A. (2008). Cognitive differences for ages 16 to 89 years (Canadian WAIS-III): Curvilinear with Flynn and Processing Speed corrections. *Journal of Psychoeducational Assessment, 26,* 382–394.

Lee, Joyce M., & Menon, Ram K. (2005, October). Growth hormone for short children without a hormone deficiency: Issues and practices. *Contemporary Pediatrics, 22,* 46–53.

Lefkowitz, Eva S., & Gillen, Meghan M. (2006). "Sex is just a normal part of life": Sexuality in emerging adulthood. In Jeffrey Jensen Arnett & Jennifer Lynn Tanner (Eds.), *Emerging adults in America: Coming of age in the 21st century* (pp. 235–255). Washington, DC: American Psychological Association.

Lehmann, Wolfgang. (2004). "For some reason, I get a little scared": Structure, agency, and risk in school-work transitions. *Journal of Youth Studies, 7,* 379–396.

Lenneberg, Eric H. (1967). *Biological foundations of language.* New York: Wiley.

Lenton, Alison, & Webber, Laura. (2006). Cross-sex friendships: Who has more? *Sex Roles, 54,* 809–820.

Leon, David A., Saburova, Ludmila, Tomkins, Susannah, Andreev, Evgueni M., Kiryanov, Nikolay, McKee, Martin, et al. (2007, June 16). Hazardous alcohol drinking and premature mortality in Russia: A population based case-control study. *Lancet, 369,* 2001–2009.

Leonard, Christiana M. (2003). Neural substrate of speech and language development. In Michelle De Haan & Mark H. Johnson

(Eds.), *The cognitive neuroscience of development* (pp. 127–156). New York: Psychology Press.

Lepper, Mark R., Greene, David, & Nisbett, Richard E. (1973). Undermining children's intrinsic interest with extrinsic reward: A test of the "overjustification" hypothesis. *Journal of Personality & Social Psychology, 28,* 129–137.

Lerner, Claire, & Dombro, Amy Laura. (2004). Finding your fit: Some temperament tips for parents. *Zero to Three, 24,* 42–45.

Lerner, Richard M., Theokas, Christina, & Bobek, Deborah L. (2005). Concepts and theories of human development: Historical and contemporary dimensions. In Marc H. Bornstein & Michael E. Lamb (Eds.), *Developmental science: An advanced textbook* (5th ed., pp. 3–43). Mahwah, NJ: Erlbaum.

Leve, Leslie D., & Chamberlain, Patricia. (2005). Association with delinquent peers: Intervention effects for youth in the juvenile justice system. *Journal of Abnormal Child Psychology, 33,* 339–347.

Levenson, Robert W., & Miller, Bruce L. (2007). Loss of cells—Loss of self: Frontotemporal lobar degeneration and human emotion. *Current Directions in Psychological Science, 16,* 289–294.

Levesque, Roger J. R. (2002). *Not by faith alone: Religion, law, and adolescence.* New York: New York University Press.

Levine, James A., Lanningham-Foster, Lorraine M., McCrady, Shelly K., Krizan, Alisa C., Olson, Leslie R., Kane, Paul H., et al. (2005, January 28). Interindividual variation in posture allocation: Possible role in human obesity. *Science, 307,* 584–586.

Levinson, Daniel J. (1978). *The seasons of a man's life.* New York: Knopf.

Levitt, Mary J. (2005). Social relations in childhood and adolescence: The convoy model perspective. *Human Development, 48,* 28–47.

Levitt, Mary J., Levitt, Jerome, Bustos, Gastón L, Crooks, Noel A., Santos, Jennifer D., Telan, Paige, et al. (2005). Patterns of social support in the middle childhood to early adolescent transition: Implications for adjustment. *Social Development, 14,* 398–420.

Levy, Becca, & Langer, Ellen. (1994). Aging free from negative stereotypes: Successful memory in China among the American deaf. *Journal of Personality & Social Psychology, 66,* 989–997.

Levy, Becca R., & Leifheit-Limson, Erica. (2009). The stereotype-matching effect: Greater influence on functioning when age stereotypes correspond to outcomes. *Psychology and Aging, 24,* 230–233.

Lewin, Kurt. (1943). Psychology and the process of group living. *Journal of Social Psychology, 17,* 113–131.

Lewis, Michael. (1997). *Altering fate: Why the past does not predict the future.* New York: Guilford Press.

Lewis, Michael, & Brooks, Jeanne. (1978). Self-knowledge and emotional development. In Michael Lewis & L. A. Rosenblum (Eds.), *Genesis of behavior: Vol. 1. The development of affect* (pp. 205–226). New York: Plenum Press.

Lewis, Michael, & Carmody, Dennis P. (2008). Self-representation and brain development. *Developmental Psychology, 44,* 1329–1334.

Lewis, Michael, & Ramsay, Douglas. (2005). Infant emotional and cortisol responses to goal blockage. *Child Development, 76,* 518–530.

Li, Qing. (2007). New bottle but old wine: A research of cyberbullying in schools. *Computers in Human Behavior, 23,* 1777–1791.

Lichtwarck-Aschoff, Anna, van Geert, Paul, Bosma, Harke, & Kunnen, Saskia. (2008). Time and identity: A framework for research and theory formation. *Developmental Review, 28,* 370–400.

Lieberman, Debra. (2006). Mate selection: Adaptive problems and evolved cognitive programs. In Patricia Noller & Judith A. Feeney (Eds.), *Close relationships: Functions, forms and processes* (pp. 245–266). Hove, England: Psychology Press/Taylor & Francis.

Lieu, Tracy A., Ray, G. Thomas, Black, Steven B., Butler, Jay C., Klein, Jerome O., Breiman, Robert F., et al. (2000). Projected cost-effectiveness of pneumococcal conjugate vaccination of healthy infants and young children. *Journal of the American Medical Association, 283,* 1460–1468.

Lillard, Angeline, & Else-Quest, Nicole. (2006, September 29). Evaluating Montessori education. *Science, 313,* 1893–1894.

Lillard, Angeline Stoll. (2005). *Montessori: The science behind the genius.* New York: Oxford University Press.

Lin, I-Fen. (2008a). Consequences of parental divorce for adult children's support of their frail parents. *Journal of Marriage and Family, 70,* 113–128.

Lin, I-Fen. (2008b). Mother and daughter reports about upward transfers. *Journal of Marriage and Family, 70,* 815–827.

Lin, I-Fen, Goldman, Noreen, Weinstein, Maxine, Lin, Yu-Hsuan, Gorrindo, Tristan, & Seeman, Teresa. (2003). Gender differences in adult children's support of their parents in Taiwan. *Journal of Marriage and Family, 65,* 184–200.

Lindauer, Martin S. (2003). *Aging, creativity, and art: A positive perspective on late-life development.* New York: Plenum.

Lindenberger, Ulman. (2001). Lifespan theories of cognitive development. In Neil J. Smelser & Paul B. Baltes (Eds.), *International encyclopedia of the social & behavioral sciences* (pp. 8848–8854). Oxford, England: Elsevier.

Lindenberger, Ulman, Lövdén, Martin, Schellenbach, Michael, Li, Shu-Chen, & Krüger, Antonio. (2008). Psychological principles of successful aging technologies: A mini-review. *Gerontology, 54,* 59–68.

Lindenberger, Ulman, & von Oertzen, Timo. (2006). Variability in cognitive aging: From taxonomy to theory. In Ellen Bialystok & Fergus I. M. Craik (Eds.), *Lifespan cognition: Mechanisms of change* (pp. 297–314). New York: Oxford University Press.

Lindfors, Kaj, Elovainio, Marko, Wickman, Sanna, Vuorinen, Risto, Sinkkonen, Jari, Dunkel, Leo, et al. (2007). Brief report: The role of ego development in psychosocial adjustment among boys with delayed puberty. *Journal of Research on Adolescence, 17,* 601–612.

Lindsay, Ronald A. (2008). *Future bioethics: Overcoming taboos, myths, and dogmas.* Amherst, NY: Prometheus Books.

Lippa, Katherine D., Klein, Helen Altman, & Shalin, Valerie L. (2008). Everyday expertise: Cognitive demands in diabetes self-management. *Human Factors, 50,* 112–120.

Lippa, Richard A. (2002). *Gender, nature, and nurture.* Mahwah, NJ: Erlbaum.

Liptak, Gregory S., Benzoni, Lauren B., Mruzek, Daniel W., Nolan, Karen W., Thingvoll, Melissa A., Wade, Christine M., et al. (2008). Disparities in diagnosis and access to health services for children with autism: Data from the National Survey of Children's Health. *Journal of Developmental & Behavioral Pediatrics, 29,* 152–160.

Little, Peter (Ed.). (2002). *Genetic destinies.* Oxford, England: Oxford University Press.

Litwin, Howard, & Shiovitz-Ezra, Sharon. (2006). The association between activity and well-being in later life: What really matters? *Ageing & Society, 26,* 225–242.

Liu, Cong, Spector, Paul E., & Shi, Lin. (2007). Cross-national job stress: A quantitative and qualitative study. *Journal of Organizational Behavior, 28,* 209–239.

Liu, David, Wellman, Henry M., Tardif, Twila, & Sabbagh, Mark A. (2008). Theory of mind development in Chinese children: A meta-analysis of false-belief understanding across cultures and languages. *Developmental Psychology, 44,* 523–531.

Liu, Hui-li, Wang, Hong-Chung, & Yang, Ming-Jen. (2006). Factors associated with an unusual increase in the elderly suicide rate in Taiwan. *International Journal of Geriatric Psychiatry, 21,* 1219–1221.

Liu, Peter Y., Swerdloff, Ronald S., Christenson, Peter D., Handelsman, David J., Wang, Christina, & Hormonal Male Contraception Summit Group. (2006). Rate, extent, and modifiers of spermatogenic recovery after hormonal male contraception: An integrated analysis. *Lancet, 367,* 1412–1420.

Liu, Ping. (2006). Community-based Chinese schools in Southern California: A survey of teachers. *Language, Culture and Curriculum, 19,* 237–246.

Lleras-Muney, Adriana. (2005). The relationship between education and adult mortality in the United States. *Review of Economic Studies, 72,* 189–221.

Lloyd-Sherlock, Peter (Ed.). (2004). *Living longer: Ageing, development and social protection.* London: Zed Books.

Lockhart, Kristi L., Chang, Bernard, & Story, Tyler. (2002). Young children's beliefs about the stability of traits: Protective optimism? *Child Development, 73,* 1408–1430.

Lockley, Steven W., Cronin, John W., Evans, Erin E., Cade, Brian E., Lee, Clark J., Landrigan, Christopher P., et al. (2004). Effect of reducing interns' weekly work hours on sleep and attentional failures. *New England Journal of Medicine, 351,* 1829–1837.

Loeb, Susanna, Fuller, Bruce, Kagan, Sharon Lynn, & Carrol, Bidemi. (2004). Child care in poor communities: Early learning effects of type, quality, and stability. *Child Development, 75,* 47–65.

Löfmark, Rurik, Nilstun, Tore, Cartwright, Colleen, Fischer, Susanne, van der Heide, Agnes, Mortier, Freddy, et al. (2008, February 12). *Physicians' experiences with end-of-life decision-making: Survey in 6 European countries and Australia.* Retrieved September 3, 2009, from http://www.biomedcentral.com/1741-7015/6/4

Loland, Sigmund. (2002). *Fair play in sport: A moral norm system.* London: Routledge.

Long, Lynellyn, & Oxfeld, Ellen (Eds.). (2004). *Coming home? Refugees, migrants, and those who stayed behind.* Philadelphia: University of Pennsylvania Press.

Longino, Charles F., Jr. (2005). The future of ageism: Baby boomers at the doorstep. *Generations, 29*(3), 79–83.

Lopez, Nestor L., Vazquez, Delia M., & Olson, Sheryl L. (2004). An integrative approach to the neurophysiological substrates of social withdrawal and aggression. *Development & Psychopathology, 16,* 69–93.

Lopez, Oscar L., Kuller, Lewis H., Becker, James T., Dulberg, Corinne, Sweet, Robert A., Gach, H. Michael, et al. (2007). Incidence of dementia in mild cognitive impairment in the cardiovascular health study cognition study. *Archives of Neurology, 64,* 416–420.

Lucas, Richard E., Clark, Andrew E., Georgellis, Yannis, & Diener, Ed. (2003). Reexamining adaptation and the set point model of happiness: Reactions to changes in marital status. *Journal of Personality and Social Psychology, 84,* 527–539.

Luciana, Monica. (2003). Cognitive development in children born preterm: Implications for theories of brain plasticity following early injury. *Development and Psychopathology, 15,* 1017–1047.

Ludden, Alison Bryant, & Eccles, Jacquelynne S. (2007). Psychosocial, motivational, and contextual profiles of youth reporting different patterns of substance use during adolescence. *Journal of Research on Adolescence, 17,* 51–88.

Ludington-Hoe, Susan M., Johnson, Mark W., Morgan, Kathy, Lewis, Tina, Gutman, Judy, Wilson, P. David, et al. (2006). Neurophysiologic assessment of neonatal sleep organization: Preliminary results of a randomized, controlled trial of skin contact with preterm infants. *Pediatrics, 117,* e909–923.

Luoh, Ming-Ching, & Herzog, A. Regula. (2002). Individual consequences of volunteer and paid work in old age: Health and mortality. *Journal of Health and Social Behavior 43,* 490–509.

Luthar, Suniya S. (2003). The culture of affluence: Psychological costs of material wealth. *Child Development, 74,* 1581–1593.

Luthar, Suniya S., Cicchetti, Dante, & Becker, Bronwyn. (2000). The construct of resilience: A critical evaluation and guidelines for future work. *Child Development, 71,* 543–562.

Luthar, Suniya S., D'Avanzo, Karen, & Hites, Sarah. (2003). Maternal drug abuse versus other psychological disturbances: Risks and resilience among children. In Suniya S. Luthar (Ed.), *Resilience and vulnerability: Adaptation in the context of childhood adversities* (pp. 104–129). New York: Cambridge University Press.

Luthar, Suniya S., & Zelazo, Laurel Bidwell. (2003). Research on resilience: An integrative review. In Suniya S. Luthar (Ed.), *Resilience and vulnerability: Adaptation in the context of childhood adversities* (pp. 510–549). New York: Cambridge University Press.

Lutsey, Pamela L., Diez Roux, Ana V., Jacobs, David R., Jr., Burke, Gregory L., Harman, Jane, Shea, Steven, et al. (2008). Associations of acculturation and socioeconomic status with subclinical cardiovascular disease in the Multi-Ethnic Study of Atherosclerosis. *American Journal of Public Health, 98,* 1963–1970.

Lutz, Donna J., & Sternberg, Robert J. (1999). Cognitive development. In Marc H. Bornstein & Michael E. Lamb (Eds.), *Developmental psychology: An advanced textbook* (4th ed., pp. 275–311). Mahwah, NJ: Erlbaum.

Lykken, David T. (2006). The mechanism of emergenesis. *Genes, Brain & Behavior, 5,* 306–310.

Lynch, Robert G. (2004). *Exceptional returns: Economic, fiscal, and social benefits of investment in early childhood development.* Washington, DC: Economic Policy Institute.

Lyng, Stephen (Ed.). (2005). *Edgework: The sociology of risk taking.* New York: Routledge.

Lynn, Richard, & Mikk, Jaan. (2007). National differences in intelligence and educational attainment. *Intelligence, 35,* 115–121.

Lynn, Richard, & Vanhanen, Tatu. (2002). *IQ and the wealth of nations.* Westport, CT: Praeger.

Lynne, Sarah D., Graber, Julia A., Nichols, Tracy R., Brooks-Gunn, Jeanne, & Botvin, Gilbert J. (2007). Links between pubertal timing, peer influences, and externalizing behaviors among urban students followed through middle school. *Journal of Adolescent Health, 40,* 181.e7–181.e13.

Lyons-Ruth, Karlen, Bronfman, Elisa, & Parsons, Elizabeth. (1999). IV. Maternal frightened, frightening, or atypical behavior and disorganized infant attachment patterns. *Monographs of the Society for Research in Child Development, 64*(3, Serial No. 258), 67–96.

Maas, Carl, Herrenkohl, Todd I., & Sousa, Cynthia. (2008). Review of research on child maltreatment and violence in youth. *Trauma, Violence & Abuse, 9,* 56–67.

Maccoby, Eleanor E. (1998). *The two sexes: Growing up apart, coming together.* Cambridge, MA: Belknap Press of Harvard University Press.

Maccoby, Eleanor E. (2000). Parenting and its effects on children: On reading and misreading behavior genetics. *Annual Review of Psychology, 51,* 1–27.

MacKay, Andrea P., Berg, Cynthia J., King, Jeffrey C., Duran, Catherine, & Chang, Jeani. (2006). Pregnancy-related mortality among women with multifetal pregnancies. *Obstetrics & Gynecology, 107,* 563–568.

Mackay, Judith, & Eriksen, Michael P. (2002). *The tobacco atlas.* Geneva, Switzerland: World Health Organization.

Maclean, Kim. (2003). The impact of institutionalization on child development. *Development and Psychopathology, 15,* 853–884.

Macmillan, Ross, & Copher, Ronda. (2005). Families in the life course: Interdependency of roles, role configurations, and pathways. *Journal of Marriage and Family, 67,* 858–879.

Madden, David J., & Whiting, Wythe L. (2004). Age-related changes in visual attention. In Paul T. Costa & Ilene C. Siegler (Eds.), *Recent advances in psychology and aging* (pp. 41–88). Amsterdam: Elsevier.

Maehara, Takeko, & Takemura, Akiko. (2007). The norms of filial piety and grandmother roles as perceived by grandmothers and their grandchildren in Japan and South Korea. *International Journal of Behavioral Development, 31,* 585–593.

Magill-Evans, Joyce, Harrison, Margaret J., Rempel, Gwen, & Slater, Linda. (2006). Interventions with fathers of young children: Systematic literature review. *Journal of Advanced Nursing, 55,* 248–264.

Magnusson, Roger S. (2004). Euthanasia: Above ground, below ground. *Journal of Medical Ethics, 30,* 441–446.

Maguen, Shira, Floyd, Frank J., Bakeman, Roger, & Armistead, Lisa. (2002). Developmental milestones and disclosure of sexual orientation among gay, lesbian, and bisexual youths. *Journal of Applied Developmental Psychology, 23,* 219–233.

Mahler, Margaret S., Pine, Fred, & Bergman, Anni. (1975). *The psychological birth of the human infant: Symbiosis and individuation.* New York: Basic Books.

Mahoney, Joseph L., Larson, Reed W., & Eccles, Jacquelynne S. (Eds.). (2005). *Organized activities as contexts of development: Extracurricular activities, after-school and community programs.* Mahwah, NJ: Erlbaum.

Malina, Robert M., Bouchard, Claude, & Bar-Or, Oded. (2004). *Growth, maturation, and physical activity* (2nd ed.). Champaign, IL: Human Kinetics.

Malone, Fergal D., Canick, Jacob A., Ball, Robert H., Nyberg, David A., Comstock, Christine H., Bukowski, Radek, et al. (2005). First-trimester or second-trimester screening, or both, for Down's syndrome. *New England Journal of Medicine, 353,* 2001–2011.

Mancini, Anthony D., & Bonanno, George A. (2006). Marital closeness, functional disability, and adjustment in late life. *Psychology and Aging, 21,* 600–610.

Mandemakers, Jornt J., & Dykstra, Pearl A. (2008). Discrepancies in parent's and adult child's reports of support and contact. *Journal of Marriage and Family, 70,* 495–506.

Mandler, Jean Matter. (2004). *The foundations of mind: Origins of conceptual thought.* Oxford, England: Oxford University Press.

Mange, Elaine Johansen, & Mange, Arthur P. (1999). *Basic human genetics* (2nd ed.). Sunderland, MA: Sinauer Associates.

Manini, Todd M., Everhart, James E., Patel, Kushang V., Schoeller, Dale A., Colbert, Lisa H., Visser, Marjolein, et al. (2006). Daily activity energy expenditure and mortality among older adults. *Journal of the American Medical Association, 296,* 171–179.

Manlove, Jennifer, Ryan, Suzanne, & Franzetta, Kerry. (2003). Patterns of contraceptive use within teenagers' first sexual relationships. *Perspectives on Sexual and Reproductive Health, 35,* 246–255.

Manly, Jody Todd, Kim, Jungmeen E., Rogosch, Fred A., & Cicchetti, Dante. (2001). Dimensions of child maltreatment and children's adjustment: Contributions of developmental timing and subtype. *Development & Psychopathology, 13,* 759–782.

Mann, Ronald D., & Andrews, Elizabeth B. (Eds.). (2007). *Pharmacovigilance* (2nd ed.). Hoboken, NJ: Wiley.

Manners, Paula Jean. (2009). Gender identity disorder in adolescence: A review of the literature. *Child and Adolescent Mental Health, 14,* 62–68.

Mannuzza, Salvatore, Klein, Rachel G., Truong, Nhan L., Moulton, John L., III, Roizen, Erica R., Howell, Kathryn H., et al. (2008). Age of methylphenidate treatment initiation in children with ADHD and later substance abuse: Prospective follow-up into adulthood. *American Journal of Psychiatry, 165,* 604–609.

Manzi, Claudia, Vignoles, Vivian L., Regalia, Camillo, & Scabini, Eugenia. (2006). Cohesion and enmeshment revisited: Differentiation, identity, and well-being in two European cultures. *Journal of Marriage and Family, 68,* 673–689.

Manzo, Kathleen Kennedy. (2007, March 14). Australia grapples with national content standards. *Education Week, 26,* 10.

Manzoli, Lamberto, Villari, Paolo, Pironec, Giovanni M., & Boccia, Antonio. (2007). Marital status and mortality in the elderly: A systematic review and meta-analysis. *Social Science & Medicine, 64,* 77–94.

Mao, Amy, Burnham, Melissa M., Goodlin-Jones, Beth L., Gaylor, Erika E., & Anders, Thomas F. (2004). A comparison of the sleep–wake patterns of cosleeping and solitary-sleeping infants. *Child Psychiatry and Human Development, 35,* 95–105.

March, John S., Franklin, Martin E., Leonard, Henrietta L., & Foa, Edna B. (2004). Obsessive-compulsive disorder. In Tracy L. Morris & John S. March (Eds.), *Anxiety disorders in children and adolescents* (2nd ed., pp. 212–240). New York: Guilford Press.

Marcia, James E. (1966). Development and validation of ego-identity status. *Journal of Personality & Social Psychology, 3,* 551–558.

Marcia, James E., Waterman, Alan S., Matteson, David R., Archer, Sally L., & Orlofsky, Jacob L. (1993). *Ego identity: A handbook for psychosocial research.* New York: Springer-Verlag.

Marcus, Gary. (2004). *The birth of the mind: How a tiny number of genes creates the complexities of human thought.* New York: Basic Books.

Marks, Amy Kerivan, Szalacha, Laura A., Lamarre, Meaghan, Boyd, Michelle J., & Coll, Cynthia García. (2007). Emerging ethnic identity and interethnic group social preferences in middle childhood: Findings from the Children of Immigrants Development in Context (CIDC) study. *International Journal of Behavioral Development, 31,* 501–513.

Markus, M. Andrea, & Morris, Brian J. (2008). Resveratrol in prevention and treatment of common clinical conditions of aging. *Clinical Interventions in Aging, 3,* 331–339.

Marlow–Ferguson, Rebecca (Ed.). (2002). *World education encyclopedia: A survey of educational systems worldwide* (2nd ed.). Detroit, MI: Gale Group.

Marmot, Michael G., & Fuhrer, Rebecca. (2004). Socioeconomic position and health across midlife. In Orville Gilbert Brim, Carol D. Ryff, & Ronald C. Kessler (Eds.), *How healthy are we? A national study of well-being at midlife* (pp. 64–89). Chicago: University of Chicago Press.

Marschark, Marc, & Spencer, Patricia Elizabeth (Eds.). (2003). *Oxford handbook of deaf studies, language, and education.* Oxford, England: Oxford University Press.

Marsiske, Michael, & Margrett, Jennifer A. (2006). Everyday problem solving and decision making. In James E. Birren & K. Warren Schaie (Eds.), *Handbook of the psychology of aging* (6th ed., pp. 315–342). Burlington, MA: Elsevier Academic Press.

Martel, Jane G. (1974). *Smashed potatoes: A kid's-eye view of the kitchen.* Boston: Houghton Mifflin.

Martin, Carol Lynn, Ruble, Diane N., & Szkrybalo, Joel. (2002). Cognitive theories of early gender development. *Psychological Bulletin, 128,* 903–933.

Martin, Joyce A., Hamilton, Brady E., Sutton, Paul D., Ventura, Stephanie J., Menacker, Fay, Kirmeyer, Sharon, et al. (2009). Births: Final data for 2006. *National Vital Statistics Reports, 57*(7).

Martin, Joyce A., Hamilton, Brady E., Ventura, Stephanie J., Menacker, Fay, Park, Melissa M., & Sutton, Paul D. (2002, December 18). Births: Final data for 2001. *National Vital Statistics Reports, 51*(2).

Martin, Mike, & Zimprich, Daniel. (2005). Cognitive development in midlife. In Sherry L. Willis & Mike Martin (Eds.), *Middle adulthood: A lifespan perspective* (pp. 179–206). Thousand Oaks, CA: Sage.

Martini, Mary. (1994). Peer interactions in Polynesia: A view from the Marquesas. In Jaipaul L. Roopnarine, James Ewald Johnson, & Frank H. Hooper (Eds.), *Children's play in diverse cultures* (pp. 73–103): State University of New York Press: Albany.

Martino, Steven C., Collins, Rebecca L., Elliott, Marc N., Strachman, Amy, Kanouse, David E., & Berry, Sandra H. (2006). Exposure to degrading versus nondegrading music lyrics and sexual behavior among youth. *Pediatrics, 118,* e430–441.

Marx, Jean. (2005, August 5). Preventing Alzheimer's: A lifelong commitment? *Science, 309,* 864–866.

Marx, Jean. (2007, January 19). Trafficking protein suspected in Alzheimer's disease. *Science, 315,* 314.

Mascie-Taylor, C. G. Nicholas, & Karim, Enamul. (2003, December 12). The burden of chronic disease. *Science, 302,* 1921–1922.

Mascolo, Michael F., Fischer, Kurt W., & Li, Jin. (2003). Dynamic development of component systems of emotions: Pride, shame, and guilt in China and the United States. In Richard J. Davidson, Klaus R. Scherer, & H. Hill Goldsmith (Eds.), *Handbook of affective sciences* (pp. 375–408). Oxford, England: Oxford University Press.

Maslow, Abraham H. (1954). *Motivation and personality.* New York: Harper.

Maslow, Abraham H. (1970). *Motivation and personality* (2nd ed.). New York: Harper & Row.

Mason, Robert A., Williams, Diane L., Kana, Rajesh K., Minshew, Nancy, & Just, Marcel Adam. (2008). Theory of Mind disruption and recruitment of the right hemisphere during narrative comprehension in autism. *Neuropsychologia, 46,* 269–280.

Masoro, Edward J. (1999). *Challenges of biological aging.* New York: Springer.

Masoro, Edward J. (2006). Are age-associated diseases an integral part of aging? In Edward J. Masoro & Steven N. Austad (Eds.), *Handbook of the biology of aging* (6th ed., pp. 43–62). Amsterdam: Elsevier Academic Press.

Masten, Ann S. (2004). Regulatory processes, risk, and resilience in adolescent development. In Ronald E. Dahl & Linda Patia Spear (Eds.), *Adolescent brain development: Vulnerabilities and opportunities* (Vol. 1021, pp. 310–319). New York: New York Academy of Sciences.

Masten, Ann S., & Coatsworth, J. Douglas. (1998). The development of competence in favorable and unfavorable environments: Lessons from research on successful children. *American Psychologist, 53,* 205–220.

Masten, Carrie L., Guyer, Amanda E., Hodgdon, Hilary B., McClure, Erin B., Charney, Dennis S., Ernst, Monique, et al. (2008). Recognition of facial emotions among maltreated children with high rates of post-traumatic stress disorder. *Child Abuse & Neglect, 32,* 139–153.

Mastro, Dana E., Behm-Morawitz, Elizabeth, & Kopacz, Maria A. (2008). Exposure to television portrayals of Latinos: The implications of aversive racism and social identity theory. *Human Communication Research, 34,* 1–27.

Masunaga, Hiromi, & Horn, John. (2001). Expertise and age-related changes in components of intelligence. *Psychology & Aging, 16,* 293–311.

Maton, Kenneth I., Schellenbach, Cynthia J., Leadbeater, Bonnie J., & Solarz, Andrea L. (Eds.). (2004). *Investing in children, youth, families, and communities: Strengths-based research and policy.* Washington, DC: American Psychological Association.

Matsumoto, David. (2004). Reflections on culture and competence. In Robert J. Sternberg & Elena L. Grigorenko (Eds.), *Culture and competence: Contexts of life success* (pp. 273–282). Washington, DC: American Psychological Association.

Matsumoto, David, & Yoo, Seung Hee. (2006). Toward a new generation of cross-cultural research. *Perspectives on Psychological Science, 1,* 234–250.

Matthews, Gerald, Zeidner, Moshe, & Roberts, Richard D. (2002). *Emotional intelligence: Science and myth.* Cambridge, MA: MIT Press.

Maughan, Angeline, & Cicchetti, Dante. (2002). Impact of child maltreatment and interadult violence on children's emotion regulation abilities and socioemotional adjustment. *Child Development, 73,* 1525–1542.

Maxfield, Molly, Pyszczynski, Tom, Kluck, Benjamin, Cox, Cathy R, Greenberg, Jeff, Solomon, Sheldon, et al. (2007). Age-related differences in responses to thoughts of one's own death: Mortality salience and judgments of moral transgressions. *Psychology and Aging, 22,* 341–353.

Mayberry, Rachel I., & Nicoladis, Elena. (2000). Gesture reflects language development: Evidence from bilingual children. *Current Directions in Psychological Science, 9,* 192–196.

Mayeux, Lara, & Cillessen, Antonius H. N. (2007). Peer influence and the development of antisocial behavior. In Rutger C. M. E. Engels, Margaret Kerr, & Håkan Stattin (Eds.), *Friends, lovers, and groups: Key relationships in adolescence* (pp. 33–46). Hoboken, NJ: Wiley.

Maynard, Ashley E. (2002). Cultural teaching: The development of teaching skills in Maya sibling interactions. *Child Development, 73,* 969–982.

McAdams, Dan P. (2006). The redemptive self: Generativity and the stories Americans live by. *Research in Human Development, 3,* 81–100.

McAdams, Dan P., Bauer, Jack J., Sakaeda, April R., Anyidoho, Nana Akua, Machado, Mary Anne, Magrino-Failla, Katie, et al. (2006). Continuity and change in the life story: A longitudinal study of autobiographical memories in emerging adulthood. *Journal of Personality, 74,* 1371–1400.

McCarter, Roger J. M. (2006). Differential aging among skeletal muscles. In Edward J. Masoro & Steven N. Austad (Eds.), *Handbook of the biology of aging* (6th ed., pp. 470–497). Amsterdam: Elsevier Academic Press.

McCloskey, Laura Ann, & Stuewig, Jeffrey. (2001). The quality of peer relationships among children exposed to family violence. *Development & Psychopathology, 13,* 83–96.

McCrae, Robert R., & Allik, Jüri (Eds.). (2002). *The five-factor model of personality across cultures.* New York: Kluwer.

McCrae, Robert R., & Costa, Paul T. (2003). *Personality in adulthood: A five-factor theory perspective* (2nd ed.). New York: Guilford Press.

McElroy, Mary. (2002). *Resistance to exercise: A social analysis of inactivity.* Champaign, IL: Human Kinetics.

McGrath, Susan K., & Kennell, John H. (2008). A randomized controlled trial of continuous labor support for middle-class couples: Effect on cesarean delivery rates. *Birth: Issues in Perinatal Care, 35,* 92–97.

McKusick, Victor A. (2007). Mendelian Inheritance in Man and its online version, OMIM. *American Journal of Human Genetics, 80,* 588–604.

McLachlan, Hugh V. (2008). The ethics of killing and letting die: Active and passive euthanasia. *Journal of Medical Ethics, 34,* 636–638.

McLanahan, Sara, Donahue, Elisabeth, & Haskins, Ron (Eds.). (2005). *The future of children: Marriage and child wellbeing.* Washington, DC: Brookings Institution.

McLeod, Bryce D., Wood, Jeffrey J., & Weisz, John R. (2007). Examining the association between parenting and childhood anxiety: A meta-analysis. *Clinical Psychology Review, 27,* 155–172.

McLeod, Peter, Sommerville, Peter, & Reed, Nick. (2005). Are automated actions beyond conscious access? In John Duncan, Peter McLeod, & Louise H. Phillips (Eds.), *Measuring the mind: Speed, control, and age* (pp. 359–372). New York: Oxford University Press.

McLoyd, Vonnie C., Aikens, Nikki L., & Burton, Linda M. (2006). Childhood poverty, policy, and practice. In William Damon & Richard M. Lerner (Series Eds.) & K. Ann Renninger & Irving E. Sigel (Vol. Eds.), *Handbook of child psychology: Vol. 4. Child psychology in practice* (6th ed., pp. 700–775). Hoboken, NJ: Wiley.

McLoyd, Vonnie C., Kaplan, Rachel, Hardaway, Cecily R., & Wood, Dana. (2007). Does endorsement of physical discipline matter? Assessing moderating influences on the maternal and child psychological correlates of physical discipline in African American families. *Journal of Family Psychology, 21,* 165–175.

McNeil, Michele. (2007, May). Rigorous courses, fresh enrollment. *Education Week, 26,* 28–31.

McPherson, Miller, Smith-Lovin, Lynn, & Cook, James M. (2001). Birds of a feather: Homophily in social networks. *Annual Review of Sociology, 27,* 415–444.

McWhinnie, Chad, Abela, John R. Z., Hilmy, Nora, & Ferrer, Ilyan. (2008). Positive youth development programs: An alternative approach to the prevention of depression in children and adolescents. In John R. Z. Abela & Benjamin L. Hankin (Eds.), *Handbook of depression in children and adolescents* (pp. 354–373). New York: Guilford Press.

Meadows, Sara. (2006). *The child as thinker: The development and acquisition of cognition in childhood* (2nd ed.). New York: Routledge.

Medscape Psychiatry & Mental Health. (2005). *Autism first-hand: An expert interview with Temple Grandin, PhD.* Retrieved July 6, 2009, from http://cme.medscape.com/viewarticle/498153

Meier, Ann, & Allen, Gina. (2008). Intimate relationship development during the transition to adulthood: Differences by social class. *New Directions for Child and Adolescent Development, 2008,* 25–39.

Meisami, Esmail. (1994). Aging of the sensory systems. In Paola S. Timiras (Ed.), *Physiological basis of aging and geriatrics* (2nd ed., pp. 115–132). Boca Raton, FL: CRC Press.

Meisami, Esmail, Brown, Chester M., & Emerle, Henry F. (2003). Sensory systems: Normal aging, disorders, and treatments of vision and hearing in humans. In Paola S. Timiras (Ed.), *Physiological basis of aging and geriatrics* (3rd ed., pp. 141–165). Boca Raton, FL: CRC Press.

Melhuish, Edward, & Petrogiannis, Konstantinos. (2006). An international overview of early childhood care and education. In Edward Melhuish & Konstantinos Petrogiannis (Eds.), *Early childhood care and education: International perspectives* (pp. 167–178). London: Routledge.

Mello, Zena R. (2008). Gender variation in developmental trajectories of educational and occupational expectations and attainment from adolescence to adulthood. *Developmental Psychology, 44,* 1069–1080.

Mellor, M. Joanna, & Brownell, Patricia J. (Eds.). (2006). *Elder abuse and mistreatment: Policy, practice, and research.* New York: Haworth Press.

Meltzoff, Andrew N. (2007). 'Like me': A foundation for social cognition. *Developmental Science, 10,* 126–134.

Meltzoff, Andrew N., & Moore, M. Keith. (1999). A new foundation for cognitive development in infancy: The birth of the representational infant. In Ellin Kofsky Scholnick, Katherine Nelson, Susan A. Gelman, & Patricia H. Miller (Eds.), *Conceptual development: Piaget's legacy* (pp. 53–78). Mahwah, NJ: Erlbaum.

Mendle, Jane, Turkheimer, Eric, & Emery, Robert E. (2007). Detrimental psychological outcomes associated with early pubertal timing in adolescent girls. *Developmental Review, 27,* 151–171.

Menesini, Ersilia, Eslea, Mike, Smith, Peter K., Genta, Maria Luisa, Giannetti, Enrichetta, Fonzi, Ada, et al. (1997). Cross-national comparison of children's attitudes towards bully/victim problems in school. *Aggressive Behavior, 23,* 245–257.

Menon, Usha. (2001). Middle adulthood in cultural perspectives: The imagined and the experienced in three cultures. In Margie E. Lachman (Ed.), *Handbook of midlife development* (pp. 40–74). New York: Wiley.

Merline, Alicia C., O'Malley, Patrick M., Schulenberg, John E., Bachman, Jerald G., & Johnston, Lloyd D. (2004). Substance use among adults 35 years of age: Prevalence, adulthood predictors, and impact of adolescent substance use. *American Journal of Public Health, 94,* 96–102.

Merrell, Kenneth W., & Gimpel, Gretchen A. (1998). *Social skills of children and adolescents: Conceptualization, assessment, treatment.* Mahwah, NJ: Erlbaum.

Mervis, Jeffrey. (2006, May 19). Well-balanced panel to tackle algebra reform. *Science, 312,* 982.

Mesquita, Batja, & Leu, Janxin. (2007). The cultural psychology of emotion. In Shinobu Kitayama & Dov Cohen (Eds.), *Handbook of cultural psychology* (pp. 734–759). New York: Guilford Press.

Messer, Karen, Trinidad, Dennis R., Al-Delaimy, Wael K., & Pierce, John P. (2008). Smoking cessation rates in the United States: A comparison of young adult and older smokers. *American Journal of Public Health, 98,* 317–322.

Michaud, Catherine, Murray, Christopher J. L., & Bloom, Barry R. (2001). Burden of disease—Implications for future research. *Journal of the American Medical Association, 285,* 535–539.

Michaud, Pierre-Andre, Chossis, Isabelle, & Suris, Joan-Carles. (2006). Health-related behavior: Current situation, trends, and prevention. In Sandy Jackson & Luc Goossens (Eds.), *Handbook of adolescent development* (pp. 284–307). Hove, East Sussex, UK: Psychology Press.

Michels, Tricia M., Kropp, Rhonda Y., Eyre, Stephen L., & Halpern-Felsher, Bonnie L. (2005). Initiating sexual experiences: How do young adolescents make decisions regarding early sexual activity? *Journal of Research on Adolescence, 15,* 583–607.

Mikels, Joseph A., Larkin, Gregory R., Reuter-Lorenz, Patricia A., & Cartensen, Laura L. (2006). Divergent trajectories in the aging mind: Changes in working memory for affective versus visual information with age. *Psychology and Aging, 20,* 542–553.

Milardo, Robert M. (2005). Generative uncle and nephew relationships. *Journal of Marriage and Family, 67,* 1226–1236.

Miller, Fiona Alice, Robert, Jason Scott, & Hayeems, Robin Z. (2009). Questioning the consensus: Managing carrier status results generated by newborn screening. *American Journal of Public Health, 99,* 210–215.

Miller, Greg. (2003, April 4). Spying on the brain, one neuron at a time. *Science, 300,* 78–79.

Miller, Greg. (2005, May 13). Reflecting on another's mind. *Science, 308,* 945–947.

Miller, Joan G. (2004). The cultural deep structure of psychological theories of social development. In Robert J. Sternberg & Elena L. Grigorenko (Eds.), *Culture and competence: Contexts of life success* (pp. 111–138). Washington, DC: American Psychological Association.

Miller, Patricia H. (2002). *Theories of developmental psychology* (4th ed.). New York: Worth.

Miller, Patricia Y., & Simon, William. (1980). The development of sexuality in adolescence. In Joseph Adelson (Ed.), *Handbook of adolescent psychology* (pp. 383–407). New York: Wiley.

Miller, Richard A. (2005, June 24). The anti-aging sweepstakes: Catalase runs for the ROSes. *Science, 308,* 1875–1876.

Miller, Suzanne M., McDaniel, Susan H., Rolland, John S., & Feetham, Suzanne L. (Eds.). (2006). *Individuals, families,* *and the new era of genetics: Biopsychosocial perspectives.* New York: Norton.

Miller, Thomas E., Bender, Barbara E., & Schuh, John H. (Eds.). (2005). *Promoting reasonable expectations: Aligning student and institutional views of the college experience.* San Francisco: Jossey-Bass.

Miller, William R., & Thoresen, Carl E. (2003). Spirituality, religion, and health: An emerging research field. *American Psychologist, 58,* 24–35.

Milosevic, Dragoslav P., Kostic, S., Potic, B., Kalašić, A., Svorcan, Petar, Bojic, Daniela, et al. (2007). Is there such thing as "reversible dementia" (RD)? *Archives of Gerontology and Geriatrics, 44,* 271–277.

Minkler, Meredith, & Holstein, Martha B. (2008). From civil rights to . . . civic engagement? Concerns of two older critical gerontologists about a "new social movement" and what it portends. *Journal of Aging Studies, 22,* 196–204.

Mintz, Toben H. (2005). Linguistic and conceptual influences on adjective acquisition in 24- and 36-month-olds. *Developmental Psychology, 41,* 17–29.

MMWR. (1996, September 27). Youth risk behavior surveillance—United States, 1995. *MMWR Surveillance Summaries, 45*(SS-4), 1–83.

MMWR. (1998, August 14). Youth risk behavior surveillance—United States, 1997. *MMWR Surveillance Summaries, 47*(SS-3).

MMWR. (2000, December 22). Blood lead levels in young children—United States and selected states, 1996–1999. *Morbidity and Mortality Weekly Report, 49,* 1133–1137.

MMWR. (2002, April 5). Alcohol use among women of childbearing age—United States, 1991–1999. *Morbidity and Mortality Weekly Report, 51*(13), 273–276.

MMWR. (2003, June 13). Varicella-related deaths—United States, 2002. *Morbidity and Mortality Weekly Report, 52,* 545–547.

MMWR. (2004, July 2). Therapeutic foster care for the prevention of violence: A report on recommendations of the Task Force on Community Preventive Services. *MMWR Recommendations and Reports, 53*(RR10), 1–8.

MMWR. (2005, January 14). Reducing childhood asthma through community-based service delivery—New York City, 2001–2004. *Morbidity and Mortality Weekly Report, 54,* 11–14.

MMWR. (2005, May 27). Blood lead levels—United States, 1999–2002. *Morbidity and Mortality Weekly Report, 54,* 513–516.

MMWR. (2006, June 9). Youth risk behavior surveillance—United States, 2005. *MMWR Surveillance Summaries, 55*(SS05), 1–108.

MMWR. (2006, October 20). ST-prevention counseling practices and human papillomavirus opinions among clinicians with adolescent patients—United States, 2004. *Morbidity and Mortality Weekly Report, 55*(41), 1117–1120.

MMWR. (2007, February 9). Prevalence of autism spectrum disorders—Autism and Developmental Disabilities Monitoring Network, six sites, United States, 2000. *MMWR Surveillance Summaries, 56*(SS01), 1–11.

MMWR. (2007, March 16). Fruit and vegetable consumption among adults—United States, 2005. *Morbidity and Mortality Weekly Report, 56*(10), 213–217.

MMWR. (2007, June 8). Assisted reproductive technology surveillance—United States, 2004. *Morbidity and Mortality Weekly Report Surveillance Summaries, 56*(SS06), 1–22.

MMWR. (2008, January 18). School-associated student homicides—United States, 1992–2006. *Morbidity and Mortality Weekly Report, 57*(2), 33–36.

MMWR. (2008, June 6). Youth risk behavior surveillance—United States, 2007. *MMWR Surveillance Summaries, 57*(SS04), 1–131.

MMWR. (2008, July 18). State-specific prevalence of obesity among adults—United States, 2007. *Morbidity and Mortality Weekly Report, 57*(28), 765–768.

MMWR. (2008, August 22). Update: Measles—United States, January–July 2008. *Morbidity and Mortality Weekly Report, 57*(33), 893–928.

MMWR. (2008, October 3). Racial/ethnic disparities in self-rated health status among adults with and without disabilities—United States, 2004–2006. *Morbidity and Mortality Weekly Report, 57*(39), 1069–1073.

Moen, Phyllis, & Spencer, Donna. (2006). Converging divergences in age, gender, health, and well-being: Strategic selection in the third age. In Robert H. Binstock & Linda K. George (Eds.), *Handbook of aging and the social sciences* (6th ed., pp. 127–144). Amsterdam: Elsevier.

Moen, Phyllis, Sweet, Stephen, & Swisher, Raymond. (2005). Embedded career clocks: The case of retirement planning. In Ross Macmillan (Ed.), *The structure of the life course: Standardized? Individualized? Differentiated?* (pp. 237–265). Greenwich, CT: Elsevier/JAI Press.

Moffat, Scott D. (2005). Effects of testosterone on cognitive and brain aging in elderly men. In Richard G. Cutler, S. Mitchell Harman, Chris Heward, & Mike Gibbons (Eds.), *Longevity health sciences: The Phoenix conference* (Vol. 1055, pp. 80–92). New York: New York Academy of Sciences.

Moffitt, Terrie E. (1997). Adolescence-limited and life-course-persistent offending: A complementary pair of developmental theories. In Terence P. Thornberry (Ed.), *Developmental theories of crime and delinquency* (pp. 11–54). New Brunswick, NJ: Transaction.

Moffitt, Terrie E. (2003). Life-course-persistent and adolescence-limited antisocial behavior: A 10-year research review and a research agenda. In Benjamin B. Lahey, Terrie E. Moffitt, & Avshalom Caspi (Eds.), *Causes of conduct disorder and juvenile delinquency* (pp. 49–75). New York: Guilford Press.

Moffitt, Terrie E., Caspi, Avshalom, & Rutter, Michael. (2006). Measured gene–environment interactions in psychopathology: Concepts, research strategies, and implications for research, intervention, and public understanding of genetics. *Perspectives on Psychological Science, 1,* 5–27.

Moffitt, Terrie E., Caspi, Avshalom, Rutter, Michael, & Silva, Phil A. (2001). *Sex differences in antisocial behaviour: Conduct disorder, delinquency, and violence in the Dunedin Longitudinal Study.* New York: Cambridge University Press.

Monastersky, Richard. (2007, January 12). Who's minding the teenage brain? *Chronicle of Higher Education, 53,* A14–A18.

Monroe, Scott M., Slavich, George M., Torres, Leandro D., & Gotlib, Ian H. (2007). Severe life events predict specific patterns of change in cognitive biases in major depression. *Psychological Medicine, 37*(6), 863–871.

Monserud, Maria A. (2008). Intergenerational relationships and affectual solidarity between grandparents and young adults. *Journal of Marriage and Family, 70,* 182–195.

Monteiro, Carlos A., Conde, Wolney L., & Popkin, Barry M. (2004). The burden of disease from undernutrition and overnutrition in countries undergoing rapid nutrition transition: A view from Brazil. *American Journal of Public Health, 94,* 433–434.

Monteiro, Carlos A., Conde, Wolney L., & Popkin, Barry M. (2007). Income-specific trends in obesity in Brazil: 1975–2003. *American Journal of Public Health, 97,* 1808–1812.

Montessori, Maria. (1966). *The secret of childhood* (M. Joseph Costelloe, Trans.). Notre Dame, IN: Fides. (Original work published 1936)

Moody, Harry R. (2001–2002). Who's afraid of life extension? *Generations, 25*(4), 33–37.

Moody, Raymond A. (1975). *Life after life: The investigation of a phenomenon—Survival of bodily death.* Atlanta, GA: Mockingbird Books.

Moore, Celia L. (2002). On differences and development. In David J. Lewkowicz & Robert Lickliter (Eds.), *Conceptions of development: Lessons from the laboratory* (pp. 57–76). New York: Psychology Press.

Moore, Ginger A., & Calkins, Susan D. (2004). Infants' vagal regulation in the still-face paradigm is related to dyadic coordination of mother–infant interaction. *Developmental Psychology, 40,* 1068–1080.

Moore, Keith L., & Persaud, Trivedi V. N. (2003). *The developing human: Clinically oriented embryology* (7th ed.). Philadelphia: Saunders.

Moore, Keith L., & Persaud, Trivedi V. N. (2007). *The developing human: Clinically oriented embryology* (8th ed.). Philadelphia: Saunders/Elsevier.

Moore, Susan, & Rosenthal, Doreen. (2006). *Sexuality in adolescence: Current trends* (2nd ed.). New York: Routledge.

Morales, Alvaro. (2008). The use of hormonal therapy in "andropause": The pro side. *Canadian Urological Association Journal, 2,* 43–46.

Morelli, Gilda A., & Rothbaum, Fred. (2007). Situating the child in context: Attachment relationships and self-regulation in different cultures. In Shinobu Kitayama & Dov Cohen (Eds.), *Handbook of cultural psychology* (pp. 500–527). New York: Guilford Press.

Morgan, Craig, Kirkbride, James, Leff, Julian, Craig, Tom, Hutchinson, Gerard, McKenzie, Kwame, et al. (2007). Parental separation, loss and psychosis in different ethnic groups: A case-control study. *Psychological Medicine, 37,* 495–503.

Morgan, Ian G. (2003). The biological basis of myopic refractive error. *Clinical and Experimental Optometry, 86,* 276–288.

Morris, Amanda Sheffield, Silk, Jennifer S., Steinberg, Laurence, Myers, Sonya S., & Robinson, Lara Rachel. (2007). The role of the family context in the development of emotion regulation. *Social Development, 16,* 361–388.

Morris, Pamela, & Kalil, Ariel. (2006). Out-of-school time use during middle childhood in a low-income sample: Do combinations of activities affect achievement and behavior? In Aletha C. Huston & Marika N. Ripke (Eds.), *Developmental contexts in middle childhood: Bridges to adolescence and adulthood* (pp. 237–259). New York: Cambridge University Press.

Morrison, India. (2002). Mirror neurons and cultural transmission. In Maxim I. Stamenov & Vittorio Gallese (Eds.), *Mirror neurons and the evolution of brain and language* (pp. 333–340). Amsterdam: John Benjamins.

Morrow, Daniel G., Ridolfo, Heather E., Menard, William E., Sanborn, Adam, Stine-Morrow, Elizabeth A. L., Magnor, Cliff, et al. (2003). Environmental support promotes expertise-based mitigation of age differences on pilot communication tasks. *Psychology & Aging, 18,* 268–284.

Morrow-Howell, Nancy, & Freedman, Marc. (2006–2007). Bringing civic engagement into sharper focus. *Generations, 30*(4), 6–9.

Moscovitch, Morris, Fernandes, Myra, & Troyer, Angela. (2001). Working-with-memory and cognitive resources: A component-process account of divided attention and memory. In Moshe Naveh-Benjamin, Morris Moscovitch, & Henry L. Roediger (Eds.), *Perspectives on human memory and cognitive aging: Essays in honour of Fergus Craik* (pp. 171–192). New York: Psychology Press.

Moshman, David. (2005). *Adolescent psychological development: Rationality, morality, and identity* (2nd ed.). Mahwah, NJ: Erlbaum.

Moshman, David, & Geil, Molly. (1998). Collaborative reasoning: Evidence for collective rationality. *Thinking & Reasoning, 4,* 231–248.

Moss, Ellen, Cyr, Chantal, & Dubois-Comtois, Karine. (2004). Attachment at early school age and developmental risk: Examining family contexts and behavior problems of controlling-caregiving, controlling-punitive, and behaviorally disorganized children. *Developmental Psychology, 40,* 519–532.

Moster, Dag, Lie, Rolv T., Irgens, Lorentz M., Bjerkedal, Tor, & Markestad, Trond. (2001). The association of Apgar score with subsequent death and cerebral palsy: A population-based study in term infants. *Journal of Pediatrics, 138,* 798–803.

Mowbray, Carol T., Megivern, Deborah, Mandiberg, James M., Strauss, Shari, Stein, Catherine H., Collins, Kim, et al. (2006). Campus mental health services: Recommendations for change. *American Journal of Orthopsychiatry, 76,* 226–237.

Mroczek, Daniel K., Spiro, Avion, III, & Griffin, Paul W. (2006). Personality and aging. In James E. Birren & K. Warner Schaie (Eds.), *Handbook of the psychology of aging* (6th ed., pp. 363–377). Amsterdam: Elsevier.

Mueller, Margaret M., & Elder, Glen H. (2003). Family contingencies across the generations: Grandparent–grandchild relationships in holistic perspective. *Journal of Marriage and Family, 65,* 404–417.

Mueller, Trisha E., Gavin, Lorrie E., & Kulkarni, Aniket. (2008). The association between sex education and youth's engagement in sexual intercourse, age at first intercourse, and birth control use at first sex. *The Journal of Adolescent Health, 42,* 89–96.

Muennig, Peter, & Woolf, Steven H. (2007). Health and economic benefits of reducing the number of students per classroom in U.S. primary schools. *American Journal of Public Health, 97,* 2020–2027.

Mukamal, Kenneth J., Lumley, Thomas, Luepker, Russell V., Lapin, Pauline, Mittleman, Murray A., McBean, A. Marshall, et al. (2006). Alcohol consumption in older adults and Medicare costs. *Health Care Financing Review, 27,* 49–61.

Mukesh, Bickol N., Dimitrov, Peter N., Leikin, Sophia, Wang, Jie J., Mitchell, Paul, McCarty, Catherine A., et al. (2004). Five-year incidence of age-related maculopathy: The Visual Impairment Project. *Ophthalmology, 111,* 1176–1182.

Mullis, Ina V. S., Martin, Michael O., Gonzalez, Eugenio J., & Chrostowski, Steven J. (2004). *TIMSS 2003 international mathematics report: Findings from IEA's Trends in International Mathematics and Science Study at the eighth and fourth grades.* Chestnut Hill, MA: TIMSS & PIRLS International Study Center, Lynch School of Education, Boston College.

Munakata, Yuko. (2006). Information processing approaches to development. In William Damon & Richard M. Lerner (Series Eds.) & Deanna Kuhn & Robert S. Siegler (Vol. Eds.), *Handbook of child psychology: Vol. 2. Cognition, perception, and language* (6th ed., pp. 426–463). Hoboken, NJ: Wiley.

Munroe, Robert L., & Romney, A. Kimbal. (2006). Gender and age differences in same-sex aggregation and social behavior: A four-culture study. *Journal of Cross-Cultural Psychology, 37,* 3–19.

Murabito, Joanne M., Pencina, Michael J., Zhu, Lei, Kelly-Hayes, Margaret, Shrader, Peter, & D'Agostino, Ralph B., Sr. (2008). Temporal trends in self-reported functional limitations and physical disability among the community-dwelling elderly population: The Framingham Heart Study. *American Journal of Public Health, 98,* 1256–1262.

Muraco, Anna. (2006). Intentional families: Fictive kin ties between cross-gender, different sexual orientation friends. *Journal of Marriage and Family, 68,* 1313–1325.

Murphy, Laura M. Bennett, Laurie-Rose, Cynthia, Brinkman, Tara M., & McNamara, Kelly A. (2007). Sustained attention and social competence in typically developing preschool-aged children. *Early Child Development and Care, 177,* 133–149.

Murray, Christopher J. L., Kulkarni, Sandeep C., Michaud, Catherine, Tomijima, Niels, Bulzacchelli, Maria T., Iandiorio, Terrell J., et al. (2006). Eight Americas: Investigating mortality disparities across races, counties, and race-counties in the United States. *PLoS Medicine, 3*(9), e260.

Murray, Lynne, Halligan, Sarah L., Adams, Gillian, Patterson, Paul, & Goodyer, Ian M. (2006). Socioemotional development in adolescents at risk for depression: The role of maternal depression and attachment style. *Development and Psychopathology, 18,* 489–516.

Musick, Kelly. (2002). Planned and unplanned childbearing among unmarried women. *Journal of Marriage and Family, 64,* 915–929.

Musick, Marc A., Herzog, A. Regula, & House, James S. (1999). Volunteering and mortality among older adults: Findings from a national sample. *Journals of Gerontology: Series B: Psychological Sciences & Social Sciences, 54B,* S173–S180.

Muter, Valerie, Hulme, Charles, Snowling, Margaret J., & Stevenson, Jim. (2004). Phonemes, rimes, vocabulary, and grammatical skills as foundations of early reading development: Evidence from a longitudinal study. *Developmental Psychology, 40,* 665–681.

Myers, David G. (2002). *Intuition: Its powers and perils.* New Haven, CT: Yale University Press.

Nair, K. Sreekumaran, Rizza, Robert A., O'Brien, Peter, Dhatariya, Ketan, Short, Kevin R., Nehra, Ajay, et al. (2006). DHEA in elderly women and DHEA or testosterone in elderly men. *New England Journal of Medicine, 355,* 1647–1659.

National Center for Education Statistics. (2007). *Digest of Education Statistics.* Retrieved September 11, 2009, from http://nces.ed.gov/programs/digest/d07/tables/dt07_041.asp

National Center for Health Statistics. (2000, September 21). Deaths: Final data for 1999. *National Vital Statistics Reports, 49*(8).

National Center for Health Statistics. (2007). Births: Final data for 2005. *National Vital Statistics Reports, 56*(6), 1–104.

National Center for Health Statistics. (2007). *Health, United States, 2007, with chartbook on trends in the health of Americans* (DHSS Publication No. 2007–1232). Hyattsville, MD: Author.

National Center for Health Statistics. (2008). *Prevalence of overweight among children and adolescents: United States, 2003–2004.* Retrieved August 2, 2009, from http://www.cdc.gov/nchs/products/pubs/pubd/hestats/overweight/overwght_child_03.htm

National Center for Health Statistics. (2009). *Health, United States, 2008 with chartbook with special feature on the health of young adults* (DHHS Publication No. 2009-1232). Hyattsville, MD: Author.

National Center for Health Statistics. (n.d.). *Difficulty in physical functioning, ages 18+: US, 1997–2007.* Retrieved September 5, 2009, from http://205.207.175.93/hdi/TableViewer/tableView.aspx?Reportid=641

National Center for Public Policy and Higher Education. (2008). *Measuring up 2008.* Retrieved August 25, 2009, from http://measuringup2008.highereducation.org/

National Heart, Lung, and Blood Institute. (n.d.). *Body mass index table.* Retrieved September 14, 2009, from http://www.nhlbi.nih.gov/guidelines/obesity/bmi_tbl.htm

National Highway Traffic Safety Administration. (2008). *Traffic safety facts: 2007 Data: Pedestrians* (DOT HS 810 994). Washington, DC: Author.

National Institute of Child Health Human Development Study of Early Child Care and Youth Development Network. (2003). Frequency and intensity of activity of third-grade children in physical education. *Archives of Pediatrics & Adolescent Medicine, 157,* 185–190.

Neave, Nick. (2008). *Hormones and behaviour: A psychological approach.* New York: Cambridge University Press.

Nelson, Charles A. (2007). A neurobiological perspective on early human deprivation. *Child Development Perspectives, 1,* 13–18.

Nelson, Charles A., de Haan, Michelle, & Thomas, Kathleen M. (2006b). *Neuroscience of cognitive development: The role of experience and the developing brain.* Hoboken, NJ: Wiley.

Nelson, Charles A., III, Thomas, Kathleen M., & de Haan, Michelle. (2006a). Neural bases of cognitive development. In William Damon & Richard M. Lerner (Series Eds.) & Deanna

Kuhn & Robert S. Siegler (Vol. Eds.), *Handbook of child psychology: Vol. 2. Cognition, perception, and language* (6th ed., pp. 3–57). Hoboken, NJ: Wiley.

Nelson, Charles A., III, Zeanah, Charles H., Fox, Nathan A., Marshall, Peter J., Smyke, Anna T., & Guthrie, Donald. (2007, December 21). Cognitive recovery in socially deprived young children: The Bucharest Early Intervention Project. *Science, 318,* 1937–1940.

Nesdale, Drew. (2004). Social identity processes and children's ethnic prejudice. In Mark Bennett & Fabio Sani (Eds.), *The development of the social self* (pp. 219–245). Hove, East Sussex, England: Psychology Press.

Nesselroade, John R., & Molenaar, Peter C. M. (2003). Quantitative models for developmental processes. In Jaan Valsiner & Kevin J. Connolly (Eds.), *Handbook of developmental psychology* (pp. 622–639). Thousand Oaks, CA: Sage.

Neugarten, Bernice L., & Neugarten, Dail A. (1986). Changing meanings of age in the aging society. In Alan J. Pifer & Lydia Bronte (Eds.), *Our aging society: Paradox and promise* (pp. 33–52). New York: Norton.

Nevin, Rick. (2007). Understanding international crime trends: The legacy of preschool lead exposure. *Environmental Research, 104,* 315–336.

Newschaffer, Craig J., Falb, Matthew D., & Gurney, James G. (2005). National autism prevalence trends from United States special education data. *Pediatrics, 115,* e277–282.

Ng, Nawi, Weinehall, Lars, & Öhman, Ann. (2007). 'If I don't smoke, I'm not a real man'—Indonesian teenage boys' views about smoking. *Health Education Research, 22,* 794–804.

Nguyen, Simone P., & Murphy, Gregory L. (2003). An apple is more than just a fruit: Cross-classification in children's concepts. *Child Development, 74,* 1783–1806.

NICHD Early Child Care Research Network. (2001). Child care and children's peer interaction at 24 and 36 months: The NICHD Study of Early Child Care. *Child Development, 72,* 1478–1500.

NICHD Early Child Care Research Network. (2003a). Do children's attention processes mediate the link between family predictors and school readiness? *Developmental Psychology, 39,* 581–593.

NICHD Early Child Care Research Network. (2003b). Does amount of time spent in child care predict socioemotional adjustment during the transition to kindergarten? *Child Development, 74,* 976–1005.

NICHD Early Child Care Research Network. (2004a). Does class size in first grade relate to children's academic and social performance or observed classroom processes? *Developmental Psychology, 40,* 651–664.

NICHD Early Child Care Research Network. (2004b). Trajectories of physical aggression from toddlerhood to middle childhood. *Monographs of the Society for Research in Child Development, 69*(Serial No. 278), vii–129.

NICHD Early Child Care Research Network (Ed.). (2005). *Child care and child development: Results from the NICHD Study of Early Child Care and Youth Development.* New York: Guilford Press.

Nichols, Sharon L., & Berliner, David C. (2007). *Collateral damage: How high-stakes testing corrupts America's schools.* Cambridge, MA: Harvard Education Press.

Nichols, Tracy R., Graber, Julia A., Brooks-Gunn, Jeanne, & Botvin, Gilbert J. (2006). Sex differences in overt aggression and delinquency among urban minority middle school students. *Journal of Applied Developmental Psychology, 27,* 78–91.

Nielsen, Mark. (2006). Copying actions and copying outcomes: Social learning through the second year. *Developmental Psychology, 42,* 555–565.

Nielsen, Mark, Suddendorf, Thomas, & Slaughter, Virginia. (2006). Mirror self-recognition beyond the face. *Child Development, 77,* 176–185.

Nielsen, Tore, & Paquette, Tyna. (2007). Dream-associated behaviors affecting pregnant and postpartum women. *Sleep: Journal of Sleep and Sleep Disorders Research, 30,* 1162–1169.

Nielson, Kristy A., Langenecker, Scott A., & Garavan, Hugh. (2002). Differences in the functional neuroanatomy of inhibitory control across the adult life span. *Psychology & Aging, 17,* 56–71.

Nieto, Sonia. (2000). *Affirming diversity: The sociopolitical context of multicultural education* (3rd ed.). New York: Longman.

Nihtilä, Elina, & Martikainen, Pekka. (2008). Institutionalization of older adults after the death of a spouse. *American Journal of Public Health, 98,* 1228–1234.

Nimrod, Galit. (2007). Expanding, reducing, concentrating and diffusing: Post retirement leisure behavior and life satisfaction. *Leisure Sciences, 29,* 91–111.

Nimrod, Galit, & Kleiber, Douglas A. (2007). Reconsidering change and continuity in later life: Toward an innovation theory of successful aging. *International Journal of Aging and Human Development, 65,* 1–22.

Nishida, Tracy K., & Lillard, Angeline S. (2007). The informative value of emotional expressions: 'Social referencing' in mother–child pretense. *Developmental Science, 10,* 205–212.

Nishina, Adrienne, & Juvonen, Jaana. (2005). Daily reports of witnessing and experiencing peer harassment in middle school. *Child Development, 76,* 435–450.

Nolen-Hoeksema, Susan, Wisco, Blair E., & Lyubomirsky, Sonja. (2008). Rethinking rumination. *Perspectives on Psychological Science, 3,* 400–424.

Nooyens, Astrid C. J., van Gelder, Boukje M., & Verschuren, W. M. Monique. (2008). Smoking and cognitive decline among middle-aged men and women: The Doetinchem Cohort Study. *American Journal of Public Health, 98,* 2244–2250.

Normile, Dennis. (2007, April 13). Japan picks up the 'innovation' mantra. *Science, 316,* 186.

Norris, Pippa. (2001). *Digital divide: Civic engagement, information poverty, and the internet worldwide.* New York: Cambridge University Press.

Nurmi, Jari-Erik. (2004). Socialization and self-development: Channeling, selection, adjustment, and reflection. In Richard M. Lerner & Laurence D. Steinberg (Eds.), *Handbook of adolescent psychology* (2nd ed., pp. 85–124). Hoboken, NJ: Wiley.

Nusselder, Wilma J., Looman, Caspar W. N., Franco, Oscar H., Peeters, Anna, Slingerland, Annabelle S., & Mackenbach, Johan P. (2008). The relation between non-occupational physical activity and years lived with and without disability. *Journal of Epidemiology and Community Health, 62,* 823–828.

O'Connor, Brian P., & St. Pierre, Edouard S. (2004). Older persons' perceptions of the frequency and meaning of elderspeak from family, friends, and service workers. *International Journal of Aging & Human Development, 58,* 197–221.

O'Connor, Thomas G. (2002). The 'effects' of parenting reconsidered: Findings, challenges, and applications. *Journal of Child Psychology & Psychiatry, 43,* 555–572.

O'Doherty, Kieran. (2006). Risk communication in genetic counselling: A discursive approach to probability. *Theory & Psychology, 16,* 225–256.

O'Donnell, Lydia, Stueve, Ann, Duran, Richard, Myint-U, Athi, Agronick, Gail, Doval, Alexi San, et al. (2008). Parenting practices, parents' underestimation of daughters' risks, and alcohol and sexual behaviors of urban girls. *Journal of Adolescent Health, 42,* 496–502.

O'Rahilly, Ronan R., & Müller, Fabiola. (2001). *Human embryology & teratology* (3rd ed.). New York: Wiley-Liss.

O'Rand, Angela M. (2006). Stratification and the life course: Life course capital, life course risks, and social inequality. In Robert H. Binstock & Linda K. George (Eds.), *Handbook of aging and the social sciences* (6th ed., pp. 145–162). Amsterdam: Elsevier.

O'Sullivan, Maureen. (2008). Home runs and humbugs: Comment on Bond and DePaulo (2008). *Psychological Bulletin, 134,* 493–497.

Oberman, Lindsay M., & Ramachandran, Vilayanur S. (2007). The simulating social mind: The role of the mirror neuron system and simulation in the social and communicative deficits of autism spectrum disorders. *Psychological Bulletin, 133,* 310–327.

Oddy, Wendy H. (2004). A review of the effects of breastfeeding on respiratory infections, atopy, and childhood asthma. *Journal of Asthma, 41,* 605–621.

Offer, Daniel, Offer, Marjorie Kaiz, & Ostrov, Eric. (2004). *Regular guys: 34 years beyond adolescence.* New York: Plenum.

Offit, Paul A. (2008). *Autism's false prophets: Bad science, risky medicine, and the search for a cure.* New York: Columbia University Press.

Ogawa, Tetsuo. (2004). Ageing in Japan: An issue of social contract in welfare transfer or generational conflict? In Peter Lloyd-Sherlock (Ed.), *Living longer: Ageing, development and social protection* (pp. 141–159). London: Zed Books.

Ogbu, John U. (2003). *Black American students in an affluent suburb: A study of academic disengagement.* Mahwah, NJ: Erlbaum.

Ogden, Cynthia L., Carroll, Margaret D., & Flegal, Katherine M. (2008). High body mass index for age among U.S. children and adolescents, 2003–2006. *Journal of the American Medical Association, 299,* 2401–2405.

Oh, Seungmi, & Lewis, Charlie. (2008). Korean preschoolers' advanced inhibitory control and its relation to other executive skills and mental state understanding. *Child Development, 79,* 80–99.

Okumoto, Kaori. (2008). Lifelong learning in England and Japan: Three translations. *Compare: A Journal of Comparative Education, 38,* 173–188.

Okun, Morris A., Pugliese, John, & Rook, Karen S. (2007). Unpacking the relation between extraversion and volunteering in later life: The role of social capital. *Personality and Individual Differences, 42,* 1467–1477.

Oldershaw, Lynn. (2002). *A national survey of parents of young children.* Toronto, ON, Canada: Invest in Kids.

Olson, Kristina R., & Dweck, Carol S. (2008). A blueprint for social cognitive development. *Perspectives on Psychological Science, 3,* 193–202.

Olson, Lynn. (2005, June 22). States raise bar for high school diploma. *Education Week, 24*(41), 1, 28.

Olson, Steve. (2004, September 3). Making sense of Tourette's. *Science, 305,* 1390–1392.

Olweus, Dan. (1992). Bullying among schoolchildren: Intervention and prevention. In Ray DeV. Peters, Robert Joseph McMahon, & Vernon L. Quinsey (Eds.), *Aggression and violence throughout the life span* (pp. 100–125). Thousand Oaks, CA: Sage.

Olweus, Dan. (1993). Victimization by peers: Antecedents and long-term outcomes. In Kenneth H. Rubin & Jens B. Asendorpf (Eds.), *Social withdrawal, inhibition, and shyness in childhood* (pp. 315–341). Hillsdale, NJ: Erlbaum.

Olweus, Dan, Limber, Sue, & Mahalic, Sharon F. (1999). *Bullying prevention program.* Boulder, CO: Center for the Study and Prevention of Violence, Institute of Behavioral Science, University of Colorado at Boulder.

Omariba, D. Walter Rasugu, & Boyle, Michael H. (2007). Family structure and child mortality in sub-Saharan Africa: Cross-national effects of polygyny. *Journal of Marriage and Family, 69,* 528–543.

Ontai, Lenna L., & Thompson, Ross A. (2008). Attachment, parent–child discourse and theory-of-mind development. *Social Development, 17,* 47–60.

Oosterman, Mirjam, Schuengel, Carlo, Slot, N. Wim, Bullens, Ruud A. R., & Doreleijers, Theo A. H. (2007). Disruptions in foster care: A review and meta-analysis. *Children and Youth Services Review, 29,* 53–76.

Orallo, Francisco. (2008). Trans-resveratrol: A magical elixir of eternal youth? *Current Medicinal Chemistry, 15,* 1887–1898.

Oregon Department of Human Services. (2006). *State of Oregon: Death with dignity act.* Retrieved September 18, 2009, from http://oregon.gov/DHS/ph/pas/index.shtml

Oregon Department of Human Services. (2008, March). *Oregon's Death with Dignity Act—2007.* Retrieved September 3, 2009, from http://oregon.gov/DHS/ph/pas/docs/year10.pdf

Orentlicher, David, & Callahan, Christopher M. (2004). Feeding tubes, slippery slopes, and physician-assisted suicide. *Journal of Legal Medicine, 25,* 389–409.

Organisation for Economic Co-operation and Development. (2006). *Education at a glance 2006: Indicator C5: Participation in adult learning.* Retrieved August 28, 2009, from http://www.oecd.org/dataoecd/46/21/37368749.xls

Organisation for Economic Co-operation and Development (OECD). (2008). *Education at a glance 2008: OECD indicators.* Paris: OECD Publications.

Organisation for Economic Co-operation and Development (OECD). (2008). *OECD health data 2008—Selected data.* Retrieved March 2, 2009, from http://stats.oecd.org/Index.aspx?DatasetCode=HEALTH

Ormerod, Thomas C. (2005). Planning and ill-defined problems. In Robin Morris & Geoff Ward (Eds.), *The cognitive psychology of planning* (pp. 53–70). New York: Psychology Press.

Ornstein, Peter A., Haden, Catherine A., & Elischberger, Holger B. (2006). Children's memory development: Remembering the past and preparing for the future. In Ellen Bialystok & Fergus I. M. Craik (Eds.), *Lifespan cognition: Mechanisms of change* (pp. 143–161). New York: Oxford University Press.

Orzeck, Pam, & Silverman, Marjorie. (2008). Recognizing post-caregiving as part of the caregiving career: Implications for practice. *Journal of Social Work Practice, 22,* 211–220.

Osborne, Jason W. (2007). Linking stereotype threat and anxiety. *Educational Psychology, 27,* 135–154.

Osgood, D. Wayne, Ruth, Gretchen, Eccles, Jacquelynne S., Jacobs, Janis E., & Barber, Bonnie L. (2005). Six paths to adulthood: Fast starters, parents without careers, educated partners, educated singles, working singles, and slow starters. In Richard A. Settersten, Jr., Frank F. Furstenberg, Jr., & Rubén G. Rumbaut (Eds.), *On the frontier of adulthood: Theory, research, and public policy* (pp. 320–355). Chicago: University of Chicago Press.

Osnes, Evind Kaare, Lofthus, Cathrine M., Meyer, Haakon, Falch, Jan A., Nordsletten, Lars, Cappelen, I., et al. (2004). Consequences of hip fracture on activities of daily life and residential needs. *Osteoporosis International, 15,* 567–574.

Otto, Beverly. (2008). *Literacy development in early childhood: Reflective teaching for birth to age eight.* Upper Saddle River, NJ: Prentice Hall.

Overbeek, Geertjan, Stattin, Håkan, Vermulst, Ad, Ha, Thao, & Engels, Rutger C. M. E. (2007). Parent–child relationships, partner relationships, and emotional adjustment: A birth-to-maturity prospective study. *Developmental Psychology, 43,* 429–437.

Owens-Sabir, Mahasin Cecelia. (2007). *The effects of race and family attachment on self-esteem, self-control, and delinquency.* New York: LFB Scholarly Publishing.

Pace, Thaddeus W. W., Mletzko, Tanja C., Alagbe, Oyetunde, Musselman, Dominique L., Nemeroff, Charles B., Miller, Andrew H., et al. (2006). Increased stress-induced inflammatory responses in male patients with major depression and increased early life stress. *American Journal of Psychiatry, 163,* 1630–1633.

Padilla-Walker, Laura M., Barry, Carolyn McNamara, Carroll, Jason S., Madsen, Stephanie D., & Nelson, Larry J. (2008). Looking on the bright side: The role of identity status and gender on positive orientations during emerging adulthood. *Journal of Adolescence, 31,* 451–467.

Padmadas, Sabu S., Hutter, Inge, & Willekens, Frans. (2004). Compression of women's reproductive spans in Andhra Pradesh, India. *International Family Planning Perspectives, 30,* 12–19.

Pagani, Linda S., Japel, Christa, Girard, Alain, Farhat, Abdeljelil, Cote, Sylvana, & Tremblay, Richard E. (2006). Middle childhood life course trajectories: Links between family dysfunction and children's behavioral development. In Aletha C. Huston & Marika N. Ripke (Eds.), *Developmental contexts in middle childhood: Bridges to adolescence and adulthood* (pp. 130–149). New York: Cambridge University Press.

Pagon, Roberta A., & Trotter, Tracy L. (2007). Genetic testing: When to test and when to refer. *Paediatrics and Child Health, 17,* 367–370.

Pahl, Kerstin, & Way, Niobe. (2006). Longitudinal trajectories of ethnic identity among urban Black and Latino adolescents. *Child Development, 77,* 1403–1415.

Palacios, Natalia, Guttmannova, Katarina, & Chase-Lansdale, P. Lindsay. (2008). Early reading achievement of children in immigrant families: Is there an immigrant paradox? *Developmental Psychology, 44,* 1381–1395.

Palfrey, John, & Gasser, Urs. (2008). *Born digital: Understanding the first generation of digital natives.* New York: Basic Books.

Palmer, Douglas J., Stough, Laura M., Burdenski, Thomas K., Jr., & Gonzales, Maricela. (2005). Identifying teacher expertise: An examination of researchers' decision making. *Educational Psychologist, 40,* 13–25.

Palmer, Raymond F., Blanchard, Stephen, Jean, Carlos R., & Mandell, David S. (2005). School district resources and identification of children with autistic disorder. *American Journal of Public Health, 95,* 125–130.

Palmore, Erdman. (2005). Three decades of research on ageism. *Generations, 29*(1), 87–90.

Palmore, Erdman, Branch, Laurence G., & Harris, Diana K. (2005). *Encyclopedia of ageism.* Binghamton, NY: Haworth.

Pan, En-ling, & Farrell, Michael P. (2006). Ethnic differences in the effects of intergenerational relations on adolescent problem behavior in U.S. single-mother families. *Journal of Family Issues, 27,* 1137–1158.

Pan, Xiaochuan, Yue, Wei, He, Kebin, & Tong, Shilu. (2007). Health benefit evaluation of the energy use scenarios in Beijing, China. *Science of the Total Environment, 374,* 242–251.

Panagiotakos, Demosthenes B., Kourlaba, Georgia, Zeimbekis, Akis, Toutouzas, Pavlos, & Polychronopoulos, Evangelos. (2007). The J-shape association of alcohol consumption on blood pressure levels, in elderly people from Mediterranean Islands (MEDIS epidemiological study). *Journal of Human Hypertension, 21,* 585–587.

Parikh, Shanti A. (2007). The political economy of marriage and HIV: The ABC approach, "safe" infidelity, and managing moral risk in Uganda. *American Journal of Public Health, 97,* 1198–1208.

Park, Denise C., & Gutchess, Angela H. (2005). Long-term memory and aging: A cognitive neuroscience perspective. In Roberto Cabeza, Lars Nyberg, & Denise Park (Eds.), *Cognitive neuroscience of aging: Linking cognitive and cerebral aging* (pp. 218–245). New York: Oxford University Press.

Park, Denise C., & Payer, Doris. (2006). Working memory across the adult lifespan. In Ellen Bialystok & Fergus I. M. Craik (Eds.), *Lifespan cognition: Mechanisms of change* (pp. 128–142). New York: Oxford University Press.

Parke, Ross D. (2002). Fathers and families. In Marc H. Bornstein (Ed.), *Handbook of parenting: Vol. 3: Being and becoming a parent* (2nd ed., pp. 27–73). Mahwah, NJ: Erlbaum.

Parke, Ross D., & Buriel, Raymond. (2006). Socialization in the family: Ethnic and ecological perspectives. In William Damon & Richard M. Lerner (Series Eds.) & Nancy Eisenberg (Vol. Ed.), *Handbook of child psychology: Vol. 3. Social, emotional, and personality development* (6th ed., pp. 429–504). Hoboken, NJ: Wiley.

Parke, Ross D., Coltrane, Scott, Duffy, Sharon, Buriel, Raymond, Dennis, Jessica, Powers, Justina, et al. (2004). Economic stress, parenting, and child adjustment in Mexican American and European American families. *Child Development, 75,* 1632–1656.

Parker, Susan W., & Nelson, Charles A. (2005). The impact of early institutional rearing on the ability to discriminate facial expressions of emotion: An event-related potential study. *Child Development, 76,* 54–72.

Parten, Mildred B. (1932). Social participation among preschool children. *The Journal of Abnormal and Social Psychology, 27,* 243–269.

Pascarella, Ernest T., & Terenzini, Patrick T. (1991). *How college affects students: Findings and insights from twenty years of research.* San Francisco: Jossey-Bass Publishers.

Pascarella, Ernest T., & Terenzini, Patrick T. (2005). *How college affects students: A third decade of research* (Vol. 2). San Francisco: Jossey-Bass.

Pastore, Ann L., & Maguire, Kathleen. (2005). *Sourcebook of criminal justice statistics, 2003* (NCJ 208756). Rockville, MD: Justice Statistics Clearinghouse/NCJRS.

Pastore, Ann L., & Maguire, Kathleen. (n.d.). *Sourcebook of criminal justice statistics online: Firearm suicide rate (per 100,000 persons in each age group), by age, United States, 1980–2004.* Retrieved April 29, 2009, from http://www.albany.edu/sourcebook/pdf/t31392004.pdf

Patel, Vimla L., Arocha, José F., & Kaufman, David R. (1999). Expertise and tacit knowledge in medicine. In Robert J. Sternberg & Joseph A. Horvath (Eds.), *Tacit knowledge in professional practice: Researcher and practitioner perspectives* (pp. 75–99). Mahwah, NJ: Erlbaum.

Patrick, Kevin, Norman, Gregory J., Calfas, Karen J., Sallis, James F., Zabinski, Marion F., Rupp, Joan, et al. (2004). Diet, physical activity, and sedentary behaviors as risk factors for overweight in adolescence. *Archives of Pediatrics & Adolescent Medicine, 158,* 385–390.

Patton, George C., Hemphill, Sheryl A., Beyers, Jennifer M., Bond, Lyndal, Toumbourou, John W., McMorris, Barbara J., et al. (2007). Pubertal stage and deliberate self-harm in adolescents. *Journal of the American Academy of Child & Adolescent Psychiatry, 46,* 508–514.

Pauli-Pott, Ursula, Mertesacker, Bettina, & Beckmann, Dieter. (2004). Predicting the development of infant emotionality from maternal characteristics. *Development & Psychopathology, 16,* 19–42.

Peden, Margie, Oyegbite, Kayode, Ozanne-Smith, Joan, Hyder, Adnan A., Branche, Christine, Rahman, A. K. M. Fazlur, et al. (Eds.). (2008). *World report on child injury prevention.* Geneva, Switzerland: World Health Organization.

Pedersen, Nancy L., Spotts, Erica, & Kato, Kenji. (2005). Genetic influences on midlife functioning. In Sherry L. Willis & Mike Martin (Eds.), *Middle adulthood: A lifespan perspective* (pp. 65–98). Thousand Oaks, CA: Sage.

Pellegrini, Anthony D., Dupuis, Danielle, & Smith, Peter K. (2007). Play in evolution and development. *Developmental Review, 27,* 261–276.

Pellegrini, Anthony D., & Smith, Peter K. (Eds.). (2005). *The nature of play: Great apes and humans.* New York: Guilford Press.

Pellegrino, James W., Jones, Lee R., & Mitchell, Karen J. (Eds.). (1999). *Grading the nation's report card: Evaluating NAEP and transforming the assessment of educational progress.* Washington, DC: National Academy Press.

Peng, Du, & Phillips, David R. (2004). Potential consequences of population ageing for social development in China. In Peter Lloyd-Sherlock (Ed.), *Living longer: Ageing, development and social protection* (pp. 97–116). London: Zed Books.

Peng, Kaiping, & Nisbett, Richard E. (1999). Culture, dialectics, and reasoning about contradiction. *American Psychologist, 54,* 741–754.

Pennington, Bruce Franklin. (2002). *The development of psychopathology: Nature and nurture.* New York: Guilford Press.

Pennisi, Elizabeth. (2007, May 25). Working the (gene count) numbers: Finally, a firm answer? *Science, 316,* 1113.

Pepler, Debra, Craig, Wendy, Yuile, Amy, & Connolly, Jennifer. (2004). Girls who bully: A developmental and relational perspective. In Martha Putallaz & Karen L. Bierman (Eds.), *Aggression, antisocial behavior, and violence among girls: A developmental perspective* (pp. 90–109). New York: Guilford.

Perfetti, Jennifer, Clark, Roseanne, & Fillmore, Capri-Mara. (2004). Postpartum depression: Identification, screening, and treatment. *Wisconsin Medical Journal, 103,* 56–63.

Perie, Marianne, Grigg, Wendy S., & Dion, Gloria S. (2005). *The nation's report card: Mathematics 2005* (NCES 2006–453). Washington, DC: U.S. Department of Education, National Center for Education Statistics.

Perlmutter, Marion, Kaplan, Michael, & Nyquist, Linda. (1990). Development of adaptive competence in adulthood. *Human Development, 33,* 185–197.

Perls, Thomas T. (2008). Centenarians and genetics. In Catherine Y. Read, Robert C. Green, & Michael A. Smyer (Eds.), *Aging, biotechnology, and the future* (pp. 89–99). Baltimore: Johns Hopkins University Press.

Perner, Josef. (2000). About + belief + counterfactual. In Peter Mitchell & Kevin John Riggs (Eds.), *Children's reasoning and the mind* (pp. 367–401). Hove, England: Psychology Press.

Perner, Josef, Lang, Birgit, & Kloo, Daniela. (2002). Theory of mind and self-control: More than a common problem of inhibition. *Child Development, 73,* 752–767.

Perreira, Krista M., Harris, Kathleen Mullan, & Lee, Dohoon. (2007). Immigrant youth in the labor market. *Work and Occupations, 34,* 5–34.

Perry, Ivan J., Whelton, Helen, Harrington, Janas, & Cousins, Bernard. (2009). The heights and weights of Irish children from the post-war era to the Celtic tiger. *Journal of Epidemiology and Community Health, 63,* 262–264.

Perry, William G., Jr. (1981). Cognitive and ethical growth: The making of meaning. In A. Chickering (Ed.), *The modern American college: Responding to the new realities of diverse students and a changing society* (pp. 76–116). San Francisco: Jossey-Bass.

Perry, William G., Jr. (1998). *Forms of intellectual and ethical development in the college years: A scheme.* San Francisco: Jossey-Bass Publishers. (Original work published 1970)

Perry-Jenkins, Maureen, Goldberg, Abbie E., Pierce, Courtney P., & Sayer, Aline G. (2007). Shift work, role overload, and the transition to parenthood. *Journal of Marriage and Family, 69,* 123–138.

Person, Ethel Spector, & Ovesey, Lionel. (1999). Psychoanalytic theories of gender identity. In Ethel Spector Person (Ed.), *The sexual century* (pp. 55–71). New Haven, CT: Yale University Press.

Peterson, Jordan B., & Flanders, Joseph L. (2005). Play and the regulation of aggression. In Richard Ernest Tremblay, Willard W. Hartup, & John Archer (Eds.), *Developmental origins of aggression* (pp. 133–157). New York: Guilford Press.

Pettigrew, Thomas F., Christ, Oliver, Wagner, Ulrich, Meertens, Roel W., van Dick, Rolf, & Zick, Andreas. (2008). Relative deprivation and intergroup prejudice. *Journal of Social Issues, 64,* 385–401.

Pettit, Gregory S. (2004). Violent children in developmental perspective: Risk and protective factors and the mechanisms through which they (may) operate. *Current Directions in Psychological Science, 13,* 194–197.

Pew Commission on Children in Foster Care. (2004). *Fostering the future: Safety, permanence and well-being for children in foster care.* Retrieved June 25, 2009, from http://pewfostercare.org/research/docs/FinalReport.pdf

Pew Research Center. (2007). *A portrait of "Generation Next": How young people view their lives, futures and politics.* Pew Research Center. Retrieved July 24, 2009, from http://people-press.org/reports/pdf/300.pdf

Pew Research Center. (2008, December 15). *Hillary's new job better known than Dow Jones Average.* Retrieved August 20, 2009, from http://pewresearch.org/pubs/1055/hillarys-new-job-better-known-than-dow-jones-average

Pfeffer, Jeffrey. (2007). Human resources from an organizational behavior perspective: Some paradoxes explained. *Journal of Economic Perspectives, 21,* 115–134.

Pfeifer, Jennifer H., Brown, Christia Spears, & Juvonen, Jaana. (2007). Prejudice reduction in schools: Teaching tolerance in schools: Lessons learned since Brown v. Board of Education about the development and reduction of children's prejudice *Social Policy Report, 21*(2), 3–17.

Phillips, Deborah A., & White, Sheldon H. (2004). New possibilities for research on Head Start. In Edward Zigler & Sally J. Styfco (Eds.), *The Head Start debates* (pp. 263–278). Baltimore: Brookes.

Phillips, Tommy M., & Pittman, Joe F. (2007). Adolescent psychological well-being by identity style. *Journal of Adolescence, 30,* 1021–1034.

Phillipson, Chris. (2006). Ageing and globalization. In John A. Vincent, Chris R. Phillipson, & Murna Downs (Eds.), *The futures of old age* (pp. 201–207). Thousand Oaks, CA: Sage.

Phinney, Jean S. (2006). Ethnic identity exploration in emerging adulthood. In Jeffrey Jensen Arnett & Jennifer Lynn Tanner (Eds.), *Emerging adults in America: Coming of age in the 21st century* (pp. 117–134). Washington, DC: American Psychological Association.

Piaget, Jean. (1932). *The moral judgment of the child* (Marjorie Gabain, Trans.). London: K. Paul, Trench, Trubner & Co.

Piaget, Jean. (1951). *Play, dreams, and imitation in childhood.* New York: Norton.

Piaget, Jean. (1962). *Play, dreams and imitation in childhood* (C. Gattegno & F. M. Hodgson, Trans.). New York: Norton. (Original work published 1945)

Piaget, Jean. (1972). *The psychology of intelligence.* Totowa, NJ: Littlefield. (Original work published 1950)

Piaget, Jean. (1997). *The moral judgment of the child* (Marjorie Gabain, Trans.). New York: Simon and Schuster. (Original work published 1932)

Piaget, Jean, & Inhelder, Bärbel. (1969). *The psychology of the child.* New York: Basic Books.

Piaget, Jean, Voelin-Liambey, Daphne, & Berthoud-Papandropoulou, Ioanna. (2001). *Problems of class inclusion and logical implication* (Robert L. Campbell, Ed. & Trans.). Hove, E. Sussex, England: Psychology Press. (Original work published 1977)

Pierce, Benton H., Simons, Jon S., & Schacter, Daniel L. (2004). Aging and the seven sins of memory. In Paul T. Costa & Ilene C. Siegler (Eds.), *Recent advances in psychology and aging* (Vol. 15, pp. 1–40). Amsterdam: Elsevier.

Pike, Gary R., & Kuh, George D. (2005). First- and second-generation college students: A comparison of their engagement and intellectual development. *Journal of Higher Education, 76,* 276–300.

Pinheiro, Andréa Poyastro (Ed.). (2006). *World report on violence against children.* Geneva, Switzerland: United Nations.

Pinker, Steven. (1999). *Words and rules: The ingredients of language.* New York: Basic Books.

Pinquart, Martin, & Silbereisen, Rainer K. (2006). Socioemotional selectivity in cancer patients. *Psychology and Aging, 21,* 419–423.

Pinquart, Martin, & Sörensen, Silvia. (2003). Associations of stressors and uplifts of caregiving with caregiver burden and depressive mood: A meta-analysis. *Journals of Gerontology: Series B: Psychological Sciences & Social Sciences, 58B,* P112–P128.

Piontelli, Alessandra. (2002). *Twins: From fetus to child.* London: Routledge.

Piotrowski, Martin. (2008). Migrant remittances and household division: The case of Nang Rong, Thailand. *Journal of Marriage and Family, 70,* 1074–1087.

Piper, Don, & Murphey, Cecil B. (2004). *90 minutes in heaven: A true story of death & life.* Grand Rapids, MI: Revell.

Pirozzo, Sandi, Papinczak, Tracey, & Glasziou, Paul. (2003). Whispered voice test for screening for hearing impairment in adults and children: Systematic review. *British Medical Journal, 327,* 967–960.

Pittaro, Michael L. (2007). School violence and social control theory: An evaluation of the Columbine massacre. *International Journal of Criminal Justice Sciences, 2*(1), 1–12.

Planalp, Sally, & Trost, Melanie R. (2008). Communication issues at the end of life: Reports from hospice volunteers. *Health Communication, 23,* 222–233.

Plank, Stephen B., & MacIver, Douglas J. (2003). Educational achievement. In Marc H. Bornstein, Lucy Davidson, Corey L. M. Keyes, & Kristin Moore (Eds.), *Well-being: Positive development across the life course* (pp. 341–354). Mahwah, NJ: Erlbaum.

Plassman, Brenda L., Langa, Kenneth M., Fisher, Gwenith G., Heeringa, Steven G., Weir, David R., Ofstedal, Mary Beth, et al. (2007). Prevalence of dementia in the United States: The Aging, Demographics, and Memory Study. *Neuroepidemiology, 29,* 125–132.

Plomin, Robert, DeFries, John C., Craig, Ian W., & McGuffin, Peter. (2003). *Behavioral genetics in the postgenomic era.* Washington, DC: American Psychological Association.

Plomin, Robert, Defries, John C., McClearn, Gerald E., & McGuffin, Peter. (2008). *Behavioral genetics* (5th ed.). New York: Worth.

Plomin, Robert, Happé, Francesca, & Caspi, Avshalom. (2002). Personality and cognitive abilities. In Peter McGuffin, Michael J. Owen, & Irving I. Gottesman (Eds.), *Psychiatric genetics and genomics* (pp. 77–112). New York: Oxford University Press.

Plutchik, Robert. (2003). *Emotions and life: Perspectives from psychology, biology, and evolution.* Washington, DC: American Psychological Association.

Pollak, Seth D., Cicchetti, Dante, Hornung, Katherine, & Reed, Alex. (2000). Recognizing emotion in faces: Developmental effects of child abuse and neglect. *Developmental Psychology, 36,* 679–688.

Pomerantz, Eva M., & Rudolph, Karen D. (2003). What ensues from emotional distress? Implications for competence estimation. *Child Development, 74,* 329–345.

Pong, Suet-ling, Dronkers, Jaap, & Hampden-Thompson, Gillian. (2003). Family policies and children's school achievement in single- versus two-parent families. *Journal of Marriage and Family, 65,* 681–699.

Porche, Michelle V., Ross, Stephanie J., & Snow, Catherine E. (2004). From preschool to middle school: The role of masculinity in low-income urban adolescent boys' literacy skills and academic achievement. In Niobe Way & Judy Y. Chu (Eds.), *Adolescent boys: Exploring diverse cultures of boyhood* (pp. 338–360). New York: New York University Press.

Portes, Alejandro, & Fernández-Kelly, Patricia (Eds.). (2008). Exceptional outcomes: Achievement in education and employment among children of immigrants. *The Annals of the American Academy of Political and Social Science, 620.*

Portes, Alejandro, & Rumbaut, Rubén G. (2001). *Legacies: The story of the immigrant second generation.* Berkeley, CA and New York: University of California Press and the Russell Sage Foundation.

Posner, Michael I., Rothbart, Mary K., Sheese, Brad E., & Tang, Yiyuan. (2007). The anterior cingulate gyrus and the mechanism of self-regulation. *Cognitive, Affective & Behavioral Neuroscience, 7,* 391–395.

Poulsen, Pernille, Esteller, Manel, Vaag, Allan, & Fraga, Mario F. (2007). The epigenetic basis of twin discordance in age-related diseases. *Pediatric Research, 61*(5, Pt. 2), 38R–42R.

Powell, Douglas H. (with Whitla, Dean K.). (1994). *Profiles in cognitive aging.* Cambridge, MA: Harvard University Press.

Powell, Douglas R. (2006). Families and early childhood interventions. In William Damon & Richard M. Lerner (Series Eds.) & K. Ann Renninger & Irving E. Sigel (Vol. Eds.), *Handbook of child psychology: Vol. 4. Child psychology in practice* (6th ed., pp. 548–591). Hoboken: Wiley.

Power, Chris, Atherton, Kate, & Manor, Orly. (2008). Co-occurrence of risk factors for cardiovascular disease by social class: 1958 British birth cohort. *Journal of Epidemiology and Community Health, 62,* 1030–1035.

Powledge, Tabitha M. (2007, October). Easing hormone anxiety. *Scientific American, 297,* 32, 34.

Powlishta, Kimberly. (2004). Gender as a social category: Intergroup processes and gender-role development. In Mark Bennett & Fabio Sani (Eds.), *The development of the social self* (pp. 103–133). Hove, East Sussex, England: Psychology Press.

Prado, Carlos G. (2008). *Choosing to die: Elective death and multiculturalism.* New York: Cambridge University Press.

Pratt, Michael W., Norris, Joan E., Cressman, Kate, Lawford, Heather, & Hebblethwaite, Shannon. (2008). Parents' stories of grandparenting concerns in the three-generational family: Generativity, optimism, and forgiveness. *Journal of Personality, 76,* 581–604.

Pratt, Michael W., & Robins, Susan L. (1991). That's the way it was: Age differences in the structure and quality of adults' personal narratives. *Discourse Processes, 14,* 73–85.

Presser, Harriet B. (2005). *Working in a 24/7 economy: Challenges for American families* (Paperback ed.). New York: Russell Sage.

Presser, Harriet B., Gornick, Janet C., & Parashar, Sangeeta. (2008). Gender and nonstandard work hours in 12 European countries. *Monthly Labor Review, 131,* 83–103.

Pressley, Michael, & Hilden, Katherine. (2006). Cognitive strategies: Production deficiencies and successful strategy instruction everywhere. In William Damon & Richard M. Lerner (Series Eds.) & Deanna Kuhn & Robert S. Siegler (Vol. Eds.), *Handbook of child psychology: Vol. 2. Cognition, perception, and language* (6th ed., pp. 511–556). Hoboken, NJ: Wiley.

Preston, Tom, & Kelly, Michael. (2006). A medical ethics assessment of the case of Terri Schiavo. *Death Studies, 30,* 121–133.

Previti, Denise, & Amato, Paul R. (2003). Why stay married? Rewards, barriers, and marital stability. *Journal of Marriage and Family, 65,* 561–573.

Proulx, Christine M., Helms, Heather M., & Buehler, Cheryl. (2007). Marital quality and personal well-being: A meta-analysis. *Journal of Marriage and Family, 69,* 576–593.

Pruden, Shannon M., Hirsh-Pasek, Kathy, Golinkoff, Roberta Michnick, & Hennon, Elizabeth A. (2006). The birth of words: Ten-month-olds learn words through perceptual salience. *Child Development, 77,* 266–280.

Pucher, John, & Dijkstra, Lewis. (2003). Promoting safe walking and cycling to improve public health: Lessons from the Netherlands and Germany. *American Journal of Public Health, 93,* 1509–1516.

Pulkkinen, Lea, Feldt, Taru, & Kokko, Katja. (2005). Personality in young adulthood and functioning in middle age.

In Sherry L. Willis & Mike Martin (Eds.), *Middle adulthood: A lifespan perspective* (pp. 99–141). Thousand Oaks, CA: Sage.

Putnam, Robert D. (2000). *Bowling alone: The collapse and revival of American community.* New York: Simon & Schuster.

Pyszczynski, Thomas A., Greenberg, Jeff, & Solomon, Sheldon. (2003). *In the wake of 9/11: The psychology of terror.* Washington, DC: American Psychological Association.

Quas, Jodi A., Bauer, Amy, & Boyce, W. Thomas. (2004). Physiological reactivity, social support, and memory in early childhood. *Child Development, 75,* 797–814.

Quinn, Paul C. (2004). Development of subordinate-level categorization in 3- to 7-month-old infants. *Child Development, 75,* 886–899.

Rabbitt, Patrick, Anderson, Michael, Davis, Helen, & Shilling, Val. (2003). Cognitive processes in ageing. In Jaan Valsiner & Kevin J. Connolly (Eds.), *Handbook of developmental psychology* (pp. 560–583). Thousand Oaks, CA: Sage.

Rabbitt, Patrick, Lunn, Mary, & Wong, Danny. (2008). Death, dropout, and longitudinal measurements of cognitive change in old age. *Journals of Gerontology Series B: Psychological Sciences and Social Sciences, 63,* P271–278.

Raikes, Helen, Pan, Barbara Alexander, Luze, Gayle, Tamis-LeMonda, Catherine S., Brooks-Gunn, Jeanne, Constantine, Jill, et al. (2006). Mother–child bookreading in low-income families: Correlates and outcomes during the first three years of life. *Child Development, 77,* 924–953.

Rakison, David H., & Woodward, Amanda L. (2008). New perspectives on the effects of action on perceptual and cognitive development. *Developmental Psychology, 44,* 1209–1213.

Raley, R. Kelly, & Wildsmith, Elizabeth. (2004). Cohabitation and children's family instability. *Journal of Marriage and Family, 66,* 210–219.

Ramchandani, Paul, Stein, Alan, Evans, Jonathan, & O'Connor, Thomas G. (2005). Paternal depression in the postnatal period and child development: A prospective population study. *Lancet, 365,* 2201–2205.

Ramey, Craig T., Ramey, Sharon Landesman, Lanzi, Robin Gaines, & Cotton, Janice N. (2002). Early educational interventions for high-risk children: How center-based treatment can augment and improve parenting effectiveness. In John G. Borkowski, Sharon Landesman Ramey, & Marie Bristol-Power (Eds.), *Parenting and the child's world: Influences on academic, intellectual, and social-emotional development* (pp. 125–140). Mahwah, NJ: Erlbaum.

Randazzo, William T., Dockray, Samantha, & Susman, Elizabeth J. (2008). The stress response in adolescents with inattentive type ADHD symptoms. *Child Psychiatry & Human Development, 39,* 27–38.

Rankin, Jane L., Lane, David J., Gibbons, Frederick X., & Gerrard, Meg. (2004). Adolescent self-consciousness: Longitudinal age changes and gender differences in two cohorts. *Journal of Research on Adolescence, 14,* 1–21.

Rauer, Amy J., Karney, Benjamin R., Garvan, Cynthia W., & Hou, Wei. (2008). Relationship risks in context: A cumulative risk approach to understanding relationship satisfaction. *Journal of Marriage and Family, 70,* 1122–1135.

Rayco-Solon, Pura, Fulford, Anthony J., & Prentice, Andrew M. (2005). Differential effects of seasonality on preterm birth and intrauterine growth restriction in rural Africans. *American Journal of Clinical Nutrition, 81,* 134–139.

Raz, Naftali. (2005). The aging brain observed in vivo: Differential changes and their modifiers. In Roberto Cabeza, Lars Nyberg, & Denise Park (Eds.), *Cognitive neuroscience of aging: Linking cognitive and cerebral aging* (pp. 19–57). New York: Oxford University Press.

Reece, E. Albert, & Hobbins, John C. (Eds.). (2007). *Handbook of clinical obstetrics: The fetus & mother handbook* (2nd ed.). Malden, MA: Blackwell.

Reed, Tom, & Brown, Mac. (2001). The expression of care in the rough and tumble play of boys. *Journal of Research in Childhood Education, 15,* 104–116.

Reese, Elaine, Bird, Amy, & Tripp, Gail. (2007). Children's self-esteem and moral self: Links to parent–child conversations regarding emotion. *Social Development, 16,* 460–478.

Register, Cheri. (2005). *Beyond good intentions: A mother reflects on raising internationally adopted children.* St. Paul, MN: Yeong & Yeong.

Regnerus, Mark D. (2005). Talking about sex: Religion and patterns of parent–child communication about sex and contraception. *Sociological Quarterly, 46,* 79–105.

Reilly, Sheena, Eadie, Patricia, Bavin, Edith L., Wake, Melissa, Prior, Margot, Williams, Joanne, et al. (2006). Growth of infant communication between 8 and 12 months: A population study. *Journal of Paediatrics and Child Health, 42,* 764–770.

Reis, Harry T., & Collins, W. Andrew. (2004). Relationships, human behavior, and psychological science. *Current Directions in Psychological Science, 13,* 233–237.

Reiss, David, Neiderhiser, Jenae M., Hetherington, E. Mavis, & Plomin, Robert. (2000). *The relationship code: Deciphering genetic and social influences on adolescent development.* Cambridge, MA: Harvard University Press.

Reiter, Russel J. (1998). Roundtable discussion: How best to ensure daily intake of antioxidants (from the diet and supplements) that is optimal for life span, disease, and general health. In Denham Harman, Robin Holliday, & Mohsen Meydani (Eds.), *Towards prolongation of the healthy life span: Practical approaches to intervention* (Vol. 854, pp. 463–476). New York: New York Academy of Sciences.

Renk, Kimberly, Donnelly, Reesa, McKinney, Cliff, & Agliata, Allison Kanter. (2006). The development of gender identity: Timetables and influences. In Kam-Shing Yip (Ed.), *Psychology of gender identity: An international perspective* (pp. 49–68). Hauppauge, NY: Nova Science.

Renkema, Lennart J., Stapel, Diederik A., Maringer, Marcus, & van Yperen, Nico W. (2008). Terror management and stereotyping: Why do people stereotype when mortality is salient? *Personality and Social Psychology Bulletin, 34,* 553–564.

Rentfrow, Peter J., Gosling, Samuel D., & Potter, Jeff. (2008). A theory of the emergence, persistence, and expression of geographic variation in psychological characteristics. *Perspectives on Psychological Science, 3,* 339–369.

Rest, James, Narvaez, Darcia, Bebeau, Muriel J., & Thoma, Stephen J. (1999). *Postconventional moral thinking: A neo-Kohlbergian approach.* Mahwah, NJ: Erlbaum.

Retting, Richard A., Ferguson, Susan A., & McCartt, Anne T. (2003). A review of evidence-based traffic engineering measures designed to reduce pedestrian-motor vehicle crashes. *American Journal of Public Health, 93,* 1456–1463.

Reuter-Lorenz, Patricia A., & Sylvester, Ching-Yune C. (2005). The cognitive neuroscience of working memory and aging. In Roberto Cabeza, Lars Nyberg, & Denise Park (Eds.), *Cognitive neuroscience of aging: Linking cognitive and cerebral aging* (pp. 186–217). New York: Oxford University Press.

Reynolds, Arthur J. (2000). *Success in early intervention: The Chicago Child–Parent Centers.* Lincoln, NE: University of Nebraska Press.

Reynolds, Arthur J., Ou, Suh-Ruu, & Topitzes, James W. (2004). Paths of effects of early childhood intervention on educational attainment and delinquency: A confirmatory analysis of the Chicago Child–Parent Centers. *Child Development, 75,* 1299–1328.

Reynolds, Heidi W., Wong, Emelita L., & Tucker, Heidi. (2006). Adolescents' use of maternal and child health services in developing countries. *International Family Planning Perspectives, 32*(1), 6–16.

Rhodes, Jean E., & Roffman, Jennifer G. (2003). Non-parental adults as asset builders in the lives of youth. In Richard M. Lerner & Peter L. Benson (Eds.), *Developmental assets and asset-building communities: Implications for research, policy, and practice* (pp. 195–209). New York: Kluwer/Plenum.

Rhodes, Marjorie, & Gelman, Susan A. (2008). Categories influence predictions about individual consistency. *Child Development, 79,* 1270–1287.

Rice, Charles L., & Cunningham, David A. (2002). Aging of the neuromuscular system: Influences of gender and physical activity. In Roy J. Shephard (Ed.), *Gender, physical activity, and aging* (pp. 121–150). Boca Raton, FL: CRC Press.

Richardson, Heidi L., Parslow, Peter M., Walker, Adrian M., Harding, Richard, & Horne, Rosemary S. C. (2006). Variability of the initial phase of the ventilatory response to hypoxia in sleeping infants. *Pediatric Research, 59,* 700–704.

Richardson, Rhonda A. (2004). Early adolescence talking points: Questions that middle school students want to ask their parents. *Family Relations, 53,* 87–94.

Richardson, Rick, & Hayne, Harlene. (2007). You can't take it with you: The translation of memory across development. *Current Directions in Psychological Science, 16,* 223–227.

Riordan, Jan (Ed.). (2009). *Breastfeeding and human lactation* (4th ed.). Sudbury, MA: Jones and Bartlett.

Ripke, Marika N., Huston, Aletha C., & Casey, David M. (2006). Low-income children's activity participation as a predictor of psychosocial and academic outcomes in middle childhood and adolescence. In Aletha C. Huston & Marika N. Ripke (Eds.), *Developmental contexts in middle childhood: Bridges to adolescence and adulthood* (pp. 260–282). New York: Cambridge University Press.

Rizzolatti, Giacomo, & Craighero, Laila. (2004). The mirror-neuron system. *Annual Review of Neuroscience, 27,* 169–192.

Rizzolatti, Giacomo, & Sinigaglia, Corrado. (2008). *Mirrors in the brain: How our minds share actions and emotions* (Frances Anderson, Trans.). New York: Oxford University Press.

Roberson, Erik D., & Mucke, Lennart. (2006, November 3). 100 years and counting: Prospects for defeating Alzheimer's disease. *Science, 314,* 781–784.

Roberto, Karen A., Allen, Katherine R., & Blieszner, Rosemary. (2001). Grandfathers' perceptions and expectations of relationships with their adult grandchildren. *Journal of Family Issues, 22,* 407–426.

Roberts, Brent W., & Caspi, Avshalom. (2003). The cumulative continuity model of personality development: Striking a balance between continuity and change in personality traits accross the life course. In Ursula M. Staudinger & Ulman Lindenberger (Eds.), *Understanding human development: Dialogues with lifespan psychology* (pp. 183–214). Dordrecht, The Netherlands: Kluwer.

Roberts, Brent W., Kuncel, Nathan R., Shiner, Rebecca, Caspi, Avshalom, & Goldberg, Lewis R. (2007). The power of personality: The comparative validity of personality traits, socioeconomic status, and cognitive ability for predicting important life outcomes. *Perspectives on Psychological Science, 2,* 313–345.

Roberts, Brent W., Walton, Kate E., & Viechtbauer, Wolfgang. (2006). Patterns of mean-level change in personality traits across the life course: A meta-analysis of longitudinal studies. *Psychological Bulletin, 132,* 1–25.

Roberts, Donald F., & Foehr, Ulla G. (2004). *Kids and media in America: Patterns of use at the millennium.* New York: Cambridge University Press.

Roberts, Leslie. (2009, February 6). Looking for a little luck. *Science, 323,* 702–705.

Robertson Blackmore, Emma, Stansfeld, Stephen A., Weller, Iris, Munce, Sarah, Zagorski, Brandon M., & Stewart, Donna E. (2007). Major depressive episodes and work stress: Results from a national population survey. *American Journal of Public Health, 97,* 2088–2093.

Rochat, Philippe. (2001). *The infant's world.* Cambridge, MA: Harvard University Press.

Roche, Alex F., & Sun, Shumei S. (2003). *Human growth: Assessment and interpretation.* Cambridge, UK: Cambridge University Press.

Rodgers, Joseph. (2003). EMOSA sexuality models, memes, and the tipping point: Policy & program implications. In Daniel Romer (Ed.), *Reducing adolescent risk: Toward an integrated approach* (pp. 185–192). Thousand Oaks, CA: Sage.

Rodgers, Joseph Lee, & Wänström, Linda. (2007). Identification of a Flynn Effect in the NLSY: Moving from the center to the boundaries. *Intelligence, 35,* 187–196.

Rodrigues, Amy E., Hall, Julie H., & Fincham, Frank D. (2006). What predicts divorce and relationship dissolution? In Mark A. Fine & John H. Harvey (Eds.), *Handbook of divorce and relationship dissolution* (pp. 85–112). Mahwah, NJ: Erlbaum.

Rogoff, Barbara. (2003). *The cultural nature of human development.* New York: Oxford University Press.

Rogoff, Barbara, Correa-Chávez, Maricela, & Cotuc, Marta Navichoc. (2005). A cultural/historical view of schooling in human development. In David B. Pillemer & Sheldon H.

White (Eds.), *Developmental psychology and social change: Research, history and policy* (pp. 225–263). New York: Cambridge University Press.

Roid, Gale H. (2003). *Stanford–Binet intelligence scales* (5th ed.). Itasca, IL: Riverside.

Roisman, Glenn I., & Fraley, R. Chris. (2006). The limits of genetic influence: A behavior-genetic analysis of infant–caregiver relationship quality and temperament. *Child Development, 77,* 1656–1667.

Roland, Erling. (2000). Bullying in school: Three national innovations in Norwegian schools in 15 years. *Aggressive Behavior, 26,* 135–143.

Romans, Sarah E., Martin, J. M., Gendall, Kelly, & Herbison, G. Peter. (2003). Age of menarche: The role of some psychosocial factors. *Psychological Medicine, 33,* 933–939.

Rönkä, Anna, Oravala, Sanna, & Pulkkinen, Lea. (2002). "I met this wife of mine and things got onto a better track": Turning points in risk development. *Journal of Adolescence, 25,* 47–63.

Roopnarine, Jaipaul L., Johnson, James E., & Hooper, Frank H. (Eds.). (1994). *Children's play in diverse cultures.* Albany, NY: State University of New York Press.

Rosano, Giuseppe M. C., Vitale, Cristiana, Silvestri, Antonello, & Fini, Massimo. (2003). Hormone replacement therapy and cardioprotection: The end of the tale? In George Creatsas, George Mastorakos, & George P. Chrousos (Eds.), *Women's health and disease: Gynecologic and reproductive issues* (Vol. 997, pp. 351–357). New York: New York Academy of Sciences.

Rose, Amanda J., & Asher, Steven R. (2004). Children's strategies and goals in response to help-giving and help-seeking tasks within a friendship. *Child Development, 75,* 749–763.

Rose, Amanda J., & Swenson, Lance P. (2009). Do perceived popular adolescents who aggress against others experience emotional adjustment problems themselves? *Developmental Psychology, 45,* 868–872.

Rose, Amanda J., Swenson, Lance P., & Waller, Erika M. (2004). Overt and relational aggression and perceived popularity: Developmental differences in concurrent and prospective relations. *Developmental Psychology, 40,* 378–387.

Rose, Steven. (2008, January 31). Drugging unruly children is a method of social control [Correspondence]. *Nature, 451,* 521.

Rosenbluth, Barri, Whitaker, Daniel J., Sanchez, Ellen, & Valle, Linda Anne. (2004). The Expect Respect project: Preventing bullying and sexual harassment in U.S. elementary schools. In Peter K. Smith, Debra Pepler, & Ken Rigby (Eds.), *Bullying in schools: How successful can interventions be?* (pp. 211–233). New York: Cambridge University Press

Rosenfeld, Barry. (2004). *Assisted suicide and the right to die: The interface of social science, public policy, and medical ethics.* Washington, DC: American Psychological Association.

Rosenfeld, Philip J., Brown, David M., Heier, Jeffrey S., Boyer, David S., Kaiser, Peter K., Chung, Carol Y., et al. (2006). Ranibizumab for neovascular age-related macular degeneration. *New England Journal of Medicine, 355,* 1419–1431.

Rosow, Irving. (1985). Status and role change through the life cycle. In Robert H. Binstock & Ethel Shanas (Eds.), *Handbook of aging and the social sciences* (2nd ed., pp. 62–93). New York: Van Nostrand Reinhold.

Rossano, Matt J. (2008). The moral faculty: Does religion promote "moral expertise"? *International Journal for the Psychology of Religion, 18,* 169–194.

Roth, David L., Ackerman, Michelle L., Okonkwo, Ozioma C., & Burgio, Louis D. (2008). The four-factor model of depressive symptoms in dementia caregivers: A structural equation model of ethnic differences. *Psychology and Aging, 23,* 567–576.

Roth, David L., Mittelman, Mary S., Clay, Olivio J., Madan, Alok, & Haley, William E. (2005). Changes in social support as mediators of the impact of a psychosocial intervention for spouse caregivers of persons with Alzheimer's disease. *Psychology and Aging, 20,* 634–644.

Rothbart, Mary K., & Bates, John E. (2006). Temperament. In William Damon & Richard M. Lerner (Series Eds.) & Nancy Eisenberg (Vol. Ed.), *Handbook of child psychology: Vol. 3. Social, emotional, and personality development* (6th ed., pp. 99–166). Hoboken, NJ: Wiley.

Rothbaum, Fred, Pott, Martha, Azuma, Hiroshi, Miyake, Kazuo, & Weisz, John. (2000). The development of close relationships in Japan and the United States: Paths of symbiotic harmony and generative tension. *Child Development, 71,* 1121–1142.

Rovee-Collier, Carolyn. (1987). Learning and memory in infancy. In Joy Doniger Osofsky (Ed.), *Handbook of infant development* (2nd ed., pp. 98–148). New York: Wiley.

Rovee-Collier, Carolyn. (1990). The "memory system" of prelinguistic infants. In Adele Diamond (Ed.), *The development and neural bases of higher cognitive functions* (Vol. 608, pp. 517–542). New York: New York Academy of Sciences.

Rovee-Collier, Carolyn. (2001). Information pick-up by infants: What is it, and how can we tell? *Journal of Experimental Child Psychology, 78,* 35–49.

Rovee-Collier, Carolyn, & Gerhardstein, Peter. (1997). The development of infant memory. In Nelson Cowan (Ed.), *The development of memory in childhood* (pp. 5–39). Hove, East Sussex, UK: Psychology Press.

Rovee-Collier, Carolyn, & Hayne, Harlene. (1987). Reactivation of infant memory: Implications for cognitive development. In Hayne W. Reese (Ed.), *Advances in child development and behavior* (Vol. 20, pp. 185–238). San Diego, CA: Academic Press.

Rovi, Sue, Chen, Ping-Hsin, & Johnson, Mark S. (2004). The economic burden of hospitalizations associated with child abuse and neglect. *American Journal of Public Health, 94,* 586–590.

Rowe, John W., & Kahn, Robert Louis. (1998). *Successful aging.* New York: Pantheon.

Rowland, Andrew S., Umbach, David M., Stallone, Lil, Naftel, A. Jack, Bohlig, E. Michael, & Sandler, Dale P. (2002). Prevalence of medication treatment for attention deficit-hyperactivity disorder among elementary school children in Johnston County, North Carolina. *American Journal of Public Health, 92,* 231–234.

Rozin, Paul. (2007). Food and eating. In Shinobu Kitayama & Dov Cohen (Eds.), *Handbook of cultural psychology* (pp. 391–416). New York: Guilford Press.

Rozin, Paul, Kabnick, Kimberly, Pete, Erin, Fischler, Claude, & Shields, Christy. (2003). The ecology of eating: Smaller portion sizes in France than in the United States help explain the French paradox. *Psychological Science, 14,* 450–454.

Rubin, Kenneth H., Bukowski, William M., & Parker, Jeffrey G. (2006). Peer interactions, relationships, and groups. In William Damon & Richard M. Lerner (Series Eds.) & Nancy Eisenberg (Vol. Ed.), *Handbook of child psychology: Vol. 3. Social, emotional, and personality development* (6th ed., pp. 619–700). Hoboken, NJ: Wiley.

Rubin, Kenneth H., Coplan, Robert, Chen, Xinyin, Buskirk, Allison A., & Wojslawowicz, Julie C. (2005). Peer relationships in childhood. In Marc H. Bornstein & Michael E. Lamb (Eds.), *Developmental science: An advanced textbook* (5th ed., pp. 469–512). Mahwah, NJ: Erlbaum.

Rubin, Lawrence C. (Ed.). (2006). *Psychotropic drugs and popular culture: Essays on medicine, mental health and the media.* Jefferson, NC: McFarland.

Ruble, Diane N., Martin, Carol Lynn, & Berenbaum, Sheri. (2006). Gender development. In William Damon & Richard M. Lerner (Series Eds.) & Nancy Eisenberg (Vol. Ed.), *Handbook of child psychology: Vol. 3. Social, emotional, and personality development* (6th ed., pp. 858–932). Hoboken, NJ: Wiley.

Ruder, Debra Bradley. (2008, September–October). The teen brain. *Harvard Magazine, 111,* 8–10.

Rueda, M. Rosario, Rothbart, Mary K., Saccomanno, Lisa, & Posner, Michael I. (2007). Modifying brain networks underlying self regulation. In Daniel Romer & Elaine F. Walker (Eds.), *Adolescent psychopathology and the developing brain: Integrating brain and prevention science* (pp. 401–419). Oxford, UK: Oxford University Press.

Rueter, Martha A., & Kwon, Hee-Kyung. (2005). Developmental trends in adolescent suicidal ideation. *Journal of Research on Adolescence, 15,* 205–222.

Ruffman, Ted, Slade, Lance, Sandino, Juan Carlos, & Fletcher, Amanda. (2005). Are A-not-B errors caused by a belief about object location? *Child Development, 76,* 122–136.

Ruiz, Sarah A., & Silverstein, Merril. (2007). Relationships with grandparents and the emotional well-being of late adolescent and young adult grandchildren. *Journal of Social Issues, 63,* 793–808.

Running, Alice, Girard, Deb, & Woodward Tolle, Lauren. (2008). When there is nothing left to do, there is everything left to do. *American Journal of Hospice and Palliative Medicine, 24,* 451–454.

Russac, Randall J., Gatliff, Colleen, Reece, Mimi, & Spottswood, Diahann. (2007). Death anxiety across the adult years: An examination of age and gender effects. *Death Studies, 31,* 549–561.

Russell, Helen. (2008). Later life: A time to learn. *Educational Gerontology, 34,* 206–224.

Rust, Tiana B., & Kwong See, Sheree. (2007). Knowledge about aging and Alzheimer disease: A comparison of professional caregivers and noncaregivers. *Educational Gerontology, 33,* 349–364.

Rutledge, Patricia C., Park, Aesoon, & Sher, Kenneth J. (2008). 21st birthday drinking: Extremely extreme. *Journal of Consulting and Clinical Psychology, 76,* 511–516.

Rutter, Michael, & O'Connor, Thomas G. (2004). Are there biological programming effects for psychological development? Findings from a study of Romanian adoptees. *Developmental Psychology, 40,* 81–94.

Rutters, Femke, Nieuwenhuizen, Arie G., Vogels, Neeltje, Bouwman, Freek, Mariman, Edwin, & Westerterp-Plantenga, Margriet S. (2008). Leptin-adiposity relationship changes, plus behavioral and parental factors, are involved in the development of body weight in a Dutch children cohort. *Physiology & Behavior, 93,* 967–974.

Ryalls, Brigette Oliver. (2000). Dimensional adjectives: Factors affecting children's ability to compare objects using novel words. *Journal of Experimental Child Psychology, 76,* 26–49.

Ryan, Michael J. (2005, June 8). Punching out in Little League. *Boston Herald.*

Ryan, Suzanne, Franzetta, Kerry, Manlove, Jennifer, & Holcombe, Emily. (2007). Adolescents' discussions about contraception or STDs with partners before first sex. *Perspectives on Sexual and Reproductive Health, 39,* 149–157.

Ryan, Suzanne, Franzetta, Kerry, Manlove, Jennifer S., & Schelar, Erin. (2008). Older sexual partners during adolescence: Links to reproductive health outcomes in young adulthood. *Perspectives on Sexual and Reproductive Health, 40,* 17–26.

Saarni, Carolyn, Campos, Joseph J., Camras, Linda A., & Witherington, David. (2006). Emotional development: Action, communication, and understanding. In William Damon & Richard M. Lerner (Series Eds.) & Nancy Eisenberg (Vol. Ed.), *Handbook of child psychology: Vol. 3. Social, emotional, and personality development* (6th ed., pp. 226–299). Hoboken, NJ: Wiley.

Sachs, Jessica Snyder. (2007). *Good germs, bad germs: Health and survival in a bacterial world.* New York: Hill and Wang.

Sackett, Paul R., Hardison, Chaitra M., & Cullen, Michael J. (2004). On interpreting stereotype threat as accounting for African American–White differences on cognitive tests. *American Psychologist, 59,* 7–13.

Sacks, Oliver W. (1995). *An anthropologist on Mars: Seven paradoxical tales.* New York: Knopf.

Saey, Tina Hesman. (2008, May 24). Epic genetics: Genes' chemical clothes may underlie the biology behind mental illness. *Science News, 173.*

Saffran, Jenny R., Werker, Janet F., & Werner, Lynne A. (2006). The infant's auditory world: Hearing, speech, and the beginnings of language. In William Damon & Richard M. Lerner (Series Eds.) & Deanna Kuhn & Robert S. Siegler (Vol. Eds.), *Handbook of child psychology: Vol. 2. Cognition, perception, and language* (pp. 58–108). Hoboken, NJ: Wiley.

Sales, Jessica, Fivush, Robyn, & Teague, Gerald W. (2008). The role of parental coping in children with asthma's psychological well-being and asthma-related quality of life. *Journal of Pediatric Psychology, 33,* 208–219.

Salkind, Neil J. (2004). *An introduction to theories of human development.* Thousand Oaks, CA: Sage.

Salmivalli, Christina, Ojanen, Tiina, Haanpaa, Jemina, & Peets, Katlin. (2005). "I'm OK but you're not" and other peer-relational schemas: Explaining individual differences in children's social goals. *Developmental Psychology, 41,* 363–375.

Salovey, Peter, & Grewal, Daisy. (2005). The science of emotional intelligence. *Current Directions in Psychological Science, 14,* 281–285.

Salthouse, Timothy A. (2000). Steps toward the explanation of adult age differences in cognition. In Timothy J. Perfect & Elizabeth A. Maylor (Eds.), *Models of cognitive aging* (pp. 19–49). London: Oxford University Press.

Salvatore, Jessica, & Shelton, J. Nicole. (2007). Cognitive costs of exposure to racial prejudice. *Psychological Science, 18,* 810–815.

Salzarulo, Piero, & Fagioli, Igino. (1999). Changes of sleep states and physiological activities across the first year of life. In Alex Fedde Kalverboer, Maria Luisa Genta, & J. B. Hopkins (Eds.), *Current issues in developmental psychology: Biopsychological perspectives* (pp. 53–73). Dordrecht, The Netherlands: Kluwer.

Samuels, S. Jay. (2007). The DIBELS tests: Is speed of barking at print what we mean by reading fluency? *Reading Research Quarterly, 42,* 563–566.

Sandberg, David E., Bukowski, William M., Fung, Caroline M., & Noll, Robert B. (2004). Height and social adjustment: Are extremes a cause for concern and action? *Pediatrics, 114,* 744–750.

Sandel, Michael J. (2007). *The case against perfection: Ethics in the age of genetic engineering.* Cambridge, MA: Harvard University Press.

Sandstrom, Marlene J., & Herlan, Rebecca D. (2007). Threatened egotism or confirmed inadequacy? How children's perceptions of social status influence aggressive behavior toward peers. *Journal of Social & Clinical Psychology, 26,* 240–267.

Sandstrom, Marlene J., & Zakriski, Audrey L. (2004). Understanding the experience of peer rejection. In Janis B. Kupersmidt & Kenneth A. Dodge (Eds.), *Children's peer relations: From development to intervention* (pp. 101–118). Washington, DC: American Psychological Association.

Santelli, John S., Lindberg, Laura Duberstein, Finer, Lawrence B., & Singh, Susheela. (2007). Explaining recent declines in adolescent pregnancy in the United States: The contribution of abstinence and improved contraceptive use. *American Journal of Public Health, 97,* 150–156.

Santesso, Diane L., Schmidt, Louis A., & Trainor, Laurel J. (2007). Frontal brain electrical activity (EEG) and heart rate in response to affective infant-directed (ID) speech in 9-month-old infants. *Brain and Cognition, 65,* 14–21.

Saper, Clifford B. (2006, November 3). Life, the universe, and body temperature. *Science, 314,* 773–774.

Sarroub, Loukia K. (2001). The sojourner experience of Yemeni American high school students: An ethnographic portrait. *Harvard Educational Review, 71,* 390–415.

Satariano, William. (2006). *Epidemiology of aging: An ecological approach.* Sudbury, MA: Jones and Bartlett.

Saul, Stephanie. (2008, July 26). Weight drives the young to adult pills, data says. *New York Times.*

Saunders, Cicely M. (1978). *The management of terminal disease.* London: Arnold.

Savin-Williams, Ritch C. (2005). *The new gay teenager.* Cambridge, MA: Harvard University Press.

Savin-Williams, Ritch C., & Diamond, Lisa M. (2004). Sex. In Richard M. Lerner & Laurence D. Steinberg (Eds.), *Handbook of adolescent psychology* (2nd ed., pp. 189–231). Hoboken, NJ: Wiley.

Saxbe, Darby E., Repetti, Rena L., & Nishina, Adrienne. (2008). Marital satisfaction, recovery from work, and diurnal cortisol among men and women. *Health Psychology, 27,* 15–25.

Saxe, Geoffrey B. (1999). Sources of concepts: A cultural-developmental perspective. In Ellin Kofsky Scholnick, Katherine Nelson, Susan A. Gelman, & Patricia H. Miller (Eds.), *Conceptual development: Piaget's legacy* (pp. 253–267). Mahwah, NJ: Erlbaum.

Saylor, Megan M., & Sabbagh, Mark A. (2004). Different kinds of information affect word learning in the preschool years: The case of part-term learning. *Child Development, 75,* 395–408.

Scambler, Douglas J., Hepburn, Susan L., Rutherford, Mel, Wehner, Elizabeth A., & Rogers, Sally J. (2007). Emotional responsivity in children with autism, children with other developmental disabilities, and children with typical development. *Journal of Autism and Developmental Disorders, 37,* 553–563.

Scannapieco, Maria, & Connell-Carrick, Kelli. (2005). *Understanding child maltreatment: An ecological and developmental perspective.* New York: Oxford University Press.

Scarf, Maggie. (2008). *September songs: The good news about marriage in the later years.* New York: Riverhead Books.

Schachter, Sherry R. (2003). 9/11: A grief therapist's journal. In Marcia Lattanzi-Licht & Kenneth J. Doka (Eds.), *Living with grief: Coping with public tragedy* (pp. 15–25). New York: Brunner-Routledge.

Schafer, Graham. (2005). Infants can learn decontextualized words before their first birthday. *Child Development, 76,* 87–96.

Schaffer, H. Rudolph. (2000). The early experience assumption: Past, present, and future. *International Journal of Behavioral Development, 24,* 5–14.

Schaie, K. Warner. (2002). The impact of longitudinal studies on understanding development from young adulthood to old age. In Willard W. Hartup & Rainer K. Silbereisen (Eds.), *Growing points in developmental science: An introduction* (pp. 307–328). New York: Psychology Press.

Schaie, K. Warner. (2005). *Developmental influences on adult intelligence: The Seattle Longitudinal Study.* New York: Oxford University Press.

Schaie, K. Warner, & Carstensen, Laura L. (Eds.). (2006). *Social structures, aging, and self-regulation in the elderly.* New York: Springer.

Schaie, K. Warner, & Willis, Sherry L. (1996). *Adult development and aging* (4th ed.). New York: HarperCollins.

Scharf, Miri, & Mayseless, Ofra. (2007). Putting eggs in more than one basket: A new look at developmental processes of attachment in adolescence. *New Directions for Child and Adolescent Development, 2007,* 1–22.

Scher, Anat. (2008). Maternal separation anxiety as a regulator of infants' sleep. *Journal of Child Psychology and Psychiatry, 49,* 618–625.

Schick, Brenda, de Villiers, Peter, de Villiers, Jill, & Hoffmeister, Robert. (2007). Language and theory of mind: A study of deaf children. *Child Development, 78,* 376–396.

Schieber, Frank. (2006). Vision and aging. In James E. Birren & K. Warner Schaie (Eds.), *Handbook of the psychology of aging* (6th ed., pp. 129–161). Amsterdam: Elsevier.

Schieman, Scott, & Plickert, Gabriele. (2007). Functional limitations and changes in levels of depression among older adults: A multiple-hierarchy stratification perspective. *Journals of Gerontology Series B: Psychological Sciences and Social Sciences, 62,* S36–42.

Schim, Stephanie Myers, Doorenbos, Ardith Zwyghuizen, & Borse, Nagesh N. (2006). Enhancing cultural competence among hospice staff. *American Journal of Hospice and Palliative Medicine, 23,* 404–411.

Schindler, Ines, Staudinger, Ursula M., & Nesselroade, John R. (2006). Development and structural dynamics of personal life investment in old age. *Psychology and Aging, 21,* 737–753.

Schmader, Toni. (2002). Gender identification moderates stereotype threat effects on women's math performance. *Journal of Experimental Social Psychology, 38,* 194–201.

Schmitt, David P., Allik, Jüri, McCrae, Robert R., & Benet-Martínez, Verónica. (2007). The geographic distribution of Big Five personality traits: Patterns and profiles of human self-description across 56 nations. *Journal of Cross-Cultural Psychology, 38,* 173–212.

Schmookler, Terra, & Bursik, Krisanne. (2007). The value of monogamy in emerging adulthood: A gendered perspective. *Journal of Social and Personal Relationships, 24,* 819–835.

Schoen, Robert, Landale, Nancy S., & Daniels, Kimberly. (2007). Family transitions in young adulthood. *Demography, 44,* 807–820.

Schoeni, Robert F., & Ross, Karen E. (2005). Material assistance from families during the transition to adulthood. In Richard A. Settersten, Jr., Frank F. Furstenberg, Jr., & Rubén G. Rumbaut (Eds.), *On the frontier of adulthood: Theory, research, and public policy* (pp. 396–416). Chicago: University of Chicago Press.

Schraagen, Jan Maarten, & Leijenhorst, Henk. (2001). Searching for evidence: Knowledge and search strategies used by forensic scientists. In Eduardo Salas & Gary A. Klein (Eds.), *Linking expertise and naturalistic decision making* (pp. 263–274). Mahwah, NJ: Erlbaum.

Schreck, Christopher J., Burek, Melissa W., Stewart, Eric A., & Miller, J. Mitchell. (2007). Distress and violent victimization among young adolescents: Early puberty and the social interactionist explanation. *Journal of Research in Crime and Delinquency, 44,* 381–405.

Schulenberg, John, O'Malley, Patrick M., Bachman, Jerald G., & Johnston, Lloyd D. (2005). Early adult transitions and their relation to well-being and substance use. In Richard A. Settersten, Jr., Frank F. Furstenberg, Jr., & Rubén G. Rumbaut (Eds.), *On the frontier of adulthood: Theory, research, and public policy* (pp. 417–453). Chicago: University of Chicago Press.

Schulenberg, John, & Zarrett, Nicole R. (2006). Mental health during emerging adulthood: Continuity and discontinuity in courses, causes, and functions. In Jeffrey Jensen Arnett &

Jennifer Lynn Tanner (Eds.), *Emerging adults in America: Coming of age in the 21st century* (pp. 135–172). Washington, DC: American Psychological Association.

Schulman, Kevin A., Berlin, Jesse A., Harless, William, Kerner, Jon F., Sistrunk, Shyrl, Gersh, Bernard J., et al. (1999). The effect of race and sex on physicians' recommendations for cardiac catheterization. *New England Journal of Medicine, 340,* 618–626.

Schulz, James H., & Binstock, Robert H. (2008). *Aging nation: The economics and politics of growing older in America* (Paperback ed.). Baltimore: Johns Hopkins University Press.

Schumann, Cynthia Mills, Hamstra, Julia, Goodlin-Jones, Beth L., Lotspeich, Linda J., Kwon, Hower, Buonocore, Michael H., et al. (2004). The amygdala is enlarged in children but not adolescents with autism; the hippocampus is enlarged at all ages. *Journal of Neuroscience, 24,* 6392–6401.

Schwartz, Amy Ellen. (2009, April 3). *Age of entry and the high school performance of immigrant youth.* Paper presented at the Biennial meeting of the Society for Research in Child Development, Denver, CO.

Schwartz, Pepper. (2006). What elicits romance, passion, and attachment, and how do they affect our lives throughout the life cycle? In Ann C. Crouter & Alan Booth (Eds.), *Romance and sex in adolescence and emerging adulthood: Risks and opportunities* (pp. 49–60). Mahwah, NJ: Erlbaum.

Schwartz, Seth J., & Finley, Gordon E. (2005). Fathering in intact and divorced families: Ethnic differences in retrospective reports. *Journal of Marriage and Family, 67,* 207–215.

Schweinhart, Lawrence J., Montie, Jeanne, Xiang, Zongping, Barnett, W. Steven, Belfield, Clive R., & Nores, Milagros. (2005). *Lifetime effects: The High/Scope Perry Preschool Study through age 40.* Ypsilanti, MI: High/Scope Press.

Schweinhart, Lawrence J., & Weikart, David P. (1997). *Lasting differences: The High/Scope Preschool Curriculum Comparison Study through age 23.* Ypsilanti, MI: High/Scope Educational Research Foundation.

Scott, Lisa S., Pascalis, Olivier, & Nelson, Charles A. (2007). A domain-general theory of the development of perceptual discrimination. *Current Directions in Psychological Science, 16,* 197–201.

Scott, Mindy E., Booth, Alan, King, Valarie, & Johnson, David R. (2007). Postdivorce father–adolescent closeness. *Journal of Marriage and Family, 69,* 1194–1209.

Scott-Maxwell, Florida. (1968). *The measure of my days.* New York: Knopf.

Seale, Clive. (2006). Characteristics of end-of-life decisions: Survey of UK medical practitioners. *Palliative Medicine, 20,* 653–659.

Sears, Malcolm R., Greene, Justina M., Willan, Andrew R., Wiecek, Elizabeth M., Taylor, D. Robin, Flannery, Erin M., et al. (2003). A longitudinal, population-based, cohort study of childhood asthma followed to adulthood. *New England Journal of Medicine, 349,* 1414–1422.

Sears, Robert R., Maccoby, Eleanor E., & Levin, Harry. (1976). *Patterns of child rearing.* Stanford, CA: Stanford University Press.

Seaton, Eleanor K., Caldwell, Cleopatra H., Sellers, Robert M., & Jackson, James S. (2008). The prevalence of perceived discrimination among African American and Caribbean Black youth. *Developmental Psychology, 44,* 1288–1297.

Sebastián-Gallés, Núria. (2007). Biased to learn language. *Developmental Science, 10,* 713–718.

Segalowitz, Sidney J., & Schmidt, Louis A. (2003). Developmental psychology and the neurosciences. In Jaan Valsiner & Kevin J. Connolly (Eds.), *Handbook of developmental psychology* (pp. 48–71). Thousand Oaks, CA: Sage.

Seifer, Ronald, LaGasse, Linda L., Lester, Barry, Bauer, Charles R., Shankaran, Seetha, Bada, Henrietta S., et al. (2004). Attachment status in children prenatally exposed to cocaine and other substances. *Child Development, 75,* 850–868.

Seki, Fusako. (2001). The role of the government and the family in taking care of the frail elderly: A comparison of the United States and Japan. In David N. Weisstub, David C. Thomasma, Serge Gauthier, & George F. Tomossy (Eds.), *Aging: Caring for our elders* (pp. 83–105). Dordrecht, The Netherlands: Kluwer.

Serpell, Robert, & Haynes, Brenda Pitts. (2004). The cultural practice of intelligence testing: Problems of international export. In Robert J. Sternberg & Elena L. Grigorenko (Eds.), *Culture and competence: Contexts of life success* (pp. 163–185). Washington, DC: American Psychological Association.

Settersten, Richard A. (2002). Social sources of meaning in later life. In Robert S. Weiss & Scott A. Bass (Eds.), *Challenges of the third age: Meaning and purpose in later life* (pp. 55–79). London: Oxford University Press.

Settersten, Richard A., & Hagestad, Gunhild O. (1996). What's the latest? Cultural age deadlines for family transitions. *Gerontologist, 36,* 602–613.

Shahin, Hashem, Walsh, Tom, Sobe, Tama, Lynch, Eric, King, Mary-Claire, Avraham, Karen, et al. (2002). Genetics of congenital deafness in the Palestinian population: Multiple connexin 26 alleles with shared origins in the Middle East. *Human Genetics, 110,* 284–289.

Shanahan, Lilly, McHale, Susan M., Osgood, Wayne, & Crouter, Ann C. (2007). Conflict frequency with mothers and fathers from middle childhood to late adolescence: Within- and between-families comparisons. *Developmental Psychology, 43,* 539–550.

Shannon, Joyce Brennfleck (Ed.). (2007). *Eating disorders sourcebook: Basic consumer health information about anorexia nervosa, bulimia nervosa, binge eating, compulsive exercise, female athlete triad, and other eating disorders* (2nd ed.). Detroit, MI: Omnigraphics.

Shapiro, Adam, & Yarborough-Hayes, Raijah. (2008). Retirement and older men's health. *Generations, 32*(1), 49–53.

Shapiro, Jenessa R., & Neuberg, Steven L. (2007). From stereotype threat to stereotype threats: Implications of a multithreat framework for causes, moderators, mediators, consequences, and interventions. *Personality and Social Psychology Review, 11,* 107–130.

Sheehy, Gail. (1976). *Passages: Predictable crises of adult life.* New York: Dutton.

Sheldon, Kennon M., & Kasser, Tim. (2001). Getting older, getting better? Personal strivings and psychological maturity across the life span. *Developmental Psychology, 37,* 491–501.

Shepard, Thomas H., & Lemire, Ronald J. (2004). *Catalog of teratogenic agents* (11th ed.). Baltimore: Johns Hopkins University Press.

Sherman, Edmund, & Dacher, Joan. (2005). Cherished objects and the home: Their meaning and roles in late life. In Graham D. Rowles & Habib Chaudhury (Eds.), *Home and identity in late life international perspectives* (pp. 63–79). New York: Springer.

Shevell, Tracy, Malone, Fergal D., Vidaver, John, Porter, T. Flint, Luthy, David A., Comstock, Christine H., et al. (2005). Assisted reproductive technology and pregnancy outcome. *Obstetrics & Gynecology, 106,* 1039–1045.

Shields, Margot. (2007). Smoking—Prevalence, bans and exposure to second-hand smoke. *Health Reports 18*(3), 67–85.

Shirom, Arie, Toker, Sharon, Berliner, Shlomo, Shapira, Itzhak, & Melamed, Samuel. (2008). The effects of physical fitness and feeling vigorous on self-rated health. *Health Psychology, 27,* 567–575.

Shuey, Kim, & Hardy, Melissa A. (2003). Assistance to aging parents and parents-in-law: Does lineage affect family allocation decisions? *Journal of Marriage and Family, 65,* 418–431.

Shushan, Gregory. (2009). *Conceptions of the afterlife in early civilizations: Universalism, constructivism, and near-death experience.* London: Continuum.

Shweder, Richard A. (1994). Are moral intuitions self-evident truths? *Criminal Justice Ethics, 13,* 24–32.

Siebenbruner, Jessica, Zimmer-Gembeck, Melanie J., & Egeland, Byron. (2007). Sexual partners and contraceptive use: A 16-year prospective study predicting abstinence and risk behavior. *Journal of Research on Adolescence, 17,* 179–206.

Siegel, Larry. (2006). *Post-publication peer reviews: Correlation is not causation.* American Academy of Pediatrics. Retrieved May 28, 2009, from http://pediatrics.aappublications.org/cgi/eletters/118/2/e430#2217

Siegel, Lawrence A., & Siegel, Richard M. (2007). Sexual changes in the aging male. In Annette Fuglsang Owens & Mitchell S. Tepper (Eds.), *Sexual health: Vol. 2. Physical foundations* (pp. 223–255). Westport, CT: Praeger/Greenwood.

Siegler, Robert S. (1996). *Emerging minds: The process of change in children's thinking.* New York: Oxford University Press.

Siegler, Robert S., & Ramani, Geetha B. (2008). Playing linear numerical board games promotes low-income children's numerical development. *Developmental Science, 11,* 655–661.

Silventoinen, Karri, Hammar, Niklas, Hedlund, Ebba, Koskenvuo, Markku, Ronnemaa, Tapani, & Kaprio, Jaakko. (2008). Selective international migration by social position, health behaviour and personality. *European Journal of Public Health, 18,* 150–155.

Silverman, Wendy K., & Dick-Niederhauser, Andreas. (2004). Separation anxiety disorder. In Tracy L. Morris & John S. March (Eds.), *Anxiety disorders in children and adolescents* (2nd ed., pp. 164–188). New York: Guilford Press.

Silverstein, Merril. (2006). Intergenerational family transfers in social context. In Robert H. Binstock & Linda K. George (Eds.), *Handbook of aging and the social sciences* (6th ed., pp. 165–180). Amsterdam: Elsevier.

Silverstein, Merril, & Parker, Marti G. (2002). Leisure activities and quality of life among the oldest old in Sweden. *Research on Aging, 24,* 528–547.

Simpkins, Sandra D., Fredricks, Jennifer A., Davis-Kean, Pamela E., & Eccles, Jacquelynne S. (2006). Healthy mind, healthy habits: The influence of activity involvement in middle childhood. In Aletha C. Huston & Marika N. Ripke (Eds.), *Developmental contexts in middle childhood: Bridges to adolescence and adulthood* (pp. 283–302). New York: Cambridge University Press.

Simpson, Sarah. (2000). Dyslexia: A developmental language disorder. *Child: Care, Health and Development, 26,* 355–380.

Sinclair, David, & Howitz, Konrad. (2006). Dietary restriction, hormesis, and small molecule mimetics. In Edward J. Masoro & Steven N. Austad (Eds.), *Handbook of the biology of aging* (6th ed., pp. 63–104). Amsterdam: Elsevier Academic Press.

Singer, Lynn T., Arendt, Robert, Minnes, Sonia, Farkas, Kathleen, Salvator, Ann, Kirchner, H. Lester, et al. (2002). Cognitive and motor outcomes of cocaine-exposed infants. *Journal of the American Medical Association, 287,* 1952–1960.

Singh, Ripudaman, Kolvraa, Steen, & Rattan, Suresh I. S. (2007). Genetics of human longevity with emphasis on the relevance of HSP70 as candidate genes. *Frontiers in Bioscience, 12,* 4504–4513.

Sinha, Jill W., Cnaan, Ram A., & Gelles, Richard J. (2007). Adolescent risk behaviors and religion: Findings from a national study. *Journal of Adolescence, 30,* 231–249.

Sirard, John R., Ainsworth, Barbara E., McIver, Kerri L., & Pate, Russell R. (2005). Prevalence of active commuting at urban and suburban elementary schools in Columbia, SC. *American Journal of Public Health, 95,* 236–237.

Sircar, Ratna, & Sircar, Debashish. (2005). Adolescent rats exposed to repeated ethanol treatment show lingering behavioral impairments. *Alcoholism: Clinical and Experimental Research, 29,* 1402–1410.

Siu, Angela F. Y. (2007). Using friends to combat internalizing problems among primary school children in Hong Kong. *Journal of Cognitive and Behavioral Psychotherapies, 7,* 11–26.

Skinner, B. F. (1957). *Verbal behavior.* New York: Appleton-Century-Crofts.

Slaughter, Virginia, & Griffiths, Maya. (2007). Death understanding and fear of death in young children. *Clinical Child Psychology and Psychiatry, 12,* 525–535.

Slessor, Gillian, Phillips, Louise H., & Bull, Rebecca. (2008). Age-related declines in basic social perception: Evidence from tasks assessing eye-gaze processing. *Psychology and Aging, 23,* 812–822.

Sliwinski, Martin J., Hofer, Scott M., Hall, Charles, Buschke, Herman, & Lipton, Richard B. (2003). Modeling memory decline in older adults: The importance of preclinical dementia, attrition, and chronological age. *Psychology & Aging, 18,* 658–671.

Slobin, Dan I. (2001). Form-function relations: How do children find out what they are? In Melissa Bowerman & Stephen C. Levinson (Eds.), *Language acquisition and conceptual development* (pp. 406–449). Cambridge, UK: Cambridge University Press.

Smedley, Keren, & Whitten, Helen. (2006). *Age matters: Employing, motivating and managing older employees.* Aldershot, England: Gower.

Smetana, Judith G. (2008). "It's 10 o'clock: Do you know where your children are?" Recent advances in understanding parental monitoring and adolescents' information management. *Child Development Perspectives, 2,* 19–25.

Smetana, Judith G., Campione-Barr, Nicole, & Metzger, Aaron. (2006). Adolescent development in interpersonal and societal contexts. *Annual Review of Psychology, 57,* 255–284.

Smith, Christian (with Denton, Melinda Lundquist). (2005). *Soul searching: The religious and spiritual lives of American teenagers.* Oxford, UK: Oxford University Press.

Smith, Deborah B., & Moen, Phyllis. (2004). Retirement satisfaction for retirees and their spouses: Do gender and the retirement decision-making process matter? *Journal of Family Issues, 25,* 262–285.

Smith, J. David, Schneider, Barry H., Smith, Peter K., & Ananiadou, Katerina. (2004). The effectiveness of whole-school antibullying programs: A synthesis of evaluation research. *School Psychology Review, 33,* 547–560.

Smith, Margaret G., & Fong, Rowena. (2004). *The children of neglect: When no one cares.* New York: Brunner-Routledge.

Smith, Peter K., & Ananiadou, Katerina. (2003). The nature of school bullying and the effectiveness of school-based interventions. *Journal of Applied Psychoanalytic Studies, 5,* 189–209.

Smith, Peter K., Mahdavi, Jess, Carvalho, Manuel, Fisher, Sonja, Russell, Shanette, & Tippett, Neil. (2008). Cyberbullying: Its nature and impact in secondary school pupils. *Journal of Child Psychology and Psychiatry, 49,* 376–385.

Smith, Peter K., Pepler, Debra J., & Rigby, Ken (Eds.). (2004). *Bullying in schools: How successful can interventions be?* New York: Cambridge University Press.

Smith, Tom W. (2005). Generation gaps in attitudes and values from the 1970s to the 1990s. In Richard A. Settersten, Jr., Frank F. Furstenberg, Jr., & Rubén G. Rumbaut (Eds.), *On the frontier of adulthood: Theory, research, and public policy* (pp. 177–221). Chicago: University of Chicago Press.

Smyth, Joshua M. (2007). Beyond self-selection in video game play: An experimental examination of the consequences of massively multiplayer online role-playing game play. *CyberPsychology & Behavior, 10,* 717–727.

Sneed, Joel R., Hamagami, Fumiaki, McArdle, John J., Cohen, Patricia, & Chen, Henian. (2007). The dynamic interdependence of developmental domains across emerging adulthood. *Journal of Youth and Adolescence, 36,* 351–362.

Sneed, Joel R., & Whitbourne, Susan Krauss. (2005). Models of the aging self. *Journal of Social Issues, 61,* 375–388.

Snijders, Rosalinde J. M., & Nicolaides, Kypros H. (1996). *Ultrasound markers for fetal chromosomal defects.* New York: Parthenon.

Snow, Catherine E. (1984). Parent–child interaction and the development of communicative ability. In Richard L. Schiefelbusch & Joanne Pickar (Eds.), *The acquisition of communicative competence* (pp. 69–107). Baltimore: University Park Press.

Snow, Catherine E., & Kang, Jennifer Yusun. (2006). Becoming bilingual, biliterate, and bicultural. In William Damon & Richard M. Lerner (Series Eds.) & K. Ann Renninger & Irving E. Sigel (Vol. Eds.), *Handbook of child psychology: Vol. 4. Child psychology in practice* (6th ed., pp. 75–102). Hoboken, NJ: Wiley.

Snow, Catherine E., Porche, Michelle V., Tabors, Patton O., & Harris, Stephanie Ross. (2007). *Is literacy enough? Pathways to academic success for adolescents.* Baltimore: Paul H. Brookes.

Snow, David. (2006). Regression and reorganization of intonation between 6 and 23 months. *Child Development, 77,* 281–296.

Snyder, James, Schrepferman, Lynn, Oeser, Jessica, Patterson, Gerald, Stoolmiller, Mike, Johnson, Kassy, et al. (2005). Deviancy training and association with deviant peers in young children: Occurrence and contribution to early-onset conduct problems. *Development & Psychopathology, 17,* 397–413.

Snyder, Thomas D., Dillow, Sally A., & Hoffman, Charlene M. (2008). *Digest of education statistics: 2007.* National Center for Education Statistics. Retrieved July 4, 2009, from http://nces.ed.gov/pubsearch/pubsinfo.asp?pubid=2008022

Snyder, Thomas D., Tan, Alexandra G., & Hoffman, Charlene M. (2004). *Digest of education statistics, 2003* (NCES 2005025). Washington, DC: National Center for Education Statistics.

Snyder, Thomas D., Tan, Alexandra G., & Hoffman, Charlene M. (2006). *Digest of education statistics, 2005* (NCES 2006-030). Washington, DC: National Center for Education Statistics.

Social Security Administration. (2009, May 8). *Popular baby names.* Retrieved June 1, 2009, from http://www.ssa.gov/OACT/babynames/

Soderstrom, Melanie. (2007). Beyond babytalk: Re-evaluating the nature and content of speech input to preverbal infants. *Developmental Review, 27,* 501–532.

Soekadar, Surjo R., Haagen, Klaus, & Birbaumer, Niels. (2008). Brain-computer interfaces (BCI): Restoration of movement and thought from neuroelectric and metabolic brain activity. In Armin Fuchs & Viktor K. K. Jirsa (Eds.), *Coordination: Neural, behavioral and social dynamics* (pp. 229–252). New York: Springer.

Sofie, Cecilia A., & Riccio, Cynthia A. (2002). A comparison of multiple methods for the identification of children with reading disabilities. *Journal of Learning Disabilities, 35,* 234–244.

Soliday, Elizabeth. (2007). Infant feeding and cognition: Integrating a developmental perspective. *Child Development Perspectives, 1,* 19–25.

Solomon, Jennifer Crew, & Marx, Jonathan. (2000). The physical, mental, and social health of custodial grandparents. In Bert Hayslip, Jr. & Robin Goldberg-Glen (Eds.), *Grandparents raising grandchildren: Theoretical, empirical, and clinical perspectives* (pp. 183–205). New York: Springer.

Sorkin, Dara H., & Rook, Karen S. (2006). Dealing with negative social exchanges in later life: Coping responses, goals, and effectiveness. *Psychology and Aging, 21,* 715–725.

Sowell, Elizabeth R., Thompson, Paul M., & Toga, Arthur W. (2007). Mapping adolescent brain maturation using structural magnetic resonance imaging. In Daniel Romer & Elaine F. Walker (Eds.), *Adolescent psychopathology and the developing brain: Integrating brain and prevention science* (pp. 55–84). Oxford, UK: Oxford University Press.

Spearman, Charles Edward. (1927). *The abilities of man, their nature and measurement.* New York: Macmillan.

Spelke, Elizabeth S. (1993). Object perception. In Alvin I. Goldman (Ed.), *Readings in philosophy and cognitive science* (pp. 447–460). Cambridge, MA: MIT Press.

Spencer, John P., Clearfield, Melissa, Corbetta, Daniela, Ulrich, Beverly, Buchanan, Patricia, & Schöner, Gregor. (2006). Moving toward a grand theory of development: In memory of Esther Thelen. *Child Development, 77,* 1521–1538.

Spooner, Donna M., & Pachana, Nancy A. (2006). Ecological validity in neuropsychological assessment: A case for greater consideration in research with neurologically intact populations. *Archives of Clinical Neuropsychology, 21,* 327–337.

Sprung, Charles L., Carmel, Sara, Sjokvist, Peter, Baras, Mario, Cohen, Simon L., Maia, Paulo, et al. (2007). Attitudes of European physicians, nurses, patients, and families regarding end-of-life decisions: The ETHICATT study. *Intensive Care Medicine, 33,* 104–110.

Sroufe, L. Alan, Egeland, Byron, Carlson, Elizabeth A., & Collins, W. Andrew. (2005). *The development of the person: The Minnesota study of risk and adaptation from birth to adulthood.* New York: Guilford.

St Clair, David, Xu, Mingqing, Wang, Peng, Yu, Yaqin, Fang, Yourong, Zhang, Feng, et al. (2005). Rates of adult schizophrenia following prenatal exposure to the Chinese famine of 1959–1961. *Journal of the American Medical Association, 294,* 557–562.

St. Petersburg-USA Orphanage Research Team. (2008). The effects of early social-emotional and relationship experience on the development of young orphanage children. *Monographs of the Society for Research in Child Development, 73*(3), 1–262.

Stacey, Phillip S., & Sullivan, Karen A. (2004). Preliminary investigation of thiamine and alcohol intake in clinical and healthy samples. *Psychological Reports, 94*(3, Pt. 1), 845–848.

Staff, Jeremy, Mortimer, Jeylan T., & Uggen, Christopher. (2004). Work and leisure in adolescence. In Richard M. Lerner & Laurence D. Steinberg (Eds.), *Handbook of adolescent psychology* (2nd ed., pp. 429–450). Hoboken, NJ: Wiley.

Stanley, Jennifer Tehan, & Blanchard-Fields, Fredda. (2008). Challenges older adults face in detecting deceit: The role of emotion recognition. *Psychology and Aging, 23,* 24–32.

Stansfeld, Stephen A., Berglund, Birgitta, Clark, Charlotte, Lopez-Barrio, Isabel, Fischer, Paul, Öhrström, Evy, et al. (2005). Aircraft and road traffic noise and children's cognition and health: A cross-national study. *Lancet, 365,* 1942–1949.

Stanton, Bonita, & Burns, James. (2003). Sustaining and broadening intervention effect: Social norms, core values, and parents. In Daniel Romer (Ed.), *Reducing adolescent risk: Toward an integrated approach* (pp. 193–200). Thousand Oaks, CA: Sage.

Stanton, Cynthia K., & Holtz, Sara A. (2006). Levels and trends in cesarean birth in the developing world. *Studies in Family Planning, 37,* 41–48.

Starkstein, Sergio E., & Merello, Marcelo J. (2002). *Psychiatric and cognitive disorders in Parkinson's disease.* New York: Cambridge University Press.

Stattin, Håkan, & Kerr, Margaret. (2000). Parental monitoring: A reinterpretation. *Child Development, 71,* 1072–1085.

Staudinger, Ursula M., & Lindenberger, Ulman. (2003). Why read another book on human development? Understanding human development takes a metatheory and multiple disciplines. In Ursula M. Staudinger & Ulman E. R. Lindenberger (Eds.), *Understanding human development: Dialogues with lifespan psychology* (pp. 1–13). Boston: Kluwer.

Staudinger, Ursula M., & Werner, Ines. (2003). Wisdom: Its social nature and lifespan development. In Jaan Valsiner & Kevin J. Connolly (Eds.), *Handbook of developmental psychology* (pp. 584–602). Thousand Oaks, CA: Sage.

Steele, Claude M. (1997). A threat in the air: How stereotypes shape intellectual identity and performance. *American Psychologist, 52,* 613–629.

Stein, Arlene. (2006). *Shameless: Sexual dissidence in American culture.* New York: New York University Press.

Stein, Theodore J. (2007). Court-ordered grandparent visitation: Welcome event or unwarranted intrusion into family life? *Social Service Review, 81,* 229–243.

Steinberg, Adria. (1993). *Adolescents and schools: Improving the fit.* Cambridge, MA: Harvard Education Letter.

Steinberg, Laurence. (2001). We know some things: Parent–adolescent relationships in retrospect and prospect. *Journal of Research on Adolescence, 11,* 1–19.

Steinberg, Laurence. (2004). Risk taking in adolescence: What changes, and why? In Ronald E. Dahl & Linda Patia Spear (Eds.), *Adolescent brain development: Vulnerabilities and opportunities* (Vol. 1021, pp. 51–58). New York: New York Academy of Sciences.

Steinberg, Laurence. (2007). Risk taking in adolescence: New perspectives from brain and behavioral science. *Current Directions in Psychological Science, 16,* 55–59.

Steinberg, Laurence. (2008). A social neuroscience perspective on adolescent risk-taking. *Developmental Review, 28,* 78–106.

Steinberg, Laurence, Lamborn, Susie D., Darling, Nancy, Mounts, Nina S., & Dornbusch, Sanford M. (1994). Over-time changes in adjustment and competence among adolescents from authoritative, authoritarian, indulgent, and neglectful families. *Child Development, 65,* 754–770.

Steiner, Meir, & Young, Elizabeth A. (2008). Hormones and mood. In Jill B. Becker, Karen J. Berkley, Nori Geary, Elizabeth Hampson, James P. Herman, & Elizabeth Young (Eds.), *Sex differences in the brain: From genes to behavior* (pp. 405–426). New York: Oxford University Press.

Stel, Vianda S., Smit, Johannes H., Pluijm, Saskia M. F., & Lips, Paul. (2004). Consequences of falling in older men and women and risk factors for health service use and functional decline. *Age and Ageing, 33,* 58–65.

Stenberg, Gunilla, & Hagekull, Berit. (2007). Infant looking behavior in ambiguous situations: Social referencing or attachment behavior? *Infancy, 11,* 111–129.

Stern, Daniel N. (1985). *The interpersonal world of the infant: A view from psychoanalysis and developmental psychology.* New York: Basic Books.

Sternberg, Betty J., Kaplan, Karen A., & Borck, Jennifer E. (2007). Enhancing adolescent literacy achievement through integration of technology in the classroom. *Reading Research Quarterly, 42,* 416–420.

Sternberg, Robert J. (1988a). *The triarchic mind: A new theory of human intelligence.* New York: Viking.

Sternberg, Robert J. (1988b). Triangulating love. In Robert J. Sternberg & Michael L. Barnes (Eds.), *The psychology of love* (pp. 119–138). New Haven, CT: Yale University Press.

Sternberg, Robert J. (1996). *Successful intelligence: How practical and creative intelligence determine success in life.* New York: Simon & Schuster.

Sternberg, Robert J. (2002). Beyond g: The theory of successful intelligence. In Robert J. Sternberg & Elena L. Grigorenko (Eds.), *The general factor of intelligence: How general is it?* (pp. 447–479). Mahwah, NJ: Erlbaum.

Sternberg, Robert J. (2003). *Wisdom, intelligence, and creativity synthesized.* New York: Cambridge University Press.

Sternberg, Robert J. (2006). The Rainbow Project: Enhancing the SAT through assessments of analytical, practical, and creative skills. *Intelligence, 34,* 321–350.

Sternberg, Robert J., Forsythe, George B., Hedlund, Jennifer, Horvath, Joseph A., Wagner, Richard K., Williams, Wendy M., et al. (2000). *Practical intelligence in everyday life.* New York: Cambridge University Press.

Sternberg, Robert J., & Grigorenko, Elena (Eds.). (2002). *The general factor of intelligence: How general is it?* Mahwah, NJ: Erlbaum.

Sterns, Harvey L., & Huyck, Margaret Hellie. (2001). The role of work in midlife. In Margie E. Lachman (Ed.), *Handbook of midlife development* (pp. 447–486). New York: Wiley.

Stevens, Judy A. (2002–2003). Falls among older adults: Public health impact and prevention strategies. *Generations, 26*(4), 7–14.

Stewart, Susan D., Manning, Wendy D., & Smock, Pamela J. (2003). Union formation among men in the U.S.: Does having prior children matter? *Journal of Marriage and Family, 65,* 90–104.

Stigler, James W., & Hiebert, James. (1999). *The teaching gap: Best ideas from the world's teachers for improving education in the classroom.* New York: Free Press.

Stiles, Joan. (2008). *The fundamentals of brain development: Integrating nature and nurture.* Cambridge, MA: Harvard University Press.

Stipek, Deborah, Feiler, Rachelle, Daniels, Denise, & Milburn, Sharon. (1995). Effects of different instructional approaches on young children's achievement and motivation. *Child Development, 66,* 209–223.

Stokstad, Erik. (2003, December 12). The vitamin D deficit. *Science, 302,* 1886–1888.

Stone, Robyn I. (2006). Emerging issues in long-term care. In Robert H. Binstock & Linda K. George (Eds.), *Handbook of aging and the social sciences* (6th ed., pp. 397–418). Amsterdam: Elsevier.

Strathearn, Lane, Li, Jian, Fonagy, Peter, & Montague, P. Read. (2008). What's in a smile? Maternal brain responses to infant facial cues. *Pediatrics, 122,* 40–51.

Straus, Murray A. (with Donnelly, Denise A.). (1994). *Beating the devil out of them: Corporal punishment in American families.* New York: Lexington Books.

Strayer, David L., & Drews, Frank A. (2007). Cell-phone-induced driver distraction. *Current Directions in Psychological Science, 16,* 128–131.

Stright, Anne Dopkins, Gallagher, Kathleen Cranley, & Kelley, Ken. (2008). Infant temperament moderates relations between maternal parenting in early childhood and children's adjustment in first grade. *Child Development, 79,* 186–200.

Strom, Robert D., & Strom, Shirley K. (2000). Goals for grandparents and support groups. In Bert Hayslip, Jr. & Robin Goldberg-Glen (Eds.), *Grandparents raising grandchildren: Theoretical, empirical, and clinical perspectives* (pp. 289–303). New York: Springer.

Stubben, Jerry D. (2001). Working with and conducting research among American Indian families. *American Behavioral Scientist, 44,* 1466–1481.

Suárez-Orozco, Carola, & Carhill, Avary. (2008). Afterword: New directions in research with immigrant families and their children. *New Directions for Child and Adolescent Development, 2008*(121), 87–104.

Suárez-Orozco, Carola, & Suárez-Orozco, Marcelo M. (2001). *Children of immigration.* Cambridge, MA: Harvard University Press.

Suárez-Orozco, Carola, Suárez-Orozco, Marcelo M., & Todorova, Irina. (2008). *Learning a new land: Immigrant students in American society.* Cambridge, MA: Harvard University Press.

Subbotsky, Eugene. (2000). Causal reasoning and behaviour in children and adults in a technologically advanced society: Are we still prepared to believe in magic and animism? In Peter Mitchell & Kevin John Riggs (Eds.), *Children's reasoning and the mind* (pp. 327–347). Hove, UK: Psychology Press.

Subrahmanyam, Kaveri, Reich, Stephanie M., Waechter, Natalia, & Espinoza, Guadalupe. (2008). Online and offline social networks: Use of social networking sites by emerging adults. *Journal of Applied Developmental Psychology, 29,* 420–433.

Subrahmanyam, Kaveri, Smahel, David, & Greenfield, Patricia. (2006). Connecting developmental constructions to the internet: Identity presentation and sexual exploration in online teen chat rooms. *Developmental Psychology, 42,* 395–406.

Suellentrop, Katherine, Morrow, Brian, Williams, Letitia, & D'Angelo, Denise. (2006, October 6). Monitoring progress toward achieving maternal and infant Healthy People 2010 objectives—19 states, Pregnancy Risk Assessment Monitoring System (PRAMS), 2000–2003. *MMWR Surveillance Summaries, 55*(SS09), 1–11.

Sugihara, Yoko, Sugisawa, Hidehiro, Shibata, Hiroshi, & Harada, Ken. (2008). Productive roles, gender, and depressive symptoms: Evidence from a national longitudinal study of late-middle-aged Japanese. *Journals of Gerontology Series B: Psychological Sciences and Social Sciences, 63,* P227–234.

Suh, Eunkook M., Diener, Ed, & Updegraff, John A. (2008). From culture to priming conditions: Self-construal influences on life satisfaction judgments. *Journal of Cross-Cultural Psychology, 39,* 3–15.

Suitor, J. Jill, Sechrist, Jori, Plikuhn, Mari, Pardo, Seth T., & Pillemer, Karl. (2008). Within-family differences in parent–child relations across the life course. *Current Directions in Psychological Science, 17,* 334–338.

Sullivan, Sheila. (1999). *Falling in love: A history of torment and enchantment.* London: Macmillan.

Sullivan, Tara M., Bertrand, Jane T., Rice, Janet, & Shelton, James D. (2006). Skewed contraceptive method mix: Why it happens, why it matters. *Journal of Biosocial Science, 38,* 501–521.

Sulmasy, Daniel P. (2006). Spiritual issues in the care of dying patients: ". . . It's okay between me and God." *Journal of the American Medical Association, 296,* 1385–1392.

Sun, Min, & Rugolotto, Simone. (2004). Assisted infant toilet training in a Western family setting. *Journal of Developmental & Behavioral Pediatrics, 25,* 99–101.

Sun, Rongjun, & Liu, Yuzhi. (2008). The more engagement, the better? A study of mortality of the oldest old in China. In Zeng Yi, Dudley L. Poston, Jr., Denese Ashbaugh Vlosky, & Danan Gu (Eds.), *Healthy longevity in China* (pp. 177–192). Dordrecht, The Netherlands: Springer.

Suomi, Steven J. (2002). Parents, peers, and the process of socialization in primates. In John G. Borkowski, Sharon Landesman Ramey, & Marie Bristol-Power (Eds.), *Parenting and the child's world: Influences on academic, intellectual, and social-emotional development* (pp. 265–279). Mahwah, NJ: Erlbaum.

Supiano, Mark A. (2006). Hypertension in later life. *Generations, 30*(3), 11–16.

Susman, Elizabeth J., Dockray, Samantha, Schiefelbein, Virginia L., Herwehe, Suellen, Heaton, Jodi A., & Dorn, Lorah D. (2007). Morningness/eveningness, morning-to-afternoon cortisol ratio, and antisocial behavior problems during puberty. *Developmental Psychology, 43,* 811–822.

Susman, Elizabeth J., & Rogol, Alan. (2004). Puberty and psychological development. In Richard M. Lerner & Laurence D. Steinberg (Eds.), *Handbook of adolescent psychology* (2nd ed., pp. 15–44). Hoboken, NJ: Wiley.

Sutcliffe, James S. (2008, July 11). Insights into the pathogenesis of autism. *Science, 321,* 208–209.

Sutton-Smith, Brian. (1997). *The ambiguity of play.* Cambridge, MA: Harvard University Press.

Suzuki, Lalita K., & Calzo, Jerel P. (2004). The search for peer advice in cyberspace: An examination of online teen bulletin boards about health and sexuality. *Journal of Applied Developmental Psychology, 25,* 685–698.

Swanson, Richard A. (2007). *Analysis for improving performance: Tools for diagnosing organizations and documenting workplace expertise* (2nd ed.). San Francisco: Berrett-Koehler Publishers.

Syed, Moin, & Azmitia, Margarita. (2008). A narrative approach to ethnic identity in emerging adulthood: Bringing life to the identity status model. *Developmental Psychology, 44,* 1012–1027.

Szinovacz, Maximiliane. (1998). Grandparent research: Past, present and future. In Maximiliane Szinovácz (Ed.), *Handbook on grandparenthood* (pp. 1–20). Westport, CT: Greenwood Press.

Szinovacz, Maximiliane E. (2000). Changes in housework after retirement: A panel analysis. *Journal of Marriage and the Family, 62,* 78–92.

Szinovacz, Maximiliane E., & Davey, Adam. (2005). Retirement and marital decision making: Effects on retirement satisfaction. *Journal of Marriage and Family, 67,* 387–398.

Taga, Keiko A., Markey, Charlotte N., & Friedman, Howard S. (2006). A longitudinal investigation of associations between boys' pubertal timing and adult behavioral health and well-being. *Journal of Youth and Adolescence, 35,* 401–411.

Talge, Nicole M., Neal, Charles, & Glover, Vivette. (2007). Antenatal maternal stress and long-term effects on child neurodevelopment: How and why? *Journal of Child Psychology and Psychiatry, 48,* 245–261.

Tallandini, Maria Anna, & Scalembra, Chiara. (2006). Kangaroo mother care and mother–premature infant dyadic interaction. *Infant Mental Health Journal, 27,* 251–275.

Tamay, Zeynep, Akcay, Ahmet, Ones, Ulker, Guler, Nermin, Kilic, Gurkan, & Zencir, Mehmet. (2007). Prevalence and risk factors for allergic rhinitis in primary school children. *International Journal of Pediatric Otorhinolaryngology, 71,* 463–471.

Tamis-LeMonda, Catherine S., Bornstein, Marc H., & Baumwell, Lisa. (2001). Maternal responsiveness and children's achievement of language milestones. *Child Development, 72,* 748–767.

Tanaka, Yuko, & Nakazawa, Jun. (2005). Job-related temporary father absence (Tanshinfunin) and child development. In David W. Shwalb, Jun Nakazawa, & Barbara J. Shwalb (Eds.), *Applied developmental psychology: Theory, practice, and research from Japan* (pp. 241–260). Greenwich, CT: Information Age.

Tang, Chao-Hsiun, Wang, Han-I, Hsu, Chun-Sen, Su, Hung-Wen, Chen, Mei-Ju, & Lin, Herng-Ching. (2006). *Risk-adjusted cesarean section rates for the assessment of physician performance in Taiwan: A population-based study.* BioMed Central. Retrieved September 9, 2009, from http://www.biomedcentral.com/1471-2458/6/246

Tang, Fengyan. (2006). What resources are needed for volunteerism? A life course perspective. *Journal of Applied Gerontology, 25,* 375–390.

Tangney, June Price, Stuewig, Jeff, & Mashek, Debra J. (2007). Moral emotions and moral behavior. *Annual Review of Psychology, 58,* 345–372.

Tardif, Twila, Fletcher, Paul, Liang, Weilan, Zhang, Zhixiang, Kaciroti, Niko, & Marchman, Virginia A. (2008). Baby's first 10 words. *Developmental Psychology, 44,* 929–938.

Tarrant, Mark, MacKenzie, Liam, & Hewitt, Lisa A. (2006). Friendship group identification, multidimensional self-concept, and experience of developmental tasks in adolescence. *Journal of Adolescence, 29,* 627–640.

Tarrant, Shira. (2006). *When sex became gender.* New York: Routledge.

Tarullo, Amanda R., & Gunnar, Megan R. (2006). Child maltreatment and the developing HPA axis. *Hormones and Behavior, 50,* 632–639.

Tay, Marc Tze-Hsin, Au Eong, Kah Guan, Ng, C. Y., & Lim, M. K. (1992). Myopia and educational attainment in 421,116 young Singaporean males. *Annals, Academy of Medicine, Singapore, 21,* 785–791.

Taylor, Alan C., Robila, Mihaela, & Lee, Hae Seung. (2005). Distance, contact, and intergenerational relationships: Grandparents and adult grandchildren from an international perspective. *Journal of Adult Development, 12,* 33–41.

Taylor, Marjorie, Carlson, Stephanie M., Maring, Bayta L., Gerow, Lynn, & Charley, Carolyn M. (2004). The characteristics and correlates of fantasy in school-age children: Imaginary companions, impersonation, and social understanding. *Developmental Psychology, 40,* 1173–1187.

Taylor, Ronald D., Seaton, Eleanor, & Dominguez, Antonio. (2008). Kinship support, family relations, and psychological adjustment among low-income African American mothers and adolescents. *Journal of Research on Adolescence, 18,* 1–22.

Taylor, Shelley E. (2006). Tend and befriend: Biobehavioral bases of affiliation under stress. *Current Directions in Psychological Science, 15,* 273–277.

Taylor, Shelley E., Klein, Laura Cousino, Lewis, Brian P., Gruenewald, Tara L., Gurung, Regan A. R., & Updegraff, John A. (2000). Biobehavioral responses to stress in females: Tend-and-befriend, not fight-or-flight. *Psychological Review, 107,* 411–429.

Teachman, Jay D. (2008a). Complex life course patterns and the risk of divorce in second marriages. *Journal of Marriage and Family, 70,* 294–305.

Teachman, Jay D. (2008b). The living arrangements of children and their educational well-being. *Journal of Family Issues, 29,* 734–761.

Teachman, Jay D., & Tedrow, Lucky. (2008). Divorce, race, and military service: More than equal pay and equal opportunity. *Journal of Marriage and Family, 70,* 1030–1044.

Teese, Robert, & Bradley, Graham. (2008). Predicting recklessness in emerging adults: A test of a psychosocial model. *Journal of Social Psychology, 148,* 105–126.

ter Bogt, Tom, Schmid, Holger, Gabhainn, Saoirse Nic, Fotiou, Anastasios, & Vollebergh, Wilma. (2006). Economic and cultural correlates of cannabis use among mid-adolescents in 31 countries. *Addiction, 101,* 241–251.

Tester, June M., Rutherford, George W., Wald, Zachary, & Rutherford, Mary W. (2004). A matched case-control study evaluating the effectiveness of speed humps in reducing child pedestrian injuries. *American Journal of Public Health, 94,* 646–650.

Thaler, Richard H., & Sunstein, Cass R. (2008). *Nudge: Improving decisions about health, wealth, and happiness.* New Haven, CT: Yale University Press.

Thelen, Esther, & Corbetta, Daniela. (2002). Microdevelopment and dynamic systems: Applications to infant motor development. In Nira Granott & Jim Parziale (Eds.), *Microdevelopment: Transition processes in development and learning* (pp. 59–79). New York: Cambridge University Press.

Thelen, Esther, & Smith, Linda B. (2006). Dynamic systems theories. In William Damon & Richard M. Lerner (Series Eds.) & Richard M. Lerner (Vol. Ed.), *Handbook of child psychology: Vol. 1. Theoretical models of human development* (6th ed., pp. 258–312). Hoboken, NJ: Wiley.

Thiele, Dianne M., & Whelan, Thomas A. (2008). The relationship between grandparent satisfaction, meaning, and generativity. *International Journal of Aging and Human Development, 66,* 21–48.

Thobaben, Marshelle. (2006). Understanding compulsive hoarding. *Home Health Care Management Practice, 18,* 152–154.

Thomas, Ayanna K., & Bulevich, John B. (2006). Effective cue utilization reduces memory errors in older adults. *Psychology and Aging, 21,* 379–389.

Thomas, David R. (2009). Vitamins and health in older persons. In Ronald R. Watson (Ed.), *Handbook of nutrition in the aged* (4th ed., pp. 15–28). Boca Raton, FL: CRC Press.

Thomas, Dylan. (1957). *The collected poems of Dylan Thomas* (6th ed.). New York: New Directions.

Thomas, Michael S. C., & Johnson, Mark H. (2008). New advances in understanding sensitive periods in brain development. *Current Directions in Psychological Science, 17,* 1–5.

Thomas, William H. (2007). *What are old people for? How elders will save the world* (Paperback ed.). Acton, MA: VanderWyk & Burnham.

Thompson, Elisabeth Morgan, & Morgan, Elizabeth M. (2008). "Mostly straight" young women: Variations in sexual behavior and identity development. *Developmental Psychology, 44,* 15–21.

Thompson, Ross A. (2006). The development of the person: Social understanding, relationships, conscience, self. In William Damon & Richard M. Lerner (Series Eds.) & Nancy Eisenberg (Vol. Ed.), *Handbook of child psychology: Vol. 3. Social, emotional, and personality development* (6th ed., pp. 24–98). Hoboken, NJ: Wiley.

Thompson, Ross A., & Nelson, Charles A. (2001). Developmental science and the media: Early brain development. *American Psychologist, 56,* 5–15.

Thompson, Ross A., & Raikes, H. Abigail. (2003). Toward the next quarter-century: Conceptual and methodological challenges for attachment theory. *Development & Psychopathology, 15,* 691–718.

Thompson, Ross A., & Wyatt, Jennifer M. (1999). Values, policy, and research on divorce: Seeking fairness for children. In Ross A. Thompson & Paul R. Amato (Eds.), *The postdivorce family: Children, parenting, and society* (pp. 191–232). Thousand Oaks, CA: Sage.

Thomson, Judith Jarvis. (1986). *Rights, restitution, and risk: Essays in moral theory* (William Parent, Ed.). Cambridge, MA: Harvard University Press.

Thomson, W. Murray, Poulton, Richie, Broadbent, Jonathan M., Moffitt, Terrie E., Caspi, Avshalom, Beck, James D., et al. (2008). Cannabis smoking and periodontal disease among young adults. *Journal of the American Medical Association, 299,* 525–531.

Thornton, Arland, Axinn, William G., & Xie, Yu. (2007). *Marriage and cohabitation.* Chicago: University of Chicago Press.

Thornton, Wendy J. L., & Dumke, Heike A. (2005). Age differences in everyday problem-solving and decision-making effectiveness: A meta-analytic review. *Psychology and Aging, 20,* 85–99.

Thurber, James. (1999). The secret life of James Thurber. In James Thurber (Ed.), *The Thurber carnival.* New York: Harper Perennial.

Tilling, Kate, Lawlor, Debbie A., Davey Smith, George, Chambless, Lloyd, & Szklo, Moyses. (2006). The relation between components of adult height and intimal-medial thickness in middle age: The Atherosclerosis Risk in Communities Study. *American Journal of Epidemiology, 164,* 136–142.

Timiras, Mary Letitia. (2003). The skin. In Paola S. Timiras (Ed.), *Physiological basis of aging and geriatrics* (3rd ed., pp. 397–404). Boca Raton, FL: CRC Press.

Tishkoff, Sarah A., Reed, Floyd A., Friedlaender, Francoise R., Ehret, Christopher, Ranciaro, Alessia, Froment, Alain, et al. (2009, May 22). The genetic structure and history of Africans and African Americans. *Science, 324,* 1035–1044.

Tither, Jacqueline M., & Ellis, Bruce J. (2008). Impact of fathers on daughters' age at menarche: A genetically and environmentally controlled sibling study. *Developmental Psychology, 44,* 1409–1420.

Titus, Dale N. (2007). Strategies and resources for enhancing the achievement of mobile students. *NASSP Bulletin, 91,* 81–97.

Tobin, Sheldon S. (1996). Cherished possessions: The meaning of things. *Generations, 20*(3), 46–48.

Tomasello, Michael. (2001). Perceiving intentions and learning words in the second year of life. In Melissa Bowerman & Stephen C. Levinson (Eds.), *Language acquisition and conceptual development* (pp. 132–158). Cambridge, UK: Cambridge University Press.

Tomasello, Michael. (2006). Acquiring linguistic constructions. In William Damon & Richard M. Lerner (Series Eds.) & Deanna Kuhn & Robert S. Siegler (Vol. Eds.), *Handbook of child psychology: Vol. 2. Cognition, perception, and language* (6th ed., pp. 255–298). Hoboken, NJ: Wiley.

Tomasello, Michael, Carpenter, Malinda, & Liszkowski, Ulf. (2007). A new look at infant pointing. *Child Development, 78,* 705–722.

Torgesen, Joseph K. (2004). Preventing early reading failure—And its devastating downward spiral. *American Educator, 28,* 6–9, 12–13, 17–19, 45–47.

Torney-Purta, Judith, Lehmann, Rainer, Oswald, Hans, & Schulz, Wolfram. (2001). *Citizenship and education in twenty-eight countries: Civic knowledge and engagement at age fourteen.* Amsterdam: International Association for the Evaluation of Educational Achievement.

Tornstam, Lars. (2005). *Gerotranscendence: A developmental theory of positive aging.* New York: Springer.

Townsend, Jean, Godfrey, Mary, & Denby, Tracy. (2006). Heroines, villains and victims: Older people's perceptions of others. *Ageing & Society, 26,* 883–900.

Toyama, Miki. (2001). Developmental changes in social comparison in preschool and elementary school children: Perceptions, feelings, and behavior. *Japanese Journal of Educational Psychology, 49,* 500–507.

Trautmann-Villalba, Patricia, Gschwendt, Miriam, Schmidt, Martin H., & Laucht, Manfred. (2006). Father–infant interaction patterns as precursors of children's later externalizing behavior problems: A longitudinal study over 11 years. *European Archives of Psychiatry and Clinical Neuroscience, 256,* 344–349.

Tremblay, Richard E., & Nagin, Daniel S. (2005). Developmental origins of physical aggression in humans. In Richard Ernest Tremblay, Willard W. Hartup, & John Archer (Eds.), *Developmental origins of aggression* (pp. 83–106). New York: Guilford Press.

Trenholm, Christopher, Devaney, Barbara, Fortson, Ken, Quay, Lisa, Wheeler, Justin, & Clark, Melissa. (2007). *Impacts of four Title V, Section 510 abstinence education programs: Final report.* Mathematica Policy Research. Retrieved September 13, 2009, from http://www.mathematica-mpr.com/publications/PDFs/impactabstinence.pdf

Trenka, Jane Jeong, Oparah, Julia Chinyere, & Shin, Sun Yung (Eds.). (2006). *Outsiders within: Writing on transracial adoption.* Cambridge, MA: South End Press.

Trickett, Edison J., & Jones, Curtis J. (2007). Adolescent culture brokering and family functioning: A study of families from Vietnam. *Cultural Diversity and Ethnic Minority Psychology, 13,* 143–150.

Trillo, Alex. (2004). Somewhere between Wall Street and El Barrio: Community college as a second chance for second-generation Latino students. In Philip Kasinitz, John H. Mollenkopf, & Mary C. Waters (Eds.), *Becoming New Yorkers: Ethnographies of the new second generation* (pp. 57–78). New York: Russell Sage.

Trimble, Joseph, Root, Maria P. P., & Helms, Janet E. (2003). Psychological perspectives on ethnic and racial psychology. In Guillermo Bernal, Joseph E. Trimble, Ann Kathleen Burlew, & Frederick T. Leong (Eds.), *Racial and ethnic minority psychology series: Vol. 4. Handbook of racial & ethnic minority psychology* (pp. 239–275). Thousand Oaks, CA: Sage.

Troll, Lillian E., & Skaff, Marilyn McKean. (1997). Perceived continuity of self in very old age. *Psychology & Aging, 12,* 162–169.

Tronick, Edward. (2007). *The neurobehavioral and social-emotional development of infants and children.* New York: Norton.

Tronick, Edward Z. (1989). Emotions and emotional communication in infants. *American Psychologist, 44,* 112–119.

Tronick, Edward Z., & Weinberg, M. Katherine. (1997). Depressed mothers and infants: Failure to form dyadic states of consciousness. In Lynne Murray & Peter J. Cooper (Eds.), *Post-partum depression and child development* (pp. 54–81). New York: Guilford Press.

Trudeau, François, & Shephard, Roy J. (2008). *Physical education, school physical activity, school sports and academic performance.* Retrieved July 2, 2009, from http://www.ijbnpa.org/content/5/1/10

Truog, Robert D. (2007). Brain death—Too flawed to endure, too ingrained to abandon. *The Journal of Law, Medicine & Ethics, 35,* 273–281.

Trzesniewski, Kali H., Robins, Richard W., Roberts, Brent W., & Caspi, Avshalom. (2004). Personality and self-esteem development across the life span. In Paul T. Costa & Ilene C. Siegler (Eds.), *Recent advances in psychology and aging* (Vol. 15, pp. 163–185). Amsterdam: Elsevier.

Tsai, James, Floyd, R. Louise, & Bertrand, Jacquelyn. (2007). Tracking binge drinking among U.S. childbearing-age women. *Preventive Medicine: An International Journal Devoted to Practice and Theory, 44,* 298–302.

Tsao, Feng-Ming, Liu, Huei-Mei, & Kuhl, Patricia K. (2004). Speech perception in infancy predicts language development in the second year of life: A longitudinal study. *Child Development, 75,* 1067–1084.

Tse, Lucy. (2001). *"Why don't they learn English?" Separating fact from fallacy in the U.S. language debate.* New York: Teachers College Press.

Tseng, Vivian. (2004). Family interdependence and academic adjustment in college: Youth from immigrant and U.S.-born families. *Child Development, 75,* 966–983.

Tucker, Joan S., Friedman, Howard S., Wingard, Deborah L., & Schwartz, Joseph E. (1996). Marital history at midlife as a predictor of longevity: Alternative explanations to the protective effect of marriage. *Health Psychology, 15,* 94–101.

Tudge, Jonathan. (2008). *The everyday lives of young children: Culture, class, and child rearing in diverse societies.* New York: Cambridge University Press.

Tudge, Jonathan R. H., Doucet, Fabienne, Odero, Dolphine, Sperb, Tania M., Piccinini, Cesar A., & Lopes, Rita S. (2006). A window into different cultural worlds: Young children's everyday activities in the United States, Brazil, and Kenya. *Child Development, 77,* 1446–1469.

Turiel, Elliot. (2006). The development of morality. In William Damon & Richard M. Lerner (Series Eds.) & Nancy Eisenberg (Vol. Ed.), *Handbook of child psychology: Vol. 3. Social, emotional, and personality development* (6th ed., pp. 789–857). Hoboken, NJ: Wiley.

Turiel, Elliot. (2008). Thought about actions in social domains: Morality, social conventions, and social interactions. *Cognitive Development, 23,* 136–154.

Twenge, Jean M., & Campbell, W. Keith. (2001). Age and birth cohort differences in self-esteem: A cross-temporal meta-analysis. *Personality and Social Psychology Review, 5,* 321–344.

Twenge, Jean M., Konrath, Sara, Foster, Joshua D., Campbell, W. Keith, & Bushma, Brad J. (2008). Egos inflating over time: A cross-temporal meta-analysis of the narcissistic personality inventory. *Journal of Personality, 76,* 875–902.

Tynes, Brendesha M. (2007). Role taking in online "classrooms": What adolescents are learning about race and ethnicity. *Developmental Psychology, 43,* 1312–1320.

Tyzio, Roman, Cossart, Rosa, Khalilov, Ilgam, Minlebaev, Marat, Hubner, Christian A., Represa, Alfonso, et al. (2006, December 15). Maternal oxytocin triggers a transient inhibitory switch in GABA signaling in the fetal brain during delivery. *Science, 314,* 1788–1792.

U.S. Bureau of the Census. (1907). *Statistical abstract of the United States: 1907* (30th ed.). Washington, DC: U.S. Government Printing Office.

U.S. Bureau of the Census. (1972). *Statistical abstract of the United States: 1972* (93rd ed.). Washington, DC: U.S. Government Printing Office.

U.S. Bureau of the Census. (1975). *Statistical abstract of the United States: 1975* (96th ed.). Washington, DC: U.S. Government Printing Office.

U.S. Bureau of the Census. (1981). *Statistical abstract of the United States: 1981* (102nd ed.). Washington, DC: U.S. Department of Commerce.

U.S. Bureau of the Census. (1989). *Statistical abstract of the United States: 1989* (109th ed.). Washington, DC: U.S. Government Printing Office.

U.S. Bureau of the Census. (2002). *Statistical abstract of the United States, 2001: The national data book* (121st ed.). Washington, DC: U.S. Department of Commerce.

U.S. Bureau of the Census. (2006). *Statistical abstract of the United States: 2007* (126th ed.). Washington, DC: U.S. Government Printing Office.

U.S. Bureau of the Census. (2007). *Statistical abstract of the United States: 2008* (127th ed.). Washington, DC: U.S. Department of Commerce.

U.S. Bureau of the Census. (2008). *Statistical abstract of the United States: 2009* (128th ed.). Washington, DC: U.S. Department of Commerce.

U.S. Bureau of the Census. (2008, December 9). *Quick guide to the American Community Survey (ACS) products in American FactFinder: 2005–2007 ACS 3-year estimates.* Retrieved June 19, 2008, from http://factfinder.census.gov/home/saff/aff_acs2007_quickguide.pdf

U.S. Bureau of the Census. (2009a). *United States—States; and Puerto Rico. GCT1703. Percent of people 65 years and over below poverty level in the past 12 months.* Retrieved September 17, 2009, from http://factfinder.census.gov/

U.S. Bureau of the Census. (2009b). *United States—States; and Puerto Rico. GCT1704. Percent of children under 18 years below poverty level in the past 12 months (for whom poverty status is determined).* Retrieved September 17, 2009, from http://factfinder.census.gov/

U.S. Bureau of Labor Statistics. (2008, January 23). *Volunteering in the United States, 2007.* Retrieved September 8, 2009, from http://www.bls.gov/news.release/archives/volun_01232008.pdf

U.S. Cancer Statistics Working Group. (2006). *United States cancer statistics: 2003 incidence and mortality.* Atlanta, GA: U.S. Department of Health and Human Services, Centers for Disease Control and Prevention and National Cancer Institute.

U.S. Census Bureau, 2005–2007 American Community Survey. (2008, August 26). *S1002. Grandparents.* Retrieved September 15, 2009, from http://factfinder.census.gov/

U.S. Department of Health and Human Services. (2004). *Trends in the well-being of America's children and youth, 2003* (No. 017-022-01571-4). Washington, DC: U.S. Government Printing Office.

U.S. Department of Health and Human Services, Administration on Children, Youth and Families. (2006). *Child maltreatment 2004.* Washington, DC: U.S. Government Printing Office.

U.S. Department of Health and Human Services, Administration on Children, Youth and Families. (2008). *Child maltreatment 2006.* Washington, DC: U.S. Government Printing Office.

U.S. Preventive Services Task Force. (2002). Postmenopausal hormone replacement therapy for primary prevention of chronic conditions: Recommendations and rationale. *Annals of Internal Medicine, 137,* 834–839.

Udry, J. Richard, & Chantala, Kim. (2005). Risk factors differ according to same-sex and opposite-sex interest. *Journal of Biosocial Science, 37,* 481–497.

Uhlenberg, Peter. (1996). The burden of aging: A theoretical framework for understanding the shifting balance of caregiving and care receiving as cohorts age. *Gerontologist, 36,* 761–767.

Umaña-Taylor, Adriana J., Bhanot, Ruchi, & Shin, Nana. (2006). Ethnic identity formation during adolescence: The critical role of families. *Journal of Family Issues, 27,* 390–414.

UNAIDS. (2008). *Report on the global AIDS epidemic 2008.* Geneva, Switzerland: Author.

Underwood, Marion K. (2003). *Social aggression among girls.* New York: Guilford Press.

Underwood, Marion K. (2004). Gender and peer relations: Are the two gender cultures really all that different? In Janis B. Kupersmidt & Kenneth A. Dodge (Eds.), *Children's peer relations: From development to intervention* (pp. 21–36). Washington, DC: American Psychological Association.

UNESCO Institute for Statistics. (2009). *Global education digest 2009: Comparing education statistics across the world.* Montreal, Quebec, Canada: Author.

United Nations. (2007). *World population ageing 2007.* New York: United Nations Department of Economic and Social Affairs, Population Division.

United Nations. (2007). *World population prospects: The 2006 revision* (Vols. 1–3). New York: United Nations, Department of Economic and Social Affairs.

United Nations Children's Fund (UNICEF). (2006). *The state of the world's children 2007: Women and children: The double dividend of gender equality.* New York: UNICEF.

United Nations Children's Fund (UNICEF). (2007). *The state of the world's children 2008: Child survival.* Retrieved June 3, 2009, from http://www.unicef.org/sowc08/docs/sowc08.pdf

United Nations, Department of Economic and Social Affairs. (2009). *Statistics and indicators on women and men: Table 1b. Composition of the population.* Retrieved July 23, 2009, from http://unstats.un.org/unsd/demographic/products/indwm/tab1b.htm

United Nations Development Programme. (2008). *Human development report 2007/2008: Fighting climate change: Human solidarity in a divided world.* Retrieved September 9, 2009, from http://hdr.undp.org/en/media/hdr_20072008_en_indicator_tables.pdf

United Nations Statistics Division. (2009, June). *Social indicators.* Retrieved June 19, 2009, from http://unstats.un.org/unsd/demographic/products/socind/child&elderly.htm

Unnever, James D. (2005). Bullies, aggressive victims, and victims: Are they distinct groups? *Aggressive Behavior, 31,* 153–171.

Uttal, William R. (2000). *The war between mentalism and behaviorism: On the accessibility of mental processes.* Mahwah, NJ: Erlbaum.

Utz, Rebecca L., Carr, Deborah, Nesse, Randolph, & Wortman, Camille B. (2002). The effect of widowhood on older adults' social participation: An evaluation of activity, disengagement, and continuity theories. *The Gerontologist, 42,* 522–533.

Vaillant, George E. (2002). *Aging well: Surprising guideposts to a happier life from the landmark Harvard Study of Adult Development.* Boston: Little Brown.

Vaillant, George E. (2008). *Spiritual evolution: A scientific defense of faith.* New York: Broadway Books.

Valentino, Kristin, Cicchetti, Dante, Rogosch, Fred A., & Toth, Sheree L. (2008). True and false recall and dissociation among maltreated children: The role of self-schema. *Development and Psychopathology, 20,* 213–232.

Valentino, Kristin, Cicchetti, Dante, Toth, Sheree L., & Rogosch, Fred A. (2006). Mother–child play and emerging social behaviors among infants from maltreating families. *Developmental Psychology, 42,* 474–485.

Valkenburg, Patti M., & Peter, Jochen. (2009). Social consequences of the Internet for adolescents: A decade of research. *Current Directions in Psychological Science, 18,* 1–5.

van den Berg, Stéphanie M., & Boomsma, Dorret I. (2007). The familial clustering of age at menarche in extended twin families. *Behavior Genetics, 37,* 661–667.

van der Heide, Agnes, Onwuteaka-Philipsen, Bregje D., Rurup, Mette L., Buiting, Hilde M., van Delden, Johannes J.M., Hanssen-de Wolf, Johanna E., et al. (2007). End-of-life practices in the Netherlands under the euthanasia act. *New England Journal of Medicine, 356,* 1957–1965.

van der Meer, Marieke. (2006). Productivity among older people in The Netherlands: Variations by gender and the socio-spatial context in 2002–03. *Ageing & Society, 26,* 901–923.

Van Gaalen, Ruben I., & Dykstra, Pearl A. (2006). Solidarity and conflict between adult children and parents: A latent class analysis. *Journal of Marriage and Family, 68,* 947–960.

Van Hoorn, Judith Lieberman, Komlosi, Akos, Suchar, Elzbieta, & Samelson, Doreen A. (2000). *Adolescent development and rapid social change: Perspectives from Eastern Europe.* Albany, NY: State University of New York Press.

Van Zundert, Rinka M. P., Van Der Vorst, Haske, Vermulst, Ad A., & Engels, Rutger C. M. E. (2006). Pathways to alcohol use among Dutch students in regular education and education for adolescents with behavioral problems: The role of parental alcohol use, general parenting practices, and alcohol-specific parenting practices. *Journal of Family Psychology, 20,* 456–467.

Vandenberg, Laura N., Hauser, Russ, Marcus, Michele, Olea, Nicolas, & Welshons, Wade V. (2007). Human exposure to bisphenol A (BPA). *Reproductive Toxicology, 24,* 139–177.

Vasan, Ramachandran S., Beiser, Alexa, Seshadri, Sudha, Larson, Martin G., Kannel, William B., D'Agostino, Ralph B., et al. (2002). Residual lifetime risk for developing hypertension in middle-aged women and men: The Framingham Heart Study. *Journal of the American Medical Association, 287,* 1003–1010.

Vaupel, James W., & Loichinger, Elke. (2006, June 30). Redistributing work in aging Europe. *Science, 312,* 1911–1913.

Veblen, Thorstein. (2007). *The theory of the leisure class.* New York: Oxford University Press. (Original work published 1899).

Veenstra, Rene, Lindenberg, Siegwart, Oldehinkel, Albertine J., De Winter, Andrea F., Verhulst, Frank C., & Ormel, Johan. (2008). Prosocial and antisocial behavior in preadolescence: Teachers' and parents' perceptions of the behavior of girls and boys. *International Journal of Behavioral Development, 32,* 243–251.

Vega, William A., Chen, Kevin W., & Williams, Jill. (2007). Smoking, drugs, and other behavioral health problems among multiethnic adolescents in the NHSDA. *Addictive Behaviors, 32,* 1949–1956.

Venn, John J. (Ed.). (2004). *Assessing children with special needs* (3rd ed.). Upper Saddle River, NJ: Pearson.

Verhaeghen, Paul, Steitz, David W., Sliwinski, Martin J., & Cerella, John. (2003). Aging and dual-task performance: A meta-analysis. *Psychology & Aging, 18,* 443–460.

Verona, Sergiu. (2003). Romanian policy regarding adoptions. In Victor Littel (Ed.), *Adoption update* (pp. 5–10). New York: Nova Science.

Verté, Sylvie, Geurts, Hilde M., Roeyers, Herbert, Oosterlaan, Jaap, & Sergeant, Joseph A. (2005). Executive functioning in children with autism and Tourette syndrome. *Development & Psychopathology, 17,* 415–445.

Viadero, Debra. (2006, February 15). Scholars warn of overstating gains from AP classes alone. *Education Week 25*(23), 14.

Viadero, Debra. (2007, April 5). Long after Katrina, children show symptoms of psychological distress. *Education Week, 26*(32), 7.

Viinanen, Arja, Munhbayarlah, S., Zevgee, T., Narantsetseg, L., Naidansuren, Ts, Koskenvuo, Markku, et al. (2007). The protective effect of rural living against atopy in Mongolia. *Allergy, 62,* 272–280.

Visser, Beth A., Ashton, Michael C., & Vernon, Philip A. (2006). Beyond g: Putting multiple intelligences theory to the test. *Intelligence, 34,* 487–502.

Vitiello, Benedetto, Zuvekas, Samuel H., & Norquist, Grayson S. (2006). National estimates of antidepressant medication use among U.S. children, 1997–2002. *Journal of the American Academy of Child & Adolescent Psychiatry, 45,* 271–279.

von Hippel, William. (2007). Aging, executive functioning, and social control. *Current Directions in Psychological Science, 16,* 240–244.

Voorpostel, Marieke, & van der Lippe, Tanja. (2007). Support between siblings and between friends: Two worlds apart? *Journal of Marriage and Family, 69,* 1271–1282.

Votruba-Drzal, Elizabeth, Coley, Rebekah Levine, & Chase-Lansdale, P. Lindsay. (2004). Child care and low-income children's development: Direct and moderated effects. *Child Development, 75,* 296–312.

Vouloumanos, Athena, & Werker, Janet F. (2007). Listening to language at birth: Evidence for a bias for speech in neonates. *Developmental Science, 10,* 159–164.

Voydanoff, Patricia. (2007). *Work, family, and community: Exploring interconnections.* Mahwah, NJ: Erlbaum.

Vu, Pauline. (2007). *Lake Wobegon, U.S.A.* Pew Research Center. Retrieved September 11, 2009, from http://pewresearch.org/pubs/403/lake-wobegon-usa

Vygotsky, Lev S. (1978). *Mind in society: The development of higher psychological processes* (Michael Cole, Vera John-Steiner, Sylvia Scribner, & Ellen Souberman, Eds.). Cambridge, MA: Harvard University Press. (Original work published 1935)

Vygotsky, Lev S. (1987). *Thinking and speech* (Robert W. Rieber & Aaron S. Carton, Eds., Norris Minick, Trans., Vol. 1). New York: Plenum Press. (Original work published 1934)

Vygotsky, Lev S. (1994). The development of academic concepts in school aged children (Theresa Prout, Trans.). In Rene van der Veer & Jaan Valsiner (Eds.), *The Vygotsky reader* (pp. 355–370). Cambridge, MA: Blackwell. (Original work published 1934)

Waddell, Charlotte, Macmillan, Harriet, & Pietrantonio, Anna Marie. (2004). How important is permanency planning for children? Considerations for pediatricians involved in child protection. *Journal of Developmental & Behavioral Pediatrics, 25,* 285–292.

Wade, Nicholas. (2006, November 7). Aging drugs: Hardest test is still ahead. *New York Times,* pp. F1, F4.

Wade, Nicholas. (2007, September 4). In the genome race, the sequel is personal. *New York Times,* pp. F1, F4.

Wadsworth, Sally J., Corley, Robin, Plomin, Robert, Hewitt, John K., & DeFries, John C. (2006). Genetic and environmental influences on continuity and change in reading achievement in the Colorado Adoption Project. In Aletha C. Huston & Marika N. Ripke (Eds.), *Developmental contexts in middle childhood: Bridges to adolescence and adulthood* (pp. 87–106). New York: Cambridge University Press.

Wagenaar, Karin, Huisman, Jaap, Cohen-Kettenis, Peggy T., & Adelemarre-van De Waal, Henriette. (2008). An overview of studies on early development, cognition, and psychosocial well-being in children born after in vitro fertilization. *Journal of Developmental & Behavioral Pediatrics, 29,* 219–230.

Wahlin, Åke, MacDonald, Stuart W. S., de Frias, Cindy M., Nilsson, Lars-Göran, & Dixon, Roger A. (2006). How do health and biological age influence chronological age and sex differences in cognitive aging: Moderating, mediating, or both? *Psychology and Aging, 21,* 318–332.

Wailoo, Michael, Ball, Helen L., Fleming, Peter, & Ward Platt, Martin. (2004). Infants bed-sharing with mothers. *Archives of Disease in Childhood, 89,* 1082–1083.

Wainright, Jennifer L., & Patterson, Charlotte J. (2008). Peer relations among adolescents with female same-sex parents. *Developmental Psychology, 44,* 117–126.

Wainright, Jennifer L., Russell, Stephen T., & Patterson, Charlotte J. (2004). Psychosocial adjustment, school outcomes, and romantic relationships of adolescents with same-sex parents. *Child Development, 75,* 1886–1898.

Wainryb, Cecilia, Shaw, Leigh A., Langley, Marcie, Cottam, Kim, & Lewis, Renee. (2004). Children's thinking about diversity of belief in the early school years: Judgments of relativism, tolerance, and disagreeing persons. *Child Development, 75,* 687–703.

Wakefield, Melanie, Flay, Brian, Nichter, Mark, & Giovino, Gary. (2003). Effects of anti-smoking advertising on youth smoking: A review. *Journal of Health Communication, 8,* 229–247.

Walden, Tedra A., & Kim, Geunyoung. (2005). Infants' social looking toward mothers and strangers. *International Journal of Behavioral Development, 29,* 356–360.

Waldfogel, Jane. (2006). What do children need? *Public Policy Research, 13,* 26–34.

Walker, Alan. (2004). *Growing older in Europe.* Maidenhead, United Kingdom: Open University Press.

Walker, Alan. (2006). Aging and politics: An international perspective. In Robert H. Binstock & Linda K. George (Eds.), *Handbook of aging and the social sciences* (6th ed., pp. 339–359). Amsterdam: Elsevier.

Walker, Elaine F. (2002). Adolescent neurodevelopment and psychopathology. *Current Directions in Psychological Science, 11,* 24–28.

Walker, Matthew P., & Stickgold, Robert. (2006). Sleep, memory, and plasticity. *Annual Review of Psychology, 57,* 139–166.

Walker, Rheeda L., & Hunter, Lora Rose. (2008). From anxiety and depression to suicide and self-harm. In Helen A. Neville, Brendesha M. Tynes, & Shawn O. Utsey (Eds.), *Handbook of African American psychology* (pp. 401–416). Thousand Oaks, CA: Sage.

Wallerstein, Judith S., & Blakeslee, Sandra. (1995). *The good marriage: How and why love lasts.* Boston: Houghton Mifflin.

Wang, A. Ting, Lee, Susan S., Sigman, Marian, & Dapretto, Mirella. (2006). Developmental changes in the neural basis of interpreting communicative intent. *Social Cognitive and Affective Neuroscience, 1,* 107–121.

Wang, Richard Y., Needham, Larry L., & Barr, Dana B. (2005). Effects of environmental agents on the attainment of puberty: Considerations when assessing exposure to environmental chemicals in the National Children's Study. *Environmental Health Perspectives, 113,* 1100–1107.

Wang, Ying, & Marcotte, Dave E. (2007). Golden years? The labor market effects of caring for grandchildren. *Journal of Marriage and Family, 69,* 1283–1296.

Wannamethee, S. Goya, & Shaper, A. Gerald. (1999). Type of alcoholic drink and risk of major coronary heart disease events and all-cause mortality. *American Journal of Public Health, 89,* 685–690.

Ward, Russell A., & Spitze, Glenna D. (2007). Nestleaving and coresidence by young adult children: The role of family relations. *Research on Aging, 29,* 257–277.

Warren, Charles W., Jones, Nathan R., Eriksen, Michael P., & Asma, Samira. (2006). Patterns of global tobacco use in young people and implications for future chronic disease burden in adults. *Lancet, 367,* 749–753.

Warshofsky, Fred. (1999). *Stealing time: The new science of aging.* New York: TV Books.

Washington, Harriet A. (2006). *Medical apartheid: The dark history of medical experimentation on Black Americans from colonial times to the present.* New York: Doubleday.

Waterhouse, Lynn. (2006). Multiple intelligences, the Mozart effect, and emotional intelligence: A critical review. *Educational Psychologist, 41,* 207–225.

Watson, John B. (1928). *Psychological care of infant and child.* New York: Norton.

Watson, John B. (1998). *Behaviorism.* New Brunswick, NJ: Transaction. (Original work published 1924)

Watts, Jonathan. (2002). Public health experts concerned about "hikikomori." *Lancet, 359,* 1131.

Waxman, Sandra R., & Lidz, Jeffrey L. (2006). Early word learning. In William Damon & Richard M. Lerner (Series Eds.) & Deanna Kuhn & Robert S. Siegler (Vol. Eds.), *Handbook of child psychology: Vol. 2. Cognition, perception, and language* (6th ed., pp. 299–335). Hoboken, NJ: Wiley.

Way, Niobe, Gingold, Rachel, Rotenberg, Mariana, & Kuriakose, Geena. (2005). Close friendships among urban, ethnic-minority adolescents. In Niobe Way & Jill V. Hamm (Eds.), *The experience of close friendships in adolescence* (Vol. 107, pp. 41–59). San Francisco: Jossey-Bass.

Way, Niobe, & Hamm, Jill V. (Eds.). (2005). *The experience of close friendships in adolescence.* San Francisco: Jossey-Bass.

Weaver, Chelsea M., Blodgett, Elizabeth H., & Carothers, Shannon S. (2006). Preventing risky sexual behavior. In John G. Borkowski & Chelsea M. Weaver (Eds.), *Prevention: The science and art of promoting healthy child and adolescent development* (pp. 185–214). Baltimore: Brookes.

Wechsler, David. (2003). *Wechsler intelligence scale for children— Fourth edition (WISC-IV).* San Antonio, TX: The Psychological Corporation.

Wechsler, Henry, Nelson, Toben F., Lee, Jae Eun, Seibring, Mark, Lewis, Catherine, & Keeling, Richard P. (2003). Perception and reality: A national evaluation of social norms marketing interventions to reduce college students' heavy alcohol use. *Quarterly Journal of Studies on Alcohol, 64,* 484–494.

Weichold, Karina, Silbereisen, Rainer K., & Schmitt-Rodermund, Eva. (2003). Short-term and long-term consequences of early versus late physical maturation in adolescents. In Chris Hayward (Ed.), *Gender differences at puberty* (pp. 241–276). New York: Cambridge University Press.

Weikart, David P. (Ed.). (1999). *What should young children learn? Teacher and parent views in 15 countries.* Ypsilanti, MI: High/Scope Press.

Weikum, Whitney M., Vouloumanos, Athena, Navarra, Jordi, Soto-Faraco, Salvador, Sebastian-Galles, Nuria, & Werker, Janet F. (2007, May 25). Visual language discrimination in infancy. *Science, 316,* 1159.

Weil, Andrew. (2007, May & June). The truth about the fountain of youth. *AARP The Magazine,* 40–41.

Weiner, Myron F., & Lipton, Anne M. (Eds.). (2009). *The American Psychiatric Publishing textbook of Alzheimer disease and other dementias.* Washington, DC: American Psychiatric Publishing.

Weisfeld, Glenn E. (1999). *Evolutionary principles of human adolescence.* New York: Basic Books.

Weizman, Zehava Oz, & Snow, Catherine E. (2001). Lexical output as related to children's vocabulary acquisition: Effects of sophisticated exposure and support for meaning. *Developmental Psychology, 37,* 265–279.

Wellman, Henry M. (2003). Enablement and constraint. In Ursula M. Staudinger & Ulman Lindenberger (Eds.), *Understanding human development: Dialogues with lifespan psychology* (pp. 245–263). Dordrecht, The Netherlands: Kluwer.

Wellman, Henry M., Cross, David, & Watson, Julanne. (2001). Meta-analysis of theory-of-mind development: The truth about false belief. *Child Development, 72,* 655–684.

Welsh, Marilyn, & Pennington, Bruce. (2000). Phenylketonuria. In Keith Owen Yeates, M. Douglas Ris, & H. Gerry Taylor (Eds.), *Pediatric neuropsychology: Research, theory, and practice* (pp. 275–299). New York: Guilford Press.

Werner, Emmy E. (1979). *Cross-cultural child development: A view from the planet Earth.* Monterey, CA: Brooks/Cole.

Werner, Emmy E., & Smith, Ruth S. (1992). *Overcoming the odds: High risk children from birth to adulthood.* Ithaca, NY: Cornell University Press.

Werner, Emmy E., & Smith, Ruth S. (2001). *Journeys from childhood to midlife: Risk, resilience, and recovery.* Ithaca, NY: Cornell University Press.

Wertsch, James V., & Tulviste, Peeter. (2005). *L. S. Vygotsky and contemporary developmental psychology.* New York: Routledge.

West, Heather C., & Sabol, William J. (2008). *Prisoners in 2007* (NCJ 224280). Washington, DC: U.S. Department of Justice.

West, Steven L., & O'Neal, Keri K. (2004). Project D.A.R.E. outcome effectiveness revisited. *American Journal of Public Health, 94,* 1027–1029.

Westerhof, Gerben J., & Keyes, Corey L. M. (2006). After the fall of the Berlin wall: Perceptions and consequences of stability and change among middle-aged and older East and West Germans. *Journals of Gerontology Series B: Psychological Sciences and Social Sciences, 61,* S240–247.

Wethington, Elaine. (2002). The relationship of turning points at work to perceptions of psychological growth and change. In Richard A. Settersten & Timothy J. Owens (Eds.), *Advances in life course research: Vol. 7. New frontiers in socialization* (pp. 93–110). Amsterdam: JAI.

Wheatley, Thalia, Milleville, Shawn C., & Martin, Alex. (2007). Understanding animate agents: Distinct roles for the social network and mirror system. *Psychological Science, 18,* 469–474.

Whelchel, Lisa. (2000). *Creative correction: Extraordinary ideas for everyday discipline.* Wheaton, IL: Tyndale House.

Whitbourne, Susan Krauss. (2002). *The aging individual: Physical and psychological perspectives* (2nd ed.). New York: Springer.

Whitbourne, Susan Krauss. (2008). *Adult development & aging: Biopsychosocial perspectives* (3rd ed.). Hoboken, NJ: John Wiley & Sons.

White, Aaron M., & Swartzwelder, H. Scott. (2004). Hippocampal function during adolescence: A unique target of ethanol effects. In Ronald E. Dahl & Linda Patia Spear (Eds.), *Adolescent brain development: Vulnerabilities and opportunities* (Vol. 1021, pp. 206–220). New York: New York Academy of Sciences.

White, Helene Raskin, McMorris, Barbara J., Catalano, Richard F., Fleming, Charles B., Haggerty, Kevin P., & Abbott, Robert D. (2006). Increases in alcohol and marijuana use during the transition out of high school into emerging adulthood: The effects of leaving home, going to college, and high school protective factors. *Journal of Studies on Alcohol, 67,* 810–822.

Whiteman, Maura K., Hillis, Susan D., Jamieson, Denise J., Morrow, Brian, Podgornik, Michelle N., Brett, Kate M., et al. (2008). Inpatient hysterectomy surveillance in the United States, 2000–2004. *American Journal of Obstetrics and Gynecology, 198,* 34.e31–34.e37.

Whiteman, Shawn D., McHale, Susan M., & Crouter, Ann C. (2007). Longitudinal changes in marital relationships: The role of offspring's pubertal development. *Journal of Marriage and Family, 69,* 1005–1020.

Whitfield, Keith E., & McClearn, Gerald. (2005). Genes, environment, and race: Quantitative genetic approaches. *American Psychologist, 60,* 104–114.

Whitlock, Janis L., Powers, Jane L., & Eckenrode, John. (2006). The virtual cutting edge: The internet and adolescent self-injury. *Developmental Psychology, 42,* 407–417.

Whitmer, Rachel A., Gunderson, Erica P., Barrett-Connor, Elizabeth, Quesenberry, Charles P., & Yaffe, Kristine. (2005). Obesity in middle age and future risk of dementia: A 27-year longitudinal population based study. *British Medical Journal, 330,* 1360.

Whitmore, Heather. (2001). Value that marketing cannot manufacture: Cherished possessions as links to identity and wisdom. *Generations, 25*(3), 57–63.

Widmaier, Eric P., Raff, Hershel, & Strang, Kevin T. (2008). *Vander's human physiology: The mechanisms of body function* (11th ed.). Boston: McGraw-Hill.

Wigfield, Allan, Eccles, Jacquelynne S., Yoon, Kwang Suk, Harold, Rena D., Arbreton, Amy J. A., Freedman-Doan, Carol, et al. (1997). Change in children's competence beliefs and subjective task values across the elementary school years: A 3-year study. *Journal of Educational Psychology, 89,* 451–469.

Wilhelm, Mark O., Rooney, Patrick M., & Tempel, Eugene R. (2007). Changes in religious giving reflect changes in involvement: Age and cohort effects in religious giving, secular giving, and attendance. *Journal for the Scientific Study of Religion, 46,* 217–232.

Willatts, Peter. (1999). Development of means–end behavior in young infants: Pulling a support to retrieve a distant object. *Developmental Psychology, 35,* 651–667.

Williams, David R. (2003). The health of men: Structured inequalities and opportunities. *American Journal of Public Health, 93,* 724–731.

Williams, Justin H. G., Waiter, Gordon D., Gilchrist, Anne, Perrett, David I., Murray, Alison D., & Whiten, Andrew. (2006). Neural mechanisms of imitation and 'mirror neuron' functioning in autistic spectrum disorder. *Neuropsychologia, 44,* 610–621.

Williamson, Rebecca A., Meltzoff, Andrew N., & Markman, Ellen M. (2008). Prior experiences and perceived efficacy influence 3-year-olds' imitation. *Developmental Psychology, 44,* 275–285.

Willingham, Daniel T. (2004/2005, Winter). Ask the cognitive scientist: Understanding ADHD. *American Educator, 28,* 36–41.

Willis, Sherry L. (1996). Everyday cognitive competence in elderly persons: Conceptual issues and empirical findings. *Gerontologist, 36,* 595–601.

Willis, Sherry L., Tennstedt, Sharon L., Marsiske, Michael, Ball, Karlene, Elias, Jeffrey, Koepke, Kathy Mann, et al. (2006). Long-term effects of cognitive training on everyday functional outcomes in older adults. *Journal of the American Medical Association, 296,* 2805–2814.

Wilson, Barbara J. (2008). Media and children's aggression, fear, and altruism. *Future of Children, 18,* 87–118.

Wilson, Robert S., Beckett, Laurel A., Barnes, Lisa L., Schneider, Julie A., Bach, Julie, Evans, Denis A., et al. (2002). Individual differences in rates of change in cognitive abilities of older persons. *Psychology & Aging, 17,* 179–193.

Wilson-Costello, Deanne, Friedman, Harriet, Minich, Nori, Siner, Bonnie, Taylor, Gerry, Schluchter, Mark, et al. (2007). Improved neurodevelopmental outcomes for extremely low birth weight infants in 2000–2002. *Pediatrics, 119,* 37–45.

Windsor, Timothy D., Anstey, Kaarin J., & Rodgers, Bryan. (2008). Volunteering and psychological well-being among young-old adults: How much is too much? *Gerontologist, 48,* 59–70.

Wingfield, Arthur, Tun, Patricia A., & McCoy, Sandra L. (2005). Hearing loss in older adulthood: What it is and how it interacts with cognitive performance. *Current Directions in Psychological Science, 14,* 144–148.

Winsler, Adam, Carlton, Martha P., & Barry, Maryann J. (2000). Age-related changes in preschool children's systematic use of private speech in a natural setting. *Journal of Child Language, 27,* 665–687.

Winstein, Keith J. (2007, October 4). DNA decoding maps mainstream future. *Wall Street Journal,* p. B3.

Wise, Phyllis. (2006). Aging of the female reproductive system. In Edward J. Masoro & Steven N. Austad (Eds.), *Handbook of the biology of aging* (6th ed., pp. 570–590). Amsterdam: Elsevier Academic Press.

Wisse, Brent E., Kim, Francis, & Schwartz, Michael W. (2007, November 9). An integrative view of obesity. *Science,* 928–929.

Witherington, David C., Campos, Joseph J., & Hertenstein, Matthew J. (2004). Principles of emotion and its development in infancy. In Gavin Bremner & Alan Fogel (Eds.), *Blackwell handbook of infant development* (Paperback ed., pp. 427–464). Malden, MA: Blackwell.

Witt, Ellen D. (2007). Puberty, hormones, and sex differences in alcohol abuse and dependence. *Neurotoxicology and Teratology, 29,* 81–95.

Wiysonge, Charles Shey, Nomo, Emmanuel, Mawo, Jeanne Ngo-Ndjan, & Ticha, Johnson M. (2006). Accelerated measles control in sub-Saharan Africa. *Lancet, 367,* 394–395.

Wolchik, Sharlene A., Ma, Yue, Tein, Jenn-Yun, Sandler, Irwin N., & Ayers, Tim S. (2008). Parentally bereaved children's grief: Self-system beliefs as mediators of the relations between grief and stressors and caregiver–child relationship quality. *Death Studies, 32,* 597–620.

Wolfe, Michael S. (2006, May). Shutting down Alzheimer's. *Scientific American, 294,* 72–79.

Wolfinger, Nicholas H. (2005). *Understanding the divorce cycle: The children of divorce in their own marriages.* New York: Cambridge University Press.

Wolraich, Mark L., & Doffing, Melissa A. (2005). Attention deficit hyperactivity disorder. In Merlin Gene Butler & F. John Meaney (Eds.), *Genetics of developmental disabilities* (pp. 783–807). Boca Raton, FL: Taylor & Francis.

Woodlee, Martin T., & Schallert, Timothy. (2006). The impact of motor activity and inactivity on the brain: Implications for the prevention and treatment of nervous-system disorders. *Current Directions in Psychological Science, 15,* 203–206.

Woodward, Amanda L., & Markman, Ellen M. (1998). Early word learning. In William Damon (Series Ed.) & Deanna Kuhn & Robert S. Siegler (Vol. Eds.), *Handbook of child psychology: Vol. 2. Cognition, perception and language* (5th ed., pp. 371–420). New York: Wiley.

Woolley, Jacqueline D., & Boerger, Elizabeth A. (2002). Development of beliefs about the origins and controllability of dreams. *Developmental Psychology, 38,* 24–41.

World Bank. (2005). *Expanding opportunities and building competencies for young people: A new agenda for secondary education.* Washington, DC: Author.

World Health Organization. (2003). *World atlas of birth defects* (2nd ed.). Geneva, Switzerland: Author.

World Health Organization. (2005). *Sexually transmitted infections among adolescents: Issues in adolescent health and development.* Geneva, Switzerland: Author.

World Health Organization. (2006). *World health statistics 2006.* Geneva, Switzerland: Author.

World Health Organization. (2008). *Suicide rates per 100,000 by country, year and sex.* Retrieved September 5, 2009, from http://www.who.int/mental_health/prevention/suicide_rates/en/index.html

Worrell, Frank C. (2008). Nigrescence attitudes in adolescence, emerging adulthood, and adulthood. *Journal of Black Psychology, 34,* 156–178.

Wright, Dave, Bradbury, Ian, Cuckle, Howard, Gardosi, Jason, Tonks, Ann, Standing, Sue, et al. (2006). Three-stage contingent screening for Down syndrome. *Prenatal Diagnosis, 26,* 528–534.

Wright, Lawrence. (1999). *Twins: And what they tell us about who we are.* New York: Wiley.

Wurm, Susanne, Tomasik, Martin, & Tesch-Römer, Clemens. (2008). Serious health events and their impact on changes in subjective health and life satisfaction: The role of age and a positive view on ageing. *European Journal of Ageing, 5,* 117–127.

Xin, Hao. (2008, August 29). Mortality survey offers mixed message. *Science, 321,* 1155.

Xu, Yaoying. (2008). *Children's social play sequence: Parten's classic theory revisited.* Retrieved June 29, 2009, from http://www.informaworld.com/10.1080/03004430802090430

Yajnik, Chittaranjan S. (2004). Early life origins of insulin resistance and type 2 diabetes in India and other Asian countries. *Journal of Nutrition, 134,* 205–210.

Yamaguchi, Susumu, Greenwald, Anthony G., Banaji, Mahzarin R., Murakami, Fumio, Chen, Daniel, Shiomura, Kimihiro, et al. (2007). Apparent universality of positive implicit self-esteem. *Psychological Science, 18,* 498–500.

Yang, Lixia, Krampe, Ralf T., & Baltes, Paul B. (2006). Basic forms of cognitive plasticity extended into the oldest-old: Retest learning, age, and cognitive functioning. *Psychology and Aging, 21,* 372–378.

Yarber, William L., Milhausen, Robin R., Crosby, Richard A., & Torabi, Mohammad R. (2005). Public opinion about condoms for HIV and STD prevention: A midwestern state telephone survey. *Perspectives on Sexual and Reproductive Health, 37,* 148–154.

Yates, Tuppett M. (2004). The developmental psychopathology of self-injurious behavior: Compensatory regulation in posttraumatic adaptation. *Clinical Psychology Review, 24,* 35–74.

Yen, Ju-Yu, Ko, Chih-Hung, Yen, Cheng-Fang, Chen, Sue-Huei, Chung, Wei-Lun, & Chen, Cheng-Chung. (2008). Psychiatric symptoms in adolescents with internet addiction: Comparison with substance use. *Psychiatry and Clinical Neurosciences, 62,* 9–16.

Yerkes, Robert Mearns. (1923). Testing the human mind. *Atlantic Monthly, 131,* 358–370.

Yeung, W. Jean, & Conley, Dalton. (2008). Black–White achievement gap and family wealth. *Child Development, 79,* 303–324.

Yeung, W. Jean, Linver, Miriam R., & Brooks-Gunn, Jeanne. (2002). How money matters for young children's development: Parental investment and family processes. *Child Development, 73,* 1861–1879.

Yoon, Carolyn, Hasher, Lynn, Feinberg, Fred, Rahhal, Tamara A., & Winocur, Gordon. (2000). Cross-cultural differences in memory: The role of culture-based stereotypes about aging. *Psychology & Aging, 15,* 694–704.

Youn, Gahyun, Knight, Bob G., Jeong, Hyun-Suk, & Benton, Donna. (1999). Differences in familism values and caregiving outcomes among Korean, Korean American, and White American dementia caregivers. *Psychology & Aging, 14,* 355–364.

Young, Elizabeth A., Korszun, Ania, Figueiredo, Helmer F., Banks-Solomon, Matia, & Herman, James P. (2008). Sex differences in HPA axis regulation. In Jill B. Becker, Karen J. Berkley, Nori Geary, Elizabeth Hampson, James P. Herman, & Elizabeth Young (Eds.), *Sex differences in the brain: From genes to behavior* (pp. 95–105). New York: Oxford University Press.

Young, Robert. (2007). *Medically assisted death.* Cambridge, UK: Cambridge University Press.

Zaccai, Julia, McCracken, Cherie, & Brayne, Carol. (2005). A systematic review of prevalence and incidence studies of dementia with Lewy bodies. *Age and Ageing, 34,* 561–566.

Zacks, Rose T., & Hasher, Lynn. (2006). Aging and long-term memory: Deficits are not inevitable. In Ellen Bialystok & Fergus I. M. Craik (Eds.), *Lifespan cognition: Mechanisms of change* (pp. 162–177). New York: Oxford University Press.

Zahn-Waxler, Carolyn, Park, Jong-Hyo, Usher, Barbara, Belouad, Francesca, Cole, Pamela, & Gruber, Reut. (2008). Young children's representations of conflict and distress: A longitudinal study of boys and girls with disruptive behavior problems. *Development and Psychopathology, 20,* 99–119.

Zal, H. Michael. (2001). *The sandwich generation: Caught between growing children and aging parents.* New York: Perseus Books. (Original work published 1992)

Zalenski, Robert J., & Raspa, Richard. (2006). Maslow's hierarchy of needs: A framework for achieving human potential in hospice. *Journal of Palliative Medicine, 9,* 1120–1127.

Zandi, Peter P., Sparks, D. Larry, Khachaturian, Ara S., Tschanz, JoAnn, Norton, Maria, Steinberg, Martin, et al. (2005). Do statins reduce risk of incident dementia and Alzheimer disease? The Cache County Study. *Archives of General Psychiatry, 62,* 217–224.

Zani, Bruna, & Cicognani, Elvira. (2006). Sexuality and intimate relationships in adolescence. In Sandy Jackson & Luc Goossens (Eds.), *Handbook of adolescent development* (pp. 200–222). Hove, East Sussex, UK: Psychology Press.

Zeifman, Debra, Delaney, Sarah, & Blass, Elliott M. (1996). Sweet taste, looking, and calm in 2- and 4-week-old infants: The eyes have it. *Developmental Psychology, 32,* 1090–1099.

Zelazo, Philip David, Müller, Ulrich, Frye, Douglas, & Marcovitch, Stuart. (2003). The development of executive function in early childhood. *Monographs of the Society for Research in Child Development, 68*(3, Serial No. 274), 11–27.

Zernike, Kate. (2005, March 12). Drinking game can be a deadly rite of passage. *New York Times.*

Zettel, Laura A., & Rook, Karen S. (2004). Substitution and compensation in the social networks of older widowed women. *Psychology and Aging, 19,* 433–443.

Zettel-Watson, Laura, Ditto, Peter H., Danks, Joseph H., & Smucker, William D. (2008). Actual and perceived gender differences in the accuracy of surrogate decisions about life-sustaining medical treatment among older spouses. *Death Studies, 32,* 273–290.

Zhan, Heying Jenny, Liu, Guangya, & Guan, Xinping. (2006). Willingness and availability: Explaining new attitudes toward institutional elder care among Chinese elderly parents and their adult. *Journal of Aging Studies, 20,* 279–290.

Zhang, Yuanting, & Goza, Franklin W. (2006). Who will care for the elderly in China? A review of the problems caused by China's one-child policy and their potential solutions. *Journal of Aging Studies, 20,* 151–164.

Zhou, Xin, Huang, Jin, Wang, Zhengke, Wang, Bin, Zhao, Zhenguo, Yang, Lei, et al. (2006). Parent–child interaction and children's number learning. *Early Child Development and Care, 176,* 763–775.

Zielinski, David S., Eckenrode, John, & Olds, David L. (2009). Nurse home visitation and the prevention of child maltreatment: Impact on the timing of official reports. *Development and Psychopathology, 21,* 441–453.

Zigler, Edward, & Styfco, Sally J. (Eds.). (2004). *The Head Start debates.* Baltimore: Brookes.

Zimmer-Gembeck, Melanie J., & Collins, W. Andrew. (2003). Autonomy development during adolescence. In Gerald R. Adams & Michael D. Berzonsky (Eds.), *Blackwell handbook of adolescence* (pp. 175–204). Malden, MA: Blackwell.

Zito, Julie Magno, Safer, Daniel J., dosReis, Susan, Gardner, James F., Magder, Laurence, Soeken, Karen, et al. (2003). Psychotropic practice patterns for youth: A 10-year perspective. *Archives of Pediatrics & Adolescent Medicine, 157,* 17–25.

Zuvekas, Samuel H., Vitiello, Benedetto, & Norquist, Grayson S. (2006). Recent trends in stimulant medication use among U.S. children. *American Journal of Psychiatry, 163,* 579–585.